The Social Science Encyclopedia

The Social Science Encyclopedia, first published in 1985 to acclaim from social scientists, librarians and students, was thoroughly revised in 1996, when reviewers began to describe it as a classic. This third edition has been radically recast. Over half the entries are new or have been entirely rewritten, and most of the balance have been substantially revised.

Written by an international team of contributors, the *Encyclopedia* offers a global perspective on the key issues with the social sciences. Some 500 entries cover a variety of enduring and newly vital areas of study and research methods. Experts review theoretical debates from neo-evolutionism and rational choice theory to poststructuralism, and address the great questions that cut across the social sciences. What is the influence of genes on behaviour? What is the nature of consciousness and cognition? What are the causes of poverty and wealth? What are the roots of conflict, wars, revolutions and genocidal violence?

This authoritative reference work is aimed at anyone with a serious interest in contemporary academic thinking about the individual in society.

Adam Kuper is an anthropologist, author of many books, regular broadcaster and contributor to the *TLS* and the *London Review of Books*. He is a Fellow of the British Academy.

Jessica Kuper retired in 2002 as senior commissioning editor in the social sciences at Cambridge University Press.

The Social Science Encyclopedia

Third edition

Edited by Adam Kuper
and Jessica Kuper

VOLUME I
A–K

Routledge
Taylor & Francis Group

LONDON AND NEW YORK

First edition published in 1985
Second edition published in 1996
Third edition published in 2004
by Routledge
2 Park Square, Milton Park, Abingdon, Oxon OX14 4RN
Simultaneously published in the USA and Canada
by Routledge
270 Madison Ave., New York, NY 10016

Routledge is an imprint of the Taylor & Francis Group

© 2004 Routledge
Typeset in Times by Taylor & Francis Books, Ltd
Printed and bound in Great Britain by
TJ International Ltd, Padstow, Cornwall

British Library Cataloguing in Publication Data
A catalogue record for this book is available from the British Library

Library of Congress Cataloging in Publication Data
A catalog record for this title has been requested.

ISBN 0–415–32096–8 (set)
ISBN 0–415–34774–2 (Volume I)
ISBN 0–415–34775–0 (Volume II)

Contents

Illustrations

Editorial preface

This is the third edition of *The Social Science Encyclopedia*. The first edition was published in 1985. The second edition, substantially revised and updated, appeared in 1996. As editors we have benefited from the opinions of reviewers and readers, from the expert advice of three successive international panels of advisory editors, and from the suggestions of many of our contributors, and in the two decades since its launch the *Encyclopedia* has established a reputation for providing authoritative, accessible and up-to-date coverage of the social sciences, in a convenient format. We would like to think that this third edition is an advance on its predecessors, but our aim remains unchanged. We have done our best to orchestrate a reliable, intelligent and interesting review of the whole gamut of ideas and findings on the individual and society that have emerged from more than a century of academic research and debate.

Each edition has drawn on hundreds of experts from many countries, representing a variety of intellectual traditions, academic specialities and points of view. Together they have contributed between 400 and 500 entries. These range from extended reviews of an entire discipline or a major research topic through a large number of concise presentations of central concepts, subfields and key biographies to relatively brief essays on specialist issues. For this edition we have generally opted to commission longer entries, covering more ground, but there are still around 500 items. Half the entries were completely recast for the second edition, or were commissioned specially for it, and the rest were revised. Over half the entries commissioned for this edition are, once again, entirely or substantially new, often on topics not covered before. Most of the remainder have been revised and brought up to date.

The second edition covered fresh debates and fields of enquiry that had emerged in the previous decade. This third edition again introduces new theoretical and topical material to reflect the state of affairs in the social sciences in the early twenty-first century. The current edition pays more attention to evolutionary thinking in the social sciences, which has influenced all fields in the past decade. Other trends are also apparent, across disciplines and influencing a variety of research programmes. Rational choice approaches and game theory have migrated from economics into political science and sociology. At the same time, economists are drawing on psychological theories to explain failures of rationality, and to gain insights into how people act when they have to make choices but lack vital pieces of information. The human rights discourse has become central to political theory, law and international relations (which is covered more fully in this edition than previously). New developments in the study of cognition and the brain now dominate many fields of psychology, and influence linguistics and anthropology. Advances in genetics have inspired fresh approaches to classic issues in psychology, provided social scientists with new models of communication and change, and provoked critical accounts of how and why genetic models have been popularized and applied to social questions. Culture theory has become an established point of reference for many social sciences, as has poststructuralism, which draws on literary theory. Both now provoke similar debates in several disciplines. The preoccupations of gender studies have been assimilated into many debates and fields of study. In the process, gender studies itself has become broader and more eclectic.

Introducing the first edition we noted that the various social science disciplines increasingly constituted a single arena of discourse. It is perhaps more accurate to say that research programmes overlap more and more. Similar debates crop up in a variety of sites, new ideas passing from one discipline to another. Today economists win Nobel Prizes for doing psychological experiments, political scientists borrow the models of economists, historians debate concepts drawn from anthropology, and sociologists, historians and geographers, as ever, range eclectically across the social sciences. Most of the philosophical and methodological entries in this *Encyclopedia* are relevant to all the social science disciplines. One consequence of this overlap and interpenetration of established disciplines is that we have found it more difficult than ever to decide who should cover certain topics. Yet perhaps precisely because there is so much interdisciplinary activity this does not matter very much, so long as competing perspectives (which often recur in a number of disciplines) are fairly presented. Anyone browsing through these pages with an open mind will soon find that certain themes recur, cropping up in the most unexpected places, and that an initial enquiry can lead from an obvious starting-point right across disciplinary boundaries to perhaps hitherto unheard of destinations, in the process presenting the reader with a number of complementary or competitive ideas.

Intellectual affiliations and ideological concerns also cross-cut disciplinary boundaries. Like its predecessors, this third edition of the *Encyclopedia* reflects the controversies as well as the common assumptions that constitute the social sciences. We have selected our contributors for their individual expertise, but inevitably they represent a very broad cross-section of opinion, and a variety of intellectual orientations. We believe this is one of the strengths of the *Encyclopedia*. The balance comes from reading further, following up cross-references, so that one perspective can be weighed against another.

Does this imply that the social sciences are not true sciences? Bits and pieces – even quite substantial chunks – of some of these disciplines certainly qualify as scientific on any of the conventional tests, just as well as many branches of biology. But since the late nineteenth century, influential voices have queried whether studies of human interactions can and should be modelled on the natural sciences. Many of the philosophical entries included here address this issue. So do the authors of a number of substantive entries, on topics ranging from political science to the sociology of science, a field that has helped to put in question the very nature of science itself. On this, and we hope on other issues too, whatever your particular interests and inclinations, the third edition of *The Social Science Encyclopedia* will help you to make up your mind.

Adam Kuper and Jessica Kuper
London, December 2003

Advisory editors

Contributors

Peter Abell, London School of Economics and Political Science
Rational Choice (Action) Theory

Steven M. Albert, Columbia University
Gerontology, Social

Jeffrey C. Alexander, Yale University
Positivism

Graham Allan, Keele University
Marriage

Brenda Almond, University of Hull
Mill, John Stuart (1806–73)

Vered Amit, Concordia University
Community

P. Anand, University of Oxford
Decision-making

Antonios Antoniou, University of Durham
Derivative Markets and Futures Markets

W. Arens, State University of New York at Stony Brook
Cannibalism; Incest

David Armstrong, King's College, University of London
Medical Sociology

J. Scott Armstrong, The Wharton School, University of Pennsylvania
Forecasting and Prediction

A. Asimakopulos, *formerly* McGill University
Microeconomics

Robert Aunger, University College London
Memes

Roger E. Backhouse, University of Birmingham
Competition

Joëlle Bahloul, Indiana University
Memory, Social

Stephen J. Ball, Institute of Education, University of London
Case Study

Michael Banton, University of Bristol
Role

Karin Barber, University of Birmingham
Popular Culture

Alan Barnard, University of Edinburgh
Genealogies; Hunters and Gatherers

Trevor J. Barnes, University of British Columbia
Economic Geography

David Barr, Imperial College, London
Liquidity; Monetary Policy

Norman Barry, University of Buckingham
Liberalism

Robert Barsky, University of Michigan,
Ann Arbor
Stagflation

Zygmunt Bauman, University of Leeds
Class, Social; Sociology

Gerd Baumann, University of
Amsterdam
Multiculturalism

William J. Baumol, New York University
and Princeton University
Capitalism

Andrew Beatty, Brunel University
Ritual

C.G. Beer, Rutgers University
Instinct

Catherine Belsey, Cardiff University
Poststructuralism

Richard Bentall, University of
Manchester
Delusions

Christopher J. Berry, University of
Glasgow
Hume, David (1711–76)

André Béteille, University of Delhi
Stratification

Wiebe E. Bijker, University of
Maastricht, The Netherlands
Technology, Sociology of

Michael Billig, Loughborough University
Prejudice

R.D. Collison Black, Queen's University
Belfast
Malthus, Thomas Robert (1766–1834)

Christopher Bliss, Nuffield College,
Oxford
Economics

David Bloor, University of Edinburgh
*Wittgenstein, Ludwig Josef Johann
(1889–1951)*

Lawrence A. Boland, Simon Fraser
University, Canada
Neo-classical Economics

Tilman Börgers, University College
London
Game Theory

John R. Bowen, Washington University,
St Louis
Religion

Peter J. Bowler, Queen's University
Belfast
Darwin, Charles (1809–82)

Pascal Boyer, Washington University in
St Louis
Symbolism

Michael Bracher, Sydney
Population Projections

Craig Brandist, Sheffield University
Hegemony

Margaret Bray, London School of
Economics and Political Science
Rational Expectations

Andrew Britton, National Institute of
Economic and Social Research, London
Macroeconomic Policy

Archie Brown, University of Oxford
Political Culture

Stanley C. Brubaker, Colgate University
Judicial Process

Ann Buchanan, University of Oxford
Social Work

Peter Bull, University of York, UK
Non-verbal Communication

Martin Bulmer, University of Surrey
Ethics in Social Research

Valerie Bunce, Cornell University
Authoritarian and Totalitarian Systems

Richard C.K. Burdekin, Claremont
McKenna College
Inflation and Deflation

Robert G. Burgess, University of
Leicester
Methods of Social Research

Peter Burke, University of Cambridge
*Annales School; Cultural History;
History*

Michael L. Burton, University of
California, Irvine
Division of Labour by Sex

W.F. Bynum, Wellcome Institute for the
History of Medicine
Medicine, History of

John C. Caldwell, Australian National
University
*Demographic Transition; Fertility;
Population History*

Craig Calhoun, New York University and
President of the Social Science Research
Council, New York
Radicalism; Social Science

Fenella Cannell, London School of
Economics and Political Science
Patriarchy

Margaret Canovan, University of Keele
Populism

Forrest Capie, City University, London
International Monetary System

James G. Carrier, Oxford Brookes and
Indiana Universities
Orientalism

Michael Carrithers, University of
Durham
Person

Paul Cartledge, University of Cambridge
*Aristotle (384–322 BCE); Plato
(c.427–c.348 BCE)*

Rosalind D. Cartwright, Rush-
Presbyterian-St Luke's Medical Center,
Chicago
Dreams; Sleep

Mark Casson, University of Reading
*Entrepreneurship; Multinational
Enterprises*

William J. Chambliss, George
Washington University
Crime and Delinquency

John Charvet, London School of
Economics and Political Science
Freedom

Victoria Chick, University College
London
Money; Money, Quantity Theory of

Dennis Chong, Northwestern University
Collective Action

Claudio Ciborra, London School of
Economics and Political Science
Transaction Costs

Eve V. Clark, Stanford University
First-language Acquisition

Lindsey M. Clark, University of Chicago
Attitudes

Margaret Clark-Plaskie, Empire State
College
Life-span Development

John Cleland, London School of Hygiene
and Tropical Medicine
Demographic Surveys

Robin Cohen, University of Warwick
Migration

Stanley Cohen, London School of Economics and Political Science
Criminology

David Colander, Middlebury College
Law of Returns

David Collard, University of Bath
Externalities

Andrew M. Colman, University of Leicester
Personality; Psychology; Social Psychology

Max Coltheart, Macquarie University, Australia
Cognitive Neuropsychology; Dyslexia

Martin A. Conway, University of Bristol
Memory

Thomas F. Cooley, Stern School of Business, New York University
Business Cycles

Colin Cooper, Queen's University Belfast
Personality Assessment; Projective Tests

Denis Cosgrove, University of California at Los Angeles
Landscape

Frank A. Cowell, London School of Economics and Political Science
Distribution of Incomes and Wealth; Human Capital; Income Distribution, Theory of

N.F.R. Crafts, London School of Economics and Political Science
Industrial Revolutions

David de la Croix, Université Catholique de Louvain, Belgium
Economic Growth

Thomas J. Csordas, Case Western Reserve University
Body

John Curtice, University of Strathclyde
Government; Public Opinion Polls

Regna Darnell, University of Western Ontario
Boas, Franz (1858–1942)

J. Davis, All Souls College, Oxford
Exchange

Stuart Davis, Indiana University
Linguistics

David V. Day, Pennsylvania State University
Industrial and Organizational Psychology

Rutledge M. Dennis, George Mason University
Racism

Donald Denoon, Australian National University
Colonialism

Quy-Toan Do, The World Bank
Asymmetric Information

R. Emerson Dobash, University of Manchester
Domestic Violence

Russell P. Dobash, University of Manchester
Domestic Violence

Patrick Doreian, University of Pittsburgh
Mathematical Models

Keith Dowding, London School of Economics and Political Science
Prisoners' Dilemma

James S. Duncan, University of Cambridge
Cultural Geography

William Dutton, University of Oxford
Information Society

Bernhard Ebbinghaus, Max Planck
Institute for the Study of Societies,
Cologne, Germany
Trade Unions

Thráinn Eggertsson, University of
Iceland
Institutional Economics

Ed Elbers, University of Utrecht
Piaget, Jean (1896–1980)

R.F. Ellen, University of Kent
Ecology

Anthony Elliott, University of the West of
England
Psychoanalysis

Richard Elliott, University of Warwick
Consumer Behaviour

Stanley L. Engerman, University of
Rochester
Cliometrics; Economic History

Thomas Hylland Eriksen, University of
Oslo
Social Anthropology

Milton J. Esman, Cornell University
Ethnic Politics

Mary Evans, University of Kent
Women's Studies

Douglas C. Ewbank, University of
Pennsylvania
Mortality

Michael W. Eysenck, Royal Holloway
College, University of London
Activation and Arousal

Walter Feinberg, University of Illinois,
Urbana-Champaign
Education

Rita Felski, University of Virginia
Cultural Studies

W.L.F. Felstiner, University of California,
Santa Barbara, and Cardiff University
Sociolegal Studies

Robert Fildes, Lancaster University
Forecasting and Prediction

Agneta H. Fischer, University of
Amsterdam
Emotion

Joshua A. Fishman, *Emeritus*, Yeshiva
University
Language and Culture

Ronald Frankenberg, Brunel University
Medical Anthropology

Colin Fraser, University of Cambridge
Group Dynamics

Lawrence Freedman, King's College,
University of London
War Studies

Christopher French, Goldsmiths'
College, University of London
Parapsychology

Bruno S. Frey, University of Zurich
Public Choice; Public Goods

Jonathan Friedman, Ecole des Hautes
Etudes en Sciences Sociales, Paris
Postmodernism

Victoria A. Fromkin, *formerly* University
of California at Los Angeles
Language

Marie Gaille-Nikodimov, CNRS, Lyon
Machiavelli, Niccolò (1469–1527)

Giulio M. Gallarotti, Wesleyan
University
Gold Standard

Leela Gandhi, La Trobe University,
Australia
Postcolonialism

David Garland, New York University
Social Control

Alan Garnham, University of Sussex
Artificial Intelligence; Connectionism

C.A. Gearty, London School of
Economics and Political Science
Human Rights

Viktor Gecas, Purdue University
Self-Concept

Ernest Gellner, *formerly* University of
Cambridge, Central European University
Reason, Rationality and Rationalism

Nigel Gilbert, University of Surrey
Computer Simulation

K.J. Gilhooly, University of Paisley
Problem-solving; Thinking

J.A. Goddard, University of Bradford
Childcare

Anne Marie Goetz, University of Sussex
Accountability

David. B. Goldstein, University College
London
Population Genetics

Jack A. Goldstone, George Mason
University
Revolutions

Erich Goode, University of Maryland
Drug Use

John Goyder, University of Waterloo
Questionnaires; Sample Surveys

Harvey J. Graff, University of Texas, San
Antonio
Literacy

Ryken Grattet, University of California,
Davis
Sociolegal Studies

Sarah Green, University of Manchester
Patriarchy

Simon Green, Birkbeck College,
University of London
Physiological Psychology

Keith Grint, University of Oxford
Industrial Sociology

Stephen Gudeman, University of
Minnesota
Economic Anthropology

Adrian Guelke, Queen's University
Belfast
Terrorism

Guang Guo, University of North
Carolina, Chapel Hill
Event–History Analysis

Claude Hagège, Ecole Pratique des
Hautes Etudes
Saussure, Ferdinand de (1857–1913)

Lesley A. Hall, Wellcome Library for the
History and Understanding of Medicine,
London
Sexual Behaviour

Thomas D. Hall, DePauw University
World-System Analysis

A.H. Halsey, Nuffield College, Oxford
Equality

Koichi Hamada, Yale University
Financial Crisis

J. Daniel Hammond, Wake Forest
University
*Chicago School; Friedman, Milton
(1912–)*

Richard Handler, University of Virginia
Culture

Ulf Hannerz, Stockholm University
City

Barbara Harrell-Bond, American
University in Cairo
Refugees

David M. Harrington, University of
California, Santa Cruz
Creativity

Meridy Harris, University of Kent
Feminist Theory; Women

S. Alexander Haslam, University of Exeter
Leadership; Stereotypes; Stigma

Haim Hazan, University of Tel-Aviv
Total Institutions

Suzette Heald, Brunel University
Rites of Passage

Albert I. Hermalin, University of
Michigan
Ageing

Paul M. Heywood, University of
Nottingham
Corruption

Richard Higgott, Warwick University
Globalization

Paul Hirst, *formerly* University of
London
Socialism

Peter S. Hlebowitsh, University of Iowa
Dewey, John (1859–1952)

Peter Holmes, University of Sussex
Planning, Economic

Simon Hornblower, University College
London
Herodotus (c.480–420 BCE)

Anthony Horsley, London School of
Economics and Political Science
Marginal Analysis

Jennifer L. Hudson, Macquarie
University, Sydney, Australia
Cognitive Behavioural Therapy

Richard Hyman, London School of
Economics and Political Science
Industrial Relations

David Ingleby, Utrecht University
*Developmental Psychology; Mental
Health*

Tim Ingold, University of Aberdeen
Pastoralism

Norman Ireland, University of Warwick
Monopoly

Alan Irwin, Brunel University
Environment, Sociology of; Risk Society

Jonathan I. Israel, Institute for Advanced
Study, Princeton, NJ
Braudel, Fernand (1902–85)

Joyce Jacobsen, Wesleyan University
Economic Man

I.C. Jarvie, York University, Canada
Philosophy of the Social Sciences

Richard Jenkins, University of Sheffield
Disability; Habitus; Social Construction

Robert Jenkins, University of Sussex
Accountability

Per-Olov Johansson, Stockholm School
of Economics
Efficiency (Economic)

Geraint Johnes, Lancaster University
Factors of Production

Christopher Johnson, University of
Nottingham
Structuralism

Nuala C. Johnson, Queen's University
Belfast
Cultural Geography

R.J. Johnston, University of Bristol
Geography; Place; Region; Spatial Analysis

Edward E. Jones, *formerly* Princeton University
Social Psychology

Grant Jordan, University of Aberdeen
Interest Groups and Lobbying

Roger Jowell, Social and Community Planning Research and City University, London
Public Opinion Polls

P.N. Junankar, University of Western Sydney, Australia
Employment and Unemployment

Stephen Kalberg, Boston University
Weber, Max (1864–1920)

S.M. Ravi Kanbur, Cornell University
Maximization; Prices, Theory of

Victor Karady, Centre National de la Recherche Scientifique, Paris
Durkheim, Emile (1858–1917)

Harry C. Katz, Cornell University
Collective Bargaining

Dennis Kavanagh, University of Liverpool
Elections; Voting

John Kay, London School of Economics and Political Science
Strategic Management

Allen C. Kelley, Duke University
Population and Resources

Douglas Kellner, University of California, Los Angeles
Frankfurt School; Habermas, Jürgen (1929–)

Philip C. Kendall, Temple University
Cognitive Behavioural Therapy

Nathan Keyfitz, Harvard University and the International Institute for Applied Systems Analysis
Demography

J.E. King, La Trobe University, Australia
Keynesian Economics

Paul Klemperer, University of Oxford
Auctions

Paul Kline, University of Exeter
Intelligence and Intelligence Testing

Edward Knotek II, University of Michigan, Ann Arbor
Stagflation

C.A. Knox Lovell, University of Georgia
Production and Cost Frontiers

Stephen M. Kosslyn, Harvard University
Mental Imagery

David R. Krathwohl, Syracuse University
Experimental Design

David A. Kravitz, George Mason University
Affirmative Action

Robert P. Kraynak, Colgate University
Hobbes, Thomas (1588–1679)

Louis Kriesberg, Syracuse University
Conflict; Conflict Resolution

P. Krishna, Brown University
World Trade Organization

Joel Kuipers, George Washington University
Identity

Krishan Kumar, University of Virginia
Anarchism; Civil Society; Futurology; Postindustrial Society; Utopianism

Howard Kunreuther, The Wharton School, University of Pennsylvania
Risk Analysis

Adam Kuper, Brunel University
Anthropology; Primitive Society

Steinar Kvale, University of Aarhus, Denmark
Interviews (Qualitative)

Reed Larson, University of Illinois, Urbana-Champaigne
Adolescence

Peter Lassman, University of Birmingham
Phenomenology

John Lazarus, University of Newcastle
Altruism and Co-operation

William Lazonick, University of Massachusetts, Lowell, and the European Institute of Business Administration (INSEAD)
Corporate Enterprise

Ronald Lee, University of California at Berkeley
Demography

Julian Leff, Institute of Psychiatry, King's College, London
Transcultural Psychiatry

David Lehmann, University of Cambridge
Fundamentalism

Daniel S. Levine, University of Texas at Arlington
Neural Networks

Paul Lewis, Cambridge University
Hayek, Friedrich A. (1899–1992)

Arend Lijphart, University of California, San Diego
Parties, Political

David T. Llewellyn, Loughborough University
Financial Regulation; Financial System; Securitization

Brian J. Loasby, University of Stirling
Firm, Theory of

Grahame Lock, Radboud University, Nijmegen, The Netherlands
Alienation; Foucault, Michel (1926–84)

George Loewenstein, Carnegie Mellon University
Behavioural Economics

Michael B. Loewy, University of South Florida
Free Trade

Karl-Gustaf Löfgren, University of Umeå, Sweden
Efficiency (Economic)

Paul A. Longley, University College London
Geographical Information Systems

Steven Lukes, New York University
Relativism

Michael Lynch, Cornell University
Ethnomethodology

David Lyons, Boston University
Utilitarianism

John Van Maanen, Massachusetts Institute of Technology
Ethnography

Dean MacCannell, University of California, Davis
Semiotics

Alan Macfarlane, University of Cambridge
Individualism

John McGarry, Queen's University, Kingston, Canada
Federalism and Federation; Secession

Henry M. McHenry, University of California, Davis
Human Evolution

C. Nicholas McKinney, Rhodes College
Experimental Economics

N.J. Mackintosh, University of Cambridge
Conditioning, Classical and Operant

David McLellan, Goldsmiths' College, University of London
Marx, Karl Heinrich (1818–83)

Andrew K. MacLeod, Royal Holloway College, University of London
Suicide

W. Bentley MacLeod, University of Southern California
Contracts

Klim McPherson, Oxford University
Epidemiology; Public Health

Denis McQuail, University of Southampton
McLuhan, Marshall (1910–80); Mass Media; Media Effects

Joseph Maguire, Loughborough University
Sport, Sociology of

Antony S.R. Manstead, Cardiff University
Emotion

Jonathan Marks, University of North Carolina at Charlotte
Genetics and Behaviour; Race

Jan Marontate, Acadia University, Canada
Art, Sociology of

Peter Marris, Yale University
Community Development

David Marsden, London School of Economics and Political Science
Labour Market Analysis

Matt Matravers, University of York, UK
Justice, Distributive; Rawls, John (1921–2002)

Carrie Matthews, University of North Carolina
Cultural Anthropology

Ruth Matthias, University of Maryland
Conservation

Andreas Mayer, Max Planck Institute for the History of Science (Berlin)
Freud, Sigmund (1856–1939)

Andrew R. Mayes, University of Liverpool
Cognitive Neuroscience

Alan Maynard, University of York, UK
Health Economics

Ken Menzies, University of Guelph, Canada
Parsons, Talcott (1902–79)

J.S. Metcalfe, University of Manchester
Evolutionary Economics

Alfred G. Meyer, University of Michigan
Communism

David Miller, University of Oxford
Political Theory

Terence C. Mills, Loughborough University
Econometrics

Robert Millward, University of Manchester
Mixed Economy; Nationalization

Patrick Minford, Cardiff Business School, Cardiff University
Capital, Credit and Money Markets

Kenneth Minogue, London School of Economics and Political Science
Burke, Edmund (1729–97); Conservatism

James H. Mittelman, American University, Washington, DC
Underdevelopment

Donald Moggridge, University of Toronto
Keynes, John Maynard (1883–1946)

Mark Monmonier, Syracuse University
Cartography

Daniela Montaldi, University of Liverpool
Cognitive Neuroscience

Margaret Moore, Queen's University, Canada
Nationalism

David L. Morgan, Portland State University
Focus Groups

Howard Morphy, Australian National University
Material Culture

Anne Friederike Müller, King's College, London
Bourdieu, Pierre (1930–2002)

Andy Mullineux, University of Birmingham
Interest; Investment; Profit

Abhinay Muthoo, University of Essex
Bargaining

Gareth D. Myles, University of Exeter
Equilibrium

J. Peter Neary, University College Dublin
International Trade

Mark Neocleous, Brunel University
Privacy

Paul Newman, Indiana University
Language

Isak Niehaus, University of Pretoria, South Africa
Witchcraft and Witch-cleansing Movements

Dany Nobus, Brunel University
Lacan, Jacques (1901–81)

Andrew Norris, University of Pennsylvania
Hegel, Georg Wilhelm F. (1770–1831)

Charles Noussair, Emory University
Optimization

Dorothy Noyes, The Ohio State University
Folklore

D.P. O'Brien, University of Durham
Classical Economics

Peter R. Odell, *Emeritus*, Erasmus University, Rotterdam
Energy

Brendan O'Leary, University of Pennsylvania
Consociation; Partition; Political Science; State

D.L. Olmsted, University of California, Davis
Structural Linguistics

Vivienne Orchard, University of Southampton
Derrida, Jacques (1930–)

Carlos P. Otero, University of California, Los Angeles
Chomsky, Noam (1928–)

J.P. Parry, London School of Economics and Political Science
Caste; Taboo

Dorothy Pawluch, McMaster University, Canada
Social Problems

Stanley G. Payne, University of Wisconsin, Madison
Fascism

Terry Peach, University of Manchester
Ricardian Economics; Ricardo, David (1772–1823)

James L. Peacock, University of North Carolina
Cultural Anthropology

David W. Pearce, University College London
Cost–Benefit Analysis; Environmental Economics; Welfare Economics

B. Guy Peters, University of Pittsburgh
Bureaucracy

Mark Philp, University of Oxford
Authority; Power

Harold Alan Pincus, University of Pittsburgh and RAND Corporation
DSM-IV

David Pion-Berlin, University of California, Riverside
Military Regimes

Henry Plotkin, University College London
Evolutionary Psychology

Ken Plummer, University of Essex
Homosexualities; Labelling Theory; Queer Theory

Christopher Pollitt, Erasmus University, Rotterdam
Public Administration

Michael Poole, Cardiff University
Business Studies

Jonathan Potter, Loughborough University
Discourse Analysis

Jean Pouillon, Paris
Lévi-Strauss, Claude (1908–)

Cliff Pratten, Trinity Hall, Cambridge
Economies of Scale

Michael Prestwich, University of Durham
Feudalism

John Purcell, University of Bath
Human Resource Management

Martha Ratliff, Wayne State University
Historical Linguistics

Alastair J. Read, University of Cambridge
Marxist History

Isaac Reed, Yale University
Positivism

R. Reiner, London School of Economics and Political Science
Police and Policing

Stanley A. Renshon, The City University of New York
Political Psychology

Jack Revell, University of Wales
Banking

John T.E. Richardson, The Open University
Cognitive Psychology; Cognitive Science

James C. Riley, Indiana University
Morbidity

Bruce Robbins, Columbia University
Intellectuals

Roland Robertson, University of Aberdeen
Sects and Cults

Mark Robinson, University of Sussex
Governance

Paul Rock, London School of Economics and Political Science
Deviance; Symbolic Interactionism

Paul Rogers, University of Bradford
Peace Studies

Paul M. Roman, University of Georgia
Alcoholism and Alcohol Abuse

Michael Roper, University of Essex
Oral History

Nikolas Rose, London School of
Economics and Political Science
Genomics

Frederick Rosen, University College
London
Bentham, Jeremy (1748–1832)

Robert Ross, University of Leiden
Slavery

Alvin E. Roth, Harvard University and
Harvard Business School
Experimental Economics

David F. Ruccio, University of Notre
Dame
Marxian Economics

Roy J. Ruffin, University of Houston,
Texas
Balance of Payments

John Rundell, University of Melbourne
Modernization

William McKinley Runyan, University
of California, Berkeley
Life History

Peter H. Russell, University of Toronto
Constitutions and Constitutionalism

Matthias Ruth, University of Maryland
Conservation

Maurice Salles, Université de Caen
Social Choice

Todd Sandler, University of Southern
California
Defence Economics

Gigi Santow, Sydney
*Life Tables and Survival Analysis; Vital
Statistics*

Austin Sarat, Amherst College
Law

Lucio Sarno, University of Warwick,
Centre for Economic Policy Research
(CEPR), International Monetary Fund
Exchange Rate

Donald Sassoon, Queen Mary College,
University of London
Social Democracy

Michael Saward, The Open University
Democracy

Lawrence A. Scaff, Wayne State
University, Detroit
Legitimacy

Philippe Schmitter, European University
Institute, Florence
Democratization

Hans Peter Schmitz, Syracuse University
International Relations

Sergio L. Schmukler, World Bank
Financial Contagion

Friedrich Schneider, Johannes Kepler
University of Linz, Austria
Informal/Shadow Economy

Peter P. Schweitzer, University of Alaska
Fairbanks
Kinship

Jacqueline Scott, University of
Cambridge
Family

John Scott, University of Essex
Networks, Social

John Sharp, University of Pretoria,
South Africa
Tribe

Wes Sharrock, University of Manchester
Actor, Social; Structure and Agency

William H. Shaw, San José State
University, California
Marx's Theory of History and Society

Ronald Shone, University of Stirling
Economic Dynamics

Oz Shy, University of Haifa
Industrial Organization

S. Siebert, University of Birmingham
Supply-side Economics

Paul Sillitoe, University of Durham
Cargo Cults

Jerome L. Singer, Yale University
Fantasy

Andrew Skinner, Glasgow University
Smith, Adam (1723–90)

Carol Smart, University of Leeds
Divorce

Peter Smith, University of Sussex
Cross-cultural Psychology

Peter K. Smith, Goldsmiths' College,
University of London
Child Development

Charles D. Spielberger, University of
South Florida, Tampa
Anger, Hostility and Aggression; Anxiety

Elizabeth A. Stanko, Royal Holloway
College, University of London
Violence

Douglas G. Steigerwald, University of
California, Santa Barbara
Consumption Function

Charles Stewart, University College
London
Syncretism

Alan A. Stone, Harvard University
Unconscious

John Stone, Boston University
Ethnicity

M. Stone, University College London
Statistical Reasoning

J.J. Suh, Cornell University
International Institutions

Patrick Sullivan, University of Illinois,
Urbana-Champaign
Adolescence

G.M.P. Swann, University of Nottingham
Research and Development (R&D)

George Symeonidis, University of Essex
Competition Policy; Markets

Conrad Taeuber, Georgetown University
Census of Population

Sidney Tarrow, Cornell University
Social Movements

J. Edward Taylor, University of
California, Davis
Agricultural Economics

Mark Taylor, University of Liverpool
Macroeconomic Theory

Alice G.B. ter Meulen, University of
Groningen, The Netherlands
Semantics

Pat Thane, University of Sussex
Social History

H.S. Thayer, City University of
New York
James, William (1842–1910)

Jonathan Thomas, University of
Warwick
Pareto Efficiency

John B. Thompson, University of Cambridge
Hermeneutics; Public Sphere

Rodney Tiffen, University of Sydney
Media and Politics

E. Ahmet Tonak, Simon's Rock College of Bard
National Accounts

Christina Toren, Brunel University
Childhood

Jean Tournon, University of Grenoble
Citizenship; Representation, Political

Peter Townsend, London School of Economics and Political Science
Basic Needs; Deprivation and Relative Deprivation; Poverty

John Toye, University of Oxford
Economic Development

Bruce G. Trigger, McGill University
State, Origins of

Stephen Trotter, University of Hull
Privatization; Regulation

Michael Twaddle, Institute of Commonwealth Studies, University of London
Imperialism

John Urry, University of Lancaster
Reference Groups

Elizabeth R. Valentine, Royal Holloway College, University of London
Mind

Peter Vallentyne, University of Missouri
Libertarianism

Frédéric Vandenberghe, University for Humanist Studies, The Netherlands
Sociology: New Theoretical Developments

Joan Vincent, Barnard College, Columbia University
Political Anthropology

Penny S. Visser, University of Chicago
Attitudes

Eftihia Voutira, University of Makedonia, Thessaloniki, Greece
Refugees

Nicholas J. Wade, University of Dundee
Sensation and Perception

Nigel Walker, University of Cambridge
Penology

Richard Wall, ESRC Cambridge Group for the History of Population and Social Structure
Household

P.A. Watt, University of Birmingham
Supply-side Economics

Martin Weale, National Institute of Economic and Social Research, London
Productivity

Gretchen R. Webber, University of Texas, Austin
Gender, Sociology of

Eric D. Weitz, University of Minnesota
Genocide

John K. Whitaker, University of Virginia
Marshall, Alfred (1842–1924)

Douglas R. White, University of California, Irvine
Division of Labour by Sex

Geoffrey M. White, University of Hawai'i, Honolulu
Psychological Anthropology

Geoffrey Whittington, International Accounting Standards Board, London
Accounting

Christine L.R. Williams, University of Texas, Austin
Gender, Sociology of

Fiona Williams, University of Leeds
Welfare State

Deirdre Wilson, University College London
Pragmatics

Michael Winkelman, Arizona State University
Shamanism

Ronald Wintrobe, University of Western Ontario
Political Economy

R. Wodak, University of Vienna
Sociolinguistics

Robert Wokler, Yale University
Rousseau, Jean-Jacques (1712–78); Social Contract

Steve Woolgar, Oxford University
Reflexivity; Science, Sociology of

Michael J. Wright, Brunel University
Consciousness; Vision

Guillaume Wunsch, University of Louvain, Belgium
Age–Sex Structure; Cohort Analysis

Kaoru Yamamoto, University of Colorado, Denver
Educational Psychology

John W. Yolton, Rutgers University
Locke, John (1632–1704)

Jock Young, Middlesex University
Social Exclusion

Michael W. Young, Australian National University
Malinowski, Bronislaw Kasper (1884–1942)

Entries listed by discipline and subject

ANTHROPOLOGY
COGNITIVE PSYCHOLOGY AND COGNITIVE SCIENCE
CRIMINOLOGY AND LAW
CULTURAL STUDIES
DEMOGRAPHY
ECONOMICS
EDUCATION
EVOLUTION
GENDER
GEOGRAPHY
HEALTH AND MEDICINE
HISTORY

INDUSTRIAL RELATIONS AND MANAGEMENT
LANGUAGE, LINGUISTICS AND SEMIOTICS
MENTAL HEALTH
METHODS OF SOCIAL RESEARCH
PHILOSOPHY
POLITICAL THEORY
POLITICS AND GOVERNMENT
PSYCHOLOGY
SOCIAL PROBLEMS AND SOCIAL WELFARE
SOCIOLOGY

ANTHROPOLOGY

Anthropology
Boas, Franz
Body
Bourdieu, Pierre
Cannibalism
Cargo cults
Caste
Childhood
Community
Cross-cultural psychology
Cultural anthropology
Culture
Darwin, Charles
Division of labour by sex
Durkheim, Emile
Ecology
Economic anthropology
Environment
Ethnicity
Ethnography
Exchange
Family
Folklore
Gender, sociology of
Genealogies
Genetics and behaviour
Habitus
Herodotus
Household
Human evolution
Hunters and gatherers

Sensation and perception

GENDER

Age–sex structure
Body
Division of labour by sex
Domestic violence
Family
Feminist theory
Fertility
Gender, sociology of
Genetics and behaviour
Homosexualities
Incest
Marriage
Patriarchy
Sexual behaviour
Women
Women's studies

GEOGRAPHY

Cartography
Cultural geography
Economic geography
Energy
Environment
Geographical information systems
Geography
Landscape
Place
Population and resources
Region
Spatial analysis

HEALTH AND MEDICINE

Age–sex structure
Ageing
Body
Childcare
Demographic transition
Disability
Epidemiology

Fertility
Genomics
Gerontology, social
Health economics
Life tables and survival analysis
Medical anthropology
Medical sociology
Medicine, history of
Mental health
Morbidity
Mortality
Population genetics
Psychoanalysis
Public health
Sexual behaviour
Sleep
Suicide
Transcultural psychiatry

HISTORY

Annales School
Braudel, Fernand
Case study
Cliometrics
Cultural history
Economic history
Feudalism
Hegel, Georg Wilhelm F.
Herodotus
Historical linguistics
History
Hume, David
Industrial revolutions
Machiavelli, Niccolò
Marx, Karl Heinrich
Marx's theory of history and society
Marxist history
Medicine, history of
Memory, social
Oral history
Population history
Postcolonialism

Psychoanalysis
Psychology
Sleep
Stigma
Suicide
Unconscious

METHODS OF SOCIAL RESEARCH

Cartography
Case study
Census of population
Cliometrics
Cohort analysis
Computer simulation
Demographic surveys
Discourse analysis
Ethics in social research
Ethnography
Ethnomethodology
Event–history analysis
Experimental design
Focus groups
Forecasting and prediction
Genealogies
Geographical information systems
Intelligence and intelligence tests
Interviews (qualitative)
Life history
Life tables and survival analysis
Marginal analysis
Mathematical models
Methods of social research
Networks, social
Oral history
Personality assessment
Philosophy of the social sciences
Population projections
Projective tests
Public opinion polls
Questionnaires
Reflexivity

Sample surveys
Spatial analysis
Statistical reasoning

PHILOSOPHY

Aristotle
Bentham, Jeremy
Burke, Edmund
Consciousness
Derrida, Jacques
Dewey, John
Foucault, Michel
Frankfurt School
Habermas, Jürgen
Hayek, Friedrich A.
Hegel, Georg Wilhelm F.
Hermeneutics
Hobbes, Thomas
Human rights
Hume, David
James, William
Justice, distributive
Locke, John
Mill, John Stuart
Mind
Phenomenology
Philosophy of the social sciences
Plato
Political theory
Positivism
Postmodernism
Poststructuralism
Rational choice (action) theory
Rational expectations
Rawls, John
Reason, rationality and rationalism
Reflexivity
Relativism
Rousseau, Jean-Jacques
Social construction
Social contract

PSYCHOLOGY

A

ACCOUNTABILITY

Accountability describes a relationship between power-holders and those affected by their actions, and consists of two key elements: 'answerability' (making power-holders explain their actions) and 'enforceability' (punishing poor or criminal performance) (Schedler 1999). Accountability is often conceived as operating along two dimensions, the vertical and the horizontal. The 'vertical' relationship between citizens and the state can be either formal (through electoral systems) or informal (through lobbying and public advocacy by associations). The 'horizontal' relationship involves one public authority scrutinizing the activities of another – for instance, legislative oversight of executive agencies, or the capacity of specialized authorities (ombudsmen, anti-corruption agencies) to investigate charges of malfeasance (O'Donnell 1999).

Qualifying adjectives are often placed in front of the term accountability to specify the *domain of activity* within which scrutiny is to take place, the *type of actors* being held to account, or a *common standard* against which performance is to be assessed. Thus 'fiscal accountability' refers to a domain of activity: the use of public resources and the formal systems of financial reporting and auditing through which spending authorities are monitored. 'Administrative accountability' refers to a specific variety of actor: bureaucrats, who are obliged to answer to elected officials and to adhere to the rules that define their reporting relationships with superiors and subordinates. 'Legal (or 'constitutional') accountability' refers to an external *standard*: it is enforced by the judiciary, which ensures that state agents neither exceed their legal authority nor derogate from their obligations towards citizens.

The creation of democratic institutions requires the establishment of rules governing relations of accountability. Which individuals, groups, or institutions are entitled to demand answers, and from whom? Which mechanisms are to be used in effecting this right? To what standards shall power-holders be held? Which agencies shall be charged with enforcing sanctions? Because societies change over time – as new actors emerge, new techniques for exercising power are deployed, and new standards for assessing performance become accepted – democratic systems must also specify the means by which the rules governing accountability relationships are to be continuously reinvented. This is perhaps the most difficult challenge facing those seeking to design systems of democratic accountability.

Indeed, the need to adapt to change has been a central feature of the recent history of accountability. Democracy's 'third wave' during the final quarter of the twentieth century (Huntington 1991) led many newly enfranchised groups to hope for a more active role in holding politicians and bureaucrats accountable – in two senses. First, in obliging public authorities to engage in frequent, non-arbitrary, transparent and interactive processes of reason-giving, in which their actions are explained and justified against commonly agreed standards of morality and effectiveness. And, second, in exercising the right to have sanctions imposed on public authorities found to have behaved immorally or performed ineffectively. These aspirations, however, have largely been unfulfilled. Developing World democracies, and indeed the more established democracies in industrialized countries, have experienced what might be called a crisis of accountability – a perception created by pervasive corruption, poor decision-making, and a feeling that public actors are unresponsive to ordinary citizens. Elections, the primary means for holding politicians accountable, are widely considered inadequate, whether because of procedural defects in voting systems or an absence of programmatic alternatives between political parties. Moreover, structural transformations in the nature of governance – which include, but are not limited to, the privatization of some state functions – have blurred lines of accountability, making it difficult to establish which actors hold ultimate responsibility for certain types of policies or services. The ongoing process of globalization has introduced a range of new power-holders, such as multinational corporations and transnational social movements, which slip through the jurisdictional cracks separating national authorities, yet whose actions have a profound impact on people's lives. The influence exercised over economic policy in poor countries by such multilateral institutions as the World Bank, the International Monetary Fund and the World Trade Organization has also reduced the regulatory autonomy of many governments. This has made lines of accountability even harder to trace.

The challenges posed by imperfect democratization and unbalanced globalization have produced a contemporary interest around the world in strengthening accountability institutions, such as electoral systems, courts, human rights commissions and auditing agencies. This is the core of the 'good governance' agenda promoted by many aid agencies. But these efforts are increasingly viewed as insufficient for the scale of accountability-related deprivations faced by the world's poor. In response, the 1990s witnessed a proliferation of accountability-seeking. Despite the undeniable diversity among governance experiments that have sought to improve accountability, and the widely differing contexts in which they have been undertaken, it is possible to discern the defining characteristics of a new accountability agenda in the making (Goetz and Jenkins 2004). Existing mainly in fragments of conceptual innovation and practical experiment, the four basic elements of this agenda are nevertheless increasingly visible: (1) a more direct role for ordinary people and their associations in demanding accountability across (2) a more diverse set of jurisdictions, using (3) an expanded repertoire of methods, and on the basis of (4) a more exacting standard of social justice.

Examples of citizens engaging more directly in accountability efforts are citizen-managed public audits of local government spending (Jenkins and Goetz 1999), participatory budgeting and spending reviews (Abers 1998), or Public Interest Litigation to prosecute, often on behalf of socially excluded groups, public and private actors for abuses of power (Dembowski 2001). Jurisdictional shifts have spurred the development of new techniques. At a global level, the International Criminal Court provides a new (though as yet not universal) arena in which abusers of power can be made to answer to their far-flung victims. At a local level, democratic decentralization makes viable new, more direct, methods for ensuring accountability. Cyberspace even offers a deterritorialized terrain for the advancement of complaints against power-holders, and a means for the pursuit of concerted mass action to demand answers and even impose sanctions such as consumer boycotts.

But it is the question of what power-holders are being held accountable *for* that is the dimension along which accountability is being most dramatically reinvented. New popular understandings of accountability are emerging that go beyond the conventional use of the term. Accountability systems are increasingly expected not just to satisfy concerns with process integrity, but also to respond to norms of social justice.

ANNE MARIE GOETZ AND ROBERT JENKINS
UNIVERSITY OF SUSSEX

References

Abers, R. (1998) 'From clientalism to cooperation: Local government, participatory policy, and civic organizing in Porto Alegre, Brazil', *Politics and Society* 26(4): 511–38.

Dembowski, H. (2001) *Taking the State to Court: Public Interest Litigation and the Public Sphere in Metropolitan India*, New Delhi.

Goetz, A.M. and Jenkins, R. (2004) *Reinventing Accountability: Making Democracy Work for the Poor*, London.

Huntington, S. (1991) *The Third Wave: Democratization in the Late Twentieth Century*, Norman, OK.

Jenkins, R. and Goetz, A.M. (1999) 'Accounts and accountability: Theoretical implications of the right to information movement in India', *Third World Quarterly* 20(3): 603–22.

O'Donnell, G. (1999) 'Horizontal accountability in

new democracies', in A. Schedler, L. Diamond and M.F. Plattner (eds) *The Self-Restraining State: Power and Accountability in New Democracies*, London.

Schedler, A. (1999) 'Conceptualizing accountability', in A. Schedler, L. Diamond and M.F. Plattner (eds) *The Self-Restraining State: Power and Accountability in New Democracies*, London.

SEE ALSO: democracy; democratization; governance; public administration

ACCOUNTING

Accounting deals with the provision of information about the economic activities of various accounting entities, the largest of which is the whole economy, for which national accounts are prepared. However, the traditional province of the accountant is the smaller unit, typically a business firm. Here, a distinction is often made between financial accounting and management accounting.

Financial accounting deals with the provision of information to providers of finance (shareholders and creditors) and other interested parties who do not participate in the management of the firm (such as trade unions and consumer groups). This usually takes the form of a balance sheet (a statement of assets and claims thereon at a point in time), and a profit and loss account (a statement of revenue, expenses and profit over a period of time), supplemented by various other statements and notes. The form of financial accounting by companies is, in most countries, laid down by statute, and the contents are usually checked and certified independently by auditors. In many countries, there are also accounting standards laid down by the accounting profession or by the independent bodies that it supports, such as the United States Financial Accounting Standards Board, which determine the form and content of financial accounts. The standards of the International Accounting Standards Board (IASB) have been adopted in an increasing number of countries in recent years, particularly for the accounts of companies whose securities are listed on public stock exchanges. This process was encouraged by the support of International Organization of Securities Commissions (the international group of securities market regulators) given in 2000 and by the decision of the European Commission to require the adoption of IASB standards from 2005 onwards for the accounts of companies listed on stock exchanges within the European Union.

The auditing and regulation of financial accounts is a natural response to the potential moral hazard problem arising from the information asymmetry that exists between managers and providers of finance. In the absence of such quality assurance, users of accounts would have little confidence in the honesty and accuracy of statements that could be distorted by management to represent its performance in the most favourable light. The issue of investor confidence in financial accounts was brought dramatically to public attention by the collapse of Enron, one of the largest and apparently most successful of corporations in the USA, in 2001. The collapse was precipitated by a dramatic downward restatement of past profits due to the inclusion of losses that had previously been treated as 'off-balance sheet', i.e. they occurred in financial vehicles that had been (incorrectly) regarded as being outside the scope of Enron's group accounts. A number of other 'accounting scandals' were revealed in the USA and elsewhere, following the Enron case. Although it is widely believed that the Enron case involved failure to follow accounting standards, rather than failure of the standards themselves, it led to a widespread call for simpler, more transparent, principles-based rather than rules-based standards. It also drew attention to the importance of strict enforcement of accounting standards, particularly by auditors. These concerns are justified by the fact that the 'scandals' are merely the extreme of a well-established practice of 'creative accounting', i.e. using any latitude provided by accounting standards to portray the performance of the reporting entity in the most favourable possible light. Some of the devices used by creative accountants are illustrated in the books by Griffiths (1995) and Smith (1996).

Management accounting is concerned with the provision of information to management, to assist with planning, decision-making and control within the business. Because planning and decision-making are inevitably directed to the future, management accounting often involves making future projections, usually called budgets. Important applications of this are capital budgeting, which deals with the appraisal of investments, and cash budgeting, which deals with the projection of future cash inflows and outflows, and the consequent financial requirements of the entity.

Management accounting is also concerned with controlling and appraising the outcome of past plans, for example by analysing costs, and with assessing the economic performance of particular divisions or activities of the entity. Because the demand for management accounting information varies according to the activities, size and management structure of the entity, and because the supply of such information is not subject to statutory regulation or audit, there is a much greater variety both of techniques and of practice in management accounting than in financial accounting. Management has, of course, direct control over the information system of the business, so that formal regulation of the management accounting system is less important. However, within large organizations, there are information asymmetries and potential moral hazard problems between different groups (e.g. between branch managers and head office), and such organizations typically have internal auditing systems to reduce such problems.

Both management accounts and financial accounts derive from an *accounting system* that records the basic data relating to the transactions of the entity. The degree to which management accounting and financial accounting information can both derive from a common set of records depends on the circumstances of the individual accounting entity and, in particular, on the form of its management accounting. However, all accounting systems have a common root in double-entry bookkeeping, a self-balancing system, based on the principle that all assets of the entity ('debits') can be attributed to an owner (a claim on the entity by a creditor or the owners' 'equity' interest in the residual assets of the entity, both of which are 'credits'). This system owes its origin to Italian merchants of the fifteenth century, but it is still fundamental to accounting systems, although records are now often kept on computers, so that debits and credits take the form of different axes of a matrix, rather than different sides of the page in a handwritten ledger. The design of accounting systems to avoid fraud and error is an important aspect of the work of the accountant.

The traditional orientation of accounting was to record transactions at their historical cost, that is, in terms of the monetary units in which transactions took place. Thus, an asset would be recorded at the amount originally paid for it. Inflation and changing prices in recent years have called into question the relevance of historical cost, and inflation accounting has become an important subject. It has been proposed at various times and in different countries that accounts should show current values, that is, the specific current prices of individual assets, or that they should be adjusted by a general price level index to reflect the impact of inflation on the value of the monetary unit, or that a combination of both types of adjustment should be employed. Intervention by standard-setting bodies on this subject has been specifically directed at financial accounting, but it has been hoped that the change of method would also affect management accounting.

Financial accounting has also been affected, in recent years, by an increased public demand for information about business activities often supported by governments. Associated with this has been demand for information outside the scope of traditional profit-oriented accounts, resulting in research and experimentation in such areas as human asset accounting, environmental (or 'green') accounting and corporate social reporting. There has also been more interest in accounting for public-sector activities and not-for-profit organizations. Recent developments in management accounting, facilitated by the increased use of computers, include the greater employment of the mathematical and statistical methods of operational research and greater power to simulate the outcomes of alternative decisions. This development has, however, been matched by a growing interest in behavioural aspects of accounting, for example studies of the human response to budgets and other targets set by management accountants. The whole area of accounting is currently one of rapid change, both in research and in practice.

GEOFFREY WHITTINGTON
INTERNATIONAL ACCOUNTING STANDARDS
BOARD, LONDON

References

Griffiths, I. (1995) *New Creative Accounting: How to Make Your Profits What You Want Them to Be*, London.
Smith, T. (1996) *Accounting for Growth: Stripping the Camouflage from Company Accounts*, 2nd edn, London.

Further reading

Arnold, J., Hope, A., Southworth, A. and Kirkham, L. (1994) *Financial Accounting*, 2nd edn, London.
Arnold, J. and Turley, S. (1996) *Accounting for Management Decisions*, 3rd edn, London.
Ashton, D., Hopper, T. and Scapens, R. (eds) (1995) *Issues in Management Accounting*, 2nd edn, London.
Parker, R.H. (1999) *Understanding Company Financial Statements*, 5th edn, London.
Whittington, G. (1992) *The Elements of Accounting: An Introduction*, Cambridge, UK.

SEE ALSO: cost–benefit analysis; financial regulation; investment; national accounts; profit

ACTIVATION AND AROUSAL

The terms activation and arousal have often been used interchangeably in the psychological literature to describe a continuum ranging from deep sleep at one end to extreme terror or excitement at the other end. This continuum has sometimes been thought of as referring to observed behaviour, but many authorities have argued that arousal should be construed in physiological terms or in terms of an internal psychological state. So far as the physiological approach is concerned, the emphasis has often been placed on the ascending reticular activating system. This system (which plays an important role in regulating states of awareness) is located in the brain-stem and has an alerting effect on the brain.

In recent years, there has been increased questioning of the usefulness of the theoretical constructs of activation and arousal. There are various reasons for this increasing scepticism, some of which are identified here. First, there are serious measurement issues. For example, there are several potential measures of arousal (e.g. heart rate; galvanic skin response), but these measures typically intercorrelate only weakly (Lacey 1967). Second, the relationship between psychophysiological and self-report measures of arousal is generally no more than moderate, indicating that there is no equivalence between the two ways of assessing arousal. Third, it has proven difficult to distinguish clearly between the constructs of activation and arousal. H.J. Eysenck (1967) proposed that the term 'arousal' should be used exclusively with reference to cortical arousal dependent on the reticular activating system, whereas 'activation' should be

used to refer to emotional or autonomic arousal. However, this proposed distinction has received only inconsistent support from relevant research, and it appears that the overlap between arousal and activation as so defined is much greater than was predicted theoretically. Fourth, and perhaps of greatest importance, it has been found that physiological processes (including those of the autonomic nervous system) are considerably more complicated than was previously thought to be the case. As a result, reliance on terms such as 'activation' and 'arousal' serves to provide a drastic oversimplification of a complex reality.

In view of the complexities and uncertainties of physiologically based approaches to arousal and activation, it may be preferable to focus on more psychologically based approaches. Some of the clearest evidence in support of such an approach has occurred in theory and research on emotion. For example, Russell (e.g. Russell and Carroll 1999) has argued that the structure of self-reported affect is two-dimensional. One dimension contrasts unpleasant with pleasant feelings, whereas the second dimension is an arousal dimension ranging from low to high. Intense positive emotion reflects high levels of pleasant feelings and high arousal, and intense negative emotion reflects high levels of unpleasant feelings and high arousal. As Russell and Carroll pointed out, most of the available evidence supports the notion that most affects can be described within a structure consisting of two orthogonal dimensions, although there has been controversy concerning the optimal placement of the dimensions within a two-dimensional space.

MICHAEL W. EYSENCK
ROYAL HOLLOWAY COLLEGE,
UNIVERSITY OF LONDON

References

Eysenck, H.J. (1967) *The Biological Basis of Personality*, Springfield, IL.
Lacey, J.I. (1967) 'Somatic response patterning and stress: Some revisions of activation theory', in M.H. Appley and R. Trumbull (eds) *Psychological Stress*, New York.
Russell, J.A. and Carroll, J.M. (1999) 'The phoenix of bipolarity: Reply to Watson and Tellegen', *Psychological Bulletin* 125: 611–17.

SEE ALSO: anger, hostility and aggression; emotion

ACTOR, SOCIAL

In a way, the issues that are centred on the nature of the social actors run along the main fault lines which fracture sociological thought into the diverse approaches, methods and theories that make it up. However, the nature of the social actor is not itself much discussed and seldom systematically worked upon. Most approaches to sociology manage without any explicit or worked out conception of the social actor. This is perhaps partly because of the anti-individualism of much sociological thought, and the associated supposition that actors can simply be assumed to act in accord with the culture or ideology that is instilled into them, in accord with their interest, or in compliance with the power that regulates them. As a result, 'the social actor' (i.e. the sociologist's conception of a member of society) is apt to be an underdeveloped and *ad hoc* construction.

The most extensive and explicit discussion of the social actor has been predominantly driven by essentially epistemological concerns. The question of the relative validity of the actor's and the (sociological) analyst's point of view on social reality has been a persistent and focal point of consideration. To many, it seems quite pivotal to the existence of sociology. If the members of society 'know how society works', then what need is there for sociology? Other questions follow. Is social reality as it appears to be for the members of society or does their perception and experience give them only a limited, partial or distorted apprehension of the true nature of social reality? Is social reality that which is revealed in (the correct) sociological theory? Is the second point of view to be (epistemologically) privileged over the first?

This question turns up in many different contexts and guises, and no more can be done here than to highlight one or two of the key ways in which it has manifested itself.

One of the guises in which the question appears, and which has provided an influential preoccupation for many years, concerns the 'rationality' of social actors. An orthodox conception of 'rationality' defines it as conduct that is in conformity with current scientific understandings (cf. Parsons 1937: 698–9). This raises issues that have to do with the effectiveness of action. If the world really works in the way that science says it does, then only action which is premised upon scientific understandings *is* rational, and therefore effective. Conversely, action that is not premised upon scientific understanding will not be capable of effectively manipulating its real (or, as they are often called, 'objective') circumstances. The 'rationality' issue neatly ties up with arguments about whether social reality is something that exists independently of our thought about it, a question that is given a vigorously affirmative answer by 'realists' of different kinds (cf. Bhaskar 1979).

A related issue is whether social scientists should construct rational models of the actor's actions. Among the pioneering sociologists, Max Weber attempted to do so, but with the aim of comparing rational strategies with actual courses of action. Weber did not suppose that social actors are necessarily rational. Whether or not a course of action was rational was a matter to be determined empirically. In economics and game theory, on the other hand, constructions of the rational actor are very generally used, the goal being to facilitate the application of explicit formal reasoning and mathematical modelling. Recently, two prominent figures (James S. Coleman (1990) in the USA and John Goldthorpe in the UK (2000)) have independently proposed the adoption of 'rational action theory' for sociology. Such appeals characteristically find little response amongst sociologists (cf. Edling 2000). It is usually argued that they are unrealistic. Individuals are not the relentlessly calculating self-interested creatures proposed in these constructions. (For much the same reason, sociologists generally are suspicious of economics.) Nevertheless, the construction of such models can be defended on the grounds that they provide an effective simplification that makes the business of theory building manageable, and that their effectiveness does not depend on a belief that they are necessarily realistic. (It may even be argued that the making of unrealistic assumptions is a *bona fide* feature of theoretical endeavour in science.) The division over rational models reflects the (unresolved) tension within sociology between the desire for general theory and for realistic presentation, but the lack of enthusiasm for rational models may also emanate from a more pragmatic concern about whether it is practical for sociology to emulate economics, game theory and the like.

It may appear obviously true to realists that social reality exists independently of our thought about it. However, other sociologists argue that social reality consists in – is constituted by – the understandings of members of society. Society exists 'in the minds' of its members and, as such, must patently be known to them. Anyone who takes the latter point of view – or, at least, is imagined to do so, as, for example, 'phenomenological' sociologists are widely supposed to do – is liable to be accused of idealism by the realists.

One way in which the realist assumption has been contested is through a denial that there is any universal standard of knowledge, or more specifically that (Western) science can be taken as the yardstick of truth. There has been a long and characteristically unsatisfactory debate over whether rationality is to be understood 'locally' instead of as a universal. One main strand of disagreement on this was provoked by Peter Winch's 'Understanding a primitive society' of 1964. By way of a discussion as to whether the magical practices of a 'primitive' tribe are to be judged as being rational in their own right, or deemed irrational because we, the scientifically informed, know that those practices cannot *possibly* work, Winch came to the conclusion that the standards of rationality are 'internal' or 'relative' to a culture.

More recently, 'postmodern' perspectives (sometimes drawing, like Winch, on the philosophy of Ludwig Wittgenstein) have also forcefully rejected the idea of universal rationality (an idea that is part of the package of 'Enlightenment reason', which is being more globally assailed (cf. Lyotard 1988)). They deny the existence of a universal rationality, or of an external reality independent of our thought. This is because (they assume) the only way in which human beings can have access to 'reality' is through language and the understandings associated with that. Nor is there any way in which we can escape our preconceptions except by embracing another set of preconceptions. (There are always people who live by different preconceptions than our own.) Reality is a 'social construction'.

Some postmodernists have argued against 'rational' conceptions of the individual not only because they resist the idea of universal rationality, but also because they share at least some aspects of Sigmund Freud's conception of the individual mind as something that is itself internally divided. The idea of the rational individual characteristically relates to the individual's *conscious* operations. However, if Freud was on the right track, then the role of consciousness in the explanation of the individual's action is greatly overrated. Individual conduct is propelled by operations in the unconscious, beyond the awareness of the individual. (Some writers would include here the impact of sociocultural structures such as the language as well as the unconscious impulses of the individual.) Consciousness is therefore doubly 'de-centred', i.e. demoted from the place it has more usually occupied in social thought. First, the actions of individuals are not be explained solely with reference to the operations of the individual consciousness, but are to an important degree to be explained rather with reference to impersonal sociocultural structures. Second, and more fundamentally, consciousness is not the sole or necessarily the dominant feature of the individual mind. Such a view culpably neglects the role of the unconscious.

Precursors of the idea of 'social construction' can be found in two traditions of US sociology where, however, the assumption is that reality is as it is perceived (or 'defined'). Their rationale is perhaps methodological rather than epistemological. It is directed towards gaining leverage in the development of empirical methods in sociology. The assumption is that whatever philosophers or natural scientists may tell us, people everywhere act in response to reality as they experience it. Therefore, *for sociological purposes*, the need is to understand the point of view from which people act, to grasp the world as they see it, an objective that is characteristically neglected and/or underestimated in sociological research. These two traditions (symbolic interaction (Blumer 1969) and ethnomethodology (Garfinkel 1967)) both assume that the central empirical task is to recover the actor's point of view. The survey method, which is a prevalent method for finding out the individual's point of view, is regarded as an ineffective way of accessing the actor's point of view *in action*. Both these schools aim to access the actor's viewpoint as it is situated in the context of action, to understand how actors are defining the situation throughout ongoing courses of action. At this level of abstraction, the two approaches may seem broadly the same, and both commonly resort to field studies in preference to the survey, but otherwise they tend to pursue their objectives in very different ways.

WES SHARROCK
UNIVERSITY OF MANCHESTER

References

Bhaskar, R. (1979) *The Possibility of Naturalism*, New Jersey.
Blumer, H. (1969) *Symbolic Interactionism*, New Jersey.
Coleman, J. (1990) *Foundations of Social Theory*, London.
Edling, C. (2000) 'Rational choice theory and quantitative analysis', *European Sociological Review*, 16(1): 1–8.
Garfinkel, H. (1967) *Studies in Ethnomethodology*, New Jersey.
Goldthorpe, J. (2000) *On Sociology*, Oxford.
Lyotard, J.-F. (1988) *The Differend*, Manchester.
Parsons, T. (1937) *The Structure of Social Action*, New York.
Winch, P. (1964) 'Understanding a primitive society', *American Philosophical Quarterly* 1: 307–24.

SEE ALSO: role; structure and agency

ADOLESCENCE

The life stage, adolescence, is most readily defined by what it is not. Adolescents are no longer children but not yet adults. They are in a transitional status: their role in society is ambiguous and their connections to adult worlds may be limited. Some anthropologists have argued that nearly all cultures have had an adolescent-like transitional period. But in most traditional groups it is short due to early marriage and assumption of adult work responsibilities (Schlegel and Barry 1991), and many of these groups provide a well-articulated path into adulthood that keeps youth connected to adults and adult institutions. Margaret Mead (1928) and Ruth Benedict (1939) described how traditional societies provided role continuity, in which youth were progressively groomed to take on the adult roles of their parents.

In Western nations this transition became longer and more discontinuous as a product of industrialization and associated societal changes in the early twentieth century. Transformations in the labour market meant that youth were less likely to follow parents' line of work. Education became increasingly important to adult employment, and hence the years youth spent in school increased – and have kept increasing with the transition to an information society. Schools separated youth from adults, which meant that youth spent more time with peers, leading to the growth of the peer group and peer culture. At the same time, improved nutrition resulted in puberty occurring earlier, which combined with later marriage created a long period during which youth experienced sexual desire without having societally acceptable paths for directing it. These changes not only made adolescence longer and more discontinuous, but also they put a greater burden on youth to find their own way, a situation that creates more frequent stress and mental health problems.

This emergence of a similar modern adolescence has since been occurring across nations of the world as they have gone through similar economic and societal changes (Brown *et al.* 2002). Shifts in labour markets and increased rates of secondary education have expanded the transitional adolescent phase and created some of the same discontinuities and stress for young people, particularly for the large numbers of youth in poor families (Dasen 1999). Caution is needed, however, in too quickly assuming that adolescence is the same across the world. Regional differences in cultures, job markets and social systems mean that young people experience different norms, choices, supports and risks. As one example, although European and US youth are expected to develop emotional independence from their families, in India that expectation remains foreign; youth cultivate strong emotional interdependency with their families into adulthood (Larson and Wilson 2004). It would be most accurate to say that there are multiple 'adolescences' across cultural groups, with wide divergences also occurring between rich and poor, and between boys and girls, in these settings.

The perspective of developmental psychology

Although the life stage of adolescence is clearly a social construction, there are physiological and cognitive dimensions of adolescence that are not solely products of social processes. Psychologists view adolescence as a developmental phase in which brain systems mature and individual youth actively adapt to their environments. Development is an interaction of bio-psychosocial processes.

A host of biological changes occur during puberty that feed into adolescents' development. The most obvious consist of a growth spurt and the development of secondary sex characteristics. Less overt changes include dramatic reorganization of parts of the brain and increased hormonal activity. There is a massive reduction in the number of connections among neurons in the cerebral cortex occurring throughout adolescence and the two hemispheres of the brain show increased ability to process information independently of each other (Spear 2000). Although major hormonal changes occur during puberty, the relationship between these changes and adolescent behaviour appears to be weak at best. Though adolescents do experience wider mood swings than adults (Verma and Larson 1999), research suggests that this is more related to stress and other psychosocial factors than to hormones (Buchanan *et al.* 1992). The important horizon for current research is to understand how these various biological changes, including increased expression of individual genetic differences during adolescence, occur in the context of environmental and social experiences: How do processes at all these different levels interact, and modify each other? (Zahn-Waxler 1996).

As children enter adolescence they also undergo cognitive changes that enable them to perceive and interact with the world in increasingly abstract and complex ways. Research shows that they become able to think about and understand abstract concepts like time, culture and love more deeply than they did as children. Although wide variability is seen across youth, many begin to approach problem-solving in more systematic ways. They are more likely to view a problem in the context of a system of elements: thinking about all possible combinations of elements in the system, changing one variable at a time within the system while holding others constant, and understanding how different variables are related to each other in any given situation. Cognitive changes also result in the ability to engage in critical thinking. Adolescents may begin to recognize inconsistencies in the world (Keating 1980). Identification of these changes in thinking has come almost exclusively from research with Western adolescents, thus it is difficult to know how universal they are and to what degree they are a result of socialization versus the maturation of brain systems. Evidence

suggests, however, that acquisition of abstract reasoning and critical thinking is partly the product of schooling. Adolescents develop and are taught the adult ways of thinking appropriate to their society (Cole and Scribner 1974).

Current psychological theory also stresses the active role that youth play in adapting to the world. They are not passively shaped by their environment; they are active agents of their own development. They respond to challenges in the environment, make choices and draw on resources available to them. This active view of youth is particularly suited to modern adolescence, in which young people face diverse and ambiguous pathways into adulthood. One useful framework conceptualizes adolescence as presenting a set of implicit psychosocial 'developmental tasks' that youth need to address. In Western societies, these tasks include coming to terms with one's sexuality, developing socially responsible behaviour, and Erik Erikson's (1968) task of achieving identity. This active view of adolescents is also used by sociologists and historians, who have studied how societal and economic changes shape the employment and role choices available to adolescents and how the choices they make in turn affect the pathways experienced by the next generation of youth (Modell 1989; Shanahan and Elder 2002).

Development in contexts

The shift to industrial and postindustrial society has resulted in adolescents' daily lives being segmented into separate spheres, and much of adolescent scholarship focuses on their experience in these different contexts. Family, peers and school are the contexts that have received most attention, and each can be seen as an arena in which cultural, societal and psychological processes interact.

The family continues to be an important context for basic emotional and identity development. But changes in the family and its relationship to society have changed and sometimes challenged how it plays this role. Longer adolescence means that young people spend a longer time dependent on their nuclear family, and smaller family sizes allow families to provide each child with more attention and resources. Yet climbing rates of divorce, increased employment demands on parents and competition for adolescents' attention from peers, media and other sources can make it more difficult for families to have a guiding role in adolescents' lives.

In most societies, teenagers today spend less time with family and more time with peers than was true in the past, and peers have more influence. Research indicates that this influence can be positive – peers are an important context for learning mutuality and pro-social behaviour. But peers can be a source of bullying and negative influence, from which teenagers acquire anti-social behaviour patterns. In many parts of the world adolescents are engaging in romantic and sexual relationships at earlier ages, which puts them at risk for sexually transmitted diseases, unwanted pregnancy and exploitative experiences. Research shows that initiation of romantic and sexual activity in early adolescence is associated with more negative outcomes (Zimmer-Gembeck et al. 2001).

Although schools are increasingly important to adolescents' preparation for adult work, educators have not yet found ways of successfully engaging all students in learning. Many Asian nations have created demanding tests to motivate and certify young people's school work, yet these exam systems also create high levels of pressure and stress on youth. In Western nations, adolescence is an age period when boredom and alienation in school increase and achievement levels fall for many youth, severely limiting the occupational choices those youth will have as adults. An important challenge for the future is to develop modes of education that allow all youth, including those with learning disabilities, to fulfil their potential so they can have desirable adult choices within the new global information society.

REED LARSON AND PATRICK SULLIVAN
UNIVERSITY OF ILLINOIS, URBANA-CHAMPAIGN

References

Benedict, R. (1939) 'Continuities and discontinuities in cultural conditioning', Psychiatry 1: 161–7.
Brown, B., Larson, R. and Saraswathi, T.S. (2002) The World's Youth: Adolescence in Eight Regions of the Globe, New York.
Buchanan, C.M., Eccles, J.S. and Becker, J.B. (1992) 'Are adolescents the victims of raging hormones? Evidence for activational effects of hormones on moods and behavior at adolescence', Psychological Bulletin 111: 62–107.
Cole, M. and Scribner, S. (1974) Culture and Thought, New York.
Dasen, P.R. (1999) 'Rapid social change and the

turmoil of adolescence: A cross-cultural perspective', International Journal of Group Tensions 29: 17–49.
Erikson, E.H. (1968) Identity: Youth and Crisis, New York.
Keating, D.P. (1980) 'Thinking processes in adolescence', in J. Adelson (ed.) Handbook of Adolescent Psychology, New York, pp. 211–46.
Larson, R. and Wilson, S. (2004) 'Adolescence across place and time: Globalization and the changing pathways to adulthood', in R. Lerner and L. Steinberg (eds) Handbook of Adolescent Psychology, New York.
Mead, M. (1928) Coming of Age in Samoa, New York.
Modell, J. (1989) Into One's Own, Berkeley, CA.
Schlegel, A. and Barry, H. (1991) Adolescence: An Anthropological Inquiry, New York.
Shanahan, M.J. and Elder, G. (2002) 'History, agency, and the life course', in L.J. Crockett (ed.) Nebraska Symposium on Motivation: 1999, Vol. 48, Lincoln, pp. 145–86.
Spear, L.P. (2000) 'The adolescent brain and age-related behavioral manifestations', Neuroscience and Biobehavioral Reviews 24: 417–63.
Verma, S. and Larson, R. (1999) 'Are adolescents more emotional? A study of the daily emotions of middle class Indian adolescents', Psychology and Developing Societies 11: 179–94.
Zahn-Waxler, C. (1996) 'Environment, biology, and culture: Implications for adolescent development', Developmental Psychology 32: 571–3.
Zimmer-Gembeck, M., Siebenbruner, J. and Collins, W.A. (2001) 'Diverse aspects of dating: Associations with psychosocial functioning from early to middle adolescence', Journal of Adolescence 24: 313–36.

Further reading

Larson, R., Brown, B.B. and Mortimer, J. (eds) (2002) 'Adolescents' preparation for the future: Perils and promise' [special issue], Journal of Research on Adolescence 12(1): 1–166.
Lerner, R. and Steinberg, L. (eds) (2004) Handbook of Adolescent Psychology, New York.

SEE ALSO: developmental psychology; life-span development

AFFIRMATIVE ACTION

Affirmative action can be defined in conceptual, legal and operational terms; no single definition is possible. The United States Commission on Civil Rights offers the following conceptual definition: affirmative action is 'a term that in a broad sense encompasses any measure, beyond simple termination of a discriminatory practice, adopted to correct or compensate for past or present discrimination or to prevent discrimination from recurring in the future'.

Legal definitions vary with jurisdiction and social domain. Many countries have enacted equal-opportunity and affirmative-action laws. These laws differ in terms of the target groups, the actions that are permitted and forbidden, penalties for violation, etc. In the USA, federal affirmative action regulations are supplemented by state and municipal laws and ordinances. Furthermore, the laws that constrain affirmative action in the workplace are related but not identical to those that control affirmative action in university and college admissions. At the federal level, the Equal Employment Opportunity Commission (EEOC) and the Office of Federal Contract Compliance Programs (OFCCP) are responsible for most equal opportunity and affirmative-action regulations and enforcement. (Details can be obtained from their websites.)

Although constrained by applicable laws, the actual practice of affirmative action is quite varied. In the USA, for example, federal work-place affirmative-action regulations require organizations to take certain actions, such as establishing anti-discrimination policies and completing an annual utilization analysis that compares the demographic distribution of the organization's workforce to the distribution in the relevant labour market. If the utilization analysis indicates that some protected group is underrepresented, the organization must establish goals and timetables for the elimination of the underrepresentation, and must specify the actions that will be taken to attain these goals. Although the law constrains those actions (e.g. they may not include explicit quotas), a great variety of procedures are permissible. Recent United States Supreme Court decisions have determined that quotas and explicit plus points are illegal in college and university admissions, but some positive weight can be given to minority status in the context of an individualized admission process.

Regardless of the law, it is clear that a large proportion of the white public in the USA equates affirmative action with quotas and preferential treatment both in the workplace and in college and university admissions. The actual extent of such preferential actions is unknown, but they evidently do occur.

The effects of affirmative action

When considering the effects of affirmative action, the interests of various stakeholders must be taken into account. The primary stakeholders are the target groups, other non-target groups, organizations that have affirmative action plans (AAPs) and society at large.

The phrase 'effects of' implies a causal relation. However, causal conclusions can rarely be drawn in affirmative-action research because scholars cannot control whether organizations have AAPs or the dimensions (e.g. race and gender) that determine who is targeted by those plans.

The purpose of affirmative action is to improve the outcomes of target groups. Research indicates that the size and even the existence of demonstrated benefits on employment have varied across time, location, target group and job level (Holzer and Neumark 2000; Smith 2001). In addition, minority status (African American or Hispanic) contributes to college and university admission only among the most selective institutions, where it increases the probability of admission by up to 10 per cent (Kane 1998). Among African Americans, admission to such selective colleges and universities is associated with an increased probability of graduation, post-baccalaureate education and professional success (Bowen and Bok 1998).

On the other hand, the use of affirmative action in the USA is associated with decreased employment outcomes for white males (Holzer and Neumark 1999, 2000). The relative paucity of 'reverse discrimination' charges filed with the EEOC suggests that these effects are due primarily to the elimination of the privileges often enjoyed by white males rather than to the use of strong preferences for female or minority applicants. Because elite universities reject so many whites and accept so few minority students, the negative impact of affirmative action on white applicants is quite small (Kane 1998). On a broader scale, the long-term effect of having a diverse student body appears to be positive for all groups and for society as a whole. Diversity in higher education is associated with individual changes in attitudes and abilities that enhance participation and success in an increasingly diverse democratic society (Bowen and Bok 1998; Gurin et al. 2004).

Opponents of affirmative action argue that workplace AAPs depress the performance of organizations, which are forced to hire less competent employees. Supporters argue that affirmative action improves organizational performance by eliminating economically inefficient discrimination and increasing workforce diversity. Research finds that organizations that use affirmative action in selection tend to hire minority individuals whose educational credentials are slightly lower than those of their white male hires. However, this difference in education does not lead to a corresponding difference in performance, perhaps because these organizations have developed superior human resource practices that enable them to identify high potential individuals and improve their capacities after they are hired. In short, workplace affirmative action does not appear to have a substantial effect, either positive or negative, on organizational performance (Holzer and Neumark 1999, 2000).

An important question is whether individuals who are selected in the context of an AAP are stigmatized by others. The discounting principle of attribution theory suggests that one's confidence in the importance of a potential cause is lower when other plausible causes are available. For example, if a Hispanic man is hired by an organization with an AAP, two plausible causes for his selection are competence and ethnicity. But if the organization does not have an AAP or if the new hire is a white male, the remaining plausible cause for selection is competence. Ratings of the new hire's competence would therefore be lower when he or she is a target group member than in other situations. Experimental research finds precisely this effect. This stigmatization can be eliminated by providing unequivocal evidence of the new hire's competence, but it is not eliminated by ambiguous evidence of competence (Heilman et al. 1998). Given the continued prevalence of negative stereotypes of racial minorities, along with the common assumption that affirmative action involves preferential selection, it is likely that stigmatization is relatively common. Although most research on stigmatization has focused on the workplace, the same logic applies to college and university admissions. Virtually all research in this area has been limited to evaluations of paper stimuli; the extent to which such stigmatization is maintained in the context of workplace interactions is unclear.

A frequent criticism of affirmative action is that it has negative psychological effects on target group members, causing them to doubt their own competence, to choose less challenging tasks, and/or lose interest in the job. These effects could be due to the discounting principle mentioned above and to the self-threatening implications of being helped (Turner and Pratkanis 1994). Laboratory experiments have shown that white female undergraduates experience self-doubt and sometimes choose less challenging tasks when they are told that they have been selected for a leadership role on the basis of their gender. The negative effect does not occur when selection is said to be based on a combination of merit and gender, and it can be eliminated by providing unambiguous evidence of the woman's competence (Heilman et al. 1998). Similar negative effects are not observed among white men, and some limited research suggests that such effects are less common among racial minorities than white women. Initial self-confidence in one's ability seems to play a critical role in determining the occurrence of such self-stigmatization. Because it is uncommon for employees to be told that they were selected solely on the basis of their demographic status, the implications of this finding for the workplace are not clear. However, Brown et al. (2000) found an inverse relation between students' suspicion that their race or ethnicity helped them get admitted to the university and their college GPA. This finding is consistent with the logic of self-stigmatization, though the observational nature of the study precludes causal conclusions. The authors speculate that it may be related to the experience of stereotype threat.

What factors predict attitudes towards affirmative action?

Most research on affirmative action has assessed the factors that predict attitudes. The two most important types of predictors are the details of the AAP and attributes of the respondent.

One of the strongest predictors of attitudes towards workplace affirmative action is AAP strength – the weight given by the AAP to demographic status in selection decisions (Kravitz 1995). Among whites, the elimination of discrimination is preferred to opportunity enhancement procedures, which in turn are preferred to weak preferences (the use of demographic status to break ties). Strong preferences are widely disliked. Racial minorities also reject strong preferences, but they distinguish to a lesser extent than whites among the weaker plans. Research on reactions to affirmative action in college admissions has not manipulated AAP strength so precisely, but whites clearly prefer that demographic status be given no weight.

A number of studies have associated attitudes towards affirmative action with respondents' demographic characteristics, notably race and gender. African Americans express the strongest support for affirmative action. Hispanics and Asians express intermediate levels of support, and whites are the least supportive. This is true in judgements of affirmative action both in the workplace (Kravitz et al. 1997) and in university admissions (Sax and Arredondo 1999). The effect of gender is weaker, with support typically somewhat higher among white women than men; evidence for gender differences among racial minorities is quite mixed.

There are positive intercorrelations among the three most consistent individual difference predictors of affirmative-action attitudes: prejudice, conservative political ideology and the belief that discrimination is no longer a problem. One of the strongest predictors of white opposition to affirmative action is prejudice against the target group (racism for AAPs that target African Americans; sexism for AAPs that target women). Opposition to affirmative action is also stronger among conservatives and Republicans than among liberals and Democrats. There is some evidence that the predictive power of both prejudice and conservatism increases with the respondent's education (Federico and Sidanius 2002). Finally, support increases with the belief that target group members continue to experience discrimination (Konrad and Hartmann 2001).

There is considerable evidence that support for affirmative action is associated with the anticipated effects of the AAP on the individual (personal self-interest) and the individual's demographic group (collective self-interest). Indeed, group interests and conflict are central to several theories of affirmative action attitudes (Krysan 2000). However, the strongest predictor is whether or not the respondent judges that the AAP is fair (Kravitz 1995). Indeed, issues of perceived fairness are implicit in virtually all the factors that influence attitudes towards affirmative action.

DAVID A. KRAVITZ
GEORGE MASON UNIVERSITY

References

Bowen, W.G. and Bok, D. (1998) The Shape of the River: Long-Term Consequences of Considering Race in College and University Admissions, Princeton, NJ.

Brown, R.P., Charnsangavej, T., Keough, K., Newman, M. and Rentfrow, P. (2000) 'Putting the "affirm" into affirmative action: Preferential selection and academic performance', Journal of Personality and Social Psychology 79(5): 736–47.

Federico, C.M. and Sidanius, J. (2002) 'Racism, ideology, and affirmative action revisited: The antecedents and consequences of "principled objectives" to affirmative action', Journal of Personality and Social Psychology 82(4): 488–502.

Gurin, P., Nagda, B.A. and Lopez, G.E. (2004) 'The benefits of diversity in education for democratic citizenship', Journal of Social Issues 60.

Heilman, M.E., Battle, W.S., Keller, C.E. and Lee, R.A. (1998) 'Type of affirmative action policy: A determinant of reactions to sex-based preferential selection?' Journal of Applied Psychology 83(2): 190–205.

Holzer, H. and Neumark, D. (1999) 'Are affirmative action hires less qualified? Evidence from employer–employee data on new hires', Journal of Labor Economics 17(3): 534–69.

—— (2000) 'Assessing affirmative action', Journal of Economic Literature 38(3): 483–568.

Kane, T.J. (1998) 'Racial and ethnic preferences in college admissions', in C. Jencks and M. Phillips (eds) The Black–White Test Score Gap, Washington, DC, pp. 431–56.

Konrad, A.M. and Hartmann, L. (2001) 'Gender differences in attitudes toward affirmative action programs in Australia: Effects of beliefs, interests, and attitudes toward women', Sex Roles 45: 415–32.

Kravitz, D.A. (1995) 'Attitudes toward affirmative action plans directed at Blacks: Effects of plan and individual differences', Journal of Applied Social Psychology 25(24): 2,192–220.

Kravitz, D.A., Harrison, D.A., Turner, M.E., Levine, E.L., Chaves, W., Brannick, M.T., et al. (1997) Affirmative Action: A Review of Psychological and Behavioral Research, Bowling Green, OH [online]: http://www.siop.org/AfirmAct/siopsaartoc.html.

Krysan, M. (2000) 'Prejudice, politics, and public opinion: Understanding the source of racial policy attitudes', Annual Review of Sociology 26: 135–68.

Sax, L.J. and Arredondo, M. (1999) 'Student attitudes toward affirmative action in college admissions', Research in Higher Education 40(4): 439–59.

Smith, J.P. (2001) 'Race and ethnicity in the labor market: Trends over the short and long term', in N.J. Smelser, W.J. Wilson and F. Mitchell (eds) American Becoming: Racial Trends and Their Consequences, Vol. 2, Washington, DC, pp. 52–97.

Turner, M.E. and Pratkanis, A.R. (1994) 'Affirmative action as help: A review of recipient reactions to preferential selection and affirmative action', Basic and Applied Social Psychology 15(1 and 2): 43–69.

Further reading

Crosby, F.J. (2004) *Affirmative Action is Dead; Long Live Affirmative Action*, New Haven, CT.

Doverspike, D., Taylor, M.A. and Arthur, W., Jr (2000) *Affirmative Action: A Psychological Perspective*, Huntington, NY.

Gutman, A. (2000) *EEO Law and Personnel Practices*, 2nd edn, Thousand Oaks, CA.

Sniderman, P.M. and Carmines, E.G. (1997) *Reaching Beyond Race*, Cambridge, MA.

SEE ALSO: education; equality; ethnic politics; human rights; justice, distributive

AGE–SEX STRUCTURE

The age–sex structure of a population is its distribution by age and sex. The classification of the population according to age and sex can be given either in absolute numbers or in relative numbers, the latter being the ratio of the population in a given age–sex category to the total population of all ages for both sexes. The age distribution is given either in single years of age or in age groups, for example 5-year age groups. Broad age groups such as 0 to 14, 15 to 59, 60 and over are also sometimes used. The grouping of ages depends on the degree of precision desired, and on the quality of the data at hand. If data are defective, as in some developing countries where people do not know their precise age, the classification by age groups is often to be preferred to the distribution by individual year of age, even if this implies a loss of information.

A graphic presentation of the age–sex structure of the population is the so-called *population pyramid*. This is a form of histogram, absolute or relative population figures being given on the axis of the abscissa, and age or age groups being represented on the ordinate. Male data are given on the left-hand side of the axis of ordinates and female data on the right-hand side. The areas of the rectangles of the histogram are taken to be proportional to the population numbers at each age or age group.

Figure 1 presents as an example the population pyramid of the Belgian population, on 1 January 2001. The y-axis refers to age and the corresponding year of birth, while the x-axis gives the absolute population numbers. As discussed below, at very young ages there are more boys than girls, due to the higher number of boys than girls at birth. At older ages, on the contrary, there are more females than males as a result of male excess mortality at all ages. Further, the age

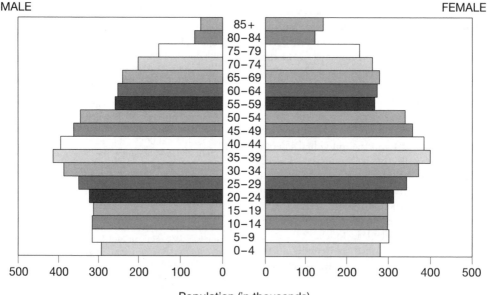

Figure 1 Population pyramid of Belgium, 1 January 2001 (absolute numbers)

Source: US Census Bureau, International Data Base

group 55 to 60 is less numerous than the adjacent groups. This is due to the postponement of births during the Second World War (birth cohorts 1940 to 1945). Postponement of births also occurred during the First World War and its impact is still to be noted in the population pyramid (age group 81 to 86). The pyramid represents an aged population, with a low proportion of young people and a high proportion of adults and older people. The base of the pyramid is narrow due to current low fertility levels.

Another useful graph shows the differential distribution of sexes by age, presenting sex ratios by age or age group. Sex ratios are obtained by dividing the number of males in each age group by the corresponding number of females. The results are often called *masculinity ratios*. Masculinity ratios tend to decrease with age. At young ages there are usually more boys than girls: approximately 105 male births occur per 100 female births. As age increases, masculinity ratios decline and become lower than 1, due to higher age-specific probabilities of dying for males than for females. On the whole, there are usually more females than males in the total population, due to excess male mortality. Masculinity ratios by age are also dependent upon the impact of migration. If migration is sex-specific, masculinity ratios will reflect this phenomenon at the ages concerned.

Demographers often speak of young or old age structures. In the former case, the proportion of young people in the population is high. In the case of an old structure, the contrary is true. Young population age structures are essentially linked to high fertility. Ageing population structures are characterized by declining fertility. The impact on age structure of a decline in mortality is much smaller than that of fertility decline, as the decrease in risks of dying affects all ages simultaneously. If decreases in risks of dying occur mainly at young ages, lower mortality will actually rejuvenate the population. In present-day low-mortality countries, probabilities of dying have reached such low levels at young ages that the impact of further decreases in mortality at these ages on the population pyramid is small. On the other hand, mortality at older ages is decreasing due to the reduction in mortality from chronic diseases, especially cardiovascular diseases. These gains in life expectancy at older ages

have now become the principal factor of population ageing in developed countries.

Internal migration can have a significant impact on population age structure at the regional level. A town may attract young adults thanks to economic or educational opportunities, for example. Pensioners tend to choose locations with an agreeable climate and good health services. Rural areas often have ageing populations as the young move to cities. *International* migration can sometimes influence the age–sex structure of the population of a whole country, such as that of Kuwait for example, where there has been an influx of largely male workers.

If fertility and mortality remain constant over time, and the population is closed to migration, a *stable* age structure will eventually result in the long run: the age distribution becomes invariant and depends solely on the age-specific fertility and mortality schedules. This property has been demonstrated by A.J. Lotka and is known as *strong ergodicity*.

GUILLAUME WUNSCH
UNIVERSITY OF LOUVAIN, BELGIUM

Further reading

Caselli, G. and Vallin, J. (2005) 'Population dynamics: Change and structure', in G. Caselli, J. Vallin and G. Wunsch (eds) *Demography: Analysis and Synthesis*, Vol. 1. *Population Dynamics*, San Diego, CA, ch. 4.
Preston, S.H., Heuveline, P. and Guillot, M. (2001) *Demography*, Oxford.

SEE ALSO: vital statistics

AGEING

Studies pertaining to ageing play a prominent and increasing role in the biological sciences, public health, social work, and the behavioural and social sciences. At the individual level, the word 'ageing' can refer to a biological process, the transitions and transformations that occur to individuals in the latter portion of their life-span, or the well-being – in terms of physical and mental health, economic conditions, work and leisure – of those at older ages, often demarcated at 60 or 65. At a societal level, the word can connote the demographic processes that determine the portion of the population at the older ages as well as the socioeconomic and cultural implications for a society that experiences changes in its age composition.

An influential World Assembly on Aging held under United Nations auspices in 1982 codified in their plan of action many of the aspects of ageing under the rubric of 'humanitarian' and 'developmental' concerns (United Nations 1983). The humanitarian issues related to the conditions of the elderly and their needs while those termed developmental related to the societal implications of older age structures, in particular the effects on production and productivity, earnings levels, and associated socioeconomic conditions and policies.

Many of these concerns are of course not new, and the perception of old age as a 'problem' for Western countries appeared in early twentieth-century literature, if not before, according to Achenbaum (1996). He also notes that the term 'gerontology', referring to the scientific study of aspects of growing older, was coined in 1908, and the term 'geriatrics' in 1914.

Nonetheless, ageing is now the focus of renewed attention, as a consequence of current and projected population trends that show large increases in the number and proportion of older people in all regions of the world. Declines in fertility and extensions of life expectancy (changes that are expected to continue) have resulted in dramatic changes in the age composition of populations. According to United Nations projections, the percentage of the population aged 60 years or older will grow from 20 per cent in 2002 to 33 per cent in 2050 in the more developed regions, and will grow from 8 per cent to 19 per cent in less developed regions over the same period (United Nations 2002). In addition, the proportion of that older age group that is age 80 or older will also increase over the coming decades, exacerbating the demand for medical and nursing care as well as services from family members and social welfare programmes.

The theoretical, substantive and methodological concerns of each of the social and behavioural sciences intersect the field of ageing on numerous – and overlapping – topics. This has led to several codifications of the multiple connections, most notably in the five editions of the *Handbook of Aging and the Social Sciences* (for the two most recent, see Binstock and George 1996, 2001) and the *Handbook of the Psychology of Aging* (most recently, Birren and Schaie 2001). (A similar series of handbooks appears for the biology of ageing; see Masoro and Austad 2001.)

Sociologists have contributed to research on ageing through the examination of age stratification, cohort succession, the life course, family and social support systems and the study of social change. Anthropologists have studied effects of culture on the definition of old age and the status of the elderly (Fry 1996). Political scientists have given attention to the political implications of old-age policies and issues of generational equity (Binstock and Day 1996). Psychologists have been prominent in developing scales of depression, cognition and other key mental states. A number of these scales have been adapted for use in large population surveys, providing important data on mental health in the older population. A relatively new specialization – demography of ageing – has appeared as a distinct speciality within the broader field of demography or population studies within the last 15 years (Martin and Preston 1994). This applies the formal tools of demography to mortality trends, levels and differentials; the determinants of age composition; and population movements. Demographers are also increasingly examining broader issues of health, work and retirement, living arrangements, and intergenerational exchanges.

Economists have played a larger role in several facets of research on ageing in recent years. They have developed useful models for investigating the connections between age composition and population growth with economic development, and for understanding the motivations and implications of intergenerational support systems (Lee 2000; Lillard and Willis 1997). They have also investigated the economic status of the elderly, patterns of labour force activity and retirement, and the consequences of different types of public and private retirement programmes (Gruber and Wise 1999).

Given the number of distinct topics in ageing addressed by the social sciences, there is no single conceptuals framework shared by all researchers, even within a single discipline (Marshall 1999). One major axis of theory and research has been the effect of economic development on the well-being of the elderly, prompted in part by an influential theory of Cowgill (1974), who held that many of the dimensions of modernization tend to reduce the status of the elderly by limiting their job opportunities, separating them from their families, and lowering their social status relative to the young. This 'modernization thesis', which has also been influenced by Goode's (1963) work on the relationship of industrialization to the rise of the 'conjugal family', has been the subject of considerable discussion and research. Two recent studies examine aspects of this thesis through a close look at the well-being of the elderly in Asia (Whyte 2003; Hermalin 2002).

An important development in recent years has been the emergence of more multidisciplinary research on ageing. A major area of intersection for social scientists and epidemiologists, biologists and public health specialists is in the study of the relationships between social factors – socioeconomic levels, social support and stress – and the physical and mental health of the elderly. Social support appears to have a significant effect on health outcomes (Marmot and Wilkinson 1999). Another example of interdisciplinary research is the emerging field of biodemography, which joins perspectives from biology and demography on several methodological and substantive issues, particularly those centring on longevity (Wachter and Finch 1997).

Methodologies have become increasingly sophisticated. Researchers draw on data from censuses, vital registration, clinical studies, administrative data and smaller-scale, specialized sample surveys, and have increasingly carried out longitudinal studies. These often take the form of panel designs. The same people are interviewed every few years and may be asked a broad range of questions dealing with finances, health, health care utilization, family support, work and other key aspects of ageing. In the case of the Health and Retirement Study in the United States, the designs and questionnaires are the product of multidisciplinary teams of economists, epidemiologists, sociologists, psychologists and public health specialists (Juster and Suzman 1995; Health and Retirement Study, n.d.). A recent report from the US National Academy of Science has stressed the importance of such designs and advocated efforts to conduct comparable studies across many countries (National Research Council 2001). Efforts now underway in Europe may be followed on the websites for the English Longitudinal Study of Ageing (2003) and the Survey of Health, Aging and Retirement in Europe (n.d.).

Government officials have given increasing attention to the potentially deleterious effects of population ageing on the welfare of the older population, and to overall economic growth and development. There has been a wide range of policy responses, which vary across countries and regions. Some responses have been demographic in character, through attempts to promote earlier marriage and higher birth rates, or by liberalizing immigration policies to bring in more workers. Other policies focus on strengthening family support for the elderly as a way of containing health and social security costs, promoting greater participation of women in the labour force, upgrading the skill levels of workers, and changing the age of retirement.

ALBERT I. HERMALIN
UNIVERSITY OF MICHIGAN

References

Achenbaum, W.A. (1996) 'Historical perspectives on aging', in R.H. Binstock and L.K. George (eds) *Handbook of Aging and the Social Sciences*, 4th edn, San Diego, CA.

Binstock, R.H. and Day, C.L. (1996) 'Aging and politics', in R.H. Binstock and L.K. George (eds) *Handbook of Aging and the Social Sciences*, 4th edn, San Diego, CA, pp. 362–87.

Binstock, Robert H. and George, Linda K. (eds) (1996) *Handbook of Aging and the Social Sciences*, 4th edn, San Diego, CA.

—— (2001) *Handbook of Aging and the Social Sciences*, 5th edn, San Diego, CA.

Birren, J.E. and Schaie, K.W. (eds) (2001) *Handbook of the Psychology of Aging*, 5th edn, San Diego, CA.

Cowgill, D.O. (1974) 'The aging of populations and societies', *The Annals of the American Academy of Political and Social Science* 415.

English Longitudinal Study of Ageing (ELSA) (2003) Retrieved 22 July 2003 from http://www.natcen.ac.uk/elsa/.

Fry, C.L. (1996) 'Age, aging, and culture', in R.H. Binstock and L.K. George (eds) *Handbook of Aging and the Social Sciences*, 4th edn, San Diego, CA, pp. 117–36.

Goode, W.J. (1963) *World Revolution and Family Patterns*, Glencoe, IL.

Gruber, J. and Wise, D.A. (eds) (1999) *Social Security and Retirement around the World*, Chicago.

Health and Retirement Study (n.d.) Retrieved 29 July 2003 from http://hrsonline.isr.umich.edu/.

Hermalin, A.I. (ed.) (2002) *The Well-Being of the Elderly in Asia: A Four-Country Comparative Study*, Ann Arbor, MI.

Juster, F.T. and Suzman, R.M. (1995) 'An overview of the health and retirement study', *The Journal of Human Resources* 30: S7–56 Supplement.

Lee, R.D. (2000) 'Intergenerational transfers and the economic life cycle: A cross-cultural perspective', in A. Mason and G. Tapinos (eds) *Sharing the Wealth:*

Demographic Change and Economic Transfers between Generations, Oxford.

Lillard, L.A. and Willis, R.J. (1997) 'Motives for intergenerational transfers: Evidence from Malaysia', *Demography* 34(1): 115–34.

Marmot, M. and Wilkinson, R.G. (eds) (1999) *Social Determinants of Health*, Oxford.

Marshall, V.W. (1999) 'Analyzing social theories of aging', in V.L. Bengtson and K.W. Schaie (eds) *Handbook of Theories of Aging*, New York, pp. 434–55.

Martin, L.G. and Preston, S.H. (eds) (1994) *Demography of Aging*, Washington, DC.

Masoro, E.J. and Austad, S.N. (eds) (2001) *The Handbook of the Biology of Aging*, 5th edn, San Diego, CA.

National Research Council (2001) *Preparing for an Aging World: The Case for Cross-National Research* (Panel on a Research Agenda and New Data for an Aging World. Committee on Population and Committee on National Statistics), Washington, DC.

Survey of Health, Aging and Retirement in Europe (SHARE) (n.d.) Retrieved 22 July 2003 from http://www.share-project.org.

United Nations (1983) *World Assembly on Aging, 1982. Vienna International Plan of Action on Aging*, New York.

—— (2002) *Population Ageing 2002*, ESA/SER.A/208, New York.

Wachter, K.W. and Finch, C.E. (eds) (1997) *Between Zeus and the Salmon*, Washington, DC.

Whyte, M.K. (ed.) (2003) *China's Revolutions and Intergenerational Relations*, Ann Arbor, MI.

Further reading

Kinsella, K. and Velkoff, V.A. (2001) *An Aging World, 2001*, US Census Bureau, Series P95/01-1, Washington, DC.

United Nations (2002) *World Population Ageing 1980–2050*, St/ESA/SER.A/207, New York.

World Bank (1994) *Averting the Old Age Crisis*, New York.

SEE ALSO: gerontology, social; life-span development; life tables and survival analysis

AGRICULTURAL ECONOMICS

The demand for food tends to be more inelastic or unresponsive to changes in prices and incomes than the demand for other goods. Therefore, shifts in supply, due for example to weather shocks or new technologies, have disproportionately large effects on agricultural prices and incomes. However, as incomes increase, the share of income spent on food eventually declines, a dynamic known as Engel's Law. In the USA, slow growth in per capita demand for agricultural products stands in contrast to the rapid growth of productivity in agriculture. This has resulted in falling prices in agriculture relative to the rest of the economy. Programmes to support the incomes of agricultural producers as they adjust to changing economic realities are a major concern of politicians as well as agricultural economists, as are efforts to minimize the costs of such programmes.

At low levels of income most of a country's population and economic activity are in agriculture. This is true of poor countries today as well as of today's rich countries in the past. Agriculture's share of total gross domestic product (GDP) was much greater than that of industry until well into the nineteenth century in France and the UK. Today, it accounts for 3 per cent of GDP in France and 1 per cent in the UK, but agriculture still accounts for as much as 60 per cent of GDP in a number of less developed countries (World Bank *Development Report 2003*).

Agriculture is closely linked with non-agricultural sectors at all levels of development. Low-income countries look to agriculture as a source of food, labour, capital (through taxation or agricultural price policies) and foreign exchange (via agricultural exports) needed for growth in the non-farm economy, and as a market for manufactures. In high-income countries, although agriculture represents a small share of total GDP, many non-agricultural activities supply inputs to farms (e.g. fertilizer and other intermediate inputs, machinery and various support services) or to process farm output. In 1997, only 2 per cent of all US jobs were in farm production but 15 per cent were in farm or farm-related sectors.

Agriculture is different from other sectors of the economy in ways that have far-reaching ramifications for research agendas and analytical approaches. The agricultural production process relies heavily on inputs from nature (land, weather). Production is carried out by farmers with unequal access to resources, from large agribusinesses (sometimes referred to as 'factories in the fields') to hundreds of millions of small farmers. Its supply is volatile, shaped by spatial, temporal and stochastic variables, including pest and weather risks that do not arise in manufacturing, where production processes are governed by engineering relationships. In most cases agricultural production decisions are made within economic units that are also households. Agricultural production involves long time lags between purchasing and applying inputs and harvesting outputs, with both the output price and quantities unknown at planting time. Farming requires land, so agriculture is dispersed over wide geographical areas. It involves a vast number of decisions by many actors. Because agricultural production is spread out, seasonal, naturally risky and involves long lags, timely access to diverse markets is critical, including markets for inputs, output, credit (to finance input costs ahead of harvests) and insurance.

Heavy government intervention in agriculture has moved resources off farms and into cities in poor countries, and has subsidized farmers in rich countries. Agricultural policies are both socially and politically driven. The dispersal of agriculture over wide geographical areas bolsters its political power in systems that elect representatives by area, such as the US Senate. The political importance of agriculture, in turn, results in the channelling of significant public resources into agricultural research. Internationally, major trade negotiations break down in the area of agriculture because most developed countries protect and/or subsidize their agricultural producers more than they protect other sectors of the economy. However, most of the world's agricultural producers (and consumers) are in less developed countries, which have a wide diversity of agricultural policies.

Early agricultural economics research emphasized farm management. As the field developed it raised its sights beyond the farm gate, on both the output side (food processing, consumer economics and retailing) and the input side (farm labour, natural resource use in agricultural production, farm credit and insurance). The issues addressed have changed over time, reflecting the continuing transformation of systems of agriculture and world markets.

J. EDWARD TAYLOR
UNIVERSITY OF CALIFORNIA, DAVIS

Further reading

Cramer, G.L., Jensen, C.W. and Southgate, D.D. (2000) *Agricultural Economics and Agribusiness*, Hoboken, NJ.

Gardner, B.L. and Rausser, G.C. (eds) (2002) *Handbook of Agricultural Economics: Agriculture and Its External Linkages*, Amsterdam.

Pardey, P.G. (ed.) (2001) *The Future of Food: Biotechnology Markets and Policies in an International Setting*, Baltimore, MD.

ALCOHOLISM AND ALCOHOL ABUSE

Beverage alcohol consumption occurs in most societies, and an extensive anthropological literature documents worldwide variations in the social patterns of alcohol use (Gefou-Madianou 1992; Heath 2000; McDonald 1997), much of it emphasizing the integrative functions served by alcohol consumption, a theme that also informs early sociological studies of the topic (Bacon 1943). Organized social research and publication in industrialized nations have, however, increasingly moved away from viewing alcohol as an integral part of community, work and family life. Modern sociological research deals almost exclusively with the problems associated with the use of alcohol. This is due in part to cultural ambivalence towards this potent yet widely available drug (Room 1976), but is also a consequence of the political and economic investments that have accumulated around the production and distribution of alcohol and the myriad of organizations involved in prevention, intervention and treatment of alcohol problems (Wiener 1980). The result is that research funding is very largely targeted on dysfunctions and problems associated with alcohol, and most research by social scientists in alcohol studies is grounded in four overlapping concerns: harm associated with alcohol consumption, the medical disease of alcohol dependence or alcoholism, the co-occurrence of both alcohol consumption and alcohol dependence with other physically and socially destructive behaviours, and the social and organizational characteristics of interventions designed to deal with problems of alcohol consumption and alcohol dependence.

This represents a narrowing of earlier interests. Since the 1960s, researchers had identified social factors in the aetiology of alcohol dependence. Trice (1966) offered a theory of individually rewarding drinking experiences followed by selective and sequential associations with drinking groups within which increasingly heavy and chronic alcohol use was socially accepted. In a similar vein, Akers (1977) developed a model of patterned rewards in social interaction wherein alcohol dependence could develop. Bacon (1973) and Mulford (1984) constructed somewhat parallel theories centred on the interaction of self- and social definitions over time as alcohol dependency and recovery evolved. Building on the work of other researchers who had examined homeless and disaffiliated alcoholics, Wiseman (1970) uncovered social patterns and social structure in the lives and interactions within these groups. She later documented patterns of social interaction in couples where the husband was a recovering alcoholic, strongly suggesting that social role relationships could develop around a spouse's chronic alcoholism and serve to prolong it (Wiseman 1991).

Despite considerable promise, these aetiological studies did not attract research support. Social theories of alcoholic aetiology may be seen as potentially supportive of controls on alcohol availability, and so they are unpopular within the drinks industry. Instead the explanation of aetiology has shifted almost exclusively towards a biomedical model of causation, based on inferred individual variations in alcohol metabolism, and often suggesting that these aberrant patterns are caused by genes. Such hypotheses are consistent with a disease model of alcoholism that has been the cornerstone of much research and practice, particularly in the USA since the Repeal of National Prohibition. (Prohibition was adopted in the USA in 1919 and repealed in 1933.) The disease model suggests that a minority of the drinking population is at risk for developing drinking problems due to biological reasons outside their control. By inference, this model implies that the vast majority of the population can drink without physical harm or social consequence, thus undermining support for the strategy of universal prohibition. Given the argument that those afflicted by the disease of alcoholism can recover through lifelong abstinence, the concept of prohibition is effectively shifted away from the entire population and focused exclusively on a small segment. It is evident that the centrality of such a model would be supported by the drinks industry, which constitutes a substantial political force in most industrialized nations.

While institutional forces have come to discourage social scientists from paying attention to the causes of alcohol problems, their expertise has been called on to examine the consequences of drinking (Gusfield 1996). Studies of these consequences have drawn attention to different social groupings and institutions over the past 75 years.

From the ending of Prohibition to about 1960 the central icon in the definition of alcohol problems was the homeless public inebriate. The social problem of alcohol, which had only recently been 'resolved' through the Repeal of Prohibition, could be seen as manageable if it was centred and contained in this small and socially isolated segment of the population. This group was managed through periodic imprisonment for short terms and came to be characterized as a 'revolving door' population because its members kept returning to jail. Social activism became oriented towards 'decriminalizing' public inebriates and directing them towards treatment for their alcoholism, which would move them in the direction of recovery and social reintegration. While legislation was passed to support decriminalization, it did not compel a high degree of public interest.

From the 1960s to the 1990s, the central symbol of the problem shifted away from a tiny segment of the drinking population towards a large majority, the hidden alcoholic in the workplace, who collectively were said to constitute 95 per cent of the alcoholic population while the public inebriates made up only 5 per cent (Roman and Blum 1987). Intervention mechanisms were developed in the form of employee assistance programmes that were designed to identify and direct employed persons with alcohol problems into newly developed systems of treatment designed specifically for 'respectable' segments of the population. The growth of such privately based treatment in the USA was substantially supported by legislatively mandated health insurance coverage.

In the 1980s and 1990s, a shift occurred away from the 'rehabilitative ideal' (Garland 2001) and towards a demonization of persons with alcohol problems. The first step was the discovery of the 'drinking driver', and the imposition of various means of social control to detect and punish such behaviour (Jacobs 1989). This led to a tendency to use alcohol impairment as the explanation of all injury, damage and death in traffic mishaps if evidence of alcohol consumption by drivers could be established.

The major factor that fostered the demonized view of the alcohol abuser was the escalation of efforts directed towards the prohibition of illegal drug traffic in the USA and the intermingling of imagery (and treatment) of alcohol and drug users. Constructive work-based programmes for alcohol problems were challenged by the rise of federal support for workplace testing for illegal drug use, and the suggested elimination of drug users from employment (Roman and Blum 1992).

As the new millennium began, the demonized imagery remains but has been supplemented by a new target population, college age youth. A substantial research investment in prevention and intervention of alcohol and drug problems in this group has been made in the USA since the early 1990s. Social scientists have been at the forefront of designing these strategies. Curiously, these strategies do not pay attention to the larger segment of youth that enters the workforce after secondary education or a brief college experience, and does not attend residential higher education. This emphasis coincides with the drawing of sharp new lines of socioeconomic stratification in the USA as well as other Western nations, and may reflect the direction of alcohol-related societal resources towards that segment of society perceived to have the greatest social value.

PAUL M. ROMAN
UNIVERSITY OF GEORGIA

References

Akers, R. (1977) *Deviant Behavior and Social Learning*, Belmont, CA.
Bacon, S. (1943) 'Sociology and the problems of alcohol: Foundations for a sociologic study of drinking behavior', *Quarterly Journal of Studies on Alcohol* 4: 399–445.
—— (1973) 'The process of addiction to alcohol', *Quarterly Journal of Studies on Alcohol* 34: 1–27.
Garland, D. (2001) *The Culture of Control: Crime and Social Order in Contemporary Society*, Chicago.
Gefou-Madianou, D. (ed.) (1992) *Alcohol, Gender and Culture*, London.
Gusfield, J. (1996) *Contested Meanings: The Construction of Alcohol Problems*, Madison, WI.
Heath, D. (2000) *Drinking Occasions: Comparative Perspectives on Alcohol and Culture*, Philadelphia.
Jacobs, J. (1989) *Drunk Driving: An American Dilemma*, Chicago.
McDonald, M. (ed.) (1997) *Gender, Drink and Drugs*, London.
Mulford, H. (1984) 'Rethinking the alcohol problem: A natural processes model', *Journal of Drug Issues* 14: 31–44.
Roman, P. and Blum, T. (1987) 'Notes on the new epidemiology of alcoholism in the USA', *Journal of Drug Issues* 17: 321–32.
—— (1992) 'Drugs, the workplace, and employee-oriented programming', in D. Gerstein and H. Harwood (eds) *Treating Drug Problems*, Vol. 2, Washington, DC.
Room, R. (1976) 'Ambivalence as a sociological explanation: The case of cultural explanations of alcohol problems', *American Sociological Review* 41: 1,047–65.
Trice, H. (1966) *Alcoholism in America*, New York.
Wiener, C. (1980) *The Politics of Alcoholism*, New Brunswick, NJ.
Wiseman, J. (1970) *Stations of the Lost*, Englewood Cliffs, NJ.
—— (1991) *The Other Half: Wives of Alcoholics and Their Social-Psychological Situation*, New York.

SEE ALSO: drug use; social problems

ALIENATION

Alienation (in German *Entfremdung*), sometimes called estrangement, is claimed to be a phenomenon of the human or social world. It is usually identified in psychological, sociological or philosophical-anthropological terms derived especially from the writings of Hegel, Feuerbach and Marx – though already in Calvin there is an account of the alienation of man from God by original sin.

In Hegel (1971 [1807]), we find in particular the claim that the sphere of Spirit, at a certain stage in history, *splits up* into two regions: into consciousness and its object, being. Thus self-consciousness 'disintegrates' and thought and reality become 'entirely estranged' one from another. In this sense the division of man from nature is considered an alienation: man is himself split into part subject and part object; 'self' is divided. This state of alienation can and will be overcome only when the division between Spirit and Nature is finally overcome.

Hegel's objective-idealist philosophy of history was challenged by Feuerbach (1936 [1841]), whose critique centred precisely on a rejection of Hegel's conception of the process of alienation. It is not that Feuerbach takes the 'separation' between subject and object to be a philosophical myth. But this separation, he argues, is assigned by Hegel the status of a 'false alienation'. For while man is real, God is an imaginary projection: 'the consciousness of God is the self-consciousness of man, the perception of God the self-perception of man'. Nor is nature a self-alienated form of the Absolute Spirit. Yet this reference to a 'false' alienation in Hegel suggests the existence of something like a 'true' alienation. And Feuerbach does indeed believe in such a thing; for it is, he argues, only in some relation of contact with the objects that man produces – in so producing them, separating them off from himself – that he can become properly self-conscious.

Marx (1975 [1844]) disagrees. He argues that it is precisely by creating a world of objects through his practical activity that man proves himself as a conscious species-being, but that under capitalism the objects produced by human labour come to confront him as something *alien*. So the product of labour is transformed into an alien object 'exercising power over him', while the worker's activity becomes an alien activity. Marx adds that man's species-being then also turns into a being alien to him, estranging him from his 'human aspect', and that man is thereby estranged from man.

Marx's early writings, including the so-called *1844 Manuscripts*, were (re)discovered in the 1930s. Thus it was that in the following period some of their themes, including that of 'alienation', found their way into political, sociological and philosophical writings of various – Marxist but also non-Marxist – authors. A psychological version of alienation theory also exists, partially derived from Hegelian notions (see below). The concept also has an ethical aspect: alienation is usually considered (whatever theory it derives from) to be a bad or unfortunate thing, deserving if possible of rectification. Alienation has been said (Sargent 1972) to be 'a major or even the dominant condition of contemporary life'. An abundant literature exists on the varied uses of the term (see Josephson and Josephson 1962).

Lukes (1967) has identified a fundamental difference between two concepts that are, he claims, often confused: that of alienation, and that – introduced by Durkheim – of anomia. For Durkheim the problem of anomic man is that he needs (but lacks) rules to live by, setting limits to his desires and to his thoughts. Marx's problem is rather the opposite: that of man in the grip of a system from which he cannot escape.

Althusser (1969 [1965]) developed a powerful critique of the notion of alienation as used by the young Marx, claiming that it was a speculative category abandoned by Marx in his later, mature works.

It may finally be noted that the term 'alienation' appears in the psychoanalytical writings of Lacan (1977 [1966]), in the context of his theory of the 'mirror stage' in child development. This stage is said to establish an initial relation between the organism and its environment, but at the cost of a 'fragmentation' of the body, the fragments being divided up against themselves. This may sound rather like a corporeal version of Hegel's notion of the divided personality; and Lacan was indeed influenced by Hegel. It is, according to Lacan, in the relation between human subject and language that 'the most profound alienation of the subject in our scientific civilization' is to be found.

GRAHAME LOCK
RADBOUD UNIVERSITY, NIJMEGEN,
THE NETHERLANDS

References

Althusser, L. (1969 [1965]) *For Marx*, London.
Feuerbach, L. (1936 [1841]) *The Essence of Christianity*, London.
Hegel, G.W.F. (1971 [1807]) *The Phenomenology of Mind*, London.
Josephson, E. and Josephson, M. (1962) *Man Alone*, New York.
Lacan, J. (1977 [1966]) *Ecrits*, London.
Lukes, S. (1967) 'Alienation and anomie', in P. Laslett and W.C. Runciman (eds) *Politics, Philosophy and Society*, Oxford.
Marx, K. (1975 [1844]) *Economic and Philosophic Manuscripts of 1844*, K. Marx and F. Engels, *Collected Works*, Vol. 3, London.
Sargent, L.T. (1972) *New Left Thought: An Introduction*, Homewood, IL.

Further reading

Blauner, R. (1964) *Alienation and Freedom: The Factory Worker and His Industry*, London.
Schaff, A. (1975) 'Alienation as a social and philosophical problem', *Social Praxis* 3.
Sykes, G. (ed.) (1964) *Alienation: The Cultural Climate of Modern Man*, 2 vols, New York.

SEE ALSO: Marx's theory of history and society

ALTRUISM AND CO-OPERATION

Gift giving and sharing are universal. Individuals in teams and groups work towards a common goal. Fishermen co-ordinate their fishing effort equitably, sharing the available catch on a fishing ground. Parents sacrifice themselves for their children. People help others in distress, give blood and may even donate a bodily organ to a stranger whilst still alive. In the Second World War some hid Jews from the Nazis at the risk of their own lives, and in 1981 IRA hunger strikers died voluntarily for their cause.

Theories of the origin of such co-operative and altruistic acts have come from both evolutionary and cultural sources (Fehr and Fischbacher 2003). Defining altruistic and co-operative acts in terms of their consequences, altruism is an act that benefits the recipient at a cost to the actor, while co-operation benefits both parties. A pair of mutually reciprocated altruistic acts whose benefits outweigh their costs can therefore make up a single co-operative exchange. While Darwinian evolution is commonly equated with a competitive struggle for existence, theories developed since the 1960s have shown that altruism towards kin (Grafen 1991), and unrelated individuals, are both favoured by natural selection under certain conditions. Kin-directed altruism is favoured since relatives have a high chance of carrying the genes predisposing the altruist to selfless behaviour. This means that if the altruist's loss of fitness is outweighed by the relative's gain (devalued by the chance that the genes in question are carried by the relative), genes predisposing individuals to altruism will be favoured overall and spread through the population. The ubiquitous favouring of close kin is probably the result of such evolutionary forces.

The problem for the evolution of altruism between unrelated individuals is cheating, since those who receive without giving do best of all. When cheating can be punished by the withdrawal of altruistic acts in the future, however, an evolutionary game theory analysis shows that tit-for-tat reciprocation (rewarding altruism with altruism and punishing selfishness with selfishness) results in greater rewards than egoism (Axelrod 1984). Reciprocation is an 'evolutionarily stable strategy', meaning that it becomes the population norm, replacing competing strategies over evolutionary time. The same approach shows that an increasing generosity in reciprocally altruistic exchanges is also evolutionarily stable.

This analysis fails to explain altruism between strangers, however, since it predicts reciprocation only when the same individuals interact frequently. If a reputation for altruism is rewarded by the trust and generosity – the 'indirect-reciprocity' – of strangers, this may benefit the altruist in the long run. Laboratory experiments provide evidence of such a process (Fehr and Fischbacher 2003). A good reputation is communicated to others through emotional and non-verbal signals that are difficult to fake, as demonstrated by laboratory experiments in which subjects can reliably predict, after a short

interaction, whether another person will co-operate or defect in a subsequent game. Although these 'commitment signals' leave the individual open to manipulation they are also precisely the characteristics sought in the kind of long-term relationships, whether romantic or commercial, that bring large rewards. Signals of commitment may have evolved for this purpose (Frank 1988).

A model combining evolutionary and cultural processes provides an alternative origin for unreciprocated altruism. In this model self-sacrifice is culturally transmitted and benefits the social group. Children adopt the commonest adult trait as their role model, a conformist strategy that is favoured by natural selection (Boyd and Richerson 1991). This model accords well with the tendency to favour individuals in one's own social group, and with ethnocentrism and xenophobia.

These evolutionary and cultural models leave open the psychological issue of what motivates an individual to behave altruistically. This question has been central to the study of human nature since classical times, philosophers disagreeing over whether egoistic or altruistic impulses are at the root of human action, and consequently over the possibilities for ethical and political obligation. Under the hedonic view all behaviour is motivated by the desire to avoid pain and secure pleasure, so that altruism is ultimately selfish. However, if all that is being claimed is that the achievement of goals is pleasurable, then hedonism might indeed explain altruism, but such an explanation misses the interesting points that the goal in this case is to help another individual, and that some cost is suffered even though goal achievement might be enjoyed. There remains the difficult question of whether altruistic acts are performed to ameliorate the suffering of others or the avoidance of the saddened mood that normally accompanies empathy for a victim. Social psychologists who have disentangled these associated motivations report conflicting results (Fultz and Cialdini 1991), although empathic individuals do tend to show more helping behaviour. In addition, people may help even when they believe they would remain anonymous if they declined to do so, demonstrating that maintaining a good reputation is not a necessary motive for altruism.

Co-operative behaviour also raises unresolved problems for rational choice theory, which predicts that behaviour is motivated by the goal of utility maximization. In social decision-making, utility depends not only on one's own choices but also on those of the other parties involved, game theory being the analytical tool for determining the rational solution. The problem for rational choice theory is that, in experiments, players generally behave more co-operatively and receive higher payoffs than rationality would predict. Psychological processes and goals other than utility maximization are therefore required to explain these results. Reputation building and commitment signalling may be a partial explanation, and may in fact lead to longer-term utility maximization. A related possibility is that players view themselves and others in the game as a single entity, a 'team', whose collective utility is the value to be maximized (Colman 2003). The idea that the welfare of others, and not just of oneself, plays a part in the motivation of co-operation is suggested by the experimental enhancement of co-operation by (sometimes quite minimal) social interaction with a stranger, in a variety of games.

A plausible evolutionary origin for these irrational departures from egoism lies in the benefit of maintaining group membership, and predicting and controlling the behaviour of others, in the small groups of early human societies (Caporael *et al.* 1989). Evolutionary psychological analysis might explain departures from rationality in terms of the kinds of social problem that early humans were selected to solve, and the kinds of reasoning it was adaptive to employ. Such an analysis has shown human reasoning to be well designed for cheater detection, for example (Cosmides and Tooby 1992).

The study of social decision-making in dyads and small, unstructured groups is a starting-point for understanding co-operation at the higher levels of structured groups, firms, institutions, communities and states (Axelrod 1997; Lazarus 2003). Many disciplines in the social sciences – psychology, anthropology, sociology, economics and political philosophy – share an interest in these questions, with trust being a recurring theme (Lazarus 2003). For example, individual decisions in economic communities governing their own use of common pool resources (CPRs), such as grazing pastures, determine how effectively individuals avoid the 'tragedy of the commons'. Successful CPR decisions involve: a clear in-group/out-group distinction; resource provision in proportion to need; sharing of costs

in proportion to ability to pay; and graded punishments for the greedy (Ostrom 1990). Political theorists have debated whether individuals can make and keep group commitments without enforcement by an external agent. Findings from both real-world and experimental CPR communities show that communication and internal sanctions are successful in maintaining group commitment to the co-operative enterprise (Ostrom *et al.* 1992).

The high personal investment that individuals are prepared to make in imposing sanctions, in both real-world and experimental CPR communities, supports Frank's (1988) commitment model. The strong emotions aroused by perceived unfairness in a co-operative endeavour, and the resultant personal cost some individuals are prepared to suffer in an attempt to restore equity, demonstrate the commitment and fairness that, in turn, bring rewards in the shape of offers of partnership and commitment from others. The strength of the sense of fairness is demonstrated by the fact that experimental subjects will take nothing rather than accept a reward they feel to be unfair.

In Western societies altruistic tendencies are enhanced by the development in childhood of empathy, moral reasoning and the ability to take the perspective of others. These traits develop most readily in children whose parents are caring and supportive, set clear standards, enforce them without punishment, encourage responsibility and are themselves altruistic.

However, these mechanisms are not universal, and norms of altruistic behaviour vary between societies, being influenced, for example, by the value given to individualism or collectivism. Within small-scale egalitarian societies, altruism may be valued more highly where there is little competition for resources or where a harsh environment favours co-operation.

JOHN LAZARUS
UNIVERSITY OF NEWCASTLE

References

Axelrod, R. (1984) *The Evolution of Cooperation*, New York.
—— (1997) *The Complexity of Cooperation: Agent-Based Models of Competition and Collaboration*, Princeton, NJ.
Boyd, R. and Richerson, P.J. (1991) 'Culture and cooperation', in R.A. Hinde and J. Groebel (eds)

Cooperation and Prosocial Behaviour, Cambridge, UK, pp. 27–48.

Caporael, L.R., Dawes, R.M., Orbell, J.M. and van de Kragt, A.J.C. (1989) 'Selfishness examined: Cooperation in the absence of egoistic incentives', *Behavioral and Brain Sciences* 12: 683–739.

Colman, A.M. (2003) 'Cooperation, psychological game theory, and limitations of rationality in social interaction', *Behavioral and Brain Sciences* 26: 139–98.

Cosmides, L. and Tooby, J. (1992) 'Cognitive adaptations for social exchange', in J.H. Barkow, L. Cosmides and J. Tooby (eds) *The Adapted Mind: Evolutionary Psychology and the Generation of Culture*, New York, pp. 163–228.

Fehr, E. and Fischbacher, U. (2003) 'The nature of human altruism', *Nature* 425: 785–91.

Frank, R.H. (1988) *Passions within Reason: The Strategic Role of the Emotions*, New York.

Fultz, J. and Cialdini, R.B. (1991) 'Situational and personality determinants of the quantity and quality of helping', in R.A. Hinde and J. Groebel (eds) *Cooperation and Prosocial Behaviour*, Cambridge, UK, pp. 135–46.

Grafen, A. (1991) 'Modelling in behavioural ecology', in J.R. Krebs and N.B. Davies (eds) *Behavioural Ecology: An Evolutionary Approach*, 3rd edn, Oxford.

Lazarus, J. (2003) 'Let's cooperate to understand cooperation', *Behavioral and Brain Sciences* 26: 169–70.

Ostrom, E. (1990) *Governing the Commons: The Evolution of Institutions for Collective Action*, Cambridge, UK.

Ostrom, E., Walker, J. and Gardner, R. (1992) 'Covenants with and without a sword: Self-governance is possible', *American Political Science Review* 86: 404–17.

Further reading

Hinde, R.A. and Groebel, J. (eds) (1991) *Cooperation and Prosocial Behaviour*, Cambridge, UK.

Ridley, M. (1997) *The Origins of Virtue*, Harmondsworth

SEE ALSO: evolutionary psychology; game theory

ANARCHISM

Anarchism is a political philosophy which holds that societies can and should exist without rulers. Anarchists believe that this will not, as is commonly supposed, lead to chaos – anarchy in the popular sense – but on the contrary to an increase in social order. Anarchists see the state as the decisive source of corruption and disorder in the body politic. They point to many examples where people freely co-operate, without coercion, to achieve common purposes. Among traditional societies they find much to interest

them in the 'ordered anarchies' of certain African tribes such as the Nuer, as well as in the workings of autonomous peasant communities such as the Russian *mir* and the self-governing cities of medieval Europe. In modern times they have hailed the anarchist experiments of the German Anabaptists of sixteenth-century Münster; the Diggers and Fifth Monarchists of the English Civil War; the popular clubs and societies of the French Revolution; the Paris Commune of 1871; the Russian soviets of 1905 and 1917; and the anarchist ventures in Catalonia and Andalusia during the Spanish Civil War.

Christ and Buddha have been claimed among earlier anarchists; and there were many social movements in both medieval Europe and medieval China that drew a fundamentally anarchist inspiration from Christianity and Buddhism. Religious anarchism continued into modern times with Tolstoy and Gandhi. But the modern phase of anarchism proper opens with the eighteenth-century Enlightenment, and can be traced equally from Rousseau's romanticism and William Godwin's rationalism. An early exponent was Godwin's son-in-law, the poet Shelley. Later advocates included the French socialist Proudhon, the German philosopher of egoism Max Stirner, the US individualist Thoreau, and the Russian aristocratic rebels Michael Bakunin and Peter Kropotkin. Anarchism was a strong current during the Russian Revolution and its immediate aftermath; the suppression of the Kronstadt rising in 1921 and the emasculation of the soviets signalled its defeat. But the ideas lived on, to surface not only in Spain in the 1930s, but also in Hungary in 1956, and in Paris in 1968, where the student radicals achieved a dazzling blend of anarchism and surrealism.

Anarchism has been incorporated into the political philosophy of a number of ecological groups, especially in Germany and the USA. It is strongly marked in such ecological Utopias as Ursula Le Guin's *The Dispossessed* (1974) and Ernest Callenbach's *Ecotopia* (1975). These in turn have been influenced by earlier anarchist 'ecotopias' such as William Morris's *News from Nowhere* (1890) and Aldous Huxley's *Island* (1962). Anarchism is usually a left-wing philosophy; but there is also a strand of right-wing anarchism, influenced particularly by the US philosopher Robert Nozick, which has been prominent in certain libertarian movements, especially in the USA.

KRISHAN KUMAR
UNIVERSITY OF VIRGINIA

Further reading

Bookchin, M. (1982) *The Ecology of Freedom*, Palo Alto, CA.
Kelly, Aileen M. (1987) *Mikhail Bakunin*, New Haven, CT and London.
Marshall, P. (1993) *Demanding the Impossible: A History of Anarchism*, London.
Miller, D. (1984) *Anarchism*, London.
Nozick, R. (1980) *Anarchy, State and Utopia*, New York.
Ritter, A. (1980) *Anarchism: A Theoretical Analysis*, Cambridge, UK.

SEE ALSO: libertarianism; state

ANGER, HOSTILITY AND AGGRESSION

Fear and rage were recognized by Darwin (1872) as universal characteristics of both humans and animals that evolved through a process of natural selection because these emotions facilitated successful adaptation and survival. Darwin observed that rage was reflected in facial expression (e.g. reddened face, clenched teeth, dilated nostrils), and in accelerated heart-rate, muscular tension and aggressive or violent behaviour. He regarded rage as intense anger that motivated 'animals of all kinds, and their progenitors before them, when attacked or threatened by an enemy' to fight and defend themselves. For Darwin, anger was a state of mind that differed 'from rage only in degree, and there is no marked distinction in their characteristic signs'.

Freud (1959 [1933]) considered aggression a fundamental instinctual drive that involves angry feelings which motivate aggressive behaviour. Freud conceptualized aggression as resulting from a biologically determined 'death instinct' (thanatos) that motivated people to destroy themselves. Because thanatos was generally inhibited by a more powerful life instinct (libido), the energy associated with this self-destructive drive was redirected and expressed in aggressive behaviour towards other persons or objects in the environment. However, when aggression could not be directly expressed because it was unacceptable and evoked intense anxiety, it was turned back into the self, resulting in depression and other psychosomatic manifestations (Alexander and French 1948).

Anger, hostility and aggression are recognized as important concepts in most contemporary theories of personality and psychopathology, and as important contributors to the aetiology of the psychoneuroses, depression and schizophrenia. However, angry feelings are frequently confounded with hostility and aggressive behaviour, and these terms are used interchangeably in the research literature. Consequently, definitions of these constructs remain ambiguous, leading to conceptual confusion and overlapping measurement operations of questionable validity (Biaggio *et al.* 1981).

Given the substantial overlap in prevailing definitions of anger, hostility and aggression, we have referred collectively to these constructs as the AHA! Syndrome (Spielberger *et al.* 1985), and have endeavoured to identify meaningful definitions for each concept. Anger refers to an emotional state that consists of feelings that vary in intensity from mild irritation or annoyance to intense fury or rage, with associated activation or arousal of the autonomic and neuroendocrine systems (Spielberger 1999). Hostility generally involves the experience of intense angry feelings, but also has the connotation of complex attitudes and behaviours that include being mean, vicious, vindictive and often cynical. As a psychological construct, aggression describes destructive or punitive behaviours directed towards other persons or objects in the environment.

Physiological correlates of hostility and behavioural manifestations of aggression have been investigated in numerous studies. However, until the 1980s, anger was largely neglected in psychological research. Recent research on anger, hostility and aggression, as well as observations of violence in daily life, provide strong evidence that anger-related problems are ubiquitous. In a series of studies, Deffenbacher and his associates (Deffenbacher *et al.* 1987) found that persons high in anger as a personality trait experienced angry feelings across a wide range of situations, and were more likely to engage in aggressive behaviour. Anger, hostility and aggression have also been found to contribute to the pathogenesis of hypertension (Crane 1981) and coronary heart disease (Spielberger and London 1982).

Substantial evidence that anger motivates hostility and a wide range of aggressive behaviours makes clear the need to assess both anger as an emotional state, and how frequently this emotion is experienced. The State-Trait Anger Scale (STAS) was constructed to assess the intensity of feelings of anger, and individual differences in anger proneness as a personality trait (Spielberger *et al.* 1985). In responding to the STAS S-Anger scale, examinees report their feelings of anger *at a particular time* by rating themselves on a 4-point intensity scale, e.g. 'I feel angry': (1) Not at all; (2) Somewhat; (3) Moderately so; (4) Very much so. Examinees indicate how they *generally* feel in responding to the STAS T-Anger scale by rating themselves on a 4-point frequency scale, e.g. 'I am a hotheaded person': (1) Almost never; (2) Sometimes; (3) Often; (4) Almost always.

Alpha coefficients of .93 and .87, respectively, for the preliminary STAS S-Anger and T-Anger scales administered to a large sample of university students provided impressive evidence of the utility of the working definitions of anger that guided selection of the items for these scales (Spielberger *et al.* 1985). The item-remainder correlations were .50 or higher for the final set of ten S-Anger and ten T-Anger items selected for the STAS. Factor analyses of the S-Anger items identified only a single underlying factor for both males and females, indicating that this scale measured a unitary emotional state that varied in intensity. In contrast, factor analyses of the ten STAS T-Anger items identified two independent yet substantially correlated factors, Angry Temperament (T-Anger/T) and Angry Reaction (T-Anger/R). The T-Anger/T items describe experiencing anger without specifying any provoking circumstance (e.g. 'I am a hotheaded person'; 'I have a fiery temper'). The T-Anger/R items describe reactions to situations in which anger was provoked by the negative evaluations of other persons (e.g. 'It makes me furious when I am criticized in front of others'). The results of a study in which hypertensive patients were compared with general medical and surgical patients with normal blood pressure demonstrated the importance of differences in trait anger assessed by the two T-Anger subscales (Crane 1981). The significantly higher STAS T-Anger scores that were found for the hypertensives, as compared with patients with normal blood pressure, were due entirely to their substantially higher T-Anger/R subscale scores.

The critical importance of differentiating between the *experience* and *expression* of anger has become increasingly apparent. Anger may be expressed in two ways: turned inward towards the self, or expressed in assaults or destructive behaviour. The Anger EXpression (AX) Scale was constructed to assess this dimension (Spielberger *et al.* 1985, 1995). In separate factor analyses of large samples of females and males, strikingly similar Anger-In and Anger-Out factors were identified for both sexes. Essentially zero correlations were found between the eight-item Anger-In (AX/In) and Anger-Out (AX/Out) scales based on these factors (Spielberger 1988). Relatively high internal consistency alpha coefficients were also found for the AX/In and AX/Out scales, ranging from .73 to .84 for diverse populations. Thus, the AX/In and AX/Out scales assess two distinct anger-expression dimensions that are internally consistent and empirically independent.

Several items were included in the original twenty-item AX Scale to assess the middle range of the anger-in/anger-out continuum, which were not included in the AX/In or the AX/Out scales. These items described controlling anger, rather than turning anger in or expressing anger towards other persons or environmental objects (e.g. 'I control my temper'; 'I keep my cool'). In subsequent research, the anger control items coalesced to form the nucleus of an anger control factor and stimulated the development of an eight-item Anger Control (AX/Con) scale. The eight-item AX/In, AX/Out and AX/Con scales were included in the expanded twenty-four-item AX Scale (Spielberger *et al.* 1988), which was combined with the twenty-item STAS to form the *State-Trait Anger Expression Inventory* (STAXI). An entirely new eight-item scale was subsequently added to assess how often a person tries to control anger-in (AX/Con-In) by reducing the intensity of suppressed anger (Spielberger 1999). The revised fifty-seven-item STAXI-2 also includes an expanded fifteen-item S-Anger scale, with three factorially derived subscales that assess Feeling Angry, Feel like expressing anger Verbally, and Feel like expressing anger Physically.

The STAXI has proved useful for assessing the experience, expression and control of anger in normal and abnormal individuals (Deffenbacher *et al.* 1987; Moses 1992), and for evaluating relations between the components of anger with a variety of disorders, including alcoholism, hypertension, coronary heart disease and cancer (Spielberger 1988, 1999).

CHARLES D. SPIELBERGER
UNIVERSITY OF SOUTH FLORIDA, TAMPA

References

Alexander, F.G. and French, T.M. (eds) (1948) *Studies in Psychosomatic Medicine: An Approach to the Cause and Treatment of Vegetative Disturbances*, New York.

Biaggio, M.K., Supplee, K. and Curtis, N. (1981) 'Reliability and validity of four anger scales', *Journal of Personality Assessment* 45: 639–48.

Crane, R.S. (1981) 'The role of anger, hostility, and aggression in essential hypertension' (Doctoral dissertation, University of South Florida, Tampa, FL, 1981) *Dissertation Abstracts International* 42, 2982B.

Darwin, C. (1872) *The Expression of Emotions in Man and Animals*, London.

Deffenbacher, J.L., Story, D.A., Stark, R.S., Hogg, J.A. and Brandon, A.D. (1987) 'Cognitive-relaxation and social skills interventions in the treatment of general anger', *Journal of Counselling Psychology* 34: 171–6.

Freud, S. (1959 [1933]) 'Why war?' in J. Strachey (ed.) *Collected Papers*, Vol. 5, London.

Moses, J.A. (1992) *State-Trait Anger Expression Inventory*, research edn, in D.J. Keyser and R.C. Sweetland (eds) *Test Critiques*, Vol. 9, Austin, TX, pp. 510–25.

Spielberger, C.D. (1988) *Manual for the State-Trait Anger Expression Inventory (STAXI)*, Odessa, FL.

—— (1999) *Professional Manual for the State-Trait Anger Expression Inventory-2 (STAXI-2)*, Odessa, FL.

Spielberger, C.D., Johnson, E.H., Russell, S.F., Crane, R.J., Jacobs, G.A. and Worden, T.J. (1985) 'The experience and expression of anger: Construction and validation of an anger expression scale', in M.A. Chesney and R.H. Rosenman (eds) *Anger and Hostility in Cardiovascular and Behavioral Disorders*, New York, pp. 5–30.

Spielberger, C.D., Krasner, S.S. and Solomon, E.P. (1988) 'The experience, expression and control of anger', in M.P. Janisse (ed.) *Health Psychology: Individual Differences and Stress*, New York, pp. 89–108.

Spielberger, C.D. and London, P. (1982) 'Rage boomerangs: Lethal Type-A anger', *American Health* 1: 52–6.

Spielberger, C.D., Reheiser, E.C. and Sydeman, S.J. (1995) 'Measuring the experience, expression, and control of anger', in H. Kassinove (ed.) *Anger Disorders: Definitions, Diagnosis, and Treatment*, Washington, DC, pp. 49–76.

SEE ALSO: anxiety; emotion

ANNALES SCHOOL

The journal *Annales d'histoire économique et sociale*, long planned, was founded in 1929 by two historians at the University of Strasbourg, Lucien Febvre and Marc Bloch, because they were unhappy with the manner in which history was studied in France and elsewhere, and wished to offer an alternative. They considered orthodox history to be too much concerned with events, too narrowly political and too isolated from neighbouring disciplines. In their attempt to construct a 'total' history, as it came to be called (total in the sense of dealing with every human activity, not in that of trying to include every detail), Febvre and Bloch were concerned to enlist the collaboration of workers in the social sciences. They were both admirers of the work of Paul Vidal de la Blache in human geography, and interested in the ideas of Lucien Lévy-Bruhl on primitive mentality, while Bloch was also inspired by Durkheim's concern with the social and by his comparative method. The first editorial board of *Annales* included the geographer Albert Demangeon, the sociologist Maurice Halbwachs and the political scientist André Siegfried.

The movement associated with the journal can be divided into three phases. In the first phase (to about 1945), it was small, radical and subversive. After the Second World War, however, the rebels took over the historical establishment. Febvre became president of the new interdisciplinary École Pratique des Hautes Études. He continued to edit *Annales: economies, sociétés, civilisations*, as it became in 1946, thus extending its range to the 'history of mentalities' practised by Febvre in his own work on the Reformation. He was aided by Fernand Braudel, whose doctoral thesis on *The Mediterranean and the Mediterranean World in the Age of Philip II* (1949) quickly made him famous. Braudel dominated the second generation of the movement, which was most truly a 'school' with distinctive concepts and methods. Braudel himself stressed the importance of the long term (*la longue durée*) of historical geography, and of material culture (*civilisation matérielle*). Pierre Chaunu emphasized quantitative methods (*l'histoire sérielle*), notably in his vast study of trade between Spain and the New World, *Seville et l'Atlantique* (1955–66). Pierre Goubert, a former student of Bloch's, integrated the new historical demography, developed by Louis Henry, into a historical community study of the Beauvais region. Robert Mandrou remained close to Febvre and the history of mentalities.

A third phase in the history of the movement opened in 1968 (a date that seems to mark the revenge of political events on the historians who neglected them). Braudel reacted to the political crisis by deciding to take a back seat and confiding the direction of the journal to younger men, notably Emmanuel Le Roy Ladurie. Le Roy Ladurie made his reputation with *The Peasants of Languedoc* (1966), a total history from the ground up in the Braudel manner, which used quantitative methods wherever possible, but he has since moved 'from the cellar to the attic', towards the history of mentalities and historical anthropology, as in his bestselling study of a fourteenth-century village, *Montaillou* (1975). The 1980s saw a fragmentation of the former school, which has in any case been so influential in France that it has lost its distinctiveness. It is now a 'school' only for its foreign admirers and its domestic critics, who continue to reproach it for underestimating the importance of political events. Some members of the *Annales* group, notably Le Roy Ladurie and Georges Duby, a medievalist, who has moved, like Ladurie, from rural history to the history of mentalities, are presently concerned to integrate both politics and events into their approach, and to provide narrative as well as analysis.

Others, notably Jacques Le Goff, Roger Chartier and Jean Claude Schmitt, have developed a new approach to the history of culture, in a wide sense of this term, including the history of rituals, gestures and ways of reading.

Since Braudel had a quasi-filial relationship with Febvre and a quasi-paternal relationship with Ladurie, the development of the *Annales* movement into a school and its fragmentation into a loosely organized group might be interpreted in terms of the succession of three generations. It also illustrates the cyclical process by which the rebels become the establishment and are in turn rebelled against. The movement is less influential than it once was. However, the journal (renamed *Annales: histoire et sciences sociales*) and the people associated with it still offer the most sustained long-term example of fruitful interaction between historians and social sciences.

PETER BURKE
UNIVERSITY OF CAMBRIDGE

Further reading

Burke, P. (1990) *The French Historical Revolution: The Annales School, 1929–1989*, London.
Clark, S. (ed.) (1999) *The Annales School: Critical Assessments*, 4 vols, London.
Fink, C. (1989) *Marc Bloch: A Life in History*, Cambridge, UK.
Review special issue (1978) 'The impact of the Annales School on the social sciences', *Review* 1.

SEE ALSO: Braudel; social history

ANTHROPOLOGY

The central issue in anthropology is human variation. In the nineteenth century, the guiding idea was that there were significant biological differences between human populations, and that these biological differences – notably in the development of the brain – explained variations in rationality, technical sophistication and social complexity. The Enlightenment belief that human history was a unified history of progress in knowledge and rationality was recast in an evolutionist idiom: there had been a steady and determined movement from more primitive to more advanced human types. Differences between populations were represented as reflecting the fact that they had achieved different levels of development. Ancient civilizations revealed by archaeology were thought to represent stages of development through which all modern societies had once progressed. There were also still some primitive human populations that closely resembled not only our own remote ancestors but also even the primate ancestors of humanity. 'Primitive' peoples – like, it was thought, the Fuegians, Australian Aboriginals and the South African Bushmen – were physically less evolved than other humans, lived in a 'primitive' society based on kinship and had a 'primitive' totemic religion. Other living populations represented intermediate stages of development between 'primitive' and 'civilized' modern peoples. In the 1880s, an alternative view became popular, which was that each human 'race' had specific inherent capacities and therefore produced more or less sophisticated cultural forms and social institutions.

A major paradigm shift occurred in the first decades of the twentieth century, which resulted in the abandonment of the 'evolutionist' approaches of the nineteenth century. In the USA, Franz Boas (1858–1942) and his students were among the pioneering critics of racial theory. They helped to establish that biological differences between extant human populations cross-cut the racial classifications; that these racial classifications were crude and unreliable, being based on a few phenotypical features; and that there were no apparent differences in intellectual capacity between populations. It was not race that caused the differences between cultures. Cultural differences were themselves the main source of human variation. Anthropologists in the Boasian mould accordingly distinguished between biological and cultural processes.

Culture was conceived as that part of the human heritage that was passed on by learning rather than by biological inheritance. There were, however, two very different views of culture. E.B. Tylor (1832–1917) and other evolutionist writers had typically treated culture or civilization as a single, cumulative attribute of humankind: some communities simply enjoyed more or less 'culture' as they advanced. The Boasian scholars were critical of these evolutionist speculations, and were more concerned with local histories and with regional distributions of cultural traits. In contradiction to the evolutionists, they insisted that cultural history did not follow any set course. A culture was formed by contacts, exchanges, population movements. Each culture was a historically and geographically specific accretion of traits. There was no necessary course of cultural development, and in consequence cultures could not be rated as more or less advanced.

In Britain, Bronislaw Malinowski (1884–1942) and A.R. Radcliffe-Brown (1881–1955) abandoned what they termed speculative reconstructions of the past and insisted rather that beliefs, customs, institutions and practices could be understood only in terms of the context of their use. Contemporary causes were sought, rather than historical origins. Inspired by the theories of Emile Durkheim (1858–1917), they situated anthropology within the social sciences, drawing particularly on sociology and social psychology.

The new schools of anthropology in Europe and North America agreed that social, cultural and biological processes were largely independent of each other. This fostered a divergence between the biological study of human beings and the study of cultural and social processes. Although Boas himself contributed to 'physical anthropology' or 'biological anthropology', this became a distinct specialism in the USA. In Europe, physical anthropology (often confusingly termed 'anthropology') developed independently of what had initially been called ethnology, the study of living populations. Some influential figures in American anthropology tried to preserve the 'four fields' approach, which linked cultural anthropology, physical anthropology, archaeology and linguistics, but increasingly the specialisms within anthropology diverged from each other. By the middle of the twentieth century the intellectual links between the four fields had become increasingly exiguous. Certainly there is some mutual influence. Archaeology has increasingly drawn on cultural and social theory, and some biological anthropologists have developed neo-Darwinian explanations of social institutions. In general, however, cultural anthropology in North America and social anthropology and ethnology in Europe can be treated in isolation from the other anthropological disciplines.

Ethnographic research

Europeans had accumulated a considerable body of information on the peoples of Asia, the Americas and Africa since the sixteenth century, but the reports were often unsystematic and unreliable. Since the eighteenth century, scholars had increasingly concerned themselves with the study of the literary and religious traditions of the East. Reliable and detailed descriptions of the peoples beyond the great centres of civilization were, however, hard to come by, and the universal historians of the Enlightenment had to rely on scattered and generally unsatisfactory sources. Even the pioneer anthropologists had to make do with decontextualized and often naïve reports of exotic customs and practices. It was only in the last decades of the nineteenth century that ethnographic expeditions began to be undertaken by professional scientists. These were typically surveys of extensive regions. Their model was the field reports of botanists and zoologists, and the ethnographies they produced typically took the form of lists of cultural traits and techniques, and included physical measurements and data on natural history. The most influential of these were often guided by questionnaires issued by metropolitan theorists, notably Lewis Henry Morgan (1818–81) and J.G. Frazer (1854–1941).

In the early twentieth century there was a shift to longer, more intensive field studies of particular, often very small, populations. Franz Boas made an extended study of the native peoples of southern, coastal British Columbia, collecting a vast archive of vernacular texts from key informants. Russian scientists made intensive studies of the Siberian peoples, and European scholars began to publish studies of small societies in the tropical colonies. Between 1915 and 1918 Bronislaw Malinowski engaged in a field study of the Trobriand Islands in Melanesia that introduced a new approach to ethnographic research. He spent 2 years in the field, working in the Trobriand language, and systematically recorded not only rules, values and ceremonies but also the daily practices of social life. Influenced by the sociology of Durkheim, he conceived of the Trobrianders as constituting a social system with institutions that sustained each other and served to meet a series of basic needs. But he did not provide a merely idealized account of the social order, insisting rather that even in small-scale and homogeneous communities social practices often diverged from the rules, and that individuals engaged in rational, strategic behaviour to maximize personal advantage.

Malinowski's method of fieldwork, which came to be termed 'participant observation', eventually became the standard mode of ethnographic research. In particular, the British school of social anthropology exploited the potential of this method and produced a series of classic ethnographies that may prove to be the most enduring achievement of twentieth-century social and cultural anthropology. (See e.g. Firth 1936; Evans-Pritchard 1937; Malinowski 1922, 1935; Turner 1957.) Soon large regions of Africa, Indonesia, Melanesia and the Amazon had been documented in a set of interlinked ethnographic studies that provided a basis for intensive regional comparison.

The ethnographies produced between about 1920 and 1970 were typically holistic in conception. The guiding notion was that the institutions of the society under study formed an integrated

and self-regulating system. As a heuristic device this was undoubtedly fruitful, since it directed attention to the links between different domains of social and cultural life, and resulted in rounded accounts of communities. However, this perspective tended to exclude history and social change. It also tended to neglect social and cultural processes that crossed borders, and it was not adapted to the investigation of the effects of the colonial institutions that impinged on local social life. From the 1960s, ethnographers increasingly began to develop historical perspectives, drawing on oral traditions as well as archival sources, particularly as more studies were undertaken in peasant societies in Europe and the Near and Far East. Sociologists had begun to undertake 'ethnographic' studies of urban populations on Malinowski's model in the 1930s, but it was not until the 1970s that social and cultural anthropologists began to do field studies on a regular basis in the cities, suburbs, factories and bureaucracies of Western societies.

Comparison and explanation

Ethnography was perhaps the most successful enterprise of social and cultural anthropology, but what was the purpose of piling up meticulous ethnographies that dealt mainly with small and remote communities? There were four possible responses to this challenge. (1) The first, historically, was the evolutionist notion that living so-called primitive peoples would provide insights into the ways of life of our own ancestors. (2) Some anthropologists believed that the evidence provided by comparative ethnography would permit the definition of the elements of a universal human nature. (3) Drawing on the social sciences (particularly after 1920), many anthropologists argued that ethnographic research and comparison would permit the development of genuinely universal social sciences, which embraced all the peoples of the world. (Virtually all research in the other social sciences was devoted to the study of modern Western societies.) (4) Humanists, often sceptical about generalizations concerning human behaviour, and critical of the positivist tradition, argued that the understanding of strange ways of life was valuable in itself. It would extend our appreciation of what it means to be human, inculcate a salutary sense of the relativity of values and extend our sympathies.

(1) The evolutionist faith was that the social and cultural history of humankind could be arranged in a series of fixed stages, through which populations progressed at different speeds. This central idea was badly shaken by the critiques of the Boasians and other scholars in the early twentieth century, but it persisted in some schools of archaeology and was sustained by Marxist writers. There have been attempts to revive a generalized evolutionist history in a more sophisticated form (e.g. Gellner 1988). There have also been detailed studies of type cases designed to illuminate evolutionary processes. Richard Lee (1979) undertook a detailed account of !Kung Bushman economic life, for example, with the explicit aim of seeking clues to the way of life of Upper Palaeolithic foraging populations. His study revealed that the !Kung could sustain a viable way of life using simply technologies in a marginal environment, and the details of !Kung social and economic organization were widely referred to as a paradigmatic example of hunter-gatherer life now and in the distant past (Lee and DeVore 1968). An influential critique has argued that on the contrary the !Kung are to be understood in terms of their particular modern history. They are the heirs of centuries of contact with Bantu-speaking pastoralists and with European colonists, and their way of life represents a defensive adaptation to exploitation (Wilmsen 1989). Others argued that the culture of the !Kung could best be understood as a local example of a specific cultural tradition, shared by pastoralist Khoisan peoples as well as other Kalahari Bushmen groups. These critiques are reminiscent of the Boasian critiques of the evolutionist theories of their day.

A related tradition, sometimes termed neo-evolutionist, was concerned rather with human universals, and with the relationships between human capacities and forms of behaviour and those of other primates. In the1970s and 1980s, the sociobiological movement gave a fresh impetus to this project, combining the ethological emphasis on human nature with a theory of selection: institutions (such as the incest taboo) could be explained in terms of their evolutionary payoff. In the 1990s, genetic determinism became fashionable. Social and cultural anthropologists were in general more impressed with the variability of customs and the speed with which cultures could change, and objected to the downplaying of cultural variation that neo-evolutionist

research programmes seemed to require (Sahlins 1976).

(2) An alternative approach to human universals was offered by the structuralism of Claude Lévi-Strauss, who argued that common intellectual processes – determined by the structure of the human mind – underlay all cultural productions (see e.g. Lévi-Strauss 1963, 1977). Lévi-Strauss was inspired by structural linguistics, but more recent approaches to the study of human cognitive universals in anthropology draw rather on cognitive studies (Sperber 1996, 2000).

(3) Social science approaches were dominant in social and cultural anthropology for much of the twentieth century. In Europe, the term social anthropology became current, reflecting the influence of the Durkheimian tradition of sociology. Ethnographic studies were typically written up in a 'functionalist' framework, which brought out the interconnections between institutions in a particular society. Attempts were also made to develop typologies of societies, religions, kinship and political systems, etc. (e.g. Fortes and Evans-Pritchard 1940). In the USA, G.P. Murdock produced a cross-cultural database to permit the testing of hypotheses about the relationships between particular variables, such as family form and economy, or between the initiation of young men and the practice of warfare, and so on (Murdock 1949). Since the mid-1980s, individualist sociologies have become more popular, but the structuralist tradition also persists. In the USA, the influence of psychology was more marked. A specialism developed that attempted to apply psychological theories in non-Western settings. Initially the main interest was in socialization, but recently there has been more emphasis upon the study of cognition (D'Andrade 1995). There is also a long and still vital tradition of regional comparison, which takes account of historical relationships and seeks to characterize local structural continuities, and more ambitious programmes of cross-cultural comparison are also being revived (Gingrich and Fox 2002).

(4) Boas and his students tended to emphasize the variety of local cultural traditions and the accidental course of their development. Some of his most creative associates, notably Edward Sapir, came to see cultural anthropology as one of the humanities, and this view characterized much of US cultural anthropology in the last decades of the twentieth century. Its leading

exponent is Clifford Geertz, who argued generally that 'interpretation' rather than 'explanation' should be the guiding aim of cultural anthropology (Geertz 1973). Anthropologists of this persuasion are sceptical about social science approaches, harbour a suspicion of typologies and reject what they describe as 'reductionist' biological theories. From the mid-1970s, poststructuralist movements in linguistics, hermeneutics and literary theory made converts. Claims for the superiority of a Western rationalist or scientific view of the world were treated with grave suspicion, and the ethnographer was urged to adopt a critical and reflexive stance (see Clifford and Marcus 1986).

Recent developments

The broad field of anthropology is sustained by its ambition to describe the full range of human variation. The ethnographic record provides a rich documentation of the social and cultural variety of human thought and institutions. Archaeology traces the full sweep of the history of the species. Biological anthropology studies human evolution and biological variation.

The uses to which these empirical investigations are put are many and diverse. Evolutionist approaches attempt to find common themes in the history of the species, or to define a common human nature, or to relate human behaviour to that of other primates. Social and psychological anthropologists engage in a dialogue with contemporary social science. They confront the models current in the social sciences with the experiences and models of people all over the world, living in very diverse circumstances. Finally, a humanist tradition aspires to provide phenomenological insights into the lived experience of other peoples.

Once criticized as the handmaiden of colonialism, anthropology is increasingly a truly international enterprise, with major centres in Brazil, Mexico, India and South Africa, where specialists concern themselves mainly with the study of the peoples of their own countries. In Europe and North America, too, there is a lively movement that applies the methods and insights of social and cultural anthropology to the description and analysis of the Western societies that were initially excluded from ethnographic investigation.

Applied anthropology developed in the 1920s,

and was initially conceived of as an aid to colonial administration. With the end of the European colonial empires, many anthropologists were drawn into the new field of development studies. Others began to apply anthropological insights to problems of ethnic relations, migration, education and medicine in their own societies. As local communities of anthropologists were established in formerly colonial societies, they too began more and more to concern themselves with the application of anthropology to the urgent problems of health, demography, migration and economic development. Medical anthropology is today probably the largest speciality within social and cultural anthropology, and a majority of US Ph.D.s in anthropology are now employed outside the academy.

ADAM KUPER
BRUNEL UNIVERSITY

References

Clifford, J. and Marcus, G. (eds) (1986) *Writing Culture: The Poetics and Politics of Ethnography*, Berkeley, CA.

D'Andrade, R. (1995) *The Development of Cognitive Anthropology*, Cambridge, UK.

Evans-Pritchard, E.E. (1937) *Witchcraft, Oracles and Magic among the Azande of the Anglo-American Sudan*, Oxford.

Firth, R. (1936) *We the Tikopia*, London.

Fortes, M. and Evans-Pritchard, E.E. (eds) (1940) *African Political Systems*, London.

Geertz, C. (1973) *The Interpretation of Cultures*, New York.

Gellner, E. (1988) *Plough, Sword and Book: The Structure of Human History*, London.

Gingrich, A. and Fox, R.G. (eds) (2002) *Anthropology, by Comparison*, London.

Lee, R. (1979) *The !Kung San: Men, Women, and Work in a Foraging Society*, Cambridge, UK.

Lee, R. and DeVore, I. (eds) (1968) *Man the Hunter*, Chicago.

Lévi-Strauss, C. (1963) *Structural Anthropology*, New York.

—— (1977) *Structural Anthropology Vol. 11*, London.

Malinowski, B. (1922) *Argonauts of the Western Pacific*, London.

—— (1935) *Coral Gardens and Their Magic*, London.

Murdock, G.P. (1949) *Social Structure*, New York.

Sahlins, M. (1976) *The Use and Abuse of Biology: An Anthropological Critique of Sociobiology*, Ann Arbor, MI.

Sperber, D. (1996) *Explaining Culture: A Naturalistic Approach*, Oxford.

—— (ed.) (2000) *Metarepresentations: A Multidisciplinary Perspective*, Oxford.

Turner, V. (1957) *Schism and Continuity in an African*

Society: A Study of Ndembu Village Life, Manchester.

Wilmsen, E. (1989) *Land Filled with Flies: A Political Economy of the Kalahari*, Chicago.

Further reading

Borofsky, R. (ed.) (1994) *Assessing Cultural Anthropology*, New York.
Kuper, A. (1994) *The Chosen Primate: Human Nature and Cultural Diversity*, Cambridge, MA.
Menagham, J. and Just, P. (2000) *Social and Cultural Anthropology: A Very Short Introduction*, Oxford.

SEE ALSO: cultural anthropology; economic anthropology; political anthropology; psychological anthropology; social anthropology

ANXIETY

Anxiety states are generally defined as unpleasant emotional reactions to anticipated injury or harm from some external danger. Charles Darwin (1872) argued that they were the product of evolution in both humans and animals, and observed that fear and anxiety vary in intensity, from mild apprehension or surprise, to an extreme 'agony of terror'. Freud regarded fear as 'objective anxiety'. The intensity of the emotional reaction was proportional to the magnitude of an external danger: the greater the external danger, the stronger the perceived threat, the more intense the resulting anxiety reaction. Freud also emphasized the experiential (phenomenological) qualities of anxiety, which he defined as 'something felt', an unpleasant emotional state characterized by subjective feelings of chronic apprehension, and by 'all that is covered by the word "nervousness"' (1924 [1895]: 79). According to Freud, the perception of danger evoked an anxiety state that served to warn the individual that some form of adjustment was necessary.

In contemporary psychiatry and psychology, anxiety refers to at least two related, yet logically different, constructs. Anxiety is most commonly used to describe an unpleasant emotional state (S-Anxiety). It may also refer to the disposition to experience anxiety as a personality trait in relatively stable individual differences (T-Anxiety). Persons high in T-Anxiety tend to see the world as a more dangerous or threatening place than is the case for most other people. They are therefore more vulnerable to stress. Consequently, they experience S-Anxiety more frequently and often with greater intensity than persons who are low in T-Anxiety.

Anxiety states can be distinguished from other unpleasant emotions, such as anger or depression, by their unique combination of experiential and physiological manifestations. An anxiety state is characterized by subjective feelings of tension, apprehension, nervousness and worry, and by activation (arousal) and discharge of the autonomic nervous system. Tension, apprehension and nervousness accompany moderate levels of anxiety. Intense feelings of fear, fright and panic are indicative of very high levels of anxiety. The physiological changes that occur in anxiety states include increased heart rate (palpitations, tachycardia), sweating, muscular tension, irregularities in breathing (hyperventilation), dilation of the pupils, dryness of the mouth, vertigo (dizziness), nausea and muscular skeletal disturbances, such as tremors and tics. Individuals who experience anxiety are generally aware of their subjective feelings, and can report the intensity and duration of these unpleasant emotional reactions.

The intensity and duration of an anxiety state will be proportional to the amount of threat that a particular situation poses for an individual, given her or his interpretation of the situation as personally dangerous. The appraisal of a particular situation as threatening will be influenced by the person's skills, abilities and past experience. The arousal of anxiety generally involves a temporally ordered sequence of events, which may be initiated by stressful external stimuli (stressors) or by internal cues that are interpreted as dangerous or threatening. Stressors are defined as situations or stimuli that are objectively characterized by some degree of physical or psychological danger. Threat denotes an individual's subjective appraisal of a situation as potentially dangerous or harmful. Appraisals of danger or threat evoke S-Anxiety, the emotional state that is at the core of the anxiety process.

Stressful situations that are frequently encountered may lead to the development of effective coping responses that quickly eliminate or minimize the danger. However, if a situation is perceived as dangerous or threatening and the individual is unable to cope with the stressor, he or she may resort to intrapsychic manœuvres (psychological defences) to eliminate or reduce the intensity of the resulting anxiety state. Psychological defence mechanisms may also modify, distort or render unconscious the feelings, thoughts and memories that would otherwise provoke S-Anxiety. To the extent that a defence mechanism is successful, the circumstances that evoke anxiety will be perceived as less threatening, and there will be a corresponding reduction in the intensity of the S-Anxiety reaction. However, defence mechanisms are generally inefficient and often maladaptive because the underlying problems that caused the anxiety remain unaltered.

While everyone experiences anxiety states from time to time, there are substantial interpersonal differences in the frequency and the intensity with which these states occur. So if we are told, 'Ms Smith is anxious', this may mean that she is anxious *now, at this very moment*, or that she *frequently* experiences anxiety. If Ms Smith is anxious right now, she is experiencing S-Anxiety as an unpleasant emotional state. If she experiences anxiety states more often than others, she is high in T-Anxiety, and may be classified as 'an anxious person'. Even though Ms Smith may be an *anxious person*, whether or not she is *anxious now* will depend on how she interprets her present circumstances.

Psychologists have identified two important classes of stressors that evoke anxiety states in people who differ in trait anxiety. Persons high in T-Anxiety are more concerned about being evaluated by others because they lack confidence in themselves and are low in self-esteem. Situations that involve psychological threats, i.e. threats to self-esteem, particularly ego-threats when personal adequacy is evaluated, are generally more threatening for persons who are high in T-Anxiety. Individuals very high in trait anxiety, e.g. psychoneurotics or patients suffering from depression, frequently experience high levels of S-Anxiety. In contrast, persons high or low in T-Anxiety generally experience comparable increases in S-Anxiety when responding to situations involving physical danger, such as imminent surgery. Prior to 1950, there were no well-established measures of anxiety, and relatively few experimental studies of anxiety in humans (May 1950), in part because there were ethical problems associated with inducing anxiety in laboratory studies. The Taylor Manifest Anxiety Scale (TMAS) (1953) was the first widely used psychometric instrument designed to assess anxiety in adults. The fifty items comprising the TMAS were selected from the Minnesota Multi-

phasic Personality Inventory (Hathaway and McKinley 1951) on the basis of a textbook description of the symptoms observed in patients suffering from anxiety neurosis (Cameron 1947), a clinical syndrome first identified by Freud (1924 [1895]). Respondents to the TMAS report whether or not each item describes how they generally feel.

Over the past 40 years, Cattell's (1966) Anxiety Scale Questionnaire (ASQ) and the State-Trait Anxiety Inventory (STAI: Spielberger 1983; Spielberger *et al.* 1970) have also been widely used to assess anxiety in research and clinical practice. Cattell (1966) pioneered the use of multivariate techniques in the assessment of anxiety, and was the first to identify trait and state anxiety as unique constructs. The forty-item ASQ, which is highly correlated with the TMAS, provides an objective measure of individual differences in trait anxiety.

The concepts of state and trait anxiety, as refined and elaborated by Spielberger (1972, 1983), provided the conceptual framework for constructing the STAI, which was intended to provide reliable, relatively brief, self-report scales for assessing state and trait anxiety in research and clinical practice (Spielberger *et al.* 1970). In developing the STAI, the initial goal was to identify a single set of items that could be administered with different instructions to assess the intensity of S-Anxiety and individual differences in T-Anxiety. However, subsequent research indicated that altering the instructions could not overcome the strong state or trait psycholinguistic connotations of the key words in a number of items (Spielberger *et al.* 1970).

Given the difficulties encountered in measuring state and trait anxiety using the same items, the best items for assessing S-Anxiety and T-Anxiety respectively were selected for the STAI (Form X). When given with trait instructions, the twenty items with the best concurrent validity, as indicated by the highest correlations with the TMAS and the ASQ, and that were stable over time, were selected for the T-Anxiety scale (Spielberger *et al.* 1970). The twenty items with the best construct validity when given with state instructions, as indicated by higher or lower scores under stressful and non-stressful conditions, were selected for the S-Anxiety Scale. Factor analyses of the STAI(-Form Y) have consistently identified distinct state and trait anxiety factors (Spielberger 1983). Since the STAI was first published more than 30 years ago (Spielberger *et al.* 1970), this inventory has been translated and adapted in sixty-two languages and dialects, and cited in more than 14,000 archival studies.

CHARLES D. SPIELBERGER
UNIVERSITY OF SOUTH FLORIDA, TAMPA

References

Cameron, N. (1947) *The Psychology of Behavior Disorders: A Bio-social Interpretation*, Boston.

Cattell, R.B. (1966) 'Patterns of change: Measurement in relation to state-dimension, trait change, lability, and process concepts', *Handbook of Multivariate Experimental Psychology*, Chicago.

Darwin, C. (1872) *The Expression of Emotions in Man and Animals*, London.

Freud, S. (1924 [1895]) *Collected Papers*, Vol. 1, London.

Hathaway, S.R. and McKinley, J.C. (1951) *The Minnesota Multiphasic Personality Inventory Manual. Revised*, New York.

May, R. (1977 version [original publication 1950]) *The Meaning of Anxiety*, New York.

Spielberger, C.D., (1972) 'Anxiety as an emotional state', in C.D. Spielberger (ed.) *Anxiety: Current Trends in Theory and Research*, Vol. 1, New York, pp. 24–49.

—— (1983) *Manual for the State-Trait Anxiety Inventory: STAI (Form Y)*, Palo Alto, CA.

Spielberger, C.D., Gorsuch, R.L. and Lushene, R.D. (1970) *STAI: Manual for the State-Trait Anxiety Inventory*, Palo Alto, CA.

Taylor, J.A. (1953) 'A personality scale of manifest anxiety', *Journal of Abnormal Social Psychology* 48: 285–90.

SEE ALSO: anger, hostility and aggression; emotion

ARISTOTLE (384–322 BCE)

Aristotle (Aristotelês) was born in 384 BCE at Stageira (also spelled Stageiros), in the Chalcidic peninsula of northern mainland Greece. His father was physician to King Amyntas III of Macedon, a kingdom that was at first merely adjacent to Chalcidice but by the time of Aristotle's death had swallowed it up and physically destroyed Stageira itself (348, later rebuilt). In 367 he joined Plato's Academy of scholars and intellectuals in Athens, leaving it only in 347 on the founder's death. After sojourns in Macedon (where he was hired by Amyntas's son Philip II to instruct his son and heir Alexander, later Alexander III the Great) and northwest Anatolia (where he married the ward of a local absolute ruler, another former pupil of Plato), and travels in the eastern Mediterranean (where he encountered Theophrastus, who was to succeed him as head of his own school), he returned to Athens in the mid-330s to found the institute for advanced study known as the Lyceum after its location within a grove devoted to Wolfish Apollo. Anti-Macedonian reaction in 323, following the death of Alexander at Babylon, compelled him to leave Athens once more, and he died in 322 at Chalcis on the neighbouring island of Euboea, thereby helping to prevent the Athenians from sinning against philosophy a second time (the first being the death sentence against Socrates in 399).

Some 500 titles of works were attributed in antiquity to Aristotle, whose extraordinary personal library passed eventually into the famous Library built at Alexandria in the early third century BCE. But only some thirty works actually survive, all composed for 'esoteric' consumption within the Lyceum rather than for 'exoteric' use, and some have been preserved solely through Arabic translations done in Baghdad or Moorish Spain. Their inelegant, jerky style probably faithfully reflects both their origin in lecture notes and Aristotle's determinedly down-to-earth manner (the fresco by Raphael known as *The School of Athens* depicts him with his hand pointing down towards the earth, in contrast to Plato next to him who points upwards to heaven). Aristotle was primarily a scientist, as that term would then have been understood, with major interests in biology and zoology, and a preoccupation with minute empirical observation and taxonomy. The generic term for his intellectual activity was *historia*, 'enquiry'.

In his social scientific writings on ethics and politics he adopted the method of beginning from the *phainomena* (that which seemed to be the case) of the sublunary perceptible world and from the *endoxa* (the reputable opinions of reputable people of intelligence and perception) entertained about it, but only so as then to go on from and beyond them in the direction of ever greater analytic precision and philosophical, including logical, refinement. He was indeed the founder of a systematic logic, which eliminated many of the sophistical puzzles that had perplexed earlier thinkers, and he extended the idea of mathematical proof to other areas of philosophical and scientific thought. He was especially concerned to clarify and systematize the principles of argument that had been worked out piecemeal and empirically in law courts and assembly debates, and in written as well as oral disputes between medical and other scientific or would-be scientific practitioners.

His early master, Plato, had believed that the visible world was merely an imperfect reflection of a reality that could be apprehended only intellectually, by a very select few. Aristotle claimed not to understand the relation between Plato's Forms and the ordinary real world of change and sense-data, and, perhaps influenced by his father's medical background, took the robustly practical view that it was the duty of the philosopher to reason out the right way for humankind in society and then to persuade rather than impose on his fellow-citizens. In his *Politics* ('Matters concerning the *polis* state-form') Aristotle's primary emphasis was characteristically not on the construction of an absolutely ideal polity so much as the improvement of existing real polities in line with precepts of demonstrable or plausibly predictable practicality.

In Aristotle's day the importance of private, in contradistinction to public, civic life was growing, partly as the scope for independent political action diminished in an era increasingly dominated by large territorial states. This to some extent explains Aristotle's preoccupation with friendship, apparent in all three of his Ethical writings, especially the *Nicomachean Ethics*; though one kind of friendship he analysed was precisely a political kind, and the *polis* or citizen-state was never far from the centre of his preoccupations. Indeed, in light of the super-session of the *polis* as a power-unit his preoccupation with it can be seen to be somewhat reactionary. On the one hand, he commented – perhaps with one wary eye to his former pupil Alexander – that, if the Greeks could achieve a single political framework of self-governance, a common *politeia*, they would rule the world. On the other hand, man as a species being was defined by him precisely as a living creature designed by its nature to achieve it full actualization within and only within the framework of the individual, small-scale *polis*. That is the full meaning of his often traduced definition of the human being as a *politikon zöon*, a 'political animal'. He and his pupils researched and wrote

up the 'constitutions' of more than 150 contemporary polities, most of them Greek *poleis*.

The second major source of tensions in Aristotle's life, between opposing epistemologies, was perhaps even more fruitful than that between different constructions of the political. He firmly asserted both the practical utility and the intellectual satisfactions of studying even the apparently lowest forms of animal life and of engaging in dissection (though not of living organisms, nor of human corpses). He extended the methods of research developed in medicine to the whole field of biology. He reflected systematically on logic and processes of reasoning, both human and – by analogy – animal. The characteristics that humans shared with animals, for example a kind of courage, became a basis for understanding, and that intellectual transformation had particularly far-reaching implications for psychology.

Being a prophet of things as they are inevitably meant embracing, and indeed seeking to justify philosophically, current Greek conceptions of the nature and status of women and the necessity of unfreedom for many, especially non-Greeks. Hence were derived Aristotle's rebarbative view that women (all women, including Greek) were biologically deformed, that is incomplete, males, and sociobiologically speaking the second sex, since their reasoning capacity was inauthoritative. Hence, too, his lame and retrogressive defence of a 'natural' form of slavery, in cases where the enslaved lacked by nature – and so irreparably – the reasoning capacity altogether and had to have it supplied for them by a master or mistress. Since such natural slaves were by definition non-Greeks, the natural slave doctrine could connote racism as well as extreme illiberalism. Aristotle also believed that money-making for its own sake was morally wrong, which led him to misprise the economic developments of his own day, though he made a better shot at properly economic analysis of pre-capitalist wages, prices and profit than any of his predecessors.

Within these limits, however, Aristotle has often been an inspiration to those who wish for a more fully participatory form of political engagement, and heed the call for a return to the Greeks' view of politics as the life and soul of the good citizen's endeavours. He was a shrewd observer of human social behaviour and accepted that social conflict was inevitable as long as there were economic differences between rich and poor of a kind that would later be analysed as due to and expressive of socioeconomic 'class'. The best way to achieve a due measure of social stability, he believed, was for there to be a sufficiently large intermediate class of middling citizens who would hold the political balance between the two extreme groups, a theory that certainly applied with force to the society of Athens within which he chose to spend the majority of his adult life as an unenfranchised resident alien. Firmly rejecting the Socratic-Platonic view that virtue is knowledge, since he was aware that people often fail to do what they know they should, he argued instead that virtue was an activity of soul lying in the mean between excess and defect – a sophisticated philosophical version of the maxim inscribed on the contemporary temple of Apollo at Delphi, 'Nothing in Excess' (*mêden agan*).

From one standpoint – one that Aristotle himself would not have rejected outright – Aristotle seems to be an intellectual consolidator, a synthesizer and sytematizer of ideas originally formulated by others rather than a minter of brand new theory. On the other hand, Aristotle opened up new fields of *historia*, made lasting contributions to methodology and technical-scientific vocabulary, and proposed critical readings and intelligent solutions of longstanding philosophical dilemmas. For those achievements, unparalleled in his own day and rarely attained since, the Stagirite fully deserves Karl Marx's accolade of 'giant thinker'.

PAUL CARTLEDGE
UNIVERSITY OF CAMBRIDGE

Further reading

Barnes, J. (1980) 'Aristotle and the methods of ethics', *Revue internationale de philosophie* 133–4: 490–511.
—— (ed.) (1995) *The Cambridge Companion to Aristotle*, Cambridge.
Cartledge, P. (2002) *The Greeks. A Portrait of Self and Others*, 2nd edn, Oxford.
Garnsey, P. (1996) *Ideas of Slavery from Aristotle to Augustine*, Cambridge, UK.
Humphreys, S.C. (1993) 'The family in Classical Athens' (1983), repr. in *The Family, Women and Death*, 2nd edn, Ann Arbor.
Konstan, D. (1997) *Friendship in the Classical World*, Cambridge, UK.
Lloyd, G.E.R. (1968) *Aristotle: The Growth and Structure of His Thought*, Cambridge, UK.
Meikle, S. (1995) *Aristotle's Economic Thought*, Oxford.
Owen, G.E.L. (1986) 'Tithenai ta phainomena' (1961),
repr. in M. Nussbaum (ed.) *Logic, Science and Dialectics*, London, pp. 239–51.
Rowe, C. (2000) 'Aristotelian constitutions', in C. Rowe and M. Schofield (eds) *The Cambridge History of Greek and Roman Political Thought*, Cambridge, ch. 18.
Rowe, C. and Schofield, M. (eds) (2000) *The Cambridge History of Greek and Roman Political Thought*, Cambridge, UK.
de Ste. Croix, G.E.M. (1983) *The Class Struggle in the Ancient Greek World*, rev. impr., London and Ithaca.
Schofield, M. (2000) 'Aristotle: An introduction', in C. Rowe and M. Schofield (eds) *The Cambridge History of Greek and Roman Political Thought*, Cambridge, UK, ch. 15.
Sorabji, R. (1995) *Animal Minds and Human Morals: The Origins of the Western Debate*, London and Ithaca.
Wood, N. and Wood, E.M. (1978) *Class Ideology and Ancient Political Theory: Socrates, Plato and Aristotle in Social Context*, Oxford.

ART, SOCIOLOGY OF

The term 'sociology of art' has been widely supplanted by the more inclusive term 'sociology of the arts'. This growing area of specialization is concerned with the visual arts, literature, music, drama, film, crafts and other art forms, which it treats from various sociological perspectives. Research focuses on processes like artistic production (or creation), mediation and the reception (or consumption), as well as the characteristics of people, networks and organizations involved with these processes.

While no single theoretical framework dominates the field, several approaches have particularly marked the sociology of the arts over the past half-century, among them Marxist and neo-Marxist approaches; symbolic interactionism; neo-structuralism and the so-called 'production of culture approach'.

The Marxist legacy in theories of the arts and society

Is art outside of society? Does art 'reflect' society? Can the arts shape social values and practices? Sociologists direct their attention to the social processes and political institutions, ideologies and other factors that situate art, and influence artists (Zolberg 1990). Seminal early work by Marxist sociologists like Theodor Adorno, Antonio Gramsci and Lucien Goldmann continues to fuel discussion about the place of class-based taste and aesthetic practices in processes of domination and resistance in society.

For example, Adorno suggested that the culture industries promoted art forms that induce passivity (such as styles of popular music), whereas avant-garde art forms stimulate critical thinking and resist commercialization. Others contend that art catering to 'low-brow' tastes and working-class values has creatively and effectively challenged hegemonic authority.

Marxist approaches to art, popular in many other parts of the world since the 1960s, had less influence in English-speaking America. Critics claimed that reflection theory – the notion that art reflects societal values and practices – is overly reductive. Another complaint was that critical theorists failed to take into account the specificity of aesthetic content and values, and seldom put their theoretical claims to empirical test. Nevertheless, some writers creatively combined Marxist aesthetics with insights drawn from psychology and semiotics (Luhmann 2000 [1995]). Questions of 'content' were addressed by examining art works as 'texts' or 'codes'. Other sociologists have studied the social conventions associated with the arts, considering, for example, the expectations of different types of readers and their effect upon the reception of literary works and films. And Marxist ideas infiltrated other perspectives. For example, contemporary work on the place of aesthetic experiences and conduct in cognition and agency draws on Adorno's complex oeuvre (Tia DeNora 2003; Witkin 2002).

The social organization of art worlds

Sociologists of the arts have devoted much attention to the social processes and institutions that structure artistic creation, mediation and reception. Drawing on symbolic interactionism, Howard Becker proposed a framework for understanding the social organization of the arts as networks of 'art worlds' (Becker 1982, http://home.earthlink.net/hsbecker/), showing how participants in elite and in popular art worlds develop creative relationships through conventions, consensus and collaboration. He associates different forms of social interaction with specific art forms, and analyses various categories of participants, some with roles that fall outside the occupational categories normally associated with the arts. In his discussion of filmmaking, for example, he considers camera equipment manufacturers, electrical technicians, scriptwriters,

camera operators, actors, directors and producers. He also proposed a typology of artists, distinguishing integrated professionals (who work within the conventions of their art world); mavericks (who know the rules of the game but choose not to follow them); folk artists (who work in artistic genres with different goals); and naïve artists (who generally work outside of aesthetic conventions).

Studies of outsider art, non-Western artistic traditions, and the efforts by non-Western artists to engage with avant-garde aesthetic movements suggest that contemporary practices are diversifying (Oguibe and Enwezor 1999; Zolberg and Cherbo 1997). However, funding opportunities and major institutions with connections to international art markets remain highly centralized in most artistic fields. Work in the arts has long been marked by rapidly changing tastes, strong seasonal variations, irregular remuneration and reliance on alternative part-time employment, features emphasised in studies of artistic labour markets and contemporary career strategies (Menger 2003).

Studies of the social organization of the arts are not only concerned with direct participants in artistic creation. Organizational structures also shape (and are influenced by) social boundaries that are important for understanding mediation and reception. Critics, gallery owners and impresarios may function as gatekeepers, participating in the processes that define and legitimate cultural practices related to the arts (Balfe 1993; Shrum 1996). Fans, connoisseurs and various types of patrons have played crucial roles in structuring both popular and high-culture art forms.

The high-culture model

Organizational structures of arts institutions and patterns of patronage are intimately connected to status distinctions. For example, beginning with successful initiatives in classical music and the visual arts, elite forms of organization that relied on not-for-profit models were extended to embrace theatre, opera and dance in the USA. This movement promoted institutional change and fostered new elites (DiMaggio 1991). Elite arts participation and philanthropy have also sometimes responded to the need to balance prestige with diversity and accessibility (Ostrower 2002).

The association of 'high culture' with elite tastes and education has attracted the attention of researchers who are concerned with the persistence of social inequalities. In his studies of the social production (and reproduction) of culture, Pierre Bourdieu developed core notions that are now used by many sociologists of the arts (sometimes rather indiscriminately), among them cultural capital, *habitus* and the value of symbolic goods (Bourdieu 1993).

The production of culture perspective, and new approaches

Richard Peterson introduced the 'production of culture' perspective in the 1970s, arguing that the symbolic content of culture (and of specific art forms) is shaped by the context in which it is produced and disseminated. For example, the interaction of music promoters, music makers and their fans was crucial for the invention of the conventions and stylistic features that came to define country music as a genre (Peterson 1997). This approach has influenced research on the arts, media and informally produced culture (Alexander 2003; Dowd 2002).

New approaches combine the 'production of culture' perspective with ideas drawn from other current sociological frameworks, including post-colonialism, neo-institutionalism and actor-network theory (Hennion 2001). Nathalie Heinich has produced an influential body of work that cuts across disciplinary boundaries, beginning with monographs about how artists and art works have gained recognition, historically and in contemporary society (Heinich 1998). She proposed that contemporary artists attain notoriety through a three-fold game of transgression (by the artist), rejection (by uninitiated publics) and the eventual integration of new values. In this process the onus is on the artist to express singularity in ways that are recognizable to art world insiders. Studies of censorship controversies and cases of vandalism and iconoclasm provide insights into social values and expectations of different cultural groups (Gamboni 1997; Marcus 1998). Studies of participation in the arts, the development of tastes and the cultural heritage movement have drawn attention to identity issues, agency and collective memory (Griswold 2000; Halle 1993; Tota 2002). Developments in other fields have penetrated the sociology of the arts, and public interest has been stimulated by commentators and policy-makers who recognize the contribution made by the arts to well-being and economic vitality in contemporary society (Florida 2002).

JAN MARONTATE
ACADIA UNIVERSITY, CANADA

References

Alexander, V. (2003) *Sociology of the Arts. Exploring Fine and Popular Forms*, London.

Balfe, J. (ed.) (1993) *Paying the Piper. Causes and Consequences of Art Patronage*, Chicago.

Becker, H. (1982) *Art Worlds*, Berkeley, CA.

Bourdieu, P. (1993) *The Field of Cultural Production*, Cambridge, UK.

DeNora, T. (2003) *After Adorno. Rethinking Music Sociology*, Cambridge, UK.

DiMaggio, P. (1991) 'The extension of the high culture model to theater, opera and the dance, 1900–1940', in M. Lamont and M. Fournier (eds) *Cultivating Differences: Symbolic Boundaries and the Making of Inequalities*, Chicago, pp. 21–57.

Dowd, T. (2002) 'Culture and commodification: Technology and structural power in the early US recording industry', *International Journal of Sociology and Social Policy* 22(1–3): 106–40.

Florida, R. (2002) *The Rise of the Creative Class and How It's Transforming Work, Leisure, Community and Everyday Life*, New York.

Gamboni, D. (1997) *The Destruction of Art. Iconoclasm and Vandalism since the French Revolution*, New Haven, CT.

Griswold, W. (2000) *Bearing Witness. Readers, Writers, and the Novel in Nigeria*, Princeton, NJ.

Halle, D. (1993) *Inside Culture. Art and Class in the American Home*, Chicago.

Heinich, Nathalie (1998) *Le Triple Jeu de l'art contemporain*, Paris.

Hennion, A. (2001) 'Music lovers. Taste as performance', *Theory, Culture, Society* 18(5): 1–22.

Luhmann, N. (2000 [1995])) *Art as a Social System*, Stanford, CA.

Marcus, G.E. (1998) 'Censorship in the heart of difference: Cultural property, indigenous peoples: Movements, and challenges to Western liberal thought', in R. Post (ed.) *Censorship and Silencing: Practices of Cultural Regulation*, Santa Monica, CA.

Menger, P.-M. (2003) *Portrait de l'artiste en travailleur. Métamorphoses du capitalisme*, Paris.

Oguibe, O. and Enwezor, O. (eds) (1999) *Reading the Contemporary. African Art from Theory to the Marketplace*, Cambridge, UK.

Ostrower, F. (2002) *Trustees of Culture. Power, Wealth and Status on Elite Arts Boards*, Chicago.

Peterson, R.A. (1997) *Creating Country Music. Fabricating Authenticity*, Chicago.

Shrum, W. (1996) *Fringe and Fortune. The Role of Critics in High and Popular Art*, Princeton, NJ.

Tota, A.L. (2002) 'Homeless memories: How societies forget their past', *Studies in Communication Scences* 1: 193–214.

Witkin, R.W. (2002) *Adorno on Popular Culture*, London.

Zolberg, V. (1990) *Constructing a Sociology of the Arts*, London.

Zolberg, V. and Cherbo, J.M. (eds) (1997) *Outsider Art. Contesting Boundaries in Contemporary Culture*, Cambridge, UK.

SEE ALSO: mass media; popular culture

ARTIFICIAL INTELLIGENCE

Research in artificial intelligence (AI) represents an attempt to understand intelligent behaviour (and its prerequisites: perception, language use and the mental representation of information) by making computers reproduce it. It has historical precedents in the work of Pascal, Leibniz and Babbage, who all devised schemes for intelligent machines that were impractical, given the mechanical components from which it was envisaged that those machines would be constructed. The existence of AI as an independent discipline, however, can be traced to the invention of the digital computer, and, more specifically, to a conference at Dartford College, New Hampshire, in 1956. At that conference, Allen Newell, Cliff Shaw and Herbert Simon (see e.g. 1957) described the use of heuristic, rule of thumb, procedures for solving problems, and showed how those procedures could be encoded as computer programs. Their work contrasted sharply with immediately preceding attempts to explain intelligent behaviour by modelling the properties of brain cells.

Newell *et al.*'s work led to the development of more sophisticated programming languages (in particular John McCarthy's LISP), and their general approach, dubbed *semantic information processing* by Marvin Minsky, was applied to fields as diverse as visual object recognition, language understanding and chess playing. The advent of larger, faster computers forced AI researchers to confront the problem of whether their programs would scale up so that they could operate in the real world, rather than on small-scale laboratory tasks. Could a program that conversed about wooden blocks on a table top be generalized so that it could talk about poverty in the developing world, for example?

Often the answer was: no. Tricks that worked in a limited range of cases would fail on other cases from the same domain. For example, ideas used in early object recognition programs were later shown to be restricted to objects with flat surfaces. Many aspects of intelligence came, therefore, to be seen as the exercise of domain-specific knowledge, which had to be encoded in detail into computer programs, and separately for each subdomain. This conception of intelligence led to the construction of *expert systems*. DENDRAL (see Lindsay *et al.* 1980), which computed the structure of complex organic molecules, and MYCIN (see Shortliffe 1976), which diagnosed serious bacterial infections, were the first such systems, and they remain among the best known. Expert systems have become commercially important, usually in the guise of sophisticated *aides-mémoires* for human experts, rather than as replacements for them. One of their principal strengths is their ability to process probabilistic information, which contributes to many kinds of diagnosis. In recent years attention has focused on discovering the detailed formal properties of such systems.

A different attack on the semantic information processing research of the 1960s came from David Marr (see, in particular, 1982). Marr argued that AI researchers had failed to provide a *computational theory* of the tasks their machines were trying to carry out. By a computational theory he meant an account of what outputs those machines were trying to produce from their inputs, and why. Marr wanted to combine evidence from neurophysiology and perceptual psychology with computational techniques from AI, and other parts of computer science, to produce a detailed and explanatory account of human vision. Although he did not wholly succeed before his untimely death in his mid-thirties, his work on the lower levels of the human visual system remains the paradigmatic example of successful research in cognitive science.

Marr's computational models contained units that were intended to mimic the properties of cells in the visual system. He, therefore, reintroduced techniques that had been sidelined by Newell *et al.*'s information processing approach. *Connectionism* is a more direct descendant of the earlier neural modelling approach. However, the units from which connectionist models are built are not based on specific classes of nerve cells, as those in Marr's models are.

Marr questioned whether traditional AI could generate *explanations* of intelligent behaviour, and connectionists asked whether it could model *biological*, and in particular human, intelligence. Not surprisingly, therefore, many AI researchers in the 1980s embraced the engineering side of the discipline, and focused their attention on its applications. This orientation was also sensible at a time when funding was more readily available for projects with short- to intermediate-term returns. Ideas from AI, albeit not always in a pure form, found their way into commercial expert systems, learning aids, robots, machine vision and image processing systems, and speech and language technology. Indeed, techniques that have their origin in AI are now widespread in many types of software development, particularly of programs that run on personal computers. Object-oriented programming was first introduced in the AI language SMALLTALK. It is now a staple of programming in languages such as C++, one of the standards for writing Windows applications.

Learning posed another problem for traditional AI. The semantic information processing approach assumed that the analysis of an ability, such as chess playing, should be at an abstract level, independent of the underlying hardware – person or machine – and independent of how the hardware came to have the ability, by learning or by being programmed. The ability to learn is itself an ability that might be modelled in an AI program, and some AI programs were indeed programs that learned. However, a vague unease that learning was not receiving the attention it deserved fostered the feeling, in some quarters, that machines could never be really intelligent unless they could learn for themselves. Furthermore, the kinds of learning modelled in AI programs were limited. For example, concept learning programs were capable only of making slightly more complex concepts out of simpler ones that were programmed into them. For some kinds of *machine induction* this kind of learning is satisfactory, and it can produce impressive results on large machines. However, it leaves questions about the limitations of such methods of learning unanswered.

Connectionism, with its techniques of pattern abstraction and generalization, has been seen by many as at least a partial solution to the problems about learning that beset traditional AI. A different approach is based on the analogy between evolution and learning, and on the idea that many types of intelligent behaviour are the product of evolution, rather than of learning in individual animals. *Genetic algorithms* were originally invented in John Holland (see 1992) who showed, perhaps surprisingly, that computer programs can be evolved by a method that parallels evolution by natural selection. The programs are broken into pieces that can be recombined according to fixed rules (as bits of genetic material are recombined in sexual reproduction). The new programs then attempt to perform the to-be-learned task, and the ones that work best are selected to enter the next round, and to leave offspring of their own. As in evolution, this process must be iterated many times if order is to emerge, in the form of a program that can carry out the required task. The use of genetic algorithms is important in the discipline of artificial life, which is broader in scope and more controversial than AI. Research in artificial life tries to create robots that behave intelligently in something approaching a natural environment. It also attempts to model social and other contextual influences on such behaviour, such as the factors that influence how flocks of birds behave. In artificial life it is typically assumed that intelligence does not lie in an individual organism, or even a group of organisms but in a broader system that includes the environment – the notion of *situated cognition*.

Many of the controversies that surround artificial life are philosophical ones, and they often parallel those generated by AI research. Two main questions have been prompted by work in AI. First, can machines really exhibit intelligence, or can they only simulate it in the way that meteorological computers simulate weather systems? Second, if there were intelligent machines, what moral issues would their existence raise? Potentially, intelligent machines are different from weather-predicting computers, since those computers do not produce rain, whereas robots could act intelligently in the real world. The moral question, like all moral questions raised by scientific advances, must be addressed by society and not specifically by AI researchers.

ALAN GARNHAM
UNIVERSITY OF SUSSEX

References

Holland, J.H. (1992) *Adaptation in Natural and Artificial Systems: An Introductory Analysis with Applications to Biology, Control, and Artificial Intelligence*, 2nd edn, Cambridge, MA.

Lindsay, R., Buchanan, B.G., Feigenbaum, E.A. and Lederberg, J. (1980) *Applications of Artificial Intelligence for Chemical Inference: The DENDRAL Project*, New York.

Marr, D. (1982) *Vision: A Computational Investigation into the Human Representation and Processing of Visual Information*, San Francisco.

Newell, A., Shaw, J.C. and Simon, H.A. (1957) 'Empirical explorations with the Logic Theory Machine: A case study in heuristics', *Proceedings of the Western Joint Computer Conference* 15: 218–30.

Shortliffe, E.H. (1976) 'A model of inexact reasoning in medicine', *Mathematical Biosciences* 23: 361–79.

Further reading

Bender, E.A. (ed.) (1996) *Mathematical Methods in Artificial Intelligence*, Los Alamatos, CA.

Chrisley, R. (ed.) (2000) *Artificial Intelligence: Critical Concepts*, vols 1–4, London.

Luger, G.F. (2002) *Artificial Intelligence: Strategies for Complex Problem Solving*, 4th edn, Harlow, UK.

Russell, S. and Norvig, P. (2002) *Artificial Intelligence: A Modern Approach*, 2nd edn, Upper Saddle River, NJ.

Winston, P.H. (1992) *Artificial Intelligence*, 3rd edn, Reading, MA.

SEE ALSO: computer simulation; connectionism; mind; problem-solving

ASYMMETRIC INFORMATION

Asymmetric information, as the adjective indicates, refers to situations in which an agent engaged in a transaction possesses information that is not available to other agents involved in the same transaction. This rather self-evident premise has nevertheless revolutionized modern economic thought since the 1970s. Take, for example, two major results in the economics and finance literature, the *first fundamental theorem of welfare economics* and the *Modigliani–Miller theorem*.

The first welfare theorem states that in a competitive economy with no externalities, prices would adjust so that the allocation of resources would be *optimal* in the Pareto sense (an environment is *competitive* when the action of any one single agent does not affect prices; there is an *externality* in the economy when the action of one single agent directly affects the welfare of other agents; finally, an allocation is said to be *Pareto* optimal if there does not exist any other allocation that makes at least one individual better off without making other agents worse off). A key assumption that must be made if the theorem is to hold is that the characteristics of all products traded on the market should be equally observed by all agents. When this assumption fails to hold, i.e. when information is *asymmetric*, prices are distorted and optimality in the allocation of resources is not achieved. Standard government interventions such as regulation of monopolies to replicate a competitive environment, or fiscal policy to alleviate the effects of externalities, are no longer sufficient to restore optimality. Similarly, in the finance literature, the Modigliani–Miller theorem concluded that the value of a firm is independent of its financial structure. The acknowledgement of asymmetric information within organizations shifted the debate on optimal financial structure from fiscal considerations to the provision of incentives to align the interests of managers and workers with the interests of stakeholders.

When two (or more) individuals are about to agree on a trade, and one of them happens to have some information that the other(s) do not have, this situation is referred to as *adverse selection*. Seminal contributions include Akerlof (1970), Spence (1973), and Rothschild and Stiglitz (1976) (in 2001, the Nobel Prize in Economic Science was awarded to Akerlof, Spence and Stiglitz 'for their analyses of markets with asymmetric information'). Each of these three papers investigates the implications of adverse selection on the product, labour and insurance markets respectively. Akerlof (1970) considers the example of a seller who has private information about the quality of a used car. A buyer would like to acquire a car, but is keen on paying a 'fair' price for it, i.e. a price that is consistent with the quality of the car. To make things more concrete, suppose that there are nine different cars, each car having 'fair' value, $100, $200...$900 respectively. As the buyer cannot observe quality, owners of low-quality cars will always claim they are selling a high-quality product worth $900. A fair price will then reflect the average quality of the market, in this case $500. However, sellers whose cars are worth more than $500 find such a price too low, and so they exit from the market. The average price must then drop to $300, inducing more exits, and so forth. Consequently, with the exception of sellers who are offering the worst-quality cars worth $100, no seller is willing to sell a car that a buyer is willing to buy! Spence (1973) refers to a similar mechanism when workers 'sell' their labour to firms and have private information about their skills, while Rothschild and Stiglitz (1976) analyse the insurance market in which it is the buyer who has the advantage of private information, since he or she knows more about his or her health or his or her driving skills than does the insurer.

The literature on adverse selection then investigates arrangements that allow segmentation of the market according to unobserved quality. There are studies, for example, of how insurance companies and banks *screen* their customers with the use of deductibles and collateral requirements (Rothschild and Stiglitz 1976); how sellers *signal* the quality of their products by offering product-warranties to customers or how workers *signal* their ability by getting academic degrees (Spence 1973). It is important to emphasize that market segmentation does not primarily come from some information inherent to, say, warranties or deductibles, but rather from a *menu of contracts* offered to agents that leads to self-selection, revealing their private information. In the examples mentioned above, such menus would be of the form *low insurance premium, high deductible* or *high insurance premium, low deductible*, and in the product market example, of the form *low price, no warranty* or *high price, 1-year warranty*. Such menus then induce careful drivers to opt for a *low premium, high deductible* contract, while less careful drivers prefer to pay a high premium and face a low deductible in case of accident. Similarly, sellers of high-quality goods will want to charge a high price but offer in exchange a one-year warranty to customers. This is a policy that sellers of low-quality goods are not willing to mimic.

On the other hand, the case in which the information asymmetry occurs *after* an agreement is obtained between individuals is called *moral hazard*. The framework often used to analyse moral hazard situations is the *principal–agent problem*, whereby one individual – the principal – wants to hire another individual – the agent – to perform a given task. However, once the contract has been signed, the agent can either take an action that the principal is unable to observe (hidden action), or obtain information about some characteristics of the environment that the principal cannot acquire (hidden information). As opposed to the previous case, in which agents were offered a menu of contracts, moral hazard situations imply that every agent is given the same contract. The contract must

therefore take into account future information asymmetries, and hence address the *incentives* problem. Analyses of the principal–agent problem follow pioneering works due to Mirrlees (1999), Holmström (1979) and Grossman and Hart (1983).

To illustrate this phenomenon, consider the example of the car insurance market developed in Mirrlees (1999). A driver (the agent) wants to buy insurance from an insurance company (the principal). The source of concern is that once the insurance contract is signed, the insurance company cannot observe whether the driver is careful enough. In the present case, there is no attempt to evaluate the skill of particular drivers, as opposed to the adverse selection situation addressed previously. The objective of the contract is to make drivers financially accountable for their misbehaviour, so to induce careful driving. How can the insurance company motivate the driver to take care? Suppose that it can put a camera in every single car to monitor the driver's behaviour. It could then contract with the driver that he or she would drive carefully (after agreeing on the definition of what 'carefully' means), and that in exchange the insurance would cover all costs due to any traffic accident. In this hypothetical world of symmetric information, such a contract would be optimal in that it transfers all uncertainty from risk-averse drivers on to risk-neutral insurance companies. However, putting a camera in every car is not (yet) feasible. If insurers nevertheless keep offering the same contract, drivers are fully insured against risks that are independent of how they drive their cars but also against risks arising from their own misbehaviour. This will probably lead to less careful driving, an increase in the number of accidents and a larger risk-premium. Drivers are the first to be harmed by such an outcome. An alternative to full coverage is accordingly desirable, in order to provide incentives to drive carefully. In short, an optimal contract in an environment with moral hazard must trade insurance off against the provision of incentives. The application of deductibles, and the prospects of increased insurance premiums following repeated accidents, are examples of measures designed to induce careful driving.

The principal–agent framework is now widely used to address issues ranging from public economics to corporate finance. What is quality control if not the alleviation of information asymmetries between management and employees by making actions observable? Stock-options, salaries paid in cash and in stocks, and merit-based salary increases are all examples of instruments that aim at providing the right incentives to constituencies of an organization, aligning their own objectives with the objectives of stakeholders.

A more complex version of the principal–agent problem may involve several agents: a seller (the principal) wants to sell a good to several buyers (the agents), but does not have information on how much buyers are willing to pay for the good. The design of the appropriate contract in this particular environment is nothing less than the starting-point of the theory of auctions. Another modification could consist of considering one agent but several principals. Such a *common agency* framework is useful to analyse a large set of situations including voters choosing their representatives, producers selling their goods through intermediaries, or even parents educating children!

Asymmetric information considerations have encompassed all fields of economics and finance. Recognizing that the presence of information asymmetries could be the source of large economic inefficiencies, considerable emphasis has been placed on the characterization of mechanisms or institutions that could alleviate the information asymmetry. The economics of information has opened new avenues for research and policy in the social sciences, which surely contributed to a better understanding and management of our economic and social environment.

QUY-TOAN DO
THE WORLD BANK

References

Akerlof, G. (1970) 'The market for lemons: Quality uncertainty and the market mechanism', *The Quarterly Journal of Economics* 89: 488–500.

Grossman, S. and Hart, O. (1983) 'An analysis of the principal–agent problem', *Econometrica* 51: 7–45.

Holmström, B. (1979) 'Moral hazard and observability', *Bell Journal of Economics* 10: 74–91.

Mirrlees, J.A. (1999) 'The theory of moral hazard and unobservable behaviour: Part I', *Review of Economic Studies* 66: 3–21.

Rothschild, M. and Stiglitz, J.E. (1976) 'Equilibrium in competitive insurance markets: An essay in the economics of imperfect information', *The Quarterly Journal of Economics* 90: 629–49.

Spence, A.M. (1973) 'Job market signaling', *The Quarterly Journal of Economics* 87: 355–74.

Further reading

Mas-Collel, A., Whinston, M.D. and Green, J.R. (1995) *Microeconomic Theory*, Oxford.

Stiglitz, J.E. (2000) 'The contributions of the economics of information to the twentieth century economics', *The Quarterly Journal of Economics* 115(4): 1,441–78.

SEE ALSO: competition; contracts; markets

ATTITUDES

The capacity to differentiate hostile from hospitable stimuli within the environment is arguably the single most important aspect of human functioning. It is perhaps no surprise, then, that the study of 'attitudes' – people's general and relatively enduring evaluative responses to objects – has long been one of the most central and most fertile domains within the field of social psychology. Indeed, the attitude has been described as 'the most distinctive and indispensable concept in contemporary American social psychology' (Allport 1935: 798).

In the decades since this bold claim, interest in the attitude construct has wavered very little. Today, a search of the psychological literature using 'attitude' as the search term yields more than 40,000 articles, chapters, books and dissertations. And this extensive literature attests to the fact that, as Allport (1935) suggested nearly 70 years ago, attitudes often exert a powerful influence on perception, cognition and behaviour, profoundly shaping people's interactions with the social world (for a review, see Eagly and Chaiken 1993).

What is an attitude?

Conceptualizations of the attitude construct have changed over the years, but most contemporary researchers define an attitude as a general, relatively enduring evaluation of an object. Attitudes are evaluative in that they reflect the degree to which our response to an object is positive and approach-oriented versus negative and avoidance-oriented. Indeed, attitudes are typically conceptualized as falling along a bipolar dimension ranging from extremely negative to extremely positive. Attitudes are general in that they reflect our overall, summary evaluation of an object (which may be based on a number of more specific positive and negative attributes of the object). Attitudes are enduring in that they are presumed to be represented in long-term memory and to exhibit at least some stability over time, rather than being fleeting evaluative responses to an object. Finally, attitudes are specific to particular objects (such as a person, a group, an issue or a concept) rather than diffuse evaluative responses (such as moods).

How are attitudes formed?

Attitudes can be derived from one or more distinct classes of antecedents. Some attitudes are based primarily on our cognitions about an attitude object. We may come to support a particular political candidate, for example, because of our beliefs about the policies he or she will promote and the skills and attributes he or she is perceived to possess. These beliefs may form an elaborate interconnected cognitive structure containing all of the knowledge that we possess about the candidate, and from this set of cognitions we may derive a positive overall evaluation of the candidate.

Other attitudes are based primarily on our affective reactions to an object. Instead of deriving our attitude towards a candidate from our beliefs about him or her, for example, we may base our overall evaluation on the feelings that we associate with him or her. A candidate who evokes feelings of pride and hope may be evaluated positively, whereas one who evokes feelings of fear or anger may be evaluated negatively.

Attitudes can also be derived from our past behaviour. Sometimes this occurs through self-perception processes. Just as we infer others' attitudes from the behaviours that they perform, we sometimes look to our own behaviour for insights regarding our attitudes (Bem 1972). When asked about our attitude towards a political candidate, for example, we may canvas our memory for relevant information. One thing that may come to mind is past behaviour relevant to the candidate. We may recall, for example, having accepted a button from one of the candidate's campaign workers, or adding our name to a petition when a co-worker was collecting signatures in support of the candidate. From these behaviours, we may infer that we hold a positive attitude towards the candidate.

Our behaviour can influence our attitudes in a second way as well. Rather than inferring our attitudes from our behaviours, sometimes we change our attitudes to bring them into line with past behaviours. One of the central themes of the attitude literature during the 1960s was the notion that people strive to maintain consistency among the elements of their cognitive system (e.g. attitudes, beliefs). According to cognitive dissonance theory, inconsistency between cognitions produces an uncomfortable state of arousal, one that people are highly motivated to reduce (e.g. Festinger 1957). For example, the knowledge that we have performed a behaviour that is incongruent with our attitude is often uncomfortable. Resolving this discomfort requires bringing these elements into harmony with one another. Because the behaviour has already been performed and cannot be undone, the easiest way to restore consistency often involves changing the attitude to make it congruent with the behaviour. And, indeed, a wealth of empirical evidence suggests that people often do modify their attitudes to bring them into line with past behaviours, consistent with cognitive dissonance theory.

Why do we hold attitudes?

Attitudes are presumed to serve important psychological functions for people (e.g. Katz 1960; Smith *et al.* 1956). Perhaps the most basic of these is a 'utilitarian' function – attitudes help us to gain rewards and avoid punishment by summarizing the positive or negative outcomes with which an object is associated, efficiently guiding our behaviour regarding the object. Without attitudes stored in memory, we would be required to assess the evaluative implications of an object each time we encounter it to determine whether to approach or avoid the object, a process that would quickly exceed our cognitive capacity and would be dangerously slow in situations that require immediate action.

Attitudes can serve one or more other psychological functions as well. Some attitudes serve a 'value-expressive' function. They enable us to affirm central aspects of our self-concept by expressing our core values. Other attitudes serve a 'social-adjustive' function, facilitating smooth social interactions with important others. Holding a positive attitude towards environmental conservation, for example, may make it easier to get along with close friends who hold pro-environment attitudes. And some attitudes serve an 'ego-defensive' function, protecting us from having to acknowledge unpleasant aspects of ourselves. We may project our own unacceptable impulses or feelings of inferiority onto out-groups, for example. By holding negative attitudes towards out-group members, we distance ourselves from these negative aspects, protecting our self-image.

What do attitudes do?

A large literature attests to both the ubiquity of attitudes and their impact on behaviour. There is clear evidence, for example, that attitudes are activated automatically upon encountering an object. Indeed, before we have finished processing the semantic meaning of an object, our brains have extracted its evaluative meaning. Evidence from psychophysiological studies suggests that almost instantly objects are categorized into things that we like versus things that we dislike.

And once an attitude has been activated, it has predictable consequences for thought and behaviour. For example, attitudes often bias our judgements regarding the logical validity of syllogisms. If the consequence of a syllogism is attitude-congruent, we perceive the syllogism to be more logically valid than if the consequence is attitude-incongruent. Attitudes also shape our interpretation of ambiguous stimuli: people on both sides of an issue have been shown to interpret an ambiguous passage of text as supporting their own position on the issue. Attitudes bias our predictions about the future as well – preferred outcomes are seen as more likely to occur. And our own attitudes shape our perceptions of other people's attitudes – we tend to overestimate the prevalence of our attitudes.

There is also plenty of evidence that attitudes motivate and guide behaviour. For example, people's attitudes towards snakes are strongly predictive of their behaviour when confronted by a snake. And attitudes towards political candidates are excellent predictors of voting behaviour. Indeed, attitudes have been shown to predict behaviour towards a diverse range of objects, including recycling, littering, alcohol, contraception and breast feeding, among many others.

An important caveat

Attitudes do not always exert powerful effects on thought and behaviour, however. In fact, from the start, inconsistencies within the attitude literature surfaced with troubling frequency. Sometimes attitudes seemed to be entirely unrelated to thought and action. By the late 1960s, the number of glaring inconsistencies in the literature had grown sufficiently large to lead some prominent scholars to question the very existence of attitudes.

Since then, tremendous strides have been made towards clarifying the nature of attitudes and identifying the conditions under which attitudes exert strong effects on cognitive and behavioural outcomes. We now recognize, for example, that attitudes influence thought and behaviour for some types of people more than others, and in some situations more than others. More recently, social psychologists have also come to recognize that some attitudes are *inherently* more powerful than others. That is, across people and situations, some attitudes exert a strong impact on thinking and on behaviour, whereas others are largely inconsequential. Similarly, some attitudes are tremendously durable, resisting change in the face of a persuasive appeal and remaining stable over long spans of time, whereas others are highly malleable and fluctuate greatly over time.

The term 'attitude strength' is often used to capture this distinction, and researchers have identified a number of specific attributes of an attitude that are associated with its strength (Petty and Krosnick 1995). For example, attitudes tend to be strong and consequential when they are deemed personally important to the attitude holder, when they are based on a large store of attitude-relevant knowledge, when they are held with great certainty, and when they are highly accessible in memory. A large literature now exists documenting the relations between roughly a dozen of these attitude attributes and the durability and impactfulness of an attitude.

PENNY S. VISSER
LINDSEY M. CLARK
UNIVERSITY OF CHICAGO

References

Allport, G.W. (1935) 'Attitudes', in C. Murchison (ed.) *Handbook of Social Psychology*, Worcester, MA, pp. 798–884.
Bem, D.J. (1972) 'Self perception theory', in L. Berko-

witz (ed.) *Advances in Experimental Social Psychology*, Vol. 6, New York, pp. 1–62.

Eagly, A.H. and Chaiken, S. (1993) *The Psychology of Attitudes*, Fort Worth, TX.

Festinger, L. (1957) *A Theory of Cognitive Dissonance*, Stanford, CA.

Katz, D. (1960) 'The functional approach to the study of attitudes', *Public Opinion Quarterly* 24: 163–204.

Petty, R.E. and Krosnick, J.A. (1995) *Attitude Strength: Antecedents and Consequences*, Mahwah, NJ.

Smith, M.B., Bruner, J.S. and White, R.W. (1956) *Opinions and Personality*, New York.

SEE ALSO: prejudice; stereotypes

AUCTIONS

Auction theory is one of economics' success stories. It is of both practical and theoretical importance: practical importance, because many of the world's most important markets are auction markets, and good auction theory has made the difference between successful auctions and disastrous ones; theoretical importance, because lessons from auction theory have led to important insights elsewhere in economics.

Auctions are not a new idea: the Babylonians auctioned wives, the ancient Greeks auctioned mine concessions and, in addition to their notorious slave auctions, the Romans auctioned everything from war booty to debtors' property. In the modern world, auctions are used to conduct a huge volume of economic transactions. Governments use them to sell treasury bills, foreign exchange, mineral rights including oil fields, and other assets such as firms to be privatized. Government contracts are typically awarded by procurement auctions, and procurement auctions are also often used by firms buying inputs or subcontracting work; in these cases, of course, the auctioneer is seeking a low price rather than a high price. Houses, cars, agricultural produce and livestock, art and antiques are commonly sold by auction. Other economic transactions, for example takeover battles, are auctions by another name.

The range of items sold by auction has been greatly increased by e-commerce, and in the last decade or so there has also been an explosion of interest in using auctions to set up new markets, for example for energy, transport and emissions permits. Although many of these markets do not look like auctions to the layman, they are best understood through auction theory. (For example, electricity markets are best described and analysed as auctions of infinitely divisible quantities of identical goods.) Probably the most famous of the new auction markets have been the auctions of mobile phone licences across the world (Klemperer 2002, 2003a).

Two basic designs of auction are most commonly used: the ascending auction, in which the price is raised successively until only one bidder remains and that bidder wins the object at the final price he or she bid; and the first-price sealed-bid auction, in which each bidder independently submits a single bid without seeing others' bids, the object is sold to the bidder who makes the highest bid, and the winner pays his or her bid.

The key result in auction theory is the remarkable *Revenue Equivalence Theorem* that tells us, subject to some reasonable-sounding conditions, that the seller can expect equal profits on average from all the standard (and many non-standard) types of auctions, and that buyers are also indifferent among them all. William Vickrey's Nobel Prize was in large part awarded for his (1961, 1962) papers that developed some special cases of the theorem, and Riley and Samuelson (1981) and Myerson (1981) offer more general treatments.

Much of auction theory can be understood in terms of this theorem, and how its results are affected by relaxing its assumptions of a fixed number of symmetric, risk-neutral bidders, who each want a single unit, have independent information, and bid independently. Myerson's (1981) paper shows how to derive optimal auctions (that is, auctions that maximize the seller's expected revenue) when the assumption of symmetry fails. Maskin and Riley (1984) consider the case of risk-averse bidders, in which case the first-price sealed-bid auction is the most profitable of the standard auctions. Milgrom and Weber (1982) analysed auctions when the assumption of independent information is replaced by one of 'affiliated' information, and showed that the most profitable standard auction is then the ascending auction. (Roughly, bidders' information is affiliated if when one bidder has more positive information about the value of the prize, it is more likely that other bidders' information will also be positive.) Models of auctions in which bidders demand multiple units lead to less clear conclusions. For practical auction design, however, it is probably most important to relax the assumptions that there are a fixed number of bidders and that they bid independently; sealed-bid designs frequently (but not always) both attract more serious bidders and are better at discouraging collusion than are ascending designs (Klemperer 1998, 2002).

The predictions of auction theory have been the basis of much empirical and experimental work. In particular, auctions have become a leading testing ground for game theory because they are particularly simple and well-defined economic institutions, constraining the extensive form of the game so tightly that sharp qualitative predictions are possible (Hendricks and Porter 1988; Kagel and Roth 1995; Laffont 1997). There has been considerable debate in this literature about whether or not bidders really fall prey to the famous 'winner's curse' – the phenomenon that if the actual value of the prize is uncertain but the same for all the bidders, the winning bidder will often lose money if he or she made her bid without allowing for the fact that winning suggests he or she is among the most optimistic bidders.

Auction theory has also been the basis of much fundamental theoretical work not directly related to auctions: by carefully analysing very simple trading models, auction theory is developing the fundamental building-blocks for our understanding of more complex environments. It has been important in developing our understanding of other methods of price formation, including posted prices, and negotiations in which both the buyer and seller are actively involved in determining the price.

There are especially close connections between the theories of auctions and perfect competition. Wilson (1977), Milgrom (1979) and others have developed conditions under which the sale price of an object whose value is the same to all bidders converges to this value as the number of bidders becomes large, even though each bidder has only partial information about the value. The fact that the auction thus fully aggregates all of the economy's information justifies some of our ideas about perfect competition and rational expectations equilibrium.

There is also a close analogy between the theory of optimal auctions and the theory of monopoly pricing; the analysis of optimal auctions is 'essentially equivalent to the analysis of standard monopoly third-degree price discrimination' (Bulow and Roberts 1989). Insights can therefore be translated from monopoly theory to auction theory and vice versa.

More recently, auction-theoretic tools have been used to provide useful arguments in a broader range of contexts – including many that do not, at first sight, look like auctions – starting with models of oligopolistic pricing, running through non-price means of allocation including queues, wars of attrition, lobbying contests, other kinds of tournaments and rationing, and extending to models in finance, law and economics, labour economics, political economy, etc. (Klemperer 2003b). It turns out that a good understanding of auction theory is valuable in developing intuitions and insights that can inform the analysis of many mainstream economic questions.

PAUL KLEMPERER
UNIVERSITY OF OXFORD

References

Bulow, J.I. and Roberts, D.J. (1989) 'The simple economics of optimal auctions', *Journal of Political Economy* 97: 1,060–90.

Hendricks, K. and Porter, R.H. (1988) 'An empirical study of an auction with asymmetric information', *American Economic Review* 78: 865–83.

Kagel, J.H. and Roth, A.E. (1995) *The Handbook of Experimental Economics*, Princeton, NJ.

Klemperer, P.D. (1998) 'Auctions with almost common values', *European Economic Review* 42: 757–69.

—— (2002) 'What really matters in auction design', *Journal of Economic Perspectives* 16(1): 169–89.

—— (2003a) 'Using and Abusing Economic Theory', *Journal of the European Economic Association* 1, :272–300 (and Alfred Marshall Lecture to European Economic Association, 2002).

—— (2003b) 'Why every economist should learn some auction theory', in M. Dewatripont, L. Hansen and S. Turnovsky (eds) *Advances in Economics and Econometrics: Invited Lectures to Eighth World Congress of the Econometric Society*, Vol. 1, Cambridge, pp. 25–55.

Laffont, J.J. (1997) 'Game theory and empirical economics: The case of auction data', *European Economic Review* 41: 1–35.

Maskin, E.S. and Riley, J.G. (1984) 'Optimal auctions with risk averse buyers', *Econometrica* 52: 1,473–518.

Milgrom, P.R. (1979) 'A convergence theorem for competitive bidding with differential information', *Econometrica* 47: 679–88.

Milgrom, P.R. and Weber, R.J. (1982) 'A theory of auctions and competitive bidding', *Econometrica* 50: 1,089–112.

Myerson, R.B. (1981) 'Optimal auction design', *Mathematics of Operations Research* 6: 58–73.

Riley, J.G. and Samuelson, W.F. (1981) 'Optimal auctions', *American Economic Review* 71: 381–92.

Vickrey, W. (1961) 'Counterspeculation, auctions, and competitive sealed tenders', *Journal of Finance* 16: 8–37.

—— (1962) 'Auction and bidding games', in *Recent Advances in Game Theory*, Princeton, NJ: The Princeton University Conference, pp. 15–27.

Wilson, R. (1977) 'A bidding model of perfect competition', *Review of Economic Studies* 44: 511–18.

Further reading

Klemperer, P.D. (1999) 'Auction theory: A guide to the literature', *Journal of Economic Surveys* 13(3): 227–86.

—— (2002) 'What really matters in auction design', *Journal of Economic Perspectives* 16(1): 169–89.

—— (2004) *Auctions: Theory and Practice*, Princeton, NJ [draft at http://www.paulklemperer.org].

SEE ALSO: bargaining; competition; experimental economics; game theory; markets

AUTHORITARIAN AND TOTALITARIAN SYSTEMS

Authoritarian systems are political regimes that are characterized by a concentration of political power in the hands of a small group of political elites who are not in any institutional sense accountable to the public. Thus, they lack those traits that distinguish liberal democratic orders – in particular, extensive civil liberties and political rights guaranteed by law, interparty competition, free, fair and regular elections, and, finally, representative government.

There are many forms of authoritarian government. Rule can be by the military or by civilian politicians, and political power can be exercised by individuals acting on their own account or as leaders of a political movement or political party. Moreover, dictatorships vary in their ideological commitments, with some leftist in terms of goals and class representation, and others rightist. Perhaps the most important distinction among authoritarian regimes, however, is on the dimensions of despotism and penetration (Mann 1986). Despotism refers to the extent to which the exercise of political power is both capricious and violent, whereas penetration refers to the extent to which the state intervenes in daily life. At one end of this continuum would be 'soft and superficial' dictatorships. This is where the reach of the state is limited, where repression is also limited, and where publics – and elites outside the inner governing circle – have some room for political and economic manœuvre. At the other end of the continuum would be 'hard and deep' dictatorships, or totalitarianism. This is where an interlocking and highly centralized party–state directorate uses terror, detailed organization and ideological indoctrination to control virtually all aspects of political, social and economic life (Friedrich and Brzezinski 1956). In the first case, there are boundaries separating politics, economics and society, whereas, with totalitarianism, such boundaries disappear.

The rise of states as forms of political organization was accompanied by the rise of authoritarianism. In this sense, authoritarianism is as old as the state itself, because it was through authoritarian political practices that states began to form (Anderson 1974; Tilly 1975). However, beginning in the eighteenth century in Europe, states began to differentiate themselves in terms of their degree of accountability to the public. This process – which eventually led in England and France, for example, to the rise of democracy – has produced a spirited set of debates about the rise of democracy versus the consolidation of authoritarian rule in fascist and communist forms (Moore 1967; Rueschemeyer *et al.* 1992; Anderson, Jr *et al.* 2001).

Debates have also flourished on three other issues. One is why some democracies evolve into authoritarian systems (Collier 1979; Luebbert 1991). Another is why some authoritarian systems collapse and give way to more liberalized political orders (Bunce 1999; Di Palma 1990). A final issue addresses the legacies of authoritarian rule and their consequences for democratic politics (Howard 2003).

VALERIE BUNCE
CORNELL UNIVERSITY

References

Anderson, P. (1974) *Lineages of the Absolutist State*, London.

Anderson, R., Jr, Fish, M., Hanson, S. and Roeder, P. (2001) *Postcommunism and the Theory of Democracy*, Princeton, NJ.

Bunce, V. (1999) *Subversive Institutions: The Design and the Destruction of Socialism and the State*, New York.

Collier, D. (1979) *The New Authoritarianism in Latin America*, Princeton, NJ.

Di Palma, G. (1990) *To Craft Democracies: An Essay on Democratic Transitions*, Berkeley, CA.

Friedrich, K. and Brzezinski, Z. (1956) *Totalitarian Dictatorship and Autocracy*, Cambridge, MA.

Howard, M. (2003) *The Weakness of Civil Society in Post-Communist Europe*, New York.

Luebbert, G. (1991) *Liberalism, Fascism or Social Democracy: Social Classes and the Political Origin of Regimes in Interwar Europe*, Oxford.

Mann, M. (1986) *Sources of Social Power*, Cambridge, UK.

Moore, B. (1967) *Social Origins of Dictatorship and Democracy*, Boston, MA.

Rueschemeyer, D., Stephens, E.H. and Stephens, J.D. (1992) *Capitalist Development and Democracy*, Chicago.

Tilly, C. (1975) *The Formation of National States in Western Europe*, Princeton, NJ.

SEE ALSO: fascism; military regimes; power

AUTHORITY

Authority involves a distinctive type of command and an associated type of compliance. It is a distinct subset of power: like coercion, persuasion, influence and manipulation, it is a way of getting others to do what they would not otherwise do (and where what they do is what you want them to do). But a command involves the exercise of authority if and only if it implicitly or explicitly claims a right to determine how the other should act *and* is able to elicit compliance which recognizes that right to command.

Coercion works by creating disincentives for some set of actions; when people respond to coercion they do so to avoid incurring costs that are threatened or actual. Persuasion works by changing the agent's view of what he or she must do to secure some objective or interest. But much social and political behaviour is difficult to explain if people are assumed to act only in response to threats and sanctions or to efforts at rational persuasion – persuading them, for example, that *x* rather than *y* course of action more fully meets their interests. In emergency situations, for example, commands are often authoritative simply because they offer clarity of direction in the midst of confusion – they provide a salient co-ordination solution and orders will be accepted so long as they fall within a reasonable range. Moreover, they are often authoritative over bystanders whose interests are not directly affected by the emergency, and who could just walk away. In such cases we are dealing neither with coercion, since there are no sanctions, nor with persuasion, since in many cases there is no occasion to provide an explanation or justification for the command. More widely, there are many cases where we simply accept the right of an individual to command us in some respect – 'all rise', 'move along now', 'don't walk on the grass', 'drink up now', 'keep to the right', and so on. In most cases there is no attempt to persuade and no threat, yet the commands produce compliance. At a more general level still, most states and social and economic institutions are able to secure people's compliance with very low levels of coercion, and without engaging in extensive deliberation and persuasion. In both cases, the suggestion is that much co-ordinated social and political behaviour can be understood as involving a distinctive type of compliance that is elicited in the exercise of authority. There are different explanations for this behaviour, with some giving greater weight to implicit coercion, information costs and risk aversion, and others to shared understandings and values, but there is wide recognition that this remains a distinctive type of social action. In understanding this relationship of command and compliance several distinctions are of value (Friedman 1973; Lukes 1978; Raz 1986, 1989).

What is it that is special about the character of the command and of the compliance that Y renders X which marks off authority from coercion and rational agreement? Essentially, a command appeals to authority when it implicitly or explicitly claims a right to determine the action of the subject of the command. A command that does not imply this right effectively implies a threat and becomes an attempt at coercion (and to that extent ceases properly to be a 'command'). The form of compliance is also distinctive. Coercion secures Y's compliance by the use of force or threats; persuasion convinces Y by appeal to arguments that an action is in Y's interests, or is, for example, morally right, or prudent; but Y complies with X's authority when Y recognizes X's right to command in a certain sphere. Y surrenders the right to make compliance contingent on an evaluation of the content of X's command, and obeys because X's order comes from an appropriate person and falls within the appropriate range. A servant who makes up her mind as to whether or not she will obey her mistress's commands depending on whether she thinks them reasonable or is concerned only to avoid penalties for failing to do so, is not responding to her mistress's authority. One who obeys the commands because she acknowledges her mistress's right to command her within a particular domain, does acknowledge – and thereby completes – her mistress's authority.

Authority is a two-tier concept: it refers to a mode of influence and compliance, and to a set of criteria that identify who is to exercise this influence over whom. For this influence to take effect it must be exercised 'within a certain kind of normative arrangement accepted by both parties' (Friedman 1973). The set of criteria can develop a certain independence from the relationship of command and compliance. Thus, someone who tries to exercise authority and fails, e.g. the Speaker calling 'Order!' in an especially unruly meeting of the House of Commons, may still be recognized as occupying a position of authority, despite the fact that in this instance he is unable to ensure that his right to compliance takes effect. Here the distinction between *de facto* and *de jure* authority is helpful (Peters 1967; Winch 1967). *De facto* authority is evidenced whenever Y complies with X in the appropriate manner; *de jure* authority exists where X has a right to Y's compliance in a given area that derives from a set of institutional rules or more general societal norms. That X has *de jure* authority does not entail that X will also have *de facto* authority. But if someone with *de jure* authority never in fact has *de facto* authority then there is room for doubt at to whether the institutional structure or societal norms have any grounding within the broader society – a royal pretender may claim the right to rule but if that right receives no institutional support or normative recognition, and no compliance, the claim to *de jure* authority seems empty. Inversely, someone can recognize another as having a right to rule even in the absence of a broader institutional or widely shared normative background of justification – so that a *de facto* authority relationship can exist without a *de jure* relationship. We have, however, to press the question of why the person who complies treats their commander's utterances as normative for them. As Hart (1961) argues, for someone to recognize that an authority exists we do seem to require the existence of some underlying 'rules of recognition' or 'marks' by which to identify those eligible to exercise it, and it seems odd to think that the act of recognition can in itself wholly confer (rather than partly respond to) such marks. But the broader sense that authority relationships may start from either end does seem to be right: developing customary compliance may generate institutional orders and societal norms within which *de jure* authority can be claimed and exercised; and the establishment of institutional orders and associated claims to authority may over time come to elicit *de facto* compliance.

One issue that concerns social scientists is the appropriate background account required to explain the existence of authority relationships. For example, MacIntyre (1967) and Winch (1967) see authority relationships as reflecting underlying common traditions, practices, sets of beliefs and norms in a society, and they see authority as functioning most effectively the higher the level of normative integration (see also Arendt 1963; Parsons 1960; Durkheim 1992 [1957]). In contrast, some game-theoretic accounts see the norms and rules of the social order as providing a co-ordination solution from which each gains – but where the gain is used to explain the resilience of the institutions and their related claims to authority, rather than being offered as an account of the motive for each act of compliance (see Hobbes 1651; Hardin 2004; see also Elster's (1989) discussion of the power of norms that suggests the limits of game-theoretic accounts). Finally, if we operate with a more deeply conflict-based account of the social and political order we will tend to explain political and social authority as the outcome of habituated obedience originally instilled through coercion, so that, although social order is imposed by force, it derives its permanence and stability through techniques of legitimation, ideology, hegemony, mobilization of bias, false consensus and so on, which secure the willing compliance of citizens through the manipulation of their beliefs (Lukes 1978; Weber 1978 [1922]). These perspectives offer different accounts of the origins, grounds and likely stability of authority relationships, but they do so while sharing an understanding of what it is for X to exercise authority over Y. Similarly, Weber's distinctions between traditional, charismatic and legal-rational authority are best understood, not as different types of authority so much as different bases upon which authority relationships may rest.

A further important distinction is that between being *an* authority and being *in* authority. The former concerns matters of belief; the latter concerns X's place in a normative order with recognized positions of *de jure* authority. When X is *an* authority, X is held to have, or successfully claims, special knowledge, insight, expertise and so on, which justifies Y's deference to X's judgement. When X is *in* authority, X claims, and is recognized as occupying, a special institutional role with a co-ordinate sphere of command (as with Weber's legal-rational authority (1978 [1922])). When Y complies with X's judgement where X is *an* authority, Y's compliance involves belief in the validity of A's judgement; whereas, when X is simply *in* authority, Y may disagree yet comply because Y recognizes X's *de jure* authority. Traditional and charismatic leaders are authoritative over belief and value; leaders in legal-rational systems are granted authority in certain spheres of action for convenience and may be authoritative over neither belief nor value. Where X is *an* authority, X's influence over Y relies on Y's continued belief in X's guaranteed judgement. Where X is *in* authority, X relies on Y continuing to recognize that X fulfils a valuable co-ordination function. Both systems may face legitimation crises when Y no longer believes X or no longer believes that X successfully co-ordinates. However, both systems may seek to maintain Y's belief through a variety of techniques: ideology, hegemony, mobilization of bias and so on (Habermas 1976 [1973]).

There is also an issue of the scope of authority, both in terms of the extent to which a given society is governed by relations of authority across a wider rather than narrow range of political, social and legal institutions, and in terms of the range within which a given individual accords to another the right to rule him or her. On the first count, there has been a tendency to use the term authoritarian regime to describe regimes that are invasive across a wide range of political, social and personal behaviour, and demand unresisting compliance no matter how intrusive the command. The analysis of such regimes in the postwar period often suggested that people's indoctrination was such that they accepted the state's claim to this scope and depth of intrusion. But the collapse of such regimes, in Central and Eastern Europe in particular, raised doubts as to how far people's compliance with the regime really had had much to do with authority rather than fear and coercion – saying and doing 'the right thing' is not equivalent to doing so for the right reason (a recognition of the right to rule) (see Kuran 1995 and Scott 1990).

The second issue, concerning the range within which an individual accords to another the right to rule, also deserves further exploration: Y's compliance with X's authority may be

1 unlimited, as when Y will accept any order issued by X as legitimate;
2 delimited, so that Y has a clear sense of the boundaries within which X may command him or her;
3 uncritical in that B makes no attempt to consider the content of the order (so long as it falls within the appropriate domain); or
4 critical, where B complies because he recognizes A's right to command, but nonetheless has reservations as to the wisdom of doing so.

Categories 1 and 2, and 3 and 4, are contrastive, but the two sets may cut across each other. In any analysis of an authority relationship we can refine the description by identifying the precise character of Y's compliance. X's charismatic authority may elicit unlimited compliance, without the compliance being uncritical, or it may be delimited but uncritical. These dimensions help clarify the dimensions of a particular relationship of authority, but they do so within a common definition of the essential character of an authority relationship.

Many writers have referred to authority as 'legitimate power'. Although this rather muddies the waters by linking a partly consensual relationship of command and compliance with a coercive implication, there is a clear case in which the phrase does make sense. If power is understood as the ability to get others to do what they would not otherwise do then, for X to have authority over individuals $Y_{1....n}$, is for X to be able to get them to act in ways they would not otherwise have acted and for him to do so through commands that are recognized as legitimate by those subject to them. This treats authority as a subset of power, and defines power as legitimate when it involves the exercise of authority and evokes the appropriate form of compliance. The term is less helpful when it is used to describe a case where X coerces Y where X's *de jure* authority over Y fails to elicit Y's compliance. This usage risks ambiguity because it fixes the content of 'legitimate' by reference to X's institutional position, and in doing so it treats all *de jure* authority as legitimate. Yet, if people are not complying appropriately then they are not responding to the claim to authority and they cannot be said to regard the exercise of power as legitimate. And while some instances (like the Speaker of the Commons) clearly can claim broader legitimacy, it is not invariably the case that institutional claims have overriding legitimacy despite being, in practice, unable to elicit the compliance of those nominally subject to them. Crumbling authoritarian orders have many institutional structures but it is questionable to regard a claim to authority as legitimizing their coercion of their recalcitrant subjects.

A final set of issues concerns the authority of the state within democratic orders. There is a basic sense that it is preferable to live in political orders that can rely on authority rather than on the continuous exercise of force and coercion (presuming that a state based wholly on free and open deliberation is implausible). Moreover, the more that this authority resides in laws, procedures, institutions and offices, rather than being attached to the personal attributes of individuals, the closer we approach to an ideal of a constitutional and procedural state, in which a high level of consensus and a high level of efficient coordination of collective action can be achieved. In many respects this ideal provided the basis for idealized views of the nineteenth-century constitutional state. But this ideal was not strongly democratic. Moreover, the tendency in many modern democratic orders to increase the accountability and regulation of those exercising power and authority within the state can threaten to erode the authority of modern democratic states. The assumption that the governed should be able to regulate and scrutinize the activities of politicians and public servants to ensure that they act in the public's interest is now unremarkable, yet there are grounds for concern that direct forms of popular accountability are fundamentally incompatible with preserving the authority of public office. Judges who are directly elected and subject to democratic recall are hard pressed to function independently of public opinion, and their authority is correspondingly undermined; civil servants who are directly accountable to the public (or who are made wholly subordinate to their political masters) become subservient to those to whom they are answerable, rather than having institutional authority by virtue of their official position and function; and politicians who become wholly subordinate to public opinion no longer exercise authority over it. Clearly, such concerns are a matter of tendency, but the suggestion raises two important issues. The first, of interest to theorists of institutional design, concerns the extent to which modern forms of democratic accountability are supportive of, rather than destructive of, political authority. The second concerns the more general issue of how far we are witnessing the evolution of the modern state into forms in which authority is more fragile and less institutionalized – and, if we are, what consequences this might have (will political systems become correspondingly more coercive, more volatile and less procedural?). Complex political systems rely on those in public office having authority to undertake the organizational and administrative tasks they face and it seems increasingly clear that many modern forms of regulation and accountability undercut that authority (see for example Anechiarico and Jacobs 1996). If it is one of the great achievements of liberal constitutional orders to have established procedures and institutions that moderate conflict and constrain the direct pursuit of interests in ways that violate norms of fairness, justice and so on, one of the pressures they face as a result of democratization is that the independence and authority of the offices that make up these institutional orders can easily be eroded (Philp 2001; Suleiman 2003).

MARK PHILP
UNIVERSITY OF OXFORD

References

Anechiarico, F. and Jacobs, J.B. (1996) *The Pursuit of Absolute Integrity*, Chicago.
Arendt, H. (1963) 'What is authority?' in *Between Past and Future*, New York.
Durkheim, E. (1992 [1957]) *Professional Ethics and Civic Morals*, ed. B.S. Turner, London.
Elster, J. (1989) *The Cement of Society*, Cambridge.
Friedman, R.B. (1973) 'On the concept of authority in political philosophy', in R.E. Flathman (ed.) *Concepts in Social and Political Philosophy*, New York.
Habermas, J. (1976 [1973]) *Legitimation Crisis*, London.
Hardin, R. (2004) *Hume*, Oxford.
Hart, H.L.A. (1961) *The Concept of Law*, Oxford.
Hobbes, T. (1651) *Leviathan*, London.
Kuran, T. (1995) *Private Truths, Public Lies: The Social Consequences of Preference Falsification*, Cambridge, MA.
Lukes, S. (1978) 'Power and authority', in T. Bottomore and R. Nisbett (eds) *A History of Sociological Analysis*, London.

MacIntyre, A. (1967) *Secularisation and Moral Change*, London.

Parsons, T. (1960) 'Authority, legitimation, and political action', in *Structure and Process in Modern Societies*, Glencoe, IL.

Peters, R.S. (1967) 'Authority', in A. Quinton (ed.) *Political Philosophy*, Oxford.

Philp, M. (2001) 'Access, accountability and authority: Corruption and the democratic process', *Crime, Law and Social Change* 36: 357–77.

Raz, J. (1986) *The Morality of Freedom*, Oxford.

—— (ed.) (1989) *Authority*, Oxford.

Scott, J.C. (1990) *Domination and the Arts of Resistance: Hidden Transcripts*, New Haven.

Suleiman, E. (2003) *Dismantling Democratic States*, Princeton, NJ.

Weber, M. (1978 [1922]) *Economy and Society*, 2 vols, eds G. Roth and C. Wittich, Berkeley, CA.

Winch, P. (1967) 'Authority', in A. Quinton (ed.) *Political Philosophy*, Oxford.

SEE ALSO: leadership; legitimacy; power

B

BALANCE OF PAYMENTS

Popular thinking on the balance of payments reflects the views of a group of seventeenth- and eighteenth-century pamphleteers (called mercantilists, because of their association with merchants) who argued that a country should export more than it imports. The most famous of these mercantilists, Thomas Mun, believed the world's trading activities constituted a zero-sum game and that the balance of trade measured the gains or losses of each country. The mercantilists coined the phrase 'a favourable trade balance'. This quaint notion seems to linger forever in the popular press even though international trade specialists have long argued there is nothing particularly favourable about exports exceeding imports.

The balance of payments is a record of all the economic transactions between the residents of one country and residents of the rest of the world during a specified time period, such as a quarter or a year. It is a bookkeeping system in which positive entries reflect incoming payments and negative entries outgoing payments. Exports of goods and services, visits by foreigners, remittances from foreigners as gifts or income receipts from home assets located in the foreign country, and investments by foreigners in the home country are the main categories of positive items; imports of goods and services, travel to a foreign country, remittances by the home country as gifts to foreigners or as income payments for foreign assets located in the home country, and home investments abroad are the main categories of negative items.

If one thinks about the balance of payments as a series of subaccounts, such as goods, services, income payments on assets, and the capital account, then it is convenient to say that the sum of all the subaccounts must be zero. The USA in the late twentieth century and early twenty-first century had a trade deficit that was counterbalanced by inflows of foreign capital. Without those inflows of foreign capital, interest rates in the USA would have been higher.

Balance of payments theory began with a brilliant 1752 essay by David Hume. Even though the balance of payments is always 'in balance', it may be balanced by drawing down on a country's assets, such as purchasing imports with a country's supply of gold or, in modern times, foreign exchange reserves. A 'deficit' simply means a loss of such reserves. Hume began his essay by pointing out how several decades ago the country was alarmed when a writer suggested that if current trends continued Britain would soon run out of gold. Hume pointed out that the prediction turned out to be completely false. He then set out to explain the mechanism of the gold standard. If two countries base their monetary systems on gold, a balance of payments deficit will be corrected by the impact of the resulting fall in the money supply at home and rise in the money supply abroad. Prices and especially wages will fall at home and rise abroad as a consequence of the redistribution of the world's money supply. As prices fall at home and rise abroad, the 'deficit' will soon be corrected by an automatic mechanism because exports would be cheaper and imports more expensive. In modern times, with large capital flows, interest rate adjustments will also play a role. The same would happen under a flexible exchange rate, because although domestic prices would not change, a country in deficit would find that its exchange rate would depreciate, causing exports to become cheaper compared to imports.

The automatic nature of the balance of payments requires that countries follow certain rules or conventions. Under a fixed exchange rate standard, countries must allow deficits to reduce the supply of money and surpluses to increase the supply of money. Thus deficits would be accompanied by downward pressure on wages and prices, and upward pressure on interest rates. Countries that operate a floating exchange rate system must not try to peg the exchange rate. If deficits are neutralized by domestic policy instruments, the causes of the deficit persist and a balance of payments crisis may erupt. But if deficits are not neutralized, the automatic adjustment works quite well in practice. The euro, the common European currency, is based on Hume's theory of balance of payments adjustment because there is a European Central Bank that determines the total supply of euros rather than the distribution of euros within Euroland. The same happens within the USA with the dollar. Should New York have a deficit and Texas a surplus, the money supply shifts from New York to Texas, which puts pressure on prices and interest rates in such a manner as to cure the disequilibrium. It is 'automatic' because New York and Texas do not have the institutions in place to increase their domestic money supplies independent of what the central monetary authority is doing.

Floating exchange rates govern the balance of payments in trade between Europe, the USA, Japan, and the UK. When exchange rates are allowed to fluctuate freely, adjustments are effected by simply changing the exchange rate instead of adjusting internal wages and interest rates. After the Second World War there was a brief experiment with a system of adjustable 'pegged' exchange rates. This broke down by 1972 when it was discovered that such a system is prone to excessive speculation, since there is little to lose from betting against a country that is losing a large fraction of its foreign exchange reserves. The floating system has worked well compared to the pre-1972 system of pegs, with its recurrent crises.

Three aspects of the balance of payments deserve emphasis. The first is that under stationary conditions there is a tendency to go through certain stages. Should a country be a young creditor country, it must have a trade surplus to finance its foreign investments abroad, and its income from foreigners will be comparatively small. Over time, however, foreign assets abroad will accumulate, causing a surplus on the income account. As time goes on this surplus can outweigh the capital outflow and bring about a state of permanent trade deficit when the country is a mature creditor country. A young debtor country could similarly start with a trade deficit and end with a trade surplus. In the late twentieth century and the early twenty-first century the USA was a young debtor country, and thus had a large trade deficit. Should current trends continue, as obligations to pay income abroad increase, the USA is likely to generate a trade surplus, without any change in the USA's competitiveness.

A second point to remember is that no matter what the composition of the balance of payments, there appears to be no link with the general rate of unemployment. The reader can confirm this by taking any country with a reasonable data base and running a correlation between imports or exports (relative to Gross Domestic Product) and the unemployment rate. It will always be the case that if there is a positive correlation of imports with unemployment, there will also be a positive correlation with exports! Similarly, if there is a negative correlation with exports, there will be a negative correlation with imports. Any correlation that is observed is accidental; what is not accidental is that the correlations between unemployment and either imports or exports should be the same because exports and capital inflows pay for imports and capital outflows.

Third, since the balance of payments is a series of accounts, some will be in deficit while others are in surplus. It is a mistake of the first order to fear deficits in one account while ignoring the surpluses in the other accounts. Indeed, deficits in a particular subaccount, such as trade, is not in itself bad because it is the other side of the coin to the surplus in other accounts. Likewise, a surplus on the trade account and a deficit in the capital account is not in itself good. Both sets of circumstances are the way in which the balance of payments reflects the many decisions of businesses and consumers to invest, save and spend according to their private interests.

The most blatant error is to suppose that a country loses on its exchanges with another country if it runs a large bilateral trade deficit.

The gain from trade consists primarily of the imports. Exports help particular industries, but imports help the country as a whole. Exports may be regarded as the price that has to be paid to purchase the imports. The invisible hand of free competition enables a country to acquire products or services that it cannot produce, or which cost more labour and capital than is required to produce the exports that pay for them.

ROY J. RUFFIN
UNIVERSITY OF HOUSTON, TEXAS

References

Hume, David (1752) 'The balance of trade', *Political Discourses*, Edinburgh.
Mun, Thomas (1664) *England's Treasure by Forraign Trade*, London.

Further reading

Friedman, Milton (1953) 'The case for flexible exchange rates', in *Essays in Positive Economics*, Chicago.
Kaminsky, G.L. and Reinhart, C.M. (1999) 'The twin crises: the causes of banking and balance of payments problems', *The American Economic Review* 89: 473–500.

SEE ALSO: exchange rate; international trade; national accounts

BANKING

The word for a bank is recognizably the same in many European languages, and is derived from a word meaning 'bench' or 'counter'. The bench in question appears to have been that of the money-changer at the medieval fairs rather than that of the usurer, and the link of banking with trade between nations and communities has been maintained. The early banks were often started as a subsidiary business by merchants, shippers, cattle drovers and, more recently, by travel agents. Other banks grew out of the business of the goldsmiths, and some of the earliest were founded for charitable reasons. In the last two centuries, however, banking has become a recognizable trade in its own right, and companies and partnerships have been founded to carry on the specific business of banking.

Each legal system has its own definition of a bank. One common element present in nearly all definitions is the taking of deposits and the making of loans for the profit of the owners of the bank, although in some cases the proviso is made that both the deposits and the loans should be short term. An economist would be more likely to seize on the fact that bankers are able to use a relatively small capital of their own to pass large sums from ultimate lenders to ultimate borrowers, taking a margin on each transaction in the form of higher interest rates for loans than for deposits. Both these approaches credit banks with only one function, the macroeconomic function of intermediation. In reality all banks perform many more functions, while some recognized banks are not particularly active as intermediaries. Many provide payment services, and most act as insurers by giving guarantees on behalf of their customers. Services of this sort could plausibly be regarded as facilitating intermediation, but there are many other services that are purely incidental – investment management, computer services and travel agency are among them. Increasingly important in many countries is the part of the bank's income that comes from fees and commission rather than from the interest margin.

Because the liabilities of banks form a large part of the accepted definitions of the money supply, banks attract government regulation on a scale that is greater than that applying to almost every other sector. This regulation can be divided into two main areas. The first is regulation for the purposes of furthering monetary policy. The other area of regulation covers prudent behaviour of banks in an effort to ensure the safe and efficient functioning of the banking system.

Monetary policy seeks to influence the behaviour of the real economy by changing various financial variables like interest rates, the stock of money, the volume of credit and the direction of credit. Since bank deposits account for a large part of the stock of money, and since bank loans are a very important part of the total volume of credit, it is only natural that banks should be the most important channel for monetary policy measures. The measures that have been imposed on banks include control of their interest rates, primary and secondary requirements on holdings of reserves with the central bank and of government securities, limitation of the amount of credit extended, and control over the direction of credit. Many of these measures built on constraints that the banks had previously observed on their own initiative for prudential reasons.

Banking is a business that depends completely on the confidence of the public, and for the most part banks have always been very careful not to endanger that confidence. After the banking crisis of the early 1930s, the self-regulation that banks had practised for prudential reasons was supplemented in most countries by an elaborate set of prudential regulations and often by detailed supervision; the same intensification of prudential regulation and supervision occurred after the 1974–5 banking crisis. The various measures adopted are often said to be motivated by a desire to protect the interests of the depositor, but an even more important motive is the need for any government to protect the stability and soundness of the entire financial system. The measures laid down in regulations are designed to prevent bank failures by ensuring that the capital and reserves are adequate to cover all likely risks of loss, and that there are sufficient sources of liquidity to meet cash demands day by day. Many sets of regulations seek to achieve these aims by detailed and rigid balance-sheet ratios, and since 1989 banks of all kinds in most developed countries have been required to observe a minimum ratio devised by bankers from the largest countries meeting at the Bank for International Settlements in Basle. Under this scheme banks must hold capital equal to at least 8 per cent of the total of risk-weighted assets, the weights ranging from zero for government securities up to 100 for normal bank loans.

The agent for carrying out monetary policy is always the central bank, which is in a specially favourable position for influencing financial flows because it is usually the banker to the government, the main domestic banks and the central banks of other countries; it thus stands at the crossroads between the banking system and the private, public and external sectors, and can influence the behaviour of all of them to various degrees by its regulations and its market operations.

There has long been a strong current of opinion which held that the central bank should not be a government department but should have some autonomy. In the USA and in Italy, the central bank is wholly or partly owned by private banks and not by the government. The Bank of England was not nationalized until 1946. In 1997 it was granted operational independence, subject only to a broad brief from the parliament.

Prudential regulation and supervision are often carried out by the central bank, but many countries, including Germany and the Scandinavian countries, have long had separate supervisory bodies; the USA has several. In 1998, the Bank of England's responsibility for banking supervision was transferred to a new statutory body, the Financial Services Authority.

Since the 1960s, the banking systems of most developed countries have changed considerably in several directions. The first major trend has been the internationalization of banking. Until the mid-twentieth century, banks conducted most of their international business through correspondent banks in the various countries, but most large and many medium-sized banks now reckon to have branches in all important international financial centres. This move was led by the large banks from the USA, and they and branches of banks from other countries have introduced new techniques and been the catalysts for change in many countries whose banking markets were previously sheltered. Banking has also become internationalized through the establishment of a pool of international bank deposits (the eurodollar market) and through syndicated lending by numbers of large banks to multinational corporations and to governments. During the recession that started in 1978, the inability of many governments and other borrowers to meet the conditions of loan repayments has been a considerable source of instability, which continued into the recession that started at the end of the 1980s. The heavy provisions that banks had been forced to make against sovereign debt in the first of the two recessions were joined by provisions against domestic loans in the second. The banking systems of developed countries were considerably weakened by these two bouts of provisions against bad loans, and their large customers turned to the capital market for a much higher proportion of their funding needs. Banks have proved very flexible in this situation by themselves acquiring subsidiaries in the securities industry and in insurance, and by the switch to non-interest income referred to earlier, but the balance of power in the financial system has moved considerably away from banking to the securities markets and to the institutional investors that are the biggest holders of most types of security.

On the domestic scene, the methods of operation of the international banking market have been adopted in what is termed wholesale banking, in which banks deal with large organizations. The technique is essentially the mobilization of large deposits through an interbank money market to provide funds for loans of up to 10 years, often at rates of interest that change every 3 or 6 months.

In retail banking, with households and small businesses, the number of personal customers has increased, especially through the payment of wages into bank accounts rather than by cash. Competition has intensified, and savings banks, building societies and co-operative banks are becoming more like the main banks in their powers and kinds of business. Electronic payment technologies increased competition, making it easier for institutions without branch networks to compete successfully with those that have branches.

JACK REVELL
UNIVERSITY OF WALES

Further reading

Chick, V. (1993) 'The evolution of the banking system and the theory of monetary policy', in S.F. Frowen (ed.) *Monetary Theory and Monetary Policy: New Tracks for the 1990s*, London.

Fabozzi, F.J., Modigliani, F. and Jones, F. (2002) *Foundations of Financial Markets and Institutions*, 3rd edn, New York.

Howells, P. and Bain, K. (2001) *The Economics of Money, Banking and Finance*, London.

Molyneux, P. (1990) *Banking: An Introductory Text*, London.

SEE ALSO: capital, credit and money markets; financial regulation; financial system; interest; securitization

BARGAINING

Bargaining is ubiquitous. Married couples are constantly in negotiation about who will do which domestic chores, or who will take the kids to the local park on a wet Sunday afternoon, and the children negotiate homework, bed times and TV rights. Government policy is typically the outcome of negotiations amongst cabinet ministers. The passage of legislation through parliament or congress may depend on the outcome of negotiations amongst the dominant political parties. National governments are often engaged in a variety of international negotiations on matters ranging from economic issues (such as the removal of trade restrictions) to global security (such as the reduction in the stockpiles of conventional armaments, and nuclear non-proliferation and test ban), and environmental and related issues (such as carbon emissions trading, biodiversity conservation and intellectual property rights). Much economic interaction involves negotiations on wages and commodity prices, and the recent wave of mergers and acquisitions provoked highly publicized and nerve-wracking negotiations over the price of these transactions. What variables (or factors) determine the outcome of this whole gamut of negotiations? That is the subject matter addressed by the modern theory of bargaining.

Consider the following situation. Aruna owns a house that she is willing to sell at a minimum price of £50,000; that is, she 'values' her house at £50,000. Mohan is willing to pay up to £70,000 for Aruna's house; that is, he values her house at £70,000. If the trade takes place, and Aruna sells the house to Mohan at a price that lies between £50,000 and £70,000, then both Aruna (the 'seller') and Mohan (the 'buyer') would become better off. This means that in this situation these two individuals have a common interest to trade. At the same time, however, they have conflicting (or divergent) interests over the price at which to trade: Aruna, the seller, would like to trade at a high price, while Mohan, the buyer, would like to trade at a low price. Any such exchange situation, in which a pair of individuals (or organizations) can engage in mutually beneficial trade but have conflicting interests over the terms of trade is a *bargaining situation*. Stated in general terms, a bargaining situation is one in which two or more players – where a 'player' may be either an individual or an organization (such as a firm, a political party or a country) – have a common interest to co-operate, but have conflicting interests over exactly how to co-operate.

There are two main reasons for being interested in bargaining situations. The first, practical reason is that bargaining situations are so important, interesting and widespread. Wherever there is an exchange, the potential for bargaining exists. This is obvious where goods are being exchanged in a market situation, but it is equally true in many social contexts. Even in the intimate and enduring relationship between a husband and wife, bargaining situations constantly recur.

In the political arena, bargaining situations crop up in a variety of forms. For example, when no single political party can form a government on its own (such as when there is a hung parliament), the party that has obtained the most votes will typically find itself in a bargaining situation with one or more of the other parties. Bargaining may sometimes be built into constitutional arrangements. In the USA, for instance, it is often required to cope with the sometimes acute divergences between the policies of the legislative and the executive arms. The second, theoretical reason for being interested in bargaining situations is that understanding such situations is fundamental to the development of an understanding of the workings of markets and the appropriateness, or otherwise, of prevailing monetary and fiscal policies.

The main issue that confronts the players in a bargaining situation is the need to reach agreement over exactly how to co-operate. Each player would like to reach some agreement rather than to disagree and not reach any agreement, but each player would also like to reach an agreement that is as favourable to him or her as possible. It is therefore always possible that the players will strike an agreement only after some costly delay, or indeed fail to reach any agreement.

Bargaining may be defined as any process through which the players try to reach an agreement. This process is typically time-consuming, and involves the players making offers and counter-offers to each other. A main focus of any theory of bargaining is on the efficiency and distribution properties of the outcome of bargaining. The former property relates to the possibility that the players fail to reach an agreement, or that they reach an agreement only after some costly delay. Examples of costly delayed agreements include: when a wage agreement is reached after lost production due to a long strike, and when a peace settlement is negotiated after the loss of life through war. The distribution property relates to the issue of exactly how the gains from co-operation are divided between the players. The principles of bargaining theory determine the roles of various key factors (or variables) on the bargaining outcome (and its efficiency and distribution properties). As such they determine the sources of a player's bargaining power.

If the bargaining process is 'frictionless' – by which I mean that neither player incurs any cost from haggling – then each player may continuously demand that agreement be struck on terms that are most favourable to him or her. So Aruna may continuously demand that trade take place at the price of £69,000, while Mohan may continuously demand that it take place at the price of £51,000. In such a case, the negotiations are likely to end in deadlock, since the negotiators would have no incentive to compromise and reach an agreement. If it did not matter *when* the negotiators agree, then it would not matter *whether* they agreed at all. In most real-life situations, however, the bargaining process is not frictionless. Haggling has a cost because bargaining is time-consuming, and time is valuable to the player. Indeed a player's bargaining power will tend to be higher the less impatient he or she is relative to the other negotiator. Aruna will be able to get a better price for her house if she is less impatient to close the deal than Mohan is.

In general, patience confers bargaining power. A person who has been unemployed for a long time is typically quite desperate to find a job, and so may be willing to accept work at almost any wage. This propensity can be exploited by potential employers, who then obtain most of the gains from employment. Consequently, an important function of minimum-wage legislation is to strengthen the bargaining power of the long-term unemployed. In general, since a player who is poor is typically more eager to strike a deal in any negotiations, poverty (by inducing a larger degree of impatience) adversely affects bargaining power. This is one reason why the richer nations of the world often obtain relatively better deals than the poorer nations in international trade negotiations. Another potential source of friction in the bargaining process comes from the possibility that the negotiations might break down due to some exogenous and uncontrollable factors. Even if the possibility of such an occurrence is small, it nevertheless may provide incentives to the players to compromise and reach an agreement. In general, a player's bargaining power is higher the less averse he or she is to risk relative to the other negotiator.

In many bargaining situations the players may have access to 'outside' options and/or 'inside' options. Aruna may be sitting on a non-negotiable (fixed) price offer on her house from another buyer; and she may also derive some 'utility' (or benefit) while she lives in it. The former is her outside option, while the latter her inside option. Should Aruna exercise her outside option, accepting the offer from another buyer, her negotiations with Mohan will be ended. In contrast, her inside option is the utility per day that she derives by living in her house while she, perhaps temporarily, disagrees with Mohan over the price at which to trade. Similarly, a married couple who are considering divorce may have outside and inside options. Their outside options are their payoffs from divorce, while their inside options are the payoffs they will enjoy from remaining married, even if their relationship has many problems. A player's bargaining power is higher the better his outside option and/or inside option.

Commitment tactics also affect the bargaining outcome. This tactic involves a negotiator taking actions prior to and/or during the negotiations that partially commit her to a particular bargaining position. For example, before a government goes to international trade negotiations it may attempt to enhance its bargaining position by making statements calculated to persuade its public that few concessions should be made. If the cost of abandoning a partial commitment of this sort is high, it enhances a player's bargaining power. Paradoxically, what may appear to be a weakness (the high cost of revoking a partial commitment) is actually a resource that enhances a bargaining position. So a government's hand is strengthened at the negotiating table because its interlocutors are aware that it will pay a high price should it renege on public commitments made to its electorate. Such tactics can, however, make bargaining difficult, if not impossible, resulting at best in costly delayed agreements. This is particularly likely in cases where two or more governments make incompatible partial commitments to their respective electorates, and their respective costs of reneging on such partial commitments are sufficiently large.

Another important determinant of the outcome of bargaining is the extent to which information about various variables (or factors) is known to all the parties in the bargaining situation. For example, the outcome of union–firm wage negotiations will typically be influenced by whether or not the current level of the firm's revenue is known to the union. A key principle is that costly delays can be mechanisms through which privately held information is credibly communicated to the uninformed party. For example, the employers may not know how tough the union is prepared to be in pressing its demands. In order to persuade the company that it is indeed tough (and so to extract a higher wage), the union may need to undertake a costly strike.

A bargaining situation is a game, in the sense that the outcome of bargaining depends on both players' bargaining strategies. Whether or not an agreement is struck, and the terms of the agreement (if one is struck), depends on both players' actions during the bargaining process. Because bargaining situations share many features with other games, the methodology of game theory has been used to develop the principles of bargaining theory.

ABHINAY MUTHOO
UNIVERSITY OF ESSEX

Further reading

Muthoo, A. (1999) *Bargaining Theory with Applications*, Cambridge, UK.
—— (2000) 'A non-technical introduction to bargaining theory', *World Economics* 1(2): 145–66.
Osborne, M. and Rubinstein, A. (1990) *Bargaining and Markets*, New York.

SEE ALSO: auctions; contracts; experimental economics; game theory; markets

BASIC NEEDS

This concept was taken up in studies of development in the 1970s, especially as a result of initiatives taken by the International Labour Office (ILO). Strictly the idea had a longer history (see, for example, Drewnowski and Scott 1966; Drewnowski 1977). The ILO was concerned about the slow rate of progress in improving conditions in the poorest countries and wanted to accelerate development programmes and anti-poverty policies alike. There was also concern that poor countries lacked the infrastructure provided by public facilities and services during the later stages of the industrialization in the twentieth century of the rich countries. Developing countries seemed to be being denied public-sector necessities that had been accepted and indeed institutionalized by their wealthier forebears. Basic needs were said to include two elements:

Firstly, they include certain minimum requirements of a family for private consumption: adequate food, shelter and clothing, as well as certain household furniture and equipment. Second, they include essential services provided by and for the community at large, such as safe drinking water, sanitation, public transport and health, education and cultural facilities....The concept of basic needs should be placed within a context of a nation's overall economic and social development. In no circumstances should it be taken to mean merely the minimum necessary for subsistence; it should be placed within a context of national independence, the dignity of individuals and peoples and their freedom to chart their destiny without hindrance.

(ILO 1976: 24–5; and see also ILO 1977)

The concept of 'basic needs' played a prominent part in a succession of national plans (see, for example, Ghai *et al.* 1977 and 1979, and, for India and Kenya, Townsend 1993) and in international reports (see, for example, UNESCO 1978; and the Brandt Report 1980). In international work poverty was perceived to have been restricted too much to the means of achieving individual or family subsistence rather than the development of facilities and services for the majority of the population. Universal or collective needs had to be recognized. Emphasis was therefore placed on the minimum facilities and the essential services, like health and education, required by local communities as a whole and not only on the resources required by individuals and families for physical survival and efficiency.

This drew heavily on the 'universal' services established over many years in the industrialized countries. Health, education, housing and community services had been established with free or heavily subsidized access. But it also drew implicitly on a number of the articles of human rights agreed in various of the Declarations and Conventions on Human Rights agreed by majorities of governments in the years after the 1939–45 war. Thus, Article 24 of the Convention on the Rights of the Child recognizes the fundamental right of the child to the enjoyment of the highest attainable standard of health and to 'facilities for the treatment of illness and rehabilitation of health. States parties shall strive to ensure that no child is deprived of his or her right of access to such health care services.' Article 26

recognizes 'for every child the right to benefit from social security'. Article 28 recognizes the right of the child to education. States parties must, among other things, therefore make 'primary education compulsory and available free to all'. Any reading of the various instruments for human rights demonstrates the consciously expressed aim of many governments to establish commonly available facilities and services – not targeted or selective services. In the mid-1970s the ILO was concerned to highlight the agreements already reached in the early postwar years and to accelerate the process of action to enable developing countries to 'catch up'.

However, proponents of the concept of basic needs seem to have had great difficulty in producing acceptable criteria for the choice and precise operational definition of those basic facilities and services. The minimum *form* of those arrangements was not unambiguously specified (Streeten 1984; Hunt 1989: 268–9). Sceptics argued that the needs of populations cannot be defined adequately just by reference to the physical needs of individuals and the more obvious physical provisions and services required by local communities. The nature of minimum facilities requires exposition as detailed and persuasive as of minimum individual nutrition. The exposition of need also depends on assumptions that have to be made about the development and functioning of societies and, in particular, how the organization of markets can be reconciled with the organization of collective utilities and services. Under the influence of monetarism and neo-liberalism the insistence on establishing free trade and a larger place for markets and for private business in plans for development involved major costs for sections of the populations of developing countries. Governments found they were expected to reduce tariffs without being offered corresponding concessions by the industrial countries (Watkins 2002).

The expectations laid upon governments during the last years of the twentieth century as well as their citizens in the development reports of the international financial agencies and by the governments of the major industrial countries came to be increasingly recognized to be illogical. To give priority to the work ethic without giving equal attention to the needs of people who cannot work and cannot be expected to work – children and disabled, sick and elderly people – and to the needs of the victims of discrimination and racism, was regarded as unbalanced as it was wrong and attracted strong opposition. For example, the disproportionately greater poverty and deprivation experienced by ethnic minorities, women, the elderly, children and people with disabilities in developing countries had not been sufficiently allowed for in formulations of development. Specialized investigation of their conditions and situation was inseparable from more general analysis and judgement. The social structure of poverty, with sections or groups in the population experiencing higher risk of poverty, some of whom are more severely impoverished than others, had to be set out, so that the extent and form of service could correspondingly be precisely identified, and the costs of bringing existing facilities up to standard estimated. This illuminates cause, but also priorities in policy. The links between the two have to be recognized, so that they can be exploited for both scientific and political or social reasons. The 'basic needs paradigm', as it has been called (Hunt 1989: 77 and 265–78; but see also Streeten 1984, Cornia 1984 and Stewart 1985), gained a good deal of support, and was also linked to the need of local communities for access to their own plots of land. Under the basic needs approach the modernization of traditional farming could be advocated, using public works programmes to invest in small- to medium-scale labour-intensive methods of farming.

One of the attractions of the 'subsistence' concept to liberal theorists was its limited scope and therefore its limited implications for socio-stuctural reform, which allowed poverty to be reconciled more easily with the individualism and free-market ethos underlying liberal-pluralism. On the other hand, the 'basic needs' concept appeared to go much further in accepting certain, albeit limited, preconditions for community survival and prosperity in all countries. This amounted to necessary structural reform to establish public-sector facilities and services to be used, if not entirely owned, by sovereign states and their entire populations, which simultaneously provided individual entitlement to those social provisions.

In the 1990s and early 2000s the influence of the concept of basic needs has waned. This has been due partly to the strong revival of neo-classical economics and theoretical attempts to reconcile basic needs with that perspective – for example, by emphasizing investment in 'human capital' rather than investment in the institutions of public service. But it has been due partly to the growing strength of alternative formulations, including what Amartya Sen has called the 'case for re-orienting poverty analysis from *low incomes* [and basic needs] to *insufficient basic capabilities*' (Sen 1992: 151, and see also p. 109, his emphasis). This change of direction in the priorities of development appealed to most economists at the time, but despite the elegance and overarching intentions of the 'capabilities' approach it has proved difficult to measure and has still to demonstrate enduring influence on development policies.

PETER TOWNSEND
LONDON SCHOOL OF ECONOMICS
AND POLITICAL SCIENCE

References

Brandt, W. (1980) *North–South: A Programme for Survival*, London.

Cornia, G. (1984) 'A summary and interpretation of the evidence', in G. Cornia and R. Jolly (eds) *The Impact of the World Recession on Children*, London.

Drewnowski, J. (1977) 'Poverty: Its meaning and measurement', *Development and Change* 8(2): 183–206.

Drewnowski, J. and Scott, W. (1966) *The Level of Living Index*, Report No. 4, Geneva.

Ghai, D.P. *et al.* (1977) *The Basic Needs Approach to Development: Some Issues Regarding Concepts and Methodology*, Geneva.

Ghai, D., Godfrey, M. and Lisk, F. (1979) *Planning for Basic Needs in Kenya*, Geneva.

Hunt, D. (1989) *Economic Theories of Development: An Analysis of Competing Paradigms*, New York.

International Labour Office (ILO) (1976) *Employment Growth and Basic Needs: A One-World Problem*, Geneva.

—— (1977) *Meeting Basic Needs: Strategies for Eradicating Mass Poverty and Unemployment*, Geneva.

Sen, A. (1992) *Inequality Re-examined*, Cambridge, MA.

Stewart, F. (1985) *Planning to Meet Basic Needs*, London.

Streeten, P. (1984) 'Basic needs: Some unsettled questions', *World Development* 12.

Townsend, P. (1993) *The International Analysis of Poverty*, New York.

UNESCO (1978) *Study in Depth on the Concept of Basic Human Needs in Relation to Various Ways of Life and Its Possible Implications for the Action of the Organisations*, Paris.

Watkins, K. (2002) *Rigged Rules and Double Standards: Trade, Globalisation and the Fight against Poverty*, Oxford.

Further reading

India (1978) *Five Year Plan 1978–83*, Delhi.
Malaysia (1986) *Fifth Malaysia Plan 1986–1990*, Kuala Lumpur.
Rowntree, B.S. (1901) *Poverty: A Study of Town Life*, London.

SEE ALSO: deprivation and relative deprivation; poverty

BEHAVIOURAL ECONOMICS

Behavioural economics – the enrichment of economics with findings and insights from other disciplines – emerged as a major force in the discipline at the end of the twentieth century. As late as 1990, one could count on one hand the number of influential behavioural economics papers published in mainstream economics journals, yet by the early twenty-first century behavioural economics was well represented in the pages of major journals, and its practitioners were on the faculty of top economics departments, and among the recipients of honours and awards such as the John Bates Clark Award and the Nobel Prize.

In fact, behavioural economics is not a new enterprise. Adam Smith presented the psyche as the site of a struggle between our passions and our efforts to see ourselves through the rational eyes of an 'impartial spectator'. Psychological speculations were common in the economics literature well into the early stages of the neo-classical revolution, and the neo-classical paradigm itself, with its core concept of utility maximization, takes individual behaviour as the foundation of analysis. However, from Freud's 'unconscious motives' to William James's rejection of self-interest as an explanation of human behaviour, psychological theories of the time were antithetical to the postulates of utility maximization (Lewin 1996), and despite attempts to reintroduce psychology into economics by, among others, Tibor Scitovsky, George Katona and Harvey Leibenstein, the gap could not be bridged as long as critics of neo-classicism offered no compelling alternative theory.

In the early 1970s two seminal papers launched the field of *behavioural decision research*, a subfield of psychology that directly contrasts actual human behaviour with the assumptions and predictions of economics. The psychologists Tversky and Kahneman (1974) proposed that – contrary to the neo-classical assumption of human rationality, but consistent with Herb Simon's notion of bounded rationality – people use simplifying heuristics to assess probabilities and update beliefs. In certain situations, reliance on such heuristics leads to systematic biases, such as the 'gambler's fallacy', or the tendency to give undue weight to information that is vivid or easily called to mind. In the second paper, Kahneman and Tversky (1979) proposed a theory of decision-making under risk. Called 'Prospect Theory', it deviates from expected utility theory in several important respects: (1) it weighs probabilities non-linearly, overweighting small probabilities and underweighting changes in probabilities in the mid-range; (2) it assumes that people care about changes in, rather than levels of, wealth; and (3) it assumes that people dislike losses much more than they like gains, a concept known as 'loss aversion'. In 1980 a third seminal paper, by Richard Thaler, applied these ideas to economics.

In the decades following the publication of these three foundational papers, progress in behavioural economics has followed a roughly predictable curve: (1) one or more behavioural economists identify a regularity, or 'anomaly', which violates economic theory; (2) mainstream economists then attempt to show the anomaly is artefactual or argue that the regularity is not anomalous, i.e. does not violate economic theory; (3) debate continues until behavioural economists prevail and go on to study the anomaly's psychological underpinnings and boundary conditions, develop formal models of the phenomenon and use the models to derive specific implications for economics.

The cycle can be illustrated with the classic case of the 'endowment effect'. First recognized by Thaler (1980), the endowment effect identifies the tendency for people to become attached to objects in their possession, an attachment that may lead them to demand a (sometimes dramatically) higher price for selling the object than what they would have paid for it. Many economists initially doubted this effect, perhaps because it poses such a fundamental challenge to the economic assumption that preferences are invariant with respect to transient endowments, and there were many empirical attempts to discredit the effect or to account for it within traditional theory. Once the dust had cleared from the field, behavioural economists began to model the effect mathematically (e.g. Tversky and Kahneman 1991), and to investigate its psychological underpinnings. Subsequent research has shown, for example, that buyers tend to focus on the money they will relinquish, while sellers focus on the object they will receive (Carmon and Ariely 2000); that people cannot predict beforehand that they will become attached to objects after they receive them (Loewenstein and Adler 1995); and that the strength of the effect depends on how one obtained the object (e.g. whether one earned it. (Loewenstein and Issacharoff 1994)). Most recently, behavioural economists have begun to examine implications of the endowment effect for real-world phenomena such as investor behaviour and boom–bust cycles in the housing market (Genesove and Mayer 2001).

New directions

Having established what seems to be a firm foothold within the profession, behavioural economics is currently heading in several interesting directions.

First, behavioural economists have begun to look past behavioural decision research, and even beyond psychology, for new insights and findings. They have drawn, for example, on social psychology and sociology to develop models of 'social preference' that incorporate motives such as aversion to unfairness (Rabin 1993) and inequality aversion (e.g. Fehr and Schmidt 1999). An especially promising source of new findings and insights is the nascent field of cognitive (as well as affective) neuroscience.

Second, behavioural economists are designing and implementing policies that draw on behavioural insights rather than depending only upon the price mechanisms of traditional economics. For example, whereas economics traditionally relies on changes in interest rates or taxation to encourage savings behaviour, behavioural economists have recently demonstrated the efficacy of changing default contributions rates in retirement plans to promote savings (which has a large impact on savings rates, contrary to standard predictions (Madrian and Shea 2001)). Alternatively, they exploit behavioural insights into self-control by, for example, persuading people that

they should commit to make savings out of *future* increments to salary (Bernartzi and Thaler 2001).

Third, having begun as a largely experimental science, behavioural economics now draws on a more diverse range of methods, including field studies and, most recently, brain imaging.

Fourth, and most controversially, behavioural economists are exploring ideas that challenge not only the core assumptions, but also the fundamental paradigm, of neo-classical economists. Virtually all of the most influential work in behavioural economics over the past decades has adopted what could be called an 'incremental' approach, adhering to the basic economic assumption of utility maximization. Emboldened by the success of their enterprise, however, and armed with new insights culled from neuroscience and other fields, many behavioural economists have begun to question whether human behaviour is in fact best modelled using the framework of maximizing utility, and have begun to explore alternative accounts. Whether such more radical variants of behavioural economics will eventually take root will depend on whether these insights can be incorporated into coherent theoretical frameworks that predict behaviour better than do the models developed by behavioural economists working within the neo-classical paradigm.

GEORGE LOEWENSTEIN
CARNEGIE MELLON UNIVERSITY

References

Bernartzi, S. and Thaler, R. (2001) 'Naïve diversification strategies in defined contribution savings plans', *American Economic Review* 91: 79–98.

Carmon, Z. and Ariely, D. (2000) 'Focusing on the forgone: Why value can appear so different to buyers and sellers', *Journal of Consumer Research* 27(3): 360–70.

Fehr, E. and Schmidt, K.M. (1999) 'A theory of fairness, competition and cooperation', *Quarterly Journal of Economics* 117(3): 817–68.

Genesove, D. and Mayer, C. (2001) 'Loss aversion and seller behavior: Evidence from the housing market', *Quarterly Journal of Economics* 116(4): 1,233–60.

Kahneman, D. and Tversky, A. (1979) 'Prospect theory: An analysis of decision under risk', *Econometrica* 47: 263–91.

Lewin, S.B. (1996) 'Economics and psychology: Lessons for our own day from the early twentieth century', *Journal of Economic Literature* 34(3): 1,293–323.

Loewenstein, G. and Adler, D. (1995) 'A bias in the prediction of tastes', *Economic Journal* 105: 929–37.

Loewenstein, G. and Issacharoff, S. (1994) 'Source-dependence in the valuation of objects', *Journal of Behavioral Decision Making* 7: 157–68.

Madrian, B. and Shea, D.F. (2001) 'The power of suggestion: Inertia in 401(k) participation and savings behavior', *Quarterly Journal of Economics* 116: 1,149–525.

Rabin, M. (1993) 'Incorporating fairness into game theory and economics', *American Economic Review* 83(5): 1, 281–302.

Thaler, R. (1980) 'Toward a positive theory of consumer choice', *Journal of Economic Behavior and Organization* 1: 39–60.

Tversky, A. and Kahneman, D. (1974) 'Judgment under uncertainty: Heuristics and biases', *Science* 185(4,157): 1,124–31.

—— (1991) 'Loss aversion in riskless choice: A reference-dependent model', *Quarterly Journal of Economics* 106: 1,039–61.

Further reading

Camerer, C. and Loewenstein, G. (2003) 'Behavioral economics: Past, present, future', in C. Camerer, G. Loewenstein and M. Rabin (eds) *Advances in Behavioral Economics*, Princeton, NJ.

Loewenstein, G. (1999) 'Experimental economics from the vantage-point of behavioral economics', *Economic Journal* 109: 25–34.

Rabin, M. (1998) 'Psychology and economics', *Journal of Economic Literature* 36: 11–46.

SEE ALSO: decision-making

BENTHAM, JEREMY (1748–1832)

Jeremy Bentham was undoubtedly one of the most important and influential figures in the development of modern social science. His numerous writings are major contributions to the development of philosophy, law, government, economics, social administration and public policy, and many have become classic texts in these fields. To these subjects he brought an analytical precision and careful attention to detail that, especially in matters of legal organization and jurisprudence, had not been attempted since Aristotle, and he transformed in method and substance the way these subjects were conceived. He combined a critical rationalism and empiricism with a vision of reform and, latterly, radical reform, which gave unity and direction to what became Philosophic Radicalism. Although he was not the first philosopher to use the greatest-happiness principle as the standard of right and wrong, he is rightly remembered as the founder of modern utilitarianism. Many of Bentham's writings were never published in his lifetime or were completed by various editors. The new edition of the *Collected Works* (1968–in progress) will replace in approximately sixty-five volumes the inadequate *Works of Jeremy Bentham* (1838–43), edited by John Bowring, and will reveal for the first time the full extent and scope of Bentham's work.

Bentham is best known for some of his earliest writings. *An Introduction to the Principles of Morals and Legislation* (printed in 1780 and published in 1789) and *Of Laws in General* (not published until 1945) are important texts in legal philosophy and, together with his critique of William *Blackstone's Commentaries on the Laws of England* in the *Comment on the Commentaries* (published first in 1928) and *A Fragment on Government* (1776), represent major landmarks in the development of jurisprudence. The *Introduction to the Principles of Morals and Legislation* was also intended to serve as an introduction to a penal code, which was an important part of a lifelong ambition, never fully realized, of constructing a complete code of laws (latterly called the *Pannomion*). At this time Bentham also turned to economic questions, which were to occupy him in various forms throughout his life. His first publication was the *Defence of Usury* (1787), a critique of Adam Smith's treatment of this subject in *The Wealth of Nations*.

From the outset of his career, Bentham was devoted to reform and especially to the reform of legal institutions. His attitude towards fundamental political reform developed more slowly. Although at the time of the French Revolution he was not part of the radical movement in England, he wrote numerous manuscripts in support of democratic institutions in France. He eventually reacted strongly against the excesses of the revolution, but earlier contacts, largely developed through Lord Lansdowne, and the publication of his *Draught of a New Plan for the Organisation of the Judicial Establishment of France* (1790), led to his being made an honorary citizen of France. One important development of this period was his friendship with Etienne Dumont, the Swiss reformer and scholar, whose French versions of Bentham's works, especially the *Traités de législation, civile et pénale* (1802), were read throughout Europe and Latin America, and earned for Bentham a considerable international reputation. Following the French Revolution much of Bentham's practical energies were devoted, in conjunction with his brother Samuel, to establishing model prisons, called Panopticons, in various countries. His main effort in England failed, and this failure, though ultimately compensated by the government, was one factor leading him to take up the cause of radical political reform. The influence of James Mill was perhaps the most important factor (there were many) in his 'conversion' to radicalism in 1809–10, and the publication of *A Plan of Parliamentary Reform* in 1817 launched the Philosophic Radicals in their quest for parliamentary reform. In the 1820s, though now in his seventies, Bentham resumed the task of codification and the construction of the *Pannomion* in response to requests from governments and disciples in Spain, Portugal, Greece and Latin America. In his massive, unfinished *Constitutional Code* (1822–), he set forth a theory of representative democracy that was a grand synthesis of many of his ideas and a classic of liberal political thought.

FREDERICK ROSEN
UNIVERSITY COLLEGE LONDON

Further reading

Dinwiddy, J. (1989) *Bentham*, Oxford.
Halévy, E. (1901–4) *La Formation du radicalisme philosophique*, 3 vols, Paris.
Hart, H.L.A. (1982) *Essays on Bentham: Jurisprudence and Political Theory*, Oxford.
Kelly, P. (1990) *Utilitarianism and Distributive Justice: Jeremy Bentham and the Civil Law*, Oxford.
Rosen, F. (1983) *Jeremy Bentham and Representative Democracy*, Oxford.
—— (1992) *Bentham, Byron and Greece: Constitutionalism, Nationalism and Early Liberal Political Thought*, Oxford.
—— (2003) *Classical Utilitarianism from Hume to Mill*, London.
Semple, J. (1993) *Bentham's Prison: A Study of the Panopticon Penitentiary*, Oxford.

SEE ALSO: utilitarianism

BOAS, FRANZ (1858–1942)

Franz Boas, born in Germany in 1858, and naturalized as a US citizen in 1892, unquestionably dominated both the intellectual paradigm and institutional development of twentieth-century US anthropology until the Second World War, presiding over the emergence of anthropology as a professional discipline based on the concept of culture, and establishing a subdisciplinary scope including cultural, physical and linguistic anthropology as well as prehistoric archaeology.

In spite of his focus on professionalism in science, Boas himself was trained in (psycho)physics in his native Germany, thereby coming into contact with the folk psychology of Wundt and the anthropology of Bastian (European folk cultures) and Virchow (anthropometry). Boas's dissertation at the University of Kiel in 1881 on the colour of sea water led to concern with the inherent subjectivity of observer perception. His work in geography with Fischer initially supported environmental determinism, but his expedition to the Eskimo of Baffin Land in 1882–3 led to a more flexible argument stressing the interaction of culture and environment.

Boas settled permanently in North America only in 1887, recognizing greater opportunities there for an ambitious young Jewish scholar. In the ensuing years, he was crucially involved in the development of US anthropology in all of its early major centres. The institutional framework for the emerging Boasian anthropology was usually collaboration between a university, ensuring the academic training of professional anthropologists, and a museum to sponsor field research and publication. Boas himself settled in New York, teaching at Columbia from 1896 until 1936. He had previously served as Honorary Philologist of the Bureau of American Ethnology, which dominated Washington and government anthropology. Through F.W. Putnam of Harvard, he organized anthropology at the Chicago World's Fair of 1892 and acquired ties to archaeological work centring at Harvard. Boas's own students established programmes elsewhere, particularly Kroeber at Berkeley, Speck at Pennsylvania and Sapir in Ottawa. By about 1920, Boasian anthropology was firmly established as the dominant paradigm of the North American discipline.

Boas's theoretical position, often characterized as historical particularism, claimed that unilinear evolution was an inadequate model for the known diversity of human cultures. Human nature was defined as variable and learned tradition. Although he was extremely interested in particular historical developments, Boas argued that progress did not necessarily follow a fixed sequence, nor was it always unidirectional from simple to complex. He further parted from evolutionary theorists like E.B. Tylor in his contention that cultural learning is basically unconscious rather than rational. Boas produced particular ethnographic examples to argue the limits of theoretical generalization in anthropology, indeed in social science generally. 'Laws' comparable to those of the natural sciences were possible in principle though usually premature in practice. The ultimate generalizations of anthropology would be psychological (1911b), but Boas's own studies rarely transcended the prior level of ethnographic description. Later students, especially Margaret Mead and Ruth Benedict, elaborated these ideas in what came to be called culture and personality.

Particular histories could not be reconstructed in detail for societies without written records. In contrast, Boas stressed the historical dimensions of synchronically observable, particular cultural phenomena. For example, distribution was the primary reconstructive method to trace the diffusion (borrowing) of folklore motifs and combinations on the Northwest Coast. Elements in a single culture had diverse sources rather than a single common origin. Boas applied this same argument to linguistic work, assuming that language was a part of culture. His scepticism about distant genetic relationships of American Indian languages was consistent with his lack of training in Indo-European philology, and brought him into frequent disagreement with his former student Edward Sapir, whose linguistic work was far more sophisticated.

On the other hand, Boas made important contributions to linguistics, being the first to establish the theoretical independence of race, language and culture as classificatory variables for human diversity (1911a). He broke with the Indo-European tradition in insisting on the 'inner form' (Steinthal) of each language in its grammatical patterning, developing new analytic categories appropriate to American Indian languages.

Boas insisted on the importance of first-hand fieldwork in living cultures, and he returned again and again to the Kwakiutl and other Northwest Coast tribes. He trained native informants to record their own cultures, and collected native language texts for folklore as well as linguistics. He was particularly concerned to record the symbolic culture of these tribes, focusing on art, mythology, religion and language, and was influential in the development of the disciplines of folklore and linguistics as well as anthropology.

Boas's own research spanned the scope of anthropology in its North American definition. In archaeology, he pioneered in Mexico and the Southwest in developing research programmes to reconstruct the history of particular cultures. In physical anthropology, he demonstrated that the head-form of descendants of immigrants can change in a single generation, thereby illustrating the essential variability and plasticity of the human form. He further developed important statistical methods for human growth studies, using longitudinal studies and family-line variation to show the role of environment in modifying heredity. Moreover, Boas was dedicated to the idea that anthropology had practical consequences for society generally, arguing, particularly in response to events in Nazi Germany at the end of his life, for the essential equality of races (defined in terms of statistical variability) and the validity of each cultural pattern.

Boas is, then, more than any other individual, responsible for the characteristic form that the discipline of anthropology has taken in North America. During his long career, he and several successive generations of students stood for a particular scope, method and theory, applied largely to the study of the American Indians. The increasing diversity of North American anthropology since the Second World War still has Boasian roots.

REGNA DARNELL
UNIVERSITY OF WESTERN ONTARIO

References

Boas, F. (1911a) 'Introduction', in *Handbook of American Indian Languages*, Washington, DC.
—— (1911b) *The Mind of Primitive Man*, New York.

Further reading

Boas, F. (1940) *Race, Language and Culture*, New York.
—— (1964 [1888]) *The Central Eskimo*, Lincoln, NB.
Cole, D. (1999) *Franz Boas: The Early Years, 1858–1906*, Seattle, WA.
Darnell, R. (2001) *Invisible Genealogies: A History of Americanist Anthropology*, Lincoln, NB.
Goldschmidt, W. (ed.) (1959) *The Anthropology of Franz Boas: Memoir of the American Anthropological Association* 89.
Harris, M. (1968) *The Rise of Anthropological Theory*, New York.
Stocking, G. (1968) *Race, Culture and Evolution*, New York.

BODY

Since the early 1970s the human body has become a vivid presence in the human sciences and interdisciplinary cultural studies. Feminist theory, literary criticism, history, comparative religion, philosophy, sociology, psychology and anthropology are all implicated in the move towards the body. It has been suggested that this widespread interest in the body may be due to the current historical moment in which 'we are undergoing fundamental changes in how our bodies are organized and experienced' such that we are seeing 'the end of one kind of body and the beginning of another kind of body' (Martin 1992: 121).

Recent scholarship (Bynum 1989; Frank 1991) appears to support this claim. The body has been typically assumed, by scholarly and popular thought alike, to be a fixed, material entity subject to the empirical rules of biological science, and characterized by unchangeable inner necessities. The new body beginning to be identified can no longer be considered a brute fact of nature. A chorus of critical statements has declared that 'the body has a history' in that it behaves in new ways at particular historical moments, that neither our personal nor social bodies are natural because they exist only within the self-creating process of human labour, and that as the existential ground of culture the body is characterized by an essential indeterminacy and flux. With biology no longer a monolithic objectivity, the body is transformed from object to agent.

Others argue that the human body can no longer be considered a 'bounded entity' due to the destabilizing impact of social processes of commodification, fragmentation and the semiotic barrage of images of body parts (Kroker and Kroker 1987). In the milieu of late capitalism and consumer culture, the body/self is primarily a performing-self of appearance, display and impression management. Fixed life-cycle categories are blurred, and the goals of bodily self-care have changed from spiritual salvation, to enhanced health, and finally to a marketable self. The asceticism of inner-body discipline is no longer incompatible with outer-body hedonism and social mobility, but has become a means towards them.

The contemporary cultural transformation of the body is also observable in the problematizing of the boundaries of corporeality itself. These include the boundaries between the physical and non-physical, between animal and human, between animal/human and machine or automaton, and between human and gods or deities. Yet another inescapable transformation of the contemporary body is being wrought by the incredible proliferation of violence: ethnic violence, sexual violence, self-destructive violence, domestic violence and gang violence. From the dissolution of self in torture and the denaturing of the body in situations of chronic political violence, from unarticulated bodily resistance to hegemonic oppression among the impoverished and again to the madness of 'ethnic cleansing' and rape as political weapons, the body is the threatened vehicle of human being and dignity.

Across these transformations, several general approaches to the body can be identified in current literature. A premise of much writing is an 'analytic body' that invites discrete focus on perception, practice, parts, processes or products. Other literature concentrates on the 'topical body', that is, an understanding of the body in relation to specific domains of cultural activity: the body and health, the body and political domination, the body and trauma, the body and religion, the body and gender, the body and self, the body and emotion, the body and technology are examples. Finally, there is the 'multiple body', with the number of bodies dependent on how many of its aspects one cares to recognize. Douglas (1973) called attention to the 'two bodies', referring to the social and physical aspects of the body. Scheper-Hughes and Lock (1987) give us 'three bodies', including the individual body, social body and body politic. O'Neill (1985) ups the ante to 'five bodies': the world's body, the social body, the body politic, the consumer body and the medical or medicalized body.

To greater or lesser degrees these approaches study the *body* and its transformations while taking *embodiment* for granted. Emphasis on embodiment problematizes conceptual dualities between mind and body, pre-objective and objectified, subject and object, culture and biology, mental and material, culture and practice, gender and sex. There is among champions of the body in contemporary theorizing a tendency to vilify what is usually called Cartesian dualism as a kind of moral abjection. Yet Descartes in part introduced the doctrine as a methodological distinction and a way to free scientific thought from subjection to theology and strict institutional supervision by the Church. The philosopher is doubtless not entirely to blame for the ontologization of the distinction, and the way it has become embedded in our thinking (cf. Leder 1990).

The possibility that the body might be understood as a seat of subjectivity is one source of challenge to theories of culture in which mind/subject/culture are placed in contrast to body/object/biology. Much theorizing is in fact heir to the Cartesian legacy in that it privileges the mind/subject/culture set in the form of representation, whether cast in terms of rules and principles by social anthropology and sociology, signs and symbols by semiotics, text and discourse by literary studies, or knowledge and models by cognitive science. In such accounts the body is a creature of representation, as in the work of Foucault (1979, 1986), whose primary concern is to establish the discursive conditions of possibility for the body as object of domination. In contrast, the body can be comprehended as a function of being-in-the-world, as in the work of Merleau-Ponty (1962), for whom embodiment is the existential condition of possibility for culture and self. If indeed the body is in a critical historical moment, the corresponding theoretical moment is the tension between representation and being-in-the-world.

THOMAS J. CSORDAS
CASE WESTERN RESERVE UNIVERSITY

References

Bynum, C.W. (1989) 'The female body and religious practice in the Later Middle Ages', in M. Feher (ed.) *Fragments for a History of the Human Body, Part One*, New York.
Douglas, M. (1973) *Natural Symbols*, New York.
Foucault, M. (1979) *Discipline and Punish: The Birth of the Prison*, New York.
—— (1986) *The Care of the Self: The History of Sexuality*, vol. 3, New York.
Frank, A. (1991) 'For a sociology of the body: An analytical review', in M. Featherstone, M. Hepworth and B.S. Turner (eds) *The Body: Social Process and Cultural Theory*, London.
Kroker, A. and Kroker, M. (1987) *Body Invaders: Panic Sex in America*, New York.
Leder, D. (1990) *The Absent Body*, Chicago.
Martin, E. (1992) 'The end of the body?', *American Ethnologist* 19 (1): 121–40.
Merleau-Ponty, M. (1962) *Phenomenology of Perception*, trans. J. Edie, Evanston, IL.
O'Neill, J. (1985) *Five Bodies: The Shape of Modern Society*, Ithaca, NY.
Scheper-Hughes, N. and Lock, M. (1987) 'The mindful body: A prolegomenon to future work in medical anthropology', *Medical Anthropology Quarterly* 1.

Further reading

Csordas, T. (ed.) (1994) *Embodiment and Experience: The Existential Ground of Culture and Self*, Cambridge, UK.
Featherstone, M., Hepworth, M. and Turner, B.S. (eds) (1991) *The Body: Social Process and Cultural Theory*, London.
Feher, M. (ed.) (1989) *Fragments for a History of the Human Body*, 3 vols, New York.
Haraway, D. (1991) *Simians, Cyborgs, and Women: The Reinvention of Nature*, New York.
Jacobus, M., Keller, E.F. and Shuttleworth, S. (eds) (1990) *Body/Politics: Women and the Discourses of Science*, New York.
Lock, M. (1993) 'The anthropology of the body', *Annual Review of Anthropology* 22.
Scarry, E. (1985) *The Body in Pain: The Making and Un-Making of the World*, New York.

BOURDIEU, PIERRE (1930–2002)

Pierre Bourdieu was probably the most influential French sociologist of the last third of the twentieth century. Synthesizing diverse philosophical and sociological traditions, his research practice and theory aimed at unveiling correspondences between social and mental structures, and at giving a historical account for their emergence – a research orientation that Bourdieu himself once called 'constructivist' or 'genetic structuralism'. He became internationally renowned for introducing or reactualising the concepts of 'practice', '*habitus*', 'capital' and 'field' in social science. Having graduated in philosophy, Bourdieu turned to anthropology and sociology during a stay in Algeria in the late 1950s. He taught at the Ecole des Hautes Etudes en Sciences Sociales (Paris) from 1964, and edited the interdisciplinary journal *Actes de la Recherche en Sciences Sociales* from 1975. In 1981 he obtained a professorship at the Collège de France, the most prestigious French academic institution, and became latterly one of the leading intellectuals in France.

At first sight, Bourdieu's work covers a bewildering range of subject-matter, including perceptions of time among Algerian peasants, matrimonial strategies in Southwestern France, students' performances at French schools and higher education institutions, cultural tastes, language, literature, museums, photography, sports, *haute couture*, housing, intellectuals, urban ghettos and the state, to name some central areas of investigation. There is, however, one main theme that runs through most of Bourdieu's analyses, namely the issue of unequal access to the dominant culture, and the sociopolitical preconditions and consequences of this inequality.

Bourdieu drew a significant amount of his material from three sites: the French region of Béarn, where he was born in 1930, the son of a lower civil servant; 1950s Algeria, where he did military service, conducted fieldwork and taught at university level; and (elite) higher education institutions in Paris, which he attended as a student and where he worked until his death in 2002. Albeit informed by philosophy (his original subject of study), Bourdieu's concepts were forged out of the practical engagement with and the critical analysis of these three fields.

Bourdieu examined Algeria, the Béarn and the French elite in terms of 'symbolic violence'. A universally shared system of values and perceptions privileges those who embody the dominant or legitimate culture, whereas those who have less access to material and cultural resources are devalued. What is more, the disadvantaged segments of the population (colonised Algerians, rural Béarnais, poor and uneducated Frenchmen) contribute to their own domination to the extent that they unquestioningly share the system of evaluation that works against them.

For instance, Bourdieu showed that, in the 1950s, with increasing urbanization, peasant families in the Béarn encouraged their daughters to marry townsmen, whom they considered to be a better match than young farmers, thus condemning their own sons to celibacy and depreciating life in the countryside still further. As this example indicates, Bourdieu looked at kinship (and social action in general) in a more dynamic, more actor-centred and more politicized framework than Lévi-Straussian structuralism, the dominant paradigm in 1960s French social science.

He elaborated on themes from Durkheim and Mauss (social systems of classification), Marx (class relations) and Weber (legitimacy, subjective representations), and orchestrated a fruitful dialogue between their points of view.

Bourdieu himself represented his own social thought as an attempt to overcome dualisms, and in particular the opposition between 'objectivism'

and 'subjectivism'. According to Bourdieu, most social action is guided neither by objective rules, nor by subjective choices. '*Habitus*', 'strategy' and 'practical sense' are the concepts that he used to express this intermediate position. *Habitus*, a term taken from Aristotelian discourse, refers to a set of dispositions that are inculcated in childhood, persist more or less unchanged over the course of a life, and incline people to act and react in specific ways that virtually always betray their social background. Relatively unaware and without following any conscious rule, people of similar social origin share homologous attitudes, categories and perceptions, and engage in similar practices.

The sense of honour of Kabyle men, and the humble attitude of Kabyle women, in Algeria, are examples of such dispositions. The *habitus* is history materialized and embodied; it is inscribed in the Kabyle house (which is organized along an opposition between a dark, damp, lower, 'female' part and a light-filled, noble, upper part) and in the (upright, male, or stooped, female) bodies of the Kabyle. Pierre Bourdieu used the Kabyle material as an illustration in *Outline of a Theory of Practice* [1972] and *The Logic of Practice* [1980], two highly influential books that summed up his social thought in mid-career, about two decades before the comprehensive presentation of his approach in *Pascalian Meditations* [1997].

Bourdieu drew on concepts derived from economics to conceptualize social action. Agents have different kinds and amounts of 'capital'. These include material resources in the original sense of the word, but also 'social capital' (social relations, networks), 'symbolic capital' (prestige, honour) and 'cultural capital'. Cultural capital takes three forms: it is materialized as books and art works in one's possession, incorporated as a certain cultivated '*habitus*' and institutionalized in the form of diplomas and degrees.

With the help of these conceptual instruments, Bourdieu analysed the workings of the French educational system. *The Inheritors: French Students and Their Relation to Culture* [1964] and *Reproduction in Education, Society and Culture* [1970], two books co-authored with Jean-Claude Passeron, showed that students from lower social classes, being less familiar with the dominant culture, are more likely to fail in school than those with a certain social and cultural capital. Notwithstanding an appearance of neutrality, the school system reproduces and legitimizes pre-existing social differences.

Generally, and with the complicity of the educational system, the dominant classes accumulate all kinds of capital. In strategies that are designed to bring about the reproduction of their social standing, they sometimes transform one kind of capital into another, for example when they invest in the education of their children. Having graduated from prestigious schools, the latter obtain leading positions in industry and the state, so converting their cultural and symbolic capital back into economic capital.

In accordance with the amount and structure of their capital, agents occupy different 'positions' in the 'social space'. In *Distinction: A Social Critique of the Judgement of Taste* [1979], Bourdieu made a fine-tuned analysis of the class visions and divisions of French society in the 1960s and 1970s. He correlated social positions with preferences for certain types of music, art and theatre, but also seemingly trivial cultural forms such as foodstuffs, table manners, sports and interior design. Such seemingly natural tastes and 'choices', Bourdieu argued, are in reality strategies that serve to differentiate oneself from (or sometimes to emulate) members of other social groups.

The social space can be seen as a juxtaposition of various 'fields', for instance the economic and the political field, or the fields of science, fine arts and literature. A field is a relatively autonomous microcosm with its own rules and logic. Agents and institutions compete with each other over a highly priced value or good that all agree is at stake, e.g. truth in the field of science, or salvation in the field of religion. Everyone employs strategies (either consciously or, more often, out of practical sense, the 'feel for the game') in order to maintain and increase their capital. The existence of a field implies struggle and a power relationship between a dominant and a dominated section within the field.

These fields have evolved historically. For instance, Bourdieu investigated the emergence of an autonomous field of the arts in the late nineteenth century. He argued that only such a historical analysis could unearth the conditions for 'understanding' art in our time, e.g. for judging artworks according to purely formal aesthetic criteria rather than appreciating their (religious, economic or decorative) function.

Bourdieu advocated a similar historization for

every scientific endeavour. In an exercise of self-reflexivity or 'participant objectivation', social scientists should question their research interests and strategies in three ways: how much are these research orientations influenced first by the scholars' social origin, and, second, by their current position in the scientific field; and do they have an 'intellectualist' bias, i.e. is sufficient attention paid to the fact that most social action is practice rather than the conscious creation of meaning or application of rules? In *Homo Academicus* [1984], Bourdieu proposed an analysis of the field of higher education in France prior to and during the events of May 1968, investigating correspondences between scholars' social and symbolic capital, their career paths, research interests and outlooks; and he included his own career and research activities in this review.

In the 1990s, Bourdieu had amassed enough scientific authority (or symbolic capital) to make his voice heard outside his own field. Obviously, there was a political agenda in Bourdieu's research virtually from the beginning. By exposing the mechanisms of domination, social science should provide weapons of defence against symbolic violence, as he argued repeatedly. From the mid-1990s however, having published *The Weight of the World* [1993], an account of the daily suffering of the disadvantaged in France, Bourdieu intervened more and more often directly in public debate, speaking out against neoliberalism and in defence of the welfare state. If these statements secured him a considerable following outside the field of social science and stirred increasing media attention, they also provoked sometimes harsh criticism from political adversaries and some peers.

Social scientists have also questioned certain of Bourdieu's central concepts. The actual impact of childhood experiences on the *habitus* has come under scrutiny. What is the influence of the plural, perhaps contradictory settings in which many humans grow up? What role do media and other discourses play in the formation of *habitus*? The notion of the *field* might be extremely pertinent for the analysis of socioprofessional domains, but possibly much less so for other social realities, such as the family. Is there necessarily conflict and domination as soon as relations between human beings are established? Is it appropriate to suspect (conscious or unconscious) interests behind expressions of friendship, compassion and solidarity? As for 'capital', how can one account for the social action of those who do not possess any at all?

Many of Pierre Bourdieu's analyses are highly pertinent criticisms of French society, where the republican ideology of egalitarianism and meritocracy often clashes with a reality of racism, class contempt and relative social immobility. His writings have had a decisive impact on the sociological study of culture and education, as well as on the anthropology of Algeria. Bourdieu's social thought offers suggestions about how to overcome theoretical impasses associated with dichotomies such as the social and the individual, free will and determinism, body and mind, structure and agency. One of the most important legacies of his work is his own *modus operandi*, i.e. the ethos of a social science that crosses boundaries between disciplines such as sociology, anthropology, philosophy and history; between different national intellectual traditions; and between the purely academic exchange of ideas and public debate.

ANNE FRIEDERIKE MÜLLER
KING'S COLLEGE, LONDON

References

Bourdieu, P. (1977 [1972]) *Outline of a Theory of Practice*, Cambridge.
—— (1984 [1979]) *Distinction: A Social Critique of the Judgement of Taste*, London.
—— (1988 [1984]) *Homo Academicus*, Stanford, CA.
—— (1990 [1980]) *The Logic of Practice*, Cambridge.
—— *et al.* (1999 [1993]) *The Weight of the World: Social Suffering in Contemporary Society*, Cambridge.
—— (2000 [1997]) *Pascalian Meditations*, Cambridge.
Bourdieu, P. and Passeron, J.-C. (1977 [1970]) *Reproduction in Education, Society and Culture*, London.
—— (1979 [1964]) *The Inheritors: French Students and Their Relation to Culture*, Chicago.

Further reading

Bourdieu, P. and Wacquant, L.J.D. (1992) *An Invitation to Reflexive Sociology*, Cambridge.
Delsaut, Y. and Rivière, M.-Ch. (2002) *Bibliographie des travaux de Pierre Bourdieu*, Pantin.
Lane, J.F. (2000) *Pierre Bourdieu: A Critical Introduction*, London.
Robbins, D. (2000) *Bourdieu and Culture*, London.
Swartz, D. (1997) *Culture & Power: The Sociology of Pierre Bourdieu*, Chicago.

SEE ALSO: habitus; sociology: new theoretical developments

BRAUDEL, FERNAND (1902–85)

Fernand Braudel was one of the most influential historians of the twentieth century. The third of the founding fathers of the so-called Annales School of French historians, he followed the lead of such pre-Second World War historians as Lucien Fèbvre and Marc Bloch in seeking to revitalize the study of history in the light of the methods and concerns of the social sciences. However, Braudel went considerably further along this path than his predecessors, developing an entirely new concept of, and approach to, historical studies. In a more systematic way than his precursors, Braudel sought to emancipate history from its traditional division into political, economic and cultural history, and to achieve a 'total' history of society. The objective was to integrate all aspects of humankind's past, placing the chief emphasis on the changing environment and lifestyle of the common person and of society as a whole. Inevitably, the new approach involved a marked de-emphasizing and distancing from the political and constitutional history, which had always been the central preoccupation of historians and which Braudel and his followers term '*histoire événementielle*'.

Braudel's most famous and important work, on the Mediterranean world in the age of Philip II, was first published in 1949 and was greeted with widespread and eventually almost universal acclaim. A revised and considerably expanded second edition was published in 1966. In this vast undertaking, Braudel transcended all political and cultural borders, as he did in all historical practice and procedure. He sought to reveal the immense scope and implications of the decline of Mediterranean society in the sixteenth century, achieving a majestic and often elegant synthesis of economic, demographic, cultural and political data and interpretation. It was by no means Braudel's intention to disregard political phenomena; rather he wished to tackle these in a new way, within the context of long- and medium-term socioeconomic trends. Thus one of his principal objectives was to throw new light on the shift in the policy concerns of Philip II of Spain away from the Mediterranean and towards the Atlantic, a change in the direction of Spanish policy-making that dates from the 1580s.

Basic to Braudel's approach was his novel categorization of history into simultaneous processes proceeding on different levels at quite different speeds. He envisaged these various trends as taking place on three main levels and, on occasion, compared the processes of historical change to an edifice consisting of three storeys. On the lowest level, he placed the slow, long-term changes in humankind's agrarian, maritime and demographic environment. On the middle level, Braudel placed the medium-term economic and cultural shifts that take place over one or two centuries rather than millennia. Finally, on his uppermost storey, he located all short-term fluctuations and 'events' in the traditional sense.

This novel approach to history is further developed in Braudel's second major work, an ambitious trilogy entitled *Civilisation matérielle et capitalisme* (1967–79) (English trans. 1973–82; *Material Civilization and Capitalism*), which deals with the evolution of the world economy and of society generally from the end of the Middle Ages to the Industrial Revolution. Despite Braudel's insistence on material factors as the determinants of social change, and his readiness to borrow concepts from Marx, including the term capitalism, which figures prominently in his later work, Braudel's system, like the work of the Annales School more generally, is in essence quite outside the Marxist tradition in that it allocates no central role to class conflict. In the view of some scholars, certain weaknesses evident in the earlier work are much more pronounced in the later study. A less secure grasp of detail, frequent errors both of fact and interpretation of data, and, generally, much less convincing evaluations detract considerably from the value of the later work. Certain historians now also see serious defects in Braudel's overall approach, running through his entire *œuvre* that, besides the two major works, includes a number of noteworthy short books and essays. In particular it is felt that Braudel's method of handling the interaction between socioeconomic and political history is unconvincing and unsatisfactory. Thus, his radical de-emphasizing of political and military power, and the impact of 'events' on socioeconomic development, gives rise in his writing to numerous, often major, distortions.

The influence of Braudel's ideas and the extent to which they have been adopted as the modern approach to historical studies varies from country to country, but has been pervasive in several European and many Latin American countries as well as in North America, but is less so now. It has been repeatedly asserted that he was 'indisputably the greatest of living historians', but it must also be said that a tendency towards uncritical adulation of his work has become fashionable in many quarters on both sides of the Atlantic. Some history departments in universities, and a number of collaborative historical research projects and publications, have professed Braudel and his approach as the guiding principle directing their studies, though this tendency, predictably perhaps, has much receded since the 1980s.

JONATHAN I. ISRAEL
INSTITUTE FOR ADVANCED STUDY,
PRINCETON, NJ

References

Braudel, F. (1967–79 [1966]) *The Mediterranean and the Mediterranean World in the Age of Philip II*, 2 vols, New York.
—— (1982, 1983, 1984 [1967–79]) *Material Civilization and Capitalism, 15th–18th Century*, vol. 1: *The Structure of Everyday Life*; vol. 2: *The Wheels of Commerce*; vol. 3: *The Perspective of the World*, London.

Further reading

Israel, J.I. (1983) 'Fernand Braudel – a reassessment', *The Times Literary Supplement* 4: 164.
Journal of Modern History (1972) vol. 44: special issue on Braudel with articles by H.R. Trevor-Roper and J.H. Hexter, and Braudel's own 'Personal testimony'.

SEE ALSO: Annales School; social history

BUREAUCRACY

The word bureaucracy is used any number of ways in ordinary discourse, as well as in the social sciences. In everyday discussions bureaucracy is usually a term of derision, implying inefficiency, buck-passing, shirking and a host of other behaviours that cast doubt on the ability of bureaucracies to provide services to clients. Although many of these characteristics may exist in large organizations in either the public or private sectors, bureaucracy is usually used to describe the permanent administration in government. Further, in addition to the other dysfunctions associated with large, formal organizations, these organizations in the public sector are assumed to attempt to promote the unjustified expansion of their own budgets (see Blais and Dion 1992), and to advance their own conceptions of policy against those of their nominal political masters.

Bureaucracy in theory

Bureaucracy was typified by Max Weber as a system of organization based on hierarchy, rules, merit recruitment and specialization of activities by its participants (Gerth and Mills 1946). Although bureaucracy is generally a term of opprobrium, in its original presentation the term was meant to represent the highest possible form of organizational development, and social modernity. Bureaucracy would be the embodiment of rational-legal authority, with governance within the organization being through law and formalized rules. Weber conceived this characterization as an 'Ideal Type', meaning that it was an intellectual model that was almost certainly unattainable in the real world, but could be used as a standard against which to compare real organizations. The assumption undergirding that conception of organization and management was that if this high level of formal rationality could be obtained then maximum efficiency in the implementation of programmes would follow.

Bureaucracy was assumed not only to be efficient but also as offering substantial normative advantages, especially for organizations in the public sector. One of the virtues of rules and hierarchy within bureaucracy is that they should ensure equality of treatment for individual cases. Traditional administrative structures, as well as many contemporary administrations in the public and private sectors, deal with cases on the basis of family or partisan affiliations. This may well lead them to treat different types of citizens very unequally. Further, within bureaucratic organizations themselves, merit recruitment assures fairer treatment of all categories of citizens. Similarly, the bureaucrat within these organizations is (presumably) willing to suspend his or her individual judgement in relationship to the characteristics of the cases that he or she confronts, and is also willing to submit to the political and/ or hierarchical authority of a superior in the organization. That submission to the policy priorities of superiors may be true even when the administration has substantial expertise in the policy and may be better situated to design policies.

The roots of the efficiency and virtue of a bureaucracy are to some extent also the sources of its weaknesses as a mechanism for administration. The emphasis on formal rules and authority produces the 'displacement of goals' described by Merton (1940). Compliance with rules rather than the achievement of goals becomes the dominant concern for individuals in a bureaucratic organization. Formalism also produces rigidity and an associated inability to adapt to changing circumstances, so that bureaucratic organizations can quickly become ossified. Likewise, hierarchy in an organization may reduce the flow of information in the organization and further reduce its capacity to relate to its environment and to maintain its effectiveness. Specialization and repetitive tasks also tend to lower the motivation of workers, and may reduce rather than increase the efficient processing of cases.

The normative virtues of a bureaucracy are perhaps even more clearly related to its normative shortcomings than are the processes and their apparently negative implications for efficiency. Most fundamentally the requirement, implicit or explicit, that a bureaucrat suspend his or her judgement makes the bureaucrat the willing servant of any cause, just or unjust – the famous defence of 'just following orders' is the extreme version. At a less extreme level the suspension of judgement, assuming that were really possible, imposes a cost on the bureaucrat and on the client. For the bureaucrat, tasks become endlessly repetitive, uninteresting and dehumanizing. For the client, any capacity to influence decisions about their future is eliminated, and he or she is left facing a mechanistic and unresponsive system.

The development of these conceptions of formal organization reflect the historical period within which they were developed. Weber's characterization, and other classical conceptions of formal organization, e.g. those of Frederick Taylor or Henri Fayol, developed at the end of the nineteenth century, at a time when it was widely assumed that structures and processes within organizations could be designed scientifically. Further, these models of organizations assumed that human beings would, and could, fit into these structures and would conform to the constraints placed upon them by the formal organization. Individuals – as workers within an organization or as clients of programmes – were not considered to be variable but as uniform inputs. While these ideas were almost certainly unrealistic at the time in which they were formulated, their inherent problems have become more apparent as time has passed.

Bureaucracy in practice

The executive branches of most contemporary governments have many of the characteristics of a bureaucracy. Most have some formalized hierarchy, and rules that govern many aspects of their behaviour such as personnel, budgeting and procurement. There are also constant attempts to routinize many aspects of behaviour within the organization. The design of the traditional public-sector organizations has approximated the bureaucracy. That design to some extent represents the absence of imagination about other forms of structuring these organizations, and also to some extent the desire to achieve some of the presumed benefits of formal bureaucracy.

As should have been predictable to the designers, bureaucratic organizations in the public sector have generated many of the dysfunctions characteristic of this form of organization. Public organizations have been criticized as being inflexible, unresponsive, slow and inefficient. Such complaints have been registered by both employees within the organizations, and the clients of public programmes. The public at large also consider bureaucracies inefficient, ineffective and expensive, even if they may have little information on which to base that assessment.

As well as generating dysfunctions, bureaucratic organizations have generated a number of attempts at change. The human relations approach to management initiated during the 1930s was an early effort, but this has continued since. The large-scale attempts at reform of the public bureaucracy (and to some extent also private bureaucracies) at the end of the twentieth century represent attempts to move away from the hierarchical, rule-based organizations of the past towards more flexible, entrepreneurial and participatory organizations. There are any number of proposals for change, involving a number of different fundamental ideas about the problems of bureaucracy and the associated opportunities for reform (Peters 2001).

Cultural changes in the industrial world have placed pressures on bureaucracies to change, and this has helped to emphasize the cultural basis of organization. In other parts of the world the formality and rigidity of bureaucratic forms of organization may not correspond well to the operative political and managerial cultures (see Hofstede 2001). In particular, norms of uniformity and neutrality that are central to the bureaucratic models are not compatible with more particularistic traditions of administration. Donor organizations are placing pressures on governments in many less-developed countries to adopt the new, debureaucratized formats for organization now becoming characteristic of the more affluent countries. The problem is that without first institutionalizing some of the bureaucratic values of probity and fairness the reforms may only justify corruption and favouritism.

Summary

The fundamental goal of bureaucracy is to institutionalize rationality and formal hierarchy as means of ensuring efficiency and equal treatment of employees and clients. That is a laudable goal, but the means chosen to achieve it have often proven to be fundamentally flawed. In particular, bureaucracies tend to ignore the nature and the individual goals of the people who work in organizations and who are served by them. It may be, however, too easy to dismiss bureaucracy. The need to create fairness and efficiency, and to balance those two virtues, remains a crucial challenge for public-sector organizations, and bureaucracy was designed as one solution to that challenge.

B. GUY PETERS
UNIVERSITY OF PITTSBURGH

References

Blais, A, and Dion, S. (1992) *The Budget-Maximizing Bureaucrat*, Pittsburgh.
Gerth, H.H. and Mills, C.W. (1946) *From Max Weber: Essays in Sociology*, New York.
Hofstede, G. (2001) *Culture's Consequences: Comparing Values, Behaviors, Institutions and Organizations across Nations*, Thousand Oaks, CA.
Merton, R.K. (1940) 'Bureaucratic structure and personality', *Social Forces* 17: 560–8.
Peters, B.G. (2001) *The Future of Governing*, revised edn, Lawrence, KA.

SEE ALSO: government; public administration; state; Weber

BURKE, EDMUND (1729–97)

Edmund Burke, the British statesman and political theorist, was born in Dublin in 1729. He came to London in 1750 and soon acquired a reputation as a philosopher and man of letters. In 1765 he was elected to the House of Commons, acting as party secretary and chief man of ideas to the Whig connection led by the Marquis of Rockingham. He wrote voluminously, and the eloquence he brought to expressing a high-minded but by no means unrealistic view of political possibilities has never been surpassed. He could bring out the universal element in the most parochial of issues.

Burke's enduring importance in articulating a political tendency is particularly evident in the *Reflections on the Revolution in France* (1790) and subsequent late works in which he defended his criticism of the Revolution against fellow Whigs who had welcomed it as an act of liberation from an odious Bourbon absolutism. Attacked as one who had betrayed the cause of liberty, Burke agreed (in the *Appeal from the Old to the New Whigs*) that consistency was the highest virtue in politics, but proceeded to theorize its complex nature. In supporting the American colonists, he argued, he was in no way committed to support every movement that raised the banner of liberty, for in his view the Americans 'had taken up arms from one motive only; that is, our attempting to tax them without their consent' (Burke 1855, *Appeal*, vol. 3). Real political consistency must take account of circumstances, and cannot be deduced from principles. And it was in terms of the contrast between historical concreteness and abstract principle that Burke interpreted the challenge posed by the revolutionaries in France.

The revolutionaries were, Burke argued, amateur politicians attempting to solve the complex problems of French society with a set of theories or what he called 'metaphysic rights'. They believed that an ideal rational constitution, in which a republic guaranteed the rights of humankind, was suitable for all societies. This belief constituted a revelation that stigmatized most existing beliefs as prejudice and superstition, and all existing forms of government as corrupt and unjust. On Burke's historical understanding of the specificity of different societies, the beliefs and practices of any society revealed their character; indeed, properly understood, they revealed a kind of rationality much more profound than the prepositional fantasies of revolutionaries. To condemn what whole societies had long believed as merely mistaken was in the highest degree superficial. Society is a delicate fabric of sentiments and understandings that would be irreparably damaged if subjected to the butchery of abstract ideas. Burke judged that, as the revolutionaries discovered that the people were not behaving according to the rationalist prescriptions, they would have increasing recourse to violence and terror. At the end of every prospect would be found a gallows. He predicted that the outcome would be a military dictatorship.

Burke's genius lay in breaking up the conventional antitheses through which politics was then understood. He had never been, he wrote, 'a friend or an enemy to republics or to monarchies in the abstract' (Burke 1855, *Appeal*, vol. 3), and this refusal to take sides on an abstractly specified principle became a dominant strain in conservatism. The real clue to wisdom politics lay not at the level of high principle but of low and humble circumstance. This was the level of actual human experience, and, at this level, there was not a great deal that governments could achieve, and most of what they could was to prevent evils rather than promote goods. No stranger to paradox, Burke insisted that one of the most important of the rights of humankind is the right to be restrained by suitable laws. Again, Burke was prepared to agree that society was indeed a contract, but he instantly qualified this conventional judgement by insisting that it was a contract of a quite sublime kind, linking the living, the dead and those yet to be born. It is in these hesitations and qualifications of conventional wisdom to which he was impelled by the excitements of his time that Burke's contribution to political understanding lies.

More philosophically, Burke adapted to political use the empiricist doctrine that the passions, especially as entrenched in and shaped by social institutions, are closer to reality than the speculations of philosophers, and especially of *philosophes*. His defence of prejudice threw down a gauntlet to the superficial rationalism of his opponents, and has sometimes been seen as expressing an irrationalism endemic to conservative thought. It is, however, an argument about the relations between reason and passion similar to that of Hegel, though in a quite different idiom.

Burke's political judgement is a conservative modification of the English political tradition and covers many areas. On the nature of representation, for example, he argued that the House of Commons was not a congress of ambassadors from the constituencies. His defence of the place of parties in British politics contributed to the acceptance and development of party government, however limited in intention it may have been (Brewer 1971). In the indictment of Warren Hastings, he stressed the trusteeship of power and property that was never far from his thoughts. But in all his political writings, Burke wrote to the occasion, and it is perilous to generalize about him too far. His personal ambitions required manœuvring in the complex world of late eighteenth-century politics, which have led some writers (e.g. Namier 1929; Young 1943) to regard him as little more than a silver-tongued opportunist. This is to do less than justice to the suggestiveness of his prose and the momentousness of the occasions to which he so brilliantly responded.

KENNETH MINOGUE
LONDON SCHOOL OF ECONOMICS AND POLITICAL SCIENCE

References

Brewer, J. (1971) 'Party and the double cabinet: Two facets of Burke's thoughts', *Historical Journal* 14.
Burke, E. (1855) *Works*, London.
Namier, L. (1929) *The Structure of Politics at the Accession of George III*, London.
Young, G.M. (1943) *Burke* (British Academy Lecture on a Mastermind), London.

Further reading

Canavan, F.P. (1960) *The Political Reason of Edmund Burke*, Durham, NC.
Cruise O'Brien, Conor (1992) *The Great Melody*, London.
White, S.K. (1994) *Edmund Burke: Modernity, Politics and Aesthetics*, Los Angeles, CA.

BUSINESS CYCLES

The term 'business cycle' refers to a collection of events that are associated with the expansion and contraction of economic activity in an economy. Business cycles are mostly commonly characterized as a set of common movements of economic aggregates (GDP, Employment, Investment, Consumption and so on). Nevertheless, the key feature of business cycles is that the changes in economic activity are widespread. Thus a recession – a contraction – is a significant decline in economic activity that is widespread across the economy and lasts for more than a few months. It will show up as measurable declines in real GDP, real income, employment, industrial production, investment and retail and wholesale sales. An expansion, by contrast, is the widespread increase in real economic activity and it is the normal state of an economy. Most recessions tend to be short-lived (in the USA the average postwar recession is about 11 months long) while the average expansion is 50 months long over the postwar period. These periods of expansion and contraction are termed cycles because they have been documented to be recurrent features of economic life for two centuries or more.

Although the existence of business fluctuations was well established, few systematic attempts had been made to document their features before Wesley Mitchell (1913, 1927) and Mitchell together with Arthur Burns (1946) and their associates at the National Bureau of Economic Research wrote down what they regarded as the most important observations about the systematic nature of business cycles. The features that they found compelling were the sequences of cycles, the phases of the cycle and the turning points. Economists were then led to consider the possibility that these features could be used to define indicators that would help to forecast economic activity over the cycle. Since the 1970s, when interest in business cycle theory entered a new phase, prompted by the pioneering work of Lucas (1977), there has been a shift in emphasis. Now it is deemed more useful to characterize the business cycle in terms of the approximately synchronous co-movement of a number of economic variables over periods of expansion and contraction. Thinking about these co-movements implied another sort of possibility as well – the possibility that these changes in economic activity can be accounted for by well-specified theoretical models.

The features of business cycles are now well documented. The business cycle is typically characterized in terms of the volatility and co-movement of key economic aggregates such as real output, consumption, employment and investment. Also of interest are the fluctuations in nominal variables like the price level, the inflation rate and interest rates. The features of business cycles, measured in this way, have been shown to be very similar across countries and over time although there are some important differences between developed economies and developing economies.

Theories of the business cycle

Business cycles have always been puzzles. Why is it that the economy enters into a contraction when it is not in the interest of any of the actors in the economy? Accordingly, most attempts to explain how business cycles occur have focused on the idea that they result from unforeseen shocks to the economic system. Random events occur that deflect the economy from a natural tendency to expand and set off a contraction in economic activity. While it is not difficult to imagine this possibility, the challenge has always been to explain how unpredictable events can lead to the persistent and widespread contraction in real output that characterize the cycle.

The recent history of business cycle theory has focused primarily on two different sources of the shocks that cause the business cycle. The first, real business cycle theory argues that business cycles are caused by shocks to technology that render existing capital and labour less (or more) productive. A second explanation is that the business cycle is caused by monetary shocks that affect real economic activity. There are other theories that describe business cycles as resulting from co-ordination failures in the economy or as resulting from expectations that are driven by beliefs that are not related to fundamental features of the actual economy.

The research on shocks as the source of business cycles has attempted to quantify the portion of the fluctuation in real output that can be explained by either real shocks or monetary shocks. This research proceeds by studying the response to shocks of artificial general equilibrium economies based on the neo-classical growth model. These artificial economies are calibrated to match the features of actual economies and to display the features of long-term growth that actual economies exhibit. The solution and simulation of these simple artificial economies has become a dominant method of research in business cycle theory. The appeal of this methodology is that it provides economists with a simple laboratory to study the ability of various theoretical constructs to explain the fluctuations observed in the data.

The major challenge for those who would explain the business cycle as resulting from shocks is to explain how those shocks get propagated and amplified. How do random events come to show up as persistent, asymmetric and widespread movements in real output and employment? Most of the candidate sources of shocks, either monetary or real, are simply not large enough to generate fluctuations with the magnitude and persistence of the business cycle.

The sources of amplification that have attracted the most attention in the literature include rigidities in nominal wages, 'stickiness' in prices, difficulties in extracting the right signals about inflation information from prices, and credit constraints, or limits on how much economic agents can borrow.

Over time, experience has tended to favour one or another of these channels as a source of propagation depending on the source of the shock and the economic environment. No one factor is necessarily dominant, and all play a role at some time or other.

THOMAS F. COOLEY
STERN SCHOOL OF BUSINESS,
NEW YORK UNIVERSITY

References

Burns, A.F. and Mitchell, W.C. (1946) *Measuring Business Cycles*, New York.
Lucas, R.E., Jr (1977) 'Understanding business cycles', in K. Brunner and A.H. Meltzer (eds) *Stabilization of the Domestic and International Economy*, vol. 5, Amsterdam, North Holland, pp. 7–29.
Mitchell, W.C. (1913) *Business Cycles*, Berkeley, CA.
—— (1927) *Business Cycles: The Problem and Its Setting*, National Bureau of Economic Research, New York.

BUSINESS STUDIES

The term 'business studies' is a loose generic title for several related aspects of enterprises and their environments, foremost among these being administration and management, accounting, finance and banking, international relations, marketing, and personnel and industrial relations. There is considerable disagreement, however, on the extent to which scholastic, managerial or professional values should predominate in the framing of the curriculum and in research and teaching objectives.

It is usual to trace modern ideas on business studies to formative developments in the USA, where the Wharton School of Finance and

Commerce was the first of twenty schools of business administration and commerce to be founded between 1881 and 1910. But it was particularly in the next two decades, when a further 180 schools were established, that the distinctive US style of business education, with a high degree of abstraction and a quantitative approach to the solution of problems, became firmly rooted (Rose 1970). Of particular interest, associated not least with the Harvard Business School, was the use of case studies as a key part of business education. Management education developed much later in Europe, originally under the tutelage of practitioners from the USA. Indeed, in Britain, it was not until 1947 that the first major centre, the Administrative Staff College at Henley, was inaugurated. There are now several leading European institutes for business and management studies. In both Europe and Japan, there have been active attempts to develop programmes that are distinctive from the original North American model, a change that has been facilitated by the considerable interest in business studies in Third World nations and by the rigorous analytical techniques that have latterly evolved in the USA.

The precise causes of the expansion of business education are open to some doubt, although processes of rationalization in modern societies and the rapid growth in numbers of managerial personnel have been signal influences. Further favourable trends have been increased international competition and investment, major technical changes, a larger scale and greater complexity of modern enterprises, and a facilitative role of governments.

However, opinion differs on whether business studies should become an empirical social science or whether, to the contrary, it should be founded on a series of prescriptive values (what should be accomplished) and ideas (what can be achieved) in actual employing organizations. A particular problem of internal coherence in business education also stems from the varied subject backgrounds of research workers and teachers, a situation that has militated against an adequate interdisciplinary synthesis.

In principle, the theoretical linkages between the main areas of business studies are examined in strategic management, although this has in practice become a highly specialized area dealing primarily with the concept in an intertemporal way (Wheelen and Hunger 2002). In substantive terms, organizational behaviour is the most obvious branch of study that connects the disparate approaches within the business field. Nevertheless, its excessive reliance on contingency theory (which implies that whether a particular organizational form is effective depends on the nature of the environmental context) has proved to be an encumbrance, since challenges to this approach have ensured that there is no longer a generally accepted model for conceptualizing business behaviour (Huczynski and Buchanan 2001).

A further critical issue in business studies is the extent to which, regardless of cultural, socioeconomic or political conditions, common administrative practices are appropriate on a worldwide scale. The earliest perspectives tended to assume a considerable uniformity, the various strands being combined in the 'industrial society' thesis in which a basic 'logic of industrialism' was seen to impel all modern economies towards similar organizational structures and modes of administration (Kerr et al. 1960). This complemented the earlier work on classical organization theory, which postulated universal traits of business management, and on studies of bureaucracy, which arrived at similar conclusions. In this approach, too, a key assumption was that there had been a divorce of ownership from control in the business enterprise that, in turn, had ensured the convergence of decision-making processes between societies with ostensibly irreconcilable political ideologies and economic systems.

More recently, however, the 'culturalist' thesis has emerged as a check-weight to these universalist approaches. This assumes great diversity in business behaviour and ideology occasioned either by variations in the 'task' environment (community, government, consumer, employee, supplier, distributor, shareholder) or, more especially, in the 'social' environment (cultural, legal, political, social). Above all, it emphasizes that each new generation internalizes an enduring strain of culture through its process of socialization, with people in different countries learning their own language, concepts and systems of values. Moreover, such deep-rooted cultural forces are continually reasserted in the way people relate to one another and ensure that organizational structures that are not consonant with culturally derived expectations will remain purely formal.

Divergence in business organization and practice can also stem from temporal as well as spatial differences between societies. Indeed, 'late development' would appear to enhance a mode of industrialization quite distinct from the earliest Western models, with the state being more predominant at the expense of a *laissez-faire* ideology, educational institutions preceding manufacturing, more substantial technical and organizational 'leaps', human relations and personnel management techniques being more advanced, and large-scale enterprises being deliberately constructed as a spearhead for economic advancement. In this respect, too, the choices of strategic elites are as important as the constraints of environment and organizational structure in determining which types of business conduct become ascendant in any given society.

Since the Second World War, business studies have been influenced by notions of 'human resource management' (Redman and Wilkinson 2001). The issue here is whether business managers have wider moral obligations, beyond seeking to enhance profitability and efficiency. 'External social responsibility' is particularly relevant to marketing policies. Various ethical questions are raised by the strategies and techniques for promoting different types of goods and services (Baird *et al.* 1990). 'Internal social responsibility' has to do with employee welfare and satisfaction, and human relations in the enterprise. More broadly, there has been a major expansion of research and teaching in the fields of personnel management and industrial relations (Poole 1999).

The structure of business studies courses often shows evidence of a tension between professional and managerial approaches. Another unresolved issue is the extent to which business studies should concentrate on the development of empirical social science, perhaps at the expense of consultancy work.

MICHAEL POOLE
CARDIFF UNIVERSITY

References

Baird, L.S., Post, P.J. and Mahon, J.F. (1990) *Management: Functions and Responsibilities*, New York.

Huczynski, A. and Buchanan, D. (2001) *Organizational Behaviour*, Harlow.

Kerr, C., Dunlop, J.T., Harbison, F.H. and Myers, C.A. (1960) *Industrialism and Industrial Man*, Cambridge, MA.

Poole, M. (ed.) (1999) *Human Resource Management*, 3 vols, London.

Redman, T. and Wilkinson, A. (2001) *Contemporary Human Resource Management: Text and Cases*, Harlow.

Rose, H. (1970) *Management Education in the 1970s*, London.

Wheelen, T.L. and Hunger, J.D. (2002) *Strategic Management and Business Policy*, New Jersey.

C

CANNIBALISM

Cannibalism, as the customary consumption of human flesh in some other time or place, is a worldwide and time-honoured assumption. This pervasive, and in many ways appealing, characterization of others has also found its place in contemporary anthropology, which has tended to accept uncritically all reports of cannibalism in other cultures as ethnographic fact. This propensity has led to the development of a variety of categories for the conceptualization of the pattern and motivation for the purported behaviour. These have included the recognition of endocannibalism (eating one's own kind) as opposed to exocannibalism (eating outsiders), and ritual in contrast to gustatory or nutritional cannibalism. Uncondoned survival cannibalism, under conditions of extreme privation, has also been noted. Yet, despite the uncounted allusions and the elaborate typologies, there is reason to treat any particular report of the practice with caution, and the entire intellectual complex with some scepticism.

This estimation is warranted for a number of reasons. Depending on time or place, written accounts of alleged cannibalism entered the historical record long after the cessation of the purported custom – often after the obliteration of the culture itself and the decimation of its population. Moreover, reporters were representatives of the very society that was then engaged in the subjugation and exploitation of the people in question. Those responsible for our contemporary impressions rarely took an unbiased view of the traditional culture, and at best relied upon informants who claimed that 'others', such as the nobility or priesthood, engaged in such reprehensible practices. Consequently, rather than reliably documenting a custom, between the early sixteenth and late nineteenth centuries the allegation of cannibalism in Western literature often merely legitimized the conquest of foreign cultures by expansionist European states.

These suspect conditions could have been rectified by modern anthropologists actually resident among presumed cannibals in the remoter regions of the world. However, contemporary reports continue to be second hand; indeed, no anthropologist has ever provided an account of cannibalism based on observation. While reasonable explanations are offered for these circumstances, for example that the practice has been discontinued or is now hidden, the overall pattern continues to be one of circumstantial rather than direct evidence. There are some recent indications from the prehistoric record of isolated instances of cannibalism based upon cut marks on bones. However, as these are rare occurrences they suggest an event rather than a custom.

Thus, is it reasonable to assume that cannibalism ever occurred? The answer is yes, but neither as often nor in the context usually assumed. There is as indicated survival cannibalism, but also an anti-social or criminal variety and sometimes subcultural cannibalism practised by a deviant segment of the population (see Parry 1982). In rare instances, 'inversion' cannibalism has also occurred. The first three types are sporadically noted in every part of the world, where they are frowned upon by the majority. The final instance, of which there are a few accounts, involves rituals in which members of a society are constrained to act for the moment in ways prohibited under ordinary moral circumstances (Poole 1983). Such occasions of inversion underscore the basic rules of society by intentional violations but should not be construed as custom in the general sense. There is a simplistic and unwarranted tendency to label non-Western societies with such restricted practices of any aforementioned type as cannibalistic. This suggests that the portrayal of others as man-eaters, rather than the deed itself, is the pervasive human trait.

W. ARENS
STATE UNIVERSITY OF NEW YORK
AT STONY BROOK

References

Parry, J. (1982) 'Sacrificial death and the necrophagous ascetic', in M. Bloch and J. Parry (eds) *Death and the Regeneration of Life*, Cambridge, UK.
Poole, F.P. (1983) 'Cannibals, tricksters and witches', in D. Tuzin and P. Brown (eds) *The Ethnography of Cannibalism*, Washington, DC.

Further reading

Arens, W. (1979) *The Man-Eating Myth*, New York.
Barker, F., Hulme, P. and Iversen, M. (eds) (1997) *Cannibalism and the Colonial World*, Cambridge, UK.
Horn, J. and Creed, B. (eds) (2001) *Body Trade: Captivity, Cannibalism, and Colonialism in the Pacific*, New York.

CAPITAL, CREDIT AND MONEY MARKETS

Production requires capital to be laid down in advance; capitalist economies have developed markets to allow the division of function between the person undertaking the production, the 'entrepreneur', and the ultimate owner of capital. The modern capital market, as this nexus of markets is called, extends across frontiers and embraces a wide variety of contracts, from debt and credit through preferential shares to ordinary equity (i.e. shared ownership). Investors of capital are able through diversification, between different types of projects and contracts, to obtain the most favourable combination of risk and return. The entrepreneur is able to tap into sources of funds that similarly offer the best combination of risk and cost.

In addition to the primary markets in debt and equity, 'derivative' markets have developed that allow investors and entrepreneurs to adjust their portfolios of assets and liabilities to a quite precise mix. This mix is defined by the events that would trigger costs and returns: through options and futures one may protect one's position against a particular event such as the outcome of an election while being exposed to, say, the economy's growth rate. (An option is a contract for someone to pay or receive a sum contingent on an event, while a future is a purchase or sale of a primary instrument made for a future date.) Banks and other financial firms that take on such option contracts are thus effectively providing a wide range of insurance to their counter-parties. Collapses of large financial institutions such as Barings and Long Term Capital Management (a hedge fund) showed that not all of them fully appreciated the total risks they were running. This has caused regulators to demand that 'Value At Risk' be assessed and limited for large financial institutions operating inside the main developed countries. Hedge funds are nevertheless in general unregulated because they operate offshore with funds from wealthy individuals who in principle wish to avoid both political interference and protection. In the past two decades there has thus been a huge expansion in the scope of financial markets, such that one can probably claim that markets are more 'complete' than ever in history, in the sense that people can buy and sell more or less the flexible bundle of contingencies that exactly suits them.

The modern theory of finance suggests that in capital markets free from controls the multitude of people buying and selling will drive the expected return on (or, seen from the other side, the cost of) investment to a risk-free rate plus a risk-premium that should reflect (besides the average investor's dislike of risk or 'risk-aversion') 'systematic' risk, by which is meant the contribution to the overall risk on a portfolio made by holding this asset. This contribution will depend on the correlation between returns on this asset and on other assets, which is taken advantage of by diversification. Since this correlation should be reasonably stable, this risk-premium ought to be stable too and invariant to the amounts of the asset being traded, provided these are small relative to the market as a whole. Furthermore if people make proper use of available information (rational expectations) then the expected return should change only when new information arrives in the market.

This theory is that of 'efficient markets', efficient in the sense that information is being reflected appropriately in market prices (and hence in expected returns). This also implies that the capital markets allocate capital in the most economical way between uses, so that government intervention could not (using the same information) improve matters. At an international level it implies extremely high capital mobility between countries. A country's entrepreneurs or government will be able to raise as much capital as they can profitably employ at a cost that will reflect the general international cost of capital adjusted for their particular risk-premium.

This smoothly functioning world of capital may seem too good to be true. Certainly in empirical testing the results have been mixed. But their interpretation is problematic (see Minford and Peel 2002: chapter 14), and the hypothesis of efficiency has not been convincingly rejected. It has certainly proved hard to make above-normal returns by investment strategies other than those that used information unavailable to the market; this suggests a fair degree of efficiency. Recent capital market crises, such as in Asia, Latin America and IT stocks, have been argued popularly to be evidence of 'bubbles' in which abnormal returns were possible. However, the country crises were connected with poor policies of monetary control and exchange rate management; the collapse of IT stocks was typical of previous stock market collapses in the context of rapid innovation (e.g. railways at the end of the nineteenth century) where prediction of returns is fraught with uncertainty. There is clearly a tension between the exploitation of information driving above-normal returns to zero and there being sufficient above-normal returns available to motivate the research into an analysis of information that makes such exploitation possible. It may well be, therefore, that the markets are 'nearly efficient' – but just inefficient enough to enable analysts to make a living. This state of affairs would justify using the theory as a working approximation.

So far we have made no mention of money. Indeed it would be quite possible to envisage this world of capital markets functioning without money. If everyone had a balance in a gigantic clearing system, whose unit was some amount of a consumer good or combination of several (a 'basket'), then money would be unnecessary. However, it is a fact that many goods are paid for by money by most people and most goods are

paid for by money by some people. The reason is to do with the cost of doing business (transactions cost). Clearing systems are typically good value for large transactions made by people with some security to offer. Money is typically good value for small transactions, and for people with no security. The costs of both sorts of exchange technology also depend on how intensively and widely they are used, the size of their network – rather like a telephone system.

Notice that money and capital markets are quite separate things. Money is a means of exchange (of anything), one way of permitting exchange in any set of markets; while capital markets trade capital and could use various means of exchange to carry out this trade, including a clearing system or money. (Cash could also be used as part of the portfolio, as a store of value, but being non-interest-bearing it would make better sense to hold a savings deposit in a bank.)

However, once money exists as the means of exchange it acquires potential importance for the functioning of the whole economy. The usual institutional set-up will be one in which money (cash) is used for a limited set of goods, while clearing systems (such as credit cards and cheques) are used for the rest, with cash as their unit of account. By this is meant that to close a balance in these systems one must produce cash or an acceptable equivalent. In the case of bank accounts, cash is virtually never used to close a balance. Rather the account continues in credit or overdraft, and bank balances are accepted as equivalent to cash. Thus credit card balances are usually settled by the transfer of bank account balances.

How does money affect the economy and capital markets in such a set-up? Money, being the unit of account, now implies a price level: the amount of money needed to pay for a basket of goods. Also the rate of interest is expressed in terms of money. While other capital contracts may not be explicitly related to money (for example, an equity simply gives one part-ownership of a firm), their prices in the market are money prices, and are related as above to the risk-free rate of interest. It follows that the government (or the central bank, if it has the authority) can either fix the quantity of money (cash that it prints), or the price level (through a conversion rule, for example as under the early gold standard, where it offers to buy goods, or print money, if their price level falls below a certain level and vice versa), or the rate of interest.

Given that people want cash in order to carry out transactions, printing money will give them more than they initially require. The oldest of theories, the quantity theory, views this requirement as related to the volume of transactions, the price level, and the period over which money turns over (basically the gap between wage payments). The latter should be sensitive to the rate of interest because non-interest-yielding cash creates an incentive to economize by more frequent payment. Hence these different policies of government are in certain conditions equivalent. Printing money creates an excess supply of money. Higher demand must then be induced by lowering the rate of interest. Lowering the rate of interest increases the demand, and this can only be met by printing more money. These two equivalent policies then raise spending on capital and consumption so that, assuming that the economy is fully employed and cannot produce extra quantities, the price level will be driven up. Direct action by government to raise the price level would have raised the price level in an equivalent fashion, and this would have raised demand for money, which would have required that extra money be printed.

This way of thinking – in which full employment was assumed to be normal – dominated economics before the First World War. Money was seen as the way to control the price level. It was considered fairly immaterial whether the control was carried out by direct printing control, or indirectly, by fixing interest rates or pegging the price level. After the First World War the Great Depression focused minds (particularly that of J.M. Keynes) on how monetary contraction could depress output and employment rather than only prices. The answer seems to be that most contract prices for goods and labour are written in money terms and are renegotiated at intervals, so that prices change only slowly. Hence sharp unexpected changes in monetary conditions (whether the gold parity, interest rates, or money printed) could have their first effect on output. When this happens, these three monetary policy interventions will have different effects. It will depend on the shocks that may hit the economy, whether policies that stabilize money supply, the price level, or interest rates are preferable. The recurring debate over whether exchange rates should be fixed or flexible can be seen in this light. (The evidence tends to suggest that a modern economy facing a wide variety of demand and supply shocks will be better served by flexible rates that permit competitiveness to adjust quickly and also allow interest rates to vary flexibly to maintain employment stability. Experience within the European Exchange Rate Mechanism has reinforced the point.) Modern thought (following the work of monetarists such as Milton Friedman and Karl Brunner) accepts such ideas for the short run while maintaining the classical position for the long run, when monetary policy should have its sole impact on prices (or if it is persistently expansionary, on inflation, in which case it will also affect interest rates as capital providers protect their returns against it). However, there is no general agreement on the precise short-run mechanisms.

Some monetary theorists have stressed that credit availability rather than cost (interest rates) is the channel by which monetary policy works. However, while this appears superficially attractive from experiences of 'credit crunches', such episodes (for example in 1980 in the USA) tend to occur when controls on credit or other capital markets are introduced. When capital markets are free of controls it is hard to see why availability of finance should be limited, given the wide variety of instruments through which capital can be made available.

PATRICK MINFORD
CARDIFF BUSINESS SCHOOL,
CARDIFF UNIVERSITY

Reference

Minford, P. and Peel, D. (2002) *Advanced Macroeconomics: A Primer*, Cheltenham.

Further reading

Allen, D.E. (1985) *Introduction to the Theory of Finance*, Oxford.
Brunner, K. (1970) 'The "monetarist" revolution in monetary theory', *Weltwirtschaftliches Archiv* 105.
Friedman, M. (1968) 'The role of monetary policy', *American Economic Review* 58.
Keynes, J.M. (1936) *The General Theory of Employment, Interest and Money*, London.
Parkin, M. and Bade, R. (1988) *Modern Macroeconomics*, London.

SEE ALSO: capitalism; derivative markets and futures markets; financial system; markets; money; securitization

CAPITALISM

'Capitalism' refers to a socioeconomic arrangement in which business firms are privately owned, are operated with minimal governmental direction, and the proprietors – the capitalists – normally provide the bulk of the financing. In addition, in an advanced capitalist economy some of those private enterprises are extremely large by historical standards, their sales exceeding the GDP of some smaller but prosperous nations. These firms are usually organized as corporations or joint-stock enterprises with limited liability, and are directed by hired managers rather than their proprietors.

Some of the earlier writers on the subject, for example historians such as Sombart (1915), Weber (1930 [1922]) and Tawney (1926), found the essence of capitalism in the acquisitive spirit of profit-making enterprise. Karl Marx (1867–94) was the first to attempt a systematic analysis of the 'economic law of motion' of capitalist society. For Marx, capitalism was a 'mode of production' characterized by two classes of producers: the capitalists, who own the means of production (capital or land), make the strategic day-to-day economic decisions on technology, output and marketing, and appropriate the profits of production and distribution; and the labourers, who own no property but are free to dispose of their labour for wages on terms that depend on the cost of creating labour power and the numbers seeking work.

The emergence of a dominant class of entrepreneurs supplying the capital necessary to activate a substantial body of workers was a critical step in the transition from feudalism to capitalism. In England, preceded by Holland, it can be dated from the late sixteenth and early seventeenth centuries. Holland's supremacy in international trade, associated with its urgent need to import grain and timber (and hence to export manufactures), enabled Amsterdam to corner the Baltic trade and to displace Venice as the commercial and financial centre of Europe. The capital thus amassed was available to fund the famous chartered companies (Dutch East India Company, 1602; West India Company, 1621) as well as companies to reclaim land and exploit the area's most important source of industrial energy – peat. It also provided the circulating capital for merchants engaged in the putting-out system who supplied raw materials to domestic handicrafts workers and marketed the product.

Dutch capitalists flourished the more because they were subject to a Republican administration that was sympathetic to their free-market, individualist values. In England, where similar economic developments were in progress in the sixteenth and early seventeenth centuries, the rising class of capitalists was inhibited by a paternalistic monarchical government bent on regulating their activities for its own fiscal purposes and power objectives and social values. Tudor state control sought to guide enclosure of the fields used in common, control food supplies, regulate wages and manipulate the currency. The early Stuarts went further in selling industrial monopolies and concessions to favoured entrepreneurs and exclusive corporations, infuriating those whose interests were thus damaged. The English capitalists carried their fight against monopolies to the Cromwellian Revolution. When the monarchy was restored in the 1660s, the climate of opinion had been moulded by religious, political and scientific revolution into an environment that favoured the advancement of capitalism and laid the foundations for its next significant phase – the Industrial Revolution.

More recent discussions of capitalism have generally been the work of economic historians (see, e.g., Landes 1969; North and Thomas 1973; Rosenberg and Birdzell 1986; and Maddison 2001). Among modern economic theorists, discussion of the subject was led by Schumpeter (1936 [1911], 1947) and has since been taken up, at least implicitly, in discussions of the mechanism of innovation, including the work of Nordhaus 1969, Nelson 1996, DeLong 2001 and Baumol 2002.

The more than half-century since the end of the Second World War has brought out both the shortcomings and accomplishments of capitalism for the general welfare. Its deficiencies are well recognized. They include instability and business fluctuations with their painful periods of unemployment and forgone output, great inequality of wealth and the harm suffered by workers and consumers when managements driven by greedy pursuit of wealth and power engage in dangerous misinformation, exploitation and general disregard of ethical standards. Capitalism is not alone in these deficiencies; for example, greed and questionable ethics far precede its birth. But in this form of economy such shortcomings seem especially egregious, particularly where abundant national wealth would appear to make possible universal improvement in living standards.

The other side of the matter – the extraordinary accomplishments of capitalism – were recognized and emphasized by Marx and Engels as early as the *Communist Manifesto* (1848), but subsequently little note was taken of them in the economic literature until Schumpeter's contribution. Capitalism has brought growth in real per capita incomes and a flood of innovation (including the marketing and widespread utilization of inventions) such as the world has never seen. Growth in per capita incomes that before the Industrial Revolution was barely discernible probably increased more than 700 per cent in the twentieth-century USA, and in some other industrial countries it exploded even faster. For the first time in history, cities were alight after dark, transport exceeded the speed of a horse, information could gird the earth almost instantaneously rather than requiring months, the voices of the dead could be heard by the living, people could fly and even reach the moon, and they could travel deep below the ocean's surface; even the humble home kitchen experienced a revolution. All this was virtually undreamed of before.

Capitalism accomplishes this via the competitive mechanism that threatens major firms with demise if they do not battle constantly and successfully in keeping up with their rivals in the introduction of new products and processes. At the same time, the smaller enterprises and individual inventors, spurred on by the success of others, typically are those that contribute the revolutionary breakthroughs that are then vastly improved in the research and development (R&D) sections of the economy's giant corporations.

The unprecedented growth and innovation accomplishment of capitalism has led nations, anxious to share in the resulting abundance, to move towards the free-market economy. Still, in no economy is the market left entirely free from governmental interference, and economists generally agree that some such types of intervention are appropriate. The result is that the world's capitalist economies vary considerably in the purity of their form of capitalism.

WILLIAM J. BAUMOL
NEW YORK UNIVERSITY AND
PRINCETON UNIVERSITY

References

Baumol, W.J. (2002) *The Free-Market Innovation Machine: Analyzing the Growth Miracle of Capitalism*, Princeton, NJ.

DeLong, J.B. (2001) *The Economic History of the Twentieth Century: Slouching Toward Utopia?* http://www.j-bradford-delong.net.

Landes, D. (1969) *Prometheus Unbound*, Cambridge, UK.

Maddison, A. (2001) *The World Economy: A Millennial Perspective*, Paris.

Marx, K. (1867–94) *Das Kapital*, 3 vols, Moscow.

Marx, K. and Engels, F. (1848) *Manifesto of the Communist Party*, London.

Nelson, R.N. (1996) *The Sources of Economic Growth*, Cambridge, MA.

Nordhaus, W. (1969) *Invention, Growth and Welfare*, Cambridge, MA.

North, D.C. and Thomas, R.P. (1973) *The Rise of the Western World*, Cambridge, UK.

Rosenberg, N. and Birdzell, L.E., Jr (1986) *How the West Grew Rich: The Economic Transformation of the Industrial World*, New York.

Schumpeter, J. (1936 [1911]) *The Theory of Economic Development*, Cambridge, MA.

—— (1947) *Capitalism, Socialism and Democracy*, New York.

Sombart, W. (1915) *The Quintessence of Capitalism*, New York.

Tawney, R.H. (1926) *Religion and the Rise of Capitalism*, London.

Weber, M. (1930 [1922]) *The Protestant Ethic and the Spirit of Capitalism*, New York.

SEE ALSO: capital, credit and money markets; markets

CARGO CULTS

Cargo cults is the name given to millenarian movements of Melanesia, which centre on a belief that specified ritual manipulations and observances will soon bring to the people involved material rewards, notably manufactured goods, and a better, more emancipated, life. The name originates from the frequent use by participants of the Pidgin word *kago* (derived from the English 'cargo') to describe the returns they intend their activities to bring, although having a wider, and in the cult context uniquely Melanesian, connotation.

These small-scale and intense cults often have messianic leaders who rise up to direct their activities, using relevant traditional belief, reinterpreting myths and manipulating associated symbols, mixing them with aspects of Christian teachings, to promulgate a syncretized and appealing message. The activities inspired and directed by these 'prophets' frequently disrupt everyday life, as they divert people from subsistence tasks (at times even forbid them), and encourage the pursuit of preparations for the coming millennium. One example is clearing airstrips, and surrounding them with bamboo landing lights, to receive the prophesied aircraft coming with cargo, sometimes to be piloted by the ancestors.

Recent manifestations of cult behaviour occurred as the year 2000 approached. It was widely believed that when the second millennium began the known world would come to a cataclysmic end with believers saved and transported to heaven where everyone would have all they wished, and unbelievers would be cast into the eternal fires of damnation. The teachings of evangelical missionaries, whose churches subscribe to similar beliefs, fuelled these beliefs. Enigmatic cargo cult-like predictions were to be heard, for example associating Bible verse numbers with credit cards – these related to a belief that when the divine cataclysm came all believers would come into possession of credit cards and would find the PIN numbers 666, after Revelation's reference to the devil's works, tattooed on their bodies, and would subsequently have access to unlimited wealth from certain slots in walls.

Early reports interpreted such cults as the actions of irrational and deluded people, even in states of temporary collective madness. Sensitive research in postwar years has refuted this dismissive conclusion, showing that cargo cults are a rational indigenous response to traumatic culture contact with Western society. Although precipitated by familiarity with, and a desire to possess, the goods of the industrialized world, they have a traditional focus and logic. They turn to time-honoured beliefs and idioms to cope with a bewildering invasion, and, although inappropriate, even comical to us in their misunderstanding of our society and their bizarre interpretation of unintelligible aspects of it (like the function of credit cards or aircraft technology), they are neither illogical nor stupid.

The newcomers had material wealth and technical capabilities beyond local people's understanding and imagination, and – for tribal societies – irresistible political and military power emanating from incomprehensible nation-states. Europeans apparently did no physical work to produce their goods, unlike the politically subjugated local population, many of whom they put to hard labour for paltry returns. Neither did Europeans share their fabulous wealth with others, a direct assault on a cardinal Melanesian value, where giving and receiving is an integral aspect of social life.

Clearly Europeans knew something, and the problem for the Melanesians was how to gain access to this knowledge. Unable to comprehend Western society and the long-term nature of education, which some interpreted as a scheme to dupe them, or the worldwide capitalist economic system and the life of a factory worker, they turned to millenarian cults. A recurring feature of these cults is a belief that Europeans in some past age tricked Melanesians and are withholding from them their rightful share of material goods. In cargo cults the Melanesians are trying to reverse this situation, to discover the ritual formula that will facilitate access to their misappropriated manufactured possessions. They conclude that material goods come from the spirit world and that the wealthy whites are stealing their share; so it is a case of manipulating rituals in order to gain access to them.

An oft-repeated aim is to secure the cargo of the ancestors, who some cultists believe will return at the millennium. They will come to right current injustices. Some cults take on a disturbing racist tone here, probably reflecting the attitudes of some Europeans, which signal people's discontent with foreign domination and feelings of impotence. With the coming of the millennium, blacks will become whites, and the whites turn black, and white domination will end. Some millenarian movements have subsequently informed wider political awareness and developments, cults evolving into more clearly defined nationalistic and more effective political movements, as is evident for example on the Vanuatuan island of Tanna where the John Frum movement has become a political force.

The relatively frequent pan-Melanesian occurrence of cargo cults in a wide range of disparate cultures, and their recurrence time and again, with modified dogma and ritual, in the same region, testify to their importance to people. In their expression of tensions, they lend themselves to a range of sociological and psychological interpretations. Although frenetic, short-lived and – to outsiders – disruptive, these cults allow Melanesians who find themselves in a confusing and inexplicable world invaded by technically superior outsiders to cope with the change, even manipulate it, as evidenced in some subsequent political developments.

PAUL SILLITOE
UNIVERSITY OF DURHAM

Further reading

Burridge, K.O.L. (1960) *Mambu*, London.
Kocher-Schmid, C. (ed.) (1999) *Expecting the Day of Wrath: Versions of the Millennium in Papua New Guinea*, Boroko: Papua New Guinea National Research Institute Monograph No. 36.
Lawrence, P. (1965) *Road Belong Cargo*, Manchester.
Lindstrom, L. (1993) *Cargo Cult*, Honolulu, Hawaii.
Sillitoe, P. (2000) *Social Change in Melanesia: Development and History*, Cambridge.

SEE ALSO: religion; sects and cults

CARTOGRAPHY

Cartography is the art and technology of making and using maps to represent locations and spatial relationships. It is an art because these representations typically, but not always, are graphic, and thus instruments of visual communication and visual aesthetics. It is also a technology because map-makers use, develop and adapt a wide variety of electronic, mechanical and photographic techniques for storing, retrieving, selecting, generalizing and displaying geographical information. These techniques can affect the appearance of graphic maps as well as the efficacy of map-making and map use. Dramatic changes in the cartographical image reflect profound changes in map-making technology over the past five centuries, particularly since 1970. Maps have become dynamic and interactive, electronic technology encourages an ever-more diverse range of specialized cartographical applications, and the Internet offers viewers a rich, ever-widening and often challenging array of map information.

Especially significant is ready access since 2000 to advanced mapping technologies originally developed for the defence and intelligence communities. New cartographical products include commercial satellite imagery with a ground resolution of 1 metre or less, lidar (light detection and ranging) terrain data that support locally precise analyses of flood hazards, and differentially corrected global positioning system (GPS) receivers that record horizontal and vertical coordinates to within a few centimetres. In addition to threatening the livelihood of map-makers invested in older technologies, the new electronic cartography poses unprecedented threats to personal privacy and national security. Suggested remedies include regulations on the use of GPS-based tracking systems and restrictions on the sale of high-resolution satellite imagery of small states with hostile neighbours.

Most geographers and other scholars regard cartography largely as map authorship, that is, the design and crafting of geographical illustrations to accompany a verbal narrative. Often there is a division of labour in expository cartography between the author-cartographer, who compiles the maps and writes the text, and a cartographical illustrator or drafter, who produces the artwork. But as word-processing and electronic-publishing technology are displacing the typesetter by making fuller use of the author's key strokes, electronic cartography is displacing the drafter who retraces the map author's delineations. Because the cartographical technician serves as a design filter, to advise authors ignorant or uncertain about map projections, symbols and generalization, electronic cartography calls for a greater awareness of graphic and cartographical principles and practices by both authors and their editors. Electronic cartography also fosters a closer integration of maps and words in multimedia and hypertext presentations as well as in traditional publishing formats of articles, books and atlases. Computers, too, are weakening distinctions between cartographical presentation and cartographical analysis, in which maps are a tool for discovering and understanding geographical patterns and for testing and refining hypotheses.

Map-making is also an institutional enterprise, in which government cartographical units compile and publish a wide variety of topographical maps, navigational charts, geographical inventories and other cartographical products essential for economic development, national defence, environmental protection and growth management. In addition, commercial firms not only serve governments as contractors but also produce a still wider range of derivative, value-added maps and cartographical databases tailored to the needs of travellers, industries, businesses, local governments and educators. Because expository cartography depends heavily on institutional cartography for source materials, map authors must be aware of the availability, utility and reliability of government and commercial maps.

Cartography is also a subdiscipline of geography in which scholars either seek more effective means of cartographical communication or treat the map, its derivation and its impact as an object of study. Most academic cartographers are concerned with training geographers and others in the design and use of maps as well as with developing improved methods of cartographical display. Studies of map design rely on a variety of approaches, including semiotic theory, psychophysics, colour theory, statistics, policy analysis and subject-testing. Because maps can be largely or subtly rhetorical, other cartographical scholars focus on mapping as a social or intellectual process and on the map's role as an instrument of power and persuasion. Despite the hyperbole of cartographical chauvinists who assert that the field is fundamentally a science, maps are subjective texts that reflect the biases of their authors and sources as well as the limitations of technology.

Around 1990, cartographical scholars, particularly historians of cartography, developed a heightened awareness of maps as instruments of oppression, empowerment and propaganda. Prime examples are place names and boundaries, which not only support territorial claims but also confirm the existence of a state or nation. Similarly, the conscious or unconscious suppression of names and features – the late J.B. Harley called these culturally or politically biased omissions 'cartographic silences' – can deny a nation's existence as well as open its territory to settlement or exploitation. In addition, maps help governments reify 'no-fly' zones, publicize travel restrictions and regulate land use. Within cities, cartographical 'redlining' contributes to the deterioration of neighbourhoods stigmatized by high crime rates, permissive 'zoning' (land-use regulations) or institutional barriers to home loans. Whether the detrimental effects of planning and zoning maps, designed to preserve neighbourhoods and support property values, are merely unintended consequences of a value-neutral technology is questionable.

Strongly persuasive or emblematic overtones undermine the naïve notion that maps are objective representations of reality. Well-known examples of ideology-laden cartography include the clever but questionably effective Nazi propaganda maps of the late 1930s, the use of Mercator's projection to exaggerate the threat of Communism during the Cold War, and the uncritical adoption of the Peters projection by Oxfam, UNESCO and other pro-Third World groups as an antidote to the Mercator projection. Although claims that the Mercator world map has been detrimental to developing nations are unsubstantiated, use of the Peters map is hardly as harmful as professional cartographers and other opponents of Peters have argued. An effective defence against persuasive, potentially misleading cartography is the use of multiple maps representing diverse viewpoints or interpretations.

MARK MONMONIER
SYRACUSE UNIVERSITY

Further reading

Dorling, D. and Fairbairn, D. (1997) *Mapping: Ways of Representing the World*, London.

Harley, J.B. (2001) *The New Nature of Maps: Essays in the History of Cartography*, Baltimore.

MacEachren, A.M. (1995) *How Maps Work: Representation, Visualization, and Design*, New York.

Monmonier, M. (1993) *Mapping It Out: Expository Cartography for the Humanities and Social Sciences*, Chicago.

—— (1996 [1991]) *How to Lie with Maps*, Chicago.

—— (2002) *Spying with Maps: Surveillance Technologies and the Future of Privacy*, Chicago.

Perkins, C.R. and Parry, R.B. (eds) (1990) *Information Sources in Cartography*, London.

Taylor, D.R.F. (ed.) (1998) *Policy Issues in Modern Cartography*, New York.

Wright, J.K. (1942) 'Map makers are human: Comments on the subjective in mapping', *Geographical Review* 32.

SEE ALSO: geographical information systems; landscape; spatial analysis

CASE STUDY

The case study is widely and variously used across the whole range of social science disciplines. It refers to both an organizing principle for and a method of social research. Simply put, case study describes any form of single unit analysis. An individual may be the focus for a case study, as in psychotherapy or medicine, but so may an organization, a group, an event or a social process. The point is that the focus is upon a naturally occurring social phenomenon rather than an experimentally constructed activity or selected sample. Thus, Smith, writing about educational research, says:

> The relative emphasis on what I call an 'intact', 'natural' or 'ongoing' group versus some kind of sampled set of pupils, teachers, classes, curricula or schools also seems very important. I believe that this is what some of the case study advocates mean by 'case'.
>
> (1990: 11)

Cases are not normally selected by criteria of typicality but on the basis of theoretical significance or particular critical qualities.

Case studies aim to achieve depth; more specifically they strive to be holistic and exhaustive. The goal is what Geertz (1973) calls 'thick description', which is so essential to an understanding of context and situation. An eclectic variety of types of data are collected and set against one another in the processes of analysis and in the representation of 'the case' in writing. Where appropriate and feasible, researchers themselves are central to the conduct of case study research. Data are collected by direct presence in the site, or face-to-face exchange with the subject. The researcher aims to share experiences with the researched, to witness events first hand, to question action within the setting. The design and conduct of case study research is responsive and creative, accommodating to the form, rhythm and possibilities of the setting. 'Any case study is a construction itself, a product of the interaction between respondents, site and researcher' (Lincoln and Guba 1990: 54). This is typically reflected in the language of case study reporting; 'case studies will rhetorically exemplify the interpersonal involvement which characterized that form of inquiry' (Lincoln and Guba 1990: 59). This contrasts with the 'stripped down, cool' style of 'scientific' reporting. Case studies are written to convey authenticity, to recapture the natural language of the setting and to evoke a vicarious response from the reader.

Case study research is frequently attacked for its lack of generalizability (Bolgar 1965; Shaunhessy and Zechmeister 1985) although in some respects the importation of generalization arguments from the field of quantitative research is based upon misunderstandings of the purposes of case study research. The case study is not premised on the generation of abstract, causal or law-like statements. Rather, it is intended to reveal the intricate complexities of specific sites or processes and their origins, interrelations and dynamics. However, the evolution of the approach and the defence against the generalization argument, the escape from what is called 'radical particularism', has led, in some fields, to the use of multi-site case study research designs. These concentrate upon a limited range of issues across a number of settings, collecting the same data and using the same analytical procedures. Firestone and Herriot (1984) examined twenty-five such studies, which ranged in scope from three sites to sixty. Both the number and the heterogeneity of sites have been used as a basis for claims about more robust generalizability. However, the basic issue of the value of breadth rather than depth applies as much when considering single as against multi-site case studies as it does when the single case study is set over and against survey research. The key question is 'What is lost and gained in the trade-off between exhaustive depth and more superficial breadth?'

STEPHEN J. BALL
INSTITUTE OF EDUCATION,
UNIVERSITY OF LONDON

References

Bolgar, H. (1965) 'The case study method', in B.B. Wolman (ed.) *Handbook of Clinical Psychology*, New York.

Firestone, W.A. and Herriot, R.E. (1984) 'Multisite qualitative policy research: Some design and implementation issues', in D.M. Fetterman (ed.) *Ethnography in Educational Evaluation*, Beverly Hills, CA.

Geertz, C. (1973) *The Interpretation of Cultures*, New York.

Lincoln, Y.S. and Guba, E.G. (1990) 'Judging the quality of case study reports', *International Journal of Qualitative Studies in Education* 3(1).

Shaunhessy, J.J. and Zechmeister, E.B. (1985) *Research Methods in Psychology*, New York.

Smith, L.M. (1990) 'Critical introduction: Whither classroom ethnography?' in M. Hammersley (ed.) *Classroom Ethnography*, Milton Keynes.

SEE ALSO: ethnography; life history; methods of social research

CASTE

Caste systems have been defined in the most general terms as systems of hierarchically ordered endogamous units in which membership is hereditary and permanent (e.g. Berreman 1960). On such a definition a whole range of rigidly stratified societies would be characterized by caste – Japan, for example, or certain Polynesian and East African societies, or the racially divided world of the US Deep South. Hindu India is generally taken as the paradigmatic example. Many scholars would argue, however, that the difference between this case and the others is far more significant than the similarities, and that the term caste should properly be applied only to this context.

The morphology of the Hindu caste system can be described in terms of three key characteristics (Bouglé 1971 [1908]), all of which are religiously underpinned by the religious values of purity (Dumont 1970 [1966]). First, there is a *hierarchy* of castes that is theoretically based on their relative degree of purity. As the purest of all, the Brahmans rank highest, and are in principle both distinct from and superior to the caste that actually wields politico-economic power. Second, as the pure can maintain their purity only if there are impure castes to remove the pollution that they inevitably incur by their involvement in the natural world, there is a *division of labour* between castes resulting in their *interdependence*. Third, pollution is contagious, and a caste must therefore restrict its contacts with inferiors in order to maintain its status. This *separation* takes many forms: a rule of endogamy precluding marital alliances with inferiors; restrictions on commensality; the outcasting of those who transgress the rules lest they pollute the rest of the group; and the phenomenon of Untouchability debarring physical contact between 'clean' and 'polluted' groups. (We even have historical reports of theoretically Unseeable castes; while in parts of traditional Kerala the relative status of non-Brahman castes was in theory precisely reflected in the number of paces distant they had to keep from the highest Brahmans.)

While the (upward) mobility of *individuals* is theoretically impossible and empirically rare, the group as a whole may lay claim to a higher status by emulating the customs and practices of its superiors, and may succeed in validating its claims by using a new-found political or economic leverage to persuade erstwhile superiors to interact with it on a new basis (the crucial test being their acceptance of its food and water). As the actors present it, however, this is not a matter of social climbing but of reasserting a traditional status quo that was temporarily disrupted. A theory of timeless stasis is thus preserved despite a good deal of actual mobility.

The system is often visualized as being like a layer-cake with each layer as an occupationally specialized group characterized by endogamy and unrestricted commensality. A better image is of a set of Chinese boxes. At the most schematic level, contemporary Hindus, following the scriptures, represent the caste order in terms of a four-fold division: Brahman, Kshatriya, Vaishya and Shudra. At the local level (the details vary considerably), the Brahmans may be subdivided into priestly and non-priestly subgroups, the priestly Brahmans into Household-priests, Temple-priests and Funeral-priests; the Household-priests into two or more endogamous circles; and each circle into its component clans and lineages, who may be the only people who will freely accept one another's food. The answer to the question 'What is your caste?' will depend on context and might legitimately be phrased in terms of any of these levels. At each level the group is referred to as a *jati*, a term that is conventionally translated as 'caste' but is more accurately rendered as 'breed' or 'species'. Groups which share a common status in relation to outsiders are internally hierarchized: all Brahmans are equal in relation to non-Brahmans, but non-priestly Brahmans are superior in relation to priestly ones, and Household-priests in relation to Funeral-priests. It will be seen that the occupationally specialized group is not necessarily coterminous with the endogamous group, which may not coincide with the unit of unrestricted commensality. It is therefore impossible to define caste by listing a series of characteristics (e.g. occupation, endogamy, etc.) common to all. The universe of caste is a relational universe, rather than one made up of a given number of fixed and bounded units.

J.P. PARRY
LONDON SCHOOL OF ECONOMICS
AND POLITICAL SCIENCE

References

Berreman, G.D. (1960) 'Caste in India and the United States', *American Journal of Sociology* 66.

Bouglé, V. (1971 [1908]) *Essays on the Caste System*, Cambridge, UK.

Dumont, L. (1970 [1966]) *Homo Hierarchicus: The Caste System and Its Implications*, London.

Further reading

Dirks, N.B. (2001) *Castes of Mind: Colonialism and the Making of Modern India*, Princeton, NJ.
Srinivas, M.N. (ed.) (2003) *Caste: Its 21st Century Avatar*, New Delhi.

SEE ALSO: stratification

CENSUS OF POPULATION

A census of population, as defined in United Nations reports, is the total process of collecting, compiling, evaluating, analysing and publishing, or otherwise disseminating, demographic, economic and social data pertaining to all persons in a country, or to a well-delimited part of a country at a specified time.

The census of population is the oldest and most widely distributed statistical undertaking by governments throughout the world. Censuses have also been developed to provide information on housing, manufactures, agriculture, mineral industries and business establishments. Many of the principles applying to the census of population apply equally to these other censuses.

It is not known which ruler first ordered a count of the people in order to assess the numbers potentially available for military service or to determine how many households might be liable to pay taxes. Population counts were reported from ancient Japan, and counts were compiled by Egyptians, Greeks, Hebrews, Persians and Peruvians. Many of these early censuses were limited as to the area covered and in some instances dealt with only a part of the population, such as men of military age. The results were generally treated as state secrets. In Europe, censuses on a city-wide basis were reported in the fifteenth and sixteenth centuries. India reported a census in 1687. Various censuses have been claimed as the first in modern times.

Data collected in a population census have often been used as the basis for the allocation of a territory to one or the other claimant governments. Census data are widely used by governments for planning and carrying out a variety of governmental functions. In some countries representation in legislative bodies and distribution of funds by the central government are significantly affected by the census results. The powers and duties of many municipalities depend on the size of their population. The private economy makes extensive use of the data for site locations, marketing strategies and many other activities. Health, education and welfare programmes depend very heavily on such data.

The oldest continuous census taking is that of the USA where a census has been taken every ten years since 1790. The UK began taking a census in 1801 and followed the 10-year pattern except in 1941 when wartime requirements led to its cancellation. The 10-year pattern is widely observed. In many countries the census is authorized anew whenever the government finds a need for the data. In a few countries censuses are taken at regular 5-year intervals. During the 1970s special efforts by the United Nations and some donor countries were directed to assisting African countries that had not previously taken a census. In 1982 the People's Republic of China completed the largest census ever taken. By 1983 virtually every country in the world had taken at least one census of population.

Early censuses often utilized household lists or similar sources as the basis of their tabulations. A modern census is one in which information is collected separately about each individual. Such practices became common during the last half of the nineteenth century.

The information assembled in a census depends in large part on the needs of the government for such information and on the availability of alternative sources. The United Nations has identified a set of topics that appear most essential. They include place where found at time of census, place of usual residence, place of birth, sex, age, relationship to head of household, marital status, children born alive, children living, literacy, school attendance, status (employer, employee, etc.). International comparability will be facilitated to the extent that national census offices utilize the standard definitions that have been developed by the United Nations.

A question that needs careful attention prior to a census is who is to be counted as part of the national and local population. Special consideration needs to be given to such persons as members of the Armed Forces, including those stationed outside the home country, migratory workers, university students, technical assistance personnel outside their home countries, long-term visitors and guest workers.

Having determined who is to be included in the census, it becomes necessary also to determine in which part of the national territory they are to be counted. The classic distinction is that between a *de facto* and a *de jure* census. In a *de facto* census people are generally counted as a part of the population of the place where they encountered the census enumerator. This differs from the practice in a *de jure* census where an effort is made to ascertain where the person 'belongs'. This may be a usual residence, a legal residence or an ancestral home. Persons who spend part of the time in one place and the remainder in one or more other places, and persons in long-stay institutions (prisons, hospitals, etc.), need to be recorded in a uniform manner within the country. Special procedures may need to be developed for persons who have no fixed place of residence, such as persons who live on the streets, nomads, refugees or illegal aliens.

Customarily two basic methods of taking the census are recognized – direct enumeration and self-enumeration. Under the former method the enumerator collects information directly from the household. Self-enumeration means that the household members are given a questionnaire with the request that they enter the appropriate information and deliver the completed form to the designated census office or to an enumerator who comes to collect the completed forms.

The law establishing the census normally makes provision for the authority of the census office and its employees to conduct the census and establishes the obligation of the residents to provide the answers to the best of their ability. There are normally legal penalties for refusal or for providing false information.

An important part of the legal provision for the census is the guarantee that the individually identifiable information will be held in strict confidence and will be used only for statistical purposes, and violation of pledge of confidentiality is a punishable offence.

The almost universal availability of computers for the processing, tabulation and printing of the data collected in the census has greatly facilitated the work of census offices. A more complete and thorough review of the raw data as well as of intermediate and final tabulations is possible, and where the research community also has access to computers the provision of summary tapes and of public use microdata sample tapes has enabled them to use the data more effectively.

The improved access of the public to the census products has greatly increased the concern over errors in the census from whatever source, whether in coverage of the population, errors by the respondents, errors in recording the information supplied by respondents, or errors made in the processing of the data, and census officials are alerted to this problem.

Computers and the development of sampling procedures have brought about significant changes in the conduct of population censuses. The effective use of computers has brought about changes in field procedures and has speeded up the tabulation and release of the results. They have led to the preparation of data for specialized purposes. They have contributed to procedures for making microdata available for research purposes, while protecting the confidentiality of the individual records.

The quality of census results has come under increasing study. The completeness of the coverage is critical for many governmental actions. Special efforts have been undertaken to ascertain the completeness of the census results. Methods of ascertaining the degree of under- or overcounting of the population of a given area have yielded valuable information. Special attention has been given to sources of data within the census operation that can yield the information required. The treatment of members of minority groups – ethnic, age, occupation, country of birth, etc. – can have profound effects on the data and public actions for or against members of the groups.

Related sources of information, such as a population register, can be used very effectively in all phases of the census. Training and supervision of the staff are critical to the success of a census. Special arrangements may be needed if the census work in essence is a part-time activity by persons who have other duties. A different set of procedures is needed if the bulk of the census is carried on by persons who are recruited for the census.

CONRAD TAEUBER
GEORGETOWN UNIVERSITY

Further reading

Alonso, W. and Starr, P. (eds) (1983) *The Politics of Numbers*, New York.

Kertzer, D. and Arel, D. (eds) (2002) *Census and Identity: The Politics of Race, Ethnicity and Language in National Censuses*, Cambridge, UK.

Mitrof, I., Mason, R. and Barabba, V.P. (eds) (1983)

The 1980 Census: Policymaking Amid Turbulence, Lexington, MA.

National Academy of Sciences, Committee on National Statistics (1993) *A Census That Mirrors America*, Washington, DC.

Shryock, H.S. and Taeuber, C. (1976) *The Conventional Population Census*, Chapel Hill, NC.

United Nations (1980) *Principles and Recommendations for Population and Housing Censuses*, New York.

SEE ALSO: demographic surveys; vital statistics

CHICAGO SCHOOL

The Chicago School refers to people and economic ideas from the University of Chicago through the last 70 years of the twentieth century. Among the individuals considered members of the Chicago School are Frank H. Knight, Jacob Viner, Henry C. Simons, Aaron Director, Milton Friedman, George J. Stigler, Gary S. Becker and Ronald J. Coase. It should be noted that there is considerable diversity in the ideas of the individuals listed here, and still more diversity across the people who taught economics at the University of Chicago. However, there are commonly held beliefs and practices that set these Chicago economists apart from others outside Chicago. In short, the Chicago economists' ideas are: (1) opposition to socialism and extensive 'social engineering', (2) the importance of political, civic and economic liberty for individuals, (3) the importance of monetary policy for macroeconomic stability, and (4) belief that economic theory coupled with empirical evidence is a powerful lens through which to view society and solve social problems.

Frank H. Knight and Jacob Viner were key figures in the 1930s and 1940s. Both taught price theory and edited the Department of Economics's *Journal of Political Economy*. Knight was philosophically inclined, tending to raise several questions for each question to which he offered an answer. Viner was a virtuoso theorist, and a daunting presence in the classroom. Henry Simons and Aaron Director were both highly influential teachers in the Economics Department and the Law School. Neither was as prolific a writer as the other individuals. Simons was most notable for his advocacy of policy reforms rooted in classical liberalism at a time when German National Socialism and Soviet Communism threatened to overwhelm free societies. Aaron Director is famous for bringing economic analysis into the heart of the Law School curriculum, especially with regard to antitrust.

Milton Friedman and George J. Stigler were the second generation of the Chicago School, and it was through their influence that Chicago economics came to have its image. Friedman and Stigler continued in the classical liberal ideological tradition established by Knight, Simons and Director. Through their teaching, price theory textbooks and articles, Friedman and Stigler spread Chicago-style price theory, with its emphasis on problem-solving and keeping mathematics the handmaiden rather than mistress of economic analysis. Friedman revived interest in the Quantity Theory of Money when it seemed to have been swept aside by the Keynesians. Stigler made extensive studies of the causes and effects of government regulation of business, showing that some regulations, thought to be important, have little actual effect, and others work to the benefit of the regulated firms. Stigler did pioneering work on the economics of information, treating information as a commodity that is bought and sold. Gary S. Becker led a revival of home economics, economic analysis of the family and other non-market institutions. He also pioneered economic analysis of racial discrimination. Ronald Coase followed Aaron Director as resident economist on the Law faculty. Coase's primary contributions are in the economics of property rights and transactions costs. His writings have had a major effect on torts theory.

For a clear view of Chicago School economics it is helpful to compare it with what it was not, or that for which it was an alternative. Following the Russian Revolution and the Great Depression many intellectuals, including economists, saw capitalism as a failed economic system. Communism and socialism were viewed as morally superior, with more equal distributions of wealth and income, and as more productive, not subject to depressions and inflations. Both advantages were thought to be based on the purposive planning of communism and socialism, in contrast to the want of central direction in capitalist societies. The economists who compose the Chicago School were defenders of capitalism.

Also, after the Second World War, economics became much more mathematical than it had theretofore been. Paul Samuelson and colleagues at the Massachusetts Institute of Technology, and economists up the Charles River at Harvard, set the standard for formalized, highly abstract economic theory. Logic and internal consistency of mathematical models trumped empirical evidence in mathematical economics. At Chicago, however, economics retained its grounding in the use of theory to solve concrete problems. This was a more pragmatic approach, letting the economic problem (e.g. explaining the effects of a regulation, or explaining pricing practices in an industry) determine the exact theoretical construct, and bringing empirical evidence to bear on the problem.

J. DANIEL HAMMOND
WAKE FOREST UNIVERSITY

Further reading

Coase, R.H. (1994) *Essays on Economics and Economists*, Chicago.
Emmett, R.B. (ed.) (1999) *Selected Essays by Frank H. Knight*, 2 vols, Chicago.
Friedman, M. (2002) *Capitalism and Freedom: Fortieth Anniversary Edition*, Chicago.
Simons, H.C. (1948) *Economic Policy for a Free Society*, Chicago.

SEE ALSO: Friedman

CHILD DEVELOPMENT

Interest in child development, and the role of society in helping to form a child's character, dates back at least to the time of Plato. However, the scientific study of childhood may be taken to date from the latter part of the nineteenth and early twentieth centuries, the first of three periods of developmental psychology delineated by Cairns (1998). Darwin's evolutionary theory provided a perspective on childhood nature, and Darwin himself described a 'biographical sketch of an infant' (1877), this being an early example of a 'case study'. In the USA, G. Stanley Hall developed a biological approach to child and adolescent development, for example in his 1908 book *Adolescence*. By contrast, J.B. Watson emphasized the importance of environmental stimuli and contingencies learnt, leading to the behaviourist approach developed further in later decades by B.F. Skinner. Yet another influence was to be the writings of Freud (1856–1939), who saw the origins of adult neuroses in child experiences. (Implications of his theory for childhood were particularly developed by his daughter, Anna Freud.)

A second period of research in child development is characterized by Cairns as extending from the 1920s to the 1940s. This period sees the early work of Jean Piaget in Geneva, and the life career of Lev Vygotsky in the then Soviet Union. These theorists set up a productive dialogue on the nature of cognitive and social-cognitive development. Piaget emphasized the role of the individual child as a cognitive thinker, and of the balance between 'assimilation' (fitting experiences to the child's existing cognitive structures) and 'accommodation' (the child adapting cognitive structures in the light of new experiences). Vygotsky emphasized more the role of language, and of the social context, as expressed in the 'zone of proximal development', in which the child learns a bit more from someone more knowledgeable than themselves. At a more empirical level, the late 1920s and 1930s saw the founding of several institutes and child welfare stations in the USA, which started to document the typical behaviours of children, especially at younger ages and in nursery school.

What Cairns calls the modern era of developmental psychology dates from 1947 to the present. This has seen a remarkable increase in methodological sophistication, an elaboration of theoretical ideas from earlier periods, and new perspectives inspired by for example computers and information technology; structuralist approaches in anthropology and sociology; and advances in behaviour genetics. Nevertheless, debates that began in the late nineteenth century continue to reverberate in the early twenty-first century.

The psychological study of child development through this modern period has tended to split into different areas of developing competence; thus, there are specialists (and specialist journals) in cognitive development, social development and language development; as well as in abnormal development. Physical development has been relatively neglected by child psychologists, although of interest in sports science and health studies. In fact physical development was given more attention in the early and middle periods, but research on the detrimental effects of institutional rearing drew attention to important adverse cognitive and social consequences. Moreover, the theoretical impact of the Piaget–Vygotsky debate led to a predominance of cognitive studies, with studies of social and language development following behind.

Research in cognitive development was strongly influenced by Piaget through the 1950s to 1970s, as his works were translated into English and as his findings were replicated in other countries. The 1970s and 1980s, however, saw mounting criticism of his findings, especially what was seen as his attempts to 'trick' children into mistakes. The predominant emphasis in US psychology was to emphasize the child's potential and achievements, rather than the failures or signs of immaturity. When Vygotsky's writings were 'discovered' by Western psychologists in the 1970s his ideas were accordingly welcomed, and his message continues to resonate.

The 1980s and 1990s saw the rise of information-processing approaches to cognitive development, as in the study of cognition generally. Besides research on, for example, memory development, there has been interest in topics such as 'metamemory' – the child's growing awareness of mnemonic strategies such as rehearsal, or having concrete reminders such as written lists. This period also saw the rise of interest in 'theory of mind', the ability to recognize that someone else can have different knowledge or emotions from oneself, and this has become a major paradigm in recent research. Specific tasks such as Sally–Anne (Sally moves an object while Anne is absent) or Smarties (pencils are put in a smarties tube) have become standard 'false belief' assessments to see if children have achieved a theory of mind.

The study of language development had been influenced by the behaviourist learning tradition, but a savage critique of Skinner's 1957 book *Verbal Behavior* by Noam Chomsky (1959) led to a more structuralist perspective with an emphasis on the innate abilities of children, such as the 'Language Acquisition Device' that processes verbal input and helps create grammatical understanding. More recently, research in this area has benefited from detailed records of children's language in context, and from beginnings of examination of development of language development in languages other than English.

Research in social development was strongly influenced by the work of John Bowlby. Taking off from a combination of psychoanalytic theory, ethological/evolutionary theory and early ideas of information processing, Bowlby's attachment theory provided a perspective on early adult–infant development that has developed into another major research paradigm (Bowlby 1988). Mary Ainsworth worked with Bowlby and developed the 'strange situation' technique in which infants are observed in a mildly stressful situation with the mother/caregiver (Ainsworth *et al.* 1978). The evidence for intergenerational transmission of security of attachment has helped develop attachment theory into a life-span perspective. It has had marked application in understanding phenomena such as child abuse, and pathological parenting. Attachment theory has not been the only perspective in parenting, and work on parenting skills and styles has also been influential.

Another major area of research in social development has been that of peer relationships. Starting with early work on children's friendships and sociometry, the 1980s saw the onset of studies of 'sociometric status', ratings of children as popular, controversial, average, neglected or rejected depending on both 'like most' and 'like least' nominations from classmates. More recently, there has been research on co-operation and competition amongst peers. Aggression has long been a focus of research, and bullying/victimization has become a major area of research since the 1990s, with a strong emphasis on school intervention programmes.

In a 1998 book, *The Nurture Assumption*, Judith Harris argued a controversial position that parents had little influence on children after the preschool years, and that peer group influence predominated. The general consensus is that there is a complex admixture of genetic and temperamental factors in the child, early socialization and parenting, and peer group and broader societal factors, necessary to explain developmental outcomes.

Methodologically, child development and developmental psychology have been eclectic. Observational methods were used widely both in the 1930s and later from the 1970s. Laboratory studies were especially influential in the 1950s to 1970s but retain a strong influence especially in cognitive development. Questionnaires, interviews and focus groups are widely used. Although most data are gathered by adult researchers, there has been recent interest in using children/adolescents as researchers too.

The easiest way of studying development is by cross-sectional comparison, in which children of different ages are compared at the same point of historical time. A more powerful but obviously time-consuming method is longitudinal study, in which a group of children are followed through development for periods ranging from months to many years. There are several large-scale longitudinal studies which now have data on representative samples over a span of 20 years or more. Such studies must also grapple with historical factors. Development takes place in a historical context; for example the rapid advent of television in the 1950s (in Western countries) had profound effects on children's time budgets and on influences on their behaviour, still a matter of controversy (and magnified by more recent developments in video, and computer games and the World Wide Web). Combining cross-sectional and longitudinal studies into 'cohort-sequential' designs (in which several cohorts of different generations are followed longitudinally) help researchers to disentangle these influences, but are exceptionally expensive in execution and correspondingly rare in actuality.

Besides examining age differences, child development researchers have considered sex differences; differences related to social class, and cultural or subcultural grouping; and differences related to individual circumstances, temperament and experience, including family constellation, family composition, and peer and school influences.

The development of particular methodological tools has a probably excessive influence on research. The major recent paradigms all reflect a popular research tool: attachment theory and the 'strange situation', theory of mind and the 'false belief' tasks, and peer relationships and the 'sociometric status' assessment. Another set of research tools – twin studies and adoption studies – has led to an expansion of behaviour genetic investigations, supported by increasingly powerful techniques of identifying particular genes and tracking gene–behaviour relationships.

Psychology remains the major disciplinary influence, but other disciplines have had and continue to have a major impact. Evolutionary theory in its more modern neo-Darwinian and sociobiological guise has led to an evolutionary developmental psychology, and ethological studies of non-human species, especially primates (monkeys and apes) has brought about not only a renaissance of observational methods, but also renewed theoretical interest in the evolution of capacities such as mind-reading and empathy (Bjorklund and Pellegrini 2002). Anthropological studies provide a welcome cross-cultural perspective to what can often be a very Western

perspective on development. Sociologists have emphasized the social construction of childhood, and Alison James and Alan Prout highlighted a challenge to conventional psychological thinking in their 1990 book *Constructing and Reconstructing Childhood*. Sociological and also feminist theorists argue that power structures in society have a major influence on the direction of research and upon what is conventionally seen as worthy of study by psychological researchers.

Traditionally the field has been dominated by 'child development', underpinned by the belief that early childhood, and perhaps adolescence, were vitally formative stages for the life-span. Both Freudian theory and behaviourism, despite opposite theoretical origins, supported this position. However, as more sophisticated developmental theories emerged, so too concepts of 'life-span development' have become particularly influential since the 1980s. Erik Erikson developed an eight-stage model of life-span development that has had wide influence in other disciplines such as history. Paul Baltes (1978) has provided major conceptual and methodological supports to a life-span approach. The role of the wider social context was elaborated by Urie Bronfenbrenner working from the microsystem (home, school) through the mesosystem (links between microsystems), exosystem (indirect influences from the local environment) to the macrosystem (general social ideology and organization) (Bronfenbrenner 1979).

As an academic discipline, child development has obvious implications for the wider society. Research informs, but does not yet provide conclusive answers to, debates in many areas such as: What is effective parenting? Should parental physical punishment be forbidden? What forms of early child day care are non-detrimental? What are the effects of divorce and family constellation on development? How can we prevent child abuse in families, and bullying in schools? What are the best methods of encouraging reading? What is the role of play in development? Does violence in the mass media affect normal children? Is adolescent turmoil inevitable? The relevance of these questions for all parents and for political argument ensures a vital role for child development research in decades to come.

PETER K. SMITH
GOLDSMITHS' COLLEGE, UNIVERSITY OF LONDON

References

Ainsworth, M.D.S., Blehar, M.C., Waters, E. and Wall, S. (1978) *Patterns of Attachment: A Psychological Study of the Strange Situation*, Hoboken, NJ.

Baltes, P.B. (ed.) (1978) *Life-span Development and Behavior (Vol. 1)*, New York.

Bjorklund, D.F. and Pellegrini, A.D. (2002) *The Origins of Human Nature: Evolutionary Developmental Psychology*, Washington, DC.

Bowlby, J. (1988) *A Secure Base: Clinical Applications of Attachment Theory*, London.

Bronfenbrenner, U. (1979) *The Ecology of Human Development*, Cambridge, MA.

Cairns, R.B. (1998) 'The making of developmental psychology', in W. Damon (series ed.) and R.M. Lerner (vol. ed.) *Handbook of Child Psychology. Vol. 1: History and Systems of Developmental Psychology*, New York, pp. 25–105.

Chomsky, N. (1959) 'A review of B.F. Skinner's *Verbal Behavior*', *Language* 35(1): 26–58.

Darwin, C. (1877) 'A biographical sketch of an infant', *Mind* 2: 285–94.

Hall, G.S. (1907) *Adolescence*, New York.

Harris, J.R. (1998) *The Nurture Assumption*, New York.

James, A. and Prout, A. (1990) *Constructing and Reconstructing Childhood*, Basingstoke.

Further reading

Slee, P. and Shute, R. (2003) *Child Development: Thinking about Theories*, London.

Smith, P.K., Cowie, H. and Blades, M. (2003) *Understanding Children's Development*, 4th edn, Oxford.

SEE ALSO: childhood; developmental psychology; life-span development

CHILDCARE

Childcare is a wide-ranging term, encompassing both the most intimate, personal care of individual children and the broader strategies of governments towards children as a whole. Here, the focus is on state policy relating to the care of children. Such policy is applied in three broad arenas. First, there is state supervision and/or support of families where children remain in the care of their parents but where doubts exist about the adequacy of that care, or where extra support is necessary. In these cases, measures such as child protection registers and respite care for disabled children are used either to intervene in or to bolster family life. Second, there is state regulation of private facilities for short-term childcare (such as child minders) away from parental supervision. This field primarily involves the use of inspection, regulation and, sometimes, direct provision. Third, there is direct state care of children who, for short or long periods, need to live apart from their families. Here, the main instruments used are foster care and various forms of residential care.

Childcare is an emotive topic in all three contexts, but especially the first. For this reason, policy change has often been scandal-driven or has been a response to perceived crises or moral panics. This has reduced the capacity for linear, coherent policy formulation and produced episodic policy development. Such development is evident in the last century and a quarter in the UK, where a burst of activity on child abuse in the late nineteenth century was followed by a relatively quiet period and then a further burst of activity on wider social welfare support for families after the Second World War, and a renewed concern with child abuse from the early 1970s onwards (Hendrick 2003). Policy debate in this latter period repeatedly invokes the names of particular abused children whose deaths prompted soul-searching in the media and amongst politicians on the adequacy of social work support (Corby *et al.* 2001).

One reason for the emotiveness of childcare policy is the triangular relationship it sets up between children, parents and the state in an arena that many regard as essentially private. In the UK, this issue emerged most explosively in the Cleveland Inquiry (Butler-Sloss 1988), which concerned sexual abuse investigations by local authority social services in relation to large numbers of children and led to claims of excessive intervention in family life. This triangular relationship makes childcare policy profoundly ideological and an arena for conflict between competing perspectives based on the primacy of the rights of parents, of the rights of children and of the duty of the state to protect all of its citizens (Fox Harding 1997). The subsequent 1989 Children Act sought to provide a balance in UK law between these competing perspectives by giving the courts an enhanced role in safeguarding the rights and safety of all the actors involved in legal interventions.

In recent decades and for a variety of reasons, there has been increased interest in the welfare and rights of children within childcare policy. First, the production of the United Nations Convention on the Rights of the Child in 1989 has enhanced the profile of children's rights issues amongst the media, pressure groups, professionals and politicians (see Franklin 2002). Second, the exponential growth of single-parent families and of other changes to family structure in advanced industrialized countries in the 1980s and 1990s has increased concern with the wider social implications of private family arrangements. Third, the early 1990s saw increased focus on the links between youth crime and family life (Goldson 2000). Such factors have made a once simplistic approach to child welfare, focused on the provision of extra resources and support, infinitely more complex. They have introduced into childcare debates concerns with the power and voice of children, with the role (and absence, in many cases) of fathers (Featherstone 2003) and with the extent to which the state should seek to promote specific family models or remain neutral as to family form.

Partly as a result of such increased complexity, a number of issues have come to dominate childcare policy. The first of these, related to what has been said above, is the adequacy of systems for detecting and dealing with child abuse. These have come in for repeated attention from government as cases of abuse both within families or private care arrangements (Laming 2003) and within the care system itself (e.g. Waterhouse 2000) have come to light. Second, there has been strong debate about the correct balance to be struck between the prevention of family problems through the provision of family support and dealing with such problems after they occur. Third, there has been debate about the extent to which government should support traditional family forms and power relationships through the tax and benefits system, and – a particularly contentious issue – through its approach to the legality of physical punishment of children by parents. Fourth, there has been debate about the adequacy of the care provided by the state itself, in view of a long record of poor outcomes (Utting 1997). Fifth, there has been a concerted attempt to reduce child poverty after a long-term increase in child poverty levels in the 1980s and 1990s.

All this activity indicates that childcare policy has become an increasingly high-profile area of government activity. In a wider context, this can partly be seen to result from the development of a 'social investment' strategy by governments in a number of countries (Lister 2003). This strategy places support for childcare at the centre of long-term social and economic goals. As part of such a strategy, measures for enforcing parental support for children sit easily alongside extra state support for day-time childcare provision that allows mothers to work and initiatives that are designed to provide extra help to disadvantaged children. In sum, a reorientation of the welfare state towards future economic competitiveness and social cohesion has meant that proposals for children and childcare have now become central to the appeal of political parties and to the actions of governments.

J.A. GODDARD
UNIVERSITY OF BRADFORD

References

Butler-Sloss, Lord Justice E. (1988) *Report of the Inquiry into Child Abuse in Cleveland 1987*, Cmnd 412, London.
Corby, B., Doig, A. and Roberts, V. (2001) *Public Inquiries into Abuse of Children in Residential Care*, London.
Featherstone, B. (2003) 'Taking fathers seriously', *British Journal of Social Work* 33: 239–54.
Fox Harding, L. (1997) *Perspectives on Child Care Policy*. Harlow.
Franklin, B. (ed.) (2002) *The New Handbook of Children's Rights: Comparative Policy and Practice*, London.
Goldson, B. (ed.) (2000) *The New Youth Justice*, Lyme Regis.
Hendrick, H. (2003) *Child Welfare: Historical Dimensions, Contemporary Debates*, Bristol.
Laming, Lord (2003) *The Victoria Climbié Inquiry: Report*, London.
Lister, R. (2003) 'Investing in citizen-workers of the future: Transformations in citizenship and the state under New Labour', *Social Policy and Administration* 37(5): 427–43.
Utting Report (1997) *People Like Us: The Report of the Review of the Safeguarding of Children*, London.
Waterhouse Tribunal (2000) *Report of the Tribunal of Enquiry into the Abuse of Children in Care in the Former County Council Areas of Gwynedd and Clwyd since 1974: Lost in Care*, London.

Further reading

Bradshaw, J. (ed.) (2002) *The Well-being of Children in the UK*, London.
Corby, B. (2000) *Child Abuse: Towards a Knowledge Base*, 2nd edn, Buckingham.
Foley, P., Roche, J. and Tucker, S. (2001) *Children in Society: Contemporary Theory, Policy and Practice*, Basingstoke.
Goldson, B., Lavallette, M. and McKechnie, J. (eds) (2002) *Children, Welfare and the State*, London.
Parton, N. (ed.) (1997) *Child Protection and Family Support*, London.
Pringle, K. (1998) *Children and Social Welfare in Europe*, Buckingham.

SEE ALSO: childhood; developmental psychology; life-span development

CHILDHOOD

For most periods of history and for most children in the world, childhood is *not* ideally cosy, protected, playful and free from adult responsibilities; in practice, a child's survival in hostile conditions is often the first challenge that the child faces (see Scheper-Hughes 1987). The UN Convention on the Rights of the Child 1976 accordingly sought to establish not 'the best' but progressive realization of the 'best possible' standards respecting the economic, social and cultural rights of children. However, the movement towards universal child and human rights reflects broadly Euro-American ideas about what it is to be a child or a person, and this raises questions about how we are to account for historical and cultural variation.

Philippe Ariès (1962 [1960]) argued that in Europe childhood began to be marked as a distinctive stage of life only in the thirteenth century. The conception of childhood altered radically in the seventeenth century with the rise of modern notions of the family and of the school, and again in the nineteenth century when children's physical and moral welfare became the focus of legislation. The modern world (and by implication the social sciences that are part of it) is 'obsessed by the physical, moral and sexual problems of childhood' (Aries 1962 [1960]: 411).

It cannot be sheer coincidence, then, that the most influential theorists in the history of psychology – Sigmund Freud and Jean Piaget – were concerned to understand childhood and how children come to be adults. Freud focused on sexual identification and the development of conscience. The child becomes a moral being via the control by guilt of sexual and aggressive impulses. Piaget (e.g. 1926, 1935) devoted his life to describing how the child cognitively constructs the concepts that allow for an effective adult engagement in the world, such as those of number, time, physical causality, measurement, etc.

Behaviourist psychologists of the 1950s and 1960s tried to show how children, like animals, are 'conditioned' to behave in certain ways through encounters with their environment, including other people, that yielded rewards and punishments. The increasing sophistication of biology-based studies of animal behaviour and cognitivist studies of humans throughout the 1960s and 1970s revealed difficulties with this type of learning theory, but the notion that children are 'conditioned' by their environment proved particularly congenial to sociologists and anthropologists in the 1950s, who were less concerned with the child as 'individual' than they were with the child as a member of a collectivity. For example, the anthropologist Margaret Mead, whose best-known works focus on childhood and adolescence, ascribed to cultural conditioning the fact that *what* children learn is culturally appropriate and *how* they learn is culturally mediated too (see e.g. Mead and Wolfenstein 1955). Data on child-rearing practices were also of special significance for those 'culture and personality' theorists who were interested in the cross-cultural applicability of psychoanalytic theory (see e.g. Whiting and Child 1953).

With the export of Piaget's ideas to the USA, however, and the increasing dominance of cognitivist explanations in psychology during the 1960s and 1970s, the idea of the child as conditioned by the environment or, more radically, as imitating adult behaviour, gave way to 'socialization' theories, according to which the child was understood to be actively engaged in knowledge processes.

Piaget was criticized by his Russian contemporary Vygotsky for failing to incorporate historical (i.e. sociocultural) parameters and social interaction in his account of childhood cognition (see e.g. Vygotsky 1962 [1934]). Others argued that Piaget did not recognize how extensive are a child's earliest cognitive abilities (see e.g. Smith *et al.* 1988), nor how early infants form a sense of an emergent self that actively shapes their interactions with others (e.g. Stern 1985). So, while the new cognitivism of the 1990s suggests that the majority of the child's abilities are given at birth (Mehler and Dupoux 1994), it is challenged by the neuroconstructivist approach. In this view, any given child's cognitive abilities are a function of its particular history and understood as 'self-organising emergent structures arising from the complex interactions between both organism and environment' (Elman *et al.* 1996: 113).

While psychological models of childhood long stressed the active and *transformative* nature of cognitive developmental processes, they have struggled to incorporate the idea that children's understanding is, always and from the very beginning of life, socially mediated. By contrast, in anthropology and sociology the child was regarded as a more or less passive receiver of collectively constituted, and adult, ideas. Since the 1980s, however, there have emerged a number of interdisciplinary approaches to the project of understanding children and childhood. They emphasize the idea of the child as an active producer as well as a product of the dynamic collective processes we characterize as 'history' (see e.g. Kessel and Siegel 1983; James and Prout 1992; Stein 1998).

Childhood is a relational category that situates children relative to infants, youths and adults, so its study requires an approach that examines not only children's lives and their ideas about themselves and the world, but also adult ideas about what it is possible for children to be and become. By the same token what is particular to adults' lives cannot be understood unless we take into account their histories as children. Children inevitably differentiate themselves from their parents and, in so doing, they establish historically specific forms of social relations that manifest at once both cultural continuity and cultural change. This approach directs attention to how children cognitively construct over time concepts that refer to domains that we have been used to think of as distinctively adult – kinship or political economy or religion (see e.g. Toren 1990). Under the stimulus of new theoretical approaches and with more sophisticated research about how children make sense of the world, the study of childhood in anthropology and sociology may come in time to have the same importance for theory in these disciplines as it has always had in psychology.

CHRISTINA TOREN
BRUNEL UNIVERSITY

References

Ariès, P. (1962 [1960]) *Centuries of Childhood*, London.

Elman, J.L., Bates, E.A., Johnson, M.H., Karmiloff-Smith, A., Parisi, D. and Plunkett, P. (1996) *Rethinking Innateness: A Connectionist Perspective on Development*, Cambridge, MA.

James, A. and Prout, A. (eds) (1992) *Constructing and Reconstructing Childhood*, London.

Kessel, F.S. and Siegel, A.W. (eds) (1983) *The Child and Other Cultural Inventions*, New York.

Mead, M. and Wolfenstein, M. (eds) (1955) *Childhood in Contemporary Culture*, Chicago.

Mehler, J. and Dupoux, E. (1994) *What Infants Know: The New Cognitive Science of Early Development*, Cambridge, MA.

Piaget, J. (1926) *The Child's Conception of the World*, London.

—— (1935) *The Moral Judgement of the Child*, New York.

Scheper-Hughes, N. (1987) *Child Survival: Anthropological Perspectives on the Treatment and Maltreatment of Children*, Dordrecht.

Smith, L.G., Sera, M. and Gattuso, B. (1988) 'The development of thinking', in R.J. Sternberg and E.E. Smith (eds) *The Psychology of Human Thought*, Cambridge, UK.

Stein, B. (ed.) (1998) *Intersubjective Communication and Emotion in Early Ontogeny*, Cambridge, UK.

Stern, D.N. (1985) *The Interpersonal World of the Infant*, New York.

Toren, C. (1990) *Making Sense of Hierarchy: Cognition as Social Process in Fiji*, London.

Vygotsky, L.S. (1962 [1934]) *Thought and Language*, Cambridge, MA.

Whiting, J.W.M. and Child, I.L. (1953) *Child Training and Personality: A Cross-Cultural Study*, New Haven, CT.

Further reading

Briggs, J.L. (1999) *Inuit Morality Play*, New Haven, CT.

James, A., Jenks, C. and Prout, A. (1998) *Theorizing Childhood*, Cambridge, UK.

Richards, M. and Light, P. (eds) (1986) *Children of Social Worlds*, Cambridge, MA.

Scheper-Hughes, N. and Sargent, C. (eds) (1998) *Small Wars: The Cultural Politics of Childhood*, Berkeley, CA.

Schieffelin, B.B. (1990) *The Give and Take of Everyday Life: Language Socialization of Kaluli Children*, Cambridge, UK.

Stafford, C. (1995) *The Roads of Chinese Childhood. Learning and Identification in Angang*, Cambridge, UK.

Toren, C. (1999) *Mind, Materiality and History: Explorations in Fijian Ethnography*, London.

SEE ALSO: adolescence; childcare; child development; developmental psychology; lifespan development

CHOMSKY, NOAM (1928–)

Noam Chomsky, language theoretician, philosopher, intellectual historian and social critic, is one of the most profound and influential thinkers of the modern period, and one of the few scientists whose works are widely read. An often repeated view is that 'judged in terms of the power, range, novelty and influence of his thought, [he] is arguably the most important intellectual alive' (*New York Times Book Review*, 25 February 1979).

After receiving a PhD in linguistics from the University of Pennsylvania in 1955, he joined the faculty at the Massachusetts Institute of Technology, where he was promoted to full professor in 1961, appointed to an endowed chair in 1966, and made Institute professor (one of a handful, most of them Nobel laureates) in 1976. Since the appearance in 1957 of his first published book, *Syntactic Structures*, he has been recognized as 'an eminent and revolutionary scholar in the field of linguistics', to quote from a representative blurb. Many of the most distinguished contemporary linguists were once his students, some of whom continue to find his work inspiring. (He has supervised close to one hundred doctoral dissertations to date.)

His most original contribution has been to open the way to the cognitive natural sciences, for which he has provided a model that is still without equal. (He received the Kyoto Prize for 'basic sciences' in 1988.) His specific model for human language, often referred to as (transformational) generative grammar, can be regarded as a kind of confluence of traditional, and long-forgotten, concerns of the study of language and mind (as in the work of Wilhelm von Humboldt or Otto Jespersen) and new understanding provided by the formal sciences in the late 1930s, specifically, recursive function theory, also known as the theory of computation. His rather unusual knowledge of philosophy, logic and mathematics also allowed him to make use of more sophisticated techniques in linguistics than were being used when he appeared on the scene (and to go on to develop, in the late 1950s, algebraic linguistics, a branch of abstract algebra that is now part of theoretical computer science).

However, his original theory of language led in due course (by 1980) to the principles-and-parameters model (greatly improved in his 'minimalist programme' of the early 1990s) and this new model – the first one ever to suggest a substantive solution to the fundamental problem of language acquisition – constitutes a radical break from the rich tradition of thousands of years of linguistic enquiry, which in a way cannot be said of early generative grammar. It is true that the entire (modern) generative grammar period appears to be in many ways a new era. In retrospect it is clear that it has brought with it quite significant changes and progress in the study of language. New areas of enquiry have been opened to serious investigation, leading to many insights and deeper understanding. Furthermore, the current rate of change and progress is rapid even by the standards of the 1960s, so that the generative grammar of the second decade of the twenty-first century may be as novel to us as present-day generative grammar would be to linguists of the not too distant past. If the thinking along the lines of the minimalist programme is anywhere near accurate, it might not be unreasonable to expect that 'a rich and exciting future lies ahead for the study of language and related disciplines', as Chomsky wrote in the mid-1990s.

One of the most important consequences of his technical work is that it provides what appears to be decisive evidence in support of epistemological rationalism, as he was quick to point out. It is no secret that Chomsky was greatly influenced by developments in philosophy from the very beginning, and that he turned to the serious study of the Cartesian tradition, which he was to revive and update, shortly after he made his revolutionary discoveries. It was these discoveries that made it possible for him to go well beyond the programmatic, non-specific insights of the Cartesians, and give substance, at long last, to central Cartesian claims, in the process reconstructing the enduring ideas of the first phase of the age of modern philosophy (a not always recognized antecedent of the cognitive revolution of the 1950s), on which Chomsky has shed much light as a very insightful intellectual historian.

For Chomsky, as for Descartes, there is no essential variation among humans (no 'degrees of humanness') apart from superficial physical aspects: a creature is either human or it is not. Racism, sexism and other inegalitarian tendencies are then a logical impossibility under this conception, if consistently applied. This conviction, which his technical linguistic work shores up to some extent, is at the root of his broader, more searching studies of human nature and society, and on the grounding of concepts of a social order in features of human nature concerning which empirical enquiry might provide some insight ('human nature' being the central notion in both of Chomsky's main endeavours). This is not to say that he, or anyone else, has been able to provide a specific model for the study of social structures, that is, a sort of 'universal grammar' (a new cognitive science) of possible forms of social interaction comparable in depth to the model he has provided for linguistic structures, something possible in principle for other cognitive domains, in his view (which provides an entirely new perspective on the humanities and the social sciences). Still, his social and political theory, which takes an 'instinct for freedom' and the associated urge for self-realization as our basic human need (as distinct from our merely animal needs) – drawing heavily on his superb sympathetic acquaintance with the modern history of social struggle and the ideals underlying it – does not lack inner coherence, is consistent with what is currently known, and compares favourably with any available alternative.

However, the bulk of Chomsky's 'non-professional' writings, which by now are voluminous, and of his numerous and well-attended talks, is devoted not to social and political theory but to a painstaking analysis of contemporary society, to which he brings the intellectual standards taken for granted in scrupulous and profound disciplines (in addition to a hard-to-match brilliance and just plain decency). Because of the broad range, the massive documentation and the incisiveness of this work he is widely recognized as the foremost critic of the foreign and domestic policies of the world's number one (and now only) superpower.

CARLOS P. OTERO
UNIVERSITY OF CALIFORNIA, LOS ANGELES

Further reading

Achbar, M. (ed.) (1994) *Manufacturing Consent: Noam Chomsky and the Media*, Montreal.
Anthony, L.M. and Hornstein, N. (eds) (2003) *Chomsky and His Critics*, Oxford.
Chomsky, N. (1986) *Knowledge of Language: Its Nature, Origin, and Use*, New York.
—— (1987) *The Chomsky Reader*, New York.
—— (1988) *Language and Problems of Knowledge*, Cambridge, MA.
—— (1993) *Year 501: The Conquest Continues*, Boston, MA.
—— (1995) *The Minimalist Program*, Cambridge, MA.
—— (1996) *Powers and Prospects: Reflections on Human Nature and the Social Order*, Boston.
—— (2000) *New Horizons in the Study of Language and Mind*, Cambridge, UK.
—— (2003) *Chomsky on Democracy and Education*, ed. C.P. Otero, London.
Epstein, S.D. and Hornstein, N. (1999) *Working Minimalism*, Cambridge, MA.
Jenkins, L. (2000) *Biolinguistics: Exploring the Biology of Language*, Cambridge, UK.
McGilvray, J. (1999) *Chomsky: Language, Mind, Politics*, Cambridge, UK.
Otero, C.P. (ed.) (1994) *Noam Chomsky: Critical Assessments*, 8 vols, London.
Smith, N. (1999) *Chomsky: Ideas and Ideals*, Cambridge, UK.
Uriagereka, J. (1998) *Rhyme and Reason: An Introduction to Minimalist Syntax*, Cambridge, MA.

CITIZENSHIP

Only a state, i.e. an internationally recognized territorial entity, can grant a person citizenship. One cannot be a citizen of an ethnic group, or of a nationality that is not organized as a state. However, a person does not have to live in a democratic state in order to qualify as a citizen. The old distinction between citizens (who belong to a republic) and subjects (who belong to a monarchy) became obsolete after democracy matured in states that retained a monarchical façade. And contemporary non-democratic states routinely term their inhabitants 'citizens'.

Citizenship is a legal status defined by each state. Rights and obligations are nowadays ascribed equally to all citizens, since it has become inexpedient to acknowledge the existence of second-class citizens, whether on the basis of place of birth or residence, property, gender, beliefs, behaviour, race or caste. 'Civil' rights protect their safety and their ability to act. Raymond Aron (1974) affirms that 'modern citizenship is defined by the Rights of Man', but ancient polities (e.g. the Roman Empire) emphasized liberties and procedural guarantees on behalf of their recognized members. In addition to these civil rights, other rights, again supposedly modern, are termed social rights or entitlements. These entitle the citizen to some level of well-being and of social (i.e. socially guaranteed and organized) security. It should not be forgotten, however, that ancient states had their own forms of entitlements. Rome famously had its *panem et circenses* (bread and circuses), but these were small-scale efforts when compared to the state socialism of some ancient empires in America or Asia. Moreover, civil rights, widely considered to be true prerequisites of democracy, have been viewed for centuries as 'natural' possessions of individuals, which had only to be protected from the state. (This is why they are often designated in negative terms. For example: 'Congress shall make no law...abridging the freedom of speech or of the press.') Social rights, in contrast, are popular aspirations that are not always enforceable, even where they are endorsed by the state, because of socioeconomic or ideological constraints. Westbrook therefore suggests that 'a civil right is thus defined in spite of ordinary politics; a social right is defined by the grace of ordinary politics' (1993: 341).

Traditional political philosophy focused on the just balance between the rights and duties of the citizenry. Contemporary theorists have argued that the social contract relates not to abstract individuals but incorporates specific human groups, especially those like the proletariat (nineteenth–twentieth centuries), or ethnic or religious minorities, or women (twentieth–twenty-first centuries). Such groups are said to require 're-cognition' and a period of preferential treatment before their members are in a position to enjoy full citizenship. However, a policy of 'differentiated citizenship' and negotiated inclusion skirts two contentious issues. The first must be decided by each state: Who is a legitimate member of the political community, to be endowed with the appropriate obligations and rights? The second issue has to be decided by each interest group, and must be resolved in the end by each individual, with all his or her overlapping group memberships. Shall we take part in a given political process, which may be democratic or otherwise, at the scale of a state or otherwise?

Citizenship, originally simply an indication of membership in a particular category of persons, has become enmeshed with the three most formidable ideological currents of modern times. Nationalism and democracy both advocate an active, dedicated citizenship. Nationalists, however, tend to reject the non-patriots. Democrats are in turn acutely suspicious of those who do not respect human rights or constitutional rules. Third, but not less important, citizenship has become bound up with the ideology of the welfare state in the third ideological current, which envisages a passive, consumerist citizenry, and which merges easily with the Hobbesian view of a profitable authority. These three conflicting ideologies are themselves internally divided on such issues as the relevance of ethnicity for the nation, and of majority rule for democracy. Because these ideological conflicts are grafted upon it, the juridical notion of citizenship is sure to remain a matter of urgent public debate for many years to come.

JEAN TOURNON
UNIVERSITY OF GRENOBLE

References

Aron, R. (1974) 'Is multi-national citizenship possible?' *Social Research* 16(4).
Westbrook, D.A. (1993) 'One among millions: An American perspective on citizenship in large polities', *Annales de Droit de Louvain* 2.

Further reading

Bellamy, R. (2000) 'Citizenship beyond the national state: The case for Europe', in N. O'Sullivan (ed.) *Political Theory in Transition*, London.
Bowden, B. (2003) 'The perils of global citizenship', *Citizenship Studies* 7(3).
Carens, J.H. (2000) *Culture, Citizenship and Community*, Oxford.
Etzioni, A. (1997) *The New Golden Rule*, London.
Faculté de Droit de Nantes (1993) *De la citoyenneté, notions et définitions*, Paris.
Habermas, J. (1992) 'Citizenship and national identity', *Praxis International* 12(1).
Kymlicka, W. (1995) *Multicultural Citizenship*, Oxford.
Magnette, P. (2001) *La citoyenneté*, Bruxelles.
Parekh, B. (2000) *Rethinking Multiculturalism: Cultural Diversity and Political Theory*, London.
Roche, M. (1992) *Rethinking Citizenship: Welfare, Ideology and Change in Modern Society*, Cambridge, UK.
Smith, R.M. (2003) *Stories of Peoplehood. The Politics and Morals of Political Memberships*, Cambridge, UK.
Taylor, C. and Gutman, A. (eds) (1992) *Multiculturalism and the Politics of Recognition*, Princeton, NJ.
Turner, B. and Hamilton, P. (eds) (1994) *Citizenship*, London.

SEE ALSO: civil society; democracy; representation, political; state; welfare state

CITY

Terms like the city, urban and urbanism relate to a wide range of phenomena, which have varied greatly through history and between world regions. Different disciplines develop their own perspectives towards urban phenomena: there is an urban anthropology, an urban economics, an urban geography, an urban sociology, etc. Conceptions of the urban community are not congruent between different languages: the English town/city distinction does not have direct counterparts even in closely related languages.

We may regard a reasonably large and permanent concentration of people within a limited territory as the common characteristic of all cities and other urban places. Scholarship has focused on the role of such communities within the wider society, and on the particular characteristics of their internal life.

The beginnings of urbanism are now usually identified with a broad type of ritual-political centre that developed apparently independently in six areas: Mesopotamia, the Nile and Indus Valleys, North China, Mesoamerica, the Andes, and Yorubaland in West Africa (Wheatley 1971). In these centres divine monarchs and priesthoods, with a corps of officials and guards, controlled the peasants of the surrounding region and extracted a surplus from them. What may have begun as modest tribal shrines were elaborated as complexes of monumental architecture: temples, pyramids, palaces, terraces and courts. We find here the early history not only of the city, but also of civilization and the state. The Yoruba towns, last of the kind to emerge independently, but the only ones still existing as ongoing concerns in a form at all resembling the original, have not exhibited the complexity of architecture and other technology of the earlier and more famous cases but show similarities of social form.

The early centres were urban especially through their capacity to organize the countryside around them, evidently mostly through symbolic control. Yet they might have small residential populations, and most of the people under their rule came to them only for major ritual events. In this sense, one may see the centres as marginally urban. Over time, however, warfare and other factors tended to lead to more secular forms of political control, as well as to greater population concentrations at the centres themselves. The same development can be discerned in European antiquity. In *La Cité antique* (1864) (*The Ancient City*), Fustel de Coulanges has described its urban beginnings as once more a complex of ritual politics, but at the height of their power, the cities of the Graeco-Roman world had elites of landowners and warriors, in control of enormous slave workforces.

These were cities of power, and cities of consumers. Commerce and industry played a minor part within them. But the ancient empires and their cities would decline, and in the Middle Ages a new urbanism came into being in Western Europe. It was mostly commercially based, and with business as the dominant element the cities developed a considerable autonomy and independence from the feudal social structures surrounding them. The Belgian historian Henri Pirenne is one of the scholars who has been concerned with these medieval European cities. Another is Max Weber, who developed an ideal type in *The City* (1958 [1921]): an urban community must have a market as its central institution, but also a fortification, an at least partially autonomous administrative and legal system, and a form of association reflecting the particular features of urban life (the guild was a conspicuous example).

This frequently quoted formulation constituted a very restrictive definition of urbanism. The distinctiveness of the town in relation to the surrounding countryside is clear, but the institutional apparatus belonged in a particular phase of European history. Weber also contrasted this occidental city with its oriental counterparts. The latter were more internally fragmented and at the same time more closely integrated into imperial administrations. As cities of power rather than of commerce, often with some emphasis on the symbolic expression of pre-eminence, the great urban centres of the East as seen by early European travellers may appear more related to the first urban forms.

Industrialism, of course, has given shape to yet other kinds of cities. One important account of the misery of the huge new concentrations of labouring people in rapidly growing cities is Friedrich Engels's in *The Condition of the Working Class in England* (1969 [1845]), based on his experience in Manchester. Another classic set of studies of urban life under industrialism was carried out by the Chicago School of sociologists – Robert E. Park, Louis Wirth and others – in the 1920s and 1930s. The Chicago sociologists drew attention to the spatial organization of the industrial city and its apparently orderly changes, and thus launched an 'urban ecology'. At the same time, they located a series of smaller-scale ethnographies of particular 'natural areas' within the wider spatial order. Thus they simultaneously pioneered the study of many topics now central to urban anthropology – ethnic quarters, youth gangs, occupations, deviant groups and public places.

In a well-known formulation, Louis Wirth (1938) described urban social contacts as 'impersonal, superficial, transitory, and segmental', and the Chicago sociologists were generally pessimistic about the possibilities of achieving a satisfying human life under urban conditions, as a great many other thinkers have also been. (Yet one celebrates the contribution of urbanism to intellectual life.) On the whole, they concerned themselves more with the internal characteristics of the city, rather than with its place in society. This probably contributed to their tendency to generalize about urbanism on the basis of their Chicago experience, instead of emphasizing that this city was a product of a particular US context, including expansive industrial capitalism as well as ethnic diversity in a somewhat unsettled state.

Partly in response to such generalizations, a considerable body of ethnographically inclined research has emphasized the great variety of forms of life that can be found under urban conditions, and not least the fact that informal social organization may indeed be quite different from the type summarized by Wirth's phrase. William F. Whyte's *Street Corner Society* (1943), describing a close-knit Italian American neighbourhood in Boston, was a noteworthy early study in this vein, and it is by now generally understood that while city life may have its share of impersonality and anonymity, it also contains a web of friendship, kinship and occupational linkages: in part, it may be a mosaic of 'urban villages'. With the growth of new subcultures and lifestyles, and a new appreciation for cultural diversity in the city, urban ethnography has been further revitalized in North America and Europe, becoming at the same time more sensitive to wider contexts of power and history (Sanjek 1998).

Similar perspectives have also been important in the study of urbanism in what became known, in the latter half of the twentieth century, as the Third World. Especially as the process of urbanization accelerated greatly in Africa, Asia and Latin America, there was first a tendency by commentators to emphasize 'disorganization', 'detribalization' and the weakening of traditional social ties generally. Later studies have tended to point to the security still provided by kinship and ethnicity, the economic and political uses to which they may be put, and the ability of urbanites to evolve new adaptations, even without significant economic means. Research on squatter settlements, especially in Latin American cities, thus often made the point that such 'informal housing' is often superior in its efficiency to large-scale public housing projects, and a wave of studies of the 'informal sector' of the urban economy (begun by Hart 1973) showed that a very large number of people in Third World urban centres make some kind of living through self-employment or less formal employment arrangements, without occupational training in formal educational structures, and with very limited material resources. This sector includes artisans, petty traders, rickshaw drivers, ice cream vendors, shoe shiners, truck pushers and a multitude of other more or less legitimate ways of supporting oneself, as well as a variety of illicit occupations.

One must not exaggerate the capacity of informal modes of organization to solve the problems of urban living, however, in Third World countries or elsewhere, and the debate on such issues is not yet concluded. What is clear is that generalizations about cities and city life must almost always be qualified. There are in fact a great many types of urban centres, each city has many kinds of inhabitants, and every urbanite engages in social contacts and activities of multiple sorts.

This diversity obviously depends to a great extent on the varying relationships between cities and society. Several different research perspectives thus concern themselves with setting urban centres in a wider context. In economic geography and regional science, different models have been developed to deal with the spatial distribution of urban functions within larger areas. Central place theory, developed by Walter Christaller (1933) in the 1930s, was a prominent early example, dealing with the location of commercial, administrative and transport centres. Geographers have also concerned themselves with the problem of classifying cities according to societal functions, and analysing their internal structure as determined by these functions. Among early well-known classifications, for example, is one showing eight types of urban communities in the USA: retail, wholesale, manufacturing, mining, transport, resort and retirement, university, and diversified. Since the 1960s, one strong interdisciplinary trend was to view urban processes especially in Western Europe and North America within the framework of the political economy of industrial capitalism. This trend, partially under Marxist inspiration, related urbanism more closely to issues of class, power and social movements (Castells 1977).

In the years since Max Weber drew his contrast between occidental and oriental cities, there have also been numerous further attempts at delineating various regional urban types, such as the Middle Eastern City or the Latin-American City. Cultural historians and other area specialists have played an important part in evolving such constructs, and they have not always been guided by a desire to arrive at a comprehensive comparative understanding of world urbanism. Because of colonialism and other kinds of Western expansion, of course, the urban forms of different regions have not all been equally autonomous in their development. Often they must be seen within the context of international centre–periphery relationships. In Africa, Asia and Latin America the large port cities that grew with Western domination – Dakar, Mumbai, Calcutta, Shanghai, Buenos Aires and others – are an example of this. A recurrent pattern in the colonial and postcolonial Third World has also been the growth of 'primate cities', which through a strong concentration of the commercial, administrative, industrial, cultural and other functions of a country or a territory become much larger and more important than any other urban centre there. Yet colonialism has also created other kinds of urban communities – mining towns, small administrative centres, 'hill stations' for resort purposes, and so forth – and its products may have coexisted with more indigenous urban traditions. Due to such variations, it would seem wiser to look at regional forms of urbanism not always as single types but as typologies in themselves, generated through an interplay of international influences and local forces of social and spatial differentiation.

As for present and future changes in urbanism, these depend in complex ways on demographic, economic, technological and other factors. The twentieth century witnessed urban growth on an unprecedented scale. 'Megalopolis' and 'conurbation' are new concepts applicable to phenomena of both the Western and the non-Western world. With increasing globalization, the growing economic and cultural importance of 'world cities' has drawn more attention since the 1980s (Sassen 2000 [1991]). Yet in some ways, new modes of transport and communication make human beings less dependent on crowding themselves in limited spaces. 'Counter-urbanization' is thus another modern phenomenon.

ULF HANNERZ
STOCKHOLM UNIVERSITY

References

Castells, M. (1977) *The Urban Question*, London.
Christaller, W. (1933) *Central Places in Southern Germany*, Englewood Cliffs, NJ.
Engels, F. (1969 [1845]) *The Condition of the Working Class in England*, London.
Fustel de Coulanges, N.D. (n.d. [1864]) *The Ancient City*, Garden City, NY (original French edn, *La Cité antique*, Paris).
Hart, K. (1973) 'Informal income opportunities and urban employment in Ghana', *Journal of Modern African Studies* 11.
Sanjek, R. (1998) *The Future of Us All*, Ithaca, NY.
Sassen, S. (2000 [1991]) *The Global City*, Princeton, NJ.
Weber, M. (1958 [1921]) *The City*, New York.
Wheatley, P. (1971) *The Pivot of the Four Quarters*, Edinburgh.
Whyte, W.F. (1943) *Street Corner Society*, Chicago.
Wirth, L. (1938) 'Urbanism as a way of life', *American Journal of Sociology* 44.

CIVIL SOCIETY

This is an old concept in social and political thought that has recently been revived, especially in Eastern Europe but also in the West. Traditionally, up to the eighteenth century, it was a more or less literal translation of the Roman *societas civilis* and, behind that, the Greek *koinónia politiké*. It was synonymous, that is, with the state or 'political society'. When Locke spoke of 'civil government', or Kant of *bürgerliche Gesellschaft*, or Rousseau of *état civil*, they all meant simply the state, seen as encompassing – like the Greek *polis* – the whole realm of the political. Civil society was the arena of the politically active citizen. It also carried the sense of a 'civilized' society, one that ordered its relations according to a system of laws rather than the autocratic whim of a despot.

The connection of citizenship with civil society was never entirely lost. It forms part of the association that lends its appeal to more recent revivals of the concept. But there was a decisive innovation in the second half of the eighteenth century that broke the historic equation of civil society and the state. British social thought was especially influential in this. In the writings of John Locke and Tom Paine, Adam Smith and

Adam Ferguson, there was elaborated the idea of a sphere of society distinct from the state and with forms and principles of its own. The growth of the new science of political economy – again largely a British achievement – was particularly important in establishing this distinction. Most of these writers continued to use the term civil society in its classical sense, as in Adam Ferguson's *Essay on the History of Civil Society* (1966 [1767]), but what they were in fact doing was making the analytical distinction that was soon to transform the meaning of the concept.

It is to Hegel that we owe the modern meaning of the concept of civil society. In the *Philosophy of Right* (1958 [1821]), civil society is the sphere of ethical life interposed between the family and the state. Following the British economists, Hegel sees the content of civil society as largely determined by the free play of economic forces and individual self-seeking. But civil society also includes social and civic institutions that inhibit and regulate economic life, leading by the ineluctable process of education to the rational life of the state. So the particularity of civil society passes over into the universality of the state.

Marx, though acknowledging his debt to Hegel, narrowed the concept of civil society to make it equivalent simply to the autonomous realm of private property and market relations. 'The anatomy of civil society,' Marx said, 'is to be sought in political economy.' This restriction threatened its usefulness. What need was there for the concept of civil society when the economy or simply 'society' – seen as the effective content of the state and political life generally – supplied its principal terms? In his later writings Marx himself dropped the term, preferring instead the simple dichotomy 'society–state'. Other writers too, and not only those influenced by Marx, found less and less reason to retain the concept of civil society. The 'political society' of Alexis de Tocqueville's *Democracy in America* (1835–40) recalled the earlier sense of civil society as education for citizenship; but Tocqueville's example did little to revive the fortunes of what was increasingly regarded as an outmoded term. In the second half of the nineteenth century 'civil society' fell into disuse.

It was left to Antonio Gramsci, in the writing gathered together as the *Prison Notebooks* (1971 [1929–35]), to rescue the concept in the early part of the twentieth century. Gramsci, while retaining a basic Marxist orientation, went back to Hegel to revitalize the concept. Indeed he went further than Hegel in detaching civil society from the economy and allocating it instead to the state. Civil society is that part of the state concerned not with coercion or formal rule but with the manufacture of consent. It is the sphere of 'cultural politics'. The institutions of civil society are the Church, schools, trade unions and other organizations through which the ruling class exercises hegemony over society. By the same token it is also the arena where that hegemony is challengeable. In the radical decades of the 1960s and 1970s, it was Gramsci's concept of civil society that found favour with those who attempted to oppose the ruling structures of society not by direct political confrontation but by waging a kind of cultural guerrilla warfare. Culture and education were the spheres where hegemony would be contested, and ended.

New life was also breathed into the concept by the swift-moving changes in Central and Eastern Europe in the late 1970s and 1980s. Dissidents in the region turned to the concept of civil society as a weapon against the all-encompassing claims of the totalitarian state. The example of Solidarity in Poland suggested a model of opposition and regeneration that avoided suicidal confrontation with the state by building up the institutions of civil society as a 'parallel society'. In the wake of the successful revolutions of 1989 throughout the region, the concept of civil society gained immensely in popularity. To many intellectuals it carried the promise of a privileged route to the post-communist, pluralist society, though they were vague about the details. Western intellectuals too were enthused anew with the concept. For them it suggested a new perspective on old questions of democracy and participation, in societies where these practices seemed to have become moribund.

Civil society, it is clear, has renewed its appeal. As in the eighteenth century, we seem to feel once more the need to define and distinguish a sphere of society that is separate from the state. Citizenship appears to depend for its exercise on active participation in non-state institutions, as the necessary basis for participation in formal political institutions. This was Tocqueville's point about American democracy; it is a lesson that the rest of the world now seems very anxious to take to heart. The question remains whether 'civil society' will simply be a rallying cry and a slogan, or whether it will be given sufficient substance to help in the creation of the concrete institutions needed to realize its goals.

KRISHAN KUMAR
UNIVERSITY OF VIRGINIA

References

Ferguson, A. (1966 [1767]) *Essay on the History of Civil Society*, ed. D. Forbes, Edinburgh.
Gramsci, A. (1971 [1929–35]) *Selections from Prison Notebooks*, trans. Q. Hoare and G. Nowell Smith, London (original edn, *Quaderni del Carcere*, 6 vols, Turin).
Hegel, G.W.F. (1958 [1821]) *Philosophy of Right*, trans. T.W. Knox, Oxford.
Tocqueville, A. de (1835–40) *Democracy in America*, ed. J.P. Mayer, trans. G. Lawrence, 2 vols, New York.

Further reading

Arato, A. and Cohen, J. (1992) *Civil Society and Democratic Theory*, Cambridge, MA.
Fullinwider, R.K. (ed.) (1999) *Civil Society, Democracy, and Civic Renewal*, Lanham, MD.
Hall, J.A. (ed.) (1995) *Civil Society: Theory, History, Comparison*, Cambridge.
Keane, J. (ed.) (1988) *Civil Society and the State*, London.
Kumar, K. (2001) *1989: Revolutionary Ideas and Ideals*, Minneapolis, MN.

SEE ALSO: citizenship; democracy; public sphere; state

CLASS, SOCIAL

In the course of the first three decades of the nineteenth century the term 'class' gradually replaced estates, ranks and orders as the major word used to denote divisions within society. The change of vocabulary reflected the diminishing significance of rank and ascribed or inherited qualities in general, and the growing importance of possessions and income among the determinants of the social position. Taken over by social theory from its original context of political debate, class came to refer to large categories of population, distinct from other categories in respect of wealth and related social position, deriving their distinctive status mainly from their location in the production and distribution of social wealth, sharing accordingly in distinctive interests either opposing or complementing other group interests, and consequently displaying a tendency to a group – distinctive political, cultural and social attitudes and behaviour. At the very early stage of the debate, class was given a pronounced economic meaning, arguably under the influence of David Ricardo, who identified the social category of labourers with the economic category of labour, understood as one of the factors of capitalist production. Political economists of the 'Ricardian socialist' school (William Thompson (1824), Thomas Hodgskin (1825) and others) developed Ricardo's suggestions into a comprehensive economic theory of class division, which was then adopted and elaborated upon by Karl Marx.

The many usages of class in social scientific theory and research are invariably influenced by Marx's magisterial vision of class division as, simultaneously, the principal source of social dynamics and the main principle of its interpretation. Even if historiosophic aspects of Marx's class theory (all history is a history of class struggle; social change occurs through class revolutions; the conflict between capitalists and workers, arising from the capitalist form of production, is bound to lead to a proletarian revolution and to a new, socialist form of production) are questioned or rejected, the enduring interest in class and, indeed, the unfaltering centrality of the category of class in social scientific discourse are due to Marx-inspired belief in a high predictive and explanatory value of (primarily economic) class in respect of both individual and collective behaviour.

The resilience to this latter aspect of Marx's theoretical legacy is in no small part due to its overall harmony with the dominant liberal world-view, which interprets individual action as, by and large, rational pursuit of interest, and assigns to 'gain' the role of the central motive of human conduct. The continuous popularity of Marx's class theory has been helped by the incorporation of these tacit premises of common sense and the resulting strategy of interpreting social antagonisms as conflicts of economic interests (that is, incompatibility of goals rationally pursued by various groups differently located within the economic process).

Defining classes as large groups united by their common location within the economic process and aspiring, against efforts of other classes, to an increased share of the surplus product, was a habit firmly established inside the classic political economy before Marx. The fateful contribution of Marx consisted in the reading into the class conflict of another dimension – the struggle for the management of social surplus. Since, within the capitalist order, the right to the surplus was the prerogative of the managers of the productive process, rational effort to amplify a class share in the surplus product must be aimed at the management of production; since, again in the capitalist system, the right to manage productive process as a prerogative of the owners of capital (or means of production), a class barred from access to the surplus can defy its deprivation only through dissociating the right to manage from the right of ownership – through the expropriation of the owners of the capital. In the succession of historical forms of class struggle, the conflict between capitalists and their workers was thus presented by Marx as the modern equivalent of *both* the conflict between precapitalist landlords and their serfs *and* the conflict between landowning aristocracy and industry-owning capitalists. Indeed, the specifically Marxist approach to class analysis of industrial society consists in conflating the two dimensions of class conflict and the tendency to interpret the first (the redistribution of surplus) as an immature manifestation, or an early stage, of the second (the management of the production of surplus).

In consequence, the Marx-inspired study of class and class conflict focuses its attention on the combat between owners of capital and industrial workers. More specifically, in this conflict, considered central for the current historical era, this study is interested in the progression of industrial workers from their objective situation as a factor in the process of capitalist production ('class in itself') to the acquisition of a consciousness of their situation and, finally, to the appropriation of a political strategy aimed at radically overcoming their subordination to capital by abolishing the capitalist mode of production itself ('class for itself').

For the Marx-inspired class theory, therefore, the major difficulty arises from the evident failure of industrial workers to make any notable advance along the line of anticipated progression. A century and a half after the essential historiosophical assumptions of Marx's class theory had been made public in the *Communist Manifesto* (1980 [1848]), the workers of the industrialized world seem to come nowhere near the threshold of the socialist transformation of society.

The gap between predictions generated by class theory and the actual tendency of historical development was brought into sharp relief in the wake of the October Revolution in Russia in 1917: a revolution claiming to fulfil the Marxist promise of socialist transformation occurred in a society little advanced in its capitalist development, while all the timid attempts at socialist revolution in truly capitalist countries with a large industrial working population failed. What, from the theoretical perspective, appeared a bewildering incongruity of historical praxis, triggered off recurring attempts among Marxist thinkers to provide auxiliary theories accounting for the failure of the anticipated historical tendency to materialize.

The first, and tone-setter, in the long chain of such auxiliary theories was Lukács's (1967 [1923]) 'false consciousness' theory. Lukács distinguished 'consciousness of class' from 'class consciousness'; the first was the empirically ascertainable state of ideas and motives of the class members arising from the experience accessible within their daily business of life, while the second could be arrived at only through a bird's-eye survey of the total situation of the society, and a rational study of the totality of the information related to the social system (Lukács was here influenced by Weber's method of 'ideal types'). In Lukács's view, there was no automatic passage from the first to the second: the information necessary to construct ideal-typical 'class consciousness' was not available within the individual experience constrained by the tasks of daily survival. The empirical consciousness of class displayed a tendency, therefore, to remain a 'false consciousness', misguided and misled as it were by the narrow horizons of individual experience – unless assisted by scientific analysis filtered into the minds of the workers through the channels of their political organizations. In Lukács's subtle revision of the original model, the passage from 'class in itself' to 'class for itself', far from being an automatic process guaranteed by the logic of capitalist economy, has now become a matter of ideological struggle. Without such battle of ideas the passage would not be probable, let alone inevitable.

Numerous suggestions have been made in the sociological literature since the mid-1960s to render the discrepancy between the objective deprivation of the workers, and the apparent lack of radical opposition to the system responsible for it, amenable to empirical study, leading eventually to the location of factors either furthering the persistence of deprivation or prompting opposition to it. An early attempt was made by Dahrendorf (1959) to analyse the problem in terms of the passage from 'quasi-groups', united only by 'latent interests', to 'interest groups', whose consciousness of the common fate renders their interests 'manifest'. Sharing of latent interests is a necessary, but insufficient, condition of the passage; the latter demands that a number of additional factors must be present. Developing this insight, Morris and Murphy (1966) suggested that class consciousness should be seen as 'a processual emergent', and that from 'no perception of status difference' to a 'behaviour undertaken on behalf of the stratum interests and ideology' lead a number of stages, each subject to a somewhat different set of factors. In a highly influential collective study of *The Black-Coated Worker*, Lockwood (1958) departed from the 'stages' or 'progression' framework heretofore dominant in post-Marxian study of class consciousness and proposed that depending on the technologically determined type of employment, presence or absence of communal living and other cultural aspects of the mode of life, different types of consciousness ('traditional', 'deferential' or 'privatized') may develop among workers, each acquiring a degree of permanence grounded in its congruence with specific conditions of life. The early study of class consciousness by Parkin (1974) prompted similar conclusions: Parkin singled out, as an attitudinal type most likely to arise from life experience of the workers, a 'subordinate' ideology, taking either a 'deferential' or 'aspirational' form, but in both cases inducing the workers to make peace with the system responsible for their subordinate position.

These auxiliary theories all assume that the life situation of the workers within the capitalist mode of production necessarily produces an anti-capitalist tendency in their consciousness. It is this assumption, and this assumption only, which renders the evident absence of anti-capitalist action problematic and gives both meaning and urgency to the study of factors responsible for the empirical departure from a theoretically grounded expectation.

Not so in the case of another large family of class theories, tracing its origin to Max Weber. Weber revised Marx's theory of class in three important respects. First, having accepted Marx's notion of class as a category articulated first and foremost within the network of economic relations, he denied to these relations the determining role in respect of the articulation of society on its sociocultural and political planes. Status groups (the nearest equivalent of the Marxist idea of class consciousness) as well as political groupings (the nearest equivalent of the Marxist idea of class action) are categories in their own right, parallel to but not necessarily overlapping with economically determined classes, and subject to their own constitutive rules and developmental logic. In short, Weber denied that economic divisions were necessarily mirrored in the cultural and political articulation of the society. Then, having related class, as an economic phenomenon, to the market (specifically, to the chances of access to marketable goods), Weber questioned the possibility of determining a priori which of the many conflicts of interests that the market may generate at various times should be assigned a paramount role. And in contrast to Marx, Weber argued that interests vary with respect to different goods and market chances. Consequently they divide the population exposed to the market in more than one way, each individual belonging in principle to a number of classes whose boundaries need not overlap. (The concept of 'housing classes', advanced by Rex (1967), is a good example of a category of economic classes articulated in relation to just one, though highly important, marketable commodity.) The relative importance attached by a given individual to each of the classes to which they belong is not, therefore, determined in advance. It may change, depending on the structure of the market situation, and no one class can be credited in advance with a capacity to command an overwhelming allegiance, displacing all other classes as the major determinant of action.

Weber's insight into the multiplicity of classes and the role of the market in their articulation has been applied, particularly by British sociologists, in a novel analysis of the self-perception of classes and their responses to class inequality. Theoretical models emerging from these analyses refuse to be constrained by the idea of a structurally assigned class consciousness organizing the field of class attitudes and opinions, and instead attempt to gear themselves, with some success, to the empirically accessible evidence of actual ideologies, policies and actions of labour. Among these developments two are perhaps most seminal. One is W.G. Runciman's (1966) concept of 'relative deprivation' (akin to Moore's concept of 'outraged justice'), according to which groups, in their effort to assess their own social position, tend to 'compare with comparable' only: that is, they do not perceive as inequality, at least not as an 'unjust' inequality, the differences between their situation and that of groups distant on the scale of possessions – but they keenly guard their parity with groups they consider their equals, and are goaded into collective action when overtaken by those occupying a lower rung of the ladder. A somewhat similar analysis of class conflicts has been advanced by Parkin (1979) in his later study, drawing on the little used concept of 'closure', introduced but left largely undeveloped by Weber. According to Parkin, the mechanism of class behaviour can best be understood in terms of a tendency to preserve, and if possible enhance, whatever privileged access to coveted market commodities a given class may possess. Subject to this tendency, rational action would consist in the policy of either 'closure by exclusion' (to prevent dilution of the privilege by an influx of those below), or 'closure by usurpation' (to acquire a share in the privileges of those above). In the light of both analyses, organized labour's notorious lack of concern with the extremes of the social distribution of surplus, the paramount importance attached in the practice of trade unions to the preservation of 'differentials', or the puzzling indifference of the same unions to the conditions of the unemployed poor (as distinct from the defence of members' jobs), are all manifestations of a sociological regularity, rather than aberrations calling for special explanations in terms of unusual factors.

The US reception of Weberian ideas pointed in a somewhat different direction. It was guided by the Weberian image of the essential multidimensionality of social differentiation, and was concerned above all with the investigation of correlation (or lack of correlation) between wealth, prestige and influence. In practice most US sociology (particularly until the 1960s) tended to assign a central role to the dimension of prestige (as exemplified by the widespread studies of social deference in relation to occupations). In the context of these practices, however, the term 'class' was employed but rarely (when used outside the Weberian current, for example by Warner or Centers, the term was given a

primarily psychological meaning). The specifically US approaches to the question of socially induced inequality are not an exact equivalent (or an alternative to) class theory, and are better analysed in their own framework, as theories of stratification (based on the master-image of gradation, rather than division).

As for class theory proper, both post-Marxian and post-Weberian approaches remain faithful to the ground premises articulated early in the nineteenth century: class is first and foremost an economic phenomenon, and class conflict is above all about the defence or the improvement of economic position, that is, of the share in the distribution of social surplus. One can say that the discursive formation of class has been shaped in its present form in the period of reinterpretation, in economic terms, of social conflicts spanning the course of West European history between the French Revolution and the 'Spring of Nation' of 1848. It was only quite recently that the rethinking of the class model of society has developed sufficiently to put in question the very premises on which the discourse of class is grounded. One of the important lines of questioning comes from the work of Foucault (1980), which revealed a close association of the modern social system, not so much with the invention of machine technology or the spread of the capitalist form of labour, as with the establishment of a new type of 'disciplinary' power, aimed directly at the control of the human body and using surveillance as its main method. From this perspective the intense social conflicts of the early nineteenth century, later interpreted as manifestations of the inchoate labour movement, are seen as the last stage of the defensive struggle against new forms of controlling power; while the economically oriented organizations of factory workers, portrayed within class theory as specimens of a mature labour movement, are seen as a product of displacing the original conflict, centred around control, on to the field of distribution.

Whatever the view of the applicability of class theory to the understanding of the past two centuries, other doubts are raised about its usefulness in the study of the current stage in social development. Habermas (1978 [1973]), Offé (1964), Gorz (1982) and Touraine (1971) among others drew attention, each in a slightly different way, to the rapidly shrinking size of the industrial labour force, to the diminishing role of bargaining between owners of capital and industrial workers in organizing the distribution of surplus, and to the growing mediation and, indeed, initiative of the state in reproducing the essential conditions of the social production of surplus. In view of these developments, it is increasingly difficult to maintain that class membership remains a major key to the mechanism of reproduction of societally inflicted deprivations (and, more generally, social differentiation as such) or, for that matter, a major explanatory variable in the study of individual and group behaviour. Thus far, however, no alternative concept of similar comprehensiveness and cogency has been proposed to replace class in the description and interpretation of socially produced inequality.

Some sociologists have attempted to replace class as the overriding determinant of identity with other criteria, notably gender, ethnicity, race or culture. On the whole, however, contemporary sociologists are not inclined to accept that one dimension of stratification subsumes all others. Identity is generally treated as multidimensional, and the ability of individuals to construct and deconstruct their social identities is acknowledged. Indeed, the degree to which this freedom is enjoyed may be seen as the most salient element in defining social status. The wider social categories, previously treated as given, are now also analysed as the products of human agency. Moreover, no principle of division or stratification is believed to apply to all members of a society. The notion of the underclass, for example, tacitly suggests that a part of the population is excluded from the 'class system'.

ZYGMUNT BAUMAN
UNIVERSITY OF LEEDS

References

Dahrendorf, R. (1959) *Class and Conflict in Industrial Society*, London.
Foucault, M. (1980) *Power and Knowledge*, ed. C. Gordon, Brighton.
Gorz, A. (1982) *Farewell to the Working Class*, London.
Habermas, J. (1978 [1973]) *Legitimation Crisis*, London.
Hodgskin, T. (1825) *Labour Defended against the Claims of Capital*, London.
Lockwood, D. (1958) *The Black-Coated Worker*, London.
Lukács, G. (1967 [1923]) *History and Class Consciousness*, London.
Marx, K. (1980 [1848]) *Communist Manifesto*, London.
Morris, R.T. and Murphy, R.J. (1966) 'A paradigm for the study of class consciousness', *Sociology and Social Research* 50 (April): 297–313.
Offé, K. (1964) 'Political authority and class structures', in D. Senghaas (ed.) *Politikwissenschaft*, Frankfurt.
Parkin, F. (1974) *Class Inequality and Political Order*, London.
—— (1979) *Marxism and Class Theory*, London.
Rex, J. (1967) *Race, Community and Conflict*, Oxford.
Runciman, W.G. (1966) *Relative Deprivation and Social Justice*, London.
Thompson, W. (1824) *An Inquiry into the Principles of the Distribution of Wealth Most Conducive to Human Happiness*, London.
Touraine, A. (1971) *The Post-Industrial Society*, New York.

Further reading

Argyle, M. (1994) *The Psychology of Social Class*, London.
Bottomore, T. (1965) *Classes in Modern Society*, London.
Giddens, A. (1973) *Class Structure of the Advanced Societies*, London.
Lasch, S. and Friedman, J. (eds) (1992) *Modernity and Identity*, Oxford.
Wright, E.O. (1996) *Class Counts: Comparative Studies in Class Analysis*, Cambridge, UK.

SEE ALSO: deprivation and relative deprivation; equality; Marx's theory of history and society; stratification; Weber

CLASSICAL ECONOMICS

The term 'classical economics', although sometimes given the rather broader meaning of any economics which is not Keynesian, is generally taken to refer to the body of economic ideas stemming from the work of David Hume, whose most important work was published in 1752, and Adam Smith, whose great *Wealth of Nations* was published in 1776. These ideas came to dominate economics particularly, but far from exclusively, in Britain throughout the last quarter of the eighteenth and the first three-quarters of the nineteenth century.

Hume's contributions principally concerned money and the balance of payments. But Smith's work is a virtual compendium of economics, focusing on the key question of economic growth, and covering division of labour, distribution, capital accumulation, trade and colonial policy, and public finance. Among their successors was T.R. Malthus; though chiefly famous for his writings on population, he covered the whole field of economic enquiry (Malthus 1820). A major impetus to the development of classical economics was provided by David Ricardo (1951–73). He read Smith's work critically and from it constructed a 'model' that, unlike Smith's work, produced fairly clear and definite predictions. Ricardo succeeded initially in attracting disciples, notably J. Mill (1821–6; see also Winch 1966) and – though he later drifted away from Ricardo's influence – J.R. McCulloch (1825) as well as Thomas De Quincey. But his influence waned after his death and the work of J. Mill's son, J.S. Mill (1848, 1963–85), is much closer to Smith in range, reliance upon empirical material and the avoidance of precise predictions.

Classical economics covered the whole field of economic enquiry, but with an emphasis on questions dealing with large aggregates – economic growth, international trade, monetary economics and public finance – rather than with the analysis of the behaviour of the maximizing individual which came to be of dominant interest after 1870. (In the field of value theory, in particular, the classical economists generally made do with various sorts of production theories emphasizing, in varying degrees, the importance of labour cost in total cost.) At the same time a fundamental premise lying behind the analysis of aggregates, and stemming from Smith, was that individuals were motivated by the pursuit of self-interest, and that their pursuit had to be limited by a framework of law, religion and custom, to ensure coincidence of private and social interest. This in turn meant that in the field of economic policy classical economics, while predisposed against government interference (partly because of the way in which such interference could be used for purely sectional interest, and partly because of a belief that decentralized individual knowledge was superior to state knowledge), was pragmatic – the necessary legislative framework could be learned only by experience and enquiry.

At the heart of the classical vision is the idea of economic growth occurring through the interaction of capital accumulation and division of labour. Capital accumulation made it possible to postpone the sale of output, permitting the development of specialization and division of labour. Division of labour in turn increased total output, permitting further capital accumulation. Economic growth would be increased by allowing capital to flow to where it was most productive; thus, other things being equal, it was desirable to remove restraints on the free allocation of resources. Division of labour itself was limited by the extent of the market. The extent of the home market depended on population and income per head. As capital was accumulated, the available labour supply found itself in greater demand and wages rose above the necessary minimum – 'subsistence', which could be either psychological or physiological. Population responded to the rise in wages by increasing; this in turn increased the labour supply, which pushed wages back towards subsistence, though, if subsistence was a psychological variable – as it was with many classical writers – population growth might well stop before wages had fallen to the old level of subsistence. As wages rose, profits fell; this might check capital accumulation, but as long as profits were above a necessary minimum, capital accumulation would continue. Output, population and capital thus all grew together. However, a brake on growth was provided by the shortage of a third input, land. With the progress of economic growth, food became more and more expensive to produce, while landlords enjoyed the benefit of an unearned rent arising from ownership of this scarce but vital resource – this aspect was particularly stressed by Malthus and Ricardo. The rising cost of food also meant that the floor below which subsistence could not fall – the minimum wage necessary to procure basic physical necessities of life – rose, and Ricardo in particular emphasized that such a rise would depress profits and might eventually stop capital accumulation and growth altogether. (Smith had believed that growth would stop only when investment opportunities were exhausted.) He then argued that repeal of the Corn Laws (restricting food imports) was urgent, since subsistence could be obtained more cheaply abroad. (Later classical economists such as McCulloch and J.S. Mill were, however, optimistic about technical progress in agriculture that could postpone any slowdown in economic growth by lowering the cost of agricultural output.)

The argument for repeal of the Corn Laws provided one part of a general classical case for freedom of trade; the desire to widen the market to maximize possible division of labour provided another. However, a more general and sophisticated argument for freedom of trade was provided by R. Torrens (1820, 1821) and Ricardo, in the form of the theory of comparative costs (later refined and developed by J.S. Mill), which showed that a country could gain from importing even those commodities in which it had a competitive advantage if it had an even greater competitive advantage in the production of other commodities – it should concentrate its scarce resources on the latter.

Balance of payments equilibrium was ensured by a mechanism that was due to David Hume, and which was also basic to classical monetary theory, the price-specie-flow mechanism. A balance of payments deficit would, through gold outflow, reduce the money supply, and thus the price level, making exports competitive and imports less attractive, and this equilibrating mechanism would continue until the gold outflow stopped and payments came into balance. The price level was thus dependent on the money supply, and the predominant classical view from Ricardo to Lord Overstone (1837) was that the note issue, as part of the money supply, should be contracted if gold was flowing out, since the outflow was a symptom of a price level that was too high. Monetary control was also necessary to dampen the effects of an endogenous trade cycle, an element introduced into classical economics, chiefly by Overstone, from the late 1830s. (A minority of classical economists, however, viewed the money supply as demand-determined.)

Classical economics represented a major intellectual achievement. The foundations that it laid in the fields of monetary and trade theory, in particular, are still with economics. Eventually it lost some of its momentum; it was always policy-oriented, and as the policy questions were settled – usually along the lines indicated by the classical analyses – and as economists came to take continuing economic growth for granted, they turned their attention to different questions requiring different techniques of analysis.

D.P. O'BRIEN
UNIVERSITY OF DURHAM

References

Hume, D. (1752) *Political Discourses*, Edinburgh.
McCulloch, J.R. (1825) *The Principles of Political Economy: With Some Inquiries Respecting Their Application and a Sketch of the Rise and Progress of the Science*, 2nd edn, Edinburgh.
Malthus, T.R. (1820) *Principles of Political Economy*, London.
Mill, J. (1821–6) *Elements of Political Economy*.
Mill, J.S. (1848) *Principles of Political Economy with Some of Their Applications to Social Philosophy*.
—— (1963–85) *Collected Works of J.S. Mill*, ed. J.M. Robson, Toronto.
Overstone, Lord (1837) *Reflections Suggested by a Perusal of Mr J. Horsley Palmer's Pamphlet on the Causes and Consequences of the Pressure on the Money Market*, London.
Ricardo, D. (1951–73) *The Works and Correspondence of David Ricardo*, eds P. Sraffa with M.H. Dobb, 10 vols, Cambridge, UK.
Smith, A. (1981 [1776]) *An Inquiry into the Nature and Causes of the Wealth of Nations*, ed. R. Campbell and A. Skinner, Indianapolis, IN.
Torrens, R. (1820) *An Essay on the External Corn Trade*, London.
—— (1821) *An Essay on the Production of Wealth*, London.
Winch, D. (ed.) (1966) *James Mill: Selected Economic Writings*, Edinburgh.

Further reading

O'Brien, D.P. (1975) *The Classical Economists*, Oxford.
Peach, T. (1993) *Interpreting Ricardo*, Cambridge.

SEE ALSO: Hume, David; Keynesian economics; macroeconomic theory; Marshall; neo-classical economics; Ricardian economics; Ricardo; Smith

CLIOMETRICS

The term 'cliometrics' (a neologism linking the concept of measurement to the muse of history) was apparently coined at Purdue University, Indiana, USA, in the late 1950s. Originally applied to the study of economic history as undertaken by scholars trained as economists (and also called, by its practitioners and others, the new economic history, econometric history and quantitative economic history), more recently cliometrics has been applied to a broader range of historical studies (including the new political history, the new social history and, most inclusively, social science history).

The historians' early interest in cliometrics partly reflects the impact of two important works in US economic history. The detailed estimates by Conrad and Meyer (1958) of the profitability of slavery before the Civil War and the quantitative evaluation of the role of the railways in economic growth by Fogel (1964) triggered wide-ranging debate, with much attention to questions of method as well as substance. While these two works, combining economic theory and quantitative analysis, attracted the most attention, other books and articles published at about the same time also highlighted the quantitative aspect, although in a more traditional (and less controversial) manner. A National Bureau of Economic Research (NBER 1960) conference volume, edited by Parker, presented a number of important studies (by, among others, Easterlin, Gallman, Lebergott and North) pushing back many important time-series on economic variables to the early nineteenth century, an effort complemented by the publication, several years later, of another NBER (1966) conference dealing mainly with nineteenth-century economic change. North (1961) combined his new estimates of pre-1860 foreign trade with a familiar regional approach to describe the basic contours of US economic growth from 1790 to the Civil War. These works had important implications for discussions of economic growth in the USA, particularly in the period before the Civil War. The concentration of major publications within a short time period, together with the start of an annual conference of cliometricians at Purdue University, organized by Davis, Hughes and others, which, with several changes of venue, still continues, generated the momentum which led to major shifts in the nature of the writing of US economic history, as well as revisions of many interpretations of past developments. The late 1950s and 1960s saw similar changes in other subfields of history, particularly political and social history, although it was in economic history that the concentration on theory, quantitative data and statistical methods was most complete.

In perhaps the most controversial work of cliometrics, Fogel (who was, with North, to win the Nobel Prize in Economics for 1993) co-authored, with Engerman, a work on the economics of US slavery, *Time on the Cross* (1974), whose conclusions as to the profitability, viability and efficiency of slavery triggered considerable debate among cliometricians and other historians. Fogel's subsequent work on slavery, *Without Consent or Contract* (1989), did not lead to a similar debate, although the basic conclusions were similar to those of the earlier work. The 1970s and 1980s saw a broadening of the interests of cliometricians from those of the earlier decades. For example, there was considerable attention given to the study of demographic and anthropometric issues, while North (see e.g. Davis and North 1971; North 1990), and various

other scholars, focused attention on the study of the development of economic institutions and organizations. An indicator of these expanding horizons is seen in the third of the NBER (1986) volumes dealing with economic history, edited by Engerman and Gallman.

The most general characteristics of cliometric work (in economic history) have been the systematic use of economic theory and its concepts to examine economic growth in the past, and the widespread preparation and formal statistical analysis of quantitative material. While none of this may seem to provide a new approach in historical studies (as is often pointed out in criticizing claims of novelty), the more explicit attention to theory and the more frequent reliance on quantitative materials and statistical procedures have had an important impact upon the manner in which historical questions have been approached and interpreted. However, cliometricians still differ in how they make use of quantitative and statistical methods. To some, the major work is the preparation of quantitative data, either of detailed information for a particular time period (based on, e.g., the samples of population, agriculture and manufacturing records drawn from the decadal federal census) or of long-period time-series (e.g. national income and wealth, wages, labour force) to be used in measuring and understanding past economic changes. These estimates require imaginative reconstructions from the available samples of past data, but do not often involve sophisticated statistical tools. Others emphasize the use of more formal statistical methods, most frequently regression analysis, to test hypotheses. Some cliometricians restrict themselves to the use of economic theory to analyse institutional and economic changes, which are difficult to describe quantitatively.

Continued interest in economic (and political and sociological) theory has led to a more frequent attempt to find historical generalizations based upon social science concepts and methods than some, more traditionally trained, historians seem comfortable with. Nevertheless, the ability to collect and examine data, from archival and published sources, furthered by the development of the computer, has permitted a considerable expansion in the amount of material relevant to questions of interest to historians, as well as better methods of organizing, analysing and testing data. The heat of earlier debates on method has apparently declined as the use of quantitative methods and theoretical constructs has become a part of the standard toolkit of historians, while cliometricians have broadened the range of questions they have discussed and the varieties of evidence utilized.

While the first cliometric studies were done principally by North American scholars and, for reasons of data availability, most frequently concerned the USA in the nineteenth century, since the mid-1970s the temporal and geographical scope has widened, as have the types of questions to which cliometric analysis is applied. Much work has been done on the colonial period, as well as the twentieth century, in the USA. Not only have the interests of US cliometricians expanded to include studies of other parts of the world, but also cliometric work has developed in a number of other countries, most particularly in Britain and other parts of Western Europe. Although, as with most attempts at categorization, a sharp dividing line is often difficult to draw, cliometric history continues to emphasize the systematic application of social science theory and the use of quantitative data and statistical analysis to understand the historical past.

STANLEY L. ENGERMAN
UNIVERSITY OF ROCHESTER

References

Conrad, A.H. and Meyer, J.R. (1958) 'The economics of slavery in the ante-bellum South', *Journal of Political Economy* 66: 95–130.
Davis, L.E. and North, D.C. (1971) *Institutional Change and American Economic Growth*, Cambridge, UK.
Fogel, R.W. (1964) *Railroads and American Economic Growth: Essays in Econometric History*, Baltimore, MD.
—— (1989) *Without Consent or Contract*, New York.
Fogel, R.W. and Engerman, S.L. (1974) *Time on the Cross: The Economics of American Negro Slavery*, Boston, MA.
National Bureau of Economic Research (NBER) (1960) Conference on Research in Income and Wealth, *Trends in the American Economy in the Nineteenth Century*, Princeton, NJ.
—— (1966) Conference on Research in Income and Wealth, *Output, Employment, and Productivity in the United States after 1800*, New York.
—— (1986) Conference on Research in Income and Wealth, *Long-Term Factors in American Economic Growth*, Chicago.
North, D.C. (1961) *The Economic Growth of the United States, 1790–1860*, Englewood Cliffs, NJ.
—— (1990) *Institutions, Institutional Change and Economic Performance*, Cambridge, UK.

Further reading

Engerman, S.L. (1977) 'Recent developments in American economic history', *Social Science History* 11: 72–89.
Kousser, J.M. (1980) 'Quantitative social scientific history', in M. Kammen (ed.) *The Past before Us*, Ithaca, NY.
Lamoreaux, N.R. (1998) 'Economic history and the cliometric revolution', in A. Molho and G.S. Woods (eds) *Imagined Histories: American Historians Interpret the Past*, Princeton, NJ.
McCloskey, D.N. (1978) 'The achievements of the cliometric school', *Journal of Economic History* 38 (1): 13–28.
McCloskey, D.N. and Hersh, G.A. (1990) *A Bibliography of Historical Economics to 1980*, Cambridge, UK.
Williamson, S.H. (1991) 'The history of cliometrics', in J. Mokyr (ed.) *The Vital One: Essays in Honor of Jonathan R.T. Hughes*, Greenwich, CT.

SEE ALSO: economic history

COGNITIVE BEHAVIOURAL THERAPY

Cognitive behavioural therapy (CBT) is based on a model that emphasizes the interrelatedness of behaviour, cognition, emotion and contextual factors. Basic to the cognitive behavioural model is the notion that cognition (e.g. attitudes, expectancies, attributions, self-talk, beliefs, schemata) is central to understanding and hence producing change in affect and behaviour (Beck 2002). The CBT model recognizes the importance of learning, the influence of contingencies and models in the individual's environment, and the role of the individual's social and interpersonal context in the development and improvement of psychological difficulties.

Cognitive behavioural interventions are typically short term, and make use of structured behavioural tasks as well as cognitive interventions to effect change, and therapists work together with their clients to evaluate problems and generate solutions. By monitoring and correcting unrealistic thoughts, the individual is able to develop a more accurate rational cognitive set and so should be in a position to modify affect and behaviour. After examining the influence of behavioural factors on the individual's psychological difficulties, the therapist and client utilize specific behavioural techniques to effect change.

Behavioural interventions may include structured reward programmes, relaxation, problem-solving, exposure tasks and the scheduling of pleasant events. The techniques that are used may vary depending on the client's specific psychological difficulty. For example, the therapist may schedule pleasant events for a client with depressed mood, or gradually expose a client experiencing excessive anxiety to particular tasks.

CBT is a major force in psychotherapy today, both in theory and in application. A number of cognitive behavioural therapies have been given empirical support in randomized clinical trials (Chambless and Ollendick 2001), and manuals now provide therapists with clear direction regarding the content of the treatments (Sanderson and Woody 1995). Well-established procedures include cognitive behavioural therapy of depression, anxiety, bulimia, marital distress and pain associated with rheumatic disease, and promising treatments have been developed in other fields, such as the treatment of children suffering from anxiety. Some of these therapies will be briefly described.

Cognitive behavioural therapy of depression (Young et al. 2001) is structured, active and typically time-limited. Learning experiences are designed to teach clients to monitor their negative thinking, to examine the evidence for and against their distorted (again often negative) thinking, to substitute more realistic interpretations, and to begin to alter the dysfunctional beliefs and lifestyle associated with distorted thinking. Behavioural strategies such as self-monitoring of mood, the scheduling of pleasant activities, graduated task assignments and role-playing exercises are integrated with more cognitive procedures designed, for example, to challenge negative thinking.

Stress inoculation training (Meichenbaum 1985) is a three-stage intervention that focuses on teaching cognitive and behavioural skills for coping with stressful situations. In the first, educational, phase, clients are taught a conceptual framework for understanding stress in cognitive terms. The second phase, skills training, teaches clients cognitive (imagery, changing irrational self-talk) and behavioural (relaxation, breathing) skills. In the final stage, clients practise the new skills in stressful situations.

Cognitive behavioural treatment for bulimia nervosa (Fairburn et al. 1993) consists of three stages of semi-structured, problem-oriented therapy. The first stage of the intervention informs the individual of the cognitive model of bulimia and explains the consequences of binge-eating, self-induced vomiting and purgative misuse. Clients are provided with alternative coping behaviours such as a pattern of regular eating. The second stage focuses on cognitive strategies to modify cognitive distortions regarding body shape, weight and eating. The final stage is designed to prevent relapse.

Cognitive behavioural therapy for children teaches the child to identify anxious reactions and to employ a number of coping skills such as relaxation strategies, cognitive restructuring and problem-solving. The programme provides clients with controlled exposure to situations that had caused them distress, and gives them opportunities to practise coping (Kendall 2000a, 2000b). Parental involvement in this therapy such as contingency management and parental anxiety treatment has also shown to be beneficial (Rapee et al. 2000).

The common thread in all these treatments is the focus on cognitive change and performance-based procedures. At this stage, the mechanisms by which positive outcomes in CBT are achieved remain unclear although some evidence indicates that behavioural techniques with or without cognitive restructuring produce changes in negative thinking and outcomes (e.g. Jacobson et al. 2000; Feske and Chambless 1995). Client factors (e.g. expectancies for change), relationship factors (e.g. therapist–client alliance) and treatment strategies (e.g. degree of focus on cognitive processing; flexibility in implementation) are being investigated in order to gain a better understanding of the process of successful psychological change.

JENNIFER L. HUDSON
MACQUARIE UNIVERSITY,
SYDNEY, AUSTRALIA
PHILIP C. KENDALL
TEMPLE UNIVERSITY

References

Beck, A.T. (2002) 'Cognitive models of depression', in R.L. Leahy and E.T. Dowd (eds) *Clinical Advances in Cognitive Psychotherapy: Theory and Application*, New York, pp. 29–61.

Chambless, D.L. and Ollendick, T.H. (2001) 'Evidence supported psychological interventions: Controversies and evidence', *Annual Review of Psychology* 52: 685–716.

Fairburn, C.G., Marcus, M.D. and Wilson, G.T. (1993) 'Cognitive-behavioral therapy for binge eating and bulimia nervosa', in C.G. Fairburn and G.T. Wilson (eds) *Binge Eating: Nature, Assessment, and Treatment*, New York.

Feske, U. and Chambless, D.L. (1995) 'Cognitive behavioral versus exposure only treatment for social phobia: A meta-analysis', *Behavior Therapy* 26: 695–720.

Jacobson, N.S., Dobson, K.S., Truax, P.A., Addis, M.E., Koerner, K., Gollan, J.K., Gortner, E. and Prince, S.E. (2000) 'A component analysis of cognitive-behavioral treatment for depression', *Prevention and Treatment* 3: n.p.

Kendall, P.C. (ed.) (2000a) *Child and Adolescent Therapy: Cognitive-Behavioral Procedures*, 2nd edn, New York.

—— (2000b) *Cognitive-Behavioral Therapy for Anxious Children: Therapist Manual*, 2nd edn, Ardmore, PA.

Meichenbaum, D. (1985) *Stress Inoculation Training*, New York.

Rapee, R.M., Wignall, A., Hudson, J.L. and Schniering, C.A. (2000) *Treating Anxious Children and Adolescents: An Evidence-Based Approach*, Oakland, CA.

Sanderson, W.C. and Woody, S. (1995) 'Manuals for empirically validated treatments: A project of the task force on psychological interventions', *The Clinical Psychologist* 48(4): 7–11.

Young, J.E., Weinberger, A.D. and Beck, A.T. (2001) 'Cognitive therapy for depression', in D.H. Barlow (ed.) *Clinical Handbook of Psychological Disorders: A Step-by-Step Treatment Manual*, 3rd edn, New York, pp. 264–308.

COGNITIVE NEUROPSYCHOLOGY

One way to learn about how a system works is to study how it behaves when a part of it is broken. People who have suffered brain damage may have problems with a specific domain of cognitive processing. Cognitive neuropsychology investigates the patterns of preserved and impaired abilities exhibited by such patients, in order to make inferences about the structure of the normal system.

For example, brain damage sometimes affects the ability to understand the meaning of words. A person may be able to recognize spoken words, and repeat them, or be able to read written words aloud, and yet still not know what these words mean. Sometimes this loss of meaning is selective. Particular patients have difficulties with words that refer to animate things, like 'kangaroo' or 'corn', while they understand words that refer to man-made objects like 'ferry' or 'hammer'. In other patients, the reverse is observed. What do these observations suggest about the way in which meaning is represented in the mind? It seems logical to infer that there are at least two separate mental systems here. One contains knowledge about animate objects, while the other contains knowledge about inanimate objects. That is a claim about intact minds, even though the data on which it is based came from studies of damaged minds.

When a patient retains normal use of some ability after brain damage, but is impaired in some other ability, these abilities are said to be *dissociated*. If Patient X is normal at ability A but impaired at ability B, and patient Y is impaired at ability A but normal at ability B, we have a *double dissociation*. Double dissociations are important data for cognitive neuropsychology because of the theoretical inferences that they license. For example, after brain damage some people lose the ability to recognize faces (this disorder is known as *prosopagnosia*) but can still recognize objects, whereas, also after brain damage, other patients can no longer recognize objects (this disorder is known as *visual agnosia*) but can still recognize faces. If there were a single mental information-processing system that carried out all forms of visual recognition – which was responsible for recognizing faces and also for recognizing objects, for example – it is very hard to see how it could happen that in one patient recognition of faces but not objects is affected, while the reverse is the case for another patient. It seems reasonable to conclude that there is a cognitive system that is used for recognizing faces but which is not important for recognizing objects, and another cognitive system that is used for recognizing objects but which is not important for recognizing faces. These dedicated cognitive systems are typically referred to as modules. A cognitive neuropsychologist would therefore say that there is a face recognition module and a separate object recognition module.

This way of studying cognition was already being practised in the second half of the nineteenth century but it fell into disrepute at the beginning of the twentieth century, and only became popular again in the early 1970s. Since then it has flourished, and many remarkable double dissociations have been discovered. This has led to the development of modular theories in many domains of cognition. Modular theories based on observations of double dissociations have been developed for reading, spelling, speaking, recognizing spoken words, sentence comprehension, attention, the planning and execution of skilled action, memory, numerical ability and calculation, and musical ability, in addition to the representation of meaning, face processing and object recognition already mentioned.

Such cognitive abilities are very basic components of cognition. In the past decade, cognitive neuropsychologists have become interested in higher-order cognitive abilities, such as problem-solving or the evaluation and acquisition of beliefs. These are studied by applying cognitive-neuropsychological methods of investigation to disorders typically thought of as belonging to psychiatry: schizophrenia, delusion and hallucination, for example. This branch of cognitive neuropsychology has come to be known as *cognitive neuropsychiatry*. Its aim is to learn something about higher-order cognitive abilities by studying individuals with impairments of these abilities.

The psychiatric disorder most intensively studied so far by cognitive neuropsychiatrists has been the delusion. A delusion is a belief that a person holds to tenaciously even though there is very good evidence that it is untrue, and even though everyone assures the deluded person that the belief is false. It is quite normal for unusual hypotheses about the world to occur to us, but we then reflect on the evidence for and against such a hypothesis, and consider the views of other people we know concerning the hypothesis, as a way of evaluating this potential belief. How does this belief evaluation process actually work? We may be able to learn something about this by studying people in whom the belief evaluation process is no longer working – that is, people with delusions. Amongst the remarkable delusions that cognitive neuropsychiatrists are studying in this way are the Capgras delusion (the belief that someone emotionally close to you has been replaced by an impostor); the Cotard delusion (the belief that you are dead); the Fregoli delusion (the belief that a group of people you know are constantly following you around, *but that you cannot recognize them* because they are always in disguise); the De Clerambault delusion (the belief that some particular famous person is secretly in love with you); and mirrored-self misidentification (the belief that the person you see when you look in the mirror isn't you, but some stranger who looks like you). Good progress is currently being made in understanding at least the first and the last of the delusions on this list.

Modular theories are typically expressed in the form of box-and-arrow flow diagrams. These specify the modules of the system and the pathways of communication between modules. Figure 2 shows a simplified version of such a model, in this case a model offering an account of the system by which objects and printed words are recognized and understood, and objects, words and nonwords named. A theory like this will emerge after numerous different double dissociations have been observed. Dissociations may also be used as evidence to refute such theories. According to Figure 2, for example, a patient who cannot access the meanings of objects that he sees will also be unable to name them. The discovery of a patient who can name objects that he cannot understand – a dissociation between object comprehension and object naming – would show that this theory is wrong.

This approach raises the old issue of the relationship between brain and mind, but in a new way. When a modular theory is represented as explicitly as is the case in Figure 2, it is natural to wonder whether the components of the diagram represent not only discrete mental information-processing subsystems but also discrete brain regions. This is not necessarily the case. Each of the components of Figure 2 could depend on a set of neurons that is distributed widely throughout the brain rather than being concentrated in some small localized brain region. But if that were generally the case, it would not be possible for brain damage to impair some components of the model while leaving others intact. Highly specific double dissociations would not be observed. Since highly specific double dissociations are in fact commonly reported in the cognitive-neuropsychological literature (some are described above), it would seem then that cognitive modules *do* typically map on to highly restricted brain regions. What has emerged from cognitive neuropsychology, then, is a picture of the mind as a highly modularized information-processing system, and it seems likely that these mental

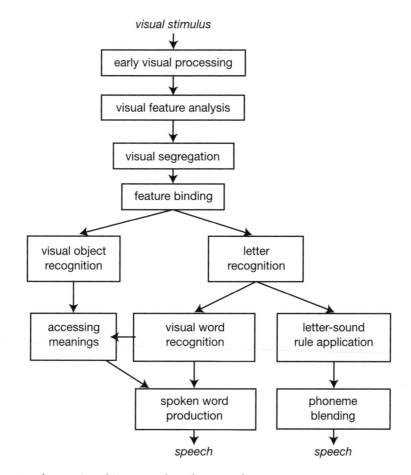

Figure 2 A system for naming objects, words and nonwords

modules are neurally realized in small localizable regions of the brain.

MAX COLTHEART
MACQUARIE UNIVERSITY, AUSTRALIA

Further reading

Coltheart, M. (1999) 'Modularity and cognition', *Trends in Cognitive Sciences* 3: 115–20.
—— (2001) 'Assumptions and methods in cognitive neuropsychology', in B. Rapp (ed.) *Handbook of Cognitive Neuropsychology*, Philadelphia.
—— (2002) 'Cognitive neuropsychology', in J. Wixted and H. Pashler (eds) *Stevens' Handbook of Experimental Psychology*, Vol. 4: *Methodology*, 3rd edn, New York.
McCloskey, M.J. (2001) 'The future of cognitive neuropsychology', in B. Rapp (ed.) *Handbook of Cognitive Neuropsychology*, Philadelphia.
Rapp, B. (ed.) (2001) *Handbook of Cognitive Neuropsychology*, Philadelphia.

SEE ALSO: cognitive neuroscience; cognitive psychology; neural networks; thinking

COGNITIVE NEUROSCIENCE

The reason that *cognitive neuropsychology* and *cognitive neuroscience* are commonly used as the names of closely related, but still distinct, sciences is a historical accident. Both sciences aim to determine how the brain (and particularly the human brain) mediates different kinds of cognition. Cognitive neuropsychology pursues this goal by studying the ways in which lesions to specific parts of the brain impair some kinds of cognition, but leave others intact. In contrast, cognitive neuroscience pursues the same goal not only by studying the effects of lesions on cognition, but also by examining the neural correlates of specific cognitive processes. Indeed, cognitive neuroscience explores how the brain mediates cognition using a convergent operations approach that, in principle, draws on all available techniques for exploring or disrupting brain activity.

The name *cognitive neuroscience* is reported to have been coined by George Miller and Michael Gazzaniga whilst taking a taxi ride in New York in the late 1970s. They were going to a meeting to consider ways to study 'how the brain enables the mind' and felt that the subject needed a name. Whether or not it did, the name cognitive neuroscience rather than cognitive neuropsychology has clearly been very widely adopted. One reason for this is probably because the neural bases of psychology have been primarily explored through the study of the effects of brain lesions since the middle of the nineteenth century and this activity has long been called neuropsychology. A second reason is that within around a decade of the legendary taxi ride several powerful functional neuroimaging techniques became available, which dramatically improved our ability to identify the neural bases of normal cognition.

The broadest aim of cognitive neuroscience is to characterize how activity in different brain regions causes different kinds of cognition (for example perception, attention, memory, thinking, emotion and social cognition). There are several more specific goals. First, as the brain is an evolved system that develops from a single cell, cognitive neuroscience needs to explain how the brain–cognition relationship matures as the brain grows as well as how the brain mediates cognition in adults. Second, as cognition differs not only between species, but also between individuals within a species, cognitive neuroscience needs to explain how differences between brains explain individual as well as species differences in cognition. Third, although an intermediate goal is to discover which brain regions mediate specific kinds of cognition, the ultimate goal is to work out how the millions of individual neurons in these regions interact to produce these kinds of cognition.

To achieve these goals many kinds of knowledge are needed. On the one hand, knowledge is needed about the chemical and electrical workings of neurons, how they influence each other and what their connections are. On the other hand, detailed knowledge of the components of cognition and how these interact is also needed. Building on these two kinds of knowledge, it is critical to know as precisely as possible how brain and cognitive activities interact.

This third kind of knowledge lies at the heart of cognitive neuroscience, which, in addition to rarely used invasive techniques such as stimulating or recording neuronal activity directly in the brains of patients, uses several much less invasive techniques to achieve this. First, since the late 1970s, the structure of intact as well as damaged brains has been imaged in living people with computed tomography, and, from the 1980s, by magnetic resonance imaging (MRI). Structural MRI has better spatial resolution and can discriminate structures only 1 mm apart. The volume of brain structures in normal and brain-damaged people can be measured using structural MRI. This not only improves estimates of brain damage, but also allows cognition to be correlated with brain structure size in people with intact brains. For example, apart from evidence that the brain tends to be larger in brighter people, there is evidence that the size of parts of the hippocampus, a structure important in memory, is larger in London taxi drivers and that in orchestral players a region of the left frontal neocortex is larger than in non-players. Furthermore, with taxi drivers and orchestral players, there is a suggestion that more years of practice enhances the effect.

Second, correlations between neural and cognitive activity can be acquired using several techniques. Since the late 1980s, positron emission tomography (PET) has been used to image blood flow changes in the brain that correlate with specific kinds of mental activity. However, since the early 1990s, functional MRI (fMRI) has rapidly become the dominant technique for exploring neural activity–cognitive function correlations because it can localize brain activations with greater precision, does not use radioactive substances and, for this reason, allows more flexible experimental designs. For example, unlike PET, fMRI can also be used with event-related studies in which brain activity associated with randomly occurring specific cognitive processes is averaged. Event-related paradigms can be used not only with fMRI, but also with the much older technique of event-related potentials (ERPs), which uses scalp-recorded electroencephalography, and the more recently developed technique of magnetoencephalography

(MEG) that records the brain's variable magnetic activity.

These techniques have disadvantages as well as advantages. PET and fMRI are good at identifying where brain activity is, but poor at determining when it occurs. In contrast, ERPs and MEG are poor at identifying where activity is, but can localize it in time to within a few milliseconds. Ideally, both kinds of techniques should be used to explore brain–cognition relationships. The techniques also measure neural activity indirectly. For example, PET measures blood flow and fMRI measures BOLD, or the blood oxygen level dependent response. Although blood flow and oxygenation are known to increase rapidly with neural activity in a specific region, precisely how this happens is not fully understood and neither are the exact neural correlates of the vascular responses. Finally, the techniques are correlational so they do not prove that brain activity causes the cognitive processes being investigated. To establish this one needs to facilitate or disrupt brain activity. This has been done historically by exploring the disruptive effects of specific brain lesions, but this has disadvantages that make interpretation difficult. For example, lesions are messy, usually damaging several functionally distinct regions, and there may be some reorganization of function following damage. Even if this does not occur, brain lesions do not indicate *when* activity in a particular structure is necessary for a cognitive process to occur.

A third kind of technique, transcranial magnetic stimulation (TMS), which can be applied to the cranium to temporarily disrupt (and sometimes perhaps facilitate) activity at specific cortical sites, avoids some of these problems. There is not time for reorganization of function to occur when TMS is applied to specific sites and stimulation is precisely timed so it is possible to determine exactly when activity in a region is necessary for a specific kind of cognition. However, TMS cannot be used to affect activity in deep brain sites selectively and it is even hard to localize its effects on the cortical surface. Good localization requires functional imaging of abnormal neural activity close in time to TMS. Such functional imaging shows that TMS not only changes activity beneath the stimulating coil, but also at distant, but connected, sites. Since the early 1990s, use of complementary techniques like these has fuelled explosive growth in cognitive neuroscience.

Computational neural network models have been used to show how large numbers of neurons in connected brain regions might interact to produce specific kinds of cognition. The networks can incorporate the known structure of each region, and not only represent and process specific information, but also show changes in the strength of the connections between specific 'neuronal' components in accordance with learning rules. Through tests of the models' predictions using available cognitive neuroscience techniques, theories about how myriad neurons in human brains interact to produce specific kinds of cognition will be improved. For example, the role of the hippocampus and other parts of the medial temporal lobes in recall of and familiarity for different types of information has been investigated by lesion and functional imaging studies. Several neural network models of how these brain regions mediate recall and familiarity, which make precise and testable predictions, now exist. Finally, with improved knowledge of the human genome, it is now possible to discover how individual genetic differences in genes that influence brain growth and function relate to cognitive differences. For example, ability to recall studied materials is significantly worse in people with a rare version of a gene that influences the efficiency of a serotonin receptor that is found in memory-related brain regions, such as the hippocampus. Work like this will expand in the future and fuller explanations of associations like this will have to be found by cognitive neuroscientists.

So far, the picture that has emerged from cognitive neuroscience is that nearly all forms of cognition comprise many processes so that cognitive acts such as perceiving depend on linked activity in several brain regions each of which processes and probably stores specific kinds of information. Thus, the brain mediates cognition in a broadly modular way in so far as representation, processing and storage of specific information is mediated by fairly focal brain regions. But it is also highly interactive because activity in many regions is influenced by activity in several other regions and coherent activity across these regions may play a key role in cognition. Exactly how neurons code information, undergo memory changes and interact in order to mediate modular and interactive processing will be a major task for cognitive neuroscience in the twenty-first century.

DANIELA MONTALDI AND ANDREW R. MAYES
UNIVERSITY OF LIVERPOOL

Further reading

Frackowiak, R.S.J., Friston, K.J., Frith, C.D., Dolan, R.J. and Mazziotta, J.C. (1997) *Human Brain Function*, London.
Frith, C.D. and Wolpert, D.M. (2004) *The Neuroscience of Social Interactions*, Oxford.
Gazzaniga, M.S., Ivry, R.B. and Mangun, G.R. (2002) *Cognitive Neuroscience: The Biology of the Mind*, 2nd edn, New York.
Kandel, E.R. and Squire, L.R. (2000) 'Neuroscience: Breaking down scientific barriers to the study of brain and mind', *Science* 290: 1,113–20.
Walsh, V. and Pascual-Leone, A. (2003) *Transcranial Magnetic Stimulation: A Neurochronometrics of Mind*, Cambridge, MA.

SEE ALSO: cognitive neuropsychology; cognitive psychology; connectionism; emotion; neural networks; sensation and perception; thinking

COGNITIVE PSYCHOLOGY

According to Drever's (1964) *Dictionary of Psychology*, 'cognition' is 'a general term covering all the various modes of knowing – perceiving, imagining, conceiving, judging, reasoning'. It picks out those forms of abstract thinking and problem-solving that are based upon the manipulation of either linguistic symbols (propositions) or iconic symbols (images). Cognitive psychology refers to the attempt to understand these various human faculties by means of systematic empirical observation and theory construction. Its origins lie in research conducted during the 1950s by Donald Broadbent, Jerome Bruner and George Miller (see Gardner 1985), although it was probably first generally acknowledged as a distinctive intellectual development with the publication of Ulric Neisser's (1967) book, *Cognitive Psychology*. It was also encouraged by cognate movements in other areas of psychology, such as the work by Jean Piaget and David Ausubel in developmental psychology and by Alan Newell and Herbert Simon in artificial intelligence. Cognitive psychology has in turn promoted developments in related areas of psychological research, of which cognitive neuropsychology is a notable example, and it is a central pillar of cognitive science.

The methods and theories of cognitive psychology have been influenced by two rather different traditions. First, cognitive psychology is the natural heir to what used to be called 'human experimental psychology', and it has incorporated (perhaps too uncritically) the behaviourist methodology that dominated psychological research earlier in the twentieth century. It therefore involves most typically the objective description of human behaviour within formal laboratory experiments. These experiments usually seek to differentiate well-articulated theoretical alternatives within an established (though relatively narrow) research paradigm. This approach encourages a degree of artificiality in cognitive research, as it has always been recognized that the degree of naturalism in a laboratory study is likely to be inversely related to the extent to which the subjects' performance can be adequately described and to which the task itself can be conceptually analysed.

Cognitive psychology also stems from the field of human factors research that developed during the Second World War in order to tackle problems concerning human–machine interaction. This work led to an interest in the control mechanisms governing intelligent behaviour, to the idea of human thought and action as consisting of discrete stages of information processing, and inevitably to the use of the structure and function of the digital computer as a metaphor in theorizing about human cognition. (This is, of course, distinct from the use of the digital computer itself as a research tool.) An early though highly influential account of such notions was contained in Miller *et al.*'s (1960) *Plans and the Structure of Human Behavior*. Research carried out within this tradition is rather more pragmatic in its orientation: it aims to produce general frameworks that are of direct benefit in the design and construction of complex systems but which may not be amenable to rigorous experimental evaluation (Reason 1987).

Human cognition is undoubtedly a complex object of study, and researchers within cognitive psychology are faced with a number of options with regard to the most fruitful way to conduct their investigations. Eysenck (1984) identified three such decisions: the pursuit of basic or applied research; the focus upon general or specific problems; and the inclusion or exclusion of the motivational and emotional states of the subjects from their domain of analysis. Eysenck observed that the contemporary emphasis was upon 'basic research into specific problems that is conducted with a total disregard for emotional and motivational factors', although he for one has certainly been concerned to address issues concerning the role of emotional and motivational factors in human cognition.

Cognitive psychology does provide sophisticated theoretical accounts based upon experimental manipulations and procedures that have been extensively employed in laboratory-based research. However, there are various respects in which it has proved difficult to relate such research to practical issues, and Eysenck (1984) pointed to three interrelated problems. First, what is studied in laboratory research may be of little relevance to ordinary human functioning; second, laboratory research has very often ignored important characteristics of the cognition of everyday life; and, third, at least some laboratory findings may not extrapolate to real-life events because of the artificiality of the experimental situation. Eysenck pointed out that the goal of laboratory-based research was not simply to mimic aspects of everyday cognitive functioning, but he concluded that genuine theoretical progress in cognitive psychology would be achieved only by means of a cross-fertilization between laboratory studies and more applied research.

Accounts of this sort given by cognitive psychologists themselves tend to assume that it is simply an empirical matter whether the cognitive processes that are being tapped in a particular psychological experiment are actually employed in the everyday task that the experiment is intended to model. Such an assumption is often made when the methods of cognitive psychology are criticized for their dubious 'ecological validity' (to use the prevalent jargon), for the latter tends to be regarded as a purely technical characteristic of particular experimental procedures. Whether or not a psychological experiment involves cognitive processes that are used in everyday life is then a matter to be settled by further empirical research. For instance, Yuille (1986) argued that laboratory-based research revealed little or nothing about the real-life functions of basic cognitive processes, but his criticisms of a purely experimental approach to the study of human cognition were based predominantly upon evidence obtained from formal laboratory experiments.

However, more radical critics have argued that the social situation of the psychological experiment is qualitatively different from the concrete tasks that confront individual human beings in their everyday lives. It is this point that is behind criticisms of the artificiality and worthlessness of laboratory experiments (Harré 1974). Some critics have pointed to the power relationships inherent in the experimental situation, and have put forward political and moral arguments concerning the effects of laboratory research upon both subjects and researchers (Heron 1981). Rowan (1981) suggested that experimental laboratory work exemplified the various forms of alienation that according to Marx would operate in any economic system where the workers (in this case, the subjects) did not own the means of production. There is thus perhaps a perverse sense in which laboratory experiments successfully (though unwittingly) capture certain aspects of the social situation of workplace, though certainly not of those situations in which individual human beings engage in autonomous and self-motivated cognition. Nevertheless, on this account, to compare the results of laboratory-based research either with the findings of applied studies or with 'natural history' observations would simply fail to set like against like (though Rowan included conventional forms of 'applied' research in his criticisms).

These criticisms are not trivial ones, and some call into question the whole enterprise of cognitive psychology. They clearly need to be addressed, perhaps by means of more sophisticated conceptual analyses, perhaps by means of theoretical developments, or perhaps by means of methodological innovations. However, many of these criticisms are already being addressed, and this in itself has led to significant advances within the field of cognitive psychology. In addition to the concern with practical applications that has always been inherent in the human factors tradition, the 1970s and 1980s saw a lively interest in accommodating mainstream research to the realities of everyday life, most obviously with regard to research on human memory (Gruneberg et al. 1978, 1988). Nowadays, most cognitive psychologists would agree that attention to the potential or actual applications of research is likely to provide a major impetus in the development and elaboration of theories and research within cognitive psychology itself.

JOHN T.E. RICHARDSON
THE OPEN UNIVERSITY

References

Drever, J. (1964) *A Dictionary of Psychology*, rev. H. Wallerstein, Harmondsworth.

Eysenck, M.W. (1984) *A Handbook of Cognitive Psychology*, London.

Gardner, H. (1985) *The Mind's New Science: A History of the Cognitive Revolution*, New York.

Gruneberg, M.M., Morris, P.E. and Sykes, R.N. (1978) *Practical Aspects of Memory*, London.

—— (1988) *Practical Aspects of Memory: Current Research and Issues*, Chichester.

Harré, R. (1974) 'Some remarks on "rule" as a scientific concept', in T. Mischel (ed.) *Understanding Other Persons*, Oxford.

Heron, J. (1981) 'Philosophical basis for a new paradigm', in P. Reason and J. Rowan (eds) *Human Inquiry: A Sourcebook of New Paradigm Research*, Chichester.

Miller, G.A., Galanter, E. and Pribram, K.H. (1960) *Plans and the Structure of Human Behavior*, New York.

Neisser, U. (1967) *Cognitive Psychology*, New York.

Reason, J. (1987) 'Framework models of human performance and error: A consumer guide', in L. Goodstein, H.B. Anderson and S.E. Olsen (eds) *Tasks, Errors and Mental Models*, London.

Rowan, J. (1981) 'A dialectical paradigm for research', in P. Reason and J. Rowan (eds) *Human Inquiry: A Sourcebook of New Paradigm Research*, Chichester.

Yuille, J.C. (1986) 'The futility of a purely experimental psychology of cognition: Imagery as a case study', in D.F. Marks (ed.) *Theories of Image Formation*, New York.

Further reading

Eysenck, M.W. and Keane, M.T. (2000) *Cognitive Psychology: A Student's Handbook*, 4th edn, Hove.

Smyth, M.M., Collins, A.F., Morris, P.E. and Levy, P. (1994) *Cognition in Action*, 2nd edn, Hove.

SEE ALSO: cognitive neuropsychology; cognitive neuroscience; cognitive science; symbolism; thinking

COGNITIVE SCIENCE

The term 'cognitive science' refers to the interdisciplinary study of information processing in human cognition. Although there are obvious precursors in the work of mathematicians such as Alan Turing and John von Neumann, of neurophysiologists such as Warren McCulloch and Walter Pitts, and of communications theorists such as Norbert Wiener and Claude Shannon, it is generally agreed that cognitive science came into being in 1956. This year marked the beginnings of genuine collaboration among research workers in artificial intelligence (Allen Newell and Herbert Simon), cognitive psychology (Jerome Bruner and George Miller) and linguistics (Noam Chomsky); Gardner (1985) has identified cognate movements in epistemology, anthropology and the neurosciences. Kosslyn (1983) has summarized the manner in which cognitive science has taken advantage of developments in these different disciplines:

> From computer science it draws information about how computers and computer programs work; from philosophy it has adopted not only many of its basic questions and a general orientation toward the mind, but many of the fundamental ideas about information representation (e.g. 'propositions'); from linguistics it draws a basic way of thinking about mental events and theories of language; and from cognitive psychology it draws methodologies and specific findings about human information-processing abilities.

Cognitive science has been inspired very much by insights within the discipline of psychology, and in particular has developed in step with the field of cognitive psychology. However, it is intrinsically at odds with much of mainstream cognitive psychology, which grew out of what used to be called 'human experimental psychology', and which has incorporated the behaviourist methodology which dominated research earlier this century. Cognitive science owes rather more to the 'human factors' tradition within cognitive psychology, which developed during the Second World War in order to tackle problems concerning human–machine interaction. An illustration of the disparity between cognitive psychologists and cognitive scientists arises in their attitudes to introspective reports of conscious experience. Cognitive psychologists tend to be suspicious of introspective reports and sceptical of their value as empirical data, whereas in cognitive science the use and analysis of such verbal 'protocols' is widely accepted (see e.g. Ericsson and Simon 1984). As an excellent case study within the field of cognitive science, Kosslyn (1983) has given an autobiographical account of his work on mental imagery, which combines systematic experimentation with introspectionist methodology.

Gardner (1985) has identified two core assumptions in contemporary research in cognitive science. The first assumption is that to explain intelligent behaviour it is necessary to incorporate the idea of 'internal' or 'mental' representations as a distinctive and irreducible level of theoretical analysis. Indeed, theories in cognitive science are often based upon the structuralist notion that internal representations intervene between experience and behaviour. Human cognition is regarded as the symbolic manipulation of stored information, and in order to understand intelligent human behaviour, it is necessary to investigate the properties of these internal representations and of the processes that operate upon them. Nevertheless, it should be noted that sociologists have argued that descriptions of mental experience are socially constructed and are at the very least problematic as explanations of behaviour (see Woolgar 1987).

The second core assumption is that the computer is a useful model of human thought and a valuable research tool. Precisely because digital computers are artefactual systems that have been specifically designed for the symbolic manipulation of stored information, the language of computer science seems to provide a convenient and congenial means of articulating notions concerning human cognition. As Kosslyn (1983) has noted, cognitive scientists have therefore borrowed much of the vocabulary that was originally developed to talk about computer functioning and use it to talk about mental representation and processing in human beings. Indeed, the language of computer science tends to function as a theoretical lingua franca among the variety of disciplines that make up cognitive science; as Levy (1987) has put it, the computational representation of models is the 'common test-bed' of cognitive science. Of course, the contemporary digital computer may not provide the best model for characterizing human information processing, and alternative system architectures may prove to be more useful (Kosslyn 1983): a very fashionable approach based upon the notion of parallel distributed processing is claimed to be much more appropriate for modelling human cognition because it is more akin to the known physiology of the central nervous system (McClelland et al. 1986). Nevertheless, the supposed functional similarity between computers and human brains provides a distinctive means of evaluating the theories of cognitive science: the computer simulation of behaviour. The point has been elegantly summarized by Kosslyn (1983):

> If the brain and computer both can be described as manipulating symbols in the same way, then a good theory of mental events should be able to be translated into a computer program, and if the theory is correct, then the program should lead the computer to produce the same overt responses that a person would in various circumstances.

A fundamental criticism of research in cognitive science is that it has tended to view cognition in abstract terms, devoid of any personal, social or ecological significance. As Gardner (1985) remarks, cognitive science tends to exclude (or at least to de-emphasize) 'the influence of affective factors or emotions, the contribution of historical and cultural factors, and the role of the background context in which particular actions or thoughts occur'. Gardner implies that this feature of cognitive science is the result of a deliberate strategic decision in order to render the problems under investigation more tractable. However, it has to be recognized that the pattern of much research within cognitive science (as in other areas of scholarly investigation) is set by existing traditions, and therefore such strategic choices have typically gone by default. The relevance of cognitive science to everyday human experience and its practical application in real-life situations will undoubtedly be enhanced by the incorporation of emotional, cultural and contextual factors into theoretical accounts of human cognition.

JOHN T.E. RICHARDSON
THE OPEN UNIVERSITY

References

Ericsson, K.A. and Simon, H.A. (1984) *Protocol Analysis: Verbal Reports as Data*, Cambridge, MA.

Gardner, H. (1985) *The Mind's New Science: A History of the Cognitive Revolution*, New York.

Kosslyn, S.M. (1983) *Ghosts in the Mind's Machine: Creating and Using Images in the Brain*, New York.

Levy, P (1987) 'Modelling cognition: Some current issues', in P. Morris (ed.) *Modelling Cognition*, Chichester.

McClelland, J.L., Rumelhart, D.E. and Hinton, G.E. (1986) 'The appeal of parallel distributed processing', in D.E. Rumelhart, J.L. McClelland and the

PDP Research Group, *Parallel Distributed Processing: Explorations in the Microstructure of Cognition*, Vol. 1, Cambridge, MA.

Woolgar, S. (1987) 'Reconstructing man and machine: A note on sociological critiques of cognitivism', in W.E. Bijker, T.P. Hughes and T. Pinch (eds) *The Social Construction of Technological Systems*, Cambridge, MA.

Further reading

Harré, R. (2002) *Cognitive Science: A Philosophical Introduction*, London.

SEE ALSO: cognitive neuroscience; cognitive psychology; connectionism

COHORT ANALYSIS

Cohort analysis (also known as longitudinal analysis) refers to studies that measure characteristics of cohorts through their lives, a cohort being a group of persons who have experienced the same life event during a specified period of time (usually 1 year). If the life event is birth, one speaks of a birth cohort, or generation. Similarly one may speak of marriage cohorts, divorce cohorts, educational cohorts, etc., life events in these cases being respectively marriage, divorce or the attainment of a certain level of education, during a particular period of time. For instance one may follow a cohort of marriages over time in order to ascertain how many couples eventually divorce, and to determine the risk of divorcing at each duration of marriage.

Cohort data are usually obtained by comparing the characteristics of a cohort at two or more points in time, using census or sample survey data. When the *same* individuals are compared, the term 'panel study' is often used. Demographic and epidemiological data on cohorts can frequently be derived from records or registers, such as vital statistics or cancer registers. Other important sources of cohort data are retrospective studies, in which respondents are asked to provide information about past characteristics and events.

Cohort data may be affected by selection effects. People die, or move, between censuses or surveys, and retrospective questions can be answered only by those who survive. Bias may be introduced if those who are lost through death or migration tend to have other characteristics that

differentiate them from those interviewed. Retrospective studies are also influenced by recall lapses.

Cohort measures may relate to the characteristics of the cohort, or to events experienced by it. For example, an inter-cohort study might compare the proportions of single people in different cohorts, or focusing on birth, compare the average number of children borne by women at the end of their reproductive period. An intra-cohort study would be concerned rather with changes in characteristics over a lifetime, or in the distribution of events by age, such as changes in the proportion surviving by age, or the distribution of deaths or probabilities of dying by age. If individual data are available, intra-cohort studies can be carried out using e.g. event–history analysis. Inter-cohort effects can in addition be taken into account by multilevel modelling, the cohort being taken as one level of analysis and the individual as the other.

Cohort studies are often undertaken in order to distinguish cohort effects (i.e. effects particular to each cohort) from age (or duration) effects and period effects. It has been shown for example that, in various developed countries, cohort effects have less left their mark on fertility trends than on mortality trends. Ordinary statistical methods are unsatisfactory here, due to the *identification problem*. Age, period and cohort (APC) are not independent variables: knowing two yields the third. The three variables cannot therefore be used simultaneously in statistical procedures that require linear independence between variables. One way out of this difficulty is to place constraints on the model, for example to suppose that one of the effects (e.g. the period effect) is nil, or that the effect of being in one age group is a particular constant. APC models, moreover, do not usually incorporate terms measuring interaction effects between age and cohort, or between period and cohort. Alternatively, the period variable (such as the year) may be used as an indicator of an underlying variable, for example yearly income per head. If data are available, one may then substitute the underlying variable for the year. This is a simple resolution of the identification problem, as the underlying variable is not a linear construct of age and cohort. The choice of the procedure or constraint must rest on supplementary information, or on an appeal to theoretical considerations: it cannot be made on purely statistical grounds.

GUILLAUME WUNSCH
UNIVERSITY OF LOUVAIN, BELGIUM

Further reading

Glenn, N.D. (1977) *Cohort Analysis, Quantitative Applications in the Social Sciences*, Beverly Hills, CA.

Wunsch, G. (2005) 'The longitudinal approach', in G. Caselli, J. Vallin and G. Wunsch (eds) *Demography: Analysis and Synthesis*, Vol. 1, *Population Dynamics*, San Diego, ch. 10.

SEE ALSO: life tables and survival analysis

COLLECTIVE ACTION

Groups often cannot be treated as unitary actors but must be regarded analytically as a collection of individuals who will make choices on the basis of their own interests. Unlike rational individuals who follow their own self-interest, a group of rational actors may fail to pursue collective action that is in their common interest.

The logic of collective action (Olson 1965), which has proved applicable to a remarkably broad range of social and economic situations, assumes that co-operation must be explained in terms of the individual's cost–benefit calculus rather than the group's, because the group is not itself rational, but can only consist of rational individuals. Groups often seek public goods that are available, once they are generated, to everyone including those who did not contribute to producing them. Because individuals can potentially receive the benefits of these public goods without having contributed, they have an incentive to let others pay for them. In the classic examples of collective action problems, such as preserving the environment, sharing a common natural resource, participating in national defence, voting in mass elections, and engaging in social protests, group members gain when all individuals do their share, but for any individual the marginal benefit of a single contribution exceeds the cost. What is best for the group therefore is not necessarily best for the individual. The study of collective action using game theory, laboratory experiments and historical cases has tried to identify the conditions under which rational actors are likely to co-operate

when they have a strong incentive to be free riders.

While the problem of collective action can assume many alternative forms, it is most often represented by a game theoretic model known as the prisoners' dilemma (Hardin 1982). The prisoners' dilemma is a non-co-operative game in which the players' choices are independent and agreements and promises cannot be enforced. A group of n individuals must decide to contribute (i.e. co-operate) or not to contribute to a collective good (i.e. defect). Depending on whether the public good is divisible, the utility of a contribution is either the additional amount of the good that is produced or it is the increase in the probability that an indivisible public good will be generated as a result of the contribution. Unanimous co-operation is preferred by everyone to unanimous defection, but the payoff structure of the game also specifies that no matter how many individuals contribute, each person does better by defecting and thereby enjoying the public good for free; in this sense, defection is a dominant strategy. However, should each rational individual choose his or her dominant strategy, the outcome – total defection – is Pareto-suboptimal, for everyone can improve his or her position if all co-operate in the supply of the public good.

A group may succeed in providing itself with some amount of the public good if it is 'privileged'; that is, if it contains a single member who receives a sufficiently large benefit from the good that it is economical for the person to pay for it even if no one else contributes. In Mancur Olson's (1965) terminology, this results in the exploitation of the great by the small. Groups that are not privileged have to devise other means to encourage contributions, either by changing the incentive structure facing individuals, or by inducing co-operative behaviour through repeated social interaction.

Many groups alter cost–benefit calculations by offering selective incentives in the form of rewards to co-operators and punishments to free riders. Members of professional organizations, for example, receive trade publications and journals, reduced fare travel packages, subsidized health insurance programmes, and other products or services. Shame, praise, honour and ostracism can likewise be viewed, in this regard, as non-material social selective incentives. Administration of a system of selective incentives, however, either by a central authority or by group members, usually entails a separate collective action problem that demands further explanation, because individuals also have an incentive not to contribute to the maintenance of such a system. The second-order collective action problem may in some cases be simpler to solve than the original problem, but the point remains that a more basic explanation is required.

Another potential selective incentive is the benefit inherent in the activity itself, in which case the motivation behind co-operation is not the outcome sought by collective action, but the process or experience of participation. Hirschman (1982) likened taking a free ride when one has an opportunity to participate in public action to declining a delicious meal in favour of a satiation-producing pill. It is undeniable that, for some people, political and organizational activity builds self-esteem and feelings of political efficacy, symbolizes political citizenship, reinforces moral convictions, and constitutes an enthralling experience. Eagerness on the part of people to engage in some forms of collective action is obviously inconsistent with claims that people always have to be dissuaded from free riding.

To the extent that the act of participation is viewed as a benefit rather than a cost, the logic of collective action is transformed. However, co-operation may still be contingent on the strategic choices of others. If expressive benefits are derived from the process rather than the outcome of participation, such benefits are nevertheless more likely to be experienced when collective action is successful. A political activist wishing to share in the excitement of a group effort cannot do so without the co-operation of other activists. Therefore, the pursuit of expressive benefits does not by itself solve the collective action problem but instead changes its structure to a co-ordination game (Schelling 1978) that presents a different set of strategic challenges.

Aside from changing the incentive structure of the prisoners' dilemma (thus removing the dilemma), co-operation in groups can be fostered, in the absence of selective incentives, by repeated social interactions that introduce long-term calculations (Taylor 1987). In iterated social interaction, a person can try to influence the behaviour of others by making his or her choices contingent upon their earlier choices. Some degree of conditional co-operation is necessary to sustain collective action among rational players. In a two-person prisoners' dilemma, for example, a person might co-operate on the first exchange and thereafter co-operate only if the other player co-operated on the previous exchange. If both players use this strategy – known as tit for tat – mutual co-operation will be the equilibrium outcome as long as future benefits are not discounted too heavily. Co-operation is therefore possible among self-interested players if they care sufficiently about future payoffs to modify their present behaviour.

One possible equilibrium in the n-person prisoners' dilemma occurs when everyone co-operates initially and continues to do so as long as everyone else does, but not otherwise. Co-operation is therefore sustained by the expectation that, as soon as one person defects, everyone else defects in retaliation. A less stringent equilibrium occurs when there is a subset of co-operators, some proportion of which co-operates contingent upon the co-operation of every other member of the subset. These equilibria, however, may be difficult to realize in practice if threats of disbanding given a single or a small number of defectors are not credible. Such is the case, for example, when the remaining co-operators can still profitably produce the collective good, so that they would have to hurt themselves in order to punish free riders. Incredible threats open the door to mass defection: if some individuals free ride on the assumption that others will continue to provide the collective good, then everybody might be so tempted and the collective good may never be produced.

Conditional co-operation is less likely to solve the collective action problem as group size increases because defection is harder to identify and deter when many people are involved. Intuitively, the members of small groups are likely to have closer personal bonds, individual contributions will have a greater impact on the likelihood of collective success, and individual defections are more readily observed. For this reason, contingent co-operation in large-scale ventures is facilitated when collective action comprises a federated network of community groups and organizations. Monitoring is feasible in these smaller groups and co-operation or defection can be rewarded or punished in the course of everyday interaction with friends and associates. Consequently, individuals who refuse to contribute to a community-wide effort may suffer damage to their reputations and lose companionship and future opportunities for beneficial exchanges with those in their immediate reference groups (Chong 1991).

Given the importance of knowledge about the motives and actions of other group members in any individual's decision to co-operate, political entrepreneurs or leaders can play a pivotal role in co-ordinating the beliefs and expectations of potential contributors. Among the main tasks of leaders is to provide information to individuals about the parameters of the collective action problem, the intentions of other individuals, the level of past contributions, and the level of contributions needed to achieve success.

There is no reason to suppose that successful collective action will be driven by a single motivation, either coercive or voluntary. Self-interested calculations based on selective material incentives and ongoing social exchange often have to be supplemented by moral and psychological considerations and co-ordinated by political leadership in order for people to contribute to collective goods. Nor is it necessary to assume that all contributors to collective action will employ the same cost–benefit calculus. Collective action frequently relies on the initiative and sacrifice of committed leaders who supply information, resources and monitoring, and lay the foundation for subsequent conditional co-operation among more narrowly self-interested actors.

DENNIS CHONG
NORTHWESTERN UNIVERSITY

References

Chong, D. (1991) *Collective Action and the Civil Rights Movement*, Chicago.
Hardin, R. (1982) *Collective Action*, Baltimore, MD.
Hirschman, A. (1982) *Shifting Involvements*, Princeton, NJ.
Olson, M. (1965) *The Logic of Collective Action*, Cambridge, UK.
Schelling, T. (1978) *Micromotives and Macrobehavior*, New York.
Taylor, M. (1987) *The Possibility of Cooperation*, Cambridge, UK.

Further reading

Axelrod, R. (1984) *The Evolution of Cooperation*, New York.
Elster, J. (1989) *The Cement of Society*, Cambridge, UK.
Rapoport, A. and Chammah, A.M. (1965) *Prisoner's Dilemma*, Ann Arbor, MI.

SEE ALSO: collective bargaining; game theory; interest groups and lobbying; prisoners' dilemma; public goods; social movements

COLLECTIVE BARGAINING

Collective bargaining is a mechanism for organized groups of workers and their employers to resolve conflicting interests and to pursue agreement over common interests. Collective bargaining typically leads to a collective bargaining agreement that codifies the results of labour–management negotiations in written form for a fixed term.

A critical influence on the process of collective bargaining is the inherent conflict of interest that prevails between employees and employers. That conflict arises out of the clash of economic interests between employees seeking, among other things, high pay and job security, and employers pursuing profits. There are also a number of common interests between employers and their employees. Both firms and their work forces can benefit, for example, from increases in productivity through higher wages and higher profits. Conflict and negotiations may therefore serve important private and social functions.

Collective bargaining is only one of a variety of mechanisms for resolving conflicts and pursuing common interests at the workplace, and it competes with these alternative employment systems. Not all employees, for example, feel that they have deep conflicts with their employers or want to join unions, and some may prefer to deal with their employers on an individual rather than a collective basis. Other employees may quit their job when dissatisfied with employment conditions rather than choosing to voice their concerns, either individually or collectively.

Employment conditions are the most important bargaining outcomes that are shaped by collective bargaining. Collective bargaining agreements commonly address, at the very least, the following sets of issues: (1) wage and fringe benefit levels, payment systems and administration; (2) job and income security; (3) physical working conditions; (4) some personnel management and plant operation practices; and (5) union and management rights and responsibilities. The scope and content of bargaining agreements within and across countries vary significantly depending on the parties' relative power and their preferences.

A key aspect of the workplace interaction between labour and management in unionized settings focuses on administration of the collective bargaining agreement. In countries such as the USA and Canada there is a grievance procedure to settle disputes that arise during the term of a collective bargaining agreement. These typically end with a decision by an impartial arbitrator. In other countries, individuals have the right to bring unresolved disputes to legally sanctioned labour courts.

In collective bargaining negotiations both sides have a strong incentive to avoid a strike as each loses income during a strike. Yet, the parties to collective bargaining are unlikely to settle on terms in negotiations that differ substantially from the terms they think would settle a strike if one were to occur. The expectation or even the possibility of a strike outcome consequently shapes negotiated outcomes whether or not a strike actually occurs. It follows that the parties' relative bargaining power, and the dynamics of collective bargaining, depend critically on whether or not labour has the legal right to strike, and on the legal penalties that may be applied where striking is deemed illegal.

In most countries, unions representing private-sector employees have the right to strike and unions representing public employees do not have that right. In the absence of the right to strike, deadlocks in public-sector collective bargaining are typically settled through administrative procedures such as fact-finding or arbitration, although in some jurisdictions these procedures are lacking. In the private sector, in contrast, arbitration is rarely used to settle bargaining occurring over the terms of a labour contract, although mediation is frequently used to facilitate voluntary settlements in both the private and public sectors.

A critical factor that shapes the form and the outcomes of collective bargaining is the structure of bargaining. Bargaining structure refers to the scope of employees and employers covered, or in some way affected, by the terms of a collective bargaining agreement. The formal bargaining structure is defined as the bargaining unit, or the negotiation unit, i.e. the employees and employers who are legally bound by the terms of an agreement. The informal bargaining structure is defined as the employees or employers who are affected by the results of a negotiated settlement, through either pattern bargaining or some other non-binding process.

The USA has a highly decentralized bargaining structure, and from the 1980s on, many US employers pressed for even further decentralization of the formal and informal structures of bargaining. In many European countries, such as Germany and Sweden, and in a number of other regions, labour contracts often cover entire industries, sectors or regions. In recent years, however, a number of European and other employers who traditionally engaged in collective bargaining at relatively centralized levels have been arguing for greater decentralization of collective bargaining in order to allow individual firms the latitude to adjust to their particular economic circumstances.

Where conflict has not overwhelmed their relationship, some labour and management have recently attempted to introduce a new approach, labelled *interest-based* collective bargaining. This approach seeks to move away from more traditional *positional* bargaining in an effort to increase the potential for greater problem-solving in negotiations. In interest-based collective bargaining labour and management try to: (1) focus on their underlying interests, (2) generate options for satisfying these interests, (3) work together to gather data and share information needed to evaluate options, (4) evaluate the options against criteria that reflect their interests, and (5) choose options that maximize their mutual interests.

There has also been pressure in recent years, in many countries, to draw higher-level industrial actors into the process of collective bargaining. For example, tripartite interactions between representatives of labour, management and government affect or supplement the collective bargaining that occurs at the sector or firm level in some European countries, and elsewhere. While in the 1960s and 1970s tripartite bargaining often focused on efforts to control inflation, in recent years the focus has shifted towards compliance with regional objectives (such as conformity with European Union policy objectives) or on efforts to stimulate international competitiveness. At the same time, there has been pressure to include more direct participation by workers and unions in decision-making and the restructuring of work. In Germany and other European countries, works councils have long provided a channel for employee input into workplace decisions that parallel and interact with collective bargaining.

The prevalence of collective bargaining is heavily influenced by the extent of union representation. The share of the workforce represented by unions has been declining in the USA since the early 1950s and in most other countries over the last 10 years or longer. As a result, the prevalence of collective bargaining has declined, leading unions to develop new strategies to organize workers and to 'revitalize' their organizations and activities. Union revitalization commonly includes efforts to change the process and outcomes of collective bargaining. A key aspect of union revitalization has been the spread of 'corporate campaigns' and the linking of collective bargaining to organizing and political strategies. Corporate campaigns are characterized by the use of media, political, financial, community and regulatory pressures to build bargaining power. Such campaigns have become a key part of the more 'strategic' collective bargaining that some unions are promoting in order to counteract the advantages management has gained through the availability of outsourcing, globalization and (in the USA and a few other countries) the use of striker replacements.

A key challenge confronting labour unions all over the globe is the increased international trade and the accelerated expansion of multinational corporations that extend product and labour markets internationally. To counteract the advantages that management gains through globalization, unions have felt the need to create cross-national unionism and collective bargaining. However, the labour movement's efforts to create these structures face substantial barriers including divergent interests (i.e. each labour movement wants the employment) and national differences in language, culture, law and union structure. While there are some recent signs of increased international co-ordination of unionism and collective bargaining, the gains on these fronts to date are extremely limited, and the obstacles remain daunting.

HARRY C. KATZ
CORNELL UNIVERSITY

Further reading

Katz, H.C. and Darbishire, O. (2000) *Converging Divergences: Worldwide Changes in Employment Systems*, Ithaca, NY.

Katz, H.C. and Kochan, T.A. (2004) *An Introduction to Collective Bargaining and Industrial Relations*, 3rd edn, Boston.

Kochan, T.A., Katz, H.C. and McKersie, R.B. (1994) *The Transformation of American Industrial Relations*, 2nd edn, Ithaca, NY.

Walton, R.E., Cutcher-Gershenfeld, J.E. and McKersie, R.B. (1994) *Strategic Negotiations: A Theory of Change in Labor–Management Relations*, Ithaca, NY.

SEE ALSO: collective action; trade unions

COLONIALISM

Modern colonialism has two distinct but related lives. The first was constituted by the historic institutions of Western European (and, briefly, Japanese) administration in Asia, Africa and the Americas. That phenomenon began in the sixteenth century and mainly ended in the middle of the twentieth. The second avatar comprises the values, attitudes and stereotypes associated with colonial rule, from which the world can only recover slowly, if at all.

When colonial empires reached their greatest extent – the first decades of the twentieth century – most scholars agreed that colonialism had a beginning and a middle, and would logically come to a complete end. Colonies were merely a novel form of empire devised and elaborated by Europeans from the sixteenth century onwards. By 1900 almost every society outside Europe had become or had been the colony of a European state. Scholars debated differences between Dutch energy and Portuguese lethargy, French assimilation and British indirect rule, but these were merely the national idioms in which a generic European colonialism was articulated. It began by force or treaty when sovereignty was seized and exercised by governors responsible to European states. When indigenous rulers were retained for the convenience of the new sovereign, they masked the reality of power. The poverty of most colonized peoples and their economies seemed to result from the distorting effects of colonial policies and programmes. And as colonial states became secure, they intruded increasingly into the lives of their subjects, and popular resentment seemed to foreshadow the end of this colonial era.

The war in the Pacific hastened the end of Dutch, British and French colonial ventures in Asia, with further consequences for Africa and the Caribbean. In 1960, as the pace of decolonization quickened, the UN General Assembly created a Decolonization Committee (the Committee of 24) embodying the views of newly independent Asian and African states, with a brief to dismantle all remaining dependencies. Over the next two decades almost every colony was released to join the UN. A few fragments survived as strategic bases, nuclear testing facilities or entrepôts, but most scholars believed that the narrative was approaching its predicted end: Western colonialism had reached its apotheosis in the sovereign states that succeeded them.

To be sure, the end was messy and incomplete. Islands with small populations or scant resources resisted the tide. Several French dependencies preferred the material benefits of continued linkage to independent poverty. New Zealand and US colonies in the Pacific also negotiated 'free association' – limited sovereignty and continuing access to the former metropolitan country. These decisions expressed an increasing scepticism about the benefits of decolonizing. Independence was expected to liberate national energies in pursuit of development and modernization. The United Nations Development Decade focused international attention on these goals, and academic centres of development studies graduated platoons of experts to find and apply technical solutions. But the connections between poverty and colonialism were, at best, blurred. If colonialism distorted economies, freedom did not always deliver prosperity. On the other hand if Japan's industrial revolution suggested the benefits of having resisted colonial annexation, surely Ethiopia, Thailand and even Tonga should have achieved similar outcomes.

In brief, no sooner did colonial governors fold their tents than every piece of conventional wisdom about colonialism came into question. The rights of nations to sovereignty begged the question of defining a nation. Most successor-states were ethnically diverse, bounded by arbitrary frontiers. They proved vulnerable to Cold War rivalries that (for their leaders) increased the attraction of authoritarian rule and a command economy. In Africa particularly, the ever-present threat of secession was reinforced by civil wars in ex-Belgian Congo and Nigeria. In some regions the power and the legitimacy of the state has declined so far that scholars now talk about 'failed states'. In the Pacific, flexibility was possible, such as the separation of the Gilbert and Ellice Islands into Kiribati and Tuvalu. But did polyglot West New Guinea have a right to separate independence from the Netherlands (as some African states argued), or were they properly part of the Indonesian nation, as Western powers insisted?

Attempts to generate solidarity for the whole Third World, or more modest efforts such as African unity, failed to reorient the ex-colonies' economic links. Their inherited bureaucracies were better equipped to control than to mobilize the populace, and their formal economies were well designed to export unprocessed commodities. New education and training institutions could not immediately cope with the aspirations of burgeoning populations. Few ex-colonies responded as planned, to strategies of agricultural intensification and economic diversification. Most of tropical Africa and some other parts of the world have performed so poorly that they have, in effect, been retired from the global economy, their cities swelling and their budgets dependent on aid. These catastrophes contrast sharply with the performance of the economic tigers of Southeast and East Asia, whose success often defies the advice of development experts. In either case, the imperatives of economic development legitimized authoritarian styles of government, which often elaborated colonial structures of control.

These disconcerting tendencies feed into postmodernist critiques of academic positivism. Rather than a mainly administrative and economic phenomenon, recent scholarship (such as Thomas 1994) emphasizes its cultural content and the capacity for colonial cultures to survive the demise of formal colonial rule. Stage theories of human progress have suffered especially badly. Colonialism was not, after all, an aberration, nor was it limited to particular times and particular places. Some see it as inherent in the Western Enlightenment, quoting (for example) John Locke's opinion that 'God gave the world to men in Common, but since He gave it them for their benefit and the greatest conveniencies of life they were capable to draw from it, [therefore He must have intended to give it] to the use of the industrious and rational.' Edward Said's seminal *Orientalism* (1978) and his *Culture and Imperialism* (1993), and the Subaltern Studies pioneered and elaborated by expatriate South Asians (Guha 1994), insist that colonialism was neither a finite era nor a particular set of institutions. Decolonization therefore requires more than the application of technical solutions to material problems. Colonial apologetics and the triumphalist narratives of anti-colonial nationalism are portrayed as two sides of the same coin, alternative stage theories of social evolution that distort rather than illuminate past and present human experience. Only their deconstruction may exorcise colonialism's diffuse influences in the minds and practices of subalterns and superiors alike.

Just as colonialism has burst its old chronological limits, so it has burst its spatial and thematic bounds. It is now closely linked with divisive ideas about gender and especially race, whether or not race is no more than a pigment of the imagination.

DONALD DENOON
AUSTRALIAN NATIONAL UNIVERSITY

References

Guha, R. (ed.) (1994) *Subaltern Studies: Writings on South Asian History and Society*, 2 vols, Delhi.
Said, E. (1978) *Orientalism*, New York
—— (1993) *Culture and Imperialism*, New York.
Thomas, N. (1994) *Colonialism's Culture*, New York.

SEE ALSO: imperialism; postcolonialism

COMMUNISM

Communism connotes any societal arrangement based on communal ownership, production, consumption, self-government, perhaps even communal sexual mating. The term refers both to such societies and practices, and to any theory advocating them. Examples of the former can be found in religious orders throughout history and in radical communities, from the sixteenth-century Anabaptists to the contemporary 'counter-culture', and the most famous example of advocacy of communism may well be the regime proposed for the guardian caste in Plato's *Republic*.

In the middle of the nineteenth century, the most radical schools of the growing socialist movement, including that of Marx and Engels, called themselves communists in order to dissociate themselves from other, allegedly less consistent, socialist groups. Hence when reference is made to that period, communism often is synonymous with the system of ideas developed by Engels and Marx, even though they often used the terms communism and socialism interchangeably. Communism in this sense connotes the sum total of Marxist doctrines; hence it is the Marxist critique of capitalism and liberal theory, and the project for the proletarian revolution, though at times it connotes specifically the ultimate goal of that revolution – the society visualized as emerging out of it, which is dimly foreseen as a society without property, without classes or a division of labour, without institutions of coercion and domination. The precise features of this society are not delineated in the writings of Marx and Engels, and among Marxists there are controversies about the degree of residual alienation and oppression (if any) that one ought to expect in the communist society of the future. Some of the hints Marx and Engels themselves gave come from their notion of a primitive communism allegedly prevailing among the savage early ancestors of the human race.

Among the earliest followers of Engels and Marx, the term fell into disuse; most Marxists around the turn of the century called themselves Social Democrats. The term was revived after the Russian Revolution of 1917 by V.I. Lenin, who renamed his faction of the Russian Marxist movement the Communist Party and compelled all those parties who wished to join the newly created Third (or Communist) International to adopt the same designation, so as to dissociate themselves from the Social Democratic parties. As a consequence, communism since then connotes that interpretation of Marxism, which considers the ideas and actions of Lenin and his Bolshevik faction to be the only correct interpretation of Marxism, and the sum total of parties that subscribe to this interpretation.

Leninism is characterized by the insistence that meaningful social change can come only through revolution, while reforms threaten to corrupt the oppressed. Further, it implies the application of Marxism to countries where capitalism is underdeveloped, hence the development of flexible political strategies, including the mobilization of peasants and ethnic minorities for revolution. Foremost, it insists on the need for a 'vanguard party' of revolutionaries-by-profession to whom correct knowledge of the laws of history and politics ('consciousness') is attributed. Within the party and its numerous auxiliary organizations designed to mobilize the working class and its presumed allies, the vanguard is expected to ensure the prevalence of enlightened consciousness over blind passion by a combination of mass initiative and bureaucratic control that Lenin called 'democratic centralism'. Finally, Leninism implies the accumulated experience of the Russian Communist Party in governing their country. Communism thus connotes the theory and practice of rule by communist parties.

Although the leaders of ruling communist parties have generally refrained from claiming that the systems they were ruling were communist, it has become customary in the Western world to refer to them as communist systems. Communism thus refers to any society or group of societies governed by communist parties.

The mature form of communist rule was developed in the USSR under the rule of J.V. Stalin. Hence communism since the 1930s has become synonymous with Stalinism or neo-Stalinism. This is a system in which the communist party proclaims itself the enlightened leadership and claims authority to speak for the entire nation. It enforces this claim through control over all organizations and associations, all forms of communication, education and entertainment, individual appointments and careers. The chief aim of these systems is rapid economic growth through crash programmes of industrialization, carried out through a centralized command economy. Communism in its Stalinist form thus is a species of entrepreneurship.

Contemporary communist societies thus bear no resemblance to the vision of communism sketched by Marx and Engels or even to that provided by Lenin in his unfinished work, *The State and Revolution*. Yet the memory of that vision lingers and has repeatedly led to attempts within communist parties to define alternatives to Leninist and Stalinist theories and practices. Contemporary communism therefore is not one single orthodoxy, but an ever growing cluster of orthodoxies and heresies, all of them backing up their arguments by reference to Engels and Marx, yet fiercely contending with each other.

Twentieth-century communism began as a dream to create an ideal society and an empowered human being. It turned into a clumsy crash programme of anti-capitalist capital accumulation, of Westernization despite the West. That project has now collapsed in the European part of the communist world; the command economies have yielded to various modes of privatization and the market, doctrinal orthodoxy and the leadership claims of communist parties have been replaced by a multiplicity of parties and ideologies. Ethnic hatreds long tabooed and suppressed have erupted into the open, tearing empires and states apart in bloody conflict. The agony of this revolutionary process has led many citizens of the formerly communist countries to look back to the rule of the communist parties with nostalgia, while for others everything connected with communism has been thoroughly and irreversibly discredited. General opinion in the 'West' considers communism to be dead, but that may be premature.

ALFRED G. MEYER
UNIVERSITY OF MICHIGAN

Further reading

Claudin, F. (1975) *The Communist Movement: From Comintern to Cominform*, London.
Daniels, R.V. (ed.) (1965) *Marxism and Communism: Essential Readings*, New York.
—— (1993) *The End of the Communist Revolution*, London and New York.
Kolakowski, L. (1978) *Main Currents of Marxism*, 3 vols, Oxford.
Meyer, A.G. (1984) *Communism*, 4th edn, New York.
Rosenberg, A. (1967) *A History of Bolshevism*, New York.

SEE ALSO: Marx's theory of history and society; social democracy; socialism

COMMUNITY

Community is one of those key words that has recurred so frequently that at times it has seemed to mean everything and thereby nothing. Thus by 1955, G. Hillary was already able to list scores of different definitions of the term that had appeared in the sociological literature. As a result, later scholars have sometimes noted the futility of taxonomic approaches to this concept or raised doubts about its analytical utility altogether. Nonetheless, in spite of the apparent plurality of references to community, concerted scholarly theorization of this concept has featured a remarkably sustained focus on a few key elements and issues. For over a century, social theorists have repeatedly used the concept of community as a vehicle to interrogate the implications of major historical transformations for the production and reproduction of social sodalities.

In the waning years of the nineteenth and the early decades of the twentieth century, as European theorists tried to grapple with the sometimes devastating displacements initiated by advanced capitalism, it seemed as if community was doomed. Yet the community being mourned was an explicitly idealized version of social solidarity. Dichotomous concepts such as Tönnies's *Gemeinschaft/Gesellschaft* (2001 [1887]) and Durkheim's mechanical/organic solidarity (1984 [1893]) presented ideal types of social formation that, if not necessarily standing for successive historical phases, could still be used to identify key shifts in the basis of social cohesion. Within the terms of these dualities, modernization was viewed as eroding the sense of collective solidarity and conformity that could be enforced and drawn on in small, face-to-face and homogenous communities and encouraging instead the atomized individualism and instrumental relationships characterizing more anonymous, differentiated and exchange oriented industrial metropolises.

Permutations of this paradigm of development then played a significant role in the development of urban sociology and anthropology during the twentieth century. Thus, in the early decades of the twentieth century, under the leadership of Robert Park, the members of the University of Chicago's Department of Sociology ('Chicago School') tended to view the rapid and unplanned expansion of the city around them in terms of alienation, 'disorganization' and a weakening of social solidarity (Park 1925; Wirth 1938). The Chicago School's model of urbanism sparked waves of subsequent work by sociologists and anthropologists that either sought to expand on the thesis of an inevitable loss of community in an urbanizing society (Stein 1960; Nisbet 1953) or alternatively to argue that a sense of collective belonging, continuity and intimacy could persist in metropolitan neighbourhoods from London to Mexico City (Young and Willmott 1957; Gans 1962; Lewis 1965).

In spite of the differences in their prognostications, these critiques as well as endorsements of urban alienation often shared a romanticized view of 'community' as arising spontaneously out of longstanding ties of kinship, ethnicity, race or religion and placed a primary emphasis on strong sentiments of allegiance. The problem with this approach to community, as Gerald Suttles pointed out, is that it tended to be dismissive of the many other forms of residential solidarities that did not conform to this portrait. By the terms of this logic, with the decline of ethnic differentiation and segregation, some local communities should have disappeared and yet some of the most vocal and self-conscious residential groupings in the USA were among the most heterogeneous (Suttles 1972: 15). Instead, Suttles suggested giving attention to the structural characteristics of local cohesion, for example the effects of government policy or administration, and an appreciation of utilitarian impetuses for the negotiation of limited spheres of trust and familiarity within complex metropolitan environments. Put most simply, community could often be a matter of making the best of circumstances not necessarily of one's own choosing rather than of prior sentimental ties.

As the twentieth century drew to a close and sociologists and anthropologists turned their attention to the social impact of yet another phase of capitalist restructuring and technological evolution, community once again featured in a bout of *fin de siècle* stock taking. In some ways this latest incarnation has taken us full circle, back to the ascribed identities and emotionally charged allegiances that earlier theorists had also associated with community but consigned to a premodern past. Now, however, these sentiments and loyalties have, as one scholar put it, been 'liberated' from Tönnies's ideal as a 'traditional, face-to-face collectivity of consociates, bound in amity' (Werbner 1997: 46) and thus rendered iconic of the translocal connections of the globalizing moment.

The liberation of community from locality or direct social interaction received one of its most significant initial impetuses from the seminal work by Benedict Anderson (1991 [1983]) on nationalism. Anderson argued that the development of nationalism relied on the capacity of a multitude of people who would never meet each other face to face, or even know of each other personally, nonetheless to imagine themselves through the mediation of mass printing as part of the same community. Anderson argued that one should not read 'imagined' as 'spurious' or 'invented', for any community that extended beyond the immediately face to face incorporates this element of imagined commonality.

While Anderson was trying to explain a historical transition that first took shape in the sixteenth century, the concept of the 'imagined community' was quickly seized on as a vehicle for explaining quintessentially contemporary collective identities. In spite of this accent on the new and the current, the term 'imagined community' has often been applied to some rather venerable categories of ascription: ethnicity, race, religion or nationality only now portrayed as likely to involve populations dispersed *across* as within national borders.

The enthusiasm for the notion of 'imagined community' has been implicated in a more general conceptual shift away from community as an actualized social form towards an emphasis on community as an idea or quality of sociality. Yet such a focus seems too partial an interrogation of the dialectic between historical social transformations and social cohesion that has continued to propel the recurring sociological fascination with the problem of community. Personal and organizational responses to such major changes are surely as likely to include the utilitarian considerations and circumstantial consociations noted by Suttles as the ideological movements exercising the attention of more recent scholarship. At the start of a century promising to be as turbulent as the last, the changing bases of sociality are likely to continue to vex scholars. The challenge will be to develop models of community that integrate the full complexity of social relations, interactions, identities, localities, ideologies and consociation.

VERED AMIT
CONCORDIA UNIVERSITY

References

Anderson, B. (1991 [1983]) *Imagined Communities*, London and New York.
Durkheim, E. (1984 [1893]) *The Division of Labor in Society*, New York.
Gans, H.J. (1962) *The Urban Villagers*, New York.
Hillary, G.A. (1955) 'Definitions of community: Areas of agreement', *Rural Sociology* 20: 86–118.
Lewis, O. (1965) 'Further observations on the folk–urban continuum and urbanization with special reference to Mexico City', in P.M. Hauser and L.F. Schnore (eds) *The Study of Urbanization*, New York.
Nisbet, R.A. (1953) *The Quest for Community*, New York.
Park, R.E. (1925) 'The city: Suggestions for the investigation of human behavior', in R.E. Park, W. Burgess and R.D. McKenzie, *The City*, Chicago, pp. 1–46.
Stein, M.R. (1960) *The Eclipse of Community*, New York
Suttles, G.D. (1972) *The Social Construction of Communities*, Chicago.
Tönnies, F. (2001 [1887]) *Community and Civil Society*, Cambridge.
Werbner, P. (1997) 'Essentialising essentialism, essentialising silence: Ambivalence and multiplicity in the constructions of racism and ethnicity', in P. Werbner and T. Madood (eds) *Debating Cultural Hybridity: Multi-Cultural Identities and the Politics of Anti-Racism*, London.
Wirth, L. (1938) 'Urbanism as a way of life', *American Journal of Sociology* 44: 1–24.
Young, M. and Willmott, P. (1957) *Family and Kinship in East London*, London.

SEE ALSO: community development

COMMUNITY DEVELOPMENT

In the context of public policy, the phrase community development has most often been used to describe projects initiated by, or with the active participation of, the inhabitants of a locality, which are intended to benefit them collectively. The projects may concern education, social welfare, health, infrastructure such as roads, wells or irrigation, farming, manufacture or commerce. While much of the benefit may accrue to individual families, the projects are intended to enhance the community as a whole, in self-confidence and political skills, for instance, even if not more tangibly.

This conception of community development was widely adopted by British, French and Belgian colonial administrations in Africa and Asia, especially after the Second World War, as a social and political as much as economic strategy for rural areas. In British Africa, for example, departments of community development were created with community development officers trained according to increasingly self-conscious principles of professional community development practice (du Sautoy 1958; Batten 1962). The stimulation of local leadership, the growth of capacity to initiate projects and organize self-help, and the learning of skills were characteristically considered more important than the achievements of any particular project. The ideal community development officer was therefore a facilitator, adviser and sensitive guide, who sought to encourage a collective capacity for initiative and organization that would then continue independently.

In practice, the community development officer's role was more ambivalent than this ideal allowed. As a government employee, he was bound to favour local initiatives that corresponded with national policy and discourage others. His intervention was often crucial in drawing local factions into co-operation and in securing resources. Hence community development remained essentially an aspect of government policy, although a variety of mutual aid and village development associations evolved independently of government – as for instance in eastern Nigeria.

After independence, community development was seen as a means of mobilizing rural people for such endeavours as mass literacy or education, as for instance in the movement for self-reliance in Tanzania, or the Harambee movement in Kenya. But the inherent ambiguity remains of a strategy intended both to encourage self-help and initiative while implementing national government's goals.

In the 1960s, the term community development came to be applied to projects in predominantly urban neighbourhoods of the USA and later Britain, where poverty and social pathologies were believed to concentrate. Like their colonial predecessors, these projects were intended both to provide practical benefits, such as improved social services, more relevant vocational training, legal aid, low-cost housing and more jobs, and, in doing so, to increase the community's sense of its collective competence. In the USA, this approach became national policy under Title II of the Economic Opportunity Act of 1964, following earlier experiments by the Ford Foundation and the President's Committee on Juvenile Delinquency (Marris and Rein 1980) and was continued in many subsequent policies, such as the Model Cities Program and Community Development Block Grants from the federal to local governments. Besides community action agencies, largely concerned with social welfare and educational programmes, community development corporations were funded to promote housing and commercial enterprises, especially in neighbourhoods of high unemployment. The Watts Labor Community Action Coalition, for instance, has, at various times, developed produce markets, a bus service, a large shopping centre and housing in a black district of Los Angeles (Hampden-Turner 1974). Apart from housing, development corporations have experienced great difficulties in sustaining viable commercial enterprises in their communities. In most instances, the attempt to fulfil social purposes, such as employment opportunities for local residents, in market settings that more experienced commercial enterprises have already judged unprofitable, proves too difficult even

with the help of subsidies. Over time, therefore, the corporations tend either to withdraw from commercial endeavours or to defer many of their original social reasons for starting them. Although both government and philanthropies have continued to fund community development projects, poverty and social disintegration in inner-city neighbourhoods have proved very difficult to alleviate (Halpern 1995).

The British Community Development Project, modelled on US community action agencies, was initiated in 1969 by the Home Office with a similar hope of stimulating self-help and innovative solutions in neighbourhoods of concentrated social problems, choosing for the experiment twelve mostly urban neighbourhoods in Britain (Marris 1987). Over time, as concern shifted from social pathology – which was neither as apparent nor as concentrated as had been assumed – to unemployment, the project had to confront the difficulty of applying very localized resources to remedy the effects of large-scale changes of economic structure.

Both the British and US projects were regarded as experimental by the governments that initiated them. Community development, in this context, was intended to discover inexpensive solutions to problems of poverty and unemployment, through self-help and innovative, more relevant and efficient use of resources already allocated. It has therefore never received funding on a scale commensurate with the problems it addressed. Its most lasting achievement, especially in the USA, probably lies in the growing sophistication and organizational capacity of neighbourhood groups in dealing with economic and physical changes that affect them.

PETER MARRIS
YALE UNIVERSITY

References

Batten, T.R. (1962) *Training for Community Development*, London.

du Sautoy, P. (1958) *Community Development in Ghana*, London.

Halpern, Robert (1995) *Rebuilding the Inner City: A History of Neighborhood Initiatives to Address Poverty in the United States*, New York.

Hampden-Turner, C. (1974) *From Poverty to Dignity: A Strategy for Poor Americans*, Garden City, NY.

Marris, P. (1987) *Meaning and Action*, 2nd edn, London.

Marris, P. and Rein, M. (1980) *Dilemmas of Social Reform*, 3rd edn, Chicago.

SEE ALSO: community

COMPETITION

The simplest meaning of the term is rivalry between alternative buyers and sellers, each seeking to pursue their own ends. It is central to economics because it provides the mechanism through which the actions of agents can be co-ordinated. It is the basis for Adam Smith's claim that every individual 'is led by an invisible hand to promote an end which was no part of his intention' (Smith 1979 [1776]: 456). It requires both a plurality of potential buyers and sellers, and a competitive attitude. Thus its opposite may be either monopoly (the usage in most modern economics) or custom and co-operation (as was the case for J.S. Mill).

When Adam Smith and the classical economists used the term competition, they referred to the process whereby prices were forced down to costs of production, and wages and profits to their 'ordinary' levels. The requirement for this was what Smith termed 'perfect liberty' in which there are no barriers to mobility and 'every man, as long as he does not violate the laws of justice, is left perfectly free to pursue his own interests in his own way, and to bring both his industry and his capital into competition with those of any other man' (Smith 1979 [1776]: 687). This is what has since been termed the long-period aspect of competition, the process whereby capital and labour are moved from one activity to another, taking considerable time. In contrast, the short-period aspect of competition concerns the way markets operate. For the classical economists, the short-period aspect of competition was summarized by the law of one price: the proposition that there cannot be two prices in the same market. It embodies a static notion of competition, for the process whereby price differences are eliminated is ignored.

Between the 1870s and the 1930s a number of economists (notably W.S. Jevons, L. Walras, F.Y. Edgeworth, V. Pareto, A. Marshall, K. Wicksell, J. Robinson and E.H. Chamberlin) developed the concept of perfect competition. Like the law of one price, and in contrast to what the classical economists understood by competition, perfect competition is a static concept. It is not a process but a type of market in which each agent is so small as to be unable to influence the price at which goods are bought and sold. Agents are price-takers. It is contrasted with imperfect competition, a state in which individual agents are sufficiently large to be able to have some control over the price of what they are buying or selling. Imperfect competition covers a variety of market structures ranging from monopoly (one seller) and monopsony (one buyer) to oligopoly (a small number of sellers) and bilateral monopoly (one buyer and one seller).

Perfect competition is a situation where most of the phenomena commonly associated with competition (brands and product differentiation, advertising, price wars – phenomena that were extensively discussed in the late nineteenth-century US literature) are absent, yet it has provided the dominant theory of competition in economic theory since the 1940s. Economists have explored, with great rigour, the conditions under which perfect competition will occur. Perfect competition has been shown to be efficient in the sense that in a perfectly competitive equilibrium it is impossible to make any individual better off without simultaneously making someone else worse off (Pareto efficiency). Perfect competition was, at least until the 1980s, the almost universally used assumption about market structure in diverse areas of economics such as international trade, inflation and unemployment, despite its implausible assumption that firms' decisions should depend only on prices and not on their beliefs about the quantity of goods they can sell.

The main reason why economists rely so heavily on models of perfect competition is that imperfect competition, in particular oligopoly, is much more difficult to analyse, one of the main problems being that in order to work out what is the best action to take, agents (usually firms) have to take into account how their competitors are likely to respond. Nowadays the most widely accepted solution to this problem is to use game theory. Using game theory economists have managed to construct theoretical models of aspects of competition such as entry deterrence, strategic investment, product variety and R&D expenditure. Economists have also learned ways to use models of monopolistic competition in international economics and macroeconomics.

While the focus of most economic theory has been on perfect competition, dynamic aspects of competition such as concerned Smith and the classical economists have not been neglected. The

Austrian School, based on the work of C. Menger, sees competition as a dynamic process of discovery, dominated by the figure of the entrepreneur. It is entrepreneurs who see the possibilities for making profits by producing new goods, or by producing existing goods in new ways. The competitive process involves the continual creation and subsequent elimination of opportunities for profit. The contrast between orthodox and Austrian conceptions of competition is shown by the debate, in the 1920s and 1930s, over whether rational (i.e. efficient) economic calculation was possible under socialism. Market socialists such as O. Lange focused on the static concept of perfect competition, arguing that it was possible to design a set of rules for a socialist economy (in which there was no private ownership of capital) that would produce the same allocation of resources as would occur in a competitive, capitalist economy. Against them, Austrians such as L. von Mises and F.A. von Hayek argued that competition in the sense of rivalry was necessary if new products and new technologies were to be discovered: that those aspects of competition that K. Marx saw as wasteful (e.g. the building of two factories, one of which was subsequently eliminated by competition) were a vital feature of capitalism that could not be emulated under socialism.

Perhaps the best-known economist working in the Austrian tradition was J.A. Schumpeter. His vision was of competition as a process of 'creative destruction'. Entrepreneurs discover new technologies, earning large profits as a result. Over time their discoveries are imitated by others, with the result that competition forces profits down. This theory fits into a longer tradition of evolutionary theories of competition, whose history goes back to the social Darwinism of the late nineteenth century in which competition was seen as eliminating the unfit. Among the most prominent modern exponents of evolutionary theories of competition are R.R. Nelson and S.G. Winter, who combined the Austrian idea that entrepreneurs explore alternative ways of responding to novel situations with the Darwinian idea that those who make good choices survive, with competition eliminating those who make bad ones.

The Austrian emphasis on innovation also results in a different attitude towards the role of numbers in competition. The standard view is that the smaller the number of firms, the less is the degree of competition. Attempts have therefore been made to measure competition by measuring variables such as concentration ratios – the share of output produced by, say, the largest five firms. Austrians, however, emphasize potential competition, which may be unrelated to the number of firms in the industry. A similar line has been pursued by W.J. Baumol who has developed the notion of a 'contestable' market. A perfectly contestable market is one in which entry and exit are absolutely costless, the result being that potential competition will keep prices low even if there are few firms in the industry.

ROGER E. BACKHOUSE
UNIVERSITY OF BIRMINGHAM

Reference

Smith, A. (1979 [1776]) *An Inquiry into the Nature and Causes of the Wealth of Nations*, eds R.H. Campbell and A.S. Skinner, Oxford.

Further reading

Archibald, G.C. (1987) 'Monopolistic competition', in J. Eatwell, M. Milgate and P. Newman (eds) *The New Palgrave Dictionary of Economics*, London.
Backhouse, R.E. (1990) 'Competition', in J. Creedy (ed.) *Foundations of Economic Thought*, Oxford.
High, J. (ed.) (2001) *Competition*, Cheltenham.
Lavoie, D. (1985) *Rivalry and Central Planning: The Socialist Calculation Debate Reconsidered*, Cambridge, UK.
McNulty, P.J. (1987) 'Competition: Austrian conceptions', in J. Eatwell, M. Milgate and P. Newman (eds) *The New Palgrave Dictionary of Economics*, London.
Morgan, M. (1993) 'Competing notions of "competition" in late-nineteenth-century American economies', *History of Political Economy* 25(4).
Schumpeter, J.A. (1976) *Capitalism, Socialism and Democracy*, 5th edn, London.
Stigler, G.J. (1957) 'Perfect competition, historically contemplated', *Journal of Political Economy* 65(1). Reprinted in G.J. Stigler (1965) *Essays on the History of Economics*, Chicago.
—— (1987) 'Competition', in J. Eatwell, M. Milgate and P. Newman (eds) *The New Palgrave Dictionary of Economics*, London.

SEE ALSO: competition policy; game theory; markets; monopoly; regulation

COMPETITION POLICY

The main objective of competition policy is to improve market efficiency by promoting or safeguarding competition between firms, and thus to minimize the resource misallocation effects of the exercise of market power. Economists usually distinguish between competition policy and regulation. Regulation refers to more direct government intervention in circumstances where effective competition is difficult or impossible because firms possess a lot of market power and are likely to abuse it.

High market concentration has traditionally been seen as a cause of concern, since it has been thought to facilitate the abuse of market power by firms. However, higher concentration need not be associated with less price competition and lower welfare. The opposite may sometimes be the case, as more intense competition reduces profit margins and the number of firms that can survive in an industry. So competition authorities should probably be less concerned with concentration than with ensuring that competition between firms is 'effective', i.e. firms do not collude or otherwise abuse their market power and there are no barriers to entry.

Design and implementation of competition policy

There are several difficulties with the design and implementation of competition policy:

1   Firm conduct that may improve one aspect of market efficiency may also worsen another. For example, a horizontal merger between two firms may result in higher prices, but it may also lead to lower current costs or lower future costs or better products.

2   In many cases, the effect of a particular business practice on efficiency may not be unambiguous in general. Examples of such practices are price discrimination, exclusive dealing agreements between manufacturers and retailers, and so on.

3   Some practices, such as tacit collusion or predatory pricing, are difficult to detect, thus making the implementation of policy difficult even in cases where the welfare implications of firm conduct are relatively unambiguous.

4   It is not always easy to know what degree of market power is acceptable in a particular industry, given the technological and other constraints faced by firms in the industry. Some degree of market power is necessary under conditions of increasing returns to

scale, so that firms can cover their fixed costs, including investment and research costs. Moreover, a firm may possess market power because it is efficient or innovative, which surely cannot be bad in itself.

5   Assessing the market power of firms (or the change in market power that has been or may be brought about by a certain action of the firms) may be complicated because of difficulties in defining the relevant product or geographical market, the absence of precise information on firms' costs and perhaps also on demand parameters, and the need to take into account market dynamics that may influence the extent to which market power is likely to persist in time.

6   The efficiency goal has not been the only objective of competition policy in practice. Other objectives may include the protection of small firms, the dispersion of economic power and the maximization of consumer welfare (as opposed to efficiency).

7   Conflicts may also arise between competition policy and other government policies, such as industrial or trade policy. For instance, competition policy may clash with a policy of supporting the creation of strong domestic firms that are able to compete with foreign firms in some sectors.

Merger policy

Competition authorities can influence market structure in particular industries by preventing certain mergers between firms from taking place. The rationale for merger policy is that a consequence of many mergers is the creation of significant additional market power. In the case of horizontal mergers, the primary concern is the rise in market share. In the case of vertical mergers, the primary concern is the possibility that vertical integration hinders the access of non-integrated firms to outlets or sources of supply.

Even when a merger creates significant market power, it can have countervailing benefits, such as current or future efficiency gains. The merger may therefore be allowed despite its effect on competition. This can be justified if the merger is thought to result in lower costs, better management, improved R&D capabilities or some other efficiency gain. Moreover, mergers may often be made necessary by exogenous changes in market conditions, such as competitive pressures due to economic integration. A merger may be allowed if it can be shown that one of the firms will otherwise go out of business.

Policy towards restrictive practices

Explicit or tacit agreements between firms to fix prices or to allocate customers or geographical areas are generally considered to be detrimental for competition and are therefore prohibited in most competition laws. There are some exceptions, the most important of which concerns agreements to co-operate in research. The major difficulty regarding horizontal restrictive practices is detection. It is not easy to distinguish between collusive and non-collusive behaviour on the basis of the information typically available to competition authorities. For instance, evidence of parallel pricing, i.e. the similarity of prices and price changes, is not sufficient for concluding that collusion exists. The exchange of information on prices, costs, etc., between firms may facilitate collusion, but it may also improve the knowledge of market conditions and thus promote competition.

Policy towards the abuse of a dominant position

Competition authorities are not so much worried by the mere existence of market power as by the possibility that market power is used in a way that eliminates, restricts or distorts competition. Business practices that may constitute abuses of market power include 'excessive' prices, strategies that deter entry or expansion of rivals, price discrimination, tying, predatory pricing and vertical restraints. Some of these practices, such as price discrimination or vertical restraints, can have ambiguous welfare effects. Others, such as introducing new products or building capacity in anticipation of a rise in demand, can be legitimate competitive actions even if they also deter entry. And still others, such as predatory pricing, are definitely welfare-reducing, but are also difficult to detect. Most competition laws therefore recognize the need for detailed investigations on a case-by-case basis when it comes to assessing whether a firm or group of firms have abused their market power.

GEORGE SYMEONIDIS
UNIVERSITY OF ESSEX

Further reading

Baker, J.B. (1999) 'Developments in antitrust economics', *Journal of Economic Perspectives* 13(1): 181–94.

Comanor, G.W., Jacquemin, K., Jenny, A., Kantzenbach, F., Ordover, E. and Waverman, L. (2002) *Competition Policy in Europe and North America*, London.

Commission of the European Communities (1997) *The Single Market Review, vol. V.2: Competition Issues*, Luxembourg.

Hay, D. (1993) 'The assessment: Competition policy', *Oxford Review of Economic Policy* 9(2): 1–26.

Kovacic, W.E. and Shapiro, C. (2000) 'Antitrust policy: A century of economic and legal thinking', *Journal of Economic Perspectives* 14(1): 43–60.

Martin, S. (2001) 'Competition policy', in M. Artis and F. Nixon (eds) *The Economics of the European Union*, 3rd edn, Oxford.

Scherer, F.M. (1994) *Competition Policies for an Integrated World Economy*, Washington, DC.

Symeonidis, G. (2002) *The Effects of Competition*, Cambridge, MA.

SEE ALSO: competition; industrial organization; markets; monopoly; regulation

COMPUTER SIMULATION

The construction of computer programs that simulate aspects of social behaviour can contribute to the understanding of social processes. Most social science research either develops or uses some kind of theory or model, for instance, a theory of cognition or a model of the class system. Generally, such theories are stated in textual form, although sometimes the theory is represented as an equation (for example, in structural equation modelling). As personal computers began to become common in the 1980s, researchers began to explore the possibilities of expressing theories as computer programs. Social processes can then be simulated in the computer. In some circumstances, it is even possible to carry out experiments on artificial social systems that would be quite impossible or unethical to perform on human populations.

The logic underlying the methodology of simulation is that a model is constructed (for example, in the form of a computer program or a regression equation) through a process of abstraction from what are considered to be the actually existing social processes. The model is then used to generate expected values, which are compared with empirical data. The main difference between statistical modelling and simulation is that the simulation model can itself be 'run' to produce output, while a statistical model requires a statistical analysis program to generate expected values.

It is necessary to think through one's basic assumptions very clearly in order to create a useful simulation model. Every relationship that is to be modelled has to be specified exactly. Every parameter has to be given a value, for otherwise it will be impossible to run the simulation. This discipline also means that the model is potentially open to inspection by other researchers, in all its detail. These benefits of clarity and precision also have disadvantages, however. Simulations of complex social processes involve the estimation of many parameters, and adequate data for making the estimates can be difficult to come by.

Another benefit of simulation is that it can, in some circumstances, give insights into the 'emergence' of macro-level phenomena from micro-level actions. For example, a simulation of interacting individuals may reveal clear patterns of influence when examined on a societal scale. A simulation by Nowak and Latané (1994), for example, shows how simple rules about the way in which one individual influences another's attitudes can yield results about attitude change at the level of a society. A simulation by Axelrod (1995) demonstrates how patterns of political domination can arise from a few rules followed by simulated nation-states. Schelling (1971) used a simulation to show that high degrees of residential segregation could occur even when individuals were prepared to have a majority of people of different ethnicity living in their neighbourhood.

Schelling's study is a good example of the kind of work involved in simulation. He modelled a neighbourhood in which homes were represented by squares on a large grid. Each grid square was occupied by one simulated household (either a 'black' or a 'white' household), or was unoccupied. When the simulation is run, each simulated household in turn looks at its eight neighbouring grid squares to see how many neighbours are of its own colour and how many of the other colour. If the number of neighbours of the same colour is not sufficiently high (for example, if there are fewer than three neighbours of its own colour), the household 'moves' to a randomly chosen unoccupied square elsewhere on the grid. Then the next household considers its neighbours

and so on, until every household comes to rest at a spot where it is content with the balance of colours of its neighbours. Schelling noted that when the simulation reaches a stopping point, where households no longer wish to move, there is always a pattern of clusters of adjacent households of the same colour. He proposed that this simulation mimicked the behaviour of whites fleeing from predominantly black neighbourhoods, and observed from his experiments with the simulation that even when whites were content to live in locations where black neighbours were the majority, the clustering still developed: residential segregation could occur even when households were prepared to live among those of the other colour.

There are a number of different kinds of computer simulation models, each appropriate for different domains and research questions. Macrosimulation models describe the future evolution of a whole system in terms of difference equations, often using the conventions of systems dynamics (Hanneman 1988). The most famous macrosimulation models are the early ones of Forester (1971) and Meadows (Meadows et al. 1972; Meadows 1992). These were complex models designed to anticipate the global effects of changes in world population, the amount of pollution, the depletion of natural resources, etc. Microanalyical models (often called, loosely, 'microsimulation' models) simulate the ageing of a survey sample in order to learn about its characteristics in the future. These models are typically used to predict tax and benefit transfer flows. For example, they may be designed to forecast how much the Treasury will need to pay out in pensions in 10 years' time. The third main type of model is the multi-agent model. These models (also called multi-agent systems) are the most active area of research at present.

The agents in multi-agent models are computer programs (or parts of programs) that are designed to act relatively autonomously within a simulated environment. An agent can represent an individual or an organization, according to what is being modelled. Agents are generally programmed to be able to 'perceive' and 'react' to their situation, to pursue the goals they are given, and to interact with other agents, for example by sending them messages. Agents are generally created using an object-oriented programming language and are constructed using collections of condition–action rules. The Schelling model described above is an early and simple example of a multi-agent model. Agent-based models have been used to investigate the bases of leadership, the functions of norms, the implications of environmental change on organizations, the effects of land-use planning constraints on populations, the evolution of language, and many other topics. (Examples of current research can be found in the *Journal of Artificial Societies and Social Simulation*, available at http://www.soc.surrey.ac.uk/JASSS/.)

While most agent-based simulations have been created to model real social phenomena, it is also possible to model situations that could not exist in our world, in order to understand whether there are universal constraints on the possibility of social life. (For example, can societies function if their members are entirely self-interested and rational?) These are at one end of a spectrum of simulations ranging from those of entirely imaginary societies to those that aim to reproduce specific settings in great detail.

A variant on agent-based modelling is to include people in place of some or all of the computational agents. This transforms the model into a type of multiplayer computer game, which can be valuable for allowing the players to learn more about the dynamics of some social setting (for example, business students can be given a game of this type in order to learn about the effects of business strategies). Such games are known as participatory simulations.

Although computer simulation can be regarded as simply another method for representing models of social processes, it encourages an emphasis on emergence, the search for simple regularities that give rise to complex phenomena, and an evolutionary view of the development of societies. These features suggest connections with complexity theory, an attempt to locate general principles that apply to all systems which show autonomous behaviour, including not only human societies but also biological and physical phenomena (e.g. Solé and Goodwin 2000).

NIGEL GILBERT
UNIVERSITY OF SURREY

References

Axelrod, R. (1995) 'A model of the emergence of new political actors', in N. Gilbert and R. Conte (eds) *Artificial Societies*, London.

Forester, J.W. (1971) *World Dynamics*, Cambridge, MA.

Hanneman, R.A. (1988) *Computer-Assisted Theory Building: Modeling Dynamic Social Systems*, Newbury Park, CA.

Meadows, D.H. (1992) *Beyond the Limits: Global Collapse or a Sustainable Future*, London.

Meadows, D.H., Meadows, D.L., Randers, J. and Behrens, W.W., III (1972) *The Limits to Growth*, London.

Nowak, A. and Latané, B. (1994) 'Simulating the emergence of social order from individual behaviour', in N. Gilbert and J. Doran (eds) *Simulating Societies: The Computer Simulation of Social Phenomena*, London, pp. 63–84.

Schelling, T.C. (1971) 'Dynamic models of segregation', *Journal of Mathematical Sociology* 1: 143–86.

Solé, R. and Goodwin, B. (2000) *Signs of Life: How Complexity Pervades Biology*, New York.

Further reading

Brown, L. and Harding, A. (2002) 'Social modelling and public policy: Application of microsimulation modelling in Australia', *Journal of Artificial Societies and Social Simulation* 5(4), http://jasss.soc.surrey.ac.uk/5/4/6.html.

SEE ALSO: artificial intelligence

CONDITIONING, CLASSICAL AND OPERANT

The Russian physiologist, Ivan Pavlov, was not the first scientist to investigate how animals learn, but he was certainly one of the first to undertake a systematic series of experiments intended to provide precise quantitative information on the subject, and it is to his work that we owe the term conditioning to describe one form of that learning. In the course of his work on the digestive system of dogs, Pavlov had found that salivary secretion was elicited not only by placing food in the dog's mouth but also by the sight or smell of food, and that eventually a dog might start to salivate at the sight or sound of the attendant who usually provided the food. These 'psychic secretions', although initially interfering with the planned study of the digestive system, provided the basis for the study of conditional reflexes for which Pavlov is now far more famous.

Pavlov's experimental arrangement was simple. A hungry dog is restrained on a stand; every few minutes, the dog receives some meat powder, the delivery of which is signalled by an arbitrary stimulus, such as the ticking of a metronome or the flashing of a light. The food itself elicits copious salivation, which is measured by diverting the end of the salivary duct through a fistula in the dog's cheek. After a number of trials on which the delivery of food is always preceded by the ticking of the metronome, the dog does not wait for the food, but starts to salivate as soon as the metronome is sounded. Food is referred to as an unconditional stimulus because it unconditionally elicits salivation; the metronome is a conditional stimulus that comes to elicit salivation conditional on its relationship to the food. By similar reasoning, salivation to food is an unconditional response, but when the dog starts salivating to the metronome, this is a conditional response, strengthened or reinforced by the delivery of food whenever the metronome sounds, and weakened or extinguished whenever the metronome occurs without being followed by food. In translation from the original Russian, 'conditional' and 'unconditional' became 'conditioned' and 'unconditioned', and the verb 'to condition' was rapidly introduced to describe the procedure that brought about this change in the dog's behaviour.

At about the same time as Pavlov was starting his work on what is now called classical conditioning, a young US research student, Edward Thorndike, was undertaking an equally systematic series of experiments that are now regarded as providing the first analysis of operant conditioning. Thorndike was more catholic in his choice of animal to study than was Pavlov, using cats, chickens and monkeys impartially. The impetus for his work was also different. While Pavlov was a physiologist who saw himself as studying the brain and how it controlled not only inborn but also acquired reflexes, Thorndike was concerned to study how animals learned in an objective and scientific manner in order to dispel the myths that he thought had arisen about the amazing feats of intelligence of which animals were capable, myths that owed much to a post-Darwinian desire to prove the mental continuity of humans and other animals.

In a typical experiment, Thorndike would place a cat in a puzzle box from which the animal could escape, and so get access to a dish of food, only by performing some arbitrary response such as pressing a catch or pulling on a piece of string. Thorndike recorded the time it took the animal to perform the required response on successive trials, and observing a gradual decline in this time, interpreted the learning in terms of his celebrated 'law of effect': the reward of escaping from confinement and obtaining food strengthened the one response that was successful in achieving this, while all other responses, being followed by no such desirable effects, were weakened.

The term operant conditioning was introduced by the US psychologist, B.F. Skinner, who refined Thorndike's procedure by the simple device of delivering food to the animal (via, for example, an automatic pellet dispenser) while it remained inside the box. In this apparatus, a rat could be trained to perform hundreds of responses, usually pressing a small bar protruding from one wall, in order to obtain occasional pellets of food. The response of pressing the bar was termed an operant because it operated on the animal's environment, and the procedure was therefore operant conditioning, which was reinforced by the occasional pellet of food, and extinguished if pressing the bar was no longer followed by food.

Although Skinner, unlike Thorndike, took over much of Pavlov's terminology, he interpreted the learning he observed in a way much more closely related to Thorndike's analysis. For Skinner, as for Thorndike, the central feature of learning and adaptation is that an animal's behaviour should be modified by its consequences. The rat presses the bar because this response produces a particular outcome – the delivery of food; when it no longer does so, the rat stops pressing the bar, just as it will also stop if pressing the bar produces some other, less desirable outcome such as the delivery of a brief shock. The schedules according to which the experimenter arranges these outcomes have orderly and appropriate effects on the animal's behaviour.

The law of effect, which summarizes these observations, is entirely in accord with common sense: parents hope and believe that rewarding children for good behaviour or punishing them for bad will also have appropriate effects, and when they are mistaken or disappointed we are more inclined to look for other sources of reward or to question the efficacy of their punishment than to question the underlying logic of the argument. Operant conditioning, therefore, although no doubt only one, rather simple form of learning or way of modifying behaviour, is surely an important and pervasive one. It is not so immediately obvious that the process of classical conditioning identified by Pavlov is of such importance. Why does the dog start salivating at the sound of the metronome? The experimenter delivers the food regardless of the dog's behaviour (this, of course, is the precise distinction between classical and operant conditioning, for in Skinner's experiments the rat gets food only *if* it presses the bar). It has been argued that salivation does actually achieve something – for example, it makes dry food more palatable and this is why the dog learns to salivate in anticipation of food. The explanation attempts to interpret classical conditioning in operant terms, for it seeks to identify a desirable consequence of salivation responsible for reinforcing the response. But the explanation is probably false. Another popular example of classical conditioning is that of blinking by a rabbit to a flash of light that signals the delivery of a puff of air to the rabbit's eye. Since this is a classical experiment, the puff of air is delivered on every trial regardless of the rabbit's behaviour. Just as in the case of the dog's salivary response, however, it seems reasonable to argue that the rabbit's eye blink serves to protect the eye from the puff of air and is therefore reinforced by this desirable consequence. The argument implies that if the experimenter arranged that on any trial on which the rabbit blinked in anticipation of the puff of air, the experimenter cancelled its delivery altogether, the rabbit would learn to blink even more readily. Here, after all, blinking has an even more beneficial consequence than usual: it completely cancels an aversive consequence. But in fact such a procedure significantly interferes with the conditioning of the rabbit's eye blink.

A more plausible interpretation, then, is that classical conditioning simply reflects an animal's anticipation of a particular consequence, not necessarily an attempt to obtain or avoid that consequence – this latter being the provenance of operant conditioning. Classical conditioning probably has its most important application in the area of emotions and attitudes: the anticipation of an unpleasant event may generate a variety of emotional changes, such as fear or alarm that are not necessarily under voluntary control. Voluntary behaviour, that is, that directly affected by its consequences, is the sphere of operant conditioning.

N.J. MACKINTOSH
UNIVERSITY OF CAMBRIDGE

Further reading

Domjan, M. and Burkhard, B. (1986) *The Principles of Learning and Behavior*, 2nd edn, Monterey, CA.
Flaherty, C.E. (1985) *Animal Learning and Cognition*, New York.
Mackintosh, N.J. (1983) *Conditioning and Associative Learning*, Oxford.
—— (1994) *Handbook of Perception and Cognition*, Vol. 9, *Animal Learning and Cognition*, New York.

CONFLICT

Among the several meanings of conflict, two are discussed here: first, conflict as a perspective explaining many aspects of social life, and, second, at greater length, as a contentious relationship exemplified in wars, revolutions or other struggles.

Conflict perspective

The conflict approach (comparable to the functionalist, exchange, symbolic-interaction, systems or other theoretical approaches) is often used to account for the maintenance of social order and also for its transformation. Theorists and researchers using this approach regard societies, organizations and other social systems as arenas for interpersonal and intergroup struggles. They use this approach to examine particular social topics such as how men dominate women or how crimes and other forms of deviance are socially defined. Although common and complementary interests are recognized, conflict theorists emphasize the incompatible ones. They also tend to stress the use of coercion in social relations. Finally, they generally assume that humans will strive to resist domination and coercion, and overt struggles consequently will arise.

Conflict theory goes back to the earliest historians and advisers of rulers, as seen in the writings of Thucydides, Machiavelli and Hobbes. Later, Marx and Engels stressed economic conditions and the resulting property relations that underlay class conflict and so accounted for the rise and coming fall of capitalism. Other conflict theorists such as Gumplowitz, Ratzenhofer and Novicow worked in the context of evolutionary thought and posited group struggles for existence. They variously stressed military power and interests – for example ethnic differences – as bases for conquest.

Contemporary conflict theorists emphasize different elements from this rich conflict tradition.

Many social scientists continue to draw from Marxism, but they differ greatly in interpreting and using it. Thus, Dahrendorf (1959) argues that authority relations, not property relations, underlie social conflicts. Gramsci (1971) stresses the cultural hegemony exercised by the ruling class as a mode of domination. Collins (1975) considers violence and other forms of coercion as important in social control, but he also draws from the symbolic-interaction tradition to stress the importance of meanings in the organization of people for struggle, both at the interpersonal and the social structural levels, as in gender relations.

Many social scientists from every discipline draw upon various aspects of the conflict perspective in studying diverse areas of social life. Thus, many analysts of international relations focus on power relations among states and the search for security by gaining power (Morgenthau 1950). Some analysts of economic development in different parts of the world stress the use of economic, political and military power to impose unequal exchanges that yield a relationship of dependency by peripheral underdeveloped countries upon the highly developed core countries (Frank 1978). Students of globalization commonly stress its inequality and the domination by small groups in the USA and other powerful capitalist countries (Rupert and Smith 2002). Finally, analysts of worker–employer relations often draw on Marxist or other ideas in the conflict perspective.

Specific social conflicts

Social scientists have always been interested in particular kinds of conflicts, such as wars, revolutions, labour relations and ethnic, religious and other communal struggles. They have developed explanations for some of these types of conflicts and also theories about social conflicts in general (Kriesberg 2003). Social scientists draw from the conflict perspective in explaining various aspects of conflicts, but many also draw on various other social science approaches (Boulding 1962).

TYPES OF SOCIAL CONFLICTS

Among the many ways in which conflicts differ, four kinds of variations are discussed here: characteristics of the adversaries, matters in contention, means used in the struggle, and the social context of the conflict.

First, adversaries in a conflict vary in their degree of organization and boundedness. At one extreme are governments, trade unions and other entities with clear procedures for deciding and for implementing policies towards antagonists. At the other extreme are entities such as social classes or ethnic communities whose boundaries may be in flux, and who lack agreed upon procedures for deciding and executing policies. Moreover, every social conflict is likely to include many adversaries: some overlapping and crosscutting, or encompassing others. For example, a government head may claim to speak for a government, a state, a people, an ideology, a political party faction and a social class. Each such claim helps constitute a corresponding adversary. Herein lies one of the bases for the interlocking character of conflicts.

Second, social conflicts differ in the goals in contention. Adversaries may contest control over land, money, power or other resources that they all value: such disputes are consensual conflicts. Alternatively, they may come into conflict about differently held values. These are dissensual conflicts. Of course, in specific conflicts both consensual and dissensual components are usually present. In addition, goals differ in their significance for the adversaries, e.g. whether they pertain to peripheral interests or to basic human needs.

Third, conflicts are waged in diverse ways. Conflict analysts usually examine struggles involving violence or other forms of coercion, whether employed or threatened, and which are relatively non-institutionalized. But an adversary often uses persuasion and even the promise of rewards to influence the other side to agree to what is being sought. In many conflicts, the adversaries adhere to such well-developed and highly institutionalized rules that they often are not regarded to be in conflict. This often is the case in electoral campaigns, where different parties seek to control the government. Certain kinds of conflicts become increasingly institutionalized and regulated over time, and that transformation is a matter of paramount significance. We can recognize such a change in labour–management conflicts in many countries during the nineteenth century (Dahrendorf 1959).

Fourth, the social contexts within which conflicts are conducted vary greatly, including families, communities, organizations, societies and regions of the world. The contexts often provide procedures of conducting and settling fights. Moreover, even for relatively non-institutionalized conflicts, external parties may intervene as partisans or as intermediaries and affect the course and outcome of the conflicts.

Aside from the theoretical approach adopted, the investigators' value orientations also greatly affect their analyses. Some analysts tend to approach a social conflict from a partisan outlook, trying to learn how to advance the goals of their side. This is the case for military strategists and many advocates of national liberation. Others want to minimize violence and look for alternative ways a fight may be waged. Still others are primarily interested in attaining a new social order, justified in terms of universal claims for justice or equity, and see conflicts as the right process towards that end. Finally, the intellectually curious may adopt a disinterested, relativistic view of social conflicts.

Judgements about social conflicts are also shaped by changing social conditions, value and belief systems, technology and paradigm-shifting conflicts. For example, in the 1950s the USA was marked by considerable elite consensus as the Cold War reigned; hence domestic conflicts were often viewed as unrealistic and disruptive, and as instigated by socially marginal individuals. However, during the late 1960s and 1970s, with the eruption of struggles regarded as legitimate by major groups in the society, conflicts were often viewed as realistic efforts to redress injustices. With later backlashes in the 1980s and 1990s, the growth of conflict resolution ideas and the lessening of the salience of ideology, the view that all contenders in a struggle should be accorded some legitimacy became more widespread. At the end of the twentieth and beginning of the twenty-first centuries, the increased salience of ethnic and religious identities and conflicts associated with them resulted in gruesome conflicts accompanied by the dehumanization and demonizing of enemies. At the same time, increasing globalization and human rights norms increased the condemnation of abusers of such rights and the likelihood of external intervention.

STAGES OF SOCIAL CONFLICTS

Social scientists often analyse social conflicts by focusing upon particular conflict stages: the conflicts' underlying bases, emergence, escala-tion, de-escalation, settlement, outcome or consequences. Different theoretical approaches are often applied to particular stages, emphasizing various combinations of factors within each party, in the relations between them, or to the social system within which they exist.

Social scientists generally find the bases of social conflicts in social conditions and processes, and not in the biological nature of humans. Those social conditions and processes that are internal to one party in a conflict may be stressed in accounting for a fight or for the means used in waging the struggle (Ross 1993). For example, feminists note the prevalence of gender role socialization that produces aggressiveness among men, and psychologists note that resentments arising from dissatisfaction from one source may be displaced upon easily targeted scapegoats. Many analysts regard the conflicts resulting from such processes as 'unrealistic'.

Most conflict analysts stress that conflicts arise from adversaries striving for the same limited matters, and an important underlying basis for such conflicts is inequality. Other conflicts may arise from differences in goals – when groups have different values but one group seeks to impose its own upon the other. Countering factors that reduce the likelihood of a conflict erupting include high levels of interdependence and shared norms.

The system within which possible adversaries act also affects the eruption of severe conflicts, e.g. by not providing legitimate means for managing them. Functionalist theorists stress the functional integration and consensual character of social systems, noting that many conflicts result from unequal rates of social change.

For a conflict to emerge, four factors must be minimally present. First, members of a potential conflict party have a sense of collective identity distinct from another group. Second, they have a sense of grievance, feeling threatened or suffering an injustice. Third, they believe another group is responsible for their grievance and formulate a goal to change those others to reduce their grievance. And they believe that they can act to induce a change in the other to achieve their goals.

Some analysts emphasize the emergence of particular ways of thinking that shape self conceptions and conceptions of others that foster conflict emergence and a more or less destructive conflict trajectory. Ideologies related to racism or to ethnonationalism are cases in point

Conflict analysts have differed about the relative importance of absolute deprivation and of relative deprivation in generating a sense of grievance (Gurr 1970). Prevailing values about what is fair and beliefs about how social conditions arise also influence the changing sense of grievance.

Many analysts have come to emphasize the group members' belief that they are able to improve their conditions, and these beliefs vary with developments in each contending party and in their relations with each other. The strength and cohesion of the dominant group is critical to the emergence and success of challengers to domination. Groups seeking to change others must also be able to mobilize to pursue their goals (Tilly 1978).

The fact that dominant groups are relatively able to attain their goals helps explain why they often initiate further demands leading to overt conflict. If a subordinate group begins to act on its belief that it can effectively challenge the status quo, the dominant group often tries to suppress the challengers.

Most studies of social conflicts focus on the use of coercion and its escalation. The coercion used in waging a conflict varies greatly in intensity and extent, but non-coercive inducements are also employed in conflicts. While coercion encompasses a variety of violent and non-violent means, non-coercion includes efforts at persuasion and positive sanctions, such as promised benefits (Kriesberg 2003).

The internal developments in each of the adversary groups, the interaction between them, and the conduct of actors not initially involved in the conflict, may all affect the escalation and de-escalation of conflicts. Internal factors, including social-psychological processes and organizational developments, may make protagonists more or less committed to the cause of the struggle. Subunits engaged in the conflict may derive power, status and economic gains in the fight, while those who suffer in the struggle, especially if they are severely harmed, may become less committed.

Second, how adversaries interact profoundly shapes a conflict's trajectory. Adversary actions can be provocatively hostile and hence escalating, or successfully intimidating and thereby de-escalating; or the actions can be conciliatory and thus de-escalating, or appeasing and thereby encouraging escalation.

Third, parties not initially involved in a conflict affect its course of development by joining in to advance their own interests or by setting limits to the conflict. Intermediaries can also mitigate the undesired aspects of conflicts by mediation, thus facilitating communication and providing face-saving options.

Every fight ends, but the end may be the prelude to a new or renewed fight. Conflict analysts are increasingly studying the nature of agreements or accommodations that mark a conflict's ending (Stedman *et al.* 2002). They also are examining the implementation of agreements and the construction of enduring peaceful relations, even after terrible violence has been inflicted and suffered by antagonists. This work includes consideration of the processes of conflict transformation and how security, justice, truth and mutual regard contribute to conflict transformation and are the products of it.

LOUIS KRIESBERG
SYRACUSE UNIVERSITY

References

Boulding, K.E. (1962) *Conflict and Defense*, New York.
Collins, R. (1975) *Conflict Sociology*, New York.
Dahrendorf, R. (1959) *Class and Class Conflict in Industrial Society*, London.
Gramsci, A. (1971) *Selections from the Prison Notebooks*, London.
Gurr, T.R. (1970) *Why Men Rebel*, Princeton, NJ.
Frank, A.G. (1978) *Dependent Accumulation and Underdevelopment*, London.
Kriesberg, L. (2003) *Constructive Conflicts: From Escalation to Resolution*, 2nd edn, Lanham, MD.
Morgenthau, H.J. (1950) *Politics among Nations*, New York.
Ross, M.H. (1993) *The Culture of Conflict*, New Haven, CT.
Rupert, M. and Smith, H. (eds) (2002) *Historical Materialism and Globalization*, London.
Stedman, S.J., Rothchild, D. and Cousens, E.M. (eds) (2002) *Ending Civil Wars: The Implementation of Peace Agreements*, Boulder.
Tilly, C. (1978) *From Mobilization to Revolution*, Reading, MA.

Further reading

Coser, L. (1956) *The Functions of Social Conflict*, New York.
Kriesberg, L. (1992) *International Conflict Resolution*, New Haven, CT.

Marshall, M.G. and Gurr, T.R. (2003) *Peace and Conflict 2003*, College Park, MD.

Powers, R.S. and Vogele, W.B. with associate editors C. Kruegler and R.M. McCarthy (1997) *Protest, Power, and Change: An Encyclopedia of Nonviolent Action from ACT-Up to Women's Suffrage*, New York and London.

SEE ALSO: conflict resolution; genocide

CONFLICT RESOLUTION

Since the end of the Second World War and especially since the 1970s, a new approach, drawing on a range of social science disciplines, has developed for the constructive resolution of conflicts. Variously called problem-solving conflict resolution, integrative negotiations or simply conflict resolution, it is increasingly being used throughout the world and is now an established field of training, research and theory building as well as of applied work.

Social conflicts are inherent in social life, and although they are often destructive, conflicts may promote desired changes or inhibit undesirable developments. Whatever its causes, almost any conflict may be conducted in a constructive fashion, with mutually satisfactory and more generally beneficial consequences (Galtung *et al.* 2002; Kriesberg 2003; Miall *et al.* 1999).

The analysis of social conflicts is a necessary preliminary to the adoption of conflict resolution strategies and techniques. Conflicts are said to occur when members of two or more groups have decided that they have incompatible objectives, irrespective of how these are being pursued. The conflict becomes manifest when: (1) members of each side have a sense of a collective 'us' in relationship to a collective 'them'; (2) members of at least one group feel aggrieved; (3) attributing responsibility for their grievance to the other group, one or both parties formulate goals to change the behaviour of the other so as to alleviate their grievance; and (4) members of the aggrieved party believe they can bring about the desired change in the antagonist.

Each of these components may have features that foster constructive resolution of the conflict. For instance, identities and conceptions of the adversary can embody tolerance and respectfulness. Grievances can be attributed to circumstances not solely of the adversary's making. Goals can be formulated so that they are attainable only by co-operation. Finally, the methods antagonists use may be regarded as legitimate by all parties, and have significant non-violent and even non-coercive elements.

Adversaries are always engaged in many interlocked conflicts, and these conflicts are nested in each other over time and social space. Consequently, changes in one set of conflicts may affect the development of other conflict relationships. The rise of a new enemy, for example, may lessen the antagonism directed towards an old foe.

Each conflict tends to move through a sequence of stages, but often regresses to an earlier stage. The stages include emergence, escalation, de-escalation and transformation, termination and then outcome, which may be the prelude to a new struggle. Diverse conflict resolution methods are varyingly effective at different conflict stages.

Some conflict resolution methods are designed to avert destructive conflicts. These include moderating the underlying conditions generating such conflicts: for example, where both parties come to recognize the basic human needs of the other (Burton 1990). The underlying conditions for conflict may also be reduced by promoting tolerance for people with differing values and by sharing desired resources equitably. Institutionalized methods of contention may be fostered that do not in themselves further exacerbate fights. Even some non-institutionalized methods can communicate readiness to negotiate a settlement and not to destroy the other group. Thus, advocates of non-violent action as a means of struggle stress how such actions can convey the commitment to what is being sought at the same time the opponents' humanity is recognized (Powers and Vogele 1997).

Other conflict resolution methods are directed at the de-escalation and transformation of destructive conflicts (Kriesberg 1992; Mitchell 2000). These also include actions to bring about internal changes in one or both sides so that their goals are less likely to be regarded as incompatible. Finally, some conflict resolution methods may help reduce a conflict's destructive prolongation. These include meetings in which dialogue is fostered, interactive problem-solving workshops (Fisher 1997) and also confidence-building measures.

Most methods of conflict resolution are designed to promote the negotiated settlement of specific social conflicts. Mediators may help to bring adversaries to the negotiating table by testing their readiness to negotiate, by devising an appropriate agenda for particular negotiating partners, and by providing an appropriate meeting venue. They may provide a safe, neutral social and/or physical space for negotiators to meet; they may convey information between adversaries who do not communicate well with each other; and they can help to break through emotional barriers, enabling people on each side to hear what the others are saying. Mediators also can suggest options, give cover for making concessions, add resources, speak up for unrepresented groups, and help to ensure the implementation of an agreement (Moore 1996).

The process of negotiation directed at maximizing mutual gain is central to conflict resolution (Lewicki et al. 1999). A major approach is interest-based negotiation (Fisher et al. 1991). Using this approach, negotiators strive to convert zero-sum conflicts into problems to be solved to the mutual advantage of the parties. With this goal in view, each party seeks to understand the other's underlying interests, then to devise options that might meet the interests of both sides, and finally to select the best options according to agreed upon standards. Agreements reached through such processes may not only reduce grievances, but also contribute to improving the adversaries' conceptions of each other. Experience with these methods also accustoms the adversaries to use non-antagonistic ways to settle their disputes.

Finally, many conflict resolution practices are increasingly relevant to peace-building after intense violence has ended. This is particularly important in the case of civil wars and other violent domestic conflicts after which the former enemies must live closely together. In this situation, constructing shared identities and developing common institutions for managing conflicts are helpful. Policies that redress past injustices and foster justice are also important, but they must be pursued with care in order to prevent a backlash, and they should not endanger other concerns, such as security.

Contemporary conflict resolution methods are used in all kinds of arenas, including interpersonal relations (as in alternative dispute resolution practices), public policy disputes about environmental issues, labour–management relations, societal intercommunal and class conflicts, and international conflicts. A variety of persons and groups use these methods, including official

representatives of the contending sides. Non-officials, who may have more or less influence and power, can also play critical roles at every conflict stage and contribute to waging conflicts constructively.

Two strategies to transform protracted conflicts are particularly noteworthy. One is the graduated reciprocation in tension-reduction (GRIT) strategy (Osgood 1962) and the other is the tit-for-tat (TFT) strategy (Axelrod 1984). In the GRIT strategy, one side unilaterally initiates a series of co-operative moves, announcing them and inviting reciprocity. The conciliatory moves are continued for an extended period, even in the absence of immediate reciprocity. In the TFT strategy one party initiates a co-operative act and then simply reciprocates the other party's actions, whether it is a co-operative action or not.

Analysts have assessed these strategies by examining actual interventions that helped to wind down dangerous confrontations. For example, a quantitative analysis comparing the GRIT and TFT explanations was made of relations between the USA and the Soviet Union, between the USA and the People's Republic of China (PRC), and between the Soviet Union and the PRC for the period 1948–89 (Goldstein and Freeman 1990). Although GRIT was proposed as a strategy for the US government to break out of the Cold War, it was in the event applied most spectacularly by a Soviet Leader, Mikhail Gorbachev, and transformed Soviet–US relations. The role of mediators, formal and informal, may also be significant. For example, President Jimmy Carter played a critical role in the negotiations between Egypt and Israel, leading to their 1979 Peace Treaty. A crucial component of the treaty was the exchange of high-priority benefits between the two countries: the return of the Sinai to Egyptian sovereignty, and the imposition of limits on Egyptian military forces in areas of the Sinai bordering Israel. External actors may also nudge, or pressure, the parties to end conflicts. For example, intervention in the form of economic and other sanctions contributed significantly to the end of apartheid in South Africa. In some cases, widely shared beliefs about human rights may encourage outside parties to impose solutions to domestic conflicts.

After destructive encounters have ended, various means may be used to sustain peaceful relations between former adversaries. For example, policies, institutions and patterns of conduct may be introduced to provide redress for past injustices, promote personal and communal security, and foster mutual respect and integration. The Truth and Reconciliation Commission (TRC) of South Africa is a widely cited instance.

Even skilled applications of conflict resolution methods do not guarantee that each and every destructive conflict can be prevented, limited or transformed, let alone brought to a permanent resolution. Nevertheless, there have been many successes, and the application of these methods may help to avoid the escalation of conflicts. It is also evident that adversaries who rely solely on force and intimidation in the prosecution of conflicts often fail disastrously, and may themselves be destroyed in the process.

LOUIS KRIESBERG
SYRACUSE UNIVERSITY

References

Axelrod, R. (1984) *The Evolution of Cooperation*, New York.
Burton, J. (1990) *Conflict: Resolution and Prevention*, New York.
Fisher, R. (1997) *Interactive Conflict Resolution*, Syracuse, NY.
Fisher, R., Ury, W. and Patton, B. (1991) *Getting to Yes: Negotiating Agreement without Giving in*, 2nd edn, New York.
Galtung, J., Jacobsen, C.G. and Brand-Jacobsen, K.F. (2002) *Searching for Peace: The Road to TRANSCEND*, 2nd edn, London.
Goldstein, J.S. and Freeman, J.R. (1990) *Three-Way Street: Strategic Reciprocity in World Politics*, Chicago.
Kriesberg, L. (1992) *International Conflict Resolution: The US–USSR and Middle East Cases*, New Haven, CT.
—— (2003) *Constructive Conflicts: From Escalation to Resolution*, 2nd edn, New York.
Lewicki, R.J., Saunders, D.M. and Minton, J.W. (1999) *Negotiation*, New York.
Miall, H., Ramsbotham, O. and Woodhouse, T. (1999) *Contemporary Conflict Resolution*, Cambridge.
Mitchell, C. (2000) *Gestures of Conciliation: Factors Contributing to Successful Olive Branches*, New York.
Moore, C.W. (1996) *The Mediation Process: Practical Strategies for Resolving Conflict*, San Francisco.
Osgood, C.E. (1962) *An Alternative to War or Surrender*, Urbana, IL.
Powers, R.S. and Vogele, W.B. (eds) (1997) *Protest, Power and Change: An Encyclopedia of Nonviolent Action from ACT-UP to Women's Suffrage*, New York and London.

Further reading

Kressel, K. and Pruitt, D.G. (1989) *Mediation Research*, San Francisco.
Kriesberg, L. (2001) 'The growth of the conflict resolution field', in F.O. Hampson *et al.* (eds) *Turbulent Peace*, Washington, DC, pp. 407–26.
Lederach, J.P. (1997) *Building Peace: Sustainable Reconciliation in Divided Societies*, Washington, DC.
O'Leary, R. and Bingham, L. (eds) (2003) *The Promise and Performance of Environmental Conflict Resolution*, Washington, DC.
http://www.campus-adr.org/Faculty_Club/academics_faculty.html>, tools and support for conflict studies instructors.
http://www.crinfo.org, the Conflict Resolution Information Source.

SEE ALSO: conflict; peace studies

CONNECTIONISM

The term 'connectionism' has been used in a variety of senses in the history of psychology. Carl Wernicke's (1874) model of language functioning, which emphasized connections between different areas of the brain, was dubbed connectionist, as was Donald Hebb's (1949) account of memory as the strengthening of neural connections. The modern use of the term is related to Hebb's, and applies to computational models of human performance that are built from neuron-like units. These models can be traced back to the work of McCulloch and Pitts (1943) on the simulation of neural functioning. Their ideas were simplified and made computationally viable by Rosenblatt (1962), in his work on *perceptrons* in the 1950s and 1960s. However, interest in perceptrons waned when Minsky and Papert (1969) showed that the best understood perceptrons had severe limitations. In particular they could not solve so-called *exclusive-OR* problems, in which a stimulus was to be classified in a particular way if it had one property or another property, but not both. More complex perceptrons were difficult to analyse mathematically, but interest in them revived in the late 1970s, with the availability of cheap computer power. Such computer power enabled a practical, rather than a mathematical, demonstration of what problems could be solved by complex *neural networks*.

Since the mid-1980s neural network computing has seen a wide variety of applications, most of which lie outside of psychology. Understanding of the formal properties of neural nets has also continued apace. But again most of this work has been done by non-psychologists. The term *connectionism*, though not strictly defined, is usually applied to the use of neural networks in psychological models of a kind made popular by Rumelhart, McClelland, Hinton and others (McClelland and Rumelhart 1986; Rumelhart and McClelland 1986). A connectionist model contains two or three groups of neuron-like units called *input units*, *hidden units* (these are optional) and *output units*. The basic property of a unit is to have a *level of activation*, corresponding roughly to a rate of neural firing. Activation is passed along the connections that link the units into a network, so that the activation of a particular unit is affected (either positively or negatively) by the activation of the units it is linked to. Passing of activation takes place in a series of cycles, one at each tick of a (computational) clock.

The stimulus that a connectionist net is currently responding to is encoded as a pattern of activation in the input units. Cycles of activation passing lead to a pattern of activation in the output units, which encodes the net's response. The hidden units, if they are included, come between the input units and the output units, and allow considerable complexity both in the responses that the net can make and in the relations between the ways it responds to different stimuli.

It is possible to construct a connectionist network in which the function of and the strengths of the connections between them are specified in advance. For example, a unit in a word identification system might correspond to a letter A at the beginning of the word, and this unit will be highly activated by a word that actually begins with A. In addition this unit will have strong positive connections to units that represent words beginning with A. However, not all connectionist models are constructed in this way. One of the most important properties of connectionist networks is that they can learn to perform tasks. But if they are to learn, all that can be specified is the methods of encoding used by the input and the output units. The interpretation of activation of the hidden units, and of the strengths of the connections between the units, cannot be predetermined. In fact, learning in such systems is defined as a change in strength of the connections.

The best-known method of learning in connectionist nets is known as *back propagation*. Initially the strengths of the connections are set at random, and an input is presented to the system. It produces a random output, but is told by its teacher (usually another part of the program) what the correct output should be. The difference between the actual output and the correct output is then used to adjust the strengths of the connections, working back from the output units to the input units (hence *back propagation*). This procedure is repeated many times for different inputs, selected from a so-called *training set*. The changes to the strengths of the connections are always (very) small, because the net must not get its response to the last input right at the expense of responding correctly to other inputs. Eventually, a set of connection strengths should emerge that allow accurate response to all the stimuli in the training set and to other stimuli from the same class, on which it might be tested. Unsupervised methods of learning are also available for connectionist nets. *Competitive learning* is the best known in psychology, but a technique called *adaptive resonance* can be shown formally to produce more stable learning outcomes.

Connectionist networks have found a variety of applications, both in psychological modelling and in the real world. In psychological modelling, the area that has seen the most successful application of pure connectionist techniques has been the identification of spoken and written words. *Hybrid* models are more popular in other domains, particularly those thought of as 'higher level'. These models combine connectionist techniques with more traditional symbolic ones. For example they may include a number of subnets that interact in ways that cannot be described in terms of passing activation and changing connection strengths. Interestingly, hybrid systems are also often used in commercial applications such as industrial process control (including robotics and machine vision) and pattern classification (see e.g. Lisboa 1992).

Although strong claims have been made for them, connectionist nets suffer certain limitations. First, despite their success in models of word identification, connectionist nets in their basic form are not able to represent sequential information, of the kind that people and animals often have to respond to, in a natural way. However, the recurrent (or sequential) nets developed by Jordan (1986) do have this capability, since they feed information from the output units back to the input units (with a time delay), so that temporal sequences may be learned. A more important limitation is that current connectionist networks appear to be incapable of explaining some of the inevitable relations between pieces of information stored in the human mind. As Fodor and Pylyshyn point out:

> You don't...get minds that are prepared to infer *John went to the store* from *John and Mary and Susan and Sally went to the store* and from *John and Mary went to the store* but not from *John and Mary and Susan went to the store*.
>
> (1988: 48)

Unfortunately it is all too easy for connectionist nets to have this property.

ALAN GARNHAM
UNIVERSITY OF SUSSEX

References

Fodor, J.A. and Pylyshyn, Z.W. (1988) 'Connectionism and cognitive architecture: A critical analysis', *Cognition* 28: 3–71.
Hebb, D.O. (1949) *The Organization of Behavior: A Neuropsychological Theory*, New York.
Jordan, M.I. (1986) 'Attractor dynamics and parallelism in a connectionist sequential machine', in *Proceedings of the Eighth Annual Conference of the Cognitive Science Society*, Hillsdale, NJ, pp. 531–46.
Lisboa, P.J.G. (ed.) (1992) *Neural Networks: Current Applications*, London.
McClelland, J.L., Rumelhart, D.E. and the PDP Research Group (1986) *Parallel Distributed Processing: Explorations in the Microstructure of Cognition*, Vol. 2: *Psychological and Biological Models*, Cambridge, MA.
McCulloch, W.S. and Pitts, W.H. (1943) 'A logical calculus of ideas immanent in nervous activity', *Bulletin of Mathematical Biophysics* 5: 115–33.
Minsky, M. and Papert, S. (1969) *Perceptrons*, Cambridge, MA.
Rosenblatt, F. (1962) *Principles of Neurodynamics*, New York.
Rumelhart, D.E., McClelland, J.L. and the PDP Research Group (1986). *Parallel Distributed Processing: Explorations in the Microstructure of Cognition*, Vol. 1: *Foundations*, Cambridge, MA.
Wernicke, C. (1874) *Der aphasische Symptomenkomplex*, Breslau.

Further reading

Hagan, M.T., Demuth, H.B. and Beal, M. (1996) *Neural Network Design*, Boston, MA.
Haykin, S. (1999) *Neural Networks: A Comprehensive Foundation*, 2nd edn, Upper Saddle River, NJ.
Levine, D.S. (1991). *Introduction to Neural and Cognitive Modeling*, Hillsdale, NJ.
McLeod, P., Plunkett, K. and Rolls, E.T. (1998) *Introduction to Connectionist Modelling of Cognitive Processes*, Oxford.

SEE ALSO: cognitive neuroscience; cognitive psychology; neural networks

CONSCIOUSNESS

Consciousness in the core sense refers to a state or continuum in which we are able to feel, think and perceive. Certain usages within the social sciences, such as class consciousness, and certain popular usages, such as consciousness raising and self-consciousness, refer to the content, style or objects of consciousness rather than the primary fact of being aware.

Consciousness is paradoxical because we have direct and immediate personal knowledge of it, but, at the same time, it seems to evade the explanatory frameworks of the social and natural sciences. Let us assume that it can be shown that a particular group of neurons in the brain fires whenever the observer sees something red, and that another group of neurons fires whenever the observer sees something green. This might explain how the observer can make different responses to different colours, but it does not seem to explain the subjective appearance of those colours. Acquisition of the appropriate linguistic usages of the term red (as a child) might explain why we can all agree that ripe strawberries and British post boxes are red, but can it explain their redness? This point is illustrated in the puzzle of the inverted spectrum (Locke 1706); suppose what you see as having the subjective quality of redness, I see as having the subjective quality of greenness. We nevertheless can agree in our use of colour names because the same (publicly describable) objects always cause similar (private) sensations for a given individual.

Philosophers have given the name *qualia* to specific sensory qualities, such as the smell of freshly baked bread, the sound of a breaking glass or the colour and texture of the bark of an oak tree. To know these things vividly and precisely, it is not good enough to be told about them, one must experience them for oneself. Consciousness thus seems to depend on a privileged observer and unique viewpoint, and this might seem to imply that subjective aspects of consciousness are outside the explanatory systems of science, which are based on shared knowledge (Nagel 1986), and, by extension, beyond all socially constructed meanings. This is the much-contested 'explanatory gap' (Levine 1983). In another formulation, the explanation of phenomenal consciousness is considered to be the 'hard problem' in the philosophy of mind (Chalmers 1996).

In recent decades there has been an energetic search for a material basis of consciousness. Compelling evidence comes from studies of patients with brain injuries. If the visual cortex on one side of the brain is destroyed following a stroke, vision is lost in the opposite half of the visual field. Such patients report a complete absence of any visual sensations from the blind hemifield. Some of these patients nevertheless can point (given a forced choice) to a visual target in the 'blind' hemifield, while denying that they see anything. Vision without conscious awareness is termed 'blindsight' (Weiskrantz 1986); different brain areas are found to be concerned with the conscious experience of seeing and the largely unconscious visual processing required for control of actions (Milner and Gooddale 1995). If certain areas of right parietal cortex are damaged, patients tend to exhibit a syndrome known as unilateral neglect. They appear not to be conscious of bodily or extra-personal space on the side opposite the lesion. The sensory input appears to be intact, because if a stimulus is applied in isolation to the neglected side, it can usually be detected. However, under everyday conditions patients may misjudge the centre of doors, eat only the right half of food on a plate or dress only the right half of the body. Bisiach and Luzzatti (1978) have shown that unilateral neglect may apply to imagined as well as real scenes. It would appear that conscious awareness of an external world, of the body and of an imagined scene requires brain processes over and above the simple registration of sensory inputs. Another key component of consciousness is deliberate or voluntary action: Luria (1973) described patients who, after massive frontal lobe lesions, were completely passive, expressed no wishes or desires and made no requests. Luria showed that this was a disturbance only of the higher forms of conscious activity, not a global paralysis or stupor. Involuntary or routine behaviours were intact or intensified, emerging sometimes at inappropriate moments, due to the loss of conscious regulation. Incidental stimuli such as the squeak of a door could not be ignored; a patient might respond involuntarily to an overheard conversation with another patient, while being unable to respond directly to questions. Shallice (1982) has proposed that frontal lobe areas are part of a 'supervisory attentional system' that controls and modulates the routine, involuntary and habitual processes of behaviour and perception. It is tempting to identify conscious thought with the operation of a unitary 'central executive' system; however, functional imaging techniques have revealed a multiplicity of brain modules and systems whose activation is correlated with different, specialized aspects of consciousness (Zeki 2003). A key question is how particular neural activations come to be associated with conscious rather than unconscious processes.

We begin in unconsciousness, so what are the developmental origins of consciousness? Vygotsky (1986) saw individual subjective awareness as secondary and derivative of social awareness; an internalization of processes and concepts derived from the wider culture via speech (Kozulin 1990). In keeping with this view, the ability to monitor one's own experiences and the intentions of others may be facets of the same developmental achievement (meta-representation). According to Perner (1991), children below the age of 4 years do not know that they have intentions and cannot accurately report upon the thought processes they use. Self-awareness may be a relatively late developmental achievement, but a broader definition of consciousness, including the beginnings of verbal communication and explicit memory, would indicate that infants first show conscious awareness at around 12–15 months (Perner and Dienes 2003), and this may require the maturation of specific brain areas.

Social, developmental and cognitive theories of consciousness are broadly compatible with a functionalist stance on the mind–body problem. Thus, Dennett (1991) has argued that there is no possible explanation of consciousness beyond that available, in principle, to the social and natural sciences; indeed, he exposes dualistic arguments as non-explanations. The paradoxes of consciousness are captivating but false, and Dennett marshals arguments to strip them of their power: qualia, for instance, are ultimately nothing more than the sum total of our reactive dispositions. Likewise, there is no 'Cartesian theatre' where conscious events are played out for us. Rather, thought is accomplished in a parallel, distributed pattern of provisional, competing scripts, described by Dennett as 'multiple drafts'. Dennett, like Vygotsky, favours the idea that consciousness is primarily a cultural construction, acquired in early development, believing that it is in evolutionary terms a recent phenomenon, unlikely to be hard-wired into our brains.

Reductive explanations of consciousness are unsatisfying to many. There is a revival of interest in cross-cultural aspects of consciousness, including trance, meditative states and religious experience (Ferrari 2003). The central importance of phenomenology and the first-person perspective has been reasserted and reinstated in the integrative theories of Varela (1999) and Velmans (2000). According to Chalmers (1996) the solution to the 'hard problem' will require the introduction of new universal and fundamental properties. Likewise, for Penrose (1994), the paradox of consciousness endures. He implies that the primacy of conscious experience places it outside the functionalist paradigm. He explains (with great clarity) that there are fundamental problems in reductive theories of computation and quantum physics, and argues (more obscurely) that there is a deep connection between the incompleteness of these theories and the problem of consciousness.

MICHAEL J. WRIGHT
BRUNEL UNIVERSITY

References

Bisiach, E. and Luzzatti, C. (1978) 'Unilateral neglect, representational schema and consciousness', *Cortex* 14.
Chalmers, D. (1996) *The Conscious Mind: In Search of a Fundamental Theory*, New York.
Dennett, D.C. (1991) *Consciousness Explained*, New York.
Ferrari, M. (ed.) (2003) 'William James's "The varieties of religious experience": Centenary essays', *Journal of Consciousness Studies* 9.
Kozulin, A. (1990) *Vygotsky's Psychology: A Biography of Ideas*, New York.
Levine, J. (1983) 'Materialism and qualia: The explanatory gap', *Pacific Philosophical Quarterly* 64: 354–61
Locke, J. (1689) *An Essay Concerning Human Understanding*, London, Bk 2, Ch. 8.
—— (1976 [1706]) *An Essay Concerning Human Understanding*, London, Bk 2, Ch. 32, Section 15.
Luria, A.R. (1973) *The Working Brain: An Introduction to Neuropsychology*, Harmondsworth.
Milner, A.D. and Gooddale, M.A. (1995) *The Visual Brain in Action*, Oxford
Nagel, T. (1986) *The View from Nowhere*, Oxford.
Penrose, R. (1994) *Shadows of the Mind*, Oxford.
Perner, J. (1991) *Understanding the Representational Mind*, Cambridge, MA.
Perner, J. and Dienes, Z. (2003) 'Developmental aspects of consciousness: How much theory of mind do you need to be consciously aware?' *Consciousness and Cognition* 12: 63–82.
Shallice, T. (1982) 'Specific disorders of planning', *Philosophical Transactions of the Royal Society of London* 298.
Varela, F.J. (1999) 'Neurophenomenology: A methodological remedy for the hard problem', *Journal of Consciousness Studies* 3: 330–50.
Velmans, M. (2000) *Understanding Consciousness*, London.
Vygotsky, L.S. (1986) *Thought and Language*, ed. A. Kozulin, Boston, MA.
Weiskrantz, L. (1986) *Blindsight*, Oxford.
Zeki, S. (2003) 'The disunity of consciousness', *Trends in Cognitive Sciences* 7: 214–18.

Further reading

James, W. (1890) *The Principles of Psychology*, New York.

SEE ALSO: mind

CONSERVATION

Decisions about conservation typically require giving answers to the following questions: What should be conserved? For what purpose should conservation activities be undertaken? Who should benefit from conservation? How should conservation take place? Since it is often difficult to find clear-cut answers to any of these questions, conservation issues frequently are controversial, require and involve extensive research, and can cause considerable public debate.

When thinking of what to conserve, we typically have in mind a particular stock, such as money in a bank account, an energy resource, a forest stand or a plant or animal species. We value these stocks because we expect that they provide benefits in the present or future. Money in an account may generate interest earnings; energy resources may contribute to a country's productivity; forest stands may supply timber, opportunities for recreation and natural habitat; and maintaining viable populations of plant and animal species may contribute to people's happiness because humans appreciate the existence of other species in their own right or make use of them in production or consumption processes. In many cases the current or future purposes of a stock may not be precisely known. For example, some species may provide substances for the cure of known or yet-to-be-encountered diseases, or they may be essential components of ecosystems, without which fundamental, undesirable environmental changes may occur.

Conserving stocks can be an important strategy to deal with current and future uncertainties and risks. Conservation of domestic energy resources or forest stands may help economies buffer themselves against declining supplies much like savings of money can help households buffer against losses of personal income. Conservation of species can similarly leave or put in place a capacity to deal with current or potential future threats to people's welfare – for example by providing substances that can be used by the pharmaceutical industry to develop new medicines, by providing blueprints for new materials in manufacturing or construction, or by maintaining diversity to buffer against adverse impacts of climate change on agricultural production.

The question of what to conserve is always closely related to questions concerning the purpose of conservation. Some reasons for conservation clearly are utilitarian by nature – we conserve because we wish to make use of the stock we conserve, or the flows or services these stocks will generate. In other cases, conservation is undertaken for purely ethical or moral reasons. For example, we may protect scenic landscapes or historical monuments because we feel that we owe future generations access to the same magnificent vistas that leave us at awe, or we engage in conservation of species diversity because we believe that humanity does not have the right to knowingly and purposely impoverish the natural world in which it exists. Utilitarian and ethical reasons for conservation are often intermingled, which adds to the complexity of many conservation decisions.

Since there are typically many ways of satisfying human needs and wants, and since each action with which these needs and wants are satisfied will entail undesired consequences, trade-offs need to be found. For example, conservation of an energy resource for future uses may reduce the ability of the present generation to satisfy its needs and wants. If, in contrast,

current uses of a resource were building up capital stocks and knowledge to enhance productivity in the future, and potentially eliminate the need for the resource in the first place, then current uses may be justified on the grounds that these uses benefit both present and future generations. In this case, conserving the resource could mean forgoing benefits today without adequate gains later. However, whether indeed full compensation of future generations for current resource use takes place is typically only knowable retrospectively.

Questions surrounding conservation also entail questions about winners and losers. Since gains and losses can occur among members within the same generation, among species and across generations, gains and losses are difficult to quantify, evaluate, judge and defend.

The question of what to conserve is also closely tied to the means of conservation. Historically, efforts to maintain, for example, species diversity and species richness have heavily concentrated on individual target populations. For example, conservation of endangered whale species has led to bans on whaling, mandates to use fishing gear that limits adverse impacts on whales while catching other species, rules for national and international maritime activity so that shipping vessels or drilling platforms minimize interference with migratory and breeding behaviours of whales, and more. Conservation efforts may infringe on the freedom of those individuals and corporations engaged in relevant activities (in the case of protection of whales, for example, this would include fishing communities, vessel operators, oil companies, etc.). In some cases (e.g. conservation of historic monuments), the costs of conservation are spread across society, irrespective of any uses of the resource by the individuals who bear the costs.

Increasingly, species conservation efforts have moved from a species focus to more of a systems orientation. According to the systems view, individual species and their populations are an integral part of an ecosystem and, without a proper functioning ecosystem, viable populations of individual species may not be sustainable. Consequently, a call for conservation of species often entails protecting ecosystems from changes that are adversarial for maintenance of viable population sizes. In these cases, conservation efforts require wide-ranging changes in society and the economy because a larger number of pathways, through which a large range of ecosystems components are affected, may need to be addressed.

However, in some cases conservation efforts come too late to avert the plight of a species. A wetland may have been lost, the amount of contiguous forest cover may already be too small, or the climate may already have changed too much to keep alive a sufficient number of individuals of a species to guarantee enough genetic diversity to sustain its populations. In such cases, *ex situ* conservation may place individuals of such species in human-created habitats (aquaria, zoos, etc.) or preserve seeds and other forms of genetic information in collections until ecosystems can be restored.

Many of the issues surrounding conservation can be, and actively are, addressed by the sciences. For example, social scientists explore conditions under which intra- and intergenerational decision-making is optimal, given current preferences and technologies, various assumptions about technological change, as well as expectations, risks and uncertainties. Most notably, economists model and analyse the trade-offs societies face when making conservation decisions. Their analyses highlight that each decision (including the one not to conserve) has opportunity costs associated with it – in any case, benefits are forgone by choosing one action over another. An optimal choice then is the one that minimizes opportunity costs.

How to define (forgone) benefits and costs, however, is a matter of considerable controversy. While many benefits and costs can easily be captured conceptually and measured empirically, some important benefits and costs are more difficult to reflect in models. For example, the price of a tree sold on timber markets reflects only a fraction of the actual value of that tree to society. A tree's contribution to water retention in soils, provision of habitat, aesthetic value or stabilization of climate are typically not reflected in its price. As a consequence, economic models that rely on market prices for the valuation of goods and services may disregard many of the costs and benefits associated with the use of environmental and human-made goods and services, and thus may generate misleading management and policy advice.

Improving our understanding of the structure and function of ecosystems, the role that individual species play in them, the drivers behind the dynamics of changes in population sizes, species diversity and richness, genetic diversity and more are rich and active areas of research in the natural and life sciences. To an increasing extent, the insights generated by that research are informing economic modelling and decision-making, and, conversely, economists' needs for data and information to better specify their models are guiding natural and life science research.

However, carrying out the best disciplinary and interdisciplinary research is not a sufficient condition for arriving at the best conservation decisions. The many fundamental uncertainties surrounding technological, socioeconomic and environmental change, the often hard-to-understand and difficult-to-predict personal and social value judgements, and existing institutional constraints that surround conservation issues will continue to challenge scientists and decision-makers alike. Constructive contributions to conservation decisions will thus continue to require balanced input from scientists and the rest of society, skills of all parties to understand and appreciate the knowledge and perspectives provided by others, willingness to communicate and collaborate, and abilities to revise conservation decisions in the light of new information.

MATTHIAS RUTH
UNIVERSITY OF MARYLAND

Further reading

Daly, H.E. and Cobb, J.B. (1994) *For the Common Good*, Boston.
Hanley, N., Shogren, J.F. and White, B. (2001) *Introduction to Environmental Economics*, Oxford.
Primack, R. (1995) *A Primer of Conservation Biology*, Sunderland, MA.
Ruth, M. (1993) *Integrating Economics, Ecology and Thermodynamics*, Dordrecht, The Netherlands.
Ruth, M. and Lindholm, J. (2002) *Dynamic Modeling for Marine Conservation*, New York.

SEE ALSO: energy; environment, sociology of; environmental economics; population and resources

CONSERVATISM

Conservatism is the doctrine that the reality of any society is to be found in its historical development, and therefore that the most reliable, though not the sole, guide for governments is caution in interfering with what has long been established. Clearly distinctive conservative doctrine emerged in the 1790s, in reaction to the rationalist projects of the French revolutionaries, and its classic statement is to be found in Edmund Burke's *Reflections on the Revolution in France* (1790). Burke's historical emphasis was itself the outcome of deep currents in European thought, currents rejecting abstract reasoning as a method for understanding the human world. The sheer flamboyance of Burke's rhetoric was necessary to bring conservatism into the world, however, since the doctrine in its purest form consists of a few maxims of prudence (concerning the complexity of things and the wisdom of caution) that, in the intellectualist atmosphere of the last two centuries, make a poor showing against the seductive philosophical pretensions of modern ideologies. These competing doctrines claim to explain not only the activity of politics, but also humankind and its place in the universe. Burke himself thought that this wider picture was supplied for us by religion, and thus he was prone to extend the reverence appropriate to divine things so that it embraced the established institutions of society. This fideist emphasis, however, ought not to conceal the fact that conservatism rests upon a deep scepticism about the ability of any human being, acting within the constraints of a present consciousness, to understand the daunting complexities of human life as it has developed over recorded time.

Conservatism construes society as something that grows, and conservatives prefer pruning leaves and branches to tearing up the roots. The latter view is taken by radicals who believe that nothing less than a revolutionary transformation both of society and of human beings themselves will serve to save us from what they believe to be a deeply unjust society. Generically, then, all are conservative who oppose the revolutionary transformation of society. Specifically, however, conservatism is one of three doctrinal partners, each of which may plausibly claim centrality in the European political tradition. One of these is liberalism, constituted by its allegiance to liberty and the values of reform, and the other is constitutional socialism, whose fundamental preoccupation with the problem of the poor leads it to construe all political problems as issues of realizing a truer community. Modern politics is a ceaseless dialogue between these three tendencies and movements.

Conservatism in this specific sense emerged from a split in the Whig Party in late eighteenth-century Britain, and it was only in the 1830s, when the present nomenclature of each of the three doctrines crystallized, that Tories began calling themselves 'conservatives'. This name failed to catch on in other countries, most notably perhaps the USA, where 'conservative' until recently connoted timidity and lack of enterprise. From the 1960s onwards, however, the tendency of US liberals (predominantly but not exclusively in the Democratic Party) to adopt socialist policies has provoked a reaction that calls itself '*neo*-conservative' in testimony to its adherence to many classical liberal positions.

As it is conservative doctrine that political parties must respond to changing circumstances, it would be not merely futile but also paradoxical to discover a doctrinal essence in the changing attitudes of any particular Conservative party. Nevertheless, conservatism is not only a doctrine but also a human disposition; many conservative temperaments have influenced the British Conservative Party, whose response to the successive problems of the modern world may give some clue to conservatism. Under Disraeli it organized itself successfully to exploit successive nineteenth-century extensions of the franchise, and its electoral viability has since largely depended upon the allegiance of the figure known to political scientists as the 'Tory workingman'. In the latter part of the nineteenth century, it rode a tide of imperial emotion and economic protection, and stood for the unity of the United Kingdom against attempts to grant self-government to Ireland. Between the two world wars, Baldwin saw it as the task of the party to educate an electorate, now enjoying universal suffrage, in the responsibilities of power. After Attlee's creation of the welfare state from 1945 to 1951, Churchill and Macmillan found conservative reasons for sustaining a welfarist consensus, but since 1976, Mrs Thatcher and a dominant wing of the party identified the expense of the welfare state in its present form as one of the emerging problems of politics.

A principle of conservatism offers little substantive guide to political action, and is vulnerable to the objection brought by F.A. Hayek: 'By its nature, it cannot offer an alternative to the direction we are moving' (*The Constitution of Liberty*, 1960). It is a mistake, however, to identify conservatism with hostility to change; the point is rather the *source* of change. It is characteristic of all radicals to seek one big change, after which a perfected community will be essentially changeless. On this basis, they often seek to monopolize the rhetoric of change. Liberals consider it the duty of an active government to make the reforms that will dissipate social evils. While refusing to erect limitation of government into an absolute principle, conservatives tend to think that, within a strong framework of laws, society will often work out for itself a better response to evils than can be found in the necessary complexities of legislation, and worse, of course, in the simple *dictat* of the legislator. Conservatism is, in this respect, a political application of the legal maxim that hard cases make bad law. It is thus a central mistake to think of conservatism as mere hostility to change. It poses, rather, the issue of where change should originate.

Like all political doctrines, conservatism is loosely but importantly associated with a particular temperament, a view of the world. It is characteristic of the conservative temperament to value established identities, to praise habit and to respect prejudice, not because it is irrational, but because such things anchor the darting impulses of human beings in solidities of custom that we often do not begin to value until we are already losing them. Radicalism often generates youth movements, while conservatism is a disposition found among the mature, who have discovered what it is in life they most value. The ideological cast of contemporary thought has provoked some writers to present conservatism as if it contained the entire sum of political wisdom; but this is to mistake the part for the whole. Nevertheless, a society without a strong element of conservatism could hardly be anything but impossibly giddy.

KENNETH MINOGUE
LONDON SCHOOL OF ECONOMICS
AND POLITICAL SCIENCE

Reference

Hayek, F.A. (1960) *The Constitution of Liberty*, London.

Further reading

Baker, K. (ed.) (1993) *The Faber Book of Conservatism*, London.
Kirk, R. (1953) *The Conservative Mind*, Chicago.
Minogue, K. (ed.) (1996) *Conservative Realism: New Essays in Conservatism*, London
Oakeshott, M. (1962) *Rationalism in Politics*, London.
O'Sullivan, N. (1976) *Conservatism*, London.

Quinton, A. (1978) *The Politics of Imperfection*, Oxford.
Scruton, R. (1980) *Meaning of Conservatism*, London.

SEE ALSO: Burke; Hayek

CONSOCIATION

The expression consociation derives from the Latin words for 'with' and 'society'. It is now used for political systems comprised of parallel communities that share power while retaining autonomy. Consociations have three key features: cross-community executive power-sharing; proportional representation and allocation in governmental posts and resources; and community self-government, especially in cultural domains, e.g. in schools with different languages of instruction. Fully fledged consociations empower community representatives with veto rights over constitutional or legal changes. Consociational theory may be traced to the sixteenth-century Protestant philosopher, Johannes Althusius (1557–1638), the early twentieth-century Austro-Marxists, Karl Renner and Otto Bauer (Bauer 2000), the Nobel Laureate, Sir Arthur Lewis, and in our times to the political scientist, Arend Lijphart (Lijphart 1968, 1969, 1977; Lustick 1997). Consociational thinking is not restricted to the academy. Politicians have refined, innovated and reinvented consociational institutions and practices in Belgium, Bosnia-Herzegovina, Canada, the Netherlands, Switzerland, Northern Ireland, the Lebanon and Macedonia. Consociations are promoted to prevent, manage or resolve conflicts, especially between communities divided by nationality, ethnicity, race, religion or language. Consociationalists and their critics differ radically over the merits of consociation, and there is much disagreement over how consociations are established, maintained or break down (McGarry and O'Leary 2004).

Critics of consociation sometimes condemn consociational ideas as futile: they claim they have no (or no long-run) impact on deeply rooted, identity-based conflicts. More frequently critics who pride themselves on their moral universalism attack consociations as perverse: they achieve the opposite of their ostensible purposes by institutionalizing the sources of conflict; by organizing a stalemate around the relevant collective identities they encourage a politics of immobilism and gridlock. They reward and reinforce politicians who mobilize existing sources of division. Such critics claim that consociationalists are primordial pessimists, who take people as they are, and not as they might be. Political integration, the creation of a common citizenship and public sphere, and the non-recognition of cultural differences in the public domain, from this perspective, is much preferred. Another standard objection to consociation is that it jeopardizes important values. Encouraging proportional representation, it is said, will lead to the likely irreversible formation of ethnic, communal or sectarian parties, thereby breaking with the possibilities afforded by a politics of programmes and interests. The use of quotas and proportional representation in affirmative action programmes or preferential policies are claimed to weaken the merit principle, creating new injustices and inefficiencies in resource allocation. The major criticism usually made against consociation is that it is undemocratic; it excludes opposition; it does not permit governmental alternations; it is a loser-takes-all system; it is elitist. Arguments in this vein usually celebrate the merits of oppositional politics. A last argument deployed against consociations is outright denial of their existence. The tactic here is to define consociation so rigidly that nowhere or almost nowhere fits the criteria. Sometimes this argument rests on the alleged incoherence of consociational ideas; sometimes, as in Marxist arguments, the illusory quality of consociation is suggested: it divides and disorganizes the working class around false identities (Kieve 1981).

Consociationalists, by contrast, understand themselves as realists, as counsellors of necessary triage, and as democrats who are aware that consociations need not (and should not) be applied in every country or every possible policy sector where identity politics manifests itself. They are just as concerned about justice as their critics. And, they submit that consociational settlements are 'naturally' recurrent phenomena – generated through negotiations by representative politicians.

Consociationalists believe that certain collective identities, especially those based on nationality, ethnicity, language and religion, are generally fairly durable once formed. To say they are likely to be durable is not to say that they are either primordial or immutable, or that they necessarily generate intense throat-cutting antagonisms, or that they are generally desirable. But,

consociationalists insist that such durable identities are often mobilized in a politics of antagonism, perhaps especially during the democratization of political systems. Politicians, parties and communities interpret their histories and futures through narratives, myths and symbols but also through realistic rather than merely prejudiced appraisals of past group antagonisms. Narratives, myths and symbols may have significant resonance and truth-content – without these traits politicians, *ceteris paribus*, would be less successful in their manipulative endeavours. Consociationalists maintain that it is their critics, 'social constructionists', and certain liberals and socialists, who are too optimistic about the capacities of political regimes to dissolve, transform or transcend inherited collective identities. They are cautiously sceptical about the current celebration of civil society as *the* or even *a* vehicle of transformation, peace-making and peace-building, and point out that in divided territories there is more than one society and their relations may be far from civil.

Consociationalists argue from a standpoint of political necessity: they do not embrace cultural pluralism for its own sake, or because they want a romantic celebration of a thousand different flowers (or weeds). Hard confrontations with reality in certain conjunctures force certain options on reasonable decision-makers in (potentially) deeply divided territories. Their claim is that in hard cases the effective choice is between consociational arrangements and worse alternatives. The worse alternatives include armed conflict, genocide and ethnic expulsion, imposed partition, or imposed control: the coercive and hierarchical imposition of one community or coalition of communities over others. Consociationalists claim that dispassionate analysis shows that the real choice in many deeply divided regions is between consociational democracy and no (worthwhile) democracy.

Majoritarian democracy – especially based on a single-party government rooted in one community – is very likely to provoke serious communal conflict in territories with two or more significantly sized communities with durable identities differentiated by nationality, ethnicity, language and religion. Elite bargaining and adjustment should be designed to achieve widespread consensus – to prevent the possibility that democracy will degenerate into a war of communities. Realists should therefore endorse a politics of accommodation, of leaving each group to their own affairs where that is possible and widely sought – 'good fences make good neighbours'. Consociation should, however, be designed to protect basic natural rights, of individuals and communities, the most important right being the right to exist. Consociation does not eliminate democratic opposition within communities, but enables such divisions and oppositions as exist to flourish in conditions of generalized security. Nothing precludes intrabloc democratic competition, and turnover of political elites, and shifts of support between parties; and in a liberal consociation nothing necessarily blocks the dissolution of historic identities if that is what voters want.

Consociations vary in the extent to which segments are included, and in the degree of opposition to the governing partners in the executive. A distinction may be made between complete, concurrent and 'pluralitarian' consociational executives. In a complete consociation all parties and all groups are included in the executive and enjoy popular support within their blocs. This is the rare case of the grand coalition – which may indeed preclude effective opposition. In concurrent executives, by contrast, the major parties, which enjoy majority support within their blocs, are included within the executive, and opposition groups exist in parliament and elsewhere. In 'pluralitarian' executives at least one of the major communities has a party in the executive that enjoys just plurality support within its bloc – implying a range of opposition parties in its bloc that are not in the executive. What matters in a consociation therefore is not wholesale inclusion of all, but meaningful, cross-community or joint decision-making within the executive. This clarification helps resolve a recurrent misunderstanding: a democratic consociation does not require an all-encompassing grand coalition in the executive (or in other institutions).

Consociational arrangements facilitate greater justice, both procedural and social, say its advocates. Groups govern themselves in agreed domains of autonomy. Distributions that follow proportional allocations may be seen as very fair: to each according to their numbers. There is also a correlation between numbers and potential power that makes such a mode of justice likely to be stable and legitimate.

Consociationalists observe that consociations may and do occur without their urgings. Variations on their formulae are continually reinvented by politicians as 'natural' creative political responses to a politics of antagonism: the outcomes of negotiated deals. Politicians, Lijphart observes, invented consociational institutions in the Netherlands in 1917, in Lebanon in 1943, in Malaysia in 1958, and British politicians did so for Northern Ireland in 1972. We can add that they were reinvented by US diplomats to end the war in Bosnia-Herzegovina at Dayton in 1995; by Lebanese and Northern Irish politicians with external promptings in 1989 and 1998 respectively; and by European Union diplomats in promoting the Ohrid agreement between Macedonian Slavs and Macedonian Albanians. The United Nations and the European Union between them have been trying to mediate a consociational and federal settlement in Cyprus. Within academic political theory, without necessarily having a full appreciation of the history of their ideas, many contemporary multiculturalists advance consociational agendas: inclusivity (cross-community power-sharing); quotas (proportionality); and group rights (autonomy) are usually advanced to remedy the participatory defects in some contemporary democracies.

BRENDAN O'LEARY
UNIVERSITY OF PENNSYLVANIA

References

Bauer, O. (2000) *The Question of Nationalities and Social Democracy*, ed. Ephraim Nimni, trans. Joseph O'Donnell, Minneapolis, MN.

Kieve, R. (1981) 'Pillars of sand: A Marxist critique of consociational democracy in the Netherlands', *Comparative Politics* 13 (April).

Lijphart, A. (1968) *The Politics of Accommodation*, Berkeley, CA.

—— (1969) 'Consociational democracy', *World Politics* 21(2): 207–25.

—— (1977) *Democracy in Plural Societies: A Comparative Exploration*, New Haven, CT.

Lustick, I.S. (1997) 'Lijphart, Lakatos and consociationalism', *World Politics* 50 (October): 88–117.

McGarry, J. and O'Leary, B. (2004) 'Introduction: Consociational theory and Northern Ireland', in J. McGarry and B. O'Leary (eds) *Essays on the Northern Ireland Conflict: Consociational Engagements*, Oxford.

Further reading

Brass, P.R. (1991) 'Ethnic conflict in multiethnic societies: The consociational solution and its critics',

Ethnicity and Nationalism: Theory and Comparison, New Delhi, pp. 333–48.

Esman, M. (2000) 'Power sharing and the constructionist fallacy', in M.M.L. Crepaz, T.A. Koelbe and D. Wilsford (eds) *Democracy and Institutions: The Life Work of Arend Lijphart*, Ann Arbor, MI, pp. 91–113.

Halpern, S. (1986) 'The disorderly universe of consociational democracy', *West European Politics* 9(2): 181–97.

Kymlicka, W. (1995) *Multicultural Citizenship: A Liberal Theory of Minority Rights*, Oxford.

—— (ed.) (1995) *The Rights of Minority Cultures*, Oxford.

McGarry, J. and O'Leary, B. (eds) (1993) *The Politics of Ethnic Conflict-Regulation: Case Studies of Protracted Ethnic Conflicts*, London, pp. 41–61.

SEE ALSO: constitutions and constitutionalism; democracy; democratization; ethnic politics; federalism and federation; multiculturalism; partition; secession

CONSTITUTIONS AND CONSTITUTIONALISM

The constitution of a state is 'the collection of rules and principles according to which a state is governed'. In antiquity the most important function of a constitution was to determine who should rule. The criterion that served as the basis for assigning political power reflected the ethos of the society. Thus each constitutional form exercised a moulding influence on virtue; the good citizen was a different being in an oligarchy, a democracy and an aristocracy (Aristotle). Although modern constitutions are far more complex, still the rules they establish for acquiring and exercising governmental power will usually embody the underlying norms and ideology of the polity.

The constitution of the modern nation-state contains three main elements. First, it establishes the principal institutions of government and the relationships among these institutions. These institutions may be structured on traditional Western lines of a division of executive, legislative and judicial responsibilities. The constitutions of one-party states give greater emphasis to the structures of the governing party, while those based on theocratic principles assign a dominant position to religious offices and institutions. Second, constitutions provide for a distribution of governmental power over the nation's territory. In a unitary state, local units of government are established as agencies of the central government. The constitution of a federal state assigns power directly to central and local levels of government. Third, constitutions provide a compendium of fundamental rights and duties of citizens including their rights to participate in the institutions of government. Some constitutions emphasize economic and social rights as much as, if not more than, political and legal/procedural rights.

In most countries there is a single document called 'the Constitution' that contains most of the significant elements of the constitutional system. But this is not the only form in which the rules of a constitution may be expressed. They may also take the form of ordinary laws such as statutes or decrees, judicial decisions or well-established customs and conventions. The UK is distinctive in that it does not have a document known as the Constitution; all of its constitutional rules are expressed more informally as statutes, judicial opinions, customs and conventions. Since the American Revolution the worldwide trend has been very much towards the codification of constitutional norms. New states established in the aftermath of revolution, the withdrawal of empire and world war have relied on a formal constitutional text to set out their basic governmental arrangements. However, even in these new nations, statutes, judicial decisions and conventions usually supplement the formal constitution.

A country may have a constitution but may not enjoy constitutionalism. Constitutionalism is a political condition in which the constitution functions as an effective and significant limit on government. Where constitutionalism characterizes a regime, the constitution is antecedent to government, and those who govern are constrained by its terms. The constitutional rules of such a regime are not easily changed – even when they are obstacles to policies supported by leading politicians. Thus, constitutional government is said to be 'limited government' (Sartori 1956). The limits imposed by a constitution are sometimes said to embody a 'higher law' – the enduring will of a people – which constitutes the basis of a legitimate check on the will of governments representing transient majorities (Corwin 1955; McIlwain 1947).

Constitutionalism may be maintained by the practice of judicial review, whereby judges with a reasonable degree of independence of the other branches of government have the authority to veto laws and activities of government on the grounds that they conflict with the constitution. Constitutionalism in the European Union has been largely promoted by the European Court of Justice, whose decisions have given the treaties on which the Union is based the status of constitutional law with supremacy over the laws of the member states (Weiler and Wind 2003). Constitutionalism may also be manifest in a formal amendment process that requires much more than the support of a dominant political party or a simple majority of the population to change the formal constitution. The British situation demonstrates, however, that neither of these practices is a necessary condition for constitutionalism. In that country the most important constitutional precepts are maintained and enforced more informally through well-established popular attitudes and the restraint of politicians (Dicey 1959).

The reality of constitutionalism depends on whether there are political forces genuinely independent of the government of the day powerful enough to insist on the government's observance of constitutional limits. Critics of those liberal democracies that claim to practise constitutionalism contend that in reality the constitutions imposing constitutional limits (e.g. the judiciary or the opposition party) are not independent of government, because they are controlled by social or economic interests aligned with the government. However, defenders of these regimes may point to occasions on which the maintenance of constitutional rules has forced political leaders to abandon major policies or even to abandon office (e.g. US President Nixon in the Watergate affair).

In countries that have formal written constitutions, whether or not they practise constitutionalism, the constitution may serve an important symbolic function. Constitutions are often employed as instruments of political education designed to inculcate public respect for political and social norms. A constitution may also be a means of gaining legitimacy, both internally and externally, for a regime. The development of codes of fundamental human rights since the Second World War has prompted many states to include such rights in their domestic constitutions in order to ingratiate themselves in the international community.

PETER H. RUSSELL
UNIVERSITY OF TORONTO

References

The Politics of Aristotle (1948), trans. E. Barker, Oxford.

Corwin, E.S. (1955) *The 'Higher Law' Background of American Constitutional Law*, Ithaca, NY.

Dicey, A.V. (1959) *Introduction to the Study of the Law of the Constitution*, 10th edn, London.

McIlwain, C.H. (1947) *Constitutionalism: Ancient and Modern*, rev. edn, Ithaca, NY.

Sartori, G. (1956) 'Constitutionalism: A preliminary discussion', *American Political Science Review* 56.

Weiler, J.H.H. and Wind, M. (eds) (2003) *European Constitutionalism beyond the State*, Cambridge, UK.

Further reading

Andrews, W.G. (1961) *Constitutions and Constitutionalism*, Princeton, NJ.

Friedrich, C.J. (1950) *Constitutional Government and Democracy*, New York.

SEE ALSO: consociation; federalism and federation; state

CONSUMER BEHAVIOUR

The study of consumers and consumption originated within economics, but since the 1960s it has become a discipline in its own right, drawing on theories and methods from psychology, sociology and anthropology as well as semiotics and literary theory. The majority of studies of consumer behaviour have addressed it at the individual level, often using experimental methods to explore cognition. More recent approaches have moved to the sociocultural level and drawn on contemporary social theory. In parallel with this development, there has been a shift away from positivist assumptions about reality towards interpretivist approaches based on the idea of the social construction of reality.

The focus of most early work was on the decision process, operationalized as a choice between competing brands. There is now general agreement on a sequential-stage model of information-processing that starts with problem recognition, followed by information search, evaluation of alternatives and finally product choice. This model of a rational consumer seeking a solution to a problem has been mirrored in much advertising that seeks to stimulate recognition of a problem and to demonstrate its solution by a specific brand. Each stage in the process has been studied in great detail and it has become clear that it is rare for a consumer to act fully rationally, particularly in searching for information and processing it to reach an optimal choice. A key variable is the degree of involvement that the consumer has with the product category. This predicts a range of behaviour from low-involvement habitual decisions at one extreme to high-involvement extensive problem-solving at the other (Celsi and Olson 1988). Involvement is a complex concept that attempts to combine perceptions of risk with the importance of the product to the individual consumer. Often the most highly involving products are those with symbolic meaning for the individual's sense of self (Laurent and Kapferer 1985). At low levels of involvement, consumers are likely to engage in very limited information search and to use simple decision heuristics such as selecting a brand whose name they recall, or buying-the-brand-last-bought. Levels of involvement have also been found to predict the amount of attention and processing that consumers will give to advertisements. In low-involvement categories, frequent repetition is required to increase levels of brand awareness, and it is brand awareness that has been found empirically to be the best predictor of purchaser behaviour in these product categories (Ehrenberg 1988).

For products in the mid-range of involvement, the evaluation process has been modelled using multi-attribute attitude theory, which predicts consumer behaviour based on an evaluation of a limited number of salient beliefs about a product's attributes and the relative importance of these attributes to the consumer. The theory of reasoned action includes an assessment of social influence on behaviour. This model has been supported by a meta-analysis of several hundred studies to predict consumer behaviour in situations where the product or service is sufficiently high-involvement to motivate cognitive processing (Sheppard *et al.* 1988).

At the high end of the dimension of involvement are products and services that are carriers of significant symbolic meaning. Here emotional processes rather than cognitive evaluation are dominant. Instead of focusing on the individual decision-maker, studies of consumer choice where involvement is high draw attention to the social and cultural context. From an interpretivist perspective, and drawing on contemporary social theory, the consumer is viewed as taking symbolic meanings into account in making consumption choices, and not making a choice simply on a judgement of the products' utilities.

These meanings also serve in the construction, maintenance and communication of social and individual identity (Elliott 1998). Possessions may be used to portray images of personality, lifestyle and social connectedness, and individuals who feel that they lack a personal quality may attempt to compensate by using symbolic resources, drawn largely from possessions. Attempts to use consumption to cope with low self-esteem have been found to be associated with dysfunctional and even addictive consumer behaviour.

Products and their symbolic meanings are deeply implicated in many areas of interpersonal behaviour and in the development and affirmation of social relationships, especially through the act of gift-giving. Every culture prescribes certain occasions and ceremonies for gift-giving and these play a significant role in consumer behaviour. Christmas and other festivals are often marked by consumption practices as much as by religious practices. Rites of passage marking changes between stages in life and social status, such as puberty, adulthood, parenthood, marriage, divorce and death, are also cultural universals that often involve gift-giving and other consumption activities. The nature of the relationships between consumers and products has some similarities with the relationships between people. Over time, brands come to be perceived as having human qualities, brand personalities that are derived largely from advertising. Consumers often choose brands that they perceive to have a brand personality that is consistent with their own self-image, and Fournier (1998) has demonstrated that some consumers develop strong, deep and durable bonds with their favourite brands. These perceived relationships are often expressed in personal rituals of purchase and usage.

At the social level, consumer behaviour can be an important element in the formation of groupings that are defined by possession and display of a product. Fashion products are widely used by teenagers in the construction of identity and in linking themselves with others. Temporary subcultural groups form through the purchase and display of styles of clothes, shoes and music that carry shared meanings inside the group. There are often also rivalries with other style groupings. Specific brand communities have also been found to coalesce around some brands of car, or motorcycle or computer, and to involve a sense of community, even a feeling of responsibility towards other people who own the same brand. These brand communities often develop their own sets of rituals and traditions that can involve attendance at meetings and other social events. They can even involve a form of brand missionary behaviour where community members will attempt to recruit new people to purchase the brand and participate in the social life around it.

At the highest levels of sociocultural analysis, consumer choice has been theorized as playing an important role in the ordering of society. Bourdieu (1984) suggests that social status is no longer simply a function of the possession of economic capital but depends on the accumulation of symbolic capital, which reflects a knowledge of taste (cultural patterns of choice and preference) and that is manifested in consumption choices and lifestyles. Going beyond the conscious action of consumer behaviour, Douglas and Isherwood (1979) identify the largely unconscious process by which the consumption of goods maintains stable social structure across cultures. Goods are used to communicate cultural categories, divisions and rankings, and their use may help to counter the inherent instability of social meanings.

RICHARD ELLIOTT
UNIVERSITY OF WARWICK

References

Bourdieu, P. (1984) *Distinction: A Social Critique of the Judgement of Taste*, London.

Celsi, R. and Olson, J. (1988) 'The role of involvement in attention and comprehension processes', *Journal of Consumer Research* 15.

Douglas, M. and Isherwood, B. (1979) *The World of Goods: Towards an Anthropology of Consumption*, London.

Ehrenberg, A. (1988) *Repeat-Buying: Facts, Theory and Applications*, London.

Elliott, R. (1998) 'A model of emotion-driven choice', *Journal of Marketing Management* 14.

Fournier, S. (1998) 'Consumers and their brands: Developing relationship theory in consumer research', *Journal of Consumer Research* 24.

Laurent, G. and Kapferer, J. (1985) 'Measuring consumer involvement profiles', *Journal of Marketing Research* 22.

Sheppard, B., Hartwick, J. and Warshaw, P. (1988) 'The theory of reasoned action: A meta-analysis of past research with recommendations for modifications and future research', *Journal of Consumer Research* 15.

SEE ALSO: consumption function; optimization

CONSUMPTION FUNCTION

The international depression of the early twentieth century undermined the existing theory that extended departures from full employment were prevented by the natural stabilization of macroeconomic forces. In response Keynes (1936) developed a theory of equilibrium at less than full employment and, in so doing, created the consumption function. As envisaged by Keynes, the function relates aggregate consumption for an economy to variables such as income and wealth. To understand the link between the consumption function and the level of employment at equilibrium, note that the dominant theory prior to Keynes stated that the interest rate would fluctuate to ensure that savings equalled the investment required to maintain full employment. By positing that consumption depended on income, Keynes was able to show that, if the level of saving was not sufficient to meet investment at full employment, the level of income would fall, thereby reducing consumption and increasing saving. The result would be equilibrium at less than full employment, in accord with the reality of the long-lasting depression.

The idea of a consumption function soon took root in economic theory. In basic form, consumption was posited to be an increasing function of income. The fraction of additional income consumed, termed the marginal propensity to consume, was estimated to be very close to one. With estimates of the marginal propensity to consume in hand, questions turned to the evolution of the marginal propensity as an economy matures. Some speculated that the marginal propensity to consume would fall towards zero, as economies develop. Research revealed that such was not the case, with mature economies consuming about 75 per cent of income.

Empirical analyses of the consumption function multiplied over succeeding decades until Lucas (1976) observed that the interplay of consumption, income and interest rates does not yield a stable function that could be identified with consumption. In response, research shifted to studies of parameters related to functions tied more closely to consumers' attempts to maximize their utility. These studies are guided by the permanent income hypothesis developed by Friedman (1957). Under the permanent income hypothesis, individuals wish to maintain a constant relation between consumption and income (as measured by permanent factors such as expected labour income) and so smooth consumption over their lifetime. Some of the smoothing is easily undertaken by saving for retirement. Another component of smoothing is quite difficult to complete as young workers are unable to borrow against future human capital. Such workers are said to be liquidity constrained. To develop an econometric framework in which to test the hypothesis, Hall (1978) linked Friedman's permanent income hypothesis to models of intertemporal choice. Hall found that the permanent income hypothesis implies that consumption is a martingale, so that only current consumption should be useful in predicting future consumption. While the permanent income hypothesis has been challenged many times (e.g. Zeldes (1989) finds that the predictions do not hold for consumers who are liquidity constrained), the hypothesis is widely believed to be a useful description of consumer behaviour.

DOUGLAS G. STEIGERWALD
UNIVERSITY OF CALIFORNIA,
SANTA BARBARA

References

Friedman, M. (1957) *A Theory of the Consumption Function*, Washington, DC.
Hall, R. (1978) 'Stochastic implications of the life cycle–permanent income hypothesis: Theory and evidence', *Journal of Political Economy* 86: 971–87.
Keynes, J.M. (1936) *General Theory of Employment, Interest and Money*, London.
Lucas, R. (1976) 'Econometric policy evaluation: A critique', in K. Brunner and A. Metzer (eds) *The Phillips Curve and Labor Markets*, Carnegie-Rochester Conference Series on Public Policy, Vol. 1.
Zeldes, S. (1989) 'Consumption and liquidity constraints: An empirical investigation', *Journal of Political Economy* 97: 305–46.

SEE ALSO: consumer behaviour

CONTRACTS

A typical market transaction between a buyer and a seller entails the buyer paying the seller an agreed upon sum in exchange for an agreed upon quantity of a good or service. Debreu (1959) has shown that if such markets are complete and competitive, then the resulting equilibrium is *Pareto efficient*. That is, there is no other allocation of resources that makes every person at least as well off, and some better off. Debreu re-

marked, however, that the complete markets assumption is very restrictive since it requires the existence of a new market whenever goods differ not only in quality, but also by the time and location of delivery. For example, a fish bought at 3 p.m. in the afternoon is a different good than if it were bought at 8 p.m. the same day. Moreover, if there are not a large number of buyers and sellers of fish for every time and location during the day, then in practice markets are very incomplete.

The purchase and subsequent delivery of fish at a given time and location is an example of what Williamson (1985) calls idiosyncratic exchange. The goal of contract theory is to understand how such idiosyncratic exchange may be governed efficiently. For example, suppose that the fish delivery is late, and occurs at 8 p.m., rather than at 3 p.m. as originally agreed upon. Anticipating that this may occur, the contract with the delivery company may require damages to be paid in the event of a late delivery. These damages play two roles. First, they provide incentives for the delivery company to be on time. Second, they provide some insurance to the restaurant against lost income due to late delivery.

Moral hazard

If the delivery company is very small, and traffic conditions make timely delivery difficult and uncertain, then such damages also pose a hardship to it. Thus one faces a trade-off – large damages provide incentives for timely delivery and insure the restaurant, but they also impose a risk upon the delivery company as a result of events that are not under its full control. This is known as the problem of *moral hazard*, and is the basis for the principal–agent model. In this model, the principal (the restaurant) offers the agent (the delivery company) a contract that optimally trades risk off against insurance.

The optimal contract has the feature that insurance should not be perfect whenever the agent can take actions that affect the probability of a loss. The problem of moral hazard is ubiquitous, and can explain why insurance programmes rarely provide complete coverage. Examples include limits on the duration of benefits in unemployment insurance programmes and the use of co-payments in health, fire and automobile insurance. In addition, it has been shown that the optimal contract is sensitive to any useful piece of information regarding performance, such as a person's employment history or driving record.

A weakness of the theory, particularly when applied to employment contracts, is that in practice contracts often ignore such information. For example, customer complaints, if infrequent, are unlikely to have an impact on a salesperson's income. One reason is the existence of actions that the agent can take or events that the agent can observe that affect the principal's pay-off, but cannot be observed by the principal and/or the courts that enforce the contract. These transactions costs are the basis for many of the recent developments in contract theory (see Hart and Holmström (1987) for a review of the moral hazard literature).

Mechanism design and asymmetric information

When dealing with complex transactions it has proven to be useful to view contracts as *mechanisms* governing exchange. A contract specifies the *rules* that determine who receives a good, and how much they should pay, rather than explicitly stating the price and quantity. This is particularly important when there is asymmetric information regarding the value of a good. For example, a potential buyer may write a contract with a seller stating that he or she will meet or exceed any competing offers. Another example would be the case of warrantees – the seller of a good, such as a car, agrees to pay any repairs required for a certain period of time after purchase.

If contracts simply specify price and quantity then, as Akerlof (1970) showed with his famous used car market example, markets may break down completely. Using the idea that contracts are a mechanism for exchange, Myerson and Satterthwaite (1983) provide a complete characterization of all possible contracts when there is asymmetric information between the buyer and the seller, a case that includes the Akerlof (1970) example. Their result shows that if there is asymmetric information it may be impossible for any contract to guarantee efficient trade. This finding requires an important qualification to the Coase (1960) theorem. (See Jackson (2001) for a review of mechanism design theory.)

Incomplete contracts

The theory discussed above is sometimes called *complete contract theory*, because contracts provide a comprehensive prescription for actions and payments as a function of future events that occur in the relationship. Yet an event may occur that contracting parties did not anticipate, or the courts may be unable to enforce the actions and payments as written in the contract. Such contracts are considered *incomplete*.

One of the early concerns of the theory of incomplete contracts had to do with the application of contract theory to the study of *property rights*. Demsetz (1967) was the first to argue that property rights are designed to provide individuals with the correct incentives to solve externality problems, such as the overuse of a common resource. Any contract governing a property right is bound to be incomplete, however, because it does not explicitly specify how property is to be used in the future, and individuals do not anticipate all the possible future uses of property when it is acquired.

Recently, this observation has been used to provide a foundation for the theory of the firm. The idea is that since ownership is a contract that allocates residual rights of control to the owner, this provides incentives for the owner to invest efficiently in the assets of the firm, and then to use these assets efficiently given information that is acquired after the investment has been made. The idea that property allocates residual control rights has its roots in an important paper by Simon (1951), who argues that the distinguishing feature of employment is that the employer (the asset owner) has the right to direct the actions of the employee as he or she wishes. Recent research explores the interplay between authority, information and its effects upon employee motivation. This research shows that increasing authority ensures that the employer is more likely to obtain the desired outcome. However, this comes at the cost of lower employee motivation. There is an optimal trade-off between authority and employee effort. (See Hart (1995) for a review of these theories.)

An alternative to the delegation of authority is the use of *relational contracts*. Consider the employer of a chef at a restaurant. The chef is required to produce excellent food, but the quality of his dishes is a matter for subjective judgement. It is therefore impossible for the courts to decide whether or not his cooking has been good enough to warrant staying in his job. In this case, the chef has an interest in cooking well, since his reputation would suffer if he was fired for cooking badly. Such behaviour can be viewed as part of a *self-enforcing contract* in which the employee agrees to perform because of the threat of punishment by the principal, while the principal agrees to reward good behaviour because of the threat of poor performance by the worker. Subjective evaluation is formally modelled as private information held by the principal (employer) and agent (employee) corresponding to each person's evaluation of performance, which may or may not agree with the other. The efficiency of the self-enforcing contract depends upon the extent to which principal (employer) and agent (employee) may agree to what constitutes acceptable performance. Consequently, performance is enhanced in environments where individuals have common values regarding work. (See MacLeod (2003) and Levin (2003) for recent results and discussions of the literature.)

Law and economics

The economic theory of contract focuses upon the interplay between transactions costs and the form of the optimal contract, with little reference to the legal enforcement of a contract. The law and economics literature addresses the properties of different legal rules that are used to assess damages when a party breaches a contract. The standard legal remedy for breach of contract is expectations damages, the requirement that the harmed party be compensated for his or her expectation from a transaction. This remedy has the desirable property that an individual will breach a contract if and only if it is socially efficient. When deciding whether or not to honour a contract, the individual compares the value that would follow performance with the value he or she would get from breaching (say selling the promised goods to another person at a higher price), less the harm to the original partner, as given by the expectation damages.

This calculation ensures that the breaching party acts efficiently. However, the breached against party, say the person receiving the goods,

may rely too much on the expectation that the trade will occur since he or she is perfectly compensated whenever there is breach. The recent literature explores the optimal design of legal rules that trade off incentives for reliance upon trade occurring against the need for efficient breach. (See Cooter and Ulen (2000) for a comprehensive review of this literature.)

W. BENTLEY MACLEOD
UNIVERSITY OF SOUTHERN CALIFORNIA

References

Akerlof, G.A. (1970) 'The market for "lemons": Quality uncertainty and the market mechanism', *Quarterly Journal of Economics* 84(3): 488–500.
Coase, R.A. (1960) 'The problem of social cost', *Journal of Law and Economics* 3: 1–44.
Cooter, R. and Ulen, T. (2000) *Law and Economics*, Reading, MA.
Debreu, G. (1959) *Theory of Value*, New Haven, CT.
Demsetz, H. (1967) 'Toward a theory of property rights', *American Economic Review* 57(2): 347–59.
Hart, O.D. (1995) *Firms, Contracts and Financial Structure*, Oxford.
Hart, O.D. and Holmström, B. (1987) 'The theory of contracts', in T. Bewley (ed.) *Advances in Economic Theory: Fifth World Congress*, Cambridge, UK, pp. 71–155.
Jackson, M.O. (2001) 'A crash course in implementation theory', *Social Choice and Welfare* 18(4): 655–708.
Levin, J. (2003) 'Relational incentive contracts', *American Economic Review* 93(3): 835–57.
MacLeod, W.B. (2003) 'Optimal contracting with subjective evaluation', *American Economic Review* 93(1): 216–40.
Myerson, R. and Satterthwaite, M. (1983) 'Efficient mechanisms of bilateral trading', *Journal of Economic Theory* 28: 265–81.
Simon, H.A. (1951) 'A formal theory of the employment relationship', *Econometrica* 19: 293–305.
Williamson, O.E. (1985) *The Economic Institutions of Capitalism*, New York.

Further reading

Laffont, J.-J. and Maritmort, D. (2002) *The Theory of Incentives*, Princeton, NJ.
MacCollel, A., Whinston, M.D. and Green, J.R. (1995) *Microeconomic Theory*, Oxford.
Milgrom, P. and Roberts, J. (1992) *Economics, Organization and Management*, Englewood Cliffs, NJ.
Salanie, B. (1997) *The Economics of Contracts: A Primer*. Cambridge, MA.

SEE ALSO: asymmetric information; bargaining; exchange; markets.

CORPORATE ENTERPRISE

Corporate size

Business corporations are of central importance to economic activity at both the national and global levels. In 2002 there were thirteen corporations in the world that had revenues in excess of $100 billion. Six were US, three Japanese, two German, one British and one British–Dutch. Of the world's fifty biggest employers – ranging from Wal-Mart, with 1,300,000 employees, to Peugeot, with 198,600 employees – eighteen were US, nine French, seven German, six Chinese, four Japanese, two British and one each Dutch, British–Dutch, Russian and Swiss. In 2002 the 500 largest corporations by revenues employed an average of 92,985 people each (Fortune 2003). Many large business corporations engage in global operations, with facilities and employees throughout the world. Nevertheless, there remain significant differences in the governance, strategy, organization and finance of these companies that reflect the home bases in which they originally developed and out of which they continue to operate. This short entry will refer to the case of the US corporate enterprise.

Corporate governance

The large business corporation is generally a *managerial* enterprise. Salaried managers who are employees of the company make resource allocation decisions. They may, and usually do, own some shares in the company, and indeed the extent of their shareholdings may constitute substantial personal wealth. But given the large number of total shares of the corporation that are outstanding, the shareholdings of these salaried managers are too small to give them, through *ownership*, control over corporate resource allocation. Rather that control is based on their progress in their careers as salaried employees, often within the corporation over which they now exercise allocative control but also perhaps by moving up and around other organizations in the business and government sectors.

It is also typically the case that no individuals or organizations that hold shares in a particular corporation have sufficiently large shareholdings to enable them, through ownership, to exercise control over the allocation of corporate. The

fragmentation of share ownership across tens or hundreds of thousands, and in some cases even millions, of shareholders in effect leaves a property vacuum that enables salaried managers to exercise allocative control. In the USA most outstanding corporate stock takes the form of common shares that, almost invariably, give the holder one vote for each share owned. Shareholders can vote on a slate of directors to sit on the board as well as resolutions to be voted on at the annual general meeting (AGM) of shareholders. The board of directors in turn monitors the allocation decisions as well as the compensation of top corporate executives, and has the right to hire and fire them. While, in principle, shareholders can elect the board of directors, the fragmentation of shareholding means that, in practice, shareholders approve a board that top management has selected. Quite apart from its fealty to incumbent management, the complexity of corporate decision-making means that board members who are not themselves full-time executives of the company have little choice but to act as a rubber stamp for management decisions. At best, the board can try to ensure that corporate executives do not engage in illegal activity; as periodic corporate scandals have revealed, however, the board does not always perform this function particularly well.

Moreover, in the USA, shareholders have little power to influence managerial decision-making directly through votes on particular issues at the AGM. More specifically, they do not have the right to put resolutions before the AGM that pertain to ordinary business decisions; such decisions are strictly the prerogative of corporate management. Shareholder resolutions to be voted upon at the AGM must pertain to *social* (as distinct from business) issues, such as corporate pollution of the environment or discrimination against certain groups of employees.

Why are shareholders willing to own assets when they exercise virtually no control over the allocation of resources that are essential for generating returns on those assets? The main reasons are *limited liability* and *share liquidity*. Limited liability protects the shareholder from responsibility for claims against the corporation for bad debts or legal transgressions. Should the corporation's managers make decisions that result in losses or lawsuits, the public shareholder cannot be held responsible. In taking an ownership stake in a business corporation, the public shareholder only risks losing the investment made in purchasing the share. Moreover, the ease with which a share can be sold on the stock market – that is, the share's liquidity – means that the shareholder can cease to be an owner of the corporation's assets at any time he or she wants, simply by making a telephone call or clicking a computer mouse.

Executives who are full-time salaried employees of the corporation therefore exercise effective control over the allocation of the corporation's resources. How they choose to allocate corporate resources will be a major determinant of the performance of the corporation. An innovative investment strategy seeks to transform the company's technological capabilities and market access with the objective of generating higher-quality, lower-cost goods services, at prevailing factor prices. An innovative strategy can give the corporation a sustainable competitive advantage, while also possibly permitting an increase in the returns to labour and capital

Corporate organization

When engaging in an investment strategy, corporate executives choose not only the technologies and markets that will characterize the business enterprise but also, over time, the organizational forms through which the company's goods and services will be produced and sold. These activities can all be performed in-house or some of them can be outsourced to other companies. Products and processes can be developed solely within the company or through strategic alliances, or, alternatively still, they can be acquired at a certain stage in development by purchasing other companies. Investments in new lines of business may build on the technological capabilities that the company already possesses and/or the markets to which it already has access, or they may be quite unrelated to the types of business activities in which the corporation is already engaged. For any given activity, even the set of skills – or what can be called the 'skill base' – in which the corporation invests may be a matter of strategic choice.

As a result, the corporation may have an organizational structure that is, among other varieties, *functional*, *multidivisional* or *conglomerate*. The functional corporation divides corporate responsibility by functions such as sales, research, manufacturing, purchasing, and fi-

nance, and then co-ordinates these functions from a head office. The multidivisional corporation divides corporate responsibility by business activity, and, in principle, allows the divisions to co-ordinate functions. The corporate headquarters of the multidivisional enterprise plans the entry and exit of the corporation from business activities while also providing the divisions with common services such as fundamental research (corporate R&D), executive training and finance. In theory, the multidivisional structure grows over time by making use of available resources in existing business activities as a basis for moving into new activities. The conglomerate corporation may look like a multidivisional corporation, except that the activities in which it engages do not have a technological or market relation to one another; the conglomerate grows over time largely by adding new companies that come under its ownership through mergers and acquisitions. It is often also the case that, because of the way in which they grow, conglomerates centralize allocative control in the corporate headquarters to the detriment of the constituent businesses whose investments needs the top corporate executives are incapable of evaluating. Such overcentralization of allocative control, however, can also characterize a multidivisional corporation, notwithstanding its more organic growth path.

Ultimately, within the corporate enterprise, products and processes are developed and utilized through the work of large numbers of people who participate in the hierarchical and functional divisions of labour. The hierarchical division of labour allocates employees to different levels of responsibility over decision-making, including the supervision, evaluation, promotion and termination of other employees. The functional division of labour allocates employees according to their productive specializations. At any point in time the structure of this hierarchical and functional skill base will depend on the prior evolution of the company's division of labour and its new investments in hierarchical and functional capabilities. In recent years, particularly in the information and communications technology (ICT) industries, many large corporations have become more vertically specialized as they have outsourced routine manufacturing activities. At the same time, the capabilities in which these corporations do make innovative investments have become more complex than previously in terms of the arrays of technologies that have to be developed and markets that have to be accessed. Moreover, in high-tech industry established corporations are generally subject to more vigorous global competition than was the case in the past.

Finally, to generate innovation from the hierarchical and functional skill bases, the corporation must create a set of incentives for employees that *integrates* their skills and efforts in the pursuit of corporate goals. The most powerful means for achieving such organizational integration is the offer to employees of stable, remunerative and creative careers within the corporation. The expectation of such career rewards creates the integrative incentives that are critical to the innovation process, while the success of the innovative process enables the corporation actually to deliver these career rewards, and thus sustain the career expectations of its employees. Conversely, a corporation that fails to deliver these rewards may undermine its organizational capabilities as employees no longer see their own individual progress and that of the corporation as intimately related. Additionally, the entry of new innovative firms that compete for experienced and talented labour may reduce the attraction for corporate employees of career paths within an established corporation.

Corporate finance

An innovative investment strategy is essential to the sustained competitive success of the corporation. Innovative strategies are costly not only because of the size of the investment in productive capabilities that must be made, but also the duration of time from when the investments are made until they have been developed and utilized sufficiently to generate financial returns. To succeed, therefore, an innovative strategy requires not only the organizational integration of an appropriate skill base, but also financial commitment to sustain the innovation process until returns are generated.

In a new firm, financial commitment will have to come from private sources such as the savings of family and friends, venture capital or possibly bank loans (including personal lines of credit such as credit cards). Additionally, the new firm may be partially financed by its employees who accept wages that are below market rates in return for an equity stake in the company (often

in the form of stock options). If the innovative strategy is successful, the firm's financiers can realize returns on the financial investment by laying claim to a share of corporate revenues. They may also be able and willing to sell ownership of the company to an existing firm or have the firm do an initial public offering (IPO) whereby public investors acquire ownership stakes, and the firm in fact becomes a public enterprise. When such transfers of ownership occur, original investors who had taken an equity stake in the firm can now recoup their investment and in many cases make substantial capital gains as well.

In the USA, a corporate enterprise that requires further funds to finance its investment strategy generally turns to the bond market, where it can secure finance at a fixed rate of interest for a period of 10, 20 or 30 years or more. In some other countries, such as Germany and Japan, the banking system is structured to enable business enterprises to rely on bank debt for committed finance, but in the USA bank loans are generally used for working capital – that is, to fund expenditures that should be quickly covered by sales revenues.

Corporate performance

Corporate performance is important to the performance of the economy as a whole. It affects the level and stability of employment and retirement incomes, as well as government budgets that depend on revenues from taxes related to corporate activities. Particularly in the USA, the financial conditions of households and governments have come to depend, directly or indirectly, on the performance of corporate stock. The S–P500, a stock market index that currently includes 423 New York Stock Exchange stocks and 74 NASDAQ stocks (plus two others listed on the American Stock Exchange), showed real total stock yields (price yields plus dividend yields divided by inflation) of −1.66 per cent per annum over the decade of the 1970s, but 11.67 percent per annum over the decade of the 1980s and 15.01 per annum over the decade of the 1990s, before recording – 9.76 per annum for the years 2000–2. Over these decades price yields rather than dividend yields became much more important in determining the total yields on corporate stocks. After a period of two decades in which soaring stock prices appeared to support the ideology that corporations should be run to 'maximize shareholder value', the recent debacle in the stock market, and the dependence of households and governments on stock market returns, have begun to raise new questions about how corporate enterprises should be governed for the sake of stable and equitable economic growth.

WILLIAM LAZONICK
UNIVERSITY OF MASSACHUSETTS, LOWELL,
AND THE EUROPEAN INSTITUTE OF
BUSINESS ADMINISTRATION (INSEAD)

Reference

Fortune (2003) http://www.fortune.com/fortune/fortune500.

Further reading

Berle, A. and Means, G. (1932) *The Modern Corporation and Private Property*, London.
Chandler, A. (1977) *The Visible Hand: The Managerial Revolution in American Business*, Cambridge, MA.
Chandler, A., Amatori, F. and Hiking, T. (eds) (1997) *Big Business and the Wealth of Nations*, Cambridge, UK.
Lazonick, W. (2004) 'Corporate restructuring', in S. Ackroyd, R. Batt, P. Thompson and P. Tolbert (eds) *Oxford Handbook of Work and Organization*, Oxford.
—— (2004) 'The innovative firm', in J. Fagerberg, D. Mowery and R. Nelson (eds) *The Oxford Handbook of Innovation*, Oxford.
Lazonick, W. and O'Sullivan, M. (eds) (2002) *Corporate Governance and Sustainable Prosperity*, New York.
Penrose, E. (1995) *The Theory of the Growth of the Firm*, 3rd edn, Oxford.
Schumpeter, J. (1942) *Capitalism, Socialism, and Democracy*, New York.

SEE ALSO: entrepreneurship; firm, theory of; industrial organization; multinational enterprises

CORRUPTION

Since the early 1990s, a series of major scandals in both the financial and especially the political worlds has resulted in close attention being paid to the issue of corruption. The collapse in late 2001 of the US energy company, Enron, which had engaged in systematic tax evasion and dubious accounting practices during its 15-year rise to global prominence, revealed a widespread web of alleged deceit and malpractice in corporate circles. In mid-2002, the even larger collapse of the telecommunications giant, WorldCom, shortly followed by that of Tyco International, raised further questions about the manipulation of balance sheets, profit and loss accounts and tax liabilities. These corporate crashes resulted not just in criminal investigations into the behaviour of their top executives, but also in a severe blow to the image of Wall Street and US capitalism more generally.

In Western Europe, meanwhile, the much acclaimed triumph of capitalism over communism following the collapse of the Soviet bloc regimes at the end of the 1980s had also been tainted by the subsequent revelation of corruption scandals involving major political figures. The most dramatic of these occurred in Italy, following the so-called '*Mani Pulite*' investigations into bribery in Milan, which in turn exposed a major network of corruption involving politicians at the highest level. Further scandals were revealed in France, notably the so-called Elf Aquitaine affair, which led to the imprisonment of a former government minister; in Germany, where a linked investigation revealed that long-term Chancellor, Helmut Kohl, had set up a secret political slush fund to channel funds to the ruling CDU; in Belgium, where the Augusta-Dassault defence contract scandal led to the conviction of former deputy premier and NATO secretary-general, Willy Claes; in Spain, where a series of high-profile scandals resulted in several ministerial resignations and the discrediting of the socialist government of Felipe González. Even in the UK, long seen as free of high-level political corruption, accusations of sleaze in government led to the creation of a Committee on Standards in Public Life.

Such events served to reinforce a growing sense of public concern about the seemingly inexorable spread of corruption. International organizations, such as the World Bank, the International Monetary Fund and the Organization for Economic Co-operation and Development, began in the 1990s to devote major attention to the issue of corruption, which was seen as a significant impediment to economic growth. Their concern was primarily with the developing world, where corruption was seen as rife. Since the mid-1990s, the independent agency, Transparency International (TI), has published an annual ranking of how corrupt countries are perceived to be, which not only supports the view that corruption is a serious issue in the developing world, but also that there are several established Western democracies in which it is seen as a significant problem. The TI rankings have helped ensure that the attention of policy-makers and opinion formers has remained focused on the question of how to combat corruption.

However, in order to combat corruption, a necessary precursor is to have a clear idea of just what it is and where it is taking place – and this is where real problems start to arise. First of all, in order to judge whether something has been corrupted, we need an understanding of its proper or un-corrupt state: whereas in some circumstances, such an understanding may be straightforward, in the case of 'politics', for instance, it is beset with difficulties. Logically, any definition of political corruption implicitly presupposes a notion of 'un-corrupt' politics and therefore our definition of politics itself will affect our understanding of what political corruption entails. On that basis, it follows that the meaning of political corruption will vary with the nature of the political system in question. In practice, much of the literature on political corruption has followed Arnold J. Heidenheimer in distinguishing between public office-centred, public interest-centred and market-centred definitions of political corruption. In fact, only the first two of these really offer *definitions*, which in turn depend on normative – and, therefore, inevitably contestable – judgements about the scope of public office, or the nature of public interest. Market-centred approaches, by contrast, tend to be more concerned with the *mechanics* of political corruption, and the circumstances under which it becomes possible. To the extent that market-centred approaches offer an explicit *definition*, it tends to be minimalist or else based on a recourse to legal norms: political corruption occurs when an agent breaks the law in sacrificing the interest of a principal to his or her own benefit.

Illegality is central to many definitions of political corruption, because it provides a basis for comparative analysis. Such an approach, however, confronts a two-fold problem: first, laws are not necessarily consistent in interpretation or application across different countries. What is illegal in one country may not be in another, leading to situations in which similar acts can be defined as corrupt or not according only to where they take place. The financing of political parties provides a good example, since the rules on party financing in some countries are much stricter than in others. For instance, until recently in the UK, unlimited private contributions (even from overseas) could be made to party funds, something which has long been proscribed in many other democracies.

Second, the recourse to legal norms in definitions of political corruption forgoes any possibility of capturing a more nebulous aspect of the phenomenon. All democracies rest on some basic principles, one of which is the public accountability of decision-making. But accountability can be enforced only if government activity is transparent: citizens cannot hold their elected leaders to account for activities they are unaware of having taken place. This truism underlines one of the central conundrums in constructing a definition of political corruption. It could be argued that one of the most damaging forms of political corruption *in a democracy* occurs when the 'democratic transcript' is betrayed: that is, when members of the political class act in such a way as to prevent or circumvent the exercise of accountability, by actively seeking to ensure that the electorate is not properly informed about a given issue. Although the concept of democracy is essentially contested, we can nonetheless construct an image of what one *should* look like (in an appraisive sense) in a way that is impossible for non-democracies. Dictatorships may make claims to legitimacy, but these can never be based on public accountability exercised through free elections. Therefore, at least one form of political corruption – a betrayal of the 'democratic transcript' – can exist only in democratic regimes.

Thus, a wide-ranging generic definition can at best provide a starting-point for identifying and analysing different *types* of political corruption, which need to be categorized according to a number of dimensions. The construction of a comprehensive taxonomy may run the risk of sacrificing analytical insight for descriptive detail, but is probably an essential first step in providing a basis for meaningful comparison. Some such attempts have been made. Syed Hussein Alatas, for instance, developed a broad-ranging typology on the basis of a minimalist definition: 'corruption is the abuse of trust in the interest of private gain'. He distinguished between 'transactive' and 'extortive' corruption. The former refers to a mutual arrangement between a donor and a recipient, actively pursued by, and to the mutual advantage of, both parties, whereas the latter entails some form of compulsion, usually to avoid some form of harm being inflicted on the donor or those close to him or her.

Other types of corruption revolve around, or are the by-products of, transactive and extortive corruption. *Defensive* corruption is obviously related inversely to the extortive type, whilst *investive* corruption involves the offer of goods or services without any direct link to a particular favour, but with a view to future situations in which a favour may be required. *Nepotistic* corruption refers to the unjustified appointment of friends or relatives to public office, or according them favoured treatment. *Autogenic* corruption involves just one person, who profits, for example, from preknowledge of a given policy outcome. Finally, *supportive* corruption describes actions undertaken to protect and strengthen existing corruption, often through the use of intrigue or else through violence. One advantage of Alatas's schema is that it offers a clear definition of corruption that is neither rulebound, nor tied to society's prevailing moral conventions or norms. Extortive and transactive corruption can be identified in both complex and simple societies, democracies and non-democracies.

In recent years, there has been a growing appreciation amongst both policy-makers and academic analysts that different forms of corruption have different causes, even if all forms of corruption are ultimately damaging. The challenge is to identify those measures that will help eradicate the most damaging forms of corruption, without creating incentive structures for new forms to arise. Organizations like the World Bank and the OECD have invested major efforts into promoting 'good governance' as a strategy for minimizing corruption, underlining the importance of accountability, transparency, responsiveness, participation, inclusiveness, high ethical standards and respect for the rule of law. In practical terms, good governance tends to be equated with market-based economies, minimum levels of regulation and low levels of state intervention and bureaucracy. In short, good governance is often seen as being equated with politically lean and economically neo-liberal economies. However, it is striking and noteworthy that those countries that have consistently scored best in TI rankings are the Scandinavian democracies with higher than average levels of taxation and state expenditure, whereas it is precisely in the far less bureaucratized environment of the USA that major financial scandals such as Enron and WorldCom have emerged.

PAUL M. HEYWOOD
UNIVERSITY OF NOTTINGHAM

Further reading

Alatas, S.H. (1990) *Corruption: Its Nature, Causes and Functions*, Aldershot.
Heidenheimer, A.J., Johnston, M. and Le Vine, V.T. (1989) *Political Corruption. A Handbook*, New Brunswick, NJ.
Rose-Ackerman, S. (1999) *Corruption and Government*, Cambridge, UK.
Transparency International, *Global Corruption Report* (published annually since 2001).

SEE ALSO: financial crisis; governance

COST–BENEFIT ANALYSIS

In terms of its practical application, cost–benefit analysis (CBA) is usually regarded as having its origins in the US Flood Control Act 1936. Without reference to the body of welfare economics that had already arisen by then, and before the introduction of compensation criteria into the literature, the Act argued that flood control projects had their social justification in a weighing up of the costs and benefits, with the latter being summed regardless of to whom they accrued. It is this reference to the social dimension of investment appraisal that distinguishes CBA from the more orthodox techniques that deal with the cash flow to a firm or single agency.

Oddly, CBA grew in advance of the theoretical foundations obtained from welfare economics that subsequently provided its underpinning. The notion that the benefits to individuals should be measured according to some indicator of consumer's surplus was well established by nineteenth-century writers, especially Dupuit and Marshall, but Hicks's work (1943) established the exact requirements for such measures. Similarly, the notion of a shadow price is crucial to CBA as, even if a project's output is marketed, CBA does not necessarily use market prices as indicators of value. Rather, reference is made to the marginal cost of providing the extra output in question. Despite the ambiguous relationship between marginal cost pricing in an economy where some sectors have unregulated pricing policies that force price above marginal cost, CBA and shadow pricing have flourished as an appraisal technique. CBA secured widespread adoption in US public agencies in the 1950s and 1960s, and was both used and advocated in Europe in the 1960s. It suffered a mild demise in the early 1970s in light of critiques based on the alleged fallacy of applying monetary values to intangible items such as peace and quiet, clean air and the general quality of life. Significantly, the post-1973 recession revived its use as governments sought value for money in public expenditure. Unease with the monetization of many unmarketed costs and benefits remained, however, resulting in a proliferation of alternative techniques such as environmental impact assessment, cost-effectiveness analysis (in which only resource costs are expressed in money, and benefits remain in non-monetary units) and some multi-objective approaches. However, none of these techniques permits a full range of decisions. For example, judgements of cost-effectiveness can only assist in the choice between two alternative courses of action. They cannot be used to compare these courses of action with the option of doing nothing. CBA retains its strength because of its ability potentially to identify optimal expenditures (where net benefits are maximized) and to secure a well-defined project ranking. However, few practitioners would argue that it has a role outside the ranking of expenditures within a given budget. That is, it has a highly limited role in comparing the efficiency of expenditures across major budget areas such as defence, education, health and so on.

As generally formulated, CBA operates with the efficiency objectives of welfare economics. The maximization of net social benefits is formally equivalent to securing the largest net welfare gain as defined by the Kaldor–Hicks compensation principle. Academic debate in this respect has centred on the appropriate choice of the measure of consumer's surplus, with the dominant advocacy being of the use of the 'compensating variation' measure introduced by Hicks (1943). Use of social prices based on consumer valuations implicitly assumes that the distribution of market power within the relevant economy is itself optimal. As this is a value judgement, it is open to anyone to substitute it with an alternative distributional judgement.

Some would argue that this apparent arbitrariness defines the inadequacies of CBA, while others suggest that no society has ever operated with disregard for distributional criteria and that distributional judgements are no less arbitrary than efficiency judgements.

Much of the practical effort in CBA has gone into actual mechanisms for discovering individuals' preferences in contents where there is no explicit market. The most successful have been the hedonic price techniques and the use of bidding techniques ('contingent valuation').

Hedonic prices refer to the coefficients defining the relationship between property prices and changes in some unmarketed variable affecting property prices. An example would be clean air, which should raise the price of a property, other things being equal. Questionnaire, or 'stated preference', techniques involve the use of questionnaires that offer hypothetical choices between different 'bundles' of attributes. The analyst considers the choices made and infers willingness to pay.

As costs and benefits accrue over time, CBA tends to adopt a discounting approach whereby future cash and non-cash flows are discounted back to a present value by use of a discount rate. The determination of the discount rate has occupied a substantial literature. In theory, one would expect consumers to prefer the present to the future because of impatience ('myopia') and expectations of higher incomes in the future (thus lowering their marginal valuation of a unit of benefit in the future). In turn, the resulting rate of time preference should be equal to interest rates ruling in the market that also reflect the productivity of capital. In practice, time preference rates and cost of capital estimates can vary significantly because of imperfections in capital markets. Moreover, the rate of discount relevant to social decisions can differ from the average of individual valuations, because choices made as members of society will differ when compared to choices made on an individualist basis. Further controversy surrounds the issue of intergenerational fairness, since positive discount rates have the potential for shifting cost burdens forwards to future generations, Thus the risks of, say, storing nuclear waste appear small when discounted back to the present and expressed as a present value. Conversely, zero discount rates may discriminate against projects that offer the highest potential for leaving accumulated capital for the use of future generations. Additionally, zero discounting can produce unacceptable outcomes, such as current generations sacrificing everything bar some minimum level of consumption in order to benefit future generations. To pursue the nuclear power example, non-investment because of the waste-disposal problem could reduce the inherited stock of energy availability to future generations, by forcing a rapid depletion of finite stock resources such as coal or oil. The intergenerational issue is thus complex and raises the fundamental issue of just how far into the future CBA should look. Because of its foundations in consumer sovereignty, there is a temptation to argue that the time horizon is set by the existing generation and, at most, the succeeding one or two generations. Recent work also suggests that there is no formal reason why 'the' discount rate should be constant over time. Discount rates should very probably decline with time.

CBA has enjoyed a revival of interest in recent years. Not only has there been a return of concern over the social value of public expenditure, but also the alternative techniques developed in the 1970s have been shown to be even more limited in their ability to discriminate between good and bad investments and policies. In particular, CBA has resurfaced through environmental economics, particularly with reference to the economic valuation of environmental costs and benefits. As an aid to rational thinking its credentials are higher than any of the alternatives so far advanced. That it cannot substitute for political decisions is not in question, but social science has a duty to inform public choice, and it is in this respect that CBA has its role to play.

DAVID W. PEARCE
UNIVERSITY COLLEGE LONDON

Reference

Hicks, J. (1943) 'The four consumers' surplus', *Review of Economic Studies* 11(1): 31–41.

Further reading

Boardman, A., Greenberg, D., Vining, A. and Weimer, D. (2001) *Cost Benefit Analysis: Concepts and Practice*, Upper Saddle River, NJ.

SEE ALSO: accounting; externalities; welfare economics

CREATIVITY

Creativity is typically defined by those who study it as the bringing into existence of new and humanly valuable ideas, objects, actions or ways of doing things. This definition identifies new and valuable products in essentially any sphere of human activity, including, for example, business, education, communication, technology, politics, philosophy, religion, entertainment, social organization and the arts and sciences as creative, while it excludes from consideration new ideas, objects, or actions in any sphere that are ineffective or inconsequential. From the perspective of history, human creativity looms large as a major cause of cultural change and enrichment, scientific advance and technological progress. Occurring in almost every sphere of human life, acts of creativity can also take many different forms. An act of creativity, for example, can involve a modest improvement in an object or way of doing things, the production of a highly valued piece of work within an existing form or genre (for example, a powerful new coming-of-age novel or an elegant new piece of computer software) or the kind of radical advance or revolution introduced by such creative geniuses as Isaac Newton, Pablo Picasso or Albert Einstein. Acts of creativity also vary widely in their range of impact, some affecting only the creative agents themselves, while others benefit people within the ambit of the creative agent's daily life, or impact even larger and more distant audiences, segments of society, professional fields or enduring human enterprises. Such variety has led some contemporary scholars to apply the term 'Big C' creativity to acts that transform or radically advance entire fields or subfields of human endeavour and the terms 'small c' or 'everyday' creativity to the cumulatively important but more humble creative acts of daily life. This dichotomous framework, while somewhat useful, seems to neglect a very large and extremely important middle range of creativity ('middle c' creativity?), which includes creative acts that have substantial social impact beyond the creative agents' immediate circle of acquaintances, but which do not transform entire fields or subfields. While some psychologists focus on Big C creativity, and a few study everyday creativity, many study socially significant creativity in the important range between these two extremes.

Despite the fact that creativity can and does occur in nearly every realm of human affairs and in every corner of the inhabited world, almost all psychological studies of creativity in the first half of the twentieth century focused on scientific, technological or artistic creativity in Europe or the USA and the individuals (usually men) who produced them. Though the fields and cultural settings included for study expanded somewhat during the second half of the century, creativity research and scholarship continues to be culturally bounded and to neglect many socially important forms of creativity.

However, the psychological study of creativity did expand considerably during the second half of the century in terms of empirically richer studies of creative people, more detailed examinations of creative processes, a new focus on ways to foster creativity, and much greater attention paid to qualities of the physical, social and cultural environment that influence creativity.

While continuing to study eminently creative historical figures, psychologists increasingly turned their energies to the study of living creative men and, notably, women who were involved in artistic, scientific and technological creativity. Investigators also examined the development and expression of creative potential in children, adolescents and young adults, childhood experiences and family backgrounds associated with later creativity, different prototypical trajectories of productivity throughout adulthood in various fields, higher than average rates of mental illness (especially depression and bipolar disorders) among certain artistically creative groups, and possible genetic influences on creativity.

The study of creative processes expanded to include the development and exploration of new tests designed to measure forms of ideational fluency and originality thought by some to be important components of creative thinking abilities, greater attention to the problem-finding or problem-making phase of creativity, increased focus on analogical and metaphorical thinking, broadly construed, as processes of possibly deep significance, and pioneering studies of the impact of affect and mood on creativity. Extremely detailed and concrete theories of creative processes were also instantiated and evaluated in the form of computer programs. Serious attention began being paid to the processes of dyadic and group creativity in artistic, scientific and business contexts, and at century's end, efforts also were being made to understand improvisational creativity in music, theatre and everyday life.

A new interest in fostering creativity emerged within segments of the educational, business and scientific research worlds during the 1950s. This interest resulted in efforts to teach schoolchildren general creative thinking abilities and attitudes, to teach group problem-solving techniques such as brainstorming to adults in organizational and business contexts, and to enhance creativity in organizational, engineering and research settings by altering the physical and social qualities of their workplaces.

An expanded concern with the influence of the social environment brought greater attention to ways in which large social systems (e.g. professions, invisible colleges, societies, nations and cultures) foster, channel or inhibit various forms of creative activity. For example, scholars became more conscious of social factors that have impeded the development and expression of women's creative potential throughout history. A series of analytically sophisticated studies of the apparent impact on eminent creativity of factors such as wars, political fragmentation, cultural heterogeneity and number of creative figures and models in preceding generations also contributed to the field's understanding of the influential roles played by macro-level historical factors. Beginning in the 1980s, heightened awareness of the impact of culture and society on creative activity led several scholars to begin developing systems-oriented theoretical models that identified and emphasized important ways in which creative people, products-in-the-making and sociocultural environments interact with one another in the course of complex creative episodes. The theoretical success and research utility of these ambitious models remains an open question.

A 'general' theory of creativity?

One of the important questions already confronting creativity scholars, and one that will probably pose an even greater challenge to future scholars, concerns the degree to which it will or will not be possible to make generalizations about creativity across different forms and fields of activity, and, therefore, whether the idea of constructing a 'general' theory or understanding of creativity is or is not a desirable or realistic scientific goal. In what respects and at what levels of abstraction, for example, are the processes involved in writing a novel, creating a new cosmological theory, composing a popular song or creating a new business the same and different? In what respects are the personality characteristics, mental abilities, motivations, family backgrounds, life histories, working environments and social systems conducive to creative work in one field or form conducive to creative work in another? For instance, though creatively effective people studied thus far tend to share personality characteristics that often distinguish them somewhat from the general population or from their less creative peers (overall, they appear to be above average in intelligence, powerfully motivated by their work, and unusually curious, open to experience, tolerant of ambiguity, imaginative, original and flexible in their thinking, independent, self-confident, willing to initiate activity in the face of uncertainty and risk, and able to work effectively over long periods of time) there is theoretical reason to expect and some empirical evidence to suggest that personality characteristics associated with creativity in different fields (in art and science, for instance) may be different in some significant ways. Will future studies of different forms and fields of creativity support the idea of a 'general' theory of creativity, or will the evidence produced necessitate the construction of a loosely connected family of form- and field-specific theories? The answer to this question may shape the future study of creativity in fundamental ways.

Future directions

In the early years of the twenty-first century, psychologists will almost surely begin using new technologies to examine the workings of the brain during various creative activities. They are also apt to begin searching within the human genome for genetic factors that influence the development of certain creative potentials and impulses. These efforts to shed light on creativity by looking more deeply into the human body should almost certainly be complemented by a corresponding turning of attention outward to instances and manifestations of creativity in diverse social and cultural settings, for human creativity is a complex and widespread phenomenon that will require a global vision and a multilayered perspective on the part of those who seek to understand its many forms and facets.

DAVID M. HARRINGTON
UNIVERSITY OF CALIFORNIA, SANTA CRUZ

Further reading

Boden, M.A. (2003) *The Creative Mind. Myths and Mechanisms*, expanded edn, New York.
Csikszentmihalyi, M. (1996) *Creativity. Flow and the Psychology of Discovery and Invention*, New York.
Eysenck, H.J. (1995) *Genius: The Natural History of Creativity*, New York.
Gardner, H. (1993) *Creating Minds*, New York.
Ghiselin, B. (1980 [1952]) *The Creative Process. Reflections on Invention in the Arts and Sciences*, Berkeley, CA.
Ludwig, A.M. (1995) *The Price of Greatness. Resolving the Creativity and Madness Controversy*, New York.
Runco, M.A. and Albert, R.S. (eds) (1990) *Theories of Creativity*, Newbury Park, CA.
Runco, M.A. and Pritzker, S.R. (eds) (1999) *Encyclopedia of Creativity*, Vols 1 and 2, San Diego, CA.
Sawyer, R.K. (2003) *Group Creativity. Music, Theatre, Collaboration*, Mahway, NJ.
Simonton, D.K. (1999) *Origins of Genius: Darwinian Perspectives on Creativity*, New York.
Sternberg, R.J. (ed.) (1999) *Handbook of Creativity*, New York.
Wallace, D.B. and Gruber, H.E. (eds) (1989) *Creative People at Work*, Oxford.

SEE ALSO: mind

CRIME AND DELINQUENCY

The terms 'crime' and 'delinquency' are emotionally loaded in everyday language, and often loosely used. People speak of all sorts of unseemly behaviour as being 'criminal', and unruly children may casually be called 'delinquents'. Although there is not a consensus on the matter, the prevailing view among criminologists is that, for scientific purposes, the term 'crime' should be restricted to those acts that are defined as violations of the criminal law. Even this more restricted definition creates difficulties when general theories of crime are sought, since it encompasses so much: government officials who plan and carry out criminal acts; corporate executives who violate health and safety laws, or engage in illegal economic transactions; juveniles who play truant from school, or who hang about in gangs;

the physical abuse of spouses and children; murder, rape, theft and robbery.

Despite the conceptual problems that inhere in the acceptance of the legal definition of crime and delinquency, there are advantages as well. For one, the legal definition provides an objective criterion for what is included in the study of crime and delinquency. To determine whether or not an act is a crime one need only look to see if a law has been passed that provides for punishment by state officials.

Another analytical advantage of limiting crime and delinquency to the legal definition is that it allows for cross-cultural comparisons. These show that some acts are defined as criminal in all state societies. Equally important, however, what is counted as a crime in one nation-state, or at one historical period, may not be a crime in another country, or at a different time. For example, murder, rape and theft are criminal acts in every state society. However, some acts of business executives or journalists that are a crime in one country are not in another. If the Secrecy Act of Great Britain were in force in the USA, and US journalists exposed governmental crime, as they presently do, then US journalists would be well represented in the prison population. Heroin addicts can obtain drugs through state-monitored programmes in some countries, while in others they face long prison sentences merely for possessing the drug. Marijuana may be purchased in special cafés in The Netherlands. In many other countries, possession of small amounts can land a person in prison for many years. Even within a country, different jurisdictions may define criminality differently: in the USA, marijuana possession is a felony for which a conviction can earn a defendant 40 years in prison in one state, while in an adjoining state it is a misdemeanour punishable by a very small fine, or it is not criminal at all.

Some acts that we now judge to be clearly criminal, such as murder and rape, were once viewed as wrongs that should be settled in accordance with the wishes of the aggrieved party, or the party's relatives, rather than as acts that should be punished by the state. In many countries, local courts still operate on this principle. In the USA, American Indian communities emphasize the importance of providing transgressors a right of passage back into legitimate roles. The anthropologist Laura Nader (1990), in her cross-cultural studies of law and crime, found that stateless societies and small communities are much more likely to invoke the principle of 'give a little, get a little', rather than 'winner take all', when members of the community deviate from accepted norms. One of the more recent innovations in criminal law in a number of Western jurisdictions is the introduction of 'restorative justice', whereby offenders and victims are brought together and encouraged to agree upon a punishment or compensation for the harm caused. If this movement gains momentum it will represent a fundamental shift in Western criminal law, away from rule enforcement and towards reconciliation between the parties in conflict (Chambliss and Seidman 1982: 28–36).

The definition of crime, and variations in what constitutes crime in time and space, is, of course, only the beginning of the systematic study of crime and delinquency by social scientists. Three sets of questions have dominated the field.

The question most often asked is 'Why do some people commit crime and others do not?' From the earliest studies of crime and delinquency in Italy, England and France, the search for an adequate answer to this question has led researchers to seek biological, sociological, psychological, economic and even geographical variables associated with, and presumably causally related to, criminal and delinquent behaviour. This quest has not been crowned with success. That is not surprising when it is realized that practically everyone commits some types of crimes in the course of a lifetime, so it may be that what is required is nothing less than a general theory of human behaviour. It is probably safe to say that the cross-fertilization of general social psychological theories of human action and social psychological theories of criminal and delinquent behaviour has yielded, to date, the most satisfactory, if partial, answers to this question.

Second, social science research on crime and delinquency has asked the sociological (as contrasted with social psychological) question, 'Why do rates and types of crimes and delinquency vary from one society or group to another?' Emile Durkheim in his study of suicide was the first to approach the study of deviant behaviour from this perspective (Durkheim 1966 [1897]). Consistent differences in crime rates between countries have been established, and it has been shown that crime rates are highest in rapidly changing societies, and in societies where discrepancies between the incomes of rich and the poor are greatest.

Third, since the mid-1980s there has been rapid growth in efforts to answer two other fundamental questions about crime and delinquency: 'What are the social forces that lead to the definition of some acts as criminal and not others?' and 'How does the criminal justice system of police, prosecutors, courts and prisons work, and what effect does it have on the perception, reporting and incidence of crime and delinquency?' These questions dovetail the study of crime and delinquency with the sociology of law, and they have provided for a great deal of valuable cross-fertilization between the fields. As might be expected, responses to these questions are strongly influenced by the theoretical traditions of Durkheim, Marx and Weber. Consensus is lacking on which paradigm is most useful but a substantial body of fascinating research has been accumulated in an effort to shed light on these important issues.

There is no reason to suppose that the future of studies of crime and delinquency will veer very far away from these basic questions. In view of the salience of crime as a political and economic issue, however, it is likely that rather more resources will be devoted to questions about the appropriateness of defining acts as criminal, and the functioning of the criminal justice system. The issue of whether using drugs should be criminalized is preoccupying most Western countries. More generally, the growth and power of what the Norwegian criminologist Nils Christie (1993) calls 'the crime industry' is deservedly receiving a great deal more attention than heretofore.

WILLIAM J. CHAMBLISS
GEORGE WASHINGTON UNIVERSITY

References

Chambliss, W. and Seidman, R. (1982) *Law, Order and Power*, rev. edn, Reading, MA.
Christie, N. (1993) *Crime Control as Industry*, London.
Durkheim, E. (1966 [1897]) *Suicide*, New York.
Nader, L. (1990) *Harmony, Ideology, Justice and Control*, Stanford, CA.

Further reading

Anderson, E. (1999) *Code of the Streets*, New York.
Beirne, P. and Messerschmidt, J. (1991) *Criminology*, New York.
Braithwaite, J. (1979) *Inequality, Crime and Public Policy*, London.
Calavota, K., Pontell, H. and Tillman, R. (1997) *Big Money Crime*, Berkeley, CA.
Chambliss, W. (2001) *Power, Politics, and Crime*, Boulder, CO.
Cohen, S. (1988) *Against Criminology*, New Brunswick, NJ.
Denton, S. and Morris, R. (2001) *The Money and the Power*, New York.
Feeley, M. (1992) *The Process is the Punishment*, New York.
Hamm, M. (2002) *In Bad Company*, Boston.

SEE ALSO: criminology; deviance; penology; police and policing; sociolegal studies

CRIMINOLOGY

Standard textbook accounts find two scriptural beginnings to the history of criminology: the 'classical school' and the 'positivist school', each one marking out a somewhat different fate for the discipline. More sophisticated criminologists have rewritten this history (Beirne 1993; Garland 1985, 1994) but the conflict between these two trajectories still remains a useful way of understanding the shape of a discipline conventionally defined as 'the scientific study of crime and its control'.

The classical trajectory dates from the mid-eighteenth century and tells of the revolutionary contribution of Enlightenment thinkers like Beccaria and Bentham in breaking with a previously 'archaic', 'barbaric', 'repressive' or 'arbitrary' system of criminal law. For these reformers, legal philosophers and political theorists, the crime question was predominantly the punishment question. Their programme was to prevent punishment from being, in Beccaria's words, 'an act of violence of one or many against a private citizen'; instead it should be 'essentially public, prompt, necessary, the least possible in given circumstances, proportionate to the crime, dictated by laws'.

Classicism presented a model of rationality: on the one side, the 'free' sovereign individual acting according to the dictates of reason and self-interest; on the other hand, the limited liberal state, contracted to grant rights and liberties, to prescribe duties and to impose the fair and just punishment that must result from the knowing infraction of the legal code and the knowing infliction of social harm.

This 'immaculate conception' of the birth of the classical school as a humanistic reform has been challenged by revisionist histories of law and the state. Dates, concepts and subjects have been reordered. Classicism is now more likely to be conceived in terms of the broader rationalization of crime control associated with the emergence of the free market and the new capitalist order. But whatever their origins, the internal preoccupations of classicism – whether they appear in utilitarianism, Kantianism, liberalism, anarchism or indeed any political philosophy at all – have never really disappeared from the criminological agenda. This is where the subject overlaps with politics, jurisprudence and the sociology of law.

A century after classicism, though, criminology was to claim for itself its 'real' scientific beginning and a quite different set of influences. This was the positivist 'revolution', dated in comic-book intellectual history with the publication in 1876 of Lombroso's *Delinquent Man*. This was a positivism that shared the more general social scientific connotations of the term (the notion, that is, of the unity of the scientific method) but which acquired a more specific meaning in criminology. As David Matza (1964, 1969) suggests in his influential sociologies of criminological knowledge, criminological positivism managed the astonishing feat of separating the study of crime from the contemplation of the state. Classicism was dismissed as metaphysical speculation. The new programme was to focus not on crime (the act) but on the criminal (the actor); it was to assume not rationality, choice and free will, but determinism (biological, psychic or social). At the centre of the new criminological enterprise was the notion of causality. No longer sovereign beings, subject to the same pulls and pushes as their fellow citizens, criminals were now special creatures or members of a special class.

The whole of the last century of criminology can be understood as a series of creative yet eventually repetitive variations on these late nineteenth-century themes. The particular image conjured up by Lombroso's criminal type – the atavistic genetic throwback – faded away, but the subsequent structure and logic of criminological explanation remained largely within the positivist paradigm. Whether the level of explanation was biological, psychological, sociological or a combination of these ('multifactorial' as some versions were dignified), the Holy Grail was a general causal theory: Why do people commit crime? This quest gave the subject its self-definition: 'the scientific study of the causes of crime'.

At each stage of this search, criminology strengthened its claim to exist as an autonomous, multidisciplinary study. Somewhat like a parasite, criminology attached itself to its host disciplines (law, psychology and, dominantly, sociology) and drew from them methods, theories and academic credibility. At the same time – somewhat like a colonial power landing on new territory – each of these disciplines descended on the eternally fascinating subjects of crime and punishment, and claimed them as their own. In this fashion, the theories, methods and substance of criminology draw on Freudianism, behaviourism, virtually every stream of sociology (the Chicago School, functionalism, anomie theory, interactionism, etc.), Marxism, feminism, rational choice theory and even postmodernism. Each of these traces can be found in any current criminological textbook; it would be difficult to think of a major system of thought in the social sciences that would not be so represented.

All the time, however, that this positivist trajectory was being established, criminologists retained their interest in questions of punishment and control. If, in one sense, all criminology became positivist, then also all criminology has always been concerned with classical matters. But instead of thinking about the limits and nature of the criminal sanction, this side of criminology (sometimes called penology) took this sanction as politically given. True, there was (and still is) an important debate about whether the discipline's subject matter should be confined to conventional legal definitions of crime or broadened to include all forms of socially injurious conduct. And the criminalization versus decriminalization debate is still very much alive, in areas such as corporate wrong-doing, pornography and drug abuse.

Questions of punishment and social control, however, became part of a more scientific discourse: the construction of empirical knowledge about the workings of the criminal justice system. Research findings were built up about the police, courts, prisons and various other agencies devoted to the prevention, control, deterrence or treatment of adult crime and juvenile delinquency. The structure and ideologies of these agencies are analysed, their working practices and relations to each other observed, their effectiveness evaluated. This is now a major part of the criminological enterprise.

Behind this work, the classical tradition remains alive in another sense. Modern criminologists became the heirs of the Enlightenment belief in rationality and progress. Their scientific task was informed by a sense of faith: that the business of crime control could be made not only more efficient, but also more humane. As reformers, advisers and consultants, most criminologists claim for themselves not merely an autonomous body of knowledge, but also the status of an applied science or even profession.

It is this simultaneous claim to knowledge and power that links the two sides of the criminological discourse: causation and control. In positivism, this is an organic link: to know the cause is to know the appropriate policy. But the history and status of this link is more complicated. The early nineteenth-century penitentiary system was dependent on theories of rehabilitation, behaviour modification and anomie well before their supposed 'discovery' by scientific criminology. There is a lively debate about Foucault's characterization of criminological knowledge as wholly utilitarian, an elaborate alibi to justify the exercise of power.

In the general climate of radical self-scrutiny that descended on the social sciences in the 1960s, criminology too began to fragment. There were three major attacks against what was visualized as the positivist hegemony. Each in its own peculiar and quite distinct way represented a revival of classicist concerns.

First, labelling theory – a loose body of ideas derived from symbolic interactionism – restated some simple sociological truths about the relativity of social rules and normative boundaries. Crime was only one form of that wider category of social action, deviance; criminology should be absorbed into the sociology of deviance. Beyond such conceptual and disciplinary boundary disputes, the whole quest for causality was regarded with scepticism. In addition to the standard behavioural question (Why do some people do these bad things?) there were a series of definitional questions. Why are certain actions defined as rule-breaking? How are these rules applied? What are the consequences of this application? These definitional questions took causal primacy: it was not that deviance led to control, but control to deviance. Social control agencies – the most benevolent as well as the most punitive –

only made matters worse. Sympathy and tolerance for society's outsiders were preferable to the conformity and scientific pretensions of mainstream criminology.

Second, this liberal criticism became harder in the 1960s onslaught on mainstream criminology. This came from what was labelled variously as conflict, new, critical, radical or Marxist criminology. Combining some strands of labelling theory and conflict sociology with classical Marxist writing about law, class and the state, this critique moved even further from the agenda of positivism. Traditional causal inquiries, particularly individualistic, were either dismissed or subsumed under the criminogenic features of capitalism. Legalistic definitions were either expanded to include the 'crimes of the powerful' (those social harms that business and the state license themselves to commit) or subjected to historicist and materialist enquiry. Labelling theory's wider category of deviance was refocused on law: the power of the state to criminalize some actions rather than others. The analytical task was to construct a political economy of crime and its control. The normative task was to eliminate those systems of exploitation that cause crime.

The third critique of the positivist enterprise came from a quite different theoretical and political direction, one that would prove more enduring. Impressed by the apparent failure of the causal quest and of progressive policies such as treatment, rehabilitation and social reform ('nothing works' was the slogan), loose coalitions appeared in the 1970s under such rallying calls as 'realism', 'back to justice' and 'neo-classicism'. Some of this was neo-liberalism – sad disenchantment with the ideals and policies of progressive criminology. Some was neo-conservativism – satisfaction about the supposed progressive failures. But politics aside, all these criminologists began turning back to classical questions. The notion of justice allowed liberals to talk of rights, equity and fairness, and to advance the Kantian-derived 'just-deserts' model of sentencing. In the face of massively escalating crime rates throughout the West, conservatives (and just about everyone else) talked about law and order, social defence, deterrence and the protection of society. The traditional positivist interest in causation seemed less important than devising rational crime control policies.

Since the early 1990s, the fragmented discourse of criminology has settled into yet another pattern. The original labelling and radical moments have all but disappeared, most of their cohort denouncing its own earlier romantic excesses in favour of what is called 'left-realist criminology'. This is more receptive to reformist social policy, and more interested in victimization and causation. 'Victimology' has become a major subfield in itself. The mainstream non-positivist position has become highly influential in various forms of managerial or administrative criminology. These emphasize 'situational crime prevention' (designing physical and social space to reduce criminal opportunity) and rest on an image of the new 'reasoning criminal' (Cornish and Clarke 1986) derived from rational choice theory. At the same time, traditional positivist enquiry remains very much alive in the form of massive birth cohort or longitudinal studies about the development of criminal careers. A more theoretically innovative direction comes from Braithwaite's neo-Durkheimian theory of reintegrative shaming (Braithwaite 1989).

Most criminologists now work in what has been separated off in the USA as the applied field of criminal justice studies. Basic theoretical debates – whether about the nature of the subject or the nature of criminality – are still alive but less prestigious. The subject remains ethnocentric: seldom engaging with the less developed world or with crimes of the state or with political violence.

The diversity in modern criminology arises from two tensions. First, crime is behaviour, but it is behaviour that the state is organized to punish. Second, crime raises matters of pragmatic public interest, but it has also created its own theoretical discourse.

STANLEY COHEN
LONDON SCHOOL OF ECONOMICS
AND POLITICAL SCIENCE

References

Beirne, P. (1993) *Inventing Criminology: The Rise of 'Homo Criminalis'*, Albany, NY.
Braithwaite, J. (1989) *Crime, Shame and Reintegration*, Cambridge, UK.
Cornish, D.B. and Clarke, R.V. (eds) (1986) *The Reasoning Criminal: Rational Choice Perspectives on Offending*, New York.
Garland, D. (1985) *Punishment and Welfare*, Aldershot.
—— (1994) 'Of crimes and criminals: The development of criminology in Britain', in M. Maguire, R.

Morgan and R. Reiner (eds) *The Oxford Handbook of Criminology*, Oxford.
Matza, D. (1964) *Delinquency and Drift*, New York.
—— (1969) *Becoming Deviant*, Englewood Cliffs, NJ.

Further reading

Christie, N. (1981) *Limits to Pain*, Oxford.
Cohen, S. (1988) *Against Criminology*, New Brunswick, NJ.
Gottfredson, M. and Hirschi, T. (1990) *A General Theory of Crime*, Stanford, CA.
Maguire, M., Morgan, R. and Reiner, R. (eds) (1994) *The Oxford Handbook of Criminology*, Oxford.
Sutherland, E. and Cressey, D. (1989) *Principles of Criminology*, Philadelphia, PA.
Young, J. and Mathews, R. (eds) (1992) *Rethinking Criminology: The Realist Debate*, London.

SEE ALSO: crime and delinquency; deviance; penology; police and policing; sociolegal studies

CROSS-CULTURAL PSYCHOLOGY

Cross-cultural psychology has emerged as a distinctive specialism within the field of psychology over the past 40 years. The principal reason for this derives from the way in which psychology as a whole has developed. A primary goal of psychology as an academic discipline has been to identify universal aspects of human behaviour. This focus of attention has led many researchers to assume that it is not especially important where a particular investigation is undertaken. Since around two-thirds of the psychologists in the world are American, it is no surprise that the majority of published studies are conducted in the USA and many of these have been based upon investigations using students as participants. Cross-cultural psychology has developed as evidence accumulates that choice of location and samples for study do affect the findings obtained. This is least true for studies of biologically determined aspects of behaviour and most true in respect of social behaviours.

Early work by cross-cultural psychologists focused on differences in cognitive abilities. For instance it was shown that those who grew up in a 'non-carpentered' world (i.e. without buildings that have straight walls and flat ceilings) had different responses to visual illusions. Differences that were found in performance on Western-designed intelligence tests were challenged on the basis that the concept of intelligence was culture-specific. Whereas in Western nations intelligence has customarily been defined in terms of the capacity to think logically, elsewhere in the world intelligence is often thought to include aspects of social sensitivity. The recent Western interest in 'emotional intelligence' acknowledges the narrowness of earlier conceptions. In a similar way, differences that were found in children's rate of progression through Piagetian stages of development were reinterpreted. Rather than showing that some children were more able than others, it was argued that a different range of environments elicits development of a differing range of abilities. By designing tests with local relevance, researchers were able to show that children without schooling performed as well or better than those who experienced schooling, whereas non-schooled children did much worse on conventional Western tests. This emphasis upon the physical and social environment as a key determinant of differing cultural emphases is espoused by those who define themselves as cultural psychologists rather than as cross-cultural psychologists. Their work takes forward the perspective of the Russian psychologist, Vygotsky. They see cultures as relatively fluid entities, constantly in a process of definition and redefinition on the basis of the myriad of social interactions that take place every day. They mostly favour qualitative modes of data analysis.

Cross-cultural psychologists take a different approach, but they too quickly become aware of the need to define the concepts and methods that are required to give a more systematic account of the different results of studies conducted in different parts of the world. A major impetus was provided by Hofstede's (1980) study of the values espoused by a very large worldwide sample of employees of the US company, IBM. Hofstede's principal innovation was to aggregate his data to the level of nation. While psychologists typically study individuals, all definitions of culture have some basis in collectivity. Hofstede chose to define culture as 'the collective programming of the mind'. He argued that while there are numerous and important variations within nations there is also sufficient in common in the educational, linguistic, legal and political structures of modern nations, that it is worthwhile to explore the value of treating nations as cultures.

Hofstede therefore averaged for each of forty nations (later fifty-three) the responses obtained to various questions and then factor analysed the country means. This led him to define four dimensions along which he concluded that the nations of the world vary, namely Individualism–Collectivism, Power Distance, Uncertainty Avoidance and Masculinity–Femininity. These four dimensions of variability, especially the first, have had a major effect on subsequent investigations by cross-cultural psychologists. Individualistic cultures are defined as those in which individuals define themselves in terms of relative autonomy from others and the freedom to make individual life choices. Collectivist cultures are those in which individuals are more prone to define their identity in terms of long-lasting group memberships that entail a variety of reciprocal obligations. Since Hofstede found that the most individualistic nations were those economically developed Western nations in which most psychological research is undertaken, this provided an impetus to determine whether studies would yield similar outcomes in collectivist nations.

Simple replication of Western studies within more collectivist nations does not always yield unambiguous results. For instance, Bond and Smith (1996) found that conformity was greater within collectivist nations when Asch's well-known study of the judgement of lines was replicated. However, they noted that in the context of an individualist culture, yielding to the majority verdict might be disparagingly categorized as conformity, but within a collectivist context, the same behaviour might be thought of as tact or sensitivity. More recent studies have not simply taken prior Western studies and repeated them elsewhere, but instead have designed investigations to be conducted in two or more locations, based upon theories advanced by Hofstede and others. The best of these studies do not simply categorize nations on the basis of Hofstede's scores, but include measures determining the predominant cultural orientations of those who are actually sampled. Care is also taken to use tasks that are locally meaningful and to conduct adequate checks on translation of materials into local languages.

Many recent studies have focused on contrasts between North America and Pacific Asia (typically represented by Japan, China or Korea). These nations are seen as exemplars of individualism and collectivism, even though Hofstede actually reported rather greater collectivism from Latin America and Africa. It has been established for instance that collectivists work harder in groups than when alone, whereas individualists show 'social loafing' (i.e. work less hard) when in groups. Collectivists see it as more fair to allocate rewards within their group equally, whereas individualists favour allocating rewards on the basis of individual merit. However, collectivists make more of a distinction between their in-group and out-groups than do individualists. If collectivists are asked to allocate rewards to persons outside their in-group, then they too favour allocation based on merit. Collectivists favour in-group harmony, seeking to preserve not just their own face but also the face of others. Individualists are more concerned to save their own face. Collectivists more often communicate in indirect, tacit ways, whereas individualists are more forthright and direct. These differences are apparent in formal negotiations and in the handling of conflicting opinions. Collectivists are also less likely to report anxiety or depression, but more likely to report somatic complaints. Individualistic parents more quickly train their children to act independently, while collectivistic parents maintain closer emotional bonds.

The reader may note that the findings summarized in the preceding paragraph (for more detail, see Berry *et al.* 1992 and Smith and Bond 1998) are expressed at the level of individuals, rather than as generalizations about cultures. This shift reflects recent developments in the field, moving it back towards the level of analysis upon which psychologists mainly focus. As many nations are in fact rather diverse, some researchers think it preferable to design measures reflecting the extent to which individuals construe themselves in ways that are individualistic or collectivistic. Whether cultural differences are adequately captured by measuring self-construals is a matter of current debate. Alternative views are that prevailing patterns of values or of beliefs may be preferable. In a major project over the past 15 years, Schwartz (1992) has surveyed the values of students and schoolteachers in more than sixty nations. He uses individual-level within-nation analyses to determine whether specific values do actually have the same meaning within each of the nations sampled. Using only those values that are found to have equivalent meanings, he then characterizes nations at the culture-level. Some consistency is found with Hofstede's dimensions, but the data also provide a richer, more differentiated picture.

The focus upon interrelating the two levels of analysis holds increasing promise of clarifying some otherwise puzzling effects. For instance, surveys show that people living in the richest countries report the greatest happiness (Diener and Diener 1995), and yet the richest individuals within particular nations are not found to be the happiest. At the level of nations, the availability of material resources offers greatest opportunities for fulfilment, but at the individual level, other more subjective factors come into play. In the study of basic emotions, there is evidence that facial expressions of emotions such as anger, sadness and joy are universally recognized (Ekman *et al.* 1987). However, cultures differ in terms of the local rules permitting or restraining the overt expression of emotions. Consequently, individual emotional experience is overlaid by the broader cultural context within which it occurs. In a similar way, there is evidence that basic personality structure has some consistency across cultures, but the behaviours that would best represent (for instance) extraversion within a particular culture would depend on local rules and circumstances (Church and Lonner 1998).

The findings of cross-cultural psychology have two major areas of practical application. First, the contrasting results obtained within collectivist nations have implications for international organizations and for multinational business. Many of the policies and strategies employed by organizations originating in Western nations are based upon assumptions about individualistic motivations. Effective operation in other parts of the world requires detailed attention to the collective aspects of local circumstance. Second, the world is currently subject to an unparalleled degree of individual mobility, whether this is in terms of tourism, higher education, business operations, emigration or asylum-seeking. Cross-cultural psychologists are increasingly active in studying the processes of short- and long-term acculturation. Early models described this process in terms of cultural assimilation, whereby migrants or their descendants were thought to gradually relinquish their culture of origin and internalize their adopted culture. A more recent influential model has been that of Berry (1997), who distinguished assimilation from what he termed integration. Integration is defined in terms of both maintenance of one's original cultural identity and internalization of one's adopted cultural identity, a pattern more consistent with the multiculturalism espoused by some governments. Studies have focused on the determinants and consequences of these different styles of acculturation, as well as separation, in which one rejects the adoption of a new cultural identity, or marginalization in which one loses both new and old sources of identity.

The work of cross-cultural psychologists indicates that we cannot fully understand human behaviour adequately simply by studying samples of individuals. We also need conceptual frameworks that enable us to measure validly how social environments around the world differ. Some progress in this direction has been achieved, but much wider sampling remains a key requirement.

PETER SMITH
UNIVERSITY OF SUSSEX

References

Berry, J.W. (1997) 'Immigration, acculturation and adaptation', *Applied Psychology: An International Review* 46.

Berry, J.W. *et al.* (1992) *Cross-Cultural Psychology: Research and Applications*, Cambridge.

Bond, R.A. and Smith, P.B. (1996) 'Culture and conformity: A meta-analysis of studies using Asch's (1952, 1956) line judgment task', *Psychological Bulletin* 119.

Church, A.T. and Lonner, W.J. (1998) 'Personality and its measurement across cultures', *Journal of Cross-Cultural Psychology* 29.

Diener, E. and Diener, M. (1995) 'Cross-cultural correlates of life satisfaction and self-esteem', *Journal of Personality and Social Psychology* 68.

Ekman, P. *et al.* (1987) 'Universals and cultural differences in judgements of the facial expressions of emotion', *Journal of Personality and Social Psychology* 53.

Hofstede, G. (1980) *Culture's Consequences: International Differences in Work-Related Values*, Beverly Hills, CA.

Schwartz, S.H. (1991) 'Beyond individualism/collectivism: New cultural dimensions of values', in U. Kim, H.C. Triandis, C. Kagitqibasi, S.C. Choi and G. Yoon (eds) *Individualism and Collectivism Theory, Method and Applications*, Thousand Oaks, CA.

—— (1992) 'Universals in the structure and content of values: Theoretical advances and empirical tests in 20 countries', in M.P. Zanna (ed.) *Advances in Experimental Social Psychology*, Vol. 25, Orlando, FL.

Smith, P.B. and Bond, M.H. (1998) *Social Psychology across Cultures*, 2nd edn, Hemel Hempstead.

Further reading

Berry, J.W., Poortinga, Y.H., Segall, M.H. and Dasen, P.R. (2002) *Cross-Cultural Psychology*, 2nd edn, Cambridge, UK.

Berry, J.W., Dasen, P.R. and Saraswathi, T.S. (eds) (1997) *Handbook of Cross-Cultural Psychology*, 2nd edn, 3 vols, Needham Heights, MA.

SEE ALSO: psychological anthropology; transcultural psychiatry

CULTURAL ANTHROPOLOGY

Cultural anthropology in a broad sense encompasses the anthropology of culture or that stream in anthropology which emphasizes culture. In a narrower sense it identifies a group or lineage of anthropologists concentrated in the USA whose guiding concept was or is culture. Key originating figures were Franz Boas and his students, especially Ruth Benedict, Alfred Kroeber and Margaret Mead. Cultural anthropology contrasts historically and, to a degree still, with social anthropology, whose heritage is British, and whose key originating figures include W.H.R. Rivers, A.R. Radcliffe-Brown and Bronislaw Malinowski. The distinction between a social and a cultural emphasis is complex and not always sharp, so many prefer the term 'sociocultural anthropology'. However, the streams do differ in perspective and emphasis, as can be illustrated by classic works. Ruth Benedict's *Patterns of Culture* (1934) described how the pueblo Indians differed from those of the plains, using Nietzsche's distinction between the Apollonian and the Dionysian. The pueblo way of life was more settled, ritualistic and static, the plains way of life more nomadic, episodic and dynamic. Where Benedict depicted guiding values (culture), social anthropology emphasized relationships.

Postwar anthropology until the 1970s broadly focused on the structure of culture in relation to the functioning of society. Despite some crosscurrents, a contrast was still evident to contemporaries between European and US approaches. Leading British and French anthropologists tended to work in the tradition of Durkheim and his school. Lévi-Strauss, Leach, Needham and other 'structuralists' elucidated the structure of collective thought manifested in varying forms – myths, language, ritual – and correlated to institutional or social systems – kinship, class, community. In the USA, Geertz treated similar topics but was more influenced by Parsons and Weber, and by the US stream of cultural anthropology. Culture, for Geertz, was initially defined as a system of symbols, ideas and values, later as a kind of text, and constituted a framework for action. He deployed this idea of culture in the study of revolutions, economic development and ecology as well as the practice of religion and art, kingship and ceremony. US cognitive anthropologists relied heavily on the behaviourist model, but were interested particularly in the structure of individual thought – cognitive paradigms. Correlated, though at a much narrower and more technical sphere, were the 'ethno scientists' or 'cognitive anthropologists' (Frake, Conklin, Goodenough) who drew on linguistics to elicit models of thought expressed through words that labelled domains of thinking. Despite enormous variation, all of these research programmes aimed to lay bare dimensions of culture. Counterpoints set out further complications or dynamic implications. Leach (1954) analysed dynamics of change in Burma. Bateson (1972) showed the contradictions between linguistic levels that created a 'double bind'. Other studies formulated dynamic processes – of ritual, theatre, communication – by which culture is created, in a word, the process of mimesis (e.g. Peacock 1968).

Beginning in the 1970s, the relative clarity of the paradigm gives way to a diversity of approaches that are difficult to summarize succinctly. One indication of the diversity was the reorganization of the American Anthropological Association after the 1970s: from a centralized governing board to myriad 'sections' defined along multiple dimensions – specialities, ethnic or gender identities, applications – allied to numerous organizations. This was associated with a multiplication of numbers of programmes – now around four hundred – in US universities alone, not to mention globally. What was the intellectual paradigm associated with these developments?

One could speak of two directions, internal and external. The internal was the reflexive dimension, inserting the anthropologist as subject into objects of study and critique from within of the discipline. The external ranged from a broadening context of understanding – for example, recognizing the influence of power and wealth on culture – to practice, as anthropologists increased their work outside academia and sought new relevancies.

Exemplifying the internal, reflexive and self-critical direction, James Clifford and George Marcus (1986) wrote about 'writing culture', analysing in a literary critical frame how anthropologists represent 'the other' and themselves. Not only style but also context and allegiance was part of this critique, especially the relation between anthropology and colonialism. Critique led to creative, experimental modes of ethnographic and historical writing. For example, Kathleen Stewart (1996) evocatively portrayed Appalachian subjects in relation to herself. Vincent Crapanzano (1980) described his relation to Tuhami, a Moroccan with whom he practised a quasi-clinical interaction. James Boon (1999) exploded boundaries, merging histories of anthropology and personal or cultural memories – of father, of coca-cola, of museums, of figures in the history of anthropology and field study.

Circling back to attempt to capture notions of culture, but also with awareness of the subjective dimensions, some cultural anthropologists have focused on the notion of 'identity' and life history (see Holland *et al.* 1998), while others have drawn on enduring but neglected linkages between culture and psychological anthropology to move past both the objectivist stance of the Geertzians and the inward look of the reflexivists (see e.g. Nuckolls 1998; Wikan 1990).

Focusing externally, Eric Wolf called for awareness of power and of capitalistic forces in history (*Europe and the People without History*), a stream illustrated by numerous works, for example Catherine Lutz's *Homefront*, and others showing the influence of the military. Such theoretical, ethnographic and, one may say, ideological discourses found parallels in practice or discourses on practice. Applied or practising anthropology was at work in virtually every sphere; anthropologists were in General Motors, in government agencies, administrators of universities, activities reflected and reinforced by the National Association of Practicing Anthropologists (NAPA) and others (WOPA, SOPA, etc.) in the USA, continuing long traditions begun with Margaret Mead and others. Also continuing such traditions from Boas, Mead and others was a call sometimes termed public or public interest anthropology for anthropologists to enter the policy arena, to shape directions of society. Action as well as rhetoric includes human rights work and environmental activism. Often it is not anthropology *per se* but anthropologists as citizens or workers in various organizational contexts who do this work, doubtless informed by backgrounds in cultural anthropology.

What about disciplines beyond anthropology? What cognate or linked directions extend from cultural anthropology? Cultural anthropology has influenced literary theory and criticism by affecting basic tenets of theory, objects of study and approaches, perhaps most significantly via the development of interdisciplinary areas of study such as cultural studies, women's and ethnic studies, religion and literature, and postcolonial studies. The disciplines of anthropology, history and literary study have tended to converge in subfields of study, particularly in the last 40 years. Examples of studies in which the three disciplines overlap and merge include Edward Said's *Orientalism*, Mary Louise Pratt's *Imperial Eyes*, Anderson's *Imagined Communities* and Lynn Hunt's edited collection *The New Cultural History*.

Cultural anthropology merges not only with literary studies and history, but also with economics, communication studies, political science, women's studies, and ethnic studies to produce cultural studies. Examining questions of representation, discourses of power, and social and political constructs and movements, cultural studies aims to connect interdisciplinary theory to lived experience.

Cultural anthropology now celebrates its first century, if one thinks of US origins, a bit longer if one traces back to European beginnings. This snapshot differs from that in the last edition, and the next will differ again: in a globalizing world, further transformations may be expected.

JAMES L. PEACOCK
CARRIE MATTHEWS
UNIVERSITY OF NORTH CAROLINA

References

Anderson, B.R. (1983) *Imagined Communities*, London.

Bateson, G. (1972) *Steps to an Ecology of Mind*, New York

Benedict, R. (1934) *Patterns of Culture*, Boston.

Boon, J.A. (1999) *Verging on Extravagance*, Princeton, NJ.

Clifford, J. and Marcus, G. (1986) *Writing Culture: The Poetics and Politics of Ethnography*, Berkeley, CA.

Crapanzano, V. (1980) *Tuhami*, Chicago.

Holland, D.C., Lachicotte, W., Jr, Skinner, D. and Cain, C. (1998) *Identity and Agency in Cultural Worlds*, Cambridge, MA.

Hunt, L. (ed.) (1989) *The New Cultural History*, Berkeley, CA.

Leach, E.R. (1954) *Political Systems of Highland Burma*, London.

Lutz, C. (2001) *Homefront*, Boston.

Nuckolls, C.W. (1998) *Culture: A Problem That Cannot Be Solved*, Madison, WI.

Peacock, J.L. (1968) *Rites of Modernization*, Chicago.

Pratt, M.L. (1992) *Imperial Eyes*, London.

Said, E.W. (1978) *Orientalism*, New York.

Stewart, K. (1996) *A Space on the Side of the Road*, Princeton, NJ.

Wikan, U. (1990) *Managing Turbulent Hearts*, Chicago.

Wolf, E. (1982) *Europe and the People without History*, Berkeley, CA.

Further reading

Borofsky, R. (ed.) (1994) *Assessing Cultural Anthropology*, New York

Clifford, J. (1988) *Histories of the Tribal and the Modern*, Cambridge, MA.

Hill, C.E. and Baba, M. (eds) (2000) *The Unity of Theory and Practice in Anthropology*, Arlington, VA.

Marcus, G.E. (1999) *Anthropology as Cultural Critique*, 2nd edn, Chicago.

Peacock, J.L. (2001) *The Anthropological Lens*, Cambridge.

SEE ALSO: culture; psychological anthropology; social anthropology

CULTURAL GEOGRAPHY

Since the 1980s cultural geography has undergone significant theoretical, methodological and empirical shifts. While the subfield has a long and important place in the intellectual and institutional history of the discipline in North America, the recent 'spatial and cultural turn' in the humanities and social sciences has repositioned the field as one of considerable import to contemporary debates in Anglo-American human geography. From the 1920s through the 1970s Carl Sauer and his students in the 'Berkeley School' (Leighly 1963; Wagner and Mikesell 1962) focused on human/environment relationships, material culture and landscape interpretation. Such concerns remain an important part of cultural geography, particularly in North America. Although the Berkeley School was not explicitly theoretical, it nonetheless drew theoretical and methodological insights from cultural anthropology and landscape history.

The 1950s and 1960s saw the sustained importation into geography of positivist theory, behavioural psychology and highly abstract quantitative methods as human geography sought to redefine itself as a spatial, model-building science. Cultural geographers' emphasis on the symbolic dimension of human activities, the relevance of historical understanding of societal processes and a commitment to an interpretative epistemology, all challenged the scientific reductionism and economism of such a positivist human geography. A new generation of cultural geographers offered an alternative vision to the model builders of what geography had to offer (Tuan 1974; Lowenthal 1961; Meinig 1979; Zelinsky 1973). This challenge remained historicist and to a large extent empiricist as well. During the 1980s there arose what some have termed a 'new cultural geography' that questioned the Berkeley School's predominant use of the term culture as a reified 'super organic' explanatory variable (Duncan 1980). It offered in its place a more sociological and political approach that attempted to understand the 'inner workings of culture' and to unpack what had been consigned to a 'black box' by earlier generations. The explicit use of theory became a hallmark of the new cultural geography, and sharply demarcated it from more traditional cultural geography. Another important change at this time was initiated by the British social geographers (Jackson 1980), who had previously dismissed cultural geography as irrelevant to contemporary urban social and political issues, but now began to turn to cultural history and the then rising field of cultural studies for inspiration. The study of 'race' and ethnicity in historic and contemporary contexts, for instance, shifted from an emphasis on spatial mapping to an exploration of cultural representations of 'race'. This merged longstanding concerns in social geography with more explicitly cultural interpretations and contributed to the development of a 'new cultural geography' (Anderson 1988; Jackson 1987; Ley 1974).

Similarly the emergence in the 1970s and 1980s of a radical human geography both invigorated cultural geographers' concern with a materialist basis for landscape interpretation (Cosgrove 1983; Daniels 1989) while simultaneously providing a focus for a broader critique of the limitations of economistic Marxist interpretations of human societies (Duncan and Ley 1982). Within cultural geography there also emerged a reassertion of the centrality of place to human geographical concerns (Agnew 1987; Entrikin 1991; Relph 1976). Feminist geographers also had a marked impact on contemporary cultural geography, highlighting the prevalence of the detached male gaze in the study of landscape and stressing the role of gender in any unpacking of the 'inner workings of culture' (Rose 1993; Nash 1996). The promotion of a geography that would value the subjective, subaltern voices and cultural specificity, and which would employ a range of source material not normally used by geographers, would open up the discipline to methods and debates prevalent in philosophy, literary theory, cultural studies and anthropology (Ley and Samuels 1978; Duncan and Duncan 1988; Gregory 1994).

During the last decade of the twentieth century, cultural concerns penetrated political, economic and social geography. Issues of discourse, power, justice, the body, difference, hybridity, transnationalism, actor-networks, resistance, transgression, performance and representation have been particularly important in contemporary approaches within cultural geography and beyond. Feminist, Marxist, critical, psychoanalytical, postcolonial and postmodern theorists have led the subfield in radically interrogating and transforming geographical conceptions of space, place and landscape (McDowell 1999; Mitchell 2000; Nast and Pile 1998; Jacobs 1996; Driver 2001; Thrift 1996; Gregory 2002).

The traditional concern of cultural geographers with human/environment relationships has been maintained, and there have been renewed and vigorous debates about how nature is constituted and understood across different traditions. Ranging from considerations of situated knowledges, environmental ethics, popular understandings of environmental issues to the unsettling of the nature/culture divide, cultural geography has been central in efforts to reconceptualize nature and to the critical examination of environmental policies (Whatmore 2002; Fitzsimmons 1989; Castree and Braun 2001; Wolch and Emel 1998).

In sum, cultural geography has increasingly influenced the broader trajectories that other branches of geography are taking. Beyond the boundaries of the discipline, it has become increasingly visible to anthropologists, historians of science, cultural historians, archaeologists and sociologists. Cross-disciplinary research and collaborative publication is a testament to this trend (e.g. Jackson *et al.* 2000).

JAMES S. DUNCAN
UNIVERSITY OF CAMBRIDGE
NUALA C. JOHNSON
QUEEN'S UNIVERSITY BELFAST

References

Agnew, J.A. (1987) *Place and Politics*, London.

Anderson, K.J. (1988) 'Cultural hegemony and the race-definition process in Chinatown, Vancouver: 1880–1980', *Environment and Planning D. Society and Space* 6: 127–49.

Castree, N. and Braun, B. (eds) (2001) *Social Nature*, Oxford.

Cosgrove, D. (1983) 'Towards a radical cultural geography: Problems of theory', *Antipode* 15(1): 1–11.

Daniels, S. (1989) 'Marxism, culture and the duplicity of landscape', in R. Peet and N. Thrift (eds) *New Models in Geography*, Vol. 2, London, pp. 196–220.

Driver, F. (2001) *Geography Militant: Cultures of Exploration and Empire*, Oxford.

Duncan, J.S. (1980) 'The superorganic in American cultural geography', *Annals of the Association of American Geographers* 70: 181–98.

Duncan, J.S. and Duncan, N.G. (1988) '(Re)reading the landscape', *Environment and Planning D. Society and Space* 6: 117–26.

Duncan, J.S. and Ley, D. (1982) 'Structural Marxism and human geography', *Annals, Association of American Geographers* 72: 30–59.

Entrikin, J.N. (1991) *The Betweenness of Place*, Baltimore, MD.

Gregory, D. (1994) *Geographical Imaginations*, Oxford.

—— (2002) *The Colonial Present*, Oxford.

Jackson, P. (1980) 'A plea for cultural geography', *Area* 12: 110–13.

—— (ed.) (1987) *Race and Racism*, London.

Jackson, P., Lowe, M., Miller, D. and Mort, F. (eds) (2000) *Commercial Cultures*, Oxford.

Jacobs, J. (1996) *Edge of Empire: Postcolonialism and the City*, London.

Leighly, J. (ed.) (1963) *Land and Life: A Selection from the Writing of Carl Ortwin Sauer*, Berkeley, CA.

Ley, D. (1974) *The Black Inner City as Frontier Outpost*, Washington, DC.

Ley, D. and Samuels, M. (eds) (1978) *Humanistic Geography: Prospects and Problems*, Chicago.

Lowenthal, D. (1961) 'Geography, experience and imagination: Toward a geographical epistemology', *Annals, Association of American Geographers* 51: 241–60.

McDowell, L. (1999) *Gender, Identity and Place: Understanding Feminist Geographies*, Cambridge.

Meinig, D.W. (ed.) (1979) *The Interpretation of Ordinary Landscapes*, New York.

Mitchell, D. (2000) *Cultural Geography*, Oxford.

Nash, C. (1996) 'Reclaiming vision: Looking at landscape and the body', *Gender, Place and Culture* 3(2): 149–69.

Nast, H. and Pile, S. (eds) (1998) *Places through the Body*, London.

Relph, E. (1976) *Place and Placelessness*, London.

Rose, G. (1993) *Feminism and Geography: The Limits of Geographical Knowledge*, London.

Thrift, N. (1996) *Spatial Formations*, London.

Tuan, Y.-F. (1974) *Topophilia: A Study of Environmental Perception, Attitudes and Values*, Englewood Cliffs, NJ.

Wagner, P. and Mikesell, M. (eds) (1962) *Readings in Cultural Geography*, Chicago.

Whatmore, S. (2002) *Hybrid Geographies: Natures, Cultures, Spaces*, London.

Wolch, J. and Emel, J. (eds) (1998) *Animal Geographies*, London.

Zelinsky, W. (1973) *The Cultural Geography of the United States*, Englewood Cliffs, NJ.

SEE ALSO: culture; landscape; place; spatial analysis

CULTURAL HISTORY

The term 'cultural history' came into use in the late eighteenth century, originally in Germany, inspired by the attempts of Herder, Hegel and others to view the different parts of culture as a whole (histories of literature, art and music go back much further). The most famous nineteenth-century example of the genre was the Swiss scholar Jacob Burckhardt's *Civilization of the Renaissance in Italy* (1860), which was concerned not so much with painting or literature as with attitudes, notably with individualism, with the admiration for antiquity, with morality and with festivals, and even the organization of the state as 'works of art'. In the early twentieth century, the Dutch historian Johan Huizinga produced a masterly study of Franco-Flemish culture, *The Waning of the Middle Ages* (1919), more or less on the Burckhardtian model (see Huizinga 1959 [1929]), while in Hamburg Aby Warburg wrote a handful of important articles and built up a marvellous library (transferred to London in 1933) devoted to the history of the classical tradition and to the science of culture (*Kulturwissenschaft*). However, these attempts to write a general history of culture found few emulators. At much the same time, between the two world wars, French attempts to go beyond political and economic history took the form of the history of collective mentalities associated with the Annales School, while in the USA attention was focused on the history of ideas.

The history of culture did not go uncriticized. Marxists in particular pointed out that the 'classical' studies of cultural history depend on a postulate that it is extremely difficult to justify, that of cultural unity or consensus. Thus Burckhardt wrote of 'the culture of the Renaissance', while Huizinga once described history as the form in which 'a culture accounts to itself for its past'. In similar fashion the non-Marxist Ernst Gombrich rejected the work of Burckhardt and Huizinga on the grounds that it was built on 'Hegelian foundations' that had 'crumbled' (Gombrich 1969).

The rise or revival of interest in a holistic history of culture goes back to the 1970s or thereabouts, a time of reaction against socio-economic determinism and archive positivism. Just as late eighteenth-century historians were inspired by Herder and Hegel, so late twentieth-century historians – especially in France and the USA – drew on cultural anthropology (especially on Clifford Geertz, whose essay on the cock-fight is cited again and again), and on cultural theory more generally. The ideas of Lévi-Strauss evoked some response from historians in the 1970s, but the influence of Elias, Bakhtin, Foucault and Bourdieu has been considerably more substantial and long-lasting, while a few brave souls are attempting to make use of Derrida.

In recent work, the term culture has extended its meaning to embrace a much wider range of activities. Historians study popular culture as well as elite culture. They are concerned not only with art but also material culture, not only with the written but also the oral, not only with drama but also ritual. The idea of political culture stretches the concept still further. Everyday life is included, or more precisely the rules or principles underlying everyday practices. It is becoming more and more difficult to discover what is not culture.

Traditional assumptions about the relation between culture and society have been reversed. Cultural historians, like cultural theorists, now claim that culture is capable of resisting social pressures or even that it shapes social reality. Hence the increasing interest in the history of representations (whether verbal or visual), the history of the social imagination, and especially the story of the construction, invention or constitution of what used to be considered social facts such as social class, nation, caste, tribe or gender.

Another approach, partly inspired by anthropology, focuses on cultural encounters, clashes or invasion. Historians have attempted to reconstruct the way in which the Caribs perceived Columbus, the Aztecs saw Cortés, or the Hawaiians viewed Captain Cook and his sailors. The point to emphasize here is the relatively new interest in the way in which the two sides understood or failed to understand one another. There is also increasing interest in the process of borrowing, 'acculturation', 'reception' and resistance, not only in cases of encounters between cultures but also between different groups within them.

PETER BURKE
UNIVERSITY OF CAMBRIDGE

References

Gombrich, E.H. (1969) *In Search of Cultural History*, Oxford.

Huizinga, J. (1959 [1929]) 'The task of cultural history', in *Men and Ideas*, New York.

Further reading

Burke, P. (2004) *What is Cultural History?* Cambridge, UK.

Chartier, R. (1988) *Cultural History*, Cambridge, UK.

Hunt, L. (ed.) (1989) *The New Cultural History*, Berkeley, CA.

SEE ALSO: Annales School; culture; oral history; social history

CULTURAL STUDIES

As the term 'cultural studies' is invoked ever more frequently to describe, justify or advertise work in the humanities and social sciences, so definitions of cultural studies are contested ever more vigorously. Does the term invoke a particular method? Object of analysis? Political orientation? Or a combination of all three? Scholars disagree not only on how to define cultural studies but also whether it should be defined at all. For some, the value of cultural studies lies in an intellectual capaciousness and free-wheeling eclecticism that defies traditional frameworks and disciplinary boundaries. As a result, attempts to delimit the field are viewed with suspicion and cultural studies is valued for its resistance to definition and categorization. Others believe that cultural studies does in fact comprise a distinctive orientation, methodology and intellectual tradition that should be distinguished from alternative approaches to questions of culture and power. According to Tony Bennett (1998), for example, the often noted skittishness about specifying the protocols of the field epitomizes the mindset of cultural studies scholars who equate political authenticity with a resistance to institutionalization and the codification of knowledge, and thereby overlook the realities of their own social positioning.

Most histories of the field trace the origins of cultural studies back to the founding of the Centre for Contemporary Cultural Studies in Birmingham, England, in 1964. Directed in turn by Richard Hoggart, Stuart Hall and Richard Johnson, the Centre brought together scholars, many of them originally trained as literary critics or sociologists, interested in developing new approaches to the study of culture. A key influence was the work of Marxist scholar Raymond Williams, with his famous dictum that 'culture is ordinary'. From its beginnings, cultural studies defined itself in a critical relationship to several fields of enquiry. Against the fastidious discriminations of literary critics, it argued that the everyday culture of ordinary individuals was worthy of serious and respectful attention. Unlike the discipline of mass communications, it did not decode the meanings of popular texts via content analysis and statistical data, but insisted that such texts, like those of high culture, were repositories of complex, multi-layered meanings mediated by form. And against the tradition of critical theory and the default position of leftist intellectuals from Theodor Adorno to Dwight McDonald, it suggested that the political functions of mass-media forms were complex and often unpredictable, and were not reducible to corporate brainwashing or a mass opiate.

While this general orientation towards popular culture still defines cultural studies, the field has undergone dramatic changes. Early work in cultural studies drew heavily on Marxist methods and concepts, typically invoking either Gramsci's notion of hegemony or Althusser's definition of ideology. Even as they awarded greater primacy and power to the cultural sphere than traditional Marxism, scholars took it for granted that class was the pre-eminent marker of social division and that society was in the last instance determined by economic structures and interests. For example, studies of (male, working-class) youth subcultures produced by researchers associated with the Birmingham Centre acknowledged the complexities of cultural identification and the power of 'resistance through ritual' but concluded that the ultimate meanings of subcultural practices were to be found in the reproduction of class hierarchies (Willis 1977).

In an often-cited essay, Angie McRobbie (1980) criticized these studies of subcultures for ignoring gender. Not only did scholars overlook the frequent misogyny of working-class male subcultures, but their equation of resistance with public displays of masculine bravado occluded the popular culture of teenage girls, which was more likely to be located in the bedroom than the street. In the 1980s, feminist scholars began to play a prominent role in cultural studies, analysing popular genres such as women's magazines, soap operas and romantic novels or focusing on aspects of culture conventionally associated with femininity, such as fashion, consumption and the body. Thanks to a general waning of intellectual commitment to socialism as well as the increasing participation of US scholars, class has almost dropped out of sight in cultural studies, while issues of gender, race and sexuality have assumed much greater importance. Scholars are also drawing on theories of globalization to analyse the transmission of mass-media forms and new technologies across geographical and cultural distance, while questioning models of cultural imperialism insufficiently attuned to the diverse ways in which texts are interpreted, used and actively remade in local environments. Australia has played a leading role in the development of cultural studies (Frow and Morris 1993) and scholars based in Australia such as Ien Ang (2001) are at the forefront of such attempts to combine cultural studies and postcolonial theory.

The mutation in the politics of cultural studies has gone along with methodological changes. In the 1970s and 1980s, the influence of structuralist and poststructuralist theories inspired a critique of the 'expressive humanism' of earlier cultural critics such as Williams. In an influential essay, Hall distinguished between 'culturalist' and 'structuralist' paradigms within cultural studies; while the former attributed authenticating power to lived experience, the latter sought to relativize and decentre such experience as a product of signifying systems. While culturalism emphasized consciousness, structuralism focused on conditions (1980). Terms such as 'discourse' and 'representation' came into general use, conveying a new emphasis on the ways in which cultural forms shape meaning rather than simply expressing pre-existing identities or socioeconomic realities. And a growing body of work on popular culture and postmodernism scrutinized the distinctive qualities of our own media-saturated, computer-wired, consumer-oriented epoch (Hebdige 1988). That is to say, cultural studies' theoretical commitment to breaking down rigid distinctions between high and popular culture is linked to historical conditions that have rendered such distinctions less viable: the idea of aesthetic autonomy seems risible now that high art is openly commodified and institutionalized, whereas popular film and television often draw on an aesthetics of shock, self-reflexivity and intertextual quotation once associated with modernism and the avant-garde.

Perhaps the key concept of cultural studies is articulation. Influentially developed in the work of Stuart Hall and Lawrence Grossberg, it provides a useful litmus test for distinguishing the methodology of cultural studies from related analyses of culture and power. An articulation is a temporary linkage, a forged connection between two or more elements that can in turn be unmade and remade. The concept of articulation thus seeks to explain how segments of the social field may join together to form temporary unities without resorting to a view of the social whole as an expressive totality whose essential features are mirrored in every one of its parts. 'The so-called "unity" of a discourse,' writes Hall, 'is really the articulation of different, distinct elements which can be rearticulated in different ways because they have no necessary "belongingness"' (1996). Religion, for example, has no necessary political connotation, but may serve disparate purposes and functions in different communities. The model of articulation can thus be distinguished from large-scale theories of capitalism, patriarchy or imperialism that assume a necessary homology between (oppressive) political systems and cultural forms. Without seeking to deny systemic forms of exploitation, cultural studies argues that the political functions of texts cannot be predicted in advance but derive from their contingent positions in changing constellations of texts, practices and interests.

This insight has obvious consequences for interpretative method. Cultural studies is more interested in consumption than production; the motives of authors or the economic interests of corporations do not determine ahead of time what a text will signify or its political functions for particular audiences. Thus textual analysis is often supplemented or even replaced by reception studies and ethnographies of readers or viewers; meanings are not inscribed in the text itself, awaiting decoding by the expert critic, but arise out of the complex interactions between audiences and texts. For example, Janice Radway's well-known ethnography of a group of romance novel readers (1984) called into question previous feminist readings of the genre, pointing out that such readings had ignored women's own understanding of why they read romance fiction. Ordinary people are not 'cultural dopes' in need of correction by enlightened intellectuals, but individuals capable of responding actively and often critically to their environment. The work of Michel de Certeau (1984) was especially influential in this regard, offering a compendium of the inventive ruses and subterranean tactics that make up the mundane practice of everyday life. This eagerness to acknowledge the agency of consumers has in turn inspired complaints that cultural studies is in danger of embracing an uncritical populism that finds symptoms of resistance anywhere and everywhere (Morris 1988).

It is noticeable, however, that recent anthologies and overviews of cultural studies often include the work of critical theorists and politically oriented literary critics who reveal little or no familiarity with the concept of articulation or the Birmingham tradition. In the USA, 'cultural studies' has increasingly come to serve as a handy synonym for any political approach to literature or culture and is often equated with a style of self-righteous ideology critique that cultural studies has in fact sought to call into question (Felski 2003). Because the institutional location of US practitioners of cultural studies is frequently the English department, much of what now passes as cultural studies is more accurately described as a hybridization of literary and cultural studies that combines an interest in popular culture and politics with a continuing reliance on techniques of close reading and a noticeable lack of interest in ethnographic research or social science methodologies.

Is cultural studies then a disciplinary, interdisciplinary or anti-disciplinary endeavour? And is it plausible for practitioners of cultural studies to cast themselves in the role of organic intellectuals and to conceive of their work as furthering the interests of oppressed groups? The institutionalization of cultural studies in publishers' lists, academic positions and scholarly journals has become a topic of concern for those who equate radical politics with a condition of marginality and believe that cultural studies is losing its connections with everyday life and real-world political struggles. Others warn against a romanticizing of resistance and an overestimation of the possible political effects of cultural studies, arguing that the field should define its goals in more modest terms as a specific form of institutional intervention. Moreover, while cultural studies has often defined itself in radical opposition to traditional literary and cultural criticism, Francis Mulhern (2000) has recently underscored the continuities between cultural studies and an older tradition of *Kulturkritik* that extends from German romanticism to the work of F.R. Leavis. Both frameworks, he argues, espouse an essentially moral and aesthetic vision of culture as a redemptive force that can help overcome the alienated condition of modernity.

Even as cultural studies continues to thrive and to attract ever more disciples, it is entering a self-reflective phase in which many of its tenets are being re-examined. Some scholars, as well as questioning the strategy of aligning oneself with 'the people' and thereby denying one's role as an intellectual, are also proposing that it no longer makes sense to assume a dichotomous distinction between high and popular culture that correlates directly to structures of power (Frow 1995). In the light of such arguments, the common political rationale for cultural studies as a way of redeeming the culture of the disenfranchised appears less compelling. There is also a new interest in aesthetics and questions of value; while such concepts were once spurned by cultural critics as irredeemably elitist, there is a growing recognition that cultural studies is heavily influenced by the aesthetic tradition and that acts of evaluation, and hence questions of value, are inescapable. In short, cultural studies has tended to justify its project by vaunting its transgressive newness, its radical difference to what has gone before; as it comes to acknowledge its own embedding in a modern intellectual and aesthetic tradition that extends from German romanticism to the historical avant-garde, it may need to rethink aspects of its role and its mission, both aesthetically and politically.

RITA FELSKI
UNIVERSITY OF VIRGINIA

References

Ang, I. (2001) *On Not Speaking Chinese*, London.
Bennett, T. (1998) *Culture: A Reformer's Science*, London.
De Certeau, M. (1984) *The Practice of Everyday Life*, Minnesota.
Felski, R, (2003) 'The role of aesthetics in cultural studies', in M. Bérubé (ed.) *Aesthetics and Cultural Studies*, New York.
Frow, J. (1995) *Cultural Studies and Cultural Value*, Oxford.
Frow, J. and Morris, M. (1993) *Australian Cultural Studies: A Reader*, Sydney.
Hall, S. (1980) 'Cultural studies: Two paradigms', *Media Culture and Society* 2(1) (January).
—— (1986) 'Cultural studies: Two paradigms', in R. Collins, J. Curran, N. Garnham, P. Scannell, P. Schlesinger and C. Sparks (eds) *Media, Culture and Society: A Critical Reader*, London.
—— (1996) 'On postmodernism and articulation', in D. Morley and Kuan-Hsing Chen (eds) *Stuart Hall: Critical Dialogues in Cultural Studies*, London.
Hebdige, D. (1988) *Hiding in the Light: On Images and Things*, London.
McRobbie, A. (1980) 'Settling accounts with subcultures: A feminist critique', *Screen Education* 34.
Morris, M. (1988) 'Banality in cultural studies', *Discourse* 10.
Mulhern, F. (2000) *Culture/Metaculture*, London.
Radway, J. (1984) *Reading the Romance: Women, Patriarchy and Popular Literature*, Chapel Hill, NC.
Willis, P. (1977) *Learning to Labour: How Working-Class Kids Get Working-Class Jobs*, Aldershot.

Further reading

Dent, G. and Wallace, M. (1992) *Black Popular Culture*, New York.
Grossberg, L. (1997) *Bringing It All Back Home: Essays on Cultural Studies*, Durham.
Grossberg, L., Nelson, C. and Treichler, P. (eds) (1992) *Cultural Studies*, New York.
Hollows, J. (2000) *Feminism, Femininity and Popular Culture*, Manchester.
Williams, R. (1965) *The Long Revolution*, London.

SEE ALSO: culture; mass media; popular culture

CULTURE

The rise to prominence of *fin de siècle* cultural studies, the general turn among humanists to what they call 'theory' (which they derive from such canonical figures as Marx, Freud, Foucault, Derrida, Bourdieu and, now, Du Bois – but less frequently from other ancestral social philosophers like Durkheim, Weber and Boas), the tremendous facility among the cleverer historians with the entire range of social scientific theory – all have conspired to create a new worry among a perpetually worried lot, anthropologists, who can be heard to complain, 'We have lost control of the culture concept.' It doesn't take much study of the history of this old, widespread and potent term to see that their lament stems from whiggish self-deception. Anthropologists never really controlled the term, even during the mid-twentieth century, when the expansion of social science led them to imagine their discipline as centrally relevant to the work of democratic welfare states in an emergent global order.

Many scholars have written histories of the culture concept (from the mid-eighteenth to the late twentieth centuries), and of its relationship to equally important 'keywords' like 'civilization' and 'race' (e.g. Williams 1958; Kuper 1999; Manganaro 2002). Such histories often take account of differing national-geographic traditions, the German, French, British and North American. They also distinguish between progressive and relativist, idealist and materialist definitions of culture. There are traditions of thought in which culture is understood to be unitary and progressive, that is, accumulative over the entire course of human history; and other, competing traditions in which culture is understood to be pluralistic and non-cumulative, so that world history is imagined to include the ceaseless rise and demise of radically different local cultures. Some scholars define culture in terms of humanity's growing mastery of nature based on technological progress and the development of objective knowledge. Others use the term to denote spiritual and aesthetic realms of human experience. These oppositions are sometimes linked to the dichotomous pairing of 'culture' and 'civilization', in which one of the two terms stands for material progress while the other refers to spiritual blossoming (and decay).

Edward Tylor famously treated 'culture or civilization' as synonyms, both denoting 'that complex whole which includes knowledge, belief, art, morals, law, custom, and any other capabilities and habits acquired by man as a member of society' (1871: 1). Tylor argued that culture progressed inevitably (according to natural law) in both the material and moral domains. Franz Boas and his students, arguing against Tylor's evolutionary positivism, saw human history in terms of the particularities of local cultural growth. But local cultures were also part of a global history, one of endless acts of borrowing (diffusion) and incorporation. Edward Sapir, for example, distinguished 'civilization', which he defined as 'any socially inherited element in the life of man' (equivalent, more or less, to the predicate of Tylor's famous definition), from

'culture', 'the expression of a richly varied yet somehow unified and consistent attitude toward life'. Sapir then made 'civilization' stand for the worldwide development and diffusion of all cultural materials, whereas 'culture' referred to the temporary, local occurrence of unique, 'harmonious' ways of life: 'Civilization, as a whole, moves on; culture comes and goes' (1949 [1924]: 309, 314–15, 317).

In the twentieth century, culture has been opposed to race in the nurture–nature debate (a debate that took on life-and-death significance in industrial genocides animated by racist ideologies). Race itself is a term as multifarious as culture. George Stocking points out that at the end of the nineteenth century, the term contained 'the residues of several...traditions of racial thought...the ethnological, the Lamarckian, the polygenist, and the evolutionist' (2001: 9). 'Race' was often synonymous with 'nation', and culture (or way of life, mentality, etc.) was imagined to be carried in the 'blood' of racial-national groups. (In such thinking, the Lamarckian inheritance of acquired characteristics allowed for the slow transfer of environmental and historical influences into what were nonetheless imagined as naturally bounded, transhistorical social groups.) In two decisive moves (carried out from the 1880s through the 1920s), Boas attacked the notions that 'race, language and culture' moved together through history, and that biological race determined mental or cultural capacity. In the resultant Boasian paradigm, it was culture, not race, that accounted for most social and historical differences between groups.

Another prominent conceptual opposition for twentieth-century anthropologists had them defending their inclusive definition of culture against the high-cultural ideals of Victorians such as Matthew Arnold, who defined culture as 'the best which has been thought and said in the world' (1868: 6). From an Arnoldian perspective, 'culture' refers to artistic and spiritual accomplishments, and there are absolute standards by which to judge and rank such accomplishments. Anthropologists saw their version of 'culture' as more useful, scientifically, than the Arnoldian approach, since anthropological culture, not conceptually confined to the products of elite institutions, can take account of the entire range of human activity. In a landmark volume, Kroeber and Kluckhohn (1952: 9) argued that another Victorian, Tylor, had established the modern, scientific definition of culture, and thus anthropology as a discrete discipline, in 1871. But Stocking countered that Tylor's approach, with its universal stages of cultural development (savagery, barbarism, civilization), had as much in common with Arnold's elitist humanism as it did with later, anthropological approaches. Tylor's concept of culture lacked many 'elements crucial to the modern anthropological usage – plurality, relativity, integration, meaningful historicity [and] behavioral determinism' (Stocking 1968: 83–4). Indeed, those were the very features that characterized the approach of Kroeber and Kluckhohn (1952: 159–79), who, according to Stocking, had misread not the consensus of the discipline at mid-century, but the course of its history.

That mid-century consensus had been elegantly formulated in Benedict's *Patterns of Culture* (1934). Benedict relied on vision metaphors: each culture is a way of seeing the world that is itself invisible, and people project the values of their culture onto reality itself, rationalizing the unconsciously held premises of their world-view as human nature or universal truth. But for Benedict, there are few, if any, human universals other than the empirical fact that the world is made up of different cultures. Benedict stressed the capacity of each culture to achieve what she called 'integration', by which she meant (echoing Sapir's notion of harmoniousness) 'a more or less consistent pattern of thought and action' (1934: 46). Drawing on Boasian historical particularism, Benedict likened the growth of a culture to the historical formation of an aesthetic style (Gothic architecture was the example she used (1934: 47)); open always to the diffusion of culture 'traits' from around the globe, a culture over time shaped the materials it took in to its 'characteristic purposes' (1934: 46). 'All the miscellaneous behaviour directed toward getting a living, mating, warring, and worshipping the gods, is made over into consistent patterns in accordance with unconscious canons of choice that develop within the culture' (1934: 48). Although Benedict tried to take account of individual agency, in her theory the causal arrow pointed primarily from culture to individuals, who, she wrote, 'are plastic to the moulding force of the society into which they are born' (1934: 254).

While Benedict's understanding of culture could accommodate definitions like that of Tylor, which stressed the social inheritance of knowledge, customs and techniques, as well as their accompanying material products, *Patterns of Culture* put values and ethos at the centre of culture. That emphasis continued through and after the Second World War, and in the 1960s and 1970s was reformulated, in the work of people like Clifford Geertz, David Schneider and Marshall Sahlins, in discussions of symbolism and semiosis. Geertz, for example, wrote that 'culture is best seen not as complexes of concrete behavior patterns...but as a set of control mechanisms – plans, recipes, rules, instructions... for the governing of behavior' (1973: 44). At issue for all three, and for the 'symbols-and-meanings' anthropology that grew out of their work, was the relationship of culture to other aspects of human society – the environment, technology and economy, social organization, and the psychic and biological imperatives of *Homo sapiens*.

The discussion was sometimes framed as the role of anthropology among the social sciences, with Schneider (1968) arguing that anthropologists should study culture as a relatively autonomous system of symbols, apart from its connection to social organization and norms, and apart from its manifestation in human action. At other times, the discussion engaged the hoary mind–body problem, set in the context of modern science and its concepts of causality. To explain human action, should analysts assess and sum the causal contribution of each 'level' of reality (the biological, environmental, psychological, social and cultural), or, taking semiosis as the defining characteristic of human beings, should they treat 'biology', 'the environment', etc., as themselves 'cultural constructs' (that is, symbolic formulations responding to a world 'out there') and then argue that human action could be nothing other than a semiotic encounter with a world unknowable apart from culture? In such a perspective, the world is real enough: as the Boasians put it, the environment, the human life cycle, social relations and tradition all constrain cultural action. But they do not determine it. Nor is there, in this perspective, an underlying 'human nature' that culture merely expresses. As Geertz put the latter position, 'there is no such thing as a human nature independent of culture....Without men, no culture, certainly; but equally, and more significantly, without culture, no men' (1973: 49).

What I have called the mid-century consensus about culture (at least among those anthropologists who privileged the term as central to anthropology), from Benedict to Schneider and Geertz, foundered at the end of the century on three problems. First, the notion of a world made up of neatly bounded cultures, as presented in *Patterns of Culture*, came to seem less and less plausible. It is customary to interpret anthropologists' critique of boundaries as their response to the changing conditions of the world they work in – specifically, to the demise of colonial societies and the emergence of 'globalization' and the consequent mass movements of people and goods across national boundaries. But anthropologists working at the time of Tylor and Boas were often acutely aware of such issues – hence the theoretical salience of a topic like 'diffusion' at that time. We might as easily attribute the heightened awareness of boundary problems to cyclic theoretical fashions as to absolute changes in the real world (cf. Brightman 1995). At bottom was an epistemological question about the nature of the anthropological object: were cultures (or societies) out there in the world, awaiting description by scientists with the correct concepts, or were they unbounded historical phenomena, unified only, as Boas had put it, 'in the mind of the observer' (1940 [1887]: 642)?

Closely linked to the boundary problem was a critique of the idea that cultures represent consensus – that they are characterized by homogeneity of habits, practices, values and ethos. In this model, 'a' group is by definition a collection of like individuals, whether the similarities among them are imagined as a function of substance (as in racialist models, where 'blood' is shared) or of rational choice (as in social contract theories). Arguing against such models, anthropologists emphasized the theoretical importance of the existence of competing voices within cultures – that is, they privileged the empirical facts of argument, ambivalence and political domination and rebellion. Again, one can attribute this theoretical development to anthropologists' growing awareness of an increasingly contested world order, or one can see it in terms of the re-emergence of dormant theoretical positions (for example, varieties of 'conflict' theory derived from Marxism, on the one hand, and of utilitarian individualism, on the other).

I suggest that while both real-world developments and cyclical theoretical trends contributed to anthropologists' *fin de siècle* critique of culture, a third issue was salient as well. By mid-century, 'culture', like many terms drawn from social science and medicine (think of such Freudian chestnuts as 'subconscious' and 'ego'), had passed into popular discourse and politics. Not only did the people anthropologists studied 'have' culture, they knew they had it, or, at least, they thought they ought to have it. Anti-racist and anti-colonial political movements throughout the world were movements of national, ethnic or racial affirmation; and the modern ideology of identity that such affirmation required was underpinned by both anthropological and humanistic notions of culture.

Anthropologists thus found themselves in the strange position of working from a theory of culture that had been borrowed and reworked by the very people they were studying (Handler 1988). In late twentieth-entury processes of cultural representation, people 'objectify' aspects of their world as 'their' culture, transforming culture even as they think they are preserving it. To discuss such activities, anthropologists must have a model of culture that can speak to people's ability to be self-conscious about (or blind to) their own cultural activities. To see culture simply as a product (those objects that can be put into a museum case, or described in ethnographies) is to ignore the fact that people's cultural activities are always accompanied by meta-cultural discussion. People at once create culture and stand aside from it, second-guessing it (in a potentially infinite regression).

All this brings us back to the question of causality in the social sciences. Geertz argued that anthropology is not a natural science in search of causal explanation, but an 'interpretive' science in search of meaning (1973: 5). (Nearly a century earlier, Boas had distinguished between natural science, in search of nomothetic laws, and historical science, or 'cosmography', in search of the historical 'truth' of individual entities (1940 [1887]).) To the degree that nineteenth- and twentieth-century social sciences have modelled themselves on what they imagine to be natural-scientific canons of causality, they have dreamed of disciplines that can explain and predict human actions. Most social scientific dreamers have been content to say that human action is so complex (emergent from so many different 'layers' of reality, from the physical to the psychic to the social to the historical) that the discovery of social scientific laws must await 'further' research. To them, the interpretive option seems to lead to an impossible world of 'uncaused' events.

Tylor, for example, thought that the Christian conception of 'free will', if interpreted to mean that humans can 'act...without cause', was 'incompatible with scientific argument'. The only scientifically sound approach to human will, he argued, was to understand it 'as strictly according with motive' (1871: 3). Human motivations are predictable (and we all presuppose that fact as we conduct our daily business) and thus, Tylor implied, we can find in them the law-like regularity of causation that science requires. Many social scientists after Tylor reinvented this conflation of 'causation' and 'motivation', taking it as the road to a scientific account of culture. The trouble, however, is that, as we should all know after Freud, motivation is itself an elusive phenomenon, semiotically constructed in processes of conceptualization and rationalization, processes in which 'mind' is never in rational control of 'culture' at the very moment when the latter (as 'plans, recipes, rules, instructions') makes action possible.

Analogously, to many symbols-and-meanings anthropologists, 'events' themselves are not discrete phenomena with discrete causes, but interpretations of interpretations – that is, activities in which cultured human beings respond, based on their own cultural knowledge, to one another. A semiotic model of culture suggests that human worlds are not natural phenomena at all. In studying them, rationality and scientific methods may well help us to gather empirical materials and explore relations among facts, but they alone won't allow us to make ultimate sense of culture. In this model, nonetheless, culture makes meaning possible, and if anthropologists can never deliver airtight causal explanations for cultural actions, they can, and routinely do, figure out what other people think they're doing. Such knowledge is not only useful, it is appropriate to the human reality of [cultured] mind, in [cultural] action, in the [culturally constructed] world.

RICHARD HANDLER
UNIVERSITY OF VIRGINIA

References

Arnold, M. (1868) *Culture and Anarchy*, London.

Benedict, R. (1934) *Patterns of Culture*, Boston.

Boas, F. (1940 [1887]) 'The study of geography', in *Race, Language and Culture*, New York.

Brightman, R. (1995) 'Forget culture: Replacement, transcendence, relexification', *Cultural Anthropology* 13.

Geertz, C. (1973) *The Interpretation of Cultures*, New York.

Handler, R. (1988) *Nationalism and the Politics of Culture in Quebec*, Madison, WI.

Kroeber, A.L. and Kluckhohn, C. (1952) *Culture: A Critical Review of Concepts and Definitions*, Cambridge, MA.

Kuper, A. (1999) *Culture: The Anthropologists' Account*, Cambridge, MA.

Manganaro, M. (2002) *Culture, 1922: The Emergence of a Concept*, Princeton, NJ.

Sapir, E. (1949 [1924]) 'Culture, genuine and spurious', in D. Mandelbaum (ed.) *Selected Writings of Edward Sapir*, Berkeley, CA.

Schneider, D.M. (1968) *American Kinship: A Cultural Account*, Englewood Cliffs, NJ.

Stocking, G.W. (1968) *Race, Culture, and Evolution: Essays in the History of Anthropology*, New York.

—— (2001) *Delimiting Anthropology: Occasional Inquiries and Reflections*, Madison, WI.

Tylor, E.B. (1871) *Primitive Culture*, London.

Williams, R. (1958) *Culture and Society: 1780–1950*, New York.

D

DARWIN, CHARLES (1809–82)

Charles Darwin is widely regarded as the founder of modern evolutionism. Although not the first to propose a theory of the transmutation of species, his *Origin of Species* (1859) sparked the debate that converted the scientific community to evolutionism. This book not only provided the basic argument for evolution, but also proposed a new mechanism of change: natural selection. Although this mechanism remained controversial until synthesized with Mendelian genetics in the twentieth century, it has now become the basis for most biologists' approach to the question. Darwin also confronted the human implications of evolutionism in his *Descent of Man* (1871), exploring the link between humans and their ape-like ancestors, and the implications of such a link for the nature of society.

Charles Robert Darwin was born in Shrewsbury, England. His father was a wealthy doctor. His grandfather, Erasmus Darwin, also a successful physician, had proposed an evolutionary theory in the 1790s. During an abortive attempt to study medicine at Edinburgh, Darwin met the Lamarckian evolutionist R.E. Grant, who aroused his interest in fundamental biological problems. Darwin then went to Cambridge, where he studied for a BA in the expectation of becoming an Anglican clergyman, but also came into contact with the botanist John Henslow and the geologist Adam Sedgwick. After taking his degree he spent five years as ship's naturalist aboard the survey vessel HMS *Beagle* (1831–6). On the voyage he studied both the geology and zoology of South America. He soon accepted the uniformitarian geology of Charles Lyell, in which all change was supposed to be slow and gradual.

He proposed important geological theories, especially on the formation of coral reefs. The fauna of the Galapagos islands (off the Pacific coast of South America) forced him to reassess his belief in the fixity of species. It was clear that closely related forms on separate islands had diverged from a common ancestor when the populations were isolated from each other.

On his return to England, Darwin spent the years 1836–42 as an active member of the scientific community in London. Family support enabled him to marry and then to set up as a country gentleman at Down in Kent. Darwin had already turned his attention to the problem of the evolutionary mechanism. He realized that evolution adapted each population to its local environment, but did not think that the Lamarckian explanation of the inheritance of acquired characteristics was adequate. He studied the techniques of artificial selection used by animal breeders and then encountered the principle of population expansion proposed in T.R. Malthus's *Essay on the Principle of Population*. This led to his theory of natural selection: population pressure created a struggle for existence in which the best-adapted individuals would survive and breed, while the least adapted would die out. The extent to which the selection theory embodies the competitive ethos of capitalism remains controversial. Darwin wrote outlines of his theory in 1842 and 1844, but had no intention of publishing at this time. Although now affected by a chronic illness, he continued his researches. He studied barnacles, in part to throw light on evolutionary problems, and also worked on biogeography. A few naturalists were informed of the evolutionary project lying behind these studies, especially the botanist J.D. Hooker. In the mid-1850s he realized the significance of divergence and specialization in evolution, and began to write an account of his theory for publication. This was interrupted by the arrival in 1858 of A.R. Wallace's paper on natural selection, which prompted Darwin to write the 'abstract' that became the *Origin of Species*.

The *Origin* aroused much controversy, but Darwin had primed a group of sympathetic naturalists, including J.D. Hooker and T.H. Huxley, who ensured that his theory would not be dismissed. By 1870 the general idea of evolution was widely accepted, although natural selection remained controversial. Both scientists and non-scientists found natural selection too harsh a mechanism to square with their religious and philosophical beliefs. Darwin himself accepted a role for Lamarckism, and this mechanism became widely popular in the late nineteenth century. Much evolutionary research was based on an attempt to reconstruct the tree of life from anatomical and palaeontological evidence, but Darwin's own later work concentrated on botany, explaining the origin of various structures in plants in terms of natural selection. He also studied the effects of earthworms upon the soil.

Darwin had become aware of the human implications of evolutionism in the 1830s, but avoided this topic in the *Origin* to minimize controversy. His *Descent of Man* of 1871 was the first detailed attempt to explain the origin of the human race in evolutionary terms and to explore the implications of this approach for human affairs. Darwin used T.H. Huxley's work as evidence that the human species was closely related to the great apes. Much of his book took it for granted that mental and social evolution were progressive. Darwin was convinced that the white race was the most advanced, while darker races were closer to the ancestral ape. Yet he also pioneered ideas about human origins that would not be taken seriously until the mid-twentieth century. He identified Africa rather than Asia as the most probable centre of human evolution and proposed that the key breakthrough separating the ape and human families was the latter's adoption of bipedalism. This freed the hands for making weapons and tools, introducing a selection for intelligence and a consequent increase in the size of the brain. He explained the moral faculties as rationalizations of the instinctive behaviour patterns that had been programmed into our ancestors because of their social life. His *Expression of the Emotions in Man and the Animals* (1872) explained many aspects of human behaviour as relics of our animal ancestry.

PETER J. BOWLER
QUEEN'S UNIVERSITY BELFAST

References

Darwin, C.R. (1859) *On the Origin of Species by Means of Natural Selection: Or the Preservation of Favoured Races in the Struggle for Life*, London.
—— (1871) *The Descent of Man and Selection in Relation to Sex*, London.
—— (1872) *The Expression of the Emotions in Man and the Animals*, London.

Further reading

Bowler, P. J. (1990) *Charles Darwin: The Man and His Influence*, Oxford.
Browne, J. (1995) *Charles Darwin: Voyaging*, London.
—— (2002) *Charles Darwin: The Power of Place*, London.
Desmond, A. and Moore, J. (1991) *Darwin*, London.

SEE ALSO: evolutionary psychology; human evolution

DECISION-MAKING

In a sense, the study of decision-making is so fundamental to social science that all of its disciplines have some claim to contribute to our knowledge of how decisions are, or should be, made. Throughout the twentieth century, some of these themes have come to be studied under the heading of a single discipline known as decision theory. Many of the key contributions come from experts in mathematics, philosophy, economics and psychology, and partly because of this strong interdisciplinary theme, the subject has not found an obvious institutional foothold in the university system. North America is an exception to this, though there is a tendency for university departments to focus on decision science, which is perhaps better understood as a branch of operations research. With these caveats in mind, an interpretation of decision theory broad enough to take in contributions from game theory's insights into strategic choice (decisions made in competition with reasoning agents) as well as those from the areas of organizational behaviour and sociology gives one access to a corpus of ideas that provide a bedrock for understanding the logic of reasoned (and sometimes seemingly unreasoned) action in most human spheres.

Mathematical and qualitative analyses of decision-making emphasize different aspects of decision-making, but there are three themes that recur. First, there are questions about the appropriate modelling of risk and uncertainty. Second, it is recognized that options need to be evaluated according to a number of different, potentially incommensurable criteria. Third, there are questions about the meaning (and truth) of the assumption that human agents are rational. A fourth issue arises in practice and concerns the apparent gap between planning (rational decision-making) and the implementation of those plans within organizations (Langley 1991). We deal with each in turn.

Decision theorists are particularly interested in how decision-makers cope with uncertainty. Probability theory provides the basic tools, but there are a number of ways in which the concept can be interpreted and each has pros and cons. The practice of using the relative frequency of an event (a ratio of successes to trials) has a long history though the first theoretical account, associated with the name of Laplace, suggested that probability was a measure of ignorance concerning equally likely events (so regarded because there was insufficient reason to make any other ascription (Weatherford 1982)). To the question, 'What should we do when relative frequencies do not exist, are undefined or are unknown?' the answer is taken to be that we can think of probability as measuring belief and infer subjective probabilities from people's choices over certain gambles. The ability to infer coherent beliefs, that is, ones which satisfy basic laws of probability, depends on the truth of certain assumptions about people's preferences and their beliefs. The experimental literature that has resulted shows that the axioms of classical decision are violated both often and systematically (Baron 1988; Kahneman and Tversky 1979).

One of the classic experiments (Ellsberg 1961) to show how and when the subjective interpretation of probability might fail also makes a direct link with the notion of uncertainty, as opposed to risk. If the term risk is reserved for situations in which probabilities can be attached to different states of the world, then it is clear that there are many situations (ranging from the adoption of some innovation through to the evaluation of environmental policy) in which even the qualitative nature of the decision problem is poorly

understood, and for which probabilities are inappropriate. There is no consensus about how to model uncertainty, as opposed to risk, though ideas in Chapter 6 of Keynes's (1921) treatise have drawn considerable attention. The fact of experimental failings does not in itself touch normative claims (this is how people should behave if only they were rational) but it turns out that many of the philosophical arguments are invalid (Anand 1993).

Turning to the second issue, that of weighing up different aspects associated with options, the customary method of evaluation in economics and finance is to use some form of cost–benefit analysis that requires the aggregation of considerations in terms of costs and benefits. Every general decision-making tool must handle situations in which different considerations must be weighed against each other even though decision-makers might object to the explicitness of certain trade-offs. An alternative, which avoids the description of attributes in monetary terms, can be found in multi-attribute utility theory (MAUT), which allows decision-makers to rate options on a number of criteria. This turns out to be a useful practical tool. Often it is impossible to be precise about the relative weights given to different criteria or the criteria scores of different actions so that extensive sensitivity analysis is required: the procedure can be time-consuming but it has the merit of contributing substantially to our understanding of the dilemmas and conflicts in a decision problem. An unexpected finding by those using such tools with decision-makers (Phillips 1984) is that the process of using them helps foster consensus and commitment, the absence of which can undermine even the most sophisticated planning systems.

The assumption that humans are rational is often the occasion for more heated debate than enlightened discussion. Some of this might be avoided if there were more clarity about what the assumption entails. The following list of definitions is undoubtedly partial but contains those that recur most frequently. An older philosophical view (which still curries favour in lay circles) is that rationality identifies things that we ought to pursue – though the rise of countries and supranational states where cultural diversity is the norm sees this view on the wane. An alternative, more widely accepted, 'instrumental' view is that rationality is about choosing means appropriate to ends, whatever the ends are. A third possibility, due to Herbert Simon (1955), is implied by the observation that human beings are not *maximizers* of anything given: that they are cognitively limited and seek only to satisfy their desires within the bounds of expectation. Another view, namely that rational agents have transitive preferences (if you prefer *a* to *b*, and *b* to *c*, then you also prefer *a* to *c*), predominates in the higher reaches of economic theory. Yet more accounts of what it is rational to do can be found in game theory. Suffice to say, the term has no unique meaning and accusations of irrationality are made at the risk of not understanding the logic that underpins a particular behaviour.

As Turner (1994) foresaw, a new discipline, known as risk studies, has emerged, though whilst decision theory makes an important contribution to its development the gulf between mathematical and institutional analyses remains. There are many aspects of good decision-making in practice about which decision theory has had little to say, such as the creative acts required to conceive of options (de Bono 1970). It is, for example, apparent that good risk communication is essential if increasingly publicized crises, from oil spills to faulty breast implants, are to be handled successfully, though there is no substantial body of theory to help with this as yet. A more methodological lesson that we might draw from this subject is the possibility that theories might be useful even if they are false.

P. ANAND
UNIVERSITY OF OXFORD

References

Anand, P. (1993) *Foundations of Rational Choice Under Risk*, Oxford.
Baron, J. (1988) *Thinking and Deciding*, Cambridge.
de Bono, E. (1970) *Lateral Thinking*, Harmondsworth.
Ellsberg, D. (1961) 'Risk ambiguity and the savage axioms', *Quarterly Journal of Economics* 75.
Kahneman, D. and Tversky, A. (1979) 'Prospect theory', *Econometrica* 47.
Keynes, J.M. (1921) *A Treatise on Probability*, London.
Langley, A. (1991) 'Formal analysis and strategic decision making', *Omega* 19.
Phillips, L. (1984) 'A theory of requisite decision models', *Acta Psychologica* 56.
Simon, H.A. (1955) 'A behavioral model of rational choice', *Quarterly Journal of Economics* 99.
Turner, B.A. (1994) 'The future for risk research', *Journal of Contingencies and Crisis Management* 2.
Weatherford, R. (1982) *Philosophical Foundations of Probability Theory*, London.

SEE ALSO: optimization; rational choice (action) theory

DEFENCE ECONOMICS

Since the beginning of the Second World War, economists have applied their tools to the study of war and the preservation of peace. Defence economics is the study of defence and peace with the use of economic analysis and methods, embracing both microeconomics and macroeconomics, and including static optimization, growth theory, distribution theory, dynamic optimization, comparative statics (i.e. the comparison of equilibria) and econometrics (i.e. statistical representations of economic models). In defence economics, agents (e.g. defence ministries, bureaucrats, defence contractors, Members of Parliament, allied nations, guerrillas, terrorists and insurgents) are characterized as rational agents who seek their well-being subject to constraints on their resources and actions. As such, agents are viewed as responding in predictable fashions to alteration in their tastes or environment. Thus, for example, a terrorist, who confronts higher prices (costs) for engaging in, say, skyjackings owing to the installation of metal detectors in airports, is expected to substitute skyjackings with a related mode of attack (e.g. kidnappings) that are relatively cheaper to perform.

When analysing the behaviour of government agents (e.g. bureaucrats or elected officials), defence economists often employ public choice methods that account for the self-interests of the agents. These agents may, consequently, trade off the welfare of their constituency in the pursuit of their own well-being, incurring costs that are not justified by defence needs.

Topics relevant to defence economics include the study of arms races, alliances and burden-sharing, economic warfare, the arms trade, weapons procurement policies, defence and development, defence industries, arms control agreements and their net benefits, the economics of treaty verification, evaluation of disarmament proposals, and defence industry conversion. Relevant studies of economic efficiency in the defence sector deal with budgeting, evaluation of alternative organizational forms, internal markets in the armed forces, recruitment, military personnel, incentive contracting and performance indicators.

During the Cold War, much of the attention of defence economists focused on the following issues: defence burdens and their impact on economic growth; defence burden sharing among allied nations; the measurement and instability of arms races; the efficient allocation of resources within the defence sector; and the regional and national impact of defence spending on income distribution. In the post-Cold War era, researchers have focused their attention on industrial conversion, the resource allocative aspects of disarmament, the economics of peace-keeping forces, the measurement of a peace dividend, and non-coventional warfare (e.g. terrorism, guerrilla war and civil wars). With recent increases in defence spending, the demand for defence has increased in importance as a topic. Econometric tools have been applied extensively to the study of defence economics.

When applying economic methods to defence economic issues, researchers must take into account the unique institutional structures of the defence establishment. Thus, for example, cost-plus contracts make more sense when one realizes that the buyer (e.g. the Ministry of Defence) may reserve the option to change the performance specification of a weapon system at a later stage. Institutional considerations are relevant to procurement practices, arms trade policies, defence industries' performance, alliance burden sharing, defence and growth, and a host of related defence economic topics.

Policy issues have centred around whether large allies shoulder the burdens of the small, and, if so, what can be done about it. Another policy concern involves the impact of defence spending on growth: that is, does defence promote or inhibit growth? For most developed countries, defence is expected to impede growth by channelling resources (including research scientists) away from investment. The outcome is less clear-cut in developing economies where military service can train personnel and build social infrastructure. The relative profitability of the defence sector has also been a policy concern, since firms tend to face little competition and may earn high profits. Another policy issue has focused on the costs and benefits of an all-volunteer military force. There is interest in examining the economic impacts of civil wars and factors determining the duration of civil wars.

TODD SANDLER
UNIVERSITY OF SOUTHERN CALIFORNIA

Further reading

Sambanis, N. (2002) 'A review of recent advances and future directions', *Quantitative Literature of Civil War, Defence and Peace Economics* 13(3) (June): 215–43.
Sandler, T. and Hartley, K. (1995) *The Economics of Defence*, Cambridge, UK.
—— (2001) 'Economics of alliances: The lessons for collective action', *Journal of Economic Literature* 39(3) (September): 869–96.

SEE ALSO: war studies

DELUSIONS

Although the notion that a bizarre or irrational belief may reflect a state of insanity has a long history (Sims 1995), most contemporary accounts of delusions have been influenced by the work of the Heidelberg school of psychiatry, particularly Karl Jaspers (1963 [1913]). Jaspers advocated a phenomenological approach in which the clinician attempts to understand mental illness by empathizing with and sharing the patient's experiences. On his view, the hallmark of psychotic illness is that it is not amenable to empathy, and is therefore ultimately *ununderstandable*. Jaspers observed that abnormal beliefs in general are held with extraordinary conviction, are impervious to counter-argument, and have bizarre or impossible content. However, he further distinguished between *delusion-like ideas*, which arise understandably from the individual's personality, mood or experiences, and *primary delusions*, which arise suddenly from a more fundamental change of personality and that are not mediated by inference. In their diagnostic manual, the American Psychiatric Association (1994) defines a delusion as simply:

A false personal belief based on incorrect inference about external reality that is firmly sustained despite what almost everyone else believes and despite what constitutes incontrovertible and obvious proof or evidence to the contrary. The belief is not one ordinarily accepted by other members of the person's culture or subculture.

The concept of paranoia has been used to describe psychotic disorders in which delusions (particularly of persecution) are the main feature. Kraepelin (1907), also a Heidelberg psychiatrist who had a major influence on the development of modern systems of psychiatric classification, initially took the view that dementia paranoides was a discrete type of psychotic disorder, but he later held that it was a subtype of dementia praecox (renamed schizophrenia by Bleuler). The American Psychiatric Association (1994) now uses the term delusional disorder to describe schizophrenia-like illnesses in which delusions are the main feature.

In most cultures, the most common type of delusion observed in clinical practice is persecutory (Ndetei and Vadher 1984). Delusions of reference (when a patient believes that apparently meaningless or innocuous events, comments or objects refer to the self) and grandiosity are also common, perhaps reflecting patients' concerns about their place in the social universe (Bentall 2003). Morbid jealousy (characterized by a delusion that a loved one is being unfaithful) and misidentification syndromes (for example, the Capgras syndrome, in which a patient believes that a loved one has been replaced by an impostor) are less often observed (Enoch and Trethowan 1979).

The social context of delusional thinking has hardly been investigated. However, in a population-based study, Mirowsky and Ross (1983) found that paranoid ideation is common in social and economic circumstances characterized by powerlessness. More recently, the role of victimization and marginalization in paranoid thinking has been highlighted by the abnormally high rates of paranoid psychosis observed in ethnic minority groups (Harrison et al. 1988). In Britain, this effect is greatest amongst Afro-Caribbeans living in predominantly white neighbourhoods (Boydell et al. 2001).

Following his analysis of the memoirs of Daniel Schreber, a German judge who suffered from a severe mental illness, Freud (1950 [1911]) suggested that paranoia is a product of homosexual longings that are unacceptable to consciousness. This theory has been disputed by other commentators, who have attributed Schreber's illness to the authoritarian childrearing practices advocated by his father (Niederland 1960).

Two further accounts of delusional thinking have been proposed in the psychological litera-ture. Maher (1974) has suggested that delusions are the product of rational attempts to explain anomalous experiences including abnormal bodily sensations; on this view the reasoning of deluded people is normal. Although perceptual abnormalities do seem to be implicated in some types of delusions (particularly the misidentification syndromes; cf. Ellis and Lewis 2001), empirical studies have failed to establish a general relationship between anomalous experiences and abnormal beliefs (Chapman and Chapman 1988).

Other psychologists have argued that reasoning processes may be abnormal in deluded patients and recent empirical studies would tend to support this view. Garety et al. (1991) have shown that many deluded patients perform abnormally on probabilistic reasoning tasks, sampling less evidence before making a decision than non-deluded controls. Taking a different approach, Bentall et al. (2001) have shown that paranoid patients have an abnormal tendency to explain negative experiences by reference to causes that are external to self. This attributional style, which seems to reflect the abnormal functioning of a normal defensive mechanism, is hypothesized to protect the deluded individual from low self-esteem. This account is consistent with the view that paranoia is a camouflaged form of depression (Zigler and Glick 1988).

There is evidence that cognitive-behavioural therapy may be effective in the treatment of some kinds of delusional beliefs (Morrison 1998).

RICHARD BENTALL
UNIVERSITY OF MANCHESTER

References

American Psychiatric Association (1994) *Diagnostic and Statistical Manual for Mental Disorders*, 4th edn, Washington, DC.
Bentall, R.P. (2003) *Madness Explained: Psychosis and Human Nature*, London.
Bentall, R.P., Corcoran, R., Howard, R., Blackwood, R. and Kinderman, P. (2001) 'Persecutory delusions: A review and theoretical integration', *Clinical Psychology Review* 21: 1, 143–92.
Boydell, J., van Os, J., McKenzie, J., Allardyce, J., Goel, R., McCreadie, R.G. and Murray, R.M. (2001) 'Incidence of schizophrenia in ethnic minorities in London: Ecological study into interactions with environment', *British Medical Journal* 323: 1–4.
Chapman, L.J. and Chapman, J.P. (1988) 'The genesis of delusions', in T.F. Oltmanns and B.A. Maher (eds) *Delusional Beliefs*, New York, pp. 167–83.
Ellis, H.D. and Lewis, M.B. (2001) 'Capgras delusion:

A window on face recognition', *Trends in Cognitive Sciences* 5: 149–56.

Enoch, M.D. and Trethowan, W.H. (1979) *Uncommon Psychiatric Syndromes*, 2nd edn, Bristol.

Freud, S. (1950 [1911]) 'Psychoanalytic notes upon an autobiographical account of a case of paranoia (Dementia Paranoides)', *Collected Papers*, Vol. 3, London, pp. 387–466.

Garety, P.A., Hemsley, D.R. and Wessely, S. (1991) 'Reasoning in deluded schizophrenic and paranoid patients', *Journal of Nervous and Mental Disease* 179: 194–201.

Harrison, G., Owens, D., Holton, A., Neilson, D. and Boot, D. (1988) 'A prospective study of severe mental disorder in Afro-Caribbean patients', *Psychological Medicine* 18: 643–57.

Jaspers, K. (1963 [1913]) *General Psychopathology*, Manchester.

Kraepelin, E. (1907) *Textbook of Psychiatry*, 7th edn, London.

Maher, B.A. (1974) 'Delusional thinking and perceptual disorder', *Journal of Individual Psychology* 30: 98–113.

Mirowsky, J. and Ross, C.E. (1983) 'Paranoia and the structure of powerlessness', *American Sociological Review*, 48: 228-39.

Morrison, A.P. (1998) 'Cognitive behaviour therapy for psychotic symptoms of schizophrenia', in N. Tarrier, A. Wells and G. Haddock (eds) *Treating Complex Cases: The Cognitive Behavioural Therapy Approach*, London, pp. 195–216.

Ndetei, D.M. and Vadher, A. (1984) 'Frequency and clinical significance of delusions across cultures', *Acta Psychiatrica Scandinavica* 70: 73–6.

Niederland, W.G. (1960) 'Schreber's father', *Journal of the American Psychoanalytic Association* 8: 492–9.

Sims, A. (1995) *Symptoms in the Mind*, 2nd edn, London.

Zigler, E. and Glick, M. (1988) 'Is paranoid schizophrenia really camouflaged depression?' *American Psychologist* 43: 284–90.

SEE ALSO: fantasy

DEMOCRACY

Democracy refers both to a political system and a political aspiration. As a name for a political system, it refers to the fact that the people themselves rule in some sense (in the modern period, indirectly, through elected representatives). As an aspiration, it stands for the desire to deepen and extend the ideal of self-government. These two approaches are often in tension. Contemporary representative democracy, for example, is sometimes criticized as remote and bureaucratic, giving rise to aspirations for more direct or participatory visions. Such tensions are part of democracy's flexibility and vibrancy as a concept.

The standard definition of democracy is 'rule by the people', from the ancient Greek (*demos* + *kratia*). This definition prompts questions concerning the identity of the people and the nature of their rule. Today, a 'people' normally means citizens of a nation-state or country – the French, the South Africans, the Peruvians, etc. But in an age of globalization, massive movements of peoples across continents, and the revival of local and secessionist movements, it has become evident that there is no obvious democratic way to decide who constitutes 'a people'. How would one conduct a vote on how to constitute the political community? Who would decide which people could take part in *that* vote?

And in what sense can the people rule? In an influential account, Jack Lively (1975) set out a sliding scale of possibilities. Rule by the people could mean that all should be involved in deciding policy and administrative procedures, or that all should be involved in *crucial* decisions. Perhaps democratic rule can involve only a select minority, normally elected representatives, in ruling? Is it enough if these representatives are chosen by, or accountable to, the people as a whole? And what if rulers are chosen by representatives of the ruled? Clearly there is wide scope for specifying democracy's meaning and requirements. Some observers regret such indeterminacy; others view it as part of democracy's value.

Varied perspectives on democracy can be brought together if we link two questions – 'Is this system a democracy or not?' and 'How democratic is it?' The first, 'threshold', question must be answered with a yes or a no. If a system operates with free and fair elections that produce representatives who then govern for a limited period, it might be agreed that the minimum requirements for democracy are met. That leaves the second, 'continuum', question, which can trace the difference between minimal electoral democracy and a system with wider and deeper citizen participation.

Historically, democracy emerged to prominence in ancient Greece, most famously in Athens, around 2500 BCE. Ancient Greek democracy was practised in city-states rather than nations or empires. It featured direct citizen participation in a face-to-face assembly making decisions for the community, rather than representation (though there were representative elements). However, women, slaves and resident foreigners were not 'citizens' and so were excluded from the public political life of the city. Only a minority of male citizens actually took part in the direct democratic assemblies and were eligible to be chosen (by 'lot' or random selection) for public offices (Finley 1985).

Aspects of democratic practice were evident in ancient Rome, and in Renaissance Italian city-states, but national and representative democracy as we know it today awaited what Robert A. Dahl (1989) calls democracy's 'second transformation' in Europe around the mid-eighteenth century. This second transformation involved a shift from the city to the nation. The increase in political scale created political communities that were much more numerous and diverse than ancient or Renaissance city-states. Population and territory could be much greater. Direct participation was now displaced by representation. The French and American revolutions set in chain a series of massive changes that resulted in the emergence of contemporary representative democracy (which to an ancient Athenian would resemble a form of oligarchy, presiding over an empire).

In the early twenty-first century, something approaching two-thirds of the countries in the world are classed as democratic. This historically unprecedented spread of popular government came about as a result of the rapid (though often difficult and halting) spread of democracy across Eastern Europe, Latin America and Africa at the end of the twentieth century and the beginning of the twenty-first century. Democracy has no serious rivals as a way of organizing political life. Its practice varies according to region, culture and degree of economic development, but democracy today basically refers to a political system where collective decisions are made by governments that are accountable to an elected legislature. There are no major restrictions on the right to vote other than age, and freedom of expression and association are constitutionally protected.

Social scientists debate such issues as whether presidential or parliamentary systems provide greater stability and popular control, and when we might regard a new democracy as having been consolidated. Different practitioners and observers have their preferred models or theories of democracy. Historically, many models are available. Liberal models stress individual freedom, a limited role for the state, and the rule of law. Socialist and social democratic models stress social equality and solidarity as a basis for healthy democracy, and prescribe a more expansive role for the state. Developmental and participatory models emphasize the importance of democracies fostering citizen capacities and efficacy, while protective models emphasize the role of the democratic state as a protection against tyranny or the transgression of citizens' rights (Held 1996).

Some models and theories have proposed tidied-up descriptions of democratic practice, such as the contemporary 'majoritarian' and 'consensus' models discussed influentially by Arend Lijphart (1999). Others have been ideal, aspirational visions, such as the contemporary deliberative and cosmopolitan models. Some have become mainstream, such as various accounts of liberal democracy, while others are radical and critical, such as Marxist or radical ecological approaches. Whatever its precise focus, any worthwhile model or theory of democracy will offer answers to six questions. These six questions represent the six core dimensions or aspects of democracy:

1 What is the appropriate political unit or political community in which democracy is to be practised, in terms of geography, population size, the terms of membership (or citizenship) and degree of cultural homogeneity?

2 What constitutional constraints should democratic majorities face, if any? What rights should be guaranteed to citizens of a democracy?

3 To what degree and over what concerns should distinct subgroups, functional or territorial, possess rights to autonomy or collective self-determination?

4 What is the appropriate balance between different forms of popular participation in the making of collective decisions, in terms of both (a) the balance between direct and representative institutions, and (b) the balance of variation within each of these two basic forms?

5 How are relations of accountability to be structured, how are 'accounts' to be given, by whom and to whom?

6 How are the respective roles of the public and the private spheres, and formal and informal modes of political activity, to be understood?

The orthodox liberal democratic model has been characterized by the advocacy or acceptance of primarily representative institutions (4). Allied with this, democratic politics has been conceived as occurring largely within the formal structure of the state (6). The formal range of the jurisdiction of that state has been defined in terms of national territorial units (1), on the basis of majority rule (2), constrained largely by guaranteed rights to expressive, associative and basic political freedoms. Elected and appointed officials exercise considerable policy discretion in the context of lines of formal and hierarchical accountability (5). Distinct territorial subgroups have tightly circumscribed autonomy (if any) from the central state within a specific scope (3).

A range of influential twenty-first-century models offer challenges to this orthodox view. The *deliberative* model stresses political talk rather than voting, debate rather than choice. Deliberative conceptions have challenged conventional views of accountability (5), emphasizing the ongoing giving of accounts, explanations or reasons to those subject to decisions, rather than more formal and periodic electoral accountability.

Advocates of the *cosmopolitan* model responded to globalization – the (contested) fact that many important economic, ecological, technological decisions are now too large to be made by individual nation-states – by arguing that democracy must be organized on global and regional levels as well as the national if politics is to keep up with transnational economic power. In this way the cosmopolitan model challenges received ideas of political community for democracy (1).

Ecological models suggest that familiar representative institutions should be adapted so that the vital interests of (in particular) non-human nature and future generations can find a 'voice'. This could work, for example, by the proxy representation of nature: interested constituencies (such as memberships of campaigning environmental groups) electing members of parliament whose task is to represent these 'new environmental constituencies' (Dobson 1996). Such a proposal reinforces the idea of representation while transforming it (4), along with our notions of who or what belongs to a 'political community' (a key aspect of dimension 1).

Advocates of a '*politics of presence*' (and the related 'politics of difference'), including many feminist and multicultural commentators, have challenged orthodox views of democratic citizenship, arguing that democrats must attend to social and cultural exclusion and inequality, such as that between the experiences of men and women, or different minority ethnic groups (Phillips 1995). Effective membership of a political community can depend on whether particular identities and perspectives are recognized (dimension 1).

Proponents of *associative* democracy seek a 'dispersed, decentralized democracy' in which the existing structures of liberal democracy would be supplemented by a range of local associations such as religious and cultural organizations, interest groups and trade unions. The role of the state would change quite dramatically, from a provider to an enabler or facilitator of services as well as a standard-setter for more decentralized systems (Hirst 1994). As such, associative models encourage us to worry less about majorities and more about local, dispersed decisions and policy delivery (2).

Democratic practice in 2050 will no doubt look very different from those of the early twenty-first century. Future democratic practices may be influenced by today's radical thinking and experimentation, including ideas about: (a) the representation of 'new constituencies', such as future generations and non-human animals; (b) the importance of deliberation and reason-giving in the shaping of government activities; (c) the importance of power being exercised from the bottom up by more educated and self-aware citizens; and there may be (d) a decline in the relative significance of national political units as compared to local, regional and global units of governance, to the point where 'shared sovereignty' becomes the norm. Each of these possibilities represents a great challenge to conventional wisdom on various dimensions of democracy. That need not presage the end of democracy, or its transgression. Since its invention, democracy as a practice and an aspiration has undergone significant change and adaptation, and we must expect that it will continue to do so.

MICHAEL SAWARD
THE OPEN UNIVERSITY

References

Dahl, R.A. (1989) *Democracy and Its Critics*, New Haven, CT.

Dobson, A. (1996) 'Representative democracy and the environment', in W.M. Lafferty and J. Meadowcroft (eds) *Democracy and the Environment*, Cheltenham, UK.

Finley, M.I. (1985) *Democracy Ancient and Modern*, London.

Held, D. (1996) *Models of Democracy*, 2nd edn, Cambridge, UK.

Hirst, P. (1994) *Associative Democracy: New Forms of Economic and Social Governance*, Cambridge.

Lijphart, A. (1999) *Patterns of Democracy*, New Haven, CT.

Lively, J. (1975) *Democracy*, Oxford.

Phillips, A. (1995) *The Politics of Presence*, Oxford.

Further reading

Axtmann, R. (ed.) (2003) *Understanding Democratic Politics*, London.

Beetham, D. (ed.) (1994) *Defining and Measuring Democracy*, London.

Benhabib, S. (ed.) (1996) *Democracy and Difference*, Princeton, NJ.

Catt, H. (1999) *Democracy in Practice*, London and New York.

Dryzek, J.S. (2000) *Deliberative Democracy and Beyond*, Oxford.

Saward, M. (2003) *Democracy*, Cambridge, UK.

SEE ALSO: citizenship; consociation; democratization; elections; freedom; government; parties, political; representation, political; voting

DEMOCRATIZATION

In its most elementary meaning, democratization refers to the process or (better) processes whereby a political regime either becomes democratic in the aftermath of some form of autocracy or becomes more democratic as the result of internal reforms.

Until relatively recently, this was not a particularly salient concern for students of politics since it was presumed that only a very small number of the world's existing polities stood any chance of becoming democratic. According to this account, after having satisfied a lengthy list of 'prerequisites', a few favoured countries had become more-or-less automatically democratic. Economic prosperity, a large middle class, a 'civic culture', Protestantism and a British colonial heritage were shown to have been strongly correlated with the advent of stable liberal democracy in the past and were considered necessary for its occurrence in the future. Since there were so few countries that could satisfy these criteria and that were not already democratic, the issue of democratization was rarely

addressed. To the extent that the process of regime transformation was taken explicitly into consideration, the preferred course was that of modest, gradual and sequential reforms over a lengthy period of time. Great Britain and the USA were the models to emulate; France and the other 'unstable' democracies on the European continent were the ones to avoid (Almond and Verba 1963; Dahl 1971; Lipset 1981).

In the mid-1970s, starting with the dramatic events of the 'Revolution of the Carnations' in Portugal, a number of countries in Southern Europe and South America began transitions from previously autocratic regimes towards what was intended to be democracy. None of them had the full set of requisites; a few had none of them. All of them had tried to consolidate liberal democracy before and failed – some of them several times. According to the usual probabilistic calculations of social science, therefore, they should have failed.

When a group of scholars working on these two regions began by questioning this pessimistic assumption (O'Donnell *et al.* 1986), 'transitology' was born and, with it, the study of democratization. It subsequently became a 'growth industry' within the discipline of political science. Drawing inspiration from a previous article by Dankwart Rustow (1970), this approach postulated that democracy was not 'produced' by socioeconomic imperatives but chosen by political agents. The outcome depended on when and whether these agents would divide into factions, form alliances, control state power and negotiate with external powers during the critical period of exceptionally high uncertainty that characterized the transition from one generic type of domination to another. Moreover, there existed multiple potential ways – alternative 'modes of transition' – that could successfully accomplish such a change in regime.

A second novel assertion was that the process of regime change could be usefully analysed by distinguishing between three stages: (1) liberalization involving the concession of greater individual rights to persons; (2) transition restricted to the period between the demise of the *ancien régime* and the installation of the first freely elected one; and (3) consolidation devoted to the efforts to find and implement stable and consensual rules for co-operation and competition between representative institutions. In their actual occurrence, these stages often overlap with each other, but their contribution to the overall process of democratization is distinctive. For example, almost all regime changes from autocracy begin with liberalization and, not a few of them, end there. The consolidation of some sets of mutually acceptable rules may begin before the transition gets under way and may even be inherited from the previous autocracy, but the consolidation of a distinctively democratic regime depends on the end of transition, i.e. on the consensus of actors that no return to the *statu quo ante* is either possible or desirable.

A third observation was that, in the contemporary historical context, regime change was relatively rarely the product of a prior and sustained mobilization of civil society and of gradual and measured reforms by elites.

This actor-centred and historically contingent approach to democratization has not gone unchallenged, but certain conclusions are widely accepted. Democracy is not necessary for economic or social development. It is not a functional requisite for capitalism, nor does it respond to some ethical imperative of social evolution. And it is not irrevocable. Transitions from autocratic or authoritarian regimes can lead to diverse outcomes, ranging from a reversion of autocracy and the development of incomplete democratic regimes to the consolidation of democracy by mutually acceptable rules and valued institutions of competition and co-operation among its major actors. Moreover, there are democracies and democracies. It is not democracy that is being consolidated, but one or another type of democracy. Many different rules and organizational forms can ensure the accountability of rulers to citizens, as well as satisfy the criteria of contingent consent among politicians and gain the eventual assent of the people.

The type of democracy will depend significantly (but not exclusively) on the mode of transition from autocracy. This very uncertain period sets the context within which actors choose the arrangements that are going to govern their future co-operation and competition by determining the identity and power relations of actors. Also, they may be compelled to make choices in a great hurry, with imperfect information about the available alternatives and without much reflection about longer-term consequences. Their fleeting arrangements, temporary pacts and improvised accommodations to crises tend to accumulate and to set precedents. Furthermore,

each type of democracy has its own distinctive way of consolidating itself – especially its own rhythm and sequence; no single path to consolidation is necessarily a guarantee for the future stability or viability of democracy. All types of democracy, in other words, have their own problems and their own vulnerabilities. In the last instance, the success of consolidation may eventually depend on cleavages in the social structure, rates and extent of economic change and cultural processes of political socialization and ethical evaluation. But these lie in the distant and unforeseeable future. What counts in the here and now are differences at the point of departure.

Current processes of transition to democracy

At this historical moment democracy (or, better, one or another type of democracy) is the only legitimate form of political domination. Only it can offer a stable consensual basis for the exercise of public authority. In the past, there were always alternative state regimes that seemed to be viable, and that were even perceived as more efficacious or desirable by certain social classes or groups. However, this convergence in aspirations does not imply a convergence in trajectories and outcomes. Neo-democracies since 1974 will attempt to adopt and adapt the current practices of previously established democracies and, hence, they will not follow (and, especially, they will not be able to repeat) the paths to democracy already trodden by these established regimes in Western Europe and North America. They will be invaded, whether they like it or not, by the most advanced institutions of present-day democracy, but without having passed through the same processes of gradualism, apprenticeship and experimentation as the democracies that preceded them.

This 'unrepeatability' of the democratization process has incalculable secondary consequences for new democracies (NDs), all connected with profound changes both in the domestic and international contexts, and with the nature of already established democracies. First, the rhythm of change in NDs will be much faster and compressed in time (but not in space where it has become much more extensive). There will be much less time for hesitation, for allowing processes to mature, for making gradual concessions or for being able to wait for a more propitious moment of economic growth or international circumstance. Second, the political actors will not be the same as before. The effective citizens of well-established democracies are organizations, not individuals. They are vastly better endowed, informed and aware than were their forerunners. They can act in multiple sites, over a wider span of issues and for more protracted periods. They can draw upon a greater variety of resources, domestic and foreign. Few NDs will begin with a full set of such 'organizational citizens', but if and when their consolidation proceeds they will acquire them. Third, most of the politicians that participate, through their respective organizations, in the process of regime change are not amateurs, but professionals. They may start out, of course, with little or no experience at the job, but they rather quickly learn to depend upon it. Fourth, domestic structures and international contexts have changed so much that the grand ideological formulas and partisan confrontations of the past are no longer convincing. The end of the Cold War and the collapse of Soviet power have also contributed more recently to a further fragmentation of symbolic identities and interest conceptions. The tacit assumption that modern democracy would lead inexorably to 'leftist' policies and an expansion of the role of the state as competing parties offered public compensation and subsidization to broader constituencies has given way to neoliberal expectations of the inverse: privatization, deregulation, monetary orthodoxy, balanced budgets, tax cuts and the overriding importance of protecting property rights and the international competitiveness of producers.

They also have to make do with generally weak political parties. Modern political parties rarely provide individual citizens with their principal element of political self-identification and they are much less significant in the process of political socialization. While they remain indispensable for the formal organization of electoral competition at all levels of government, they have lost a great deal in terms of militants, followers, internal participation, programmatic coherence and credibility with the general public. At the same time, NDs benefit (and suffer) from the coincidence that they emerged almost at the same time that an enormous variety of 'new social movements' were emerging in established democracies, and penetrating their political processes.

Transitions to democracy rarely happen without the simultaneous presence of other demands and other processes of profound change in socioeconomic structures and cultural values. The circumstances that lead to the demise of autocracies are varied, but invariably involve crises and deficiencies in several institutions and spheres of society. It will be difficult to restrict the agenda of regime change only to political transformations. In favoured (but rare) cases, the *ancien régime* may have already accomplished some of the necessary tasks, for example it may have established national identity and boundaries, imposed civilian control over the military, increased the efficiency of the fiscal system, privatized inefficient state enterprises and/or stabilized the value of national currency. Normally, however, the inverse is the case and neodemocrats inherit an accumulation of problems in different social, economic and cultural domains, along with the inevitable problems of political structure and practice.

The empirical cases of democratization in Southern Europe and South America have taught us that it is possible (but not necessarily easy) to move from various types of autocracy to various types of democracy without necessarily respecting the preconditions or prerequisites that political science has long considered indispensable for a task of such magnitude and difficulty. It is possible to achieve this transition without violence or the physical elimination of the protagonists of the previous autocracy; without having attained a high level of economic development; without effecting a substantial redistribution of income or wealth; without the prior existence of a national bourgeoisie; without a civic culture; without (many) democrats.

The present wave of democratization will probably leave behind more cases of consolidated democracy dispersed over a wider area than all previous waves, but some polities will be dragged by the undertow back to autocracy. It is also very likely to produce a profound sense of disenchantment and disillusionment, when people discover that modern democracy does not resolve many of the palpable inequalities and unhappinesses of this world. We are still far from 'the end of history'. The triumph of democracy in the last decade of the twentieth century will lead ineluctably to a renewed criticism of democracy well into the twenty-first century.

PHILIPPE SCHMITTER
EUROPEAN UNIVERSITY INSTITUTE,
FLORENCE

References

Almond, G.A. and Verba, S. (1963) *The Civic Culture: Political Attitudes in Five Nations*, Princeton, NJ.
Dahl, R. (1971) *Polyarchy. Participation and Opposition*, New Haven, CT.
Lipset, S.M. (1981) *Political Man. The Social Base of Politics*, extended edn, Baltimore, MD.
O'Donnell, G.O, Schmitter, P.C. and Whitehead, L. (eds) (1986) *Transitions from Authoritarian Rule*, Baltimore, MD.
Rustow, D. (1970) 'Transitions to democracy: Toward a dynamic model', *Comparative Politics* 2: 337–63

Further reading

Diamond, L. (1999) *Developing Democracy: Toward Consolidation*, Baltimore, MD.
Di Palma, G. (1990) *To Craft Democracies. An Essay on Democratic Transitions*, Berkeley, CA.
Gunther, R., Puhle, H.-J. and Diamandouros, N.P. (1995) *The Politics of Democratic Consolidation. Southern Europe in Comparative Perspective*, Baltimore, MD.
Huntington, S. (1991) *The Third Wave. Democratization in the Late Twentieth Century*, Norman, OK.
Linz, J.J. and Stepan, A. (1996) *Problems of Democratic Transition and Consolidation: Southern Europe, South America and Post-Communist Europe*, Baltimore, MD.
Przeworski, A., Alvarez, M.E., Cheibub, J.A. and Limongi, F. (2000) *Democracy and Development: Political Institutions and Material Well-Being in the World, 1950–1990*, Cambridge, UK.
Rueschemeyer, D., Huber Stephens, E. and Stephens, J.D. (1992) *Capitalist Development and Democracy*, Cambridge, UK.

DEMOGRAPHIC SURVEYS

Surveys, censuses and vital registration systems are the three main sources of demographic information. Demographic surveys are distinguished from other types of sample survey by their focus on the forces of population change: births, deaths and migration. Their role has been particularly important in regions that still lack reliable vital registration systems: most of Africa and the Middle East, much of Asia and some Central and South American countries. It was in these poorer regions of the world following the Second World War that demographic surveys blossomed in response to the planning needs of newly independent countries and international concerns about rapid population growth.

At its most simple, the protocol for a demographic survey consists of one page only: a list of household members with age and sex of each to provide data on population composition; questions for women on children ever born and surviving, and date of most recent birth to yield cohort and current fertility; number of deaths of household members by age and sex in the past 12 or 24 months to give mortality estimates; and place of residence of each household member x years ago to chart population mobility. All too often, however, this simple straightforward approach provided estimates that were very clearly defective. In many poor, largely illiterate countries, ages and dates have little social significance and are poorly reported. Reports on children ever born suffered from omission, particularly of those who died at very young ages. Recent deaths of household members also tended to be underreported, partly because the death of a key member may lead to the dissolution of the household.

One reaction to this situation was the multiround or panel survey that, it was thought, would greatly facilitate accurate dating of recent births, deaths and migrations. This approach allows enumerators to check household members against the list enumerated in the previous round and thus identify additions (births and in-migrants) and omissions (deaths and out-migrants). A related development was the dual-record system in which vital events recorded in repeated surveys were reconciled with events detected by continuous registration, often performed by a local schoolteacher. The popularity of such prospective data-collection systems peaked in the 1960s and early 1970s but their record of delivering high-quality data at reasonable cost and timeliness was poor and they have been less commonly used since that time (Blacker 1977). Their single most enduring achievement is India's sample registration system, based on the dual-record principle, which has provided reliable data on fertility and mortality at national and state levels for over 30 years.

A second reaction to data quality problems is associated particularly with the British demographer, William Brass. He advocated the retention of simple single-round surveys but developed new ways of indirect estimation of vital rates from answers to questions that placed little reliance on respondents' abilities to recall dates. For instance he demonstrated that recent trends in childhood mortality can be derived from mothers' reports on the number of children surviving and deceased, and that trends in adult mortality can be based on answers about the survival of parents. He also pioneered ways of correcting defective data (Brass 1996). These techniques are still widely used.

The third reaction, however, was destined to become the dominant form of demographic sample survey. This was essentially a high-quality elaboration of the single-round strategy and is best illustrated by the methods of the World Fertility Survey (WFS). The hallmarks of the WFS approach included a lengthy, but carefully translated, questionnaire administered verbatim to small samples of women by well-trained female interviewers who worked in teams under close and constant supervision. Central to the questionnaire was a set of standard questions on lifetime fertility, followed by a complete pregnancy history in which dates (or ages) of each child born, its sex, survival status and (where applicable) age at death were recorded. This central material was complemented by a complete marriage history, information on contraceptive knowledge and use, breast feeding, fertility preferences and socioeconomic characteristics. A typical respondent would be required to answer about eighty questions in an interview that lasted some 30 minutes.

Under the WFS programme, sixty-two nationally representative surveys were conducted between 1974 and 1986. Though expensive in terms of fieldwork costs and technical assistance, it was successful in generating reasonably reliable trend data on fertility and child mortality. Moreover by providing information on some of the direct determinants of fertility and mortality, such as marriage, contraception and breast feeding, it went far beyond the provision of information on vital rates and yielded data of direct relevance to health and family-planning programme managers.

Under the successor to the WFS, the Demographic and Health Survey (DHS), the range of topics covered in the questionnaire has steadily widened to include, for instance, child morbidity and health care, knowledge of HIV/AIDS, and sexual conduct and condom use outside of marriage. A greater readiness to collect biological data is also apparent. Anthropometric measures of children are now routinely obtained in DHS enquiries to obtain indicators of stunting and wasting. Recent surveys in Africa have collected blood specimens for HIV testing and thus are beginning to make a contribution to HIV surveillance in that region that, hitherto, has been based on testing of pregnant women at antenatal clinics in unrepresentative samples of health facilities. Between 1985 and 2003, about 150 nationally representative DHSs were completed in nearly seventy low-income countries. Many countries have conducted a series of DHSs, thus permitting unusually rich trend analyses.

The main limitations of the WFS/DHS type of survey are two-fold. First sample sizes are generally small: in the range of 5,000–8,000 women/ households. This size severely curtails geographical disaggregation of results. Ideally programme managers require information at district level rather than the provincial or regional level. The size of sample is also too small to sustain analysis of adult mortality, though indirect estimation from questions on the survival of siblings may overcome this weakness. Second, the complexity of the design, particularly in terms of data management and processing, implies high cost and continued reliance on international technical assistance. The continuation of DHS or similar surveys is almost totally dependent on the willingness of the United States Agency for International Development to provide financial support.

The focus of both WFS and DHS has been on low-income countries. In more affluent industrialized countries, demographic surveys are not needed to monitor trends in fertility or child mortality but specialist surveys on fertility and family formation have proved useful in augmenting evidence from vital registration. In the 1990s the Economic Commission for Europe co-ordinated some twenty Fertility and Family Surveys, and in the USA six rounds of the National Survey of Family Growth were conducted between 1973 and 2002. Demographic data are also generated from labour force, health and household expenditure surveys.

JOHN CLELAND
LONDON SCHOOL OF HYGIENE
AND TROPICAL MEDICINE

References

Blacker, J.G.C. (1977) 'Dual record demographic surveys: A reassessment', *Population Studies* 31(3): 585–97.

Brass, W. (1996) 'Demographic data analysis in less developed countries, 1946–1996', *Population Studies* 50(3): 451–68

Further reading

Cleland, J. (1996) 'Demographic data collection in less developed countries, 1946–1996', *Population Studies* 50(3): 433–50.
Cleland, J. and Scott, C. (eds) (1987) *The World Fertility Survey: An Assessment*, Oxford.
Demographic and Health Survey (2003) http://www.measuredhs.com.

SEE ALSO: census of population; vital statistics

DEMOGRAPHIC TRANSITION

Demographic transition describes the movement of death and birth rates in a society from a situation where both are high to one where both are low. In the more developed economies, it was appreciated in the nineteenth century that mortality was declining. Fertility began to fall in France in the late eighteenth century, and in Northwest and Central Europe, as well as in English-speaking countries of overseas European settlement, in the last three decades of the nineteenth century. Fertility levels were believed to have approximated mortality levels over much of human history, but the fact that fertility declined later than mortality during demographic transition inevitably produced rapid population growth. In France this situation appeared to have passed by 1910, as birth and death rates once again drew close to each other, and by the 1930s this also seemed to be happening in the rest of the countries referred to above.

Thompson (1929) grouped the countries of the world into three categories according to their stage in this movement of vital rates (later also to be termed the vital revolution). This process was to be carried further by C.P. Blacker (1947), who discerned five stages. The final stage was characterized not by a return to nearly stationary demographic conditions but rather by a declining population, a possibility suggested by the experience of a range of countries in the economic depression of the 1930s. However, it was a paper published in 1945 by Notestein, the director of Princeton University's Office of Population Research, which introduced the term demographic transition. Notestein implied that the transition would take place in all societies and began to explore the mechanisms that might explain the change. He argued that the mortality decline was the result of scientific and economic change, and was generally welcomed. However, fertility had been kept sufficiently high to avoid population decline in high-mortality countries only by a whole array of religious and cultural mechanisms. As the mortality rate fell, these were no longer needed and fell into abeyance. Notestein also believed that the growth of city populations, and economic development more generally, created individualism and rationalism that undermined the cultural props supporting uncontrolled fertility.

Demographic transition theory is less a theory than a body of observations and explanations. Coale (1973) has summarized research on the European demographic transition as indicating the importance of the diffusion of birth control behaviour within cultural units, usually linguistic ones, with diffusion halting at cultural frontiers. Caldwell (1976) has argued that high fertility is economically rewarding to the decision-makers, usually the parents, in pre-transitional societies. Should changes in the social relations between the generations mean that the cost of children outweighs the lifelong returns from them, then fertility begins to fall. The Chicago Household Economists (see Schultz 1974) place stress on the underlying social and economic changes in the value of women's time as well as on the changing marginal value of children.

After the Second World War there was a baby boom, which led to doubts being cast on the prediction that the transition necessarily ended with near-stationary population growth. However, by the 1970s this was regarded as an aberrant phenomenon related largely to a perhaps temporary movement towards early and universal marriages. By this time the demographic transition's claim to be globally applicable had received support from fertility declines (usually assisted in developing countries by government family-planning programmes) in most of the world, though with major exceptions in Africa and the Middle East.

Although demographic transition refers to the decline of both mortality and fertility, social scientists have often employed it to refer almost exclusively to the latter phenomenon. The world's first persistent fertility decline began in Northwest and Central Europe and in English-speaking countries of overseas European settlement (North America and Australasia) in the second half of the nineteenth century. Some demographers used the term second demographic transition for subsequent large-scale movements of this type, such as the somewhat later fall of the birth rates in Southern and Eastern Europe or the fertility decline in much of Latin America and Asia from the 1960s. However, the term second demographic transition is now usually applied to the fertility decline that followed the baby boom in developed countries and which began first in those countries that participated earliest in the first demographic transition (Northwest and Central Europe and the English-speaking countries of overseas European settlement). Between the mid-1960s and early 1980s, fertility fell by 30–50 per cent in nearly all these countries. In consequence, by the early 1980s fertility was below the long-term replacement level in virtually all these countries, and in the rest of Europe as well. In both developed and developing countries these fertility falls had been greatly assisted by the new contraceptives available from the 1960s (the pill, injectables and the IUD), and easier access to sterilization and abortion.

Philippe Ariès (1980) wrote of 'two successive motivations for the decline of the Western birth rate'. While the first had aimed at improving the chances of the children in achieving social and occupational advancement in the world, the second was parent-oriented rather than child-oriented and had in fact resulted in the dethroning of the child-king (his term). Aries and others agreed that in a faster changing world parents were now planning for their own futures as well as those of their children, that the process had been accelerated by later and fewer marriages, and the trend towards most women working outside the home, and that it had been facilitated by the development of more effective methods of birth control, such as the pill and IUD, and readier resort to sterilization. Henri Leridon (1981) wrote of the second contraceptive revolution, Ron Lesthaeghe and Dirk van de Kaa (1986) of two demographic transitions, and van de Kaa (1987) of the second demographic transition.

The last two decades of the twentieth century witnessed a new phenomenon, very low fertility, with fertility falling in some countries to between one-half and two-thirds of that required for replacement. This occurred in the 1980s in Central Europe (Germany and Austria), from the later 1980s in Southern Europe (Italy, Spain and Greece) and from the early 1990s in Asia

(Japan, Hong Kong, Macao, Singapore and Taiwan). From the 1990s the economic shock of the collapse of communism was followed by a massive fall in fertility in all Eastern Europe, except Albania, and in the trans-Caucasian republics (Georgia and Armenia). Marriages were postponed and fertility within marriage declined. Women's education and employment, liberal economics, the welfare state and the consumption society were all blamed. Demographic analysis suggested that the annual fertility rates exaggerated the fertility decline during a period of rising ages at marriage, and that average completed family size, although well below replacement level, would in nearly all cases be above the very low fertility level (Bongaarts 2002).

By 2000 fertility was falling widely even in sub-Saharan Africa and the Middle East, so that it was possible to refer to a global fertility transition (Bulato and Casterline 2001). Mortality decline continued more persistently in developed countries than had been anticipated but was checked by AIDS in sub-Saharan Africa. The United Nations (2003) forecast a world population around 8.9 billion in 2050, and there was a possibility that human numbers might never exceed 10 billion.

JOHN C. CALDWELL
AUSTRALIAN NATIONAL UNIVERSITY

References

Ariès, P. (1980) 'Two successive motivations for the declining birth rate in the West', *Population and Development Review* 6(4).

Blacker, C.P. (1947) 'Stages in population growth', *Eugenics Review* 39.

Bongaarts, J. (2002) 'The end of fertility transition in the developed world', *Population and Development Review* 28.

Bulato, R.A. and Casterline, J.B. (eds) (2001) 'Global fertility transition', supplement to *Population and Development Review* 27.

Caldwell, J.C. (1976) 'Toward a restatement of demographic transition theory', *Population and Development Review* 2(3–4).

Coale, A.J. (1973) 'The demographic transition', in International Population Conference, Liege, *Proceedings*, Vol. 1.

Leridon, H. (1981) 'Fertility and contraception in 12 developed countries', *International Family Planning Perspectives* 7(2).

Lesthaeghe, R.J. and van de Kaa, D.J. (1986) 'Twee demografische transities?', in D.J. van de Kaa and R. Lesthaeghe (eds) *Bevolking: Groei en Krimp*, Deventer, The Netherlands.

Notestein, F.W. (1945) 'Population: The long view', in T.W. Schultz (ed.) *Food for the World*, Chicago.

Schultz, T.W. (ed.) (1974) *Economics of the Family: Marriage, Children, and Human Capital*, Chicago.

Thompson, W.S. (1929) 'Population', *American Journal of Sociology* 34.

United Nations (2003) *World Population Prospects: The 2002 Revision*, New York.

van de Kaa, D.J. (1987) 'Europe's second demographic transition', *Population Bulletin* 42(1).

SEE ALSO: population history; population projections

DEMOGRAPHY

Demography is the analysis of population variables. It includes methods, theory and substantive results, in the fields of mortality, fertility, migration and resulting population numbers. Demographers collect data on population and its components of change, and construct models of population dynamics. They contribute to the wider field of population studies that relate population changes to non-demographic – social, economic, political or other – factors. In so far as it reaches into population studies, demography is interdisciplinary: it includes elements of sociology, economics, biology, history, psychology and other fields. Its methods include parts of statistics and numerical analysis. Public health officials and actuaries have had their part in its development. Most demographers have professional knowledge of one or more of these disciplines.

Population variables are of two kinds – stock and flow. The important source of information on stock variables is national censuses, whose modern form goes back to the seventeenth century in Canada, Virginia, Sweden and a few other places, and which are now carried out periodically in nearly all countries of the world. Among the cross-sectional information collected in censuses are age and sex distribution, labour force status and occupation, and birthplace.

The flow variables, the components of population change, include birth and death registrations, initiated before the nineteenth century in Sweden and in Britain, and now routine in all industrial countries. Efforts to attain completeness are slowly making their way elsewhere. Migration statistics, collected at national frontiers, are less available and less reliable than birth and death registrations. Much additional information on both stocks and flows is collected by sample surveys, some with global coverage.

These four sources (censuses, vital registration, migration records and sample surveys) differ in the ease with which they may be instituted in a new country. Censuses and surveys are the easiest to initiate. With care the completeness of a census can reach 97 per cent or more. It is true that a large number of enumerators have to be mobilized (over 100,000 in the USA in 1980, over 5 million for China's 1982 census), but that is easier to arrange than the education of the entire population to the need for birth registration. The USA first attained 90 per cent complete birth records in the first quarter of the twentieth century; contemporary poor countries are unlikely to reach this level of completeness until their residents come to have need for birth certificates. Migration statistics will not be complete as long as many of those crossing international borders can conceal their movement from the immigration authorities. Apart from illegal crossings there is the difficulty that migrants are a small fraction of those passing national boundaries, the majority being tourists, persons travelling on business, commuters and other non-immigrants. US sentiment that people ought to be able to leave their country of residence without hindrance is so strong that outgoing residents are not even stopped at the border to be asked whether they intend to return.

The special characteristics of demography are the quantitative and empirical methods that it uses. Once data in the form of censuses and registrations are available, demographic techniques are needed for valid comparisons among these. Mexico has a death rate of 6 per thousand, against France's 10; this does not signify that Mexico is healthier, but only that it has a younger population age distribution as a result of high fertility; standardized comparison consists in finding what Mexico's death rate would be if it had France's age distribution but retained its own age-specific rates.

Partly for purposes of comparing mortality, but originally more for the conduct of pension and insurance business, life tables were developed in The Netherlands and in Britain during the course of the eighteenth century. The first technical problem that actuaries and demographers solved was how to go from statistics of deaths and of populations exposed to risk of death to calculate the probabilities of dying. With data in finite age intervals the probabilities are not uniquely ascertainable, and a variety of methods for making life tables are currently in use.

The concerns of public health have led to the improvement of mortality statistics along many lines, including drawing up the International List of Causes of Death, now in its ninth revision. Unfortunately uniformity in applying the classification among physicians in all countries is still a distant goal. One object of the International List is the making of cause-related tables. The expectation of life in the USA in 2001 was 77 years. If all deaths from cancer were eliminated this would be increased by about 3 years; elimination of all heart disease would increase the expectation by over 15 years.

Increasing populations have lower proportions of deaths than stationary populations. In effect the age distribution pivots on the middle ages as population growth slows. A sharp drop in the birth rate does not show its full effect immediately; births remain high as the large cohorts of children already born themselves come into childbearing; population growth thus has a kind of momentum. Replacement is the condition where each child is replaced in the next generation by just one child, so that ultimately the population is stationary. After birth rates fall to bare replacement a population can still increase by 60 per cent or more.

Births are not as sensitive to the pivoting of age distribution as are deaths, since the fertile ages, intermediate between childhood and old age, are a relatively constant fraction of a population. Fast-growing countries have more children below reproductive age but fewer old people. But births can be greatly affected by a bulge of individuals in the reproductive ages.

The pioneer in demographic methods and models was Alfred J. Lotka, who in a series of papers extending from 1907 to 1948 showed how to answer a number of questions that are still being asked. A central one was, 'How fast is a given population really growing, as determined by its age-specific birth and death rates in abstraction from its age distribution?' Any population that grows at a fixed rate for a long period develops a stable or fixed-age distribution that Lotka showed how to calculate, and its increase when it reaches this stage is its intrinsic rate.

After a long period of neglect, Lotka's work came to be applied and further developed during the 1960s. It turned out that his approach could help the estimation of birth and death rates for countries of known age distribution but lacking adequate registration data. His demographic equations have also played a central role in biology and evolutionary theory.

The techniques of birth and death analysis have been carried over to migration, especially in the form of Markov chains that describe movement or transition between countries, and other areas, just as they describe transition between life and death. Such Markov chains are capable also of representing transitions between the married and single condition, among working, being unemployed and leaving the labour force, and many other sets of states. A literature has now been built up in which changes of state, including migration, are represented by matrices. The first extensive calculation of this kind was due to P.H. Leslie in the 1940s.

Preindustrial populations tend to grow slowly; their high birth rates are offset by high deaths. The movement of a population from this condition to one of low birth and death rates as it modernizes is known as the demographic transition. Since the fall in the birth rate typically lags behind the fall in the death rate, very large increases can occur during the transition. Britain's population multiplied four-fold between the censuses of 1801 and 1901. Contemporary less developed countries have increased even more rapidly, although population growth rates are now declining in most parts of the world.

The effect on fertility of rising income is contrary to what has often been thought: that people want children and will have as many as they can afford – a view commonly attributed to Malthus, although Malthus's writings, after the first edition of his *Essay*, are much more subtle than this. Economists and sociologists have developed elaborate theories to explain why fertility has tended to decline at the same time that individuals have grown more prosperous. Central themes are the rising opportunity costs of childrearing for women as their options in the labour market improve; the desire of parents to invest more in each child as their incomes rise; the rising direct costs of children and their declining labour contributions; and the increasing proportions of births that survive to adulthood as mortality declines. Great controversy remains about the importance of improved contraceptive technology and organized family-planning programmes in bringing about fertility decline.

Not long ago, it was believed that over the course of the demographic transition, fertility would decline to the level of replacement, or about 2.1 births per woman, and then stabilize. However, average fertility in the industrial populations has been well below replacement levels at round 1.5 births per woman since the 1980s. The USA, with fertility close to replacement in recent years, is anomalous. There is an active debate about the extent to which this subreplacement fertility in industrial populations is real and persistent rather than an artefact generated by the progressive postponement of childbearing by women who will ultimately have more births. The mean age at which women give birth has been rising by 0.1 to 0.4 years every calendar year in many European populations over recent decades, causing a downward 'tempo' distortion that obscures the underlying 'quantum' of fertility. Similar changes have occurred in many Third World countries, particularly in East Asia, where birth rates have dropped below replacement. In fourteen Asian nations, fertility was below replacement level in 2003, including China with 1.7 births per woman and Japan with 1.3 births per woman. Consequently, many demographers now expect that fertility in Third World nations will also tend to drop below replacement as they move through the transition.

The modernization that brings down the birth rate affects subgroups of national populations at different times. In consequence the demographic transition shows itself as differential fertility: the rich, the urban and the educated have for a time lower birth rates than the poor, the rural and the illiterate in cross-sections taken during the transition. Such differentials close up as incomes generally rise and income distributions narrow.

Mortality also declines over the course of the demographic transition. Starting from high levels, initial improvements come from reductions in contagious and infectious diseases. Subsequent improvements are due to reductions in chronic and degenerative diseases, notably heart disease and cancer. Since 1840, the national record level of life expectancy each calendar year has risen at a remarkably regular pace of 0.25 years of life per year of time, for a gain of 40 years. Japan currently has the highest life expectancy at 81 years, the population average. The individual record is 122 years, set by Madame Calmant of France. For the future, the human genome project and stem cell research promise continuing gains. But how low can mortality fall, and how high can life expectancy rise? Some analysts believe there is a biological limit to attainable life expectancy at around 85 years. Most demographers, however, believe that life expectancy will continue to rise, noting that there has been no deceleration so far, and indeed that death rates are declining more rapidly at extreme old ages than in the past, indicating that if there is a limit, we are not yet near it. Recent experiments with other species such as nematodes, Medflies and mice show that life-span is highly plastic, and can be dramatically increased by manipulating genes, through caloric restriction, or in other ways. Despite this generally favourable picture, however, there have been serious setbacks. In the 1980s and 1990s, more than 60 million people were infected by HIV/AIDS worldwide, of whom 40 million are still alive. In sub-Saharan Africa, HIV/AIDS has become the leading cause of death. For other reasons, the countries of Eastern Europe and the former territories in the Soviet Union have experienced stagnating or declining life expectancy over the past two or three decades, predating the difficulties of the transition to market economies. Male life expectancy in the Russian Federation is now 60 years, equal to its level in the early 1950s and similar to that of India.

As people live longer, there is increasing interest in the health and functional status of the older population: What is the quality of the added years? Although the rolls of government-run disability programmes have swelled in most industrial nations, this mainly reflects increasing wealth, changing standards and the incentives created by the programmes, not adverse trends in the functional status of older workers. There is increasing evidence that at the ages over 60, disability rates have declined quite strongly in the 1980s and 1990s, and there is some evidence that this trend has held throughout the twentieth century in the USA.

During the demographic transition, in addition to the decline in fertility and mortality that was already described, and acceleration then deceleration of the growth rate, there are also important changes in the age distribution of the population that can be tracked through the dependency ratios. The Child Dependency Ratio is the ratio of the population under age 20 to the working aged population age 20 through 64. The Old Age Dependency Ratio is the ratio of those

65 and over to the working age population. Their sum is the Total Dependency Ratio. These age boundaries are somewhat arbitrary; different ones are sometimes used. Before the transition, the Child Dependency Ratio is high, and Old Age Dependency Ratio is very low. During the first phase of the transition, while mortality falls and fertility remains high, the Child Dependency Ratio rises. Once fertility begins to fall, there is a period of 50 years or so in which both the Child Dependency and Total Dependency Ratios fall, and the proportion in the working ages rises. Other things equal, these demographic changes may add about half a per cent per year to the growth rate in per capita income, an outcome called the 'demographic bonus'. This phase comes to an end when fertility ends its decline, typically around the same time that the Old Age Dependency Ratio begins to rise. In this final phase, which lasts another 50 years or so, there is substantial population ageing, and the Total Dependency Ratio returns to roughly its pretransitional levels – but is now composed of a low Child Dependency Ratio and high Old Age Dependency Ratio, the reverse of the pretransitional situation. The Less Developed Countries as an aggregate entered the bonus phase around 1970, and will remain in it until around 2030. Between 2000 and 2050, their median age is projected to rise from 25 to 38. The industrial nations experienced baby booms after the Second World War, making differentiation of the phases difficult. However, they will move definitively into the ageing phase by 2010, as their large baby boom generations grow old. By 2050, there will be about one elderly person for every two workers, and the median age will have reached 45. The entire process of the transition takes about 150 years.

Population forecasts of some kind are indispensable for virtually any kind of economic planning, whether by a corporation or a government. One of the most important uses of population forecasts in modern times is to assess the financial soundness of public pension systems such as the Social Security system in the USA. Professional demographers describe their statements on future population as projections, the working out of the consequences of a set of assumptions. Users believe that the assumptions are chosen by the demographers because they are realistic, and they accept the results as forecasts. Forecasting has gone through many styles, start-

ing with extrapolation of population numbers by exponential, logistic or other curves. More acceptable is extrapolating age-specific rates of fertility, mortality and net migration, and assembling the population from the extrapolated values of these. Based on this approach, the United Nations forecasts that global population size will reach 8.9 billion by 2050, with virtually the entire projected increase taking place in the Less Developed Countries, which gain 1.8 billion, or 43 per cent. In recent years, there has been a growing interest in estimating the uncertainty of population forecasts so that policy-makers will know the range of future possibilities, and know how much confidence to place in the central forecast. For example, a careful analysis of the performance of United Nations forecasts over the past 50 years indicates there is a 95 per cent probability that the actual population in 2050 will fall between 8.2 and 10.2 billion.

Demographers also consider the consequences of demographic change. One important topic is the relationship between rapid population growth and economic development in the Less Developed Countries. To some it seems obvious that rapid population growth must lead to slower growth in per capita income by making it more difficult to increase the amount of physical and human capital per worker, by pressing increasingly on the natural resource base including land, and by giving less time to achieve technological advance. However, there are also potential beneficial effects of a larger or more rapidly growing population, including more rapid institutional change, a larger market fostering greater division of labour, heightened incentives for innovations, and a younger work force that might be more mobile and innovative. The empirical evidence is mixed, and controversy reigns.

A related topic is the relation of a deteriorating planetary environment to population growth. How far are the loss of forests, emissions of carbon dioxide and other greenhouse gases with consequent danger of global warming, thinning of the ozone layer, and declining catches in the fishing areas off Western Europe due to population increase, to what extent due to expanding economies, and to what extent due to inadequate environmental regulation? Here also there is strong disagreement. However, there is some degree of consensus that the most serious problem is population pressure on renewable resources such as those listed above that are outside of the economic market, and for which the market therefore cannot guide use. By contrast, most non-renewable resources, such as minerals and fossil fuel, are governed by the market, and the past record of substitution of inputs in production and consumption in response to market signals suggests that shortages of non-renewable resources will not pose serious economic problems (except perhaps for fossil fuels).

There is also much concern about the economic consequences of population ageing, particularly as this impacts government budgets through public pensions, publicly provided health care and publicly provided long-term care. This concern is well founded. The public pension programmes of many industrial nations are already under financial pressure due to early retirement and generous benefits. As Old Age Dependency Ratios double or more in the next half century, the costs per worker will also double. The same is true for costs of health care, although here the problem is compounded by growth in costs per person at a more rapid rate than the growth in per capita output. Only for long-term care is the picture somewhat brighter, due to the improving health and functional status of the elderly. In the face of demographic projections that imply future insolvency, many governments are restructuring their pension programmes, although there is often strong popular resistance.

Concern about population ageing has been met on the one hand by pronatalist policies that seek to improve the lot of the working mother or provide financial incentives for childbearing, and on the other hand by proposals to admit more immigrants. Because most immigrants are in the young working ages, they improve the Total Dependency Ratio and ease the burden of providing for the elderly. They also often have higher fertility than the receiving population, and alleviate ageing in this way as well. However, the fiscal consequences of immigrants are mixed, because their children require costly education, because they typically have lower incomes and therefore pay less in taxes while qualifying more often for need-based government programmes, and because they too eventually grow old and claim government benefits. The bottom line is that the fiscal impacts, whether positive or negative, are quite small. Furthermore, demographic analysis and projection

shows that the effects of immigration on the population age distribution are far more modest than is generally thought, and that only massive and accelerating rates of immigration could have a substantial and enduring effect on the Old Age Dependency Ratio. Studies have also examined the effect of immigrant workers on the wages and unemployment rates of domestic workers. The usual conclusion is that such effects are very small.

The richness of demography is in part due to the commitment of scholars from many disciplines. Actuaries developed much of the early theory, and statisticians and biostatisticians add to their work the techniques of numerical analysis and determination of error. Sociologists see population change as both the cause and the result of major changes in social structures and attitudes; they study the increase of labour force participation by women, of divorce, of single-person households, the apparently lessening importance of marriage, and the decline in fertility rates. Economists see fertility rising and falling as people try to maximize utility, and study the economic consequences of population change. Biologists employ an ecological framework relating human populations to the plant and animal populations among which they live and on which they depend, and are increasingly probing the determinants of ageing and mortality schedules. Psychologists have brought their survey and other tools to the study of preferences of parents for number and sex of children. Historians, in a particularly happy synthesis with demography, are putting to use the enormous amount of valuable data in parish and other records to gain new insights on what happened to birth and death rates during the past few centuries.

NATHAN KEYFITZ
HARVARD UNIVERSITY AND THE INTERNATIONAL
INSTITUTE FOR APPLIED SYSTEMS ANALYSIS
RONALD LEE
UNIVERSITY OF CALIFORNIA AT BERKELEY

Further reading

Keyfitz, N. (1977) *Applied Mathematical Demography*, New York.

Lee, R. (2003) 'The demographic transition: Three centuries of fundamental change', *Journal of Economic Perspectives* 17(4) (autumn).

Preston, S.H., Heuveline, P. and Guillot, M. (2000) *Demography: Measuring and Modeling Population Processes*, Oxford.

Shryock, H.S. and Siegel, J.S. (1976) *The Methods and Materials of Demography*, 2 vols, Washington, DC.

DEPRIVATION AND RELATIVE DEPRIVATION

During the last decades of the twentieth century widening inequality in the distribution of resources, higher rates of unemployment and deteriorating conditions in the inner cities concentrated attention in Europe and elsewhere upon the general extent and exact meaning of 'deprivation'. The idea was used not only in the analysis of social conditions, but also in the definition of human rights, for example the Universal Declaration of Human Rights and the Convention on the Rights of the Child, and in the construction of government policies, especially anti-poverty policies, and policies to allocate resources to inner-city areas. One practical problem, still relevant to urban and rural areas, local government and access to health care is the selection of insufficiently representative indicators of deprivation to discriminate exactly enough between small areas in equitably allocating resources.

Deprivation may be defined as a state of observable and demonstrable disadvantage relative to the local, national and even international community to which an individual, family, group or nation belongs. It is objective rather than subjective. The idea has come to be applied to conditions (that is, physical, environmental and social states or circumstances) rather than resources and to specific and not only general circumstances, and therefore can be distinguished from the concept of poverty. For purposes of scientific exposition and analysis both ideas are important and their relationship has to be clarified (Townsend 1993: Chapters 2 and 4).

Deprivation takes many different forms in every known society. People can be said to be deprived if they lack the types of diet, clothing, housing, household facilities and fuel, and environmental, educational, working and social conditions, activities, services and facilities that are customary, or at least widely available and approved, in the societies to which they belong (Townsend 1979: 413). They fall below standards of living that can be demonstrated to be attained by a majority of the national population or which are socially accepted or institutiona-

lized. Severe deprivation (sometimes described as 'absolute' deprivation – especially in comparing extreme conditions in developing and highly industrialized countries) should be distinguished from lesser forms of deprivation, on the grounds that there is usually a continuum, from excess, abundance and sufficiency through to extreme deficiency, which can be identified for each form of deprivation. But severe deprivation has been shown also to apply to substantial percentages of the populations of some highly industrialized societies.

Measures of subjective rather than objective deprivation are often found to be easier and cheaper to produce, and there is a long history of studies showing differences between the two. Subjective deprivation can be collective or social and not only individual (Townsend 1979: 46–9). All three versions of the concept have value in the exposition and analysis of social structure and social change.

People can interpret their own conditions differently from what is demonstrable and observable. They may experience resentment or dissatisfaction about conditions that are average or better than average in the surrounding society. This interpretation may of course be fostered by people sharing their race, gender, ethnic minority or other group affiliation. The term 'relative deprivation' was first coined by Samuel Stouffer and associates at the Research Division of the Information Branch of the US Army to explain why some objectively better-off soldiers experienced greater dissatisfaction and discontent than soldiers who were less well-off (Stouffer *et al.* 1949: 125). They were found to have compared their situation either with some previous experience of their own in the past or were comparing their own situation negatively with the presumed prosperity of neighbours or other groups. There are various relative deprivation models. The idea was taken up by Merton (1949) and other sociologists (Runciman 1966: 10, and 1989: 36 and 97; Townsend 1979: 46–53, and Townsend 1987) to explain both differences of feeling between groups and differences between feelings and reality (reviewed by Gurney and Tierney 1982). But 'relative' deprivation must apply to objective and not just subjective states.

The idea that deprivation takes a variety of forms is widely agreed. A review of the entire programme of work on the 'cycle' of deprivation, financed by the Social Science Research Council in the UK, concluded, 'In using the term deprivation, then, we are essentially referring to the wide range of states or categories of deprivation' (Brown and Madge 1982: 39). An earlier study had taken the view that deprivation covers 'all the various misfortunes people can suffer in society'. These involve conditions and experiences

> becoming more unacceptable to society as a whole....The word deprivation, as it is commonly used, appears to imply a situation that is unacceptably below some minimum standard, even though more general inequality may be accepted as at least inevitable, if not desirable. If inequality can be seen as a hill, deprivation is a ravine into which people should not be allowed to fall.
>
> (Berthoud 1976: 175 and 180)

What may be discerned in mapping out the scientific future of the subject is the desirability of distinguishing between 'material' and 'social' deprivation. People may not have the material goods of modern life or the immediately surrounding material facilities or amenities. On the other hand, they may not have access to ordinary social customs, activities and relationships as well as collectively provided services. These social characteristics are more difficult to establish and measure, and the two sets of conditions may be difficult in practice to separate.

In ordinary speech people recognize the problems of those who lead restricted or stunted social lives and they feel sorry for them or criticize those who appear to impose restrictions upon them. The concept of 'social deprivation' provides a useful means of generalizing the condition of those who do not or cannot enter into ordinary forms of family and other social relationships. However, operational measures of that concept are much less developed than of the corresponding concept of material deprivation. Some of the same problems arise with the more restricted concept of 'social exclusion' (Gordon et al. 2000).

If material and social deprivation can be distinguished then subcategories of both concepts can also be developed. This is helpful in explaining social conditions and particularly in explaining paradoxes of the apparent coexistence of prosperity and deprivation. Thus, if there are different forms of deprivation then some people

will experience multiple deprivation and others only a single form of deprivation. This has a number of logical and predictable consequences. It will be difficult to disentangle the relative importance of different forms of deprivation on health, personality and social pathology. Measures of deprivation are still too rough and ready, and depend on the use of particular indicators, whose scope and representativeness is greatly, if often unwittingly, exaggerated. Empirically the pattern of deprivation will include many paradoxes. People with prosperous home conditions can be deprived at work, and vice versa. Some people who are materially deprived will be less socially deprived than their conditions would lead observers to expect.

Indicators of deprivation are sometimes direct and sometimes indirect, sometimes representing conditions or states and sometimes representing victims of those conditions or states. From a sociological perspective it is important to distinguish between the measurement of deprivation in different areas and the kind of people experiencing that deprivation. Otherwise there is a danger of treating age, ethnicity and single parenthood as causes of the phenomenon under study. It is wrong in principle to treat being black or old and alone or a single parent as part of the definition of deprivation. Even if many such people are deprived it is their deprivation and not their status that has to be measured. And many people having that status are demonstrably not deprived.

PETER TOWNSEND
LONDON SCHOOL OF ECONOMICS
AND POLITICAL SCIENCE

References

Berthoud, R. (1976) *The Disadvantages of Inequality: A Study of Deprivation*, London.

Brown, M. and Madge, N. (1982) *Despite the Welfare State*, London.

Gordon, D., Adelman, L., Ashworth, K., Bradshaw, J., Levitas, R., Middleton, S., Pantazis, C., Patsios, D., Payne, S., Townsend, P. and Williams, J. (2000) *Poverty and Social Exclusion in Britain*, York.

Gurney, J.N. and Tierney, K.J. (1982) 'Relative deprivation and social movements: A critical look at twenty years of theory and research', *Sociological Quarterly* 23.

Merton, R.K. (1949) *Social Theory and Social Structure*, New York.

Runciman, W.G. (1966) *Relative Deprivation and Social Justice*, London.

—— (1989) *A Treatise on Social Theory, Vol. 2: Substantive Social Theory*, Cambridge, UK.

Stouffer, S.A., Suchman, E.A., De Vinney, L.C., Star, S.A. and Williams, R.M. (1949) *The American Soldier: Adjustments during Army Life*, Princeton, NJ.

Townsend, P. (1979) *Poverty in the United Kingdom*, London.

—— (1987) 'Deprivation', *Journal of Social Policy* 15(2): 125–46.

—— (1993) *The International Analysis of Poverty*, New York.

SEE ALSO: basic needs; class, social; equality; poverty; reference groups

DERIVATIVE MARKETS AND FUTURES MARKETS

A financial instrument that is derived from, or is written on, some other asset is known as a derivative and is traded on a derivatives market. The asset on which the derivative is written can be a commodity or a financial asset. While trading in derivatives based on commodities has a much longer history, the value of trading in these instruments is greatly outweighed by the value of trading in derivatives on financial assets.

The main forms of derivative instruments are forward, futures, options and swaps contracts. Forward and futures contracts involve two parties contracting to trade a particular asset at some point in the future for a price agreed now. Options contracts give the buyer the right, but not the obligation, to buy from, if it is a call option, or sell to, if it is a put option, the writer of the contract a particular commodity or asset at some point in the future for a price agreed now. Swaps contracts involve two parties contracting to exchange cash flows at specified future dates in a manner agreed now. Forward, swaps and some types of options are traded on over-the-counter markets where the details of the contract are tailored to the specific needs of the two parties. In contrast, some other options contracts and futures are traded through organized exchanges where trading takes place at a specified location and contracts are standardized. The standardized nature of futures and exchange traded options enhances the liquidity of these markets. Almost all futures and traded options contracts are settled not by delivery of the asset but by the parties to the contract taking an offsetting position.

Trading of derivatives based on commodities through organized exchanges dates back to the nineteenth century, with the establishment of the Chicago Board of Trade in 1848 and the introduction of futures trading there in the 1860s. However, it was not until the 1970s that trading in financial derivatives through organized exchanges began. Derivative markets represent one of the major advances in financial markets since this time. The early 1970s saw the breakdown of the Bretton Woods fixed exchange rate regime. The move to floating exchange rates, together with other major changes in the global economy in the early 1970s, led to increased volatility in both exchange rates and interest rates. Such volatility is a source of uncertainty for firms and led to a demand for financial instruments that would assist risk management. Financial futures and exchange traded options were developed to help meet this demand. By the beginning of the twenty-first century the volume of trading had increased substantially (the volume in US exchanges alone had reached almost 600 million contracts by 2001), as had the geographical location of derivative exchanges and the types of instrument on which contracts are written. For example, in addition to currencies and interest rate futures, futures are written on stock indexes (since 1982) and in 2000 the London International Financial Futures and Options Exchange (LIFFE) began trading futures on individual stocks.

Derivative instruments are now widely used as a means of risk management (hedging). As an example, consider a firm that is selling overseas, and is due to receive payment in a foreign currency in 3 months' time. Changes in exchange rates over the next 3 months could lead to the amount of domestic currency received being much less than anticipated, possibly rendering the sale a loss-making enterprise. By using currency futures the firm can remove the uncertainty associated with exchange rate movement and lock in an exchange rate for the currency to be received. When futures are used to hedge, the risk associated with the position is transferred from the hedger to the counter-party to the trade. This counter-party may be another hedger with opposite requirements or a speculator. Speculators are willing to take on the risk in the expectation that they can profit from the activity.

In addition to their hedging role, derivatives also fulfil a price discovery role. Futures prices, for example, provide a forecast of expected future asset prices. Futures prices thus provide important information that can assist the planning of both individuals and companies. While derivative markets provide important benefits in the form of hedging and price discovery, they have also been criticized. This criticism is largely due to the fact that they are attractive to speculators who, some argue, may have a destabilizing impact on the market for the underlying asset. However, there is little evidence to suggest that this negative view of derivatives is justified.

ANTONIOS ANTONIOU
UNIVERSITY OF DURHAM

Further reading

Cuthbertson, K. and Nitzche, D. (2001) *Financial Engineering: Derivatives and Risk Management*, Chichester, UK.
Hull, J.C. (2000) *Options, Futures and Other Derivatives*, 4th edn, Upper Saddle River, NJ.
Kolb, R.W. (2003) *Futures, Options and Swaps*, 4th edn, Oxford.

SEE ALSO: capital, credit and money markets

DERRIDA, JACQUES (1930–)

Jacques Derrida's writings, produced over the course of more than 40 years, have been influential across the range of humanities and social sciences. His philosophical stance has been misleadingly characterized as a form of postmodernist relativism, but he may be more usefully situated within the poststructuralist, or postphenomenological traditions (although periodization and genetic location of this kind are resisted and problematized throughout Derrida's work). His writings sustain an important dialogue with the work of Hegel, Husserl, Heidegger and Nietzsche.

Derrida was born in El-Biar, Algeria, on 15 July 1930. He studied under the Hegel scholar, Jean Hyppolite, at the École Normale Supérieure in Paris, and went on to teach there for 20 years, from 1964 to 1984. In 1983, he was elected to the École des Hautes Etudes en Sciences Sociales and was amongst the founders of the Collège International de Philosophie in Paris, becoming its first director in 1984. From 1975 onwards, Derrida has taught for part of each year in the USA, principally within literature departments: first at Yale, then from 1987 onwards at the

University of California at Irvine, and since 1992 at the Cardozo School of Law, New York City.

Derrida's first work was a translation of and introduction to Husserl's *Origin of Geometry* (1989 [1962]). Husserl's concern with the origins of ideal objects such as the concepts of geometry, and, more broadly, the historicity of reason, is interrogated by Derrida in terms of a thematics that acts as the starting-point for subsequent works. Derrida first came to widespread attention in 1966, on the occasion of a Baltimore conference, and on publishing three major works simultaneously in 1967: a study of Husserl, *Speech and Phenomena*, and two books of essays, *Writing and Difference*, and *Of Grammatology*. The paper given at Johns Hopkins, 'Structure, sign and play in the discourse of the human sciences', inaugurated Derrida's US trajectory and influence, and marks the inception of the critique of structuralism and, consequently, the beginning of 'poststructuralism', in so far as this term can be taken as indicating a transitional historical moment. This paper (reprinted in *Writing and Difference*) also marks the beginning of the misunderstanding of Derrida's work as advocating interpretive 'free play' of meaning, and its appropriation as a literary critical style and method of reading by his US epigones. Both here and in *Of Grammatology*, Derrida focuses on the work of the structural anthropologist, Claude Lévi-Strauss, reading it in terms of its unavoidable dependence on precisely the philosophical tradition that it claims to sidestep or supersede. He also examines the work of the linguist, Ferdinand de Saussure, and the philosopher, Jean-Jacques Rousseau, in terms of the binary opposition between speech and writing, writing being generally subordinated to speech, which is regarded as the direct expression of self-present consciousness. Derrida also unpicks Saussure's theory of the linguistic sign, which forms the basis of structuralism, in terms of the repression of its materiality or exteriority. With this diagnosis of *logocentrism*, Derrida begins an engagement with structuralism that registers its theoretical import and significance, while demonstrating the impossibility of simply going beyond metaphysics.

The premises of these works already entail much of what is at stake in Derrida's output. Crucially, the term *deconstruction*, whose fortunes have been excessive and surprising, as he has himself commented, at first represented a translation of Heidegger's *Destruktion*, a dismantling rather than a destruction of the tradition of Western metaphysics, and here functions in terms of the overturning of hierarchical conceptual oppositions and a reinscriptive transformation of these oppositions. Neither method nor organizing concept itself, deconstruction is best understood as a strategy for approaching the 'unthought' of Western philosophy, characterized as a 'metaphysics of presence', whether ultimate epistemological foundation or determinate and fully determinable meaning. Derrida has produced close readings of thinkers such as Plato, Leibniz or, in the collection, *Margins of Philosophy* (1982 [1972]), the ordinary language philosopher J.L. Austin, as well as Heidegger, Husserl, Hegel and Aristotle. His aim is to trace and tease out themes and ideas that have been consistently, perhaps unavoidably, repressed in the Western philosophical tradition. He has also examined the work of writers such as Mallarmé, Sollers, Artaud and Jabès, in a move that has added to the rejection of Derrida's work as 'literary' rather than 'philosophical' by, in particular, some Anglophone analytic philosophers.

Derrida introduces a series of neologistic 'marks' or mobile terms, often taken from the texts on which he is writing, reinscribing them strategically within his own argument and text. Thus the coinage *différance* is brought in to convey both difference and deferral of meaning as structuring principle and the non-saturability of context. This double strategy, of displacement *and* reinscription is not simply a method of textual close reading in order to unravel and lay bare aporias and contradictions. Nor is it, on the other hand, a form of critique in the Kantian sense: in other words, a clearing of the ground as a prelude to laying the foundations for an alternative method. Other terms employed in this way in Derrida's work include dissemination, aporia, trace, supplement, iterability and undecidability, but he continually moves on, creating new ones. This reworking has been misunderstood, and deconstruction widely extrapolated as a method that can be applied, almost mechanically. Many of Derrida's works of the 1980s and 1990s readdress this problem.

Some commentators have contrasted an early versus a late Derrida, one more rigorous and philosophical, the other more stylistically and hermeneutically experimental (each valued differently by, for example, Christopher Norris and Richard Rorty). This stems from the technical and stylistic radicality of texts such as *Glas* from 1974 and *The Post-Card* (1987 [1980]). Derrida's key early US expositor, Jonathan Culler, has argued that deconstruction's radical potential can only be tamed and defused by its institutionalization (Culler 1983). Nonetheless, deconstruction has re-emerged within a series of contexts from architecture and postcolonial studies to education, critical legal studies and ethics. Since 1990, including notably his *Spectres of Marx* (1994 [1993]), Derrida's published work has been concerned with political and ethical themes of justice, responsibility and hospitality, suggesting to some commentators that his work has taken an 'ethical turn'. In fact, these concerns and thematics are present throughout his work, perhaps most crucially in *Of Spirit: Heidegger and the Question* (1991 [1987]) and *Memoirs for Paul de Man* (1989 [1988]), and they recur regularly in the work of twenty years collected in *Du droit à la philosophie* (1990).

VIVIENNE ORCHARD
UNIVERSITY OF SOUTHAMPTON

References

Culler, J. (1983) *On Deconstruction: Theory and Criticism after Structuralism*, Ithaca, NY.
Derrida, J. (1973 [1967]) *Speech and Phenomena*, Evanstan, IL.
—— (1974 [1967]) *Of Grammatology*, Baltimore, MD.
—— (1978 [1967]) *Writing and Difference*, Chicago.
—— (1982 [1972]) *Margins of Philosophy*, Chicago.
—— (1986 [1974]) *Glas*, Lincoln, NE.
—— (1987 [1980]) *The Post-Card*, Chicago.
—— (1989 [1962]) *Edmund Husserl's Origin of Geometry: An Introduction*, Lincoln, NE.
—— (1989 [1988]) *Memoirs for Paul de Man*, New York.
—— (1990) *Du droit à la philosophie*, Paris.
—— (1994 [1993]) *Spectres of Marx*, London.
Derrida, J. et al. (1991 [1987]) *Of Spirit: Heidegger and the Question*, Chicago.

Further reading

Norris, C. (1987) *Jacques Derrida*, London.

SEE ALSO: poststructuralism

DEVELOPMENTAL PSYCHOLOGY

Developmental psychology studies change in psychological structures and processes during the life cycle. Although traditionally focused on childhood and adolescence, it has extended its scope to adulthood and old age as well.

Two factors stimulated the rise of developmental psychology towards the end of the nineteenth century. First, Darwin's claim of continuity between humans and nature revived the discussion among philosophers such as Locke, Kant and Rousseau regarding the origins of mind. It was hoped that the study of childhood would unlock the secrets of the relationship between animal and human nature. Darwin himself kept notebooks on the development of his first child, setting a trend that was to be followed by many of the great names in the discipline.

Given Darwin's role in the genesis of developmental psychology, it is hardly surprising that biological views, in which development is regarded as the unfolding of genetically programmed characteristics and abilities, have been strongly represented in it. (Indeed, the etymological root of the word development means 'unfolding'.) Typical of such views are Stanley Hall's theory that development recapitulates evolution, Sigmund Freud's account of the stages through which sexuality develops, Arnold Gesell's belief in a fixed timetable for growth, John Bowlby's notion of attachment as an instinctive mechanism and Chomsky's model of inborn language-processing abilities. Since 1990 the field of 'behavioural genetics' (see Plomin *et al.* 2001) has received a boost from the spectacular advances in molecular biology that have made possible the identification of the approximately 30,000 genes in human DNA. However, most of the evidence for genetic influences on individual differences in development still comes from more traditional quantitative studies involving twins and adopted children: there have been few successes up to now in identifying the genes responsible for specific traits, though this field is still in its infancy.

However, those who place their faith in the influence of the environment have also had a major influence on developmental psychology. Behaviourism, which attributes all change to conditioning, may have failed to account satisfactorily for many developmental phenomena, but its attempts to imitate the methodology of the natural sciences have left an indelible imprint on the discipline. Most developmental psychologists now eschew extreme nature or nurture viewpoints and subscribe to one form or other of interactionism, according to which development is the outcome of the *interplay* of external and internal influences.

The second factor that stimulated the growth of developmental psychology was the hope of solving social problems. Compulsory education brought about a growing realization of the inadequacy of traditional teaching methods and a call for new ones based on scientific understanding of the child's mind. The failures of nineteenth-century psychiatry prompted a search for the deeper causes of mental disturbances and crime, widely assumed to lie in childhood. The application of developmental psychology to these social problems led to the creation of cognitive, emotional and social subdisciplines, with the unfortunate side-effect that the interrelatedness of these facets of the person has often been overlooked.

In the field of *cognitive development*, the contribution of the Swiss psychologist Jean Piaget (1896–1980) has been unparalleled, though by no means unchallenged. Piaget developed his own form of interactionism (constructivism) in which the child is biologically endowed with a general drive towards adaptation to the environment or equilibrium. New cognitive structures are generated in the course of the child's ongoing confrontation with the external world. Piaget claimed that the development of thought followed a progression of discrete and universal stages, and much of his work was devoted to mapping out the characteristics of these stages. His theory is often regarded as a biological one – yet for Piaget the developmental sequence is not constrained by genes, but by logic and the structure of reality itself.

Full recognition of Piaget's work in the USA had to await a revival of interest in educational problems during the mid-1950s and the collapse of faith in behaviourism known as the cognitive revolution that followed in 1960. Subsequently, however, developmental psychologists such as Jerome Bruner challenged Piaget's notion of a solitary epistemic subject and revived ideas developed in Soviet Russia half a century before by Lev Vygotsky (1896–1934). As a Marxist, Vygotsky had emphasized the embeddedness of all thought and action in a social context; for him, thinking was a *collective* achievement, and cognitive development largely a matter of internalizing culture. His provocative ideas exert an increasing fascination on developmental psychologists. Others, however, maintain Piaget's emphasis on the child as solitary thinker, and seek to understand the development of thought by reference to computer analogies or neurophysiology.

The study of *social and emotional development* was mainly motivated by concerns over mental health, delinquency and crime. The first serious developmental theory in this area was that of Sigmund Freud; invited to the USA by Stanley Hall in 1909, his psychoanalytic notions were received enthusiastically for a time. For Freud, however, the origin of psychopathology lay in the demands of civilization (above all the incest taboo), and no amount of Utopian social engineering could – or should – hope to remove these. From 1920 onwards, US psychology increasingly abandoned Freud in favour of the more optimistic and hard-nosed behaviourism.

However, the emotional needs of children were of scant interest to behaviourists, and it was not until the 1950s that John Bowlby (1907–90) established a theoretical basis for research on this topic by combining elements of psychoanalysis, animal behaviour studies and system theory into attachment theory. Bowlby's conception of the biological needs of children was informed by a profoundly conservative vision of family life, and his initial claims about the necessity of prolonged, exclusive maternal care were vigorously challenged in the rapidly changing society of the 1960s and 1970s. Nevertheless, his work helped to focus attention on relationships in early childhood, which have now become a major topic in developmental psychology. New awareness of the rich and complex social life of young children has undermined the traditional assumption that the child enters society (becomes socialized) only *after* the core of the personality has been formed.

Critics of developmental psychology point to its tendency to naturalize middle-class, Western ideals as universal norms of development, to its indifference to cultural and historical variations, and to the lack of a unified theoretical approach. However, its very diversity guarantees continued debate and controversy, and its own development shows no signs of coming to a halt.

DAVID INGLEBY
UTRECHT UNIVERSITY

Reference

Plomin, R., Defries, J.C., McClearn, G.E. and McGuffin, P. (2001) *Behavioral Genetics*, 4th edn, New York.

Further reading

Burman, E. (1994) *Deconstructing Developmental Psychology*, London.
Dehart, G.B., Sroufe, L.A. and Cooper, R.G. (2004) *Child Development: Its Nature and Course*, 5th edn, Boston.

SEE ALSO: adolescence; childhood; first-language acquisition; life-span development; Piaget

DEVIANCE

Although the term 'deviance' has been employed for over 300 years, its sociological meanings are rather recent and distinct. In the main, sociologists and criminologists have taken deviance to refer to behaviour that is banned, censured, stigmatized or penalized. It is more extensive than crime, crime being no more than a breach of one particularly serious kind of rule, but it includes crime and its outer margins are unclear and imprecise. What exactly deviance comprises, what it excludes, how it should be characterized, and whether it should be studied at all are not settled, and some sociologists have proceeded either as if its definition is unimportant or, indeed, as if its very indefiniteness is what chiefly distinguishes it. There have been sociological studies of very diverse groups in its name, including the deaf, the blind, the ill, the mad, dwarves, stutterers, strippers, prostitutes, homosexuals, thieves, murderers, nudists, robbers and drug addicts, and it is perhaps not remarkable that sociologists disagree about whether all these roles are unified and what it is that may be said to unify them. There is little guidance within their own discipline or in lay definitions.

Commonplace interpretations themselves are often elastic and local. What is called deviant can shift from time to time, subject to subject and place to place, its significance being highly contingent. What is deviant in public space may not be deviant in a space that is private. What is deviant when committed by an old person or a woman may not be so when done by a young man. To complicate matters further, common sense and everyday talk do not seem to point to an area that is widely and unambiguously recognized as deviant. It is not even evident that people use the word 'deviance' with any great frequency. Instead, they allude to specific forms of conduct without making it clear whether they are claiming that there is a single, overarching category that embraces them all. They may talk of delinquents, addicts, glue-sniffers, fundamentalists, thieves, traitors, liars and eccentrics, but they rarely mention *deviants*. It may only be the sociologist who finds it interesting and instructive to clump these groups together under a solitary title.

The apparent elusiveness and vagueness of the idea of deviance has elicited different responses from sociologists. Some have refrained from attempting to find one definition that covers every instance of the phenomenon. They have instead used *ad hoc* or implied definitions that serve the analytic needs of the moment and suppress the importance of definition itself. Others, like Liazos, have questioned the intellectual integrity of the field, alleging that it may contain little more than an incoherent jumble of 'nuts, sluts and preverts [*sic*]'. Some time ago, Phillipson described the analysis of deviance as 'that antediluvian activity which sought to show oddities, curiosities, peccadilloes and villains as central to sociological reason'. And Sumner has argued that the sociology of deviance has had its day, and that what was once analysed as a facet of a pluralistic world of interpretations should instead be replaced by 'censure', the ideological construction of a politically fractured society.

A number of sociologists have chosen to represent Phillipson's 'antediluvian activity' as important precisely because its subject is so odd: the inchoate character of deviance becoming a remarkable and interesting property of the phenomenon rather than a mere weakness in its description. Matza, for example, held that 'plural evaluation, shifting standards, and moral ambiguity may, and do, coexist with a phenomenal realm that is commonly sensed as deviant'. His book, *Becoming Deviant* (1969), proceeded to chart the special contours of that realm by following the passage of an archetypal deviant across its 'invitational edge' and into the interior. In such a guise, deviance is taken to offer a rare glimpse of the fluid and contradictory face of society, showing things in unexpected relief and proportion. Garfinkel (1967), Goffman (1963) and others took to the deviant margins precisely because they were held to offer new perspectives through incongruity, perspectives that might jolt the understanding and make the sociologist 'stumble into awareness'. Deviants, they claimed,

are required to negotiate problems of meaning and structure that are foreign to everyday life, and their study may usefully encourage the sociologist to view the world as anthropologically strange. Indeed, some sociologists have implicitly turned the social world inside out, making deviance the centre and the centre peripheral. They have explored the odd and the exotic, giving birth to a sociology of the absurd that dwells on the parts played by indeterminacy, paradox, contingency and surprise in social life.

Absurdity was perhaps given its fullest recognition in a number of essays by structuralists and phenomenologists. They asserted that deviance was distinguished by its special power to muddle and unsettle social reality, to upset systems of thought and challenge conventional methods of classification. Deviant matters were treated as things out of place, or as things that made no sense. Scott (1972) argued, 'The property of deviance is conferred on things that are perceived as being anomalous.' The meaninglessness of deviance was thus forced to become its defining quality rather than a simple lack of intellectual or substantive coherence.

Lacking analytic clarity, everyday currency or the precise meanings explicit in the law, the idea of deviance could in effect become what the sociologist chose to make of it, and it came to refract the wider disagreements, problems and pursuits of sociology at large. A list of examples should reveal a little of that diversity.

Probably the most elementary definition of deviance defines it as behaviour that is *statistically infrequent*. A contrast may be traced between the normal, which is common, and the abnormal or deviant, which is uncommon. That definition has been deployed characteristically in clinical or psychological analysis that relied on counting instances of behaviour: normal distribution curves are drawn, and the deviant is that which falls towards the poles. Those who wet their beds with unusual frequency, who are very tall or very short, who read obsessively or not at all, are deviant for practical numerical purposes. It is a definition that serves well enough for certain purposes, but it can sometimes fail to make sense of deviance as it is presented and controlled in everyday life. Thus, the statistically infrequent may have little social consequence whilst the statistically frequent may well be treated as aberrant and exposed to regulation, disapproval and stigma. Crime itself is an example. The issue may be further complicated in social life because assumptions about frequency and normality may be only tenuously related to the actual incidence of an activity. Domestic violence, sexual assault and child abuse are both more common than many people suppose, for instance. It may thus be *beliefs* about statistical incidence that are occasionally more significant than the incidence itself.

A second major strand of sociological thought is *Marxism*, but many Marxists relegated deviance to the margins of analysis. Deviation was commonly thought to be a process that is relatively trivial in a world dominated by the massive structures of political economy. It used to be said that little can be gained from studying deviance that cannot be achieved more directly, efficiently and elegantly from the analysis of class and state. Some, like Hirst (1975), Bankowski *et al.* (1977), actually reproached Marxist and radical sociologists of deviance for discussing unsuitable problems. Marxists, they once claimed, should concentrate on the class struggle.

When Marxists *did* explore deviance, they tended to stress its bearing on the class struggle and the state. Thus Hill (1961), Thompson (1975), Hobsbawm (1965) and Reiman (1990) developed a social history of crime that emphasized popular opposition to capitalist formations. Latterly, under the influence of crime surveys and feminist criticism, 'Left Realists' defined crime and deviance as intraclass as much as interclass phenomena, although they retain their stress on the role played by class structure in fomenting aspiration and depressing attainment (Lea and Young 1984). Most recently, they have come to represent crime and deviance as so abundant that they have become 'normal' features of societies increasingly fearful and preoccupied with the exclusion of demonized 'others' (Taylor 1999; Young 1999).

Perhaps the most important sociological framework for discussing deviance was symbolic interactionism, which focused on the processual character of social life and the centrality of deviant identity as an emergent feature of moral careers. Deviance was redefined as a moving transaction between those who made rules, those who broke rules and those who implemented rules. Deviance was held to be *negotiated* over time, its properties reflecting the practical power and assumptions of those who propelled it from phase to phase. At the very core of the negotiating process are deviants themselves, and their conduct responds to the attitudes that are taken towards them at various junctures. Becoming deviant entails a recasting of the self and a redrafting of motives. It entails a supplying of accounts, meanings, purposes and character. In that process, deviant and conventional identities are manufactured, and the interactionist sociologists of deviance furnished portrait after portrait of hustlers, police officers, prostitutes, delinquents and drug users. Their work continues although it became overshadowed by more recent theories.

In retrospect, it is clear that the chief importance of the word 'deviance' was connotative rather than denotative. It signified the break made in the 1960s by sociologists who sought symbolically to distance themselves and their work from what was taken to be the excessive positivism and correctionalism of orthodox criminology, introducing in its place a more fully sociological and 'appreciative' approach. In the American Society for the Study of Social Problems and the British National Deviancy Conference, in the writings of Howard Becker (1963), David Matza and Stan Cohen, there was an attempt to champion a new beginning for criminology, a beginning that conceived rule-breaking processes to be meaningful and emergent, that did not judge or refrain from making conventional moral and political judgements, and that attached importance to the consequences of the signifying work performed by audiences and by representatives of the state in particular. What was actually studied tended, in the main, to be much the same as before, although there was a new attention to rule making and rule enforcement.

The effects of the new sociology of deviance were profound. They fed into orthodox criminology and made it rather less analytically threadbare and empiricist. But, conversely, the sociology of deviance itself began to take on some of the political and moral preoccupations it had once derided. In the 1980s, especially, civil disorder, social disorganization, crimes against women and children, and victim surveys persuaded many sociologists that correctionalism and social intervention were not really inappropriate responses to the sufferings of victims, and of female, young and black victims above all. The distinctions between crime and deviance, and between criminologists and sociologists of deviance, blurred and faded, no longer seeming to be of such great interest, and the very word deviance itself acquired a somewhat dated ring. Many criminologists now incorporate symbolic interactionist ideas as the taken-for-granted constituents of their analysis, not perhaps referring to them by name, but absorbing them in a new generation of theories.

PAUL ROCK
LONDON SCHOOL OF ECONOMICS
AND POLITICAL SCIENCE

References

Bankowski, Z., Mungham, G. and Young, P. (1977) 'Radical criminology or radical criminologist?' *Contemporary Crises* 1.
Becker, H. (1963) *Outsiders*, New York.
Garfinkel, H. (1967) *Studies in Ethnomethodology*, Englewood Cliffs, NJ.
Goffman, E. (1963) *Stigma*, Englewood Cliffs, NJ.
Hill, C. (1961) *The Century of Revolution*, Edinburgh.
Hirst, P. (1975) 'Marx and Engels on law, crime and morality', in I. Taylor, P. Walton and J. Young (eds) *Critical Criminology*, London.
Hobsbawm, E. (1965) *Primitive Rebels*, New York.
Lea, J. and Young, J. (1984) *What Is to Be Done about Law and Order?* London.
Matza, D. (1969) *Becoming Deviant*, Englewood Cliffs, NJ.
Phillipson, M. (1974) 'Thinking out of deviance', unpublished paper.
Reiman, J. (1990) *The Rich Get Richer and the Poor Get Prison*, Boston.
Scott, R. (1972) 'A proposed framework for analyzing deviance as a property of social order', in R. Scott and J. Douglas (eds) *Theoretical Perspectives on Deviance*, New York.
Taylor, I. (1999) *Crime in Context*, Cambridge.
Thompson, E. (1975) *Whigs and Hunters*, London.
Young, J. (1999) *The Exclusive Society*, London.

Further reading

Downes, D. and Rock, P. (2003) *Understanding Deviance*, Oxford.
Hall, S. and Jefferson, T. (eds) (1976) *Resistance through Rituals*, London.
Smart, C. (1977) *Women, Crime and Criminology*, London.
Sumner, C. (1994) *The Sociology of Deviance: An Obituary*, Buckingham.

SEE ALSO: crime and delinquency; criminology; disability; labelling theory; social exclusion; social problems; stigma

DEWEY, JOHN (1859–1952)

John Dewey was born in 1859. He was a child of preindustrial New England, born and raised in Burlington, Vermont, where his father was a storekeeper, and where Dewey himself would grow to maturity and eventually attend the University of Vermont at age 16 (Wirth 1989). Graduating in 1879, Dewey became a high school teacher. Within 3 years, however, he entered into a doctoral programme at Johns Hopkins University. Dewey took only 2 years to complete his doctoral studies, which culminated with a dissertation on Kant's psychology. His first academic appointment was at the University of Michigan as an instructor of psychology and philosophy. In 1884 he moved to the University of Chicago, where he put a great deal of energy into the development of a laboratory school that allowed him to test his school-related ideas against the actual experience of teaching children (see *The School and the Society*, 1902). But in 1905, in a squabble over the leadership of the laboratory school, Dewey left Chicago for Columbia University. He remained at Columbia until his retirement and died in New York City at the age of 92.

During his long life, Dewey engaged in a philosophy that not only addressed traditional philosophical pursuits in logic, ethics, political science, religion, psychology and aesthetics, but also spoke to issues in the public arena. Dewey, for instance, had substantive things to say about issues related to the suffragette movement, labour unions, birth control, world peace, social class tensions and societal transformations in Mexico, China and Russia (Dworkin 1954). A complete corpus of Dewey's work has been captured in a thirty-seven volume edition edited by Jo Ann Boydston (1979).

Although Dewey started his career in the field of psychology while still under the philosophical influence of German idealism, he soon came to know and appreciate the work of the US pragmatists, William James, Charles Peirce and George Herbert Mead, who inspired a social psychology that examined human behaviours. Dewey eventually made his own contributions to US pragmatism by stressing the role that the scientific method could play in improving the human condition, and by openly committing his philosophy to the values and aims of democracy.

To Dewey, democracy was less of a political concept than a moral one. When married to a method of enquiry (essentially found in science), democracy represented a moral method of understanding. Dewey, in this sense, became the chief axiologist for US pragmatism, a role that likely led George Herbert Mead to observe that 'in the profoundest sense John Dewey is the philosopher of America' (quoted in Morris 1970: 8).

Dewey's social philosophy focused on the worth of the individual in the context of the collective, and aimed to empower the judgements of the common people. Scientific enquiry was favoured because it represented a method of deliberation that provided provisional answers to situational or emergent problems. These emergent problems comprised the main focal points for enquiry. To Dewey, problems were always seen as opportunities for growth and improvement. He believed that by subjecting the problems of the present to a method of enquiry, humanity could reconstruct and improve itself.

Dewey's programme for US pragmatism yoked together science, democracy and education (Dewey 1916). He bridged conserving and transforming agendas by fashioning a method of understanding within a democratic ethic. He argued that education should always be responsive to the organic interplay between the nature of the learner, the values of the society and the world of knowledge embodied in organized subject matter (Tanner and Tanner 1990). Despite a variety of criticisms, some of which was overtly ideological, Dewey continues to attract a diverse scholarly audience.

PETER S. HLEBOWITSH
UNIVERSITY OF IOWA

References

Boydston, J.A. (1979) *The Complete Works of John Dewey*, Carbondale, IL.
Dewey, J. (1902) *The School and the Society*, Chicago.
—— (1916) *Democracy and Education*, New York.
Dworkin, M. (1954) *Dewey on Education*, New York.
Morris, C. (1970) *The Pragmatic Movement in American Philosophy*, New York.
Tanner, D. and Tanner, L.N. (1990) *The History of the School Curriculum*, New York.
Wirth, A. (1989) *John Dewey as Educator*, Lanham, MD.

Further reading

Dykhuizen, G. (1973) *The Life and Mind of John Dewey*, Carbondale, IL.
Mayhew, K. and Edwards, A. (1936) *The Dewey School*, New York.
Rockefeller, S. (1991) *John Dewey*, New York.
Westbrook, R. (1991) *John Dewey and American Democracy*, Ithaca, NY.

SEE ALSO: education

DISABILITY

Even though at least 5 per cent of the populations of the industrialized nations can be categorized as disabled, disability, compared to other forms of disadvantage, was relatively slow to capture the imagination of social scientists. With the exception of a few pioneer studies, using an interactionist sociology of deviance approach, it was not until the 1990s that disability research significantly progressed beyond descriptive studies reflecting the demands of policy, advocacy or demographic monitoring.

This change happened partly because disability has become more visible socially. People are living longer, resulting in an increase in age-related physical impairments. Advances in medical technology pose ever more difficult questions about the survival of babies born with serious impairments. 'Community care' policies mean that disabled people are less likely to be confined in institutions of seclusion. Finally, the development of a politicized disability movement – and its intellectual manifestation in disability studies (e.g. Davis 1997; Barnes *et al.* 1999) – means that disabled people are resisting stigmatization, questioning the provision that others make for them, and creating a space within which to theorize the issues.

Perhaps the most fundamental and controversial issue is definition. Medical conventional wisdom distinguishes between *impairment*, the absence or defect of a limb, organ or bodily mechanism, *disablement* or *disability*, the reduction or loss of function or ability consequent upon impairment, and *handicap*, the disadvantage or constraint that follows from disability. Social conditions may intervene to make an impairment more or less disabling, while handicap is likely to be due in large part to social factors, rather than an inevitable consequence of disability. Handicap can also result from a non-disabling impairment such as disfigurement.

This medical model has been challenged for neglecting the social construction of disablement and the active role of scientific medicine in that process. An increasingly influential alternative conventional wisdom rejects the category of handicap, and sees disability as wholly the product of social processes of exclusion and marginalization. The focus of attention is upon disabling environments and the inadequate nature of political and other responses to impairments (Oliver 1996; Swain *et al.* 1993).

Yet more recently, however, a reaction to this thoroughgoing social model of disability – reflecting not least what many disabled people themselves have been saying – has begun to reinstate a recognition of the embodied realities of impairment. Thomas, for example, discussing women's experience of disability, has argued for the need to recognize that 'impairment effects' are to some extent independent of social construction (Thomas 1999).

Various themes are now well established in the critical social science literature dealing with disability: how people with disabilities manage and respond to their stigmatization, the reproduction of disadvantage and disability in the complex interaction between disability, poverty and social exclusion, and disability and sexuality, for example. Reflecting the influence of the disability movement, perhaps the most significant social science development has emphasized the *meaning* of disability for people with disabilities and their experiences and testimony, and asserts the epistemological primacy of their own voices. An eloquent contribution to this literature is anthropologist Robert Murphy's personal account of his own paralysis and gradual assumption of an identity as 'disabled' (Murphy 1990).

The latter raises complex issues. Intellectual disability, for example, presents a specific set of difficulties and research questions. On the one hand, 'community care' and 'normalization' philosophies, as they apply to people with intellectual disabilities, problematize the cultural construction and imposition of 'normality' (Chappell 1992). On the other hand, how we may best document and understand the social experiences of people's intellectual disabilities is a question of some methodological and epistemological moment (Brechin and Walmsley 1989).

Another important emergent field in which epistemology and interpretation are at issue is the comparative cross-cultural study of disability (Ingstad and Whyte 1995). Nor is this a matter of purely intellectual concern. For developing nations, disability is a pressing practical concern, rooted in dietary deficiencies, inadequate health care, public health problems and poor social provision. In turn, disability makes its own contribution to poverty and underdevelopment. In this respect, as in so many others, disability continues to pose theoretical, methodological and ethical challenges to the social sciences.

RICHARD JENKINS
UNIVERSITY OF SHEFFIELD

References

Barnes, C., Mercer, G. and Shakespeare, T. (eds) (1999) *Exploring Disability: A Sociological Introduction*, Cambridge.

Brechin, A. and Walmsley, J. (eds) (1989) *Making Connections: Reflecting on the Lives and Experiences of People with Learning Difficulties*, London.

Chappell, A.L. (1992) 'Towards a sociological critique of the normalisation principle', *Disability, Handicap and Society* 7.

Davis, L.J. (ed.) (1997) *The Disability Studies Reader*, New York.

Ingstad, B. and Whyte, S.R. (eds) (1995) *Disability and Culture*, Berkeley.

Murphy, R.F. (1990) *The Body Silent*, New York.

Oliver, M. (1996) *Understanding Disability: From Theory to Practice*, Basingstoke.

Swain, J., Finkelstein, V., French, S. and Oliver, M. (eds) (1993) *Disabling Barriers – Enabling Environments*, London.

Thomas, C. (1999) *Female Forms: Experiencing and Understanding Disability*, Buckingham.

SEE ALSO: social exclusion; stigma

DISCOURSE ANALYSIS

Discourse analysis refers to a lively but theoretically contested crossroads between several social science disciplines. Here social and cognitive psychologists have come into creative but sometimes rather uncomfortable contact with sociologists, philosophers, rhetoricians, linguists and literary theorists as they rework their theoretical ideas in the terrain of discourse (itself a contested notion). To further the confusion, discourse analysis is sometimes treated as a generic term to refer to virtually all work on language use in its social or cognitive context and at other times as a label for specific bodies of work, or as a contrast to text linguistics or conversation analysis. It is perfectly possible to have two books on discourse analysis that have no overlap in content at all.

At the boundary of cognitive psychology and linguistics there is work done in the tradition of discourse processes. Discourse analysis is here defined as the study of linguistic units that are larger than the sentence, and the hope is that some of the successes of linguistic analysis with smaller units could be repeated in this domain. Work in this tradition considers the way that individual utterances or sentences cohere into spoken or written discourse, and the relation between such patterning and the psychological phenomena involved in representing and comprehending such organizations. For example, it might ask whether there is a regular grammar underlying a written narrative, and it might consider whether the reader is using a cognitive representation such as a script or schema to recover the sense from the narrative.

Another distinctive area of discourse analysis has been developed principally using the example of classroom interaction. Sinclair and Coulthard (1975) attempted to provide a systematic model that would account for some of the typical interaction patterns that take place in teaching in terms of initiation–response–feedback (IRF) structures. For example:

Teacher: What's the capital of Austria?
   (*Initiation*)
Pupil: Berne, Miss.
   (*Response*)
Teacher: Close, Jenny, have another go.
   (*Feedback*)

The ambition was to provide a model that would ultimately account for discourse structure in a range of settings such as doctor–patient interactions, news interviews and committee meetings. Despite some success in characterizing features of rather formal kinds of classroom interaction, this model has encountered a series of difficulties that are mainly a consequence of applying a basically linguistic approach to the complex social practices taking place in classrooms and similar locations.

If linguistic forms of analysis take the upper hand in these first two areas, a separate tradition of discourse analysis has been more driven by developments in sociology and literary theory. The ambition here is rather different. Instead of being primarily concerned with extending linguistics, or connecting it to cognition, it is attempting to provide an alternative way of doing social science that is much more responsive to the idea that talk and writing – whether in an interview, a questionnaire or an everyday conversation – is oriented to action.

In its simplest form, this tradition started with the observation that, when researching a complex social domain such as science, there are wide variations in the accounts given by different scientists and even by the same scientist in different settings. Rather than treat this as a methodological problem to be resolved by 'triangulation' from the different accounts, or by the use of ethnographically acquired knowledge of the setting, these discourse analysts endorsed the virtue of taking such variation as a research topic in its own right. In an influential study Gilbert and Mulkay (1984) showed how a group of biochemists constructed versions of their social world using two very different 'interpretative repertoires', or interrelated vocabularies of terms, metaphors and tropes. The 'empiricist repertoire' predominated in research papers and was used by scientists to warrant their own beliefs in the manner of textbook science; the 'contingent repertoire' was a much more fragmentary set of notions that were used in informal settings to explain away beliefs seen as false in terms of social, political and psychological influences. Work of this kind has not only focused attention on the workings of scientists' texts but also raised questions about the literary forms with which social scientists construct and authorize their own versions of reality.

This approach has been reworked by social psychologists who have built a more explicit theoretical grounding that has increasingly drawn on thinking in ethnomethodology and conversation analysis. This tradition of work is sometimes called 'discursive psychology' to separate it from other traditions of discourse analysis. One key work focused on the systematic basis of constructionism, and in particular the way descriptions in talk and texts are assembled to appear neutral, factual and independent of the speaker (Potter 1996). For example, it considers the way current affairs filmmakers, barristers in court cases and everyday phone callers construct their category entitlements to offer versions and manage issues of responsibility and upshot in what they are describing. Another has focused on the way psychological constructions become an object in interaction, and are used for interactional purposes. For example, Edwards (1997) shows the way participants in relationship counselling sessions construct the nature of their marriage, their past actions, their partners and their own motives, using a wide range of psychological resources, and how these suggest different outcomes in terms of blame for the relationship breakdown and responsibility for personal change within the relationship.

The significance of discourse analysis, here, is that discourse is the medium through which the 'inner world' of psychology and the 'outer world' of events, social organizations and histories is put together for the purposes of action. This work raises profound issues about the nature of cognition and psychology, about the relationship between psychology and institutions, and about the most productive way to conduct social science.

JONATHAN POTTER
LOUGHBOROUGH UNIVERSITY

References

Edwards, D. (1997) *Discourse and Cognition*, London and Beverly Hills, CA.

Gilbert, G.N. and Mulkay, M. (1984) *Opening Pandora's Box: A Sociological Analysis of Scientists' Discourse*, Cambridge, UK.

Potter, J. (1996) *Representing Reality: Discourse, Rhetoric and Social Construction*, London.

Sinclair, J. and Coulthard, M. (1975) *Towards an Analysis of Discourse: The English Used by Teachers and Pupils*, Oxford.

Further reading

Jaworski, A. and Coupland, N. (eds) (1999) *The Discourse Reader*, London.

Phillips, L.J. and Jorgenson, M.W. (2002) *Discourse Analysis as Theory and Method*, London.

Schiffrin, D. (1994) *Approaches to Discourse*, Oxford.

van Dijk, T.A. (1997) *Discourse Studies: A Multidisciplinary Introduction*, 2 vols, London.

Wetherell, M., Taylor, S. and Yates, S. (eds) (2001) *Discourse Theory and Practice: A Reader*, London.

Wood, L.A. and Kroger, R.O. (2000) *Doing Discourse Analysis: Methods for Studying Action in Talk and Text*, London.

SEE ALSO: pragmatics; sociolinguistics

DISTRIBUTION OF INCOMES AND WEALTH

The distribution of income is usually understood by economists in two main senses: the distribution of income among *factors* (sometimes known as the *functional* distribution of income), and the distribution of income among *persons* (alternatively known as the *size* distribution of income).

The distribution of income among factors is an integral part of the economic analysis of relative prices, output and employment. In this sense there are several theories of income distribution corresponding to different theoretical and ideological stances on these central issues. However, these various analyses usually focus on the same basic economic concepts: employment of the factors of production – land, labour and capital – and the rates of remuneration of their services – rent, wages and profit. This tripartite classification is by no means the only functional decomposition that is useful in economic theory; in some analyses, for example, a finer subdivision is attempted, distinguishing specifically between interest and profits as rewards to 'waiting' and 'entrepreneurship' respectively, or distinguishing between rewards to different types of labour. In many practical applications the characteristics of national data make it expedient to subdivide the functional categories simply as income from work and income from property. When these categories are applied to the income of an individual, household or subgroup of the population, a third type must be added, transfer income, although items in this category, such as welfare payments and alimony, net out when the economy as a whole is considered. Some macroeconomists gave much attention to the supposed constancy or stability of the share of wages in national income. This interest now appears to have been somewhat misplaced, since it is clear that over long periods this share does change significantly. In many industrialized countries during the twentieth century it increased, and now stands at about three-quarters to four-fifths.

The distribution of income among persons – the size distribution – and the distribution of wealth may both be thought of as particular applications of a statistical frequency distribution, although they are often represented by other statistical devices such as the Lorenz curve (which in the case of income distribution graphs indicate cumulative proportions of income received against cumulative proportions of income receivers). The frequency distribution of each quantity is generally positively skewed with a long upper tail indicating the presence of relatively small numbers of very well-off people. The dispersion of these frequency distributions, which can be measured in a number of ways, is taken as an indicator of the inequality of the size distributions of income and of wealth.

During the third quarter of the twentieth century the size distribution of income was noted almost everywhere for two remarkable qualities: the great inequality of personal incomes that is revealed, and the stability of the distribution over time. This was true even though the exact shape of the size distribution is significantly affected by the particular definition of income one employs (for example whether one includes transfer incomes and incomes received in 'kind' rather than cash, and deducts personal taxes), and the definition of the income-receiving 'unit' (for example whether one looks at the distribution of income among households, or incomes among persons). However, it is clear that from around the late 1970s income inequality rose sharply in many industrialized countries: this increase in inequality affected both wages and income from capital. It is also clear that in the early part of the twentieth century there was a reduction in top incomes from capital so that over the century the profile of income shares of the richest followed a U-shaped pattern (Piketty and Saez 2003).

A point underlying the last remark is that while the composition of personal incomes in the lower tail of the distribution has changed substantially as the scope of government transfers has altered, it is still true to say that in most Western-style economies the component of personal income that comes from various forms of property is primarily associated with the upper tail of the distribution. In order to understand the size distribution of *incomes* in the upper tail, therefore, it is important to examine the size distribution of wealth.

One of the most difficult problems in analysing the wealth distribution within any community with reasonably extensive holdings of private property is to decide exactly what one means by wealth. This is not a point of semantics, nor is it one of purely arcane, theoretical interest. While *marketable* wealth – including financial assets such as stocks and cash balances, and physical assets such as land, houses and jewellery – is fairly readily recognizable for what it is, other forms of wealth may also need to be taken into account in estimating the people's effective command over economic resources.

These include various pension rights, which represent substantial *future* claims against economic goods (and are thus in that sense substitutes for cash or negotiable securities that have been held as a precaution against old age), but which may have little or no immediate surrender value. As is the case with the size distribution of incomes, estimates of the distribution of wealth are sensitive to assumptions one makes about the definition of wealth itself and the 'units' of population among whom the wealth is distributed. Moreover, parts of the wealth distribution are also very sensitive to different methods of valuing the components of wealth and to short-term changes in the prices of assets. However, it is virtually incontestable that the size distribution of wealth is much more unequal than the size distribution of income – the share of wealth held by the top 1 per cent varies from about 15–35 per cent, for example, whereas their income share is usually less than 10 per cent (Davies and Shorrocks 2000). Furthermore, it is clear that a substantial proportion of this implied inequality in the distribution of wealth is attributable to the effects of inheritance, rather than to the process of wealth accumulation that takes place during the course of people's lives (Harbury and Hitchens 1979).

Finally, if one switches one's attention from the analysis of the size distribution of income (or wealth) within national economies to the size distribution in the world as a whole, not only do the problems of measurement and comparison become much greater, so also does the dispersion. However one resolves the difficult practical questions of defining and quantifying personal or household incomes on this intercountry basis, it is clear that income inequality within national economies is usually much smaller than the income inequality that persists between countries.

FRANK A. COWELL
LONDON SCHOOL OF ECONOMICS
AND POLITICAL SCIENCE

References

Davies, J.B. and Shorrocks, A.F. (2000) 'The distribution of wealth', in A.B. Atkinson and F. Bourguignon (eds) *Handbook of Income Distribution*, Vol. 1, Amsterdam, Chapter 11, pp. 605–67.

Harbury, C. and Hitchens, D.M.W.N. (1979) *Inheritance and Wealth Inequality in Britain*, London.

Piketty, T. and Saez, E. (2003) 'Income inequality in the

United States, 1913–1998', *Quarterly Journal of Economics* 118: 1–39.

Further reading

Atkinson, A.B. and Harrison, A.J. (1978) *Distribution of Personal Wealth in Britain*, Cambridge, UK.
Durlauf, S. and Quah, D. (1999) 'The new empirics of economic growth', in J.B. Taylor and M. Woodford (eds) *Handbook of Macroeconomics*, Amsterdam, Chapter 4, pp. 231–304.
Pen, J. (1971) *Income Distribution*, London.

SEE ALSO: income distribution, theory of

DIVISION OF LABOUR BY SEX

The sexual division of labour is a basic structural element in human social organization. Humans are the only primates who have a highly developed sexual division of labour in food production. They also are the only primates that share food on a regular basis. However, there is substantial variability in the sexual division of labour across societies and the female contribution to food supply in foraging societies is far greater than was once believed,

Evidence for the original human division of labour comes from two sources: primate ethology and the ethnology of foragers. Male specialization in hunting is consistent with the tendency of male terrestrial primates to specialize in defence, a specialization that gives a selective advantage to larger males. Sexual dimorphism is a consequence of this original division of labour. However, while it is true that in foraging societies men tend to hunt and women to gather, early studies of foragers greatly underestimated the importance of female gathering. They therefore exaggerated the dependence of wives on their husbands. Modern studies of foragers (Lee and DeVore 1968) show that women's gathering often contributes more than half of the subsistence calories.

The rise of cross-cultural and cross-national research makes it possible to estimate the relative frequencies of allocations of male and female effort to various tasks. As a result of Murdock's work (Murdock 1937; Murdock and Provost 1973) we now have cross-cultural codes on sexual division of labour for fifty tasks. These codes confirm earlier generalizations about near-universals. Tasks done by males in more than 95 per cent of the sample societies include hunting

large land animals, metal-working, wood- and bone-working, boat building, and trapping. Tasks done by females in more than 95 per cent of the sample include only cooking and care of infants. Patterns of sexual division of labour appear to have only a partial basis in biology, and most tasks exhibit high variability. This is especially true of the important food-production tasks pertaining to agriculture and the care of domesticated animals.

These variations, however, fall within constraints of a relative rather than universal nature. Many researchers have sought rules of consistency in the variable allocation of tasks. While earlier researchers emphasized the male strength advantage, research in the 1970s placed more emphasis on constraints due to the reproductive specialization of women. Brown (1970) emphasized the compatibility of women's tasks with simultaneous childcare responsibilities. Women's tasks are likely to be relatively close to home, not dangerous, and interruptible. Burton *et al.* (1977) proposed that these relative constraints produce entailments within production sequences. Women tend to take on additional tasks within production sequences in an order that begins with tasks closer to the home and ends with tasks farther afield. Men take on additional tasks in the opposite order, from the more distant to those closer to home. Burton and colleagues found entailment chains for the following production sequences: animal tending, animal products, textiles, fishing and agriculture. An example from agriculture: if women clear the land, they also prepare the soil; if the latter, they also plant, tend crops and harvest. If they tend crops, they also fetch water, and if they plant, they also prepare vegetables for cooking.

Women also seem to participate in more tasks in less complex societies. For example, women build houses in nomadic societies but not in sedentary societies, and female participation in pottery-making declines with increasing population density. For crafts, the explanation for these changes seems to be the evolution of occupational specialization, which displaces craft activity from the domestic arena to the workshop. Agricultural intensification is accompanied by dramatic decreases in female contributions to farming. For Boserup (1970) agricultural intensification results from population pressure and introduction of the plough, and pulls men into agriculture to meet the increased demand for labour. Ember (1983) suggested a second mechanism in the shift to male farming: women are pulled out of farming into the household economy by increased time spent on food processing, household chores and childcare. Burton and White (1984) carried this work further with a model of four factors – a short growing season, presence of the plough, processing of cereal crops and high dependence on domesticated animals – which lead to the displacement of women's labour from agriculture to the domestic and less economically visible activities.

The four-factor intensification model accounts for many empirical observations concerning female subsistence participation: that it is higher in tropical climates and in horticultural societies, and that it is higher with root crops than with cereal crops, for these attributes are correlated with a long rainy season, low dependence on domesticated animals and absence of the plough. While Burton and White's four factors account for a high percentage of the variance, a smaller portion of the variance is attributable to historical processes, which they link, using network autocorrelation analysis, to the Bantu societies of Africa. Guyer (1988) further develops the theme of historical factors of assignment of new African crops by gender.

Finally, several researchers following Boserup (1970) hypothesized that agricultural intensification has a negative impact on female control of economic resources. This research suggests that high female subsistence contributions are a necessary prerequisite to female control of economic resources, and to women's freedom of choice in life events. In searching for other consequences of the sexual division of labour, Heath (1958) and several other researchers (e.g. Burton and Reitz 1981) found that low female subsistence contributions lead to monogamy. Such studies shed light on puzzles such as the rise of monogamy and decline in women's status, originally noted by nineteenth-century theorists. However, White and Burton (1988) showed that the sexual division of labour has little effect on polygyny, given statistical controls for the effects of residence patterns and warfare.

MICHAEL L. BURTON
DOUGLAS R. WHITE
UNIVERSITY OF CALIFORNIA, IRVINE

References

Boserup, E. (1970) *Woman's Role in Economic Development*, New York.
Brown, J.K. (1970) 'A note on the division of labor by sex', *American Anthropologist* 72.
Burton, M.L. and Reitz, K. (1981) 'The plow, female contribution to agricultural subsistence, and polygyny', *Behavior Science Research* 16: 275–305.
Burton, M.L. and White, D.R. (1984) 'Sexual division of labor in agriculture', *American Anthropologist* 86.
Burton, M.L., Brudner, L.A. and White, D.R. (1977) 'A model of the sexual division of labor', *American Ethnologist* 4.
Ember, C.R. (1983) 'The relative decline in women's contribution to agriculture with intensification', *American Anthropologist* 85.
Guyer, J. (1988) 'The multiplication of labor', *Current Anthropology* 29: 247–72.
Heath, D. (1958) 'Sexual division of labor and cross-cultural research', *Social Forces* 37.
Lee, R.B. and DeVore, I. (1968) *Man the Hunter*, Chicago.
Murdock, G.P. (1937) 'Comparative data on the division of labour by sex', *Social Forces* 15.
Murdock, G.P. and Provost, C. (1973) 'Factors in the division of labor by sex: A cross-cultural analysis', *Ethnology* 12.
White, D.R. and Burton, M.L. (1988) 'Causes of polygyny: Ecology, economy, kinship and warfare', *American Anthropologist* 90: 871–87.

Further reading

Bossen, L. (1989) 'Women and economic institutions', in S. Plattner (ed.) *Economic Anthropology*, Stanford, CA, pp. 318–50.
Hawkes, K.(1996) 'Foraging differences between men and women: Behavioral ecology of the sexual division of labour', in S. Shennan and J. Steele (eds) *Power, Sex and Tradition: The Archaeology of Human Ancestry*, London, pp. 283–305.

SEE ALSO: gender, sociology of; women

DIVORCE

Divorce is the legal procedure by which marriage can be formally ended. Not all societies permit divorce but in the majority of Western countries, not only is divorce possible but also legal constraints and obstacles to divorce have been gradually reduced since the middle of the twentieth century. It is usually possible to divorce on the grounds of incompatibility, and it is no longer necessary to prove that a spouse has committed a matrimonial offence such as adultery or desertion. The fact that divorce is now easier to obtain has, however, led to a belief that divorce itself is easy. Moreover, the idea that couples divorce simply because they are incompatible masks the seriousness of problems that may exist within the institution of marriage. Such problems may include violence, economic deprivation and cruelty to children. It is a mistake to imagine that couples divorce for casual reasons, although the fact that people know that divorce is available may alter the way they deal with marital problems.

In the European Union (EU), Denmark and Finland had the highest rates of divorce in 2000 (2.7 divorces per 1,000 population) with the UK close behind (2.6 per 1,000). This was at a time when the EU average was 1.9 divorces per 1,000 population. The USA has the highest divorce rate of all developed societies and in 1998 it was at 4.3 divorces per 1,000 population, but interestingly this figure was down from 4.7 in 1990, and the rate of increase in divorce has also been slowing in European countries like the UK. This has led commentators to suggest that rather than an inevitable and inexorable rise in divorce, a plateau effect may be occurring.

It has become clear that divorce is associated with poverty because, at the very least, the same resources that once went into one household have to be shared across two. This problem is exacerbated if the main wage earner repartners and has additional children. Evidence suggests that the resulting hardship is most acutely felt by divorced mothers who still typically retain the care of children. This is because they may not be able to return to the labour market or because they can do so only on a part-time basis, often returning to lower-status, more poorly paid jobs than those they held before their marriage. Many lone mothers tend to become reliant on state support for a period of time, or on inadequate wages. In addition, in countries where health care is based on private insurance, divorced women often find they lose access to decent health care provision because it is typically attached to a husband's employment and/or record of contributions. Divorced wives may also lose entitlement to their husbands' occupational pension schemes and so, later in life, they are forced to become reliant on low state provisions or their own partial contributions. Divorce therefore 'stores up' long-term poverty for many women if they have left the labour market to care for children and if they do not remarry (Glendinning 1992; Maclean 1991).

Although the economic consequences of divorce remain important, the focus of recent policy has switched to the equally important question of which parent the children should live with, and how often a child should see the 'non-residential' parent. The welfare of children is the main priority of most divorce legislation in Western democracies, but ideas about how best to meet their welfare needs have changed over time and are open to constant redefinition. It is perhaps correct to suggest that in the 1960s and 1970s it was assumed that children's welfare was best served by continuing to live with their primary carer, and the primary carer was almost inevitably the mother. This reflected the division of labour that was typical in families and which is still the norm. It was also expected that parents would remarry, typically with fathers starting new families elsewhere and having limited contact with their first families, and with mothers remarrying and introducing a stepfather into the household. It was usual to read in the sociological literature about 'reconstituted' families, meaning that, after a breakdown, remarriage would make the family whole again.

This situation has begun to change (although it is important to note that mothers are still predominantly the primary carers of children). Policy-makers initially paid special attention to children because of the concern that divorce caused children to become delinquent or antisocial, or to fail in school. These concerns are still real, but longitudinal research (especially in the USA) now suggests that divorce cannot be isolated as a cause of these social problems and that as divorce is 'normalized' children can manage the process if their parents can be supportive. More recently attention has turned to the situation of fathers after divorce. Fathers' rights movements have argued that past policy has ignored the importance of fathers to their children and that it should become the norm for parents to share their children after divorce. Legal systems in Europe, the USA, Australia and New Zealand are all starting to adjust in order to take account of this changed emphasis. It is seen as increasingly important for children's welfare that they retain 'real' relationships with fathers and even that they should live with them half the time.

These developments may lead to extensive changes to post-divorce family life. More children may find they have two homes and that they move regularly between families. This is likely to alter children's experiences of family life. It may well also indicate the demise of the reconstituted family, since step-parents are less likely to take the place of biological parents if children retain close ties with their natural parents. While this situation may seem to be an ideal solution to conflicts over who gets the children on divorce, little research has yet been carried out to check whether children thrive if they are shared in this way (Smart *et al.* 2001).

CAROL SMART
UNIVERSITY OF LEEDS

References

Glendinning, C. (1992) *The Costs of Informal Care*, London.
Maclean, M. (1991) *Surviving Divorce*, London.
Smart, C., Neale, B. and Wade, A. (2001) *The Changing Experience of Childhood: Families and Divorce*, London.

Further reading

Childhood: A Global Journal of Child Research (2003) Vol. 10(2), a Special Issue on New Perspectives on Childhood and Divorce.
Clark, D. (ed.) (1991) *Marriage, Domestic Life and Social Change*, London.
Gibson, C. (1993) *Dissolving Wedlock*, London.
Maclean, M. and Eekelaar, J. (1997) *The Parental Obligation*, Oxford.

SEE ALSO: domestic violence; marriage

DOMESTIC VIOLENCE

There have been three historical periods during which the problem of domestic violence has become a public issue and been responded to by reformers and agencies of the state – 1870s, 1910s and 1970s to present. At each of these junctures, the problem was publicly recognized, statistics were gathered, explanations were proffered and policy reforms were introduced. On each occasion, the move to public recognition and reform was led by a vigorous women's movement.

The issue has been variously described as wife-beating and, more recently, as violence against women, woman abuse or domestic violence. Research findings show that across time and across cultures violence in marital and marital-like relationships is overwhelmingly asymmetrical, with men using violence against their female partners. While much of this violence remains unreported, current findings from crime statistics, victim surveys and depth-interviews reveal that of women who have ever been married or cohabited, about one-quarter have experienced violence from a male partner at some time during their life. The nature of the violence ranges from slapping and shoving to domestic homicide. The most common form is punching and kicking, resulting in injuries such as bruising, broken bones and teeth, and cuts. Evidence further suggests that this physical violence is usually accompanied by other acts of aggression, coercion and intimidation, referred to as the 'constellation of abuse'. In addition, sexual violence may also occur.

Across societies, homicide in domestic settings is, for the most part, the killing of wives, uxoricide. This often occurs in the context of a history of sustained violence by the man against his female partner. Occasionally women kill husbands and the rate of these acts varies across societies, but this usually occurs in the context of a history of male violence directed at the woman. While death is an unusual outcome of domestic assaults, it nonetheless represents an important proportion of all the homicides of women, and in some societies uxoricide accounts for a considerable proportion of all homicides. The evidence about domestic violence tells a common story, of a problem that is serious and widespread in most societies and of violence perpetrated by males against females.

Various explanations have been proposed by social scientists to account for this violence: social and individual pathologies; interactional, situational and family dynamics; and institutional, cultural and ideological forces. In many of these perspectives, male power, domination and control are emphasized to varying degrees. Historical, anthropological and contemporary research consistently reveals that conflicts associated with the use of violence typically include male concerns about power and authority, jealousy and sexual possessiveness, and the domestic labour of women (e.g. food preparation and childcare). Men's individual backgrounds and learning experiences have been shown to be important.

Domestic violence is a problem that has simultaneously involved researchers, social activists and policy-makers. Activists have introduced the problem into the public agenda, secured its definition as a social problem and engaged the state in the process of policy-making. Researchers have added systematic knowledge and policy-makers have engaged in efforts to respond with measures intended to reduce or eliminate the problem and/or to provide support to its victims. The women's movement has been at the forefront in recognizing the problem internationally, providing the major response in the form of refuge or shelter for abused women and their children, and engaging the state in seeking reforms.

In addition to studying the nature of violence, social scientists have investigated the responses of the state and community. These include short-comings of traditional responses as well as the effectiveness of innovative policies and pro-grammes. In this respect, initial attention was focused primarily on housing and refuge provi-sion for abused women and criminal justice responses to violent men and the women they victimized. Evidence has shown that housing and shelter provide important sanctuaries for women and children but that traditional justice responses have not usually been effective in reducing violence or supporting victims. There is now a climate of change in law and law enforcement in some countries and research suggests that legal innovations can be effective. Social and health-care services show a similar history of ineffective responses followed by innovations, public policy and academic research.

Within the social sciences, the disciplines of sociology, criminology and psychology have to date provided the greatest amount of research and scholarship. Anthropology, evolutionary psy-chology, medicine and nursing also study the problem and offer additional explanations and evidence.

RUSSELL P. DOBASH
R. EMERSON DOBASH
UNIVERSITY OF MANCHESTER

Further reading

Browne, A., Williams, K. and Dutton, D. (1999) 'Homicide between intimate partners: A 20-year review', in M.D. Smith and M.A. Zahn (eds) *Homicide*, London, pp. 149–64.
Dobash, R.E. and Dobash, R.P. (1979) *Violence against Wives*, New York.
—— (1992) *Women, Violence and Social Change*, London.
—— (1998) (eds) *Rethinking Violence against Women*, London.
—— (2000) *Changing Violent Men*, London.

Hanmer, J. and Itzin, C. (eds) (2000) *Home Truths about Domestic Violence*, London.
Mirrlees-Black, C. (1999) *Domestic Violence: Findings from a New British Crime Survey Self-Completion Questionnaire*, London.
Mullender, A. (1996) *Rethinking Domestic Violence: The Social Work and Probation Response*, London.

SEE ALSO: childcare; divorce; social problems; violence

DREAMS

Despite their power to bewilder, frighten or amuse us, dreams remain an area of human behaviour little understood and typically ignored in models of cognition. As the methods of introspection were replaced with more self-con-sciously objective methods in the social sciences of the 1930s and 1940s, dream studies dropped out of the scientific literature. Dreams were not directly observable by an experimenter and sub-jects' dream reports were not reliable, being prey to the familiar problems of distortion due to delayed recall, if they were recalled at all. More often dreams are, of course, forgotten entirely, perhaps due to their prohibited character (Freud 1955 [1900]) or state-specific nature. Altogether, these problems seemed to put them beyond the realm of science.

The discovery that dreams take place primarily during a distinctive electrophysiological state of sleep, rapid eye movement (REM) sleep, which can be identified by objective criteria, led to a rebirth of interest in this phenomenon. When REM sleep episodes were timed for their duration and subjects woken to make reports before major editing or forgetting could take place, it was determined that subjects accurately matched the length of time they judged the dream narrative to be ongoing to the length of REM sleep that preceded the awakening. This close correlation of REM sleep and dream experience was the basis of the first series of reports describing the nature of dreaming: that it is a regular nightly, rather than occasional, phenomenon, and a high-frequency activity within each sleep period occur-ring at predictable intervals of approximately every 60 to 90 minutes in all humans throughout the life-span. REM sleep episodes and the dreams that accompany them lengthen progressively across the night, with the first episode being shortest, of approximately 10–12 minutes dura-tion, and the second and third episodes increasing to 15–20 minutes. Dreams at the end of the night may last as long as 45 minutes, although these may be experienced as several distinct stories due to momentary arousals interrupting sleep as the night ends. Dream reports can be retrieved from normal subjects on 50 per cent of the occasions when an awakening is made prior to the end of the first REM period. This rate of retrieval is increased to about 99 per cent when awakenings are made from the last REM period of the night. This increase in ability to recall appears to be related to an intensification across the night in the vividness of dream imagery, colours and emotions. The dream story itself in the last REM period is furthest from reality, containing more bizarre elements, and it is these properties, coupled with the increased likelihood of spontaneous arousals allowing waking review to take place, that heighten the chance of recall of the last dream. The distinctive properties of this dream also contribute to the reputation of dreams being 'crazy'. Reports from earlier dreams of the night, being more realistic, are often mistaken for waking thoughts.

Systematic content analysis studies have established that there are within-subject differences between dreams collected from home versus laboratory-monitored sleep periods, with home dreams being on the whole more affect-laden. This calls into question the representativeness of laboratory-collected dreams, particularly when subjects have not been adapted to the laboratory and the collections are carried out only for a limited period. More often, between-group comparisons are being made. Here clear differences have been reported between the home-recalled dreams of males and females, old and young, rich and poor, and between those of different ethnic groups living in the same geographical area. These differences reflect the waking sex-role characteristics, personality traits and sociocultural values and concerns of these groups. These findings raise the question of whether dreams make some unique contribution to the total psychic economy, or merely reflect, in their distinctive imagistic, condensed language and more primitive logic, the same mental content available during wakefulness by direct observation or interviewing techniques.

The question of uniqueness of dream data and function may well be answered differently for home- and laboratory-retrieved dreams. Home dreams are so highly selected, whether from dream diaries or those recalled in response to questionnaires, that they yield culturally common material much like the study of common myths. In the laboratory, where the database includes all of the dreams of a night in sequence and where experimental controls can be instituted to ensure uniform collection, the yield is more individual and varied. Despite this, the question of dream function has continued to be an area of controversy in modern sleep research since the mid-1950s. It has been approached empirically through studies of the effects of dream deprivation with little progress. Neither awakenings at REM onset to abort dreams nor nights of drug-induced REM sleep deprivation have been followed by reliable deficits in waking behaviour or the appearance of dream-like waking hallucinations.

It is possible that these studies have not been carried out long enough or that the dependent measures have not been appropriately designed. Other studies have proceeded by manipulating the pre-sleep state to heighten a specific drive, such as thirst or sex, or to introduce a problem requiring completion, such as a memory task and testing for the effects on dream content or subsequent waking behaviour. Again, effects have been small and rarely replicable. The laboratory setting and experimenter effects have been implicated in masking the very phenomenon the studies were designed to reveal, being more powerful stimuli than the experimental manipulation itself (Cartwright and Kaszniak 1978).

Seldom have theoretical models of dream function been tested. These have varied widely in the psychological processes implicated. Learning and memory have been prominent, as in the Hughlings Jackson (1932) view that sleep serves to sweep away unnecessary memories and connections from the day. This has been revised by Crick and Mitchison (1983) and stated as a theory that dream sleep is a period of reversed learning. However, the opposite view that dreaming has an information-handling, memory-consolidating function (Hennevin and Leconte 1971) is also common. Other writers stress an affective function. Greenberg and Pearlman (1974) and Dewan (1970) hold that, during dreaming, reprogramming of emotional experiences occurs, integrating new experiences and updating existing programmes. The modern psychoanalytically oriented view is an adaptation of Freud's conception of dreams as safe ways for unconscious drive discharge to take place (Fisher 1965; French and Fromm 1964). Beyond the issue of what psychological process is involved is the further problem posed by those who deny that studies of dream content can make any headway without taking into account their latent as well as their manifest content. This requires obtaining waking associations to each dream to plumb their function fully. Such a design would produce confounding effects on subsequent dreams.

Despite the theoretical morass and methodological problems rife in this field, systematic headway in understanding dreams has been made. One such advance came from a groundbreaking longitudinal collection of home and laboratory dreams of boys and girls by Foulkes (1982). These were analysed to explore the age- and sex-related changes in dream structure and content in terms of the cognitive and other aspects of the developmental stages of these children. Another advance came in the area of methodology with the development of standardized content analysis systems (Hall and Van de Castle 1966) and rating scales (Winget and Kramer 1979). Another improvement in design combines the advantages of the methods of the laboratory with the reality of a field study by predicting dream-content differences in the laboratory-retrieved dreams among groups of persons differing in response to a major affect-inducing life event. For example, Cartwright (1991) has shown that those who dream directly of the emotionally disturbing person (the former spouse in a divorcing sample) more often made a good waking adjustment to the change in marital status.

Another new thrust came from the development of home monitoring equipment for the collection of dreams that avoids the problems associated with the invasion of the dreamer's privacy by the laboratory technician and the change to an unfamiliar environment (Mamelak and Hobson 1989; Lloyd and Cartwright 1995). This is proving useful in tracking images from presleep experience into sleep onset to trace the origins of dreams.

The study of dreams is ready to move beyond the descriptive. Many factors have been amassed about this distinctive mental activity, without any clear understanding of its basic nature. Many points of view on dream function still compete (see Moffitt *et al.* 1993). The hypothesis that dreaming is involved in organizing new experience into long-term memory and regulating emo-

tion are both the focus of current research. How is a dream put together into a dramatic format without the contribution of any voluntary intent of the dreamer? How are the new perceptions formed that often express in such highly economical terms a coming together of old memories and current waking experiences? Do dreams have effects despite the fact that they are forgotten? What do these processes tell us about how the mind works? Dreams are a difficult challenge. They deserve our best response.

ROSALIND D. CARTWRIGHT
RUSH-PRESBYTERIAN-ST LUKE'S
MEDICAL CENTER, CHICAGO

References

Cartwright, R. (1991) 'Dreams that work', *Dreaming* 1.

Cartwright, R. and Kaszniak, A. (1978) 'The social psychology of dream reporting', in A. Arkin, Antrobus, J.S. and Ellman, S.J. (eds) *The Mind in Sleep*, Hillsdale, NJ.

Crick, F. and Mitchison, G. (1983) 'The function of dream sleep', *Nature* 304.

Dewan, E. (1970) 'The programming "P" hypotheses for REM sleep', in E. Hartmann (ed.) *Sleep and Dreaming*, Boston, MA.

Fisher, C. (1965) 'Psychoanalytic implications of recent research on sleep and dreaming. II. Implications of psychoanalytic theory', *Journal of American Psychoanalytical Association* 13.

Foulkes, D. (1982) *Children's Dreams*, New York.

French, T. and Fromm, E. (1964) *Dream Interpretation: A New Approach*, New York.

Freud, S. (1955 [1900]) *The Interpretation of Dreams, Standard Edition of the Complete Psychological Works of Sigmund Freud*, ed. J. Strachey, Vols 4 and 5, London.

Greenberg, R. and Pearlman, C. (1974) 'Cutting the REM nerve: An approach to the adaptive role of REM sleep', *Perspectives in Biology and Medicine* 17 (4): 513–21.

Hall, C. and Van de Castle, R. (1966) *The Content Analysis of Dreams*, New York.

Hennevin, E. and Leconte, P. (1971) 'La fonction du sommeil paradoxal: faits et hypothèses', *L'Ann. Psychologique* 2.

Jackson, J.H. (1932) *Selected Writings of John Hughlings Jackson*, ed. J. Taylor, London.

Lloyd, S. and Cartwright, R. (1995) 'The collection of home and laboratory dreams by means of an instrumental response technique', *Dreaming* 5: 63–73.

Mamelak, A. and Hobson, J.A. (1989) 'Nightcap home-based sleep monitoring system', *Sleep* 12: 157–66.

Moffitt, A., Kramer, M. and Hoffman, R. (1993) *The Functions of Dreaming*, New York.

Winget, C. and Kramer, M. (1979) *Dimensions of Dreams*, Gainesville, FL.

Further reading

Cartwright, R. and Lamberg, L. (2000) *Crisis Dreaming*, San Jose, CA.

Domhoff, W. (2003) *The Scientific Study of Dreams*, Washington, DC.

Pivik, T. (2000) 'Psychobiology and dreaming', in M. Kryger, T. Roth and W. Dement (eds) *Principles and Practice of Sleep Medicine*, 3rd edn, Philadelphia, pp. 463–519.

Solms, M. (1997) *The Neuropsychology of Dreams*, Hillsdale, NJ.

SEE ALSO: fantasy; Freud; sleep; unconscious

DRUG USE

The concept 'drug' is both socially constructed and concretely real. Drugs are physical entities with fixed properties and objective, measurable effects. However, it is also the case that the definition of a drug depends on the perspective of the definer. Certain definitions are relevant only within specific social contexts. Put another way, the physical properties and effects of specific substances may or may not be relevant, depending on the observer's definitional and conceptual framework.

Of all definitions of drugs, the one most widely accepted in the social sciences is substances that are *psychoactive*. That is to say, they influence the mind in significant ways. Among other things, drugs have an impact on mood, emotion, feeling, perception and thinking processes. This definition excludes substances that are 'drugs' within a medical context, such as penicillin and antibiotics, but which are not psychoactive. On the other hand, it includes substances that strongly influence the mind but which are legally obtainable and, as a result, may not be widely regarded as drugs by the general public, such as alcohol and tobacco cigarettes.

The ingestion of mind-altering substances is practised in virtually every society, and everywhere a significant proportion of the population take at least one drug for psychoactive purposes. This has been true for a significant stretch of human history. Fermentation is one of the earliest of human discoveries, predating even the fashioning of metals. Humans have been ingesting alcoholic beverages for more than 10,000 years. Strands of the marijuana plant have been found by archaeologists embedded in Chinese pottery in sites estimated to date back some ten millennia. Dozens of plants containing chemicals that influence the workings of the mind have been smoked, chewed or sniffed by people all over the world: coca leaves, the opium poppy, marijuana, the psilocybin (or 'magic' mushroom), *Amanita muscaria*, the peyote cactus, quat leaves, nutmeg, coffee beans, the yagé vine and tea leaves. During the past century or so, hundreds of thousands of psychoactive chemicals have been discovered, isolated or synthesized by scientists, physicians or technicians. Thousands have been marketed for medicinal purposes.

According to the journal, *Pharmacy Times*, over 3 billion prescriptions for pharmaceutical drugs were written each year during the twenty-first century in the USA alone, roughly one in six or seven of which are psychoactive. In the USA, in 2001, over eight out of ten of the population aged 12 and older drank alcohol one or more times in their lives; two-thirds had done so during the previous year; and just under half during the past month. One-quarter of all Americans are current smokers of tobacco cigarettes. One-third have at least tried marijuana, 9 per cent had used it in the past year, and 5 per cent in the past month (SAMHSA 2002). Systematic studies conducted in Australia, Canada, the UK and the Netherlands indicate comparable levels of psychoactive drug use (Australian Institute of Health and Welfare 2002; Nolin 2002; Ramsay *et al.* 2001; Abraham *et al.* 1999). Each year, the United Nations issues its report, *Global Illicit Drug Trends*, and the European Union publishes annual reports on use in its member states, which all indicate extremely high levels of drug consumption. Drug-taking is clearly a widespread and extremely common activity.

When psychoactive chemicals are ingested, they are generally being used 'in a culturally approved manner' (Edgerton 1976), with little or no negative impact on the user or on society. However, drugs are also often taken in a culturally unacceptable or disapproved fashion. A proscribed drug may be taken instead of an approved one, or a drug may be taken too frequently, or in the wrong circumstances, for the wrong reasons, or with undesirable consequences. The use, possession or sale of certain drugs, taking drugs in certain contexts, or the ingestion of drugs for disapproved motives, have been regarded as crimes in nearly all modern states.

While the possession and sale of certain psychoactive substances have been criminalized in societies all over the world, exactly how the government deals with drug offenders varies enormously. In the USA, law enforcement – that is, arrest and incarceration (the 'supply side' strategy) – is the dominant drug policy. In contrast, in Western Europe, Canada and Australia, treatment (or the 'demand side' strategy) is becoming, increasingly, the dominant drug policy. In the latter countries, where drug possession and sale are still *de jure* illegal, the problems caused by intemperate drug consumption is handled as a medical rather than a criminal matter. This approach has come to be referred to as the 'harm reduction' policy.

It must be emphasized that drug use is not a unitary phenomenon. There exist, to begin with, different types of drugs, classified according to their action. Drugs are commonly categorized on the basis of their impact on the central nervous system (the CNS), that is, the brain and the spinal column.

Some drugs speed up signals passing through the CNS; pharmacologists refer to them as stimulants. Stimulants include cocaine (both in powder and 'crack' form), the amphetamines, Ritalin (methylfenidate) and caffeine (which is an extremely weak stimulant). Nicotine, the principal psychoactive ingredient in tobacco cigarettes, also has a stimulating effect, but some of its other effects are sufficiently distinct as to merit a separate classification.

Other drugs retard, slow down or 'depress' signals passing through the CNS, and are referred to as depressants. The two major types of depressants include narcotics or narcotic analgesics (such as opium, morphine, heroin, codeine, fentanyl, oxycodone and methadone), which dull the sensation of pain; and sedatives or 'general depressants' (such as alcohol, barbiturates, methaqualone, Xanax and Valium), which are anti-anxiety agents. Rohypnol (flunitrazepam), a sedative, and GHB, a strong general depressant, are increasingly being used among youth for recreational purposes. (Both are frequently referred to as 'date rape' drugs because of their soporific properties.)

A wide and miscellaneous range of psychoactive substances may be used to treat mental disorder or mental illness. The two major types are the antipsychotics (or phenothiazines, such as Thorazine, Stelazine and Mellaril), which are administered to schizophrenics, and antidepressants (or the 'mood elevators' such as Prozac,

Elavil and Zoloft), which are administered to the clinically depressed. Antipsychotics and antidepressants are almost never used recreationally, that is, for the purpose of getting 'high'.

Hallucinogens or 'psychedelics', such as LSD, mescaline and psilocybin, are capable of producing dramatic perceptual changes (although they very rarely produce genuine hallucinations).

Three widely used recreational drugs cannot be classified according to the usual typologies. The illicit drugs most widely used to produce intoxication or to achieve a 'high' are the cannabis products, marijuana and hashish. Roughly half of all episodes of illicit drug use worldwide are with cannabis. Ecstasy or MDMA (a chemical analogue of amphetamine) produces a 'noetic' action – the feeling that familiar phenomena are new. In addition, many users describe the drug's effects as empathogenic, that is, it stimulates the feeling of closeness, intimacy and compassion with their companions. And lastly, PCP, once used to tranquillize animals and sometimes classified as a hallucinogen, together with ketamine, form a category that are referred to as 'disassociative anesthetics', that is, they generate a sense in the user of being removed from reality, in addition to numbing a variety of sensations, including pleasure and pain.

Even the same psychoactive substance may be taken for different reasons by different individuals (or by the same person at different times). Attaining religious or mystical insight or ecstasy, healing the mind or body, suppressing fatigue, hunger or anxiety, enhancing pleasure, facilitating interpersonal intimacy, following the dictates of a particular group or social circle, and establishing an identity as a certain kind of person include some of the more commonly expressed motives for psychoactive drug use. A drug's psychoactive properties may be central to the user's motive for taking it, or they may be incidental. The intoxication or 'high' may be pursued as an end in itself, or the drug may be taken for instrumental purposes, that is, to attain a specific and separate goal, such as alleviating pain. Of the many varieties of drug use, perhaps the three most common and important are: (1) legal recreational use; (2) illegal recreational use; and (3) legal instrumental use, mainly medical. Each of these varieties attracts different users and has different consequences. It is a fallacy to assume that the pharmacological properties of a drug dictate the consequences of its use: factors such as the motives of the user, the social context in which use is embedded, the social norms surrounding use, and methods of use or 'route of administration' all play a role in influencing the impact of the use of psychoactive substances.

Legal recreational use

Legal recreational use refers to the use for pleasurable purposes of a psychoactive drug whose possession and sale are not against the law. In Western nations, this refers to alcohol and tobacco consumption. In the USA, there has been an effort to redefine alcohol as a drug in the educational curricula, but much of the public does not see alcohol as a 'drug'. However, in the pharmacological sense – that is, in terms of its effects – alcohol is psychoactive. It is used for the purpose of altering the user's consciousness, it can produce a physical dependence or 'addiction', in heavy, long-term, chronic users, and it causes or is associated with a wide range of medical maladies. Many estimates place the proportion of alcoholics at roughly one drinker in ten, and argue that alcoholism is the West's most serious drug problem. Smoking tobacco cigarettes containing nicotine produces a 'low-key high', generates an addiction (or a pattern of continued use in spite of efforts to quit), and kills more users than all other drugs combined. With respect to its effects, tobacco is unquestionably a drug, albeit a legal one (Horgan et al. 2001).

Illegal recreational use

In the generation following the early 1960s, Western Europe and North America experienced an unprecedented rise in the recreational use of illegal psychoactive drugs. The most widely used of these have been the cannabis products, marijuana and hashish. In a number of Western countries, there are as many episodes of cannabis use as episodes of use for all other illegal drugs combined. Of all illegal drugs, cannabis is the one that users are most likely to consume regularly, and least likely to abandon or use only episodically. As a general rule, however, legal drugs such as alcohol and cigarettes have far higher 'continuance rates' than is the case for illegal drugs, marijuana included (Sandwijk et al. 1991). Hallucinogens, such as LSD, tend to be taken on an experimental or episodic basis, and are extremely rarely taken heavily or abusively.

As with alcohol, the vast majority of cannabis users take the drug on a moderate, controlled fashion, but some illegal drugs do attract heavy, chronic, abusive users. In the USA, the number of heroin addicts has been estimated at a half a million. In the past decade the number of registered addicts in the UK has increased tenfold. It has been estimated that there are as many as several million daily cocaine users in the USA. At the same time, the vast majority of one-time or experimental users of all illegal substances either abandon the drug after a few trials or use it moderately, in a controlled fashion, on a once-in-a-while basis (Zinberg 1984).

Legal instrumental use

The *medical use* of psychoactive drugs in the Western world has undergone dramatic changes over the course of the twentieth century. Throughout the nineteenth century, preparations containing psychoactive substances such as morphine and cocaine were freely available and were widely used to cure or treat medical and psychiatric ailments. Legal controls on the sale of these nostrums, or even on their basic ingredients, were practically non-existent (Berridge and Edwards 1998 [1986]; Musto 1999). In contrast, the twentieth century has witnessed an avalanche of legal controls on psychoactive substances for medical purposes. In Western countries, the primary mode of dispensing drugs for medical and psychiatric purposes is via medical prescription.

In the 1950s, it was discovered that the phenothiazine drugs suppress the symptoms of mental disorder, especially schizophrenia. Since that time, the administration of antipsychotic drugs, such as Thorazine, Stelazine and Mellaril, to mental patients has been increasing dramatically. There were just under 560,000 resident patients in publicly funded mental hospitals in the USA in 1955; today, there are roughly 75,000. Some three-quarters of all individuals diagnosed as mentally disordered are taking phenothiazine drugs on an outpatient basis. While the number of admissions to mental hospitals more than doubled since the 1950s, the length of stay of mental patients then was 6 to 8 months while today it is 2 weeks. Mentally disordered individuals who once would have been confined to mental institutions are now outpatients.

In the USA, there was an immense flood of calls during the 1980s and 1990s for the full legalization or decriminalization of all currently illegal psychoactive substances, including cocaine and heroin. The pro-legalization argument is based on three assumptions: one, that use and abuse will not increase when legal controls are removed; two, that the currently illegal drugs are not as harmful as those that are legal, nor as harmful as legislators and the public believe; and, three, that criminalization is both ineffective and counter-productive (Nadelmann 1989). Calls for legalization have receded since the late 1990s. Many of those formerly in favour of full legalization now endorse a programme that has come to be referred to as 'harm reduction' (Nadelmann 1998).

The vast majority of the American public is strongly opposed to full legalization, and legislators, even were they convinced of the proposal's feasibility, would be voted out of office were they to support it. Moreover, the assumption that legalization would produce no increase in use or abuse is not entirely convincing, since: (1) There is a strong correlation between cost and use. Criminalization keeps the cost of illegal drugs high, which depresses consumption. (2) Current abusers and heavy users confirm that they would use substantially more were their substances of choice readily available. (3) Where psychoactive substances are or were readily available, for instance in the case of physicians and other medical workers, or among military personnel during the US War in Vietnam, use has been almost invariably high. (4) During the period of national alcohol Prohibition in the USA, the consumption of alcohol declined by more than half (Lender and Martin 1987). (5) Where risk-taking activities remain beyond the reach of the law, a certain proportion of individuals will engage in them (motorcyclists refusing to wear helmets, motorists not wearing seat belts). When those same activities are legally controlled, a much lower proportion continue to take these risks. (6) Continuance rates for legal drugs tend to be strikingly higher than they are for illegal drugs. (7) In the USA, legislation outlawing the sale of alcoholic beverages to persons under the age of 21 has been accompanied by a significant decline in the number of alcohol-related automobile fatalities in this age group.

While prohibition keeps consumption below what it would be in the absence of anti-drug laws (this is referred to as 'relative deterrence'), this does not mean that drug use could be drastically reduced or eliminated by an escalation in the harshness of penalties. After all, illicit drug use remains high in spite of prohibition. Moreover, prohibition has its costs too. In fact, lower drug use may be bought at a very high price. Criminalization has almost certainly produced higher rates of drug-related crime, disease and violence than would be the case under almost any conceivable system of drug legalization. In other words, as measured by the criterion of containment, legal controls may have been successful. However, when their indirect effects or unanticipated consequences are taken into account, legal controls may be judged to have been a serious failure.

Notwithstanding public opposition to full drug legalization, support does exist for more humane drug policies. Public opinion polls indicate that, even in the USA, a majority or near-majority of voters support reform on issues such as the legalization of marijuana as medicine; not dealing with marijuana users as criminals; and prioritizing treatment over law enforcement for addicts. There may therefore be a 'third way', located somewhere between the current punitive policy and full legalization, which would gain public support and prove most effective. In one form or another, harm reduction strategies are in place in Canada, Australia, the UK, the Netherlands, Switzerland and indeed in much of Western Europe. The results are generally positive. Such strategies include: distinguishing between 'hard' (heroin, cocaine and amphetamines) and 'soft' (mainly cannabis products) drugs; legalizing marijuana as medicine; arresting hard drug dealers but treating addicts and abusers; launching or expanding needle exchange and condom distribution programmes; expanding methadone maintenance; experimenting with heroin maintenance. In addition, strategies to reduce alcohol and tobacco consumption (for instance increasing taxes, eliminating advertising, enforcing the laws against sale to minors, eliminating vending machines, enforcing drunk driving laws) could lower the death rate from drug consumption. Some form of harm reduction might be explored for the USA.

ERICH GOODE
UNIVERSITY OF MARYLAND

References

Abraham, M., Cohen, P.D.A., van Til, R.-J. and deWinter, M.A.L. (1999) *Licit and Illicit Drug Use in the Netherlands, 1999*, Amsterdam.

Australian Institute of Health and Welfare (2002) *2001 National Drug Strategy Household Survey*, Canberra.

Berridge, V. and Edwards, G. (1998 [1986]) *Opium and the People: Opiate Use in Nineteenth-Century England*, 2nd edn, New Haven, CT.

Edgerton, R.B. (1976) *Deviance: A Cross-Cultural Perspective*, Menlo Park, CA.

Horgan, C., Skwara, K.C. and Strickler, G. (2001) *Substance Abuse: The Nation's Number One Health Problem*, Princeton, NJ.

Lender, M.E. and Martin, J.K. (1987) *Drinking in America: A History*, rev. and exp. edn, New York.

Musto, D.F. (1999) *The American Disease: Origins of Narcotic Control*, 3rd edn, New York.

Nadelmann, E.A. (1989) 'Drug prohibition in the United States', *Science* 245.

—— (1998) 'Commonsense drug policy', *Foreign Affairs* 77.

Nolin, P.C. (2002) *Cannabis: Our Position for a Canadian Public Policy*, Ottawa.

Ramsay, M., Baker, P., Goulden, C., Sharp, C. and Sondhi, A. (2001) *Drug Misuse Declared in 2000: Results from the British Crime Survey*, London.

Sandwijk, J.P., Cohen, P.D.A. and Musterd, S. (1991) *Licit and Illicit Drug Use in Amsterdam*, Amsterdam.

Substance Abuse and Mental Health Services Administration (SAMHSA) (2002) *Results from the 2001 National Household Survey on Drug Abuse*, Rockville, MD.

Zinberg, N.E. (1984) *Drugs, Set, and Setting: The Basis for Controlled Intoxicant Use*, New Haven, CT.

Further reading

DuPont, R.L. (1997) *The Selfish Brain: Learning from Addiction*, Center City, MN.

Goode, E. (2005) *Drugs in American Society*, 6th edn, New York.

Inciardi, J.A. (ed.) (1999) *The Drug Legalization Debate*, Thousand Oaks, CA.

MacCoun, R.J. and Reuter, P. (2001) *Drug War Heresies: Learning from Other Vices, Times, and Places*, Cambridge, UK, and New York.

Musto, D.F. and Korsmeyer, P. (2002) *The Quest for Drug Control: Politics and Federal Policy in a Period of Increasing Substance Abuse, 1963–1981*, New Haven, CT.

Walton, S. (2001) *Out of It: A Cultural History of Intoxication*, London.

SEE ALSO: alcoholism and alcohol abuse; DSM-IV; social problems

DSM-IV

DSM-IV is the fourth edition of the American Psychiatric Association's Diagnostic and Statistical Manual of Mental Disorders. Originally published in 1994, portions were revised in 2001 and published as DSM-IV-TR (Text Revision). The DSM-IV is a categorical classification that groups mental disorders based on primarily phenomenological features which are organized into specifically defined sets of criteria. Although developed primarily for its utility in clinical practice, the DSM-IV is also used in training, research and medical record keeping.

Attempts to classify mental illness date back thousands of years (e.g. Egyptian and Sumerian references to senile dementia, melancholia and hysteria date back to 3000 BCE), and a variety of approaches has been applied. While some systems were based on a large number of narrowly defined conditions, others were established on more inclusive, broad conceptualizations. Classification systems have also differed in the extent to which classification of disorders should be based on aetiology, the course of the illness or the descriptive presentation of symptom patterns. In the later half of the nineteenth century, Emil Kraepelin developed a classification that combined aspects of various systems: he studied groups of patients whose disorders had the same course, in order to determine their shared clinical symptomotology. Kraepelin's (1917) general methodology has been largely retained in the development of the current DSM system.

Other classification systems were developed in the USA prior to the publication of the DSM-I in 1952; however, the DSM system was the first to emphasize clinical utility. DSM-I was a variant of the World Health Organization's (1948) *International Classification of Diseases, Injuries, and Causes of Death*, 6th edn (later editions are entitled *International Classification of Disease (ICD)*), which was the first edition of the ICD to include a section on mental disorders. The relationship with the ICD system has continued; revisions were closely timed and recent efforts have ensured a greater compatibility between the two systems. The DSM-III (published in 1980) represented a major shift in the approach to psychiatric diagnosis and for the first time included explicit criteria (rather than glossary definitions), multiaxial assessment and a descriptive approach that was neutral with regard to aetiology. The major innovation of the DSM-IV lies in its documentation and explicit reliance on empirical data in the revision process, the inclusion of over one thousand health and mental professionals in the development of the manual, expanded text sections describing symptom presentations that may vary according to age, gender and cultural differences, and the inclusion of more specifiers, subtypes and course modifiers. A three-step process was utilized in the development of the DSM-IV: comprehensive literature reviews, data reanalyses and focused field trials.

The DSM has four principal components: (1) the classification itself (the organized list of categories and coding procedures), (2) specific criteria for defining each category, (3) explanatory text, and (4) a series of appendices providing additional information relevant to researchers, clinicians and administrators. The DSM-IV disorders are grouped into sixteen major diagnostic classes, beginning with mental disorders Usually First Diagnosed in Infancy, Childhood, or Adolescence. Although almost all disorders in the DSM are neutral in regard to aetiology, the next three sections of the manual – Delirium, Dementia, Amnestic, and Other Cognitive Disorders; Mental Disorders Due to a General Medical Condition; and Substance-Related Disorders – are by definition based on aetiology and are listed before the remaining disorders because of their importance in differential diagnosis. These disorders were formerly referred to as Organic Disorders. The term organic has been eliminated from the DSM because of the erroneous implication that all other disorders in the system have no organic basis. The remaining disorders (except for Adjustment Disorders, which vary in their presentation, but are reactions to stressful events) are grouped based on common presenting symptoms. They are Schizophrenia and Other Psychotic Disorders; Mood Disorders; Anxiety Disorders; Somatoform Disorders; Factitious Disorders; Dissociative Disorders; Sexual and Gender Identity Disorders; Eating Disorders; Sleep Disorders; Impulse-Control Disorders Not Elsewhere Classified; Adjustment Disorders; and Personality Disorders. An additional section describes conditions that may be a focus of clinical attention (e.g. bereavement, relational problems) but which are not considered mental disorders.

DSM-IV utilizes multiaxial assessment to ensure a comprehensive assessment of the individual's general health, environmental/psychosocial context and functional level. Axis I includes all mental disorders except Mental Retardation and the Personality Disorders, which are listed on

Axis II. General Medical Conditions (i.e. any condition listed in the ICD outside of the mental disorders section) are listed on Axis III. Psychosocial and environmental stressors (e.g. occupational or economic problems) are listed on Axis IV, while Axis V is used to record a Global Assessment of Functioning score (i.e. the clinician's assessment of the individual's level of occupational, social and psychosocial functioning; this information is helpful in planning a treatment regimen and in predicting likely treatment outcome).

In addition to the criteria set for each disorder, explanatory text describes diagnostic features (e.g. examples of criteria); subtypes and specifiers; recording procedures; commonly associated features and disorders; specific culture, age and gender features; prevalence rates; typical lifetime pattern and evolution of the disorder; familial pattern; and differential diagnosis pointers. Work groups conducted systematic literature reviews to update the explanatory text for DSM-IV-TR. In addition, several errors were corrected and a number of ambiguities were clarified. In order to avoid disruption of clinical communication or research efforts, no revisions were made in the structure of the classification or the specific criteria for each disorder.

Numeric codes for each disorder or condition listed in the manual are provided, and are derived from those used in the ICD, 9th edn, Clinical Modification (ICD-9CM), the official coding system in the USA (US Government Department of Health and Human Services 1979). Since the ICD-9CM is updated regularly, the DSM-IV-TR also included several coding modifications. An appendix lists all disorders with the *International Statistical Classification of Diseases and Related Health Problems*, 10th edn (ICD-10), codes as well (World Health Organization 1992). The ICD-10 is used in most other countries. Thus, the complete compatibility of DSM-IV with both systems facilitates medical record keeping and statistical comparison both in the USA and internationally.

Several caveats in the use of the DSM-IV are noted. First, although the inclusion of specific criteria sets aids in the diagnosis of mental disorders, the criteria are provided as guidelines and require specialized clinical training in their application. Also, additional information beyond that needed to make a diagnosis is necessary in the formulation of an appropriate treatment plan. Special consideration should be given when the clinician is unfamiliar with the cultural reference of the individual that he or she is evaluating; a clinician may mistake thoughts or actions that are an accepted and typical part of that person's culture as symptoms of a mental disorder.

The manual is intended to be comprehensive and reflect current knowledge but may not include all conditions for which individuals seek treatment, or for which research may be appropriate. Inclusion in the manual of a mental disorder does not imply that the condition meets legal or other non-medical criteria for what constitutes disability, mental disease or a mental disorder. Clinical diagnosis in itself does not necessarily have a one-to-one relationship with issues of control, competence, criminal responsibility, disability or impairment or treatment.

HAROLD ALAN PINCUS
UNIVERSITY OF PITTSBURGH
AND RAND CORPORATION

References

American Psychiatric Association (1952) *Diagnostic and Statistical Manual of Mental Disorders*, 1st edn, Washington, DC.
—— (1968) *Diagnostic and Statistical Manual of Mental Disorders*, 2nd edn, Washington, DC.
—— (1980) *Diagnostic and Statistical Manual of Mental Disorders*, 3rd edn, Washington, DC.
—— (1994) *Diagnostic and Statistical Manual of Mental Disorders*, 4th edn, Washington, DC.
Diagnostic and Statistical Manual of Mental Disorders, 4th edn: Text Revision, DSM-IV-TR. American Psychiatric Association, Inc., Washington, DC, 2000.
Kraepelin, E. (1917) *Lectures on Clinical Psychiatry*, 3rd edn, New York.
US Government Department of Health and Human Services (1979) *International Classification of Diseases*, 9th edn, Clinical Modification, Washington, DC.
World Health Organization (1948) *International Classification of Diseases, Injuries, and Causes of Death*, 6th edn, Geneva.
—— (1992) *International Statistical Classification of Diseases and Related Health Problems*, 10th edn, Geneva.

SEE ALSO: mental health; transcultural psychiatry

DURKHEIM, EMILE (1858–1917)

Emile Durkheim was the founding father of academic sociology in France and the most influential early theoretician of archaic or primitive societies. A Jew from northeast France, Durkheim followed the educational and ideological path of the positivist generation of great Republican academics. He was educated at the *Ecole Normale Supérieure*, taking a teacher's degree in philosophy and a doctorate (1893). After a short period as a *lycée* teacher, he spent a year in German universities studying social theory. On his return, he was appointed the first ever lecturer in 'social science and pedagogy' in a French university, at Bordeaux (1887). In 1902 he transferred to the Sorbonne, where he held a chair for the rest of his life.

Durkheim's seminal teaching and publications included *The Division of Labor in Society* (1933 [1893]), *The Rules of Sociological Method* (1938 [1894]), *Suicide* (1952 [1897]), and work on socialism, family organization, the scope and development of German social theories. He attracted a cluster of gifted young scholars – mostly philosophers but also historians, economists and jurists (including Mauss, Hubert, Simiand, Fauconnet, Richard and Bouglé) – with whom he founded the *Année sociologique* (1898). This was an essentially critical journal intended to cover the whole range of emerging social disciplines (social geography, demography, collective psychology, social and economic history, history of religion, ethnology and sociology proper). It was to become instrumental in developing and promoting a synthetic theory of social facts that overrode earlier disciplinary divisions.

Durkheim's later work included studies and lecture courses on the sociology of education, morality and moral science, pragmatism, family sociology, history of the social sciences, vital statistics and several other topics, but after the birth of the *Année* he was primarily concerned with the study of archaic societies, and especially with primitive religion and social organization. The problem of social cohesion in so-called polysegmentary societies that, according to Durkheim, were based on mechanical solidarity (as against the organic solidarity of modern societies, based on a division of labour) had been a major theme in his doctoral thesis (1893), but there it lacked any significant ethnological underpinning. Durkheim developed an intense interest in primitive society much later, after reading contemporary British 'religious anthropologists', above all Robertson Smith and Frazer. This resulted in a reorientation of his work towards the study of 'collective representations' and, more specifically, of religion, from 1896 onwards.

There were two sets of reasons, theoretical and methodological, for this shift. First, religion was considered to serve an essential social function, creating a strong community of beliefs and providing a basis for social cohesion. The sacred and the profane became the two essential categories in Durkheim's sociology, which ordered the system of social facts. Second, primitive religion, either because it was believed to be more simple and consequently easier to study, or because it appeared to be functionally interconnected with most other 'social facts' (like economy, law, technology and so on, which had gained a measure of functional autonomy in the course of later development), seemed to provide the key to a theory of social order. The religious system of archaic societies thus became a privileged topic of research for Durkheim and for some of the most gifted scholars of his cluster, notably Mauss, Hubert and Hertz. One out of four review articles published in the *Année* was dedicated to social anthropology, and primitive societies now supplied, for the first time in French intellectual history, a central topic in public philosophical debate, which soon engaged other leading academics, such as the philosophers Bergson and Lévy-Bruhl.

In his anthropological work, Durkheim never surmounted the basic ambiguity of his approach to 'primitives', who were regarded either as prototypes, or as exemplifying the simplest imaginable occurrences of observable social types, or both at the same time. Moreover, he was initially sceptical about the heuristic utility of ethnographic data, and believed that preference should be given to historical documents over ethnographic information. His attitude changed, however, especially with the publication of more professional ethnographies, like those by Spencer and Gillen (on the Australian aborigines), Boas (on the Kwakiutl Indians) and the Cambridge scholars of the expedition to Torres Straits. He discussed all these new studies in painstakingly detailed critical reviews. They also supplied the data for his own contributions to the contemporary international debate concerning archaic societies. These fall broadly under two thematic headings: social organization and belief systems (and various combinations of the two).

The essay on *Incest: The Nature and Origin of the Taboo* (1963 [1898]) obeyed to the letter his own prescription, 'Explain the social fact by other social facts.' Social institutions could not be explained by invoking instinctive behaviour. They must be accounted for purely in terms of social causes. Incest and exogamy derived from the nature of the elementary, that is, uterine, clan. Respect for the clan's totem manifested itself by a religious aversion to the blood of fellow clanspeople and, by extension, to sexual contact with the clan's women. The prohibition of incest was accompanied by prescriptions concerning interclan marriage. Some modern writers on kinship (for example Lévi-Strauss 1969 [1949]) recognize their debt to Durkheim, though they have submitted his theory to substantial criticism. Similarly, in his essays on totemism (1963 [1902]) and Australian kinship (1905a), Durkheim seemed clearly to anticipate much later structuralist approaches. He identified, beyond the social categories of kinship, truly logical categories that, he suggested, could be understood as 'mathematical problems' (Durkheim 1905a). He went further in the exploration of such logical categories in a famous study, written together with Mauss, *Primitive Classification* (1963 [1903]). This essay related ideas about space among some Australian and North American tribesmen to their social organizations. Durkheim and Mauss argued that men 'classified things because they were divided into clans'. The model of all classification (especially of spatial orientation) is the society, because it is the unique whole (or totality) to which everything is related, so that 'the classification of things reproduces the classification of men'. Primitive classifications generated the first concepts or categories, enabling men to unify their knowledge. They constituted the first 'philosophy of nature'. Durkheim and Mauss suggested that in these classifications could be discerned 'the origins of logical procedure which is the basis of scientific classifications'. Durkheim would systematize these intimations in his last great work, which focused on the social functions of religion proper.

The Elementary Forms of Religious Life (1915 [1912]) was the culmination of Durkheim's anthropological studies. His focus upon Australians (and to some extent on American Indians) was grounded on the methodologically essential (and still ambiguous) assumption that their clan system was the most 'elementary' observable. The elementary religion is that of totemic clans.

It contains the germ of all essential elements of religious thought and life.

Durkheim starts from the proposition that religious experience cannot be purely illusory and must refer to some reality. The reality underlying religious practice is society itself. Religion is 'above all a system of ideas by which individuals represent the society they belong to'. Moreover, 'metaphorical and symbolic as it may be, this representation is not unfaithful'. Certain types of 'collective effervescence' produce religious beliefs, or help to reconfirm beliefs and values of religious relevance. The type of religion is also determined by social structure. For example, the cult of the 'great god' corresponds to the synthesis of all totems and to the unification of the tribe.

Religion also helps to interpret or represent social realities by means of their projection in a special symbolic language. Thus, mythologies 'connect things in order to fix their internal relations, to classify and to systematize them'. They represent reality, as does science. The function of religion is ultimately social integration, which is effected by 'constantly producing and reproducing the soul of the collectivity and of individuals'. Symbolism is the very condition of social life, since it helps social communication to become communion, that is, 'the fusion of all particular sentiments into one common sentiment'.

Durkheim's religious anthropology has been severely criticized by field researchers, yet without ceasing to inspire scholars concerned with archaic religions. At the time, his sociology of religion had an immediate public appeal in consequence of the conflict then raging between the Church and the Republican State. The study of primitive religion allowed Durkheim to adopt a purely scientific posture, while offering a historical criticism and a sociological evaluation of contemporary religious institutions. (He once described the Catholic Church as a 'sociological monster' (1905b).)

Ethnographic evidence drawn from primitive societies also led to heuristic generalizations concerning the nature of social cohesion, its agents and conditions. Ethnology, moreover, lent itself more easily than other established disciplines (like history or geography) to Durkheimian theorizing, because it was an intellectually weak and institutionally marginal branch of study. Durkheim's theoretical anthropology, together with the work of his followers and debating partners (such as Lévy-Bruhl, Mauss, Hubert and Hertz), contributed decisively to the birth of French academic field anthropology between the two world wars. A later generation of French anthropologists, including Griaule, Métraux, Dumont and Lévi-Strauss, continued to exploit Durkheim's heritage, while critically re-evaluating it. As a consequence of its Durkheimian roots, French social anthropology never broke with the other social sciences, and retained a penchant for high-level generalization.

VICTOR KARADY
CENTRE NATIONAL DE LA
RECHERCHE SCIENTIFIQUE, PARIS

References

Durkheim, E. (1905a) 'Sur l'organisation matrimoniale des sociétés australiennes', *L'Année sociologique* 8.
—— (1905b) 'Conséquences religieuses de la séparation de l'église et de l'état', republished in E. Durkheim (1975) *Textes*, Paris.
—— (1915 [1912]) *The Elementary Forms of Religious Life*, London.
—— (1933 [1893]) *The Division of Labor in Society*, London.
—— (1938 [1894]) *The Rules of Sociological Method*, London.
—— (1952 [1897]) *Suicide*, London.
—— (1963 [1898]) *Incest: The Nature and Origin of the Taboo*, New York.
—— (1963 [1902]) 'Sur le totémisme', in *Année sociologique*, vol. v, 1900–1901, pp. 82–121.
Durkheim, E. and Mauss, M. *Primitive Classification*, Chicago.
Lévi-Strauss, C. (1969 [1949]) *The Elementary Structures of Kinship*, London.

Further reading

Alexander, J.C. (1988) *Durkheimian Sociology: Cultural Studies*, Cambridge, UK.
Besnard, P. (ed.) (1983) *The Sociological Domain: The Durkheimians and the Founding of French Sociology*, Cambridge, UK.
Besnard, P., Borlando, M. and Vogt, P. (eds) (1993) *Division de travail et lien social, la thèse de Durkheim un siècle après*, Paris.
Lukes, S. (1972) *Emile Durkheim: His Life and Work. A Historical and Critical Study*, London.
Pickering, W.F.S. (1984) *Durkheim's Sociology of Religion. Themes and Theories*, London.

DYSLEXIA

The general meaning of dyslexia is an impairment of the ability to read. Such impairments can arise in either of two ways: (1) There are cases of people who learned to read normally and reached a normal level of skill in reading, and who subsequently suffered some form of damage to the brain, a consequence of which was a reduction or even loss of their reading ability. This is often referred to as acquired dyslexia. (2) There are cases of people who fail to learn to read adequately in the first place and who never reach a normal level of skill in reading. The condition from which they suffer is known as developmental dyslexia. (An alternative terminology is to use the words *alexia* for acquired dyslexia, and *dyslexia* for developmental dyslexia.)

A parallel term is dysgraphia, the general meaning of which is an impairment of the ability to spell (in writing or aloud). This too can be an acquired or a developmental disorder, so that acquired and developmental dysgraphia are distinguished. The terms *agraphia* and *dysgraphia* are sometimes used to express this distinction.

Current progress in understanding the nature of acquired and developmental dyslexia and dysgraphia is being achieved largely through taking seriously the obvious fact that neither reading nor spelling is an indivisible mental activity: each relies on the correct functioning of a considerable number of independent cognitive subsystems. It follows that impairment of any one of the various cognitive subsystems involved in reading will produce some form of dyslexia. The particular form of dyslexia that will be seen will depend upon the particular cognitive subsystem, which is imperfect. Theories about which cognitive subsystems actually underlie reading and spelling thus permit one to offer interpretations of the different sets of symptoms manifest in different varieties of dyslexia and dysgraphia.

The idea that there are different forms of dyslexia that vary according to which particular reading subskill is impaired is now completely accepted in relation to acquired dyslexia. Although the evidence for the existence of different forms of developmental dyslexia is also very strong, this evidence is still sometimes ignored, particularly by purveyors of treatment packages for children with reading difficulties. If there are different forms of developmental dyslexia then it is likely that each form will require a different treatment, but many such packages provide a single method of treatment meant for all dyslexic children.

What is the cause of developmental dyslexia? This question is often raised but it is badly put, for two reasons. First, if there are different forms of developmental dyslexia there can't be a single cause for the disorder as a whole. Second, even for a particular form, there won't be a single cause but a chain of causes. Current evidence indicates that in some children an early link in this chain is genetic. In others, an early link will be inappropriate teaching methods. Such early links in the causal chain are *distal causes* (Jackson and Coltheart 2001) of developmental dyslexia. The final link in the causal chain – the *proximal cause* (Jackson and Coltheart 2001) of a child's poor reading – is the lack of competence in whichever reading subskill or subskills the child has been unable to acquire properly.

MAX COLTHEART
MACQUARIE UNIVERSITY, AUSTRALIA

Reference

Jackson, N. and Coltheart, M. (2001) *Routes to Reading Success and Failure*, Hove.

Further reading

Coltheart, M. (2001) 'The cognitive psychology of acquired dyslexia', in N.J. Smelser and P. Baltes (eds) *International Encyclopedia of the Social and Behavioral Sciences*, Kidlington.

Rapp, B., Folk, J.R. and Tainturier, M.-J. (2001) 'Word reading', in B. Rapp (ed.) *The Handbook of Cognitive Neuropsychology*, Hove.

Tainturier, M.-J. and Rapp, B. (2001) 'The spelling process', in B. Rapp (ed.) *The Handbook of Cognitive Neuropsychology*, Hove.

E

ECOLOGY

The concept of ecology finds its historical origins in Darwin's 'web of life', although such a non-Aristotelian view of the relationship between entities had been increasingly common since the eighteenth century. The term itself (*Ökologie*) we owe to Ernst Haeckel (1834–1919). By the opening years of the twentieth century, crude generalizations and theory had been translated into empirical studies, beginning with the natural history of plants.

Ecology might briefly be described as the study of relations between living species, associations of different species, and their physical and biotic surroundings through the exchange of calories, material and information. As such it has been centrally concerned with the concept of adaptation and with all properties having a direct and measurable effect on the demography, development, behaviour and spatio-temporal position of an organism. Within this framework, the main preoccupations of contemporary biological ecology have been with population dynamics, energy transfer, systems modelling, nutrient cycles, environmental degradation and conservation; and, since the 1970s, especially with the application of neo-Darwinian thinking to socioecology.

In the social sciences, the concept of ecology in the strict sense was introduced first into human geography, via biogeography, and many geographers came to redefine their subject in explicitly ecological terms. By the 1930s, the Chicago School of urban sociology was describing its conceptual orientation as 'human ecology'. Such an epithet was claimed to be justified on the grounds that analogies were drawn directly from the biological lexicon to explain spatial relationships, such as 'succession' for the movement of different class groups through urban areas. For a short time Chicago ecology was extremely influential, but it finally floundered on its own naïve analogies, crude empiricism and functionalist inductivism.

A number of the most fruitful applications of ecological approaches in the human and social sciences have been associated with anthropology. This has been so despite the dual intellectual dominance of Emile Durkheim (1858–1917) and Franz Boas (1858–1942) during the first three decades of the twentieth century, which had thoroughly crushed a nineteenth-century concern with environmental determinism. But although environmental issues were considered for the most part peripheral, and the environment accorded a constraining rather than a determinant role, there have been a number of important studies dealing with environmental interactions in this tradition. The general theoretical position is set out clearly in Daryll Forde's (1934) *Habitat, Economy and Society*.

The first really explicit use of the concept of ecology in anthropology is found in the work of Julian Steward during the 1930s (Steward and Murphy 1977). In Steward's theory the concept of cultural adaptation becomes paramount, and the key adaptive strategies of a particular culture are located in an infrastructural core of social institutions and technical arrangements directly concerned with food-getting activities. The recognition of distinctive adaptive strategies provided the basis for the delineation of cultural types, which Steward maintained evolved multilineally, rather than in the unilinear fashion subscribed to by many nineteenth-century thinkers. Steward's work has been very influential (and has found admirers in other disciplines), but his theory of cultural ecology entailed an interpretation of the concept of adaptation, together with a fundamental division between organic and superorganic levels of explanation, and between a core of key adaptive traits and a neutral periphery, which more recent writers (Ellen 1982) have been inclined to reject.

Advances within biological ecology linked to the notion of ecosystem, the empirical measurement of energy flow and the employment of the language of cybernetics and systems theory, led during the 1960s to a new formulation of ecological problems in the social sciences: in archaeology, geography and also in anthropology. The prominence given by Steward to the superorganic level of organization was passed over in favour of a view of human behaviour in many respects functionally equivalent to that of other animals. The description of ecological interactions became more sophisticated, involving computations of carrying-capacity, estimates of energy intake, output and efficiency for different groups and activities. There also developed an interest in the way in which cultural institutions might serve to regulate certain systems of which human populations are part. All of these trends are demonstrated in the seminal work of Rappaport (1968), undertaken on a Maring clan from Highland New Guinea.

Sustained interest in the theoretical problems of systems approaches, plus an increasing number of detailed empirical analyses of particular cases, has, however, bred scepticism concerning simplistic notions of adaptation and system, and the more extreme proposition that certain kinds of small-scale society have built-in mechanisms for maintaining environmental balance through homeostasis (Ellen 1982; Moran 1990). Recent work has emphasized much more how people actually cope with environmental hazards (Vayda and McCay 1975), employing the methods of economic individualism, including evolutionary (Winterhalder and Smith 1981) and event (Vayda 1983) ecology. In contrast, Ingold (1986a, 1986b) has explicitly attempted to disaggregate post-Stewardian general ecology, and speaks instead of humans being simultaneously involved in a field of ecological relations and a field of consciousness that cannot be reduced to adaptionist or other Darwinian explanations. He provides a persuasive anthropological critique of the organism–environment distinction through borrowings from ecological psychology and phenomenology. The emphasis on how different cultures represent and 'construct' their worlds, the questioning of the objective notion of system, new knowledge of the extent to which people modify their biological surroundings and the growing literature on historical ecology (Crumley 1993) have all led to the emergence of a critical questioning of what is meant by the terms 'nature' and 'environment' (e.g. Croll and Parkin 1992; Ellen and Fukui 1996).

The other major impact of ecological concepts in the social sciences has been in relation to political environmentalism, and to environment and development. Under the guidance of figures such as Garrett Hardin and Kenneth Boulding, economic thinking has been placed in a broader biospheric context, and the 'growth model' rejected both in relation to advanced industrial and developing societies. Practical concern for biodiversity loss, environmental degradation, the profligate use of finite resources, and the calculated advantages of 'alternative' technologies and 'indigenous' environmental knowledge (e.g. Richards 1985, 1986) have spawned theories of sustainable development (Oldfield and Alcorn 1991; Redclift 1989). In turn, concepts of sustainability and environmentalist rhetoric and practice have themselves been the subject of critical interrogation (e.g. Milton 1996).

R.F. ELLEN
UNIVERSITY OF KENT

References

Croll, E. and Parkin, D. (eds) (1992) *Bush Base: Forest Farm: Culture, Environment and Development*, London.

Crumley, C. (ed.) (1993) *Historical Ecology: Cultural Knowledge and Changing Landscapes*, Santa Fe.

Ellen, R.F. (1982) *Environment, Subsistence and System: The Ecology of Small-Scale Formations*, Cambridge, UK (new edn 2002).

Ellen, R.F. and Fukui, K (eds) (1996) *Redefining Nature: Ecology, Culture and Domestication*, London.

Forde, C.D. (1934) *Habitat, Economy and Society*, London.

Ingold, T. (1986a) *The Appropriation of Nature: Essays on Human Ecology and Social Relations*, Manchester.

—— (1986b) *Evolution and Social Life*, Cambridge, UK.

Milton, K. (1996) *Environmentalism and Cultural Theory*, London.

Moran, E.F. (ed.) (1990) *The Ecosystem Approach in Anthropology: From Concept to Practice*, Ann Arbor, MI.

Oldfield, M.L. and Alcorn, J. (eds) (1991) *Biodiversity: Culture, Conservation and Ecodevelopment*, Boulder, CO.

Rappaport, R.A. (1968) *Pigs for the Ancestors: Ritual in the Ecology of a New Guinea People*, New Haven, CT (new edn 1984).

Redclift, M. (1989) *Sustainable Development: Exploring the Contradictions*, London.

Richards, P. (1985) *Indigenous Agricultural Revolution: Ecology and Food Production in West Africa*, London.

—— (1986) *Coping with Hunger: Hazard and Experiment in an African Rice-Farming System*, London.

Steward, J. and Murphy, R.F. (1977) *Evolution and Ecology*, Urbana, IL.

Vayda, A.P. (1983) 'Progressive contextualism: Methods for research in human ecology', *Human Ecology* 11: 265–81.

Vayda, A.P. and McCay, B.J. (1975) 'New directions in ecology and ecological anthropology', *Annual Review of Anthropology* 4.

Winterhalder, B. and Smith, E.A. (eds) (1981) *Hunter-Gatherer Foraging Strategies: Ethnographic and Archaeological Strategies*, Chicago.

SEE ALSO: environment; landscape; population and resources

ECONOMETRICS

Econometrics is that branch of economics that, broadly speaking, aims to give empirical content to economic relations. Although the term 'econometrics' appears to have first been used as early as 1910, it was Ragnar Frisch, one of the founders of the Econometric Society in 1931, who established it as a subject in the sense in which it is known today. Econometrics can be defined generally as the application of mathematics and statistical methods to the analysis of economic data. By emphasizing the quantitative aspects of economic problems, econometrics seeks to unify measurement and theory in economics. Theory without measurement can have only limited relevance for the analysis of actual economic problems, as it then becomes just a branch of logic. The converse, however, must lack any theoretical framework to allow for the interpretation of statistical observations, and so is unlikely to result in a satisfactory explanation of the way in which economic forces interact with each other. Hence neither 'theory' nor 'measurement' on their own is sufficient to enable us to further our understanding of economic phenomena. The unification of the two thus lies at the heart of econometrics.

It is important to distinguish econometrics from statistics. What distinguishes the former from the latter is that econometricians tend to be preoccupied with problems caused by violations of the standard assumptions made by statisticians, since, owing to both the nature of economic relationships and the lack of controlled experimentation, these assumptions are seldom met. 'Patching up' statistical methods to deal with situations commonly encountered in empirical economics has created a large battery of extremely sophisticated techniques. Unfortunately, such techniques can founder on the quality, or lack of it, of the data available. In practice, good econometrics depends on both theory and data: 'the art of the econometrician consists in finding the set of assumptions which are both sufficiently specific and sufficiently realistic to allow him to take the best possible advantage of the data available to him' (Malinvaud 1966: 514).

What are these techniques and the assumptions that go with them? The workhorse of econometrics is the multiple linear regression model, in which a dependent, or endogenous, variable is a linear function of a set of independent (or exogenous) variables, plus an unobserved error term capturing all the myriad other influences on the endogenous variable. The coefficients of this linear function are unknown, but may be optimally estimated by the technique of ordinary least squares using a sample of observed data on all of the variables if the error term satisfies a set of 'classical' regression assumptions. These are, most notably, that the error has constant variance, that errors are independent of each other across observations, and that each of the exogenous variables are independent of the errors. If, as well, the error term is normally distributed, hypotheses concerning the coefficients may be tested, thus enabling competing economic theories, which place different sets of restrictions on the values taken by the coefficients, to be examined.

So far, this is a standard set-up in statistics, but, as was emphasized earlier, the lack of controlled experimentation in most areas of economics typically results in one or more of these assumptions being violated. In such cases ordinary least squares becomes a suboptimal estimation technique, producing estimates that can be biased and having incorrect measures of precision attached to them. For example, the presence of non-constant error variance, known as heteroskedasticity, requires the use of weighted least squares, where each observation is deflated by an amount proportional to its error variance. When dealing with time-series data, the errors are often dependent through time. Such autocorrelation is now typically dealt with by introducing lagged values of both the endogenous and exogenous variables, thus making the model dynamic, in the sense that a change in an exogenous variable will have not just a contemporaneous impact on the endogenous variable but also secondary effects through time. The assumption of independence between an exogenous variable and the error term is violated when the underlying model exhibits simultaneity – a type of 'feedback' between the endogenous and the supposedly exogenous variable that necessitates systems methods of estimation based on structural (multiple-equation) models of an economy or a particular sector. Non-normally distributed errors may be a consequence of a few 'outlying' observations that may be dealt with by introducing artificial exogenous variables, known as dummies, or it may reflect an intrinsic property of the process generating the data, thus necessitating more complex models and estimation techniques. Such properties are often exhibited by financial data such as stock returns and exchange rate changes. Non-normality is often related to a breakdown of the linear model assumption. Consequently, non-linear models estimated by techniques such as maximum likelihood are now increasingly common in econometrics.

Violations of the classical assumptions of regression both destroy the optimality of ordinary least squares estimation and require its replacement by computationally expensive techniques, at least until recently. Econometrics is thus also characterized by the numerous tests that have been developed of whether the assumptions hold or not in a particular application. Popular examples of such diagnostic tests are the Durbin–Watson test for residual autocorrelation, White's test for heteroskedasticity, Jarque and Bera's test for non-normality, and the RESET test for incorrect functional form.

These diagnostic tests have shown in stark relief the almost endemic presence of misspecification in simple regression models in econometrics and this has led to major methodological debates and improvements in modelling strategies. The approach of beginning with a simple model, subjecting it to diagnostic checking and then, on the discovery of one or more misspecifications, attempting to generalize the model to eradicate the problems has been shown to be an extremely flawed approach. The methodology that now holds sway (but which still has some critics) is the alternative strategy of beginning with a model general enough to show no misspecification but which is necessarily overparameterized. It is then progressively simplified using sequences of nested hypothesis tests, all the while diagnostic checking to ensure that no misspecifications begin to creep in as the model becomes more specific – this is known as ensuring congruence with the data. This approach is referred to as a general-to-specific (or *gets*) modelling strategy and is now being used as the basis for automated model-selection methodologies.

Different areas of economics have developed their own distinct brands of econometrics in response to the type of statistical problems encountered. Macroeconomics and finance typically use time-series data that are subject to trends and other forms of non-stationarity. Methods of dealing with trending and co-trending time-series have led to major developments in the field of time-series econometrics and these have been influential in developing theories and methodologies for forecasting economic and financial time-series. Microeconomics, on the other hand, usually employs large cross-sectional data sets, and sometimes panels of observations on a group of individuals observed over several time periods – this is also the case in the rapidly advancing field of growth economics. Such data require their own special techniques of model estimation and analysis, such as qualitative response models and truncated and censored regression techniques. Consistently embodying the formation of expectations is also a perennial topic for econometricians, most popularly seen in the various methods of incorporating rational expectations.

Recent developments in econometrics have increasingly harnessed the power of modern computer technology. The ability to develop highly computer-intensive techniques has enabled approaches that, in the past, were simply too expensive or difficult to perform to now come within the reach of researchers. This is particularly so in Monte Carlo simulation of the performance of testing procedures and in the computation of Bayesian densities. Non-parametric techniques, in which flexible functional forms are estimated, are also becoming increasingly popular.

Excellent discussions of the current state of econometrics and the challenges that it faces may be found in the centenary volume of the *Journal of Econometrics* and the September 2002 issue of the *Journal of Economic Surveys*.

TERENCE C. MILLS
LOUGHBOROUGH UNIVERSITY

References

Journal of Econometrics 100 (2001).
Journal of Economic Surveys 16(4) (2002).
Malinvaud, E. (1966) *Statistical Methods of Econometrics*, Amsterdam.

Further reading

Baltagi, B.H. (2001) *A Companion to Theoretical Econometrics*, Oxford.
Clements, M.P. and Hendry, D.F. (2002) *A Companion to Economic Forecasting*, Oxford.

SEE ALSO: macroeconomic policy; macroeconomic theory

ECONOMIC ANTHROPOLOGY

Economic anthropologists study how humans maintain and express themselves through material goods and services. During the twentieth century, ethnographic research was usually carried out in 'non-Western' contexts, but the field of economic anthropology embraces all societies. Today, economic anthropologists also study industrial societies and mixed economic forms, especially in contexts of differential power and conflicting ideologies.

As a discipline, economic anthropology has both descriptive and theoretical dimensions. How can they be brought together? Ethnographers have provided rich studies of property systems, technologies, forms of production, non-market exchanges, consumption, non-modern monies, gifting, bridewealth, dowry and other topics. Recently they have focused on postsocialist transitions, gender, resistance to development, modern money, household economies and globalization. Whatever the focus, their studies also characteristically explore the social and cultural context, including households, tribes, states and religious ideologies, which influence the economic processes. This contextual material often overflows the normal categories of economy.

Major theories in economics are also brought to the crucible of economic anthropology. Contemporary macroeconomics has had little influence, partly because the ethnographic contexts rarely resemble developed, market economies. But microanalyses of price and rational-actor models have been influential, as is evident in anthropological studies of decision-making in agriculture and in domestic groups, and in numerous studies of markets and bargaining behaviour, as well as some work on fisheries and irrigation systems. Neo-classical economists usually start with assumptions about actor rationality, calculation and optimization that do not always fit observational and social approaches in anthropology. For example, microeconomic theorists often find that habitual behaviours and cultural norms are difficult to explain, except as constraints on market-like behaviour. Economic anthropologists remain divided on the importation of neo-classical assumptions and theory.

In the 1960s and 1970s, Marxist anthropologists raised important questions about the origin and use of surplus in society, and about the impact of changing technologies on social forms. They identified several modes of production in ethnographic situations (based on the control and use of labour), and explored the interrelations or articulation of these modes in local and international systems. In the 1980s and 1990s, Marxist influence fostered an interest in the interaction of world-systems and local economies, and promoted the treatment of practices, rituals and ideologies as reflections of, or expressions of resistance to, dominant economies.

Karl Polanyi and his associates, who developed a more institutional approach to economics, insisted that the market-based economy is not universal and that material life in many societies is embedded in social relationships. The Polanyi school emphasized the importance of economic processes such as reciprocity and redistribution, which fitted in with the long-established interest of anthropologists in social exchange and gift-giving. Debates between the followers of Polanyi and supporters of microeconomics went on for many years, and in some respects the issues separating the two approaches remain current. The Polanyi school seemed to decline in prominence during the 1980s, but with the rise of postsocialist economies it has gained renewed attention.

A different approach, cultural economics, began to develop in the 1980s, when some anthropologists looked at consumption and exchange as expressive modes of behaviour. Others explored the economic models that people construct. Such local models are often formed by projecting images of the body or social group onto the earth, crops or natural forces. Anthropologists have also analysed Western economic theories in light of their cultural assumptions, rhetoric and context of production. By showing how Western economics uses metaphors, local notions of the self, and images from other domains, these anthropologists blur the line between modern and non-modern knowledge, challenge neo-classical claims to universality, and point to a different way of studying economic systems.

The various theoretical perspectives and disparate ethnographic reports are partly cross-cut by a dialectic or interaction of incommensurate realms. Everywhere, people face the practical choice between producing for the self and producing for others. In the first case, which might be called the 'community realm' of economy, material activities take a reproductive form that supports group independence and identity. In the second case, termed the 'market realm' of economy, production is primarily intended to produce goods to exchange for what people need and desire. Real economies are complex, shifting combinations of the two, and individuals are often pulled in both directions.

The community realm of economy forms around many types of association, such as households, compound groups, lineage segments, agglomerations of kinfolk, religious sodalities and settled villages, as well as states, clubs and industrial organizations. Such communities are frequently stacked one inside another, with each undertaking distinct tasks. People may participate simultaneously in several communities that overlap in membership and functions. Each community holds a 'base', in which members share, consisting of items such as knowledge, a heritage of practices, land and material resources, as well as the deceased or spirits. Fracturing mutuality leads to loss of the base. People are connected to and through the base, which is integral to their identity, so that loss of the base means dissolution of communal relationships. Rules of inheritance, access, use and disposal, as well as assertions of power, determine the allocation of the resources of the base between members. Communal rules of distribution express a variety of values from equality to adequacy, and from prominence to power. For example, game caught by a hunter may be distributed to a chief or headman, to a mother's brother and grandmother, and to other members of the community in support of their welfare. Likewise, in many industrial societies, a family shares the contents of its refrigerator but provides unequal access to and control over its income. Citizens of a modern state may have equal access to small parks, but unequal access to medical benefits and old-age pensions, which fall in the communal realm of economy.

The market realm is based on impersonal trade and competition among buyers and sellers. Markets are arenas, contained within shared rules and spaces (or communal norms) defining who may participate, the nature of legitimate transactions, and what may be transacted. According to the major theory of economy, the market promises efficiency in the allocation of resources, but it never pledges adequacy in meeting the needs of all. Thus, the two economic realms revolve about different, incommensurate values.

Many of the economies that anthropologists once studied gave prominence to the communal realm, but ethnographers found that even within the communal economy there were generally also impersonal exchanges that allowed individuals to explore the wider world and to secure special items. By contrast, in market economies today many exchanges are leavened with communal features that temper the competitive element, as in the cases of oligopolies, corporations, unions and households. Networks link people between firms and within buyers' markets; product advertising often promises a fresh identity and communal affiliation to purchasers. Today, most theories used in economic anthropology must be blended to make sense of these practical and mixed situations. But economic anthropology suggests that there is an inherent and ever-present tension between the two realms of material life and values. This tension will probably remain a central focus of economic anthropology.

STEPHEN GUDEMAN
UNIVERSITY OF MINNESOTA

Further reading

Akin, D. and Robbins, J. (eds) (1999) *Money and Modernity*, Pittsburgh.
Gudeman, S. (2001) *The Anthropology of Economy*, London, UK.
Narotzky, S. (1997) *New Directions in Economic Anthropology*, London.
Wilk, R. (1996) *Economies and Cultures*, Oxford.

SEE ALSO: exchange

ECONOMIC DEVELOPMENT

A central question in the study of economic development has turned out to be 'In what precisely does the economic development of a society consist?' For about 20 years after 1945, the accepted view was that the prolonged and steady increase of national income was an adequate indicator of economic development. This was held to be so because it was generally believed that such an increase could be sustained over long periods only if specific economic (and social) processes were at work.

These processes, which were supposed to be basic to development, can be briefly summarized as follows:

1   The share of investment in national expenditure rises, leading to a rise in capital stock per person employed.

2   The structure of national production changes, becoming more diversified as industry, utilities and services take a larger relative share, compared with agriculture and other forms of primary production.

3   The foreign trade sector expands relative to the whole economy, particularly as manufactured exports take a larger share in an increased export total.

4   The government budget rises relative to national income, as the government undertakes expanded commitments to construct economic and social infrastructure.

Accompanying these structural changes in the economy, major changes of social structure also occur:

5   The population expands rapidly as death rates fall in advance of declining birth rates. Thereafter, a demographic transition occurs in which improved living conditions in turn bring the birth rate down, to check the rate of overall population increase.

6   The population living in urban areas changes from a small minority to a large majority.

7   Literacy, skills and other forms of educational attainment are spread rapidly through the population.

This conceptualization of economic development as the interrelation of capital accumulation, industrialization, government growth, urbanization and education can still be found in many contemporary writers. It seems to make most sense when one has very long runs of historical statistics to look back over. Then the uniformity that this view implies is most likely to be visible. One doubt has always been whether generalizing retrospectively from statistics is not an ahistorical, rather than a truly historical, approach. It presupposes some theory of history that links the past to the future. The theory may not be transparent, or it may be excessively mechanical and deterministic.

Another major doubt about the adequacy of the view of development described in processes 1–7 centres around the question of income distribution. If the basic development processes described above either do not make the distribution of income more equal, or actually worsen the degree of inequality for more than a short period, some theorists would argue that economic development has not taken place. They prefer to distinguish economic growth from economic development, which by their definition cannot leave the majority of the population as impoverished as they originally were. For them, indicators of economic growth and structural change must be complemented by positive improvement in the Gini coefficient or in physical indices of the quality of people's lives.

The latter can be of various kinds. They can focus on the availability of basic needs goods – food, shelter, clean water, clothing and household utensils. Or they can focus on health, as measured in life expectation tables and in statistics of morbidity. The availability and cost of education opportunities are also very relevant. Although the distribution of income may be a good enough starting-point, the distribution of capabilities (to use a concept expounded by Sen 1999) is the true objective. Similar kinds of consideration arise when one examines the role of political liberty in economic development. Is rapid growth and structural change induced by an oppressive, authoritarian regime true development? Those who object to the 'costs' of the development strategies of the former Soviet Union or the People's Republic of China do not think so. From a libertarian standpoint, they refuse to accept the standard account of economic development as sufficiently comprehensive. In particular, the public availability of adequate information has increasingly been argued to be a crucial factor in safeguarding the well-being of poor people.

If economic development is a product of many factors, it is difficult to know how to weight all of the different indices involved, in order to arrive at a single measure of the degree of development in this extended sense. Perhaps it cannot be done, and perhaps, if policy rather than the construction of international league tables is our main concern, this failure is not very important. The United Nations Development Programme's *Human Development Report* series (UNDP 1990–) provides an equally weighted amalgam of per capita income, life expectancy and literacy as its index of human development.

Linked with these questions about the meaning and measurement of development is the problem of conceptualizing the process of development. Perhaps the most famous of all models of this process is the classic capital accumulation model of Sir Arthur Lewis (1954). This attempts to capture the simultaneous determination of income growth and income distribution. It assumes that within traditional, technologically backward agriculture surplus population exists (surplus in the sense that their marginal product in agriculture is zero). It also assumes that the wage rate in the industrial sector does not rise as the surplus agricultural population is transferred gradually into industrial employment. The transfer of labour from agriculture to industry at a constant wage rate (which may or may not involve physical migration, but usually does) permits industrial capitalists to receive an increasing share of a rising national income as profit. They then reinvest their profits in activities that progressively expand the share of industry in the national output. Thus Lewis explained what he regarded as the central puzzle of economic development, namely to understand the process that converted economies which habitually saved and invested 4–5 per cent of

the national income into economies which save and invest 12–15 per cent.

The Lewis model can be elaborated to explain other stylized facts of development. If labour transfer involves physical migration to towns, urbanization will follow. If capitalists are defined as those with an accumulation mentality (as Lewis does), they can operate in the public as well as the private sector, and expansion of the government share in national output can be understood in these terms. If industrial employment in some sense requires labour to be healthy and educated, these major social interventions may accelerate the demographic transition.

Much of the subsequent literature on economic development can be read as an extended commentary on the Lewis model. First, neoclassical economists have criticized the assumptions of the model, questioning whether labour in the agricultural sector does have a zero marginal product, and whether labour transfer can be effected without raising the real wage rate. Second, the Lewis model's account of rural–urban migration has stimulated a large literature proposing alternative theories. Third, the Lewis model's sharp focus on physical capital formation has been strongly questioned. Some critics have gone so far as to deny that physical capital formation is necessary at all to economic development. A less extreme view is that human capital formation or investment in the acquisition of good health and skills is a prerequisite, rather than an inevitable consequence, of the successful operation of physical capital. A balance is therefore required between physical and human investments to ensure that an economy raises its level of technological capability in advance of a physical investment drive. At the same time, human capital investment will be wasted if it outruns the pace of physical capital accumulation.

The sectoral destination of investment in the Lewis model also provoked a strong reaction. The Lewis model's focus on investment in the modern industrial sector was seen as inimical to the development of agriculture. Increasingly, the failure of agricultural development was identified as a cause of slow growth and unequal income distribution in developing countries (as argued by Lipton 1977). The debate about sectoral investment balance was subsumed into the analysis of project appraisal, as pioneered by Little and Mirrlees (1974) and others. This provides, in principle, a calculus of social profitability of projects in all sectors of the economy, while still basing the rationale for the social pricing of labour on the Lewis conception of agriculture–industry labour transfer.

The Lewis model recognized the possibilities of state capitalism as well as private capitalism. The infrequency in practice with which such potential has been realized has led to demands that governments confine themselves to their so-called 'traditional functions' and the creation of an incentive and regulatory framework for the promotion of private enterprise. This has been one of the major thrusts of the counter-revolution in development thinking and policy of the 1980s (Toye 1993). The reorientation of the public sector has been one of the major policy thrusts of IMF and World Bank programmes of structural adjustment in developing countries.

The other has been the reform of their foreign trade regimes. Foreign trade plays a minor role in the Lewis model and other early models of economic development. This reflected the pessimism of many pioneers (such as Singer 1950) about the tendency of the terms of trade of primary commodity producers to decline. It also responded to a belief that, historically, isolation from the world economy had spurred development in Meiji Japan and interwar Latin America. More recently, the expansion of manufactured exports has been seen as a major element in the astonishingly successful development performances of East Asian countries like South Korea and Taiwan. Whether this kind of trade expansion experience validates liberal trade and finance policies, or an intelligent and selective style of government intervention in these markets (as argued by Wade 1990), remains controversial.

The concessional transfer of finance and technical assistance from developed to developing countries fitted well with the Lewis emphasis on physical capital formation as the key to growth and income distribution. More recently, the effectiveness of aid has been questioned. It is common now to see more clearly the complexities of the aid process, and to stress the many lessons that have been learned from hard experience to improve the likelihood of aid achieving its desired objectives (e.g. Cassen and Associates 1986; Lipton and Toye 1990). It is now increasingly argued that aid will be beneficial only in a 'good policy environment' (Dollar and Pritchett 1999).

Somewhat greater agreement exists on the facts of recent economic development than on the methods of bringing it about. That many poor countries have experienced much economic growth and structural change since 1945 is widely accepted. Few still claim that growth in developed countries systematically causes increased poverty in other, poorer countries. A weaker version of this thesis is that there is an ever-widening gap between richest and poorest, which can arise when the welfare of the poorest is constant or rising. Even this weaker version is disputable, on the grounds that countries are ranged evenly along a spectrum of wealth/poverty, and thus to split this spectrum into two groups of rich and poor in order to compare group statistics of economic performance can be somewhat arbitrary. There is also the important point that increasing income inequality between countries may be compatible with decreasing inequality between people, if income growth is concentrated in one or two very large poor countries, such as China and India.

But, although the overall record of economic growth at least need not give cause for deep gloom, certain geographical regions do appear to have markedly unfavourable development prospects. Such regions include sub-Saharan Africa and some parts of South Asia, the Middle East and Central and South America. The reasons for their poor prospects vary from place to place. Some are held back by severe pressure of population on cultivable land; some by inability to generate indigenous sources of appropriate technical progress; some by the persistence of intense social and political conflict; some by unenlightened policy-making (especially concerning oil and mineral rents); and some by the continuing failure to evolve a worldwide financial system that does not tend to amplify the inherent unevenness (over place and time) of economic development. The Asian financial crisis of 1997–9 is a recent testimony to the latter problem (Stiglitz 2002).

It is also true that the rapid increase in the world's population makes it possible for the *absolute* number of people whose consumption falls below a given poverty line to increase, even when the *percentage* of the world's people who are poor on this definition is falling. This is what seems to be happening at the moment. Despite all the evidence of widespread economic development, theoretical and practical work on poverty alleviation still has, therefore, great urgency and relevance.

JOHN TOYE
UNIVERSITY OF OXFORD

References

Cassen, R.H. and Associates (1986) *Does Aid Work?* Oxford.

Dollar, D. and Pritchett, L. (1999) *Assessing Aid: What Works, What Doesn't and Why*, New York.

Lewis, W.A. (1954) 'Economic development with unlimited supplies of labour', *The Manchester School* 22(2).

Lipton, M. (1977) *Why Poor People Stay Poor*, London.

Lipton, M. and Toye, J. (1990) *Does Aid Work in India?* London.

Little, I.M.D. and Mirrlees, J.A. (1974) *Project Appraisal and Planning for Developing Countries*, London.

Sen, A.K. (1999) 'The possibility of social choice', *American Economic Review* 89.

Singer, H.W. (1950) 'The distribution of the gains between investing and borrowing countries', *American Economic Review* 40.

Stiglitz, J. (2002) *Globalization and its Discontents*, London.

Toye, J. (1993) *Dilemmas of Development: Reflections on the Counter-Revolution in Development Economics*, 2nd edn, Oxford.

United Nations Development Programme (UNDP) (1990–) *Human Development Report*, New York.

Wade, R. (1990) *Governing the Market*, Princeton, NJ.

Further reading

Chang, H.-J. (2003) *Re-thinking Development Economics*, London.

Thirlwall, A.P. (2003) *Growth and Development with Special Reference to Developing Economies*, 7th edn, Basingstoke.

Todaro, M.P. (2003) *Economic Development in the Third World*, 8th edn, Boston.

SEE ALSO: economic dynamics; economic growth; industrial revolutions

ECONOMIC DYNAMICS

Comparative statics considers an economic system's equilibrium that is then disturbed by some exogenous change (shock) and a new equilibrium is attained, and the resulting equilibrium is compared with the old one. There is a presupposition that an equilibrium exists, but equally important is that it can be attained. The transition from one equilibrium to another is not considered. How the economic system moves from one equilibrium to another is the subject matter of economic dynamics. By its very nature such dynamics involves the passage of time: either continuously or in terms of discrete time. Economic systems evolve over time. The economic system may be microeconomic or macroeconomic. At the microeconomic level, economic dynamics is concerned with how the decisions of individuals or firms respond with the passage of time. At the macroeconomic level, the concern is how macroeconomic variables – such as income, inflation, unemployment and money supply – change over time. Although a new equilibrium exists, is it stable, in the sense that the system will approach it? Or is it unstable, in the sense that the system moves away from the equilibrium over time? The stability of dynamic systems is most important and dictates to a large extent the transition of the system.

The movement of a system over time is portrayed in terms of its trajectory. If the system is stable and it is disturbed (the system receives a shock) then the trajectory will move from the old equilibrium to the new one. If it is unstable, then the trajectory, starting from the old equilibrium, will move away from it and never reach the new equilibrium. It may be that the system cycles around the new equilibrium. The subject matter of economic dynamics is to investigate the dynamic properties of economic systems and establish whether they are or are not stable or even whether they are cyclical. Sometimes all that can be investigated is the conditions that will make the system stable, unstable or cyclical. However, in doing this what matters is whether the economic system is a continuous one or a discrete one. The dynamic properties of these two systems are not the same, and certainly one should not impute the stability of a discrete system from its continuous equivalent: one can be unstable while the other is stable.

In the early days of economics only simple dynamic systems were considered. In microeconomics, for example, the most important was the cobweb model. This referred in particular to the market for agricultural products. Demand at time t was related to the price at time t, but the supply was related to the *expected* price at time t. Farmers, in the simplest model, assumed the expected price at time t was what it was in the previous period, namely at time t-1. This made the demand and supply market *time dependent*, in the sense that the price at time t becomes dependent on the price in time t-1. This in turn means that the quantity demanded and supplied in time t also depended on the price in time period t-1. Agricultural markets tended to over-react and so lead to cyclical phenomena. But the important question was whether the cycles converged or diverged from the equilibrium. Cobweb phenomena are not confined to agricultural markets, but these are the most important where such dynamic behaviour occurs.

In terms of macroeconomics, the earliest dynamic system to be investigated was the multiplier-accelerator model. In this model, consumption depends on lagged income whilst investment is related to the change in income over the *past* period. This leads to a solution in which income at time t depends on income at time t-1 *and* time t-2. The cobweb model involved a first-order system while the present model involves a second-order system, and as such involves much more complex behaviour. The properties of first- and second-order systems, both in discrete time and continuous time, became an important research topic in economic dynamics.

Economic systems, however, became much more complex as economists began to set up quite sophisticated economic models. In fact, one of the most characteristic developments in economics post-1945 was mathematical economic modelling. In the early years these were largely static, but with the development of computerization and sophisticated mathematical software, there is now a move towards more dynamic systems. This development coincided with a greater emphasis on non-linear systems. Linear systems, assuming they have an equilibrium, have only one. Furthermore, the properties of linear systems can be looked into with a wealth of mathematical results. On the other hand, non-linear systems can have, and often do have, more than one equilibrium solution. More difficult is to establish the stability or otherwise of non-linear systems. To do this phase diagrams and phase portraits have become an important tool of analysis.

Even though the stability of economic systems is important, when considering this it is essential to know whether such a system involves only past values of the state variables or whether future values are involved. Put simply, if you look at the state of where a system is now, it may depend only on the past state the system went through to get there. For instance, in the cobweb model we referred to earlier, the expected price now depended on what the price was in the previous period. When expected values depend only on past values, then we have *backwards-looking expectations*, and only the history of the model matters in determining its equilibrium state now and the stability of that equilibrium. On the other hand, we can readily have a system that depends on future expected values. For instance, wage contracts now may be set based on what is expected in the future rate of inflation. In this case we have *forwards-looking expectations*. Methodologically, early economic systems were dominated by analogies to physical systems, and these were all backwards looking. With the rise of monetarism and the rational expectations revolution, forwards-looking expectations became more important. Modelling these, however, is more difficult than modelling backwards-looking ones. Whether a system involves backwards-looking expectations or forwards-looking expectations (or even both!), such systems are inherently dynamic. The expected value of a variable at time t is either related to past values, future values or both.

The moment one considers the dynamic adjustment of markets, the question arises: Do markets adjust at the same rate and if they do not, does this matter? A rise in autonomous investment will lead to a rise in income and through the multiplier will lead to a rise in consumption and to further rises in income over time. This reflects dynamic adjustment in the goods market. Each round will take time and the whole process can take many years. In the money market, a rise in the money supply will lead to a fall in the rate of interest. This dynamic adjustment can be very quick indeed. The same applies to disequilibria in the foreign exchange market. What we observe here is differential adjustment speeds. Asset markets are quick to adjust while the market for goods and services is sluggish. This directs our attention to the trajectory that the economy takes from one equilibrium state to another. Because forces in the goods market and forces in the money market operate at the same time in no way means that they have the *same* force. On the contrary, the force acting on interest rates in the money market is far quicker and far greater in the early stages than those acting on income from the goods market. This can lead to asset prices overreacting to shocks in the economy: to the situation of *overshooting*.

Such overshooting is typical of exchange rate adjustments. In a fully employed economy, increases in aggregate demand become translated into increases in prices. Disequilibrium in the foreign exchange market leads to changes in the exchange rate. The exchange rate can adjust very quickly, but prices take a much longer period to adjust. So what we observe is overshooting of exchange rates.

With the growing interest in economic dynamics, economists have turned their attention to the stability of non-linear systems, as well as linear ones, modelling both backwards- and forwards-looking expectations, considering chaotic systems and the problems surrounding bifurcations, and more recently to stochastic dynamic systems.

RONALD SHONE
UNIVERSITY OF STIRLING

Further reading

Ferguson, B.S. and Lim, G.C. (1998) *Introduction to Dynamic Economic Models*, Manchester.
Gandolfo, G. (1997) *Economic Dynamics*, study edn, Amsterdam.
Medio, A. and Lines, M. (2001) *Nonlinear Dynamics*, Cambridge, UK.
Shone, R. (2001) *An Introduction to Economic Dynamics*, Cambridge, UK.
—— (2002) *Economic Dynamics*, 2nd edn, Cambridge, UK.

SEE ALSO: economic development

ECONOMIC GEOGRAPHY

Economic geography is a subdiscipline within human geography concerned with describing and explaining the production, distribution, exchange and consumption of goods and services within an explicitly spatial economy. Institutionalized during the late nineteenth century, economic geography arose in large part because of its potential contribution to European colonialism (Barnes 2000). Early economic geographers provided a global inventory of tradable resources and their conditions of production (Chisholm 1889), and offered intellectual justifications for the marked differences in levels of economic development between colonized and colonizing countries based upon environmental determinism (Huntington 1915).

After the end of the First World War, economic geographers increasingly looked inwards, and practised a regional approach that involved delineating a place's unique economic character. Employing a standardized typology based upon such categories as production, transportation, markets and so on, facts were carefully compiled and organized for a particular region. By comparing different typologies, the peculiarities of a given place were then immediately revealed.

Following the Second World War, economic geography's 'space cadets' mounted a 'quantitative and theoretical revolution', transforming the discipline into spatial science (Barnes 2000). Led by graduate students and young professors, the movement was defined by the use of increasingly sophisticated statistical techniques, and the importation of rigorous abstract theories and models drawn from at least four different sources. From neo-classical economics came general models of competition and rational choice theory. From physics came gravity, potential and entropy models that, in turn, were used to explain patterns of spatial interaction. From the recouping of a hitherto forgotten nineteenth-century German location school came a series of location models: von Thunen's theory of agricultural location, Weber's theory of industrial location, and Lösch and Christaller's central-place theory. Finally, from geometry came a slew of axioms, lemmas and theorems that could be used to underpin a set of explanatory spatial morphological laws (Bunge 1962). More generally, economic geographers who practised spatial science believed that an autonomous set of spatial forces regulated the geography of the economy. Using the scientific method these forces could be uncovered, and their operation reduced to laws.

From the mid-1970s, spatial science was increasingly criticized by an emerging group of radical economic geographers. They argued that spatial science's main mistake was assuming that the spatial was separate from the social, governed by independent geographical laws. In contrast, radicals argued that the spatial had no meaning outside of the dominant mode of production, capitalism, which determined all economic geographical relations. As David Harvey (1982), the movement's pre-eminent spokesperson, argued, if economic geographers were to understand capitalism's changing economic landscape they needed to grasp the basic tensions within the non-spatial core of the capitalist system itself, and not search for the chimera of autonomous geographical laws. For Harvey this was possible only by returning to Marx. In particular, by making use of Marx's idea of the 'annihilation of space by time'. Harvey (1982) provided a brilliant reconstruction of capitalism's geography of accumulation.

The political economy approach that Harvey introduced into economic geography in the mid-1970s remains the dominant paradigm. Subsequently, it has been elaborated and constructively criticized in at least five different ways, thereby defining the current agenda of the discipline.

First, in the mid-1980s Doreen Massey (1984) embellished Harvey's argument by suggesting that just as the spatial is socialized once it is embedded within capitalism, so capitalist social relations are spatialized by the same move. 'Geography matters,' as she crisply put it. To show that it matters, Massey (1984) developed an original theoretical framework based on the idea that a place's character is a result of the specific combination of past layers of investment found there. That character, however, reacts back and recursively influences future rounds of investment. Places for Massey, then, are not passive, as they sometimes appear in Harvey's work, but active, energetically determining an economy's spatial division of labour. More generally, Massey's conception of the relationship between a place and economy became the basis of the British 'localities project' that subsequently generated an enormous amount of research and debate within economic geography, especially in the UK (Cooke 1989).

Second, there was an attempt to flesh out the institutional structure that comprised Harvey's capitalist social relations, and then used empirically to understand the industrial restructuring, including deindustrialization, which occurred in advanced industrial economies from the 1970s. A key theoretical source was the French Regulationist school, and their conceptualization of an older mass-production form of industrialization, Fordism, that was superseded by a newer, flexible production type, post-Fordism (Tickell and Peck 1992). The concept of post-Fordism has proven to be especially useful, and it has been deployed in understanding the geographical restructuring of particular industrial sectors such as automobile manufacture, the emergence and maintenance of high-tech regions such as Silicon Valley, and the persistence of specialized geographical agglomerations – 'industrial districts' – found, for example, in the Veneto region, Italy.

Third, stemming from Harvey's concern with the geography of accumulation, there is work on the processes and spatial consequences of investment at the regional and international scales. At the international level, emphasis is on analysing the strategies and effects of transnational corporations, the geographical and social networks through which investment flows (e.g. Chinese business networks on the Pacific Rim), and the emergence of both a new international division of labour and growth complexes particularly in Southeast and East Asia (Dicken 1998).

Fourth, there is increasing examination of services including retail, financial and producer. In each case, though, there is a shift away from Harvey's pure political economy, towards a more catholic approach, which recognizes other factors, especially culture. The 'new retail geography', for example, attempts to link the recent corporate restructuring in retailing with an analysis of the culture of consumption (Wrigley and Lowe 2002). Work on the financial services, and their centres such as the City of London, stresses both technological change in communications, and new cultures of work and consumption (Leyshon and Thrift 1996). Research on producer services highlights dense geographically proximate interrelations characterized by high degrees of trust, tacit knowledge, and common cultural references and institutions (Thrift 2000).

Finally, attempts have been made to broaden the agenda of economic geography to include gender and race. Feminist economic geographers seek both to criticize what they see as the phallocentric basis of the discipline, to offer a series of case studies that demonstrate that gender matters (MacDowell 1991), and to use feminist theory to rethink the very idea of the economy (Gibson-Graham 1996). Works that explicate racialization within economic geography are less numerous, but there are analyses of racialized labour markets, particular entrepreneurial activities, and even forms of capitalism (e.g. Yeung and Olds 2000).

Economic geography is a vibrant, diffuse discipline, frequently taking ideas conceived in one discipline, and refashioning them for a *geographical* world. Such a task seems especially pertinent in a world in which the geographical is ever more important.

TREVOR J. BARNES
UNIVERSITY OF BRITISH COLUMBIA

References

Barnes, T. (2000) 'Inventing Anglo-American economic geography: 1889–1960', in E. Sheppard and T. Barnes (eds) *A Companion to Economic Geography*, Oxford.

Bunge, W. (1962) *Theoretical Geography*, Lund.

Chisholm, G. (1889) *Handbook of Commercial Geography*, London.

Cooke, P. (1989) *Localities: The Changing Face of Urban Britain*, London.

Dicken, P. (1998) *Global Shift: Transforming the World Economy*, 3rd edn, London.

Gibson-Graham, J.K. (1996) *The End of Capitalism (As We Knew It): A Feminist Inquiry into Political Economy*, Oxford.

Harvey, D. (1982) *The Limits to Capital*, Chicago.

Huntington, E. (1915) *Civilization and Climate*, New Haven, CT.

Leyshon, A. and Thrift, N. (1996) *Money/Space: Geographies of Monetary Transformation*, London.

MacDowell, L. (1991) 'Life without father Ford: The new gender order of post-Fordism', *Transactions: Institute of British Geographers* 16.

Massey, D. (1984) *Spatial Divisions of Labour: Social Structures and the Geography of Production*, London.

Thrift, N. (2000) 'Performing cultures in the new economy', *Annals, Association of American Geographers* 91.

Tickell, A. and Peck, J. (1992) 'Accumulation, regulation and the geographies of post-Fordism: Missing links in regulationist research', *Progress in Human Geography* 16.

Wrigley, N. and Lowe, M. (2002) *Reading Retail: A Geographical Perspective on Retailing and Consumption Spaces*, London.

Yeung, H. and Olds, K. (2000) *Globalization of Chinese Firms*, London.

Further reading

Sheppard, E. and Barnes, T. (eds) (2000) *A Companion to Economic Geography*, Oxford.

ECONOMIC GROWTH

Economic growth is the process by which per capita income rises over time. Growth theory attempts to model and understand the factors behind this process. It is a particularly challenging area of research because growth is extremely uneven in space as well as in time.

Over the past millennium, world per capita income increased thirteen-fold, from $435 per person per year around the year 1000 to $5,700 nowadays (see Maddison 2001). This contrasts sharply with the preceding millennia, when there was almost no advance in per capita income. Per capita income started to rise and accelerate around the year 1820 and it has sustained a steady rate of increase over the last two centuries. One of the main challenges for growth theory is to understand this transition from stagnation to growth and in particular to identify the main factor(s) that triggered the take-off.

The rise in per capita income did not happen everywhere in the world. The gap between the leading regions and the poor ones has actually increased over time. Citizens from Western Europe were three times richer than African citizens around the year 1820: now they are thirteen times richer. To understand why countries differ so dramatically in standards of living one needs to identify the factors behind the success or the failure of the growth process in different parts of the world.

The first key factor in the growth process is the accumulation of physical capital. For capital steadily to drive growth, the output of an economy needs to be proportional to the stock of capital used in production. In this case, growth will be proportional to investment. This accumulation through investment may come about either through local saving or by investment from abroad. A theoretical argument against this view claims that marginal returns to capital are decreasing, i.e. one cannot increase production per worker indefinitely simply by increasing the stock of capital per worker. If machines per employed person grow at a constant rate, the growth of output will eventually fall to zero. Workers, whose number is bounded by the active population, cannot deal with many machines with the same efficiency as they cope with fewer machines. The debate on this issue is still very lively (see, e.g., McGrattan 1998).

While decreasing marginal returns on capital may make it impossible to sustain growth by investment alone, it remains true that capital is one of the most important determinants of growth in the medium-run. McGrattan (1998) finds a strong positive relationship between average rates of investment and growth in post-war data for a large cross-section of countries. The typical example of such a relationship is the emergence of the East Asian tigers, which managed to catch up with the rich countries in the second half of the twentieth century essentially by accumulating capital. However, Zambia's experience provides a counter-example. If all aid to that country had been invested, and if investment had gone into growth, Zambia's income per capita would actually be $20,000 p.a instead of $600 p.a. (Easterly 2002).

Since physical capital cannot be the engine of growth when marginal returns are decreasing, something else must account for rising per capita income over time. Technological change can help to deal with this problem by making labour more efficient, i.e. better able to work with many machines. Such technological change is labelled 'labour-saving technical progress'. Neo-classical growth theory assumed that technological change was exogenous to the economic system. Advances in knowledge, e.g. in basic science, led to technological progress. Growth theorists, however, have pointed to the importance of what they termed a research and development sector, which either invents new goods or increases the quality of existing goods (see Barro and Sala-I-Martin 1995). This theory attributes a pre-eminent role to the R&D sector in generating growth, and makes a crucial link between innovation and market power. Indeed, the incentive to innovate is provided by monopoly rights on the new goods, which grant extra profits to research firms. Such models also open up interesting policy debates, essentially on the optimal patent protection laws, and the optimal level of subsidies required to stimulate research.

Accumulating human capital is the other way to sustain a growth process. Indeed, even if a country cannot indefinitely increase its supply of labour, it can enhance the quality of labour. This quality is referred as 'human capital'. Human capital can be accumulated in two ways: during the early stage of life by going to school and spending on education; during the working life by accumulating experience (learning-by-doing) or by on-the-job training. Investment in formal education has increased substantially all over the world. In England, for example, the number of years spent at school went from two on average in 1820 to more than fourteen today. In developing countries, school enrolments grew rapidly between 1960 and 2000. However, many poor countries experienced an educational boom but did not start to grow more quickly. In general, empirical studies stress the lack of correlation between educational attainment and growth performance. The accumulation of human capital is a necessary condition for growth, but does not seem to be a sufficient condition.

Another key determinant of economic growth is demographic. The initial view was that a high rate of population growth could not be supported by a corresponding increase in investment, thus lowering growth of income per capita. This negative relationship between population and economic growth calls for population control policies. More recent empirical literature finds that there is in general a non-significant correlation in cross-country studies. From these studies it is also clear that the impact of population growth has changed over time and varies with the level of development. The composition of the population as well as age-specific variables are relevant to growth. In particular, a reduction in the death rates of workers does not have the same effect as reductions in the death rates of dependants, young or old.

Institutions are often blamed or acclaimed for their role in promoting growth. Acemoglu et al. (2002) argue that relatively rich countries colonized by European powers in 1500 are now relatively poor and vice versa. They explain this 'reversal of fortune' by the types of institutions imposed by the European settlers. 'Extractive' institutions were introduced in the relatively rich countries for the benefit of the settlers rather than in order to increase general prosperity. In the relatively poor areas, there were fewer incentives to plunder, and so less to prevent the development of investment-friendly institutions. As a result, the decline or rise of those countries is rooted in a major – exogenous – institutional change linked to colonization. A number of authors have also related the poor performance of many developing countries to governance issues: corruption, ethnic fragmentation, wars, etc.

To be complete, growth theory should not only be able to account for successful growth experiences, but should also explain why some economies have experienced relative and also sometimes absolute periods of decline. Kindleberger (1996) defends the view that economies, like human bodies, go through a life-cycle, in the course of which 'vitality' varies, depending on how entrepreneurial each generation is. The Venetian Maritime Republic declined when leaders started to devote more time to consumption rather than investing in the improvement of shipping techniques, the discovery of new routes, etc. Florence and its famous banking sector declined when Lorenzo the Magnificent delegated power over the Medici bank branches as he spent more time on luxury and pleasure. In order to capture the idea that rich regions tend to rest on their laurels, and are inclined to favour consumption over investment in knowledge, we can use habit consumption models (see de la Croix 2001). This approach suggests that desire to consume depends positively on past consumption (either of the individual, or of his or her parents, or of the society as a whole). The point eventually comes when the new generation in the richer regions develop living standards that are incompatible with the continuing investment in knowledge that is required to maintain economic leadership. This reduces the growth rate in comparison with that of other regions. At some point in this process of decline, consumption falls to a low level once again, and a new growth cycle may start.

The relationship between growth and inequality has now at last also begun to attract attention. The question is two-fold. First, does inequality evolve along with economic growth? The 'Kuznet curve' would suggest that inequality first increases, then decreases in the course of the growth process. Second, is inequality good or bad for growth? Most of the existing literature on inequality and growth concentrates on the channels by which inequality affects growth, through the accumulation of physical capital. For example, in countries with many poor people, there is a high demand for redistribution policies, which in turn lead to tax distortions that retard growth. Inequality can also influence growth because of its effects on the accumulation of human capital. Finally, demographic variables must be taken into account in assessing the effects that economic growth may have on income distribution (see de la Croix and Doepke 2003).

DAVID DE LA CROIX
UNIVERSITÉ CATHOLIQUE
DE LOUVAIN, BELGIUM

References

Acemoglu, D., Johnson, S. and Robinson, J. (2002) 'Reversal of fortune: Geography and institutions in the making of the modern world income distribution', *Quarterly Journal of Economics* 117: 1,231–94.

Barro, R. and Sala-I-Martin, X. (1995) *Economic Growth*, New York.

de la Croix, D. (2001) 'Growth dynamics and education spending: The role of inherited tastes and abilities', *European Economic Review* 45: 1,415–38.

de la Croix, D. and Doepke, M. (2003) 'Inequality and growth: Why differential fertility matters', *American Economic Review* 93(4) (September).

Easterly, W. (2002) *The Elusive Quest for Growth, Economists' Adventures and Misadventures in the Tropics*, Cambridge, MA.

Kindleberger, C.P. (1996) *World Economic Primacy 1500–1990*, Oxford.

McGrattan, E. (1998) 'A defense of AK growth models', *Federal Reserve Bank of Minneapolis Quarterly Review* 4 (autumn): 13–27.

Maddison, A. (2001) *The World Economy, a Millennial Perspective*, Paris.

SEE ALSO: economic development

ECONOMIC HISTORY

Economic history, as a combination of two disciplines, has had a rather varied evolution. Whereas in Britain and most other European countries economic history has been regarded as a separate discipline, such an academic distinction has not existed in the USA where, indicating the dual nature of the subject, economic historians can be found in either the history department or the economics department. Since the 1960s there has been a marked change in the study of economic history, first in the USA, then elsewhere, with the expansion of quantification and social science model building, changes that have affected other subdisciplines of history. Economic history in the USA has now become dominated by scholars trained as economists.

The definition of a field of study can be a rather uncertain thing, although there are generally two somewhat overlapping approaches to delimiting a discipline. One definition relates to the set of questions being studied. Economic history can be defined as the study of the economic aspects of the past, or as the study of the solution to the problems of the allocation and the distribution of goods and services that arise from the problem of scarcity. The second definition is based on the methods, techniques and concepts applied by scholars in studying problems. Applications of the basic tools of economics to historical problems would thus be considered to fall within the discipline. Given these two, at times inconsistent, definitions, it is sometimes difficult to be precise on the boundaries of economic history. This has become particularly so since the 1960s, where the basic concepts of economic analysis have been applied to wider sets of issues, and to problems that were until recently generally held to be outside the province of economics and of economic history.

Although the works of some earlier economists, including Smith, Steuart and Malthus, contained historical data, the modern evolution of economic history in Britain from the latter part of the nineteenth century dates from the Irish historical economists, Cliffe, Leslie and Ingram, and the first of the Oxbridge economic historians, Rogers, Toynbee and Cunningham. Toynbee's student, Ashley, who was also influenced by the German, Schmoller, came to hold the first chair in economic history in the English-speaking world, at Harvard in 1892, before returning to Britain. The first chair in economic history in Britain went to Unwin at Manchester, followed by a London School of Economics (LSE) chair to Cunningham's student, Knowles, in 1921, with chairs over the decade between 1928 and 1938 to Clapham (Cambridge), Clark (Oxford), Power (LSE), Tawney (LSE) and Postan (Cambridge). The acceptance of economic history as a field of study was marked by the founding of the Economic History Society in 1926; publication of the *Economic History Review* began in 1927.

The development of economic history in the USA lagged behind that in Britain, with more attention in the earlier part of the twentieth century given to the histories prepared for the Carnegie Institution, dealing with agriculture, manufacturing, transportation and commerce, among other issues. These scholarly writings and document collections are still central in the work of many contemporary economic historians. There was no 'historical school' in the British sense, but the US 'institutional school' filled its role as critic of economy theory and was to play a key role in influencing the study of economic history and its offshoot, business history. The latter emerged with the appointment of Gras to a chair at the Harvard Business School in 1927. Also important in influencing the development of economic history in the USA was the founding of the National Bureau of Economic Research in 1920. Among the founders was the Harvard economic and business historian, Gay, but most influential was its long-time director of research, Mitchell, and his student, Kuznets, with their emphasis on data collection and the, studies of business cycles and economic growth. The Economic History Association was founded in 1940; its journal, the *Journal of Economic History*, began publication in 1941. The work of most US (and British) economic historians prior to the

Second World War, however, still reflected primarily the historian's orientation.

Economic history, being at the intersection of two disciplines, has often been involved in debates about methods and techniques. Before the 1960s, however, these debates were most frequently between economic historians and economists, and were concerned with the relative usefulness of abstract theory as contrasted with detailed institutional knowledge in understanding the past world and in prescribing policies for the contemporary situation. The German and English historical schools of the late nineteenth century arose primarily in reaction to what was felt to be the extreme abstractions of Austrian and Ricardian economic theory, with their extensive claims in regard to the universal applicability of economic theory as a guide to understanding past (and present) developments. Further, at this time the prescriptions of economic historians often pointed to the desirability of a wider range of state interference in the economy than was advocated by theoretical economists, a position buttressed by their claims of knowledge obtained from detailed examination of 'real' historical developments. Following Toynbee in Britain, there was often a social reform purpose central to historical studies. The classic *Methodenstreit* between Menger and Schmoller, which also raised questions about the usefulness and importance of induction and deduction as basic scientific approaches, is indicative of these debates with economists. Related points on the applicability of theoretical constructs arose in other debates between economic historians and economists, such as those at Cambridge between Marshall and Cunningham, and the 1920s series of articles, by Clapham and Pigou, on 'Empty Economic Boxes' (e.g. Clapham 1922; Pigou 1922).

There were some critiques stressing the advantages of the use of economic theory in the study of history. Heckscher's 1928 address to the International Historical Congress was not unique, nor was it the first, although it remains among the clearest examples of 'A plea for theory in economic history' (Heckscher 1929). Clapham's *Encyclopedia of the Social Sciences* essay (Clapham *et al.* 1931) sounded the call of the quantitatively oriented, with its reminder of the importance of 'the statistical sense, the habit of asking in relation to any institution, policy, group or movement the questions: how large?

how long? how often? how representative?' Yet it seems safe to say that prior to the Second World War most economic historians fought their interdisciplinary battles mainly against economic theorists, and, in their own work, more often followed the style and methods of historians rather than those of economists. As historians, the economic historians did broaden the range of questions and approaches to reflect some of the concerns of economists, but the work remained closer to the historical mainstream than it was to be in subsequent years.

In the USA, beginning in the late 1950s and 1960s, there occurred a significant shift in the training and interests of economic historians. The work of the post-1950s generation of economic historians, including Davis, Fogel, Gallman, North and Parker, as well as others trained as economists, generally falls under the rubric of the new economic history, but is also known as econometric history and cliometrics. It contains three different, and not always compatible, aspects, features seen somewhat in earlier works of economic historians, but not to such a pronounced degree. The first feature, one that reflected the interests of many social scientists in the post-Second World War period, was a heightened concern with problems relating to the long-term economic growth of nations (in the sense of an increase in the measured output of goods and services per capita). These studies rested more heavily on economic analysis and quantitative measures than did earlier work. The questions to be studied by economic historians were often guided by a search for messages to those nations currently underdeveloped, and the economic histories of the developed nations were regarded as case studies to be looked at for the secrets of their success. This focus on growth was to be found among economic historians in Britain and elsewhere in Europe, with important works by Rostow (1960) and by Deane and Cole (1962) on British growth in the eighteenth and nineteenth centuries helping to shape subsequent studies.

A second important influence was a growing reliance upon quantitative constructs, such as measures of aggregate national income, as a means both of describing the past and of posing questions for study. Economic history has always been quantitatively oriented because much of the basic data, such as prices and wages, are numerical. There had been a major multinational collection of price data under the auspices of the International Scientific Committee on Price History in the 1930s. In explaining the increased attention to statistical measurement, the crucial role of the National Bureau of Economic Research can be seen. It was the direct contribution of Kuznets (1941), in making national income an operational construct, which led to much of the work in preparing estimates of national income and of output and input by the industrial sector for the late nineteenth and twentieth centuries that was undertaken beginning in the 1930s. It was only in, and after, the 1950s that detailed estimates, based on census data, of US national income from 1839 onwards, and of British national income in the nineteenth century, were generated, and even later before similar estimates were presented for other countries and, in some cases, for earlier times. Quantitative work, both by cliometricians and what might be called more traditional economic historians, greatly expanded after the 1960s with the development of the computer. The increased analysis of quantitative data by economic historians mirrors the expansion of econometrics as a tool used by economists, as well as the greater occurrence of quantification within other fields of historical study.

The third feature of recent work in economic history is the systematic use of economic analysis, particularly the application of conventional neo-classical supply and demand analysis. It should be noted that the claims to scientific history of the economic historians who used these methods differs from the claims of earlier scholars. To the earlier writers, scientific history meant the uncovering of the laws of motion of the social system, providing a key to understanding the past as well as predicting the future. Recently it has meant applying the tools of economics to answer specific questions that fit into the broader historical picture. As the critique of neo-classical economics has emerged among economists, however, so has criticism of its use in the study of historical problems. Similarly, the concern among economists with issues related to income distribution and power relations in society, whether influenced by neo-classical or Marxist models, has been reflected in the work of economic historians who have utilized census manuscripts, tax lists and probate records to provide a fuller historical record of the course of inequality over the past centuries. The general attempt to expand the tools of economic analysis to what have been regarded as exogenous elements in the study of economic history has many applications: in the study of institutional changes, the examination of causes of technological change, the analysis of the causes and consequences of demographic movements (including both fertility and mortality changes), and the determination of the varieties of labour control to be found in different economies and over time.

In the post-Second World War period leadership in the new approach to economic history has been in the USA, with other nations generally following after a period of years. Yet the more traditional approaches to economic history, updated somewhat in method and approach, have continued to flourish in Britain and elsewhere, and economic history has retained its status as a separate discipline in Britain and other countries. In the USA, economic historians have again made the critique that mathematical economic theory has become too abstract and divorced from real-world issues, and that economics would benefit from reintroducing a more historical and empirical bent to the discipline, a practice that has, however, developed successfully in various fields of applied economics. Thus economic history has continued to contribute to both economics and to history.

STANLEY L. ENGERMAN
UNIVERSITY OF ROCHESTER

References

Clapham, J.H. (1922) 'Of empty economic bogies', *Economic Journal* 32.
Clapham, J.H., Pirenne, H. and Gras, N.S.B. (1931) 'Economic history', in E.R.A. Seligman (ed.) *Encyclopedia of the Social Sciences*, Vol. 5, New York.
Deane, P. and Cole, W.A. (1962) *British Economic Growth, 1688–1959*, Cambridge, UK.
Heckscher, E.F. (1929) 'A plea for theory in economic history', *Economic Journal*, Historical Supplement 4.
Kuznets, S. (1941) *National Income and its Composition, 1919–1938*, New York.
Pigou, A.C. (1922) 'Empty economic boxes: A reply', *Economic Journal* 32.
Rostow, W.W. (1960) *The Stages of Economic Growth*, Cambridge, UK.

Further reading

Cole, A.H. (1968) 'Economic history in the United States: Formative years of a discipline', *Journal of Economic History* 28.
Coleman, D.C. (1987) *History and the Economic Past: An Account of the Rise and Decline of Economic History in Britain*, Oxford.
Fishlow, A. and Fogey, R.W. (1971) 'Quantitative economic history: An interim evaluation', *Journal of Economic History* 31.
Harte, N.B. (ed.) (1970) *The Study of Economic History. Collected Inaugural Lectures, 1893–1970*, London.
Hudson, P. (ed.) (2001) *Living Economic and Social History*, Glasgow.
Koot, G.M. (1987) *English Historical Economics, 1870–1926: The Rise of Economic History and Neomercantilism*, Cambridge, UK.
Maloney, J. (1985) *Marshall, Orthodoxy and the Professionalisation of Economics*, Cambridge, UK.
North, D.C. (1968) 'Economic history', in D.L. Sills (ed.) *International Encyclopedia of the Social Sciences*, Vol. 6, New York.
Wright, C.D. (1905) 'An economic history of the United States', *American Economic Review*, Papers and Proceedings, Part 11(b).

SEE ALSO: cliometrics; industrial revolutions

ECONOMIC MAN

Who is economic man, where did he come from and where has he ventured forth, and how might he be revised into a more crowd-pleasing form? Schumpeter refers to the concept of economic man as one 'particularly effective in promoting the critics' mirth or wrath' (1954: 887n). Indeed, the concept continues to bring down wrath on the heads of economists, even as economic man continues to lurk in the pages of economics textbooks as an omnipresent but somewhat unsatisfactory teaching tool.

The idea of man as a rational calculator of gains and losses, and generally interested in monetary gain, potentially in opposition to the view of man as driven by whim and emotion, can be traced back in philosophical writings to the ancients. Schumpeter (1954: 156) identifies an early precursor in Frigerio's *L'economo prudente* (1629), but others have traced the notion back further to Plato, Aristotle and St Augustine, viewing their discussions as related to these opposing views of human motivation. Indeed, the earliest use of a closely related terminology, as it appears in Carey, indicates the continuing dualism within man: 'We have the politico-economical man, on one hand influenced solely by the thirst for wealth, and on the other...under the control of the sexual passion' (1858: 29). However, a fuller statement of the idea in a form that was subsequently highly influential on the development of economic thought was first created by Mill (1836), who described this hypothetical person of narrow and well-defined motives in some detail. In 1880 Bagehot refers to 'economical man' (1880: 83) and in 1888 the first appearance in print of the current favoured version, 'economic man' (Ingram 1888: 155), occurs. The older-sounding Graeco-Latin version 'Homo oeconomicus' (with the other common variant being Homo economicus) does not appear until Pareto (1906)).

Generally economic man is characterized formally by a complete set of ordered preferences, perfect information about the world, and infinite computing power to calculate with. Using these innate resources, he maximizes his welfare subject to external constraints. Although we need not know what his welfare depends on – indeed, it is irrelevant – it is generally a well-being that does not depend on the well-being of others. He need not be motivated solely by money; for instance, Mill's version desired accumulation, leisure, luxury and procreation (Persky 1995: 223). The key to the characterization of economic man is his selection technique for making choices rather than what the choices are. And clearly here the roots of economic man lie to large extent in Bentham's pleasure versus pain 'calculus' – as further developed along mathematical lines to regard trade-offs on the margin by Jevons, for there must be both trade-offs and a well-defined set of preferences between alternatives, i.e. a utility function, in order for this framework to be both non-tautological and potentially tractable using mathematical tools.

How seriously should we take this depiction of economic man in terms of its potential coincidence with actual human behaviour? Certainly, economists do not always take this depiction seriously. Marshall wrote critically of the unrealism inherent in the attempts that have 'been made to construct an abstract science with regard to the actions of an "economic man", who is under no ethical influences and who pursues pecuniary gain warily and energetically, but mechanically and selfishly' (1890: vi). However, because Marshall viewed economics as mainly being the study of the side of life, i.e. business matters, where business is 'more clearly marked off from other concerns of life' (1890: 5), he was willing to consider man as being more deliberate in his calculations in regards to business matters – and hence more correspondent in this realm to

economic man. Mill as well thought of political economy in general as concerned with an abstraction of man that 'does not treat of the whole of man's nature as modified by the social state' (1836: 321).

However, Friedman sparked much controversy by opining that hypotheses, even if generated in a purely deductive framework, with potentially unrealistic assumptions, are still useful if they are consistent with observed phenomena. Indeed, in this viewpoint, an 'alternative hypothesis is more attractive than [another] not because its "assumptions" are more "realistic" but rather because it is part of a more general theory that applies to a wider variety of phenomena...has more implications capable of being contradicted, and has failed to be contradicted under a wider variety of circumstances' (Friedman 1953: 192). Under this canopy, economic man's usefulness is measured against his ability to explain and predict rather than against an 'aesthetic' viewpoint regarding the realism of the assumptions underlying his characterization. In addition, this viewpoint sets no a priori limitation on the range of human behaviour over which economic man is allowed to roam.

Non-economists, not surprisingly, find this strategy particularly unsatisfying and this viewpoint unpersuasive. Philosophers Hollis and Nell point out that

> there is no question of testing an economic theory against the actual behaviour of the rational producer or consumer. Producers and consumers are rational precisely insofar as they behave as predicted and the test shows only how rational they are.
>
> (1975: 55)

Nevertheless, the positivist strategy has been quite successful in leading the economists' late twentieth-century colonization of various topics that were previously considered off-limits to economists.

For instance, Downs extends the conception of economic man into the field of political science. He makes the novel assertion that both voters and governments act as maximizing economic agents (contrary to the view of political citizens and states as disinterested ruling bodies), assuming that 'homo politicus...approaches every situation with one eye on the gains to be had, the other eye on costs, a delicate ability to balance them, and a strong desire to follow wherever rationality leads him' (Downs 1957: 7–8).

Becker, one of the most celebrated of the 'economic imperialists', has gone even farther, creatively applying the economic man approach to such topics as crime, discrimination and marriage. He suggests expansively that 'all human behavior can be viewed as involving participants who maximize their utility from a stable set of preferences and accumulate an optimal amount of information and other inputs in a variety of markets' (Becker 1976: 14) and calls departures from the strictly economic approach, acknowledgements of 'defeat in the guise of considered judgement' (Becker 1976: 12).

In the quest to move beyond economic man, two main lines of potential reformulation have developed. One reformulation, perhaps into 'semi-economic man', stresses the limits on human reason, including the amount of time available for gathering information, and computational ability, and leads to the concept of 'bounded rationality' or 'satisficing' (Simon 1957). Much recent work in the subfield of behavioural economics, influenced in addition by the intersections between psychology and economics explored by Tversky, Kahneman and Thaler, among others, can be seen in the spirit of this viewpoint, and in addition questions the very nature of human rationality as tied to perception, e.g. the different weighting that humans place on choices depending on how they are framed and the social context in which they appear.

The second reformulation, led by the recent feminist economist movement, asks how much economic man, rather than being the universal person *homo* is the specific male *vir* – and a European white male to boot. Some authors, such as Burggraf, assert that women are becoming more like men as the separation between paid and unpaid, 'caring' labour is weakened, that 'there is an economic woman, *femina economica*, who calculates the value of her time and talents in alternative roles and occupations, and increasingly goes where the returns are greatest, a female who follows the same market signals as men' (1997: 22). Others argue that women act differently from men, and in particular act less selfishly. McCloskey characterizes the difference thus: that *vir economicus* routinely defects from social arrangements when it suits his convenience, 'dumping externalities on the neighbors.

Femina economica, by contrast, would more often walk down the beach to dispose of her McDonald's carton in a trash bin...because she feels solidarity with others' (1993: 79). Hence a satisfactory reformulation must first take into account that *Homo economicus* is 'the brainchild of Western man's philosophical traditions' and 'bears the markings of his fathers' profoundly gendered social and cultural lives' (Williams 1993: 145) in order to move beyond this narrow formulation.

The frequency of appearance of economic man, both in sarcastic and earnest usage, continues practically unabated since the late 1800s. However, his continued appearance does not imply acceptance of the tenets of his being. His underpinnings, as with much of economics, are continually in question even as additional edifices are placed upon his limbs.

JOYCE JACOBSEN
WESLEYAN UNIVERSITY

References

Bagehot, W. (1880) *Economic Studies*, London.

Becker, G. (1976) *The Economic Approach to Human Behavior*, Chicago, IL.

Burggraf, S.P. (1997) *The Feminine Economy and Economic Man*, Reading, MA.

Carey, H.C. (1858) *Principles of Social Science*, Philadelphia, PA.

Downs, A. (1957) *Economic Theory of Democracy*, New York.

Friedman, M. (1953) *Essays in Positive Economics*, Chicago, IL.

Hollis, M. and Nell, E. (1975) *Rational Economic Man*, Cambridge, UK.

Ingram, J.K. (1888) *A History of Political Economy*, New York.

McCloskey, D.N. (1993) 'Some consequences of a conjective economics', in M.A. Ferber and J.A. Nelson (eds) *Beyond Economic Man*, Chicago, IL.

Marshall, A. (1890) *Principles of Economics*, London.

Mill, J.S. (1836) 'On the definition of political economy; and on the method of investigation proper to it', *London and Westminster Review*.

Pareto, V. (1906) *Manuale di Economia Politica*, Milan.

Persky, J. (1995) 'The ethology of *Homo economicus*', *Journal of Economic Perspectives* 9(2): 221–31.

Schumpeter, J.A. (1954) *History of Economic Analysis*, London.

Simon, H. (1957) *Models of Man*, New York.

Williams, R.M. (1993) 'Race, deconstruction, and the emergent agenda of feminist economic theory', in M.A. Ferber and J.A. Nelson (eds) *Beyond Economic Man*, Chicago, IL.

SEE ALSO: optimization; rational choice (action) theory

ECONOMICS

In the draft of the introduction to his monumental study of the history of economic analysis, Joseph Schumpeter (1954) writes as follows:

> This book will describe the development and the fortunes of scientific analysis in the field of economics, from Graeco-Roman times to the present, in the appropriate setting of social and political history and with some attention to the developments in other social sciences and also in philosophy.

Few contemporary economists view their subject as stretching back continuously to Graeco-Roman civilizations, and some would regard a close association with history or philosophy as unnecessary, if not positively undesirable. Yet Schumpeter's account takes up nearly 200 pages before reaching Adam Smith's *The Wealth of Nations*, which is where economics began according to a vulgar view.

There is no great contradiction here. A reading of Schumpeter shows that he, as much as any other commentator, recognizes that the study of economic questions underwent radical changes of method, and an accelerated pace of development, in the late eighteenth century. Yet contemporary historians of economic thought agree with Schumpeter in not attributing the beginning of modern economics to the European Enlightenment, still less to the Scottish Enlightenment and Adam Smith. On examination the mercantilist and liberal writers turn out to share as much in common as they have differences. As in other cases, a sharper contrast exists between modern and early thinkers together, and their premodern predecessors. (On mercantilism, see Magnusson 1994.)

What began, whenever it began, and accelerated in the late eighteenth century, was not the description, not even the analysis, of economic institutions and questions, all of which are ancient. It was a redefinition of the centre of focus for such studies. A part justification of the simple belief that it all began with *The Wealth of Nations* is that the way in which Smith defined the subject is, in broad outline at least, recognizably the same as the subject defines itself today. To be specific:

1 The Renaissance idea that man is part of nature is sovereign. This frees economic analysis to apply rationalist and reductionist methods in order to attack economic 'superstitions', such as the belief that true wealth consists in the possession of gold.

2 Economics is liberated from morality, but not in the direction of an amoral political economy of nation-state power, which the mercantilists and others had explored. Rather many simple 'moral' views are discredited, often by the device of showing that their intentions fail to translate into moral outcomes. A phrase frequently used by Adam Smith captures this change of philosophy perfectly. Mercantilist restrictions are *unreasonable*. This means, of course, that like all institutions they are subject to critical rational review, and that they fail that test.

3 If economics is not about selecting policies to promote the power of the sovereign, then what is it about? A view characteristic of the liberal individualism of the seventeenth and eighteenth centuries, again inherited by the modern discipline, has it that it is about the individual (or the individual family) and about the proper field, conceived as a wide one, for the pursuit of self-interest. The understanding that self-interest may be a socially constructive force is what separates the economist from the one who derives his views on economic issues solely from common sense. Equally, the understanding that self-interest may need to be channelled or even constrained to achieve good social outcomes is essential to a sophisticated economic insight.

4 This last tension, between the field for liberal policy, even *laissez-faire*, and the field for intervention, makes economics essentially concerned with policy. True there exist economic questions that are inherently abstract; questions addressed to the formalized issues that considerations of preference, decision and equilibrium throw up. Yet policy is never far away. As an illustration of the point, consider that no one would ever have wasted time on determining what is the level of normal prices if normal price was not

considered as, at least potentially, an input to economic policy.

Description and analysis sound like science, but what of policy? Can there be a science of policy? Is indeed economics itself a science? The question is often asked thoughtlessly, without the enquirer having a clear notion of what counts as a science. Yet it conceals serious issues. Obviously economics is not physics, however physics may be conceived. Biology, or even climatology, seem to be closer cousins. Economics has models, data and, certainly, simplifying assumptions. But it also concerns itself with values, with what is good or bad in economic states. Science is usually conceived of as value free; not in the sense that subject matter is chosen at random, but with the meaning that it concerns itself with what is, not with what ought to be.

Economics has tried to wriggle around this dilemma for most of its modern history. If there can be no ought to be, how can there be policy? And without policy, will not economics reduce to a kind of descriptive anthropology of economic life? If, on the other hand, values enter into economic discourse – a higher gross national product is good, fluctuations are bad, etc. – how is economics to escape from a mire of relativism in which its values are shown to be just one of many possibilities?

The question was posed most sharply by Professor Lionel Robbins, who asked by what right economists maintained that the abolition of the Corn Laws in nineteenth-century Britain was a good thing. While it was good for manufacturers, and possibly for their workers, it was surely bad for landlords. Who were economists to say that landlords' losses counted for less than the gains of manufacturers?

Showing that history was on the side of the manufacturers would hardly settle the matter. History after all was on the side of Cortés and against the South American aborigines at one time, but few people today regard that as settling the value issues. A different tack was tried by Kaldor (1939), and a similar argument explored by Hicks. An economic change could be regarded as an improvement, argued Kaldor, if it carried the potential of making everyone in the economy better off. This fascinating argument, and its problems, almost define what the modern field of welfare economics is about.

The assumption that individual tastes are sovereign was not contentious for economists, although others might question it. Preferred by all had to mean better. Making individual self-interest basic to welfare evaluation goes back to Pareto and beyond. Hicks (1969 [1959]) is a striking challenge to this view. Later investigation showed that even if the sovereignty of individual preference is conceded, there remain serious conceptual problems for welfare evaluation. The most fundamental statement of these difficulties is the hugely influential work of Arrow (1963), which shows that a social welfare function derived from individual preferences, according to weakly constrained principles, implies the dictatorship of one individual over the ranking of at least three possibilities. Arrow's axioms for the social welfare function have proved controversial (see Sen 1979), but there is no trick solution to a problem that just reformulates itself when the question is redefined.

Some economists have elected to throw away value neutrality and to investigate the implications for policy of specific value weights. Others have relied upon the important and useful fact that several important results in economic theory are 'value neutral' in the sense that they hold true for all value weights. An example would be the very general result of public finance theory which says that lump-sum taxation imposes less cost on those taxed (has a lower excess burden), for a given revenue collected, and regardless of how the burden of taxation is distributed, than any other form of taxation (see Atkinson and Stiglitz 1980: Chapter 11).

This is not to say that one can easily manœuvre around the problem that economic pronouncements are heavily value-laden. Lump-sum taxation completely severs the link between efficiency and distribution, and creates a Utopian world in which economic institutions function perfectly to take the economy to its utility possibility frontier, while leaving the policy-maker to select a point on that frontier. In general, efficiency and distribution are more closely bound together when policy is designed with feasible taxes and other instruments to hand. Modern economics has made much of *incentive compatibility*, which means the design of institutions, including taxation, but much more as well, so that the individual agents involved will find it in their self-interest to do what the policy-maker intends. (On incentive compatibility and the associated concept of mechanism design, see Fudenberg and Tirole 1991: Chapter 7.)

Policy design as conceived by modern economic theory is hugely more complicated and sophisticated than its eighteenth-century ancestor, with its sometimes simple 'get rid of irksome interference' approach. The role of the state and how it should best operate are well modelled in the context of the design of systems of taxation and regulation. Outside those particular areas, policy design needs a good deal of improvement, a point to which I shall return.

A good measure of how economics has grown and changed over its recent centuries of history is provided by the story of GNP (gross national product) or its equivalents. Before the twentieth century it would be no exaggeration to say that there was no well-developed flow concept of economic well-being. The wealth of nations, or regions or peoples, were the object of comment and investigation. Naturally, wealth and income, as the writings of Cantillon, Petty and Quesnay confirm, are closely related concepts. Yet they part company in the short run, as when a depression lowers incomes substantially while little affecting wealth. To record fluctuations in national income at all precisely demands a systematic collection of statistics, via a census of production, which had to wait until the mid-twentieth century to become reality.

Before that happened, the theory of national income as a concept and as a measure of economic welfare had been developed. Pigou (1955) is a good short exposition. The theoretical framework was implemented in modern GNP accounting, which has graduated in half a century from an academic exercise to perhaps the most important objective and indicator of government policy.

It is no surprise that the success of GNP accounting in measuring the level of activity for the economy has been followed by deep criticism of GNP as an objective of policy. More than one type of issue is involved and limitations of space prohibit a full discussion here. Yet two basic points are frequently encountered. They can be briefly labelled consumerism and the environment. In short the consumerism argument says that GNP is biased towards a market notion of human welfare that overweighs capitalist lifestyle and consumption and underweighs non-market activities and lifestyle. Thus transport to commute to work, and health costs associated with

commuting, enter into GNP, while the value of home-grown vegetables does not. Similar arguments become even more heated where the environment and finite resources are concerned. Modern industrial production based on the burning of fossil fuels boosts GNP. Yet the cost that is the reduction of the levels of those fuels remaining in the ground is not deducted from GNP. There are no easy answers to any of these issues; yet their existence shows the change in focus of economic thought among professionals and non-professionals alike.

Probably the ideological side to economics explains why the subject has been prone to controversy and to discord between competing schools. In the Anglo-Saxon world, however, the predominant method has become the neo-classical approach. Most economists would agree with that view even when some would regret the fact. But what exactly is neo-classical economics, and what are the alternatives that have failed while the neo-classical variety has flourished?

In summary, neo-classical economics is built on the assumption that efficient markets arrive at an equilibrium in which the separate actions of rational maximizing agents are made consistent via market-equilibrium (or market-clearing) conditions. In the absence of externalities, it is then a *theorem* that the resulting allocation of resources is efficient in the sense of Pareto. This is the so-called first fundamental theorem of welfare economics. The second fundamental theorem states that any Pareto efficient allocation can be made a market equilibrium when suitable lump-sum transfers place each agent on the right budget constraint. These two results fully clarify the relationship between efficiency and market equilibrium for competitive economies.

Such a clear intellectual framework makes it easy to classify the main lines of attack for anti-neo-classical economics. These concern:

1   Motivation: are real-life economic agents maximizers who concentrate mainly on economic self-interest?
2   Information: are these agents well informed about prices – current and future – and about technology, and even about their own tastes?
3   Calculation: even given the information, and the objective, how can agents calculate the right action? And how can the market, or the market-maker, calculate the equilibrium?

and finally:

4   Do markets function as the neo-classical model has it, or are they subject to price rigidities, imperfect competition or monopoly, market failure or missing markets?

Some of these arguments are old, some more or less modern. The economist's assumption about the motivation of 'economic man' have always seemed absurd, and immoral as well, to many outsiders. Thornstein Veblen articulated passionately the problems with the computational abilities implied by the assumption that economic agents maximize. Keynes's theory, on one interpretation, is partly about the macroeconomic effects of sticky prices. The idea that imperfect information is crucial to market failure may have been mentioned in the nineteenth century, but until recent years there is no analysis of the idea worthy of the name. Imperfect competition, especially duopoly, was analysed by Cournot amazingly ahead of his time in the middle of the nineteenth century, and analysis continued ever since. The idea that markets may be *missing*, as opposed to just not functioning well, is certainly modern, and is tied up with the again modern concept that sources of information and transaction costs should be modelled explicitly.

Now we come to a powerful paradox. As models developed from the shortcomings of neo-classical theory listed above become increasingly refined and sophisticated, they frequently and typically emerge from the work of economists of the neo-classical stable. Indeed the neo-classical critique of neo-classical economics has become an industry in its own right. In this situation a truly anti-neo-classical economics has not been easy to construct. Akerlof (1984) is one of the most interesting attempts to do so, and the frequently 'neo-classical' nature of approaches based on highly 'non-neo-classical' assumptions is suggestive.

It must of course be easy to construct an entirely non-neo-classical economics if one is willing to ditch enough baggage. In particular, theories in which agents behave according to more or less arbitrary rules produce radically different conclusions. But do such theories count as theories in economics? This debate tends to separate theory and empirical investigation. *Ad hoc* behavioural assumptions are hard to moti-

vate or to formalize. Yet empirical studies have sometimes forced economists to recognize them as fact. A notable case in point is choice under uncertainty. Some evidence is solidly against the most powerful and appealing theoretical model. Yet the evidence seems to indicate what may be going on, and formalization of that has been attempted (see Machina 1987).

If there is little truly anti-neo-classical economics but mainly neo-classical economics in need of more refinement and sophistication, where does that leave the Keynesian Revolution? Keynes (1973) saw himself as correcting a (neo)classical economics, the root specifications of which he was to a great extent willing to accept. Specifically, he argued that his unemployment could be encountered in a competitive economy in some kind of equilibrium. How far he was correct is a controversial question. A modern North American school of New Keynesian thinkers maintains that Keynesian economics can only be made to work by introducing the specific modelling of market imperfections, information asymmetries and missing markets (see Blanchard and Fischer 1989).

Certainly the treatment of expectations differs notably between Keynes and his modern successors in macroeconomic theory. Keynes argued for the subjectivity and irrationality of expectations concerning the future. Some modern theorists, by contrast, have gone to the opposite extreme by studying *rational expectations* – expectations as efficient and perfect as it is possible to be in the circumstances (see Begg 1982). Although taken to its logical limit, this approach soon becomes mathematically elaborate and even indeterminate, there lies at the bottom of the debate some fundamental questions concerning Keynes's economics that have asserted themselves from the start of the Keynesian Revolution.

With the flexible output prices assumed by Keynes, the theory asserts that an increase in effective demand will generate an increased output from the supply side by raising output prices relative to wage costs – i.e. by inflation, which cuts the real wage. How will this do when workers become aware of the fall in their living standards even when employed? There are various answers, none completely satisfactory. Keynes's discussion suggests that price inflation coordinates real wage cuts for all workers that they cannot achieve acting on their own, but will willingly accept when generalized because imposed by price inflation. New classical macro-economists argued that output could not be increased by a boost to effective demand, as workers willing to accept a cut in their real wage could have taken it anyway. Hence only inflation surprises would increase output from the supply side. With rational expectations the scope for policy using inflation surprises would be severely limited. These arguments contained a germ of truth, as with the conclusion that rapid and expected inflation is soon discounted and has few real effects. Experience has shown that Keynesian effects continue to exist but that their scope is shorter run than the many earlier Keynesian theorists assumed. Unemployment, however, has proved to be a growing problem for industrial countries, leading some to conclude that structural factors and dual labour markets may now be more important than the demand side.

The intricacies of rational expectations analysis provides an example of the growing use, and eventual dominance, of mathematics in economic theorizing. Economics today is an applied mathematical subject to an extent unimaginable a century ago. This is not because the mathematically literate have conspired to squeeze out their less advantaged colleagues. Rather, mathematics is a natural language for economic reasoning. Obviously mathematics, including the differential calculus, lends itself to maximization. Yet for all the arguments ever since Veblen, maximization is seldom vital; it often serves to provide a definiteness that could in principle be provided by alternative means. More important, however, is the power of mathematics in dealing with systems in which many influences make themselves felt simultaneously – a typical situation for social science models. Solving simultaneous equations really requires mathematics, and anyone who thinks that they can do it intuitively is practising self-deception.

Another great merit of mathematical reasoning is that it facilitates connections between theoretical and empirical work. For all the hostility of Keynes himself to mathematical economics and econometrics, the Keynesian revolution served to bring theoretical and applied economics closer together than had ever previously been the case. The development of national income accounting is a leading instance of this point. Yet economics and econometrics, though always second cousins, have never married. Rather, they have developed sufficiently separately to retain distinctive methods and styles. Hence the Econometric Society, at its regular conferences in different parts of the world, divides its programmes into economics and econometrics. Some resent this but no one could claim it to be an absurd division.

Growing specialization within economics does not affect only econometrics and is a result of the huge growth of the discipline and the proliferation of journals. Today economists tend to be development economists, labour economists, game theorists or specialists in other fields. The generalist hardly exists. Also, as a general category, *economist* is now more like *architect* than *man of letters*. It defines a profession. And clearly the number of people who can be said to earn a living by the practice of economics has increased massively since the Second World War. The total cannot easily be known but 200,000 worldwide would be a reasonable guess.

The story of the last 60 years has been one of the growing professionalization of economics. Prior to the Second World War there was nothing like an agreed syllabus for the subject. That means no agreement even within countries, not to speak of between countries, concerning what a properly trained economist should know, what books he or she should definitely have read, and so on. That frequently entailed disorganized amateurism and unnecessary originality. On the positive side, however, that early undeveloped period of the subject made it possible for a few exceptional thinkers to build whole branches of the discipline from the ground, giving them a personal shape as they did so. Arrow on general equilibrium, Friedman on consumption function theory and Schultz and Lewis on economic development are just some random examples.

These last three instances are selected from early names on the list of thirty-five winners of the Bank of Sweden Nobel Prize in Economics, 1969–2003. That list is good at indicating the manner in which economics (and econometrics too) has changed and developed over the years, always finding new concepts and new techniques on which to test itself. An old joke has it that in economics the questions never change, only the answers. That is surely untrue. Recently the author examined a 2003 undergraduate macroeconomics examination, imagining himself once again a 1960s undergraduate. Some questions are incomprehensible to those pretended eyes; others could have been answered, but mainly irrelevantly. The largest changes that separates the two vintages of undergraduate are institutional. The world of the 1960s was a world overwhelmingly of fixed exchange rates and capital controls. A very few economists worried about inflation. They were all on the political right and appeared to be somewhat cranky.

To return to the Nobel Prize list, all the first twenty names are mainstream in the sense that their economics (or in two instances econometrics) is addressed to types of issues that are, and have always been, clearly inside the boundaries of the discipline. After 1990 several 'offbeat' (for want of a better term) scholars appear on the list. Fogel and North (1993) bring cliometrics (quantitative economic history) and institutions. Akerlof, Spence and Stiglitz (2001) receive the award for their work on imperfect information and missing markets. This is an example of the 'neo-classical' approach to 'non-neo-classical' assumptions already mentioned above. A year later Kahneman and Vernon-Smith are given the award for work on experiments designed to throw light on 'real-life' decision-making based on psychological and behavioural models.

The Nobel awards only confirm the manner in which economics is ceaselessly changing and reforming itself as new ideas and fields emerge, and old ones are radically reassessed and reformulated. Thus the old field of industrial organization has been transformed completely by the infusion of formal theory models based on game theory (see Tirole 1988). Economic growth theory has enjoyed a renaissance founded in endogenous technical progress and explicit optimization (see Barro and Sala-i-Martin 1995). Some fields that hardly existed 20 years ago are now huge. For instance auction theory is now a speciality in its own right, with some important practical applications (see Klemperer 1999).

How successful is economics in the early twenty-first century? In a crude ecological sense, economics is undoubtedly successful. It is reproducing itself with an impressive efficiency. It is now a worldwide profession, with a standard of training to great extent agreed. It is much like medicine in that respect. On the test of its power as a problem-solving method, the success of economics is more questionable. The subject has spent much of the last 20 years writing itself out of policy relevance. This is particularly marked with macroeconomics, where policy ineffective-

ness theorems are central to a still-influential mode of thought. Recently models for good macroeconomic policy have returned, specially in connection with theories of how central banks should operate. What is claimed for policy is now more modest, but good central banking is seen as crucial. Incidentally, central banks are now huge employers of postgraduate economists, as are competition regulators. Neither of these were major employers of economists 25 years ago.

It is true that the subject has always recognized that policy may be unable to improve on the market. With Adam Smith, however, that view owed more to scepticism about the usefulness of policy interference than to a faith in the perfection of unregulated markets as such. Recently, however, a belief in the efficiency of markets, sometimes, but not always, qualified by the recognition of imperfect information and similar problems, has attracted many and enthusiastic adherents.

The sometimes unfortunate effects of ill-considered deregulation exercises in the West may be blamed in part on intellectual fashion. Economists have continued to struggle with a hugely important class of problems that may be called structural adjustment. This includes how to treat economies in serious macroeconomic disequilibrium, and how to advise economies making the wide and dangerous transit from central-planned socialism to free-market capitalism. Economists are bitterly divided on the first question; witness Stiglitz (2002) and its reception. Equally lacking any clear consensus is the issue of transition, the question of how the ex-Soviet economies of Eastern Europe should adjust (or should have adjusted) to the fall of communism. That reform, which has required the creation of markets more than their liberalization, found economists somewhat empty-handed. The result has too often been a flood of inconsistent advice based on partial models inspired by Western economies. It is too soon to write the history of the reform of ex-Soviet economies and economic thought but it must be hoped that some deep lessons will have been learnt from an experience that underlines the fact that economics, for all its modern reach and power, remains a subject embedded in particular historical experiences and presumptions.

CHRISTOPHER BLISS
NUFFIELD COLLEGE, OXFORD

References

Akerlof, G.A. (1984) *An Economic Theorist's Book of Tales*, Cambridge, UK.

Arrow, K.J. (1963) *Social Choice and Individual Values*, 2nd edn, London.

Atkinson, A.B. and Stiglitz, J.E. (1980) *Lectures on Public Economics*, London.

Barro, R.J. and Sala-i-Martin, X. (1995) *Economic Growth*, New York.

Begg, D.K.H. (1982) *The Rational Expectations Revolution in Macroeconomics*, Deddington Banbury, Oxfordshire.

Blanchard, O.J. and Fischer, S. (1989) *Lectures on Macroeconomics*, Cambridge, MA.

Fudenberg, D. and Tirole, J. (1991) *Game Theory*, Cambridge, MA.

Hicks, J.R. (1969 [1959]) 'Preface and a manifesto', in K.J. Arrow and T. Scitovsky (eds) *Readings in Welfare Economics*, American Economic Association Series, London, pp. 95–7.

Kaldor, N. (1939) 'Welfare propositions of economics and interpersonal comparisons of utility', *Economic Journal* 49: 549–52.

Keynes, J.M. (1973) *The General Theory*, London.

Klemperer, P. (1999) 'Auction theory: A guide to the literature', *Journal of Economic Surveys* 13: 227–86.

Machina, M.J. (1987) 'Choice under uncertainty: Problems solved and unsolved', *Journal of Economic Perspectives* 1: 121–54.

Magnusson, L. (1994) *Mercantilism: The Shaping of an Economic Language*, London.

Pigou, A.C. (1955) *Income Revisited*, London.

Schumpeter, J.A. (1954) *History of Economic Analysis*, New York.

Sen, A.K. (1979) *Collective Choice and Social Welfare*, Amsterdam.

Stiglitz, J. (2002) *Globalization and Its Discontents*, New York.

Tirole, J. (1988) *The Theory of Industrial Organization*, Cambridge, MA.

ECONOMIES OF SCALE

The economies of scale are the reductions in average unit costs associated with increases in the scale of production of goods or services. The scale at which unit costs cease to fall, or fall only slowly, is defined as the minimum optimum scale. The economies of scale are an important determinant of the structure of industries. If the minimum optimum scale represents a substantial proportion of an industry's output, the industry will tend to have a concentrated structure. The motor industry is an example of an industry in which the economies of scale are large. In terms of firms operating in the industry, it evolved a concentrated structure in all the advanced industrial countries and with globalization the concentration has increased. The manufacture of clothing is an example of a trade in which the economies of scale are smaller. There are many firms and factories operating in the industry.

The economies of scale relate to changes in the scale of production along different *dimensions* of scale. Examples of the dimensions of scale are the capacity of a plant or factory, the output of distinct products, the number of units produced in a production run by firms that produce a range of products in batches and the overall scale of a company. Reductions in unit costs associated with increases in the scale of multiproduct firms have been distinguished from the economies of scale and labelled 'the economies of scope'. The relationships between the scale of firms, their expenditure on R&D, and the effectiveness of the R&D in producing improved and new products and processes are of increasing importance.

The main sources of economies of scale are increasing specialization, indivisibilities, increasing dimensions of plant and the benefits of increased resources. Examples of indivisibilities are the cost of designing and developing a product, such as an aircraft, car or computer programme, setting up a production line for a product or for a batch of a product, the capacity of a machine tool and a TV advert. A firm that cannot fully utilize the item to which the indivisible cost relates, or spread the cost over as large an output as its rivals, is at a disadvantage. However, it may be able to damp down its cost disadvantage by, for example, acquiring a second-hand machine tool, or by using a different type of promotion in place of TV advertising. For some types of plant, such as tanks and pipelines, and over certain ranges of size, the capacity – the potential output – increases approximately in proportion to the volume and faster than the capital cost that increases in proportion to the surface area. The sources of diseconomies of scale are the increasing complexity of production and organization, management and motivation. As the output of a plant increases, the average unit cost of transporting the product to markets rises.

For a limited range of processes it is possible to base estimates of the economies of scale on engineering relationships, for example for the capital and operating costs and capacity of boilers. For other processes engineers and accountants can make hypothetical estimates of the costs for producing in the least-cost way and given the existing technology. These approaches to measuring the economies of scale are more difficult to apply to estimating the relationships between scale and the costs of selling and marketing, and the cost and effectiveness of management, R&D and innovation. Attempts have been made to estimate the economies of scale for establishments and firms by statistical analyses of actual costs and scale. These data usually relate to establishments making different combinations of products and with equipment acquired at different points in time and incorporating different technologies, so the extent to which the analyses identify the economies of scale is obscure. Another approach to assessing, or at least checking, the importance of the economies of scale in an industry is to examine changes in its structure. If many small firms are entering, establishing themselves and producing an increasing share of the output of an industry this suggests the economies of scale are limited.

Estimates have been made of the economies of scale for many manufacturing industries. These estimates and the changing structure of industries indicate that there are large economies of scale in many, but not all, manufacturing industries. In the service sector there are economies of scale but it is difficult to estimate their magnitude. There are many fixed costs for advertising, meeting regulatory requirements and opportunities for risk spreading by, for example, banks and insurance firms, but also scope for smaller firms to specialize in areas where they are not at a cost disadvantage.

The economies of scale can change through time. One example is the development of mini-steel mills using scrap that, depending on the price of scrap, can compete with much larger works converting iron ore to steel. The introduction of computer-controlled machinery has reduced the set-up costs in the vehicle, engineering and book-printing industries, and reduced the economies of long production runs.

Adam Smith (1776) described the organization of the pin industry and drew attention to the benefits of specialization. Austin Robinson (1931) described and analysed the determinants of the optimum scale, distinguishing the optimum for production, marketing, finance and dealing with risks and fluctuations. Bain (1956) pioneered quantifying the economies of scale. Stigler (1958) proposed the use of the survivorship method of estimating the economies of scale. Haldi and Whitcomb (1967) developed the engineering ap-

proach to estimating the economies of scale. Pratten (1971 and 1988) estimated the economies of scale in a wide range of manufacturing industries. Scherer *et al.* (1975) concentrated on estimating the economies of scale in industries in which each firm operated many factories or plants often located in a number of countries.

CLIFF PRATTEN
TRINITY HALL, CAMBRIDGE

References

Bain, J.S. (1956) *Barriers to New Competition*, Cambridge, MA.
Haldi, J. and Whitcomb, D. (1967) 'Economies of scale in industrial plants', *Journal of Political Economy* 75: 373–85.
Pratten, C. (1971) *The Economies of Scale in Manufacturing Industry*, Cambridge.
—— (1988) 'A survey of the economies of scale', in *Studies on the Economics of Integration. Research on the Cost of Non-Europe: Basic Findings*, Vol. 2, Brussels, Ch. 2, pp. 11–165.
Robinson, A. (1931, revised 1958) *Structure of Competitive Industry*, Cambridge.
Scherer, F.M., Beckenstein, A., Kaufer, E. and Murphy, R.D. (1975) *The Economies of Multi-Plant Operation*, Cambridge, MA.
Smith, A. (1776) *The Wealth of Nations*, London.
Stigler, G.J. (1958) 'The economies of scale', *Journal of Law and Economics* 1: 54–71.

SEE ALSO: factors of production; production and cost frontiers; productivity; research and development (R&D)

EDUCATION

Educational research is very largely applied research, and in practice it deals particularly with activities related to learning, usually within the context of the schools. The problems studied and the methods employed vary a great deal, but while earlier, philosophical studies focused on the *aims* of education, modern research on education by social scientists (notably educational psychologists) has been concerned rather with questions of *means*.

In the early twentieth century, curriculum reformers cited research by Edward Thorndike, which showed that learning in one field was not easily transferred to another field (Thorndike 1906). They concluded that the school curriculum should be more specifically related to the tasks that students would be expected to perform upon graduation. This was an appealing argument in a rapidly changing society, which was moving from a predominantly rural way of life to a dominantly urban, industrial economy, and which was attracting high numbers of immigrants.

More generally, Thorndike's work signified an important moment in educational scholarship, for it was one of the first studies to link educational research and the national political and economic agenda. One great issue in the USA was that of equality of opportunity, and the very definition of a notion of fairness. Some insisted that it was up to the schools rather than to the market to assign status and to reward intelligence and motivation. For other researchers, the national interest was the greatest priority. In the 1920s, psychologists began to argue that intelligence tests could determine which nationalities, ethnic groups and races were best fitted to serve the developing industrial order, and their findings were used to support moves to restrict immigration in the 1920s. Researchers also argued that the curriculum should be differentiated according to the needs of industry, and that students should be assigned to particular programmes according to their native intelligence.

Educational research continued to be interwoven with political and economic policy debates throughout the twentieth century. For example, in the late 1950s and early 1960s, when US political leaders were concerned about the space race with the Soviet Union and the so-called missile gap, a series of reports by the well-known educator, and former President of Harvard, James B. Conant (1959), focused on the 'lagging' academic quality of education in the USA. This inspired research on how to design curriculum units and change teaching strategies and school procedures in order to produce more scientists and engineers. New ways of teaching mathematics and science were developed, and influential educators, such as the psychologist Jerome Bruner, proposed that the teaching of science, mathematics and other academic programmes should begin in the lower grades (Bruner 1960).

In the mid-1960s, social pressure built up over civil rights, and the failure of schools to achieve racial equality. At the same time, the strains engendered by the Vietnam War created a backlash against the rigidity of the Conant era reforms (Illich 1970; Silberman 1970). Drawing on the work of Jean Piaget, some researchers argued

that the curriculum should allow more room for the individual expression of interests. There should be a better match between the developmental patterns found among children and the structure and pacing of the curriculum. Critics complained about permissiveness, but it was argued that these reforms promoted individual expression and participatory democracy.

The Civil Rights movement and the reforms that it motivated also led to renewed scrutiny of the relationship between education and equality. James Coleman (1968) analysed data from thousands of US schools to find out the extent to which different factors affect school achievement across racial lines. He found that the class and racial characteristics of the student body had an important influence on individual achievement. Coleman's research was cited in support of the bussing of children across racially distinct neighbourhoods, which had been undertaken by local authorities (or sometimes imposed by the courts) in an effort to achieve greater racial balance in the student body. Other contemporary studies explored the effectiveness of preschool programmes in raising the achievement levels of blacks and other children from lower socioeconomic classes.

In an important article on equality of educational opportunity, Coleman (1973) suggested that what really mattered was not what resources were spent on different children, but rather whether or not the outcome, the pattern of achievement, is similar among different racial groups and minorities. Had this conception of equal opportunity been widely accepted, it might have mandated the allocation of unequal resources in some cases in order to achieve equal results. While this step was not taken, educational policy-makers and politicians in the USA did begin to assign federal resources to special groups, such as handicapped people, blacks, women and non-native speakers of English; legal efforts were intensified to redress racial imbalance in schools; and affirmative action programmes were introduced in an attempt to increase the opportunities available to minority students and women in universities and professional schools.

On the other hand, there were also conservative challenges to compensatory policies, such as Head Start, which had developed in response to the demands of the Civil Rights movement. The most publicized was an article by Arthur Jensen

(1969), which claimed that most compensatory programmes had failed, and that children of different intellectual ability should therefore be taught differently. In the fierce debate that followed the publication of Jensen's article, questions were raised about the whole concept of measurement as applied to intelligence, and about the appropriateness of such tests for culturally distinct, minority children. Other arguments concerned the very nature of equality of opportunity. If equality of opportunity means that everyone is to be given the same chances, then presumably differences in ability alone should be allowed to determine outcomes. However, if the major 'measure' of 'ability', that is, IQ tests, is put into question, so too is the justification for different outcomes. Some critics also argued against the use of surrogate 'intelligence' tests to select students for elite colleges and universities (Lemann 1999).

Other arguments were deployed to justify differential outcomes, and to argue against the use of 'extraordinary' measures to achieve educational equality. These arguments were often based on the view that governmental intervention creates unrealistic expectations and increases frustration, and may even cause violence. It was admitted that environmental factors might be important, but it was then argued that the most significant aspect of environment, the habits, discipline and foresight developed through class culture, were extremely difficult to change. Radical scholars countered that there was a structural relationship between a student's habits, attitudes and achievement, and the employment opportunities that were available to children from certain social classes. Bowles and Gintis (1976) argued that schooling provided very little mobility, even when research controlled for IQ scores, and that schools largely served to reproduce and legitimize the personality characteristics required by the hierarchical relations found in advanced capitalistic countries. Other Marxist studies also attempted to shift the focus of educational research from the individual to the larger social, historical, cultural and political context of schooling (Apple 1982; Giroux 1981). These studies were often inspired by the work of Pierre Bourdieu on the connection between educational structures and social class in France (see, e.g., Bourdieu and Passeron 1977 [1970]; cf. Freire 1973 for a Marxist analysis of education in Brazil).

Other critical perspectives include race theory (hooks 2003) and feminist scholarship. Some feminist studies focus on questions of gender-specific learning styles, knowledge and moral reasoning (e.g. Gilligan 1982), while others challenge the competitive ethos of schools and argue that they should foster caring communities of learning (e.g. Noddings 1984).

In the early 1980s, as unemployment rates in the USA, Britain and Western Europe hit post-depression records, political and business leaders, concerned about growing competition from Japan and other emerging industrial nations, steered the education debate to focus on the issue of foreign competition. Some critics argued that the schools had failed to produce sufficient highly trained students to allow advanced nations like the USA to remain competitive. The consequence was intense competition across North America and Europe to raise the school performance of children. The priority for educational policy-makers was now the production of more highly trained workers, scientists and engineers. Educational research began to focus on developing computer literacy, and increasing the pool from which future scientists and engineers can be drawn. There were calls to tighten the curriculum, to raise standards for admission into and matriculation out of high school, and to reduce the 'frills' in the public schools.

These developments seem to signal a return to the era of Conant, but whereas Conant focused on the high school and called for a differentiated curriculum, the present reforms are more concerned with the grade (or elementary) schools, and aim to set minimum achievement standards for all schools. A little noticed result has been the development of a new and international industry in educational testing. Test scores are now widely reported and commented upon. Nations judge their schools by how well they do in comparison to other nations, and this concern trickles down to local governments and school boards.

In the USA the federal government has threatened schools that fail to meet these standards with punitive measures, even though research has shown that, given the present rate of achievement growth, the target standards are highly unrealistic (Linn 2003). The determination of the federal government to develop performance standards has led to the increased use of standardized tests, a movement that has gained momentum in virtually every industrially developed nation. Side by side with this central direction, somewhat anomalously, efforts are being made to introduce market ideology into the schools, for example by the provision of vouchers that would provide parents with funds that would allow them to choose between public, private and religious schools for their children (Chubb and Moe 1990).

One of the great difficulties with research that relies exclusively on standardized test scores is that what counts as educational success tends to be decided by politicians and business leaders. The views and experiences of staff and students are discounted. In contrast, ethnographic studies offer a corrective to this top-down specification of the process of education. Ethnographic studies in the field of education range from apolitical explorations of the way in which children from different cultural groups learn to read (Heath 1983); to an exploration of the way in which teachers and students interact to renegotiate the meaning of 'success' (McDermott 1974); to quite politicized explorations of the way in which working-class adolescent boys structure their experience to reproduce their working-class status (Willis 1977); to studies of how working-class girls cope in a deindustrialized economy (Weis 1993). Unfortunately, it is often difficult to generalize from ethnographic studies, and they do not easily fit into the wholesale world of educational policy-making, where input and output standards provide a seemingly neat measure for improvement. Moreover, the replication of ethnographic studies can be expensive, time-consuming and sometimes is impossible to achieve. In consequence, ethnographic studies remain a boutique industry in a world where the gold standard is some idealized version of laboratory research, of the kind Thorndike was engaged in, and which the big-time testers and curriculum designers strive to emulate (National Research Council 2002).

The applied nature of educational research, and its failure to develop an independent research programme, suggest that its future direction will depend on political and economic developments. One of the last attempt to provide an independent focus for the study of education was developed by the US philosopher, John Dewey (see Boydston 1979). After Dewey, educational philosophy took a different turn, one that until quite recently emphasized the analysis of concepts and linguistic clarity, and to a lesser extent the role and place of scientific method in educational research and evaluation. Recently there has been a resurgence of interest in Dewey's ideas on education (e.g. Garrison 1997). In the field of education itself, Dewey's work has been coupled, sometimes in a rather vague way, with the ideas on child development of Piaget or Vygotsky, to justify a shift in emphasis from the acquisition of accurate knowledge to the study of the way in which learners construct understanding and solve problems (Phillips 2000). This intellectual movement is usually called constructivism. Constructivism is a term that covers a multitude of positions, but in general it indicates a turn away from an emphasis on 'right' answers and 'objective' knowledge to a concern with the subjective processes that make knowledge possible. Constructivists are accordingly concerned to model the mental structures that are exhibited in the acquisition of 'knowledge' and 'skills', and scholars who take this position tend to agree that the aim of education should not be only the acquisition of accurate knowledge. Education should also, perhaps primarily, foster understanding, and develop the ability to solve problems

Growing religious, racial and ethnic diversity, and increasing global mobility, have led to a renewal of debates on assimilation and citizen education (Gutmann 1987; Callan 1997; Feinberg 1998; McDonough and Feinberg 2003). However, the deeper questions about education involve the understanding of intergenerational continuity and change, and the normative concerns that guide the process of social and cultural reproduction. It is possible to specify some of the factors that such a research programme would involve. They would include an analysis of the kind of knowledge that is valued and reproduced in a given society; the institutional arrangements to protect and transmit such knowledge; the methods used to identify and train those who will bear that knowledge in the future; and the way in which knowledge is distributed among different groups in the society. Such a programme would maintain the interdisciplinary character of educational studies, but would provide a focus that has been lacking. It would also provide a perspective from which to appraise present educational practice (see Feinberg 1983).

WALTER FEINBERG
UNIVERSITY OF ILLINOIS,
URBANA-CHAMPAIGN

References

Apple, M. (1982) *Education and Power*, London.

Bourdieu, P. and Passeron, J.-C. (1977 [1970]) *Reproduction in Education, Society and Culture*, London.

Bowles, S. and Gintis, H. (1976) *Schooling in Capitalist America: Educational Reform and the Contradictions of Economic Life*, New York.

Boydston, J. (ed.) (1979) *The Complete Works of John Dewey*, Carbondale, IL.

Bruner, J. (1960) *The Process of Education*, Cambridge, MA.

Callan, E. (1997) *Creating Citizens*, Oxford.

Chubb, J.E. and Moe, T.M. (1990) *Politics, Markets and America's Schools*, Washington, DC.

Coleman, J.S. (1968) 'The concept of equality of educational opportunity', *Harvard Educational Review* 38.

—— (1973) 'Equality of opportunity and equality of results', *Harvard Educational Review* 43.

Conant, J.B. (1959) *The American High School Today*, New York.

Feinberg, W. (1983) *Understanding Education: Toward Reconstruction of Educational Inquiry*, Cambridge, UK.

—— (1998) *Common Schools/Uncommon Identities: National Unity and Cultural Difference*, New Haven, CT.

Freire, P. (1973) *Pedagogy of the Oppressed*, New York.

Garrison, J. (1997) *Dewey and Eros: Wisdom and Desire in the Art of Teaching*, New York.

Gilligan, C. (1982) *In a Different Voice: Psychological Theory and Woman's Development*, Cambridge, MA.

Giroux, H.A. (1981) *Ideology, Culture and the Process of Schooling*, Philadelphia, PA.

Gutmann, A. (1987) *Democratic Education*, Princeton, NJ.

Heath, S.B. (1983) *Ways with Words: Language, Life and Work in Communities and Classrooms*, Cambridge, UK.

hooks, b. (2003) *Teaching Community: A Pedagogy of Hope*, London.

Illich, I. (1970) *Deschooling Society*, New York.

Jensen, A.R. (1969) 'How much can we boost IQ and scholastic achievement?' *Harvard Educational Review* 39.

Lemann, N. (1999) *The Big Test: The Secret History of the American Meritocracy*, New York.

Linn, R. (2003) 'Presidential address, American Educational Research Association' (unpublished).

McDermott, R. (1974) 'Achieving school failure: An anthropological approach to illiteracy and social stratification', in G. Spindler (ed.) *Education and Cultural Process*, New York.

McDonough, K. and Feinberg, W. (eds) (2003) *Citizenship and Education in Liberal Democratic Societies: Teaching for Cosmopolitan Values and Collective Identities*, Oxford.

National Research Council (2002) *Scientific Research in Education*, Washington, DC.

Noddings, N. (1984) *Caring: A Feminist Approach to Ethics and Moral Education*, Berkeley, CA.

Phillips, D.C. (ed.) (2000) *Constructivism in Education: Opinions and Second Opinions on Controversial Issues* (Ninety-ninth Yearbook of the National Society for the Study of Education), Chicago.

Richard, J., Herrnstein, R.J. and Murray, C. (1994) *The Bell Curve: Intelligence and Class Structure in American Life*, New York.

Silberman, C. (1970) *Crisis in the Classroom: The Remaking of American Education*, New York.

Thorndike, E. (1906), *The Principles of Teaching Based on Psychology*, New York.

Weis, L. (1993) 'High school girls in a de-industrialized economy', in L. Weis (ed.) *Class, Race, and Gender in American Education*, Albany, NY, pp. 183–208.

Willis, P. (1977) *Learning to Labor: How Working Class Kids Get Working Class*, Teakfield, UK.

Further reading

West, C. (1993) *Race Matters*, Boston.

SEE ALSO: affirmative action; Dewey; educational psychology

EDUCATIONAL PSYCHOLOGY

The enduring difficulties that face both the academic and the professional sectors of educational psychology are due to three factors. First, educational psychology mirrors all the propensities and peculiarities of psychology. Second, and perhaps as a consequence, no distinctive approach or unified understanding of the field has evolved. Third, despite the professed concern with educational problems in general, the primary focus has in fact been schooling, as if all educational concerns are localized in schools.

Psychology in general has placed an enormous emphasis on quantification. Within educational psychology this trend has given rise to a huge testing industry, making tests, selling tests, giving tests, scoring tests, interpreting scores, categorizing and labelling people on the basis of scores, coaching test taking, doing research on and with tests, and so on. These activities have become so widespread, particularly in schools, as to make them a hallmark of the whole field, and educational psychologists have become effectively technicians of tests, measurements and evaluation, especially in the cognitive domain dealing with intelligence, aptitude and achievement (USA) or attainment (UK). The technical bias is so pervasive as to blind many practitioners to the damage that may be done to the test subjects (Hanson 1993).

This preoccupation with the tools of research has, of course, affected the substance. Persons *qua* persons tend to be diminished even as they are counted, aggregated, classified, labelled and treated. Not surprisingly, many significant questions have been ignored – for instance, how to handle young children's napping and sleeping patterns, and their disruptions; what they dream, and how that affects their life awake; how one's temperament contributes to the formation of a world-view; how to help a person develop courage and a sense of honour; or what nurtures maturity, integrity and wisdom.

Substantively, educational psychology remains a hodgepodge. Indeed, a cursory survey of graduate programmes reveals large portions of courses devoted to research design and analysis, measurements and evaluation, and computer applications. Side by side with these are courses on learning, development (mostly focused on child–adolescent phases), personality formation and pathology. The last category is heavily dependent upon the psychiatric tradition of diagnosis and classification. Among the relevant areas of enquiry that are normally absent from such courses are group dynamics, the process of teaching or the nature of curriculum. It is still rarer for such a course to pay attention to other disciplines. On the level of theory, what is typically found is a doctrinaire adherence to a single fashionable approach. In the 1950s the Skinnerian school was dominant, to be replaced, in turn, by the approaches of Piaget, Chomsky, Vygotsky and others.

There is little sense of the history of the field, and perhaps in consequence it is hardly surprising that the same mistakes tend to be repeated both in theory and in practice. One error has been to view the school experience in a linear, causal fashion, within its narrowest and most immediate context, without interpreting it in interactional, systemic terms against the broader backdrop of human meaning. As important as schooling has become, particularly to the young, an educational psychology that centres its attention exclusively upon this process is unlikely to achieve that rounded understanding of the person in the world that is required if we are to provide appropriate support, assistance and guidance (Bronfenbrenner 1979; Ianni 1989).

KAORU YAMAMOTO
UNIVERSITY OF COLORADO, DENVER

References

Bronfenbrenner, U. (1979) *The Ecology of Human Development*, Cambridge, MA.
Hanson, F.A. (1993) *Testing Testing*, Berkeley, CA.
Ianni, F.A.J. (1989) *The Search for Structure*, New York.

Further reading

Kozulin, A. (2001) *A Sociocultural Approach to Education*, Cambridge, MA.

SEE ALSO: education; intelligence and intelligence testing

EFFICIENCY (ECONOMIC)

In a restricted sense, economic efficiency is often taken to mean that resources or inputs should be used so as to produce an output in the cheapest possible way. It is the cost of a combination of inputs that is of interest, not the use of a single input. The economically efficient input combination is the one that yields a specified output level at the least possible cost. The use of a single input (e.g. energy) can, of course, be further reduced, but so much extra is then needed of other inputs that the total cost increases. Alternatively, one can speak of efficiency when a firm produces as much as possible (maximizes output) at a specified total cost. This illustrates the fact that the concept of efficiency is used in different production contexts. Similarly, one can speak of efficiency in consumption. Individuals who aim at achieving the highest possible level of utility, subject to their income, will allocate their income between goods in such a way that the marginal rate of substitution between any two goods (the satisfaction derived from an extra unit of the first commodity divided by the satisfaction derived from an extra unit of the second commodity) is equal to the ratio between their prices. This is the criterion for efficiency in consumption.

The concept of economic efficiency, as attributed to the Italian economist Vilfredo Pareto (1848–1923), is usually interpreted in a broader sense. Pareto specified a condition of optimal or efficient allocation of resources that is referred to as the *Pareto condition*. According to this criterion, a policy change is socially desirable if everyone is made better off by the change (the weak Pareto criterion), or at least some are made better off, while no one is made worse off (the strong Pareto criterion). When the possibilities for making such policy changes have been exhausted, society is left with an allocation of commodities that cannot be altered without someone being made worse off. Such an allocation is called *Pareto-optimal* or *efficient*.

Under certain conditions, a market economy will be Pareto efficient. The important relationship between competitive equilibria and Pareto-optimality is that, when a competitive equilibrium exists, it attains Pareto-optimality. This result, which is known as the *First Theorem of Welfare Economics*, provides a strong argument for the advocates of a pure market economy. The result says that the perfect market economy simultaneously yields efficiency in production and consumption.

PER-OLOV JOHANSSON
STOCKHOLM SCHOOL OF ECONOMICS
KARL-GUSTAF LÖFGREN
UNIVERSITY OF UMEÅ, SWEDEN

Further reading

Johansson, P.-O. (1991) *An Introduction to Modern Welfare Economics*, Cambridge, UK.
Pareto, V. (1971) *Manual of Political Economy*, London.
Varian, H.R. (2002) *Intermediate Microeconomics: A Modern Approach*, 6th edn, New York.

SEE ALSO: Pareto efficiency; welfare economics

ELECTIONS

In politics elections are a device whereby popular preferences are aggregated to choose an office-holder. Choice by elections is now almost inseparable from representative democracy (Lipset 1960; Schumpeter 1942).

Election systems provide guidelines on such matters as who votes and how, frequency of election, how votes are counted, who stands for office and so on. In the twentieth century, most states granted the vote to all (with a few exceptions) adult resident citizens. Over time, the suffrage has been extended from estates to individuals, and in the past century to large categories formerly excluded on grounds of race, sex and property qualifications. The change has also been to equality or 'one man one vote one value' (Rokkan 1970).

In most states, responsibility for registering eligible voters lies with the government. A significant exception is the USA, where states leave registration to individuals. This partly explains why the turnout in presidential elections since 1960 has averaged 60 per cent, compared to over 80 per cent in many Western states. But US voters have more opportunities to cast votes, in federal, state, local and primary elections, and in long ballots. At the other extreme, political and cultural pressures may produce remarkable turnouts and verdicts, for example 99.9 per cent turnout in the former German Democratic Republic in 1964.

Elections have several functions. These include designating, directly or indirectly, the government; providing feedback between voters and government; demonstrating public support for or repudiation of a regime; providing a means for the recruitment of political leaders; and making the government answerable to the electorate. Functions may differ in states that have elections without choice, where a party's hegemonic or monopolistic position makes the outcome a foregone conclusion (Hermet *et al.* 1978).

In some countries (Belgium, Italy, Denmark and The Netherlands, for example) it is not the election but the interparty bargaining following the election that determines the composition of government. Where the party system provides a choice between alternative potential majorities, voters do have such a choice. The impact of elections on policies depends in part on a programmatic disciplined majority party being in government. Until recently, the British two-party system was admired for providing a model of 'responsible party government'. More direct popular verdicts on issues may be made through referendums.

The nature of the electoral choice in each state is shaped by three sets of factors. The first is the *object* of election, which may be to choose a constituency representative, party list or president. The second is the *party system*, or pattern of voting alignments (Lijphart 1995), which in turn is shaped by cleavages in society, the electoral system and the manœuvres of elites. The third is the *electoral system*, particularly those provisions which aggregate votes and translate them into seats, that is, rules for counting and weighing votes.

A distinction may be drawn between the absolute majoritarian system, as in France, in which the winner has to achieve at least half the votes; the plurality (first past the post) system in many English-speaking countries; the various forms of proportionalism, including the pure proportional representation (PR) in The Netherlands (where 0.67 per cent of the vote gives a group a seat in the legislature); and those that combine elements of different systems (for example, Germany has PR for half the seats, subject to a party gaining at least 5 per cent of the vote).

Proportionalism was introduced early in the twentieth century in divided societies to provide guarantees to minorities that felt threatened by universal suffrage or majority rule. Proportionalism furthers the goals of representativeness but, in the absence of a clear party majority, makes the choice of government less certain.

The British plurality system has usually achieved certainty in choice of the government while sacrificing representativeness. In the general elections of 2001, Labour won 63 per cent of the seats in the House of Commons with 41 per cent of the votes. The two systems maximize different values; most Western states have opted for proportionalism, subject to qualifications.

We lack a good typology of elections. One may distinguish between degrees of choice, which in turn depends on the number of effective parties and the prospects of turnover in government. The USA has two parties, The Netherlands and Denmark a dozen. Italy, Sweden and Norway have had very long spells of dominant one-party rule, and there has been only one change in France since 1958.

There are limits to the decisiveness of elections as authoritative arbiters of policy. Incumbents of the bureaucracy and judiciary, and leaders of powerful interests, who are not elected by the voters, constitute checks. The debate about the relative influence of socioeconomic factors or party political factors (and therefore elections) has not been conclusive. The influence of the government depends on the power centralization in society. In pluralist and market societies the government is only one decision-maker among others, and competitive elections and majority rule are only two elements in representative democracy. Competitive elections do not ensure the political responsiveness of an elite; they have to operate in favourable conditions. There are alternative methods of facilitating popular choice and eliciting and demonstrating popular consent (for example, acclamation, seniority, rotation and elite bar-

gaining), but election is still the birthmark of a government claiming to be democratic.

DENNIS KAVANAGH
UNIVERSITY OF LIVERPOOL

References

Hermet, G., Rose, R. and Rouquié, A. (eds) (1978) *Elections without Choice*, Paris.
Lijphart, A. (1995) *Electoral Systems and Party Systems*, Oxford.
Lipset, M.S. (1960) *Political Man: The Social Bases of Politics*, New York.
Rokkan, S. (1970) *Citizens, Elections, Parties*, New York.
Schumpeter, J.A. (1942) *Capitalism, Socialism and Democracy*, New York.

Further reading

Colomer, J. (ed.) (2003) *Handbook of Electoral System Choice*, London.
Dummett, M. (1997) *The Principles of Electoral Reform*, Oxford.
LeDuc, L., Niemi, R.G. and Norris, P. (eds) (2002) *Comparing Democracies: Elections and Voting in Global Perspective: New Challenges in the Study of Elections and Voting*, London.
Rose, R. (ed.) (2000) *International Encyclopedia of Elections*, London.

SEE ALSO: democracy; parties, political; voting

EMOTION

William James wrote that he would 'as lief read verbal descriptions of the shapes of the rocks on a New Hampshire farm' as toil again through the classic works on emotion, which lacked a 'central point of view, a deductive or generative principle'. Over one hundred years after James's (1884) famous essay in *Mind*, we are still debating the issues he posed, in particular the role of physiological changes in emotions, and the central components that determine an emotion. Since James, many theories of emotion and definitions of emotion have been advanced, but there is still a lack of consensus on central issues. This diversity of views is due partly to an upsurge during the past two decades of interest in emotion from scholars in different disciplines, each advocating a particular perspective on emotions. In this respect the area of emotion research has changed from a situation in which psychologists and physiologists dominated the field, to a multidisciplinary endeavour in which sociologists, anthropologists and philosophers are also heavily engaged.

The issues that preoccupy modern emotion theory are in certain respects similar to those that arose from James's theory of emotion. Three major disputes may be distinguished. The first concerns the role of physiological changes in emotion. James advocated what has come to be called a *peripheral theory* of emotion, in which he argued that the perception of an arousing stimulus causes changes in peripheral organs such as the viscera (heart, lungs, stomach and so on) and the voluntary muscles, and that emotion is quite simply the perception of these bodily changes. To use James's own example, it is not that we tremble and run because we are afraid; rather, we are afraid because we tremble and run. This view clearly implies that there should be as many discrete patterns of physiological activity accompanying emotion as there are discernible emotional states. Cannon (1927) published what was widely regarded as a devastating critique of James's theory, although subsequent research has shown that some of Cannon's objections were ill founded. Although Cannon's critique weakened the influence of James's peripheral theory of emotion, this theory has by no means been completely discarded. In particular, the idea that the perception of bodily changes may elicit an emotion still inspires various contemporary researchers. Indeed, there is experimental evidence (e.g. Strack *et al.* 1988) that the mere induction of a posture or facial expression can elicit or enhance emotional feelings. However, evidence for the existence of discrete physiological patterns that differentiate the various emotions is still rather weak and this limits the extent to which James's ideas are accepted by modern researchers.

The essence of Cannon's critique was that the visceral changes that occur during emotion are too non-specific to serve as the basis for differentiated emotional experience. This point led later researchers to abandon the search for an explanation of emotion couched exclusively in terms of bodily changes, and to consider more carefully the role played by cognitive factors – the individual's interpretation of external and internal events.

There are several theories that pay attention to cognitive factors, and the question of the precise role played by cognition in emotion is a second major issue in current emotion theory and research. A classic theory is Schachter's (1964) two-factor theory. Schachter reasoned that the mere awareness of bodily changes does not necessarily result in emotional experience: emotion is the joint product of two factors, namely a general state of physiological arousal, and the cognition that this arousal is caused by an emotional stimulus. The arousal creates the condition necessary for any emotion to be experienced, while the cognition determines which emotion is actually experienced. Thus the same physiological arousal could, in principle, be experienced as any of a variety of emotions, depending on cognitive factors. Although this theory has an appealing elegance and simplicity, there is little evidence to support its central proposition (Manstead and Wagner 1981; Reisenzein 1983).

Cognitive theories of a different nature have been proposed by Lazarus and his associates (Lazarus and Folkman 1984) and by others (e.g. Frijda 1986). What such theories have in common is the view that emotions are temporally extended processes in which cognitions are one of the central components. More specifically, people appraise their circumstances with respect to their well-being, and these appraisals elicit different emotions. This means that different emotions can be distinguished by different appraisal patterns. Indeed, there is abundant evidence that emotions are associated with different patterns of appraisal. For example, anger is associated with the appraisal of a negative event caused by another person who is held responsible for this; anxiety is characterized by a negative event with an uncertain outcome, and which is mainly situationally caused; guilt is linked to the appraisal of a negative event for which one blames oneself.

Although there is an emerging consensus about the major dimensions of these appraisal patterns (see Roseman and Smith 2001), debates in the 1980s and 1990s centred on the question of whether the role of appraisal really is a causal one (Parkinson and Manstead 1992). Much of the empirical evidence does not rule out a different conclusion, namely that appraisal is the result of the emotion, rather than its cause. Zajonc's (1980) paper was influential in questioning the extent to which cognitions are necessary precursors of emotion. He reasoned that there are good grounds for thinking that affective reactions to stimuli sometimes precede cognitive responses. Zajonc's own programme of experimental research on the 'mere exposure effect', in which he showed that we have a tendency to like stimuli as a function of how frequently we have been exposed to them, even when we are not consciously aware of this exposure, is an example of how evaluative responses to stimuli seem to occur in the absence of any elaborate cognitive analysis (for a recent review, see Zajonc 2004). This sort of reasoning has led to a growth in research on unconscious processes in emotion.

Another experimental example of how people may be influenced by affective processes despite being unaware of them comes from research by Winkielman, Berridge and Wilbarger (see Berridge 2004). These investigators used subliminal exposures of happy or angry faces to trigger different affective responses in their participants. The participants did not report any change in subjective emotion, but when they were given a drink they evaluated it more positively if they had been exposed to the happy face than if they had been exposed to the angry one. Such effects were most apparent among thirsty participants. Berridge (2004) regards this sort of finding as evidence of 'unconscious' liking, and he proposes a number of brain mechanisms that might be responsible for this phenomenon.

The third major issue governing current emotion research is concerned with its social and cultural aspects. An important question that generates much theorizing and research is whether emotions are universal or culturally specific phenomena. The advocates of basic emotions (e.g. Ekman 1992) claim that there are a few basic emotions (among others fear, anger, sadness, happiness and disgust) that are expressed in similar ways across cultures and can therefore be recognized universally. Evidence for this claim comes mainly from studies on facial expressions: photographs showing faces posing particular emotional expressions appeared to be correctly recognized by people from a great variety of cultures (Ekman 1982). However, both theoretical and methodological objections have been raised against this view (Russell 1994). A related controversy concerns the extent to which facial behaviour is reflective of subjective emotion. For example, whereas Ekman and his colleagues (e.g. Ekman et al. 1990) hold that there will be good correspondence between smiles and subjective happiness, others (e.g. Fridlund 1991) propose that smiles reflect social

and motivational factors, rather than subjective state.

The opposite of the basic emotions view is defended by theorists who argue that emotions are social constructions. Harré (1986), for example, reasons that in order to gain more insight into emotions, we have merely to study the emotion vocabularies of different cultures. Although there is evidence that the richness, size and content of emotion language differs from one culture to another, there is little support for the view that emotion language is the major determinant of what we feel. However, emotions are certainly influenced by social and cultural factors. Research, much of it conducted by sociologists (e.g. Hochschild 1983) and cultural anthropologists (e.g. Lutz 1988), has shown how culture socializes our emotions by means of emotion rules, beliefs about emotions, emotion rituals and so on. Thus, the answer to the question of the cultural specificity versus universality of emotions seems to lie somewhere in the middle: there are both cross-cultural similarities and differences in emotions. What one finds depends on the level of analysis and the specific aspects of emotions that are taken into account (Mesquita and Frijda 1992).

Despite the evidence that social factors impact on emotion, much research on emotion tends to treat it as an intraindividual phenomenon, whether it is seen as being driven primarily by physiological processes that have been shaped by evolutionary pressures or by cognitive processes that are potentially malleable. What both types of account appear to underestimate is the role played by emotion in social relations: how emotions are shaped by, and in turn shape, interpersonal, intragroup and intergroup relations (see Parkinson et al. 2004).

AGNETA H. FISCHER
UNIVERSITY OF AMSTERDAM
ANTONY S.R. MANSTEAD
CARDIFF UNIVERSITY

References

Berridge, K.C. (2004) 'Unfelt affect and irrational desire: Springing from the brain', in A.S.R. Manstead, N.H. Frijda and A.H. Fischer (eds) Feelings and Emotions: The Amsterdam Symposium, New York.

Cannon, W.B. (1927) 'The James–Lange theory of emotions: A critical examination and an alternative theory', American Journal of Psychology 39.

Ekman, P. (ed.) (1982) *Emotion in the Human Face*, 2nd edn, Cambridge, UK.

— (1992) 'An argument for basic emotions', *Cognition and Emotion* 6.

Ekman, P., Davidson, R.J. and Friesen, W.V. (1990) 'The Duchenne smile: Emotional expression and brain physiology', *Journal of Personality and Social Psychology* 58.

Fridlund, A.J. (1991) 'Sociality of solitary smiling: Potentiation by an implicit audience', *Journal of Personality and Social Psychology* 60.

Frijda, N.H. (1986) *The Emotions*, Cambridge, UK.

Harré, R. (ed.) (1986) *The Social Construction of Emotions*, Oxford.

Hochschild, A.R. (1983) *The Managed Heart: Commercialization of Human Feeling*, Berkeley.

James, W. (1884) 'What is an emotion?' *Mind* 5.

Lazarus, R.S. and Folkman, S. (1984) *Stress, Appraisal and Coping*, New York.

Lutz, C. (1988) *Unnatural Emotions: Everyday Sentiments on a Micronesian Atoll and their Challenge to Western Theory*, Chicago.

Manstead, A.S.R. and Wagner, H.L. (1981) 'Arousal, cognition and emotion: An appraisal of two-factor theory', *Current Psychological Reviews* 1.

Mesquita, B. and Frijda, N.H. (1992) 'Cultural variations in emotions: A review', *Psychological Bulletin* 112.

Parkinson, B. and Manstead, A.S.R. (1992) 'Appraisal as a cause of emotion', in M.S. Clark (ed.) *Review of Personality and Social Psychology*, Vol. 13, Newbury Park, CA.

Parkinson, B., Fischer, A.H. and Manstead, A.S.R. (2004) *Emotions in Social Relations: Cultural, Group, and Interpersonal Perspectives*, Philadelphia.

Reisenzein, R. (1983) 'The Schachter theory of emotion: Two decades later', *Psychological Bulletin* 94.

Roseman, I.J. and Smith, C.A. (2001) 'Appraisal theory: Overview, assumptions, varieties, controversies', in K.R. Scherer, A. Schorr and T. Johnstone (eds) *Appraisal Processes in Emotion: Theory, Methods, Research*, New York.

Russell, J.A. (1994) 'Is there universal recognition of emotion from facial expression? A review of cross-cultural studies', *Psychological Bulletin* 115.

Schachter, S. (1964) 'The interaction of cognitive and physiological determinants of emotional state', in L. Berkowitz (ed.) *Advances in Experimental Social Psychology*, Vol. 1, New York.

Strack, F., Martin, L.L. and Stepper, S. (1988) 'Inhibiting and facilitating conditions of the human smile: A non-obtrusive test of the facial feedback hypothesis', *Journal of Personality and Social Psychology* 54.

Zajonc, R.B. (1980) 'Feeling and thinking: Preferences need no inferences', *American Psychologist* 35.

— (2004) 'Exposure effects: An unmediated phenomenon', in A.S.R. Manstead, N.H. Frijda and A.H. Fischer (eds) *Feelings and Emotions: The Amsterdam Symposium*, New York.

Further reading

Frijda, N.H. (1986) *The Emotions*, Cambridge, UK.

Oatley, K. (1992) *Best Laid Schemes*, Cambridge, UK.

SEE ALSO: activation and arousal; anger, hostility and aggression; cognitive neuroscience

EMPLOYMENT AND UNEMPLOYMENT

The concepts of employment and unemployment are most easily defined for a developed capitalist economy that has a market for wage labour. Employment is defined as working for at least one hour a week for some payment, either for a wage or for profit, or commission, or without pay in a family business. However, this definition usually excludes people (mainly women) who provide unpaid household services. Unemployment is defined in terms of not being employed while being available and looking for work. In less developed countries, where wage labour is not a predominant form of employment, the concept of unemployment becomes 'fuzzy': the line between employment in the informal sector (selling cigarettes on the street corners) and unemployment is not clearly defined (Turnham 1993). In most economies people may not 'look for work' when there are no obvious vacancies available and drop out of the labour force (i.e. the participation rate varies). Since the concept of unemployment may not be well defined labour economists sometimes use the concept of employment–population ratios (or the not-employed to population ratio).

In OECD countries, the postwar decades have seen a growth of the service sector and a relative decline of the industrial and agricultural sectors. At the same time, there has been a growth in part-time female employment and a decline in full-time male employment. Further, there has been an increase in white-collar employment and a decline in blue-collar employment. Wage inequality has also increased. After a short period of full employment in the 1950s and 1960s, most of the OECD economies have faced increasing unemployment and long-term unemployment (the latter defined, at present, as continuous durations of unemployment of 12 months or more). This has led to economists (e.g. Matthews 1968) asking whether this period was unusual and whether the norm for developed capitalist economies is of periods of high unemployment. The only OECD countries that appear to have avoided the problems of high unemployment have been Japan, and to a lesser extent the USA. However, the USA appears to have lowered its unemployment rate at the expense of increasing the 'working poor' and creating an underclass, and by a growth of informal sector activities like hustling on the streets.

In conventional economics, employment is determined by demand for labour and supply of labour. Demand for labour is determined in the same way as the demand for non-human inputs (e.g. raw materials, or capital): by firms maximizing profits. Labour supply is determined by individuals maximizing utility and making a choice between leisure and work (where work is considered to be a necessary evil). In this paradigm wages clear the labour market and unemployment is purely voluntary. In Keynesian and post-Keynesian theories wages do not adjust instantaneously to clear the labour market and involuntary unemployment eventuates. Employment is determined by labour demand: the excess of labour supply at the market wages is called unemployment.

Full employment is defined as a state where the demand for labour equals the supply, at existing wage rates. More recently, the concept of the NAIRU has been proposed: this is the non-accelerating inflation rate of unemployment (Johnson and Layard 1986). This level of unemployment, sometimes called the 'natural' rate of unemployment, is often thought of as the full employment level. Many economists argue that the labour market operates in such a way as to make the present level of unemployment depend on the previous history of the time path of unemployment: the idea of *hysteresis* in the labour market that leads to unemployment rates increasing with time in a 'ratchet' fashion. The reasons for hysteresis are thought to be the lower probability of the long-term unemployed finding work because of decreased search by them due to a loss of self esteem; because of skill atrophy; and because employers use unemployment as a signal of poor qualities. In addition, in the macroeconomic sphere the long-term unemployed have no impact on wage bargaining and the NAIRU increases. In contrast to this view, new classical economists argue that employment and unemployment follow a random path; exogenous shocks simply perturb the 'natural' rate. For the few countries for which we have data spanning a long period (say over 50 years) there is no obvious trend in the unemployment rate (see Layard *et al.* 1991).

Unemployment is usually separated into the following components: seasonal, frictional (due to temporary mismatch between workers and vacancies), cyclical (due to aggregate demand changes) and structural (due to long-term changes in the economic structure, including technological change). Sometimes hidden unemployment (people who leave the labour force in times of recession) is distinguished from open unemployment. Underemployment is the situation where workers who are placed on short-time working, or who can only find part-time work, would prefer full-time work.

The major explanations of unemployment (and fluctuations in unemployment) are as follows: aggregate demand, technological and structural change, wage rigidity, information problems, and aggregate supply (see Junankar 2000). Some economists have postulated that unemployment in OECD countries has been caused by the growth of low-wage Newly Industrialized Countries (Korea, Singapore, Thailand, etc.), which are taking away markets from the richer high-wage economies (see Krugman and Lawrence 1994; and *Economist* 1994).

Keynesians explain unemployment in terms of a shortfall in the aggregate demand for goods and services, together with a labour market where wages do not adjust instantaneously. Marx and Schumpeter argued that technological and structural change were inherent in a capitalist economy, and due to the volatility of investment unemployment would also be cyclical. In an interesting development of such ideas, Davis *et al.* (1996) discussed job creation and job destruction that took place simultaneously due to changing technology, demand, etc. Marx also argued that the industrial reserve army (unemployment) would act as a brake on wage growth as well as controlling the 'pretensions of the workers'. Neoclassical economists explain unemployment in terms of misinformation in the labour market that leads some unemployed people not to accept wage offers in the (sometimes mistaken) belief that a better wage offer is just around the corner. This is made possible by the availability of unemployment benefits. In some versions this is simply an optimizing strategy where the unemployed are carrying out an intertemporal substitution of leisure. In some recent versions, firms are supposed to create jobs and put up vacancies, and unemployed workers are searching in a market with imperfect information. 'Matching functions' are set up that are productive matches between unemployed workers searching for jobs and firms posting vacancies looking for appropriate employees (Petrongolo and Pissarides 2001). In other versions, unemployment is due to random supply shocks. However, it is not explained why these 'random' shocks hit a number of countries simultaneously.

Most theories of unemployment focus on reasons for wages not adjusting downwards in textbook fashion in the face of excess supply (unemployment). Neo-classical theories tend to emphasize the 'rigidities' introduced by unions, unemployment benefits and minimum wage legislation. An alternative explanation, the 'insider–outsider' hypothesis, has wage bargaining conducted between employers and unions such that they only concern themselves with the employed labour force (the insiders), while the unemployed (the outsiders) are ignored (Lindbeck 1993).

In the 1980s and 1990s, theories of employment and unemployment focused on emphasizing the distinctive properties of the labour market and the role of wages in providing incentives to offer more or higher-quality (more productive) labour services (Solow 1990). It was argued that higher than market clearing wages are set by employers either to get a more skilled labour force (adverse selection models), or to provide the workers with an incentive to be more productive. These efficiency wage models suggest that where wages are set higher than necessary, workers who do not perform adequately would be fired (the 'shirking' model). The threat of unemployment, or of having to find a poorly paid job, gives workers an incentive to be productive. In another version, higher wages decrease turnover. Consequently, employers have a more stable (and so more productive) workforce (see Akerlof and Yellen 1986). Akerlof has also suggested that social custom plays a part, and that a partial gift-exchange takes place: workers get paid a wage higher than necessary and workers provide more (better) labour services than they are required to.

In some recent work, using experimental economics methods, various authors have discussed the role of 'fairness' and 'reciprocity' in much of human behaviour that influences decisions on effort, wages, etc. Many economists have argued that the labour market is distinctive, since social considerations influence the way that a labour market operates (Akerlof and Yellen 1986; Fehr and Gachter 2000; Junankar 2000; Solow 1990). Much of this recent work throws doubt on the self-regulating features of a labour market: employers do not cut wages in times of unemployment, wages are set above market clearing rates to get higher productivity, workers are willing to accept lower wages but employers do not hire these workers, etc. (Agell 1999).

Unemployment imposes severe costs on the economy in terms of lost GDP (both now and in the future), costs to the government in terms of lost revenues, loss of earnings for the unemployed individuals and families, and a loss in terms of physical and mental illness, social disruption and crime in society (Junankar 1986).

Many OECD governments have given up their commitment to full employment, either on the basis that they believe that the free market would eventually solve the problem, or that the danger of inflationary forces is too great to introduce explicit policies for full employment. Recent pronouncements tended to stress the advantages, or supposed necessity, of more flexible labour markets (i.e. increased downwards flexibility of wages, fewer constraints on employers in hiring and firing practices, weakening of the powers of the unions, etc.). The major policy interventions have been in introducing labour market training programmes, the use of private-sector agencies to provide labour market assistance, improving the efficiency of labour market exchanges, and de-regulation of the labour markets.

P.N. JUNANKAR
UNIVERSITY OF WESTERN SYDNEY, AUSTRALIA

References

Agell, J. (1999) 'On the benefits from rigid labour markets: Norms, market failures, and social insurance', *Economic Journal* 109(453): F143–64

Akerlof, G.A. and Yellen, J.L. (eds) (1986) *Efficiency Wage Models of the Labor Market*, Cambridge, UK.

Davis, S.J., Haltiwanger, J.C. and Schuh, S. (1996) *Job Creation and Job Destruction*, Cambridge, MA.

Economist (1994) 'The global economy: A survey', 1 October, 233(7,883): Survey 1–42.

Fehr, E. and Gachter, S. (2000) 'Fairness and retaliation: The economics of reciprocity', *Journal of Economic Perspectives* 14(3): 159–81.

Johnson, G.E. and Layard, P.R.G. (1986) 'The natural rate of unemployment: Explanations and policy', in O. Ashenfelter and R. Layard (eds) *Handbook of Labor Economics*, Amsterdam.

Junankar, P.N. (1986) *Costs of Unemployment: Main Report*, Luxembourg.

—— (ed.) (2000) *Economics of Unemployment: Causes, Consequences and Policies*, 4 vols, Cheltenham.

Krugman, P.R. and Lawrence, R.Z. (1994) 'Trade, jobs and wages', *Scientific American* 270(4): 22–7.

Layard, R., Nickell, S. and Jackman, R. (1991) *Un-employment: Macroeconomic Performance and the Labour Market*, Oxford.

Lindbeck, A. (1993) *Unemployment and Macroeconomics*, London.

Matthews, R.C.O. (1968) 'Why has Britain had full employment since the war?' *Economic Journal* 78: 555–69.

Petrongolo, B. and Pissarides, C.A. (2001) 'Looking into the black box: A survey of the matching function', *Journal of Economic Literature* 39(2): 390–431.

Solow, R. (1990) *The Labour Market as a Social Institution*, Oxford.

Turnham, D. (1993) *Employment and Development: A Review of the Evidence*, Paris.

Further reading

Junankar, P.N. (2000) 'Are wage cuts the answer? Theory and evidence', in S. Bell (ed.) *The Unemployment Crisis in Australia: Which Way Out?* Cambridge, UK.

Marsden, D.W. (1999) *A Theory of Employment Systems: Micro-foundations of Societal Diversity*.

Mortensen, D.T. and Pissarides, C.A. (1999) 'New developments in models of search in the labor market', in O.C. Ashenfelter and D. Card (eds) *Handbook of Labor Economics*, Vol. 3, Amsterdam.

SEE ALSO: collective bargaining; inflation and deflation; macroeconomic policy; stagflation

ENERGY

The ability of any society to survive depends on its continuing access to energy in appropriate quantities and at acceptable costs. The transformation since the mid-nineteenth century of a world that then consisted mainly of peasant economies largely subsistent in their organization, to one now comprising postindustrial, industrial and industrializing economies well-nigh exclusively, has led to a global use of energy in the early twenty-first century that is over thirty-five times greater than it is estimated to have been in 1860. Figure 3 shows what a remarkably consistent rate of growth in energy use there has been over the whole of this period (at about 2.0 per cent per year), except for the years between 1950 and 1973 when, for reasons that will be discussed below, the rate of growth was almost 5 per cent per year.

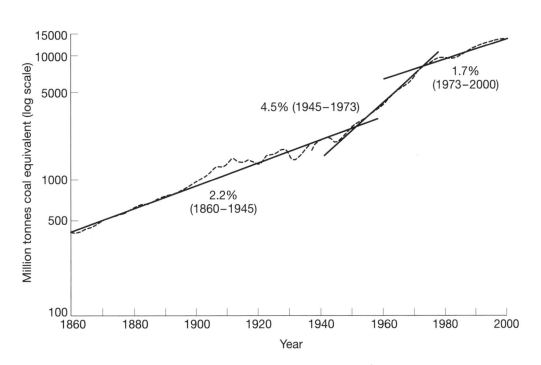

Figure 3 Trends in the evolution of world energy use, 1860–2000

Source: © PRO 2003

The demand for energy

Though attitudes to the world energy situation and outlook in the third quarter of the twentieth century became oriented to the idea that the then period of rapid energy growth represented the norm, it was, on the contrary, nothing more than a temporary combination of time-coincident factors that produced an energy growth rate so much higher than the long-term trend.

Between 1950 and 1973 virtually all the world's nations happened to be in the most highly energy-intensive period of development. First, the rich countries of the Western economic system were going through the later stages of the industrialization process, with an emphasis on products such as motor vehicles, household durable goods and petrochemicals – with high-energy inputs. As a result, the use of energy on the production side of their economies greatly increased. Simultaneously, the increase in energy use on the demand side was even more dramatic. This was the consequence of a number of interrelated factors, viz. the mass use of motor cars, the suburbanization of cities, the switch from public to private transport, the expanded availability of leisure time, the 'annihilation of space' in the public's use of such time, the mechanization of households by the use of electricity-intensive equipment and the achievement of much higher standards of comfort (by heating and/or cooling) in homes and other buildings.

Second, many of the same factors positively influenced the rate of growth in energy use in the centrally planned economies of the former Soviet Union and Eastern Europe. This was particularly the case in respect of those countries' industrialization, with its special emphasis on the rapid expansion of heavy, energy-intensive industry. To a smaller, but, nevertheless, a still significant extent, consumers in the centrally planned economies also increased their levels of energy use as a result of higher living standards and changes in lifestyle. Additionally, however, the centrally planned economies were very inefficient in their use of energy, partly because of technical inefficiencies and partly because the price of energy was kept very low, so enhancing the rate of growth in their use of energy.

Third, by 1950 most developing countries had introduced policies of industrialization, accompanied by rapid urbanization, in pursuit of higher living standards. The sort of industry that was established was, moreover, either energy-intensive heavy industry, such as iron and steel and cement, or relatively energy-intensive industry, such as textiles and household goods. The urbanization process also meant that the former rural inhabitants abandoned their low-energy ways of living (in which most of the energy required was collected rather than purchased), for lifestyles in the city environment that were, no matter how poor the living standards achieved, much more demanding in their use of commercial energy.

It was thus the temporal coincidence of these basic societal change factors in most countries of the world that caused the high rate of growth in energy use in the 1950s and 1960s. In addition, however, the energy growth rate was further increased by the continuing decline in the real price of energy during that period. This can be seen in Figure 4 in which the evolution of the real price of Saudi Arabian light or equivalent crude oil (measured in terms of the 1974 value of the US dollar) over the period from 1950 is illustrated. From this one can see that the value of a barrel of oil fell by almost 60 per cent from 1950 to 1970. This decline in the oil price brought about a falling market price for other forms of energy throughout the world, and most especially in the Western industrial countries with their open – or relatively open – economies. In these countries local energy production (such as coal in Western Europe and oil and natural gas in the USA) either had to be reduced in price to enable it to compete, or it went out of business. Thus, both the actual decline in the price of energy and the perception created among energy users that energy was cheap, getting cheaper and so hardly worth worrying about in terms of the care and efficiency with which it was used created conditions in which the careless and wasteful consumption of energy became a hallmark of both technological and behavioural aspects of societal developments – with the consequential evolution of systems of production, transport and consumption that were unnecessarily too energy-intensive.

The impact of higher prices

Post-1970 changes in the price of oil (also shown in Figure 4), and hence in the price of energy overall, brought these attitudes to an end, so that the use of energy has since been curbed. The

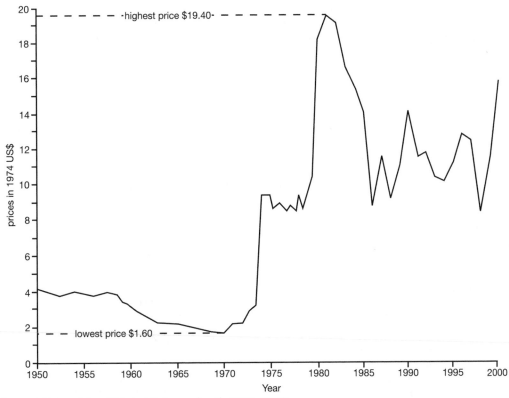

Figure 4 Price of Saudi/Dubai light crude oil, 1950–2000

Source: © PRO 2003
Note: Shown in 1974 US$ values; the actual lowest price in 1970 was less than $1.50 per barrel compared with over

results of this change have (as shown in Figure 3) been dramatic. The rate of increase between 1973 and 2000 has fallen back to only 1.7 per cent per annum – well below the long-term historic rate of 2.2 per cent per year.

The most important element in this reduction in the rate of growth has been the fall in the energy-intensity of economic activities in the industrialized countries. For Western European countries, for example, the energy-intensity of economic growth from 1973 to 1982 declined to little more than half that of the preceding 10 years, and since 1982 the ratio has fallen by another 30 per cent. There have been both technological and behavioural components in this change; the latter include consumers' decisions to save energy through the expenditure of effort and money on insulating their homes and on living with lower temperatures, and on their use of more efficient motor cars. It is, however, the technological improvements that have been the more

important in saving energy: through more efficient processes in factories, more efficient lighting in offices, the development of motor vehicles, planes and ships that give more kilometres per litre of fuel and the expansion of inherently more energy-efficient systems of electricity production.

Nevertheless, both the behavioural and the technological aspects of more effective energy use still have far to go before the pre-existing energy inefficient systems of the period of low- and decreasing-cost energy are finally replaced, even in the richer countries where the required investment funds and other inputs (of knowledge, managerial and technical expertise, and so on) are available.

The diffusion of more effective energy-using systems to the modern sectors of most Third World countries is an even slower process because of the scarcity of the capital and the managerial inputs required. Change is, however, taking place under the stimulus of the high foreign exchange cost of energy (particularly oil) imports to the developing world's economies concerned. Thus, enhanced levels of energy-use efficiency are now being achieved in many such countries. This is most notable in the case of China, now second only to the USA in total energy use, where an 8–9 per cent annual economic growth rate has been sustained over the past decade by a less than 3 per cent per annum increase in energy consumption. Nevertheless, as the percentage of world energy use in these countries is steadily increasing under the joint impact of expanding populations and of economies that are going through the most energy-intensive period of development, the Third World is becoming increasingly important for the longer-term evolution of global energy demand.

The countries that until recently had centrally planned economies lie somewhere in between the industrialized and the Third World countries in respect of energy use and prospects patterns. To date, they have not done as well as the market economies in saving energy, but the importance of energy conservation has now become generally recognized by the postcommunist governments of the countries concerned so that the implementation of measures in these countries has been given a much higher priority. Indeed, over the past decade improvements in energy use efficiency in the former Soviet Union and the associated centrally planned Eastern European countries have contributed significantly to the 25 per cent decline in their annual energy use.

The supply of fossil fuels

Meanwhile, on the supply side the search for a higher degree of energy self-sufficiency by nations in all parts of the world became a key element in energy policy-making after 1973. This was because of widely shared fears for recurring supply problems, emerging from the dependence on oil from the Middle East and a few other OPEC countries. This has caused a reversal of what had hitherto been an increasingly concentrated geography of energy production in the 1945 to 1973 period, when the prolific and extremely low-cost oil resources of the Middle East, North Africa and a few other countries (including Venezuela, Nigeria and Indonesia) undermined the economic production of many energy sources in most other parts of the world.

Thus, not only did hitherto important energy-producing regions, such as Western Europe (where the economy had been built on the use of indigenous coal), become dependent on oil imports from the low-cost countries, but also so did much of the developing world, where the rapid increase in the required supply of energy was easier to secure on the basis of oil imported through the aegis of the international oil companies, rather than through efforts to expand the indigenous production of energy.

It was only in the case of the few countries, including the USA and China, which protected their indigenous energy supply industries to a high degree, that the contribution of low-cost imported oil was restricted to a relatively small part of total energy supply. By the early 1970s, however, even the USA, with its wealth of energy resources, finally had to reduce the degree to which it protected its indigenous production. This reflected its need to reduce the energy cost disadvantage it had come to suffer compared with competing industrial nations where energy costs were related to the cheap oil available from the Middle East.

This situation changed drastically, however, once OPEC increased the price of oil – as shown in Figure 4. The approximately five-fold real price increase of OPEC oil between 1970 and 1975 and the subsequent further doubling of the price by 1981 removed economic restraints on investment in locally available energy resources, so there was thus a general reappraisal of the prospects for indigenous energy production in most countries. Some developments were possible in the short term, notably in the USA where underutilized capacity in already established energy supply industries was quickly brought into production. In Western Europe a massive stimulus was given to the efforts to exploit North Sea oil and gas, while the hitherto deteriorating prospects for the continent's coal industry were temporarily reversed. Similar developments occurred elsewhere in the non-communist world and produced the changes, shown in Table 1, of the relative importance of OPEC exports to non-OPEC energy supplies by 1986, with the continuity in the changes clearly evident for a further 13-year period to 1999, in spite of a near 30 per cent increase in energy use.

In essence, OPEC's contribution to the non-communist world's energy supply has fallen dramatically. Other oil supplies came to exceed

Table 1 Sources of energy used in the non-communist world (excluding the OPEC countries) in 1973, 1986 and 1999

	1973		1986		1999	
	Mtoe*	% of total	Mtoe*	% of total	Mtoe*	% of total
Imports of OPEC oil	1,480	36.5	674	16.2	1,128	20.4
Other energy supply of which	2,565	63.5	3,474	83.8	4,413	79.6
Oil	810	20.0	1,318	31.8	1,556	28.1
Natural gas	795	19.5	865	20.9	1,251	22.6
Coal	825	20.5	1,049	25.3	1,228	22.2
Other	135	3.5	242	5.5	378	6.8
Total energy supply	4,045		4,148		5,541	

Source: Derived by the author from *UN Energy Statistics* (Series J) and BP's *Annual Statistical Review of World Energy*.

Note: * million tons oil equivalent

imports of OPEC oil by a very wide margin. By 1986 OPEC's oil exports even became less important than locally produced natural gas and coal.

The process of a geographically more dispersed pattern of energy production seems likely to continue as long as the price of OPEC oil remains above the cost of alternatives, and as long as oil supplies from most OPEC countries continue to be perceived as unreliable. Thus the low-cost, but high-price, oil reserves of the OPEC countries have become 'the energy source of last resort'. This involved real economic costs for the world economy as a result of the higher-than-necessary price of energy inputs to both production and consumption activities – so reducing economic growth in most parts of the world in the 1980s.

The changes in energy supply and demand conditions have, however, since survived the reversal of the upwards trend in prices, as also shown in Figure 4. From 1982 to the late 1990s there was a more or less continuing downwards trend in the oil price, so that by 1998 the price was back to its level of the mid-1970s. Yet supplies remained plentiful, while global demand for energy continued to grow only slowly, as shown in Figure 3. Increasing geological knowl-edge, technical innovations and rising efficiency in production methods have eliminated the earlier fears of scarcity of fossil fuels and have made the international supply system much more competitive.

While there are some residual concerns for the security of oil and even gas supplies – largely related to geopolitical factors – a new issue has now emerged to dominate a continuing concern for energy, viz. the regional and global environmental impacts of the use of increasing volumes of fossil fuels. In particular, the widely perceived global warming consequence of carbon dioxide emissions is now central to policies that seek to constrain energy use. While increases in taxes are generally agreed to be the most effective way of achieving this objective, political considerations inhibit this solution. Such constraints do, moreover, imply limitations on the supply required, much to the consternation of the countries whose economies depend greatly on fossil fuel exports and that, therefore, question the validity of the hypothesized relationship between anthropogenic CO_2 emissions and climate change.

Alternative energy sources

Prospects for the exploitation of renewable energy sources attracted much attention in the

1970s and 1980s through fears of scarcity of fossil fuels: alternative energy prospects are now, by contrast, related principally to environmental considerations. Thus, there are enthusiastic lobbies for the rapid expansion of benign energy systems based on solar, wind, water, wave and biomass energy potential. There has been an increasingly significant response to this enthusiasm by energy policy-makers in most parts of the world, mainly in the form of more research and development funds. However, apart from a continued slow expansion of hydroelectricity production (a long-established source of energy), only modest success has been achieved to date in 'commercializing' the potential contribution of the benign energy sources. This is partly because of the long gestation period required for technical innovation, partly because their successful utilization depends on locating and exploiting appropriate physical geographical conditions, and partly because their use also depends on changes in the structure of societies and the reorganization of national energy supply networks. Collectively, these constitute a set of formidable problems so that the contribution of such sources of energy to the world's now slowly rising total energy needs still seems unlikely to grow very quickly until well on into the twenty-first century. This prospect is shown in Figure 5.

Nuclear power developments are incorporated into the 'alternative energies' component in Figure 5. These initially secured the support of many governments as a means of reducing dependence on imported oil. Nuclear power expansion has thus been generously, even extravagantly, funded (partly, at least, because it was linked to the development of the major powers' nuclear arsenals). There has thus been a ten-fold expansion in nuclear electricity production since the mid-1970s, albeit from a very small initial level of output. Nevertheless, in spite of all the efforts and money devoted to it, nuclear power globally remains no more important than hydroelectricity and it still contributes only 2.5 per cent to the world's total energy supply. A few governments and other authorities still remain convinced of nuclear power's potential, but cost escalation, public concern for the safety of the reactors and of the irradiated waste products from the power stations, and, most important of all, its inability to compete effectively with electricity from fossil fuels in most countries where nuclear power is a practicable proposition

(from the standpoints of available finance and technology) have combined severely to undermine the prospects for its further development. It thus also seems destined to make little additional contribution to world energy supplies in the early twenty-first century, even though it is now also presented as a source of energy that produces little by way of CO_2 emissions.

As shown in Figures 5 and 6, growth in energy use will continue to be modest and in this context the contribution of fossil fuels will remain dominant. The relative importance of coal, oil and natural gas will, however, change quite significantly. Plentiful supplies, consumer preferences and its more acceptable use from the environmental point of view will make natural gas the world's single most important energy source by 2040: with its cumulative use over the century greater than that of coal, oil and renewables.

The poor world's energy problem

Outside the framework of the discussion of energy as presented above is one element that remains important for large parts of the world, viz. the supply of locally available energy in societies that remain largely or partly subsistent in their economic organization. The per capita use of energy in such societies is small, as it depends on the immediately available supply of combustible materials (such as wood and dung) that can provide for cooking and heating needs. Collectively, however, this pattern of energy use in the world is still large, given the numbers of people involved in such societies. Overall, it is estimated still to account for almost 20 per cent of total energy used in Latin America and to over 90 per cent in some of the poorest countries of Africa. In almost all of the latter countries the local scarcity of wood is becoming an increasingly difficult problem. The short-term solution requires 'energy-farming' and new, albeit simple, technological developments that bring improved efficiencies in the use of the combustible materials.

For the longer term, however, the objective must be to bring electricity to the estimated 2,000 million of the world's present population of 6,000 million that do not yet have access to light and power. Though traditional electricity distribution systems from centralized production facilities are gradually being extended, high

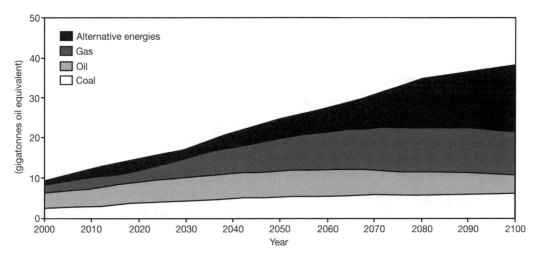

Figure 5 Trends in the evolution of energy supplies by source in the twenty-first century

Source: © PRO 2003

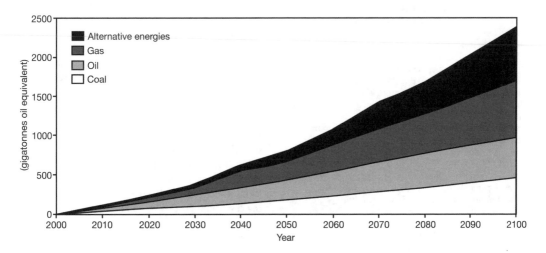

Figure 6 Cumulative supplies of energy by source in the twenty-first century

Source: © PRO 2003

capital costs constrain the speed of such developments in poor countries. Under these circumstances localized electricity production, based on solar power together with more compact and efficient generators using small volumes of liquid or gaseous hydrocarbons, seem likely to offer hope for a more rapid expansion of electrification. This massive poor-world energy supply problem that still exists at the beginning of the twenty-first century urgently needs to be accorded as much attention as that which is given to the problems of the energy sources that are required for intensive use in the developed world and in the modernized sectors of the developing countries' economies.

PETER R. ODELL

EMERITUS, ERASMUS UNIVERSITY, ROTTERDAM

Further reading

Adelman, M.A. (1995) *The Genie out of the Bottle: World Oil since 1970*, Cambridge, MA.
Beck, P. (1994) *Prospects and Strategies for Nuclear Power*, London.

Blake, G., Pratt, M., Schofield, C. and Allison-Brown, J. (eds) (1998) *Boundaries and Energy: Problems and Prospects*, London.
Claes, D.H. (2001) *The Politics of Oil Producer Cooperation*, Oxford.
Clark, J.G. (1990) *The Political Economy of World Energy*, London.
Davis, J.D. (1984) *Blue Gold: The Political Economy of Natural Gas*, London.
Gillespie, K. and Henry, C.M. (eds) (1995) *Oil in the New World Order*, Gainesville.
Gordon, R.L. (1987) *World Coal: Economics, Politics and Prospects*, Cambridge, UK.
Grimston, M.C. and Beck, P. (2002) *Double or Quits? The Global Future of Nuclear Energy*, London.
Grubb, M. (1991 [1990]) *Energy Policies and the Greenhouse Effect*, Aldershot.
—— (1995) *Renewable Energy Strategies for Europe*, London.
International Energy Agency (1997) *Energy Technologies for the 21st Century*, Paris.
Lazarus, M., Greber, L., Hall, J., Bartels, C., Bernow, S., Hansen, E., Raskin, P. and Von Hippel, D. (1993) *Towards a Fossil Free Energy Future*, Stockholm.
Mounfield, P.R. (1991) *World Nuclear Power*, London.
Noreng, Ø. (1997) *Oil and Islam*, Chichester.
Odell, P.R. (1986) *Oil and World Power*, Harmondsworth.
—— (2001) *Oil and Gas: Crisis and Controversies, 1961–2000*, Brentwood.
Office of Technology Assessment (US Congress) (1992) *Fuelling Development: Energy Technologies for Developing Countries*, Washington, DC.
Schipper, L. and Meyers, S. (1992) *Energy Efficiency and Human Activity*, Cambridge, UK.
Schumacher, D. (1985) *Energy: Crisis or Opportunity*, Basingstoke.
Simon, J.L. and Khan, H. (eds) (1984) *The Resourceful Earth*, Oxford.
Smil, V. and Knowland, W.E. (1980) *Energy in the Developing World: The Real Crisis*, New York.
World Energy Council (1995) *Global Energy Perspectives to 2050 and Beyond*, London.

SEE ALSO: conservation; environmental economics; population and resources

ENTREPRENEURSHIP

The term 'entrepreneur' seems to have been introduced into economic theory by Cantillon (1931 [1755]) and was first accorded prominence by Say (1803). It was variously translated into English as merchant, adventurer or employer, though the precise meaning is the undertaker of a project. John Stuart Mill (1848) popularized the term in Britain.

In the neo-classical theory of the firm, entrepreneurial ability is analogous to a fixed factor endowment because it sets a limit to the efficient size of the firm. The static and passive role of the entrepreneur in the neo-classical theory reflects the theory's emphasis on perfect information – which trivializes management and decision-making – and on perfect markets – which do all the co-ordination that is necessary and leave nothing for the entrepreneur.

According to Schumpeter (1934), entrepreneurs are the prime movers in economic development, and their function is to innovate or carry out new combinations. Five types of innovation are distinguished: the introduction of a new good (or an improvement in the quality of an existing good); the introduction of a new method of production; the opening of a new market, in particular an export market in new territory; the 'conquest of a new source of supply of raw materials or half-manufactured goods'; and the creating of a new type of industrial organization, in particular the formation of a trust or some other type of monopoly.

Schumpeter is also very clear about what entrepreneurs are not: they are not inventors, but people who decide to allocate resources to the exploitation of an invention; they are not risk-bearers: risk-bearing is the function of the capitalist who lends funds to the entrepreneur. Essentially, therefore, Schumpeter's entrepreneur has a managerial or decision-making role.

This view receives qualified support from Hayek (1937) and Kirzner (1973), who emphasize the role of entrepreneurs in acquiring and using information. Entrepreneurs' alertness to profit opportunities, and their readiness to exploit these through arbitrage-type operations, makes them the key element in the market process. Hayek and Kirzner regard entrepreneurs as responding to change – as reflected in the information they receive – while Schumpeter emphasizes the role of entrepreneurs as a source of change. These two views are not incompatible: a change effected by one entrepreneur may cause spill-over effects, which alter the environment of other entrepreneurs. Hayek and Kirzner do not insist on the novelty of entrepreneurial activity, however, and it is certainly true that a correct decision is not always a decision to innovate; premature innovation may be commercially disastrous. Schumpeter begs the question of whether someone who is the first to evaluate an innovation, but decides (correctly) not to innovate, qualifies as an entrepreneur.

Knight (1921) insists that decision-making involves uncertainty. Each business situation is unique, and the relative frequencies of past events cannot be used to evaluate the probabilities of fixture outcomes. According to Knight, measurable risks can be diversified (or laid off) through insurance markets, but uncertainties cannot. Those who take decisions in highly uncertain environments must bear the full consequences of those decisions themselves. These people are entrepreneurs: they are the owners of businesses and not the salaried managers that make the day-to-day decisions.

Leibenstein (1968) regards the entrepreneur as someone who achieves success by avoiding the inefficiencies to which other people – or the organizations to which they belong – are prone. Leibenstein's approach has the virtue of emphasizing that, in the real world, success is exceptional and failure is the norm.

Casson (1982) defines the entrepreneur as someone who specializes in taking decisions where, because of unequal access to information, different people would opt for different strategies. Casson shows that the evaluation of innovations, as discussed by Schumpeter, and the assessment of arbitrage opportunities, as discussed by Hayek and Kirzner, can be regarded as special cases. Casson also shows that if Knight's emphasis on the uniqueness of business situations is used to establish that differences of opinion are very likely in all business decisions, then the Knightian entrepreneur can be embraced within his definition as well. Because the definition identifies the function of the entrepreneur, it is possible to use conventional economic concepts to discuss the valuation of entrepreneurial services and many other aspects of the market for entrepreneurs.

Perhaps the aspect of entrepreneurship that has attracted most attention is the motivation of the entrepreneur. Hayek and Kirzner take the Austrian view that the entrepreneur typifies purposeful human action directed towards individualistic ends. Schumpeter, however, refers to the dream and will to found a private dynasty, the will to conquer and the joy of creating, while Weber (1930) emphasizes the Protestant Ethic and the concept of calling, and Redlich (1956) the role of militaristic values in the culture of the entrepreneur. Writers of business biographies have ascribed a whole range of different motives to people whom they describe as entrepreneurs. For many students of business behaviour, it seems that the entrepreneur is simply someone who finds adventure and personal fulfilment in the world of business. The persistence of this heroic concept suggests that many people do not want a scientific account of the role of the entrepreneur.

Successful entrepreneurship provides an avenue of social advancement that is particularly attractive to people who are denied opportunities elsewhere. This may explain why it is claimed that immigrants, religious minorities and people denied higher education are overrepresented among entrepreneurs. Hypotheses of this kind are difficult to test without carefully controlled sampling procedures. The limited evidence available suggests that, in absolute terms, the most common type of entrepreneur is the son of an entrepreneur.

MARK CASSON
UNIVERSITY OF READING

References

Cantillon, R. (1931 [1755]) *Essai sur la nature du commerce en générale*, ed. H. Higgs, London.
Casson, M.C. (1982) *The Entrepreneur: An Economic Theory*, Oxford.
Hayek, F.A. von (1937) 'Economics and knowledge', *Economica* 4.
Kirzner, I.M. (1973) *Competition and Entrepreneurship*, Chicago.
Knight, F.H. (1921) *Risk, Uncertainty and Profit*, ed. G.J. Stigler, Chicago.
Leibenstein, H. (1968) 'Entrepreneurship and development', *American Economic Review* 58.
Mill, J.S. (1848) *Principles of Political Economy*, London.
Redlich, F. (1956) 'The military enterpriser: A neglected area of research', *Explorations in Entrepreneurial History* 8.
Say, J.-B. (1803) *Traité d'économie politique*, Paris.
Schumpeter, J.A. (1934) *The Theory of Economic Development*, Cambridge, MA.
Weber, M. (1930) *The Protestant Ethic and the Spirit of Capitalism*, London.

Further reading

Brown, J. and Rose, M.B. (eds) (1993) *Entrepreneurship, Networks and Modern Business*, Manchester.
Acs, Z.J., Carlsson, B. and Karlsson, C. (1999) *Entrepreneurship, Small and Medium Sized Enterprises and the Macroeconomy*, Cambridge, UK.

SEE ALSO: corporate enterprise; leadership

ENVIRONMENT, SOCIOLOGY OF

During the early1990s, it became commonplace to observe that sociology had been slow (compared, for example, to economics) to engage with environmental problems or to consider their significance for the discipline. Thus, in a widely reported speech, the chair of the UK Economic and Social Research Council in 1991 lamented the 'disappointing' and 'slender' contribution of sociologists to the study of the environment (Newby 1991). One explanation for this can be found in the disciplinary origins of sociology and, especially, the desire to demarcate a 'science of the social' that could avoid biological explanations for human behaviour. Early theorists (such as Spencer, Comte and, later, Marx) drew to varying degree upon 'natural' explanations of social action and change. However, twentieth-century sociology characteristically separated 'society' from 'nature' or, as in debates over 'race' and gender, specifically set out to undermine claims to a 'natural' basis for human behaviour and diversity. The wish to avoid biological determinism may have left the discipline in a weak position to respond to the environmental agenda as it emerged from the 1960s onwards. Certainly, for most of the twentieth century environmental issues remained marginal to mainstream discussions and debates within sociology.

One early call for sociological engagement with the environment came from Catton and Dunlap in the 1970s, who undertook a 'crusade' (Hannigan 1995) on behalf of the 'New Environmental (or, later, Ecological) Paradigm' (Catton and Dunlap 1978). As Dunlap subsequently described it, rather than continuing in the Durkheimian tradition of dealing only in 'social facts', they argued that it had become necessary to acknowledge the 'ecosystem-dependence' of human society (Dunlap 1997). In promoting the study of the human–environment relationship, these early environmental sociologists were calling for an analysis both of the resource constraints on societal growth (Meadows *et al.* 1972) and of the impact of society on the environment.

Although the discipline as a whole may have been slow to engage with environmental issues, it is important not to neglect the much broader stream of environmental writing that has direct sociological relevance. Several strands of 'green thought' have been significant for environmental sociology. One can be traced through the early writings of Petr Kropotkin to the 'social ecology' of Bookchin. This approach stresses the connection between 'man's domination of nature' and 'man's domination of man' (Bookchin 1980). Linked to this, writers such as Barry Commoner were from the 1960s emphasizing the relationship between environmental destruction and capitalist society. Very importantly, eco-feminism has explored the manner in which the attempted mastery of nature by men is closely associated with the domination of women (Merchant 1980). Environmental sociology has also drawn on other critical concerns about modernity. For example, Shiva (1988) has brought together a critique of science, patriarchy, development and the environment. Meanwhile, more specific areas of environmentalist action (anti-nuclear protests, Love Canal and other toxic sites in the USA, worldwide pesticides campaigns) have both raised issues about the logic of industrial development and generated an 'environmental justice' movement. Finally, the sociological significance of the UN Brundtland Commission and its concept of 'sustainable development' should not be neglected, particularly since the definition of sustainability adopted by the Commission encompasses both intergenerational equity and a concern with the social roots of environmental destruction (notably, world poverty).

Since the 1990s, explicit sociological attention to the environment has been more prominent. One starting-point for this has been a lively discussion over the theoretical relationship between 'society' and 'nature'. For early contributors such as Dunlap and Catton, the social and natural worlds impact upon one another: they represent separate but closely interacting domains. However, taking their lead from Latour (1992) and the sociology of scientific knowledge, other sociologists have advocated a constructivist (or constructionist) approach to the environment. Constructivism takes different forms but ultimately suggests that the environment does not simply 'impact' upon society but that such impacts must in some way be 'constructed'. Whilst realism emphasizes the 'reality' of environmental problems, constructivism draws attention to the social processes by which people become aware of, select and act upon the environment.

Although these positions are often presented as irreconcilable, realists have noted that an element of social construction is intrinsic to all environmental claims (Dickens 1996). Meanwhile, some sociologists have advocated a 'co-construction' perspective whereby a simple realist-constructivist dichotomy is avoided: the point is not to separate society from nature but to explore their hybrid and dynamic relations (Burningham and Cooper 1999; Irwin 2001). For example, rather than simply presenting global warming as a scientifically defined problem, or else viewing the issue as a matter of discourse and agenda-setting, it becomes important to combine 'social' and 'natural' forms of investigation, while accepting that the 'social' and the 'natural' are not necessarily fixed, unchanging or separable from one another.

A recurrent topic in contemporary environmental sociology is 'environmental knowledge'. This in turn reflects some of the difficulties encountered by both environmentalist and governmental bodies when attempting to identify, define and gauge environmental threats. Yearley, for example, has considered the extent to which science can be an unreliable and insufficient friend to environmentalist groups (1991). Brown and Mikkelsen (1997) observe the emergence of a 'popular epidemiology' as lay-people develop their own forms of experience and understanding. Feminist scholars also have challenged the uses of modern science in environmental disputes and the relationship between science and 'situated knowledge' (Haraway 1991). The point throughout has not been to dismiss or undermine science but instead to consider the fundamental uncertainties of environmental knowledge and the difficulties of achieving environmental action.

The sociology of the environment brings together an array of theoretical and political perspectives, not all of which are narrowly 'sociological' in focus or orientation. This lack of theoretical integration should not necessarily be seen as a weakness, since the sociology of the environment raises profound questions about the very definition of the discipline and the best role for sociology in engaging with real-world challenges.

ALAN IRWIN
BRUNEL UNIVERSITY

References

Bookchin, M. (1980) *Towards an Ecological Society*, Montreal.

Brown, P. and Mikkelsen, E.J. (1997) *No Safe Place: Toxic Waste, Leukemia and Community Action*, Berkeley and Los Angeles.

Burningham, K. and Cooper, G. (1999) 'Being constructive: Social constructionism and the environment', *Sociology* 33(2): 297–316.

Catton, W.R. and Dunlap, R.E. (1978) 'Environmental sociology: A new paradigm', *The American Sociologist* 13: 41–9.

Dickens, P. (1996) *Reconstructing Nature: Alienation, Emancipation and the Division of Labour*, London and New York.

Dunlap, R.E. (1997) 'The evolution of environmental sociology: A brief history and assessment of the American experience', in M. Redclift and G. Woodgate (eds) *The International Handbook of Environmental Sociology*, Cheltenham and Northampton, MA, pp. 21–39.

Hannigan, J.A. (1995) *Environmental Sociology: A Social Constructionist Perspective*, London and New York.

Haraway, D. (1991) *Simians, Cyborgs and Women*, London.

Irwin, A. (2001) *Sociology and the Environment*, Cambridge.

Latour, B. (1992) *We Have Never Been Modern*, London.

Meadows, D.H., Meadows, D.L., Randers, J. and Behrens, W.W., III (1972) *The Limits to Growth*, Washington, DC.

Merchant, C. (1980) *The Death of Nature: Women, Ecology and the Scientific Revolution*, San Francisco.

Newby, H. (1991) 'One world, two cultures: Sociology and the environment', BSA bulletin, *Network* 50: 1–8.

Shiva, V. (1988) *Staying Alive: Women, Ecology and Survival in India*, London.

Yearley, S. (1991) *The Green Case: A Sociology of Environmental Issues, Arguments and Politics*, London.

Further reading

Goldblatt, D. (1996) *Social Theory and the Environment*, Cambridge.

Macnaghten, P. and Urry, P. (1998) *Contested Natures*, London, Thousand Oaks, New Delhi.

Redclift, M. and Benton, T. (eds) (1994) *Social Theory and the Global Environment*, London and New York.

World Commission on Environment and Development (1987) *Our Common Future*, Oxford and New York.

SEE ALSO: conservation; ecology; energy; environmental economics; landscape

ENVIRONMENTAL ECONOMICS

Environmental economics has its origins in the writings of Gray (the early 1900s), Pigou (1920s) and Hotelling (1930s), but did not develop as a coherent discipline until the 1970s, the era of the first environmental revolution. There are three central features of environmental economics.

First, human well-being is seriously affected by environmental degradation and the depreciation of natural resources. These linkages can be as obvious as the scarcity of fuelwood because of deforestation, landslides brought about by loss of vegetation cover, and mortality and morbidity due to contaminated water supplies. Or they can be more subtle and complex, as with the effects of certain trace gases on the stratospheric ozone layer and the resulting increase in ultraviolet radiation that affects human health (skin cancers and cataracts) through to marine productivity. That part of environmental economics that deals with demonstrating the *size* of such effects involves *economic valuation*, the process of placing money values on human preferences for, or against, environmental change.

Second, the *causes* of environmental degradation are invariably to be found in the workings, or failures, of the economic system. Such failures generally encompass *market failure*, the inability of free-market systems to account adequately for the third-party effects of economic activity (externalities); and *intervention failure*, the environmental degradation brought about by government interventions in the working of the economy. Examples of the former include conventional externality situations – such as upstream pollution of a river affecting downstream users – but need to be extended to *global missing markets*. An example of a global missing market is the carbon stored in tropical forests. If the forest is cleared by burning (to convert the land for agricultural use), then the carbon is released as carbon dioxide, contributing to the greenhouse effect and hence global warming. There are currently only limited markets in carbon storage, so the 'owner' of the forest has no incentive to conserve it to prevent the warming damage. This situation is changing as polluters pay for afforestation, forest conservation and emission reduction to offset their own emissions of carbon dioxide (such trades are known as 'joint implementation'). Intervention failures are commonplace, as with the detrimental effects on the environment of the Common Agricultural Policy (e.g. lost hedgerows) and the underpricing of irrigation water, energy and fertilizers in many countries. The underpricing encourages wasteful use and hence creates environmental problems.

Third, the *solutions* to environmental problems are often most efficiently found in correcting the economic causes of degradation. Thus, underpricing of products and resources causes environmental degradation. The solution is therefore to charge the right price by imposing environmental taxes equal to the marginal external costs involved. Ideally, such taxes should equal the marginal externality at the optimum point. In practice, measurement problems result in approximations to such ideal taxes. An alternative to a tax is a *tradeable permit or quota*. These involve issuing quotas for pollution or resource use (e.g. fish catches) equal to the desired level, and then allowing holders of the quotas to buy and sell them. Such markets have emerged in practice for sulphur dioxide permits in the USA, and for fisheries in a number of the world's main fishing grounds. In general, the choice of an *economic instrument*, such as a tax or tradeable permit, can be shown to be cheaper, and hence more cost effective, than the alternative command and control regulation.

In the area of natural resource economics, issues such as the optimal rate at which to deplete an exhaustible resource, and the optimal harvest rate for renewable resources, have been analysed in great detail. Renewable resource problems probably dominate current work in resource economics due to concerns about overuse of fisheries, deforestation, excess use of groundwater and so on. Indeed, global problems such as ozone layer depletion and global warming can be thought of as renewable resource issues – an excessive use of the world's 'sinks' for everyday pollutants.

In recent years, *sustainable development* has absorbed a lot of attention from environmental economists. Sustainable development involves making sure that economic development paths do not make future generations worse off because of current policies. This non-declining utility definition has been shown by several authors to involve leaving the next generation a capital stock no less than that possessed by the current generation. This constant capital rule has two variants. If all capital is substitutable, then it does not matter if environmental capital (oil, forests, ozone layer) is lost so long as other forms of capital (roads, machinery, education) are built up. This is the weak sustainability rule. If, however, it is not possible to substitute between forms of capital – if, for example, some forms of environmental capital are 'special' – then not only must the overall stock of capital be kept constant but so, too, must the stock of critical environmental capital. In this way sustainable development becomes an added rationale for natural resource conservation.

Finally, the early 1990s witnessed the emergence of *ecological economics*, an as yet ill-defined body of thought that stresses ecological limits to economic activity, the essential nature of environmental assets, and the presence of discontinuities and thresholds in economic-ecological systems. The policy prescriptions of ecological economics appear not to differ very much from those of environmental economics.

From being a somewhat fringe activity in the 1970s environmental economics has emerged as one of the most exciting and socially relevant disciplines of the 1990s. It is still a young science, and much more is to come.

DAVID W. PEARCE
UNIVERSITY COLLEGE LONDON

Further reading

Pearce, D.W., Markandya, A. and Barbier, E. (1989) *Blueprint for a Green Economy*, London.
Perman, R., Ma, Y., McGilvray, J. and Common, M. (1999) *Natural Resource and Environmental Economics*, 2nd edn, Harlow.

SEE ALSO: conservation; energy; environment, sociology of; population and resources

EPIDEMIOLOGY

Epidemiology is a multidisciplinary science that formally assesses the causes, natural history and treatment of disease, using mainly statistical techniques. It originates in the study of epidemics of communicable diseases, but is now more concerned with chronic disease and health care delivery, a change of emphasis strongly influenced by the relative burden of diseases and consequent costs. The objectives of epidemiology are to minimize the unwanted (and avoidable) consequence of diseases by researching and informing appropriate policy to promote prevention, and to help determine appropriate treatment.

Epidemiology is primarily the science of the causes of disease. It is concerned to study the variation in the incidence of (or mortality from) diseases with respect to person, time and place, so that patterns can be observed from which the component parts of a biologically plausible aetiological process can be constructed. This involves special studies using statistical methods, social observation and understanding, as well as biological knowledge. Epidemiology forms a basic science for public health, preventive medicine, health services research and health promotion.

Key early figures in the development of epidemiology include John Snow (1813–58), who removed the handle from the Broad (now Broadwick) Street water pump in Soho, London, and at a stroke confirmed the method of transmission of cholera, because people unable to draw the water, which was contaminated by raw sewage, no longer contracted cholera (Snow 1949). Florence Nightingale (1820–1910), another pioneering figure, emphasized in her practice the importance of systematic observation of patients in order to learn about the distinctive features of a disease course.

Thomas McKeown (1979) identified and discussed the broad determinants of disease, and found that the role of organized medicine in alleviating this burden was much smaller than was commonly supposed. Archie Cochrane (1972) identified the extent of knowledge about outcomes consequent upon treatment, which he argued needed much more rigorous and systematic evaluation in medical practice by randomized controlled trials of treatments. Randomized trials, where feasible, allow the only certain method of distinguishing between real causal effects and incidental associations. Richard Doll and Bradford Hill successfully elucidated the relationship of tobacco with disease by identifying a cohort of doctors who answered periodic questions about their smoking habits. This enabled Doll and Hill to make a rigorous comparison of their death rates over the next 40 years (Doll and Hill 1964). These seminal studies have, among other things, encouraged the formal construction of systematic reviews of epidemiological evidence to bring together all randomized studies of particular treatments (Maynard and Chalmers 1997) and epidemiological studies of disease associations (Eggar *et al.* 2001) in as unbiased manner as is feasible.

Contemporary epidemiology studies vital statistics on disease incidence and mortality. Sometimes cross-sectional studies are undertaken to look at particular patterns of disease prevalence and population characteristics. More often, case control studies are used to investigate the relationships of past exposure to putative risk factors and a disease. Final assessment of causal relationships often has to await prospective cohort studies in which individuals who have been exposed to specific risks are compared with those who have not. In exceptional circumstances, randomized controlled trials are used to compare outcomes between those allocated to a particular exposure.

The most useful measure of risk is the *relative risk*. This measure simply compares the incidence of a disease among groups of subjects exposed to a risk factor with that among those not exposed. For instance, the relative risk of lung cancer among heavy cigarette smokers, compared with people who have never smoked, is around twenty. In other words, the annual incidence of lung cancer among heavy smokers (male or female) is twenty times as high as among similar people who have never smoked. In contrast, a relative risk of two might describe the potency of moderate obesity with respect to coronary heart disease or, indeed, environmental tobacco smoke and lung cancer. This number is an aggregated statistic. In circumstances where the relative risk for a risk factor and a disease varies importantly the phenomenon is called *effect modification*. There is no intrinsic reason to suppose constant relative risks across heterogenous populations, but often effect modification is much less important than the aggregate effect itself.

An alternative measure of risk is the *attributable risk per cent*. This measures the amount of disease that is attributable to the risk factor being considered. For example, how much would the incidence of lung cancer be decreased if nobody had ever smoked? The answer is that around 86 per cent of the current incidence of lung cancer is attributable to cigarette smoking. In contrast, the highest determined relative risk for breast cancer is around three, for women with an early age of starting periods compared with very late, and also a late age of first pregnancy, and a late menopause. The magnitude of the attributable risks depends not only on the relative risks but also on the prevalence of risk factors. In this case, the attributable risk percents are no higher than 15 per cent for each risk factor. Moreover, the risk factors themselves are not readily amenable to incidental change. For breast cancer, the main control emphasis is on treatment and population screening.

The role of epidemiology becomes increasingly difficult as the larger effects are found and validated. The smaller effects, with relative risks of around 1.5, are exceptionally difficult to establish, because of measurement errors and the problem of confounding. In the absence of randomized controlled trials, the epidemiologist cannot distinguish between an association of exposure with an unknown risk factor, or a direct causal relationship, or both. A noteworthy instance was the confusion that developed in the monitoring of the safety of hormone replacement therapy (HRT) for women with menopausal symptoms. Most large observational cohort studies comparing coronary heart disease rates among users of HRT with non-users found about half the incidence among HRT users. Even when adjustments were made for known differences between these groups, the difference seemed to stand. Ultimately a prospective randomized controlled trial demonstrated that, in the short term, heart disease rates were actually higher among HRT users than among non-users. It turned out that subtle selection effects had caused the apparent protection in observational studies (Michels and Manson 2003). This episode is a potent reminder of the difficulties that attend non-experimental inferences.

On the other hand, small effects are of paramount importance for common diseases. They represent the rule and not the exception, and their recognition presents the best hope for the prevention of disease. Most chronic diseases are not particularly amenable to treatment. Progress can be made only by way of constructive synergy between epidemiology, statistical science, the social sciences and biology. For instance, the study of genes that predispose to cancer may give rise to more precise estimates of other risks.

KLIM MCPHERSON
OXFORD UNIVERSITY

References

Cochrane, A.L. (1972) *Effectiveness and Efficiency*, Oxford.

Doll, R. and Hill, A.B. (1964) 'Mortality in relation to smoking: Ten years' observation of British doctors', *British Medical Journal* 269.

Eggar, M., Davey Smith, G. and Altman, D. (2001) *Systematic Reviews in Health Care*, London.

McKeown, T. (1979) *The Role of Medicine: Dream, Mirage or Nemesis?* Oxford.

Maynard, A. and Chalmers, I. (eds) (1997) *Non-random Reflections on Health Services Research. On the 25th anniversary of Archie Cochrane's Effectiveness and Efficiency*, London.

Michels, K.B. and Manson, J.E. (2003) 'Postmenopausal hormone therapy: A reversal of fortune', *Circulation* 107: 1,830–3.
Snow, J. (1949) *Snow on Cholera*, Cambridge, MA.

Further reading

Ashton, J. (ed.) (1994) *The Epidemiological Imagination*, Buckingham.
Buck, C., Llopis, A., Najera, E. and Rerris, M. (eds) (1989) *The Challenge of Epidemiology: Issues and Selected Readings*, Buckingham.

SEE ALSO: morbidity; mortality; public health

EQUALITY

'We hold,' wrote Thomas Jefferson (1743–1826), 'these truths to be sacred and undeniable; that all men are created equal and independent.' No natural scientist *qua* scientist could do other than dismiss such a statement as either meaningless or empirically false. Equality for a mathematician is a concept of some complexity in relation, for example, to identity or correlation, but one of no moral significance. Social scientists by contrast are latecomers to a debate about equality that is unresolved because it adds to the mathematician's complexity the further complications of moral argument. Equality refers to the principles on which human society ought to, as well as might, be based. Jefferson's was a moral declaration, not an empirical description. Social science attempts to explore the empirical validity of such declarations. The question is whether, and in what sense, social, political and economic equalities are possible. The answer is tentative, requiring the determination of the origins of inequality, the significance of inequality, and the viability of action intended to establish equality. All three aspects are disputed.

Traditional discussion of the origins of inequality turned on a crude distinction between nature and society. Modern recognition of cultural evolution complicates that distinction and tends to substitute a more elaborate matrix out of the consequences of interaction between genetic and environmental influences. But in neither simple nor sophisticated discussion is there denial of natural inequalities, the Jeffersonian declaration notwithstanding. Humans are not clones, and Mendelian genetics guarantees variation. Dispute, however, continues in important areas of scientific ignorance. For example, there is not adequate scientific evidence to settle the dispute between those who believe in the genetic basis of differences between ethnic or racial or class groups in educational attainment or performance in intelligence tests, and those who hold such differences to be socially created. Resolution of such disputes is, in principle, possible through the further advance of empirically tested theories of the interaction between heredity and environment.

Meanwhile dispute about the significance of natural differences continues its long history. Plato confidently argued from natural to political inequality. Hobbes in *Leviathan* (1934 [1651]) expressed the opposite view:

> Nature hath made man so equall, in the faculties of body, and mind; as that though bee found one man sometimes manifestly stronger in body, or of quicker mind than another; yet when all is reckoned together, the difference between man, and man, is not so considerable, as that one man can thereupon claim to himself and benefit, to which another may not pretend, as well as he.

Hobbes's formulation still defines the debate. Egalitarian claims, especially with respect to race and gender, are more strident now than they were in the seventeenth century, and we would now say that Hobbes was making empirical propositions from both genetics and sociology, the one referring to natural differences and the other (about claiming and pretending) referring to the social psychology of human perceptions of social rights. But the central assertion is fundamentally about the values that ought to be reflected in the actual relations of men and women in society.

In this sense the debate, turning as it does on ethical priorities between such values as equality, liberty and fraternity, may never be finally resolvable. There have been, to be sure, notable contributions to greater conceptual clarity as to the meaning of terms. John Rawls (1971) adopts the device of the 'original position' – an 'if so' story of the rational choices that might be expected from an individual contemplating different societies with known different equalities or inequalities of positions but an unknown placement for the contemplator – to illuminate the problems of value choice. Brian Barry (1973) takes the discussion further to demonstrate how a small adjustment to Rawls's social and psychological assumptions opens the possibility of a crucial shift of preference towards egalitarian rather than liberal forms of society. Arneson (1999) opposes Rawls's view of equality of opportunity. But no amount of conceptual clarification, sophisticated or erudite, solves the problem of evaluation.

The social sciences can, however, note the provenance of different priorities. One mundane but momentous perspective recurs down the ages – the recognition of mortality. Thus Horace (65–8 BCE) wrote: 'Pale death kicks his way equally into the cottages of the poor and the castles of kings.' And James Shirley (1596–1666) reminds us that

> Death lays his icy hand on kings
> Sceptre and crown
> Must tumble down
> And in the dust be equal made
> With the poor crooked scythe and spade.

This attitude is integral to Christian social teaching, which dominated the evaluation of equality at least until the eighteenth century. It was not that natural inequalities between individuals were denied so much as deemed irrelevant in discussing the rights and wrongs of dictatorship or democracy, freedom or slavery. Christians were not only 'equal before the Cross' but, as the early Church Fathers insisted, would, if they eschewed sin, live like brothers without inequalities of property and power. Sin, since the fall of Adam, had created earthly inequality. Political inequality might be necessary to protect order and restrain evil, but it did not arise, as Plato had imagined, from natural inequality. Political inequality in Christian tradition must be endured but by no means implied a necessary respect or admiration for the rich and the powerful. On the contrary, position in the next world was typically held to be threatened by privilege in this. 'He hath put down the mighty from their seat and hath exalted the humble and meek,' says the Magnificat.

The break with Christian attitudes of submission to inequality dates from the eighteenth century, with the decline of religious belief and the beginnings of a secular optimism with respect to the possibility of social transformation. Egalitarianism as a movement is commonly associated with Rousseau. But Rousseau, though believing that the evils of unfreedom and inequality were socially created, was a remorseless pessimist. He held that freedom was impossible except in a community of equals, but held out no hope of social transformation towards equality. In this sense he was a child of Christianity, and if the early socialists (Fourier, Proudhon, Saint-Simon, Robert Owen, William Thompson) were his intellectual children they were also crucially different in entertaining the hope of progress. Modern egalitarianism derives from this form of sociological optimism, and it was encouraged by, if by no means identical with, either the Hegelian idealist or Marxist materialist theories of the inevitability of social transformation. Hegel's elaborate analysis of the relation between masters and slaves, and Marx's development of it into a prediction of the future history of the working class, hold out the possibility of a community of equals.

However, egalitarianism does not presuppose either the Hegelian or the Marxist theory of history. Its more fruitful contemporary discussion in the social sciences proceeds on assumptions of openness or voluntarism as opposed to necessitous history. These debates are the substance of the third aspect of the equality problem – the viability of deliberate social action aimed at reducing inequality. One theoretical approach deserves mention here because it avoids both liberal evolutionist determinism and the alternative Marxist historicism. This is T.H. Marshall's (1950) interpretation of the development of citizenship in advanced industrial societies. Marshall shows in the case of Britain how the basic equality of membership in a society, which is rooted in the civil rights established in the eighteenth century, was extended to include political rights in the nineteenth century and certain social rights in the twentieth century, when citizenship and class have been at war as opposing principles of social distribution. Marshall's analysis also brings out the important truth that the forces that influence the distribution of life-chances are neither mechanical nor irreversible. Class displaced feudal status with formal equality of market relations, as well as ushering in new inequalities of social condition. Citizenship promotes unequal rewards as well as equal rights, for example state scholarships to selective university admission and universal political franchise. More generally, it may be noted that no social goal, equality, efficiency, liberty, order or fraternity, may be regarded as absolute. Public policies are perforce compromises aiming at optimal balance between desired ends.

Three illustrations of the limits to egalitarianism are prominent in the form of arguments against the viability of egalitarian theory.

The first illustration concerns the immutability of occupational hierarchy, postulating a *de facto* necessity for some jobs to be more distasteful, unrewarding and injurious to health than others. Given that life-chances are largely determined by the individual's occupation, a hierarchy of social advantage seems to be inescapable, and equality, as opposed to equality of opportunity, therefore unobtainable. But, egalitarians reply, a less inegalitarian society is not sociologically impossible. It is not difficult to imagine a wide range of counteracting social policies. Apart from progressive taxation and levies on wealth, there could be national service specifically designed to direct the advantaged to a period of distasteful labour. The obvious rejoinders are lodged in the name of liberty and economic efficiency, again emphasizing the relativist character of claims for any social principle. Value choice is always the nub of the issue.

A second illustration may be had from Christopher Jencks's *Inequality* (1972), which essentially argues the importance of educational reform as an instrument of egalitarianism and stresses the role of chance or luck in the unequal distribution of income and occupational status. Schooling explains only 12 per cent of the variance in US incomes. But Jencks's argument is flawed in that his evidence is about the distribution of individuals over a given structure of occupations and wages. The explanation of inequality of income accruing to jobs is not what would explain who happens to hold those jobs. Whether the inequality of the job structure is immutable remains an open question. So does that of educational inequality. Here the debate remains fierce. Two notable contributions have been made recently by Peter Saunders (1999) and Adam Swift (2000), the former arguing against and the latter defining precisely what is meant by equality in the educational context.

Finally, there is the alleged obstacle of genetic differences between races and classes of which Jensen (1972) has been an outstanding proponent. As to classes, and against Jensen's marshalling of the evidence from studies of twins reared apart, there is the opposed conclusion of Schiff (1982) from his studies of cross-class adopted children in France. As to race, it has to be said that we do not yet have the techniques or the data to measure definitively the genetic and environmental influences on race–IQ differences. Nor does the answer really matter, for there are more important issues of equality and justice in present-day society that do not have to wait upon further advances in the social sciences.

A.H. HALSEY
NUFFIELD COLLEGE, OXFORD

References

Arneson, R. (1999) 'Against Rawlsian equality of opportunity', *Philosophical Studies* 93: 77–112.
Barry, B. (1973) *The Liberal Theory of Justice*, Oxford.
Hobbes, T. (1934 [1651]) *Leviathan*, Everyman edn, London.
Jencks, C. (1972) *Inequality*, New York.
Jensen, A. (1972) *Genetics and Education*, London.
Marshall, T.H. (1950) *Citizenship and Social Class*, Cambridge, UK.
Rawls, J. (1971) *A Theory of Justice*, Cambridge, MA.
Saunders, P (1999) 'On the meaning and measurement of inequality', *Acta Sociologica* 42(3): 241–50.
Schiff, M. (1982) *L'Intelligence gaspillée*, Paris.
Swift, A. (2000) 'Class analysis from a normative perspective', *British Journal of Sociology* 51(4): 662–79.

Further reading

Letwin, W. (ed.) (1983) *Against Equality: Readings on Economic and Social Policy*, London.
Parfit, D. (1998) 'Equality and priority', in A. Mason (ed.) *Ideals of Equality*, Oxford.
Runciman, W.G. (1966) *Relative Deprivation and Social Justice*, London.
Tawney, R.H. (1952) *Equality*, 4th rev. edn, London.

SEE ALSO: affirmative action; class, social; deprivation and relative deprivation; distribution of incomes and wealth; income distribution, theory of; justice, distributive; Rawls; social contract; stratification

EQUILIBRIUM

In a static context, two distinct but related definitions of equilibrium can be given. The first defines equilibrium as a position of balance in the economy; the equality of demand and supply is an equilibrium under this definition because the forces of supply are balanced by the forces of demand. Alternatively, equilibrium can be defined as being achieved when no agent in the economy has any incentive to modify their chosen action or chosen strategy. This latter definition is derived from that used in the theory of games and is illustrated by the equilibrium of an oligopolistic market in which all firms are satisfied with their choice of output level. It is easily seen that these definitions are related. When supply is equal to demand, it is also true that no firm will wish to produce any more or less since each will have sold its profit-maximizing quantity. Similarly, each consumer will have been able to carry out their chosen consumption plan and this will be utility-maximizing. In the context of a competitive economy, the two definitions are identical: as shown by Arrow and Debreu (1954), the equilibrium of the competitive economy can be represented as the equilibrium point of a suitably defined game. For dynamic economies, the tradition since Hicks (1946) has been to divide time into discrete periods. When markets are balanced within a period, a temporary equilibrium is achieved. An equilibrium for the economy is a sequence of temporary equilibria.

Despite the existence of research into the economics of disequilibrium, the concept of equilibrium remains at the heart of economic analysis. Much effort is directed towards proving the existence of equilibrium in economic models and demonstrating the welfare properties of equilibrium. Equally important are the analysis of the uniqueness and stability of equilibrium and the determination of how changes in exogenous parameters affect the equilibrium. Positions of equilibrium are also contrasted to those of disequilibrium.

This emphasis upon equilibrium can be given several explanations. Historically, the economy was viewed as self-correcting so that, if it were ever away from equilibrium, forces existed that move it back towards equilibrium. In the long run, equilibrium would then always be attained. Although such adjustment can be justified in simple single-market contexts, both the practical experience of sustained high levels of unemployment and the theoretical study of stability (Arrow and Hahn 1971) have shown that it is not justified more generally. The present justifications for focusing upon equilibrium are more pragmatic. The analysis of a model must begin somewhere, and the equilibrium has much merit as a starting-point. Sometimes the focus can be justified by showing that the equilibrium is the outcome of playing the underlying game cor-

rectly. In addition, even if the final focus is on disequilibrium, there is much to be gained from comparing the properties of points of disequilibrium to those of equilibrium. Finally, no positions other than those of equilibrium have any obvious claim to prominence.

GARETH D. MYLES
UNIVERSITY OF EXETER

References

Arrow, K.J. and Debreu, G. (1954) 'Existence of equilibrium for a competitive economy', *Econometrica* 22.
Arrow, K.J. and Hahn, F.H. (1971) *General Competitive Analysis*, Amsterdam.
Hicks, J. (1946) *Value and Capital*, Oxford.

Further reading

Benassy, J.-P. (1982) *The Economics of Market Disequilibrium*, New York.
Hahn, F.H. (1973) *On the Notion of Equilibrium in Economics*, Cambridge, UK.

SEE ALSO: economic dynamics; game theory

ETHICS IN SOCIAL RESEARCH

Social research ethics involves the consideration of the moral implications of social science enquiry. Ethics is a matter of principled sensitivity to the rights of others, in such a way that human beings who are being studied by social scientists are treated as ends rather than as means. Such ethical issues frequently also lead to consideration of the politics of research, the place of the investigator in the power structure, and the wider social impact of research. Those conducting social research need increasingly to be aware of the ethical and political implications of their actions.

The protection of human subjects is enshrined in the doctrine of informed consent, first developed in biomedical research. This stipulates that the voluntary consent of the human subject is essential, and this should be freely given without duress, and knowing and understanding what the research involves. Most social research, whether by experimental, social survey or observational methods, respects this principle, but there have been occasional sharp controversies where experimental or observational subjects have been left in ignorance of research, or have had research misrepresented to them. In observing the principle, most social scientists do not follow the formal procedures used in medical research such as signed consent forms.

A related controversy has concerned the use of deception in social research. The majority of social scientists are open about their purposes and aims, but in rare cases deception has been used on the grounds that, because of practical methodological or moral considerations, research could not otherwise be carried out. (Such studies include research on obedience to authority, and sexual deviance.) Objections to deception include its degrading and false character, its harmful social consequences, harm to the investigator, the creation of suspicion among subjects, and the breach of informed consent.

Research may in certain circumstances impinge upon the privacy of research subjects (that is, the freedom of the individual to decide how much of the self to reveal to others, when and to whom). Some information about the individual may be sensitive. Some settings (for example jury rooms, Cabinet meetings) may be entirely closed to outsiders. The wider dissemination of research results may affect subjects adversely. Such problems may be handled by obtaining informed consent or by various forms of making data anonymous. In the latter case, for example, the location in which research was carried out may be concealed and the identities of particular individuals hidden under pseudonyms. A distinction may be made between the circumstances under which data are collected, and their subsequent storage, dissemination, analysis and reanalysis. Issues of confidentiality are raised by the latter, though also impinging upon collection. What will happen to data once collected? To whom will they be available? What repercussions might there be for the individual in providing certain data to a social researcher?

The importance of these questions has been intensified by the advent of the electronic computer, with immensely powerful means of large-scale data storage and retrieval. This has a major impact upon census data and large-scale social survey data. Various techniques have been developed to ensure that individual identities cannot be linked to published information. These include the deletion of individual identifiers such as name, address or local area of residence; the suppression of tables containing small numbers of cases; and processes of random error injection. In addition to physical security, technical means exist for making anonymous the data held in computer files, including the separation of identifiers from the main body of data and their linkage by suitable codes. Randomized response is a method of ensuring the confidentiality of data while it is being collected.

The ethical issues raised by research go wider than the treatment of research subjects and handling of data once collected. The social impact of research has been of concern and controversy both within particular societies (as in the Moynihan Report on black families in the USA) and internationally (as in Project Camelot in Chile in the 1960s). There is increasing concern about the sponsorship of research (Who pays? For whom, and in whose interest, is research conducted?), the negotiation of research access (especially the role played by gatekeepers, who may give or withhold permission), and about the possible adverse effects of the publication of research results on certain weaker groups or lower-status sections of society. The investigator can rarely control any of these factors, but awareness of them can help to produce more effective work. Particular care is also required to review the ethical implications of action research and applied research leading to social intervention (for example of some of the large-scale social experiments for social policy). Consideration of these broader issues leads on to an examination of the political role of social science research and its place in the society in which it is carried out.

There is no agreed theory of research ethics with which to evaluate the merits of undertaking particular pieces of research. It is difficult to determine whether, and if so to what extent, research subjects may be harmed by particular research practices. One widespread approach is in terms of a utilitarian risk/benefit calculus, but this leaves several issues unresolved. Both risks and benefits are difficult to predict and to measure, harm to the individual can only with difficulty be weighted against societal benefits, and the investigator is usually the judge in his own case. Another approach is in terms of situational ethics, where the investigator weighs up the morally appropriate course of action in the actual research context. A different approach is in terms of absolute moral principles to be followed in all situations. No approach receives universal approval, and ethical decision-making in research remains ultimately a matter of individual judgement as well as professional controversy.

One practical consequence both of the societal impact of research and the indeterminacy of ethical decision-making about research has been a move towards greater regulation. Many professional associations of social scientists have their own ethical codes, to which members are expected to adhere. Various forms of peer review by a researcher's own department or institution are a more rigorous and direct form of oversight. The Institutional Review Boards established by universities in the USA are one example of efforts to prevent unethical behaviour by social researchers.

MARTIN BULMER
UNIVERSITY OF SURREY

Further reading

Barnes, J.A. (1980) *Who Should Know What? Social Science, Privacy and Ethics*, Cambridge, UK.
Beauchamp, T.L., Faden, R.R., Wallace, R.J., Jr and Walters, L. (eds) (1982) *Ethical Issues in Social Science Research*, Baltimore, MD.
Homan, R. (1991) *The Ethics of Social Research*, London.

ETHNIC POLITICS

More than 80 per cent of contemporary states that comprise the United Nations are ethnically plural, in that they contain two or more mobilized ethnic communities. These communities compete, sometimes by civic methods, sometimes by violence, for hegemony (control of the state apparatus), for autonomy (ranging from regional self-government to secession), or for incorporation into the society and polity on more favourable terms. Interethnic relations may vary from stratificational (one group dominating the others politically and economically), to segmentational (each party controlling significant resources and institutions). In the contemporary era, ethnic politics implicate the state, because the state has become the principal allocator of the values that affect the relative power, status, material welfare and life-chances of ethnic collectivities and their individual constituents. The values at stake may be political – control of territory, citizenship, voting rights, eligibility for public office, symbols of the state and respect for a group's collective identity; economic – access to higher education, employ-

ment, land, capital, credit and business opportunities; or cultural – including the position of religion and the relative status of language in education and in government transactions.

Ethnic politics may be generated by the grievances of territorially concentrated peoples, demanding independent statehood or greater autonomy for their homeland and more equitable representation in the central government; or by immigrant diasporas asking for more equitable terms of inclusion in the polity, combined often with claims for recognition and official support for their distinctive cultural institutions. These initiatives often trigger counter-mobilization within ethnic groups that consider themselves native sons committed to the ethnic status quo and that feel threatened by the demands of recent immigrants.

The state has the principal responsibility for managing or regulating ethnic conflicts. Its strategies may be directed in three ways: first, at maintaining pluralism by coercive domination of subordinated ethnic communities or by consensual processes such as federalism and power sharing; second, at eliminating pluralism by genocide, expulsion (ethnic cleansing) or induced assimilation; or, third, at reducing the political salience of ethnic solidarity by cultivating cross-cutting affiliations, delegitimizing ethnic organizations and ethnic political messages, and promoting individual participation and integration into the mainline economy and polity. Ethnic conflicts are seldom settled or resolved; though specific issues may be successfully compromised, the parties remain to focus their grievances and demands on other issues. Thus ethnic politics is a continuing feature of ethnically divided states. Ethnic activism is promoted either by perceived threats to a community's dignity, status, rights or opportunities; or to newly discovered possibilities to rectify an unsatisfactory status quo.

Government policies may contribute to stimulating and rewarding ethnic mobilization, as well as to mitigating ethnic conflict. Complicating interethnic relations is the inevitability of factions within ethnic communities, each competing for available resources, for support within their constituency and for the right to represent it to outsiders. Factional conflicts within ethnic communities may result in expedient, often tacit, understandings and coalitions with counterparts across hostile ethnic boundaries or with representatives of the state.

Many ethnic disputes spill over the borders of individual states, especially where ethnic kinfolk inhabit neighbouring states. Domestic ethnic conflicts thus intrude into international relations, prompting intervention by other states, by sympathizers with one of the parties to the dispute, and by international organizations attempting to mediate, restore and maintain order or mitigate the suffering of civilians and refugees. Violent ethnic conflicts including full-scale civil wars have emerged as a major source of international instability that preoccupies national politicians and attentive publics; they have strained the diplomatic, financial and operational capacities of the United Nations.

Liberals, Marxists and modernizers, despite their differences, have joined in perceiving ethnic solidarity as the residue of earlier stages of human development and in predicting and advocating its early disappearance in favour of more rational forms of association. They continue to treat it as a dangerous and essentially illegitimate phenomenon. Others explain the resurgence of politicized ethnicity and thus ethnic politics variously as, first, the search for community in increasingly bureaucratized and impersonal industrialized societies; second, more reliable sources of security and material opportunity than class-based organizations or weak, unrepresentative Third World governments; third, efficient vehicles for mobilization and representation of individual and collective interests in modern societies; or, fourth, the consequence of the disintegration of colonial empires and multiethnic states that leave ethnic collectivities as their residual legatees. These explanations relate to the ongoing dispute between 'primordialists', who argue that collective ethnic identities are deeply rooted historical continuities nurtured by early socialization and collective memories, and reinforced by collective sanctions; 'instrumentalists', who hold that ethnic identities are exploited cynically by ethnic entrepreneurs to justify their pursuit of political and material gain; and 'social constructionists', who consider ethnic solidarities to be imagined or invented categories, fluid and opportunistic, moulded by changing circumstances.

Self-determination is the ideology that legitimizes ethnic activism on behalf of peoples who demand independence or increased territorial autonomy. Multiculturalism legitimates cultural distinctiveness and self-management of cultural institutions. Demands for non-discriminatory inclusion of individuals regardless of ethnic, religious or racial origins are inspired by universalistic liberal principles. State nationalism may either confirm the super-ordinate position of a dominant ethnic community, or claim a higher-order allegiance to the state that attempts to amalgamate and supersede traditional loyalties in an ethnically plural society.

MILTON J. ESMAN
CORNELL UNIVERSITY

Further reading

Danspeckgruber, W. (ed.) (2002) *Self-Determination of Peoples: Community, Nation, and State in an Interdependent World*, Boulder, CO.

Esman, M.J. (1994) *Ethnic Politics: Conflict and Coexistence in the Modern State*, Ithaca, NY.

Gurr, T.R. and Harff, B. (1994) *Ethnic Conflict in World Politics*, Boulder, CO.

Horowitz, D.L. (1985) *Ethnic Groups in Conflict*, Berkeley, CA.

Moynihan, D.P. (1993) *Pandaemonium: Ethnicity in International Politics*, New York.

Rothschild, J. (1970) *Ethnopolitics: A Conceptual Framework*, New York.

Schermerhorn, R.A. (1970) *Comparative Ethnic Relations: A Framework for Theory and Research*, New York.

Smith, A.D. (2001) *Nationalism: Theory, Ideology, History*, Cambridge, UK.

SEE ALSO: affirmative action; consociation; ethnicity; genocide; multiculturalism; nationalism; race

ETHNICITY

Ethnicity is a fundamental category of social organization that is based on membership defined by a sense of common historical origins and which may also include shared culture, religion or language. It can be distinguished from kinship in so far as those relationships arise largely as a result of biological inheritance. The term is derived from the Greek word *ethnos*, which may be translated as 'a people or nation'. One of the most influential definitions of ethnicity can be found in Max Weber's *Economy and Society* (1968 [1922]) where he describes ethnic groups as 'human groups (other than kinship groups) which cherish a belief in their common origins of such a kind that it provides a basis for the creation of a community'.

The boundaries of ethnicity often overlap with related or similar concepts, like race and nation.

Most social scientists regard the idea of 'race' as a highly problematic concept despite lingering popular beliefs that regard 'races' as biological groups with a distinct genetic composition. There is no scientific evidence to support these notions. The term nation implies a self-conscious ethnic group mobilized with the goal of creating or preserving a political unit in which it is the predominant or exclusive political force. According to Weber (1968 [1922]), 'a nation is the political extension of the ethnic community as its members and leadership search for a unique political structure by establishing an independent state'.

In those societies that have been influenced by large-scale immigration, like the USA, Argentina, Australia and Canada, the study of ethnic groups forms a central theme of their social, economic and political life. Systematic research on US ethnic groups can be traced to the sociologists of the Chicago School during the 1920s, led by W.I. Thomas and Robert Ezra Park (Lal 2002), who were concerned with the processes of ethnic group assimilation into the dominant white, Anglo-Saxon, Protestant (WASP) mainstream. Park's race relations cycle, which outlined a sequence of stages consisting of 'contact, competition, accommodation and assimilation', implied that successive immigrant groups would be gradually absorbed into a relatively homogeneous US society. The underlying assumption of ethnic group theory was that these long-term trends would result in the disappearance of separate ethnic communities as they merged into a US melting pot.

This unilinear model gave way to more pluralistic conceptions of ethnicity in the USA in which various dimensions of assimilation were identified by sociologists like Milton Gordon (1964). Gordon distinguished between cultural assimilation (acculturation) and structural assimilation, the former signifying the adoption of the language, values and ideals of the dominant society, while the latter reflected the incorporation of ethnic groups into the institutions of mainstream society. While cultural assimilation did not necessarily result in an ethnic group's inclusion within the principal institutions of society, structural assimilation invariably meant that assimilation on all other dimensions – from personal identification to intermarriage – had already taken place.

Scholarly concern with ethnicity and ethnic conflict became increasingly salient in the second half of the twentieth century. Inadequate assumptions about the nature of modernization and modernity have been demonstrated by the pattern of social change under capitalism, socialism and in the developing world. The expectation that modernity would result in a smooth transition from *Gemeinschaft* (community) to *Gesellschaft* (association), accompanied by the gradual dissolution of ethnic affiliations, simply did not fit the facts. Some social scientists argued that there was a primordial basis to ethnic attachments (Horowitz 2002; Connor 2002), while others explained the apparent persistence of ethnicity in more instrumental terms, as a political resource to be mobilized in appropriate situations that may be activated by power (Jenkins 2002) or guided by cultural factors (Avruch 2002). Not only has ethnicity failed to recede in industrial and postindustrial societies. Ethnic divisions also have continued to frustrate the efforts at democratization and economic growth in large sectors of the Third and Fourth Worlds. The collapse of the political regimes of the Communist Bloc unleashed an upsurge in ethnic and national identity, some of which filled the void created by the demise of Marxism, while other elements of the same development, notably in the former Yugoslavia, turned into bloody ethnonational conflicts (Sekulic 2002).

The focus of research on ethnicity has shifted away from studies of specific groups to the broad processes of ethnogenesis, the construction and perpetuation of ethnic boundaries, the meaning of ethnic identity, the impact of globalization (Berger and Huntington 2002) and the importance of transnationalism (Levitt and Waters 2002). While traditional patterns of international migration continue to play an important role in the generation of ethnic diversity, they have been modified and changed by political and economic factors in complex and unpredictable ways. In the USA large numbers of Mexican migrants, both legal and unauthorized, have contributed to the growth of the Latino population into the largest single minority group (Bean and Stevens 2003). In Germany, the central economic component of the European Union, the relations with immigrants and ethnic minorities will be a crucial element in determining the progress and stability of the emerging political structure, no matter whether it becomes a superstate or remains a loose federation (Alba *et al.* 2003).

A central concern of social scientists has been the attempt to understand the nature of ethnic conflict and violence. The continuation of ethnic warfare and genocide in societies as diverse, and remote from each other, as Bosnia and Burundi (Avruch 2002; Lemarchand 2002), suggests that these forms of ethnic division have not lost their power to mobilize human groups and to undermine such 'rational' considerations as economic profits and losses. Ironically, the failure to understand the power of ethnic affiliations under Marxist regimes was repeated by the advocates of hegemonic global capitalism until the events of 11 September 2001 forced a dramatic reappraisal of the diverse and complex sources of contemporary identity. Some social scientists have long argued against a narrow focus on material factors and emphasized the fundamental nature of the ethnic bond (Greenfeld 2001; Connor 2002; Smith 2003) in explaining the stubborn resilience of nations and nationalism.

A wide variety of theoretical perspectives can be found supporting contemporary studies of ethnicity and ethnic conflict (Hutchinson and Smith 1996; Guibernau and Rex 1997). Some, like rational choice theory, are methodologically individualistic and apply a cost–benefit formula to account for ethnic preferences and to explain the dynamics of ethnic group formation. These have been criticized on the grounds that they fail to appreciate the collective dynamics of much ethnic behaviour and underestimate the irrational side of ethnic violence. Other common perspectives focus on ethnic stratification: theories employing neo-Marxist perspectives stress the economic components underlying much ethnic discrimination; while those following the tradition of scholars like Weber and Furnivall provide a more pluralistic interpretation of differences in ethnic power. In general, these originate from conquest and migration, and are used to account for the hierarchical ordering of ethnic and racial groups. Further theories point to social-psychological factors, like prejudice and ethnocentrism, as important explanations for the persistence of ethnicity.

Two highly controversial arguments centre on genetic imperatives, which operate through the mechanism of kin-selection, and form part of the application of sociobiological thinking to ethnic relations; and neo-conservative theories that concentrate on cultural characteristics, which, it is asserted, are disproportionately distributed among certain ethnic groups. Such theories have been vigorously challenged because of their deterministic, if not racist, implications. The heat of the debate reinforces the conclusion that no one theory provides a generally accepted and comprehensive paradigm to explain the complexity of ethnic group formation or the persistence of ethnic conflict in the new millennium.

JOHN STONE
BOSTON UNIVERSITY

References

Alba, R., Schmidt, P. and Wasmer, M. (2003) *Germans or Foreigners?* London.

Avruch, K. (2002) 'Culture and ethnic conflict in the New World Disorder', in J. Stone and R. Dennis (eds) *Race and Ethnicity*, Malden, MA.

Bean, F. and Stevens, G. (2003) *America's Newcomers and the Dynamics of Diversity*, New York.

Berger, P. and Huntington, S. (eds) (2002) *Many Globalizations*, New York.

Connor, W. (2002) 'Beyond reason: the nature of the ethnonational bond', in J. Stone and R. Dennis (eds) *Race and Ethnicity*, Malden, MA.

Gordon, M. (1964) *Assimilation in American Life*, New York.

Greenfeld, L. (2001) *The Spirit of Capitalism*, Cambridge, MA.

Guibernau, M. and Rex, J. (eds) (1997) *The Ethnicity Reader*, Cambridge.

Horowitz, D. (2002) 'The primordialists', in D. Conversi (ed.) *Ethnonationalism in the Contemporary World*, London.

Hutchinson, J. and Smith, A. (eds) (1996) *Ethnicity*, Oxford.

Jenkins, R. (2002) 'Rethinking ethnicity: Identity, categorization and power', in J. Stone and R. Dennis (eds) *Race and Ethnicity*, Malden, MA.

Lal, B. (2002) 'Robert Ezra Park's approach to race and ethnic relations', in J. Stone and R. Dennis (eds) *Race and Ethnicity*, Malden, MA.

Lemarchand, R. (2002) 'Burundi: Ethnic conflict and genocide', in J. Stone and R. Dennis (eds) *Race and Ethnicity*, Malden, MA.

Levitt, P. and Waters, M. (eds) (2002) *The Changing Face of Home*, New York.

Sekulic, D. (2002) 'The creation and dissolution of the multinational state', in J. Stone and R. Dennis (eds) *Race and Ethnicity*, Malden, MA.

Smith, A. (2003) *Chosen Peoples*, Oxford.

Weber, M. (1968 [1922]) *Economy and Society*, New York.

Further reading

Stone, J. and Dennis, R. (eds) (2002) *Race and Ethnicity*, Malden, MA.

SEE ALSO: ethnic politics; multiculturalism; nationalism; race

ETHNOGRAPHY

Ethnography is a term that carries several historically situated meanings. In its most general sense, it refers to a study of the way of life and ideas that a given group of people more or less share. The term is double-edged and has implications for both the method of study and the result of such study. When used as a method, ethnography typically refers to fieldwork (alternatively, participant-observation) conducted by a single investigator who 'lives with and lives like' those who are studied, usually for a year or more. When used as a result, ethnography ordinarily refers to the written representation of a culture. Contemporary students of culture emphasize the latter usage and thus look to define ethnography in terms of its topical, stylistic and rhetorical features.

There are three moments (discernible activity phases) associated with ethnography. The first moment concerns the collection of information or data on a specified culture. The second refers to the construction of an ethnographic report; in particular, the compositional practices used by an ethnographer to fashion a cultural portrait. The third moment of ethnography deals with the reading and reception that an ethnography receives across relevant audience segments both narrow and broad. Each phase raises distinctive issues.

The greatest attention in the social sciences has been directed to the first moment of ethnography – fieldwork. This form of social research is both a product of and a reaction to the cultural studies of the mid- to late nineteenth century (Stocking 1987, 1992). Early ethnography is marked by considerable distance between the researcher and researched. The anthropologists of the day based their cultural representations not on first-hand study but on their readings of documents, reports and letters originating from colonial administrators, members of scientific expeditions, missionaries, adventurers and, perhaps most importantly, faraway correspondents guided by questions posed by their stay-at-home pen-pals. Not until the early twentieth century did ethnographers begin to enter, experience and stay for more than brief periods of time in the strange (to them) social worlds about which they wrote. Bronislaw Malinowski (1922: 1–25) is most often credited with initiating by example a modern form of fieldwork that requires of the ethnographer the sustained, intimate and personal acquaintance with 'what the natives say and do'.

There is, however, a good deal of variation in terms of just what activities are involved in fieldwork and, more critically, just how such activities result in a written depiction of culture. Current practices include intensive interviewing, count-and-classify survey work, participation in everyday routines or occasional ceremonies engaged in by those studied, the collecting of samples of native behaviour across a range of social situations, and so on. There is now a rather large literature designed to help novice or veteran fieldworkers carry out ethnographic research (e.g. Bernard 1994; Davies 1998; Ellen 1984).

Yet much of the advice offered in fieldwork manuals defies codification and lacks the consensual approval of those who produce ethnographies. Fieldnotes, for example, are more or less *de rigueur* in terms of documenting what is learned in the field but there is little agreement as to what a standard fieldnote – much less a collection of fieldnotes – might be (Sanjek 1990). Moreover, how one moves from a period of lengthy *in situ* study to a written account presumably based on such study is by no means clear. Despite 70 or so years of practice, fieldwork remains a sprawling and quite diverse activity.

The second moment of ethnography – writing it up – has by and large been organized by a genre labelled 'ethnographic realism' (Clifford and Marcus 1986; Van Maanen 1988). It is a genre that has itself shifted over time from a relatively unreflective, closed and general (holistic) description of native sayings and doings to a more tentative, open and partial interpretation of native sayings and doings (Geertz 1973). Yet realism remains a governing style for a good deal of ethnography, descriptive or interpretative. It is marked by a number of compositional conventions that include, for example, the suppression of the individual cultural member's perspective in favour of a typified or common denominator 'native's point of view', the placement of a culture within a timeless ethnographic present and a claim for descriptive or interpretive validity based on the author's 'being there' (fieldwork) experience.

Some ethnographers, though by no means all, express a degree of dissatisfaction with ethnographic realism (Marcus and Fischer 1986).

Partly a response to critics located outside ethnographic circles who wonder just how personal experience serves as the basis for a scientific study of culture, some ethnographers make visible – or, more accurately, textualize – their discovery practices and procedures (Agar 1980). *Confessional ethnography* results when the fieldwork process itself becomes the focus in an ethnographic text. Its composition rests on moving the fieldworker to centre stage and displaying how the writer comes to know a given culture. While often carefully segregated from an author's realist writings, confessional ethnography often manages to convey a good deal of the same sort of cultural knowledge put forth in conventional realist works but in a more personalized fashion (e.g. Rabinow 1977).

Other genres utilized for ethnographic reporting are available as well. *Dramatic ethnographies*, for example, rest on the narration of a particular event or sequence of events of apparent significance to the cultural members studied. Such ethnographies present an unfolding story and rely more on literary techniques drawn from fiction than on plain-speaking, documentary techniques – 'the style of non-style' – drawn from scientific reports (e.g. Shore 1982). *Critical ethnographies* provide another format wherein the represented culture is located within a larger historical, political, economic, social and symbolic context than is said to be recognized by cultural members, thus pushing the writer to move beyond traditional ethnographic frameworks and interests when constructing the text (e.g. Nash 1979). Even self- or auto-ethnographies have emerged in which the culture of the ethnographer's own group is textualized. Such writings offer the passionate, emotional voice of a positioned and explicitly judgemental fieldworker and thus obliterates the customary distinction between the researcher and the researched (e.g. Young 1991).

A good deal of the narrative variety of ethnographic writing is a consequence of the post-1970s spread of the specialized and relatively insular disciplinary aims of anthropology and, to a lesser degree, sociology. Growing interest in the contemporary idea of culture – as something held by all identifiable groups, organizations and societies – has put ethnography in play virtually everywhere. No longer is ethnography organized simply by geographical region, society or community. Adjectival ethnographies have become

common and sizeable literatures can be found in such areas as medical ethnography, organizational ethnography, conversation ethnography, school ethnography, occupational ethnography, family ethnography and many more. The results of the intellectual and territorial moves of both away and at-home ethnography include a proliferation of styles across domains and an increase in the number of experimental or provisional forms in which ethnography is cast.

The expansion of ethnographic interests, methods and styles is a product of the third moment of ethnography – the reading of ethnographic texts by particular audiences and the kinds of responses these texts appear to generate. Of particular interest are the categories of readers that an ethnographer recognizes and courts through the topical choices, analytic techniques and composition practices displayed in a text. Three audience categories stand out. First, collegial readers are those who follow particular ethnographic domains most avidly. They are usually the most careful and critical readers of one another's work and the most familiar with the past and present of ethnography. Second, general social science readers operate outside of ethnographic circles. These are readers attracted to a particular ethnography because the presumed facts (and perhaps the arguments) conveyed in the work help further their own research agendas. Third, there are some who read ethnography for pleasure more than for professional enlightenment. Certain ethnographic works attract a large, unspecialized audience for whom the storytelling and allegorical nature of an ethnography is salient. Such readers look for familiar formats – the traveller's tale, the adventure story, the investigative report and, perhaps most frequently, the popular ethnographic classics of the past – when appraising the writing. Ironically, the ethnographer charged with being a novelist *manqué* by colleagues and other social scientists is quite likely to be the ethnographer with the largest number of readers.

For each reader segment, particular ethnographic styles are more or less attractive. Collegial readers may take in their stride what those outside the field find inelegant, pinched and abstruse. The growing segmentation across collegial readers suggests that many may be puzzled as to what nominal ethnographic colleagues are up to with their increasingly focused research techniques and refined, seemingly indecipherable, prose styles. This creates something of a dilemma for ethnographers for it suggests the distance between the general reader and the ethnographic specialist as well as the distance between differing segments of ethnographic specialists themselves is growing. While ethnography itself is in little or no danger of vanishing, those who read broadly across ethnographic fields may be fewer in number than in generations past. This is a shame, for strictly speaking an unread ethnography is no ethnography at all.

JOHN VAN MAANEN
MASSACHUSETTS INSTITUTE OF TECHNOLOGY

References

Agar, M. (1980) *The Professional Stranger*, New York.
Bernard, H.R. (1994) *Research Methods in Cultural Anthropology*, 2nd edn, Newbury Park, CA.
Clifford, J. and Marcus, G.E. (eds) (1986) *Writing Culture*, Berkeley, CA.
Davies, C.A. (ed.) (1998) *Reflexive Ethnography: A Guide to Researching Selves and Others*, London.
Ellen, R. (ed.) (1984) 'Ethnographic research: A guide to general conduct', *Association of Social Anthropologists Research Methods Series No. 1*, London.
Geertz, C. (1973) *The Interpretation of Cultures*, New York.
Malinowski, B. (1922) *Argonauts of the Western Pacific*, London.
Marcus, G.E. and Fischer, M. (1986) *Anthropology as Cultural Critique*, Chicago.
Nash, J. (1979) *We Eat the Mines and the Mines Eat Us*, New York.
Rabinow, P. (1977) *Reflections on Fieldwork in Morocco*, Berkeley, CA.
Sanjek, R. (ed.) (1990) *Fieldnotes*, Ithaca, NY.
Shore, B. (1982) *Sala'ilua: A Samoan Mystery*, New York.
Stocking, G.W. (1987) *Victorian Anthropology*, New York.
—— (1992) *The Ethnographer's Magic*, Madison, WI.
Van Maanen, J. (1988) *Tales of the Field*, Chicago.
Young, M. (1991) *An Inside Job*, Oxford.

Further reading

Taylor, S. (ed.) (2001) *Ethnographic Research*, London.
Willis, P. (2000) *The Ethnographic Imagination*, Cambridge, UK.

SEE ALSO: case study; interviews (qualitative); life history; Malinowski; methods of social research

ETHNOMETHODOLOGY

The term 'ethnomethodology' was coined in the 1950s by Harold Garfinkel to describe a distinctive orientation to the production of social order. His major work *Studies in Ethnomethodology* (Garfinkel 1967) helped establish ethnomethodology as a subfield of sociology. Harvey Sacks, along with Emanuel Schegloff and Gail Jefferson (Sacks *et al.* 1974; Sacks 1992), later developed a distinctive line of ethnomethodological research – later named 'conversation analysis' – on the detailed interactive practices that produce and co-ordinate communicative actions. Ethnomethodology originated within sociology, and it is sociological in its fundamental orientation to professional and non-professional practices, but it also has made inroads into anthropology, sociolinguistics, computer-supported co-operative work, management studies, and social studies of science, among other fields.

The word 'ethnomethodology', which recently was added to the *Oxford English Dictionary*, literally means 'people's methods'. As Garfinkel (1974) acknowledges, ethnomethodology is linked to the anthropological ethnosciences: investigations of native methods of measurement and calculation, indigenous classification systems, and other culturally specific procedures and category schemes. The domain of ethnomethodology is much broader than, for example, ethnobotany, as it includes virtually any ordinary or specialized method. In many cases, ethnomethodologists study commonplace activities in their own native societies.

Ethnomethodology is not a social scientific method in any straightforward sense, though many studies associated with that field make use of similar procedures. Often, ethnomethodological studies employ ethnographic interviews, participant observation and analyses of detailed records of continuous activities 'in real time'. Audio- and video-tapes recorded *in situ* have indispensable practical value for investigating the way activities are assembled over time through collaborative, often improvisational, sequences of discourse and embodied practice. However, the burden on the student not only is to master a set of social science techniques, but also to give an account of the methods studied – the ordinary and specialized methods that constitute social activities. When studying such methods, ethnomethodologists attempt to master the relevant skills, bodies of knowledge and discursive practices. Unlike formal methodological accounts written to instruct novices in a practice or to justify scientific findings or administrative decisions, ethnomethodological descriptions include context-sensitive details of how plans, rules, algorithms, recipes, maps, guidelines, maxims, protocols, proverbs, etc., are used (as well as disused, misused or abused) in actual conduct. Such descriptions are not anti-formalistic, in the sense of rejecting the relevance of rules, algorithms and so forth. Instead, they address the way participants *situate* rules, plans and so forth within singular scenes and courses of action (see Garfinkel 2002: Ch. 6 on 'Instructions and instructed actions'; and Suchman 1987).

The subject matter of ethnomethodology includes *methodological* inquiries as well as *methodic* practices. Garfinkel's programme makes no exception for social scientific methods, and some of his earliest studies delve into social science research practices such as coding interview responses and analysing official records (Garfinkel 1967: Chs 4, 6). These studies demonstrate that *ad hoc* judgements grounded in common-sense knowledge of the social world are crucial for constituting data points, assigning instances to nominal categories and interpretatively relating 'findings' to relevant social contexts. Starting in the 1970s, Garfinkel and some of his students turned their attention to the natural sciences. The first of these studies to be published was an investigation of a tape recording of the 'discovery' of the first pulsar visible in the optical spectrum. By closely following the sequence of characterizations of the possible 'pulse' as it built up over time on the astronomers' instrument monitor, Garfinkel *et al.* (1981) developed a genealogy in which the 'cultural object' of the pulsar – the variably characterized 'potter's object' that developed through a sequence of runs with the equipment – became identified as an astrophysical phenomenon with an objective position and space, and a specific pulse rate.

Like other ethnomethodological studies, investigations of laboratory practices and high-tech workplaces focus on quotidian details. Of course, the sciences already include extensive literatures on methodology. In order to have something to say that is not already part of the large professional literatures on methodology, it is necessary to delve into more obscure, and sometimes contentious, features of scientific practice that are not mentioned in formal methodological prescriptions and reports. There also is a difference in perspective. Ethnomethodologists not only write *accounts* of method, they examine the phenomenon of *accountability*. This does not mean that they hold the practices studied to some external normative standard of accountability; rather, it means that they delve into the issue of how practical methodological accounts (descriptions, prescriptions, rules and evaluations) arise from and reflexively feed back into the organization of conduct they make accountable. Moreover, they examine the way conduct is organized to anticipate, facilitate or, in some instances, foreclose or evade conventional coding schemes and administrative categories. Such practices sometimes result in problems for social science investigations that use organizational documents as factual records, but for ethnomethodologists they are of primary interest *as constitutive practices* rather than as sources of good or bad data.

There is some resemblance between ethnomethodological and social constructionist approaches in sociology, social problems research and social studies of science. Both approaches take a strong interest in tacit, 'street level', situated conduct; and both emphasize the mundane work that sets up and maintains the 'objective' accountability of social and natural orders. However, ethnomethodologists tend to avoid the generalized scepticism about 'facts' and 'objectivity' that runs through so much constructionist work. It is not that ethnomethodologists assume a 'realist' or 'positivist' orientation, but that they attempt to avoid the polarities of the realist-constructionist debate. In a recent collection of his papers, Garfinkel (2002) takes up Durkheim's fundamental rule of method that 'the objective reality of social facts' is sociology's 'fundamental principle' (Durkheim 1982 [1895]: 45). Garfinkel radically revises Durkheim's 'aphorism', as he calls it, so that 'the objective reality of social facts' becomes ethnomethodology's fundamental *phenomenon*. While respecting the idea that there are social facts – regular, recurrent, orders of conduct that persist despite changes in cohort – this slight change in wording respecifies the 'facts' as 'accomplishments'. Although placed in the domain of 'accomplishment' (actions produced and made accountable in organized scenes of conduct), the 'social facts' do not become mere constructions, in the sense of becoming uncertain, unpredictable or random. The initial regularities that Durkheim observed become no less regular and predictable, even while being placed in a contingent relation to the actions that sustain them.

MICHAEL LYNCH
CORNELL UNIVERSITY

References

Durkheim, E. (1982 [1895]) *The Rules of Sociological Method*, New York.
Garfinkel, H. (1967) *Studies in Ethnomethodology*, Englewood Cliffs, NJ.
—— (1974) 'On the origins of the term ethnomethodology', in R. Turner (ed.) *Ethnomethodology*, Harmondsworth.
—— (2002) *Ethnomethodology's Program: Working Out Durkheim's Aphorism*, Blue Ridge Summit, PA.
Garfinkel, H., Lynch, M. and Livingston, E. (1981) 'The work of a discovering science construed with materials from the optically-discovered pulsar', *Philosophy of the Social Sciences* 11.
Sacks, H. (1992) *Lectures on Conversation*, 2 vols, Oxford.
Sacks, H., Schegloff, E.A. and Jefferson, G. (1974) 'A simplest systematics for the organization of turn-taking in conversation', *Language* 50(4).
Suchman, L. (1987) *Plans and Situated Actions*, Cambridge, UK.

Further reading

Button, G. (1991) *Ethnomethodology and the Human Sciences*, Cambridge, UK.
Heritage, J. (1984) *Garfinkel and Ethnomethodology*, Oxford.
Livingston, E. (1987) *Making Sense of Ethnomethodology*, London.
Lynch, M. (1993) *Scientific Practice and Ordinary Action: Ethnomethodology and Social Studies of Science*, New York.
Lynch, M. and Sharrock, W.W. (2003) *Harold Garfinkel*, 4 vols, London.
Sudnow, D. (2001 [1978]) *Ways of the Hand: A Rewritten Account*, Cambridge, MA.

SEE ALSO: discourse analysis; phenomenology; reflexivity

EVENT–HISTORY ANALYSIS

Event–history analysis refers to the techniques of life tables and a class of statistical models. These techniques examine the occurrence of an event over time, and attempt to identify factors that influence the occurrence of the event. Other names for event–history analysis include survival analysis, duration models, discrete models and hazard models. The classic example of an event–history analysis is a human mortality study in which a sample of individuals are followed from birth until death, and in which the factors that influence death are related to the risk of mortality at different ages. Social scientists have studied a wide variety of phenomena along these lines, including marriage, divorce, human birth, job change, failure and merger of business firms, democratization of a nation, and so on.

The relationship of life table analysis to event–history analysis is like that of a scatter plot to linear regression, or a crosstab to logistic regression. Life table analysis is usually the first step in event–history analysis. Event–history regression analysis shares many features with other regression analysis. It has a single equation with the hazard or risk of the event at a certain time (hazard model), or the length of time since 'birth' to 'death' (accelerated failure time model or AFT models), on the left side of the equation, and predictors on the right side. In a hazard model, for instance, the predictors would predict the rate of the occurrence of the event at a given time.

Event–history analysis has a strong time dimension. The event happens over time; the value of the predictors can change over time; and the influence of the predictors can also change over time. As in linear regression, the hazard model also has an intercept. Because of the time dimension, however, the intercept is a function of time. This time-varying intercept is called the baseline hazard. The baseline hazard can be modelled parametrically by assuming that it follows a certain distribution, e.g. Weibull, or non-parametrically, via the Cox proportional hazard model (1972), which has been considered an important advance and has been implemented in all major commercial statistical packages. Piece-wise exponential models and discrete time models are two popular alternatives to the Cox model. Piece-wise exponential models use continuous time and are based on the same principle as life tables. They model the baseline hazard by cutting the entire time span under study into a number of short intervals and assuming that the hazard within each interval is constant. Piece-wise exponential models can be estimated readily by any computer procedure that handles Poisson regression. A discrete time model assumes that time is discrete by describing time in terms of days, months or years. It breaks up the event–history data in such a way that the estimation becomes 'a logistic regression'. It can easily incorporate time-varying covariates, and can be estimated by any computer package that does logistic regression. The

AFT models treats the length of time as a function of a set of predictors. This offers an interpretation of the event–history data which differs from that presented by the hazard model.

So far we have only discussed situations in which each observation concerns a single event, and the observations are independent. Advances in event–history analysis have yielded theories and techniques that handle clustered survival data, such as the mortality of households of children (Guo and Rodríguez 1992), and repeated survival data, like individuals' employment history.

Texts on event–history analysis first appeared in the early 1980s (Cox and Oakes 1984; Kalbfleisch and Prentice 1980; Lawless 1982; for social science applications, see Tuma and Hannan 1984; Lancaster 1990). About two dozen books on the topic have since been published, mainly by biostatisticians. Social scientists with a moderate amount of training in statistical theory will find that Allison (1995) provides a good combination of statistical theory, examples and computer programming.

GUANG GUO
UNIVERSITY OF NORTH CAROLINA,
CHAPEL HILL

References

Allison, Paul D. (1995) *Survival Analysis Using the SAS System: A Practical Guide*, Cary, NC.
Cox, D. (1972) 'Regression models and life tables', *Journal of the Royal Statistical Society* B34.
Cox, D. and Oakes, D. (1984) *Analysis of Survival Data*, London.
Guo, G. and Rodríguez, G. (1992) 'Estimating a multivariate proportional hazards model for clustered data using the EM algorithm, with an application to child survival in Guatemala', *Journal of American Statistical Association* 87: 969–76.
Kalbfleisch, J. and Prentice, R. (1980) *The Statistical Analysis of Failure Time Data*, New York.
Lancaster, T. (1990) *The Econometric Analysis of Transition Data*, Cambridge, UK.
Lawless, J.F. (1982) *Statistical Models and Methods for Lifetime Data*, New York (2nd rev. edn, 2003, Hoboken, NJ).
Tuma, N. and Hannan, M. (1984) *Social Dynamics: Models and Methods*, Orlando, FL.

SEE ALSO: life tables and survival analysis

EVOLUTIONARY ECONOMICS

The central concern of an evolutionary economic analysis is to explain why and how the economic world changes, its subject matter is the dynamics of structural change and adaptation, and its purpose is to make sense of the immense variety of behaviour that forms the rich tapestry of historical change. Evolution does not mean change *simpliciter* but change in the relative frequencies of specified entities within a population and subject to the operation of specific interconnected processes. This is a dynamic theme, to which the historical record in terms of cultural and economic change speaks with great eloquence and persistence (Landes 1968; Mokyr 1991, 2002). The ever-changing structure of the economic fabric, as witnessed in the growth and decline of activities, firms, cities, regions and nations, reflects evolution operating at different levels and with different speeds, as does the emergence over time of completely new areas of economic activity. The displacement of gas by electricity, the spread of robotic tools in the workplace, the displacement of corner shops by supermarkets, the growth of part-time relative to full-time employment, and the shifting balance of employment between agriculture, manufacturing and services in their different ways draw upon the same mechanism, whose mainspring is variety in behaviour. That is the fundamental fact, which makes any evolutionary social science the investigation of adaptation and interaction in the context of the changing knowledge held by individuals and organizations (Dopfer 2000).

As with modern evolutionary theory, the process is applicable at many different levels of economic activity depending on what we take to be the appropriate units of selection. But whatever the level, the three fundamental issues are the same, the specification of variety in behaviour, the identification of the selection mechanisms which resolve that variety into economic change, and the analysis of feedback and other novelty-inducing mechanisms that shape and regenerate variety over time. Inherently this involves a population perspective in which any idea of representative behaviour only has a statistical not a substantive meaning. What is representative of any population is an emergent consequence of interaction within and between populations, and it cannot be specified; a priori, it is an outcome of evolution and as a consequence changes over time. Before illustrating these remarks more fully it is useful to remember Lewontin's (1982) famous requirements for an evolutionary theory, namely entities possessing different characteristics or behavioural traits; a mechanism that assigns differential fitness to entities as they interact with other rival entities in a selection environment; and heritability, the transmission through time of the behavioural traits. We should dispose of this last point first because, *contra* naïve views on evolution, no reference to any genetic mechanism is involved or implied. What is important is stability and persistence of behaviour over time, that tomorrow's behavioural traits are correlated with those of today. Thus, inertia is an important conserving element in the picture and it will be obvious that evolution cannot occur in a world where individuals or organizations behave randomly. As to the origins of variety in economic behaviour, there is a natural emphasis on matters of technology, organization and management, that is, upon the knowledge of how to act in order to acquire beneficial behavioural traits. The entrepreneur is fully at home in an evolutionary world, and perhaps no other, for the very definition of entrepreneurship entails variety in behaviour of individuals or organized groups. Does evolution entail rationality? Apparently not. In a world in which knowledge is costly to acquire, and computational competence is bounded and individual, there is little ground for invoking omniscient optimization as a behaviour yardstick. There is nothing amiss with the idea that individuals seek the best outcome of any set of options, but such calculations as are involved are necessary local solutions, not global solutions. Here lies a powerful source of differential behaviour; individuals know different things, they live in the same world but perceive (imagine?) different worlds. Hence, it is not surprising that evolutionary analysis finds the idea of bounded rationality to be of central importance; that it specifies behaviour in terms of stable rules that themselves evolve over time; and, that it insists upon the benefits gained from the study of the internal working of organizations (Nelson and Winter 1982). Since the foundation of many of these issues is the acquisition of individual knowledge and the correlation of that knowledge across individuals via social processes, it is evident that there are close affinities with the emerging field of evolutionary epistemology and its application to the development of science and technology (Hull 1988; Plotkin 1994; Ziman 2000). Nor is the intentionality of economic behaviour an evolutionary problem; quite the contrary, it helps us to understand how economic variation is guided and channelled while underpinning the central point of individuals and organizations behaving differently (Hodgson 1993). The simple point to grasp is that the sources of economic variety are far richer than the sources of biological variety. In the economic and cultural field, the role of intentional design must here be given its due weight, a reflection of the crucial role of variety generation in maintaining evolutionary processes and, indeed, of the Lamarckian element that follows from the role of experience in shaping what is known and believed as the causes of action.

A typical, if basic, picture of economic microevolution is as follows. It concerns a population of rival firms each producing one or more products, each product with its own methods of production as dictated by the firm's technology, organization and management rules. The firm is a vehicle for many co-ordination activities, which ultimately result in the production of saleable output, co-ordinating activities which evolutionists call replicators, for they result in the firm generating, sequentially, copy after copy of its own behaviour. What is replicated is a series of instructions for action, an analogue code containing the information to permit the repetition of an activity. The firm interacts in markets with other firms to sell its products and purchase production inputs, and the result of these multiple market interactions determines the economic quality of its products, the prices at which it can sell them and the economic costs of their production. Users are continually comparing one product with another, and switching their allegiance to what they perceive to be better quality and price combinations, while firms deploy their profits in part to accumulate additional productive and marketing capabilities. In short, underlying differences in the rules of behaviour lead to different prices, costs and levels of profitability, which provide the basis for dynamic change: the general capital market rule being that the more profitable firms expand at the expense of less profitable rivals. To put it more accurately, there is market selection *for* products and their methods of production and consequent selection *of* the rival firms (Sober 1984). It is these differential rates of increase in the rate at which the different activities are operated that corresponds to the notion of economic fitness. If we imagine such a process to run in unchanged circumstances, the frequency distribution of output will concentrate on the firms with lower costs and superior products, and it will gradually eliminate other less efficient and effective firms according to the prevailing rules of bankruptcy. This is the process of dynamic competition, premised on genuine rivalry, which is the mainspring of the restless capitalism of the modern world (Andersen 1994; Metcalfe 1998).

Evolution and market concentration go hand in hand, which means that competition destroys the very variety on which it depends. Thus, if economic evolution is not to cease, mechanisms must be in play to regenerate that variety. Contrary to some perceptions, evolution is a three-stage process in which the development of further variety plays a central role (Foster and Metcalfe 2001). Innovation is thus a central component of the macroevolutionary story, and economists have learned to think of this in terms of guided variation within existing technological activities, together with the less frequent emergence of conceptually new productive opportunities. What is important for present purposes is the dependence of innovative creativity on feedback from the selection process. Internally generated profits are a principal source of the funds for such risky activity, while experience gained in pursuing particular activities is a major stimulus to push the pattern of improvement in particular directions. Conceiving of innovations as random mutations, as in genetics, is not entirely misplaced but this is certainly not the whole story. In this regard, innovation can gain a self-reinforcing momentum as the process of competition reveals fresh possibilities, and that, in the presence of such positive feedback, small historical events can have lasting consequences. In making sense of variety, evolution also makes sense of history. It is for these reasons that the evolution of useful knowledge must not be separated from the evolution of the economy more generally. Moreover, evolving economies cannot be equilibrium economies for as long as knowledge knows no equilibrium. They are highly ordered economies as a consequence of market and bureaucratic processes but that order is contingent and open, and stimulates the further growth of knowledge and fresh variation through recursive practice. We see here the central importance of market institutions to an evolutionary perspective, not in terms of the efficient allocation of known resources but in terms of openness to change and the facilitation of adaptation. What is characteristic of market capitalism is that every position is in principle open to challenge and that there are powerful incentives to organize and make those challenges.

Implicit in the above is a dual perspective on economic evolution. Much of it is concerned with the traditional role of markets as co-ordination mechanisms. It is in market interactions that the profitability of different activities and their underpinning replication codes is determined, and with this the resources to invest and innovate in the corresponding activities. This involves competition within and between industries; it is an external view of evolution taking the unit of selection in relation to its environment. Equally important is an internal perspective concerning the process of conjecture formation and selection, which takes place within organizations and defines how the relevant bundles of routines, the replication rules, evolve over time. Internal and external processes interact at different speeds and at different levels in complex intriguing ways. What happens within the community of science, for example, as it selects from novel hypotheses, provides material that firms can adopt and adapt as they seek sustainable competitive advantages. In turn the development of practice stimulates the search for further scientific understanding. These coupled processes take place at different rates within different, specialized organization structures and these different velocities of change are central to the evolutionary perspective and the uneven, ongoing structural change, which is the leitmotiv of an evolutionary process.

Many scholars have found an evolutionary perspective in economics to be appealing. Cut free from any dependence on biology in general and neo-Darwinism in particular, and with a rich array of computational powers at its disposal, there is an extensive agenda to be explored, an agenda that ultimately reduces to a question of the processes which generate and which limit the generation and spread of economic variation. In this it tackles one of the oldest of philosophical questions, the manner in which order and structure emerge from diverse behaviour. If not universal Darwinism, then at least a broader picture of evolution and its place in shaping the past, the present and the future.

J.S. METCALFE
UNIVERSITY OF MANCHESTER

References

Andersen, E.S. (1994) *Evolutionary Economics: Post Schumpeterian Contributions*, London.

Dopfer, K. (2000) *Evolutionary Economics: Programme and Scope*, Dordrecht.

Foster, J. and Metcalfe, J.S. (2001) *Frontiers of Evolutionary Economics*, Cheltenham.

Hodgson, G. (1993) *Economics and Evolution*, London.

Hull, G. (1988) *Science as a Process*, Chicago.

Landes, D. (1968) *The Unbound Prometheus*, Cambridge, UK.

Lewontin, R. (1982) *Human Diversity*, New York.

Metcalfe, J.S. (1998) *Evolutionary Economics and Creative Destruction*, London.

Mokyr, J. (1991) *The Lever of Riches*, Oxford.

—— (2002) *The Gifts of Athena*, Princeton, NJ.

Nelson, R. and Winter, S. (1982) *An Evolutionary Theory of Economic Change*, Cambridge, MA.

Plotkin, H. (1994) *The Nature of Knowledge*, London.

Sober, E. (1984) *The Nature of Selection*, Cambridge, MA.

Ziman, J. (ed.). (2000) *Technological Innovation as an Evolutionary Process*, Cambridge.

Further reading

Dennett, D.C. (1995) *Darwin's Dangerous Idea*, London.

Dosi, G. (2000) *Innovation, Organization and Economic Dynamics*, Cheltenham.

Potts, J. (2000) *The New Evolutionary Macroeconomics: Complexity, Competence and Adaptive Behaviour*, Cheltenham.

Saviotti, P. (1996) *Technological Evolution, Variety and the Economy*, Cheltenham.

Witt, U. (2003) *The Evolving Economy*, Cheltenham.

EVOLUTIONARY PSYCHOLOGY

Herbert Spencer's *Principles of Psychology* of 1855 was the first text on evolutionary psychology. But its associationist heart was married to an incorrect evolutionary theory, that of Lamarck. It was Darwin's *Origin of Species* (1859), which declared behaviour to be, like any other corporeal trait, subject to selection and conservation as a species attribute, an instinct, if it added to the survival and reproductive fitness of the individual, that was the true beginnings of evolutionary psychology. In his first book, humans received almost no mention from Darwin, but in *Descent of Man* (1871) he devoted a number of chapters to the comparison of human intellect in its various forms to that of other primates, and indeed to other mammals more widely. These were wholly anecdotal in form and set the precedent for his successor, Romanes.

Early psychology was exposed to evolutionary theory largely through William James's *Principles of Psychology* of 1890, which supported the notion of human instincts, and took a generally functionalist line. The first true evolutionary psychologist was James Mark Baldwin, who played an important role in developing evolutionary epistemology (the idea that knowledge is gained by the same processes that drive the transformation of species but embodied in different mechanisms), and the concept of organic selection. Baldwin believed that an adequate theory of the mind had to be compatible with the theory of evolution, but he was forced to leave US academic life in 1908 and he was succeeded in his chair by John Watson, arch anti-theorist of twentieth-century psychology. It was only after the poverty of behaviourism had been overturned by the cognitive revolution of the 1960s that psychologists began to think again about unobservable causes, clearing the path for a revival of evolutionary thought. Other important precursors were ethology, based upon the Darwinian approach to instincts and emotions using a comparative framework; and sociobiology, centred upon the theoretical shift to the gene as the crucial unit of evolution, rather than the individual or social group, which was the most important change to evolutionary theory for half a century. Neither ethology nor sociobiology were originally intended as disciplines relating to humans, but some came to believe that psychology was a special case of both. The case made was unconvincing, but both had shown how compelling evolutionary theory could be in explaining behaviour. If it were proving so powerful a tool in understanding the behaviour of bees and baboons, why should it not provide insights into the human mind?

Konrad Lorenz's insight into constraints on learning provided an influential example of the application of evolutionary theory to psychological questions. In 1965, in response to criticisms that he dichotomized all behaviour into either that which is innate and instinctive and that which is learned, he noted that since all learning increases the fitness of the learner, learning itself must be the adaptive product of evolution. Nurture has nature. Collapsing the learned-instinct distinction into the singularity of evolved modifiability, Lorenz advanced a powerful form of evolutionary Kantianism. The study of learning was then dominated by general process theory and there was no evidence at all that learning is adaptive in outcome, but the evidence from non-humans was soon to appear and gathered pace (Gould and Marler 1987). It became incontrovertibly clear that learning is constrained, and that those constraints are caused by neural networks being skewed to acquire information advantageous to the learner. Where Lorenz began, others followed.

From the 1980s cognitive developmentalists, using a dishabituation method allowing them to determine what caught the attention of infants, were able to establish that humans acquire a range of knowledge, including intuitive physics, number, causation and the differences between inanimate and animate entities, at ages far earlier than had previously been thought. An earlier, and parallel, development concerned the acquisition of language. The previously dominant position in psychology that language is acquired by the same learning processes and mechanisms that underlie other forms of knowledge gain, epitomized by B.F. Skinner and Jean Piaget amongst others, was overthrown by the linguist Noam Chomsky and his followers. Generative or transformational grammar is a theory of language acquisition based on the central idea that all human languages are based upon a single universal grammar that is present in the human brain at birth. Language is an innate organ of mind, and the acquisition of language is the result of learning mechanisms different from those used to acquire other forms of knowledge. Developmental, computational and neurological evidence is now overwhelmingly in favour of such a view. If language is innate, then why, asked some, should it not be seen as an evolved instinct (Pinker 1994)? And if language is an evolved and innate organ of mind, why should other cognitive capacities, such as the attribution of intentional mental states to others, the so-called Theory of Mind, not be viewed in the same way?

This general approach, the notion that human intelligence (in the wide, not the psychometric, sense) is based upon innate, specialized and constrained, knowledge structures, has been labelled the new rationalism (Fodor 1998). The central question of classical epistemology, whether knowledge is innate (the position of rationalists such as Plato and Descartes) or not (the empiricist position of the likes of Locke and Hume), has now been settled. The empiricists

were quite wrong, even if Plato was not entirely correct.

Given the stature of its predecessors (ethologists were the first ever to be awarded the Nobel Prize for the study of behaviour, and sociobiology was recognized as a major theoretical advance in evolutionary theory), released from the theoretical muteness of behaviourism, encouraged by an increasing evolutionary presence in anthropology, and assisted by the advances in animal and developmental cognition, it was inevitable that an evolutionary psychology would be born. Two of the most important midwives were Daly and Wilson's (1988) book on murder and Barkow et al.'s (1992) edited volume on the adapted mind. The former was a survey of statistics on incidents of extreme violence. The authors claimed that their figures could only be consistently explained by assuming the operation of behavioural causes rooted in genes, as expressed in selfish-gene theory. This was virtually 1970s sociobiology, but exercised by psychologists, specifically to explain a particular form of human behaviour. The central role of gene conservation and transmission (the so-called 'need' for genes to propagate themselves, which is an unhelpful caricature of selfish-gene theory) is an important theme of evolutionary psychology.

The Barkow et al. volume advanced another seminal approach pioneered by Tooby and Cosmides (1990, for example), Buss and others in earlier papers. This advances a view of the human mind compatible with contemporary psychology, yet echoing the ethological conceptions of the 1950s. It is concerned specifically with psychological mechanisms that are adaptive products of evolution. It is based on a series of premises: these are (1) that the brain is a computer designed to generate behaviour appropriate to environmental circumstances, (2) that these neural circuits were designed by natural selection to solve problems in the environment of our ancestors, and (3) different psychological mechanisms are the result of different complexes of neural circuits specializing in solving different adaptive problems. This is sometimes described as the 'Swiss-army knife' model. So the mind is a set of adaptations, but the explanation for them 'lies completely in the past, starting one generation ago, and extending back across phylogenetic time to include the history of selection that constructed those designs' (Tooby and Cosmides

1990: 78). In other words, within our skulls there is a Stone Age mind.

The Swiss-army knife school of evolutionary psychology makes a very strong assumption that prior environments cause present mechanisms, which invokes Bowlby's notion of the environment of evolutionary adaptedness (EEA). This is a problem, not because the notion of adaptation is invoked (most evolutionary psychologists are well aware of the dangers of unthinking adaptationism) but because there was no single EEA that began around 2 million years ago and extended across the Pleistocene to end with the agricultural revolution of around 12,000 years ago. Some psychological adaptations, such as the association learning that underlies causal judgements, predate the Pleistocene by hundreds of millions of years, so the EEA really extends across all evolutionary time. Some of the conditions thought to be important selection pressures in hominid evolution, such as social group living, are widespread amongst most primates, and hence must extend back at least 25 million years, and likely longer than that. During the Pleistocene itself there were rapid, repeated and massive changes of climate. There had to be constants, of course. Tooby and Cosmides provide a list of such constants, for example choosing who to mate with, recognizing faces, sharing resources, defending oneself, nurturing children, acquiring appropriate communication skills including language, and many others. All are present today, but it is unclear just how much the circumstances that tap into these cognitive and emotional resources might have altered, if at all.

There is another problem, which is that there is genuine dispute as to the extent to which domain-general learning processes might be constrained by developmental experience to look like domain-specific processes and mechanisms. This is an empirical issue, which theory alone will not resolve. Few psychologists now believe that humans are born as blank slates; what is at issue is just how much is written on the slate at birth or shortly after, and just what is doing the writing. The inevitable development of neurogenetics in the future, and improved understanding of the psychological ties to neurological states and structures in the coming decades, will answer these questions. Other criticisms concern claims that evolutionary psychology avails itself of a simplistic approach to modern evolutionary theory, which has itself evolved into a highly complex, multicausal and multilevel theory; and that often the claims of evolved adaptations lack sufficient weight of evidence.

Even when appropriate, most of these criticisms are correctable features of evolutionary psychology. Some critics, however, claim that evolutionary psychology is fatally flawed by a failure to understand that human culture is a force wholly different from that of biological evolution, that it simply cannot be encompassed within any form of evolutionary theory, and that culture is a powerful determinant of what humans do, and even shapes psychological mechanisms. Evolutionary psychologists recognize culture's power, but whether it lies outside the explanatory framework of a natural science is at the very least debatable. Even social constructions, entities like religions, ideologies, money, laws and a host of other social facts that rule our lives and often cause our deaths, which exist only because the members of a social group agree that they exist in the form that they do, must be explicable in terms of psychological mechanisms (Plotkin 2002), and at least some of these must be products of evolution.

Evolutionary psychology is a small subdiscipline within the wider body of contemporary psychology. Most psychologists care little about evolutionary biology. However, evolution is the central theorem of biology. No science of mind will be complete that does not take evolution into account, even if some current evolutionary approaches are incomplete or at fault. Even evolutionary psychology's most consistent and influential critic put it thus:

It would be the most extraordinary happening in all intellectual history if the cardinal theory for understanding the biological origin and construction of our brains and bodies had no insights to offer to disciplines that study the social organizations arising from such evolved mental power.

(Gould 1991: 51)

HENRY PLOTKIN
UNIVERSITY COLLEGE LONDON

References

Barkow, J.H., Cosmides, L. and Tooby, J. (eds) (1992) *The Adapted Mind: Evolutionary Psychology and the Generation of Culture*, Oxford.

Daly, M. and Wilson, M. (1988) *Homicide*, New York.

Darwin, C. (1859) *The Origin of Species by Means of*

Natural Selection, or the Preservation of Favoured Races in the Struggle for Life, London.

—— (1871) *The Descent of Man and Selection in Relation to Sex*, London.

Fodor, J. (1998) *In Critical Condition*, Cambridge, MA.

Gould, J.M. and Marler, P. (1987) 'Learning by instinct', *Scientific American* 256: 62–73.

Gould, S.J. (1991) 'Exaptation: A crucial tool for an evolutionary psychology', *Journal of Social Issues* 47: 43–65.

Lorenz, K. (1965) *Evolution and Modification of Behavior*, Chicago.

Pinker, S. (1994) *The Language Instinct*, London.

Plotkin, H. (2002) *The Imagined World Made Real: Towards a Natural Science of Culture*, London.

Spencer, H. (1855) *Principles of Psychology*, 2 vols, London.

Tooby, J and Cosmides, L. (1990) 'The past explains the present: Emotional adaptations and the structure of ancestral environments', *Ethology and Sociobiology* 11: 375–424.

Further reading

Broughton, J.M. and Freeman-Moir, J.M. (1982) *The Cognitive-Developmental Psychology of James Mark Baldwin*, Northwood, NJ.

Duchaine, B., Cosmides, L. and Tooby, J. (2001) 'Evolutionary psychology and the brain', *Current Opinion in Neurobiology* 11: 225–30.

Richards, R.J. (1987) *Darwin and the Emergence of Evolutionary Theories of Mind and Behavior*, Chicago.

SEE ALSO: genetics and behaviour; human evolution; population genetics

EXCHANGE

Exchange is interesting for five reasons: it is the means by which useful things pass from one person to another; it is one of the ways in which people create and maintain social organization; it is always regulated by religion, law, convention and etiquette; it is always meaningful because it carries a symbolic load, and is often a metaphor for other kinds of activities; finally, in many societies people speculate about its origins, about the motives for and the morality of it, about its consequences and what its essence might be. It is rare to find a scholar who gives equal attention to each of these aspects of the topic.

Exchange is universal: we know of no peoples who admire individuals who do not exchange, or who expect a category of people to refrain from it. Although people in industrial and market-organized countries sometimes imagine the attractions of self-sufficiency, and try to achieve it, it would be a new creation if they succeeded. It is true that in every social group some individuals are more engaged in exchange than others, but it is probably a mistake to imagine that some peoples exchange more than other peoples.

People distinguish among kinds of exchange: in English-speaking countries they talk of altruism, barter, charity, commerce, gifts, taxation and theft, among others. These distinctions are based on expectations of return: whether there should be one, whether it should be immediate or after a period of time, whether it should be equivalent or greater or less. This too is universal, although the kinds available to different peoples are variable. People also categorize kinds of goods as being more suited to one kind of exchange than another: some peoples have goods which are exchanged only as gifts (greetings cards in many countries, *vaygua* in the Trobriands, and so on). They also prohibit the exchange of certain kinds of goods: in Christian thought, for instance, the purchase of spiritual office is distinguished as a named sin (simony). People also often categorize kinds of exchange as particularly suited to kinds of relationships: friends and family should give gifts in Britain, judges and litigants should not. Where a kind of exchange is reserved to a kind of relationship, people may try to establish the relation by making the exchange. Marcel Mauss (1954 [1925]) noted that a refusal to accept a gift, or to return one, caused great offence, and could be equivalent to a declaration of war.

Social scientists, and in particular anthropologists, have tried to identify systems of exchange. They have done this in various ways. The pioneer was Mauss, who explored gift-giving as a type of exchange based on three obligations: to *give*, to *receive* and to *return*; these are still taken to be the key principles. Mauss's archetypal gift was one so heavily laden with symbolic meaning and consequence that it involved the 'total social personality' of the exchangers (who might be either individuals or groups of people), and success or failure in making exchanges affected their social standing. The potlatch (in which groups try to overwhelm competitors with gifts) was thus interested, but not directly profit-motivated. This is the first attempt to identify a non-market system of exchange by the principles on which the exchanges are made. Malinowski's (1922) exploration of *kula* exchanges between a number of Melanesian islands showed that ceremonial goods circulated by reciprocal gift-giving in the *kula* ring affording the opportunity for trade and establishing peace between neighbouring islands as well as maintaining hierarchy on particular islands: some people were more successful in the *kula* than others. Studies suggest that the ring was less systematic than Malinowski thought (Leach and Leach 1983). In later elaborations, deriving also in part from the work of Karl Polanyi (1944), the principle of reciprocity has been taken to identify a kind of economy: some economies are based principally on reciprocity, others on markets, others on the redistributive activities of chiefs and governments. Sahlins (1972) is noted for his unique attempt to show that different principles were consequential, and were not just *amusettes folkloriques*: economies performed differently as a result. This was especially important because economists and others attempted to show that forms of rational profit-seeking underlay all exchange, and that the differences shown in the ethnographic record were either imperfections (this a term of art of economists) or a manifestation of false consciousness.

The attempt by Lévi-Strauss (1969 [1949]) and his followers to link formal structures of kinship and marriage to systems of exchange of women has proved most fruitful in kinship studies.

The principle of rational exchange was the basis of exchange theory, derived from the work of von Mises, and elaborated in sociology by Homans (1961) and Blau (1964), and in anthropology by Barth (1966) and Bailey (1969). The attractiveness of such theories derived in part from the shock of describing all social activity as profit-motivated. It also probably derived from the apparent ease with which market principles diffused so quickly in the 1950s and 1960s. This process was widely recorded, perhaps most successfully in the analysis by Bohannan and Bohannan (1968) of the decline of Tiv categories of exchange, when confronted with national markets: the apparent success of 'the modern economy' seemed to justify the adoption of a modern economics to explain everything. Anthropologists and some economists are now less sure. It is possible that some valuable lines for future research have already been established: these include Appadurai's (1986) investigations of the ways that things change meaning as they change hands, and Strathern's (1988) work on symbolism; Gregory's (1982) exploration of the distinction between *gift* and *commodity*, and work by

economists and others on the mixed motives with which people engage in exchange, even in so-called market economies.

J. DAVIS
ALL SOULS COLLEGE, OXFORD

References

Appadurai, A. (ed.) (1986) *The Social Life of Things*, Cambridge, UK.
Bailey, F.G. (1969) *Stratagems and Spoils: A Social Anthropology of Politics*, Oxford.
Barth, F. (1966) *Models of Social Organisation*, London.
Blau, P.M. (1964) *Exchange and Power in Social Life*, New York.
Bohannan, P. and Bohannan, L. (1968) *Tiv Economy*, Evanston, IL.
Gregory, C.A. (1982) *Gifts and Commodities*, London.
Homans, G.C. (1961) *Social Behaviour: Its Elementary Forms*, London.
Leach, J.W. and Leach, E.R. (eds) (1983) *The Kula: New Perspectives on Massim Exchange*, Cambridge, UK.
Lévi-Strauss, C. (1969 [1949]) *The Elementary Structures of Kinship*, London.
Malinowski, B. (1922) *Argonauts of the Western Pacific*, London.
Mauss, M. (1954 [1925]) *The Gift*, London.
Polanyi, K. (1944) *The Great Transformation*, New York.
Sahlins, M.D. (1972) *Stone Age Economics*, Chicago.
Strathern, M. (1988) *The Gender of the Gift*, Berkeley, CA.

Further reading

Davis, J. (1992) *Exchange*, Milton Keynes.
Thomas, N. (1991) *Entangled Objects: Exchange, Material Culture, and Colonialism in the Pacific*, Cambridge, MA.

SEE ALSO: economic anthropology

EXCHANGE RATE

The nominal bilateral exchange rate is the price of one currency in terms of another currency, as established by the foreign exchange market. Each currency is associated with at least one country and it is generally the case that the domestic currency is used for domestic transactions. Exchange rates, by defining the relative price of currencies, facilitate the role of money as a medium of exchange in international trade and financial transactions.

The exchange rate is expressed as the domestic price of the foreign currency, which is the number of units of domestic currency that are needed to purchase one unit of foreign currency (say euros per dollar). Under this definition, an increase in the exchange rate is referred to as a *depreciation*, whereas a decrease is termed an *appreciation*. This definition is inverted (foreign price of domestic currency) for a few currencies, such as the UK sterling.

The definition of the exchange rate given above is for a nominal bilateral exchange rate. A distinction can be made between *nominal* and *real* exchange rate. The real exchange rate is the nominal exchange rate adjusted for relative price levels. At time t, let the nominal bilateral exchange rate be denoted as $S(t)$, the price level of the domestic country be denoted as $P(t)$, and the foreign price level be denoted as $P^*(t)$. Then the real bilateral exchange rate is given by $Q(t) = S(t) P^*(t)/P(t)$. While the nominal exchange rate is the price of a currency typically quoted in the foreign exchange market and listed in financial newspapers, the real exchange rate is viewed as an important indicator of a country's international competitiveness because it gives a measure of the purchasing power of the domestic currency in foreign goods markets. Movements in the real exchange rate can, therefore, influence the competitive position of goods and services produced in different countries, and, thereby, the pattern of international trade flows. The real exchange rate is also used for making international comparisons of income levels and sometimes for setting exchange rate parities among countries in a currency union.

Another distinction is between *bilateral* and *effective* exchange rate. The effective exchange rate gives the price of the domestic currency in terms of a weighted basket of other currencies. The effective exchange rate can also be expressed in nominal or in real terms; in the latter case, the relative price adjustment is a weighted average of relative prices for each of the currencies in the basket considered.

Transactions in foreign exchange have a timing component (spot, forward) and a commitment component (outright, contingent). Several *derivatives contracts*, whose price is dependent, *inter alia*, upon the value of the currencies underlying the contract and the time to maturity, characterize transactions in the foreign exchange market. *Spot* exchange rate transactions are outright transactions involving the exchange of two currencies at a rate agreed on the date of the contract for 'value' or delivery (cash settlement)

within two business days. *Outright forwards* are transactions involving the exchange of two currencies at a rate agreed on the date of the contract for value or delivery at some time in the future (more than two business days later). *Foreign exchange swaps* are transactions that involve the actual exchange of two currencies (principal amount only) on a specific date at a rate agreed at the time of conclusion of the contract (the short leg), and a reverse exchange of the same two currencies at a date further in the future at a rate (generally different from the rate applied to the short leg) agreed at the time of the contract (the long leg). Foreign exchange swaps typically involve firms in two different countries, each of which finds it easier (less costly) to borrow in the domestic country. If, however, each party wishes to borrow the foreign currency at the foreign interest rate, then a swap may create gains for both parties. Forward instruments (outright forwards and foreign exchange swaps and options) far exceed spot transactions. The declining spot market share is caused by the rapid increase of the turnover of derivatives contracts in foreign exchange markets in recent years.

Exchange-traded business is regularly collected and documented by the Bank for International Settlements (BIS) from individual foreign exchange markets. The BIS provides a triennial *Central Bank Survey of Foreign Exchange and Derivatives Market Activity*, which represents the most reliable source of information of foreign exchange market activity with a geographical coverage of over forty countries.

Exchange rate economics is a branch of international finance, which is itself a branch of international economics. The focus of exchange rate economics is on, *inter alia*, the study of the international parity conditions that link exchange rates, interest rates and forwards exchange rates; the theory and empirical evidence on which economic variables determine the level of the exchange rate; the building of econometric models designed for forecasting exchange rates; the determinants of currency crises, for example when a country has to abandon a fixed exchange rate regime; the ability of policy-makers to carry out operations designed to affect the level of the exchange rate (official foreign exchange market intervention); the effects of the institutional features of the foreign exchange market and the role of the trading mechanism in influencing the determination of the exchange rate.

LUCIO SARNO
UNIVERSITY OF WARWICK
CENTRE FOR ECONOMIC POLICY RESEARCH (CEPR)
INTERNATIONAL MONETARY FUND

Further reading

Sarno, L. and Taylor, M.P. (2001) *The Microstructure of the Foreign Exchange Market: A Selective Survey of the Literature*, Princeton Studies in International Economics 89, International Economics Section, Princeton University.
—— (2002) *The Economics of Exchange Rates*, Cambridge, UK, and New York, USA.

SEE ALSO: international monetary system; international trade

EXPERIMENTAL DESIGN

Experiments involve introducing a planned intervention (usually referred to as a treatment) into a situation. The goal is to infer the association of the intervention or treatment with a particular change in the initial situation, or with a specific outcome.

Good experimental design facilitates this inferential process in three ways:

First, the experimental design should translate all aspects of one's hypothesis – the statement of expected relation of treatment to outcome – into operational terms. These set out what participants will be used in what situation, what behaviours will be observed or measured, what equipment and procedures are involved, and so on. This translation permits the hypothesis to be tested empirically.

Second, the design should rule out plausible alternative explanations for the observed change (see Rindskopf 2000). For example, an experimental group might be tested, exposed to a treatment, and then tested again, using the same test, some improvement in performance being observed. However, this improvement might be due simply to the fact that the subjects have become familiar with the test. This is a faulty design, since it leaves open the possibility of an alternative explanation for the outcome.

Third, a good design makes it easier to relate the change to other variables, yielding a better understanding of the relationship. For example, the experiment might be designed to measure the relative success of the treatment with men versus women, and with older versus younger subjects.

The logic of experimental design

The first step in experimental design is to translate expectations expressed in a hypothesis into operational terms. For example, given the hypothesis 'the preparation of an outline promotes the writing of a good essay or report', the experimenter must specify what level of preparation would be considered 'outlining', and what aspects of the report or essay would be expected to show improvements. The accuracy of this translation is critical. If what passes for the preparation of an outline is vaguely defined, or atypical, or the writing measure is inaccurate or insensitive, misleading conclusions could result.

Following operationalization, the experimenter must create a situation in which the treatment can occur as intended and changes can be sensed. Sometimes the condition of the experimental subjects before and after the intervention is compared. In other instances, experimental subjects may be compared with an untreated comparable group, termed a control group. In still other instances, the posttreatment condition is compared with estimates of the untreated state derived, for example, from test norms or from statistical predictions calculated from previously available data.

The experimental design should rule out alternative explanations that may be important rivals to that which the experimenter has in mind. For example, if a control group is used, the experimenter should be aware that the groups may not have been equivalent to begin with, or that dropouts may have made them non-equivalent at the end. Alternative explanations common to many studies have been identified (see below) but some may be unique to a study. For example, if subjects are allowed to complete a test at home, their score may reflect their ability to seek help rather than their own unaided achievement.

Assuming that the data support one's expectations, these steps in the logic follow: since the results were as predicted; and since there is no reasonable explanation for the phenomenon other than the treatment (others having been ruled out by one's design); then the hypotheses escaped disconfirmation. While it is impossible to test the hypothesis in every conceivable situation, one infers from this that similar predictions would prove accurate in like instances. With each such confirmation, confidence in the hypothesis increases. However, a single negative instance that cannot be satisfactorily explained away is considered adequate for disconfirmation. The hypothesis may then be rejected or (more usually) modified and tested again.

Experimental control

It is difficult to provide adequate experimental control to protect against every possible alternative explanation. Further, protection usually comes at a price. For example, if an experiment is conducted in a laboratory this allows greater control, but in the social sciences, laboratory circumstances are rarely like those to which one hopes to generalize. Natural circumstances may, however, permit too little control.

Zimbardo *et al.* (1981) supply an interesting example of this dilemma and its solution. They hypothesized that the paranoid behaviour frequent in elderly people was due to not realizing they were experiencing the gradual loss of hearing that is common in old age. An expensive longitudinal design in which subjects were followed over time would have been inconclusive because of the subjects' varying social experiences. In addition, it would involve the unethical behaviour of withholding information on hearing loss in order to see if the paranoid behaviour developed. The researchers devised a creative experimental design. Posthypnotic suggestion produced a temporary, unnoticed hearing loss in college student volunteers. To eliminate rival alternative explanations, two control groups of similar subjects were established. One received the posthypnotic suggestion of a hearing loss of which they would be aware. Another received a neutral posthypnotic suggestion. This was done in order to show that the hypnotic process did not itself induce paranoid behaviour. All subjects were exposed to similar controlled social experiences following hypnosis. The paranoia was shown to follow only unnoticed induced hearing loss.

But the use of a laboratory-like setting may bring with it its own risks for the validity of one's inferences. Impressed by the scientific laboratory, subjects may try to please the researcher. Moreover, the researchers, knowing which was the experimental group and which was the control group, may have unintentionally cued subjects to

produce appropriate behaviour (Rosenthal 1976). The naturalness or appropriateness of the intervention may also be questioned, as might the choice of subjects. In the case of the hearing loss study, doubts may be raised as to whether the hypnotically induced hearing loss is equivalent to that which occurs in older people, and also as to whether college students would react in the same way as the elderly.

Nearly every design choice involves trade-offs in using resources in one way, to firm up the design logic, when those same resources might have been used in another way, to control something else. Part of the art of design is to find the balance between a setting that is realistic enough to allow generalization of the results as broadly as one wishes while permitting sufficient control to allow valid inferences to be made.

The criteria of good design

A good design reduces uncertainty that the variables are indeed linked in a relationship and that the linkage has generality. Showing that they are linked requires internal validity – the power of the study to link the treatment with the outcome (Krathwohl 1998). A study has strong internal validity when: the explanation advanced for the relationship is credible, the translation of variables into operational terms is faithful to that originally intended, a relationship is demonstrated in the data, rival explanations for the relationship are eliminated, and the results are consistent with previous studies (Krathwohl 1998). Reichardt (2000) describes a typology of strategies for eliminating rival explanations. (Shadish *et al.* (2002) and their followers confine the definition of internal validity to linking the operationalized cause to the operationalized effect. The definition used here and in many texts assumes appropriate construct operationalizations and therefore the study links the constructs. This, as Cronbach (1982) and others have noted, is the relation of interest.)

To demonstrate that the results of an experiment can be generalized requires external validity (Krathwohl 1998). The aim is to show that the results will apply to other persons, places and times, and not just to the very particular conditions that governed the experimental situation. Strong external validity exists when: the generality implied by the hypothesis, or inferred from it, is consistent with the choices made in operationalizing the study; the results found were those expected; no design choices limited generalization; and the same results would be expected were the study operationalized and designed in alternative ways.

A successful design makes the best use of all available resources, time and energy. The experimenter fits the design to the problem rather than changing the definition of the problem to suit the requirements of a design. The designer chooses an appropriate balance between internal and external validity, bearing in mind that the strengthening of internal validity may be bought at the cost of reducing external validity. The researcher anticipates the alternative explanations that are most plausible to the audience and uses designs that eliminate them. Finally, the investigator observes ethical standards, and copes with resource limitations and institutional and social constraints. Altogether, this list constitutes a complex but manageable set of criteria for effective experimentation (Krathwohl 1998).

Alternative explanations (threats to validity)

Certain common conditions provide plausible alternative explanations of an outcome that challenge the treatment. These are termed 'threats to validity'. Shadish *et al.* (2002) list nine such threats. A sample, and their remedies:

1 *Testing*: pretreatment testing may affect posttreatment testing, especially if the same test is used. A control group provides protection since its results on a second test would not be affected by the intervention, but would show the effect of retesting itself. (Also, see Lee 2000 on gathering data unobtrusively.)
2 *Selection*: those selected for the experimental group differ from their controls. For example, all volunteers may be assigned to the experimental group while everyone else becomes the control group. One remedy is to use only volunteers, and to assign them randomly to experimental and control groups.
3 *Testing by treatment interaction*: subjects sensitized to aspects of a treatment by pretesting may react differently to posttesting. To avoid this risk, it might be better to test only once, after treatment.

Shadish *et al.* (2002) also list five threats to external validity and fourteen threats to construct validity, the latter being concerned with reasons why inferences about the constructs involved in the study may not be correct.

Common designs

SINGLE INDIVIDUAL OR GROUP DESIGNS

Single individual or group designs are often called time-series designs. Relationships are inferred from the pattern of treatment and responses observed over time.

1 For static situations: premeasure, treat, postmeasure.
2 For situations with a regular pattern: observe it, treat and determine if the pattern was disturbed.
3 For situations with either an irregular pattern, or for an especially conclusive demonstration, relate the pattern of change to that of treatment, intentionally varying the timing, length and strength of the treatment and of such other factors as affect outcome.

These configurations are also referred to as *AB*, *ABA* or *ABABA* designs (*A* is the untreated condition, *B* the treated). *ABABA* and more complex designs are useful only where the change under the *B* condition is impermanent. (For information on such designs, see Franklin *et al.* 1997.)

MULTIPLE GROUP DESIGNS

These designs may involve both multiple experimental groups and multiple control groups. (In the experiment described above by Zimbardo, two control groups were used.) Groups are alike as far as possible except for the conditions to which change is to be attributed or that are to be controlled. Assuring group equivalence is usually achieved by randomly assigning subjects. On the average this will make them equivalent on every count, from length of eyelashes to motivation.

The simplest, yet very effective, design involves posttesting only. Let R indicate random assignment of subjects to groups, O a test or observation, and X treatment. Then it is diagrammed as:

$R \qquad X \qquad O$
$R \qquad \qquad O$

To assure that the groups were equivalent at the outset, a pre-test may be added:

R   O   X   O
R   O   O

However, this introduces a possible alternative explanation, which is not only that the subjects have learned from pretesting, but also have been sensitized to what is important in the treatment. For better control, the Solomon four group design combines the previous two:

R   X   O
R   O
R   O   X   O
R   O   O

Designs in which groups are not created by random assignment of subjects (same designs as above without the R) are designated quasi-experimental designs. (Their strengths and weaknesses are explored in Chapter 8 of Shadish et al. 2002.)

Where non-equivalence might affect the outcome, individuals can be assigned to 'blocks' or strata on the basis of one or more characteristics (for example blocks of high, middle and low ability) and persons in each block are randomly assigned to treatments. The matched-pairs design is an extreme form of blocking.

Factorial designs

Factorial designs permit analysis of the simultaneous effects of two or more treatments or related variables by providing a group for each possible combination. For instance, a study might be designed to work out whether it is easier, or quicker, to memorize prose if important passages are presented in bold, in italics or underlined, and if they are printed in black or red. This study would require six groups – a 2 × 3 factorial design (see Table 2).

From this design one could learn which emphasis, format or colour was best alone, and if these factors interact (the 'interaction effect'), what combination of format and colour is best. If

Table 2 A 2 × 3 factorial design

	Bold	Italics	Underlining
Black type			
Red type			

a pretest were given this would be called a repeated-measures 2 × 3 factorial design.

Other designs

The variety of designs is limited mainly by the experimenter's ingenuity. Complex designs used mainly in the natural sciences and engineering such as the factorial, Latin and Graeco-Latin square, nested and split plot designs are sometimes useful in social science studies (see Montgomery 2000).

DAVID R. KRATHWOHL
SYRACUSE UNIVERSITY

References

Cronbach, L.J. (1982) *Designing Evaluations of Educational and Social Programs*, San Francisco.

Franklin, R.D., Allison, D.B. and Gorman, B.S. (eds) (1997) *Design and Analysis of Single-Case Research*, Mahwah, NJ.

Krathwohl, D.R. (1998) *Methods of Educational and Social Science Research: An Integrated Approach*, 2nd edn, New York.

Lee, R.M. (2000) *Unobtrusive Methods in Social Research*, Buckingham, UK.

Montgomery, D.C. (2000) *Design and Analysis of Experiments*, 5th edn, New York.

Reichardt, C.S. (2000) 'A typology of strategies for ruling out threats to validity', in L. Bickman (ed.) *Research Design: Donald Campbell's Legacy*, Vol. 2, Thousand Oaks, CA.

Rindskopf, D. (2000) 'Plausible rival hypotheses in measurement, design, and theory', in L. Bickman (ed.) *Research Design: Donald Campbell's Legacy*, Vol. 2, Thousand Oaks, CA.

Rosenthal, R. (1976) *Experimenter Effects in Behavioral Research*, New York.

Shadish, W.R., Cook, T.D. and Campbell, D.T. (2002) *Experimental and Quasi-experimental Designs for Generalized Causal Inference*, Boston.

Solomon, R.L. (1949) 'An Extension of Control Group Design', *Psychological Bulletin* 46.

Zimbardo, P.G., Anderson, S.M. and Kabat, L.G. (1981) 'Induced hearing deficit generates experimental paranoia', *Science* 212.

Further reading

Winer, B.S., Brown, D.R. and Michels, K.M. (1991) *Statistical Principles in Experimental Design*, Burr Ridge, IL.

EXPERIMENTAL ECONOMICS

There was a time when the conventional wisdom was that, because economics is a science concerned with complex, naturally occurring systems, laboratory experiments had little to offer economists. But experimental economics has now become a well-established tool of economic research. The initial impetus for this transformation came from studies of individual-choice behaviour. As economists focused on microeconomic theories that depend on individuals' preferences, the fact that these are difficult to observe in natural environments made it increasingly attractive to look to the laboratory to see if the assumptions made about individuals were in fact descriptive of their behaviour. The publication in 1944 of von Neumann and Morgenstern's *Theory of Games and Economic Behavior* accelerated the interest in experimentation. The expected utility theory they presented gave a new focus to experiments concerned with individual choice, while the predictions of game theory – and how these depend on the rules of the game – sparked a wave of experimental tests of interactive behaviour. This has blossomed into large literatures on topics as diverse as bargaining behaviour, the provision of public goods, co-ordination and equilibration, auction theory, learning, and the effects of different rules of market organization.

Formal tests of economic theories of individual choice go back at least as far as L.L. Thurstone (1931), who used experimental techniques common in psychology to investigate whether the indifference curve representation of preferences could coherently describe individuals' choices (he concluded that it could). Expected utility theory made more pointed predictions, which allowed more powerful tests, and while some early experiments (e.g. Mosteller and Nogee 1951) supported the conclusion that utility theory could serve as an adequate approximation of behaviour, others, such as Allais (1953), identified systematic violations of expected utility theory. There have since been hundreds of experiments designed to explore further systematic violations of utility theory, and of the alternative-choice theories that have been proposed to account for various parts of the experimental data.

In the 1970s, the psychologists Daniel Kahneman and Amos Tversky systematically explored how decision-making heuristics introduce a number of biases in human behaviour, adding considerable richness to our understanding of how the assumption of idealized rationality may or may not be a useful approximation. One influential part of their work, prospect theory, summarized their results in a form that could be viewed as an alternative to expected-utility theory (Kahneman and Tversky 1979). Kahneman shared the 2002 Nobel prize in economics (Amos Tversky passed away in 1996). More recently, studies of individual choice behaviour have focused not only on choices involving risky alternatives, but also choices made over time, with studies focusing on robust but 'irrational' behaviours that lead to problems of self-control, or procrastination, such as arise in consumption and savings behaviour (see e.g. Laibson 1997; Loewenstein and Elster 1992; Thaler 1987 for three strands of this work). Much of this work is surveyed in Camerer (1995).

An early game-theoretic experiment, conducted by Melvin Dresher and Merrill Flood in 1950 (Flood 1958), first introduced the much studied game that subsequently came to be called the prisoners' dilemma. They observed that, even in a game with a unique equilibrium, the observed behaviour may deviate from the game-theoretic prediction. But these experiments also confirm the game-theoretic prediction that the incentives for individuals to act in their own interest may in some circumstances make it difficult to achieve the gains available from co-operative action. One body of experimental research that pursues this investigation concerns the provision of public goods; this literature is surveyed by Ledyard (1995).

A different kind of problem emerges in games having multiple equilibria, in which the players must co-ordinate their expectations and actions. Early experiments on co-ordination were reported by Thomas Schelling (1960). Bargaining presents an important class of problems in which co-ordination of expectations is of the essence, and it is a subject in which there has been considerable interplay between theory and experiment. Self-interest is not the only driving force shaping behaviour in such games. Experimental results suggest that considerations of fairness often play an important role: subjects are willing to forgo some monetary gains in order to avoid being treated unfairly. For various experiments and models of fairness, see Fehr and Schmidt (1999) and Bolton and Ockenfels (2000). Surveys of experiments concerning co-ordination and bargaining may be found in Ochs (1995) and Roth (1995a).

Experiments are particularly useful for isolating the effects of the rules of the game by which markets are organized. (For example, cattle and flowers are auctioned by different rules, but are also very different commodities, so one cannot isolate the effect of the different rules by relying only on field studies of cattle and flower auctions.) Chamberlin (1948) introduced a design, now widely used by experimenters, to create markets for artificial commodities in which the reservation prices of buyers and sellers can be controlled by the experimenter. Chamberlin's design permits experiments in which different rules of market organization (e.g. different forms of auction) can be compared while holding all else constant.

Vernon Smith and Charles Plott expanded on Chamberlin's 1948 design to investigate different rules of market organization. Smith (1962) famously showed that in a *double oral auction* (in which buyers and sellers can both propose prices to the market) there is a strong tendency for prices to converge to a competitive equilibrium. Smith received the other half of the 2002 Nobel Prize in economics. Kagel (1995) and Kagel and Levin (2002) survey the large modern literature on auctions, Sunder (1995) considers markets for commodities (such as financial securities) in which information plays a dominant role, and Holt (1995) surveys experiments in industrial organization generally.

Much modern work has gone into understanding when equilibrium predictions will be descriptive, and when they will not. Experimental evidence has helped spark an interest in theories of learning and adaptation (see e.g. Roth and Erev 1995), in contrast to theories of static equilibrium. There has also been growing use of experiments as an engineering tool, to help test new market designs (see e.g. Roth 2002).

A general overview of experimental economics, including details of its early history, may be found in Roth (1995b).

C. NICHOLAS MCKINNEY

RHODES COLLEGE

ALVIN E. ROTH

HARVARD UNIVERSITY AND

HARVARD BUSINESS SCHOOL

References

Allais, M. (1953) 'Le Comportement de l'homme rationnel devant le risque: critique des postulats et axiomes de l'école américaine', *Econometrica* 21.

Bolton, G. and Ockenfels, A.A. (2000) 'ERC: A theory of equity, reciprocity, and competition', *American Economic Review* 90.

Camerer, C. (1995) 'Individual decision making', in J. Kagel and A.E. Roth (eds) *Handbook of Experimental Economics*, Princeton, NJ.

Chamberlin, E.H. (1948) 'An experimental imperfect market', *Journal of Political Economy* 56(2).

Fehr, E. and Schmidt, K. (1999) 'A theory of fairness, competition, and cooperation', *The Quarterly Journal of Economics* 114.

Flood, M.M. (1958) 'Some experimental games', *Management Science* 5.

Holt, C.A. (1995) 'Industrial organization: A survey of laboratory research', in J. Kagel and A.E. Roth (eds) *Handbook of Experimental Economics*, Princeton, NJ.

Kagel, J.H. (1995) 'Auctions: A survey of experimental research', in J. Kagel and A.E. Roth (eds) *Handbook of Experimental Economics*, Princeton, NJ.

Kagel, J.H. and Levin, D. (2002) *Common Value Auctions and the Winner's Curse*, Princeton, NJ.

Kahneman, D. and Tversky, A. (1979) 'Prospect theory: An analysis of decision under risk', *Econometrica* 47.

Laibson, D. (1997) 'Golden eggs and hyperbolic discounting', *Quarterly Journal of Economics* 62.

Ledyard, J. (1995) 'Public goods: A survey of experimental research', in J. Kagel and A.E. Roth (eds) *Handbook of Experimental Economics*, Princeton, NJ.

Loewenstein, G. and Elster, J. (1992) *Choice over Time*, New York.

Mosteller, F. and Nogee, P. (1951) 'An experimental measurement of utility', *Journal of Political Economy* 59.

Ochs, J. (1995) 'Coordination problems', in J. Kagel and A.E. Roth (eds) *Handbook of Experimental Economics*, Princeton, NJ.

Plott, C. and Smith, V. (1978) 'An experimental examination of two exchange institutions', *Review of Economic Studies* 45.

Roth, A.E. (1995a) 'Bargaining experiments', in J. Kagel and A.E. Roth (eds) *Handbook of Experimental Economics*, Princeton, NJ.

—— (1995b) 'Introduction to experimental economics', in J. Kagel and A.E. Roth (eds) *Handbook of Experimental Economics*, Princeton, NJ.

—— (2002) 'The economist as an engineer: Game theory, experimentation, and computation as tools for design economics', *Econometrica* 70.

Roth, A.E. and Erev, I. (1995) 'Learning in extensive-form games: Experimental data and simple dynamic models in the intermediate term', *Games and Economic Behavior* 8.

Schelling, T.C. (1960) *The Strategy of Conflict*, Cambridge, MA.

Smith, V. (1962) 'An experimental study of competitive market behavior', *Journal of Political Economy* 70.

Sunder, S. (1995) 'Experimental asset markets: A survey', in J. Kagel and A.E. Roth (eds) *Handbook of Experimental Economics*, Princeton, NJ.

Thaler, R. (1987) 'The psychology of choice and the assumptions of economics', in A.E. Roth (ed.) *Laboratory Experimentation in Economics: Six Points of View*, Cambridge.

Thurstone, L.L. (1931) 'The indifference function', *Journal of Social Psychology* 2.

Further reading

Loewenstein, G. and Prelec, D. (1992) 'Anomalies in intemporal choice: Evidence and an interpretation', *Quarterly Journal of Economics* 107.

SEE ALSO: auctions; bargaining; game theory; prisoners' dilemma

EXTERNALITIES

Economic externalities are (positive or negative) goods or services generated by an economic activity whose costs or benefits do not fall upon the decision-taking agent. Pollution is a leading and important example. They may, alternatively, be thought of as residuals, the difference between 'social' and 'private' costs and benefits. The divergence was first popularized and elaborated by Pigou in *The Economics of Welfare* (1920) and is believed to be a major reason for market failure: for example, the market will overproduce goods with high external costs. For that reason a main principle of cost–benefit analysis is that *all* costs and benefits, no matter to whom they accrue, should be included. Popular discussion rightly emphasizes external costs associated with production, but one should not entirely ignore positive production effects (apples and honey) or effects on the consumption side, either positive (attractive dress) or negative (radio noise).

Various policies are, in principle, available for dealing with externalities. For example, the extent of an activity may be *regulated*, as in the case of the discharge of industrial effluent into estuaries. Using partial equilibrium analysis the regulation should set the amount of discharge at an optimum, that is, where marginal social cost and benefit are equal to one another. This is, of course, very difficult to calculate, so rough rules of thumb are used instead. Economists often argue for the direct use of *pricing*: the agent is charged a tax (or paid a subsidy) equal to the value of the externality at the margin. The congestion tax is an example of this. Such taxes and subsidies are referred to as Pigouvian: they are intended to internalize the externality. Internalization may also come about spontaneously by the *merger* of two units inflicting large externalities upon one another (as in industrial integration).

The tax–subsidy solution is often objected to on the ground that it is open to injured parties to bring an action in tort against the offending agent. If agents know this to be the case, they will take expected compensation for damages into account and externalities will automatically be internalized. On this view not only would Pigouvian taxes not be needed but also they would, if imposed, lead to an overrestriction of activity (Coase 1960). Property rights are seen to be crucial, as they define rights to compensation: defenders of the market system therefore argue that externalities do not constitute market failure provided that property rights are adequately delineated. The direction of compensation naturally depends on the initial distribution of legal rights.

The alternative solutions are closely related to one another. Take the case of a major oil spillage that fouls beaches and destroys fishing and wildlife. If spillages are to be 'banned' the fine must be at least equal to the Pigouvian tax. If there is to be a legal contest, it will have to be fought between states and oil companies rather than through improvised groups of holiday-makers, workers in the fishing industry and wildlife enthusiasts. And fines/compensation must not give an outcome that is totally unreasonable in relation to the optimum (possibly, though not certainly, zero) amount of spillage.

DAVID COLLARD
UNIVERSITY OF BATH

Reference

Coase, R.H. (1960) 'The problem of social cost', *Journal of Law and Economics* 3.

Further reading

Pearce, D.W. (ed.) (1978) *The Valuation of Social Cost*, London.

SEE ALSO: cost–benefit analysis

F

FACTORS OF PRODUCTION

Factors of production, or (in more modern terminology) 'inputs', are the things that are used in the process of producing goods or services. An early typology of inputs was provided by Jean-Baptiste Say, whose classification separately defined land, labour and capital as factors of production.

A distinction is often made between flow inputs (which are embodied in the final product and cannot therefore be used more than once in the act of production) and stock inputs (which can be used repeatedly). The distinction is somewhat artificial, however, because stock inputs characteristically depreciate in value over time, and this depreciation can itself usefully be regarded as a flow.

All factors of production can, in principle, be hired by the producer. In a non-slavery society, labour can be hired – at a per period cost defined by the wage – but not bought. Capital may, at the discretion of the producer, be bought rather than hired; it remains the case, however, that producers implicitly pay a rent ('user cost') on the capital under their ownership, because by using that capital they forgo the opportunity to hire it out to a third party. Land, likewise, may be bought or rented; in the former case producers implicitly pay a rent in order to use land as a factor of production, because they forgo the opportunity to earn a landlord's income.

Labour will in general be hired by a profit-maximizing producer up to that point where the wage is just offset by the value of the marginal revenue product of labour. Similar conditions apply to other factors of production. A change in production technology that disturbs the productivity of any factor of production will generally alter the equilibrium employment of each input. Likewise a change in the price of any input (for example, the wage or the user cost of capital) will, so long as inputs are to some degree substitutable, cause a change in the mix of factors of production employed.

Simple models of the production process typically employ two factors of production, often labour and capital. The first of these is defined to be variable in the short run, while the second is assumed fixed. In effect, the minimum timescale within which the latter input can be varied defines the length of the short run. Given information about the producer's objective function, this allows a distinction to be drawn between the behaviour of the producer, which is optimal in the short run, and that which is optimal in the long run.

The precise manner in which factors of production are converted into outputs is modelled by means of a production function. The simplest type of production function in common use postulates that the production of a single type of output is determined by a geometric weighted average of the various inputs employed. This is known as a Cobb–Douglas production function, and its parameters may statistically be estimated by means of a regression that is linear in natural logarithms. The Cobb–Douglas function can be shown to produce downwards sloping and convex isoquants – a characteristic that is conventionally deemed attractive because it establishes the existence of unique interior solutions to the constrained optimization problems characteristic of neo-classical economics.

The more general constant elasticity of substitution (CES) and transcendental logarithmic (or 'translog') production functions have become increasingly popular among applied economists. The Cobb–Douglas is a special case of both of these. The translog function adds to the list of explanatory variables used in a Cobb–Douglas type regression a full set of logged quadratic terms and interaction terms between the logged inputs.

An appealing property of all the production functions described above is their implication that the marginal product of variable inputs (eventually) falls as the employment of those inputs increases. This ensures the finiteness of the equilibrium level of output of the individual firm, regardless of demand conditions. The translog specification of the production function is particularly appealing because, depending upon the estimated parameters, it is consistent with the popular presumption that the long-run average cost curve is U-shaped.

The production technology described by these functions is closely related to the way in which the producer's costs are determined. Given the prices of the various factors of production, producers use their knowledge of the production technology to decide, for each level of output, what mix of inputs optimizes their objective function (usually profits). Once this input mix is chosen, the total cost of production at each output level is straightforwardly calculated as the product of the vectors of input prices and input quantities.

Further analytical problems are posed by firms that produce many distinct types of output. Multiproduct firms of this type might exist because of synergies that arise from the co-ordinated production of different goods and services. These synergies may in turn arise from characteristics possessed by inputs that can simultaneously be put to more than one use. In the case of firms that produce more than one type of output, output cannot be represented as a scalar, and so the technology of production is best understood by investigating the dual problem: that is by estimating a (quadratic, CES or hybrid translog) multiproduct cost function.

The efficiency with which factors of production are converted into outputs varies from producer to producer. Where the market is less than perfectly competitive, different producers can exploit scale efficiencies to different extents, and some producers might be more technically efficient than others. Techniques such as data

envelopment analysis and stochastic frontier analysis have been devised in order to evaluate the relative efficiency of producers.

The simplistic view of labour as a homogeneous variable input has been relaxed in recent work that views skilled labour as an investment in 'human capital'. Such an investment takes time, and so in the short run skilled labour may be fixed. However, where more than two inputs are employed, the distinction between the short and long run becomes blurred. Indeed, an issue that has remained underdeveloped in the economics research programme concerns the application of methods commonly used in the literature on product differentiation to the case of heterogeneous factors of production.

GERAINT JOHNES
LANCASTER UNIVERSITY

Further reading

Heathfield, D.F. and Wibe, S. (1987) *An Introduction to Cost and Production Functions*, Basingstoke.
Jorgenson, D. (2000) *Econometrics: Econometric Modeling of Producer Behavior*, Cambridge, MA.

SEE ALSO: economies of scale; law of returns; production and cost frontiers; productivity

FAMILY

Is there a global revolution going on in how we think about ourselves, and how we form ties and connections with others, that is fundamentally shifting our understanding of family? Social theorists point to demographic changes going on in advanced Western industrial nations, notably the rise in divorce, the delay of marriage, the increase of cohabitation, the dissociation of childbirth and marriage. They also cite the challenge that gender egalitarianism and the labour market has posed for traditional gender roles, especially in terms of women's increased participation in education. Elisabeth Beck-Gernsheim is not alone in insisting that 'of all the changes shaking the world today, none is more important to us than those which affect the core of our personal life – sexuality, love and marriage, relationships and parenthood' (Beck-Gernsheim 2002: vii).

The revolutionary transformations of family and personal life have provoked resistance, particularly from religious fundamentalists. Recently, two US political scientists, Ingelhart and Norris, have taken issue with Samuel Huntington's thesis about democracy being the cultural fault-line dividing the West and Islamic world. Using data from the World Values Survey, a study of attitudes across some seventy nations, they conclude that the 'true clash of civilizations' is about sex and family values, and changes in the role of women (Ingelhart and Norris 2003).

Large claims about revolutionary change and cultural divides, which derive from grand theories of modernization and globalization, are likely to be overly general. More specific claims may be made as a result of empirical work that examines the nature and consequences of particular aspects of family change and continuity, but apparently empirical statements often go far beyond what is known. And both the theoretical and the empirical literature is frequently coloured by ideology (liberal or conservative).

The strength of convictions about what constitutes an ideal family poses considerable challenges for social science. For example, there has been a good deal of research in both Europe and North America on the consequences of family diversity and family disruption for both children and adults. However, the results are often highly contentious. According to one review, there is no doubting the fact that, on average, separation, divorce and stepfamily living put individuals at risk in comparison with those who stay in 'intact' family households (Pryor and Trinder 2004). Yet household structure and separation explain only a small amount of the variance in outcomes, for both adults and children. More significant are the processes, diverse experiences and the meanings of these experiences for family members. Citing the historian John Gillis's distinction between the families we live with and the families we live by (Gillis 1997), Pryor and Trinder point to the gap between the day-to-day realities of family life for children and their parents, and the scripts provided for families, by their communities and culture.

There is no denying that in many societies the scripts have become less binding. Beck and Beck-Gernsheim refer to this process as 'institutional individualization' (Beck and Beck-Gernsheim 2002). They suggest that within the family institution, there is a normalization of diversity. Previously deviant family forms – single-parent families, cohabiting parents, lesbian and gay families, postdivorce families – have now become more normal and more acceptable. Certainly, any contemporary study of families must take seriously the enormous variations in family life across time and place. Authors go out of their way to use the plural 'Families' to deliberately avoid the misleading static and universal terminology of 'the Family'.

The concept of 'marriage' illustrates this complexity. Marriage has a very different meaning for someone growing up in Europe or North America today than it had for previous generations, when cohabitation and divorce were relatively rare. Patterns of cohabitation vary enormously from group to group, in part reflecting different religious traditions. In some societies, cohabitation is an acceptable prelude or alternative to marriage, in others it may be widely regarded as a sin. In some parts of Europe, childbirth is predominantly within the marital union, whereas in others, notably in Scandinavia, reproduction and marriage are becoming increasingly distinct.

Why are people excluding themselves from formal marriage and does it matter? The demographer Kathleen Kiernan has surveyed the evidence of changing partnership and parenting patterns in Europe and in the USA. She concludes that the anxiety expressed in the literature stems mainly from the fact that at the present time cohabiting unions are more fragile than marital unions. However, the difference between the two types of unions may be largely due to the stronger and more committed partnerships being selected into marriage. If the general trend and future course of cohabitation is for parents who live together to eschew marriage, then cohabitation, other things being equal, will become a more durable alternative (Kiernan 2004: 31). More generally it is important to bear in mind that the prevalence and dominance of particular family arrangements shift over time.

Within the USA there has been a marked ideological divide that may be loosely described as the 'families in distress' theory versus the 'families in transition' argument. Those championing the families in distress theory cite evidence which suggests that lone-parent families are detrimental to the well-being of children as compared to intact families (Elliott and Umberson 2004). These researchers call for public policies that support the 'traditional' family, such as a pro-marriage tax. Others argue that the process of legitimizing diverse family structures helps to demythologize marriage and the nuclear family, and that this may help children to blossom in a variety of family structures. The debate is unlikely to be easily resolved. Research on the effects for children of family diversity, family disruption, the changing work–family balance, or family versus public arrangements for childcare, is often highly contentious. Much of the existing literature on family and child well-being needs to be deconstructed in order to examine how ideals of family and childhood shape not only the questions asked, but also the answers found.

Even if family disruption does cause adverse outcomes for children, it could be for a variety of reasons. Disruption involves much more than changes in the composition of the family. What matters for children? Is it a fall of economic status? The loss of a father figure? An erosion of social contact? A reduction in parental care? Do all of these things matter? And is what matters different for different children? We can glean some answers from studies that examine the impact of childhood experiences on later adolescent and adult transitions and outcomes. Yet often such studies provide limited information about children's own actions, perspectives and choices. It is only recently that researchers have asked questions about how children influence parental behaviour and family environment.

Studying families is not an easy task. It is not simply ideological passions that make it so difficult. Even understanding the dynamics of a single family is highly complex. There is increasing recognition that family life is very different from the perspective of each different family member. Even within the same family, children have very different socialization experiences, deriving from what psychologists call the non-shared family environment. Recent research on child development strives to unpack the relative influence of heredity or genetic factors and shared and non-shared environments on later outcomes. The focus on genetics does not downplay the importance of family environment. Rather it emphasizes that current understanding of the interaction between genetics and family environment is very limited. More generally, research on genetics and new reproductive technologies throws up many issues that are politically sensitive and ethically problematic.

Gender is also a sensitive topic in family research. Family life is certainly very different depending on the respondent's gender. Too often in the past, the study of families has been undertaken almost exclusively from the viewpoint of women. Certainly feminists were right to express concern that women were being 'imprisoned' in families (conceptually speaking) and needed to be liberated to give them voice. If women were seen only in terms of family, this misrepresents the multidimensional nature of women's lives. Similarly, the female bias in much family research has been a problem for understanding the complex lives of men as partners, as fathers and as carers. This bias is gradually being corrected and there is an increasing focus on men within families. But gender stereotypes are hard to break down. For example, very little is known about male victims of domestic violence.

It is not only assumptions about how the private sphere of family life intersects with gender that are being re-examined. There is an increasing body of work that examines the changing interrelationships of gender, family and work. How important are men and women's preferences for combining family and work in the twenty-first century? Cross-national research is helpful in answering such questions. A snapshot picture at the start of the new millennium would show the majority of mothers and fathers in paid work in most industrialized countries. Yet while there is much in common in the trends across countries, the socioeconomic context in which family choices are formed differs profoundly across nations. Given these structural differences, how important are individual preferences? Catherine Hakim concludes that, in Britain and Spain, lifestyle preference groups will become the principal characteristic differentiating a largely unisex labour force. She writes: 'the debate is now about how each family organises their division of labour in a situation where there are no rigid rules or fixed guidelines and all options are open'. However, that assertion is tempered by her next claim that 'the challenge is for national governments to reorganise fiscal policy, family policy and employment policy so as to avoid discriminating against any preference group' (Hakim 2003: 262). Evidently gender egalitarianism in family and work preference is still some way off.

Perhaps the most fundamental changes have less to do with family structure or family economy than with family and sex. Certainly, sex is central to our understanding of the family as a social institution (Treas 2004). As the starting-point for procreation, sex supplies new family members and sustains the family lineage across time and generations. Sexuality is the basis for mate recruitment and pair bonding, and, because sexuality goes to the core of family relations, families have a stake in the regulation of sexual behaviour. And in many parts of the world there has been a marked trend towards greater permissiveness. Particularly in Europe and North America, the lives of young people follow a less predictable course, no longer fulfilling traditional expectations that marriage precedes sex and having babies. Because the age at which young people have their first sexual experience has tended to decline, while age at first marriage has risen, there is now a gap between youth and committed partnership. At least in the USA and Britain, this results in high rates of teen pregnancy and of sexually transmitted disease. These changes pose further challenges for families, but the socialization task of families is increasingly difficult because of inconsistencies between the values families are supposed to uphold and changing cultural norms and consumption practices.

More generally, there is a problem with characterizing the freer sexual choice associated with individualism as a global revolution that is changing the core of our family ties and kinship relations. The notion that the family institution is individualized may be useful for emphasizing the normalization of family diversity. However, one thing we do know from family research is that family relations matter. The evidence from family research clearly demonstrates the continuing importance of interdependency.

JACQUELINE SCOTT
UNIVERSITY OF CAMBRIDGE

References

Beck, U. and Beck-Gernsheim, E. (2002) *Individualisation. Institutionalised Individualisation and its Social and Political Consequences*, London.

Beck-Gernsheim, E. (2002) *Reinventing the Family*, Cambridge, UK.

Elliott, S. and Umberson, D. (2004) 'Recent demographic trends in the US and implications for well-being', in J. Scott, J. Treas and M. Richards (eds) *The Blackwell Companion to the Sociology of Families*, Oxford, pp. 34–53.

Gillis, J.R. (1997) *A World of Their Own Making: Myth, Ritual and the Quest for Family Values*, Cambridge, MA.

Hakim, C. (2003) *Models of the Family in Modern Societies*, Aldershot.

Ingelhart, R. and Norris, P. (2003) *Rising Tide: Gender Equality and Cultural Change around the World*, New York.

Kiernan, K. (2004) 'Changing European families: Trends and issues', in J. Scott, J. Treas and M. Richards (eds) *The Blackwell Companion to the Sociology of Families*, Oxford, pp. 17–33.

Pryor, J. and Trinder, L. (2004) 'Children, families and divorce', in J. Scott, J. Treas and M. Richards (eds) *The Blackwell Companion to the Sociology of Families*, Oxford, pp. 322–39.

Treas, J. (2004) 'Sex and family: Changes and challenges', in J. Scott, J. Treas and M. Richards (eds) *The Blackwell Companion to the Sociology of Families*, Oxford, pp. 397–415.

SEE ALSO: divorce; domestic violence; household; kinship; marriage; sexual behaviour

FANTASY

Fantasy, our capacity to 'give to airy nothing a local habitation and a name', has long intrigued poets, playwrights and painters but only during the twentieth century has the phenomenon become a formal area of scientific enquiry in psychology. In current usage the term is almost synonymous with daydream. Within the area of experimental or clinical study, however, the term fantasy has a broader significance, as it deals not only with imaginary activity spontaneously produced as part of the ongoing stream of thought (daydreams) but also with products of thought elicited upon demand from a clinician in response to inkblots or ambiguous pictures. It also refers to literary or artistic representations of the mental processes.

Fantasy refers to the human being's remarkable ability to create an 'as if' world either spontaneously or upon demand. It is possible that people at one time were more prone to regard their own fleeting imagery or brief daydreams as actual visions, as omens, or as appearances of deities, much as they responded to nocturnal dreams (Jaynes 1977). Prophetic visions, such as Ezekiel's 'wheel' or John's Apocalypse, probably represent literary expressions of elaborate daydreams or fantasies used for expository or hortatory purposes.

In 1890 William James in *The Principles of Psychology* devoted portions of several chapters, including the famous one on the 'stream of thought', to issues closely related to fantasy processes. James called attention to what he termed the reproductive and memorial facets of imagery, or the degree to which the image is of an object recently perceived or one called forth from the distant past. The fantasy presumably may represent a response to a stimulus perceived momentarily that triggers off a complex associative process in the ongoing stream of thought. In James Joyce's novel *Ulysses* the young Stephen, gazing seawards from his tower apartment, first sees the waves whose foamy curves remind him of a childhood song, then of his mother's death, his refusal (as a lapsed Catholic) to pray, and finally these associations generate a vivid fantasy of her confronting him in her graveclothes to denounce him (Singer 1994).

Psychoanalytic contributions

Freud's elucidation of the structure and interpretative possibilities of the phenomenon of nocturnal dreaming, based largely on remarkable self-observation and intensive clinical work, also led quite naturally to explorations of other dreamlike phenomena, such as daydreams. Freud (1962 [1908], 1962 [1911]) speculated on the psychological significance of the daydream in papers like 'Creative writers and daydreaming'. The free-association process of psychoanalysis itself also led to patients' frequent reports of memories of childhood fantasies or recent daydreams.

The most important fantasies from a technical psychotherapeutic sense were those involving the relationships between analyst and patient. Throughout the twentieth century psychoanalysts have made regular use of reports of spontaneous fantasies and published many papers in which myths or popular stories and literature were interpreted as outgrowths of fantasy.

Projective methods

With the indications of the widespread nature of human fantasy processes emerging from psychoanalysis and other psychiatric efforts, there was gradually an attempt to find procedures that could elicit fantasies from individuals providing significant diagnostic evidence ultimately for treatment plans and specific therapeutic interventions as well as for research purposes. The most prominent projective methods were the Rorschach Inkblots and the Thematic Apperception Test. They have been subject to literally hundreds of research studies that to some degree

have also contributed to general personality research and to diagnostic understanding.

The *Rorschach Inkblots* represent an attempt to use spontaneous associations made to the ambiguous nature of the blots as a means of identifying structural properties of the personality, such as tendencies towards imaginativeness, emotional impulsivity, indications of anxiety or cognitive organization and self-control. Hermann Rorschach observed that associative responses to the ambiguous inkblots that involved reports of humans in action ('two men playing patty cake') were linked systematically not only to a considerable tendency to engage in fantasy but also to a capacity for self-restraint and inner control. Extensive research studies have generally supported this observation (Singer and Brown 1977). These so-called M responses to the Rorschach Inkblots do seem to reflect an adaptive capacity for restraint, self-knowledge and creative thought.

The *Thematic Apperception Test*, in which the respondent makes up stories to simple pictures (such as a boy staring at a violin) that are somewhat ambiguous, has also proven to be a significant indicator of fantasy. This measure has been perhaps even more precisely analysed in the work of David McClelland because of its linkage to motivation following its original development by Henry A. Murray of Harvard University. The scoring of these fantasy-like stories for indications of motives such as *achievement*, *power*, *affiliation* and *intimacy* needs has proven to predict the social behaviour of individuals in other settings to a considerable degree (McClelland 1961, 1992).

Current research methods and theoretical considerations

Psychologists under the influence of behaviourism were at first reluctant to study ephemeral thought processes or fantasies. Since the 1950s there has been an accelerating interest in such inner processes, furthered by the emergence of many improved methods for studying the nature of fantasy processes as they emerge in the course of normal ongoing thought (Klinger 1990; Singer 1966, 1993). The methods currently in active use by researchers include questionnaire surveys; self-recordings of daydreams under controlled conditions; laboratory studies of daydreams and fantasies that emerge during a variety of simple or complex task performances; psychophysiological measurement of brain functions or eye movements during the process of creating fantasies; and the assessment of fantasies as they occur naturally through having individuals carrying paging devices or bleepers that signal randomly when an individual must immediately report ongoing thought or fantasy.

What have we learned by the application of these methods? The questionnaire approaches allow us to sample the self-reports of hundreds of individuals about the frequency, content and patterns of their fantasy; it is possible to conclude that daydreaming and the generation of fantasies is a normal process, one that occurs almost daily in every individual. Three general styles of fantasizing have been identified: one involves more positive and future-oriented explorations, a second more guilt-ridden or unpleasant and frightening considerations of past events or future possibilities, and the third pattern involves the ability to sustain elaborate fantasies or to organize one's private imagery into consistent story-like structures. Questionnaire studies have also brought various cultural differences in the content of fantasies with such differences often reflecting phenomena such as the relative upwards mobility of a sociocultural group in this society. Sexual fantasies are nearly universal in Western society if, however, not nearly as frequent as one might think from popular literature or film. There is no evidence that fantasy is in itself a sign of serious emotional disturbance; on the contrary severely disturbed individuals such as schizophrenics or extremely impulsive or aggressive individuals are often characterized by less varied or rich fantasy lives and more by single-minded and limited fantasy tendencies (Klinger 1990; Singer 1976).

Laboratory studies have shown the persistent and ubiquitous nature of human fantasy, even under conditions in which the individual is performing a relatively demanding task. For example, individuals may be sitting in small booths listening to signals presented to them via earphones and must be constantly pressing buttons to show that they comprehend the targeted signals as they appear as fast as one per second. If they are interrupted every fifteen seconds and must report on extraneous thoughts it turns out that even while processing signals quite accurately over an hour's time, they still generate a fantasy as often as 50 per cent of the time. It is

possible to show that certain types of individuals, who on questionnaires report more fantasy tendencies, are often more inclined to report fantasies during such precisely measured laboratory interruptions.

Other types of laboratory studies have demonstrated that when individuals are engaged in a fantasy activity their eyes tend to become unfocused and relatively motionless, particularly if there are movements or other visual signals presented in front of them. This would suggest that the visual images, which are the predominant characteristics of human fantasy for most people, involve the same brain system as that of normal vision when processing externally generated stimuli. There are also research suggestions that particular types of brain waves, such as alpha rhythms or theta rhythms, may be the ones most prominently in evidence during waking fantasy activity.

Studies making use of paging devices are able to capture the way that fantasies occur during ordinary day-to-day activities. Extensive work in this area has been carried out especially by Russell Hurlburt, Mihailyi Csikszentmihalyi and Eric Klinger (1990). These studies also show how closely daydreams or fantasies are linked to fundamental motivational processes called 'current concerns', both short- and longer-term unfulfilled intentions.

Early theorizing about the nature of fantasy processes was strongly influenced by Sigmund Freud's important insight that linked the human being's capacity to delay gratification, a vitally significant step in our adaptive development, to our imaginative capacity. While certainly, as Freud suggested, the daydreams of the poet can be transformed into artistic productions, there is much less evidence for his position that only 'unsatisfied wishes are the driving power behind fantasies' or as he put it another time 'happy people never daydream' (1962 [1908]).

The research evidence since the late 1960s suggests rather that daydreaming is a fundamental human capacity that not only can reflect our unfulfilled wishes, of course, but also is inherent in our normal and healthy adaptive approach to exploring the physical and social environment through playing out mentally a series of possible scenarios. A more useful conclusion from current evidence would be that unhappy people are more likely to have unhappy daydreams and that people who are functioning effectively will be characterized by a great variety of daydreams, the majority of which are more likely to involve playful and fanciful explorations of possible futures as well as some consideration of the negative alternatives in life. For the most part, most fantasy tends to be more realistic and geared to relatively mundane, practical issues in the individual's life.

Another influential conception introduced by Sigmund Freud was that the daydream or fantasy could partially discharge a drive, such as sex or aggression, and thus reduce the likelihood of an impulsive act. This *catharsis* theory has been extremely influential among literary individuals or persons in film and television. It is widely used as an explanation for encouraging children or adults to watch a variety of violent sports activities or films or encouraging children's exposure to violent fairy tales, with the notion that such exposure will reduce the likelihood of overt aggressive action. The evidence from dozens of laboratory studies of adults and children and from field studies of children exposed to violence in film and television overwhelmingly suggests that vicarious fantasy *increases* tendencies towards aggressive behaviour rather than reducing them. Our human fantasy capacity involves not a drainage of drive but a preparation for action. Those persons, however, who have developed a varied and complex imaginative life are often also more likely to recognize the unreality of many of their wishes; they can envisage a host of self-defeating consequences of impulsive action.

The current approach to fantasy and daydreaming processes casts such phenomena within a broader context of modern cognitive, affective and social scientific research. Human beings are viewed as continuously seeking to make sense of the novelty and complexity of their environment. They seek to organize and label experiences, and form them into meaningful structures called schemata or scripts. At the same time they seek to anticipate possible futures. Fantasy represents the effort (influenced by religious symbols, folk legends, popular literature and, increasingly, films and television) of individuals to rehearse their memories and to create possible futures. Studies of early imaginative play in children point to the origins of the fantasy process where the dilemmas or cognitive complexities of the big world (social and physical) are miniaturized or re-enacted in a controlled play form. Adults continue this process privately through their mental imagery and interior monologues. Nocturnal dreams as well as daydreams reflect this continuing effort and suggest the inherent creativity of almost all individuals. Artists are especially adept at noticing such fantasies and incorporating them into their productions. Psychotherapists from a variety of schools have increasingly also encouraged the fantasy and imagery capacities of their clients as resources in the treatment process.

JEROME L. SINGER
YALE UNIVERSITY

References

Freud, S. (1962 [1908]) 'Creative writers and day-dreaming', in *Standard Edition of the Complete Psychological Works of Sigmund Freud*, ed. J. Strachey, Vol. 9, London.

—— (1962 [1911]) 'Formulations regarding the two principles in mental functioning', in *Standard Edition of the Complete Psychological Works of Sigmund Freud*, ed. J. Strachey, Vol. 12, London.

James, W. (1890) *The Principles of Psychology*, New York.

Jaynes, J. (1977) *The Origin of Consciousness in the Breakdown of the Bicameral Mind*, New York.

Klinger, E. (1990) *Daydreaming*, Los Angeles, CA.

McClelland, D.C. (1961) *The Achieving Society*, Princeton, NJ.

—— (1992) 'Is personality consistent?' in R.A. Zucker, A.I. Rabin, J. Aronoff and S.J. Frank (eds) *Personality Structure in the Life Course: Essays on Personology in the Murray Tradition*, New York.

Singer, J.L. (1966) *Daydreaming: An Introduction to the Experimental Study of Inner Experience*, New York.

—— (1976) *Daydreaming and Fantasy*, Oxford.

—— (1993) 'Experimental studies of ongoing conscious experience', Ciba Foundation Symposium 174, Experimental and Theoretical Studies of Consciousness, London.

—— (1994) 'William James, James Joyce and the stream of consciousness', in R. Fuller (ed.) *Behaviour and Mind*, London.

Singer, J.L. and Brown, S. (1977) 'The experience-type: Some behavioral correlates and theoretical implications', in M.C. Rickers-Orsiankina (ed.) *Rorschach Psychology*, Huntington, NY.

Further reading

Antrobus, J.S. (1999) 'Toward a neuocognitive processing model of imaginal thought', in J.A. Singer and P. Salovey (eds) *At Play in the Fields of Consciousness*, Mahwah, NJ.

Klinger, E. (1999) 'Thought flow: Properties and mechanisms underlying shifts in content', in J.A. Singer and P. Salovey (eds) *At Play in the Fields of Consciousness*, Mahwah, NJ.

Singer, D.G. and Singer, J.L. (1990) *The House of*

Make-Believe: Children's Play and the Developing Imagination, Cambridge, MA.

SEE ALSO: delusions; dreams; projective tests

FASCISM

Of all the major terms in twentieth-century political usage, fascism has tended to remain one of the most vague. At the popular level, it has become during the past two generations little more than a derogatory epithet employed to denigrate a bewildering variety of otherwise mutually contradictory political phenomena. It has been applied at one time or another to virtually every single form of twentieth-century radicalism or authoritarianism, as well as many more moderate phenomena. More specifically, in terms of political regimes, there has developed since the 1930s a broad tendency to refer to any form of right-wing authoritarian system that is not specifically socialist as fascist. In this usage the Italian regime of Benito Mussolini is used as terminological prototype for all non-Marxist or non-socialist authoritarian systems, however they may differ from Italian Fascism or among themselves.

Rigorous scholarly and historical definition of fascism, however, refers to the concrete historical phenomena of the European fascist movements that emerged between the two world wars, first in the Italian Fascist and German National Socialist movements founded in 1919–20 and then among their numerous counterparts in many European countries. An adequate political and historical definition of fascism must define common unique characteristics of all the fascist movements in Europe during the 1920s and 1930s while at the same time differentiating them from other political phenomena. Such a criterial definition must specify the typical fascist negations, fascist doctrine and goals, and the uniqueness of fascist style and organization.

The uniqueness of fascism lay in its opposition to nearly all the existing political sectors, left, right and centre. It was anti-liberal, anti-communist (as well as anti-socialist in the social democratic sense) and anti-conservative, though willing to undertake temporary alliances with other groups, primarily rightist.

In their ideology and political goals, fascist movements represented the most intense and radical form of nationalism known to modern Europe. They aimed at the creation of a new kind of nationalist authoritarian state that was not merely based on traditional principles or models. Though fascist groups differed considerably among themselves on economic goals, they all hoped to organize some new kind of regulated, multiclass, integrated national economic structure, diversely called national corporatist, national socialist or national syndicalist. All fascist movements aimed either at national imperial expansion or at least at a radical change in the nation's relationship with other powers to enhance its strength and prestige. Their doctrines rested on a philosophical basis of idealism and voluntarism, and normally involved the attempt to create a new form of modern, self-determined secular culture.

Fascist uniqueness was particularly expressed through the movements' style and organization. Great emphasis was placed on the aesthetic structure of meetings, symbols and political choreography, relying especially on romantic and mystical aspects. Fascist movements all attempted to achieve mass mobilization, together with the militarization of political relationships and style, and with the goal of a mass party militia. Unlike some other types of radicals, fascists placed strong positive evaluation on the use of violence, and strongly stressed the masculine principle and male dominance. Though they espoused an organic concept of society, they vigorously championed a new elitism and exalted youth above other phases of life. In leadership, fascist movements exhibited a specific tendency towards an authoritarian, charismatic, personal style of command (the *Führerprinzip*, in German National Socialist parlance).

Radical rightist groups shared some of the fascists' political goals, just as revolutionary leftist movements exhibited some of their stylistic and organizational characteristics. The uniqueness of the fascists, however, lay in their rejection of the cultural and economic conservatism, and the particular social elitism of the right, just as they rejected the internationalism, nominal egalitarianism and materialist socialism of the left. The historical uniqueness of fascism can be better grasped once it is realized that significant political movements sharing all – not merely some – of these common characteristics existed only in Europe during the years 1919–45.

Fascists claimed to represent all classes of national society, particularly the broad masses.

Marxists and some others, conversely, claimed that they were no more than the tool of the most violent, monopolistic and reactionary sectors of the bourgeoisie. Both of these extreme interpretations are not supported by empirical evidence. In their earliest phase, fascist movements drew their followers from among former military personnel and small sectors of the radical intelligentsia, in some cases university students. Though some fascist movements enjoyed a degree of backing from the upper bourgeoisie, the broadest sector of fascist support, comparatively speaking, was provided by the lower middle class. Since this was one of the largest strata in European society during the 1920s and 1930s, the same might also have been said for various other political groups. In both Italy and Germany, a notable minority of party members were drawn from among urban workers. In Hungary and Romania, primary social backing came from university students and poor peasants, and there was also considerable agrarian support in some parts of Italy.

A bewildering variety of theories and interpretations have been advanced since 1923 to explain fascism. Among them are, first, theories of socioeconomic causation of various kinds, primarily of Marxist inspiration; second, concepts of psychocultural motivation related to social psychology and personality and social structures; third, the application of modernization theory, which posits fascism as a phase in modern development; fourth, the theory of totalitarianism, which interprets fascism as one aspect of the broader phenomenon of twentieth-century totalitarianism; and, finally, historicist interpretations, which attempt multicausal explanation in terms of the major dimensions of central European historical development in the early twentieth century.

The only fascist movements to establish independent regimes of their own were those of Benito Mussolini (1922–43) and Adolf Hitler (1933–45), and only in the latter case did the movement's leader achieve complete power over the state. The other countries in which fascist movements were strongest were Austria (Austrian National Socialists), Hungary (Arrow Cross), Romania (Iron Guard) and Spain (Spanish Phalanx). In general, fascism had most appeal in countries defeated or destabilized by the effects of the First World War. Though fascist movements appeared in every single European country during these years (and also, very faintly, in the countries of the Western hemisphere and

Japan, paralleled by more vigorous expression in South Africa), very few of them enjoyed any degree of success. In nearly all countries antifascists were generally much more numerous than fascists. The extreme radicalism and calls to war and violence of the fascists limited their appeal, as did the non-rationalist, voluntarist nature of their doctrines. The great expansion of military power by Hitler's Germany was mainly responsible for the broader influence and historical importance achieved by fascism for a few years. Similarly, the complete defeat of Germany and Italy in the war condemned fascism to such total political destruction and historical discredit that all attempts at revival have enjoyed only minuscule support since 1945.

STANLEY G. PAYNE
UNIVERSITY OF WISCONSIN, MADISON

Further reading

Griffin, R. (1991) *The Nature of Fascism*, London.
—— (ed.) (1995) *Fascism*, Oxford.
—— (ed.) (1998) *International Fascism. Theories, Causes and the New Consensus*, London.
Laqueur, W. (1996) *Fascism: Past, Present, Future*, Oxford.
Larsen, S.U., Hagtvet, B. and Myklebust, J.P. (eds) (1980) *Who Were the Fascists: Social Roots of European Fascism*, Bergen-Oslo.
Payne, S.G. (1995) *A History of Fascism, 1914–1945*, Madison, WI

SEE ALSO: nationalism; populism; radicalism; terrorism

FEDERALISM AND FEDERATION

Federalism is a normative political philosophy that recommends the use of federal principles, i.e. combining joint action and self-government (King 1982). 'Federal political systems' is a descriptive catchall term for all political organizations that combine what Daniel Elazar called 'shared rule and self-rule'. Federal political systems, thus broadly construed, include federations, confederations, unions, federacies, associated states, condominiums, leagues and cross-border functional authorities (Elazar 1994). Federations are very distinct federal political systems (Watts 1998). In a genuinely democratic federation there is a compound sovereign state, in which at least two governmental units, the federal and the regional, enjoy constitutionally separate competencies – although they may also have concurrent powers. Both the federal and the regional governments are empowered to deal directly with their citizens, and the relevant citizens directly elect (at least some components of) the federal and regional governments. In a federation the federal government usually cannot unilaterally alter the horizontal division of powers: constitutional change affecting competencies requires the consent of both levels of government. Therefore federation automatically implies a codified and written constitution, and normally is accompanied at the federal level by a supreme court, charged with umpiring differences between the governmental tiers, and by a bicameral legislature – in which the federal as opposed to the popular chamber may disproportionately represent the smallest regions. Elazar emphasized the 'covenantal' character of federations, i.e. the authority of each government is derived from a constitution and convention rather than from another government.

Federations vary in the extent to which they are majoritarian in character, but most constrain the power of federation-wide majorities. They constrain the federal demos, though there is extensive variation in this respect (Stepan 2001: 340–57). The USA, Australia and Brazil allow equal representation to each of their regions in the federal chamber, which means massive over-representation for the smaller ones. Other federations also overrepresent less populous units, but not to this extent. Federations differ additionally in the competencies granted to the federal chamber. Some, such as the US Senate, are extremely powerful. It is arguably more powerful than the House of Representatives because of its special powers over nominations to public office and in treaty-making. Others including those in Canada, India and Belgium are weak. Constitutional change can be blocked by individual regions in some instances, although normally a veto requires a coalition of regions. A federation is majoritarian to the extent that it lacks consociational practices of executive power-sharing, proportionality principles of representation and allocation, cultural autonomy and veto-rights; and it is majoritarian to the extent that it lacks consensual institutions or practices – such as the separation of powers, bills of rights, and courts and monetary institutions insulated from immediate governing majorities. A majoritarian federation concentrates power-resources at the federal level and facilitates executive and legisla-tive dominance either by a popularly endorsed executive president or by a single-party premier and cabinet.

The federal principle of separate competencies says nothing about how much power each level enjoys. Regions in some federations may enjoy less de facto power than those in decentralized unitary states. The constitutional division of powers (even as interpreted by the courts) is not always an accurate guide to policy-making autonomy and discretion enjoyed by different tiers. Some powers may have fallen into abeyance, or the superior financial and political resources of one level (usually the federal) may allow it to interfere in the other's jurisdiction. A better indicator of the degree of autonomy enjoyed by regions may be the proportion of public spending that is under the control of the respective levels (for such measurements (see Lijphart 1979: 504).

A key distinction is that federations can be multinational/multiethnic or mononational in character. In the former, the boundaries of the internal units are usually drawn in such a way that at least some of them are controlled by national or ethnic minorities. In addition, more than one nationality may be explicitly recognized as co-founders and co-owners of the federation. The first such federation was Switzerland, established in its current form in 1848, and the second, Canada, established in 1867. The Indian subcontinent was divided after decolonization into the two multiethnic federations of India and Pakistan. Africa has two federations, Nigeria and Ethiopia, while South Africa appears federal in all but name. The communist Soviet Union, Yugoslavia and Czechoslovakia were organized as multinational federations, and the Russian Republic (RSFSR), one of the constituent units of the Soviet Union, was itself organized along federal lines. These communist federations did not bestow genuine democratic self-government on their minorities, and fell apart in the early 1990s, although Yugoslavia continued as a dyadic federation incorporating Serbia and Montenegro until 2003, when its state structure was further decentralized and it was renamed Serbia and Montenegro. Bosnia became a multinational federation under the internationally enforced Dayton Agreement of 1995, with one of its units itself being another binational federation of Bosniacs and Croats. Belgium has recently evolved into a federation, and both Euro-optimists and pessimists think that the European Union (EU) is moving in the same direction. Multinational federations have been proposed for a significant number of other divided societies, including Afghanistan, Burma, China, Cyprus, Georgia, Indonesia and, most recently, Iraq.

National federations may be nationally or ethnically homogeneous (or predominantly so), or they are organized, often consciously, so as not to recognize more than one official nationality – often this happens in such a way that the state's national and ethnic minorities are also minorities in each of the constituent units. The intention behind national federalism is nation-building, the elimination of internal national (and perhaps also ethnic) differences. The founding and paradigmatic example of a national federation is the USA. Its model was adopted by the Latin American federations of Mexico, Argentina, Brazil and Venezuela. Germany, Austria, Australia and the United Arab Emirates are also national federations. US and US-educated intellectuals often propose national federations as a way to deal with ethnic heterogeneity in postcolonial and postcommunist societies.

Federations can also be distinguished according to their level of democracy. Some, such as Canada, the USA and Belgium, should be seen as maturely democratic; others, such as Malaysia and Nigeria, as partially democratic; and others, such as the communist federations of the Soviet Union, Yugoslavia and Czechoslovakia, as not democratic. There is an increasingly popular view in the academic literature on federalism that this distinction is unimportant. A number of prominent US academics thus interpret the failings of the communist federations as an indictment of (multinational) federalism *per se* (Brubaker 1996; Bunce 1999; Leff 1998; and Roeder 1991). In these accounts, it is structure that counts. Democracy matters crucially, however, as does the type of democratic system. One cannot extrapolate the fate of democratic federations, in which there is genuine self-government and in which groups can freely express their grievances and aspirations, from the record of failed authoritarian or totalitarian states (McGarry and O'Leary 2003). Indeed, some defenders of federalism argue that a genuine federation is necessarily democratic and that it does not make sense to describe the Soviet Union and similar states as 'federal'.

Federations should be distinguished from con-federations, although the two are sometimes confused. A federation is generally understood as a compound state with citizenship and a single international personality while a confederation is a union or alliance of (independent) states, established usually for a limited set of purposes such as defence or economic co-operation. Federal governments have a direct role in the lives of their citizens, while confederations normally interact with the citizens of their member-states indirectly through the governments and bureaucracies of these states. As confederations are much looser unions than federations, they are more likely to have decision-making rules based on unanimity. It is also (formally) easier to leave a confederation than a federation. The distinction between federation and confederation, however, is not as clear as it once was. Some federations allow their regions a role in international relations. Both Canada and Belgium permit constituent units with French-speaking populations to sit in La Francophonie, the league of French-speaking states (see also Leonardy 2000). As a result of a recent ruling by Canada's Supreme Court, there is now a constitutional process by which each of the provinces can secede, while the Badinter Commission on the Former Yugoslavia ruled that its constituent units had the right to leave the collapsing Yugoslav federation. From the other direction, the EU, which originated as a confederation, has been developing federal characteristics. Since the Maastricht Treaty, there has been EU citizenship, and the Brussels bureaucracy is increasingly having an impact on the lives of these citizens. The EU's dominant decision-making rule is shifting from unanimity to majority rule, a process that will be hastened as a result of the Treaty of Nice and the expansion of the EU eastwards. It may be in this space between federalism and confederalism that the solution to some ethnic conflicts, such as Cyprus's, Iraq's and Georgia's, are to be found.

JOHN MCGARRY
QUEEN'S UNIVERSITY, KINGSTON, CANADA

References:

Brubaker, R. (1996) *Nationalism Reframed*, Cambridge, UK.

Bunce, V. (1999) *Subversive Institutions: The Design and the Destruction of Socialism and the State*, Cambridge.

Elazar, D. (1994) *Exploring Federalism*, Tuscaloosa, AB.

King, P. (1982) *Federalism and Federation*, London.

Leff, C.S. (1998) *The Czech and Slovak Republics: Nation Versus State*, Boulder, CO.

Leonardy, U. (2000) 'Treaty-making powers and foreign relations of federated entities', in B. Coppieters, D. Darchiashvili and N. Akaba (eds) *Federal Practice: Exploring Alternatives for Georgia and Abkhazia*, Brussels, pp. 151–68.

Lijphart, A. (1979) 'Consociation and federation: Conceptual and political links', *Canadian Journal of Political Science* 12(3): 499–515.

McGarry, J. and O'Leary, B. (2003) 'Federation as a method of ethnic conflict regulation', in S.J.R. Noel (ed.) *From Power-Sharing to Democracy: Post-Conflict Institutions in Ethnically Divided Societies*, Montreal.

Roeder, P. (1991) 'Soviet federalism and ethnic mobilization', *World Politics* 43 (January): 196–232.

Stepan, A. (2001) *Arguing Comparative Politics*, Oxford.

Watts, R. (1998) 'Federalism, federal political systems, and federations', *Annual Review of Political Science* 1: 117–37.

SEE ALSO: constitutions and constitutionalism; partition; secession; state

FEMINIST THEORY

Fundamental to feminist theory is a concern with distortion and absence in past and prevailing structures, especially as they affect women, and an insistence on listening to the voices of the marginalized, the excluded and the misrepresented in order to overturn conventional assumptions that underpin unequal power relationships. Adopting a sceptical and irreverent approach to established systems of knowledge, the common aim of all feminist theory is the exposure and eradication of the multiple strands of bias in social structures and cultural production. To this end it adopts two simultaneous approaches, that of critique (deconstruction) and re-vision (construction). Feminist theory is both multidisciplinary and interdisciplinary, characteristics that inform feminist thought across the entire spectrum of intellectual endeavour.

While feminist endeavour has a long history, feminist theorizing began with the first individuals who challenged the subordinate position of women in society. Amongst the earliest recognized figures in this tradition are those women of the Enlightenment whose voices were raised against women's exclusion from education and from politics, especially the basic right to vote:

for example, in the eighteenth century, Olympe de Gouges in France, Mary Wollstonecraft in England, and Maria W. Stewart in the USA. However, it is the collective voices of women organizing the women's suffrage campaigns in the late nineteenth and early twentieth centuries that constitute the beginnings of feminist theory, identified retrospectively as the 'first wave' of feminism in the West. Familiar figures of that era are the Pankhursts in Britain, and Sojourner Truth, Susan B. Anthony and Elizabeth Cady Stanton in the USA.

By the mid-twentieth century the work of Virginia Woolf (1929) and Simone de Beauvoir (1953 [1949]) had extended the women's rights discourse beyond the demand for women's equality with men to include an interrogation of the very notion of gender difference as natural. Their writing had a profound influence on the feminist theory generated by the Women's Liberation Movement (WLM) in the 1970s. The question of gender as a social construction became crucial to the 'second wave' of feminist scholarship, with its assumption of women's universal oppression, and its objective of working together for women's liberation in a new social order. Critiques of 'sexuality', 'reproduction', 'the family' and 'work' generated by grassroots activism and 'consciousness-raising' groups were distinguishing themes of the WLM in the 1970s. Over the next two decades, the deconstruction of gendered behaviour became a crucial strand in feminist theorizing.

Despite the apparent consensus in the 1970s that 'sisterhood' was both global and powerful, and that 'patriarchy' was the common cause of women's oppression, exploitation and subordination, feminist theory has always included a variety of different approaches and perspectives. Nonetheless, by the late 1970s, the body of scholarship generated by the WLM was challenged by black feminists on the grounds that the assumption of universality upon which feminist theory was based was false (Combahee River Collective 1982). They pointed out that what masqueraded as feminist theory was no more than an unself-conscious reflection of white, middle-class European perspectives, and was therefore both racist and classist. The experience of black women fell outside some of its major premises, and indeed contradicted many of them. For example (white, Western) feminist theory assumed that the family was a crucial site of oppression, whereas for black women combating racism, the family was a potential refuge. While abortion appeared to offer liberation to white, middle-class women, and to present a straightforward issue of choice, it was not so for black women in a racist society that threatened and denigrated the black family unit. At the same time, the post-Civil Rights generation of black women writers in the USA did much to reclaim a black feminist tradition that had been suppressed for centuries by the imposed silence of black women through slavery and their exclusion from suffrage and public office, and by the negative stereotypes of black women that prevailed in Western culture.

This critique not only challenged the prevailing assumptions on which feminist theory had hitherto been based, but also paved the way for a more complex and inclusive future agenda, a 'third wave', which was informed and shaped by the perspectives of white, black, 'Third World' and 'minority' women from around the globe. Crucial to the new era of feminist theory was the explosion of the myth that 'women' constituted a natural, homogenous group. Feminism was forced to confront the reality of the multiple differences among women and to acknowledge that women's oppression is the result of interlocking systems in which race, gender, class, age and sexuality form the nexus.

By the mid-1980s, in line with wider postmodern emphases on culture and representation as significant social signifiers, feminist theory 'turned to culture'. Coinciding with a growing preoccupation with 'difference' and 'diversity', identity politics challenged Western feminism's initial confidence in women's universal solidarity as a viable solution to oppression. Furthermore while 'second wave' feminists had proclaimed that 'the personal is political', in the 1980s and 1990s 'the political' began to take on an exclusively 'personal' look, becoming increasingly a matter of private and individual lifestyle choice. Feminist theory seemed no longer connected to grassroots activism, and as the twentieth century drew to a close, cultural analysis and the fragmentation of the category 'women' appeared to have deflected attention away from the material conditions of women's lives. A new *postfeminist* discourse (popular especially amongst younger women) treats feminism as not just *passé* but redundant, and appears to challenge the need for feminist theory. At best feminism is credited with

having achieved its goal: women are equal and liberated. At worst it is considered an oppressive orthodoxy of political correctness. This was to threaten the very foundations of feminist theory.

Where does that leave feminist theory in the twenty-first century? Is the revolution over? Current feminist scholarship suggests not. Feminist voices from 'developing' countries offer insightful analyses of the continuing struggles and innovative and courageous organization among women faced with oppressive cultural practices and threatened by global economic trends (Mies and Shiva 1993) while in the 'developed' world 'the new feminism' challenges feminist theory's recent neglect of the socioeconomic conditions that subordinate and oppress women globally (Walter 1999). Both sources argue that there is as much need now as there was in previous decades for a consideration of the unequal material conditions which exploit and subordinate women. The agenda of feminist theory in the twenty-first century must continue to include all those issues yet unresolved from previous decades as well as the particular challenges that globalization, new reproductive technologies, and bioethics now pose for women, for men and indeed for children.

MERIDY HARRIS
UNIVERSITY OF KENT

References

Beauvoir, S. de (1953 [1949]) *The Second Sex*, Harmondsworth.
Combahee River Collective (1982) 'A black feminist statement', in C. Moraga and G. Anzaldua (eds) *This Bridge Called My Back: Writings by Radical Women of Color*, Watertown, MA, pp. 210–18.
Mies, M and Shiva, V. (1993) *Ecofeminisms*, London.
Walter, N. (1999) *The New Feminism*, London.
Woolf, V. (1929) *A Room of One's Own*, London.

Further reading

Collins, P.H. (1991) *Black Feminist Thought*, New York.
Coppack, V., Haydon, D. and Richter, I. (1955) *The Illusions of Post-feminism: New Women, Old Myths*, Basingstoke.
Evans, M. (1997) *Introducing Contemporary Feminist Thought*, Cambridge, UK.
Greer, G. (1999) *The Whole Woman*, London.
Harding, S. (1991) *Whose Science? Whose Knowledge?* Milton Keynes.
Humm, M. (1992) *Feminisms: A Reader*, Hemel Hempstead.

Jackson, S and Jones, J. (eds) (1998) *Contemporary Feminist Theories*, Edinburgh.

Kemp, S. and Squires, J. (eds) (1997) *Feminisms*, Oxford.

Mohanty, C.T., Russo, A. and Torres, L. (1991) *Third World Women and the Politics of Feminism*, Bloomington, IN.

Rowbotham, S. and Linkogle, S. (2002) *Women Resist Globalisation*, London.

Shiva, V. (1998) *Biopiracy*, Totnes.

Walter, N. (ed.) (1999) *On the Move: Feminism for a New Generation*, London.

SEE ALSO: gender, sociology of; patriarchy; women; women's studies

FERTILITY

Fertility (also referred to as natality) always refers in demographic usage to the achievement of live births. This is in keeping with its Latin etymological derivation from *ferre* (to bear) but in contrast to the verb, fertilize, which relates to conception. In English-language social science, the capacity to bear children is described as fecundity and the fact of giving birth as fertility. This is the reverse of the usage in French and other Romance languages. It also conflicts with much popular, medical and biological usage where infertility means not childlessness but infecundity or sterility (confusingly, the last can be employed in both senses even by demographers).

In spite of the biblical advice to be fruitful and multiply, a precept found in many preindustrial societies, the maximization of fertility is usually constrained by competing social objectives. Fertility is usually not favoured outside marriage partly because it may interfere with achieving the desired marriage. It may be discouraged soon after the birth of another child, because of the risk to health and life of both mother and children. Having children may be thought inappropriate for grandmothers, because of the conflict between grandmaternal and maternal duties. Traditionally these constraints have been embedded in religion and mores rather than being expressed solely in terms of conflicting roles and danger to health.

Fertility may be expressed as a measure of the behaviour of a society, a couple or an individual. In theory, reproductive measures are just as valid for individual males as females, but estimates for the former are rarely attempted because the fact of a man's fathering a child is less obvious to the community and may be unknown to the progenitor himself. The most meaningful measure of a woman's reproduction is the number of births she experiences between menarch (or puberty) and menopause. For the whole society, the average for all women is known as completed fertility. However, this measure can be determined only in retrospect, a quarter of a century after the peak in fertility for most women completing their reproductive spans, and societies frequently demand more immediate measures that are necessarily those for aggregate populations of different ages for a specified period (usually one year and hence described as an annual rate). The most common aggregate measure is the crude birth rate or the number of live births per year per thousand population. For national populations, this varied in 2002 from 55 in Niger to 8 in Latvia and Ukraine. The crude birth rate can prove to be an unsatisfactory measure in a society where immigration or other social changes have distorted the distribution of the population by sex or age, and more statistically refined measures relate births only to women of specified age or marital condition. The general fertility rate is the ratio of the births during a year to the total number of women 15–49 years of age. The relating of births to women of a specific age, or age range, for a specified period (usually one year), is termed the age-specific birth rate (or fertility rate) and its sum over the whole reproductive age range is the total fertility rate, which in a society characterized by constant fertility over several decades is an annual measure of the same magnitude as completed fertility. The total fertility rate ranged in 2002 from 8.0 in Niger to 0.9 in Hong Kong and Macao and 1.1 in the Czech Republic, Ukraine and Armenia. It was 1.2 in Spain, 1.3 in Italy, Russia and Japan, but as high as 2.1 in the USA. Attention may be confined to married women, so as to determine marital age-specific birth rates and the total marital fertility rate. If only female births are related to mothers of each age, then the cumulative measure is known as the gross reproduction rate. Because the effective measure of reproduction for societies is not live births but surviving children, a measure known as the net reproduction rate has been devised. This may be defined as the ratio of female births in the next generation to those in this generation in conditions of constant fertility and mortality. It therefore measures the eventual multiplication of the population of a society from one generation to the next, once the age structure changes so as to conform with these stable conditions. If the society maintains a rate of unity for a considerable period (half a century or more in societies that were previously growing rapidly) it will become stationary, while a lower rate will imply eventually declining population size, and a higher rate, a growing population. In 2002, levels below unity were recorded by all European countries, except Albania, fourteen East Asian countries (including China), nine Caribbean countries, and also Canada, Australia, New Zealand and Mauritius. By 2002 the populations of twenty-two countries were declining, with Russia losing almost 200 thousand people per year. With the exceptions of Georgia and Kazakhstan, all these countries were in Europe, with half in Eastern Europe. Births within marriage may be described as nuptial or legitimate and those outside as exnuptial or illegitimate.

The female reproductive span varies between women and between societies (or the same society at different dates), but approximately spans ages from around 15 years to the late forties. If fertility were in no way constrained, not even by the institution of marriage or by the practice of breast feeding, which tends to depress fertility, completed family size would be around 15 (Bongaarts (1982) employs 15.3 in his model). The total marital fertility rate of the Hutterites, a religious community in the western USA opposed to deliberate fertility control, was in the late 1920s at least 12.4 – a level employed by Coale (1967) in his model – but this figure was almost certainly rising because of the reduction of the period of breast feeding. Where breast feeding is of traditional duration (2 years or more) the following completed family sizes are found if deliberate control of marital fertility is not practised. First, where female marriage is early and widow remarriage is common, as until recently among the Ashanti of West Africa (who practise only short periods of postpartum abstinence), around 8. Second, where female marriage is early and widow remarriage is discouraged, as in India prior to the family-planning programme, around 6.5. Third, where female marriage is late and there are no strong feelings about widow remarriage, as in Western Europe before the Industrial Revolution, around 6. The term natural fertility has been employed to describe the level of fertility, and its structure by female age,

found in societies that do not deliberately restrict marital fertility (but in which sexual abstinence may be practised after childbirth and terminal sexual abstinence after becoming a grandmother).

Contemporary interest in fertility has developed in response to the decline in fertility in all industrialized and most other societies, and the possibility of further reduction in developing countries. The latter has been assisted by family-planning programmes that have now been instituted by a majority of Third World governments (beginning with India in 1952). The determinants of fertility have been classified (by Davis and Blake 1956) as, first, intercourse variables (age at first entrance to sexual union; the proportion of women never entering a union; the period spent after or between unions; voluntary and involuntary abstinence, and frequency of intercourse); second, conception variables (subfecundity or infecundity; contraception and sterilization); and, third, gestation variables (spontaneous or induced abortion). The list does not separately identify the duration of breast feeding, which was undoubtedly the major determinant of marital fertility in most traditional societies. Nor does it include sexual activity outside stable unions. Bongaarts (1982) has demonstrated that only four factors – the proportion of the female reproductive period spent in a sexual union (in many societies the period of marriage), the duration of postpartum infecundability (that is, the period without menstruation or ovulation plus any period beyond this of postpartum sexual abstinence), the practice of contraception and its effectiveness, and the extent of induced abortion – provide 96 per cent of the explanation of the variance in fertility levels in nearly all societies.

Beginning in France in the late eighteenth century, and becoming more general in industrialized countries from the late nineteenth century, fertility has fallen in economically developed countries so that nearly all appear likely to attain zero or declining population growth. This has been achieved largely through the deliberate control of marital fertility, in most countries by contraception (before the 1960s by chemical or mechanical means as well as rhythm, abstinence and withdrawal or coitus interruptus, and subsequently increasingly by the use of the pill, intra-uterine devices and sterilization), supplemented by different levels of abortion. Abortion is the single most important factor in fertility control.

Globally about one quarter of all pregnancies are terminated by abortion, which constitutes two-fifths of all fertility control. Its practice has become increasingly legal except in Latin America and Africa. By 2003 fertility was clearly low or declining in every major world region except sub-Saharan Africa (where, however, birth rates had begun to fall in Southern Africa, parts of tropical Africa and in most cities). Fertility also remained high in parts of the Middle East and Southwest Asia but nearly everywhere some decline had taken place. Increasingly the relationship between the sexual act and conception has been weakened, and this has allowed a weakening in the relation between sexual activity and marriage.

JOHN C. CALDWELL
AUSTRALIAN NATIONAL UNIVERSITY

References

Bongaarts, J. (1982) 'The fertility-inhibiting effects of the intermediate fertility variables', *Studies in Family Planning* 13.
Coale, A.J. (1967) 'Factors associated with the development of low fertility: an historic summary', in *Proceedings of the World Population Conference, Belgrade, 1965*, Vol. 2, New York.
Davis, K. and Blake, J. (1956) 'Social structure and fertility: An analytical framework', *Economic Development and Cultural Change* 4.

Further reading

Basu, A. (ed.) (2003) *The Sociocultural and Political Aspects of Abortion: Global Perspectives*, Westport, CT, and London.
United Nations (1965) *Population Bulletin of the United Nations*, No. 7-1963, with Special Reference to Conditions and Trends of Fertility in the World, New York.
Wrong, D.H. (1977) *Population and Society*, 4th edn, New York.

SEE ALSO: demographic transition; morbidity; population projections; vital statistics

FEUDALISM

There is no agreement on a definition of feudalism. The word can be used in very general terms to describe the totality of the economic and political relationships of medieval European society and of similar societies elsewhere. If such a view is taken, stress is normally laid upon the exploitation of the peasantry by the exaction of labour services in a closed, or natural, economy. The institution of the manor is of great importance; the main social relationships are seen in terms of lordship exercised over both people and land. Frequently such a definition becomes so wide as to be little more than synonymous with medieval, and so loses any real value, but even when used more carefully, there are still considerable problems.

During the medieval period, the economy underwent such transformations as to make the application of a single model of feudalism very dangerous. Money was far more important than was once thought, and production for the market more widespread. There were wide variations, both chronological and geographical, in the degree of the subjection of the peasantry. In England many labour services were commuted in the twelfth century, when feudalism could be thought to have been at its apogee, only to be reimposed in the thirteenth century. At best, society was only partly feudal, and it is significant that in his definition of feudalism one of its greatest historians, Marc Bloch (1961 [1939–40]), allowed for 'the survival of other forms of authority, family and state', alongside the structures of feudal lordship. Attempts at redefinition of the broad concept of feudalism, seeing small-scale peasant production under the political constraints of aristocratic lordship as the key element, have not proved satisfactory.

The alternative tradition to that which seeks a general model of feudalism is one that centres upon a specific type of landholding in return for military service. The word feudalism is derived from the Latin *feudum* (fief), the land held by a knight in return for service usually performed on horseback for 40 days. It is possible to provide a much more satisfactory description and explanation for feudalism in such terms. The system had its origins in the collapse of public authority in the ninth century as the Carolingian Empire declined. Men commended themselves to lords, who granted them lands as fiefs. The knight and the castle were central to this feudalism, in which lordship resulted from the man, or vassal, performing a specific ceremony known as homage to his lord. The system evolved gradually, save in countries such as England and southern Italy, where it was imported by the Normans in the eleventh century. Fiefs came to be held in primogeniture, and the rights of the lord to certain dues, or feudal incidents, were given increasing definition. A lord could, for example, demand aid from his vassals to help pay for the knighting of his eldest son, and payment was expected when the son of a vassal succeeded his father in his estates. A complex legal system developed: the jurisdictional rights of lords over their tenants were an important element in a feudal society.

Such a definition is largely satisfactory, provided that it is understood that no society was ever wholly feudalized. In the case of England, the king was never solely dependent upon his feudal cavalry, but relied extensively upon mercenaries and infantry levies. The last effective feudal summons was issued in 1327, but in the first half of the thirteenth century the levels of service had been radically reduced, so that the quotas of knights came to bear little relationship to the feudal landholding structure. Castles were initially an integral part of the feudal organization of the country, but when Edward I came to build his great castles in Wales in the late thirteenth century, he used paid workmen and employed paid troops as garrisons. Such castles can hardly be described as feudal. The system of hiring soldiers by means of contracts and the issue of livery in the later Middle Ages has been described as 'bastard feudalism', but the true feudal elements of landed fiefs, heritability and homage were all absent. Yet the legal aspects of feudalism in England long outlasted the military utility of the system; there was even a revival of feudal techniques of money-raising in the early seventeenth century.

If it is only with care that the term feudalism in a strict sense can be applied to a Western European country in the Middle Ages, then it is only with great difficulty that it can be used with reference to different regions and periods. Medieval Byzantium and Islam, with the *pronoia* and *iqta* respectively, had types of land grants that were not entirely dissimilar to fiefs. The *iqta* could only exceptionally be passed on by a holder to his children, but by the twelfth century the Byzantine system was moving towards the heritability that characterized Western feudalism. The legal structure of European feudalism was largely lacking in these parallel systems. Japan is frequently cited as developing something very akin to the military feudalism of Western Europe, but an economy based on rice production, and a wholly different cultural and legal tradition, made for contrasts as well as similarities. For those who are influenced by Marxist theories,

however, feudalism represents a stage through which most societies must pass in the course of their development. Such a view involves using an extremely general definition of feudalism, with its attendant difficulties.

Many of the arguments of scholars over feudalism have been the result of a failure to agree upon definitions. No one word, no single model, can ever sum up the complex and varying structures of medieval societies. As a term describing a very specific set of relationships within the noble and knightly classes of medieval Europe, feudalism is convenient, but the word should only be used with great circumspection.

MICHAEL PRESTWICH
UNIVERSITY OF DURHAM

Reference

Bloch, M. (1961 [1939–40]) *Feudal Society*, London.

Further reading

Brown, E.A.R. (1974) 'The tyranny of a construct: Feudalism and historians of medieval Europe', *American Historical Review* 79: 1,963–88.
Brown, R.A. (1973) *Origins of English Feudalism*, London.
Ganshof, F. (1961) *Feudalism*, New York.
Postan, M.M. (1983) 'Feudalism and its decline: A semantic exercise', in T.H. Aston, P. Coss, C. Dyer and J. Thirsk (eds) *Social Relations and Ideas: Essays in Honour of R.H. Hilton*, Cambridge, UK.

SEE ALSO: state

FINANCIAL CONTAGION

The series of international financial crises that erupted since the mid-1990s in emerging economies attracted the attention of economists, policy-makers and the financial press, generating a large literature on crises and contagion. Perhaps the growing interest in these crises, which saw the sharp devaluation of currencies and/or the collapse of banking systems, is due to the fact that they had severe economic consequences that engulfed a number of countries. For example, the crisis that originated in Thailand in 1997 was rapidly transmitted to Indonesia, Malaysia, Korea and the rest of East Asia. A similar, but less strong, financial series of financial shocks followed the Mexican devaluation of 1994. The 1998 crisis in Russia had much larger contagious effects, affecting not only other emerging markets but also developed countries.

The recent concern with financial contagion goes back to the debt crises of the 1980s and was given a fresh impetus by the attacks on the European Monetary System in the early 1990s. Economists then tried to determine whether crises are due to unsound economic fundamentals or to imperfections in capital markets (which may lead, for example, to self-fulfilling expectations that can trigger crises). The questions in the contagion debate are similar to those raised in the debates about financial crises, but the understanding of contagion is at a much earlier stage.

While there is no generally accepted definition of contagion, it can be broadly understood as referring to the spill-over of financial problems from one country to others. As in the case of domestic crises, this transmission of crises across countries may be due to economic fundamentals (economic links between countries) or to capital market imperfections. Some economists prefer to use the term contagion in a more restricted sense, to describe those spill-over effects (or simultaneous movements in different countries) that are not related to economic fundamentals (Masson 1999). Both these definitions of contagion exclude more or less simultaneous crises in different economies that are due to common shocks. For example, a drop in oil prices might generate crises in oil-producing countries, no matter which country is hit first. Studies of contagion are concerned rather to understand how a domestic crisis in one country leads to crises elsewhere.

It is useful to clarify that, although contagion has been studied particularly in the context of crises, contagion can also take place during 'good' times. For example, some commentators associate the high capital flows to developing countries (which led to overborrowing) and the financing of the technological firms (which led to a generalized asset bubble) to the 'irrational exuberance' that characterized many economies during the late 1990s.

Three broad channels of contagion have been identified in the literature: real links, financial links and herd behaviour. 'Real links' are usually associated with trade links. When two countries trade between themselves, or if they compete in the same external markets, a devaluation of the exchange rate in one country will reduce the other country's competitive advantage. As a consequence, both countries are likely to end up devaluing their currencies in order to rebalance their external sectors (see Gerlach and Smets 1995). Real links probably contribute some regional effects to financial crises.

The recent crises, however, have had such widespread effects across countries and regions that it has been difficult to demonstrate that real links explain the transmission of shocks. Moreover, the magnitude of recent swings in asset prices is not closely related to any real link among economies. Financial markets have reacted so strongly that some economists pointed to spill-over effects that were not explained by real channels.

In the absence of real links among economies, 'financial links' might also connect countries. One example of financial links is when leveraged institutions face 'margin calls' (Calvo 1998). When the value of their collateral falls, due to a negative shock in one country, banks and mutual funds need to raise liquidity to meet future redemptions and to increase their reserves. They then sell assets in countries that are still unaffected by the initial shock. This mechanism transmits the shock to other economies. (The literature provides different examples of financial links. For example, Allen and Gale (2000) concentrate on the overlapping claims that different regions of the banking system have on one another. Kaminsky and Reinhart (2000) emphasize the role of common bank creditors in spreading the initial shock. Kodres and Pritsker (2002) focus on investors who engage in cross-market hedging of macroeconomic risks.)

Even when there are no real or financial links, both domestic and international financial markets might transmit shocks across countries due to herd behaviour or panics. At the root of this herd behaviour is asymmetric information. (Because information is costly, many investors are imperfectly informed.) In the context of asymmetric information, what other market participants are doing might convey information to which an uninformed investor does not otherwise have access (Calvo and Mendoza 2000). Investors may then attempt to infer future price changes by observing how other markets are reacting. A change in Thailand's asset prices, for instance, might provide useful information about future changes of asset prices in Indonesia or Brazil. Rigobon (1998) shows that investors also face a signal extraction problem when making their investment decisions. This fosters herd behaviour and may induce panics.

There are different approaches to testing for the presence of contagion. Most (though not all) tests can be grouped into four categories: (1) unexplained correlations; (2) contagious news; (3) increasing probabilities; and (4) clustering of extreme returns.

(1) The studies that try to understand contagion with reference to changes in correlations examine whether the return correlations across countries increase during times of crisis, which would indicate that investors sell assets across countries regardless of the fundamentals. A key issue in this literature is how to measure correlations at a time that shocks are very large (Forbes and Rigobon 2002; Corsetti *et al.* 2002).

(2) The studies that analyse news try to determine what types of news move markets; ask whether such movements occur in the absence of significant news; and examine whether and in what ways news from one country is transmitted across borders (Baig and Goldfajn 1999; Kaminsky and Schmukler 1999).

(3) The papers that focus on probabilities ask whether the probability of having a crisis in one economy increases when crises occur somewhere else, and attempt to establish how these probabilities are affected by real and financial links (Eichengreen *et al.* 1996).

(4) The studies that analyse the clustering of extreme events examine whether very large negative or positive asset returns across countries occur around the same time (Bae *et al.* 2003).

Is there any consensus about the ultimate cause of contagion? This is a very hard question to answer. Different papers point in different directions. Some claim that contagion is explained by real links (Forbes 2004; Glick and Rose 1999). Others prefer a financial explanation, but while Frankel and Schmukler (1998) and Kaminsky *et al.* (2000) highlight the role of mutual funds, Caramazza *et al.* (2000) and Van Rijckeghem and Weder (2001) stress the role of commercial banks in spreading crises across countries. Yet other economists are persuaded that the key to understanding recent episodes of contagion is herd behaviour (e.g. Kaminsky and Schmukler 1999). Even if all these factors are present in the cross-country transmission of crises, an even more difficult problem remains, which is to determine the relative importance of each component. One issue on which most

economists would probably agree is that some countries are particularly susceptible to contagion. Where the economic fundamentals are solid, the probability of being hit by an external shock is substantially diminished.

To sum up, economists and policy-makers once debated whether high fiscal deficits or high current account deficits were good predictors of crises. The recent crises have shown that countries with very different characteristics may be the victims of external shocks. The strong cross-country contagion effects and the wide extent of the recent crises have shifted the focus of the debate to the role of domestic and international financial markets. Nowadays, countries are working not only to prevent domestic financial crises, but also to avoid the spill-over effects of foreign crises. Besides improving the economic fundamentals, the policy options are far from clear.

SERGIO L. SCHMUKLER
WORLD BANK

References

Allen, F. and Gale, D. (2000) "Financial contagion', *Journal of Political Economy* 108: 1–33.

Bae, K.H., Karolyi, A. and Stulz, R. (2003) 'A new approach to measuring financial contagion', *Review of Financial Studies* 16(3): 717–63.

Baig, T. and Goldfajn, I. (1999) 'Financial market contagion in the Asian crisis', *IMF Staff Papers* 46(2): 167–95.

Calvo, G. (1998) 'Understanding the Russian virus', mimeo, October.

Calvo, G. and Mendoza, E. (2000) 'Rational contagion and the globalization of securities markets', *Journal of International Economics* 51(1): 79–113.

Caramazza, F., Ricci, A. and Salgado, R. (2000) 'Trade and financial contagion in currency crises', *IMF Working Paper* 00/55, March.

Corsetti, G., Pericoli, M. and Sbracia, M. (2002) 'Some contagion, some interdependence: More pitfalls in testing for contagion', *IMF Seminar Series* 2,003(74): 1–28.

Eichengreen, B., Rose, A. and Wyplosz, C. (1996) 'Contagious currency crises', *Scandinavian Journal of Economics* 98(4): 463–84.

Forbes, K. (2004) 'The Asian flu and Russian virus: The international transmission of crises in firm-level data', *Journal of International Economics* 63(1): 59–92.

Forbes, K. and Rigobon, R. (2002) 'No contagion, only interdependence: Measuring stock market co-movements', *Journal of Finance* 57(5): 2,223–61.

Frankel, F. and Schmukler, S. (1998) 'Crisis, contagion, and country funds', in R. Glick (ed.) *Managing Capital Flows and Exchange Rates*, Cambridge, UK.

Gerlach, S. and Smets, F. (1995) 'Contagious speculative attacks', *European Journal of Political Economy*
11: 45–63.

Glick, R. and Rose, A. (1999) 'Contagion and trade:
Why are currency crises regional?' *Journal of International Money and Finance* 18(4): 603–17.

Kaminsky, G., Lyons, R. and Schmukler, S. (2004)
'Managers, investors, and crises: Mutual fund strate-
gies in emerging markets', *Journal of International
Economics*, forthcoming.

Kaminsky, G. and Reinhart, C. (2000) 'On crises,
contagion, and confusion', *Journal of International
Economics* 51(1): 145–68.

Kaminsky, G. and Schmukler, S. (1999) 'What triggers
market jitters? A chronicle of the Asian crisis',
Journal of International Money and Finance 18:
537–60.

Kodres, L. and Pritsker, M. (2002) 'A rational expectations model of financial contagion', *Journal of
Finance* 57: 769–99.

Masson, P. (1999) 'Contagion: Monsoonal effects,
spillovers, and jumps between multiple equilibria',
in P.R. Agenor, M. Miller, D. Vines and A. Weber
(eds) *The Asian Financial Crisis: Causes, Contagion
and Consequences*, Cambridge, UK.

Rigobon, R. (1998) 'Informational speculative attacks:
Good news is no news', mimeo, Massachusetts
Institute of Technology, January.

Van Rijckeghem, C. and Weder, B. (2001) 'Sources of
contagion: Is it finance or trade?' *Journal of International Economics* 54(2): 293–308.

Further reading

Corsetti, G., Pesenti, P. and Roubini, N. (1999) 'What
caused the Asian currency and financial crisis?'
Japan and the World Economy 11(3): 305–73.

Dornbusch, R., Claessens, S. and Park, Y.C. (2000)
'Contagion: Understanding how it spreads', *World
Bank Research Observer* 15(2): 177–97.

Kaminsky, G., Reinhart, C. and Végh, C. (2002) 'The
unholy trinity of financial contagion', *Journal of
Economic Perspectives* 17(4): 51–74.

Kawai, H., Newfarmer, R. and Schmukler, S. (2004)
'Financial crises: Nine lessons from East Asia', *Eastern Economic Journal*, forthcoming.

http://www1.worldbank.org/contagion.

SEE ALSO: financial crisis; financial system

FINANCIAL CRISIS

A financial crisis is defined as a sharp, sudden,
ultra-cyclical deterioration of almost all financial
indicators: hikes in short-term interest rates; falls
in the price of assets (stock, real estate, land);
and a rise in the number of commercial insolven-
cies as well as failures of financial institutions
(Goldsmith 1982). The process of a financial
crisis is often described as a succession of several
phases: a displacement (exogenous shock), a
speculative mania (with euphoria, overtrading
and excessive gearing), financial distress, and,
finally, catastrophe (see, e.g., Kindleberger 1989;
Minsky 1986).

The first phase begins with an exogenous
shock to the economic system, some unexpected
change that alters profit opportunities and induces changes in investment. It may be the
outbreak of war, the end of a war or political
revolution. It may be a more narrowly economic
event, such as the discovery of a new resource, a
major innovation or a good harvest or a bad one.
It may be narrowly financial, such as the unexpected success of a security issue, or the
conversion of debt to lower interest rates, which
encourages those who profited from these wind-
falls to try to maintain their returns in new
investments. Whatever the event that perturbs
the system, it alters investment opportunities and
leads usually to speculation for capital gains.

If the change is sufficiently pervasive, euphoria and overtrading are likely to follow. The
objects traded depend on the nature of the
shock, and may consist of many things: commodities, stocks, bonds (foreign or domestic),
railways, factories, mines, office buildings,
houses, land, foreign currencies, or indeed virtually anything that is of substantial value. In the
modern capital market, participants can exploit
extended or 'leveraged' profit opportunities with
increased risks by trading in derivatives such as
futures and options. Rising prices lead to further
price increases called 'bubbles', which mean that
the price of assets rises to a level that is way out
of line with their underlying value. The success
of early investors induces others to participate.
As more funds are borrowed, interest rates rise,
and some marginal buyers may be forced to
liquidate their holdings. Others, anticipating that
the price of assets is peaking, cash in their gains.
Prices stop rising, may level off or start to slip.
There follows a period called 'financial distress',
as the confident expectation that prices will
continue to climb gives way to doubt. If expectations of a price rise are replaced by expectations
of a fall, a financial crisis is likely. A rush from
real or financial assets into money drives down
the prices of those assets and in acute cases leads
to bankruptcy of individuals or concerns still
holding them with borrowed funds, and even to
bank failures.

There are abundant examples of financial
crises in modern economic history. Among well-

known earlier cases are the tulip mania in The Netherlands (1637) and the South Sea Bubble in Britain (1719). During the nineteenth century, the British economy experienced business cycles that recurred approximately every 10 years. The great depression that started with the stock market crash in 1929 affected most of the world. Nor are financial crises a peculiarity of European and North American economies. A boom in the Japanese economy during the First World War was interrupted by a severe stock market crash in 1920 and a devastating earthquake in 1923. To reduce the unfavourable impact to the credit system, the Bank of Japan extended loans as a lender of last resort, and so probably weakened the discipline of the banking sector. The loans extended after the earthquake were not recovered, and there was a run on the banks when the finance minister announced a bank failure (erroneously) in the Diet. These bank-runs and credit collapse are now known as the 'financial crisis' of 1927. In their wake, the government tightened banking regulation.

'Black Monday' in the New York Stock Exchange (NYSE) in October 1987 created a similar fear of financial instability. This crisis was allegedly triggered by the concern about the future dollar exchange rate. The stock market crash was transmitted to the stock markets the world over. The NYSE adopted a new trading rule after Black Monday, popularly known as the 'circuit breakers', a change that helped to mitigate the effect of the crash of October 1997.

Examples of significant excessive lending have been loans by international syndicates of banks, notably to Mexico, Brazil and Argentina. This was initiated by easy money in the USA beginning in 1970, and accelerated by rises in oil prices in 1973 and 1979 that increased not only the surplus of oil-producing countries as supplier of funds, but also the need for loans by non-oil-producing countries. Suddenly, interest rates in the US market jumped upwards. Some governments of borrowing countries became insolvent, or at least they claimed to be so.

In the USA, when inflation pushed market interest rates above Regulation Q, the maximum ceilings on the deposit interest rates in the 1970s, the Savings and Loans Associations (S–Ls) suddenly lost saving customers. Deregulation of interest rates was implemented to help S–Ls, but it backfired. S–Ls that were protected by the Federal Deposit Insurance Corporation (FDIC) engaged in risky investments, and more than a thousand S–Ls found themselves in financial difficulties. Eventually they were to be rescued by tax money, through the Resolution Trust Corporation (RTC), which was estimated to be in excess of US$80 billion in 1992. (The relative intensity of disturbances to the financial sector in Japan since the early 1990s is at least comparable to, and probably more serious than, the S&L crisis in the USA.)

The transmission of a financial crisis from one country to another is termed contagion. In 1998, Russia's financial distress caused confusion in the world capital market that bankrupted the Long-term Capital Market (LTCM) Fund. The most conspicuous example is the Asian financial crisis that started in 1997. In July 1997, bahts (the Thai currency) suddenly depreciated, and this led to the attacks on other Asian currencies of Malaysia, Indonesia and Korea in a domino fashion. This is a typical example of the process of contagion of a financial crisis. Sudden changes in asset values caused turbulence in the macroeconomic climate of these nations. The IMF intervened and prescribed remedies similar to those that were applied during the Latin American crisis, urging governments to correct budget imbalances and to work to improve the balance of payments. This has been criticized on the grounds that in Asian crises sudden changes in expectations and asset values were crucial triggers, while the budget balances and the balance of payments were not so problematic as they were in Latin America. More fundamentally, Stiglitz and others criticize the IMF's prescription of free trade and free capital movement (what is called the 'Washington Consensus'). This may not always be the most effective, or the fairest, way of rescuing countries suffering a financial crisis (Chang 2001).

Whether financial distress ends in a financial crisis depends on a variety of factors, including the fragility of the earlier extensions of credit, the speed of the reversal of expectations, the disturbance to confidence produced by some financial accident (such as a spectacular failure or revelation of swindles), regulation of the banking industry, and the degree of the financial community's confidence in the central bank's role as a lender of last resort.

Expectations are important. Conventional views (e.g. Kindleberger 1989; Minsky 1986) explicitly recognize the role of irrational expectations and group psychology in critical stages of a financial crisis. Economic agents may exhibit 'herd behaviour', motivated by rumour, fear and panic, rather than making the reasoned choices that rational expectations economists expect. Nevertheless, the economics of asymmetric information helps to explain how bank-runs and financial panics happen even where agents have rational expectations. For example, a bank-run can be characterized as the process where the very expectations by the public that bank reserves may run out becomes a self-filling prophecy, leading to bank-runs even if there is no fundamental weakness in the business of the bank.

A central bank may support a market in times of crisis as a lender of last resort. There is, however, an incentive problem in using a lender of last resort: the more a financial market knows it will be helped in emergency, the more likely it is that financial institutions will take chances and lend to risky borrowers. This is the 'moral hazard' phenomenon: an agent that is insured is apt to be less careful. Monetary authorities should probably leave room for uncertainty as to whether they will rescue markets and banks in difficulty. Intervening in the financial market today may prompt risky behaviour that increases the risk of a crisis tomorrow.

An international financial crisis requires an international lender of last resort, a role played by the IMF during the recent financial crises in Latin America and Asia. Opinions differ, however, regarding the way the IMF should have intervened in the crisis, and what kind of conditionality it should have imposed on the loans that it extended.

KOICHI HAMADA
YALE UNIVERSITY

References

Chang, H.-J. (ed.) (2001) *Joseph Stiglitz and the World Bank: The Rebel Within*, London.
Goldsmith, R.W. (1982) 'Comment on Hyman P. Minsky, *The Financial Instability Hypothesis*', in C.P. Kindleberger and J.P. Laffargue (eds) *Financial Crises, Theory, History and Policy*, Cambridge, UK.
Kindleberger, C.P. (1989) *Manias, Panics and Crashes: A History of Financial Crises*, New York.
Minsky, H.P. (1986) *Stabilizing an Unstable Economy*, New Haven, CT.

Further reading

Feldstein, M. (ed.) (1991) *The Risk of Financial Crisis*, Chicago.
Kindleberger, C.P. (1986) *The World in Depression, 1929–39*, rev. edn, Berkeley, CA.

SEE ALSO: financial contagion; financial regulation; financial system

FINANCIAL REGULATION

In all countries, banks, financial institutions and financial services are regulated and supervised more than virtually all other industries. The three core objectives of regulation and supervision are:

1 to sustain systemic stability,
2 to maintain the safety and soundness of financial institutions, and
3 to protect the consumer.

The ultimate economic rationale for regulation depends on various market imperfections and failures (especially externalities and asymmetric information), which, in the absence of regulation, produce suboptimal results and reduce consumer welfare.

More specifically, six components of the economic rationale for regulation and supervision in banking and financial services can be identified:

1 Potential systemic problems associated with *externalities*.
2 The correction of *market imperfections and failures*.
3 The need for *monitoring* of financial firms and the economies of scale that exist in this activity.
4 The need for consumer *confidence*, which also has a positive externality.
5 The potential for *grid lock*, with associated adverse selection and moral hazard problems.
6 *Moral hazard* associated with the preference of governments to create safety net arrangements: lender of last resort, deposit insurance and compensation schemes.

Two generic types of regulation and supervision are identified: (1) *prudential regulation*, which focuses on the solvency and safety and soundness of financial institutions, and (2) *conduct of business regulation*, which focuses on how financial firms conduct business with their customers.

The case for prudential regulation and supervision of financial firms is that consumers suffer losses in the event of an insolvency of a financial firm with which they conduct business, and that there is a systemic interest in the solvency of finance firms and most especially banks. Consumers are not generally in a position to judge the safety and soundness of financial firms.

Conduct of business regulation and supervision, on the other hand, is concerned with the way in which financial firms conduct business with their customers. It focuses upon mandatory information disclosure, the honesty and integrity of firms and their employees, the level of competence of firms supplying financial services and products, fair business practices, the way financial products are marketed, etc. Conduct of business regulation can also establish guidelines for the objectivity of advice, with the aim of minimizing those principal–agent problems that can arise when principals (those seeking advice) and agents either do not have equal access to information, or expertise to assess it. Overall, conduct of business regulation is designed to establish rules and guidelines about appropriate behaviour and business practices in dealing with customers.

Externalities: systematic issues

Regulation for systemic reasons is warranted when the social costs of failure of financial institutions (particularly banks) exceed private costs, and such potential social costs are not incorporated in the decision-making of the firm. The key systemic point is that banks are potentially subject to runs, which may have contagious effects. The externality is that the failure of an insolvent bank can cause depositors of other banks to withdraw deposits (see Diamond and Dybvig 1983).

Market imperfections and failures

The second economic rationale for financial regulation relates to market imperfections and failures. If financial services were conducted in perfectly competitive markets (i.e. there were no information problems, externalities, conflicts of interest, agency problems, etc.) there would be no case for regulation, and any regulation that was imposed would be a net cost to the consumer. *Per contra*, if there are market imperfections and failures but no regulation, the consumer pays a cost because the unregulated market outcome is suboptimum.

The ultimate rationale for regulation designed to protect the consumer is, therefore, to correct for market imperfections or market failures that would compromise consumer welfare in a regulation-free environment. There are many market imperfections and failures, particularly in retail financial services that offer a rationale for regulation. These include *inter alia* problems of inadequate information on the part of the consumer; problems of asymmetric information (consumers are less well informed than are suppliers of financial services); agency costs (asymmetric information can be used to exploit the consumer); and problems of ascertaining quality at the point of purchase. In many ways financial products are sufficiently different from other goods and services to warrant consumer protection regulation (see Llewellyn 1999).

In a regulation-free environment these imperfections impose potential costs on the consumer. An informed judgement about the purchase of financial products and services cannot be made unless consumers know the true costs of the product, the precise nature of the product or contract, the basis upon which a financial product is offered (e.g. whether the firm is a tied agent or independent adviser), or what the benefit is to an agent (e.g. commission).

Economies of scale in monitoring

Because of the nature of financial contracts between financial firms and their customers, there is a need for continuous monitoring of the behaviour of financial firms. There are several characteristics of some financial products that require a continuous process of monitoring of the suppliers of products: it is often the case that long-term contracts are involved, principal–agent problems can arise, the quality of a financial product cannot be ascertained at the point of purchase, and there is often a fiduciary role for the financial institution, etc. Above all, the value of a product is determined by the behaviour of the supplier after products have been purchased and contracts committed to. This is particularly significant for long-term contracts since the consumer is unable to exit at low cost.

Because most (especially retail) customers are not in practice able to undertake such monitoring, an important role of regulatory agencies is to monitor the behaviour of financial firms on behalf of customers. In effect, consumers delegate the task of monitoring to a regulatory agency. There are potentially substantial economies of scale to be secured through a collective authorization (via 'fit and proper' criteria), and supervising and monitoring of financial firms.

'Lemons' and confidence

A fourth economic rationale for regulation in financial services relates to questions of consumer confidence. The existence of asymmetric information can, under some circumstances, reduce consumer demand for financial services and contracts. In a situation where consumers know there are good and bad products or firms but, due to insufficient and credible information, are unable to distinguish them at the point of purchase because the quality is revealed only after the lapse of time, the demand for some products may decline. Under some circumstances, risk-averse consumers may exit the market altogether. In its extreme form (Akerlof's lemons) the market breaks down completely. This is because the perceived costs of purchasing a low-quality product are valued highly, and consumers may forgo the possibility of purchasing what might be a high-quality product because of the high risk and high cost of unwittingly purchasing a poor product. In such a situation, consumers do not purchase products they believe might be beneficial because they are unable to distinguish high- and low-quality products. An additional role of regulation, therefore, is to set *minimum* standards and thereby remove 'lemons' from the market.

The grid lock problem

It is sometimes argued that financial firms have a rational interest (reputation, etc.) in not behaving against consumers' interests. However, under some circumstances (where long-term contracts are involved, when value cannot be determined at the point of purchase, when firms adopt a short-term time horizon, etc.) firms may gain in the short term by bad behaviour in the knowledge that the consumer may be unaware of this for some considerable time. There are circumstances when, without the intervention of a regulator, a *grid lock* can emerge. The detection of hazardous behaviour may occur only in the long run. In such a situation two problems can emerge: *adverse selection* and *moral hazard*. In the former, good firms may be driven out of business by the bad as the latter undercut the former. The *moral hazard* danger is that good firms are induced to behave badly because they either see bad behaviour in others, or have no assurance that competitors will behave well. In its extreme case, all firms end up behaving badly and knowingly so because they suspect that this is what their competitors will be doing. One role for regulation, therefore, is to set common minimum standards that all firms know will be applied equally to all competitors. Regulation can have a positive and beneficial effect of breaking a *grid lock* by offering a guarantee that all participants will behave within certain standards.

Moral hazard

There is also a moral hazard rationale for regulation, and this is linked to 'safety net' arrangements: deposit insurance and lender of last resort. The existence of a lender of last resort can have *adverse incentive* effects and induce banks into excessive risk-taking. Deposit insurance or protection (even when it is limited as it is in the UK) creates four potential moral hazards. First, consumers may be less careful in the selection of banks and may even seek high-risk institutions on the grounds that, if the bank does not fail, they receive the higher rates of interest on offer, and if it does fail compensation will be received. Second, the financial firm may be induced to take more risk because depositors are protected in the event that the institution fails. Third, risk is subsidized in that, because of deposit insurance, depositors do not demand an appropriate risk premium in their deposit interest rates. Fourth, the existence of deposit insurance may induce banks to hold lower levels of capital. The lender of last resort role (i.e. the possibility that failed banks may be rescued) may also create similar, though perhaps less extensive, moral hazards.

The moral hazard rationale for regulation is, therefore, that regulation can be constructed so as to remove the probability that the moral hazard involved with insurance and compensation schemes will be exploited.

While there is an economic rationale for regulation in finance, this does not mean that optimum regulation has no bounds. There is a cost to regulation and, in one way or another, the consumer pays the cost. Regulation is necessarily about trade-offs and making judgements, particularly when considering costs and benefits.

DAVID T. LLEWELLYN
LOUGHBOROUGH UNIVERSITY

References

Diamond, D.V. and Dybvig, P. (1983) 'Bank runs, deposit insurance and liquidity', *Journal of Political Economics* 91: 401–19.
Llewellyn, D.T. (1999) *The Economic Rationale of Financial Regulation*, London.

Further reading

Goodhart, C.A.E., Hartmann, P., Llewellyn, D., Rojas-Suárez, L. and Weisbrod, S. (1998) *Financial Regulation: Why, How and Where Now?* London.
Gowland, D. (1990) *The Regulation of Financial Markets in the 1990s*, Aldershot.

FINANCIAL SYSTEM

The financial system plays a pivotal role in an economy by facilitating saving and borrowing, transferring resources from savers to investors and financing real economic activity. The financial system comprises a set of *financial markets*, *institutions* and *Exchanges*, which, to some extent, are in competition with each other. Financial institutions are intermediaries between ultimate savers and borrowers, and operate by issuing their own liabilities as a means of funding their loans to borrowers. They offer savers a choice of instruments through which to save. Financial institutions are categorized as banks and other deposit-taking institutions such as, in the UK, building societies; long-term investment institutions (such as life assurance companies, pension funds and investment or unit trusts) and, in some countries, public-sector institutions that are often created in order to finance particular types of investment projects. These different types of institution specialize in different types of assets and liabilities.

Financial markets are categorized as either *primary* (where companies raise new long-term funds for the financing of their expenditure by, for instance, issuing new securities), or *secondary* in which existing securities are traded. The stock exchange is a major example of a secondary market. Exchanges, on the other hand, perform a similar function to secondary markets except that

transactions are often with the Exchange itself. Financial futures markets often operate in this way. In both secondary markets and Exchanges ultimate buyers and sellers often deal via either brokers or market-makers (dealers). In the former case the broker does not take part in the transaction itself (in that it does not buy or sell) but simply puts the buyer in touch with the seller. Market-makers act differently in that they 'make a book' by standing ready to buy what ultimate sellers are selling and sell to ultimate buyers what they want to buy.

Five major roles are performed by the financial system, though the way these roles are performed varies from one country to another:

1 It performs *financial intermediation* services (channelling funds from one set of agents to another), which means that, by intermediating between different transactors (e.g. savers and borrowers), resources are transferred from those who have excess financial resources to those who wish to borrow.
2 It provides a wide range of other *financial services* such as payments services, insurance, fund management, etc.
3 It creates for consumers a wide range of *assets and liabilities* with different characteristics so that their particular preferences can be satisfied.
4 It engages in *asset transformation* through financial firms having assets and liabilities with different characteristics that, in the process, enables risks to be shifted to those who are more willing and able to accept them.
5 Through pricing signals (such as interest rates) it creates incentives for the *efficient allocation of resources* within the economy.

These are clearly important roles for they impinge on every aspect of the economy and, because of (5), may also have an impact on the overall efficiency of the economy.

While the role and functions of financial systems are universal, financial systems in different countries vary considerably in structure and operation. In particular, the relative role of organized markets and financial institutions varies between countries. However, the basic functions of the financial system are universal in that they apply to all systems. These universal functions are:

- To manage the *payments and settlements system*.
- To provide mechanisms for the *borrowing and lending* of funds so as to remove short-term budget constraints.
- The provision of mechanisms for the *pooling of funds* and the financing of large-scale projects beyond the capability of individual savers.
- To bridge different *portfolio preferences* of ultimate suppliers and borrowers of funds. For instance, in general, savers prefer short-term assets while borrowers prefer long-term liabilities.
- The provision of mechanisms for the *transfer of financial (and hence real) resources* over time, space and agents.
- To *allocate funds to their most efficient use* in an economy as, for instance, indicated by risk-return criteria. This requires markets and institutions to accurately assess risks of borrowers and to reflect these risks in the interest rates charged to borrowers.
- As most financial transactions involve the future, and the future is necessarily uncertain, a central function of the financial system is to enable agents to *manage uncertainty* by creating risk-sharing facilities.
- To *price risk* and enable risks to be transferred between different agents according to their ability and willingness to absorb them.
- To offer facilities and markets enabling wealth-holders to *change the structure of their portfolios* of assets and liabilities.
- To deal with problems of *asymmetric information* and the resolution of the resultant issues of moral hazard and adverse selection. A central problem is that not all transactors have the same information or abilities to assess available information. This creates potential moral hazard whereby those with superior information can use it to the disadvantage of counterparties to a transaction. Financial systems have evolved various techniques to deal with this problem and thereby enable transactions to take place.
- To offer a range of *specialist financial services* that are demanded in society (insurance, financial advice and fund management, for example).

The financial system performs some of these roles by issuing different types of assets and liabilities. Financial instruments are essentially of three different types: debt, equity and insurance. Debt contracts (such as a bank loan) require the borrower to repay the loan on specified terms irrespective of his or her performance. If an investment project financed by a loan is not successful, the borrower is not absolved from paying interest and repaying the loan. This means that, except in the extreme case of default and bankruptcy, the risk is borne by the borrower. However, it also means that the lender does not share in the upside potential of the project if the project being financed performs even better than was initially anticipated. This is because in a debt contract the terms of the loan are fixed in advance. In an equity contract, on the other hand, the return to the lender is determined by the performance of the borrower: if the project performs well both the lender and borrower share the gain, but equally both share the downside risk that the project performs badly. In contrast to debt contracts, the lender and borrower share the risks. A major example of an equity contract is when a company issues shares (often referred to as equities) that are bought by investors. If the company performs well, high dividends may be paid, and usually the secondary market price of the shares rises. In this way both the company and the shareholders gain. Conversely, if the company performs badly the company may choose not to pay a dividend. However, the company is never required to repay equity capital to shareholders.

An insurance contract is where a risk-averse transactor pays a premium in order to shift risk to others. The simplest example is when an insurance company charges a premium to a transactor in return for which it compensates the transactor in the event that the risk materializes. The insurance company is able to do this because of the law-of-large-numbers. It knows, for instance, that while a small number of houses will be destroyed by fire in any one year, because it has insured a very large number of houses it has spread its risk. In this way it can offer insurance contracts because it is able to diversify its risks to a greater extent than can those who seek insurance. More complex insurance-type contracts include forwards and options contracts. A transactor can therefore protect himself against a future price rise by, for instance, engaging in a forwards transaction or buying a futures contract that guarantees the transaction price at a specified future date. For instance, a company with a known commitment to pay foreign currency to a supplier of goods in 3 months' time is subject to an exchange rate risk. If its own currency depreciates in value over the 3 months, the domestic currency value of its foreign currency commitment will rise. It can protect itself by buying the foreign currency forwards today, at a price agreed today, but for delivery to take place in 3 months' time. As it is locked into the agreed price, it has removed the risk of domestic currency depreciation. An options contract offers the same risk transfer facility except that this requires the transactor to pay a premium at the outset in order to have the option (but not the obligation) to transact at a specified price at some future date. Whether the option is exercised by the buyer of the option at the future date depends on whether the market price at that time is above or below the price (strike price) agreed within the options contract at the outset. Options exist in many commodities and financial instruments, and are either call options (an option to buy) or put option (an option to sell). In all these cases, risk-averse transactors (i.e. those who do not wish to take risk) are able to protect against the uncertainty of the future.

Overall, the financial system deals in risks of various types and enables the preferences of transactors with different risk profiles and appetites to be met. An issue arises as to why one transactor is prepared to accept the risks that are being transferred from another (the counterparty). There are three main reasons. First, the counter-party might be a speculator who is willing to take the risk in order to make a speculative profit. In the case above, the counter-party believes that the currency being sold forwards will not decline but will rise in the 3 months, in which case, if the judgement proves to be correct, a speculative profit will be earned. This amounts to the two counterparties having different risk appetites. Second, the counter-party (e.g. an insurance company) might be more able to absorb the risk because it has the advantages of economies of scale and an ability to diversify risks to a greater extent than can the insured agent. A third possibility is that two transactors have equal and opposite risks, and both wish to remove the risk. Thus, one counter-party that has a commitment to supply foreign currency in the future buys the foreign currency forwards from a

transactor who has an equal liability to sell foreign currency in the future. By transacting with each other both have removed risk as both now have a guaranteed price.

These basic functions (both individually and collectively) impinge on all aspects of the economy and are central to its performance. It follows that the efficiency of the financial system in performing these universal functions is potentially vital to the efficiency of the economy as a whole. The efficiency of a financial system is important for an economy because it can determine the cost of intermediation (as measured, for instance, by the difference between deposit and lending interest rates of financial institutions), the incentives to save and invest, the efficiency of the allocation of scarce resources in an economy, the extent to which risks can be shifted away from those who do not want to take them, and the discipline on borrowers to behave appropriately after funds have been borrowed. The banking system in particular has a pivotal role in the economy that distinguishes it from all other industries. It is in this sense that banking (and the financial system generally) are unique and special amongst industries.

DAVID T. LLEWELLYN
LOUGHBOROUGH UNIVERSITY

Further reading

Heffernan, S. (1995) *Modern Banking in Theory and Practice*, London.

Merton, R. (1990) 'The financial system and economic performance', *Journal of Financial Services Research* (December): 263–99.

Saunders, A. and Cornett, M. (2001) *Financial Markets and Institutions*, Boston.

SEE ALSO: banking; capital, credit and money markets; financial contagion; financial crisis; financial regulation

FIRM, THEORY OF

The role of specialization in economic progress was emphasized by Adam Smith. Now specialized activities need to be co-ordinated, either by conscious integration within an organization or through market relationships; the effects of both organizational forms and market structures on economic performance are topics that date back at least to Smith. However, few economists have tried to treat the firm simultaneously as an organization and as a component of an industry or market. Marshall (1919, 1920) was one of the few, and business enterprise was at the core of his theory of economic development (Raffaelli 2003). The problems of the firm were problems of acquiring, generating and using knowledge: knowledge of production methods, existing and potential markets, and of ways to construct an organization and encourage initiative among its members. The firm's customers, suppliers and competitors, including potential competitors, at once constrained its actions and provided opportunities to those who could perceive and exploit them; those opportunities were enhanced by the development of trade connections. For the analysis of this complex evolutionary process the methods of static equilibrium offered some useful guidance, but could be misleading if rigorously pressed; there was no substitute for the detailed investigation of particular organizational and market arrangements, in relation to the technical conditions and demand characteristics of each case.

Marshall's successors ignored his advice, and the study of the firm disintegrated. The major activities of firms were defined away by the assumption of fully specified demand and cost functions, and the 'theory of the firm' became a set of exercises in constrained optimization, by which equilibrium price and output were derived for a series of market structures – perfect and imperfect competition, oligopoly and monopoly – and the effects of change read off from shifts in demand or cost curves. Cournot's (1990 [1838]) analysis was reinvented. Robinson's *The Economics of Imperfect Competition* (1933) epitomized the triumph of the formal model, and with it the dominance of problems generated within the theoretical structure, for the origins of imperfect competition theory lay in the logical impossibility of reconciling increasing returns (statically defined) with perfectly competitive equilibrium. Both were concepts that Marshall had avoided.

Chamberlin's (1933) conception of monopolistic competition was substantially different. Whereas Marshall had insisted that elements of competition and monopoly were usually blended in practice, Chamberlin set out to blend them in theory, and tried to incorporate both product variation and selling costs within a formal analysis that used the method (though often not the language) of static equilibrium. Despite his limited success, he provided the primary inspiration for the strong US tradition in industrial economics, though some of its practitioners borrowed their welfare criteria from Robinson. Chamberlin's approach was also distinguished by his attention to oligopoly, which steadily increased over the years. His insistence that oligopolistic behaviour (like all rational choice) depends on expectations, and that there could be no general theory of oligopoly because there could be no general theory of expectations, has haunted theorists ever since.

There are many specific models of oligopoly, though most restrict themselves either to relationships within the group (as, for example, the dominant firm and kinked demand models) or to the barriers, natural or artificial, against new entrants, and do not attempt to deal with both issues together – an example of economists' aversion to multilevel analysis. Andrews (1949) exceptionally tried to develop a non-formal theory of competitive oligopoly, in which the threat of cross-entry and the desire of managers to show themselves worthy of promotion might combine to ensure good value for the customer's money – especially if the customer was another firm – but neither his methods nor his conclusions were acceptable. However, the situational determinism that is apparently so effective in producing general solutions for other market structures will not deliver equivalent results for oligopoly, and the application of game theory, still heavily dependent on Cournot (updated by Nash) for its equilibrium concepts, has multiplied the possibilities. This has prompted some game theorists to look to psychology to improve their predictive ability and their understanding, but not yet to organizational factors, as Simon has urged.

Instead of examining a standard firm in different market structures, Baumol (1959) proposed to deduce the effects of different managerial objectives in oligopoly. He assumed that a firm's decision-makers sought to maximize not profit, but sales revenue; Williamson (1963) subsequently proposed a managerial utility function, and Marris (1964) favoured growth. In all three models, decision-makers were constrained not only by market opportunities but also by their shareholders: in the first two through the need to provide an acceptable profit, and in the third through the risk of takeover. Each model generated some plausible contrasts to the results of profit maximization; yet, despite assuming oligopoly, none attempted to deal seriously with interdependence, and, though invoking organizational factors to justify their choice of managerially oriented objectives, none offered any analysis of organizational influences on behaviour.

In 1937 Coase had argued that firms came into existence when formal organization could undercut the costs of market transactions, but his implicit invitation to examine how and when this might be possible has elicited a tardy and sparse response, which has been dominated by Williamson (1975, 1985). Most economists have preferred to extend market analysis into the firm, explaining the boundaries of the firm as incentive-compatible solutions to various kinds of hold-up problem but paying scant attention to the fundamental uncertainties of technology and markets, and none at all to internal organization (see Milgrom and Roberts 1992). Though Williamson also relies on efficiency arguments, he believes that bounded rationality often precludes the *ex ante* assurance of incentive compatibility, and insists that firms make extensive use of hierarchical fiat.

Yet even Williamson has very little to say about the actual problems and processes of decision-making, which are the focus of what is usually called (in economics) behavioural theory. This theory is characterized by its emphasis on the inadequacy of knowledge, and on the limited ability of people to make use even of what knowledge they think they have. Simon's (1976) proposal to substitute procedural for substantive rationality makes obvious sense at a time of much concern over control systems, information systems, techniques of planning, and the machinery of government. To Simon's (1978) problem of how to decide what to do should be added the prior question of how to decide what to think about – a question that might also be addressed to economists analysing the firm. Cyert and March's (1963) study of short-term decision-making has not been widely followed up, but Nelson and Winter (1982) have shown how the approach may be incorporated in an evolutionary theory of technical change.

The development of evolutionary reasoning has revived interest in the firm as an agent of discovery and progress. This was a key element in Schumpeter's (1943) theory of economic development through 'creative destruction', but Schumpeter is not usually thought of as a theorist of the firm. However, Casson (2003 [1982]) depicts the entrepreneur as the creator of an organization, facing some of the problems discussed by Marshall. Meanwhile, studies of innovation and technical change have increasingly recognized the need to investigate how organizational form as well as market structure influences the generation, transmission and exploitation of knowledge, and also the effects of these processes on markets and organizations. For this purpose there is no better definition of a firm than Penrose's (1959) 'pool of resources the utilisation of which is organised in an administrative framework' and no better application of that definition than the historical studies of Chandler (1962, 1990).

Capabilities now challenge transaction costs as the basis for analysing the firm, and evolutionary and cognitive psychology offer a theoretical explanation of the common observation that capabilities are domain specific; thus firms, like species, exemplify Smith's theory of the division of labour. The capabilities of a firm reside in its institutions as well as its skills. These institutions embody the consequences, intended and unintended, of boundedly rational choice: co-ordination, in firms as well as markets, reflects spontaneous order as well as conscious design. Indeed, we may be returning to Marshall's conception of a population of specialized firms generating variety within an evolutionary process that both respects and exploits the nature of human beings and the characteristics of the human mind – especially its ability to create and apply patterns. If so, we should remember Marshall's recognition of interfirm linkages – a theme explored by Richardson (1972) – and the importance of markets as a pool of resources offering variety (Langlois 1992). Firms and markets would then feature as complementary and competitive institutions that both shape and are shaped by the course of evolution.

BRIAN J. LOASBY
UNIVERSITY OF STIRLING

References

Andrews, P.W.S. (1949) *Manufacturing Business*, London.

Baumol, W.J. (1959) *Business Behavior, Value and Growth*, New York.

Casson, M. (2003 [1982]) *The Entrepreneur: An Economic Theory*, Oxford.

Chamberlin, E.H. (1933) *The Theory of Monopolistic Competition*, Cambridge, MA.

Chandler, A.D. (1962) *Strategy and Structure*, Cambridge, MA.

—— (1990) *Scale and Scope*, Cambridge, MA.

Coase, R.H. (1937) 'The nature of the firm', *Economica* ns 4.

Cournot, A. (1990 [1838]) *Researches into the Mathematical Principles of the Theory of Wealth*, New York.

Cyert, R.M. and March, J.G. (1963) *A Behavioral Theory of the Firm*, Englewood Cliffs, NJ.

Langlois, R.N. (1992) 'Transaction cost economics in real time', *Industrial and Corporate Change* 1.

Marris, R.L. (1964) *The Economics of 'Managerial' Capitalism*, London.

Marshall, A. (1919) *Industry and Trade*, London.

—— (1920) *Principles of Economics*, 8th edn, London.

Milgrom, P. and Roberts, J. (1992) *Economics, Organization and Management*, Englewood Cliffs, NJ.

Nelson, R.R. and Winter, S.G. (1982) *An Evolutionary Theory of Economic Change*, Cambridge, MA.

Penrose, E.T. (1959) *The Theory of the Growth of the Firm*, Oxford.

Raffaelli, T. (2003) *Marshall's Evolutionary Economics*, London.

Richardson, G.B. (1972) 'The organisation of industry', *Economic Journal* 82.

Robinson, J.V. (1933) *The Economics of Imperfect Competition*, London.

Schumpeter, J.A. (1943) *Capitalism, Socialism and Democracy*, London.

Simon, H.A. (1976) 'From substantive to procedural rationality', in S.J. Latsis (ed.) *Method and Appraisal in Economics*, Cambridge, UK.

—— (1978) 'On how to decide what to do', *Bell Journal of Economics* 9.

Williamson, O.E. (1963) *Economics of Discretionary Behavior: Managerial Objectives in a Theory of the Firm*, Englewood Cliffs, NJ.

—— (1975) *Markets and Hierarchies: Analysis and Anti-Trust Implications*, New York.

—— (1985) *The Economic Institutions of Capitalism: Firms, Markets, Relational Contracting*, New York.

Further reading

Langlois, R.N., Yu, T.F. and Robertson, P. (eds) (2002) *Alternative Theories of the Firm*, 3 vols, Cheltenham.

SEE ALSO: competition policy; corporate enterprise; industrial organization; transaction costs

FIRST-LANGUAGE ACQUISITION

Children hear language all around them from birth on; adults and older children talk to them, and this talk is critical to first-language acquisition. When infants acquire a first language, they learn one of the most complex social skills of their lives. They attain adult levels of skill in some domains by the age of 5 or 6, in others not until the early teens. How do they learn a system that requires mastery of a sound system, a huge vocabulary, syntactic constructions, meanings, and rules for usage in many different settings from everyday exchanges to giving instructions to telling stories? The degree to which language skills could be innate versus learnt in this complex task has long intrigued psychologists, linguists and philosophers. In their efforts to answer this question, researchers have kept detailed longitudinal records of how children advance from babbling to words to complex utterances, and carried out a variety of experimental studies to track children's errors and the stages they go through along the way (Tomasello and Bates 2001; Bloom 1994). Researchers have also turned their attention to similarities and differences in the acquisition of a variety of languages besides English, from Korean and Japanese to West Greenlandic, Walpiri, Finnish, Samoan, Kaluli, and many more (Slobin 1985, 1992, 1997).

When children start to talk (anywhere from 12 to 18 months), they usually produce just one word at a time. But they soon combine two or more, moving from utterances like *Raisin* to *More raisin* to *Me want raisin*. They use nouns to pick out objects, often in such roles as agent, patient or location, and verbs to pick out events. They mark information as 'given' versus 'new' in conversation, and later also come to mark grammatical relations like Subject-of and Direct-Object-of through inflections or word order. To do all this, children must learn how to modulate the meanings of nouns and verbs. To learn inflections, they must identify stems and endings in words, and the meanings of each, together with any variants in form. For example, the plural of *cat* in English is pronounced [kats] (with an 's' sound) while the plural of *dog* is [dogz] (with a 'z'). Learning variants can take time. In addition, some common words may be irregular. Compare regular *cat/cats* or *dog/dogs* in English with *mouse/mice*, *child/children* or *sheep/sheep*; or regular *jump/jumped* or *look/looked* with *go/went*, *sit/sat* or *bring/brought*. Children are pattern makers; they often regularize irregulars to produce plurals like *foots* and *mans*, and create past-tense verb forms like *comed*, *buyed* and *hitted*, before learning the irregular forms (Clark 2003). English contains few inflections, but in more highly inflected languages, children learn case, gender and number marking on nouns and adjectives, as well as marking for tense, aspect, person and number on verbs.

Most children start to produce word combinations and inflections around age 2. In the next few months, they elaborate their utterances: they add demonstratives, articles and quantifiers (*that, the, some*); adjectives (*stuck, wet*); auxiliary and modal verbs (*do, be, can, will*). They add adverbs and prepositional phrases (*there, in the cupboard; loudly, in a hurry*); adverbial clauses (*They were tired WHEN THEY GOT HOME*); relative clauses (*the boy WHO WAS WATCHING THEM*); and complements (*They wanted TO RUN AWAY, She said THAT SHE WAS COMING*) (Clark 2003). But children also take time to acquire syntactic constructions. Many of their early productions may omit the appropriate conjunction (*before, while*) or complementizer (*that, to*), or contain the wrong one for the meaning intended. Utterance forms and their functions are not always well co-ordinated during acquisition.

Acquisition of vocabulary plays a major role in language acquisition. Children learn words very rapidly, moving from a vocabulary of 100–400 words at age 2 to around 14,000 by age 6. By the time they are adults, they may have up to 50,000 (or more) at their disposal. During acquisition, children identify word-forms and quickly map meanings on to them (Bloom 2001). They analyse complex words into stems and affixes, and use these, when needed, to coin words with new meanings (the verb *to scale* for adult 'weigh', the nouns *sander* for one who grinds pepper or *far-see-er* for 'telescope'). Such coinages emerge from around age 2 onwards to fill gaps in the child's current vocabulary (Clark 1993). But words work only if people recognize what is being said, and children try hard to produce recognizable versions. Their earliest words may bear little resemblance to adult forms (consider [ga] for *squirrel*), so to get words right, children must listen and store what they hear, hone their articulatory skills and identify the relevant sounds in each word attempted. When they produce words, they must match their own forms to the adult versions (stored in memory), moving closer with practice, for example, from simple consonant–vowel combinations (e.g. [do] for *dog*), to adding final consonants (e.g. [dog]),

and managing consonant clusters (e.g. from [kai] to [krai], for *cry*). By age 3, much of what children say can be readily understood (Clark 2003).

Learning the structure of a language makes up only part of acquisition. Children must also learn how to *use* their language appropriately. For instance, they need to learn how to make requests and what counts as polite. And by age 4, many children distinguish among *Give me some cake, Can I have some cake? Could I have some cake please?* and *That cake looks very good, doesn't it?* They must also learn how to persuade, how to give instructions, and how to ask for information appropriate to the problem. As their knowledge of form and meaning expands, they also begin to master such skills as storytelling. Lastly, children can learn two languages just as readily as one (McLaughlin 1984). But the point at which they start on the second may make a difference. The earlier they start, the more the acquisition of a second or third language looks like acquisition of the first. In addition, how well a second or third language is learnt depends in part on the social value it carries in the larger community.

Finally, throughout acquisition, adults (the experts) offer children essential information about the conventions of the language to be acquired. They may direct children's attention to the details of a language by repeating children's erroneous utterances in conventional form and so displaying a more appropriate version for what a child apparently intended, or they offer direct instruction by telling children how to ask for something, how to apologize, or how to make a request. In short, adult speech to children displays the conventional forms of the language in use and thereby also demonstrates how the words and expressions of a language partition conceptual spaces in the world being talked about (Bowerman and Levinson 2001; Clark 2003).

EVE V. CLARK
STANFORD UNIVERSITY

References

Bloom, P. (ed.) (1994) *Language Acquisition: Core Readings*, Cambridge, MA.
—— (2001) *How Children Learn the Meanings of Words*, Cambridge, MA.
Bowerman, M. and Levinson, S.C. (eds) (2001) *Lan-*

guage *Acquisition and Conceptual Development*, Cambridge, UK.

Clark, E.V. (1993) *The Lexicon in Acquisition*, Cambridge, UK.

—— (2003) *First Language Acquisition*, Cambridge, UK.

McLaughlin, B. (1984) *Second-Language Acquisition in Childhood*, 2 vols, 2nd edn, Hillsdale, NJ.

Slobin, D.I. (ed.) (1985, 1992, 1997) *The Crosslinguistic Study of Language Acquisition*, 5 vols, Hillsdale, NJ.

Tomasello, M. and Bates, E. (eds) (2001) *Language Development: The Essential Readings*, Oxford.

SEE ALSO: developmental psychology

FOCUS GROUPS

In a focus group, the researcher collects qualitative data by asking a set of participants to discuss a specific topic. The focus therefore comes from the researcher, while the 'group' provides the data through their conversation. Focus groups were originally developed in the 1940s by Paul Lazarsfeld and Robert Merton (Merton *et al.* 1990), but they were far more popular in marketing research until they re-emerged in social science research during the 1980s. A search of electronic databases indicates that over a thousand social science articles using focus groups now appear every year.

The principal advantage of focus groups is the opportunity they provide to hear a variety of people exchange views with reference to a specific issue. As the participants discuss the researcher's questions, their conversation shows the range of their perspectives on these topics. In the best focus groups, this discussion also sheds light on not just *what* the participants feel, but *why* they feel the way they do, providing insights into the sources and meanings of different experiences and opinions (Morgan 1997).

Focus groups not only generate qualitative data, but they can also be of use in the development of surveys and other questionnaires, in generating content for social service programmes, in creating various forms of media, in evaluating programmes, and in contributing to participatory action research. However, they also have their limitations. A form of interview, focus groups provide data on attitudes and self-reports but not on actual behaviour. They produce a range of perspectives, rather than in-depth information about any of the individual participants.

Every focus group project requires four basic decisions:

- Who will be interviewed?
- What questions to ask?
- How to conduct the interview?
- How to analyse the data?

The need to take care about who will be interviewed follows from the importance of maintaining both a well-focused discussion and a good group dynamic. At the most basic level, the participants must be capable of discussing the issues that are relevant for the researcher, and it is therefore obviously a good idea if the people in the group are interested in the topic under discussion. Generating an active conversation also requires a set of participants who feel comfortable discussing the topic with each other.

The classic approach to group composition in focus groups is segmentation, i.e. the sorting of participants into sets of homogeneous groups. Segmentation has two advantages. First, it is easier for the participants to interact comfortably when they share similar perspectives on the issue under discussion, especially when it is a sensitive topic – and focus groups are commonly used to investigate difficult issues such as domestic violence, sexuality and substance abuse (see Farquhar and Das 1999). Second, dividing the full set of groups into homogeneous subsets allows the researcher to compare the perspectives of these different segments. It is important to emphasize, however, that segmentation is most effective when the participants are separated into homogeneous groups according to their perspectives on the topic itself (Fern 2001), rather than on the basis of purely demographic factors such as gender and age that may have little to do with the actual subject matter of the research.

The composition of the focus groups needs to be settled before decisions are made about what questions to ask, since the interview content must be well matched to group composition. Less structured approaches usually employ a few, broad, open-ended questions that emphasize the participants' point of view, and this approach is especially useful for exploratory research. More structured approaches put a larger number of more specific questions that emphasize the researcher's point of view. In either case, many different kinds of questions may be appropriate for generating discussions (see Krueger 1998; Krueger and Casey 2000).

The interviewer in a focus group is known as the 'moderator'. It is a common misconception that the moderator somehow produces the data in a focus group when in fact it is the participants who provide the data. Of course, the moderator is an important factor in this process, but other factors such as group composition, the interview questions, and the overall context of the research may be just as important. Focus groups are actually relatively 'robust' with regard to moderating, as long as the participants are responding to a set of questions that genuinely interest them, since this level of engagement is sufficient to ensure an effective discussion.

Approaches to moderating can also be either less or more structured. The goal in less structured focus groups is often to explore the participants' perspective, so the moderator plays a less central role and is mainly concerned with facilitating the group's own conversation. For example, a researcher who was constructing a survey questionnaire on a well-defined topic would want to concentrate on hearing the participants' ways of expressing the topic in their own words, in order to craft meaningful survey items. More structured focus groups are typically driven by the researcher's agenda, so the moderator takes a more active role, keeping the discussion focused on the topic and moving the group through the full set of interview questions.

The final step in any focus group project is to analyse the data. Typically, the data in focus groups are captured via audio recordings and then transcribed. The procedures for analysis are then similar to those applied to many other forms of qualitative or textual data. Because the data come from a relatively small number of people who were usually chosen in a non-representative fashion, there is seldom any point in doing a statistical analysis. One unique consideration in focus groups is that the data are provided by *groups* of individuals. Consequently, if the analysis labels something an 'important theme', then that theme should not only occur in almost every group but also provoke a response from almost everyone in each of those groups.

One interesting recent development in the analysis of focus groups draws attention to the interactive processes that occur during the discussion, using conversation analysis and discourse analysis. These tools are particularly useful for investigating how group participants both use and challenge elements of the 'dominant discourse'. For example, Wilkinson and Kitzinger (2000) examine the ways that cancer patients deal with advice that they should respond to their illness by 'thinking positively', while Hollander (2002) locates alternative discourses that question whether women truly are the 'weaker sex'.

It is important to remember that social science researchers have been using this method on a significant scale only for the past two decades. As a result, a coherent tradition of methodological research on focus groups is still being developed (Morgan 1993, 2001).

DAVID L. MORGAN
PORTLAND STATE UNIVERSITY

References

Farquhar, C. with Das, R. (1999) 'Are focus groups suitable for "sensitive" topics?' in R. Barbour and J. Kitzinger (eds) *Developing Focus Group Research*, Thousand Oaks, CA.

Fern, E.F. (2001) *Advanced Focus Group Research*, Thousand Oaks, CA.

Hollander, J.A. (2002) 'Resisting vulnerability: The social reconstruction of gender in interaction', *Social Problems* 49(4).

Krueger, R.A. (1998) *Developing Questions for Focus Groups*, Vol. 3 in D. Morgan and R. Krueger (eds) *Focus Group Kit*, Thousand Oaks, CA.

Krueger, R.A. and Casey, M.A. (2000) *Focus Groups: A Practical Guide for Applied Research*, 3rd edn, Thousand Oaks, CA.

Merton, R K., Fiske, M. and Kendall, P.L. (1990) *The Focused Interview*, 2nd edn, New York.

Morgan, D.L. (1993) 'Future directions for focus groups', in D.L. Morgan (ed.) *Successful Focus Groups: Advancing the State of the Art*, Thousand Oaks, CA.

—— (1997) *Focus Groups as Qualitative Research*, 2nd edn, Thousand Oaks, CA.

—— (2001) 'Focus group interviews', in J. Gubrium and J. Holstein (eds) *The Handbook of Interview Research*, Thousand Oaks, CA.

Wilkinson, S. and Kitzinger, C. (2000) 'Thinking differently about thinking positive: A discursive approach to cancer patients' talk', *Social Science and Medicine* 50(6).

Further reading

Morgan, D.L. (1998) *Planning Focus Groups*, Vol. 2 in D. Morgan and R. Krueger (eds) *Focus Group Kit*, Thousand Oaks, CA.

SEE ALSO: interviews (qualitative)

FOLKLORE

Folklore is a metacultural category used to mark certain genres and practices within modern societies as being not modern. By extension, the word refers to the study of such materials. More specific definitions place folklore on the far side of the various epistemological, aesthetic and technological binary oppositions that distinguish the modern from its presumptive contraries. Folklore therefore typically evokes both repudiation and nostalgia.

The concept emerges fully in the context of nineteenth-century nationalism, building on such precursors as 'pagan', 'superstition', 'custom' and 'antiquities'. 'Folk' and 'folklore' develop in close parallel to 'primitive' and 'anthropology'. The latter point to the colonial other of the modern nation-state; the former, to its internal other. While both disciplines connect forms of culture to kinds of people, it can be said that anthropology concentrates on the people and folklore on the forms. Institutionally, folklore scholarship is more closely bound to the arts and humanities than to the social sciences. Nonetheless, these forms have been used to define a category of people, the 'folk', variously contrasted to elites, outsiders, the masses or the working class.

While the 'primitives' of anthropology have traditionally been studied by emphatically metropolitan scholars, the relationship between Us and Them is more ambiguous in folklore. Folklore is a political discourse situating certain populations – peasants, minorities, workers and immigrants – within the nation-state. Useful to governments, it is still more important to these 'marked' populations as they strive for integration, allowing them to represent themselves in a voice the metropolis is willing to hear. In the university context, folklore has always been precariously situated and ritually impure, for its concepts and vocabulary circulate freely between the academy, government agencies, social movements, commercial enterprises and voluntary associations. Here I review seven overlapping definitions of folklore and the uses, scholarly and otherwise, to which they have been put.

Survival

Folklore is the residue of a past form of life. The word 'Folk-Lore', coined in 1846 by the English antiquarian William Thoms, marks a primarily epistemological definition of folklore as a kind of knowledge dependent on tradition and habit rather than rational enquiry. This definition follows on medieval theologians' account of peasant belief as 'superstition', the unthinking reproduction of pagan practice. By the time of E.B. Tylor's evolutionary anthropology (1871), folklore was clearly defined as 'survival': not cohesive primitive culture but its leftovers, found in social backwaters and even among educated people in those aspects of life that do not fall under rational scrutiny. This zone of belief and custom was the principal focus of nineteenth-century English folklore scholarship. While few folklorists today believe it possible to reconstruct a lost past by extrapolating from contemporary practices, the idea that folklore provides a privileged window into ancient mysteries persists with unabated vigour among neo-pagan and New Age movements, and others seeking an epistemological vacation from the ugliness of modern rationality.

National tradition

Folklore is the historical core of national culture. Against the evolutionary narrative of modernity's triumph stands what Dundes calls the 'devolutionary' narrative of cultural decay, put forward by the Romantic opposition (1975). But romantic nostalgia was quickly recuperated into a modernizing project: the nation-state. Herder and others argued that oral poetry, most famously represented by Homer and surviving in the songs of European peasants, was both mechanism and archive of the collective interactions through which the *Volk* and their language emerge in history (Bauman and Briggs 2003). Macpherson's Ossian poems for Scotland (1760), Lönnrot's *Kalevala* for Finland (1835), the *Barzaz-Breiz* of de La Villemarqué for Brittany (1839), and Longfellow's *The Song of Hiawatha* for the USA (1855) were recreations of a presumed lost national unity intended to foster such unity in the present. All of these texts, along with such encyclopedic prose narrative collections as the Grimms' *Kinder-und Hausmärchen* (1819), have been both denounced as fabrications and defended as the authentic utterance of a people. Believing themselves the legitimate inheritors of the national tradition, the romantic compilers manipulated that tradition in the service of its political fulfilment. The oral tradition could provide the basis for an autonomous national literature; more importantly it could be used to claim that it was the *vox populi*, not that of a middle-class minority, calling for national independence. The very compilation of the great anthologies, archives and ethnographic museums was a process of nation-building, fostering ongoing interaction between provincial intellectuals.

Less familiar is the place of folklore in well-established states. From the time of Philip II of Spain to that of Napoleon, states distributed ethnographic questionnaires to local officials in search of resources for economic and cultural development as well as a fuller knowledge of the populations to be governed. The idea of the folk was also invoked to counter religious and class divisions. James I and VI's *Book of Sports* (1618) put local festivals in the service of English national integration. In eighteenth-century Europe, the idealization of rural popular cultures developed in tandem with the surveillance and repression of urban ones. By the nineteenth century, the 'folk' was being put forward as an explicit alternative to an emerging working-class identity, with paternalist elites cultivating participatory local traditions.

By the twentieth century, folklore (and in particular dance and costume) had become so ubiquitous a means of representing the 'people' as to be thoroughly ambiguous politically. The festival practices through which Catalans expressed nationalist refusal of Franco's Spain in the 1960s and 1970s were cultivated by that very regime in the 1940s and 1950s to display 'provincial' adherence to the centralist project. The folk dances performed during the Cold War by anti-communist Eastern Europeans in the USA were often learned from the performances of the Moiseyev Dance Company, touring from the Soviet Union (Shay 2002). Nationalist intellectuals in the former Yugoslav countries argue that the conflicts of the 1990s arose from socialist repression of national traditions, while their critics point out the intense institutionalization and popularization of these national 'folklores' by that very socialist state, as well as the subsequent nationalist use of folklore to incite and legitimate genocide (Colovic 1994).

Oral tradition

Folklore is verbal art transmitted across time and space by word of mouth. Paradoxically, nation-alists had also to be comparativists, and as they sought the Ur-forms of local tales they discovered not only apparent cognates within related languages, but also diffusion across linguistic and racial boundaries. The structural features of oral narrative and the mechanism of oral transmission became the most continuous and productive questions in academic folklore research. The Grimms' comparative philology was formalized in the 'Finnish method', resulting in Aarne and Thompson's *The Types of the Folk-Tale* (3rd edn, 1961) and Thompson's monumental *Motif-Index of Folk Literature* (1955–8). Vladimir Propp's *Morphology of the Folk Tale* (1928) provided a formalist alternative, and Lévi-Strauss's structuralism an extreme means of reducing the diversity of international oral tradition to a universal underlying schema.

Another line of scholarship considers orality as a distinct mode of generating text. Parry and Lord argued that oral epic was not memorized, but composed in performance through the use of rhythmic formulae (Lord 2000 [1960]). Boasian linguistic anthropology provided another source for the US study of 'verbal art as performance' in the 1970s. In contrast to the focus on 'competence' in Chomsky's linguistics, the performance approach privileged the social interactions in which new meanings and expressive possibilities emerge. The performance approach treated oral tradition not as inert reiteration but creative, strategic communication, features that the Civil Rights movement and the folksong revival had demonstrated in practice. Focusing on the expressions of indigenous groups and racial minorities, the performance approach and the 'ethnography of communication' that followed defend the complexity and worth of non-literate expression (Hymes 1975; Bauman and Briggs 2003).

Face-to-face culture

Folklore is vernacular culture acquired through informal interaction. In the 1970s, orality became too narrow a framework for US scholars, who needed to address the use of new media by 'folk' populations and, indeed, to defend a disappearing disciplinary subject (Kirshenblatt-Gimblett 1998a). European scholars had always attended to both popular literacy and material culture, but they too needed a framework to replace nationalism. The prevailing definition became 'artistic communication in small groups' (Ben-Amos 1971); the reference to traditionality disappeared. Everyone has folklore: it is the ground of everyday expression out of which institutionalized and individualized forms develop. This view allowed folklore to be distinguished from mass as well as high culture, and privileged not the pure but the creole. It had deep roots in the USA, where the American Folklore Society was founded in 1888 in explicit opposition to evolutionary anthropology, positing that European settlers, Africans brought by force, indigenous peoples and recent immigrants all have lore that is shaped by historical processes. This levelling definition continues to be useful in the USA, where applied folklorists teach doctors that both Hmong refugees and WASPs may engage in non-institutional healing practices.

Community culture

Folklore is the set of practices defining community membership. European folklorists had already noted the differentiation of peasant costume in the modern period: increasing prosperity and communications strengthened rather than weakened the outward signs of local identity. 'Folklife' scholars observed that US regional and sectarian groups carried this tendency still further (Yoder 1990), and the proliferating subcultures of contemporary society turn music, costume and cuisine into badges of identity. In sympathy with this self-fashioning, US folklorists since the 1970s have tended to write ethnographies according the same integrity and plenitude to 'folk groups' within Western societies as functionalist anthropology once granted to the 'primitive'. Another view defines folklore as 'differential identity', or shibboleth, arguing that much of what we call folklore takes shape in conflict and commerce rather than community intimacy. More recently, US folklorists have embraced perforce the prevailing equation of culture and identity, their professional situations increasingly fostering the study of particular group 'cultures' rather than cultural practices as such. Here they have explored the conscious cultivation of tradition by both new groups seeking adherents and threatened groups trying to hold on. Many suspect institutional multiculturalism of wanting to trivialize difference into empty emblems, noting that the 'traditional costume' worn at an 'ethnic festival' is a very

different matter from the Muslim headscarf worn to school.

Cultural resistance

Folklore is counter-hegemonic culture. Classic Marxism conceives of folklore as a feudal survival that must give way to a new proletarian consciousness. Gramsci opened the way to a more complex view by arguing that folklore was at least distant from mainstream culture, and that its inertia could be read as resistance. Southern Italian and Latin American folklorists have followed this line of reasoning in studies of popular religion. Labour historians have identified more activist adaptations of traditional culture by peasants and workers in their struggles for autonomy. Prominent in the USA has been the political use of folksong in labour unions, African American institutions and the Civil Rights movement, all fostering the wider folksong revival; more recently, urban legend and rumour have been explored for their critical content (Fine and Turner 2001). Subsequent research has returned to older 'folklore' and discovered coded expressions of resistance in the expressions of dominated groups (Abrahams 1992; Scott 1990). Feminists have questioned the unity of the small group and pointed out that the apparent irrationality of laments, lullabies and children's games allows the expression of subversive messages (Radner and Lanser 1993).

Market niche

Folklore is a mode of cultural production within modernity. Scholars have turned from the condemnation of 'fakelore' or 'folklorismus' to a serious examination of the commodification of tradition in tourism and other industries. Once the romantic slogan against modernity's alienation, 'authenticity' has become a certification according scarcity value to folklore (Bendix 1997). But general demand necessitates increased production, and categories such as 'folk art' and 'folk music' have become recognized stylistic niches, continually generating new work. The heritage industry recycles old forms, turning rubbish into museum pieces, productive activity into tourist performance, and lifeworld into theme park (Kirshenblatt-Gimblett 1998b). Local culture has become a key resource for economic development not just in developing countries but in depopulating rural and industrial zones of the

West: folklorists both study and participate in this phenomenon.

Folklore today

Like anthropology, folklore in the last third of the twentieth century undertook a reckoning with its past, confronting fascist and Stalinist legacies, and meeting the challenges of new social movements. A large scholarship now examines the history of the concept and its political mobilization. Both state folklore institutes in former socialist countries and university departments in the West continue to redefine themselves. Often they repudiate the stigmatized 'F-word'. Europeans have turned to 'ethnology', a label allowing folklore to merge with cultural anthropology. Americans are tempted by the adjectives 'world' and 'multicultural', the globalized equivalents of the nation-state's 'folk'.

While 'folklore' has a separate life outside the academy in Europe, US folklorists have found relative prosperity in retaining close ties between academic and public work. The climate is more populist: the Clinton administration put folklorists in charge of the National Endowments of the Arts and of the Humanities to appease both the conservative right and the multicultural left. Today the American Folklore Society represents the largest, most heterogeneous body of self-identified folklorists in the world, with about 2,200 members. Most but not all have graduate training in the field. Slightly less than half are employed in a range of university departments, including fifteen or so programmes in folklore (or an updated label). The rest work in government and non-profit institutions, either in documentation and interpretation (organizing festivals, curating exhibitions, producing radio shows) or in cultural intervention (designing refugee support services, training medical students in cross-cultural communication, providing technical assistance to community organizations). Sometimes it appears that nothing holds them together but the scarlet letter F. But as culture and identity become key concepts in global political struggles, they find increasing urgency in that survival.

DOROTHY NOYES
THE OHIO STATE UNIVERSITY

References

Abrahams, R. (1992) *Singing the Master: The Emergence of African American Culture in the Plantation South*, New York.

Bauman, R. and Briggs, C. (2003) *Voices of Modernity: Language Ideologies and the Politics of Inequality*, Cambridge, UK.

Ben-Amos, D. (1971) 'Toward a definition of folklore in context', *Journal of American Folklore* 84.

Bendix, R. (1997) *In Search of Authenticity: The Formation of Folklore Studies*, Madison, WI.

Colovic, I. (1994) *Bordell der Krieger: Folklore, Politik, und Krieg*, Osnabrück.

Dundes, A. (1975) *Analytic Essays in Folklore*, The Hague.

Fine, G.A. and Turner, P. (2001) *Whispers on the Color Line: Rumor and Race in America*, Berkeley.

Hymes, D. (1975) 'Folklore's nature and the sun's myth', *Journal of American Folklore* 88.

Kirshenblatt-Gimblett, B. (1998a) 'Folklore's crisis', *Journal of American Folklore* 111.

—— (1998b) *Destination Culture. Tourism Museums, and Heritage*, Berkeley.

Lord, A. (2000 [1960]) *The Singer of Tales*, Cambridge, MA.

Radner, J. and Lanser, S. (1993) *Feminist Messages. Coding in Women's Folk Cultures*, Urbana, IL.

Scott, J. (1990) *Domination and the Arts of Resistance: Hidden Transcripts*, New Haven, CT.

Shay, A. (2002) *Choreographic Politics. State Folk Dance Companies, Representation and Power*, Middletown, CT.

Yoder, D. (1990). *Discovering American Folklife: Studies in Ethnic, Religious, and Regional Culture*, Ann Arbor, MI.

Further reading

Bendix, R. and Welz, G. (eds) (1999) *Cultural Brokerage: Forms of Intellectual Practice in Society*, special issue, *Journal of Folklore Research* 36.

Dundes, A. (ed.) (1999) *International Folkloristics*, Lanham, MD.

Feintuch, B. (ed.) (2003) *Eight Words for the Study of Expressive Culture*, Urbana, IL.

SEE ALSO: memory, social; oral history; popular culture

FORECASTING AND PREDICTION

The terms 'forecasting' and 'prediction' are used interchangeably in the literature. Forecasting is needed when there is uncertainty about decisions related to the future. Many decisions involve uncertainty, and in these cases formal forecasting and prediction procedures (referred to as 'forecasting' below) should prove useful. Forecasting procedures can also help to assess the uncertainty surrounding a forecast, enabling decision-makers to account for risk. Our description concentrates on economic and business forecasting, although many of the conclusions apply to other topics, for instance forecasting natural phenomena such as earthquakes or changes in the world climate.

With some notable exceptions, research on forecasting began in earnest around 1960. Brown (1959) introduced exponential smoothing, still one of the most widely used forecasting methods. In 1981, the International Institute of Forecasters was founded, a multidisciplinary society of researchers from statistics, economics and psychology. Also, in the 1980s, the *Journal of Forecasting* and the *International Journal of Forecasting* were launched. In the late 1990s a 'Principles of Forecasting' project was established, with publications (Armstrong 2001), and a website, http://www.forecastingprinciples.com.

Forecasting methods

Forecasting methods can be classified into two principal groups, those based primarily on judgemental sources of information and others that use statistical sources. Makridakis *et al.* (1998) provide details on most of these methods. While progress in forecasting has been achieved through application of structured and quantitative techniques, many managers continue to depend on subjective forecasts when it comes to making important decisions. In practice, unaided judgement sometimes provides accurate forecasts, but greater accuracy is usually achieved when decision-makers adopt a systematic approach to analysing available information. The challenge is to develop procedures that most effectively blend quantitative and judgemental methods (see Armstrong and Collopy 1998).

Judgementally based approaches

Intentions studies ask people to predict their behaviour in various situations. For example, potential customers could be asked how likely it is that they will buy a particular new product. Intention studies are widely used, and they are particularly useful when there is limited data on past behaviour.

Role-playing facilitates forecasts by showing how people behave in conditions that simulate the anticipated situation. Subjects make substantially different decisions depending on the roles they are assigned in these exercises (Armstrong 2001: Ch. 2). Role-playing studies prove to be much more accurate than expert opinions (or any other technique) in forecasting decisions made in conditions where there is conflict, as in labour–management negotiations, buyer–seller conflicts, or conflicts among countries (Green 2002).

Another approach is to ask experts to predict how others will behave in given situations. The accuracy of expert forecasts can be improved by using structured methods, such as the Delphi procedure, which gives better results than standard committee procedures (Rowe and Wright 2001). Delphi is an iterative survey procedure in which experts provide independent forecasts for a problem, receive anonymous feedback on forecasts made by other experts, and then make another forecast for the same event. This process can continue for two or more rounds of estimates. Delphi freeware is available at the http://www.forecastingprinciples.com website.

Conjoint analysis is a method of collecting and analysing consumer judgements. It allows forecasters to examine how the features of a situation (such as a new product design) affect intentions (to purchase the product). Each situation provides a bundle of features that have been varied according to an experimental plan. The relative importance of the different features can then be identified by relating them to the data on intentions, using various statistical methods. Conjoint analysis has been applied extensively in forecasting sales of new products.

Statistical approaches

Extrapolation methods use only historical data to make predictions. One can extrapolate over time ('tomorrow's weather will be...') or make cross-sectional forecasts ('Will our next employee be more successful than average?'). The extrapolation of time-series is widely used for short-term forecasts of inventory and production. The most popular and cost effective of these methods are based on exponential smoothing, which gives more weight to recent data.

The last 30 years have seen substantial research on developing new methods of extrapolation. These include the Box–Jenkins procedure (Box *et al.* 1994 [1976]), state space methods (Harvey 1990) and non-linear methods such as neural networks (Zhang *et al.* 1998). While their value applied to economic problems remains uncertain, they hold more promise for physical systems where well-established deterministic non-linear models are informative.

Armstrong (2001: Ch. 8) reviewed research on extrapolation. Some important principles for effective forecasting are: (1) seasonally adjust data; (2) use simple methods; (3) extrapolate when historical trends are consistent; (4) be more conservative in the extrapolation of trends as uncertainty about the forecast increases (e.g. forecast smaller changes from the most recent value); and (5) use long time-series when developing a forecasting model.

Quantitative extrapolation methods typically assume that present trends will continue, or, more precisely, that the causal forces that have affected a historical series will continue to operate in the same way in the future. When these forces change, forecast errors tend to be large, and the effects may be disastrous (Armstrong 2001: Ch. 9). One useful safeguard is the principle that trends should be extrapolated only when they coincide with the informed expectations of managers. In general, judgemental extrapolations are preferable to quantitative extrapolations when there have been large changes in the series, and where decision-makers have relevant knowledge. Quantitative extrapolations have an advantage when the data are ample and large changes are expected. Quantitative methods are also less expensive than judgemental ones when an organization has to produce many forecasts.

Expert systems formalize the procedures that experts use when forecasting. Protocols are commonly used to discover the rules used by asking an expert to talk about the way in which he or she proceeds. Alternatively, the rules might be inferred by regressing an expert's forecasts against the data used by the experts, a procedure called judgemental bootstrapping. Rule-based forecasting makes use of guidelines from research on forecasting, together with domain information. This approach gives differential weights to forecasts that employ different extrapolation methods. Expert systems and rule-based forecasting have been shown to be more accurate than traditional extrapolations for many types of data (Armstrong 2001: Chs 6, 9 and 10).

Data-based multivariate models infer causality from the data. Much research has been done to apply these models to economic time-series. They have had some success in credit assessment, where a cross-sectional set of descriptor variables are used to assess customer credit risk (Thomas 2000), and have now almost totally replaced judgemental approaches in this field, both because of their effectiveness and for legal reasons. There is, however, little evidence to suggest that data-based methods improve the accuracy of time-series forecasting.

Econometric models draw on economic theory to select variables, specify directions of relationships and select functional form. They can also be used to constrain estimates of relationships. The resulting models can be estimated by analysing time-series, longitudinal or cross-sectional data. They are widely used in macroeconomic and market forecasting (see Allen and Fildes 2001). Research has also begun to identify the reasons that some econometric models fail to provide accurate forecasts (Clements and Hendry 2002). Forecasts based on econometric models rely heavily on the judgemental expertise of the model builder. The expert's preliminary model-based estimates are often informally adjusted. In macroeconomic forecasting these adjustments lead to improved accuracy (Fildes and Stekler 2002).

Econometric models can relate forecasts directly to planning and decision-making, and they can incorporate the effects of decision variables as well as variables that represent key aspects of the environment. They are therefore appropriate when one needs to forecast what will happen under different assumptions about the environment, or when considering different strategies (Fair 2002).

Econometric methods are most useful when: (1) strong causal relationships are expected; (2) these relationships are known or can be estimated from data; (3) large changes are expected to occur in the causal variables over the forecast horizon; and (4) the changes in the causal variables can be accurately forecasted or controlled, especially with respect to their direction. If any of these conditions does not hold, econometric methods are unlikely to be more accurate than simple extrapolations. Empirical comparisons suggest that on balance they do outperform extrapolation (Allen and Fildes 2001). Above all, it is essential that the selection of causal variables is based upon theory and on domain knowledge, and that the model captures the primary characteristics and relationships in the data.

Selection of methods

A key issue in forecasting, which is of both practical and theoretical importance, is how to select the most appropriate and reliable forecasting procedure in particular cases. Among the considerations that must be kept in mind are: (1) the amount and type of data available; (2) whether the factors likely to determine future developments are well understood; and (3) whether large changes are expected in these factors (Armstrong 2001: Ch. 12).

In selecting forecasting methods one should compare the accuracy of forecasts delivered by alternative methods as applied to similar situations in the past. Significant progress has been made in testing procedures (Armstrong 2001: Ch. 12). One area of research compares the results produced by various extrapolative and econometric methods. First, a suitable measure of performance has to be agreed upon. The use of the mean square error is now thought inappropriate as it is not invariant to scale and is influenced by outliers. Measures judged against a benchmark, such as the median relative absolute error, resolve these problems.

Assessing uncertainty

Forecasting may also be used to assess uncertainty. Early approaches to this issue generally relied upon the fit to historical data, and this may provide a reasonable approximation for prediction intervals, especially for cross-sectional data. Where time-series are concerned, however, the historical fit typically leads to prediction intervals that are too narrow, and so may mislead decision-makers (see Chatfield 2001). The best approach is to simulate the actual forecasting procedure and to make forecasts for holdout data. The distribution of forecast outcomes can then be used to assess uncertainty. In the case of a 5-year forecast, for example, assess the accuracy of many 5-year forecasts.

Conclusions

Forecasting has flourished since the 1960s, in part due to the growth in data and increased computing power, but also following the development of new methods and new procedures for evaluation. The importance of such new developments is exemplified by the award of the 2003 Nobel Prize in economics to Clive Granger for his contribution to time-series econometrics and Rob Engle for his work on assessing uncertainty. The impact of forecasting research has been further enhanced by its concentration upon empirical testing of alternative approaches as exemplified by the M-Competition studies (Ord et al. 2000), an approach that is readily understood by decision-makers facing uncertainty. Research has begun to address the conditions under which various methods are most appropriate, an agenda that should prove useful both in producing practically useful findings and in improving forecasting methods.

J. SCOTT ARMSTRONG
THE WHARTON SCHOOL,
UNIVERSITY OF PENNSYLVANIA
ROBERT FILDES
LANCASTER UNIVERSITY

References

Allen, P.G. and Fildes, R.A. (2001) 'Econometric forecasting', in J.S. Armstrong (ed.) *Principles of Forecasting*, Boston, MA.

Armstrong, J.S. (ed.) (2001) *Principles of Forecasting*, Boston, MA.

Armstrong, J.S. and Collopy, F. (1998) 'Integration of statistical methods and judgment for time series: Forecasting: Principles from empirical research', in G. Wright and P. Goodwin (eds) *Forecasting with Judgment*, Chichester.

Box, G.E., Jenkins, G.M. and Reinsel, G. (1994 [1976]) *Time Series Analysis for Forecasting and Control*, 3rd edn, San Francisco.

Brown, R.G. (1959) *Statistical Forecasting for Inventory Control*, New York.

Chatfield, C. (2001) 'Prediction intervals', in J.S. Armstrong, (ed.) *Principles of Forecasting*, Boston, MA.

Clements, M.P. and Hendry, D.F. (2002) 'Explaining forecast failure in macroeconomics', in *A Companion to Economic Forecasting*, Oxford.

Fair, R.C. (2002) *Predicting Presidential Elections and Other Things*, Stanford, CA.

Fildes, R. and Stekler, H. (2002) 'The state of macroeconomic forecasting (with discussion)', *Journal of Macroeconomics* 24: 435–505.

Green, K.C. (2002) 'Forecasting decisions in conflict situations: A comparison of game theory, role-playing, and unaided judgement', *International Journal of Forecasting* 18: 321–44 (with commentary, pp. 345–95).

Harvey, A.C. (1990) *Forecasting, Structural Time Series Models, and the Kalman Filter*, Cambridge, UK.

Makridakis, S., Wheelwright, S. and Hyndman, R.J. (1998) *Forecasting Methods and Applications*, New York.

Ord, K., Hibon, M. and Makridakis, S. (2000) 'The M3 competition (with commentary)', *International Journal of Forecasting* 16: 433–519.

Rowe, G. and Wright, G. (2001) 'The Delphi technique as a forecasting tool', in J.S. Armstrong, (ed.) *Principles of Forecasting*, Boston, MA.

Thomas, L.C. (2000) 'A survey of credit and behavioural scoring: Forecasting financial risk of lending to consumers', *International Journal of Forecasting* 16: 149–72.

Zhang, G.P., Patuwo, B.E. and Hu, M.Y. (1998) 'Forecasting with artificial neural networks. The state of the art', *International Journal of Forecasting* 14: 35–62.

Further reading

Clements, M.P. and Hendry, D.F. (eds) (2001) *A Companion to Economic Forecasting*, Oxford.

SEE ALSO: futurology

FOUCAULT, MICHEL (1926–84)

Michel Foucault, born in a prosperous bourgeois family at Poitiers, was successively a university teacher (professor at Clermont-Ferrand and at Paris-Vincennes) and, from 1970, professor of the history of systems of thought at the Collège de France.

Among the central categories of his thought – which developed and changed from the early 1960s to the 1980s – are those of the *episteme* (a so-called assemblage of social knowledge conventions), as well as the epistemic break (historical discontinuity); of the method called the *archaeology of knowledge*, which makes a study of such epistemic systems; of the *discourse* or discursive formation (an organized body of social thought); of the *dispositif* (which came to displace the concept of episteme in Foucault's analyses and which, unlike the episteme, includes non-discursive as well as discursive elements) together with the associated notion of the *genealogical* method; and of *biopower* (the typically modern form of power exercised over bodies reduced to docility – for example in the mental health system, in prison regimes or in the Church confessional); of power in relation to the *production of truth*; and of *parrhesia*, or truth-telling, which Foucault took to be his task and indeed duty, thus distancing himself from the alternative roles of prophet or sage.

What especially interests Foucault is a study of the historical conditions of the emergence of the modern subject, which is at one and the same time an expression of Kantian freedom and autonomy, and an object of study for the social and behavioural sciences.

At first sight – and on account of the title of his chair at the Collège de France – one might take Foucault to be engaged in a kind of history of ideas. In fact, he refuses any such simple characterization of his work. His *The Archaeology of Knowledge* (1972 [1969]) is indeed directed against the discipline called 'the history of ideas', which he takes to be something like a totalizing project that tries to rewrite the past in order to produce an artificially unified object of study. In the same book he criticizes certain aspects of his own earlier work, for example the presupposition of the existence of a 'general subject of history' contained in *Madness and Civilization* (1967 [1961]). In *The Order of Things* (1970 [1966]) Foucault claims that humankind – 'man' – is a modern invention and moreover likely, in that guise, to disappear. Such an assertion may suggest an interpretation of Foucault as a structuralist, for he takes this idea of *man*, in the contemporary sense, to be a product of nineteenth-century structures of knowledge. But in *The Archaeology of Knowledge* he had already turned against the structuralist leanings of his earlier texts.

The problem in this connexion appears to lie in the use made in those texts of the concept of *episteme*, which, as a contingent historical 'a priori', determines the manner in which the world is generally experienced by a given epoch. But can a study of the history of the appearance and disappearance of epistemic formations itself make use of the concept of *episteme* as an *explanatory* tool? If not, what instruments can help to explain epistemic 'eruptions' and 'ruptures'? Foucault came to insist that such explanations must be rooted in 'the regime of materiality', meaning the *institutions* in which the material relations structuring discursive events are embodied.

Knowledge therefore has to be accounted for in terms of institutions, and of the events that take place within these institutions – events of a technical, economic, social and especially political nature. But institutions cannot function without the exercise of *power*. Thus Foucault turns next to an examination of the question of power; this, being institutional, is not and cannot be personal in origin or character. But he also takes a distance from the Marxist conception: unlike Marxists he puts the emphasis not on some 'mechanistic' process whereby social and political power is explained in terms of economic ownership, but rather on what he calls the 'strategies' of power. In order to avoid any sort of anthropocentrism, he explains that by the term 'strategy' he means not the conscious plan or design of some human individual or group but 'the effect of a strategic position'.

The merely descriptive – and structuralist – notion of the *episteme* is now subordinated to a properly historical conception of the emergence or 'eruption' of new epistemic configurations, including new sciences, a conception that is indeed (see above) avowedly materialist.

Power, he argues, is located in strategies that are operative at every level: they cannot be reduced to the power of, for example, the state or of a ruling class. Power, he adds, is productive (and in particular productive of knowledge). He talks about a 'microphysics of power', power disseminated throughout the whole of society. There are of course clashes between the multifarious and multilevelled strategies of power. What is not clear is how the outcome of such clashes and similar processes is to be explained, given that no general mechanism of the generation of power is offered. Foucault has thus been criticized for providing, at the theoretical level, no more (though no less) than a *metaphysics* of power.

This critique does not detract from the interest of the detailed studies carried out by him (often in collaboration with pupils): for instance, his study of prisons and imprisonment, *Discipline and Punish* (1977 [1975]) and of *The History of Sexuality*, Vol. 1 (1979 [1976]).

Foucault's metaphysics of power – if such it is – is in any case, as we have seen, a microphysics. This point is worth underlining in the light of the subsequent exploitation made of his work by the so-called '*nouveaux philosophes*' (André Glucksmann and others), who drew on some of its themes or vocabulary in order to produce a violently anti-Marxist metaphysics of the state – otherwise called a theory of totalitarianism – which reintroduces the idea, rejected by Foucault, of a single centre of power (see Glucksmann 1977).

In some of his later texts Foucault turned to an explicit consideration of matters of ethics, in particular in connexion with the theme of power. There is no society, he insists, without power relations, that is to say, without the subjection of free individuals – or without resistance to that subjection. Ethics enters when it is a matter of the exercise of power not just over others, but over oneself. Thus, for instance, there is an essential difference between ancient Greek and Christian ethics, the former being oriented around a conception of self-mastery, the latter rather around a vision of the self-denial of the flesh (*Care of the Self* (1998 [1984])). And in his late essay on 'What is Enlightenment?' Foucault claims that the Enlightenment project is one of a 'critical ethos', namely of permanent self-creation in autonomy – an ethos that can be 'reactivated' as a critique of our own historical era (in Rabinow 1984 [1982]).

In the years following his death from an AIDS-related illness, Foucault's reputation has if anything grown. Texts continue to be published from his literary remains (*Abnormal*, 2003 [1999]; *Dits et ecrits*, 3 vols, 1994–2001; *Essential Works of Foucault, 1954–1984*, 3 vols, 1997–2001); and there is now an enormous secondary literature.

GRAHAME LOCK
RADBOUD UNIVERSITY, NIJMEGEN,
THE NETHERLANDS

References

Glucksmann, A. (1977) *Les Maitres penseurs*, Paris.
Rabinow, P. (1984 [1982]) *The Foucault Reader*, Harmondsworth.

Further reading

Deleuze, G. (1988) *Foucault*, Minneapolis.
Dreyfus, H. and Rabinow, P. (1982) *Michel Foucault: Beyond Structuralism and Hermeneutics*, Brighton.
Foucault, M. (1977) *Language, Counter-Memory, Practice*, ed. D. Bouchard, Oxford.
—— (1979) *Power, Truth, Strategy*, eds M. Morris and P. Patton, Sydney.
—— (1980) *Power/Knowledge*, ed. C. Gordon, Brighton.
Sheridan, A. (1981) *Michel Foucault: The Will to Truth*, London.
White, H. (1979) 'Michel Foucault', in J. Sturrock (ed.) *Structuralism and Since*, Oxford.

FRANKFURT SCHOOL

The Frankfurt School refers to the work of members of the *Institut für Sozialforschung*, which was established in Frankfurt, Germany, in 1923 as the first Marxist-oriented research centre affiliated with a major German university. Under its director, Carl Grunberg, the Institute's work in the 1920s tended to be empirical, historical and oriented towards problems of the European working-class movement, although theoretical works by Karl Korsch, Georg Lukács and others were also published in its journal, *Archiv für die Geschichte des Sozialismus und der Arbeiterbewegung*.

Max Horkheimer became director of the Institute in 1930, and gathered around him many talented theorists, including Erich Fromm, Herbert Marcuse and T.W. Adorno. Under Horkheimer, the Institute sought to develop an interdisciplinary social theory that could serve as an instrument of social transformation. The work of this era was a synthesis of philosophy and social theory, combining sociology, psychology, cultural studies and political economy. The results appeared in its own journal, *Zeitschrift für Sozialforschung* (1932–41), which contains a rich collection of articles and book reviews still worth reading.

The first major Institute project in the Horkheimer period was a systematic study of authority, an investigation into individuals who submitted to irrational authority in authoritarian regimes, which culminated in a two-volume work, *Studien über Autorität und Familie* (1936). Fascism was a major interest during the 1930s and the Institute members wrote a series of studies of German fascism including Franz Neumann's *Behemoth* and a number of studies by Herbert Marcuse collected in the volume *Technology, War, and Fascism* (Kellner 1998).

Most members of the Institute were both Jews and Marxist radicals, and were forced to flee Germany after Hitler's ascendancy to power. The majority emigrated to the USA and the Institute became affiliated with Columbia University from 1931 until 1949, when key members returned to Frankfurt. From 1936 to the present, the Institute referred to its work as the 'critical theory of society'. For many years, 'critical theory' stood as a code for the Institute's Marxism and was distinguished by its attempt to found a radical interdisciplinary social theory rooted in Hegelian-Marxian dialectics, historical materialism and the Marxian critique of political economy and theory of revolution. Members argued that Marx's concepts of the commodity, money, value, exchange and fetishism characterize not only the capitalist economy but also social relations under capitalism, where human relations and all forms of life are governed by commodity and exchange relations and values.

Horkheimer (1972 [1937]) claimed in a key article 'Philosophie und kritische Theorie' [Traditional and critical theory] that since 'the economy is the first cause of poverty, theoretical and practical criticism has to direct itself primarily at it'. Institute members were convinced that the capitalist economy was driving bourgeois society to catastrophe through its underlying cycle of production, anarchy, depressions, unemployment and wars. They believed that increasing tendencies towards bureaucratization and social rationalization were destroying the features of individuality and freedom that the capitalist system extolled as its prize creation.

Horkheimer (1972 [1937]) wrote that critical theory's

> content consists of changing the concepts that thoroughly dominate the economy into their opposites: fair exchange into a deepening of social injustice; a free economy into monopolistic domination; productive labour into the strengthening of relations which inhibit production; the maintenance of society's life into the impoverishment of the people's.

The goal of critical theory is to transform these social conditions, and provide a theory of 'the historical movement of an epoch that is to come to an end'.

Critical theory produced theoretical analysis of the transformation of competitive capitalism into monopoly capitalism and fascism, and some members hoped to be part of a historical process through which capitalism would be replaced by socialism. Horkheimer claimed that

> The categories which have arisen under its influence criticize the present. The Marxist categories of class, exploitation, surplus value, profit, impoverishment, and collapse are moments of a conceptual whole whose meaning is to be sought, not in the reproduction of the present society, but in its transformation to a correct society.

Critical theory is thus motivated by an interest in emancipation and is a philosophy of social practice engaged in 'the struggle for the future'. Critical theory must remain loyal to the 'idea of a future society as the community of free human beings, in so far as such a society is possible, given the present technical means'.

In a series of studies carried out in the 1930s, the Institute for Social Research sketched out theories of monopoly capitalism, the new industrial state, the role of technology and giant corporations in monopoly capitalism, the cultural industries and the decline of the individual. It articulated theories that were to be central to social theory for the next several decades. Rarely, if ever, has such a talented group of interdisciplinary workers come together under the auspices of one institute. They managed to keep alive critical social theory during a difficult historical era and provided aspects of a neo-Marxian theory of the changed social reality and new historical situation in the transition from competitive capitalism to monopoly capitalism.

During the Second World War, the Institute split up due to pressures of emigration and war. Adorno and Horkheimer moved to California, while Lowenthal, Marcuse, Neumann and others worked for the US government as their contribution in the fight against fascism. Adorno and Horkheimer worked on their collective book, *Dialectic of Enlightenment* (1972 [1947]), which contains implicit critiques of Marxism, as well as fascism and consumer capitalism. Departing from the Marxian theory of history, they presented a philosophy of history that traced the fate of the Enlightenment from the beginning of scientific thought with the Greeks to fascist concentration camps and the cultural industries of US capitalism. They showed how Western rationality served as instruments of domination and how 'Enlightenment' turned into its opposite, mystification and oppression. The book criticized Enlightenment scientism and rationalism, and implicitly implicated Marxism within the 'dialectic of Enlightenment'.

After the Second World War, Adorno, Horkheimer and Pollock returned to Frankfurt to reestablish the Institute in Germany, while Lowenthal, Marcuse and others remained in the USA. In Germany, Adorno, Horkheimer and their associates published a series of books and became a dominant intellectual current in Germany. At this time, the term 'Frankfurt School' became widespread as a characterization of their version of interdisciplinary social research and of the particular social theory developed by Adorno, Horkheimer and their associates. They engaged in frequent methodological and substantive debates with other social theories, most notably 'the positivism dispute', where they criticized

more empirical and quantitative approaches to social theory and defended their own more speculative and critical brand of social theory. The German group around Adorno and Horkheimer was also increasingly hostile towards orthodox Marxism and were in turn criticized by a variety of types of 'Marxism-Leninism' and 'scientific Marxists' for their alleged surrender of revolutionary and scientific Marxian perspectives.

During the 1960s, Herbert Marcuse aligned himself with the student movement and became a guru of the New Left, leading to critical exchanges of letters with Horkheimer and Adorno (see Kellner 1984 and Marcuse 2001). Habermas emerged in the 1970s as one of the world's major philosophers and social theorists, and the Frankfurt School became influential in a variety of disciplines ranging from philosophy and social theory to art history and media studies.

The Frankfurt School became known for their theories of 'the totally administered society' or 'one-dimensional society', which theorized the increasing power of capitalism over all aspects of social life and the development of new forms of social control. During the 1950s, however, there were divergences between the work of the Institute relocated in Frankfurt and the developing theories of Fromm, Lowenthal, Marcuse and others who did not return to Germany, which were often at odds with both the current and earlier work of Adorno and Horkheimer. Thus it is misleading to consider the work of various critical theorists during the postwar period as members of a monolithic Frankfurt School. Whereas there were both a shared sense of purpose and collective work on interdisciplinary social theory from 1930 to the early 1940s, critical theorists frequently diverge thereafter, and during the 1950s and 1960s the term the 'Frankfurt School' can really be applied only to the work of the Institute in Germany.

It is accordingly not possible to characterize the Frankfurt School as a whole. Their work spanned several decades and involved a variety of thinkers who later engaged in sharp debates with one another. Rather one should perceive various phases of Institute work. (1) The empirical-historical studies of the Grunberg era; (2) attempts in the early to mid-1930s to establish a materialist interdisciplinary social theory under Horkheimer's directorship; (3) attempts to develop a critical theory of society during the exile period from about 1937 to the early 1940s; (4) the dispersion of Institute members in the 1940s and new directions sketched out by Adorno and Horkheimer in *Dialectic of Enlightenment*; (5) the return of the Institute to Germany and its work in Frankfurt during the 1950s and 1960s; (6) the development of critical theory in various ways by Fromm, Lowenthal, Marcuse and others who remained in the USA; (7) the continuation of Institute projects and development of critical theory in Germany by Jürgen Habermas, Oskar Negt, Alfred Schmidt and others in the 1970s and 1980s; (8) contributions to critical theory by younger theorists and scholars currently active in Europe and the USA.

In surveying the field of critical theory, one observes a heterogeneity of theories, theorists and projects loosely connected by commitment to interdisciplinary social theory, and an interest in social critique and transformation, all influenced by the work of theorists like Adorno, Horkheimer, Marcuse, Habermas or others. Critical theorists tend to be critical of empirical and quantitative social theory and more sympathetic to theoretical construction, social critique and social transformation. It continues to be an active, though frequently marginal, tendency of social theory and continues to influence a wide range of disciplines and theorists throughout the world.

DOUGLAS KELLNER
UNIVERSITY OF CALIFORNIA, LOS ANGELES

References

Horkheimer, M. (1972 [1937]) 'Traditional and critical theory', in *Critical Theory*, New York.
Horkheimer, M. and Adorno, T.W. (1972 [1947]) *Dialectic of Enlightenment*, New York.
Kellner, D. (1984) *Herbert Marcuse and the Crisis of Marxism*, London and Berkeley.
—— (ed.) (1998) *Herbert Marcuse: Technology, War and Fascism, Collected Papers of Herbert Marcuse, Volume 1*, London and New York.
Marcuse, H. (1998) *Technology, War and Fascism*, London and New York.
—— (2001) *Toward a Critical Theory of Society*, London and New York.
Neumann, F. (1966) *Behemoth. The Structure and Practice of National Socialism 1933–1944*, New York.

Further reading

Jay, M. (1973) *The Dialectical Imagination*, Boston, MA.
—— (1984) *Adorno and the Frankfurt School*, London.
Kellner, D. (1989) *Critical Theory, Marxism and Modernity*, Baltimore, MD.
Marcuse, H. (1984) *One-Dimensional Man*, Boston, MA.
Wiggershaus, R. (1994) *The Frankfurt School*, Cambridge, UK.

SEE ALSO: Habermas; Marx's theory of history and society

FREE TRADE

Free trade refers to an arrangement whereby international trade proceeds without tariffs or quotas on imports, subsidies to exports, or other types of government intervention that serve to alter the volume or composition of trade. When international trade takes place in the presence of such interventions, protection is said to occur. Arguments in favour of free trade typically derive from Ricardo's (1817) theory of comparative advantage, which shows that all nations, even those that are at an absolute disadvantage in the production of all goods, will nevertheless benefit from trade. This benefit takes the form of increased world production due to specialization in production and increased choices in the allocation of goods that may be consumed. More precisely, if social welfare corresponds to the welfare of individuals irrespective of their location, then because free trade guarantees that no production and/or consumption distortions are present, a worldwide perfectly competitive equilibrium yields a globally Pareto-optimal allocation. This conclusion follows directly from the first theorem of welfare economics, the hypotheses of which are satisfied under free trade. Thus, arguments in support of global free trade are primarily based upon its normative properties.

Dating back to the work of Samuelson (1939, 1962), theoretical models illustrating the efficiency gains that arise from free trade have typically been static in nature. While empirical estimates of these efficiency gains have, in a number of instances, been non-trivial, recent theoretical work on the links between trade and economic growth suggest that these static estimates most likely understate, perhaps significantly, the efficiency gains that emanate from free trade. In particular, the removal of trade barriers, be they tariffs or quotas, tends to increase the volume of trade as well as the level of international competition that producers face.

Over time, this in turn eliminates the economic profits that are earned under protection and so drives out inefficient producers while leaving behind the most efficient producers who are then able to exploit scale economies and therefore produce at a lower per unit cost.

A related source of dynamic efficiency gains occurs as increased international competition forces domestic firms to innovate, which in turn raises their productivity. These innovations may occur in order that domestic producers do not lose market share to foreign producers and/or remain competitive with potentially more efficient international producers. To the extent that trade flows capture the strength of these pressures, as Grossman and Helpman (1991) suggest, the removal of trade barriers, by raising the level of trade, raises the flow of technological spill-overs from one country to another. Since these spill-overs raise the productivity of capital and labour, it follows that trade liberalization will increase not just an economy's level of income, but its rate of growth as well. As the welfare effects stemming from increasing the rate of growth of output far outweigh those stemming from increasing the level of output, increasing technological spill-overs represent an important new argument for the removal of trade barriers.

A third argument offered in support of free trade is one based upon political realities. Inasmuch as the benefits of removing trade barriers are typically diffuse whereas the costs of doing so, to certain industries say, are typically concentrated, the latter often play a larger role in the political process than do the former. If so, then trade policy is being formulated along the line being advocated by special interest groups. Rather than succumb to such pressures, one can argue that national welfare would be enhanced by letting free trade serve as the nation's policy without exceptions. Whether or not political commitment of this sort is possible in practice is not obvious, however.

Despite the general stance of economists in support of free trade, or, failing that, freer trade, the profession does argue one case where protection may be warranted. When a nation is large enough that its actions can affect the world price for certain goods, it may be optimal, from a purely nationalistic, as opposed to a global, welfare point of view, to impose a positive tariff. In such cases, the imposition of a tariff reduces the world price of the import that is subject to it.

The resulting improvement in the terms of trade, that is the value of domestic goods in terms of foreign goods, can sometimes be large enough at the margin to more than offset the production and consumption distortions associated with the tariff. As the tariff is increased from zero say, the marginal benefit declines while the marginal cost rises. The 'optimal tariff' is such that it equates these two values. Along a similar line, it follows that, for export sectors, the 'optimal subsidy' is in fact negative since a tax on exports raises the world price of exports and so again causes an improvement in the terms of trade for the exporting country.

Although the theoretical arguments behind the 'optimal tariff' are clear, in practice such policies may be quite difficult to implement. For one, only a few countries are large enough relative to world markets to be price setters and so be in a position to impose such tariffs. Second, were a country to pursue this policy, it would very likely be subject to retaliation by other large countries thereby triggering a so-called 'tariff war'. In such a case, Johnson (1953–4) has shown that all participants will in fact experience a lower level of welfare than had they chosen free trade initially. Simply put, trade policy among nations with market power corresponds to a prisoners' dilemma. International co-ordination that settles on free trade is the globally (and nationally) preferred outcome.

A second argument offered for protection, but not one that is generally accepted by economists, is based upon the presence of market failures. Examples of this include the so-called 'infant industry' model and the existence of large and persistent differences between urban and rural wage rates in developing countries. In cases such as these, for one reason or another there is a wedge between private and social marginal benefits (or costs) in either production or factor markets. When this occurs, the imposition of a tariff, by raising the price of the import, also raises domestic production of the good. If the production increase raises the social benefits enough to cover the loss of private producer and consumer surpluses, then (again from a purely nationalistic welfare point of view) the tariff may be desirable. However, as Bhagwati (1971) and Corden (1974) have shown, attacking an internal market failure with trade policy is not a first-best response since, in effect, the tariff is adding an additional distortion beyond that due to the original market failure. Rather, welfare can be increased beyond this second-best solution by correcting the market failure at its source. For example, if marginal social benefits exceed marginal private benefits, then output can be increased by subsidizing production. Of course, if financing the subsidy itself is distorting, the case against using tariffs is weakened. Nevertheless, more often than not the net benefits of the direct approach exceed those of the indirect approach. Thus, it is preferable to adhere to free trade in these cases as well.

Despite the arguments in favour of free trade noted here, global free trade most certainly does not exist. Indeed, even nations that routinely espouse free trade frequently do not behave as such when they perceive their national interests are at stake, or, as often happens, even when the benefits of free trade exceed the costs since the former are diffuse while the latter are concentrated and so impact the political process to a greater extent. In light of this, the increasing number and size of free-trade areas (FTA), such as the European Union (EU) and the North American Free Trade Agreement (NAFTA), has been viewed by some as a positive step in the direction of global free trade. This position reflects the fact that for trade between member nations of the FTA, tariffs are set to zero. However, because there often exist other barriers to trade within FTAs and they do not set tariffs to zero for trade with countries outside of the FTA, whether they in fact improve the prospects for complete world free trade is unclear. If one views the FTA as a single economy, and if the FTA is large enough to influence world prices (as may be the case for both the EU and NAFTA), then, absent co-operation between FTAs, tariff wars could become more likely with the growth of FTAs. If so, then the goal of global free trade would appear to become less likely. Ultimately, whether global free trade ever does come to pass may well depend upon the ability of the World Trade Organization to confront the many competing interests and interest groups that comprise it internally and lobby it externally.

MICHAEL B. LOEWY
UNIVERSITY OF SOUTH FLORIDA

References

Bhagwati, J.N. (1971) 'The generalized theory of distortions and welfare', in J.N. Bhagwati, R.W. Jones, R.A. Mundell and J. Vanek (eds) *Trade, Balance of Payments and Growth*, Amsterdam.

Corden, W.M. (1974) *Trade Policy and Economic Welfare*, Oxford.

Grossman, G.M. and Helpman, E. (1991) *Innovation and Growth in the Global Economy*, Cambridge, MA.

Johnson, H.G. (1953–4) 'Optimum tariffs and retaliation', *Review of Economic Studies* 21: 142–53.

Ricardo, D. (1817) *On the Principles of Political Economy and Taxation*, Vol. 1 of *The Works and Correspondence of David Ricardo*, ed. P. Sraffa (1952) Cambridge, UK.

Samuelson, P.A. (1939) 'The gains from international trade', *Canadian Journal of Economics and Political Science* 5.

—— (1962) 'The gains from international trade once again', *Economic Journal* 72.

SEE ALSO: international trade; World Trade Organization

FREEDOM

Freedom in its original meaning in the ancient Greek and Roman languages referred to the status of a man as not being a slave (Mulgan 1984). To be a free man was not to be subject to a master. A reasonable corollary of this is that the free man is his own master. He, and not another, is in charge of his life. This twin idea constitutes the core element in the concept of freedom. The various disputes about the idea of freedom in the philosophical literature arise from a focus on one or other of these two aspects. The first aspect is negative in form – the absence of another's controlling will – while the second is positive in that it refers to the presence of the person's own active will in directing himself. Isaiah Berlin in his famous lecture *Two Concepts of Liberty* (1969) designates these two aspects as two concepts. He admits that they are at no great logical distance from each other but nevertheless thinks that they lead to very different political consequences. Negative freedom supports a liberal society while positive freedom gives sustenance to totalitarianism. However, if we have here not two different concepts, but two interconnected aspects of the one concept, Berlin's claims must be rejected.

If we focus on the negative side, we can see that the generic idea is that of not being constrained by the will of another. Several puzzles arise: first, is it better to describe the constraint as operating on what a person actually wants or on his options (Benn and Weinstein

1971)? If we adopt the former, we seem to have to say that, if a person wants above all to e.g. practise his or her Catholic religion, he or she is free if he or she can do so even though no other option is available to him or her. However, if we adopt the latter formula, it seems that a person has a high degree of freedom if he or she has many unrestricted options even though what he or she above all wants to do is not among them. The way to resolve this problem is to say that what concerns us in respect of freedom is both a person's being able to do what he or she wants (what he or she has already chosen) and from the perspective of the person as chooser in his or her having significant options among which to choose. The latter is, however, clearly a feature of the positive aspect of freedom – a person's being in charge of his or her life – and shows us just how intimately connected not being constrained by another will and being in charge of one's own life really are.

Second, for Berlin and many others, freedom-destroying constraint can arise only from the actions of other human beings. Yet, some theorists argue that lack of means or capacity, which is not attributable to others, constitutes a lack of freedom: if I am not rich enough to dine at the Ritz, then I am not free to dine there. Berlin says that lack of freedom and lack of capacity or means are quite distinct notions and should not be confused. Others distinguish between formal and effective freedom: I am formally free to dine at the Ritz but not effectively free to do so (Swift 2001). Again, the way to deal with this issue is on the positive side of the concept. In so far as the negative aspect emphasizes a person's non-subjection to the will of others, Berlin must be correct. But having more means and greater capacities extends a person's possibilities and gives him greater potential control over his life. So, they expand our potential freedom on the positive side.

Other issues raised on the negative side are:

1. Whether the making of credible threats of non-trivial penalties for non-compliance with another's will counts as a constraint at all, since a person may ignore the threat and do the action (Steiner 1975).
2. Whether man-made laws that are general in form and hence do not prescribe or proscribe particular goals are coercive, since they only require the agent to pursue whatever goals he or she has in a certain manner, e.g. by not killing or stealing (Hayek 1960).
3. Whether the unintended consequences of deliberate actions or policies that in fact limit the opportunities of others count as constraints on an agent's freedom (Cohen 1979).

On the positive side, the basic issue is whether there is anything more to being self-directing than doing whatever one wants. However, to be a human being is to be capable of forming conceptions of what is most important to one and of how one should live one's life (Taylor 1979). Acting on desires that conflict with such self-understandings constitutes a failure of the self to determine itself in accordance with its conception of its nature and ends. Such self-understandings may have different contents: as a rational self aspiring to live in accordance with objective moral reason; as a communal self dedicated to the ends of one's community or nation; as a poet, artist, producer; and so on.

However, by a rational self one may mean simply the capacity to evaluate one's desires by reasons that reflect a plurality of values. In this sense, being a rational self is an integral part of being a self-determining human being. The type of rational self that Berlin picks out as leading down a slippery path to totalitarianism involves a belief in objectively valid reasons governing moral and political conduct or what he calls a monism of value. Since reasons are objectively valid, every human being as a rational being must will them. Coercing him or her into observing them is only forcing him or her to be free, as Rousseau says (1968 [1762]). If one is, like Berlin, a pluralist about values, the supposed obnoxious implications of rational self-determination do not arise.

Freedom as self-determination is often called autonomy in contemporary literature, and one should recognize that such freedom is a matter of degree (Christman 1989). One can be more or less autonomous according to the extent to which one subjects one's conduct to reflective evaluation, and forms values that permeate one's life. A normal adult human being is unavoidably a reflective and rational being because he or she can and does give and demand reasons for human beings to act in one way or another. However poor and uneducated, a person always has the capacity to form a will through choice over some areas of his or her life and can increase the extent of his or her self-mastery through acquiring greater material and mental resources.

Very few adult human beings want to be subject to the will of another unless they do so freely by accepting an authority in some respect, e.g. the authority of a military superior. In this sense, freedom is probably a basic good for human beings. Nevertheless, we still need to distinguish freedom as an empirical property of human relations and of inner autonomous states of a human being from value questions about the worth of freedom in relation to other values and about the proper distribution of freedom between persons. However, if freedom as not being subject to another's will is a basic good for each person and freedom as autonomy is the defining human characteristic, then one obvious answer to the value questions is the liberal one according to which freedom is a higher-order value that regulates the acceptability and limits of other values and that such freedom has the same worth for each person (Rawls 1972).

The negative and positive aspects of freedom have been the basis of political ideals of a free person and society. Thus the republican ideal of freedom is standardly said to hold that a person is free only by actively participating in the self-government of a state that is itself not subject to another (Miller 1991). By contrast, the liberal ideal of freedom is usually taken to affirm that a person is free only if he or she enjoys rights that protect his or her choice of how to live from constraint by others including the state. At the same time, republicanism is associated with the ancient world and liberalism with the modern (Constant 1819).

These oppositions are misleading. It is not true that the ancients had no interest in the negative aspect of liberty (Wirszubski 1950; Mulgan 1984), nor that the moderns have no interest in political participation. In regard to the latter, there is not only a strong liberal commitment to democracy as a necessary component in a free society, but also a powerful idealist tradition in which rational self-determination is said to be fully achievable by an individual only through his or her participating in the formation of rational laws for his state (Rousseau 1968 [1762]; Kant 1965 [1797]; Hegel 1992 [1821]). It is true that it is precisely against the latter tradition that

Berlin launches his enormously influential polemic claiming that it is responsible for the perversion of the idea of freedom into its opposite in the totalitarian regimes of the twentieth century.

However, we should take this attack as a criticism of a distorting and corrupt practice rather than of the underlying ideas. If we grasp the negative and the positive as aspects of the one core concept of freedom, we can see easily enough that these political ideals are not to be radically opposed to each other but can and should be combined: negative with positive; republican with liberal; ancient with modern; and idealist with empirical.

JOHN CHARVET
LONDON SCHOOL OF ECONOMICS
AND POLITICAL SCIENCE

References

Benn, S.I. and Weinstein, W.L. (1971) 'Being free to act and being a free man', *Mind* 80.
Berlin, I. (1969) 'Two concepts of liberty', in *Four Essays on Liberty*, Oxford.
Christman, J. (ed.) (1989) *The Inner Citadel*, Oxford.
Cohen, G.A. (1979) 'Capitalism, freedom and the proletariat', in A. Ryan (ed.) *The Idea of Freedom*, Oxford.
Constant, B. (1819) 'Of the liberty of the ancients compared with that of the moderns', *Constant's Political Writings*, Cambridge.
Hayek, F. (1960) *The Constitution of Liberty*, London.
Hegel, G.W.F. (1992 [1821]) *The Philosophy of Right*, Cambridge.
Kant, I. (1965 [1797]) *The Metaphysical Elements of Justice*, New York.
Miller, D. (ed.) (1991) 'Introduction', in *Liberty*, Oxford.
Mulgan, R. (1984) 'Liberty in ancient Greece', in Z. Pelczynski and J. Gray (eds) *Conceptions of Liberty in Political Philosophy*, London.
Rawls, J. (1972) *A Theory of Justice*, Oxford.
Rousseau, J.-J. (1968 [1762]) *The Social Contract*, Harmondworth.
Steiner, H. (1975) 'Individual liberty', in *Aristotelian Society Proceedings*, Oxford.
Swift, A. (2001) *Political Philosophy*, Cambridge.
Taylor, C. (1979) 'What's wrong with negative liberty?' in A. Ryan (ed.) *The Idea of Freedom*, Oxford.
Wirszubski, C. (1950) *Libertas as a Political Idea in Rome*, Cambridge.

Further reading

Feinberg, J. (1980) 'The idea of a free man', in *Rights, Justice and the Bounds of Liberty*, Princeton.
MacCallum, G. (1967) 'Negative and positive freedom', *Philosophical Review*.
Mill, J.S. (1854) *On Liberty*, Everyman edn, London.

Skinner, Q. (1998) *Liberty before Liberalism*, Cambridge.

SEE ALSO: democracy; human rights; liberalism

FREUD, SIGMUND (1856–1939)

Sigmund Freud was the inventor of a new therapeutic and theoretical approach to the psychical unconscious for which he coined the term 'psychoanalysis' (1896). While the origins of Freudian psychoanalysis are to be found in the clinic, in the experimental and therapeutic use of hypnotic suggestion for the understanding of nervous diseases, psychoanalysis was to have manifold epistemological, cultural and political ramifications throughout the twentieth century.

Freud was born on 6 May 1856 in the small Moravian town of Freiberg, the son of the wool merchant Jacob Freud and his wife Amalia. In 1859, the family moved first to Leipzig and one year later to Vienna. In 1873, after attending the gymnasium, Sigmund Freud enrolled as a medical student at the University of Vienna. For 6 years, between 1876 and 1882, he worked in Ernst Brücke's physiological laboratory on the histology of the nervous system. Financially pressed, Freud then took a junior post at the General Hospital in Vienna, where his mentor was Theodor Meynert, one of the leading brain anatomists of the time.

In 1885 Freud received a grant to visit Berlin and Paris, where he worked at the La Salpêtrière hospital under the eminent neurologist Jean-Martin Charcot, whose studies on hysteria and hypnotism were causing debate and controversy in the international medical community. Charcot attempted to demonstrate that hysterical symptoms in male and female patients (such as paralyses and contractures) could be reproduced experimentally under hypnosis. Hippolyte Bernheim, who held a chair at the medical faculty of the University of Nancy, opposed Charcot, claiming that the connection between a pathological condition (hysteria) and the techniques of hypnotism was an artefact, since anybody could be hypnotized. Bernheim insisted that hypnotic suggestion was the most powerful therapeutic technique, and it was he who coined the term 'psychotherapy'.

Freud became a follower of Charcot, whose new lectures he translated, and on his return to Vienna he found himself in opposition to Mey-

nert and most of the medical establishment in Vienna. His first attempts at replicating the Parisian experiments with Viennese patients in front of the Viennese medical society were not very successful. In 1886, after having settled as a physician and opened his private neurological practice, he also started translating Bernheim's books, partly for strategic reasons, and following a visit at Nancy in 1889 he joined the new hypnotic movement that aimed to spread Bernheim's therapeutic techniques across Europe.

In Vienna, Freud was allied by the physician Josef Breuer who, during the early 1880s had developed the 'cathartic method' in his treatment of a patient named Bertha Pappenheim (later immortalized by Freud as 'Anna O'). Breuer's method was similar to those employed by the French practitioners of hypnotism. Together Breuer and Freud published a short paper, which led to the book *Studies on Hysteria* (1893–5), which records Freud's gradual transition from the application of the hypnotic techniques of Paris and Nancy and the development of new psychotherapeutic practices. The last chapter on therapeutic technique described the modifications he had introduced in the hypnotic treatment. The technique of hypnotic suggestion aimed to remove a specific symptom by way of the explicit directions of the hypnotist. Freud replaced this first with the 'pressure technique', in which he placed his hands on the patients' foreheads and urged them to report the thoughts or images that came to mind in response to his questions. Later he introduced the technique of free association.

During the same period, Freud withdrew almost entirely from academic life, and established a close friendship and collaboration with the Berlin physician Wilhelm Fliess. Freud's letters (1985) reveal the theoretical and therapeutic processes that led up to the invention of psychoanalysis. After working for several years on a project on neurasthenia, in collaboration with Fliess, and later on a *Project of a Scientific Psychology* (1950 [1895]), he largely abandoned these studies and turned to the investigation of dreams, jokes and slips of the tongue. Here again, Freud could build on research traditions originating in the second half of the nineteenth century, extending them in novel and original ways. Although *The Interpretation of Dreams* (1900–1) still preserves traces of the *Project*, especially with its outline of a topographical model of the mind, divided into the Conscious, the Preconscious and the Unconscious, Freud now set out the first extended exposition of the psychoanalytic method. Analysing his own dreams as well as those of his patients, friends and family, Freud proposed a new theory and a technique for the general understanding of dreams. His main thesis was that the dream is the fulfilment of a repressed wish (with an aggressive or sexual tendency). The uncovering of such wishes typically led to resistance and a refusal of psychoanalysis. The technique, demonstrated at length in Chapter 2, consists of splitting up the manifest dream content into various elements. The underlying latent wish was revealed by way of the subject's free association to every single element of the dream. Two related works (*The Psychopathology of Everyday Life* [1901] and *Jokes and Their Relation to the Unconscious* [1905b]) were conceived along similar lines.)

In 1905, Freud published *Three Essays on the Theory of Sexuality*, a short work in which he proposed a developmental theory of infantile sexuality. While Freud had believed in the early 1890s that experiences of sexual seduction in childhood were universally the basis of neurosis, he later concluded that the seductions had not actually taken place, but were fantasies (1985: 264). This major turning point in Freud's conception of infantile sexuality was not made public until 1905, but Freud began to hint at the differences between the technique of psychoanalysis and other therapeutic approaches. While other psychotherapies aim to recover real-life events, psychoanalysis finds its primary material in the fantasy-life of the patient, and in the intersubjective process that accompanies the treatment. 'Resistance' and 'transference' became the two basic concepts for the direction of the cure, 'transference' referring to the patient's special affective attachment to the person of the analyst during the psychoanalytic session.

From the first publications of his ideas about psychoanalysis, Freud and his writings became the subject of either strong criticism or passionate defence, and this polemical context needs to be taken into account when the gradual development of his theories and techniques is discussed. Freud's own relations with his close collaborators, such as Breuer and Fliess, were always intense and conflictual. The same holds true for his relationship with many of the collaborators who joined Freud at the beginning of the twentieth century. In Vienna, a group consisting of physicians (Alfred Adler, Wilhelm Stekel) and laymen (Otto Rank) met regularly at Freud's home every Wednesday evening in order to discuss case histories, and to test the extension of psychoanalysis to the realms of literature, art and cultural history. The second pillar of the psychoanalytic movement was the Burghölzli hospital at Zurich, where the director Eugen Bleuer and his assistant Carl Gustav Jung combined the technique of free association with the association test, a method derived from experimental psychology, in order to establish a new way to diagnose mental illnesses. His link with this prestigious psychiatric institution enabled Freud to launch the first psychoanalytic journal (the *Jahrbuch für Psychoanalytische und Psychopathologische Forschungen*) and to attract a number of new disciples (such as Karl Abraham, Max Eitingon and Sandor Ferenczi). The International Psychoanalytic Association (IPA) was officially founded in 1910, but it was dogged by conflicts that soon led to major ruptures. In 1913, Adler and Stekel left the Vienna society, and, in 1914, Jung and many members of the Swiss group separated from Freud.

A number of Freud's most important psychoanalytic contributions were written during these years of initial international recognition, and in the context of debates and divisions inside and outside the psychoanalytic community. These publications included the famous case histories of the Rat Man and of Little Hans (1909), the first child analysis, which were crucial for the unfolding of the concept of the Oedipus complex, a term coined by Freud in response to the use made of the notion of complex by the Swiss group. Between 1911 and 1915 he published a couple of technical papers, as a surrogate for a planned but never written treatise on the psychoanalytic method. In 1914, he published the first longer account of the history of psychoanalysis, *On the History of the Psychoanalytic Movement*, a polemical diatribe in which he settled his scores with the dissidents Adler and Jung. Two other works conceived in this period appeared in the same context: the anonymously published *Totem and Taboo* (1913 [1912–13]), in which Freud reaffirmed the Oedipus complex with a daring speculation about the killing of a primal father by his sons, and the case history of the Wolf Man (1918 [1914]), which aimed to refute Adler and Jung on clinical grounds.

During the First World War Freud resumed the quest for the coherent theoretical framework that he had adumbrated in the *Project* and in the final chapter of *The Interpretation of Dreams*. He worked on a series of twelve metapsychological essays, only five of which were published. At the same time he published the *Introductory Lectures on Psycho-Analysis* (1916–17), a popular introduction to the basic concepts of psychoanalysis.

Major theoretical revisions were introduced in *Beyond the Pleasure Principle* (1920), in which Freud postulated the existence of a death instinct, and *The Ego and the Id* (1923), where the earlier topographical model of the mind was replaced by a structural division into id, ego and superego. By the early 1920s Freud was ill with cancer of the jaw, and he had to undergo several operations, and now the preservation of his legacy and the formation of a new generation of analysts became of great concern to him. Between 1918 and 1924 he took his daughter Anna into analysis, in order to prepare her for these future tasks. With his increasing fame, most of his later writings turned to the application of psychoanalysis to grand issues of cultural and political philosophy. *The Future of an Illusion* (1927) is a psychological unmasking of religion. *Civilization and Its Discontents* (1930) argues that there is an unsurmountable antagonism between human instincts and cultural constraints. Political matters, rarely addressed by Freud in explicit manner, came to the foreground in the last years of his life. In 1933, he published an exchange of letters with Albert Einstein under the title *Why War?* At the same time he started working on his last major book, *Moses and Monotheism*, which he completed in 1939 after having escaped the Nazi regime and moved to London. At once a reaffirmation of the murder of the primal father, a parable of the history of the psychoanalytic movement, and a theory of history, the book stirred up controversy with its thesis that Moses was an Egyptian, and its argument that the deferred memory traces of his murder inspired his people to embrace monotheism. Freud died in London on 23 September 1939.

ANDREAS MAYER
MAX PLANCK INSTITUTE FOR
THE HISTORY OF SCIENCE (BERLIN)

References

Freud, S. (1953–74) *Standard Edition of the Complete Psychological Works of Sigmund Freud*, 24 vols, London.
—— (with J. Breuer) (1893–5) *Studies on Hysteria*, Vol. 2.
—— (1896) 'Further remarks on the neuro-psychoses of defence', in Vol. 3, pp. 159–88.
—— (1900–1) *The Interpretation of Dreams and on Dreams*, Vols 4 and 5.
—— (1901) *The Psychopathology of Everyday Life*, Vol. 6.
—— (1904 [1903]) 'Freud's psycho-analytic procedure', in Vol. 7, pp. 249–56.
—— (1905a) *Three Essays on the Theory of Sexuality*, in Vol. 7, pp. 125–243.
—— (1905b) *Jokes and Their Relation to the Unconscious*, Vol. 8
—— (1909) *Two Case Histories ('Little Hans' and the 'Rat Man')*, Vol. 10
—— (1913 [1912–13]) *Totem and Tabou. Some Points of Agreement between the Mental Lives of Savages and Neurotics*, in Vol. 13, pp. 1–164.
—— (1914) 'On the history of the psycho-analytic movement', in Vol. 14, pp. 3–66.
—— (1918 [1914]) 'For the history of an infantile neurosis', in Vol. 17, pp. 3–122.
—— (1939 [1934–8]) *Moses and Monotheism*, in Vol. 23, pp. 3–139.
—— (1950 [1895]) *Project of a Scientific Psychology*, in Vol. 1, pp. 283–397.
—— (1985) *The Complete Letters of Sigmund Freud to Wilhelm Fliess, 1887–1904*, ed. J.M. Masson, Cambridge, MA.

Further reading

Ellenberger, H.F. (1970) *The Discovery of the Unconscious*, London.
Forrester, J. (1997) *Dispatches from the Freud Wars. Psychoanalysis and Its Passions*, Cambridge, MA.
Jones, E. (1953–7) *The Life and Work of Sigmund Freud*, 3 vols, London.
Mannoni, O. (1971) *Freud. The Theory of the Unconscious*, London.
Rieff, P. (1959) *Freud. The Mind of the Moralist*, New York.
Sulloway, F.J. (1979) *Freud: Biologist of the Mind*, New York.

SEE ALSO: dreams; psychoanalysis; unconscious

FRIEDMAN, MILTON (1912–)

One of the most influential US economists of the twentieth century, Milton Friedman was born in Brooklyn, NY, on 31 July 1912. Friedman's parents were immigrants from a town in what today is the Ukraine. He spent his youth in Rahway, NJ, and at age 16 enrolled in Rutgers University. There one of his teachers was Arthur F. Burns, later to be Chairman of the Board of Governors of the Federal Reserve (1970–8).

Burns also served as Research Associate, Director of Research, and President of the National Bureau of Economic Research, a private organization that has been responsible for the development of many of the quantitative measures of economic performance in use today. Recommended by Burns, Friedman became a member of the research staff of the National Bureau in 1937, and remained affiliated to it through his career. In 1948 Burns persuaded Friedman to undertake a monetary research programme for the National Bureau. From this work Friedman produced *A Monetary History of the United States* (Princeton, NJ, 1963) and *Monetary Trends in the United States and the United Kingdom* (Chicago, 1982) (both with Anna J. Schwartz). *A Theory of the Consumption Function* (Princeton, NJ, 1957) was also a National Bureau publication. Equally important, Burns introduced Friedman to the economics of Alfred Marshall, and Marshall's *Principles of Economics* (first published in 1890) was to be a keystone for Friedman's scholarship and teaching.

Friedman graduated from Rutgers in 1932 with a major in economics but took more credits in mathematics than economics, and won the Bradley Mathematics Prize. At the University of Chicago he took courses from two legendary professors, Frank H. Knight and Jacob Viner, but two other people whom he met were more important to his professional and personal life. One was the economic statistician Henry Schultz. Schultz gave Friedman his start as a researcher in applied economics and statistics. The other was a fellow graduate student, Rose Director, who in 1938 became Friedman's wife. Rose Director, both personally and through her brother Aaron Director, a University of Chicago economist, influenced Friedman's development of a classical liberal view of the role of government.

Henry Schultz arranged for Friedman to receive a fellowship from Columbia University after the first year at Chicago. Aside from a generous stipend in the middle of the Great Depression, the primary attraction of going to Columbia was the presence on their faculty of the mathematical economist and statistician Harold Hotelling. At Columbia Friedman also took courses from Burns's mentor Wesley C. Mitchell and from John M. Clark. Mitchell and Clark were important figures in the US institutionalist movement.

These several personal associations from Friedman's education were bases for many of Friedman's later accomplishments. He is known as a tireless and effective advocate for a relatively unfettered private sector and fettered government. A simple formulation of Friedman's dictum is that to protect liberty and foster prosperity, private decision-making is preferable to government decision-making except for tasks where government has a demonstrable advantage. This position is presented in detail in *Capitalism and Freedom* (Chicago, 1962) and *Free to Choose* (New York, 1980), written with Rose D. Friedman.

With his training in statistics from Schultz and Hotelling, Friedman became a statistician as well as an economist, and for the decade from 1935 until his appointment to the University of Chicago faculty in 1946 was engaged as much in statistical analysis as in economics. His work from 1935 to 1937 on sampling techniques for a study of consumer purchases at the National Resources Committee, a New Deal agency concerned with national economic planning, was the seed for *A Theory of the Consumption Function* (Princeton, NJ, 1957). The puzzle that he solved in that book was reconciling evidence on the relationship between income and consumer purchases. One set of studies showed the proportion of income spent on consumer goods declining with increases in family income. Other evidence showed a constant ratio of consumption to income as average aggregate income increased over time. Friedman's reconciliation was grounded in the concept of 'permanent income'. The idea was that families' decisions about expenditures are based not on their income of the moment but rather on their expectation of future income. Thus, if this year's income is abnormally low, expenditures will be an abnormally high percentage of income. If this year's income is abnormally high, expenditures will be a small percentage of income.

Friedman is the most prominent advocate of what came to be known as monetarism. This is the idea that monetary policy is powerful, for good or for ill, and that since inception of the Federal Reserve in 1914 much of US monetary policy's effect has been for ill. Monetarism is contrasted most frequently with Keynesian fiscalism. Several issues were debated in the 1960s' and 1970s' heyday of these two macroeconomic doctrines. One was the power of monetary policy compared with that of fiscal policy. Keynesians regarded monetary policy as weak and fiscal policy as powerful. Friedman argued that fiscal policy has little power unless supported by monetary policy. Another important aspect of the Keynesian–monetarist debate was over 'fine tuning', whether central bankers and Congress have the foresight and political leeway to make appropriate changes in policy to offset recessions and inflations before they occur. Friedman argued that they are unable to do so, especially in the case of fiscal policy. If fine tuning is tried, mistimed and miscalibrated policy moves will make business cycles more pronounced rather than less. A third issue in the Keynesian–monetarist debate was the Phillips curve trade-off between inflation and unemployment. Friedman challenged the Keynesian idea that inflation is necessary to keep unemployment at acceptable levels. Simultaneous with a similar analysis by Edmund Phelps, Friedman argued in his 1967 Presidential Address to the American Economic Association that attempts to obtain lower unemployment with inflationary monetary policy cause the terms of the Phillips curve to worsen. Increasingly high inflation rates are required to keep unemployment lower than the rate determined by underlying conditions in the labour markets.

Milton Friedman's approach to economics is to rely heavily on empirical evidence to decide which among the many plausible theoretical hypotheses best explain phenomena of interest. This approach is another feature that set him apart from many of his Keynesian opponents, who relied more exclusively on theory. Friedman's power of persuasion, from the force of his reasoning and evidence, with substantial help from the tides of history, moved the conventional wisdom closer to his positions by the 1980s. The importance of monetary policy, and the importance of orienting that policy towards preventing inflation, became accepted views, as part of a general movement away from the presumption that governments can engineer away all social problems. Preference for socialism over capitalism ceased to dominate discussion of public affairs in the ivory tower, the halls of government and on main street.

J. DANIEL HAMMOND
WAKE FOREST UNIVERSITY

Further reading

Friedman, M. and Friedman, R.D. (1998) *Two Lucky People: Memoirs*, Chicago.

SEE ALSO: Chicago School

FUNDAMENTALISM

The term 'fundamentalism' is usually used, in secular intellectual parlance, to refer to religious cultures or communities characterized by (1) intolerance towards those who depart from a strict version of one or another religious tradition; (2) codes of behaviour that, when compared with codes prevailing in the mainstream of one or another religious tradition, or in the mainstream of society, are particularly concerned with external details of the body such as dress and hair; with dietary regulations such as kosher meat and bans on alcohol; and with unusually frequent attendance at religious services; (3) ostentatiously stringent, meticulous, conformity to these external details; (4) obsessive prudishness, and ferocious opposition to the permissive society or the 'commodification of the body'; (5) persons with whom the speaker does not wish to be associated. In addition, there are many predominantly political perceptions in which fundamentalists are depicted as members or supporters of violent and secretive organizations bent upon the overthrow of secular, or simply Western, power and culture in the name of the establishment of a universal religious order. In the popular UK and US media the picture is a caricature, and is often associated exclusively with Islam, or at least with certain spokesmen for Islam or for certain Islamic tendencies.

In social science parlance, in contrast, fundamentalism is constructed in terms of aims, goals, ideology and structure, in the context of a social movement or set of movements. Social scientists prefer not to deal with the more violent fringes of religious fundamentalism, probably because they regard them as, precisely, atypical fringes, and also because, being conspiratorial organizations rather than movements or institutions, they are not readily explainable in the structural terms (viz. social structures, demography, migration and the like) that social science favours. When social scientists use the term they tend to underplay fundamentalist obsessions with sex, and fundamentalist intolerance, rather emphasizing issues of doctrine and enunciated purpose.

It is not possible to provide a definition of fundamentalism that would neatly include some and exclude other movements: attempts at such comprehensive definition in practice start out from an intuitive stereotype based on predetermined, named examples, and end up by enumerating exceptions and complications.

The solution to such difficulties is to abandon the use of the term fundamentalism as a label defining *all the features* of particular movements, and instead use it as a description of certain characteristics that may appear in them.

Lists of characteristics, such as those offered by the authoritative Chicago *Fundamentalism Project*, often amount to saying only that fundamentalist movements are the same as any religious movement 'but more so' (viz. Almond *et al.* 1991). World religious traditions (i.e. Christianity, Islam and Judaism) would not be religious if they did not concern themselves with morality, refer to holy texts, view their members in some sense as elect or chosen, surround themselves with boundaries and impose behavioural requirements, or if they allowed their leaders to be elected by their followers. The claim here, in contrast, is that fundamentalism and charismatic movements represent a new meaning of religion, a new way of being religious, which has arisen in the contemporary period. This means taking account of the pejorative connotations of fundamentalist movements by defining the field in relation to their evident *troubling* character – in short, by asking what it is in these movements that unsettles the modern mind-set. (We know well what it is in the modern mind-set that so unsettles them.)

The unsettling aspects of fundamentalist movements' elements arise less because of frontal attacks on modernity, than because fundamentalists exhibit so many modern features. Fundamentalist railing against sexual permissiveness points to the evidence of the dangers of disease and family break-up which that permissiveness brings. Fundamentalist attacks on modern science proclaim that the discoveries of science are already present in sacred texts or consecrated commentaries on them, such as the Talmud. Fundamentalism claims that divine healing succeeds where modern science fails. Fundamentalism even wins elections – as it did in Algeria in 1992, and as it might in Egypt, Iraq or Tunisia (though not in Iran) if free elections were allowed. In Israel fundamentalism achieves a respectable share of the Jewish vote and the Islamist party achieves a significant share of the Arab vote. In the USA, near-fundamentalist Christian pressure groups exercise great influence over the political parties because of the number of voters they can mobilize, and have exerted influence on appointments to the Supreme Court, science research policy, US development aid policy (by more or less prohibiting funding of population programmes accused of promoting abortion) and US policy on Israel – this last because of their belief that Israeli victory will bring the Final Days.

The claim that fundamentalism is a product of modernity does not mean that its followers are predominantly poor and outcast. Indeed, the comforting implication that the influence of fundamentalism can be reduced by improving the lot of the disinherited is probably misguided. Likewise, the observation that fundamentalist movements use modern technology is incidental.

The modernist character of fundamentalism is also visible in the ability of the movements to develop a theory of history, for in so doing they are clearly distinguished from traditional or popular forms of religion (which so often they despise or attack as the work of the devil): such a theory is a prerequisite for the fundamentalist development of new versions of 'original' Jewish, Christian or Islamic society that is then implanted on varying scales in varying places. This fits in with the concentration of certain – but not all – Jewish and Islamic fundamentalists on bringing secularized Muslims and Jews back to their heritage, and back to a stringent version of that heritage – a quasi-conversion process that has evident similarities with Pentecostalism's central concern with expansion and conversion.

Another feature shared with Pentecostal movements, and which further confirms fundamentalism's modernity, is 'globality' – the ability to straddle geographical, political and linguistic frontiers, though this is more a feature of Islamic and Jewish movements than of Christian fundamentalists, who tend to remain within the USA.

Israel and France are among the few countries in the world where hostility to fundamentalism is openly espoused in political programmes. In the USA, political opposition to fundamentalism is directed only at Muslims: the Christian and Jewish varieties are off-limits for any politician seriously seeking election at any level. In Israel a successful party in the 2003 elections (Shinui) based its programme entirely on fierce hostility directed against the Jewish ultra-Orthodox, and in France hostility and fear directed against a variety of 'sects', led to the passing of a *loi anti-sectes*, in 2000, and underlies periodic rows over prohibition of headscarves in schools, on the grounds that they constitute 'up-front' (*ostentatoires*) symbols of religious affiliation by Muslim girls.

One reason why social scientists do not regard Pentecostals, or, for example, Hindu Nationalists as fundamentalists, let alone Catholic traditionalists, is that they do not share the fundamentalists' esoteric approach to texts. By 'esoteric' is meant the use of a text to find meaning behind or within the letters and numbers: ultra-Orthodox Jews, for instance, pay particular attention to 'numerology', or *gematria* as it is called in Hebrew, building on the additional significance of the Hebrew alphabet as numbers. Also, fundamentalist interpretations of texts reject modern scientific or academic methods, which they regard as anti-religious, so there is no rational basis on which conflicting interpretations can be settled: the authoritative interpretation is that which is given by the most authoritative individual. Jewish Talmudists engage in a kind of ritualized disputing about obscure points, but when it comes to making a ruling, they follow their own Rabbi, just as Christian fundamentalists and charismatics rely implicitly on their pastor or senior authority. The direct access to the text by individuals, and the notion of textual inerrancy so often observed by sociologists and proclaimed by fundamentalists, therefore mean, paradoxically, that all followers share the same interpretation.

A second reason to separate fundamentalists from evangelical Christians is that the latter have an entrepreneurial approach to church organization, encouraging missionary and even fissiparous activity. Third, evangelicals are expressive and encourage spontaneity in worship, whereas the culture of fundamentalism is much more controlling and austere. Also, fundamentalists concentrate spiritual power in a central leadership, while evangelicals spread spiritual gifts, albeit separating them from institutional power. Nonetheless, the two share certain features such as concentration of institutional power, a rejection of established forms of religious power, and a strong concern with the control of women's sexuality.

A further central and distinguishing fundamentalist feature is the constant pressure to multiply rules and prohibitions, and to thicken frontiers. In contrast to mainstream religion, where these matters tend to stagnate, a fundamentalist community or movement is in a constant process of tightening up, of extending the scope of rules, keeping followers in a state of uncertainty and so enhancing the power of the leadership.

DAVID LEHMANN
UNIVERSITY OF CAMBRIDGE

Reference

Almond, G., Sivan, E. and Appleby, R.S. (1991) 'Fundamentalism, genus and species', in M. Marty and R.S. Appleby (eds) *Fundamentalisms Comprehended*, Chicago.

Further reading

Ammerman, N.T. (1987) *Bible Believers: Fundamentalists in the Modern World*, New Brunswick, NJ.
Atran, S. (2003) *In Gods We Trust: The Evolutionary Landscape of Religion*, New York.
Boyer, P. (2001) *Religion Explained: The Human Instincts That Fashion Gods, Spirits and Ancestors*, London.
Friedman, M. (1994) 'Habad as messianic fundamentalism: From local particularism to universal Jewish mission', in M. Marty and R.S. Appleby (eds) *Accounting for Fundamentalism*, Chicago.
Kepel, G. (2002) *Jihad: The Death of Political Islam*, London.
Laurence, B. (1990) *Defenders of God: The Fundamentalist Revolt against the Modern Age*, London.
Sivan, E. (1991) 'The enclave culture', in M. Marty and R.S. Appleby (eds) *Fundamentalisms Comprehended*, Chicago.
Soloveitchik, H. (1994) 'Rupture and reconstruction: The transformation of contemporary orthodoxy', *Tradition* 28(4): 64–130.

SEE ALSO: religion; sects and cults

FUTUROLOGY

Futurology is not so much a social science as a social movement that sprang up in Europe and North America in the late 1950s, and has since spread throughout the world. Its pretensions are scientific: to predict future developments in society by an intensive study of past and present trends. In this it follows the lead given by the first systematic futurological exercise, H.G. Wells's *Anticipations* (1901). From Wells, too, it takes its strongly technological bias, as reflected in the *chef d'œuvre* of the movement, Herman

Kahn and Anthony Wiener's *The Year 2000* (1967). But beyond this general orientation there is no agreement on scientific method, as revealed by the variety of techniques practised by its numerous acolytes. These range from imaginative, one-off shots, like Michael Young's satirical *The Rise of the Meritocracy* (1958) and Dennis Gabor's *Inventing the Future* (1963), through the civilized speculations of Bertrand de Jouvenel's *The Art of Conjecture* (1967), to the solemn computer-based team reports such as the EC's *Europe 2000* projections, and the Club of Rome's *The Limits to Growth* (1972). A notable contribution from Eastern Europe in the latter vein is the report of Radovin Richta's Czech team, *Civilization at the Crossroads* (1967). Somewhere in the middle come the projections and speculations of experts working from their home disciplinary bases, as in the collections edited by Daniel Bell, *Towards the Year 2000* (1968), and Robert Jungk and Johan Galtung, *Mankind 2000* (1969). The centrality of technology in futurological thinking is underlined by the movement's frequent reference to Erich Jantsch's *Technological Forecasting in Perspective* (1967), which is for many the Old Testament, if not the Bible, of futurology. Other popular techniques include a kind of team game known as Delphi forecasting, where experts revise their initial forecasts in the light of forecasts by other members of the team. The results are understandably not usually very exciting.

Most products of futurology, again following Wells, breathe a spirit of confidence, not to say complacency. They look forward to a 'postindustrial society' or even a 'superindustrial society', where the fruits of applied science have produced an era of leisure and abundance. The basic expectation seems to be that the future will be the present writ large. Some form of extrapolation is the method common to most futurologists, and given that the movement received its main impetus in the prosperous years of the 1960s, it is hardly surprising that the future appears largely as a bigger and better version of the 1960s, above all in the technological sphere. Differences of ideology and values are played down, in the belief that the technological imperative largely commands social systems. Here futurology shows its kinship with certain kinds of science fiction and Utopianism, but an added and somewhat spurious dimension of serious science is given by the team and think-tank basis of much of its activities. This has made it attractive to governments, the more especially as it appears to offer the materials for long-range planning, and also because much of the thinking has been about 'the unthinkable', namely the prospect and possibility of nuclear war. Large private corporations have shown interest for the same reasons, and some, such as Shell, Unilever and Xerox, have themselves gone in for large-scale exercises in futurology.

In the wake of the oil crisis of 1973, and the world recession of the later 1970s, something of the gloss disappeared from futurological speculation. There was greater readiness to include the thinking of alternative and radical futurologists, especially those of an ecological persuasion. Groups such as Friends of the Earth, and magazines like *The Ecologist*, saw many of their ideas taken up in mainstream futurological journals such as *Futures* and *The Futurist*. In addition to the physical limits to growth indicated by the Club of Rome report, there was a new awareness of the 'social limits to growth', as persuasively discussed in Fred Hirsch's book of that name (1977). The world after 1989 confirmed that change of mood. Fears about nuclear war have revived. The rosy glow that hovered over the millennial year 2000 has now dissipated in the presence of a 'new world disorder' that has followed the collapse of communism. Thinking about the future is now more likely to take the form of debates about 'globalization' and its attendant inequalities than of scientific and technological forecasting. But in the euphoric projections of a world united by information technology and the World Wide Web we can discern the same kind of optimism as fired the earlier futurologists.

KRISHAN KUMAR
UNIVERSITY OF VIRGINIA

Further reading

Clarke, I.F. (1979) *The Pattern of Expectation 1644–2001*, New York.
Cooper, R.N and Layard, R. (eds) (2002) *What the Future Holds*, Cambridge, MA.
Nisbet, R. (1988) *The Making of Modern Society*, Brighton.
Wagar, W. (1992) *A Short History of the Future*, London.

SEE ALSO: forecasting and prediction; Utopianism

G

GAME THEORY

Game theory is concerned with the choices made by people who pursue their individual objectives, but who interact with each other, so that the degree to which any one of them achieves his or her objectives depends not only on their own choices, but also on everybody else's choices. Interactions of this sort are called 'strategic games' or simply 'games'. The participants in strategic games are referred to as 'players'. The choices that they make in a game are referred to as 'strategies'. Strategic games are pervasive in human and animal life.

Game theory seeks to predict people's choices in strategic games. Much of game theory is based on the paradigm of rationality that has a long tradition in economics. The predominance of this paradigm can be explained by the fact that the development of game theory has been advanced mostly by economists. An important definition of rationality in games is due to John Nash. According to this definition, a player in a game acts rationally if he or she maximizes his or her expected utility taking as given and fixed the strategy choices of all other players. Here, the notion of utility is that of von Neumann and Morgenstern, the founders of game theory. A collection of choices by players that satisfies this rationality definition for each player is called a *Nash equilibrium* (Nash 1950).

The notion of Nash equilibrium has been developed further, mainly with the purpose of refining it so that it can be applied to games that are dynamic and involve sequences of choices. This has led, in particular, to the development of the concepts of 'subgame-perfect equilibrium' and 'perfect Bayesian equilibrium'. These con-cepts form today the cornerstones of applied game theory (Gibbons 1992: Chs 2 and 4).

When game theory is applied, researchers first seek to find a stylized representation of the situation that they want to study as a strategic game. Then they find out which predictions the notions of equilibrium referred to above imply. Finally, they compare the predictions of game theory to the behaviour that is observed in practice.

The most important areas of scientific research to which game theory has been applied are economics, political science and biology. Here, we shall restrict ourselves to applications of game theory to economics and political science.

In economics, the area to which game-theore-tic methods were historically applied first is oligopoly theory. An oligopoly is a market in which a relatively small number of firms compete with each other for customers. The 'Cournot model' of oligopolistic competition (Tirole 1988: 218–21) focuses on choice of the quantity of produced output. The main findings of research about this model are that in a Nash equilibrium firms make lower profits than they would if they co-ordinated their choices and formed a cartel. This finding can explain the rationale for firms' tendency to seek cartel agreements with their rivals. As such agreements are not in the interest of customers, the Cournot model also provides a framework in which the need for competition policy can be understood.

Other models of oligopolistic interaction focus on prices as firms' strategic variable (Tirole 1988: 214–16). A main finding is that in Nash equilibrium firms that produce very similar products will set their prices almost equal to unit costs, provided that there are no major economies or diseconomies of scale, and provided that capacity constraints don't play a role. This finding indicates that it is not so much the number of firms that matters for the effectiveness of competition, but the extent to which any one firm's customers could be served by a competitor with similar cost structure and product quality.

Another line of research in oligopoly theory has been the study of dynamic interaction between firms. This has shown that firms can maintain some form of implicit collusion even without explicit cartel agreements. Prices are maintained at a high level by the understood threat that any attempt to undercut will be punished by a price war. Price wars of this type have been found in empirical studies (Porter 1983).

A further area of economics to which game theory has been applied is the theory of bargaining (Osborne and Rubinstein 1990: Chs 3 and 5). Prices and wages, for example, are often negotiated between two partners. By applying game theory to this type of situation economists have sought to study what determines each side's bargaining power, and also what determines the success or failure of negotiations. A major finding is that an important determinant of an organization's bargaining power is the loss that it incurs if agreement is delayed. On the other hand, threats to break off negotiations influence the agreement only to the extent to which they are credible, i.e. offer a return that is higher than can be expected from the negotiation. Finally, the probability that bargaining partners will succeed in finding an agreement will most importantly depend on the extent to which they are fully informed about each other. If bargaining partners are fully informed about each other, and thus understand the range of agreements that is in their mutual interest, breakdown of negotiations will not occur.

Game theory has also been used in economics to gain a better understanding of issues first raised in the economics of information. A typical application of game theory occurs in the 'theory of signalling'. This theory shows that costly investments, for example into educating oneself, can be economically useful even if they do not directly raise the productivity of the person or organization making the investment. Their use can be informational, in the sense that they are used to credibly signal hidden characteristics, such as intelligence or persistence, to potential trading partners, such as employers (Gibbons 1992: 183–210).

A classical application of game theory in political science occurs in the theory of strategic voting. As an example, consider 'plurality voting' where voters can vote for one of several candidates, and the candidate who receives the largest number of votes wins (Myerson and Weber 1993). If there are more than two candidates, then this game has many Nash equilibria. The reason is that voters' views about which alternatives have a realistic chance of winning can be self-confirming. If everybody thinks that candidate A has no chance of winning, then nobody will vote for A, and therefore A will not win.

Game theory has also been used to study the likely behaviour of politicians in a democratic society. If politicians are primarily concerned with winning elections, and if politics is widely viewed as one-dimensional, say on a 'left' to 'right' scale, then some simple game-theoretic models predict that politicians will cluster in the middle of the political spectrum (Osborne 1993).

In other areas of political economy game theory has been used to study the advantages and disadvantages of various institutional arrangements. For example, monetary policy is, in many countries, delegated to an independent central bank, which is largely removed from democratic control. Game-theoretic analysis suggests that the motivation for such an arrangement is an effort by government to make a binding commitment to controlling inflation. Without independence of the institution that implements monetary policy, investors and consumers would expect that the government would give in to the temptation of inflationary measures in recessions (Cukierman 1992).

In addition to predicting behaviour for given rules of a game, game theory can also be used to analyse the optimal choice of the rules of a game. Two typical areas in which game theory has been used in this way are the theory of voting, where game theory has been used to analyse which voting rules serve society's interests best, and the theory of auctions, where game theory has been used to analyse which auction rules lead to the highest revenue for the seller, or to the best allocation of objects to potential buyers.

We focus here on the application of game theory to the design of optimal auctions. Insights from game theory have recently been used worldwide for the design of auctions of government bonds, auctions of government licences for mobile telephone companies, and auctions in the energy sectors (McMillan 1994). One major set of results that have emerged from game-theoretic analysis has concerned the potential advantages of open auctions over sealed-bid auctions. In open auctions bidders can observe others' bids, and also the point at which other bidders withdraw from bidding. If asymmetric information among bidders is an issue, then the observability of bids and withdrawal points is potentially advantageous. Buyers can adjust their behaviour in the light of the information that they deduce from other buyers' behaviour. This may lead to higher efficiency of the allocation of object to buyers as well as higher revenues for the seller (Milgrom and Weber 1982).

A major current development in game theory is a move away from the orthodox paradigm of rationality towards more psychologically motivated theories of behaviour (Camerer 2003). As this development progresses, one can hope for further development of new applications of game theory, for example to the optimal design of incentive contracts.

TILMAN BÖRGERS
UNIVERSITY COLLEGE LONDON

References

Camerer, C. (2003) *Behavioral Game Theory*, Princeton, NJ.

Cukierman, A. (1992) *Central Bank Strategy, Credibility and Independence: Theory and Evidence*, Cambridge, MA.

Gibbons, R. (1992) *A Primer in Game Theory*, New York.

McMillan, J. (1994) 'Selling spectrum rights', *Journal of Economic Perspectives* 8: 145–62.

Milgrom, P. and Weber, R. (1982) 'A theory of auctions and competitive bidding', *Econometrica* 50: 1,089–122.

Myerson, R. and Weber, R. (1993) 'A theory of voting equilibria', *American Political Science Review* 87: 102–14.

Nash, J.F. (1950) 'Equilibrium points in n-person games', *Proceedings of the National Academy of Sciences of the United States of America* 36: 48–9.

Osborne, M. (1993) 'Candidate positioning and entry in a political competition', *Games and Economic Behavior* 5: 133–51.

Osborne, M. and Rubinstein, A. (1990) *Bargaining and Markets*, San Diego, CA.

Porter, R. (1983) 'A study of cartel stability: The joint executive committee, 1880–1886', *RAND Journal of Economics* 14: 301–14.

Tirole, J. (1988) *The Theory of Industrial Organization*, Cambridge, MA.

Further reading

Selten, R. (1975) 'Re-examination of the perfectness concept for equilibrium points in extensive games', *International Journal of Game Theory* 4: 25–55.

SEE ALSO: altruism and co-operation; auctions; bargaining; collective action; competition; equilibrium; experimental economics; prisoners' dilemma; rational choice (action) theory; rational expectations

GENDER, SOCIOLOGY OF

The sociology of gender began as an academic specialization in the 1970s and has experienced tremendous growth and development since that time. The concept of gender was first developed to distinguish anatomical and reproductive differences between men and women from the social meanings and cultural practices that are associated with those biological differences. More recently, gender scholars have argued that the basic biological distinctions of 'male' and 'female' are themselves reflections of social and cultural understandings. Currently, the term gender is used to refer to any discourse, social organization or cultural practice that distinguishes men from women.

Historical background

The sociology of gender emerged from the second wave of the feminist movement in the 1970s. Prior to that time, the term 'sex roles' was used by sociologists to refer to the different social expectations placed on men and women in society. According to the then dominant structural functionalist school, women were socialized to fit expressive, maternal roles, while men were socialized to have instrumental attributes that suited them for positions in the public sphere of work and politics (Parsons and Bales 1955). This implied that the social differences between men and women were harmless, and even beneficial to society. Feminist writers insisted, however, that 'sex roles' privileged men and were themselves the product of male domination.

Marxist theory was an important influence on the early sociology of gender. Marxism shifted the focus from conformity to conflict, and, more specifically, Friedrich Engels had tied the historic rise of male domination to industrialization and, ultimately, to capitalism. Feminist sociologists in the 1970s elaborated this critique through an examination of the ways in which patriarchy both reinforced and was bolstered by capitalism (e.g. Hartmann 1976).

Feminist sociologists began using the term gender instead of sex roles because it suggested a more dynamic and conflict-ridden social process of differentiation. The use of the term gender also appealed to feminist sociologists because it suggested that individuals might resist social pressures to conform to what are conventionally thought to be traditional male and female roles. In 1967, Garfinkel published a case study of 'Agnes', a biological male who was able to pass as a woman. This case study was especially important to gender scholars because it highlighted how the social perception of a person as either a man or a woman could be manipulated by clothing, mannerisms and social performances (e.g. Kessler and McKenna 1978). It denaturalized gender and reinforced the notion that one's biological sex may or may not match with one's social presentation of self.

Using the concept of gender, empirical sociologists in the 1980s explored the ways that society imposed gender differences on men and women. They documented different patterns in men's and women's employment and pay, education, political participation and family duties (e.g. Reskin 1988; Hochschild 1989); demonstrated how women faced discrimination, violence and restricted opportunities (e.g. Epstein 1988); and examined sexist stereotypes of women conveyed through art and culture (e.g. Thorne 1983).

Also in the 1980s, scholars began to explore the harmful consequences of gender for men. While acknowledging the privileged status of men and masculinity in society, sociologists began questioning the unrealistic expectations that may be placed on men, especially in the arenas of work, relationships and sports (e.g. Williams 1989; Messner 1992; Rubin 1983).

During the 1980s, many Western societies, including the USA and Britain, experienced a backlash against feminism and a more general resistance to social change. Some sociologists now began to investigate the gratifications and benefits that follow from gender conformity, noting that particular groups benefited from the institutionalization of gender differences. Consequently, sociologists now pay greater attention to the variations in the meanings and practices associated with gender in different historical and social contexts. Differences of race, class and sexual orientation have proved to be especially important in delimiting the specific role that gender plays in promoting social change or fostering conformity in particular situations (e.g. Glenn 1992; Klatch 1987; Stein 1997).

Current theories in the sociology of gender

Multiple theories have been offered to explain gender in society. West and Zimmerman (1987) explain gender differentiation with reference to the idea of 'doing gender'. This approach suggests that gender is malleable and contextual, and that it emerges out of social interactions. Essentially we all 'do gender' repeatedly whenever we interact with one another. Doing gender may seem natural because our interactions include taken-for-granted assumptions about how we should behave, but in fact it is through repetition that gender is reproduced. By exposing these assumptions as socially constructed, this approach dispels biological determinism as the basis for everyday behaviour. In addition, the notion of 'doing gender' enables us to see our own complicity in reproducing gender differentiation, treating gender not as something imposed from some outside source but as something we are all engaged in. This also opens the possibility that individuals may foster social change by recognizing their forms of behaviour and monitoring or changing them.

Patricia Hill Collins (1991) offers a version of 'standpoint theory' that treats gender from a black woman's point of view. (She terms this the outsider-within perspective.) Collins claims that a unique black women's standpoint exists, as a result of their unique experiences of oppression. While white women have been oppressed predominantly for reasons of gender, black women have been subjected to multiple systems of race, class and gender oppression. Collins uses the term 'matrix of domination' to describe the interlocking systems of race, class and gender, and claims that because of their situation black women will comprehend the mutually reinforcing relationships between these systems. She argues that there is not a monolithic 'woman's experience' and that not all women are similarly situated within various social institutions. The matrix of domination impacts differentially on women, and some women actually benefit from gender differentiation.

Psychoanalytic theory is a third significant perspective in the sociology of gender. Although many gender sociologists have been reluctant to consider the unconscious and internalized aspects of gender, others argue that institutionalized gender differences shape men's and women's relational capacities, emotional needs and unconscious desires, and that these processes are critical for understanding the intractability of gender inequality. Nancy Chodorow (1978) drew upon psychoanalytic theory to understand why many women yearn to be mothers, despite the many drawbacks of the role. Jessica Benjamin (1988) uses the theory to understand the apparent willingness of many women to submit to male-dominated heterosexuality. These studies suggest that there may be a link between individual desires and structured inequality.

Robert Connell's (1987) concept of hegemonic masculinity addresses four levels of the reproduction of gender inequality: power, division of labour, bodily cathexis and cultural discourse. The concept of hegemony is used to indicate that masculinity and femininity are not static roles or identities but rather social and cultural ideals that are exalted by both men and women, and which then legitimize the gender order as a whole. However, different versions of the ideals of masculinity and femininity compete for dominance. Connell's multidimensional approach facilitates a gender analysis of institutional arrangements as well as individual interactions, while recognizing that gender is also historically constituted and in flux. This perspective also draws attention to the permeation of all levels of society by gender differentiation, and indicates the ways in which individuals may be involved in the creation of male domination while simultaneously resisting it.

Future challenges for the sociology of gender

The sociology of gender faces several intellectual challenges. Incorporating international perspectives is one of these, an especially urgent concern in the post-11 September 2001 era. The sociology of gender has drawn mainly from Western feminist viewpoints that have been criticized for failing to acknowledge their colonialist links to the Third World. Western reliance on Third World women's labour in housework and childcare is one example. A major theme in this growing body of scholarship is globalization and its consequences for different forms of gender inequality around the world (Hondagneu-Sotelo 2001).

The growing transgender movement presents another challenge. Expanding our conception of gender, this movement is beginning to stimulate research on intersexuality and transgender experience. Gender theorizing can no longer represent dichotomous conceptions of men/women, male/female or masculine/feminine (Fausto-Sterling 2000).

Finally, despite the fact that social changes over the past 30 years have undermined traditional roles for men and women, gender inequality persists and creates dilemmas, especially for people who seek to organize and experience their lives in more egalitarian ways. For example, research has documented the competing and contradictory claims placed on women who seek to balance home and workplace responsibilities (Williams 2000). So far, however, sociologists have been reluctant to recommend solutions to these social problems.

CHRISTINE L.R. WILLIAMS
AND GRETCHEN R. WEBBER
UNIVERSITY OF TEXAS, AUSTIN

References

Benjamin, J. (1988) The Bonds of Love: Psychoanalysis, Feminism, and the Problem of Domination, New York

Chodorow, N. (1978) The Reproduction of Mothering: Psychoanalysis and the Sociology of Gender, Berkeley, CA.

Collins, P.H. (1991) Black Feminist Thought: Knowledge, Consciousness, and the Politics of Empowerment, New York.

Connell, R.W. (1987) Gender and Power: Society, the Person and Sexual Politics, Cambridge, UK.

Engels, F. (1972 [1884]) The Origin of the Family, Private Property, and the State, New York.

Epstein, C.F. (1988) Deceptive Distinctions: Sex, Gender, and the Social Order, New Haven, CT.

Fausto-Sterling, A. (2000) Sexing the Body: Gender Politics and the Construction of Sexuality, New York.

Garfinkel, H. (1967) Studies in Ethnomethodology, Englewood Cliffs, NJ.

Glenn, E.N. (1992) 'From servitude to service work: Historical continuities in the racial division of paid reproductive labor', Signs 18: 1–43.

Hartmann, H. (1976) 'Capitalism, patriarchy, and job segregation by sex', Signs 1: 137–69.

Hochschild, A. (1989) The Second Shift, New York.

Hondagneu-Sotelo, P. (2001) *Domestica: Immigrant Workers Cleaning and Caring in the Shadows of Affluence*, Berkeley, CA.

Kessler, S. and McKenna, W. (1978) *Gender: An Ethnomethodological Approach*, New York.

Klatch, R. (1987) *Women of the New Right*, Philadelphia.

Messner, M. (1992) *Power at Play: Sports and the Problem of Masculinity*, Boston.

Parsons, T. and Bales, R.E. (1955) *Family, Socialization, and Interaction Process*, Glencoe, IL.

Reskin, B. (1988) 'Bringing the men back in: Sex differentiation and devaluation of women's work', *Gender and Society* 2: 58–81.

Rubin, L. (1983) *Intimate Strangers: Men and Women Together*, New York.

Stein, A. (1997) *Sex and Sensibility: Stories of a Lesbian Generation*, Berkeley, CA.

Thorne, B. (1983) *Language, Gender, and Society*, Rowley, MA.

West, C. and Zimmerman, D. (1987) 'Doing gender', *Gender and Society* 1: 125–51.

Williams, C. (1989) *Gender Differences at Work*, Berkeley, CA.

Williams, J. (2000) *Unbending Gender: Why Family and Work Conflict and What to Do About It*, Oxford.

SEE ALSO: division of labour by sex; feminist theory; homosexualities; patriarchy; queer theory; women; women's studies

GENEALOGIES

Genealogies comprise verbal or diagrammatic representations of people's relationships by 'blood' or marriage. Their study, especially in relation to other aspects of kinship, has long been important for social anthropologists.

Significant anthropological interest in genealogies began with W.H.R. Rivers (e.g. 1914). In his fieldwork in the Torres Straits, in India and in the Pacific, they provided him with both a means to understand the relationships between individuals and a means to work out the complexities of relationship terminology usage. The latter was important because of his belief in the conservative nature of such terminologies. He believed that embedded in their structures would be clues to the social organization of earlier times, and late in his life he also looked to such terminological structures for clues as to the connections between ethnic groups.

It is important to distinguish genealogical relationship from biological relationship. In anthropology, genealogies are always taken to indicate social relationships, which may or may not be truly biological. They may include, for example, presumed relatives, adoptive relatives or fictive relatives. Their extent is determined by what is culturally relevant, but they always include relatives on both sides of a given family; and it should be possible to match one person's genealogy up with another to produce a 'map' of kin relationships that connect family to family. It is thus also important for a fieldworker to distinguish a person's genealogy from his or her pedigree. The latter is a subjective account provided by an informant and often emphasizes important kin relationships (such as descent from a unilineal ancestor) over less important ones (see Barnard and Good 1984). Thus, genealogies lie somewhere between the biological 'facts' of reproduction (whose objective truth is anthropologically irrelevant) and indigenous statements of how individuals are related.

There are a number of common problems in the collecting of genealogies. Informants 'collapse' them (forgetting unimportant ancestors), treat sibling relationships as genealogically equivalent (especially if they are terminologically equivalent), or claim ties that are not recognized by other members of the community. Where marriages are between close kin, the same person may legitimately be traced as a relative through more than one genealogical tie, and one of these ties (not always the closer) may be given precedence. Widespread adoptions, fictive egocentric kin relationships (like god-parenthood) or culturally specific equivalents to 'kinship' (like namesake-equivalence or age-mate equivalence) may complicate things further. However, in spite of all this, anthropologists generally agree that there is something universal about the 'genealogical grid', which consists of all socially significant relationships through parenthood and marriage, whatever the specific meaning of 'parenthood' and 'marriage' in any given society. Without the recognition of such a device, the comparative study of relationship terminologies would be impossible.

ALAN BARNARD
UNIVERSITY OF EDINBURGH

References

Barnard, A. and Good, A. (1984) *Research Practices in the Study of Kinship*, London.

Rivers, W.H.R. (1914) *Kinship and Social Organisation*, London.

Further reading

Barnes, J.A. (1967) 'Genealogies', in A.L. Epstein (ed.) *The Craft of Social Anthropology*, London.

SEE ALSO: kinship

GENETICS AND BEHAVIOUR

Since human genetics is driven principally by medical issues, it is not surprising that human behavioural genetics commonly adopts the methodological assumptions of medical genetics – for example that variation is abnormal or pathological, and that the genotype (hereditary constitution) strongly predicts and determines the phenotype (outward expression) of the feature. For much of the genetic diversity in the human species, however, this is probably not the case. The alleles of the ABO blood group paradigmatically are all normal, and produce different normal (albeit simple) phenotypes. More complex phenotypes may themselves be the result of the interaction of different alleles whose joint effect might not be predictable from their individual actions – as, for example, in the vigour of hybrid crops. Behavioural phenotypes are also commonly far more difficult to score objectively.

Consequently, search for genes affecting human behaviour tends strongly to pathologize the behaviour – a case in point being the infamous claim that an extra Y chromosome causes hyper-aggressive behaviour. In modern studies we often find, for example, schizophrenia, alcoholism and homosexuality discussed together as if they were all 'genetic diseases' (McGuffin *et al.* 2001). (In fact the claims linking each of those to particular genes have not stood up well.) Likewise, variation in the 'aggression gene' (monoamine oxidase A, MAOA) is associated not with boxers, gang molls or premedical students – all of whom are arguably very aggressive – but with small kindreds of mildly mentally retarded spousal abusers (Brunner 1995).

Why genetics will not start a revolution in understanding human behaviour

Ecologists in the 1960s recognized two broadly stereotypical strategies for species to exploit their environments successfully (MacArthur and Wilson 1967). The first is to reproduce rapidly and saturate the environment (called an *r-strategy*, related to the reproductive rate); the second is to reproduce slowly and adapt to it over the course of one's lifetime (called a *K-strategy*, related to the environment's carrying capacity). The first strategy is necessarily accompanied by a short life-span, little parental investment in any offspring, and little opportunity to adapt or to learn; the second by longer life-span, high investment by a parent in few offspring, and great flexibility in behaviour. The first strategy can be seen as the successful general adaptation of insects; the second of mammals.

Obviously humans fall on the mammalian end of that spectrum. Thus, an initial question is answered: How extensive is the genetic contribution to human behaviour, in the context of the animal kingdom? Not very extensive at all; humans have evolved quite different life-histories compared to the insects, and even among the mammals humans are on the far end of the K-strategy. Thus, the human evolutionary strategy is to be behaviourally flexible through an extended lifetime of learning, and genetics is consequently unlikely a priori to play a significant role in understanding human behaviour, simply from the standpoint of evolution.

We may now ask another question: Within the human species, how are patterns of genetic variation related to patterns of behavioural variation? Genetic variation is patterned clinally (varying gradually with geography), and the bulk of genetic variation is located within groups, not between them. The reasons for this seem to be that differentiation into self-designated groups is quite recent; those groups have porous boundaries; human groups are in various forms of genetic contact; and the environmental problems tracked by the structure of the gene pool vary themselves gradually over space.

The major features of behavioural variation, on the other hand, are of the sort that finds one group of people eating with chopsticks, proscribing first-cousin marriage as incestuous, or wearing saris; and another eating with forks, preferentially marrying cross-cousins, or wearing hoop skirts. In other words, human behaviour principally varies from group to group, and it is the structure of the variation encountered in human behaviour that is generally encapsulated in the term 'culture'. This between-group variation in thought and deed is commonly very discrete (as in languages, food preferences and other general markers of 'ethnicity'). The fact that the pattern of variation in the two categories – genetics and behaviour – is so different makes it unlikely that the former could be a major cause of the latter. Further, as studies of immigrants have shown comprehensively that people can adopt virtually all aspects of their new 'culture' in a single generation, it follows that most variation in human behaviour, being cultural, is also not genetic.

An empirical consideration of evolution and genetics strongly implies that genetics is at best a very minor influence over human behaviour. Consequently, the domain of human behavioural genetics must be seen as an exceedingly narrow one in the overarching question of how and why human beings think and do different things.

On the other hand, the question of the innateness of behaviours, especially those relating to social or economic inequalities, is an ancient one. It justifies, for example, the existence of hereditary aristocracies, on the grounds that the ruling class is simply better, smarter or more civilized on account of their natural properties. It also impinges upon the issue of free will, and whether particular events could have been otherwise, or were simply fated to have occurred as they did, with the principal actors essentially 'programmed' to do or to think as they did. To the extent that science is a source of authoritative knowledge in modern society, it is not surprising that we commonly turn to genetics with these questions. Unfortunately, authoritative answers are difficult to come by.

The two conflicts-of-interest in human behavioural genetics

Unlike most other scientific endeavours, the study of human behavioural genetics is burdened from the start with reasons to be especially sceptical of its claims. The brief vogue of Social Darwinism late in the nineteenth century demonstrated the political value to the dominant classes of justifying economic and social hierarchies as being rooted in natural differences. To the Social Darwinists, people had what they deserved as a result of the 'survival of the fittest' (Herbert Spencer's phrase). While there was not necessarily a theory of heredity underlying the ideas of the Social Darwinists, the advocates of eugenics in the USA held specifically genetic differences to be at the root of social and economic inequalities. This provided a scientific justification in the USA for involuntary sterilization of the poor and the restriction of immigration, and in Germany for genocide.

The historical legacy of these political-scientific movements lies in acknowledging that science rationalized the prejudices of the dominant classes, and rationalized as well as abrogating the rights of the underclasses. Whether the geneticists of the age were ingenuously replicating their cultural values in their scientific work, or were more duplicitously pandering to the wealthy and powerful, is less important than the extraction of a general rule: Innatist theories of human behaviour have political consequences by implicitly naturalizing social and economic disparities. This gives human behavioural genetics a conflict of interests (against simply discovering the truth), for there is a powerful incentive to generate an ideology that will justify political action.

A second conflict of interests is the reciprocal relationship between the funding levels in the science and its apparent productivity level. When a distinguished geneticist says 'We used to think our fate was in the stars. Now we know, in large measure, our fate is in our genes', it is simultaneously a political statement and a grant proposal, in addition to being a possibly true scientific statement. Although it only ever claimed to account for a tiny percentage of the phenomenon in question, the 'gay gene' (Hamer *et al.* 1993), which was never subsequently found, was front-page news across the world. While some have greeted this claim as liberating and politically valuable for advocates of gay rights (using the innatist claims about race as a model), this strategy has been criticized both on the basis of new understandings about race, and a critical approach to the genetic evidence (Halley 1994; Braman 1999). Consequently, it is far from clear just how much weight to place on the pronouncements of human behavioural genetics, and very little can be taken at face value (Beckwith and Alper 1997).

Twin studies

Certainly the most resonant data, as well as the most mythologized, involve the study of twins, especially those separated at birth and reunited as adults. Biologically, identical twins are genetic clones of one another. Consequently they hold out the hope of being a natural laboratory for the study of the inheritance of behaviours. However, as identical twins are generally raised together, and have their 'sameness' reinforced by being groomed and dressed alike, their environments are also extremely similar, thus undermining the natural experiment. If identical twins are reared in randomized environments, then the experiment might succeed.

The pioneer in these studies was Sir Cyril Burt, a twentieth-century British psychologist who claimed to have tracked down scores of identical twins raised separately, and to have found that their IQs were extraordinarily similar, thus validating his assumption that intelligence is largely innate. It was determined after his death, however, that the statistics underlying the claim were fabricated, as were Burt's field assistants'. Burt's notes were destroyed upon his death, and it is unclear how many – if any – sets of identical twins reared apart he actually studied (Tucker 1997).

The basis for such an experiment has since come under scrutiny as well. Many twins raised apart are actually in separate domiciles, but with relatives; adoptive parents are carefully screened by agencies. In neither case can the environments be considered randomized; to the extent that the environments are correlated, the true contribution of genetics will be obscured and likely overestimated (Lewontin *et al*. 1984).

The major study of twins reared apart now comes from a US psychologist named Thomas Bouchard. With initial funding from a right-wing organization called the Pioneer Fund (Tucker 2002), Bouchard popularized the study of identical twins reared apart, now focusing on their amazing resemblances. One such pair were both named Jim by their adoptive parents, married women named Linda, then married women named Betty, named their sons and dogs the same, and so forth (Holden 1980). Another pair ended up working as volunteer firemen, sporting droopy moustaches and wearing similar-style eyeglasses. These amazing similarities have been represented as evidence for the predominance of genetics in behaviour (de Waal 1999), and for the psychic contact of twins (Begley 1987). Most likely they are neither, but simply demonstrate the unreliability of anecdotal information, particularly in such a symbolically and mythologically charged circumstance.

Intelligence

The study of the inheritance of intelligence was initiated by Francis Galton (1869), who crudely (by modern standards) found that 'prominence' ran in families. By the end of the nineteenth century he had founded a movement devoted to improving the human race genetically through state control of (or at least restrictions upon) breeding. The US geneticist Charles Davenport (1911) believed that crime, backwardness, unemployment and other anti-social characteristics were manifestations of the action of a single Mendelian gene, for 'feeblemindedness' – a term that had already been in common use among social workers. This was apparently supported by family studies, most prominently that of the pseudonymous Kallikaks (Goddard 1912), in which an eighteenth-century ancestor fathered a line of degenerates through his illegitimate child with a 'nameless feebleminded tavern girl' and subsequently fathered a line of respectable citizens after marriage.

With the collapse of the eugenics movement after the Second World War, human genetics reconstructed itself as a biomedical field, rather than as a biosocial field, largely following Lionel Penrose in the UK and James Neel in the USA (Kevles 1985). While geneticists all but abandoned the issue, a group of psychologists continued to pursue it. They maintained that the scalar quantity of IQ reflected a broad behavioural repertoire of innate intelligence. The presumptively genetic basis of stupidity thus came to the fore again in 1969, with the work of psychologist Arthur Jensen (another major beneficiary of the Pioneer Fund, see above). Jensen argued that because of the high measured 'habitability' of intelligence – presumably a measure of its innateness – social programmes designed to ameliorate the discrepancies in measured IQs between US whites and blacks were doomed to failure. The same argument would be made by Jensen's successors, in *The Bell Curve* (Herrnstein and Murray 1994).

Heritability, however, is a concept from animal and plant husbandry that has been misused in this context. It was devised to measure the susceptibility of a population to a regime of artificial selection, and is defined as the ratio of the variance of a trait that is associated specifically with genetic variation to the total phenotypic variance in the trait (Sober 2001). Since the total phenotypic variance (i.e. the denominator) incorporates environmental influences, heritability is not, and cannot be, a measure of the innateness of a trait. It is, rather, a description of a population in a particular context. Some classic examples may be useful here.

> If two identical plots of soil are sown with seed, and one plot receives uniform sunlight and water, and the other does not, it stands to reason that plants will grow differently in the two plots. In the first, plants will grow to varying heights; since the environment is largely uniform, most of the difference in plant height within the first plot will be due to genetic differences among the plants. The heritability will thus be high. In the second plot, plants will be stunted but still variable. Since again the environment is uniform, the differences in height are again due to heredity, and the heritability is high. But the difference between the two plots in average plant height is entirely due to the environmental difference between them, in spite of the high heritability.
>
> (Lewontin 1970)

> There is some genetic variation for digit number in human extremities. Some people have genetic polydactyly or syndactyly; nevertheless the human body is strongly programmed to have five digits at the end of each limb. However, most people who have too few fingers or toes have lost them to accidents. There is very little variance in digit number associated with genetic variation. Consequently, although the genetic programming is very strong, the heritability is very low.
>
> (Block 1995)

> Wearing earrings had a very high heritability until about 1970, when it ceased to be so strongly negatively associated with the Y chromosome. Nowadays it has a very low heritability.
>
> (Block 1995)

Thus the measurement of the heritability of IQ says nothing about the extent to which it is genetically programmed, nor about the causes of a measured difference between two populations. It is simply a descriptive (and poorly named) statistic of a single population (Layzer 1974; Hartung 1980).

Perhaps the most ominous prospect of contemporary behavioural genetics would be the identification of alleles that augment aspects of intelligence. It is unclear whether we should even expect to find such variation after eons of selection for our large brain, and the intelligence it confers upon our species. Such alleles might well be subject to balancing selection, producing the 'intelligence phenotype' only in heterozygotes. Even if such genetic variants are identified, we would expect them to be distributed the way most genetic variation is – widely, across all populations. Moreover, basic human genetics dictates that such genetic variants will also be accompanied physiologically by pleiotropic effects – a slightly greater risk of neurological disease, for example.

The most valuable work in the study of behaviour and human genetics is most likely to come from the study of quantitative trait loci, or QTLs. A less deterministic causal model of behaviour is generally used here, in which associations are sought between DNA regions and continuously varying features, rather than the discrete diseases that are studied with so much more fanfare.

JONATHAN MARKS
UNIVERSITY OF NORTH CAROLINA
AT CHARLOTTE

References

Beckwith, J. and Alper, J.S. (1997) 'Human behavioral genetics', *The Genetic Resource* 11.

Begley, S. (1987) 'All about twins', *Newsweek* (23 November): 58–69.

Block, N. (1995) 'How heritability misleads about race', *Cognition* 56.

Braman, D. (1999) 'Of race and immutability', *UCLA Law Review* 46.

Brunner, H.G. (1995) 'MAOA deficiency and abnormal behaviour: Perspectives on an association', in Ciba foundation symposium 194: *Genetics of Criminal and Antisocial Behaviour*, Chichester.

Davenport, C.B. (1911) *Heredity in Relation to Eugenics*, New York.

de Waal, F.B.M. (1999) 'The end of nature versus nurture', *Scientific American* 281(6).

Galton, F. (1869) *Hereditary Genius*, London.

Goddard, H.H. (1912) *The Kallikak Family: A Study in the Heredity of Feeble-Mindedness*, New York.

Halley, J.E. (1994) 'Sexual orientation and the politics of biology: A critique of the argument from immutability', *Stanford Law Review* 46.

Hamer, D., Hu, S., Magnuson, V.L., Hu, N. and Pattatucci, A.M.L. (1993) 'A linkage between DNA markers on the x chromosome and male sexual orientation', *Science* 261.

Hartung, J. (1980) 'On the geneticness of traits: Beyond $h^2 = V_g/V_p$', *Current Anthropology* 21.

Herrnstein, R. and Murray, C. (1994) *The Bell Curve*, New York.

Holden, C. (1980) 'Identical twins reared apart', *Science* 207.

Kevles, D.J. (1985) *In the Name of Eugenics*, Berkeley, CA.

Layzer, D. (1974) 'Heritability analyses of IQ scores: Science or numerology?' *Science* 183.

Lewontin, R.C. (1970) 'Race and intelligence', *Bulletin of the Atomic Scientists* 26.

Lewontin, R.C., Rose, S. and Kamin, L.J. (1984) *Not in Our Genes*, New York.

MacArthur, R.H. and Wilson, E.O. (1967) *The Theory of Island Biogeography*, Princeton, NJ.

McGuffin, P., Riley, B. and Plomin, R. (2001) 'Toward behavioral genomics', *Science* 291.

Sober, E. (2001) 'Separating nature and nurture', in D. Wasserman and R. Wachtbroit (eds) *Genetics and Criminal Behavior*, New York.

Tucker, W.H. (1997) 'Re-reconsidering Burt: Beyond a reasonable doubt', *Journal of the History of the Behavioral Sciences* 33.

—— (2002) *The Funding of Scientific Racism: Wickliffe Draper and the Pioneer Fund*, Urbana, IL.

Further reading

Alper, J.S. and Beckwith, J. (1993) 'Genetic fatalism and social policy: The implications of behavior genetics research', *Yale Journal of Biology and Medicine* 66.

SEE ALSO: evolutionary psychology; genomics

GENOCIDE

Genocide is a twentieth-century word for an age-old phenomenon, the killing of a defined population group. The word was coined during the Second World War by Raphael Lemkin, a Polish-Jewish jurist. Lemkin was looking for a word that would convey the full dimension of the Nazi murder of Jews, though he also was deeply conscious of precedents, especially the killing of Armenians in 1915 and 1916 by the Young Turk government of the Ottoman Empire. Lemkin joined the Greek word for a group, '*genus*', with the Latin suffix for murder, '-*cide*', to create the word genocide. He launched a one-man diplomatic campaign to convince the newly formed United Nations that it should develop a treaty that would outlaw genocide. The General Assembly passed an initial resolution in favour of such a treaty in 1946, and the final Convention on the Prevention and Punishment of the Crime of Genocide was approved on 9 December 1948. It came into effect in January 1951 with the ratification by the requisite number of states. Since then, more than 140 states have signed the Genocide Convention (as it is commonly known).

The Convention defines genocide as the 'intent to destroy, in whole or in part, a national, ethnical, racial or religious group, as such'. It goes on to delineate the acts that constitute genocide:

1 Killing members of the group.
2 Causing serious bodily or mental harm to members of the group.
3 Deliberately inflicting on the group conditions of life calculated to bring about its physical destruction in whole or in part.
4 Imposing measures intended to prevent births within the group.
5 Forcibly transferring children of the group to another group.

Two points are critical here. First, the Genocide Convention is designed to prevent attempts at the *physical annihilation* of a group, not the mere repression of its culture. The drafters of the Convention sought to reserve the word genocide for what is sometimes called the 'crime of crimes', the wholesale slaughter of a particular group. Hence, the five acts listed above are clearly subordinate to the overall definition, the 'intent to destroy, in whole or in part', a defined population group. Second, *intent* is the critical criterion. Genocide is not an accident, or a natural catastrophe, or an unintended by-product of war. It is a deliberate act, and if some kind of body (most often a state) seeks to destroy a group, it can be charged with genocide even if it fails fully to accomplish its goal. The drafters were well aware that it would be very difficult to prove intent to kill a group completely, since individuals or isolated communities had often survived killing operations. Hence, the Convention states that the intent to destroy a group 'in part' constitutes a genocide.

The UN's definition of genocide has its flaws, which scholars and activists debate vociferously. The major omission, on which most (but certainly not all) scholars agree, is the limitation of the victim group to those defined by nationality, ethnicity, race or religion. Many of the worst atrocities of the twentieth century were committed against groups defined by their political orientation or social class. The deportations and killings of wealthy peasants and former landlords in the Soviet Union and China, the mass killings of political opponents in Indonesia, Argentina and Chile – none of these massive violations of human rights can be called genocides under the

UN Convention. The most recent research (Schabas 2000) has demonstrated that virtually all the drafters of the Genocide Convention, including the representatives of the USA, favoured excluding political and social groups from the category of victims of genocide. The sense among the drafters was that political and social identities are less stable and are so often a matter of choice, while individuals are most often born into racial, ethnic, national and religious groups, and therefore have little or no choice about such identities. Nonetheless, scholars like Helen Fein and Frank Chalk and Kurt Jonassohn have sought to broaden the UN definition to encompass victim groups defined by their political commitments and social-class backgrounds (Fein 1990; Chalk and Jonassohn 1990).

Scholars and activists have also criticized the definition for ignoring other aspects of repression, such as efforts to prohibit a group's language or religious practices, sometimes called ethnocide. Indeed, the Convention in its final version did narrow Lemkin's broader and looser definition that had encompassed cultural repression. Moreover, the clause concerning abduction indicates a certain lack of consistency in the UN's definition. Unless practised on a truly massive scale, it is not at all clear how the forced removal of children results in physical annihilation. The lack of clarity here has contributed to a huge controversy in Australia, where the long-running policy of forcibly removing 'mixed-race' children from their families has been termed a genocide. A range of scholars has promoted a variety of additional terms, such as politcide, democide, ethnocide and gendercide, in an effort to capture the variety of massive human rights violations (Rummel 1994). The value of such linguistic inflation is questionable, and it is worth emphasizing that only the UN Convention definition has meaning in international law.

Historical examples of genocide abound. Some of the earliest cases occur in the Bible. The Book of Joshua records numerous instances in which the Israelites completely destroy the populations they encounter. The Roman destruction of Carthage is often cited as another case. But in the modern period, genocides became more systematic, more widespread and more deadly. In the twentieth century, genocides were produced mostly by states that sought to create homogeneous populations of one sort or another. They are part of revolutionary drives to remake the social order, to 'purify' the population of groups, conceived in racial, national or religious terms, which hold on to different ways of life and are demonized as the enemies that threaten the well-being of the dominant group. Genocides are terribly violent acts that entail high levels of face-to-face brutality. They are never antiseptic, factory-like processes of death, not even in the Holocaust. While modern genocides are typically initiated by states, they require the mobilization of substantial segments of the population to carry out the work of killing. Generally, people are mobilized around the ideologies of extreme nationalism and racism, even in communist countries where, for example, ideas of Great Russian or Khmer superiority become dominant at genocidal moments. Invariably, the killings, with very rare exceptions, are the work of men, who are sometimes forced to follow along, but many of whom also derive pleasure from their ability to transgress wildly the normal parameters of behaviour and to so dominate people that they exercise the power over life and death.

Most modern genocides have occurred in the context of war or vast domestic upheaval, when old rules no longer apply and conditions of instability both heighten the sense of insecurity and open up visions of great transformations, of finally laying to rest internal social divisions and creating a prosperous, harmonious future. The First World War was the landmark event because it created a culture of killing and revealed what highly organized states could accomplish. It is no surprise that the first modern genocide, that of the Armenians, occurred in the context of total war when the Young Turk rulers were threatened by the Allied powers and demonized the Armenian population as traitors. At the same time, the Young Turks imagined a vast, homogeneous pan-Turkic empire, which could only be accomplished, they believed, through the deportation and massacre of Armenians. Similarly, Jews in Nazi Germany were subject to the most severe discrimination in the 1930s, but it was only in the context of total war that the Nazis unleashed the Holocaust.

Three kinds of genocides emerged in the modern period: (1) colonial genocides, (2) genocides as by-products of more general and massive violations of political and social rights, and (3) genocides in which mass killings based on ethnicity, nationality, religion or race move to the very core of state policies.

(1) Colonial genocides developed from the fifteenth century onwards as Europeans and (later on) North Americans established their domination around the globe. The entire encounter between the West and the rest of the world was most definitely *not* a genocide. In most instances, Europeans were interested in the labour power of indigenous peoples and established their political control by working through existing social and political structures. In the case of the Americas, the vast proportion of Native Americans died as a result of their exposure to diseases against which they had no immunological protection. But there were *individual cases* of genocide within the huge and complex process of European expansion, as of the California Indians in the 1840s and the Aboriginal populations in Tasmania and in Queensland, Australia. Sometimes, these actions were carried out by settlers without the express approval of their states, but colonial states also rarely intervened to put a halt to such excesses.

(2) Especially in the case of twentieth-century communist regimes, genocides have taken place around the margins of larger processes of forced social transformations. In the Soviet Union, China and Cambodia, repressions and killings were directed mostly at political opponents and at those social classes deemed by their very nature to be hostile to the cause of socialism, such as landlords, aristocrats, wealthy peasants, capitalists and the middle class. However deadly these actions, they would not qualify as genocides under the UN definition. Nonetheless, a number of communist states also carried out deportations and killings of particular ethnic and national groups, such as Chechens and Tatars in the Soviet Union in the 1940s and Muslim Chams and Vietnamese in Cambodia. In these instances, communist states 'racialized' nationality, ethnicity and even class because they charged every member of the group, no matter what any individual had actually done, with being an enemy of the state. Typically, these were groups that refused to abandon their religious beliefs and customs, or tended to be involved in small businesses and trade, economic practices that were anathema to communist regimes. In all of these instances, the killing of ethnic, national, religious or racial groups constituted a relatively small proportion of the overall repressive and murderous activities of the state.

(3) Genocides take on truly massive proportions when racism or extreme nationalism becomes the guiding principles of the state (though not all racial states engage in genocide: witness South Africa and the Jim Crow USA). The infamous, though not exclusive, examples are the late Ottoman Empire under the Young Turks, Nazi Germany, the former Yugoslavia and Rwanda. In all of these instances, the state promised its followers a future of unbounded happiness and prosperity once the supposed enemy group – Armenians in the Ottoman Empire, Jews in the Third Reich, Croats and Muslims in Yugoslavia, Tutsis under a radical Hutu government – was eliminated. At the same time, moderate members of the dominant group who opposed the genocides were also killed. No genocide occurs divorced from other human rights violations.

For almost 40 years, the Genocide Convention lay in abeyance. The drafters had envisaged an international criminal court that would prosecute (and hopefully deter other) perpetrators, but the emergence of the Cold War blocked any possibilities for its development. The international community did nothing and sometimes actively abetted genocides or near-genocides in places like Sri Lanka, East Timor and Guatemala. In the 1990s, the UN and the major powers even ignored clear warnings about the impending genocide in Rwanda and engaged in half-hearted actions that only further endangered Bosnian Muslims in the former Yugoslavia. Finally, public outcry and, especially, the fear that these genocides would further undermine the international order pushed the UN and the USA into action. The Security Council empanelled two special tribunals to prosecute war crimes, crimes against humanity, and genocide committed in Rwanda and the former Yugoslavia. Both tribunals, for the first time in history, rendered verdicts of genocide, and also significantly expanded the scope of human rights law by prosecuting instances of rape as a 'crime against humanity'. At the end of the decade, most of the world's states (though not the USA) had signed on to the International Criminal Court (ICC), finally fulfilling some of the hopes of the 1940s. The ICC will no doubt be the venue of prosecution for future crimes of genocide. Whether it will have a deterrent effect remains to be seen.

ERIC D. WEITZ
UNIVERSITY OF MINNESOTA

References

Chalk, F. and Jonassohn, K. (1990) *The History and Sociology of Genocide: Analyses and Case Studies*, New Haven, CT.

Fein, H. (1990) 'Genocide: A sociological perspective', *Current Sociology* 38: 1–126.

Rummel, R.J. (1994) *Death by Government*, New Brunswick, NJ.

Schabas, W.A. (2000) *Genocide in International Law*, Cambridge.

Further reading

Bartov, O. (1996) *Murder in Our Midst: The Holocaust, Industrial Killing, and Representation*, New York and Oxford.

Chandler, D.P. (1999) *Voices from S-21: Terror and History in Pol Pot's Secret Prison*, Berkeley and Los Angeles.

Dadrian, V.N. (1997) *The History of the Armenian Genocide: Ethnic Conflict from the Balkans to Anatolia to the Caucasus*, 3rd edn, Providence, RI.

Gellately, R. and Ben, K. (eds) (2003) *The Specter of Genocide: Mass Murder in Historical Perspective*, Cambridge.

Herbert, U. (ed.) (2000) *National Socialist Extermination Policies: Contemporary German Perspectives and Controversies*, Providence, RI.

Kiernan, B. (1996) *The Pol Pot Regime: Race, Power, and Genocide in Cambodia under the Khmer Rouge, 1975–79*, New Haven, CT.

Kuper, L. (1981) *Genocide: Its Political Use in the Twentieth Century*, New Haven, CT.

Mamdani, M. (2001) *When Victims Become Killers: Colonialism, Nativism, and the Genocide in Rwanda*, Princeton, NJ.

Melson, R. (1992) *Revolution and Genocide: On the Origins of the Armenian Genocide and the Holocaust*, Chicago.

Weitz, E.D. (2003) *A Century of Genocide: Utopias of Race and Nation*, Princeton, NJ.

SEE ALSO: ethnic politics; partition; racism

GENOMICS

Genomics refers to the study of the structure, functions and interactions of all the genetic information in the genome. The term became widely used in the late twentieth century, taking its place alongside 'genetics', a word coined in 1903 by William Bateson to describe the science of heredity (the study of the mechanisms by which characteristics were transmitted from generation to generation in living organisms). Genetics became a major field of scientific research in the first half of the twentieth century, following the rediscovery of Gregor Mendel's work on the inheritance of characteristics in peas. The word 'gene' was adopted in 1909 to characterize a unit of inheritance, then hypothetical, which was passed down from one generation to the next. The gene was also thought of as a 'unit of development' that determined the development of characteristics in an individual over a lifetime. Biologists began to think that 'genes' were located on chromosomes, which were thread-like entities in the nucleus of living cells. (They were called chromosomes, from the Greek word for colour, because they were visible under a microscope when stained.) Humans were found to have forty-six chromosomes, comprising twenty-two pairs of 'autosomal' chromosomes and two sex chromosomes, conventionally designated XX for females and XY for males. Attempts were made to identify the precise places on each chromosome that were responsible for each specific hereditary characteristic.

Chromosomes were found to contain DNA, composed of four nucleotides, adenine, thymine, cytosine and guanine (A, T, C, G), known as 'bases'. It was postulated that DNA carried its information in the form of a code made up of the sequences of these bases. The major scientific breakthrough came with the identification of the 'double helical' structure of DNA, reported in the classic paper of 1953 by Francis Crick and James Watson. In this structure, paired strands of DNA are 'antiparallel', running in opposite directions to one another, held together by bonds between pairs of bases. The nature of the bonds ensures that A always pairs with T, and C always pairs with G. This provides a 'copying mechanism' for the genetic material: when the two strands become separated, each reassembles another strand upon itself with the same sequence as its former partner, producing two identical double helices. In the early 1960s, researchers concluded that the code comprised triplets of bases, and each of the sixty-four possible triplets coded for one of the twenty amino acids that made up proteins (Kay 2000). A series of triplets thus specifies a series of amino acids that make up a protein, and the total DNA sequence in the chromosomes of an organism makes up its genome.

In the 1980s, a project was sketched out for the 'decoding' of the human genome, base pair by base pair. This was the endeavour that became known as the Human Genome Project (HGP) (Cook-Deegan 1994). A range of scientific and technological advances, from the discovery of restriction enzymes that cut DNA at specific points on the basis of the precise DNA sequence, through Polymerase Chain Reaction techniques for the rapid reproduction of millions of copies of any given DNA segment, to the development of computers with massive processing power, made it possible to trace particular genes to specific chromosomes. It was also possible to compare sequences in individuals with or without specific diseases, either by identifying the coding sequence itself, or by linkage studies that trace known genetic markers that were inherited along with a particular condition or characteristic. The HGP received massive funding from the US government and later from the European Community and the UK's large charitable foundation, the Wellcome Trust. Many were sceptical about the project, but commercial companies recognized that genome mapping might generate discoveries about the genetic basis of disease that could be patented and used as the basis for the development and marketing of therapies. One particular company, Celera Genomics, invested in massive computer power in an attempt to beat the publicly funded HGP to the map of the human genome. After political intervention and much diplomacy, both public and private ventures announced their completion of the preliminary draft of the human genome on the same day, 11 February 2001, the Celera team publishing their sequence in *Science* and the public team in *Nature*. While some commentators claimed that scientists had now decoded the 'code of codes' – 'the instruction manual to make a human' – the reality was more complicated. The medical, biological, personal, social and cultural implications of this breakthrough are still uncertain.

Assessments of these implications are heavily shaped by the history of eugenics, the movement that set out to improve the quality of the human population by encouraging the reproduction of those with desirable qualities and/or curtailing the reproduction of those with qualities thought undesirable. Eugenic ideas were taken up in many countries in the first half of the twentieth century, in information campaigns to ensure that people made 'wise choices' in marriage partners, in genetic counselling for those who were thought at risk of producing defective children, and in the development of family allowances in France. They also inspired more coercive policies, such as attempts to curb immigration from

'lower races' to the USA. In the 1920s and 1930s, laws were passed in the Nordic countries, Latin America and elsewhere enabling sterilization of those thought to be carrying inherited deficiencies threatening the quality of the population. Eugenics in the Nordic countries was an element in programmes of social welfare, and carried out in the name of economic prosperity and social progress (Broberg and Roll-Hansen 1996). But eugenics took murderous form when fused with the virulent nationalism and political absolutism of the Nazi state: some 200,000 mentally ill or physically disabled people were murdered between 1939 and 1945 in the name of eugenics (Burleigh 1994; Proctor 1988).

Conscious of this history, geneticists in the second half of the twentieth century sought to distance themselves from eugenics, espousing the principles of individual autonomy and informed choice, and engaging in 'non-directive genetic counselling'. Critics still argued that the combination of counselling with the availability of abortion embodied a belief that some human beings were more desirable than others. More generally, social scientists were largely critical of any account of social processes or psychological characteristics that made reference to genetics. Such accounts were seen as implying a genetic determinism that banished social, environmental and cultural factors to a secondary place in explaining phenomena such as intelligence, social stratification, family forms, sexual orientation or the origins of mental illness. Polemical disputes ensued, often framed in terms of 'nature versus nurture' or 'heredity versus environment'. Eugenics had been supported by many progressive and socialist thinkers in the 1920s and 1930s, but now progressives usually emphasized 'environmental' factors, because this implied that social divisions were the products of cultural factors and of history, and hence amenable to transformation. Those 'on the side of heredity' were considered to be conservatives who were liable to believe that differences between ethnic groups, classes and races, or attributes such as intelligence, sexuality, personality, mental illness, were inherited, unalterable and not affected by social, cultural or environmental influences.

Following the mapping of the human genome, and the prestige and high profile it has given to genomics, some commentators have expressed concern about the widespread acceptance of genetic determinism. This is a viewpoint that essentializes human characteristics, marginalizes social factors, explains social phenomena such as illness and crime as being the result of inherited biological traits, and leads to policies that focus upon individual reformation rather than social change (Nelkin and Lindee 1995). Some disability activist organizations argue that developments such as preimplantation genetic diagnosis, which allow potential foetuses to be screened for genetic defects outside the womb, enshrine the belief that some lives are better than others, and that, in the phrase associated with eugenics, 'some lives are not worth living' (Kerr *et al.* 2002). However, these negative assessments are contested by others, often relatives of individuals who suffer from devastating diseases that have a clear genetic component – for example the dystrophies, or devastating disorders of connective tissue and skin that lead to a painful early death of affected children. They increasingly demand investment in genomic research into these conditions, raising funds, donating tissues for genotyping, and sometimes even patenting genomic discoveries and using funds raised in this way to finance research. These new forms of activism, coupled with new obligations upon individuals to understand factors affecting their health and to take responsibility for their own well-being and that of their families, have been termed 'biosociality' (Rabinow 1996). New ideas of rights and obligations are also being developed, and theories proposed of 'genetic' or 'biological' citizenship (Heath *et al.* 2003; Rose and Novas 2003).

The current genomic era differs in many ways from its genetic predecessor. The idea of the human genome as a 'parts list to make a human' was linked to the belief that there were around 100,000 genes in the human genome, each of which coded for a particular characteristic. It seemed possible that each disease was linked to a particular mutation or variant form of a gene. But when the first maps were published in February 2002, it appeared that there were only around 31,000 sequences coding for chains of amino acids in humans. This compares with 20,000 sequences in the genome of a nematode worm and 26,000 for an average plant. (A modern jet aeroplane contains more than 200,000 unique parts.) Predictions that 'the gene for' every human trait would be identified, from homosexuality to a sense of humour, were confounded. In the age of 'postgenomics' attention is shifting to functional genomics and proteomics. The idea that one gene produces one protein, and that one mutation equals one disease, has been largely discarded. Perhaps the very idea of 'a gene' – a 'unit' of both inheritance and development – is losing credibility (Fox Keller 2000). The large-scale projects undertaken in many countries (most notably Iceland) for the genome mapping of whole populations, in combination with databases of medical and genealogical records, have identified some variations that seem to increase risk of diseases such as stroke and type 2 diabetes, but have not yet produced the great advances predicted. There are certainly some 'single gene disorders' such as Huntington's Disease and cystic fibrosis, but they tend to be rare. Most common diseases such as diabetes, cancer and heart disease have a much more complex aetiology involving variants at multiple genomic locations, each of which have only a small effect. Nonetheless, there is considerable commercial investment in research on the genomics of disease. This has given rise to important disputes concerning intellectual property. The question is being asked whether private companies should have the right to hold patents on genetic sequences linked to specific diseases, and to control access to information that is required for the development of tests and therapeutics.

The focus of most genomic research and development is now on multigenic processes, on gene–gene and gene–environment interactions. In place of determinism a new way of thinking has developed about the risk of developing a disease, the key term being 'susceptibility'. Susceptibility is not usually analysed at the level of single genes, but in terms of the small variations at the molecular level that affect the details of the proteins for which a particular gene codes. These are termed single nucleotide polymorphisms or SNPs. While all humans share some 99.9 per cent of their genetic material, individuals differ from one another by a single base in approximately 0.1 per cent of the 3 billion base pairs of the human genome. (For example, an A is substituted by a C at a particular point in the sequence.) There may be over 2 million functionally significant SNPs. Research is being undertaken to map them and to correlate combinations of SNPs in many different coding sequences that, in their interactions, increase the likelihood of a disease developing in particular environmental conditions.

The pharmaceutical industry is a major player in these developments. One key area – often misleadingly termed 'personalized' genomic medicine – is pharmacogenetics. This seeks to use SNP data to identify which drugs, in what doses, are most likely to work for particular patients with specific diseases. Currently many drugs either do not work in particular individuals or cause significant adverse effects. Such ineffective or harmful drugs are a major cost to health services, and adverse drug reactions account for a significant proportion of morbidity and mortality in developed countries. The advances made by pharmacogenetics make it more likely that in future individuals will need to undergo a genetic test, from a specialist, their general practitioner or even their pharmacist, prior to being prescribed a drug. Some have suggested that babies should be genetically profiled at birth, with the profile stored on an electronic database for future use in medical decisions. Presymptomatic genetic testing or screening is already able to identify individuals who are not currently 'ill' but have susceptibilities or increased probabilities of developing a particular disease, including certain varieties of Alzheimer's and hereditary breast cancer. There is controversy as to whether genetic testing should be undertaken when there are no known therapeutics available. The genomic conception of 'presymptomatic illness' coupled with the possibility of presymptomatic treatment raises further ethical and social questions when extended to psychiatric and behavioural conditions.

'Genetic exceptionalism' in general is misplaced, and much genetic information is no different in principle from other information. However, recent developments are likely to lead to a considerable increase in genetic testing in the name of health, and genomic information on susceptibilities has clear implications for an individual's conception of their own future health and life-span, for their relations with their kin with whom they potentially share genetic status, and for reproductive decisions. It also may have consequences for insurability, employability and individual rights.

Genomic medicine is also sparking a new debate about the idea of 'race'. This is because SNPs are apparently differentially distributed across population groups. If this turns out to be the case, it will imply that certain groups are especially susceptible to particular diseases. Some argue that these distributions of SNPs map reasonably well onto the nineteenth-century racial classifications – white (Caucasian), black (African), yellow (Asian), red (Native American), and correlate highly with popular ideas of race and with self-definitions of ethnicity. Although many researchers and activists still insist that race is a biologically meaningless concept, others claim that a race-blind genomic medicine cannot address the racialized health inequalities that beset not just the USA but a globalized world.

Developments in the field of human genomics clearly have major social, political, economic, legal and ethical implications, but these are distinct from those commonly associated with the genetic explanations of human differences, conduct and pathologies that were current for much of the twentieth century (Kevles and Hood 1992). Governments no longer attempt to manipulate the genetic stock of populations in order to gain advantage in the struggle between nations. Instead these developments are undertaken in the name of health and life, and involve alliances between private companies, biomedical researchers, health policy-makers and individuals and their support groups. The belief that heredity is destiny has been replaced by the belief, perhaps equally misplaced, that genomic information will enable individuals to take control of their own fate by intervening in their own genomic make-up. These are not merely shifts in biology or medicine. Genomics has the capacity to transform our understandings of who we are, how we should act, and what we may hope for.

NIKOLAS ROSE
LONDON SCHOOL OF ECONOMICS
AND POLITICAL SCIENCE

References

Broberg, G. and Roll-Hansen, N. (eds) (1996) *Eugenics and the Welfare State. Sterilization Policy in Denmark, Sweden, Norway, and Finland*, Ann Arbor, MI.

Burleigh, M. (1994) *Death and Deliverance: 'Euthanasia' in Germany 1900–1945*, Cambridge, UK.

Cook-Deegan, R. (1994) *The Gene Wars: Science, Politics and the Human Genome*, New York.

Fox Keller, E. (2000) *The Century of the Gene*, Cambridge, MA.

Heath, D., Rapp, R. and Taussig, K.S. (2003) 'Genetic citizenship', in *Blackwell's Companion to Political Anthropology*, Oxford.

Kay, L. (2000) *Who Wrote the Book of Life? A History of the Genetic Code*, Stanford, CA.

Kerr, A., Shakespeare, T. and Varty, S. (2002) *Genetic Politics: From Eugenics to Genome*, London.

Kevles, D. and Hood, L. (1992) *The Code of Codes: Social and Scientific Issues in the Human Genome Project*, Cambridge, MA.

Nelkin, D. and Lindee, M.S. (1995) *The DNA Mystique: The Gene as a Cultural Icon*, New York.

Proctor, R. (1988) *Racial Hygiene: Medicine under the Nazis*, Cambridge, MA.

Rabinow, P. (1996) 'Artificiality and enlightenment: From sociobiology to biosociality', in *Essays on the Anthropology of Reason*, Princeton, NJ.

Rose, N. and Novas, C. (2003) 'Biological citizenship', in A. Ong and S. Collier (eds) *The Blackwell Companion to Global Anthropology*, Oxford.

SEE ALSO: evolutionary psychology; genetics and behaviour

GEOGRAPHICAL INFORMATION SYSTEMS

Geographical information systems (GIS: geographic information systems in the USA) are integrated computer systems for the capture, storage, updating, manipulation, analysis and display of all forms of geographically referenced information. We can think of GIS as:

- a software product, acquired to perform well-defined functions (*GIS software*);
- digital representations of aspects of the world (*GIS data*);
- a community of people who use these tools for various purposes (the *GIS community*); and
- the activity of using GIS to solve problems or advance science (*doing GIS*) (Longley *et al.* 2001).

The first GIS, the Canada Geographic Information System, was a natural resource inventory, designed by Roger Tomlinson in the mid-1960s. In the same decade, the DIME (Dual Independent Map Encoding) system was developed for the US Census. It gradually became apparent to early GIS developers that the same basic needs were present in many different application areas. The modern history of GIS dates from the early 1980s, when the price of sufficiently powerful computers fell below $250,000 and typical software costs fell below $100,000.

Today's GIS is a complex of software, hardware, databases, people and procedures, connected by networks, and set in an institutional context (see Figure 7). The Internet provides society's information exchange *network*, and may be used to connect archives, clearinghouses, digital libraries and data warehouses. GIS *hardware* takes a range of forms, including desktop computers, laptops, personal data assistants, in-

Six Parts of a GIS

- **Hardware**
- **Software**
- **Data**
- **People**
- **Procedures**
- **Network**

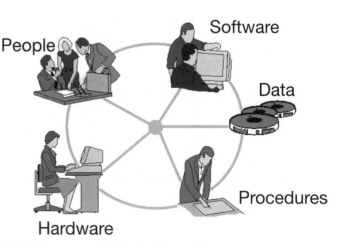

Figure 7 The six component parts of a GIS (Courtesy ESRI, Redlands, CA)

vehicle devices and cellular telephones. GIS *software* is sold by a number of vendors, and may be tailored to particular needs (e.g. simple mapping, network analysis) and applications (e.g. utility management, defence). The creation and maintenance of GIS *databases* is a major industry, which dwarfs the hardware and software industries in terms of expenditure and employment size. People are fundamental to the design, programming and maintenance of GIS, and are often trained through academic or vocational courses.

GIS are useful tools, but Longley *et al.* (2001: Chs 1 and 2) illustrate how their usage can raise profound, and sometimes frustrating, issues of design, data and methods. Resolution of these issues is central to *geographical information science* (GISc: Goodchild 1992). GISc studies the fundamental conceptual, measurement and analysis issues arising from the creation, handling, storage and use of geographically referenced information.

GIS remains fundamentally concerned with creating workable real-world applications. But the advent of GISc has brought heightened awareness of the need for sensitivity to, and depth of understanding of, all aspects of geographical information. It also emphasizes the relative importance of core organizing principles, techniques and management practices, over more transitory skills in using particular software systems. GIS remains a very exciting area of activity, which has very much to offer students interested in tackling the geographical dimension of real-world problems.

PAUL A. LONGLEY
UNIVERSITY COLLEGE LONDON

References

Goodchild, M.F. (1992) 'Geographical information science', *International Journal of Geographical Information Systems* 6: 31–45.

Longley, P.A., Goodchild, M.F., Maguire, D.J. and Rhind, D.W. (2001) *Geographic Information Systems and Science*, Chichester.

Further reading

CASA (1999) The GIS Timeline, http://www.casa.ucl.ac.uk/gistimeline/ (an excellent summary of the history of GIS).

SEE ALSO: cartography; spatial analysis

GEOGRAPHY

Geography is an academic discipline whose main concerns are describing and understanding areal differentiation in the distribution of various phenomena across the earth's surface. It focuses on the interrelationships among three main concepts – environment, space and place – and has traditionally been divided into physical geography, human geography and regional geography respectively, with the first two each containing a substantial number of separate systematic subfields.

As an academic discipline, with a major presence in universities and similar institutions, geography is little more than a century old. It was introduced, in Germany and elsewhere, to provide a source of ordered information about places; such material was of particular value to the mercantile classes plus the civil services and armed forces of imperial nations. Geography was also promoted as an important subject in school education in a number of countries, to advance both 'world knowledge' and the ideological bases of many national identities. As a set of practices, however, geography is very much older, comprising subject matter that incorporated exploration and discovery, cartography and chorography (or 'place description').

With the development of universities as research as well as teaching institutions, geographers sought coherent frameworks for their discipline that would establish it as the equal of the burgeoning sciences and social sciences. This stimulated proposed definitions of the discipline's content and methods, many of which had roots in the work of a small number of nineteenth-century German and French scholars. The most notable statements in the English language were probably Hartshorne's *The Nature of Geography* (1939) and Wooldridge and East's (1951) *The Spirit and Purpose of Geography*, although those prospectuses were largely rejected in the 1960s. For many until then, geography's goal was to identify and provide accounts of the various regions on the earth's surface – defined at a variety of spatial scales – although some, such as the influential US geologist-cum-geographer William Morris Davis, promoted physical geography as the study of landscape evolution and processes (as an underpinning for analyses of regional mosaics) and others, following Carl Sauer, a US cultural geographer, promoted the study of cultural landscape evolution.

For a variety of reasons, some related to the subject's strengths in the relevant country's school system (as in the UK), geography became a very popular university discipline in several European countries (Dunbar 2002). From the 1960s on, research achievement as the major criterion for career advancement provided the context for a rapid growth of research output and much experimentation with alternative epistemologies, methodologies and subject matters. Geography is now an extremely broadly based discipline. Most academic departments of geography are catholic in their subject matter coverage, with individual scholars having close links with a wide range of others in the social, environmental and natural sciences, as well as the humanities (Johnston and Sidaway 2004).

Subject matter and divisions

Areal differentiation of the contents of the earth's surface covers both the physical environment and its many human-generated modifications created in the struggle to exist and enhance material and cultural living standards. The various approaches to its study have loosely coalesced around three major themes.

ENVIRONMENT

The 'natural' environment of an area comprises the land surface (relatively few geographers study the oceans), the hydrology of the water bodies on that surface, the fauna and flora that occupy it, the soils that form a thin layer at the surface, and the atmosphere immediately above. All are linked in complex environmental systems – an area's flora, for example, influence the climate above it and the formation and erosion of soils beneath. Many physical geographers focus on one aspect of the environmental complex only, however, in detailed searches for understanding its genesis and continual change, but increasingly research is being undertaken by groups who span a range of substantive interests, thus facilitating system-integrated analyses (Gregory 2000).

The separate focuses are represented by the various subdivisions of physical geography, with most individuals associated with one of them. Most subdivisions are linked to allied disciplines, to which some physical geographers claim more affinity than they do to the rest of their 'home' subject. The largest subdivision has traditionally been *geomorphology*, the study of landforms at a variety of spatial scales, and the processes that create them. Many geomorphologists pay particular attention to the role of water as a landscape-forming agent, thereby creating close ties with hydrology; others, especially those interested in the longer-term processes of landform genesis, have closer affinities with other specialists (notably geologists), as illustrated by the work of glaciologists and those interested in relatively long-term environmental change. Smaller groupings are those of *climatologists* (with links to meteorology), *biogeographers*, who focus much more on plants than on animals and so associate with ecologists and botanists rather than zoologists, and those concerned with soils, who have links with pedologists

Although most physical geographers work within just one of these subdisciplinary groupings, there is increasing recognition of the importance of studying the interactions among the various components of the environmental complex – as illustrated by the current concern with rapid environmental change. Indeed, environmental changes – understanding the past and predicting the future – have become a central focus of much earth systems science, especially over the most recent geological era – the Quaternary. Within this, the impact of human occupancy of the earth's surface, soils and atmosphere on the operation of geomorphological, hydrological, glacial, biological and atmospheric processes has come to centre stage, with much debate over the environment's ability to sustain human life in the long if not the short term (Turner *et al.* 1990).

Whereas study of the physical environment is almost exclusively the preserve of physical geographers, there has always been interest in the physical landscape among human geographers, mainly those concerned with the analysis of landscapes as part of the milieu of human life. To some, interpretation of physical landscapes is central to human endeavour, and so popular conceptions of how 'the earth works' (of the hydrological cycle, for example) are important sources of geographical understanding. To others, the concept of nature itself is a social construction and so interpretations of the physical world are part of the ideological superstructure of society. Indeed, they argue that 'nature' cannot be separated from 'culture': rather the two are continuously interacting on each other, thereby creating new hybrid forms

SPACE

While physical geographers have focused their studies on the 'natural' environment, human geographers' main concern has been the occupation and use of that resource base. Land use was a major topic of interest for several decades, at a variety of scales (e.g. the difference between urban and rural areas at one scale and the agricultural use of different fields at another). Much descriptive work chronicled what was done where, with generalized explanations suggested through relationships with the physical environment.

In the late 1950s, the influence of pioneering geographical work in Scandinavia and Germany, plus spatially oriented studies by economists and sociologists, stimulated promotion of an alternative perspective for human geography focusing on the spatial organization of human activity. The goal was a scientific reconstruction of the discipline, whose rationale was to be the identification of the laws of both individual spatial behaviour and the spatial patterns in the distributions of their artefacts. Distance is an impediment to human behaviour, because it takes time and costs money to cross space in the movement of goods, people and ideas. To minimize such costs, both locational decision-making and interaction patterns are organized on distance-minimizing principles, producing spatial organizations (of, for example, the pattern of settlements in an area) that ensure least-effort solutions. Human geography was presented as a 'discipline in distance', with distance (or space) the key concept distinguishing it from other social sciences: spatial concepts formed the discipline's theoretical base (Johnston and Sidaway 2004).

Numerous attempts were made in the 1960s and 1970s to codify this approach to human geography and identify its fundamental concepts. Haggett (Haggett *et al.* 1978), for example, divided the discipline's subject matter into: point patterns (such as farm buildings in an agricultural area); hierarchical point patterns (such as shopping centres of various sizes and importance within an urban region); line patterns (notably transport networks); movement patterns (such as the flows of people, goods or information along

networks); surfaces of variations in a continuous phenomenon (such as population densities and land values within an urban area); and diffusions over space (such as the spread of a disease along a network, across a surface and/or down a hierarchy). To this can be added territories, the divisions of continuous space into discrete entities – whether nation-states, ghettos or personal spaces within an open-plan office. Others sought the fundamental basic concepts of a spatial discipline, such as direction, distance, connectiveness and, perhaps, boundary.

The goal was to identify spatial laws, which involved adopting a methodology based on the quantitative evaluation of hypotheses. Both physical and human geographers switched from describing patterns cartographically to analysing them statistically and modelling them mathematically. The discipline developed a strong quantitative core in the 1970s, with considerable hope that it could attain scientific respectability through its methods and the generality of its findings (Harvey 1969).

This new geography of the 1960s and 1970s was introduced at a time of rapid growth in the study of geography in English-speaking universities. The 'quantitative and theoretical revolutionaries' promoted their view of the discipline in a context of expansion: the large number of staff positions and research studentships enabled them to 'take over' the discipline very substantially, and to advance their particular view of what geography studies, and how. This rapid expansion stimulated application of the new ideas to a wide range of subject matters. Prior to the 1960s, human geography had some important subdisciplines (such as historical geography), but to a considerable extent it was divided by areal rather than sectoral interests (i.e. it was divided according to practitioners' interests in the geography of certain parts of the world: regional geography). This changed rapidly, and the incipient sectoral divisions soon achieved predominance over disciplinary practice.

Those subdisciplines are cross-cutting. Four of the most enduring reflect links with the main other social sciences: economic geography with economics; social geography with sociology; political geography with political science; and cultural geography with anthropology. Practitioners of the first two were more numerous in the 1960s and 1970s. The others grew more slowly, and later; the link with anthropology has been much stronger in the USA than elsewhere. There were also subdivisions of the subdivisions, notably the several distinct areas of specialization within economic geography: industrial geography, agricultural geography, transport geography, retail geography, and the geography of service industries, for example.

A second set involved the separation of urban from rural geography (with the latter largely distinct from agricultural geography). Urban geography was the focus of much of early quantitative and theoretical work. It had its own subdivisions: urban social geographers who studied residential segregation in cities, for example, were largely separate from those who studied economic aspects of urban places (such as the group influenced by the ideas encapsulated in 'central-place theory' regarding the spatial organization of shopping centres and of the spatial behaviour of individuals who visited them).

By the mid-1970s, therefore, human geographers interested in the study of spatial organization were divided into a number of interdependent subgroups, each with strong links outside the discipline. Their commonality within geography was defined by the procedures that they used rather than the subjects that they studied, and by their emphasis on distance as a key concept. (There were other, smaller, subdisciplines, such as population and medical geography.) This work continues, and the strength of the subdivisions is marked by the proliferation of academic journals concentrating on the specialist parts of geography (Johnston 2003).

During the 1970s, however, unease about the discipline's fragmentation grew and a number of geographers, many of a Marxian persuasion, argued that society should be studied as a whole (Harvey 1973). Areal differentiation is an outcome of the processes of uneven development that involves interacting social, political and cultural as well as economic factors, so important theoretical work by Harvey (1982) and others promoted the study of spatial organization as both an outcome of and a constraint to processes of capitalist development and underdevelopment. This stimulated a very different orientation to the study of space, and much debate over whether spatial patterns are contingent outcomes of social, economic, political and other processes or whether they are complicit in the production and reproduction of geographies of uneven development. Work in Marxian and realist moulds was concerned with elucidating general processes of uneven development rather than statistically analysing patterns of development and of spatial behaviour within them. This led to conflict over epistemology and methodology.

The growth of interest in what has variously been termed a political economy, radical, structural and realist approach to uneven development, in its many forms and at a variety of spatial scales, occurred during a period of very rapid socioeconomic and political change (Peet and Thrift 1989). During the 1980s, in particular, substantial economic restructuring involved considerable rewriting of the map of uneven development. There were major sociocultural shifts, too, with the promotion of 'enterprise societies' and attacks on welfare states, with nationalism growing as a response to several forms of political hegemony in many parts of the world. This rapidly changing scene attracted much geographical attention.

PLACE

Geography emerged in the nineteenth century as an academic discipline that disseminated knowledge about places; it involved the collection, collation and presentation of information about different parts of the world. As it matured, so its practitioners perceived the need for more sophisticated methods of working than mere collecting, mapping and cataloguing: they wanted an intellectual framework that allowed them to advance knowledge as well as order information.

Various attempts were made to create such a framework. Considerable support went in the early decades of the twentieth century to *environmental determinism*, whose basic argument was that human occupancy of and action upon any part of the earth is determined by its physical character. This was widely discredited by the 1930s, and replaced by *regional geography*, whose rationale was description of the individual character of each region (a defined area of the earth's surface, delimited according to certain criteria). Individuals identified themselves as regional geographers of defined areas – usually of continental or subcontinental scale – and their major publishing activities involved describing those areas, often in substantial regional texts.

Regional geography was methodologically weak, however – over the defining criteria, the means of determining regional boundaries, and descriptive protocols, for example. Much of it was strongly influenced by the environmental determinism paradigm; most regional geographies started with descriptions of the area's physical environment, as the context for, if not determinant of, patterns of human occupancy. This approach was increasingly discredited by the 1960s, being condemned as little more than 'mere description', as fact gathering and presentation in woolly analytical frameworks – unscientific and not respectable for a putative scientific discipline. It languished with the rapid growth in the number of geographers adhering to other approaches, although some still identified their role as describing and analysing the world's complex mosaic of places for wide audiences. (Those audiences were for long schoolchildren, taught by the graduates of university departments. Few geography graduates become teachers now, and few school syllabuses emphasize regional geography.)

The study of place was substantially devalued within geography, but was then revived – albeit in a different form – from the 1970s on. This renewed interest was initially promoted by those – many of them historical or cultural geographers – who were disenchanted with the spatial science paradigm and its search for laws of patterns and behaviour. Such laws, they argued, denied individual free will and thereby denigrated human individuality, culture and decision-making (Gregory 1978). Similar criticisms were addressed at some of the early Marxian work on uneven development, which implied that capitalist processes were structural determinants within which individuals had few degrees of freedom to act. Neither spatial science nor structural Marxism corresponded with some geographers' perceptions of the empirical world, which contained much cultural, social and political variation that could not be ascribed to economic determinants, however important material concerns were as impulses to human behaviour.

This alternative view, which became associated with the cultural turn in other social sciences in the 1980s, was linked to several contemporary intellectual developments. The rise of feminism, for example, not only demonstrated the oppression of women in most societies and the male dominance in the construction of academic disciplines such as geography (Rose 1992), but also showed that different groups within society have different perspectives, depending on their position therein: there is no predominant view, though one may dominate academic and other discourse. Similarly, reactions to imperialism – cultural as well as economic and political – showed how the map of the world and the construction of understandings of its various parts was structured by the ideological goals of hegemonic groups and their creation of geopolitical maps. The growth of ecological and environmental movements, promoting different interpretations of the relationships between peoples and environments, similarly advanced alternative conceptions of how society could be organized.

Difference rather than similarity became a focus of geographical scholarship, therefore. Place was central to this because of its role as a constraining factor in cultural development and its importance to constructions of the world. People learn who and what they are in places, and develop notions of self-identity (their 'sense of place') within such milieux, where new residents are socialized into the dominant construction of that place and what it means to be part of it. An important component of place-identity construction involves its opposition to that which it is not: part of what characterizes one place is its difference from others – mainly but not only its neighbours. People in places develop images of other places and their residents, and act accordingly.

Much of this work on place is not antithetic to that on the processes of uneven development, therefore, although it is largely opposed to spatial science. It enriches the political economy approach by stressing the importance of people and their positions within society as strong influences on what they do – whether in very local contexts or as world politicians, and even with rapidly globalizing economic organization and improvements in communication technologies that are 'destroying' distance. Understanding the spatial organization of the world and its many component parts requires full appreciation of the nature of the people who are continually reconstructing that world, in particular their place-contingent views of both their place in the world and those of all others. Places are thus the arenas within which individuals are nurtured, their identities and attitudes to 'others' defined, and the foundations for their economic, cultural, social and political behaviour laid down.

Approaches and methods

Geography has thus been characterized since the Second World War by three main approaches to its subject matter and, within human geography at least, considerable debate about their merits and disadvantages (Johnston and Sidaway 2004). In addition, there has been debate within each approach over the relative advantages and disadvantages of different methods.

As both physical and human geography moved from a descriptive to an analytical stance, so the attractions of the positivist approach to science became seductive, with its emphasis on testable hypotheses leading to the formulation of laws and the derivation of theories – not only for its 'scientific' charisma and status but also its potential applied value in re-engineering environments and (the spatial organization of) societies. This approach was strongly associated with quantification, and a belief that statistical regularities provide empirical proof of the existence of theoretically suggested cause-and-effect relationships. Thus measurement and the statistical manipulation of data replaced verbal and cartographic description as dominant geographical procedures.

As with any discipline adopting and adapting procedures developed elsewhere, this switch to the positivist epistemology involved much trial and error. By the late 1960s, some geographers had realized that statistical procedures developed in other disciplines could not readily be adopted for geographical work because of the particular features of spatial data sets: spatial autocorrelation was recognized as an impediment to drawing causal inferences from many analyses of spatial data, and led to sophisticated development of spatial statistical methods, for example. Whether geographers have identified many strong regularities indicative of the operation of causal laws is doubted by some; however, especially in human geography, many intriguing findings have been reported, but such is the complexity of the physical and human contexts that it is very difficult to disentangle the general from the locally particular. Many of the hopes of the early disciples of the 'quantitative and theoretical revolution' have been dashed on the difficulties of successfully testing hypotheses, although they have provided much sophisticated description of the world.

The measurement-based approach to the discipline involved experimentation and innovation in means of collecting data in the field, both of the operation of processes in the physical environment and from individuals pursuing their spatial behaviours. These have been assisted by major revolutions in the technology of data capture, storage, display and analysis, in which geographers have played important pioneering roles. The first involved the field of *remote sensing*, usually, but far from exclusively, associated with imaging the earth from space. Vast quantities of data are generated by sensors in satellites and other airborne carriers, and geographers have been at the forefront of developing means of interpreting the information provided – through large-memory computing devices – in order to portray detailed environmental variations over time and space. Remote sensing has provided not only much new material with which to analyse the earth but also many technical puzzles over how to transform and interpret that material in the pursuit of research goals.

Most geographical data refer to two- (or three-) dimensional contexts. These have traditionally been represented in map form, but developments since the late 1970s in *geographical information systems* (GIS) have very significantly advanced the ability to store, integrate, visualize and analyse such spatial data in computer systems. The presentation of spatially referenced data and their analysis, through the ability to layer data sets on to each other (for example rainfall observations at individual sites on to topographic maps), substantially enhances both the ability to suggest hypotheses for empirical testing and the conduct of those tests (Longley *et al.* 1999). These are embedded into wider systems for collecting and analysing spatial data – often termed geoinformatics and/or geographical information science; at the same time, there have been very substantial improvements in the sophistication of various methods of spatial analysis.

Reaction to the deterministic cast of much of the argument for a spatial science of human behaviour led to explorations in what became widely known as humanistic geography, which emphasized individuality and difference rather than conformity and similarity. A range of epistemologies was investigated – including phenomenology, idealism, existentialism and pragmatism (Jackson and Smith 1984) – but the main impact of this work was its opposition to the alternative paradigm being promoted, especially in the early 1970s.

The emphasis in this humanistic work was on interpretation – both interpretation of the world by those acting in it and interpretation of their actions and the outcomes (landscapes, for example) by geographers. The enterprise was strongly hermeneutic, therefore. Geographers were exploring the interpretations behind people's actions, often, especially in the case of historical work, through the study of texts, both written and visual (i.e. maps, works of art, and landscapes), and then transmitting those interpretations to their own readers. Key to much of this hermeneutic work was language, since most understandings are transmitted through words, which are very imperfect because of their openness to differences in interpretation (Barnes and Duncan 1992). The importance of language and difference in the later postmodernism project has been important to this approach to geography, with its very strong antagonism to notions of grand theory and totalizing explanation. Place is central to this, because much learning of language and its nuances is place-bound.

The methods of humanistic geography are those of interpretation, therefore, which raises a variety of issues relating to sources of information and their treatment. As already indicated, some of those sources are texts that must be interpreted in the context of their production (the language and ideology of the time and place, for example); others involve collecting material directly from the individuals concerned, involving research that is ethnographic in character, with associated ethical and other concerns.

The implicit determinism of the positivist approach to human geography and the voluntarism of its humanistic counter were together the focus of a third major approach to the discipline, also initiated in the early 1970s. As indicated above, much of this work was Marxist-inspired and presented capitalist economic processes as underpinning the ever-changing map of uneven development. Some early work was overly determinist also, however, and portrayed a set of sociospatial processes that individuals and collectivities were largely impotent to combat. Within a few years, however, that structural thinking was being married with the arguments for difference and individuality within a humanistic one. This generated a rich and sophisticated framework for appreciating how space, place

and nature are constructed, reconstructed and acted within by knowing individuals, operating within the limits of their own appreciation and constrained by the structural imperatives of the mode of production. The perspectives of postmodernism have added to this, emphasizing difference and individuality.

As with the humanistic approach, the structuralist/realist relies very heavily on textual interpretation. It is not as antagonistic to the use of quantitative data, however, though little of it involves sophisticated analysis of such material. More importantly, its goal is to identify not only specific causes but also general processes that underpin them, and which cannot be apprehended empirically. In some ways, this is similar to approaches to the understanding of large-scale environmental systems whose empirical complexities, which reflect locally contingent factors, obscure the underlying fundamental physical laws and their interactions.

Applying geography

Geography was invented as an academic discipline because of its potential applied value in promoting world understanding. Since then, the importance of an applied stance has varied, in part at least because of the demands made on the discipline, and indeed on academia in general; in some societies, of course, such as the USSR and Eastern Europe between 1945 and 1989, the practice of geography was almost entirely determined by the demands of the state apparatus.

The applied value of geography was particularly appreciated in the Second World War with the ability of geographers to provide information about other countries; their cartographic and photogrammetric skills were widely employed in intelligence work. From the 1950s on, the role of geographical work, first in data collection and later in their analysis and use in prescription, as in the preparation of town and regional plans, was increasingly recognized and some of the technical developments since (as in GIS) have been oriented to practical applications: indeed, some argue that one of the geographer's most important roles is to add value to data, which can then be 'sold' to spatial decision-makers, while US geographers have identified GIS and related skills as important 'selling' points for a geographical education (NAS-NRC 1997).

The growing concern over environmental issues – local, regional, national and global – has attracted much attention. Geographers' stress on both the processes that operate in the physical environment and the impact of human activity on those processes and their outcomes has generated much work, in the conduct of environmental impact assessments, for example, and in the moves towards sustainable development at a variety of scales.

Much of this work sees geographers applying the methods and goals of the positivist approach in seeking solutions to a variety of perceived problems, in engineering social futures on the basis of scientific understanding. This technocratic view has been challenged by others, who see such work as promoting the status quo within society, thereby maintaining its many inequalities and injustices, and sustaining both the capitalist mode of production and the state apparatus whose goal is to promote and legitimize what is perceived as an unjust system. For such critics, there are other applied roles for geographers, in promoting awareness of the nature of the changing world in which we live (both self-awareness and awareness of others) and in advancing the cause of emancipation, whereby people are enabled to obtain control over society and steer it towards their own ends. Each is a contested political goal; all involve geography as the servant of particular causes.

Summary

Geography is a large and vibrant academic discipline, with roots in the sciences, the social sciences and the humanities. It comprises a number of overlapping communities of researchers and teachers, advancing understanding of environment, space and place in a great variety of ways.

The differences among these communities in their approaches to the discipline ensure continued debate about the relative merits of alternative perspectives. Alongside them, however, there is a great deal of substantial research that is advancing our appreciation of how the physical environment is constructed and operated, of how human life is organized spatially, and of how places are created and recreated as the milieux within which most people are socialized.

R.J. JOHNSTON
UNIVERSITY OF BRISTOL

References

Barnes, T.J. and Duncan, J.S. (eds) (1992) *Writing Worlds: Discourse, Text and Metaphor in the Representation of Landscape*, London.

Dunbar, G.S. (ed.) (2002) *Geography: Discipline, Profession and Subject since 1870*, Dordrecht.

Gregory, D. (1978) *Ideology, Science and Human Geography*, London.

Gregory, K.J. (2000) *The Nature of Physical Geography*, 2nd edn, London.

Haggett, P., Cliff, A.D. and Frey, A.E. (1978) *Locational Analysis in Human Geography*, 2nd edn, London.

Hartshorne, R. (1939) *The Nature of Geography: A Critical Survey of Current Thought in the Light of the Past*, Lancaster, PA.

Harvey, D. (1969) *Explanation in Geography*, London.

—— (1973) *Social Justice and the City*, London.

—— (1982) *The Limits to Capital*, Oxford.

Jackson, P. and Smith, S.J. (1984) *Exploring Social Geography*, London.

Johnston, R.J. (2003) 'Geography: A different sort of discipline?' *Transactions of the Institute of British Geographers* NS28.

Johnston, R.J. and Sidaway, J.D. (2004) *Geography and Geographers: Anglo-American Human Geography since 1945*, 6th edn, London.

Longley, P.A., Goodchild, M.F., Maguire, D.J. and Rhind, D.W. (eds) (1999) *Geographical Information Systems: Principles, Techniques, Applications, and Management*, 2nd edn, 2 vols, New York.

NAS-NRC (1997) *Rediscovering Geography: New Relevance for Science and Society*, Washington, DC.

Peet, R. and Thrift, N.J. (eds) (1989) *New Models in Geography: The Political-Economy Perspective*, 2 vols, Boston, MA.

Rose, G. (1992) *Feminism and Geography: The Limits of Geographical Knowledge*, Cambridge, UK.

Turner, B.L., Clark, W.C., Kates, R.W., Richards, J.F., Mathews, J.T. and Meyer, W.B. (eds) (1990) *The Earth as Transformed by Human Action: Global and Regional Changes in the Biosphere over the last 300 Years*, Cambridge, UK.

Wooldridge, S.W. and East, W.G. (1951) *The Spirit and Purpose of Geography*, 2nd edn, London.

Further reading

Abler, R.F., Marcus, M.G. and Olson, J.M. (eds) (1992) *Geography's Inner Worlds: Pervasive Themes in Contemporary American Geography*, New Brunswick, NJ.

Agnew, J., Mitchell, K. and Toal, G. (eds) (2003) *A Companion to Political Geography*, Oxford.

Anderson, K., Domosh, M., Pile, S. and Thrift, N.J. (eds) (2003) *Handbook of Cultural Geography*, London.

Chorley, R.J., Beckinsale, R.P. and Dunn, A.J. (1964, 1973, 1991 and 2003) *The History of the Study of Landforms*, London.

Gaile, G. and Willmott, C.J. (2004) *American Geography at Century's End*, New York.

Gregory, K.J. (2000) *The Nature of Physical Geography*, 2nd edn, London.

Johnston, R.J., Gregory, D., Pratt, G. and Watts, M.J. (eds) (2000) *The Dictionary of Human Geography*, 4th edn, Oxford.

Johnston, R.J. and Sidaway, J.D. (2004) *Geography and Geographers: Anglo-American Human Geography since 1945*, 6th edn, London.

Johnston, R.J. and Williams, M. (eds) (2003) *A Century of British Geography*, Oxford.

Lee, R. and Wills, J. (eds) (1997) *Geographies of Economies*, London.

Livingstone, D.N. (1992) *The Geographical Tradition: Episodes in the History of a Contested Enterprise*, Oxford.

Rhoads, B.L. and Thorn, C.E. (eds) (1996) *The Scientific Nature of Geomorphology*, New York.

Sheppard, E.S. and Barnes, T.J. (eds) (2000) *A Companion to Economic Geography*, Oxford.

Thomas, D.S. and Goudie, A.S. (eds) (2001) *The Dictionary of Physical Geography*, 2nd edn, Oxford.

Unwin, T. (1992) *The Place of Geography*, London.

GERONTOLOGY, SOCIAL

Gerontology, defined as the scientific study of processes associated with ageing, is a relatively new field. The term first appeared only a 100 years ago. Multidisciplinary approaches to ageing, which take into account the conjoint biological, social and psychological features of ageing, first appeared only over the last 50 years. Finally, the National Institute of Aging, a branch of the US National Institutes of Health, is only 25 years old.

Growing interest in the scientific investigation of ageing is driven first of all by an increase in life expectancy, so that people born in more developed countries today can expect to live 40 years more than they would have, had they been born at the turn of the century. Additionally, declining fertility (which reduces the number or young people entering a population) and increasingly effective medical care (which reduces death rates at all ages) have led to an increase in the proportion of older people alive at any given time. By 2030, the proportion of people aged 65 or greater will reach 20 per cent in most European and North American countries. The same trends apply in less developed countries. These countries have become old before they have become rich and face epidemics of chronic disease with underdeveloped pension, social welfare and health care systems.

Ageing is the maturation and senescence of biological systems. With each additional decade of life, adults will see slowing in reaction time, psychomotor speed and verbal memory; declines in strength and walking speed; a decreased rate of urine flow; loss of skeletal muscle; and greater mortality, among many other changes. But they will also see declines in addictive behaviours and crime, and reduction in severe psychiatric disorders; continuing increases in vocabulary; greater selectivity in friendship and increased contact with close family; less need for novel stimuli; and increases in wealth, leisure time and altruistic behaviours, also among many other changes. The popular understanding of ageing mostly stresses negative changes, but social gerontology stresses both types of change, as its charge is to examine ageing in its full complexity.

When people think of old age, they first think of years or some other indicator of the passage of time (for example in societies where people do not use year-based calendars, these indicators might include the number of harvests completed, number of ritual cycles conducted, or number of relocations of dwellings). But even in contemporary cosmopolitan cultures, 'old age' is not simply a matter of chronological age. Survey results show that the age at which people are considered 'old' varies according to one's own age (the older one is, the later old age is said to begin), gender (women date the start of old age to later ages) and socioeconomic status (old age is said to begin at younger ages among minorities, perhaps out of recognition of shorter life expectancies).

Similarly, when people are asked to group social statuses, chronological age is only one factor affecting ratings. Such cultural dimensions as productivity, vulnerability, and reproductive potential also matter, so that respondents group old people and children together in some cases, over against people of middle age. This finding is consistent with research on the 'infantilization' of older people. 'Baby talk' is often applied to older people with cognitive impairment or other disabilities, and terms typically reserved for children are often applied to older people. The reverse is also true: younger adults who are not active, not interested in new experiences or travel, not willing to switch careers, or who are slow, deliberate or narrow-minded, are often called 'old'. This use of language suggests a social component in our understanding of ageing. People are old not just because of their age but also because of their behaviour, their health, their attitudes, their choices and even their politics. Thus, in US society, adults can refuse to 'grow up', and people can insist on 'not acting their age'. This can take a variety of forms: not leaving a parent's home, not marrying at an appropriate age, refusing to establish clear career goals, marrying someone much younger than you are, buying consumer products associated with a different age stratum.

Even this brief discussion of the use of age criteria to label behaviours suggests that attitudes towards ageing and old age are mostly negative. Old age is seen as a time of decline, withdrawal and vulnerability. In this view, ageing is not welcome, and little should be expected of older people, except perhaps to ease decline, provide care and protect people from exploitation or danger related to their increased vulnerability. These are the elements of 'ageism': assumptions of disability, lack of ability or vulnerability (and hence need for protection) based on age, rather than actual competencies.

The pervasiveness of ageism should not be underestimated. The older person who misses a word because of a hearing problem is considered too old for conversation and patronized with simplified language. Words may be put in his or her mouth and his or her opinion ignored. Older people who forget a name are called 'senile', dissatisfaction with illness-related activity restrictions is called 'crankiness', and expressions of sexual interest make one a 'dirty old man or woman'. Even medical personnel are not above recourse to ageist stereotypes.

The perspective of social gerontology is valuable for identifying the full significance of ageism. If missing a word is considered a feature of 'getting old', families (and older people themselves) may not take advantage of tertiary treatments available to manage hearing loss, such as hearing aids. Losing track of names may indicate mild cognitive impairment, not just ageing, and people with mild cognitive impairment may benefit from cognitive prostheses, environmental modification, anti-dementia drugs or increased supervision by family members. 'Crankiness' may be depression, or genuine dissatisfaction with unpalatable symptoms, a complaint against undesirable housing or simply a bad mood, any of which would otherwise be understood as features of daily life for people of any age. From a public health perspective, these expressions of ageism are doubly damaging. They falsely label potentially treatable medical conditions (such as mem-ory or hearing loss) as 'ageing', and also turn everyday complaints, dissatisfactions, interests and behaviours into pseudo-medical ageing syndromes (the so-called 'second childhood').

Negative perceptions or misunderstandings of ageing also apply to the social dimensions of later life. The actual preferences and experience of older people are often quite different from those portrayed in the media, and very different from the stereotypes commonly assumed by younger people. Decades of research in social gerontology have conclusively shown a number of important social facts: Most older people in the USA do not prefer to live with adult children. Life satisfaction and morale do not decline after retirement. Older people on the whole are not socially isolated. Adult children do not abandon elders and do not pack them off to nursing homes. Finally, older people are more likely to provide than to receive economic support from adult children. Each one of these findings has been confirmed in a variety of nationally representative, longitudinal surveys. Yet the claims of isolation, neglect and dependence persist. The origin of such claims may lie in skewed perceptions based on the minority of older adults who are, in fact, dependent on others for daily care (15–20 per cent, depending on definition), or who are demented (6 per cent for people aged 75–84, 20 per cent for people aged 85+) or living in nursing homes (4 per cent, and declining in the USA). But the tenacity and pervasiveness of the claims suggest that negative perceptions of old age generally may be at work.

Social gerontology allows us to recognize the true contours of the ageing experience. It also highlights new opportunities in social life associated with an increasingly old society. The great increase in life expectancy means that people, as adults, can expect to have relationships with parents that extend as much as 50 or 60 years. Similarly, the ageing of populations means that people are likely to spend more time in parent care than in child care. These factors will likely change family experience in fundamental ways and present new challenges for intergenerational relationships. This perspective is important to keep in mind when examining debates about the supposed competition between the 'young' and 'old' over resources, such as tax revenues. Should funds be spent on preschool or nursing homes? Subsidies for college tuition or late-life medical care? The perspective of social gerontology reminds us that 'young' and 'old' are not two separate groups or interests in society, but rather the same people at different points in the life-span. The most productive approach, which emerges from the social gerontology perspective, is to view allocation decisions from the stand-point of the entire life-span.

STEVEN M. ALBERT
COLUMBIA UNIVERSITY

Further reading

Albert, S.M. and Cattell, M.G. (1994) *Old Age in Global Perspective*, New York.
Butler, R.N. (1987) 'Age-ism: another form of bigotry', *The Gerontologist* 9(4): 243–6.
Calkins, E., Boult, C., Wagner, E.H. and Pacala, J.T. (1999) *New Ways to Care for Older People: Building Systems Based on Evidence*, New York.
Callahan, D. (1987) *Setting the Limits: Medical Goals in an Aging Society*, Washington, DC.
Rubenstein, R. (ed.) (1990) *Anthropology and Aging: Comprehensive Reviews*, Dordrecht, pp. 11–39.
Suzman, R.M., Willis, D.P. and Manton, K.G. (eds) (1992) *The Oldest Old*, New York.
Teresi, J.A., Lawton, M.P., Holmes, D. and Ory, M. (eds) (1997) *Measurement in Elderly Chronic Care Populations*, New York.

SEE ALSO: ageing

GLOBALIZATION

Globalization has become one of the most over-used and underspecified concepts in the lexicon of modern social science. It is faddish, multi-faceted and complex: but it describes something that is real (see Held *et al.* 1999; Held and McGrew 2000; Higgott and Payne 2000). There are historical continuities between the processes commonly referred to as globalization in the early twenty-first century with transformations in ages gone by (especially those of the late nineteenth century). Nevertheless, the last three decades of the twentieth century witnessed un-paralleled economic liberalization, mass air travel, telecommunications, ecological change and the large-scale development of transnational actors and international organizations both public and private in nature. The term globalization is shorthand for what has happened.

There is no settled definition of globalization, merely a range of more or less plausible under-standings. At a most basic level, it can be seen as a set of complex and contingent economic, technological, political, social, cultural and beha-vioural processes and practices that increasingly transcend jurisdictional and territorial barriers. These processes may be moving in the same direction over time, but they do not necessarily progress in concert, and their effects may differ from place to place. They are also not irreversi-ble. Indeed, the very manner of their develop-ment may provoke resistance.

Most common understandings equate globali-zation with internationalization. Internationaliza-tion, in turn, is often a synonym for increased interdependence and exchanges across borders and between countries, exchanges that are most readily identified and measured in the economic domain. Economic explanations of globalization stress the impact of the deregulation (reduction of barriers or freeing up) of trade in goods, services and financial flows, increased economic integration and the privatization of public assets. In consequence, globalization is often seen as being synonymous with 'liberalization'. But this may be to exaggerate the economic dimension of globalization. Although trends in political and social affairs are less easy to quantify than in the economic domain, they may be no less signifi-cant. Globalization is also generally taken to imply an increased flow of ideas, knowledge, experiences and information. Many commenta-tors therefore treat it as a cultural process, and equate globalization with the Westernization of culture in many parts of the world, and so with local crises of identity. The most abstract and difficult understanding of globalization sees it as progressive 'deterritorialization'. Driven by the revolution in technology, geography, space, place, distance and borders cease to be significant barriers to communication. This is not the same as saying that territory no longer matters. Clearly it does, especially with regards to the availability of resources or questions of identity. Rather it is to suggest that for many people there is an added dimensions to their life – that of superterritori-ality (Scholte 2000).

Globalization comes about in a number of ways – for example two-way interaction, emula-tion, one-way telecommunications and institu-tional isomorphism. However, three factors are generally emphasized:

- The ascendancy of a secular, rationalist and techno-scientific conception of knowledge.
- The role of 'capitalism' as a system of economic production, distribution and

exchange. (Over the last century, the enhancement of the mobility of capital, technology, production, sales and management practices has created a new global division of labour.)

- Governments have developed a regulatory environment and structure of multilateral institutions, especially in the economic domain, which have fostered globalization.

Throughout the 1990s, analysts and practitioners alike argued over the significance of globalization. The debate ranged from the 'hyperglobalists' (cf. Ohmae 1990), who depicted a world economy well on the way to profound integration, through to the 'sceptics' (Hirst and Thompson 1999), who argued that globalization is but an ideology of the modern global corporate elite and that the global economy was barely more open at the end of the twentieth century than it was at the end of the nineteenth. The evidence available now refutes the position of the global sceptics. International trade, foreign direct investment and other economic, technological, cultural and social cross-border transfers are now greater than in any previous era. But the argument, at the other extreme, that the state is in terminal decline as the principal site of authority and sovereignty, also flies in the face of the evidence.

Globalization and the state

Since 1945, institutions (of greater or lesser effectiveness) have emerged to act as *de facto* and, at times, *de jure* sites at which standard setting and policy harmonization is developed on international (that is transborder) public policy issues. These include:

- the international trading regime (GATT/WTO);
- the international financial system (the Bretton Woods institutions, notably the IMF and the World Bank Group);
- a panoply of public regimes such as the Organization for Economic Co-operation and Development (OECD) and the International Labour Organization (ILO), and also public-cum-private regimes such as the Bank for International Settlements (BIS), the International Organization of Securities Commissions (IOSCO), or the Internet Corporation for Assigned Names and Numbers (ICANN);
- quasi-formalized activities such as meetings of the G7/8, and the array of bodies and specialized agencies in the UN System such as the UN Development Programme, the UN Environment Programme and the UN Conference on Trade and Development.

States, institutions and even individuals are not powerless in the face of globalization. Policy matters, and the persistence of states (as opposed to growing limitations on their sovereign capabilities), ensure that they remain the principal, if not the only, agents of policy change. Nowadays, governments have to accommodate not only to the structural constraints imposed by globalization, especially the shifting balance in the relationship between state authority and market power. They must also accommodate to new, non-state actors, finding voice in the global policy process. Key non-state actors, coming from the market and civil society sectors respectively, include multinational corporations (MNCs), non-governmental organizations (NGOs) and even prominent individuals. They now interact in a more overlapping way under conditions of globalization than in the past. MNCs and NGOs have existed for a long time, but it is only in the closing decades of the twentieth century that their numbers have grown dramatically. As of the late 1990s there were in excess of 45,000 transborder corporations (MNCs) and nearly 20,000 transborder NGOs. Many of these bodies (be it an MNC like General Motors or Toyota, an international regime like the WTO, or an NGO like Greenpeace or Save the Children) consider that they have a global remit.

What does the presence of these new actors mean for contemporary global governance and policy-making? There is a range of competing views. Conservative and realist analysts of globalization (those scholars and policy-makers who privilege the central role of states in international affairs) argue that changes notwithstanding, globalization has done nothing fundamental to undermine the sovereignty of the nation-state. Marxists and radical critics see globalization simply as capitalism by another name. Hyperglobalists, especially beneficiaries of the new 'wired world', linked into the global economy in a flexible fashion, argue that we are witnessing a revolution that is transforming not only the relationship between the state and the economy, but also relationships within civil society. For them, the meta-trends of technological change and a new ethos of openness may be expected to continue the integration of world markets, which would have the happy effect of bringing about the new beginnings of a global civilization. (These varying views are reflected in the essays in Held and McGrew 2002.)

This optimistic view was widespread in the 1980s and first half of the 1990s, but in the late twentieth century a range of alternative voices began to make themselves heard. Most prominently articulated by a range of global social movements, NGOs and prominent political actors in the developing world, this opposition – often inaccurately described collectively as the 'anti-globalization movement' – gained momentum in the wake of the 1997 financial meltdown in East Asia and its subsequent spread to Latin America and Russia. It was given a further impetus by the defeat of the Multilateral Agreement on Investment (MAI) in 1998, and the highly-publicized opposition to the WTO in Seattle in 1999 and in Cancun in 2002.

Opposition to globalization is often dismissed as irrational and fuelled by ignorance. This is especially the case in the economic domain, where there is strong empirical and theoretical evidence to support the argument that market-led, open, liberalized economic activity delivers economic aggregate welfare more rapidly than any other form of economic organization. The economic efficiency argument is difficult to contest. But good economic theory is all too often naïve politics. The standard neo-classical economic argument fails to take account of the manner in which unfettered economic activity creates losers as well as winners. Whether the relationship between increased inequality and globalization is causally related or merely correlated is theoretically very important. But theory matters less than perception. Correlation alone is sufficient to make it an issue of the utmost political importance. It is this perceived correlation, and the mismatch between economic and political globalization, which inclines the dispossessed to identify globalization as the cause of their plight.

Current developments

Explanations (or, more precisely, interpretations) of the impact of globalization come themselves to influence the international agenda, and to shape the policies that are adopted in order to manage the contemporary global political and economic orders. Events also alter perceptions of the challenges presented by globalization. In the last quarter of the twentieth century globalization was seen primarily as an economic phenomenon. In the early twenty-first century, especially following the destruction of the World Trade Center in New York, security questions have been increasingly emphasized. The ability of non-state actors, intent on the use of violence, to operate freely across frontiers, often with impunity, is as salient an illustration of globalization as is the ability of capital to flow freely around the world in an era of financial deregulation. Advances in technology are at the core of both processes.

Economic globalization has yet to gain political legitimacy. Perhaps the crucial issue is the uneven spread of globalization and the degree to which the discrepancies between 'winners' and 'losers' have been exacerbated in the closing decades of the twentieth century. An overall rise in aggregate economic welfare has been accompanied by a growth in global income gaps since the end of the Second World War. Indicators also demonstrate that connectivity in North America and Western Europe is far higher than in Asia, Africa, Latin America and Eastern Europe. By 2000, for example, Internet populations by region were North America, 160 million; Europe, 70 million; Asia/Oceania, 42 million; and Africa and Latin America combined, 8 million. The future of globalization will therefore be contested in the political arena. In this respect, the issues raised by globalization are as old as the contest over how societies are organized and governed. The perennial questions – 'who gets what, how and when' – remain the very stuff of politics. The difference today is that these contests can no longer be conducted within hermetically sealed borders of territorially defined states. They will be, and are, increasingly conducted at a global level.

RICHARD HIGGOTT
WARWICK UNIVERSITY

References

Held, D. and McGrew, A. (eds) (2000) *The Global Transformations Reader*, Cambridge, UK.
—— (2002) *Governing Globalisation*, Cambridge, UK.
Held, D., McGrew, A., Goldblatt, D. and Perraton, J.

(1999) *Global Transformations: Politics, Economics and Culture*, Cambridge, UK.

Higgott, R.A and Payne, A.J. (eds) (2000) *The New Political Economy of Globalization*, 2 vols, Cheltenham.

Hirst, P. and Thompson, G. (1999) *Globalisation in Question*, 2nd edn, Cambridge, UK.

Ohmae, K. (1990) *The Borderless World*, London.

Scholte, J.A. (2000) *Globalisation: A Critical Introduction*, London.

Further reading

Cohen, R. and Kennedy, P. (2000) *Global Sociology*, New York.

SEE ALSO: international institutions; international trade; mass media; migration; multinational enterprises; world-system analysis; World Trade Organization

GOLD STANDARD

A gold standard represents a system of monetary organization in which gold fulfils the functions of a central money. Gold becomes the main store and measure of value as well as a central medium of exchange. In this respect, a gold standard is a metallist rule for organizing money since a metal, in this case gold (but historically various other metals have been used), becomes the foundation for managing a money supply. More generally, a metallist rule is a subset of a commodity rule whereby some good or goods serve the functions of money. Interestingly, the history of humankind has been marked by a reliance on commodity standards: often relying on metals of some kind, but other kinds of commodities such as precious stones and agricultural commodities were commonly used as well. In fact, it is only after the Second World War that commodity standards have ceased to be the foundation of national monetary regimes. Although it has fallen out of use as a means of managing national money after the war, historically this type of monetary system has prevailed at both the national level (practised most widely as a form of organizing national money from the 1850s up to the First World War) and the international level (especially 1880–1914 and 1947–71). National and international monetary organization is now founded on a fiat standard (paper money) where the value and acceptability of monies does not derive from the intrinsic value of some commodity like metal, but derives instead from the decrees of governments.

Although there has not been a uniform method of practising a gold standard, such an organization of money at the national level has traditionally been oriented around several fundamental practices. First, money is defined in terms of some fixed quantity of gold. For example, in 1879 a US dollar was defined as 23.22 grains of fine gold. Since one fine ounce of gold equalled 480 grains, then one fine ounce of gold was equal to 20.67 dollars. All denominations of money are defined in either multiples or fractions of the central unit of account (in this case the dollar), hence all money has a clear correspondence to some quantity of gold. Traditionally, these domestic par values have been kept stable over time. Second, individuals enjoy perfect interconvertibility between gold money and non-gold monies (principally notes) at rates that are legally determined. In this respect, notes ultimately represent claims on gold itself. Hence both notes and gold become widely acceptable as means of clearing debts and making purchases to unlimited amounts (i.e. acquire legal tender). This has become known as the practice of domestic convertibility.

Third, coins made of metals other than gold can circulate only as token money (small-denomination coin). These coins normally possess an intrinsic value that is significantly below their nominal value. Fourth, monetary authorities stand ready to coin all gold brought to them (usually for a slight charge referred to as seigniorage) and stand ready to convert notes into gold at legally specified rates. Fifth, individuals can hold gold in whatever form they choose (bullion or coin) and can freely import and export gold in whatever amounts they desire. Sixth, international reserves are held principally in gold. Hence gold becomes a central reserve and vehicle currency between nations that are practising gold standards. Finally, monetary authorities institute a rule that links the creation of money (i.e. growth in the money supply) to the stock of gold. In this latter respect, a gold standard (or any metallist standard for that matter) represents a classic 'rule' governing the management of a money supply.

At the international level, the currencies of nations practising gold standards become interchangeable at fixed exchange rates that derive from the respective domestic pars. Gold fulfils the function of an international numeraire in that it becomes the foundation for international transactions. Historically, such an international regime has arisen both spontaneously (as in the period 1880–1914) and been actively created and managed by economically powerful nations (as the USA did in creating and maintaining the Bretton Woods regime, 1947–71).

Advocates of a gold standard have traditionally supported such a regime as a means of escaping the unstable and inflationary effects of discretionary fiat monetary regimes where growth in the money supply is free from binding rules and subject to the whims of monetary and political elites. This support for a gold standard is all the more enhanced by a preference for fixed over flexible exchange rates. Critics of the gold standard have argued that such a regime is too rigid to allow for the management of the business cycle (i.e. it does not allow authorities the luxury of inflating out of depression), and that developments in the money supply are overly dependent on the vagaries of mining. The case against a gold standard is enhanced by a preference for flexible over fixed exchange rates.

GIULIO M. GALLAROTTI
WESLEYAN UNIVERSITY

Further reading

Bordo, M. (1999) *The Gold Standard and Related Regimes: Collected Essays*, Cambridge.

Bordo, M. and Capie, F. (1993) *Monetary Regimes in Transition*, Cambridge.

Bordo, M. and Schwartz, A. (1984) *A Retrospective on the Classical Gold Standard*, Chicago.

de Cecco, M. (1974) *Money and Empire: The International Gold Standard, 1890–1914*, Totowa, NJ.

Eichengreen, B. (1992) *Golden Fetters: The Gold Standard and the Great Depression*, New York.

Eichengreen, B. and Flandreau, M. (1997) *The Gold Standard in Theory and History*, New York.

Gallarotti, G. (1995) *The Anatomy of an International Monetary Regime: The Classical Gold Standard 1880–1914*, New York.

SEE ALSO: exchange rate; money

GOVERNANCE

Governance is a term that applies to the exercise of power in a variety of institutional contexts, the object of which is to direct, control and regulate activities in the interests of people as citizens, voters and workers. For political scientists, governance refers to the process of political management that embraces the normative basis of political authority, the style in which public affairs are conducted, and the management of public resources. It is a broader concept than government, which is specifically concerned with the role of political authorities in maintaining social order within a defined territory and the exercise of executive power. Three terms are central to most definitions of governance: accountability, which denotes the effectiveness with which the governed can exercise influence over their governors; legitimacy, which is concerned with the right of the state to exercise power over its citizens, and the extent to which those powers are perceived to be rightly exercised; and transparency, which is founded on the existence of mechanisms for ensuring public access to decision-making.

Governance is not restricted to the formal political realm; it also operates at the level of the firm or the community. Corporate governance is concerned with the processes by which corporate entities are governed, namely the exercise of power over the direction of the enterprise and mechanisms for ensuring executive accountability and the regulation of corporate actions. In more localized contexts, governance can refer to endogenously evolved sets of rules or authority structures within particular communities that play a role in resource management and in the maintenance of social order.

The concept of governance has attracted considerable attention from international aid donors concerned with political and administrative obstacles to successful economic development in developing countries. Attention centres on a perceived crisis of governance stemming from the pursuit of narrow self-interest, corruption and the loss of legitimacy, all of which undermine the effectiveness of states as development actors. Policy concern with governance has also raised questions about the appropriate role of international institutions such as the World Bank and the United Nations in global economic and political management, and the nature and legitimacy of their mandate.

In the developed world, there are two main sources of pressure shaping ideas about governance. One stems from problems of governability manifest in a breakdown of law and order, and despondency with formal political institutions that raises concerns about the manner in which the institutions of government should interact with citizens. A second set of influences derive from a neo-liberal political agenda that advocates a diminished role for the state and transforming it from a provider of services to a purchaser and regulator.

Proposals for bringing about improved governance centre on mechanisms to promote the decentralization of power and responsibility, and to increase consultation and participation in decision-making. In developing countries, proposals for better governance often imply a return to liberal democratic politics and controls on executive power, along with civil service reform and bureaucratic reorientation with a view to increasing the accountability, legitimacy and effectiveness of public management. This is challenged by an alternative view which suggests that strong government is essential for political stability, which in turn provides the best guarantee of successful development.

MARK ROBINSON
UNIVERSITY OF SUSSEX

Further reading

Minogue, M., Polidano, C. and Hulme, D. (eds) (1998) *Beyond the New Public Management: Changing Ideas and Practices in Governance*, Cheltenham.
Pierre, J. (ed.) (2000) *Debating Governance: Authority, Steering, and Democracy*, Oxford.
Turner, M. and Hulme, D. (eds) (1997) *Governance, Administration and Development: Making the State Work*, Basingstoke.

SEE ALSO: accountability; government

GOVERNMENT

The study of government lies at the heart of political science, but there is little unanimity within the discipline about how it should be studied or about the types or forms that exist. Indeed, the term itself has a multiplicity of distinct, if related, meanings. Only an overview of the confusion and controversy can be given here.

Following Finer (1974) we can discern four different meanings of the term government. First, government refers to the process of governing, that is, the authoritative exercise of power. Second, the term can be used to refer to the existence of that process, to a condition of ordered rule. Third, the government often means the people who fill the positions of authority in a society or institution, that is, the offices of

government. Finally, the term may refer to the manner, method or system of government in a society, that is, to the structure and arrangement of the offices of government and the relationship between the government and the governed.

The existence of some institution of sovereign government is a distinguishing feature of the state. The study of such sovereign governments has been a major preoccupation of political scientists. But not all governments are sovereign. The authority and even the existence of local and regional governments often depend on powers granted to them by a state-wide sovereign government. Meanwhile, any institution, such as a trade union, a church group or a political party, which has a formal system of offices endowed with the authority to make binding decisions for that organization, can be said to have a government. Equally, government (in the sense of ordered rule) may exist in the absence of the state. A number of anthropological studies have revealed the existence of societies in which conflict is resolved by a variety of processes without resort to the coercive powers of a formalized state (see, e.g., Evans-Pritchard 1940). Indeed, in any society there are many social situations (such as a bus or theatre queue) where potential conflict over an allocative decision is avoided by a non-coercive social process.

Sovereign government in advanced societies is normally regarded as consisting of three distinct sets of offices, each set having a particular role: first, the role of the *legislature* is to make the law. Second, the *executive* (also sometimes confusingly referred to as the government) is responsible for the implementation of the law and in most advanced polities has come to play a predominant role in the formulation of proposals for new laws. Third, the *judiciary*, meanwhile, is responsible for the interpretation of the law and its application in individual cases.

Classification schemes

The precise arrangement of the offices of government varies from state to state. Ever since Aristotle, the study of government attempted to classify the varieties of governments according to different types. The purpose of such classification exercises has varied, and has included both a desire to make normative statements about the best type of government and positive statements concerning the behavioural implications of different governmental structures. But all the classification exercises have in common an attempt to produce conceptual categories that make it possible to make meaningful generalizations about government in the face of a bewildering variation in the ways governments are organized.

Classifications of government are legion, yet some common threads can be discerned. Classifications have tended to concentrate on two criteria: the arrangement of offices, which is more narrow in conception; and the relationship between the government and the governed.

The first criterion has produced two classification schemes that are in wide currency among political scientists, particularly among students of democratic government. The first classification scheme is based on the relationship between the executive and the legislature. In a parliamentary system, the executive is dependent for its continuance in office upon maintaining the support of the legislature. Members of the executive are commonly also members of the legislature. While a prime minister may be the most powerful member of the executive, important decisions within the executive are usually made collectively by a group of ministers. In a presidential system, the executive is independent of the legislature. Members of the executive are not normally also members of the legislature, while the ultimate source of decision-making authority within the executive lies with one person – the president. The second classification scheme concentrates on the distribution of power between different levels of government. In a unitary state, all authority to make laws is vested in one supreme legislature whose jurisdiction covers the whole country. While it may permit local legislatures to exist, they do so only on the sufferance of the main legislature. In a federal state, there exist local legislatures that have at least a measure of guaranteed autonomous decision-making authority. That authority may well be protected by giving the judiciary the right to declare unconstitutional laws made by one level of government that encroach on the rights and powers of another, with the consequence that the judiciary acquires an enhanced role *vis-à-vis* both the executive and the legislature Both forms of government can be distinguished from a confederation, where a group of states combine for certain purposes but with each state formally at least retaining its sovereignty.

Classifications based on the second criterion –

the relationship between the government and the governed – have commonly concentrated on the extent to which governments attempt to achieve their aims by coercion of their citizens rather than persuasion, and on the extent to which limits are placed on the legitimate authority of government. The precise formulation of classification schemes based on this criterion varies widely, but not uncommonly a distinction is drawn between, at one extreme, liberal democratic government and, at the other, totalitarian governments. Under liberal democratic government, government is seen as primarily responsive to the wishes of society, and clear limitations are placed upon its ability to coerce society or to mould it in any particular way. Totalitarian governments have few limits placed upon them and are seen as instruments whereby society may be changed.

Liberal democracy has become the single most common form of government following the collapse of the Berlin Wall in 1989. But which should be the preferred form of liberal democratic government is itself the subject of dispute. One conception, which is often labelled 'majoritarian', argues that once it has been elected a government should have the authority to pursue its policy programme but then be clearly accountable to the electorate at the next election for the actions it has taken. An alternative perspective, labelled a 'consensus' or 'proportional', emphasizes the need for the diversity of public opinion to be represented in the legislature and even in the executive. The former conception favours single-party executives that are powerful *vis-à-vis* the legislature; the latter argues for multiparty coalition executives whose ability to act without the approval of the legislature is limited.

The scope of government

Scholars are not only interested in the form that government takes, but also its scope. This both widened and deepened in all advanced societies during the course of the twentieth century, with governments taking on increasing responsibility, in particular for the welfare needs of their citizens, albeit to varying degrees. Debate continues about how far this growth was a necessary means of alleviating the undesirable consequences of advanced capitalism and how far it reflects ever rising public expectations of what government should do. But towards the end of the century it was increasingly argued that this growth might have reached its limits, both because of the apparent inefficiency of the state compared with the private sector and because of the burden it was imposing on the productive economy.

Studying government

The study of government has undergone a number of changes in the period since the Second World War. Originally the study of government grew out of the study of constitutional law. It was characterized by a concentration on the formal institutions of government and upon constitutional provisions, while individual countries tended to be studied in isolation rather than in a comparative framework. However, under the influence of the behavioural revolution, from the 1960s onwards scholars paid increasing attention to how governments actually operate, to institutions outside the formal apparatus of the state but which play a vital role in its operation (such as political parties and pressure groups), and to explicitly comparative study. This perspective suggested that how government operated in practice depended more on how people behaved politically and what their political attitudes were rather than formal institutional rules. Particularly influential in the development of comparative study were approaches derived from systems theory, especially structural-functionalism. These facilitated comparative study, including of developing as well as advanced societies, by advancing a conceptual language based upon the functions that are performed within any society, and thus a language that could be applied to the study of government anywhere.

More recently, however, thanks to the work of the 'new institutionalist' school, there has been a renewed interest in the role and influence of the formal rules and institutions of government. It is argued that these rules and institutions do make a difference because they have an independent influence on both political behaviour and policy outcomes. As a result normative debates about the merits of different constitutional designs have acquired a new impetus, albeit one that means they are increasingly being informed by empirical evidence about what impact different designs actually have in practice. At the same time, however, the continued influence of the older behavioural tradition has been exemplified by a renewed interest in the influence of 'social capital' in determining the effectiveness of government (Puttnam 1993). The debate between these two perspectives can doubtless be expected to continue.

JOHN CURTICE
UNIVERSITY OF STRATHCLYDE

References

Evans-Pritchard, E.E. (1940) *The Nuer*, Oxford.
Finer, S.E. (1974) *Comparative Government*, Harmondsworth.
Puttnam, R.D. (1993) *Making Democracy Work*, Princeton, NJ.

Further reading

Almond, G.A. and Coleman, J.S. (eds) (1960) *The Politics of the Developing Countries*, Princeton, NJ.
Easton, D. (1965) *A Systems Analysis of Political Life*, New York.
Esping-Andersen, G. (1999) *Social Foundations of Postindustrial Economies*, Oxford.
Lijphart, A. (1999) *Patterns of Democracy*, New Haven.
Shugart, M.S. and Carey, J.M. (1992) *Presidents and Assemblies*, Cambridge, UK.

SEE ALSO: bureaucracy; democracy; governance; public administration; state

GROUP DYNAMICS

Group dynamics was originally the term used, from the 1930s to the early 1950s, to characterize the study, by Kurt Lewin and his followers, of changes in group life. Gradually the term lost its restricted reference and came to be more or less synonymous with the study of small groups. This broader sense will be used here.

A small group consists of from three to about thirty persons, every one of whom can recognize and react to every other as a distinct individual. The members are likely to manifest: perception of group membership; sustained interaction; shared group goals; affective relations; and norms internal to the group, which may be partially organized around a set of roles. Those are the most commonly invoked defining criteria of small social groups.

By the end of the first decade of the twentieth century about twenty social scientific articles on small groups had appeared and many of the subsequent concerns of small group research had been identified. In 1898 Triplett reported laboratory and field experiments on the effect of the presence of others on individual performance. Within the next half-dozen years: Cooley wrote about the importance of the primary group; Simmel discussed some of the consequences of group size; Taylor, the apostle of scientific management techniques, started to examine pressures on individuals to conform to group norms regarding productivity; Terman studied group leaders and leadership. From about 1920 onwards, the rate of publication started to increase. The 1930s saw the appearance of three classic lines of research: the work of Lewin *et al.* on different styles of leadership; the best-known parts of the programme of research at the Western Electric Company's Hawthorne plant, together with Mayo's selective and misleading popularization of their findings; reports by Moreno and others of sociometric techniques designed to represent choices, preferences or patterns of affect in a group.

By the late 1930s, the developing study of group processes was seen, in the USA at any rate, as part of the defence of conventional democratic practices in the face of authoritarian threats, and high hopes and expectations continued through the 1940s to the heyday of small-group research in social psychology, the 1950s and early 1960s. During that period Bales produced his category system for the relatively detailed description of group interaction processes, the sensitivity or experiential group appeared on the scene, and those not preoccupied with experiential groups increasingly studied laboratory experimental ones. In the 1970s research output abated somewhat as did some of the sense of excitement and enthusiasm. Mainly via laboratory experiments, a variety of delimited issues, often refinements of earlier topics, provided successive focuses for attention. These included co-operation and competition; aspects of group cohesion; leadership styles; social influence processes, including a new interest in minority influence; group decision-making and group polarization; personal space and density; and interpersonal attraction. Increasing methodological sophistication was claimed and the absence of major theoretical advances bemoaned.

Initially the study of group dynamics, in the original, narrow sense, was held to offer answers to a number of democracy's problems but even-

tually the most tangible legacies of the group dynamics movement were the spawning of, first, group-centred training groups and, then, individual-centred experiential groups. This shift from a concern with the world's problems to the soothing of personal anxieties perhaps was symptomatic of the failure of the study of small groups to fulfil its potential (Steiner 1974). All too often, narrow questions were studied with increasingly restricted methods, leading, at best, to mini-theories that failed to sustain interest in the issues. Some of the reasons for this reflect North American experimental social psychology more generally. But the nature of the groups studied must have been a contributing factor. In practice, the study of small groups came to be concerned not with families, friends, committees and the multitude of social groups that mediate between individual and society but with small collectivities of student strangers meeting for no more than an hour. Indeed, it is likely that a majority of groups studied manifested few, if any, of the defining properties of actual social groups (Fraser and Foster 1984). In the late 1970s and early 1980s, the field seemed to be in the doldrums.

Over the past two decades there have been some signs of revival (Levine and Moreland 1998; Hogg and Tindale 2002). It is sometimes claimed that the volume of research on groups has increased substantially, although that claim may largely depend on lumping the burgeoning interest in intergroup conflict and prejudices together with the largely different traditional concerns of intragroup dynamics. Academic social psychologists, however, have generated new theoretical ideas for the investigation of standard topics (e.g. Turner 1991), made substantial progress on some well-worked problems, such as team performance, generated some fruitful new issues, such as group memory, and shown some interest in selected real-world issues, including crowding, the operation of social support, and even relations between 'dynamics within groups and dynamics between groups' (Brown 2000). These advances have all depended predominantly on research in social psychologists' laboratories rather than in the worlds of lay-people. But what may be the most important change in the study of small groups is that the dominance of social psychology is no longer as obvious as it had been. The study of real-world social groups is increasingly being tackled by researchers from other domains, such as the family, the jury and, especially, the area of organizations and work, where many of the most productive developments regarding leadership, group effectiveness and the like are now located. It remains to be seen whether these changes, within and beyond social psychology, have been sufficient to create a study of group dynamics that can adequately illuminate the major part played by small social groups in the relations between individuals and the societies they live in.

COLIN FRASER
UNIVERSITY OF CAMBRIDGE

References

Brown, R. (2000) *Group Processes*, 2nd edn, Oxford.
Fraser, C. and Foster, D. (1984) 'Social groups, nonsense groups and group polarization', in H. Tajfel (ed.) *The Social Dimension: European Developments in Social Psychology*, Vol. 2, Cambridge, UK.
Hogg, M. and Tindale, S. (eds) (2002) *Blackwell Handbook of Social Psychology: Group Processes*, Oxford.
Levine, J.M. and Moreland, R.L. (1998) 'Small groups', in D.T. Gilbert, S.T. Fiske and G. Lindzey (eds) *The Handbook of Social Psychology*, Vol. 2, 4th edn, New York.
Steiner, I.D. (1974) 'Whatever happened to the group in social psychology?' *Journal of Experimental Social Psychology* 10.
Turner, J.C. (1991) *Social Influence*, Buckingham.

SEE ALSO: leadership

H

HABERMAS, JÜRGEN (1929–)

Jürgen Habermas has been the most prolific and influential representative of the second generation of the Frankfurt School. He has not only continued the theoretical tradition of his teachers Adorno and Horkheimer and his friend Marcuse, but also significantly departed from classical critical theory and made many important contributions to contemporary philosophy and social theory. In particular, he has opened critical theory to a dialogue with other philosophies and social theories such as the hermeneutics of Gadamer, systems theory and structural functionalism, empirical social sciences, analytic and linguistic philosophy, and theories of cognitive and moral development. He has been synthesizing these influences into a theory of communicative action, which presents the foundation and framework of a social theory that builds on the tradition of Marx, Weber and classical critical theory, but also criticizes his predecessors and breaks new theoretical ground.

Habermas was born on 18 June 1929 in Düsseldorf, and grew up in Gummersbach, Germany. His father was head of the Bureau of Industry and Trade, and his grandfather was a minister and director of the local seminary. The young Habermas experienced the rise and defeat of fascism, and was politicized by the Nuremberg trials and documentary films of the concentration camps shown after the war. Habermas began his university studies in Göttingen in 1949 and finished a dissertation of *Das Absolute und die Geschichte* in 1954. In the 1950s, he absorbed – and was strongly influenced by – Lukács's *History and Class Consciousness* and Adorno and Horkheimer's *Dialectic of Enlightenment*, which he first read in 1955. He studied the young Marx and the young Hegelians with Karl Löwith, one of Germany's great scholars and teachers.

Habermas resolved to work with Adorno and Horkheimer, because he believed that they were establishing a dialectical and critical theory of society from within a creative and innovative Marxist tradition. He therefore moved to the Frankfurt Institute for Social Research, where he wrote his first major book *Strukturwandel der Öffentlichkeit* (1962). Combining historical and empirical research with the theoretical framework of critical theory, Habermas traced the historical rise and decline of what he called the 'bourgeois public sphere' and its replacement by the mass media, technocratic administration and depoliticization. This influential work continues to animate discussion concerning problems of representative democracy in contemporary capitalist societies and the need for more participatory, democratic and egalitarian spheres of sociopolitical discussion and debate.

In the 1960s, Habermas taught at the universities of Heidelberg (1961–4) and Frankfurt (1964–71). At this time he also became more interested in politics and with others in 1961 published *Student und Politik*, which called for university reforms, and *Protestbewegung und Hochschulreform* (1969), which continued his concern with university reform and also criticized what he saw as the excesses of the German student movement in the 1960s. Habermas was also engaged in intense theoretical work during this period. His *Theorie und Praxis*, which appeared in 1963 (*Theory and Practice*, 1973), contained theoretical papers on major classical and contemporary social and political theorists, as well as anticipations of his own theoretical position. *Zur Logik der Sozialwissenschaften* in 1967 contained a detailed and critical summary of contemporary debates in the logic of the social sciences. *Erkenntnis und Interesse* in 1968 (*Knowledge and Human Interests*, 1971) traced the development of epistemology and critical social theory from Kant to the present. He also published several collections of essays: *Technik und Wissenschaft als Ideologie* (1968); *Arbeit-Erkenntnis-Fort-schritt* (1970); and *Philoso-phische-politische Profile* (1971).

During the 1970s Habermas intensified his studies of the social sciences and began restructuring critical theory as communication theory. Key stages of this enterprise are contained in a collection of studies written with Niklas Luhmann, *Theorie der Gesellschaft oder Sozialtechnologie* (1971); *Legitimationsprobleme im Spätkapitalismus* (1973); *Zur Rekonstruktion des Historischen Materialismus* (1976); and essays collected in several other books. In these works, Habermas sharpened his critique of classical Marxism and his critical theory predecessors. He attempted to develop his own reconstruction of historical materialism, a critical theory of society, and a philosophical theory rooted in analyses of communicative action. During much of this period, since 1971, Habermas was director of the Max Planck Institute in Starnberg where he involved himself in various research projects and was in close touch with developments in the social sciences. After a series of disputes with students and colleagues, he resigned in 1982 and returned to Frankfurt where he served as Professor of Philosophy and Sociology until his retirement in 2002.

In 1981, Habermas published his two-volume *magnum opus*, *Theorie des kommunikativen Handelns*. This impressive work of historical scholarship and theoretical construction appraised the legacies of Marx, Durkheim, Weber, Lukács and Western Marxism, including critical theory, and criticized their tendencies towards theoretical reductionism and their failure to develop an adequate theory of communicative action and rationality. Habermas also generated his own analysis of the importance of communicative action and rationality for contemporary social theory. The book points both to his continuity with the first generation of the Frankfurt School and his significant departures. *Theorie des kommunikativen Handelns* also manifests Habermas's continued interest in the relationship

between theory and practice with his discussion of new social movements. The concluding section is a testament to his interest in systematic social theory with a practical intent in his summation of the current status of critical theory. The work as a whole thus sums up Habermas's theoretical work in the 1970s and points to some issues and topics that constitute future projects.

After 1981 Habermas continued to develop his theory of communicative action with reference to moral discourse and legal and political discourse. *Moral Consciousness and Communicative Action* (1990) contains contributions towards developing a discourse ethics, while *Faktizität und Gultung* (1992) articulates a discourse theory of law, democracy and rights. *Postmetaphysical Thinking* (1992) contains articles that articulate Habermas's attempts to reformulate modern theory in terms of a theory of communicative action that overcomes the metaphysical presuppositions of the philosophical tradition. *Between Facts and Norms* (1992) draws on the legal and political theories of Rawls, Dworkin and others to provide theories of democratic legitimation of formal law and distributive justice in the governance of contemporary societies. *The Future of Human Nature* (2003) questions whether there are postmetaphysical answers to the quest for the 'good life' and takes on the vexed issue of human cloning.

In addition, Habermas has published collections of essays commenting on contemporary political, cultural and historical events such as *The New Conservativism* (1989) and he edited a collection of *Observations on 'The Spiritual Situation of Our Time'* (1984). *The Past as Future* (1994) collects lectures, interviews and reviews on issues of German unification, the Gulf War and German history, while *The Postnational Constellation* (2001) deals with the European Union, globalization, the future of democracy and other sociopolitical challenges of the day. Habermas has consistently criticized relativizing attitudes towards the Holocaust and dealt critically with the complex problems of German history, including fascism.

Perhaps *The Philosophical Discourse of Modernity* (1987) has been his most controversial book. In this systematic reflection on philosophy and discourses of modernity from the Enlightenment to the present, Habermas launched an attack on French postmodernist theory (especially Derrida and Foucault) and its predecessors

(Nietzsche, Heidegger and Bataille). In this text and other essays of the period, Habermas defended the heritage of modernity, Enlightenment and reason.

A vast number of books and articles have appeared that defend or criticize Habermas, and he often responds to collections of books containing essays on his work, such as *Habermas and Modernity* (Berstein 1985). A collection of interviews, *Autonomy and Solidarity* (Dews 1992), also provides answers to his critics and insights into his life and intellectual development. *The Past as Future* (1994) provides interviews in which Habermas answers critics and expresses his views on contemporary political and intellectual developments. Habermas thus continues to be highly productive and controversial as he enters his seventh decade and he has emerged as one of the great intellectual figures of our time.

DOUGLAS KELLNER
UNIVERSITY OF CALIFORNIA, LOS ANGELES

References

Berstein, R. (ed.) (1985) *Habermas and Modernity*, Cambridge, UK.
Dews, P. (ed.) (1992) *Autonomy and Solidarity: Interviews with Jürgen Habermas*, London.

Further reading

Holub, R. (1991) *Jürgen Habermas: Critic in the Public Sphere*, London.
McCarthy, T. (1978) *The Critical Theory of Jürgen Habermas*, London.
Matusktik, M.B. (2001) *Jürgen Habermas. A Philosophical-Political Profile*, Lanham, MD.

SEE ALSO: Frankfurt School; hermeneutics; phenomenology; public sphere; sociology: new theoretical developments

HABITUS

With a philosophical pedigree stretching from Hegel to Husserl, the notion of the *habitus*, although used by Weber, Durkheim and Mauss, has established itself in contemporary social science through the work of Norbert Elias, and, most notably, Pierre Bourdieu, who is often mistakenly taken to be the concept's originator.

The first extensive sociological reference to habitus is in Elias's work on 'the civilizing process' during the 1930s, in which it refers to human 'second nature': habits of doing and being that influence our behaviour even when alone. Deriving from early socialization, these embodied, thoughtless habits underpin the order and complexity of everyday social life.

The concept is central to Bourdieu's attempt to develop a sociology of human practice that avoids both individualistic voluntarism and structuralist determinism. In his work it owes much to Elias, referring to an area of human being that is neither conscious nor unconscious, neither wholly social nor wholly individual. Residing in embodied individuals, it has its roots in primary and secondary socialization. It is constituted in and by typically unreflexive processes of habituation and habit-formation.

The habitus is made up of classificatory schemes and practical dispositions, the two being intimately implicated in each other. Both are in a state of ongoing adjustment to the objective conditions of the social world of which the acting subject is a constituent. These schemes and dispositions, particularly the basic practical taxonomies in which classification and disposition most intimately coincide, are transposable from one social domain to another, as the logic of practice characteristic of a group or culture.

Embodiment is fundamental to the habitus. The body represents the point of view on which the most influential practical taxonomies – up:down, back:front, female:male, etc. – are centred. For Bourdieu the body, via the habitus, is a mnemonic device within and on which the foundations of culture are inscribed. The habitus is also constitutive of *hexis*, the socially and culturally distinctive physical style of being in the world (stance, movement, gesture).

Socially competent performances are, however, generated by the habitus without the actors necessarily appreciating what they are doing. Bourdieu is explicit that the habitus is not a set of rules governing behaviour, nor does it work through processes of conscious ratiocination. Rather, it is a framework within and out of which actors, to some extent thoughtlessly, improvise practices as a consequence of the interaction between their culturally specific dispositions and classificatory schema, and the constraints, demands and opportunities of any specific social field or domain. A particular habitus will have origins in and most affinity with particular fields. It is in these encounters that internal subjectivity is adjusted and fine tuned to the objective external world. This adjustment is one of the key processes by means of which the social world is reproduced.

In Bourdieu's own work this concept has been applied to a range of topics, from formal education, to cultural consumption, to peasant marriage strategies. In its translation into Anglophone sociology it seems to have been largely subsumed within an anthropologized model of culture. Although it can be criticized as overly dismissive of conscious decision-making and residually deterministic, it offers an intriguing model of the social and cultural constitution of individual practice.

RICHARD JENKINS
UNIVERSITY OF SHEFFIELD

Further reading

Bourdieu, P. (1990) *The Logic of Practice*, Cambridge, UK.
Bourdieu, P. and Wacquant, L. (1992) *An Invitation to Reflexive Sociology*, Cambridge, UK.
Elias, N. (2000) *The Civilizing Process: Sociogenetic and Psychogenetic Investigations*, rev. edn, Oxford.
Jenkins, R. (2002) *Pierre Bourdieu*, rev. edn, London.

SEE ALSO: Bourdieu

HAYEK, FRIEDRICH A. (1899–1992)

Friedrich August von Hayek was one of the most influential intellectuals of the twentieth century. He made major contributions to a variety of disciplines, including economics (Hayek 1931, 1948), politics (Hayek 1944), psychology (Hayek 1952), the philosophy of the social sciences (Hayek 1955) and social theory and political philosophy (Hayek 1960, 1982). He was awarded the Nobel Prize in Economics in 1974.

Hayek was born in 1899 in Austria. He studied at the University of Vienna, earning doctorates in law and political science, and also pursuing interests in economics and psychology. In the 1920s, Hayek was drawn into the intellectual circle of the prominent Austrian economist Ludwig von Mises and in 1927 was selected to become the first director of the Austrian Institute for Business Cycle Research. Hayek's research on business cycles, later published as *Prices and Production* (1931), led in 1932 to his appointment as Tooke Professor of Economic Science and Statistics at the London School of Economics. It was during his tenure as Tooke Professor that Hayek was a major participant in celebrated

controversies over macroeconomics and monetary theory, and also concerning the possibility of socialist state planning. In 1950, Hayek moved to the University of Chicago, joining its Committee for Social Thought as Professor of Social and Moral Sciences. He returned to Europe in 1962, first as Professor of Economics at the University of Frieburg and then, after his retirement in 1967, as Emeritus Professor at the University of Salzburg. Hayek died in 1992, aged 92.

Hayek's most fundamental contribution to economics, to which he was led by his participation in the so-called socialist calculation debate of the 1930s, stemmed from his recognition that the sophisticated division of labour that characterizes modern industrial societies also implies an extensive division of knowledge, that is to say, far from being given to one person in its entirety, knowledge of the production possibilities afforded by the extant technology, of consumers' preferences, and of the availability of resources, is fragmented and dispersed among the myriad actors who populate such societies. It followed, according to Hayek, that the fundamental economic problem facing a modern society is that of co-ordinating the individual plans of its inhabitants so that most of them are able successfully to implement their preferred actions, when the knowledge on which such a possibility depends is scattered throughout the economy rather than being given to any one individual in its totality. The principal task of economic theory, on this view, is to explain how the market economy facilitates the remarkable degree of plan co-ordination that is observed in practice.

Hayek's initial account of how market economies generate orderly allocations of resources focused on the role of prices in communicating the dispersed or 'local knowledge' referred to above and is to be found, along with his initial statement of the explanatory puzzle, in his book *Individualism and Economic Order* (1948). Hayek argued that when individuals act on the basis of their local knowledge, they generate changes in relative prices that inform other people of the significance of that local knowledge for the relative scarcities of resources. For Hayek, then, prices act as 'knowledge-surrogates', enabling people to adjust their behaviour to circumstances about which they have little or no direct awareness.

However, as Hayek himself realized, the information provided by price signals is insufficient to enable people to co-ordinate their plans with one another, for different people may interpret a given price in a variety of different ways, yielding a host of mutually incompatible plans. It was only in his post-1960 writings on social theory and political philosophy that Hayek was finally able to provide a convincing answer to the question of how socioeconomic order is possible in decentralized market economies. In this later work, Hayek argued that the dissemination of knowledge required for plan co-ordination is facilitated not only by price signals but also by a network of both formal and informal social rules (such as the laws of property, tort and contract, and norms of honesty and promise-keeping respectively). These rules, Hayek contended, are repositories of social knowledge, embodying the collective wisdom of society about how people should respond to various situations. And it is the fact that different people interpret price signals by reference to the same abstract social rules that enables them to form reliable expectations of each other's future conduct, thereby facilitating the formation of mutually compatible plans.

For Hayek, then, the market order (or catallaxy, as he also terms it) is an example of a spontaneous order, that is, it is an unintended consequence of people's rule-guided behaviour, the product of human action but not of human design. Hayek's later work in social theory and political philosophy was devoted to exploring in some detail the nature and origins of the institutions conducive to the generation of such spontaneous orders. Hayek identified private property and the laws of property, tort and contract, as the indispensable institutional prerequisites for the market order. He also attempted to explain how the institutions that underpin the catallaxy arise, developing an evolutionary theory according to which the institutions in question are themselves the unintended outcome of a process of cultural selection. For Hayek, those institutions and rules that survive the test of time do so because they enable people to deal effectively with the problems posed by the limitations of their knowledge so as to achieve their individual goals (Hayek 1960, 1978, 1982).

Hayek's early research in economics and his later investigations in social theory and political philosophy can thus be seen to form a more coherent body of work than might at first glance appear to be the case. Hayek's insight that the primary question of economic order is one of

knowledge also informed his later writings on political philosophy and social theory, where he examined how the social rules and institutions of a liberal polity provide both the information required for private citizens to co-ordinate their plans and so achieve their individual goals in peace and harmony. And it was in this later work on the role of social institutions and rules in shaping people's expectations and guiding their actions that Hayek was finally able to provide a convincing answer to the question, first posed in his narrow technical work on economics, of how socioeconomic order is possible in decentralized market economies.

PAUL LEWIS
CAMBRIDGE UNIVERSITY

References

Hayek, F.A. (1931) *Prices and Production*, London.
—— (1944) *The Road to Serfdom*, Chicago.
—— (1948) *Individualism and Economic Order*, Chicago.
—— (1952) *The Sensory Order*, London.
—— (1955) *The Counter-Revolution of Science*, Glencoe, IL.
—— (1960) *The Constitution of Liberty*, Chicago.
—— (1978) *New Studies in Philosophy, Economics and the History of Ideas*, Chicago.
—— (1982) *Law, Legislation and Liberty*, London.

SEE ALSO: freedom; liberalism

HEALTH ECONOMICS

Health economics is concerned with how society's scarce resources are allocated amongst competing activities that improve the health of citizens.

Many inputs affect the length and quality of an individual's health. In a world of scarce resources it is necessary to target interventions so that the cost of producing health is minimized and health gain is maximized. At the individual level, this can be modelled in a human capital framework (Grossman 1972). The Grossman model facilitates the investigation of links between inputs (such as health care, education, income distribution and housing) and the output, improvements in health status. This work demonstrates the importance of education and other non-health care variables in the production of health.

Health care is always and everywhere rationed. In consequence, patients are denied access to (or simply not offered) care from which they would benefit and that they would like to have. The policy issue is not whether to ration but how to ration. What criteria should be used to determine patient access to care (Maynard and Bloor 1998)?

One way of rationing care is by price. Access to care is granted only to those who are willing and able to pay for it. However, most countries have removed the price barrier to care, and ration on the basis of need. In this context, need is defined as the patient's ability to benefit per unit of cost. In prioritizing competing investments in health care it is accordingly necessary to identify what 'works' (i.e. what is clinically effective), and what works at least cost (i.e. what is cost effective). If society's goal is to maximize health gains from the huge public expenditures on health (in the UK, for example, the National Health Service budget runs to £60 billion), resources have to be targeted in relation to the relative cost-effectiveness of competing interventions. One consequence is that some therapies that have benefits will not be funded if their cost-effectiveness is poor. Patients will suffer pain and discomfort, and even die, despite the availability of clinically effective – but not cost-effective – treatments.

The rationale for creating public health care systems is a desire to reduce inequalities in quality-adjusted life expectancy between different social groups. This may involve discriminating in favour of the poor, or against the old who have had a 'fair innings' (Williams 1997). Such discrimination may involve transferring resources from the efficient treatment of the old to the inefficient treatment of young, chronically ill patients.

Funding of health care is dominated by implicit ideological goals. The political right favour methods such as private insurance and user changes that shift the financial burden away from the more affluent. The political left favour progressive taxation, which transfers funding burdens to the rich. However, ideological debates divert attention from the significant inefficiencies in the provision of health care that dominate all health care systems, private and public (Culyer and Maynard 1997: Ch. 5).

Evaluating the cost-effectiveness of competing therapies is a major challenge. At present many therapies are of uncertain clinical and cost-effectiveness (Maynard and Chalmers 1997). The role of the economist is to identify, measure and value what is given up (the opportunity cost) and what is gained (improved length and quality of life for the patient). Often such studies are poorly designed, executed and reported, even though there are excellent guides to best practice in the economic evaluation in health care (Drummond et al. 1997; Gold et al. 1997).

Databases that collect and review the evidence base are now accessible on the World Wide Web. For instance, the Cochrane Collaboration is an international effort to identify what is known in therapeutic areas, with groups worldwide updating their conclusions every 6 months to keep up with the explosion of medical publications (http://www.cochrane.org). The University of York's Centre for Reviews and Dissemination also has a database open to the public (http://nhscrd.york.ac.uk) that logs and critically appraises economic evaluations.

Medical practitioners dominate the provision of health care, but there are large variations in practice, and in the incidence of medical errors, and the measurement of outcomes is typically poor (see Fisher 2003; Kohn et al. 1999). The use of economic incentives to manipulate clinical behaviour at the margins is increasingly evident in the remuneration systems of the USA (Robinson 2001) and the UK (Maynard and Bloor 2003). However, contracts of employment are never complete, and the enforcement of purchasers' intentions lead to costly performance management of uncertain efficiency.

The inefficient use of health care resources is clearly unethical: it deprives patients of care from which they could benefit. The role of health economics is to generate evidence about the costs and benefits of achieving health and health care goals. However, it is no good knowing what works, if practitioners fail to adopt such interventions. The hope must be that a rigorous application of health economics will improve the efficiency and equity of health and health care across the world.

ALAN MAYNARD
UNIVERSITY OF YORK, UK

References

Culyer, A.J. and Maynard, A. (eds) (1997) *Being Reasonable about the Economics of Health: Selected Essays by Alan Williams*, Cheltenham.

Drummond, M.F., O'Brien, B., Stoddart, G.L. and

Torrano, G.W. (1997) *Methods of Economic Evaluation of Health Care Programmes*, Oxford.

Fisher, E.S. (2003) 'Medical care: Is more always better?' *New England Journal of Medicine* 349(17): 1,615.

Gold, M.R., Siegel, J.E., Russell, L.B. and Weinstein, M.C. (eds) (1997) *Cost Effectiveness in Health and Medicine*, New York.

Grossman, M. (1972) *The Demand for Health*, New York.

Kohn, L.T., Corrigan, J.M. and Donaldson, M.S. (eds) (1999) *To Err is Human: Building a Safer Health Care System*, Washington, DC.

Maynard, A. and Bloor, K. (1998) *Our Certain Fate: Rationing in Health Care*, London.

—— (2003) 'Do those who pay the piper call the tune?' *Health Policy Matters* 8, York, UK (http://www.york.ac.uk/depts/hstd/pubs/hpmindex.htm).

Maynard, A. and Chalmers, I. (eds) (1997) *Non Random Reflections on Health Services Research*, London.

Robinson, J. (2001) 'The theory and practice of physician incentive payments', *Milbank Fund Quarterly* 79(2): 200.

Williams, A. (1997) 'Intergenerational equity: An exploration of the "fair innings" argument', *Health Economics* 6(2): 117–32.

SEE ALSO: medical sociology; public health

HEGEL, GEORG WILHELM F. (1770–1831)

Vilified for years as an irrational, reactionary warmonger, Hegel is increasingly recognized as one of the most insightful and rigorous political philosophers in the Western tradition, one who puts the modern experience of freedom at the very centre of his thought. While many of the various charges levelled against Hegel can be traced back to Rudolph Haym's polemical 1857 *Hegel und Seine Zeit*, in the Anglo-American context, where the distrust of Hegel has perhaps been most intense, the main culprit is Karl Popper's widely read 1945 *The Open Society and its Enemies*. As its title perhaps suggests, this book was composed as 'a contribution to the war effort' against Nazi Germany – hardly an impartial approach to a German philosopher. But though Walter Kaufmann demonstrated 50 years ago how incompetent and irresponsible its attacks on Hegel are, too many political philosophers still quietly accept its claims that Hegel was a racist who celebrated war, glorified the state at the expense of individual rights or personal development, and in general anticipated both Prussian power politics and Nazi totalitar-

ianism. On top of all this, his identification of the real and the actual (*wirklich*) is often assumed to imply quietism in the face of the best of all possible worlds. That this strange and anachronistic blend is hardly consistent is presumably written off as proof of the irrationality of Hegel's dialectical style of thought. And it is true that the fact that Hegel's main texts on political philosophy are lecture notes that presuppose familiarity with his *Logic* is – along with the notorious difficulty and obscurity of Hegel's prose – a major reason such charges could gain the currency they have. The influence of that speculative logic is also, however, the source of much of the strength and insight of Hegel's social and political thought.

Hegel was born in 1770 in Stuttgart, a duchy of Württemberg, at that point a part not of anything we might name *Germany* but rather of the Holy Roman Empire. He studied theology and classics in the seminary at Tübingen, where he forged close friendships with Friedrich Hölderlin, the future great romantic poet, and with Friedrich Schiller, who would emerge at an extraordinarily young age as the heir apparent to Kant and Fichte. Both these men would influence Hegel profoundly. The three friends shared enthusiasms for the French Revolution and for the beautiful community they attributed to ancient Athens, as well as an eagerness to avoid a soulless and repressive modernism in a land that was only just casting off its feudal past. This desire to unite the harmony of the ancients with the revolutionary freedom of the moderns flavoured Hegel's eager youthful reading of Rousseau, whose work in many ways sets out the parameters of his own mature political philosophy. Throughout his writings Hegel is concerned with finding a way to relate the individual to the greater community that escapes the alienation and 'positivity' of an externally imposed law backed only by utilitarian considerations and the threat of force. His initial attempts in this regard centre on *love*, *life* and some form of *Volksreligion* as modes of experience that attain this moment of community without the sacrifice of individuality. In his mature political philosophy Hegel would use the less religious language of *freedom* to characterize the state of being at home in another (*Beisichselbstsein in einem Anderen*) in which we are neither opposed by an alien, hostile world nor engulfed in an unmediated totality that is equally inhospitable to the claims of individual fulfilment. Hegel argues that this state is attainable only in a modern polity that the individual can recognize as the precondition and expression of its own freedom.

There are obvious debts here not only to Rousseau's theory of the general will, but also to Kant's development of that theory in his own account of moral freedom as autonomy. But Hegel is consistently deeply dissatisfied with Kant. He regards Kant's limitation of knowledge to the phenomenal realm and his denial of our access to things in themselves as being productive of a hopelessly compromised mode of knowledge, 'like attributing to someone a correct perception, with the rider that nevertheless he is incapable of perceiving what is true but only what is false'. And he argues that its final product is an alienation from the unknowable world that encourages a romantic and ultimately nihilistic celebration of the individual's whims and fancies. For the individual to rise above those whims and recognize what it really wills requires that it not be determined by any ends that it has not freely chosen. This commitment to freedom as rational self-determination precludes appealing to immediately given feelings, desires, traditions and other forms of authority – including the conventions of our common life. While this seems to leave the will prey to precisely the decisionism that Hegel despises in romantics like Friedrich Schlegel, he argues ingeniously that in willing itself – that is, willing to be free – the free will also wills its necessary preconditions. These include a variety of legal, political and social institutions, most importantly those upon which Hegel focuses in the *Philosophy of Right*: the modern nuclear family, civil society and state. Nor are these institutions mere means to an end, since the actualization (*Verwirklichung*) of the free will would be incomplete if it did not take a real worldly form.

This effectively does away with the Kantian distinction between the legal and the moral, which is replaced by an interpretation of political institutions and customs as ethical or *sittlich* goods, goods of habit (*ethos*, *Sitte*) as well as intent. To take two examples of central importance to Hegel, neither the rights of property-owning personhood nor those of subjective moral choice are extraneous to the free will: without private property, individuals lack the ability to objectify themselves in the external world, and

without the right of subjective moral volition they cannot recognize something to be good *for them*, a product of their own will with which they are at home. For all of his admiration for the ancient Greeks, Hegel decisively prefers the modern world: where the Greek world may have been objectively good, it was not an *autonomous* world, as it did not allow for and require the individual's freely given consent. Actual freedom is both an institutional and a subjective achievement. Hence earlier peoples were not as free as moderns, lacking as they did a number of the requisite institutions (such as trial by jury, parliamentary government, freedom of conscience and of the press, a constitutional monarch) as well as an appreciation of the necessity of the subject's affirmation of them. On the one hand, this makes history and the philosophy of history an integral part of political philosophy. On the other, this places great emphasis upon our overcoming of our alienation from modern life, as we will not truly be free until we affirm as well as inhabit the modern polity. As Hegel puts it, 'the universal does not attain validity or fulfillment without the interest, knowledge, and volition of the particular [and its] conscious awareness'. He concludes that such awareness requires more than philosophical appreciation of the rational essence of world history: in a striking break from Rousseau's doctrine of the general will that anticipates de Tocqueville's celebration of US participatory government, Hegel argues that we require a *mediated* relationship between the individual and the state that leaves room for more manageable modes of co-operation in which the individual can knowingly and effectively take on work of public importance and its private interests can be integrated into public goods. Perhaps because Hegel's analysis of what he terms *civil society* is one of the first and most profound attempts to analyse the dynamic of modern capitalism, he recognizes that it is not enough to be a *Bürger*, one must also be a citizen. But the two must be intertwined with one another, if citizenship is not to assume the aspect of a hobby that distracts one from one's 'real' work.

Hegel's influence has been extraordinary, ranging from Marx's analysis of alienated labour and the history of class conflict through to the so-called Frankfurt School's critique of instrumental reason and the Dialectic of Enlightenment. His analysis of capitalism and the poverty it inevitably generates is one of the most important early instances of social as opposed to political theory. Via Alexander Kojeve's lectures in Paris in the 1930s, Hegelian themes were absorbed by Sartre, Lacan and Merleau-Ponty, decisively influencing their contributions to existentialism, psychoanalysis and phenomenology. Another set of Hegelian concerns have more recently been crucial to the 'communitarian' critique of Rawlsian liberalism and the 'politics of recognition' of Taylor, Honneth and Fraser. Even as a defining opponent Hegel has been important: Bertrand Russell and G.E. Moore gave birth to Anglo-American analytic philosophy in rebellion against the Hegelian orthodoxy of late nineteenth-century Britain, and much contemporary poststructuralism and postmodernism takes Hegel as its great adversary. Modern philosophy of religion and of history are similarly inconceivable without Hegel. In many ways this has been an inheritance of misinterpretation. To take one all too common instance: it speaks volumes that most social scientists would associate Hegel with a conception of *dialectic* in which anything one might analyse can be easily broken down to a cookie-cutter triad of thesis, antithesis and synthesis. But these were never used as terms of art by Hegel himself, who described 'this monotonous formalism' as 'a lifeless schema'. This schema was nonetheless attributed to Hegel by Heinrich Chalybaus, whose bowdlerization of Hegel was passed on to millions by Marx. If Hegel remains crucial to understanding the intellectual history of the nineteenth and twentieth centuries, it is, as a number of able scholars are now demonstrating, not simply because of his influence upon it but because he gives us the tools to demonstrate the false steps taken in it.

ANDREW NORRIS
UNIVERSITY OF PENNSYLVANIA

Further reading

Franco, P. (1999) *Hegel's Philosophy of Freedom*, New Haven, CT.
Hegel, G.W.F. (1991) *Elements of the Philosophy of Right*, ed. A.W. Wood, Cambridge, UK.
Pinkard, T. (2000) *Hegel: A Biography*, Cambridge, UK.
Schnädelbach, H. (2000) *Hegels praktische Philosophie: Ein Kommentar der Texte in der Reihenfolge*, Berlin.
Stewart, J. (1996) *The Hegel Myths and Legends*, Evanston, IL.

HEGEMONY

The term 'hegemony' derives from the ancient Greek ἡγεμονία (*igemonia*) meaning 'leadership' or 'guidance'. The *Oxford English Dictionary* defines it as leadership, predominance, preponderance; especially the leadership or predominant authority of one state of a confederacy or union over the others, and notes that the term was originally used in reference to the states of ancient Greece, whence it was transferred to the German states, and so to other modern applications.

The notion of hegemony entered modern social theory by way of debates among Russian Marxists at the end of the nineteenth century, when it became apparent that the Russian bourgeoisie was too weak to mount a serious challenge to Tsarism. The small but growing and organized proletariat would therefore need to play a leading role in the bourgeois revolution. The future Menshevik leaders Axelrod and Martov both spoke about the need for social democrats to win hegemony (*gegemoniia*) in the struggle against absolutism, and in his 1902 book *What is To Be Done?* Lenin developed this position into an argument that the proletariat should fight for leadership of all the oppressed and exploited in Russia. By 1911 Lenin was arguing that the 'idea of hegemony is one of the core positions of Marxism' (1963: 17, 215; 1968: 20, 283). 'As the only completely revolutionary class in contemporary society,' the proletariat 'must be the leader, the hegemon…in the struggle of all toilers and the exploited against the oppressors and exploiters. The proletariat is revolutionary only to the extent that it is conscious of and puts into practice this idea of hegemony' (Lenin 1963: 17, 231–2; 1968: 20, 308). Hegemony here clearly involves adoption of a wider political perspective than the consideration of merely economic or corporate interests; thus

> because there was 'hegemony' in the past, from the sum of professions, specialisms and guilds (*tsekhi*) there arose a class, for it is precisely consciousness of the idea of hegemony, precisely the embodiment of that idea through their activity, that transforms the sum of guilds into a class.
>
> (Lenin 1963: 17, 58; 1968: 20, 112)

The notion of hegemony was further refined in the Comintern debates of the early 1920s through contrasts with corporatism and dictatorship. In the struggle for a socialist revolution the industrial proletariat must win hegemony over the peasantry and the urban poor in their common struggle against exploitation and oppression, but enforce its dictatorship over hostile classes such as the aristocracy and the bourgeoisie; conversely, the bourgeoisie is able to exercise hegemony over the proletariat if the latter accepts a separation of economic and political struggles in its class practice (Anderson 1976: 17–18).

The idea of hegemony was given a specific inflection in the prison writings of the Italian Communist Party Leader Antonio Gramsci. Gramsci discussed how, in forging a class alliance of all the oppressed and exploited, the proletariat might achieve hegemony through yielding concessions of an 'economic-corporative kind' (1971: 161; 1975: 1,591) to other kindred groups, but should not shrink from using force against the bourgeoisie. He also significantly broadened the concept in a discussion of the mechanisms whereby the bourgeoisie rule over the proletariat in relatively stable capitalist societies. Here he drew upon the dialectic of force and consent, violence and civilization, state and civil society, discussed by Machiavelli in *The Prince*. Gramsci's principal innovation was, however, an elaboration of the relationship between hegemony and culture, an innovation made possible through a combination of Marxism with theories of linguistic and cultural dominance, with particular reference to studies of the relationship between regional dialects and the formation of a national language.

The work of dialectologists and linguistic geographers such as J. Gilliéron, T. Frings, J. Baudouin de Courtenay, A. Meillet, G.I. Ascoli and M. Bartoli became especially important for Marxist theorists of hegemony in the 1930s. In the work of Soviet linguists such as Ivanov and Iakubinskii (1932) and Zhirmunskii (1936), hegemony was explicitly linked to the relationship between the national language and social dialects. Zhirmunskii, for instance, argued that economic and social domination leads to ideological domination, and that 'the ruling class's cultural hegemony in turn conditions linguistic hegemony' (1936: 15–16). Drawing on Ascoli's analysis of linguistic change and substrata, and Bartoli's analysis of patterns of linguistic innovation, Gramsci argued that hegemony depends on the exertion of prestige by a predominant over a subordinate social group. Linguistic change was related to the hegemony (*egemonia*), that is the fascination or binding (*fascino*) and prestige (*prestigio*), exerted by the predominant sign community (Lo Piparo 1979). Just as a subordinate society adopts linguistic features from a dominant society, so, Gramsci argues, subordinate social groups adopt and 'verbally affirm' the world-view of their rulers. When a class rules against the interests of the subordinate class, a 'substratum' of the latter's 'own' perspectives persists. Such a hegemonic practice leads to a 'contradictory' consciousness among the subordinate class, and in 'normal' times to political passivity (Gramsci 1971: 327, 333; 1975: 1,378, 1,385–6). However, when interests are shared by the dominant and subordinate classes, the latter's perspective is strengthened and systematized through adoption of the perspectives of the predominant group. Bourgeois and proletarian hegemonies thus operate according to different principles, but each needs to be constantly renewed and modified in the face of challenges and pressures. The struggle between bourgeois hegemony and proletarian counter-hegemony is thus a crucial dimension of the class struggle.

Drawing on Gramsci, Raymond Williams argues that hegemony denotes the ways in which 'the relations of domination and subordination' appear as 'practical consciousness', that is, as 'a saturation of the whole process of living'. 'Pressures and limits of what can ultimately be seen as a specific economic, political and cultural system' appear to be 'the pressures and limits of simple experience and common sense' (Williams 1977: 110). In much contemporary social and cultural theory, however, the term is used more loosely, often with an exclusively cultural resonance, as in Laclau (1985). Here the philosophy of language underlying Gramsci's work on hegemony is effaced and replaced by a poststructuralist theory that uncouples language from the extra-discursive world, and hegemony from its moorings in productive relations.

CRAIG BRANDIST
SHEFFIELD UNIVERSITY

References

Anderson, P. (1976) 'The antinomies of Antonio Gramsci', *New Left Review* 100: 5–78.

Gramsci, A. (1971) *Selections from the Prison Note-books*, London.

—— (1975) *Quaderni del carcere*, Turin.

Ivanov, A.M. and Iakubinskii, L.P. (1932) *Ocherki po iazyku*, Moscow.

Laclau, E. (1985) *Hegemony and Socialist Strategy: Towards a Radical Democratic Politics*, London.

Lenin, V.I. (1963) *Collected Works*, 4th edn, London.

—— (1968) *Polnoe sobranie sochinenii*, 5th edn, Moscow.

Lo Piparo, F. (1979) *Lingua, intellettuali, egemonia in Gramsci*, Rome.

Williams, R. (1977) *Marxism and Literature*, Oxford.

Zhirmunskii, V.M. (1936) *Natsional'nyi iazyk i sot-sial'nye dialekty*, Leningrad.

SEE ALSO: Marx's theory of history and society; power

HERMENEUTICS

Hermeneutics is a term used to describe the views of a variety of authors who have been concerned with problems of understanding and interpretation. Some of the themes of hermeneutics were introduced to English-speaking social scientists by the writings of Max Weber. As a participant in the methodological debates that occurred in Germany during the late nineteenth and early twentieth centuries, Weber was familiar with the views of philosophers and historians such as Wilhelm Dilthey, Heinrich Rickert and Wilhelm Windleband, who all argued that the study of the social and historical world requires the use of methods that are different from those employed in the investigation of natural phenomena. These arguments were reflected in Weber's own emphasis on the concept of understanding (*verstehen*).

While Weber played an important role in introducing many social scientists to the ideas of hermeneutics, the latter tradition stretches back to a period well before Weber's time. Hermeneutics derives from the Greek verb *hermēneuein*, which means to make something clear, to announce or to unveil a message. The discipline of hermeneutics first arose, one could say, with the interpretation of Homer and other poets during the age of the Greek Enlightenment. From then on, hermeneutics was closely linked to philology and textual criticism. It became a very important discipline during the Reformation, when Protestants challenged the right of tradition to determine the interpretation of the holy scriptures. Both classical scholars and theologians attempted to elaborate the rules and conditions that governed the valid interpretation of texts.

The scope of hermeneutics was greatly extended by Wilhelm Dilthey (in the nineteenth century). A historian as well as a philosopher, Dilthey was aware that texts were merely one form of what he called 'objectifications of life'. So the problem of interpretation had to be related to the more general question of how knowledge of the social-historical world is possible. Such knowledge is based, in Dilthey's view, on the interrelation of experience, expression and understanding. Cultural phenomena, such as texts, works of art, actions and gestures, are purposive expressions of human life. They are objectified in a sphere of conventions and values that are collectively shared, in the way that a person's attitude may be objectified in the medium of language. To understand cultural phenomena is to grasp them as objectified expressions of life; ultimately it is to re-experience the creative act, to relive the experience of another. While reorienting hermeneutics towards a reflection on the foundations of the *Geisteswissenschaften* or 'human sciences', Dilthey's writings preserved a tension between the quest for objectivity and the legacy of romanticism.

The key figure in twentieth-century hermeneutics is Martin Heidegger. Whereas in Dilthey's work the hermeneutical problem is linked to the question of *knowledge*, in Heidegger's it is tied to the question of *being*: problems of understanding and interpretation are encountered while unfolding the fundamental features of our 'being-in-the-world'. For Heidegger, 'understanding' is first and foremost a matter of projecting what we are capable of. This anticipatory character of understanding is a reformulation, in ontological terms, of what is commonly called the 'hermeneutical circle'. Just as we understand part of a text by anticipating the structure of the whole, so too all understanding involves a 'pre-understanding' that attests to the primordial unity of subject and object. We are beings-in-the-world, familiar with and caring for what is ready-to-hand, before we are subjects claiming to have knowledge *about* objects in the world.

Heidegger's work has implications for the way that the human sciences are conceived, as Hans-Georg Gadamer has attempted to show. In *Truth and Method*, Gadamer (1975 [1960]) establishes a connection between the anticipatory character of understanding and the interrelated notions of prejudice, authority and tradition. The assumption that prejudices are necessarily negative is itself an unjustified prejudice stemming, in Gadamer's view, from the Englightenment. It is an assumption that has prevented us from seeing that understanding always requires pre-judgement or 'prejudice', that there are 'legitimate prejudices' based on the recognition of authority, and that one form of authority which has a particular value is tradition. We are always immersed in traditions that provide us with the prejudices which make understanding possible. Hence there can be no standpoint outside of history from which the totality of historical effects could be grasped; instead, understanding must be seen as an open and continuously renewed 'fusion' of historical 'horizons'.

Gadamer's provocative thesis was challenged in the mid-1960s by Jürgen Habermas and other representatives of 'critical theory'. While acknowledging the importance of Gadamer's hermeneutics for the philosophy of the human sciences, Habermas attacked the link between understanding and tradition. For such a link underplays the extent to which tradition may *also* be a source of power that distorts the process of communication and which calls for critical reflection. Appealing to the model of psychoanalysis, Habermas sketched the framework for a 'depth-hermeneutical' discipline that would be oriented to the idea of emancipation.

The debate between hermeneutics and critical theory has been reappraised by Paul Ricoeur (1981). As a hermeneutic philosopher concerned with critique, Ricoeur has tried to mediate between the positions of Gadamer and Habermas by re-emphasizing the concept of the text. In contrast to the experience of belonging to a tradition, the text presupposes a distance or 'distanciation' from the social, historical and psychological conditions of its production. The interpretation of a text, involving both the structural explanation of its 'sense' and the creative projection of its 'reference', thus allows for the possibility of establishing a critical relation *vis-à-vis* 'the world' as well as the self. Ricoeur shows how the model of the text and the method of text interpretation can be fruitfully extended to the study of such varied phenomena as metaphor, action and the unconscious.

As recent debates have indicated, the issues that for centuries have been discussed under the rubric of hermeneutics are still very much alive.

The appreciation of texts and works of art, the study of action and institutions, the philosophy of science and social science: in all of these spheres, problems of understanding and interpretation are recognized as central. While few contemporary hermeneutic philosophers would wish to draw the distinction between the natural sciences and the *Geisteswissenschaften* in the way that their nineteenth-century predecessors did, many would nevertheless want to defend the peculiar character of social and historical enquiry. For the *objects* of such enquiry are the product of *subjects* capable of action and understanding, so that our knowledge of the social and historical world cannot be sharply separated from the subjects who make up that world.

JOHN B. THOMPSON
UNIVERSITY OF CAMBRIDGE

References

Gadamer, H.-G. (1975 [1960]) *Truth and Method*, London.
Ricoeur, P. (1981) *Hermeneutics and the Human Sciences: Essays on Language, Action and Interpretation*, Cambridge, UK.

Further reading

Palmer, R.E. (1969) *Hermeneutics: Interpretation Theory in Schleiermacher, Dilthey, Heidegger, and Gadamer*, Evanston, IL.

SEE ALSO: Habermas; Weber

HERODOTUS (C.480–420 BCE)

Herodotus of Halicarnassus, modern Bodrum in western Turkey, was the author of the first fully surviving prose work of history, in nine 'books' or subdivisions. The ostensible subject is the Persian wars against the Greeks of 500–480 BCE, fought in western Asia Minor and mainland Greece, but the chronological and geographical sweep is far wider. He wrote in Greek but was himself only half-Greek: his mother was Carian, from one of the indigenous non-Greek ('barbarian') peoples of western Asia Minor. Plutarch (in AD c.100) called Herodotus *philobarbaros*, 'barbarian-lover', and it is Herodotus' preoccupation with and pioneering analysis of non-Greek cultures which gives his *History* its importance for the anthropologist. 'Common blood, language, religion, customs' are invoked by some Athenian speakers as the defining constituents of 'Greek-ness', *to Hellenikon* (8. 144, said to a Macedonian king; a remarkably precocious general theory about ethnicity is implicit here). Two of his books stand out from this point of view: the 'oldest people' of all, the soft Egyptians (in most ways the cultural reverse of the Greeks), are the subject of book 2, while the hard Scythians, the 'youngest' people (and the mirror of Athens: Hartog 1980), take up much of book 4. It will be seen already that Greece and in particular Athens (Fowler 2003) are the norm by which the foreign 'other' is measured; and that within the category 'barbarian', Egypt and Scythia are the conceptual poles.

Herodotus spent time at imperial democratic Athens in its glory days under Pericles, and then moved further west again to settle in south Italy at Thurii. His text contains some indisputable forward allusions to the Peloponnesian War between Athens and Sparta of 431–404 BCE, and one important passage (6. 98) shows that he was aware of the death of the Persian King Artaxerxes (424): in the three royal generations ending with Artaxerxes, he says, Greece suffered more misery than in the previous twenty, partly from the Persian wars themselves, partly from the disputes among the leading Greek states for hegemony. This establishes both Herodotus' rough compositional date, and his impartiality; it can also be seen (Fornara 1971) as offering the political key to his work, namely a warning against fratricidal strife between Greek and Greek. Otherwise we have few reliable biographical facts about his life that are not extrapolations from his writings (the Italian and even the – surely formative – Athenian periods have been doubted): sceptics ancient and modern have wondered if the liberal use of the first-person singular, and especially the explicit and implicit claims to wide travel, are merely the expression of a literary persona (Fehling 1989). To put it in the language of Michel Foucault, such sceptics are claiming that Herodotus has a strong and distorting 'author-function'. But no liar could be as good as Herodotus would need to be. We can still agree that he forced the facts from time to time through his love of schematism and patterning, and the need to subordinate a vast bulk of material to organizing principles, of which reciprocity/requital (Gould 1989) and symmetry/opposition (Redfield 1985) are the chief. (On requital, *tisis*, see also Hornblower 2003 discussing 8. 104–6.) It is a further disquieting, and not

yet fully understood or explained, feature of Herodotus' *History* that the small-scale stories artfully strewn along the path of his main narrative line exhibit similarities of structure and detail with biblical stories and with folk-tales (see Griffiths 1987 for an example: Demokedes the doctor from Kroton and the story of Joseph and Potiphar).

Herodotus' *History* is a literary achievement at the highest level: he is, a recently-discovered poem from Halicarnassus calls him, the 'pedestrian [i.e. prose] Homer' (Lloyd-Jones 1999). He is, like his model, easy, readable, charming, open-minded and capable at no notice of effecting a non-disconcerting switch from chatty and light-hearted to solemn and profound.

Herodotus' open-mindedness deserves a further word. His apparently naïve fondness for giving unadjudicated alternatives, and his pronounced intellectual permeability, has always struck some readers as uncritical and even gullible, especially by comparison with his younger contemporary Thucydides, who described the Peloponnesian War in eight 'books' and who illuminates Herodotus' achievement by contrast. The tunnel-visioned Thucydides is in constant though unavowed reaction against Herodotus. War and politics are now the focus, and ethnography dwindles to nearly nothing, though the Thracians, the northern neighbours of Greece, elicit some interesting comment of this sort from a man who was himself of part-Thracian royal descent. Above all Thucydides asserts and narrates seamlessly, saying virtually nothing about his sources. Like those of Herodotus, these sources are largely oral, and both men may have given recitations of highly finished parts of their work and to that extent display typical traces of orality; but, unlike his predecessor, Thucydides gives no hostages to fortune by citing them specifically. Thucydides closes down, Herodotus opens up. In the terminology of the Russian critic Mikhael Bakhtin, we may characterize the Herodotean approach as dialogic as opposed to monologistic (Bakhtin 1981). The old fable of the hedgehog and the fox, known to Herodotus, is relevant here: 'the fox knows many things, the hedgehog one big thing' (cf. Herodotus 4. 46. 2 with Redfield 1985: 108: the Scythians know 'one very big thing', the art of not being conquered). Thucydides, like Dostoyevsky, was a hedgehog, Herodotus a fox (Berlin 1967: 2). Herodotus' greater intellectual hospitality and his calm refusal of petty partisanship perfectly qualified him, it might be thought, to be a great anthropologist or an ethnographer.

There is much in this, though we must not forget that Herodotus had predecessors and contemporaries now partially or wholly lost. Hecataeus of Miletus anticipated his ethnography in certain respects. On the classic account of Jacoby 1956 [1913], the three 'Hecataean' ingredients of an ethnographic *logos* or account were geography, customs, marvels, to which, by a move of cardinal importance and originality and under the influence of the momentous events of his own half-century, Herodotus added a fourth: political history. This structure is particularly clear in the (compositionally early?) book 2, Egypt. Again we know, from a poem published from papyrus only in 1992, that the great poet Simonides had already bridged the gap between epic and historiography by narrating episodes from the Persian Wars in verse, which owes much to Homer (Boedeker and Sider 2001) and which draws a parallel between Trojan and Persian Wars (cf. also above for the problem of biblical precedents). Herodotus' intellectual activity generally, and his understanding of human diversity in particular, owe much to progress and speculation in technical areas like medicine; but the identification of precise 'influences' is a delicate operation (see Thomas 2000 for a nuanced and cautious attempt). The famous 'constitutional debate' (3. 80–2), implausibly set in the Persia of the 520s but surely written in the 420s, sorts political systems into the only logical possibilities: rule by one, rule by few, rule by many. This typology had a long future – but it also had a past, and an unexpected one, in a poem written by Pindar 50 years earlier to celebrate a victory in a horse-race (*Pythian* 2. 86-8). Nevertheless the virtuosity of the sustained detail of the three arguments in Herodotus is characteristic of its 'own' day, the late fifth-century age of the sophists or itinerant teachers who could, as contemporaries noted, make the worse cause appear the better. Such essentially forensic techniques were, at the very least, useful tools for the 'father of anthropology', a discipline which starts from the premise that there is more than one legitimate way of doing or saying things. 'Custom is king of all' said Herodotus in what is, as it happens, his only actual quotation from Pindar (3. 38).

But is Herodotus really doing anthropology or ethnography at all? James Redfield has distinguished between tourists, who do not mind being foreigners and make no attempt to fit in, and ethnographers, who 'characteristically align themselves with the natives against their own people' and do not believe that there are such things as superior societies (Redfield 1985: 100). Herodotus, like most Greeks, was on Redfield's analysis a great tourist, confident in his own higher cultural morale. The tourist–ethnographer distinction is a helpful one. But as more work is done on the literary texture of the *History*, the clearer it becomes (Pelling 1997) that the East–West, Greek–barbarian stereotypical opposition with which the *History* begins (1. 1–5) is subverted almost from the outset. Thus one main theme of the *History* is the way Persians gradually come to understand their main opponents the Spartans (Lewis 1977: 148). Herodotus has many levels and literary registers; he is the supreme 'anthropologist as author' (to borrow Geertz's phrase (1988)) and he can be properly understood only by respecting both halves of that formulation.

SIMON HORNBLOWER
UNIVERSITY COLLEGE LONDON

References

Bakhtin, M. (1981) *The Dialogic Imagination. Four Essays*, ed. M. Holquist, Austin, TX.

Berlin, I. (1967) *The Hedgehog and the Fox: An Essay on Tolstoy's View of History*, London.

Boedeker, D. and Sider, D. (eds) (2001) *The New Simonides*, New York.

Fehling, D. (1989) *Herodotus and His 'Sources': Citation, Invention and Narrative Art*, trans. G. Howie, Leeds.

Fornara, C. (1971) *Herodotus: An Interpretative Essay*, Oxford.

Fowler, R. (2003) 'Herodotus and Athens', in P. Derow and R. Parker (eds) *Herodotus and His World*, Oxford.

Geertz, C. (1988) *Works and Lives: The Anthropologist as Author*, Stanford.

Gould, J. (1989) *Herodotus*, London.

Griffiths, A. (1987) 'Democedes of Kroton', in H. Sancisi-Weerdenburg and A. Kuhrt (eds) *Achaemenid History 2*, Leiden.

Hartog, F. (1980) *The Mirror of Herodotus*, Berkeley, CA.

Hornblower, S. (2003) 'Panionios and Hermotimos', in P. Derow and R. Parker (eds) *Herodotus and His World*, Oxford.

Jacoby, F. (1956 [1913]) 'Herodot', in *Griechische Historiker*, Stuttgart.

Lewis, D.M. (1977) *Sparta and Persia*, Leiden.

Lloyd-Jones, H. (1999) 'The pride of Halicarnassus', *Zeitschrift für Papyrologie und Epigraphik* 124.

Pelling, C. (1997) 'East is east and west is west: Or are they? National stereotypes in Herodotus', *Histos* 1 (http://www.dur.ac.uk/Classics/histos/1997/pelling.html).

Redfield, J. (1985) 'Herodotus the tourist', *Classical Philology* 80.

Thomas, R. (2000) *Herodotus in Context*, Cambridge.

Further reading

Good recent translations of Herodotus are by D. Grene (1989), Chicago; the Oxford World's Classics translation by R. Waterfield (1998), which has perceptive introduction and notes by C. Dewald; and the Penguin translation of A. de Selincourt revised with notes by J. Marincola (1996).

Bakker, E., de Jong, H. and van Wees, H. (eds) (2002) *Brill's Companion to Herodotus*, Leiden.

Derow, P. and Parker, R. (eds) (2003) *Herodotus and His World*, Oxford.

Harrison, T. (2000) *Divinity and History*, Oxford [on religion in Herodotus].

HISTORICAL LINGUISTICS

Credit for founding the field of historical linguistics is usually given to Sir William Jones, a scholarly British judge, who in 1786 observed that Sanskrit, Latin and Greek had striking similarities in their roots and word structures that could only be explained by descent from a common, unknown, ancestral language. This view is now universally accepted by experts in the field. In the following century, European scholars developed a rigorous analytic methodology for linguistic comparison, enjoyed great success in reconstructing aspects of this common ancestor, 'Indo-European', and began to apply their methods to other families of languages (see chapters by Collinge in Koerner and Asher 1995).

Historical linguists today continue to expand their understanding of family relationships through the discovery of correspondences between sounds in like environments in sets of words with comparable meanings (the 'comparative method'). 'Cognate' words in different languages are presumed to reflect divergent forms of what was once a single word in the ancestor language. So, for example, cognate pairs in English and Latin show a relationship between an initial *k-* sound in Latin (spelled with a *c*) and an initial *h-* sound in English, both of which can be traced back to an original **k-* sound in the common ancestor, 'Proto-Indo-European'. (The asterisk is used to indicate a reconstructed,

hypothetical source.) This resulted in cognate 'doublets' when English borrowed a word directly from Latin that had not undergone the regular Germanic change of *k-* to *h-* (yielding inherited *hill* alongside Latinate *culminate*):

Indo-European
*kel- 'to be prominent, hill'
*kerp- 'to gather, pluck'
*kaput- 'head'

Latin	English
culmen 'top' (> Eng. *culminate*)	hill
carpere 'to pluck' (*carpe diem*)	harvest
caput 'head' (> Eng. *decapitate*)	head

Moving forwards in time from these earlier hypothesized states, or from early textual attestations, historical linguists also track the evolution of individual linguistic features in particular languages or language families to the present day.

Theoretical and methodological discussions that are part of this research programme address the role of (1) 'basic vocabulary' (words less likely to be borrowed from other languages) in distinguishing contact effects from inheritance; (2) analogical reformation in word structure change; (3) surface pattern reinterpretation in phrase and sentence structure change; and (4) 'grammaticalization' in lexical change – a process whereby a semantically robust word (like the Old English verb *willan* 'to wish', for example) may over time turn into a grammatical word (in this case, the Modern English future marker *will*).

Not surprisingly, historical linguistics complements other types of historical studies. Historical linguists and philologists (who study ancient languages through texts) are natural partners. Historical linguists are also often involved in deciphering ancient writing systems with the goal of elucidating older stages of the spoken languages they represent. And recently there has been fruitful collaboration between linguists, archaeologists (Renfrew 1987) and geneticists (Cavalli-Sforza 2000), since they pursue independent but potentially converging sources of evidence about history before written records, or 'prehistory' – especially as it pertains to the relationships between groups of people, the locations of ancient homelands, and migration patterns.

As a scientific as well as a humanistic enquiry, historical linguistics has taken the natural and physical sciences as its models from the beginning. For example, the family tree model itself, the comparative method, the 'punctuated equilibrium' model of species change (Dixon 1997), and the 'founder principle' in population genetics (Mufwene 2001) have all been appropriated from biology. The principle of 'uniformitarianism' – processes of change are 'uniform' throughout time, so changes happening in the present must be essentially the same as unobservable changes in the past – was taken from geology (Joseph and Janda 2003, 'Introduction'), and an older (now discredited) idea that dating languages is possible because the set of inherited words in a language disappears at a constant rate was inspired by carbon-14 dating (Swadesh 1971).

Since the middle of the twentieth century, historical linguistics has expanded to address the social context of language change: What are the necessary preconditions for change? What triggers any specific change? How should we apportion responsibility for language change between children (who arrive at new grammars by induction) and adults (who may choose one variant over another under pressure of social forces)? How do multilingualism and language contact confound the idealized picture of the 'family tree', with its cleanly diverging branches? What unites these questions is their focus on very recent change or change-in-progress under complex historical and social conditions that can still be recovered. These processes can be studied both for their own sake and for their potential to explain changes that took place in the distant past.

MARTHA RATLIFF
WAYNE STATE UNIVERSITY

References

Cavalli-Sforza, L.L. (2000) *Genes, Peoples, and Languages*, Berkeley, CA.

Dixon, R.M.W. (1997) *The Rise and Fall of Languages*, Cambridge.

Joseph, B.D. and Janda, R.D. (eds) (2003) *The Handbook of Historical Linguistics*, Oxford.

Koerner, E.F.K. and Asher, R.A. (eds) (1995) *Concise History of the Language Sciences: From the Sumerians to the Cognitivists*, New York.

Mufwene, S. (2001) *The Ecology of Language Evolution*, Cambridge.

Renfrew, C. (1987) *Archaeology and Language: The Puzzle of Indo-European Origins*, Cambridge.

Swadesh, M. (1971) *The Origin and Diversification of Language*, Chicago.

Further reading

Hock, H.H. and Joseph, B.D. (1996) *Language History, Language Change, and Language Relationship*, Berlin.

Milroy, J. (1992) *Linguistic Variation and Change*, Oxford.

Thomason, S.G. and Kaufman, T. (1988) *Language Contact, Creolization, and Genetic Linguistics*, Berkeley, CA.

Trask, L. (2000) *The Dictionary of Historical and Comparative Linguistics*, Edinburgh.

HISTORY

History has some claim to be considered one of the world's oldest professions, and the subject was taught in some European universities, from Oxford to Göttingen, in the seventeenth and eighteenth centuries (Gilbert 1977). However, the rise of history as an academic discipline in the West coincided with the rise of the social sciences in the nineteenth century. The relation of historians to these subjects was often one of rivalry and conflict. Inspired by the work of Leopold von Ranke (1795–1886), historians were moving away from the 'history of society' that some of them had practised in the eighteenth century and concentrating their attention on the production of narratives of political events firmly based on official documents. They tended to define their discipline by contrast to the social sciences, especially to sociology, although they were often interested in geography as a 'handmaid' to their subject, while a handful of economic historians, such as Gustav Schmoller (1838–1917), had an interest in economic theory. Karl Lamprecht (1856–1915) in Germany and James Harvey Robinson (1863-1936) and others in the USA advocated a new kind of history that would pay considerable attention to culture and society, and also draw on the concepts and theories of social scientists, but these historians were isolated among their professional colleagues. At the end of the century, the conventional wisdom of the historian's craft, expressed in philosophical form by Wilhelm Dilthey (1833–1911), Wilhelm Windelband (1848–1915), Heinrich Rickert (1863–1936) and Benedetto Croce (1866–1952), was that history was concerned with unique events (leaving the establishment of general laws to the social sciences), and that historians tried to understand the past from within (while social scientists attempted to explain it from outside). For their part, sociologists such as Auguste Comte (1798–1857) and Herbert Spencer (1820–1903) regarded historians as at best collectors of raw material for theorists to utilize.

This intellectual landscape had not changed very much by the middle of the twentieth century. In England, for example, the views associated with Dilthey and Croce were reiterated with force by R.G. Collingwood (1889–1943), the one philosopher of history to be taken seriously in the English-speaking world (perhaps because he doubled as a historian of Roman Britain). There had been a few rebellions against the hegemony of political narrative, but in 1950 they could not yet be described as successful. Marxist historians had not yet produced many important works – the exceptions include Jan Romein's *De lage landen bij de zee* (1934) and Emilio Sereni's *Capitalism in the Countryside* (1947). Only in two areas was change truly visible. Economic historians had become a significant group within the profession, with their own journals, such as the *Economic History Review*, their own heroes, such as the Belgian Henri Pirenne (1862–1935) and the Swede Eli Heckscher (1879–1952), and their own debates, which often had more in common with debates among economists than with those of their fellow historians. In France, a broader approach to history, inspired by Lucien Febvre (1878–1956) and Marc Bloch (1886–1944), and associated with the journal *Annales*, had begun to attract attention, and a remarkable work on the Mediterranean world in the age of Philip II was published in 1949 by Fernand Braudel (1902–85), particularly original in its exploration of what the author called 'geo-history', a historical geography influenced by the work of Vidal de la Blache but rather more deterministic.

Retrospectively, the 1950s now appear to be something of a historiographical turning point. Serious Marxist history finally came on-stream, generally produced outside the Communist Bloc (by Eric Hobsbawm and Edward Thompson in England, Pierre Vilar in France, etc.), but occasionally within it – an outstanding example being the work of the Polish economic historian Witold Kula (1916–88). In France, the Annales group, under Braudel's leadership, came to dominate the profession, both intellectually and institutionally. In the USA, France and elsewhere, the 'new economic history', like economics, became increasingly ambitious in its aims, and quantitative

in its methods. It was sometimes taken as a model for other kinds of history. Historical demography, for instance, which emerged as a subdiscipline in the 1950s (inspired by increasing concern with contemporary population growth), is a form of quantitative social history (Wrigley 1969). Other social historians and historical sociologists also took a quantitative turn at this time, though some resisted; E.P. Thompson's classic study *The Making of the English Working Class* (1963) contains a characteristically savage critique of what the author called 'sociology', more exactly the quantitative historical sociology of Talcott Parsons's follower Neil Smelser, who had recently written about the Industrial Revolution. Quantification also played an important role in the 'new political history', practised in the USA in particular, whether the emphasis fell on election results, voting patterns in Congress or attempts to count strikes and other forms of protest (Bogue 1983). Similar methods were applied to religious history, particularly in France, with statistics for annual confession and communion taking the place of voting figures. For example, in his original and controversial book on 'baroque piety and dechristianization', Michel Vovelle studied some 30,000 wills from eighteenth-century Provence, using them as indexes of views of death and of changes in religious attitudes (Vovelle 1973). His work offered a possible link between cliometrics and another concern of the 1950s, 'psychohistory'. In France, following the tradition of Durkheim and Lucien Lévy-Bruhl (1857–1939), interest in historical psychology focused not on individuals but on collective mentalities, as in a series of studies by Philippe Ariès (1914–84) on changing attitudes to childhood and to death over the centuries. A few bold spirits, among them the French medievalist Jacques Le Goff, attempted to study mentalities in the manner of Claude Lévi-Strauss, emphasizing binary oppositions in general and the opposition between nature and culture in particular. In the USA, on the other hand, where the ideas of Sigmund Freud were more deeply embedded in the culture than elsewhere, some historians and psychoanalysts attempted to study the motives and drives of religious and political leaders such as Martin Luther, Woodrow Wilson, Lenin and Gandhi, while a president of the American Historical Association invited his colleagues to consider psychohistory as their 'next assignment' (Langer 1958).

With few exceptions, historians failed to respond to Langer's invitation. What some of them did do in the 1970s, like their colleagues in related disciplines, to some extent as a reaction to the events of 1968, was to reject determinism (economic or geographical), as they rejected quantitative methods and the claim of the social sciences to be scientific. In the case of history, this rejection of the work of the previous generation was accompanied by new approaches to the past, four in particular, which can be summed up by four slogans in four languages: 'history from below', *microstoria*, *Alltagsgeschichte* and *histoire de l'imaginaire*.

First, 'history from below' is an ambiguous term, and both meanings are important: not only the history of ordinary people in the past but also history written from the point of view of ordinary people. It is perhaps the most important change in the discipline this century, a true Copernican Revolution in historical writing that compensates for the inadequacies of a tradition of elitist historiography that ignored the experiences, the culture and the aspirations of dominated groups (Guha 1982). This shift has encouraged and has in turn been encouraged by the rise of 'oral history', giving ordinary people an opportunity to describe their experience of the historical process in their own words. However, the practice of history from below has turned out to be much less simple than was originally thought, largely because of differences between different kinds of dominated group – the working class, the peasantry, the colonized and, of course, women. It was around the 1970s that the movement for women's history became generally visible, thanks to the rise of women's studies and feminism, and the result was to undermine any assumption of the unity of the 'subordinate classes'. In the second place, the study of the working class, or of women, or of popular culture, in isolation from the study of the middle class, or men, or elite culture, is now generally considered to be misleading, and attention is turning to the relations between these different groups.

Second, *microstoria* or microhistory may be defined as a concern with the past at the level of a small community, whether village, street, family or even individual; an examination of 'faces in the crowd', which allows concrete experience to re-enter social history. This approach was put on the historical map by Carlo Ginzburg's *Cheese and Worms* (1976), a study of the cosmos of a sixteenth-century Italian miller, as revealed in his replies to interrogations by the Inquisition, and by Emmanuel le Roy Ladurie's *Montaillou* (1975), which was also based on inquisitorial records, and which were used to produce a portrait of a fourteenth-century village that the author himself compared to community studies such as Ronald Blythe's *Akenfield*. These two books were not only bestsellers but also exemplary in the sense of inspiring a school or at least a trend. Condemned by more traditional historians as a kind of antiquarianism and as a dereliction of the historian's duty to explain how the modern world emerged, microhistory has been defended by one of its leading practitioners, Giovanni Levi (1991), on the grounds that the reduction of scale reveals how political and social rules often do not work in practice and how individuals can make spaces for themselves in the interstices between institutions.

Third, *Alltagsgeschichte* or 'the history of the everyday' is an approach that developed, or was at least defined, in Germany, drawing on a philosophical and sociological tradition that includes Alfred Schutz (1899–1959) and Erving Goffman (1922–82), Henri Lefebvre (1901–91) and Michel de Certeau (1925–86). Like microhistory, with which it overlaps, the history of the everyday has been important as a way of reinserting human experience into social history, which was perceived by some of its practitioners as becoming increasingly abstract and faceless. The approach has been criticized for its concern with what the critics call 'trivialities', as well as for ignoring politics, but it has been defended, in much the same way that microhistory has been defended, on the grounds that it shows how trifles may be clues to important, subterranean changes (Lüdtke 1982).

Fourth, *histoire de l'imaginaire* or the history of mentalities might be defined as the everyday version of intellectual history or the history of ideas, in other words the history of habits of thought or unspoken assumptions rather than of ideas that have been consciously formulated by philosophers and other theorists. This approach, which originated in France in the 1920s and 1930s, has recently gone through something of a revival. As not infrequently happens in these cases, however, what is revived is not quite the same as what had existed earlier. Historians working in this area show an increasing concern with 'representations' (literary, visual or mental), and also with what French historians, following Jacques Lacan and Michel Foucault, call the *imaginaire* (perhaps best translated as the 'imagined' or the 'imagination' rather than the 'imaginary'). With this shift has come what is often called a new emphasis on the construction, constitution or 'social production' not only of different forms of culture – the 'invention of traditions', for example – but also of states and societies, which are now often viewed not as hard or objective structures, but rather as 'imagined communities' (Anderson 1991; Hobsbawm and Ranger 1983). In other words, historians like their colleagues in other disciplines are experiencing the effects of the 'linguistic turn'.

It is worth noting that all four of the approaches just described are linked in some way to social anthropology, since anthropologists are concerned with 'the native's point of view' and work in small communities, observing everyday life and studying modes of thought or belief systems. Indeed, a number of historians practising these approaches would describe themselves as historical anthropologists, and introduce their work with references to E.E. Evans-Pritchard, to Victor Turner, or, most often, to Clifford Geertz (Walters 1980).

Despite the importance of these four linked trends, they are not sufficient to describe recent changes in historical writing (let alone to characterize the work of more traditional historians). As was only to be expected, there are movements in different and even in opposite directions. While some scholars try to observe social change through the microscope, others, in the spirit of the 'total history' preached and practised by Fernand Braudel, try to look at the world as a whole. The best-known representative of this approach, apart from Braudel himself, is Immanuel Wallerstein, a sociologist of Africa turned historian of capitalism, in a series of volumes on 'the modern world-system'. Marxist in inspiration, these influential volumes draw on the economics of development and world-systems theory in order to show connexions between the rise of Venice and Amsterdam, and the underdevelopment of Eastern Europe and South America (Wallerstein 1974–). As might have been predicted, other attempts to see the history of planet earth as a whole have adopted an ecological viewpoint, examining, for instance, the consequences of the encounter between Europe and America as a 'Columbian exchange' of plants, animals and, not least, diseases, and so 'placing Nature in History' (Crosby 1972). Braudel's geohistory has come to look rather static in the light of current concerns with the interaction between the landscape and its human and animal populations (Cronon 1990; Worster 1988).

At the same time as these new developments, and in reaction to some of them, readers of history have witnessed two revivals, the revival of politics and the revival of narrative. There have been many pleas by historians to put politics back into history, if not to restore its former dominance. In some respects the climate of the 1980s and 1990s has been favourable to a revival of politics, since the general rejection of determinism has made room for discussions of strategy and tactics that we may call 'political'. However, under the influence of the trends discussed above, political history has been reconstructed to include what Michel Foucault described as 'micro politics' – in other words, strategies and tactics at the level of the village or the family as well as that of the state. Even diplomatic history, necessarily focused on states, has widened its concerns to include an interest in mentalities and in rituals.

More frequently discussed and more controversial is the trend towards the revival of narrative and of the history of events once so forcefully dismissed by the leaders of the Annales School (Stone 1979). As in the case of politics, the term 'revival' is somewhat misleading. The history of events used to be written as if the past included nothing else, whereas today's historians, like some sociologists and anthropologists, are explicitly concerned with the relation between events and structures (whether these structures are 'social' or 'cultural', if that distinction still makes sense). As for narrative, it has returned in a new form, or more exactly a variety of new forms, since at least a few historians (like their sociological and anthropological colleagues) are conscious of their use of rhetoric, interested in literary experiment, and even – like some contemporary novelists – in transgressing the traditional boundaries between fact and fiction (White 1978). One of these new forms is the narrative of small-scale events, a technique commonly deployed by microhistorians, and a considerable contrast to the traditional 'Grand Narrative' that emphasized key events and dates such as 1066, 1492, 1789, 1914, and so on.

Another is the story told from more than one viewpoint, in order to accommodate differences in the perception of events from above and from below, by opposite sides in a civil war, and so on (Price 1990). Given current interest in encounters between cultures, it is likely that this 'dialogic' form of narrative will be practised more and more frequently in the future. Since this article takes the form of a monologue, this is perhaps the moment to draw attention to the fact that it has itself been written from a particular point of view, that of a middle-class Englishman, and that – like most articles in this volume – it is especially though not exclusively concerned with developments in the West.

PETER BURKE

UNIVERSITY OF CAMBRIDGE

References

Anderson, B. (1991) *Imagined Communities*, rev. edn, London.

Bogue, A.G. (1983) *Clio and the Bitch Goddess: Quantification in American Political History*, Beverly Hills, CA.

Cronon, W. (1990) 'Placing nature in history', *Journal of American History* 76.

Crosby, A.W. (1972) *The Columbian Exchange: Biological and Cultural Consequences of 1492*, Westport, CT.

Gilbert, F. (1977) 'Reflections on the history of the professor of history', in *History: Choice and Commitment*, Cambridge, MA.

Guha, R. (1982) 'Some aspects of the historiography of colonial India', in *Subaltern Studies* I, Delhi.

Hobsbawm, E.J. and Ranger, T.O. (eds) (1983) *The Invention of Tradition*, Cambridge.

Langer, W.L. (1958) 'The next assignment', *American Historical Review* 63.

Levi, G. (1991) 'On micro-history', in P. Burke (ed.) *New Perspectives on Historical Writing*, Cambridge.

Lüdtke, A. (1982) 'The historiography of everyday life', in R. Samuel and G. Stedman Jones (eds) *Culture, Ideology and Politics*, London.

Price, R. (1990) *Alabi's World*, Baltimore.

Stone, L. (1979) 'The revival of narrative', *Past and Present* 85.

Vovelle, M. (1973) *Piété baroque et déchristianisation en Provence au 18e siècle*, Paris.

Wallerstein, I. (1974–) *The Modern World System*, New York.

Walters, R.G. (1980) 'Signs of the times: Clifford Geertz and historians', *Social Research* 47.

White, H.V. (1978) *Tropics of Discourse*, Baltimore.

Worster, D. (ed.) (1988) *The Ends of the Earth: Perspectives on Modern Environmental History*, Cambridge.

Wrigley, E.A. (1969) *Population and History*, London.

Further reading

Burke, P. (ed.) (2001) *New Perspectives on Historical Writing*, 2nd edn, Cambridge, UK.

Iggers, G.G. (1984) *New Directions in European Historiography*, 2nd edn, Middletown, CT.

HOBBES, THOMAS (1588–1679)

Thomas Hobbes is one of the most important figures in the development of modern science and modern politics. As a contemporary of Bacon, Galileo and Descartes, he contributed to the radical critique of medieval Scholasticism and classical philosophy that marked the beginning of the modern age. But he alone sought to develop a comprehensive philosophy – one that treated natural science, political science and theory of scientific method in a unified system. He published this system in three volumes, under the titles *Body* (1655), *Man* (1657) and *Citizen* (1642). In the course of his long career, Hobbes also published treatises on mathematics, on free will and determinism, on the English common law system, and on the English Civil War. Although his work covered the whole of philosophy, Hobbes made his greatest contribution to modern thought in the field of political philosophy. On three separate occasions, he presented his theory of man and the state; the most famous of his political treatises, the *Leviathan* (1651), is generally recognized as the greatest work of political philosophy in the English language.

In all branches of knowledge, Hobbes's thought is characterized by a pervasive sense that the ancient and medieval philosophers had failed to discover true knowledge, and that a new alternative was urgently needed. It is this sense that defines Hobbes as a modern thinker and gives his work its originality, verve and self-conscious radicalism. In natural science (metaphysics and physics), he rejected the Scholastic and Aristotelian ideas of abstract essences and immaterial causes as nothing more than vain and empty speech. The nature of reality is matter in motion, which implied that all phenomena of nature and human nature could be explained in terms of mechanical causation. In the theory of science, Hobbes dismissed the disputative method of Scholasticism and classical dialectics as forms of rhetoric that merely appealed to the authority of common opinion and produced endless verbal controversies. The correct method of reasoning combined the resolutive-compositive method of Galileo and the deductive method of Euclidean geometry. By combining these, Hobbes believed that every branch of knowledge, including the study of politics, could be turned into an exact deductive science.

In political science proper, Hobbes was no less radical in his rejection of the tradition. He opposed the republicanism of classical antiquity, the ecclesiastical politics of medieval Europe, and the doctrine of mixed-monarchy prevalent in seventeenth-century England. All of these doctrines, Hobbes claimed, were seditious in intent or effect, because they were derived from 'higher' laws that allowed people to appeal to a standard above the will of the sovereign. Hobbes blamed such appeals, exploited by ambitious priests and political demagogues, for the political instability of his times, culminating in the English Civil War. The solution he proposed was political absolutism – the unification of sovereignty in an all-powerful state that derived its authority not from higher laws but from *de facto* power and the consent of the people, and that aimed at nothing higher than security or self-preservation.

With these three teachings – mechanistic materialism, exact deductive science and political absolutism – Hobbes sought to establish science and politics on a new foundation that would produce certain knowledge and lasting civil peace.

From the first, Hobbes's philosophical system generated controversy. In the seventeenth century, Hobbes was treated as a dangerous subversive by all who believed in, or had an interest in, the traditional order. Christian clergymen condemned his materialist view of the world as atheistic and his mechanistic view of man as soulless; legal scholars attacked his doctrine of absolutism for placing the sovereign above the civil laws; even kings, whose power Hobbes sought to augment, were wary of accepting the teaching that political authority rested on force and consent rather than on divine right (Mintz 1962). In the eighteenth and nineteenth centuries his defence of absolute and arbitrary power ran counter to the general demand for constitutional government, but Hobbes was treated more favourably in the twentieth century. Although some scholars noted parallels between Hobbes's Leviathan state and modern tyrannies (Collingwood 1942), most clearly recognize that Hobbes's political sovereign, whose primary goal is to secure civil peace, is vastly different from the

brutal and fanatical heads of totalitarian states (Strauss 1959). Hobbes's image has also been reshaped by a new appreciation for his role as a founder of the modern Enlightenment (Johnston 1986; Kraynak 1990; Reynolds and Saxonhouse 1995).

Scholarly studies of Hobbes generally fall into four groups, each reflecting the perspective of a contemporary school of philosophy as it probes the origins of modernity. The first, guided by the concerns of contemporary analytical philosophy, argues for the primacy of method and logic in Hobbes's system and views his politics as a set of formal rules that serve as utilitarian guidelines for the state (McNeilly 1968; Watkins 1965). A second group has examined Hobbes's theory of political obligation from a Kantian point of view. According to this interpretation, Hobbes's argument for obedience goes beyond calculations of utility by appealing to a sense of moral duty in keeping the social contract, and by requiring citizens to have just intentions (Taylor 1938; Warrender 1957). Developed by Marxist scholars, a third interpretation uses Hobbes to understand the ideological origins of bourgeois society and to provide a critical perspective on bourgeois liberalism by exposing its Hobbesian roots (Coleman 1977; Macpherson 1962). The fourth interpretation reflects the concerns of the natural-law school. According to the foremost scholar of this school, Hobbes is the decisive figure in transforming the natural-law tradition from classical natural right to the modern theory of natural 'rights'; Hobbes accomplished this revolution by asserting that the right of self-preservation, grounded in the fear of violent death, is the only justifiable moral claim (Strauss 1936). Despite the disagreements among scholars, all see Hobbes as a major figure in the founding of modernity.

ROBERT P. KRAYNAK
COLGATE UNIVERSITY

References

Coleman, F.M. (1977) *Hobbes and America: Exploring the Constitutional Foundations*, Toronto.

Collingwood, R.G. (1942) *The New Leviathan*, Oxford.

Johnston, D. (1986) *The Rhetoric of Leviathan: Thomas Hobbes and the Politics of Cultural Transformation*, Princeton.

Kraynak, R. (1990) *History and Modernity in the Thought of Thomas Hobbes*, Cornell.

McNeilly, F.S. (1968) *The Anatomy of Leviathan*, London.

Macpherson, C.B. (1962) *The Political Theory of Possessive Individualism*, Oxford.

Mintz, S.I. (1962) *The Hunting of Leviathan*, Cambridge, UK.

Reynolds, N.B. and Saxonhouse, A.W. (1995) *Three Discourses: A Critical Modern Edition of Newly Identified Work of the Young Hobbes*, Chicago.

Strauss, L. (1936) *The Political Philosophy of Hobbes*, Chicago.

—— (1959) 'On the basis of Hobbes's political philosophy', in *What is Political Philosophy?* New York.

Taylor, A.E. (1938) 'The ethical doctrine of Hobbes', *Philosophy* 13.

Warrender, H. (1957) *The Political Philosophy of Hobbes: His Theory of Obligation*, Oxford.

Watkins, J.W.N. (1965) *Hobbes's System of Ideas: A Study in the Political Significance of Philosophical Theories*, London.

Further reading

Skinner, Q. (1997) *Reason and Rhetoric in the Philosophy of Hobbes*, Cambridge, UK.

Sorell, T. (ed.) (1996) *The Cambridge Companion to Hobbes*, Cambridge, UK.

Tuck, R. (1989) *Hobbes*, Oxford.

SEE ALSO: social contract; state

HOMOSEXUALITIES

Homosexuality is a category invented as an object of scientific investigation by a Hungarian doctor, Benkert, in 1869, amidst a flurry of attempts to classify sexuality (Foucault 1979). It is hence a distinctively modern term. By contrast, same-sex erotic experiences have existed across time and space with varying degrees of visibility, frequency and social organization. In different parts of the world, homosexualities assume widely divergent forms from male cult prostitution to female romantic friendships; they may be patterned by age as in ancient Greece or some societies like the Sambia people of the New Guinea Highlands; by gender as in the North American Berdache; or by class, as in master–slave relations in antiquity (Greenberg 1988). There is no unitary experience.

It is not quite clear when the distinctive modern or Western form emerged. Some connect it to the rise of capitalism, others to the emergence of a modern medicine, still others to the emergence of major urban centres. However it emerged, throughout the past two centuries, homosexuality has been seen negatively – as sin, sickness or crime. Until the 1970s, the dominant mode of thinking about homosexuality in the West was clinical: caused by degeneracy, biological anomaly or family pathology, and treatments ranging from castration to psychoanalysis were advocated. While such approaches do still continue, since 1973 the American Psychiatric Association has officially removed homosexuality from its nomenclature. Homosexuality is no longer officially a sickness, though there are many studies that still suggest it is a biological anomaly (Murphy 1997).

Male homosexuality has also been illegal in most European countries and US states; not until the 1960s – a decade after the decriminalizing proposals of the British Wolfenden Report and the US model penal code of 1955 proposed by the American Law Institute – did the legal situation start to change.

Throughout this time of hostility, there were always challenges. Magnus Hirschfield established the Institute for Sexual Science in Berlin in 1897 and campaigned for acceptance of homosexuality till the 1930s when the Nazis started their policy of extermination (Plant 1986). Others – Carpenter and Wilde in England, Gide and Genet in France – were pursuing literary defences. It was not until the period after the Second World War that a substantial body of published research suggested the ubiquity and normality of homosexual experience. The Kinsey Reports in 1948 and 1953 suggested that 37 per cent of men had some postadolescent homosexual orgasm and 4 per cent had a preponderance of such experience (13 per cent and 3 per cent, respectively, for women). Kinsey also suggested there was a continuum of homosexual–heterosexual attraction (on a scale of 1 to 6) and that homosexuality was to be found in all walks of life.

There was a progressive build-up of homophile organizations through the twentieth century, but it is the New York Stonewall Riots of 27–8 June 1969 that is generally considered to symbolize the birth of the modern international Gay and Lesbian Movement (Adam 1995 [1987]). The scientifically imposed term 'homosexual' was shifted to the self-created ones of 'lesbian' and 'gay'; pathological medical rhetoric was converted to the political language of 'gay is good'; a wide array of organizations for gays and lesbians became widespread in most large cities; and millions of gay men and women started to 'come out' and identify positively with the category 'gay'. Over the next 25 years, the gay and lesbian community was to become a visible and powerful social community, political lobby and 'pink economy' on a global scale.

A striking, and unexpected, development was the arrival of AIDS and HIV infection around 1981. Although AIDS concerns many people, in the Western world it has had a disproportionate impact upon gay men – both as sickness and as symbol. As sickness, many gay men in major cities (like San Francisco) have found their lives disrupted by a life-threatening disease, and have developed self-help institutions of support to cope with this AIDS crisis. Lesbians, too, have been involved in developing major programmes of community care. But as symbol, AIDS has been used as part of a conservative backlash to renew the stigmatizing attacks on homosexuality that were so prevalent in the earlier part of the twentieth century. At times, it has looked as if homosexuality was about to become 'remedicalized' as disease. But, ironically, in resisting these attacks the lesbian and gay communities appear to have become stronger, more visible and more political (Kayal 1993).

Since the late 1960s there has been a major development in research, writing and publication around homosexuality – the rise of 'lesbian and gay studies' (Nardi and Schneider 1998; Richardson and Seidman 2002). In the 1970s, psychologists debunked the 'sick homosexual' and refocused on homophobia – the fear of homosexuality. Sociologists initiated a debate on the homosexual role, the ways in which 'homosexualities' were always 'socially constructed', and the processes through which people came to identify themselves as gay. Historians and anthropologists researched homosexualities in different settings across the world (Duberman *et al.* 1989). Feminist scholars shaped many important debates on a wide range of matters like sexuality, female relationships, literary texts and race. On all these areas, debates, conflicts and international conferences have proliferated (Altman *et al.* 1989). By the late 1980s a younger generation was bringing a new and challenging strategy: 'queer' theory, 'queer' politics and 'queer' lifestyles.

Most significantly, whilst there is a bold confidence in gay studies and the lifestyle has become more and more accepted, in many countries throughout the world, gays and lesbians are still prosecuted – even tortured and killed – and increasingly political struggles for

lesbian and gay rights have emerged internationally (Altman 2000; Baird 2001). Of marked interest, here, has been the continuing role that all world religions play in condemning homosexuality and resisting change. All the same, there has been a growing movement towards the recognition of lesbian and gay partnerships and marriages, despite protestations.

KEN PLUMMER
UNIVERSITY OF ESSEX

References

Adam, B. (1995 [1987]) *The Rise of a Lesbian and Gay Movement*, 2nd edn, Boston, MA.
Altman, D. (2000) *Global Sex*, Chicago.
Altman, D., Vance, C., Vicinus, M. and Weeks, J. (eds) (1989) *Which Homosexuality?* London.
Baird, V. (2001) *The No-Nonsense Guide to Sexual Diversity*, London.
Duberman, M., Vicinus, M. and Chauncey, G. (eds) (1989) *Hidden from History: Reclaiming the Gay and Lesbian Past*, New York.
Foucault, M. (1979) *The History of Sexuality*, Vol. 1, *An Introduction*, London.
Greenberg, D. (1988) *The Construction of Homosexuality*, Chicago.
Kayal, P.M. (1993) *Bearing Witness: Gay Men's Health Crisis and the Politics of Aids*, Oxford.
Kinsey, A., Pomeroy, W.B. and Martin, C.E. (1948) *Sexual Behavior in the Human Male*, Philadelphia.
Kinsey, A., Pomeroy, W.B., Martin, C.E. and Gebhard, P.H. (1953) *Sexual Behavior in the Human Female*, New York.
Murphy, T.F. (1997) *Gay Science: The Ethics of Sexual Orientation Research*, New York.
Nardi, P. and Schneider, B. (eds) (1998) *Social Perspectives in Lesbian and Gay Studies*, London.
Plant, R. (1986) *The Pink Triangle: The Nazi War against Homosexuals*, New York.
Richardson, D. and Seidman, S. (2002) *Handbook of Lesbian and Gay Studies*, London.

SEE ALSO: gender, sociology of; queer theory; sexual behaviour

HOUSEHOLD

The defining characteristic of household membership is the occupation of living space that is reserved for the exclusive use of that household. In certain populations, however, many other ties may unite members of the household including the pooling of incomes, the taking of at least one main meal together, responsibility for the socialization of the young and the welfare of all members, while the household may even serve as the locus of production. Households are likely to have been largest and most complex when they fulfilled all of these functions. When more of such activities took place elsewhere, as was increasingly likely from the late nineteenth century, the ties between household members were loosened and it became more feasible to live in smaller residential groups or even alone. In increasing numbers of households since the 1960s, it is no longer the case that members of the household take even one main meal together. In Britain the definition of the household as a unit of co-residence and house-keeping was replaced in 1983 with a more flexible definition referring to co-residence in combination with either the sharing of one meal a day or the sharing of living accommodation (*Social Trends* 1984 and 1985).

In 2001, 29 per cent of all British households contained just one person, 12 per cent of the population lived alone and households on average contained 2.4 persons (*Social Trends* 2002). Such small households are not at all unusual in developed populations. For example, an average household size of at least three persons was recorded for only three West European countries at the beginning of the 1990s: Portugal, Spain and the Irish Republic (Begeot *et al.* 1993). In the past larger households were more common. In preindustrial England the average was 4.75 persons per household and less than 6 per cent of households consisted of persons living on their own (Laslett and Wall 1972). Households were somewhat larger still in rural parts of Denmark in 1787 and in Norway in 1801 (averages of 5.0 and 5.5 persons per household respectively) and considerably larger (over 7.0 persons per household) in many Austrian populations of the seventeenth and eighteenth centuries, and in northern Sweden in the seventeenth century (Lundh 1995; Wall *et al.* 1983). An average of over 9.0 persons per household was reached by a Russian serf population in the early nineteenth century (Czap 1983).

Differences in the kinship structure of the household sometimes underlay these differences in household size. In much of Northwestern Europe nuclear family households comprising parents and unmarried childen predominated, even before industrialization, while complex households involving the co-residence of two or more related couples were more readily formed in parts of Southern and in Eastern Europe. Within Western Europe the composition of

households also varied considerably in terms of the numbers of children and servants present and the frequency with which unmarried persons headed households (Wall 1991). In the USA there remain marked ethnic and racial variations in household structure. Yet one common trend across white, black and Hispanic households is the decline in married couples with children. By 1998, only a third of black households were maintained by married couples and only 16 per cent of these had children. About half of the white and Hispanic households were maintained by married couples but children are markedly more common in Hispanic households (36 per cent) than in white households (24 per cent) (Casper and Bianchi 2002).

In the case of England two factors in particular account for the fact that in the early twenty-first century households are much smaller than those of preindustrial times: the decline in marital fertility and the virtual elimination from the household of the resident domestic and farm servants. The incidence of farm service for men declined markedly in most areas of England in the latter part of the eighteenth and early part of the nineteenth centuries, while domestic service (largely performed by women) persisted into the early decades of the twentieth century. The number of children per household (including households where there were no children) fell from 2.1 in 1911, little above the level typical of preindustrial times, to 1.8 in 1921, 1.3 in 1947 and 0.9 in 1981.

Demographic change explains many of the modifications that have occurred in the composition of the household. For example, the fall in fertility of the late nineteenth and early twentieth centuries initiated an immediate decline in the size of the average household and later made it less likely that parents approaching old age would still have unmarried children resident in their households (Wall 1994). Another demographic change to have a profound impact on household and family patterns of elderly people in the postwar period has been the greater improvement in female than in male life expectancy. This has prolonged the period that women spend as widows and therefore at risk of living on their own, while ensuring that many more elderly men than in the past have a spouse to provide primary care in their old age. In England in the eighteenth century, the structure of the household responded to demographic change

(Wall *et al.* 1983). An earlier age at first marriage and higher proportions marrying than in the late seventeenth century, together with a fall in adult mortality, increased the proportions of households headed by married couples and led to an expansion in the size of the child population and in the average size of the household. Population growth, by making labour relatively more abundant and therefore cheaper, may also have encouraged farmers in arable areas to switch in the eighteenth century from the use of resident male labour (servants) to labourers who had households of their own and could be employed on a more casual basis.

However, improvements in living standards over the course of the twentieth century, and particularly since the 1950s, have enabled many more people to live alone, who in earlier times would have either lived with relatives or lodged with a non-relative. Variations in the standard of living also exert important but indirect influences on household patterns through alternatively lowering or raising the age at first marriage or cohabitation, thereby increasing or decreasing the pace of household formation. Nevertheless, in England neither urbanization nor industrialization appears to have promoted a major modification in the structure of the household. Even in the middle of the nineteenth century, there were no major differences between the structure of urban and rural households, apart from the greater number of lodgers attached to urban households. The modest increase between pre-industrial times and the middle of the nineteenth century in the number of relatives in the household other than members of the immediate family of the household head was at one time thought to be associated with industrialization (Anderson 1971). However, this increase is now known to have occurred in both rural and urban areas in response to demographic, as well as economic, change (Wall *et al.* 1983).

The impact of cultural influences on the household is less easy to measure. No written rules or customs recommended the formation of specific types of households, identified an appropriate age for children to leave the parental home, or ordered that elderly people should be cared for in the households of their children. Yet the relative uniformity of household and family patterns in the English past, despite contrasting economic and demographic circumstances, implies that residence patterns were influenced by norms, even if these were never written down, and no penalties applied if the norms were not followed.

RICHARD WALL
ESRC CAMBRIDGE GROUP FOR THE HISTORY
OF POPULATION AND SOCIAL STRUCTURE

References

Anderson, M. (1971) *Family Structure in Nineteenth Century Lancashire*, Cambridge, UK.

Begeot, F., Smith, L. and Pearce, D. (1993) 'First results from West European censuses', *Population Trends* 74.

Casper, L. and Bianchi, S. (2002) *Continuity and Change in the American Family*, London.

Central Statistical Office (1984, 1985 2000) *Social Trends* 14, 15, 32.

Czap, P. (1983) 'A large family: The peasant's greatest wealth', in R. Wall, J. Robin and P. Laslett (eds) *Family Forms in Historic Europe*, Cambridge, UK.

Laslett, P. and Wall, R. (eds) (1972) *Household and Family in Past Time*, Cambridge, UK.

Lundh, C. (1995) 'Households and families in pre-industrial Sweden', *Continuity and Change* 10.

Wall, R. (1991) 'European family and household systems', in Société de Démographie Historique (ed.) *Historiens et populations: Liber amicorum Étienne Hélin*, Louvain-la-Neuve.

—— (1994) 'Elderly persons and members of their households in England and Wales from pre-industrial times to the present', in D. Kertzer and P. Laslett (eds) *Aging in the Past: Demography, Society and Old Age*, Los Angeles, CA.

Wall, R., Robin, J. and Laslett, P. (eds) (1983) *Family Forms in Historic Europe*, Cambridge, UK.

Further reading

Gershuny, J. and Robinson, J. (1998) 'Historical changes in the household division of labour', *Demography* 25(4): 537–52.

Murphy, M. (2000) 'The evolution of cohabitation in Britain 1960–1995', *Population Studies* 54: 43–56.

Rose, D. (2000) *Researching Social and Economic Change: The Uses of Household Panel Studies*, London.

US Bureau of the Census (2001) *America's Families and Living Arrangements*, Washington, DC.

Wall, R. (1995) 'Historical development of the household in Europe', in E. Van Imhoff (ed.) *Household Demography and Household Modelling*, New York.

SEE ALSO: family

HUMAN CAPITAL

Human capital is the stock of acquired talents, skills and knowledge that may enhance a worker's earning power in the labour market. A distinction is commonly made between *general* human capital – which is considered as affecting potential earnings in a broad range of jobs and occupations – and *specific* human capital, which augments people's earning power within the particular firm in which they are employed but is of negligible value elsewhere. An example of the former would be formal education in general skills such as mathematics; an example of the latter would be the acquired knowledge about the workings of, and personal contacts within, a particular firm. In many cases human capital is of an intermediate form, whether it be acquired 'off the job', in the form of schooling or vocational training, or 'on the job', in terms of work experience.

In several respects the economic analysis of human capital raises problems similar to that of capital as conventionally understood in terms of firms' plant and equipment. It is likely to be heterogeneous in form; it is accumulated over a substantial period of time using labour and capital already in existence; further investment usually requires immediate sacrifices (in terms of forgone earnings and tuition fees); its quality will be affected by technical progress; the prospective returns to an individual are likely to be fairly uncertain; and the capital stock will be subject to physical deterioration and obsolescence. Nevertheless there are considerable differences. Whereas one can realize the returns on physical or financial capital either by receiving the flow of profits accruing to the owner of the asset or by sale of the asset itself, the returns on human capital can usually be received only by the person in whom the investments have been made (although there are exceptions, such as indentured workers), and usually require further effort in the form of labour in order to be realized in cash terms. The stock of human capital cannot be transferred as can the titles to other forms of wealth, although the investments that parents make in their children's schooling and in informal education at home are sometimes taken as analogous to bequests of financial capital.

While the idea of investment in oneself commands wide acceptance in terms of its general principles, many economists are unwilling to accept stronger versions of the theory of earnings determination and the theory of income distribution that have been based on the pioneering work of Becker (1964) and Mincer (1958). This analysis generally assumes that everywhere labour markets are sufficiently competitive, the services of different types of human capital sufficiently substitutable and educational opportunities sufficiently open, such that earnings differentials can be unambiguously related to differential acquisition of human capital. On the basis of such assumptions estimates have been made of the returns (in terms of increased potential earnings) to human investment (measured in terms of forgone earnings and other costs) by using the observed earnings of workers in cross-sectional samples and in panel studies over time. The rates of return to such investment have usually been found to be in the range of 10–15 per cent. However, it should be emphasized that such estimates often neglect the impact of other economic and social factors, which may affect the dispersion of earnings.

FRANK A. COWELL
LONDON SCHOOL OF ECONOMICS
AND POLITICAL SCIENCE

References

Becker, G.S. (1964) *Human Capital*, New York.
Mincer, J. (1958) 'Investment in human capital and personal income distribution', *Journal of Political Economy* 66.

Further reading

Mincer, J. (1974) *Schooling, Experience and Earnings*, New York.
Neal, D. and Rosen, S. (2000) 'Theories of the distribution of earnings', in A.B. Atkinson and F. Bourguignon (eds) *Handbook of Income Distribution*, Vol. 1, Amsterdam, Chapter 4.
Willis, R.J. (1986) 'Wage determinants: A survey and reinterpretation of human capital earnings functions', in O. Ashenfelter and P.R.G. Layard (eds) *Handbook of Labor Economics*, Vol. 1, Amsterdam, Chapter 10.

SEE ALSO: distribution of incomes and wealth; labour market analysis

HUMAN EVOLUTION

Evolution

The term 'evolution' implies transformation through a sequence of stages. Although the term is a general one that is used in many fields of study (Lewontin 1968), in biology it is a fundamental unifying theory. Biological evolution specifically refers to *genetic* transformation of populations between organisms and their environment (Dobzhansky *et al.* 1977). The fact that life evolved is accepted by almost all modern biologists, although the exact mechanisms by which organic evolution occurs are the subject of intense research.

Principles of evolution

The benchmark for the beginning of research on biological evolution is the 1859 publication of Charles Darwin's *The Origin of Species*, although evolutionary ideas were common before that date. Darwin and Alfred Russel Wallace independently developed the idea of natural selection as the chief mechanism of causing life to evolve. The key feature of natural selection is that it is indirect: inherited variability exists in all species and the best-adapted variants tend to leave more offspring so that through time there is gradual change. In this view, evolution is not directed by the processes that create the inherited variability, but rather by how that variability is shaped or pruned through time by natural selection.

Natural selection is a major feature of the synthetic theory of evolution, a term used to describe the modern view of the mechanisms of organic evolution. This synthesis was forged in the first half of the twentieth century by combining the theory of natural selection, Mendelian genetics and other features to explain how life evolves. There has never been complete agreement on all aspects of the synthetic theory, however, with current controversy centring on topics such as the importance of random processes, the mechanisms of speciation and the extrapolation from observable genetic changes over a short time span to explain long-term evolutionary variation (Ridley 2003).

At the core of the synthetic theory of evolution are the processes that result in genetic transformation from generation to generation. These processes occur in two phases: first, the production and arrangement of genetic variation by gene mutation, chromosomal changes, genetic recombination and gene migration, and, second, the reduction of genetic variation by natural selection and genetic drift. Genetic variability is ultimately produced by gene mutation, which is a chemical change in the DNA molecule. Most mutations are deleterious or relatively neutral to the survival of the organism. Mutations with small effects probably accumulate and eventually have a greater role in evolution than macromuta-

tions. Mutation rate has little relationship with evolutionary rate. Genetic recombination is also a source of genetic variation, but at a different level. Whereas gene mutation is a change in the DNA molecule, genetic recombination is the formation of different combinations of genetic factors that occur during the sexual cycle from the formation of the sex cells to fertilization. Theoretically this process can create nearly an infinite number of different organisms simply by reshuffling the immense amount of genetic differences between the DNA of any two parents. Gene migration or flow is a source of new variability at the population level. A local population, for example, can undergo profound genetic change by the introduction of genes from other populations.

The second phase of genetic transformation is the reduction of genetic variation that is done primarily by natural selection. As far more sex cells are fertilized than can possibly survive and reproduce there is immense loss of potential life at each generation. In humans it is estimated that only about 12 per cent of all fertilized eggs survive, grow to adulthood and reproduce. The loss is probably mostly selective: genetic variants that do not survive to reproduce are lost because of deleterious mutations or combinations of genetic factors that tend to decrease vitality. Even resistance to disease often has a genetic component that can be selected. Simple chance may also be a factor in loss of genetic variability from generation to generation, a process called genetic drift. The importance of this random factor in evolution has been controversial ever since Sewall Wright proposed it in the 1930s. Since the 1980s it has become widely accepted that most evolutionary change at the molecular level is driven by random drift. However, most molecular evolution has no visible morphological or physiological effects; it consists of changes between synonymous coding states in the DNA and changes in non-coding (perhaps 'junk') regions of the DNA. The formation of new species involves mechanisms which reproductively isolate populations that were once part of the same species. In animals this usually requires physical isolation and no gene flow between populations that then undergo divergent genetic change. Naturalistic studies show that this can occur relatively rapidly in small isolated populations.

A common misunderstanding of evolution is that it occurs because of mutations that arise and directly change the genetic composition of a species through the generations. This view, called the mutation theory of evolution, was common in the early part of the twentieth century, but is now discredited for complex organisms. Genetic variability in species is immense as has been shown by biochemical research showing that a large percentage of genetic loci have one or more mutant variants. According to the synthetic theory, the direction of genetic change is determined by the selection and random loss of this vast store of existing genetic variability.

Another common misunderstanding of the synthetic theory of evolution is that it explains why the organic world evolved in the way that it did. The *pattern* of evolution revealed in the fossil record and by inference from living organisms cannot be predicted by the processes of production and reduction of genetic variation any more than human history can be explained by the processes by which individuals learn from birth to death.

Human evolution

There are twenty-one living orders of mammals. The one in which humans are classified (primates) may have originated in the late Cretaceous (*c.*70–65 million years, Myr) but only by Eocene times (54–35 Myr) do primates of the modern aspect become abundant (Martin 1990; Hartwig 2002). These Eocene forms resemble modern lemurs and tarsiers. By middle Eocene to early Oligocene times (42–24 Myr) there are primates that share some derived characteristics seen in the group containing modern monkeys, apes and people (Anthropoidea). Not until the Miocene (24–5 Myr) are there fossils that have traits shared uniquely with the superfamily containing apes and people (Hominoidea). Although some middle to late Miocene (*c.*16–8 Myr) hominoids have a chewing apparatus that looks like early members of the human family (Hominidae), the resemblance is probably due to the fact that the common ancestor of the great apes and people also shared these traits. The earliest fossils that are probably on the human evolutionary branch are in African strata dating between 6 and 5 Myr and perhaps slightly older. These include *Sahelanthropus tchadensis* (Brunet *et al.* 2002), *Orrorin tugenensis* (Senut *et al.* 2001) and *Ardipithecus ramidus* (Halle-Selassie 2001). All of these are quite ape-like except for a few critically important unique features shared only with later hominids. *Sahelanthropus* comes from Chad, is associated with fauna that occurs elsewhere between 7 and 6 Myr, and has a canine complex more like later hominids than like that seen in apes. *Orrorin* is from Kenyan strata dated to about 6 Myr, has an ape-like canine, but a thigh that is reported to be adapted to bipedality like later hominids. *Ardipithecus* comes from 5.8 to 4.4 Myr layers in Ethiopia, and has several unique features shared with later hominids (e.g. less projecting and broader canine, short cranial base, toe with bipedal features). By 4.2 Myr the first member of the genus *Australopithecus* occurs in the form of *A. anamensis* associated with a tibia that is specialized for bipedality and whose craniodental morphology is intermediate between *Ar. ramidus* and later hominid species.

The next oldest hominid species, *A. afarensis* (3.8–3 Myr), is also quite ape-like in dental and cranial anatomy, but does share more derived features with later hominids than does *A. anamensis*. The most conspicuous of these traits include a much broader deciduous molar, smaller canine, less ape-like premolar, and larger cheek-teeth. The brain size relative to body size is much closer to modern apes than to modern people, being less than one-half the relative size of *H. sapiens*. The body below the head (postcranium) is reorganized away from the common plan seen in all other primates and shares the uniquely human bipedal pattern. Some primitive traits are retained in the postcranium, such as long and curved toes, which may imply a retention of greater tree-climbing ability than that seen in *H. sapiens*.

Australopithecus afarensis was highly dimorphic with males weighing about 45 kg and females 29 kg (McHenry and Coffing 2000). This level of sexual dimorphism implies that, by analogy with other mammalian species, *A. afarensis* was not monogamous. The forelimbs of the male were relatively very large, perhaps exceeding the dimorphism of living gorillas and orangs. This may imply strong sexual selection and male–male competition analogous to the role played by the large male canine in other mammalian species.

Between 3 and 2 Myr ago the fossil record reveals a diversification of hominid species. In East Africa, *A. aethiopicus* appears by 2.5 Myr as a species combining the primitive traits of *A. afarensis* with specialized features related to heavy chewing. These specialized features include huge cheek-teeth and heavily buttressed crania for chewing musculature. In South Africa, *A. africanus* appears at about 3.0 Myr and persists to perhaps 2.4 Myr, but dating is uncertain. This species is similar to *A. afarensis* except that it is more derived towards *Homo* in key respects relating to its anterior dentition, reduced muzzle, fingers and encephalization. Cheek-tooth size is much larger than that of *A. afarensis*.

Beginning sometime between 2.4 and 2.1 Myr the genus *Homo* appears. Its appearance is marked by reduction in cheek-tooth size from that seen in earlier hominid species, expansion of the brain, and the appearance of stone-tool culture. It is known from fossil deposits in South and East Africa. Variability is high and there is a strong case to be made that more than one species of *Homo* existed before 1.8 Myr, including *H. habilis* and *H. rudolfensis*. By 1.8 Myr a new species of *Homo* appears in East Africa that in many ways resembles *H. erectus* of Asia.

Other species of hominid apparently coexisted with *Homo*. In South Africa, *A. robustus* overlapped in time and geography with early *Homo*. This species shared with *Homo* many derived characteristics relative to earlier species of hominid including encephalization, loss of a muzzle, bending of the base of the skull, and human-like hand morphology. At the same time it possessed highly derived morphology related to heavy chewing, including massive cheek-teeth, huge jaws and strong buttressing for the chewing muscles. In East Africa, *A. boisei* appeared by 2.3 Myr with a similar combination of *Homo*-like traits with an adaptation for even more extreme heavy chewing. Both of these species, *A. robustus* and *boisei*, are often referred to as 'Paranthropus' or 'robust' australopithecines. Their robustness was in chewing-related features only, however. Both species were quite petite in body size with males about 40–50 kg and females 32–4 kg (McHenry and Coffing 2000).

The first appearance of human populations outside of Africa appears to be soon after the appearance of early *Homo* in Africa. Fossil *Homo* from the Dmanisi site in the Republic of Georgia are most likely older than 1.7 Myr and are very much like those found in Africa attributed to *H. erectus/habilis*. *H. erectus* occupied parts of tropical Asia perhaps as early as 1.8 Myrs. The exact chronology is still uncertain, but sometime after this and before 0.5 Myr some populations had adapted to life in the temperate climatic zone of North Asia. Larger-brained species of archaic *Homo* begin to appear in Africa by 600,000 years ago and in Eurasia somewhat later. The Neanderthals dominate Europe and West Asia from approximately 30,000 to 40,000 years ago. *H. sapiens* appears first in Africa sometime before 100,000 years ago. By about 50,000 years ago populations of our species spread out of Africa to Asia and then Europe, apparently replacing or genetically swamping local archaic *Homo* populations. America was settled by immigrants from Asia who migrated across a landbridge connecting Siberia and Alaska perhaps at 20,000 to 15,000 years ago, although the successful colonization of most of the Americas began only 12,000 years ago. People first reached some of the Pacific islands several thousand years ago from the east, reaching the Marquesas Islands by about AD 300 and New Zealand by about AD 1200.

Technological development in human evolution appears to be erratic in pace, but it certainly shows a pattern of acceleration. Relatively crude stone tools persist for over 1.5 Myr. Finely worked blade tools are much more recent. Humans have had agriculture, cities and writing for less than one-quarter of 1 per cent of their evolutionary development as a separate mammalian lineage.

Behaviour

Human locomotor behaviour probably evolved from an ape-like ancestor with a short back, a flat chest and a highly mobile shoulder and forelimb adapted to climbing and suspending the body below tree branches (Fleagle 1999). Like modern apes (but unlike monkeys) this hypothetical ancestor was relatively awkward and energetically inefficient at walking on the ground either quadrupedally or bipedally. But as has happened to many other primate groups, terrestrial travel was taken up with greater and greater frequency. Why our ancestors took up bipedality instead of quadrupedality is unknown, but certainly the unique ape-like body plan made either gait equally efficient in terms of energetic cost at normal speeds. Free hands for carrying makes bipedality more advantageous. Fossil evidence at about 5 Myr shows that bipedality had been established in the human evolutionary lineage, but before that time the palaeontological record is not yet complete enough.

The evolutionary history of human feeding behaviour is documented by fossil dental remains spanning millions of years. The earliest hominid dentitions and habitats were similar to modern African apes, so it is probable that our lineage did not become differentiated as a result of a change in diet. It is more likely that our lineage emerged as a consequence of the adoption of a unique mode of locomotion in order to move between more widely dispersed forest patches. At least by 4 Myr the dentition of hominids changed for the common ape-like pattern to one with large and thickly enamelled cheek-teeth, and powerful chewing muscles. Microscopic studies of dental scratches show that these early humans were probably not eating seeds and grass, nor were they crushing bones. By about 2.4 Myr ago meat eating was certainly practised as evidenced by bone remains with stone tool-cut marks. Relative cheek-tooth size reduces fairly gradually from 2 Myr to the present, which may be because preliminary food preparation to some extent took over the function of the grinding teeth.

Many other aspects of human behavioural evolution are related to the fact that absolute brain size tripled and relative brain size more than doubled over the last 2.5 Myr of human evolution. Human fossils dating between about 6 and 2.5 Myr ago have endocranial volumes the size of modern chimpanzees, although relative to body size they are slightly larger.

The biological evolution of most aspects of human behaviour are much more difficult to document. The basic method of enquiry involves comparisons with other living animals. From this perspective it is clear that spoken symbolic language is the most significant uniquely human attribute in the organic world. Field studies of monkeys reveal that they possess a form of vocal symbolic communication, but there is a vast, quantitative gap in speech capabilities between human and non-human primates. Probably the expansion of the brain in the last 2.5 Myr tracts behavioural changes related to the acquisition of speech, and the remarkable acceleration in technological innovations beginning with the Upper Palaeolithic at about 50,000 years ago marks the final acquisition of modern language capabilities (Klein 1999).

The primary difficulty in the way of studying the biological evolution of human behaviour is determining the genetic component of behaviour. Often the only genetic component is genetically conditioned developmental plasticity. There is a genetic basis for the development of the neurophysiology required for speech, for example, but a great deal of plasticity in the kind of language that is learned. There is a genetic basis for most aspects of human sexuality, but an enormous flexibility in how it is expressed. One method for approximating the extent of genetic contribution to specific behaviours is by comparing differences between identical twins (and hence genetically identical individuals) with the difference among unrelated individuals. Twin studies are complicated by the fact that most twins are raised in the same environment and that the sample of identical twins raised apart is still very small.

One theoretical breakthrough in the study of behavioural evolution came in 1964 with the publication of W.D. Hamilton's 'The genetical evolution of social behavior'. He suggested that even genetically controlled behaviours that were detrimental to an organism's survival could be favoured by natural selection because of what has become known as kin selection. Kin selection refers to the 'selection of genes because of their effect in favoring the reproductive success of relatives other than offspring' (Barash 1982: 392). Kin selection theory has been successfully employed to explain several aspects of the social behaviour of non-human animals, especially social insects, but the application of this and other sociobiological theories to the evolution of human social behaviour has not yet resulted in universally accepted principles. The great extent of human behavioural plasticity makes the search for evolutionary principles difficult, but a great deal of research on this topic is currently being pursued. It is even more difficult, if not impossible, to establish that there is a genetic basis that would account for any systematic divergence in behaviour between human groups.

HENRY M. MCHENRY
UNIVERSITY OF CALIFORNIA, DAVIS

References

Barash, D.P. (1982) *Sociobiology and Behavior*, New York.

Brunet, M. *et al.* (2002) 'A new hominid from the upper Miocene of Chad, Central Africa', *Nature* 418: 145–51.

Darwin, C. (1859) *On the Origin of Species by Means of Natural Selection*, London.

Dobzhansky, T., Ayala, F.J., Stebbins, G.L. and Valentine, J.W. (1977) *Evolution*, San Francisco.

Fleagle, J.G. (1999) *Primate Adaptation and Evolution*, 2nd edn, San Diego, CA.

Halle-Selassie, Y. (2001) 'Late Miocene hominids from the Middle Awash, Ethiopia', *Nature* 412: 178–81.

Hamilton, W.D. (1964) 'The genetical evolution of social behavior', *Journal of Theoretical Biology* 12.

Hartwig, W.C. (2002) *The Primate Fossil Record*, Cambridge.

Klein, R.G. (1999) *The Human Career*, 2nd edn, Chicago.

Lewontin, R.C. (1968) 'Concept of evolution', *International Encyclopedia of the Social Sciences*, New York.

McHenry, H.M. and Coffing, K. (2000) '*Australopithecus* to *Homo*: Transformations in body and mind', *Annual Review of Anthropology 2000* 29: 125–46.

Martin, R.D. (1990) *Primate Origins and Evolution*, London.

Ridley, M. (2003) *Evolution*, 3rd edn, Boston.

Senut, B. *et al.* (2001) 'First hominid from the Miocene (Lukeino Formation, Kenya)', *C.R. Acad. Sci. Paris, sciences de la terre et des planets* 332: 137–44.

Further reading

Aiello, L. and Dean, C. (1990) *An Introduction to Human Evolutionary Anatomy*, San Diego, CA.

Delson, E., Tattersall, I., Van Couvering, J.A. and Brooks, A.S. (2000) *Encyclopedia of Human Evolution and Prehistory*, 2nd edn, New York.

SEE ALSO: Darwin; evolutionary psychology; genetics and behaviour; population genetics; population history

HUMAN RESOURCE MANAGEMENT

Human resource management (HRM) is now the term most commonly used in academic circles to encompass the range of policies and practices used by 'modern' organizations in the management of employees. The shortened term human resource (HR) is increasingly found to describe the personnel department, director or manager. UK practice is beginning to follow the USA in this respect. The terms, however, are both confused and confusing. HRM as a term was first used by Miles (1965) in the *Harvard Business Review* to differentiate the human relations school that focused on managerial leadership from the creation of 'an environment in which the total resources of [the organization] can be utilized' (1965: 150). This meant finding a means of utilizing the untapped resources of all organizational members, be it skills, tacit knowledge, commitment or competences. This presumption that certain forms of management can release or empower employees to work more effectively for the organization took hold in the 1980s and 1990s as industrial relations problems receded and many firms found that better management of their existing resources was required to meet more competitive markets.

In 1984 two books were published in the USA that established HRM but simultaneously revealed a fundamental division in the meaning of the term. Beer *et al.* (1984) emphasized, like Miles, the 'soft' elements of HRM, arguing that an integrated set of approaches focused on the individual employee linked to the strategic needs of the company could create what became known as high-value work systems. Fombrun *et al.* (1984), however, developed the 'matching model' where the organization's approach to its employees derived from and fitted the wider business strategy. This was taken further by Schuler and Jackson (1987) to suggest that firms in different market segments will develop very different types of HRM systems. A firm in a price-sensitive market with relatively low-skilled workers is unlikely to invest heavily in training and development to empower the employees. This has been described by Storey (1992) in the definitive UK book as 'hard' HRM. As Legge (1989) has noted, the first is *human* resource management, the second human *resource* management.

This distinction between the optimistic soft model and the potentially exploitative hard version is sometimes linked with the notions of loose–tight to assess the extent to which HR policies are closely linked to corporate and business strategies. It is generally agreed that HRM requires a tight link to the strategy of the firm, whereas a loose connection is seen to typify personnel management, the term which predated HRM. Personnel management was restricted to the supply-side concerned to ensure that the right labour was available. In contrast HRM operates more on the demand side and involves all managers, not just the specialists. Here all factors that impinge on the performance of the worker – the design of jobs and relations with others, the types of contracts and pay systems, and the use of forms of individual and group communication, consultation and representation systems – are all designed in the light of strategic need to maximize economic outcomes whether by the soft or hard approach to labour force management.

The final distinguishing characteristic of HRM is that it is concerned with the internal policies and practices of the organization at the micro-level and tends to ignore or take for granted wider macro-issues of societal culture, the political economy and the role of the state. At the micro-level, however, by the link with business strategy and focus on performance it does offer the prospect of a new theoretical sophistication (Boxall and Purcell 2002; Bratton and Gould 2003).

JOHN PURCELL
UNIVERSITY OF BATH

References

Beer, M., Spector, B., Lawrence, P. R., Quinn Miles, D. and Walton, R.E. (1984) *Managing Human Assets*, New York.

Boxall, P.F. and Purcell, J. (2002) *Strategy and Human Resource Management*, London.

Bratton, J. and Gould, J. (2003) *Human Resource Management: Theory and Practice*, London.

Fombrun, C.J., Tichy, N.M. and Devanna, M.A. (1984) *Strategic Human Resource Management*, New York.

Legge, K. (1989) 'Human resource management: A critical analysis', in J. Storey (ed.) *New Perspectives in Human Resource Management*, London.

Miles, R. (1965) 'Human relations or human resources?' *Harvard Business Review* 43(4).

Schuler, R.S. and Jackson, S.E. (1987) 'Organizational strategy and organizational level as determinants of human resource management practices', *Human Resource Planning* 10.

Storey, J. (1992) *Developments in Human Resource Management: An Analytical Review*, Oxford.

SEE ALSO: industrial and organizational psychology; industrial relations; strategic management

HUMAN RIGHTS

The strands of thought that come together to make up 'human rights' are far older than the descriptive label that we now attach to them, and it is only through unearthing the various layers of meaning that lie behind the phrase that we can come to a proper appreciation of the depth of its contemporary resonance. The first strand, respect for the dignity of the person, finds expression in the emphasis on love, solidarity with others and tolerance that is a recurring theme in all the basic texts of world civilization. The Bible, the Koran, the New Testament and the Buddhist and Hindu texts are in this sense all at least partly human rights documents. More directly in point from ancient times are the writings of the Greek Stoics and the Platonists. It was a follower of the first of these traditions, Epictetus of Hierapolis, who saw the possibility of freedom as a universal human attribute, while it was the originator of the second, Plato, who first speculated about the existence of eternal veritudes, encompassing a world of reality beyond our sight from which all truth flowed. This Platonic version of reality commended itself to the Christian Church, which neatly incorporated it into its world-view via the work of the Egyptian scholar Plotinus, writing in the third century of the Christian era. The eternal truths remained, as did the basic human rights that flowed from them, but the authority of the mind was supplanted by the disciplining power of the Church: it was the priest rather than your own patterns of thought that told you what human rights were and how far they extended in specific situations. (Relics of this premodern approach to rights are still to be seen in the often excellent work of the mainstream Christian churches on human rights, and in the occasional scholarly anxiety that human rights cannot exist without some religious base (Perry 1998).)

The next important layer, just above the ancient texts and the Roman church, introduces the idea of the rule of law and originates with Magna Carta, signed by King John of England, under duress and at the behest of his chief barons, at Runnymede in 1215 (Bradley 2001). The document hardly qualifies as a ringing endorsement of human dignity; nor does it in any sense 'democratize' the feudal system of government that then prevailed. But it does epitomize the idea of government under the law and (what this inevitably entails) the rejection of absolute power, whatever its alleged source or justification. The particular English contribution to human rights lies in the historical continuity of the nation's internal commitment to the rule of law, from its medieval beginnings at Runnymede through the turbulent seventeenth century wars with the Stuart kings to a resting place at the start of the eighteenth century that emphasized both the authority of law and the independence of the judicial branch, two foundation stones upon which much of political modernity (epitomized in the nation-state) was later to build. Outside the nation-state but for the same reason, the development of an embryonic system of international law by Grotius is also seen as a contribution to human rights (Freeman 2002: Ch. 2). The idea of the rule of law matters to our subject because history shows that human dignity suffers without the control of governmental and private power by reference to some set of rules external to the wielder of such power. If impunity is rightly seen as the greatest enemy of human rights, then the best guarantor we have against its spread is a properly functioning system of law, with remedies available for wrongs done and judges on hand fearlessly to enforce them.

The third great theme in human rights has long been in an ambiguous relation with the subject, both bringing it to a higher level of achievement and threatening to subvert it at the same time. This is the notion of representative government, encompassing also the protection of those civil and political rights that make such self-rule possible. Present in ancient times, and sporadically butting into history from time to time, it comes into its own as an idea in eighteenth-century France, when Kant's reworking of the Christian ethic into a shape we would describe today as 'human rights' was matched by Rousseau's original and (for its time) incendiary set of speculations on the 'General Will' and the fundamental nature of human freedom. The successful American and French revolutions with which the eighteenth century closed guaranteed that these ideas would flourish, and the United States Declaration of Independence (1776) and the French Declaration of the Rights of Man and Citizen (1789) have rightly entered the pantheon of fundamental human rights instruments. In the nineteenth century, the range of classes and persons able to participate in representative government expanded, so much so that by the end of the third decade of the twentieth century it was possible to talk of the democratic era and to refer to many states then organizing themselves on the principle of universal mass suffrage. Inspired by the radical thoughts of Rousseau and the actions of the French and American revolutionaries, self-government has over time come to be seen as a highly effective way of improving the dignity of all, and together with the rule of law, as an essential feature of any properly functioning human rights culture (as we would call it today).

The democratic ideal can also be presented as majority rule, however, and such an approach does not sit so easily with human rights. Led by Jeremy Bentham, the early nineteenth-century utilitarians savaged the language of human rights as amounting to no more than 'nonsense upon stilts', a reckless form of idealistic daydreaming that got in the way of their search for the happiness of the greatest number (Waldron 1987: Ch. 3). Such critics also asked what happened when the rhetoric of rights got into the wrong hands: the French revolution might have proclaimed a new era of rights, but the state Terror that quickly followed showed that the General Will could be as dangerous as any king with the wrong ventriloquist in control behind the scenes. When Marx joined in, savaging the declaration of the rights of man as bourgeois nonsense and a recipe for rampant individualism (Waldron 1987: Ch. 5), it looked as though the death-knell of the subject had been sounded. It is certainly true that neither of the two big political ideas of modernism, democracy and socialism, were rooted in any kind of language of rights or fundamental freedoms, the first because it had been purged of such foundations by the utilitarians, the second because Marx ensured that such universals were never to get even the thinnest of footholds. But these new twin orthodoxies contained their own explosive contradictions. Both the inevitable democratic connection with an ethic of majoritarianism and the Marxist certainty about the way the world was bound to go relegated the individual to the smallest of small footnotes, to the majority will in the first instance, to historical inevitability in the second. In each case, a large theory rooted in celebration of the dignity of man and woman, and the potential for human achievement, ended up by providing an intellectual framework for morally sanctioned repression.

Hitler and Stalin proved the point at a cost of millions of lives. The re-ignition of human rights in the latter half of the twentieth century owes itself entirely to the way in which these two rulers hurtled recklessly through the windows into amorality that each of the political systems they had inherited had left unlocked and half-opened. Hitler came to power in an entirely orthodox, democratic way and remained hugely popular until defeat became a probability. Stalin exploited Lenin's disregard of his people for the sake of the perfect future that was bound to come. Searching for a way to explain why the

Second World War was worth fighting, and after it the Cold War, it is hardly surprising that the leaders of Britain and the USA, and then of Western Europe, returned to the old, unsoiled language of fundamental rights (Simpson 2001). Starting with the Atlantic Charter in 1941, the war-time movement towards a new language of rights culminated in the Universal Declaration of Human Rights signed in 1948. The document contains an eloquent affirmation of the levels of civilization of which the human race is capable. It includes not only civil and political rights but meaningful social and economic ones as well, such as the right to work, to social security, to education, to rest and leisure and 'freely to participate in the cultural life of the community'. But while this mission statement for humanity is rich in its reflection of what is entailed by the principle of respect for human dignity, it is less convincing on the relationship between democratic government and human rights. If the outcomes of the political process are so clearly ordained, what is the point of the 'right to take part in the Government of [one's] country, directly or through freely chosen representatives' (Mandel 1998)? Just as seriously, the strand to human rights that started with Magna Carta and is epitomized in an uncompromising adherence to the rule of law is absent from the Declaration, there being no mechanism for the document's enforcement in international law.

The story of international human rights in the Cold War period follows the fault-lines already evident in the Universal Declaration (Sieghart 1986). The content of human rights races ahead with covenants being agreed on civil and political rights, and on economic, social and cultural rights in 1966, and with further breakthroughs being achieved on discrimination against women (1979), on the right to development (1986) and on the rights of the child (1989). The goal of human dignity is being exceptionally well served. But the enforcement mechanisms for the implementation of these norms in a world still divided up between hostile blocs of nation-states continued to lag well behind the pace. During this period it was only where rights were enforced by a regional authority (such as the European Court of Human Rights, overseeing the European Convention on Human Rights) or were made part of a country's internal law (such as in Germany, France and from 1982 Canada) that they were able to flourish in a manner appropriate to their

high-blown claims. The concept of democratic government itself was also dragged into the Cold War quarrel, with Soviet Bloc countries coming to regard democratic government (and the civil and political rights that go with it) not only as at odds with social and economic rights but also as a Western trick designed to bring the whole Soviet version of freedom crashing down. Indeed, during the 1970s – the era of Helsinki, the emigration of Soviet Jews and Dr Sakharov – the same might well have been said in Moscow of the human rights movement itself.

It is a cliché to say that the world changed forever in 1989, but it is certainly true of the subject of human rights. Where once they occupied a small tent in the no man's land that divided the two great Cold War ideologies, believers in the independent integrity of human rights now found their patch of land being visited in ever-increasing numbers. First it was the dissidents and peace activists from the former Soviet Bloc for whom the idea of human rights had been a cry of resistance to oppression. Then it was their former rulers and indeed socialists worldwide for whom the new discourse of human rights had become an increasingly attractive substitute for a Marxism that seemed now in permanent decline. Rooting around for a fresh rhetorical basis for their commitment to collective bargaining, trade unions also found in the language of social and economic rights a more attractive explanation for their activities than a mere assertion of industrial muscle linked to their members' selfishness. A new tranche of supporters came as enthusiasts for the market system, and getting fully into their post-Cold War stride, set about dismantling the social democratic forms that they now viewed as unnecessary concessions to prevent a revolution that would in fact (it was now clear) never come. The impact of this new privatized version of 'freedom' on the poor, the old, the unemployed and others without means became a concern even for those who did not object to the market in principle, and for these squeamish capitalists a commitment to human rights became a tempting means of having it both ways.

As the language took off, many other groups joined the fray. Political activists everywhere characterized their goals as human rights – outcomes to which they had a right not towards which they were (merely) determined to struggle. The trend towards greater globalization that began in earnest in the late 1990s confirmed the strength of the idea of human rights as perhaps the only ethical barrier to a worldwide, voracious and highly divisive brand of supranational capitalism (Evans 2001; Alston 2003). That the subject is as much part of history as any other, and is seen by some as lacking a clear philosophical foundation, is neither here nor there. Of course, it helps if some basic foundation for human rights can be pointed to and believed in, and important building work of this sort has been done by Jürgen Habermas (Habermas 2001) and Steven Lukes (Ishay 1997: 233–47). But contemporary appreciation of the value of human rights does not demand a commitment to a set of objective truths lying outside the person and beyond our language towards an understanding of which we are all obliged to strive (Douzinas 2000). Rather at very least the idea provides us with a way of saying things, a perspective on human relations, which stresses our judgement as to what it is that is valuable to us about being human: respect for others; the dignity of the individual; fairness; the avoidance of cruelty; and the importance of solidarity and community. A believer in religious truth can feel as at home in human rights as a socialist, a postmodernist and a political activist. Its mutatable character perfectly chimes with the uncertainty that is so much a part of contemporary intellectual enquiry, its lack of confidence in its own foundations a strength rather than a weakness.

Human rights today stands for a belief in human dignity in the face of the capitalist tendency to reduce individuals to mere parts of a productive chain (Klug 2000). It argues for the rule of law rather than rule by man or market power. And it asserts that a government based on the democratic principle and the independent rule of law is the likeliest to achieve the maximum amount of human dignity without a lapse into revolutionary chaos. Human rights is socialism without ideology, religion without God. Seen in this light, allegations of the cultural specificity of human rights talk fade away, the consequence of poor exposition of the idea rather than any underlying imperialist inclination (Hastrup 2001). Most importantly, across the industrial and the developing world, the language of human rights opens doors for victims by helping them to articulate their plight in a way that the powerful can understand. It gives leverage to

opponents of unregulated globalization across the world by providing a powerful set of phrases with which to condemn the way in which market power impacts on the many (Rees and Wright 2000). And because the critique is couched in the language of human rights, rather than in talk of communism or religious fundamentalism, the powerful – who only very rarely these days deny the idea entirely – feel bound to listen. Even the very richest of the world's peoples have difficulty in wholly disregarding allegations of hypocrisy and double standards, and it is in exploiting the opportunities this honesty occasionally throws up that human rights does its most effective, practical work.

No idea as powerful and as potentially subversive as human rights can expect to be left untouched by those whom it would seem in the abstract to be most critical of. Since the English liberal revolution of 1689, attempts have been made to slim down what is entailed in human rights so as to render the concept of use only in constructing the free market and meaning nothing else besides. This line of thought has never achieved dominance though it has occasionally allowed the more intellectual and extreme of the devotees of the free market to claim to have human rights on their side (Nozick 1974). More recently, the strides that have been made in the legalization of rights, both internally within many nation's domestic legal systems and externally through the promulgation of a variety of international human rights standards, have seemed at times not only beneficially to entrench the subject but also, and more negatively, to some extent to tame it. The question has been less what human dignity requires than the narrower one of whether this or that subclause in the document under scrutiny has been properly fulfilled. The legalization of rights is therefore both evidence of the subject's success and also at the same time the bringer of a new danger, namely that the spirit of human rights is drained of life and the subject made into just another lawyer's game of interpretation. This is a particular risk where the written down version of rights contains many exemptions and caveats, resulting in attacks on human rights being afterwards interpreted as in compliance with them. The problem is particularly evident where human rights charters include exemptions for national security and the like, allowing government action against civil liberties and political freedom generally to be presented as necessitated rather than contradicted by the prevailing rights discourse: the nineteenth-century critique along these lines has a strong contemporary resonance.

There seems little doubt that the subject of human rights will continue to burgeon in the coming decades. Indeed it is not at all obvious what competition it faces in the contemporary market-place of ideas critical of the current status quo. Its knack of managing to be both part of and at the same time (somewhat) opposed to the prevailing capitalist model gives it a purchase across the globe and in all sectors of society that no other ideas can presently match. Whether the subject flourishes as well as grows depends on how it develops, and this in turn hinges on how effectively it achieves a balance between its three parts of respect for human dignity, legality and democracy.

The international standards on human rights that currently exist constitute an extensive guide to the requirements of human dignity. Of course more can be done, on the disabled for example and displaced persons, but generally speaking the standards are there, and they are likely to remain into the foreseeable future, expanding as and when they are required. Problems arise, however, in the realm of legality, with the enforcement mechanisms for the promulgation of these standards still being somewhat underdeveloped. Not only are the international procedures for applying the human rights norms rather tentative, but there is as yet no easy way to guarantee the translation of these standards into domestic law; for all the battering it has taken in the era of globalization, the nation-state still rules so far as the world of enforceable legal norms is concerned. The third strand to the historical idea of human rights, a commitment to democratic government, has also drifted away from the core of the subject since its post-1945 rejuvenation (Gearty 2003). Although a simplistic commitment to democracy can slip into tyrannical majoritarianism, a fresh awareness of the value of properly constructed democratic rule as a way of delivering human rights outcomes, particularly in the social and economic field, is vital to the future health of the subject. To be truly effective, standard setting by human rights experts needs both a properly functioning system of law and a receptive domestic polity. With this triad of strong supports there is no reason why the idea

of human rights should not continue to prosper for many decades to come.

C.A. GEARTY
LONDON SCHOOL OF ECONOMICS
AND POLITICAL SCIENCE

References

Alston, P. (ed.) (2003) *The United Nations and Human Rights. A Critical Appraisal*, Oxford.

Bradley, A.W. (2001) 'Magna Carta and the protection of human rights in Europe: The challenge of the 21st century', *Law and Justice* 146: 5–27.

Douzinas, C. (2000) *The End of Human Rights*, Oxford.

Evans, T. (2001) *The Politics of Human Rights: A Global Perspective*, London.

Freeman, M. (2002) *Human Rights. An Interdisciplinary Approach*, Cambridge.

Gearty, C.A. (2003) 'Reflections on civil liberties in an age of counter-terrorism', *Osgoode Hall Law Journal* 30.

Habermas, J. (2001) *The Postnational Constellation*, Cambridge.

Hastrup, K. (2001) *Legal Cultures and Human Rights: The Challenge of Diversity*, The Hague.

Ishay, M.R. (ed.) (1997) *The Human Rights Reader*, London.

Klug, F. (2000) *Values for a Godless Age. The Story of the United Kingdom's New Bill of Rights*, London.

Mandel, M. (1998) 'A brief history of the new constitutionalism, or "How we changed everything so that everything would remain the same"', *Israel Law Review* 32(2) (spring).

Nozick, R. (1974) *Anarchy, State and Utopia*, Oxford.

Perry, M.J. (1998) *The Idea of Human Rights, Four Inquiries*, New York.

Rees, S. and Wright, S. (2000) *Human Rights and Corporate Responsibility*, London.

Sieghart, P. (1986) *The Lawful Rights of Mankind*, Oxford.

Simpson, A.W.B. (2001) *Human Rights and the End of Empire. Britain and the Genesis of the European Convention*, Oxford.

Waldron, J. (ed.) (1987) '*Nonsense upon stilts.*' *Bentham, Burke and Marx on the Rights of Man*, London.

Further reading

Campbell, T., Ewing, K.D. and Tomkins, A. (eds) (2001) *Sceptical Essays on Human Rights*, Oxford.

Dworkin, R. (1984) 'Rights as trumps', in J. Waldron (ed.) *Theories of Rights*, Oxford.

Gearty, C.A. and Tomkins, A. (eds) (1996) *Understanding Human Rights*, London.

SEE ALSO: affirmative action; citizenship; freedom; relativism; social contract

HUME, DAVID (1711–76)

The second son of a minor landowner in the Scottish Borders, Hume is now recognized as a major philosopher. That recognition, however, was only attained in the twentieth century and in his own lifetime he was best known as a historian and as an essayist on politics, economics and religion. His writings on the last of these brought him considerable notoriety, such that he was not appointed to a professorship at both Edinburgh (his Alma Mater) and Glasgow. Despite his unorthodoxy, Hume was famously 'clubbable' and one of that group of scholars, including Adam Smith (a particular friend), who together constitute the Scottish Enlightenment.

Hume's great philosophical work, *A Treatise on Human Nature* (1739–40), which he described in his brief autobiography as falling 'dead born' from the press, comprised three parts – Of the Understanding, Of the Passions, Of Morals. The overall aim of the book was to establish a 'science of man', to put moral philosophy (the human and social sciences) on a new footing. This science was to follow the 'experimental method', namely, based upon experience derived from cautious observation of human life. Each part of the book has had an impact on the development of the social sciences.

Hume accepts Locke's argument that there are no innate ideas and its consequence that knowledge must come from experience. Experience comes in the form of perceptions, which Hume divides into impressions and ideas, with the former prior to and 'livelier' than the latter. Simple ideas can be made more complex by the imagination in accordance with some universal principles of association. He identifies three such principles – resemblance, contiguity of time and place, and cause and effect. It is Hume's account of the last of these that is most significant. While, in principle, anything may be the cause of anything this is not how the world appears; it is experienced as regular not random. Hume analyses the source of this experiential regularity with the example of two billiard balls, where a moving ball hits a stationary one that then moves. All that is evident to experience is contiguity (the balls touch) and priority (the second moves only after contact). To say further that this is a causal relation we also need a third element – constant conjunction. We only *infer* a cause here because this sequence is not unique but has always recurred.

This analysis is significant for two reasons. First, there is no necessary guarantee that this will apply in the future; the only necessity lies in the customary association built up from past sequences. Custom is also the basis upon which we suppose the future will be like the past. For Hume this is sufficient to guide life; we can predict with confidence that the stationary ball will move when hit. Second, Hume thinks this analysis applies as equally to the human as it does to the natural sciences. The principles of human nature exhibit a constancy and uniformity no less secure than when two balls collide.

The source of this uniformity in human nature is the passions, the subject of Part 2 of the *Treatise*. Here a key point is that it is the passions that constitute human motives. The negative implication of this is that reason has no motivating power; it is restricted to assessing relations between ideas and is properly, in a notorious phrase, the 'slave of the passions'. In many ways Hume is here repeating the gist of Hobbes's analysis but what stops him being a Hobbesian is his different account of morality.

Part 3 of the *Treatise* intimates two powerful ideas in the history of social science. First, according to Hume it is evident that humans are not the complete egoists that Hobbes claims and morality has a genuine foundation in human nature, in the form of sentiments (like pity or generosity). In the course of arguing that these natural sentiments are a description of how humans behave Hume remarks, in a passage that has generated enormous controversy, that from a descriptive account no prescriptive conclusions can legitimately be drawn. There is logical gap, in other words, between 'facts/is' and 'values/ought' – a position that has been termed 'Hume's law'. This is, however, more a case of retrospective labelling than it is of textual exegesis and, taking his work as a whole, Hume himself seems to bridge that gap.

Second, while Hume demurs from a full subscription to Hobbes's analysis, he does allow that humans are of 'confined generosity' and that fact, when combined with relative scarcity, establishes what John Rawls has called – with open indebtedness to Hume – the 'circumstances of justice'. Hume regards justice as 'artificial', by which he means conventional or arrived at by a mutual agreement as to common advantage – an argument that has been taken up by contemporary game theorists. These agreements or conventions comprise three rules – stability of possession, its transfer by consent and promise keeping. These rules are general and inflexible. It is better for society as a whole that a wealthy miser keeps a large legacy than the rules are broken in order to give the money to a more deserving recipient. It is 'better' because it is more useful (social stability is sustained) and Hume's account is thus an important forerunner of utilitarianism, though it differs from the later Benthamite version. One expression of this difference is Hume's use of the principle of 'sympathy' to account for the virtuousness of justice. According to this principle (itself a demonstration of the uniformity in human nature), by converting the idea we have of a stranger's pain at being robbed into an impression, we share the unease and, on broadly utilitarian principles, we label the injustice suffered 'wrong'.

In simple face-to-face societies acting justly could be easily policed but as society developed it became more complex (such that it contained strangers) and, consequently, there was a need to establish governments. In his post-*Treatise* writings, Hume elaborated upon this process of social development. He contrasted his own commercial society with earlier ruder or less-refined societies. Initially government was in the hands of individuals who possessed the leadership qualities necessary for success in warfare. Over time obedience to this individual (and his heirs once property was stably transmitted) became a matter of habit. Hume believed that government rested on opinion because it was only on that basis that the few could govern the necessarily more powerful many. Contrary to the orthodoxy of the principles of a social or original contract (as articulated by Locke, for example) people consent to be ruled because they think/opine their rulers entitled to their obedience *not* because they have bestowed that entitlement.

In a series of contemporaneously influential essays Hume defended commercial society against its moral critics. In commercial societies industry, knowledge and humanity were indissoluble. This meant that these societies were more prosperous so more and better consumable goods were available; they were, consequently, more powerful because their resources were greater and they were less barbaric and generally more 'civilized'. Indeed, in explicit contradiction of the critics, a refined or luxurious society was more virtuous than one committed to the principles of 'ancient frugality' as supposedly represented by Sparta and the early era of the Roman Republic. In these essays Hume also participated in other contemporary debates on the nature of money, the principles of taxation and trade and the dangers of public credit. These have been regarded as prescient, in particular his essay on money has been hailed by Milton Friedman and others as a classic statement of the 'quantity theory'.

Hume's most famous (and most lucrative) writing was his *History of England* (1754–62). His apparently sympathetic treatment of the Stuarts caused him to be called a Tory but his approach transcended party labels. Hume was a supporter of the Hanoverian succession but, as his essay on the original contract demonstrated, he wished to debunk the high-blown rhetoric that accompanied it (Duncan Forbes labelled him a 'scientific Whig'). The *History* that, in later volumes, eventually went back to the Anglo-Saxons, incorporated his wider theoretical concerns. For example, he included information on prices to underwrite his views on the money supply and rate of interest, and traced how true liberty – liberty under law – missing in earlier times, emerged gradually along with the growth of commerce.

Throughout Hume's life and writings religion was a preoccupation. He decried enthusiasm and especially superstition (a considerable ingredient in all religions). He undermined the evidential basis for belief in miracles – it was on the balance of probabilities always more likely that the testimony of the witness of a miracle was mistaken than the reported event occurred. Most devastatingly of all (so much so that he only wished the work – *Dialogues Concerning Natural Religion* – published posthumously) he assailed the dominant Argument from Design. Since we have experience of only one universe, we are in no position to know whether or not it has been well designed. Effectively, this conclusion is indicative of his philosophy as a whole, which he himself identified as 'mitigated scepticism'.

CHRISTOPHER J. BERRY
UNIVERSITY OF GLASGOW

References

Forbes, D. (1975) *Hume's Philosophical Politics*, Cambridge.

Friedman, M. (ed.) (1956) *Studies in the Quantity Theory of Money*, Chicago.

Hobbes, T. (1991 [1651]) *Leviathan*, ed. R. Tuck, Cambridge.

Hume, D. (1963) *Hume on Religion*, ed. R.Wollheim, London.

—— (1983 [1754–62]) *History of England*, 6 vols, Indianapolis.

—— (1985) *Essays: Moral, Political and Literary* (1777 edn), ed. E. Miller, Indianapolis.

—— (2000 [1739–40]) *A Treatise of Human Nature*, eds D. and M. Norton, Oxford.

Rawls, J. (1972) *A Theory of Justice*, Oxford.

Further reading

Baier, A. (1991) *A Progress of Sentiments*, Cambridge, MA.

Norton, D.F. (ed.) (1993) *The Cambridge Companion to Hume*, Cambridge.

Rotwein, E. (ed. and intro.) (1970) *Hume: Writings on Economics*, Madison, WI.

Whelan, F. (1985) *Order and Artifice in Hume's Political Philosophy*, Princeton, NJ.

HUNTERS AND GATHERERS

'Hunters and gatherers' or 'hunter-gatherers' constitute a category of peoples vastly more significant in anthropological theory than their present-day numbers might suggest. For many, the category includes fishing peoples and shellfish eaters as well as those who subsist entirely by hunting herbivores and by gathering wild plants. In 10,000 BCE, the world's population consisted solely of hunters, gatherers and fishermen. By AD 1500, with the spread of pastoralism and agriculture, this total was down to 1 per cent. By AD 1900 it was a mere 0.001 per cent (Lee and DeVore 1968).

In recent decades, academic hunter-gatherer studies have seen a resurgence of interest, while 'pure' hunting-and-gathering peoples have dwindled in number. To reconcile this seeming contradiction, hunter-gatherer specialists have come to be less strict in their definitions. Until the 1990s many used to regard only full-time hunter-gatherers as members of the category. Today part-time hunter-gatherers or even recent former hunter-gatherers (people whose grandparents were pure hunter-gatherers) are often included.

The nature of hunting-and-gathering society

Hunter-gatherers today include small, scattered groups on several continents, and they usually live in contact with non-hunter-gatherers. Well-known examples include the Australian Aborigines, the African Bushmen and Pygmies, and the Inuit or Eskimo of northern North America. Also included are various other northern peoples of North America and Siberia, small tropical groups scattered throughout South Asia and Southeast Asia, and some South American groups, both in the Amazon basin and on the far southern tip of the continent. In each of these cases, there are a great diversity of languages, cultures and social structures. Diversity occurs within regions too, especially in practices of utilization of local environments.

Nevertheless, some cultural aspects seem to travel. Australian Aborigines share common beliefs about a deity called the Rainbow Serpent, similar rituals and a highly structured universe in which human social organization is believed to be a part. Likewise, Bushmen across Southern Africa share similar monotheistic beliefs, virtually identical 'medicine dance' rituals and a general flexibility in both belief and social life, while maintaining quite different patterns of settlement and seasonal migration according to the diverse microenvironments they inhabit.

Moreover, a number of common features (some also typical of small-scale cultivating societies) can be identified as shared among the great majority of hunter-gatherer peoples, and these distinguish hunter-gatherers from most other peoples of the world. One may quibble over details, but there are some ten of these (Barnard 1999). They include one essentially ecological attribute: (1) large territories for the size of population, coupled with notions of territorial exclusivity.

Then there are five primarily social attributes: (2) a nested social organization with the band as the primary unit, and further units both within and beyond the band; (3) a lack of social stratification except with regard to gender and age; (4) gender differentiation in activity and in rituals to mark initiation into adult roles; (5) culturally significant mechanisms for the redistribution of accumulated resources; and (6) universal kinship, that is, the recognition of 'kin' beyond the band to the limits of human interaction.

The next three concern ideology and cosmology: (7) structures that relate humans to animals or to animal species; (8) a world order based on even, as opposed to odd, numbers; and (9) a world order founded on symbolic relations within and between levels of social and symbolic structure.

The remaining factor operates in all three of these spheres: (10) flexibility. Arguably, it is that flexibility, whether in exploitation of the environment, in social structure or even in symbolic spheres, which has enabled hunter-gatherers to adapt to changing circumstances even in the twentieth and twenty-first centuries.

Hunter-gatherers in the history of anthropological thought

Hunter-gatherers have been part of anthropological theory since the earliest times. At least since the eighteenth century, and the dawn of an evolutionary thinking in which peoples were classified according to economy, they were hailed as exemplars of 'natural man' or the closest modern human beings could come to this idealized form of humanity. Adam Smith (1978 [in lectures delivered in 1762–3]), for example, spoke of an 'Age of Hunters', which marked the earliest stage of human society, before the development of other means of subsistence and economic pursuits associated with the later stages (the 'Age of Shepherds', 'Age of Agriculture' and 'Age of Commerce'). Eighteenth-century thinkers debated on matters such as whether hunting preceded gathering and on the place of fishing in such an evolutionary scheme.

Nineteenth-century writers, such as Lewis Henry Morgan (1877), similarly saw hunter-gatherers as early, and also as low in evolutionary development – 'savages' as opposed to 'barbarians' or 'civilized peoples'. Morgan believed hunter-gatherers lacked a sense of property, and it was this feature that is emphasized in his evolutionary scheme.

Through most of the twentieth century, evolutionist thinking continued to dominate thinking of hunter-gatherer society. Meanwhile, through the late nineteenth and early twentieth centuries fieldwork studies of living hunter-gatherers, and eventually archaeological studies too, increased

awareness at least in academic circles of the skills hunter-gatherers possess in order to deal with their harsh environments, and the diversity that exists between hunter-gatherer societies, and the specifics of kinship systems, age and gender relations, ritual, folklore, etc., in many parts of the world.

Hunter-gatherer studies since the 1950s

In the late 1950s and early 1960s, a resurgence of interest in hunter-gatherers hit anthropology worldwide. This was partly due to Julian Steward's book *Theory of Culture Change* (1955), an evolutionist tract that gave prominence to the classification of hunter-gatherers by social organization (patrilineal band societies versus composite band societies – the latter with larger and more fluid group structures). Steward's model proved problematic, but his theoretical work spurred fieldworkers to work among hunter-gatherers in many diverse parts of the world, from the Arctic to the Kalahari. Among these (working in the Kalahari) was Richard Lee, who along with Irven DeVore organized, in Chicago in 1966, perhaps the most important anthropology conference ever held: 'Man the Hunter'. This has been followed, from 1978 at roughly 3-year intervals, by an ongoing series of conferences held in Paris, Moscow, Osaka, Edinburgh and other cities, and known as the International Conferences on Hunting and Gathering Societies (CHAGS for short).

Lee (1992) has suggested six key issues in hunter-gatherer studies since 'Man the Hunter': (1) evolutionism, (2) optimal foraging strategies, (3) woman the gatherer, (4) world-view and symbolic analysis, (5) hunter-gatherers in prehistory, and (6) hunter-gatherers in history (Lee 1992). Since the early 1990s, two newer areas have grown in significance and are worth adding to his list: (7) relations with outsiders and (8) indigenous voices. Let us take the last three.

Hunter-gatherers in history poses perhaps the most interesting set of problems. This is especially apparent in the so-called 'Kalahari debate', between those who see Kalahari Bushmen as exponents of a hunting-and-gathering culture and essentially isolated until recent times (the traditionalists), and those who see Bushmen as an underclass and part of a larger social system (the revisionists). Although it had been simmering for some time before, the Kalahari debate proper erupted with the publication of Edwin Wilmsen's *Land Filled with Flies* in 1989. The debate was played out mainly between 1990 and 1995 in the journal *Current Anthropology*. In traditionalist Lee's ethnography adaptation is seen in a dynamic and theoretical way. Lee takes foraging for granted, as a basic and adaptive way of life. He also takes for granted the fact that Bushman society is a relevant unit of analysis, in spite of the presence of members of other, non-hunter-gatherers (Herero and Tswana) within their territories. The Bushmen and their cattle-herding neighbours seem to occupy different ecological niches. Extreme revisionists like Wilmsen de-emphasize cultural continuity in favour of greater concern with the integration of hunter-gatherers into Southern African politico-economic structures taken as a whole.

The last two issues are closely related and follow logically from the interest in hunter-gatherers in history. With regard to relations with outsiders, a number of recent studies have concentrated on relations between hunter-gatherers and their immediate neighbours, such as subsistence herders and horticulturalists. Other studies have looked beyond to relations with the state and other bureaucratic entities, and this seems to be the main direction in which the field of hunter-gatherer studies is going. Finally, 'indigenous voices' have appeared. This is partly a result of increasing pressures on indigenous population throughout the world, as well as a reflection of increasing awareness of their plight in the face of new and serious threats to their lands and livelihoods in many developing countries.

ALAN BARNARD
UNIVERSITY OF EDINBURGH

References

Barnard, A. (1999) 'Modern hunter-gatherers and early symbolic culture', in R. Dunbar, C Knight and C Power (eds) *The Evolution of Culture*, Edinburgh.

Lee, R.B. (1992) 'Art, science, or politics? The crisis in hunter-gatherer studies', *American Anthropologist* 94: 31–54.

Lee, R.B. and DeVore, I. (1968) 'Problems in the study of hunters and gatherers', in R.B. Lee and I. DeVore (eds) *Man the Hunter*, Chicago.

Morgan, L.H. (1877) *Ancient Society*, New York.

Smith, A. (1978 [lectures delivered 1762–3]) *Lectures on Jurisprudence*, Oxford.

Steward, J.H. (1955) *Theory of Culture Change*, Urbana, IL.

Wilmsen, E.N. (1989) *Land Filled with Flies: A Political Economy of the Kalahari*, Chicago.

Further reading

Biesele, M., Hitchcock, R.K. and Schweitzer, P.P. (eds) (2000) *Hunter-Gatherers in the Modern World*, New York.

Burch, E.L., Jr and Ellanna, L.J. (1994) *Key Issues in Hunter-Gatherer Research*, Oxford.

Gowdy, J. (1998) *Limited Wants, Unlimited Means: A Reader on Hunter-Gatherer Economics and the Environment*, Washington, DC.

Kelly, R.L. (1995) *The Foraging Spectrum: Diversity in Hunter-Gatherer Lifeways*, Washington, DC.

Lee, R.B. and Daly, R (eds) (1999) *The Cambridge Encyclopedia of Hunters and Gatherers*, Cambridge.

Panter-Brick, C., Layton, R.H. and Rowley-Conwy, P. (eds) (2001) *Hunter-Gatherers: An Interdisciplinary Perspective*, Cambridge.

SEE ALSO: pastoralism; primitive society

IDENTITY

Within the academy, approaches to identity differ largely in relation to the relative emphasis on the individual versus the social. Within psychology and adjacent disciplines, identity may refer to an intrapsychic, subjective sense of continuous being, and secondarily to a sense of oneself in a social and collective framework. In this view (associated with Erik Erikson and others) identity is something individuals develop over time: infants lack it, adolescents struggle to find it, and adults come to rely on it to guide their choices. Adults experiencing deficiencies in this sense may be said to have an 'identity crisis'. The evidence for the existence of this sense of oneself is derived mostly from introspection, interviews and experiments. An important focus of this approach is on *continuity and discontinuity* of identity over time.

At the other pole of analysis, a more sociologically oriented way of looking at identities examines them as *types* of individuals, such as professor, daughter, European or Hindu, arrayed within an institutional field. While these identities are shared and classify a person as a position in a particular group, any given individual may possess several of them at a time, selectively invoking them as *roles* depending on the context. This approach examines identity from an extra-individual, social perspective, asking with whom and how these identities are shared. Evidence for these identities is derived from classical sociological documentary and survey methods; this approach was articulated in anthropology by Ralph Linton (1936), in terms of a distinction between 'status' and 'role'.

Unlike the idea of identity, the concept of self harbours connotations of continuity, and in common parlance, the self *is* what one is in a privileged sense. While some argue that there are varieties of self, together these kinds of self make up an intrapsychic, integated and more or less continuous identity. Yet another term is *role*, defined as the expected behaviour associated with a social position. Analysis of roles focuses on its types, and how they are enacted and function in social situations. One *plays* a role; it is something one enacts. Identities alone are concerned with media by which distinctiveness and differentiation are established – one holds 'identity cards' to distinguish oneself from others. In English, one does not talk about 'self' cards, nor 'role' cards.

Most other approaches fall between these two poles, and attempt to integrate a macrosociological approach with a more individual or intrapsychic perspective on identity. One such effort is the sociohistorical approach of Anthony Giddens (1991). For Giddens, identity is variably negotiable depending partly on the historical epoch in which one operates, traditional, modern, postmodern or globalized. According to Giddens, in traditional societies, identities are passed down from one generation to the next, and one grows into them. If the identity does not fit, then another is provided, but relatively little negotiation is involved. In the modern order, identity is an ongoing reflexive undertaking – a project that we continuously negotiate, reflect on and revise. A key genre through which we carry out this endeavour is the biographical narrative. This is because modern identity requires a flexible, revisable story that we tell ourselves and others about who we are, how we got here and how we project our future identity. Thus identity is not something imposed, or a fixed set of behavioural features; rather it is a symbolic construct by which we perpetually situate ourselves in space and time. It is not infinitely malleable, however; it is constrained by cognitive, social and cultural limits on narrative coherence. Among these narrative constraints are the need for continuity, classification and contrast. Stability in identity is largely derived from the capacity to keep the narrative going.

An important question is the extent to which constructions of identity are subjective and internal, or external and 'objective'. Emphasizing the individual's subjective feelings, Tanya Luhrmann (2001) states that 'simply described, a person's identity is his or her psychologically salient individuality, the way he or she feels different or similar to other people'. On the other hand, there are obviously key areas in one's identity that are in the custody of others. Charles Taylor (1992), for example, sees a common theme of competing demands for recognition of the legitimacy or value of different identities. This 'politics of recognition' – exemplified in nationalism, ethnic politics, feminism and multiculturalism – is an outgrowth of the modern valuation of self and ordinary life, but depends on the acknowledgement of others. It is not clear, however, to what extent such recognition is a requirement in modern life. Many contemporary communities of practice (in work, play and other activities) seem to operate perfectly well without being accompanied by conscious, or at least explicit, identification at all. Just because people engage in common forms of work, periodically align their interests in political contexts, or even share distinctive forms of DNA, need not imply or require a subjective sense of common identity.

Postcolonial scholars argue that a fundamental disruption in identity occurred when Europeans invaded non-Western countries, colonized their societies and began to displace local conceptions of self. Colonial subjects began to model themselves on their colonizers, learning about their pasts, speaking their languages and internalizing their aspirations for the future. Even as the colonial subjects' identification with their own pasts diminished, their mobility within colonial and postcolonial society remains problematic, leading to frustration and a 'double consciousness'. While they increasingly participate in mainstream society, they nonetheless identify with traditions of critique, resistance and subversion (Nandy 1983).

Scholars of postmodernity contend that the time–space compression associated with telecommunications, air travel and international global commerce are key to understanding identity (Harvey 1989). As computers, television and other devices of simulation and virtual reality bring previously disparate worlds into rapid, intense financial, aesthetic and emotional interaction with one another, constructing an identity requires flexibility. Turkle (1995) describes the mostly male world of virtual reality, Internet-based games in which players from many different countries construct identities and interact violently in vivid, intense, virtual environments, with its virtual systems of accountability. Identities are 'in a state of continuous construction and reconstruction' where 'the test of competence is not so much the integrity of the whole but the apparent correct representation appearing at the right time, in the right context, not to the detriment of the rest of the internal "collective"' (Harvey 1989: 256–7). The flexible self is made up of individual fragments that interact with each other and the outside world in a state of continuous cycling and reconstruction. Given the multiple possibilities for identity constantly clamouring for adoption, it should be no surprise that the quest for identity so often takes a negative, oppositional form.

If postmodern manipulations of identity with computer-assisted simulacra can be a source of ludic pleasure, so-called 'identity theft' through manipulation of credit cards, bank accounts, credit histories, and even health, insurance, legal and educational records is an increasingly common means of causing very real pain and destruction. The media through which modern identities are inscribed – paper records, photographs, drawings, paintings – are giving way to digital simulacra that can be used not only for personal and/or criminal gain, but also for governmental surveillance and control. The hit film *The Matrix* draws on such real and imagined fears. It describes a world in which not only the fixed inscriptions of identity, but the very day-to-day experiences by which we reflexively monitor our identities, are under the power of a vast 'matrix' of central control.

While discussions about the possibilities for technological and social displacements of identity have multiplied, Brodwin (2002) asks whether this very process does not signal a growing movement to stabilize, inscribe and essentialize identity using genetic technology. In courtrooms, laboratories, even parliamentary chambers, the use of such evidence is increasingly debated, evaluated and often found authoritative. 'Why,' he wonders, 'is [genetic evidence] so easily accepted by some groups, but the target of suspicion by others?' Genetically based identity claims are likely to challenge the reflexive anti-essentialism of contemporary social science.

JOEL KUIPERS
GEORGE WASHINGTON UNIVERSITY

References

Brodwin, P.E. (2002) 'Genetics, identity, and the anthropology of essentialism', *Anthropological Quarterly* 75(2): 323–30.
Giddens, A. (1991) *Modernity and Self-Identity: Self and Society in the Late Modern Age*, Stanford, CA.
Harvey, D. (1989) *The Conditions of Postmodernity*, New York.
Linton, R. (1936) *The Study of Man: An Introduction*, New York.
Luhrmann, T. (2001) 'Identity in anthropology', in N.J. Smelser and P.B. Baltes (eds) *International Encyclopedia of the Social and Behavioral Sciences*, Amsterdam and New York, pp. 7,154–9.
Nandy, A. (1983) *The Intimate Enemy: Loss and Recovery of Self Under Colonialism*, Delhi.
Taylor, C. and Gutmann, A. (1992) *Multiculturalism and 'the Politics of Recognition': An Essay*, Princeton, NJ.
Turkle, S. (1995) *Life on the Screen: Identity in the Age of the Internet*, New York.

Further reading

Gleason, P. (1983) 'Identity: A semantic history', *Journal of American History* 69(4): 910–31.
West, C. (2001) *Race Matters*, New York.

SEE ALSO: multiculturalism; person; role; self-concept

IMPERIALISM

Imperialism has acquired so many meanings that the word ought to be dropped by social scientists, complained Professor Hancock in 1950. 'Muddle-headed historians in Great Britain and America use this word with heaven-knows how many shades of meaning, while Soviet writers are using it to summarize a theory and wage a war.' Alas, these errors continue, even after the collapse of the Soviet Union. Autocratic rule over a diversity of otherwise roughly equal peoples goes back in time at least as far as the Indo-European empire of Alexander the Great, but nowadays imperialism is also used as a label for the triumph of (mostly Western European) monopoly finance capital over a still larger array of non-European peoples at the end of the nineteenth century, a very different kind of empire indeed. For some writers, the term is simply synonymous with capitalism in general. Demythologizing imperialism is therefore a slippery but necessary task.

Marxist theories of imperialism were first fleshed out during the 1900s and 1910s principally to explain why the expected final collapse of capitalism was taking so long to happen. Later the outbreak of the First World War, and the promptness with which European working peoples attacked one another rather than their bosses, added fresh urgency to thought. Nationalism, in retrospect, seems to have had something to do with this, as well as the autonomy of political choice at the time of outbreak of war from anything approaching economic rationality. But Marxist writers mostly looked elsewhere for explanations. Just before the war, Rosa Luxemburg provided in *Die Akkumulation des Kapitals* (1913) an analysis of imperialism that is still read respectfully because of its pioneer probing of articulations between expanding capitalism and precapitalist social formations outside Europe. But during and after the First World War it was her advocacy of the mass revolutionary strike in order to speed up the final collapse of capitalism, otherwise given a new lease of life by imperialist expansion, that excited more immediate attention.

Marx himself had seen the expansion of capitalism outside its original heartlands as both a less important phenomenon and a more benign one than Luxemburg: it was a marginal matter, in at least two senses. Luxemburg, however, considered that capitalism could survive only if it continually expanded its territory. One problem with this view, as Mommsen (1981) pointed out, was that

Rosa Luxemburg's basic adherence to Marx's complicated and controversial theory of surplus value, which by definition accrued to capitalism alone, prevented her from considering whether, if the consumer capacity of the masses were increased, internal markets might

not afford suitable opportunities for the profitable investment of 'unconsumed', i.e. reinvest-
able, surplus value.

Another defect was that Luxemburg undoubtedly
misunderstood the significance of the enormous
rise in overseas investment at the start of the
twentieth century. Along with Hobson before and
Lenin subsequently, she assumed that it was
closely associated with colonial annexations. In
fact, as Robinson and Gallagher (1961) pointed
out, it diverged widely from it. Hilferding had
taken a slightly different view. In *Das Finanzkapi-
tal* (1910), he was more concerned to explain why
capitalist crises had become less frequent (there
had not been one since 1896), and he argued that
free trade had been replaced by finance capital,
whose dominance and ability to intervene with
state help anywhere in the world had temporarily
delayed the final catastrophe. But it was the
British journalist and free-trader Hobson, with
his wide array of attacks upon overseas investment and colonial annexations in *Imperialism*
(1902), whom Lenin used most extensively in
his own famous study of *Imperialism, The Highest Stage of Capitalism* (1917). This was written
in order not only to explain the First World War
but also to attack the reformism of Karl Kautsky,
who had suggested that the coming final collapse
of capitalism might be still further delayed by the
emergence of an 'ultra-imperialism' stopping for
the time being further intraimperialist wars. In
retrospect, Lenin's work on imperialism reads
more like a tract than a treatise, but its subsequent importance was of course vastly increased
by the success of Lenin's faction in seizing power
in Russia in 1917; for many years afterwards it
retained unquestionable status as unholy writ.

Shortly after the Russian Revolution, Lenin
also latched on to one of the greatest uses of
imperialism as political ideology, namely as a
weapon against non-communist empires. This
tendency was continued by Stalin, who told the
Twelfth Congress of the Russian Communist
Party in 1923:

Either we succeed in stirring up, in revolu-
tionizing, the remote rear of imperialism – the
colonial and semi-colonial countries of the
East – and thereby hasten the fall of imperialism; or we fail to do so and thereby strengthen
imperialism and weaken the force of our
movement.

Such statements reversed Marx's original view
that imperialism was good for capitalism but
only of marginal importance in its development,
and substituted a new conventional wisdom that,
first, imperialism was bad news for all backward
areas of the world and, second, imperialism was
of utterly central importance to the development
of capitalism itself.

The first view was widely popularized by the
underdevelopment school associated with André
Gundar Frank, and subsequently attacked from
both right and left. The second view led to an
oddly focused debate among historians over the
colonial partition of Africa at the close of the
nineteenth century, the 'theory of economic imperialism' being something of a straw man in this
debate, as imperialism (on most Marxist views)
did not arise until after the Scramble for Africa
had taken place; even after this date Lenin was
clearly wrong about the direction of most overseas investment, let alone its political significance. Only in the case of South Africa (and
possibly Cuba) is there even a plausible case for
economic imperialism being closely identified
with colonial annexation: the South African War
indeed was popularly called '*les Boers contre la
Bourse*' in continental Europe at the time.

Other difficulties with Marxist views of imperialism derive from Lenin's use of Hobson's
Imperialism (1902). Hobson was a very bitter
critic of British overseas investment, but for very
un-Marxist reasons. He was a free-trade liberal
who saw colonial annexations and wars as a
hugely expensive way of propping up the power
and profits of a very small class of *rentier*
capitalists, who pursued profit abroad to the
detriment of investment at home. Only by
manipulating the masses by appealing to their
patriotism did this small class of capitalists get
away with this (in his view) huge confidence
trick and, ideally, social reform should increase
the purchasing powers of the masses and
thereby render imperialism powerless. Lenin
ignored Hobson's theories and simply used his
facts. In retrospect, the facts about the coincidence of overseas investment with colonial
annexation appear very wrong-headed, his theories much less so. Hobson's views on under-
consumption were later taken up and given
some seminal twists by John Maynard Keynes,
while his intuitions about connections between
overseas annexations and metropolitan social
structures were later taken up by Joseph

Schumpeter and Hannah Arendt (for her analysis of the origins of Fascism).

Schumpeter wrote his essay *Zur Soziologie der Imperialismen* (1951 [1919]) as an explicit attack upon Marxist theories of imperialism. Capitalism itself he considered to be essentially anti-imperialist in nature, and such monopolistic and expansionist tendencies characterizing pre-1914 capitalism he put down to the malevolent influence of an anachronistic militarism surviving from the European feudal past. Schumpeter defined imperialism as 'the objectless disposition on the part of a state to unlimited forcible expansion'. The basic trouble with this particular formulation is that while the European colonial annexations of the late nineteenth and early twentieth centuries were certainly sometimes this, they were not always so. Similarly, while much European overseas investment in the late nineteenth century did not go to areas of European colonial annexation, sometimes it did. Furthermore, while the theory of economic imperialism may well still be a straw man as far as the debate about the causes of the Scramble for Africa is concerned, it would be absurd to suggest that the partitioners themselves did not believe that there was *something* economically useful about Africa. Imperialism needs to be demythologized, not simply wished away.

Probably imperialism is best defined in some median manner. As the etymology of the word itself denotes, imperialism is closely concerned with empires and colonialism, but this is not necessarily always the case. In the Americas the Monroe Doctrine (1823) vetoed new formal empires by European countries – but not subsequent 'dollar diplomacy' by the USA, sometimes supported by the overt use of force, sometimes with mere threats and unequal financial practices. Capitalism, too, is not necessarily linked with territorial imperialism, although it has been sometimes so linked. In these circumstances, imperialism is probably best separated analytically from both capitalism and colonialism, and treated principally as the pursuit of intrusive and unequal interests and concerns in other countries supported by significant degrees of coercion.

Thus defined, imperialism as formal empire (or 'colonialism') may well be largely a thing of the past, except for colonies that are of strategic importance (*colonies de position*), or areas that have oil. But imperialism as informal empire (or 'neo-colonialism', to employ Nkrumah's terminology) probably has an assured future ahead of it – both in areas liberated from white-minority rule, and in the territories that were freed from Soviet communism after 1989.

MICHAEL TWADDLE
INSTITUTE OF COMMONWEALTH STUDIES,
UNIVERSITY OF LONDON

References

Hancock, W.K. (1950) *Wealth of Colonies*, Cambridge, UK.
Mommsen, W.J. (1981) *Theories of Imperialism*, New York.
Robinson, R. and Gallagher, J. (1961) *Africa and the Victorians: The Official Mind of Imperialism*, London.
Schumpeter, J.A. (1951 [1919]) *Imperialism and Social Classes*, Oxford.

SEE ALSO: colonialism; partition

INCEST

Incest, defined as sexual relations between close kin (usually members of the same nuclear family), has received relatively scant theoretical attention compared to its prohibition – the incest taboo. The latter arrangement has been the subject of numerous and often contradictory explanations by almost all the major figures in Western social science, including Freud (1950), Engels (1942), Durkheim (1963) and Lévi-Strauss (1969 [1949]), as well as a host of other contributors to the present. This ambition has prevailed because the prohibition has been assumed to provide the basis for a distinctly human form of social organization, and thus allowing for the emergence of culture itself. Consequently any general theory of society must initially provide an explanation for the existence of the incest taboo. Incest itself has been assumed to be a natural human inclination to be guarded against. Yet this conclusion is in itself a profound theoretical statement about human nature – and one that has gone unconsidered. It is apparent, though, that the prohibition and the deed can be understood only in relation to each other.

In some form or another, the incest prohibition or avoidance has characterized all human societies for the overwhelming majority of its members. (Exceptions to this rule are accounted for below.) Recognizing this fact sociological explanations have noted that the rule effectively excludes sexual competition among members of the nuclear family, and in addition precludes the role confusion that would result from reproduction by father and daughter, mother and son, or brother and sister. At a more general level, the prohibition of these kinds of sexual activities requires that at maturity children will seek external partners, creating a series of social alliances among families. As such society itself – a series of linked co-operative groups – comes into existence as the consequence of these exchanges. Such functional explanations for the incest prohibition highlight obvious advantages of the custom. However, it is equally important to note that these arguments do not account for the origin of the prohibition, as opposed to its contemporary consequences.

From a biological perspective it has been argued that nuclear family inbreeding has deleterious effects on offspring. This assumption is borne out by contemporary genetics, but there is no evidence that human beings instituted the incest prohibition to achieve this purpose. Freud's famous scenario, of the primeval human horde in which the patriarch dies at the hands of his own sons for his monopoly of all available females, is a compelling image, and instructive in understanding human psychological development. However, there is no evidence from either human history or primate studies to substantiate such an argument. (Indeed primatology indicates the very opposite arrangement.)

In sum, these arguments merely assume without evidence that humans instituted the incest prohibition to prevent the deed, and that we are naturally inclined to engage in it. The implication subsumed here is that our social arrangements are morally superior to natural inclinations.

In the late nineteenth century, the moral philosopher Edward Westermarck (1894) took an entirely different tack in suggesting that humans were naturally (i.e. instinctually) inclined to avoid incest. The reasonable reaction at the time – to which Westermarck was unable to respond satisfactorily – was: Why then do all societies have the prohibition? However, we are now aware of some societies in which incest is not explicitly prohibited, but nevertheless does not occur. Moreover, ethnographic studies from China (Wolf and Huang 1980), the Middle East (McCabe 1983) and Israel (Shepher 1983) demonstrate that children raised together make for unappealing or unsatisfactory marriage partners.

Finally, both field and controlled laboratory studies of primates and other mammals also indicate mate preference for individuals other than those raised together in either the wild or captivity. In the former instance, this outcome is achieved by either male or female troop transfer, so that the evolutionary disadvantages of inbreeding are unintentionally avoided. Since this social arrangement is a feature of all contemporary primate societies, it is assumed to have characterized our last common ancestor of some 400,000 years ago (Maryanski and Turner 1992). In the latter instance of laboratory experimentation – where this natural outbreeding option was prevented – a severe depression in normal mating and reproductive rates was the result (McGuire and Getz 1981).

If incestuous inbreeding is indeed naturally avoided then why does it exist for humans in the form of the uncondoned variety, as in our society? Moreover, there is every indication that the incidence of such behaviour is greater than previously assumed (Herman 1981). There are also numerous other cultures, such as Pharaonic Egypt, where incestuous marriages were characteristic of royalty. (These may have been purely symbolic arrangements; sex and reproduction were not necessarily at issue, especially for the males who had numerous other wives and sexual partners.) In addition, there is the now well-documented example of the Greek ethnic minority in Roman Egypt (first to fourth century AD) that regularly engaged in sibling marriage to prevent reproduction with the indigenous population (Hopkins 1980).

Although separate in space and time, and different in their own ways, these incestuous episodes suggest that our species has the unique cultural capacity to overcome evolutionary inclinations against inbreeding and its negative consequences. Thus, in accounting for the existence of incest in any and all of its forms, we must look to human culture as opposed to human nature. In effect human beings have invented incest. In recognition of this inclination most societies have generated rules against incest while proclaiming that the culprit lurks in our animal nature rather than our human imagination. Interestingly (but perhaps not surprisingly) the most popular theories attempting to account explicitly for the prohibition and implicitly the deed have followed a similar mystifying path by merely assuming that culture is superior to nature. There is enough evidence from history and ethnography to indicate that this is not always the case.

W. ARENS
STATE UNIVERSITY OF NEW YORK
AT STONY BROOK

References

Durkheim, E. (1963) *Incest*, New York.
Engels, F. (1942) *The Origin of the Family, Private Property and the State*, New York.
Freud, S. (1950) *Totem and Taboo*, New York.
Herman, J. (1981) *Father–Daughter Incest*, Cambridge, MA.
Hopkins, K. (1980) 'Brother–sister marriage in Roman Egypt', *Comparative Studies in Society and History* 22.
Lévi-Strauss, C. (1969 [1949]) *The Elementary Structures of Kinship*, London.
McCabe, J. (1983) 'FBD marriage', *American Anthropologist* 85.
McGuire, M. and Getz, L. (1981) 'Incest taboo between sibling microtus ochrogaster', *Journal of Mammalogy* 62.
Maryanski, A. and Turner, H. (1992) *The Social Cage*, Stanford, CA.
Shepher, J. (1983) *Incest*, New York.
Westermarck, E. (1894) *The History of Human Marriage*, London.
Wolf, A. and Huang, H. (1980) *Marriage and Adoption in China, 1845–1945*, Stanford, CA.

Further reading

Arens, W. (1986) *The Original Sin*, New York.
Fox, R. (1980) *The Red Lamp of Incest*, New York.
Kuper, A. (1994) *The Chosen Primate*, Cambridge, MA.

SEE ALSO: Freud; sexual behaviour

INCOME DISTRIBUTION, THEORY OF

While economists have not always given such primacy to an explicit discussion of distributional questions, income distribution theory has almost always been central to the analysis of economic systems. The theory deals not only with the functional distribution of income but also with the size distribution of income.

Orthodox economic theory treats questions of income distribution as an integral part of the neo-classical analysis of prices, output mix and resource allocation. Briefly, each competitive firm takes the price it can get for its output and the prices it must pay for inputs as given in the market: it selects its level of output and adjusts its demand for inputs so as to maximize profits at those prices. Each household likewise takes as given the prices it must pay for goods and services, and the prices paid to it for goods and services (for example the labour services supplied by members of the household): it adjusts the quantities of the goods and services demanded or supplied in the market so as to maximize satisfaction within the limitations imposed by its budget. All these prices adjust so as to clear the markets: aggregate supply is at least as great as aggregate demand for every good and service. The reward to any factor of production – whether it be a particular type of labour, a natural resource or the services of capital equipment – is determined by its market clearing price. If the technology changes, or the stock of natural resources alters, or if there is a shift in the preference patterns of households, this will shift the pattern of supply and/or demand in one or more markets, and in general prices of goods and factors alter accordingly to clear the markets anew. The functional distribution of income is thus apparently automatically determined by the market mechanism, Moreover, the details of the distribution of income between persons or between households can be readily worked out within this framework: the time pattern of consumption and saving by households, and the educational investments that people make in themselves or in their offspring – each of which plays a significant role in the size distribution of incomes that is realized – can each be analysed as particular cases of the household's optimization problem.

However, one other piece of information is required for a complete theory of income distribution within this framework: the system of property rights that prevails within the community. The importance of this as regards the size distribution of income is obvious: the question of who owns which natural resources, of who owns the capital equipment and of who is entitled to a share in the profits of the firms is central to the determination of household incomes. Household budgets are determined jointly by these property rights and the market prices, and may be dramatically affected by a change in the pattern of ownership, or by a shift in the *system* of ownership (for example from a system of private property to one of state ownership). But this system of ownership will *also* affect the market prices and thus the functional distribution of income. For if households' rights of ownership are changed, the consequent change in household budgets will change the pattern of demand for goods and services, and hence the market prices of consumption goods and of labour and other resources. Thus orthodox theory might be criticized for evading one of the principal issues of income determination, by passing the question of property rights on to the historian or the political philosopher.

However, the neo-classical orthodoxy has been challenged not only because of such shortcomings, but also on account of its restrictive assumptions concerning the economic processes involved. Because these assumptions lie at the heart of the theory rather than being merely convenient simplifications, many economists have questioned the relevance of various aspects of the standard account of income distribution. We may cite three particular examples that have led to the construction of useful alternative theories.

First, note that the orthodox theory neglects barriers to competition and the exercising of monopoly power as being of secondary or transitory importance in the competitive market story. It has been argued that restraints on competition – in the form of segmentation of the labour market and outright discrimination – are of major importance in analysing the lower tail of the size distribution of earnings; and monopoly power may be particularly important in the upper tail, for example, in the determination of earnings in professions with restricted entry. Monopolistic pricing by firms has also been seen as of prime importance in the *functional* distribution of income (see e.g. Kalecki 1939). Indeed such power has an important part to play in the Marxian concept of exploitation and of theories of distribution that are based on struggle between the classes representing different factors of production. The assumption of pure competition is also likely to be inadequate in analysing economics that have a substantial public sector.

A second feature of the orthodox approach that many theorists find unsatisfactory is the assumption of perfect information by individuals and firms. Indeed it is argued that uncertainty is itself a potent force generating inequality in both earned and unearned income alike, in that the rich not only are better able to bear risk but also may have superior information that can be exploited in the stock market and the labour

market. Moreover, some of the barriers to competition may have been erected by firms in response to such uncertainty. Hence considerable interest has developed in the distributional implications of theories of output, employment and the structure of wages that explicitly incorporate imperfect information.

The third point arises from the second: the predominant interest of the neo-classical orthodox theory of income distribution in smooth adjustments to market clearing equilibria is considered by some writers to be inappropriate to a theory of the functional distribution of income. As a response to this, economists who are strongly influenced by J.M. Keynes's approach to macroeconomics have developed a number of alternative theories of the functional distribution of income-using components of the Keynesian system, for example the work of Kaldor (1956) and Pasinetti (1961). Key features of such alternative theories are rule-of-thumb savings decisions by capitalists and workers, and a rigid technique by which labour and capital are combined to produce output.

FRANK A. COWELL
LONDON SCHOOL OF ECONOMICS
AND POLITICAL SCIENCE

References

Kaldor, N. (1956) 'Alternative theories of distribution', *Review of Economic Studies* 23.

Kalecki, M. (1939) *Essays in the Theory of Economic Fluctuations*, London.

Pasinetti, L.L. (1961) 'Rate of profit and income distribution in relation to the rate of economic growth', *Review of Economic Studies* 29.

Further reading

Atkinson, A.B. (1983) *The Economics of Inequality*, 2nd edn, London.

Piketty, T. (2000) 'Theories of persistent inequality and intergenerational mobility', in A.B. Atkinson and F. Bourguignon (eds) *Handbook of Income Distribution*, Vol. 1, Amsterdam, Chapter 8, pp. 429–76.

SEE ALSO: distribution of incomes and wealth; equality

INDIVIDUALISM

Individualism is a modern word. Its first recorded use is in 1840 when it was used in the English translation of de Tocqueville's *Democracy in America*. In a later work Tocqueville

(1956 [1856]) noted that 'Our ancestors had not got the word "Individualism" – a word which we have coined for our own use, because in fact in their time there was no individual who did not belong to a group, no one who could look on himself as absolutely alone.' In modern societies, such as the USA, 'Men being no longer attached to one another by any tie of caste, of class, of corporation, of family, are only too much inclined to be preoccupied only with their private interests...to retire into a narrow individualism.' The contrast between societies based on the group and the individual was part of the nineteenth-century attempt to understand the massive changes brought about in the wake of the French and Industrial Revolutions. All the founding fathers of the modern social sciences – Marx, Durkheim, Weber, Tönnies, Simmel and others – reflected on the new relations between the individual and the group. For example, Maine (1861) noted that the 'unit of an ancient society was the Family, of a modern society the individual'. It was generally agreed that the separation of the spheres of life, economics from society, religion from politics and so on, had not only given the individual more liberty, in Mill's sense, but also destroyed both meaning and warmth.

Thus individualism came to be seen as the essential feature of 'modernity'. Bell (1976) wrote that the 'fundamental assumption of modernity...is that the social unit of society is not the group, the guild, the tribe or the city, but the person'. The belief in the primacy of the individual was not only powerful, but also peculiar. Dumont (1977) argued that

> among the great civilizations the world has known, the holistic type of society has been overwhelmingly predominant. Indeed it looks as if it had been the rule, the only exception being our modern civilization and its individualistic type of society.

The heart of the matter is summarized by Gellner (1988): 'a society emerged in which single individuals could apparently carry the entire culture within themselves, unaided'.

These views need to be qualified in various ways. First, it is clear that all human societies have the concept of the separate 'person'. As Mauss wrote, 'it is plain...that there has never existed a human being who has not been aware, not only of his body, but also at the same time of

his individuality, both spiritual and physical' (quoted in Carrithers et al. 1985). Furthermore, anthropologists have noted that many of the features of individualism are to be found in societies ranging from the simplest hunting-gathering societies to the most complex civilizations, such as Japan over the last thousand years. An over-stark contrast between the 'West' and the 'rest' is not justified.

It is also clear that the watershed theory of individualism is too simple. Although it is usually conceded that there was a long individualistic tradition in Western civilization, somehow linked to Christianity, it is often assumed that the eighteenth century, with the rise of market capitalism, saw a new order of things. Yet, whether we look at the property system of Anglo-Saxon England where Maitland (1921) found a system compatible with 'the most absolute individualism' of ownership, or the medieval philosophy of Ockham and his successors, or, many centuries earlier, the extreme individualism of much Greek philosophy, it is clear that there is no clear progressive story. Again, too simple a dichotomy between the 'past' and the 'present' is not warranted.

This makes the future much less easy to predict. Some believe that the trend is towards heightened individualism and egotism. The greater division of labour and the penetration of market values, the spread of political concepts of equality and innate human rights will lead to increased individualism as de Tocqueville predicted. Others argue that we are now moving towards a global village where, in Donne's words, 'no man is an island'. We will be electronically, if not organically, returned to a holistic society. Some writers, for instance Foucault, Derrida and Lacan, have questioned the very notion of an independently constituted individual. Developments in medical technology, particularly organ transplants and reproductive technology, have indeed made the boundaries between individuals much less precise than they once were. The future of individualism is as contested as its meaning and value.

ALAN MACFARLANE
UNIVERSITY OF CAMBRIDGE

References

Bell, D. (1976) *The Cultural Contradictions of Capitalism*, New York.

Carrithers, M., Collins, S. and Lukes, S. (eds) (1985) *The Category of the Person*, Cambridge, UK.

Dumont, L. (1977) *From Mandeville to Marx*, Chicago.

Gellner, E. (1988) *Plough, Sword and Book*, London.

Maine, H. (1861) *Ancient Law*, London.

Maitland, F.W. (1921) *Domesday Book and Beyond*, Cambridge, UK.

Tocqueville, A. de (1956 [1856]) *Ancien Régime*, trans. M. Patterson, Oxford.

Further reading

Lukes, S. (1973) *Individualism*, Oxford.

Macfarlane, A. (2002) *The Making of the Modern World*, London.

Morris, B. (1991) *Western Conceptions of the Individual*, Oxford.

SEE ALSO: identity; person; self-concept

INDUSTRIAL AND ORGANIZATIONAL PSYCHOLOGY

Industrial and organizational (I/O) psychology is the scientific study of work behaviour. As a specialized subdiscipline of general psychology, it is distinguished by a concern with human behaviour within organizations. The industrial label is a holdover from the early twentieth century when the primary context for studying work behaviour was in heavy industry and manufacturing organizations. The organizational aspect of I/O has grown in prominence over the years and was officially added to the name in 1973. The three primary areas of study that define I/O are personnel (or industrial) psychology, organizational (or applied social) psychology and the investigation of the work environment. The field of I/O psychology is considered to be an applied science.

Personnel psychology

Individual job performance is at the core of personnel psychology. Personnel psychologists are largely concerned with recruiting and selecting employees who are predicted to perform effectively in a job; training employees in the job skills that they require in order to perform effectively; appraising individual job performance; and also making personnel decisions based on job performance data about promotion, termination and compensation. The personnel psychologist must be able to assess the key demands of a job as well as the knowledge, skills, abilities and other individual characteristics (KSAOs) required to successfully meet those demands.

Various tools and processes are used by the personnel psychologist to assess individual and job characteristics. Job analysis is a broad term that is used to describe systematic procedures for examining, documenting and drawing inferences about duties, responsibilities and activities, and other aspects of the work context. Job analysis focuses on identifying the most important and frequently occurring tasks, and the KSAOs that are required for the performance of those tasks. Individual assessment, often in the form of aptitude or personality testing, is used to identify the capacities and limitations of applicants in meeting the demands of the job. Two particular individual aptitudes that personnel psychologists have found to be related to job performance across a broad range of contexts are cognitive ability (intelligence) and conscientiousness (one of the so-called 'Big Five' personality factors, along with extraversion, agreeableness, emotional stability and openness to experience).

Job performance is at the heart of all of I/O because it serves as the ultimate criterion to evaluate work-related practices, interventions and other related factors. The personnel psychologist has to formulate, conceptualize, identify and measure important dimensions of job performance. An important distinction is made between task performance (i.e. activities that transform raw materials into organizational products or services) and contextual performance, which contributes to organizational effectiveness through its effects on the psychosocial context of work. The three primary forms of contextual performance are personal support (e.g. helping others by offering suggestions), organizational support (e.g. defending or promoting the organization) and conscientious initiative (e.g. making an extra effort despite difficult conditions). Other relevant aspects of job performance that have been studied by personnel psychologists include organizational citizenship behaviour (which is conceptually very similar to contextual performance), and counterproductive behaviour (defined as behaviour that is intentional and contrary to the interests of an organization).

Personnel psychologists need expertise in psychometrics (mental measurement) because of the frequency with which testing and other individual assessment is conducted under their direction. In the USA, especially, they must also be very familiar with federal, state and local Equal Employment Opportunity laws, due to the likelihood of litigation associated with issues such as pre-employment testing, promotion and termination. Personnel psychology is closely related to the field of human resource management (HRM).

Organizational psychology

Organizational psychology (which is closely related to the field of organizational behaviour in the management sciences) is largely concerned with the social environment of work. Specific topics in organizational psychology include job attitudes (e.g. job satisfaction, job identification and organizational commitment), work motivation, leadership, work groups and teams, and organization development, all matters that have to do with interpersonal processes. Although the historical focus of I/O research, theory and practice has been the individual, there is increasing recognition that important work-related constructs occur at different organizational levels. The multilevel nature of the behavioural phenomena raises specific conceptual and measurement issues, and technical skills in multilevel modelling are rapidly becoming especially important to organizational psychologists.

Organizations increasingly use team-based approaches to work. Organizational psychologists therefore tend to conduct research, or base practical applications, on groups and teams. They draw on a tradition of research in social psychology dealing with interpersonal dynamics, which they apply to the study of task work, work flow and work processes.

Organizational psychologists should have sound backgrounds in social psychology and related topics, particularly in areas of attitude theory and measurement, judgement and decision-making, motivational theories and processes, as well as group dynamics and organizational theory. Expertise in multivariate statistics and structural modelling are also important.

Work environment

The study of work environments covers such issues as work design, stress, career dynamics, human factors and ergonomics, organizational climate and culture, work–life balance, and diversity. These issues are of great importance to I/O psychologists because a proper alignment or fit between work environments and the characteristics of people in those environments is a key to the well-being and optimal performance of both individuals and organizations. This area is known as person–environment fit.

The context can support other I/O practices, or it can impede their contribution. For example, individuals can receive extensive and well-designed training, but if the work environment does not support the transfer of training back to the job, there is little likelihood of lasting change for either the individual or the organization.

The I/O approach to the study of work environments is inherently psychological because it typically focuses on how organizational participants experience and make sense of their social and physical environments. However, social as well as structural factors affect the way in which people experience the work environment. Task perceptions and attitudes are influenced by social information, although the impact of social information is less than that of objective task characteristics. Structural factors such as organizational structure, technology and the physical environment are also relevant.

The three areas of I/O are typically interrelated. The work environment is defined by the people; the people make the place. The people in an organization are usually there because of recruitment and selection processes that are part of personnel psychology. Job attitudes and perceptions of the organizational climate are determined in large part by conditions in the work environment. Training can be conducted to enhance the skills needed for effective leadership. In turn, leadership training can serve as a catalyst for change in an organization, which is a form of organization development. Personnel psychology, organizational psychology and the work environment form a system of interrelated influences. I/O psychology accordingly considers work behaviour from a systems perspective that includes workers, jobs and the broader work environment.

DAVID V. DAY
PENNSYLVANIA STATE UNIVERSITY

Further reading

Borman, W.C., Ilgen, D.R. and Klimoski, R.J. (eds) (2003) *Handbook of Psychology: Industrial and Organizational Psychology*, Vol. 12, Hoboken, NJ.

Dunnette, M.D. and Hough, L.M. (eds) (1990) *Handbook of Industrial and Organizational Psychology*, Vols 1–4, 2nd edn, Palo Alto, CA.

Guion, R.M. (1999) *Assessment, Measurement, and Prediction for Personnel Decisions*, Mahwah, NJ.

SEE ALSO: human resource management; industrial organization; industrial relations; industrial sociology

INDUSTRIAL ORGANIZATION

A subfield of microeconomics, the study of industrial organization is concerned with markets, and in particular markets for consumer products and services. It begins with the observation that a large number of industries are concentrated. In other words, the number of active firms in many branches of industry is not very large, often ranging from one to four. Research on industrial organization accordingly pays special attention to imperfectly competitive firms in a given industry, and to imperfectly competitive producers of inputs and intermediate goods.

The intellectual history of the field can be traced back to studies by Edward Mason (1939) and Joe Bain, whose ideas are found in his textbooks on industrial organization (1956, 1968 [1951]). Mason and Bain argued that the classroom assumption of price-taking behaviour, which defines competitive markets, did not match the markets they observed. However, earlier theoretical analyses of imperfect competition date back to Cournot (1927 [1838]), Bertrand (1883), Hotelling (1929) and Chamberlin (1933). On the policy side, the need to understand how markets operate dates back to the early anti-trust regulation in the USA, the Sherman Act of 1890, the Clayton Act of 1914 and the Robinson–Patman Act of 1936.

Theoretical and empirical studies in industrial organization usually focus on the organization of markets rather than on commercial enterprises, but in the past two decades researchers have begun to consider how markets are affected by the internal organization of the firm, analysing problems such as span of control, hierarchy, monitoring, incentives and compensation. Current industrial organization research combines rigorous mathematical modelling with empirical testing.

Industrial organization research has traditionally been described as relying on the *Structure–Conduct–Performance paradigm*. The *structure* is based on consumer preferences, firms' technologies and production cost configurations, as well as on other market conditions such as entry barriers and the initial number of active producers. Market *conduct* describes firms' choice of actions such as pricing, R&D, quality, advertising, standards, entry deterrence, collusion, cartel formation, vertical integration and mergers. Advances and simplifications made in game theory provided appropriate tools with which industrial organization researchers could analyse and describe how these strategies are chosen in imperfectly competitive markets. These game theory tools have been widely used in industrial organization theory since the 1980s. In particular, the dynamic game-theoretic tools provided some explanations of the dynamic development of industries by providing a rigorous language for describing static and dynamic behaviour as well as strategic interactions among firms maximizing long-term profits. Clearly, market conduct is not only affected by some exogenously-given market structure conditions. Indeed, choices made by enterprises can feed back and cause changes in the market structure. For example, when incumbent firms attempt to create barriers to the entry of new firms, they will influence the number of active firms and hence market structure. Also, if firms invest heavily in R&D, they affect the available technologies and, in consequence, the cost structure. Finally, the third component of this paradigm, the market *performance*, involves analysing the welfare consequences of market conduct and market structure. The welfare analysis generates policy recommendations leading in some instances to anti-trust legislation (Hovenkamp 1999).

Current industrial organization research does not necessarily follow the Structure–Conduct–Performance paradigm. Instead, a common methodology would be to construct an oligopoly model by first describing the strategies available to each existing firm and potential entrants, as well as the precise timing according to which each firm, as well as the consumer, is entitled to make their decisions. Researchers then establish the equilibrium levels of these decision variables, which could be prices, quantities, R&D expenditure, quality, advertising expenditure, collusion, etc. If the research is empirical in nature, the researcher generally runs regressions on collected data, such as time-series, and estimates the number value of the parameters of the model. These parameters should be useful in predicting changes in demand and supply in response to certain policy changes, including deregulation of the industry.

The performance part of industrial organization research asks about the impact on welfare of production outcomes, supply and consumption generated by the strategic interaction of profit-maximizing firms. Since industrial organization research most commonly involves a partial equilibrium modelling (as opposed to general equilibrium modelling), the researcher has to compute industry profit and consumer welfare separately. The social welfare function is then most commonly defined as a weighted sum of aggregate consumer surplus and aggregate industry profit. Regulators as well as anti-trust and competition authorities often have to balance the trade-off between the loss (gain) of consumer surplus and the gain (loss) in industry profit associated with mandating a certain policy instrument (Viscusi *et al.* 1995).

Research topics that are generally classified as coming within the field of industrial organization include: quantity and price competition, price discrimination, product differentiation, entry barriers, entry deterrence, mergers, research and development and the patent system, persuasive and informative advertising, non-linear pricing, quality, durability, warranties, bundling and tying, internal organization of firms, outsourcing and subcontracting, optimal contracts under imperfect information, vertical integration and dealerships.

In the past two decades, industrial organization researchers have also investigated a wider variety of markets. This expansion followed and enhanced the extensive waves of market deregulations and privatizations that turned the so-called natural monopolies and public utilities into free markets. Industrial organization theory then had to find ways to avoid costly duplication of infrastructure that earlier constituted the justification behind the natural monopoly concept. The solution was termed access pricing, which allows competitors to share their infrastructure with competitors, and vice versa. The role played by industrial organization theory is to determine how access pricing affects market competition and market prices, and so consumer welfare. Almost all deregulated industries make use of similar alliances, such as code-sharing

agreements in the airline industry and access pricing for shared infrastructure in telecommunication industries (Laffont and Tirole 2001). Alliances are now also observed in almost all areas of public transportation and public utilities.

A second impetus for widening the scope of industrial organization research came from the rapid introduction of standard-dependent products, which we now describe as network industries (Shy 2001). Hardware such as audio and video cassettes and players, DVDs, TV broadcasting standards, as well as software dependent on a particular operating system, made products incompatible across standards. The reliance on incompatible standards created consumer switching costs. The purpose of the research on network industries is to determine the incentives that firms have to develop compatible or incompatible standards, and the effect of standardization on prices, quality and consumer welfare. More recently, researchers have analysed information goods and services in the digital era (Shapiro and Varian 1999), and examined the rapid changes in the extension of copyright protection to information products.

Finally, industrial organization research is now also being applied in the banking industry (Freixas and Rochet 1997). Although the banking industry is heavily regulated in most countries, and is typically not fully competitive, the modern approach portrays banks as profit maximizers that utilize fees as well as lending and borrowing risk management as their strategic variables.

OZ SHY
UNIVERSITY OF HAIFA

References

Bain, J. (1956) *Barriers to New Competition*, Cambridge, MA.
—— (1968 [1951]) *Industrial Organization*, New York.
Bertrand, J. (1883) 'Review', *Journal des savants* 68: 499–508. Reprinted in J. Friedman, and A. Daughety (eds) (1988) *Cournot Oligopoly*, Cambridge.
Chamberlin, E. (1933) *The Theory of Monopolistic Competition*, Cambridge, MA.
Cournot, A. (1927 [1838]) *Researches into the Mathematical Principles of the Theory of Wealth*, New York.
Freixas, X. and Rochet, J.C. (1997) *Microeconomics of Banking*, Cambridge, MA.
Hotelling, H. (1929) 'Stability in competition', *Economic Journal* 39: 41–57.
Hovenkamp, H. (1999) *Federal Antitrust Policy: The Law of Competition and Its Practice*, St Paul, MN.

Laffont, J.J. and Tirole, J. (2001) *Competition in Telecommunication*, Cambridge, MA.
Mason, E. (1939) 'Price and production policies of large-scale enterprise', *American Economic Review* 29(1), Supplement: 61–4.
Shapiro, C. and Varian, H. (1999) *Information Rules*, Boston.
Shy, O. (2001) *The Economics of Network Industries*, Cambridge.
Viscusi, W.K., Vernon, J. and Harrington, J. (1995) *Economics of Regulation and Antitrust*, Cambridge, MA.

Further reading

Carlton, D. and Perloff, J. (1999) *Modern Industrial Organization*, London.
Church, J. and Ware, R. (1999) *Industrial Organization: A Strategic Approach*, New York.
Martin, S. (2002) *Advanced Industrial Economics*, Oxford.
Scherer, F.M. (1970) *Industrial Market Structure and Economic Performance*, Chicago.
Schmalensee, R. and Willig, R. (1989) *Handbook of Industrial Organization*, Amsterdam.
Shy, O. (1996) *Industrial Organization: Theory and Applications*, Cambridge, MA.
Sutton, J. (1991) *Sunk Costs and Market Structure*, Cambridge, MA.
Tirole, J. (1988) *The Theory of Industrial Organization*, Cambridge, MA.
Waterson, M. (1984) *Economic Theory of the Industry*, Cambridge.

SEE ALSO: competition policy; corporate enterprise; firm, theory of; industrial and organizational psychology; industrial relations; industrial sociology; regulation

INDUSTRIAL RELATIONS

The concept and the study of industrial relations originated in the USA in the early twentieth century, and soon extended to Britain. Until the 1980s, however, they have been unfamiliar outside English-speaking countries. The meaning of industrial relations is imprecise, and both the scope of the subject and its disciplinary status have long been debated. The term entered public discourse in 1912, when the US Senate in the aftermath of violent industrial conflicts appointed a Commission on Industrial Relations with a wide-ranging investigative brief. Its agenda was comprehensive: a heterogeneous catalogue of aspects of what was conventionally described as 'the labour question'. However, the notion of industrial relations soon acquired a rather narrower meaning: the processes and institutions through which employment is managed, such as trade unions and employers' associations, collective negotiations and agreements, labour legislation and organized conflict.

This definition provided the basis for the development of academic research and teaching, on both sides of the Atlantic, in the decades between the two world wars. In both Britain and the USA, the impetus was primarily pragmatic and reformist. Early academic writers on union–management relations (the Webbs and Cole in Britain, Hoxie and Commons in the USA) were for the most part sympathetic to labour and regarded trade unions as a positive force for social improvement; their perspectives converged with those of progressive employers and civil servants. Their common belief was that social peace could be encouraged by a better understanding of the sources of industrial conflict and the mechanics of collective regulation.

The Second World War enhanced interest in industrial relations: trade unions played a key role as guarantors of national consensus, while the demands of military production increased the importance of conflict avoidance. In the USA this was reflected in the creation of a War Labor Board, employing many young scholars who went on to manage a postwar expansion of industrial relations institutes and degree programmes. In Britain a similar though more modest extension of the subject received a further boost in the 1960s, when industrial relations problems became widely perceived as an important source of relative economic decline.

Early writers on industrial relations came from a variety of academic backgrounds: sociology, economics, law, psychology and history. But as the study became increasingly institutionalized, many in the field proclaimed industrial relations as a discipline in its own right. The most notable exponent of this view was the American economist John Dunlop, whose *Industrial Relations Systems* appeared in 1958. 'An industrial-relations system,' he argued, 'is to be viewed as an analytical subsystem of an industrial society on the same logical plane as an economic system' (Dunlop 1958: 5). Its defining characteristic was 'the full range of rule-making governing the work place'. The analysis of the rules of employment, the actors (employers, workers and their organizations, and governments) involved in their formulation and administration, and the contextual influences (technological, economic and political) required, in Dunlop's view, a distinctive theoretical apparatus that identified industrial relations as a separate discipline.

To some extent, insistence on the subject's disciplinary credentials stemmed from a specifically US style of academic politics. Most British exponents have been content to regard the subject merely as an interdisciplinary field of study. Dunlop's work was, however, influential in Britain in at least three respects: by stimulating debates about the precise definition of industrial relations; by encouraging the proliferation of formal models of industrial relations as an interactive system; and by inspiring theoretical analysis, notably in the writings of Allan Flanders (1970), which located 'job regulation' as the central object of analysis.

It is noteworthy that industrial relations developed as an academic subject almost exclusively in the English-speaking world. Such translations as *relations industrielles*, *industrielle Beziehungen* or *relazioni industriali* have always appeared self-conscious and artificial: in continental Europe the study of job regulation has normally been rooted within (and thus often fragmented between) such (sub)disciplines as labour law, industrial sociology and labour economics. One possible explanation is the relative autonomy of management–union relations within the Anglo-American world. In both Britain and the USA, the state was far less actively involved in the formative process of industrialization than in most of Europe, and the individualistic common-law tradition militated against systematic legal regulation of employment. The consequence was a considerable degree of discretion for employers (and, to a lesser extent, workers and unions) in determining the terms and conditions of employment. In more regulated societies, by contrast, the processes of industrial relations were more obviously integrated within broader sociopolitical dynamics; to study them in isolation seemed futile.

From the 1970s, the study of industrial relations was beset by some disarray. The reasons were partly intellectual and partly material. US systems' approaches to the subject were strongly influenced by structural-functionalist sociology (Dunlop based his model explicitly on Parsons's *Social System*); it assumed an inherent bias towards order and stability. Mainstream writers argued that mature industrial relations systems inevitably functioned to contain and routinize conflict, often inferring a logic of capitalist development diametrically opposed to that of Marx. British writers in the field developed an analogous thesis, usually termed industrial relations pluralism. This challenged conceptions of industry based on the functional integration of interests, but also rejected any idea of class polarization. Following the ideas of such political theorists as Schumpeter, Dahl and Dahrendorf, the dominant British school of the 1960s and 1970s argued that economic interests were multiplex and cross-cutting, creating scope for negotiated accommodation through appropriate institutional arrangements. Collective bargaining was an effective recipe, not for eliminating industrial conflict but for rendering it manageable.

The challenges to conservative orthodoxies in the social sciences from the late 1960s made their mark in industrial relations also. Three aspects of this radicalization may be noted: first, a reassertion of the importance of class in the analysis of employment issues; second (post-Braverman), an insistence that any study of the world of work must attend to the dynamics of the labour process, not merely the wage-centred agenda of collective bargaining; third, the argument that processes of employment regulation must be analysed as part of a far broader political economy of capitalism. Such questioning of the prevailing intellectual foundations of the study of industrial relations undermined its academic coherence.

Material developments reinforced these challenges. The incidence of industrial disputes, which in most developed economies had fallen sharply in the 1950s and early 1960s, began to rise substantially; arguments for the institutionalization of conflict lost their plausibility. The changing structure of the economy and of employment also eroded the relevance of a field of study founded largely on the situation of male manual workers in manufacturing industry: traditional notions of industrial relations did not readily connect with the expanding milieux of work (female, white-collar, service-sector). In the 1970s, the traditional assumption of a substantial disjuncture between the worlds of politics and industrial relations also lost its purchase: Western governments increasingly attempted to regulate wage bargaining, often pursued new initiatives in individual and collective labour law (a process that German scholars termed juridification), and in some cases – at least in the 1980s – imposed new restrictions on trade union organization and collective bargaining.

Employers also challenged the established institutions and procedures. This was most obvious in the USA, where many leading employers successfully attacked union organization in order to create a union-free workforce, replacing collective bargaining by internal company mechanisms of communication and employee involvement. Increasingly, firms gave their industrial relations departments a new title: human resource management (HRM). By the 1990s, US academics had in large measure followed suit: the number of chairs, institutes and courses in industrial relations has declined, to be overtaken by a rapid growth in HRM (Kaufman 1993). In Britain this process was far less dramatic, but still significant. Union membership declined substantially after the Conservative election victory of 1979, the coverage of collective bargaining falling below half the workforce by the end of the 1980s, and the number of strikes fell dramatically. Many former industrial relations scholars switched allegiance to more managerially popular concerns, and textbooks and degrees were relaunched under the HRM label.

In its heyday, the study of industrial relations derived its appeal and seeming coherence from a historically conditioned convergence of orientations among trade unionists, leading employers and public policy-makers. In Britain and the USA, this basis has broken down: academics are forced to choose between an explicitly managerial focus on employment policy and a more critical social science approach to the analysis of work (Kelly 1998). Paradoxically perhaps, the prospects for revival in the field seem greatest in countries with no academic industrial relations tradition: interest in cross-disciplinary analysis of employment regulation has been expanding in many countries of continental Europe – both West and East – and also in many 'less developed' economies (Hyman 1995). It is also significant that the concept of industrial relations has now entered the official vocabulary of the European Union (EU 2002)

RICHARD HYMAN
LONDON SCHOOL OF ECONOMICS
AND POLITICAL SCIENCE

References

Dunlop, J.T. (1958) *Industrial Relations Systems*, New York.

EU (2002) *Report of the High-Level Group on Industrial Relations and Change in the European Union*, Brussels.

Flanders, A. (1970) *Management and Unions*, London.

Hyman, R. (1995) 'Industrial relations in Europe: Theory and practice', *European Journal of Industrial Relations* 1.

Kaufman, B.E. (1993) *The Origins and Evolution of the Field of Industrial Relations*, Ithaca, NY.

Kelly, J. (1998) *Rethinking Industrial Relations*, London.

Further reading

Hyman, R. (1989) *The Political Economy of Industrial Relations*, London.

SEE ALSO: human resource management; industrial organization; industrial and organizational psychology; industrial sociology; trade unions

INDUSTRIAL REVOLUTIONS

The term 'industrial revolution' is of fundamental importance in the study of economic history and economic development. The phrase is, however, full of pitfalls for the unwary, partly because it has been used with several different meanings, and has, of course, generated a good deal of controversy.

An early use of 'industrial revolution' referred to what are best seen as periods of industrial growth with quite limited implications for overall economic development. Well-known examples include Carus-Wilson (1941) on the thirteenth and Nef (1932) on the sixteenth centuries. This usage is now seen as unhelpful and is generally disparaged.

Still very much extant is thinking of 'industrial revolution' in the sense of technological revolution, as does Freeman (1987). This approach is often used by researchers concentrating on science and technology to describe developments that they feel had widespread economic and social ramifications. This school of thought envisages successive technological or (if you will) industrial revolutions. These would typically include the famous inventions of the period 1750–1850 based on steam power, the so-called second industrial revolution of the late nineteenth and early twentieth centuries involving new chemicals, electricity and automobiles, and the information technology revolution of the years after 1970.

Among economists and economic historians 'industrial revolution' most frequently relates to a fundamental part of the experience of economic development, namely the spread of industrialization in the economy as a whole. Since Kuznets (1966), this has been associated with the onset of modern economic growth. Econometric research has confirmed the existence of systematic patterns of change in the structure of economies as real incomes rise (Chenery and Syrquin 1975), although it is widely recognized that countries have not followed identical routes to modernity (O'Brien 1986). Industrialization is typically accompanied by acceleration in economic growth, increases in investment in both physical and human capital, and improvements in technology and urbanization.

Perhaps the most common use of all refers to the classic and pioneering example of industrialization that occurred in Britain during the late eighteenth and early nineteenth centuries, famously described by Rostow (1960) as featuring a spectacular take-off into self-sustained growth. It now seems more probable that this episode was characterized by particularly rapid changes in economic structure but quite slow growth (Crafts 1985). In this sense the British industrial revolution not only subsumed technological innovation in industry but also embraced much wider organizational changes in agriculture, finance, commerce, trade, etc. Indeed the term 'industrial revolution' is a metaphor that should not be taken literally in this context.

A large literature has sought the ultimate causes of the first industrial revolution and has produced a great variety of hypotheses, many of which are unpersuasive, although hard completely to refute (Hartwell 1967). What is generally accepted is that British industrialization resulted from prowess in technology and investment but ultimately depended on the institutions of a market economy that had their origins in the distant past (Mokyr 1993). While the structural changes and their implications for living standards can fairly be described as revolutionary, this does not detract from the point that the industrial revolution was the culmination of evolutionary changes that had been proceeding for centuries.

N.F.R. CRAFTS
LONDON SCHOOL OF ECONOMICS
AND POLITICAL SCIENCE

References

Carus-Wilson, E.M. (1941) 'An industrial revolution of the thirteenth century', *Economic History Review* 11.

Chenery, H.B. and Syrquin, M. (1975) *Patterns of Development, 1950–1970*, London.

Crafts, N.F.R. (1985) *British Economic Growth during the Industrial Revolution*, Oxford.

Freeman, C. (1987) *Technology Policy and Economic Performance*, London.

Hartwell, R.M. (ed.) (1967) *The Causes of the Industrial Revolution in England*, London.

Kuznets, S. (1966) *Modern Economic Growth: Rate, Structure and Spread*, New Haven, CT.

Mokyr, J. (ed.) (1993) *The British Industrial Revolution: An Economic Perspective*, Oxford.

Nef, J. (1932) *The Rise of the British Coal Industry*, 2 vols, London.

O'Brien, P.K. (1986) 'Do we have a typology for the study of European industrialization in the nineteenth century?' *Journal of European Economic History* 15.

Rostow, W.W. (1960) *The Stages of Economic Growth*, Cambridge, UK.

Further reading

Ashton, T.S. (1948) *The Industrial Revolution, 1760–1830*, London.

Maddison, A. (1982) *Phases of Capitalist Development*, Oxford.

More, C. (2000) *Understanding the Industrial Revolution*, London.

SEE ALSO: economic development; economic history; technology, sociology of

INDUSTRIAL SOCIOLOGY

Although industrial sociology's origins lie in the ideas of Marx, Weber and Durkheim, and perhaps beyond, as a discrete subject it really began only between the world wars, came to fruition in the late 1960s and early 1970s, and subsequently fragmented into myriad forms. Industrial sociology remains important, though it often masquerades under different labels, such as the sociology of work and organizational behaviour, or has become merged along with some elements of industrial relations into human resource management.

The history of industrial sociology can be read against the changing backdrop of the founding authorities. It might seem obvious that Marx, with his theory of proletarian revolution generated by alienation and exploitation, would prevail during the interwar period, when mass unemployment and economic crisis prevailed, but in fact Marx's influence was minimal: the limited success of the communist revolutions shifted the focus of many Marxists from industry to culture. Paradoxically, the Marxist approach to industrial sociology, primarily embedded in the Labour Process perspective (Thompson 1983) that developed in the 1970s, traces its roots to the same period when Taylor's 'scientific management' theory suggested that managers should separate the conception of work (a managerial task) from its execution (an employee's task). Taylor also suggested that economic incentives, channelled through individuals not groups, were the 'one best way' to motivate workers, and that, wherever possible, jobs should be deskilled to enhance productivity and reduce labour costs. It was Braverman's (1974) seminal work, *Labor and Monopoly Capital*, which argued that managerial control, premised upon Taylorism, was the benchmark of capitalist management, and from this point Marxists became increasingly interested in the employment relationship. The hegemony of the Labour Process approach disintegrated during the 1980s, with the New Right's political dominance, but it still remains an important strand of industrial sociology. However, much of it has transmuted to focus on management rather than the workers, its Marxist origins are now radically diluted, and it often operates under the umbrella term of 'Critical Management' (Alvesson and Willmott 2003).

Earlier on, the ideas of Durkheim, particularly his *The Division of Labor* (1933) with its notion of norms and solidarity, were more influential than Marx's. It was also the issue of social solidarity that led Elton Mayo (1946) to interpret the results of the interwar Hawthorne experiments as evidence of an irrational desire on the part of workers to form small groups. These experiments comprised a series of experimental, survey and anthropological approaches to worker behaviour. The results, considerably criticized then and now (Gillespie 1991), were nevertheless instrumental in the development of the Human Relations approach. Taylor's assertion, that the best way to manage people at work was by keeping them isolated from one another, had apparently been dealt a death blow, but since

individual contracts and payment systems came back into favour during and after the 1980s we must assume that Taylorism's death was much exaggerated. So too was Durkheim's, for although his influence waned during the 1970s it was never extinguished. It first found a home in the writings of Fox and Flanders (1969), and then provided an important foundation for the development of organizational symbolism (Turner 1990), thence into organizational culture and gender (Gherardi 1995), and finally into the role of emotion in organizations (Fineman 2003; Goleman 1999).

The interpretation of industrial phenomena, including symbols, was also at the heart of Weber's approach to industrial sociology. Disputing Marx's materialist explanation of the rise of capitalism, Weber (1948) argued that ideas also played a crucial role, particularly those associated with the Protestant work ethic. However, Weber's most telling analysis was reserved for his account of bureaucracy, and the crucial significance of rationality in the domination of 'legal rational' forms of authority, that is, those where legitimacy was rooted in formal rules and procedures. Subsequently challenged, originally by Gouldner (1954), and later in the attempts to debureaucratize work by reducing managerial hierarchies during the 1980s and 1990s, Weber's dire warnings about the decreasing significance of the individual within the 'iron cage of bureaucracy' still remain pertinent. Weber's triple heritage, in which ideas, interpretation and domination by experts prevail, later formed the crux of a series of non-Marxist approaches, ranging from the more phenomenologically oriented work of Silverman (1970) through to the rather more middle line taken by Goldthorpe *et al.* (1969) and more recently back to the role of bureaucracy (du Gay 2000).

Since the early 1990s, three new themes have emerged. First, the patriarchal overtones of much traditional industrial sociology have stimulated the rise of a feminist line of research. In this approach the assumption that 'work' can be reduced to blue-collar men employed in factories is sharply contrasted to, and linked with, both the unpaid domestic work of women and the rise of part-time women employed in clerical or service jobs. This has also stimulated an interest in the role of the work/life balance (HBR 2000; Rapaport *et al.* 2003). Furthermore, the very idea of technology as neutral and deterministic is shown to be an important element in the perpetuation of patriarchy (Wajcman 1991). Second, the collapse of communism, the globalization of industry (Stiglitz 2003), the shift from Fordism to post-Fordism, the developments of surveillance technology and the rise of unrestrained individualism in the 1980s, ushered in a renewed concern with the roles of expertise, norms, rationality and self-domination, often explicitly linked to the ideas of Foucault and other postmodernists (Fulop and Linstead 1999; Fevre 2003; Webster 2002). Third, the assumption that occupation and production are the keys to social identity has been challenged by counter-arguments suggesting that consumption patterns are the source of individual identity (du Gay 1995). Industrial sociology has certainly been transformed from its origins, but it retains an axial position in explaining contemporary life.

KEITH GRINT
UNIVERSITY OF OXFORD

References

Alvesson, M. and Willmott, H. (2003) *Critical Management*, London.
Braverman, H. (1974) *Labor and Monopoly Capital*, London.
Du Gay, P. (1995) *Consumption and Production at Work*, London.
—— (2000) *In Praise of Bureaucracy: Weber, Organization and Ethics*, London.
Durkheim, E. (1933) *The Division of Labor*, New York.
Fevre, R. (2003) *The New Sociology of Economic Behaviour*, London.
Fineman, S. (2003) *Understanding Emotion at Work*, Sage.
Fox, A. and Flanders, A. (1969) 'The reform of collective bargaining: From Donovan to Durkheim', *British Journal of Industrial Relations* 2.
Fulop, L. and Linstead, S. (1999) *Management – A Critical Text*, London.
Gherardi, S. (1995) *Gender, Symbolism and Organizational Cultures*, London.
Gillespie, R. (1991) *Manufacturing Knowledge*, Cambridge, MA.
Goldthorpe, J.H., Lockwood, D., Bechhofer, F. and Platt, J. (1969) *The Affluent Worker*, London.
Goleman, D. (1999) *Working with Emotional Intelligence*, New York
Gouldner, A.W. (1954) *Patterns of Industrial Bureaucracy*, New York.
Harvard Business Review (HBR) (2000) *Harvard Business Review on Work and Life Balance*, Boston.
Mayo, E. (1946) *The Human Problems of an Industrial Civilization*, London.
Rapaport, R., Bailyn, L., Fletcher, J.K. and Pruitt, B.H. (2003) *Beyond Work–Family Balance*, New York
Silverman, D. (1970) *The Theory of Organizations*, London
Stiglitz, J.E. (2003) *Globalization and Its Discontents*, London.
Thompson, P. (1983) *The Nature of Work*, London.
Turner, B. (1990) *Organizational Symbolism*, Berlin.
Wajcman, J. (1991) *Feminism Confronts Technology*, Cambridge, UK.
Weber, M. (1948) *From Max Weber*, eds H.H. Gerth and C.W. Mills, London.
Webster, F. (2002) *Theories of the Information Society*, London.

Further reading

Alvesson, M. and Deetz, S.A. (2000) *Doing Critical Management Research*, London.
Grint, K. (1998) *The Sociology of Work*, 2nd edn, Cambridge, UK.
Watson, T.J. (1995) *Sociology: Work and Industry*, London.

SEE ALSO: industrial and organizational psychology; industrial organization; industrial relations; information society; trade unions

INFLATION AND DEFLATION

Milton Friedman's famous proposition that inflation is always and everywhere a monetary phenomenon has much historical support (e.g. Friedman 1992; Burdekin and Weidenmier 2001). The rarity of sustained declines in consumer prices since the 1930s has, until recently, led economists to pay much less attention to deflation, however. Nevertheless just as inflation is the result of excess money growth, deflation implies insufficient money growth. That is, instead of too much money chasing too few goods we have too little money chasing too many goods. Consider the classical equation of exchange that equates the money supply multiplied by the velocity of circulation (the number of times the average currency unit changes hands in a given year) with the economy's gross domestic product (quantity of output produced multiplied by the price level). If the velocity of circulation and output are constant, there is a one-to-one relationship between a change in the money supply and a change in prices. That is, if the money supply doubles, prices double too (or, if the rate of money supply growth doubles, the rate of inflation doubles).

Of course, everything else will not be constant in practice. In fact, during inflationary times, velocity typically rises as people strive to unload currency faster before its purchasing power is eroded by higher goods prices. This reinforces the effects of faster money supply growth on inflation because, at the same time that more money is being printed, people want to hold even less of it than they did before the inflationary process began. In the extreme case of 'hyperinflation' (defined by Cagan 1956 as instances where the inflation rate exceeds 50 per cent per month), money holdings decline precipitously and the inflation rate significantly outstrips the rate of money supply growth. Conversely, under deflation, velocity is likely to fall as people hold onto their money more. After all, what is the rush to go out and buy non-essential goods and services? If you wait, the same funds will buy more and more goods and services over time if prices continue to decline. Thus, money demand rises as money supply falls, again exaggerating the effects of the money supply change on the aggregate price level. To the extent that expectations of deflation discourage current spending, deflation could, in fact, become self-sustaining as business activity declines. According to Keynes (1924): 'The wise man will be he who turns his assets into cash, withdraws from the risks and the exertions of activity, and awaits in country retirement the steady appreciation promised him in the value of his cash.'

The demand for money is also influenced by the economy's output level. If output rises, money demand should rise too as increased production generates more income and spending power. This would put downwards pressure on prices. The effects of inflation and deflation on output are less clear-cut than the effects on velocity, however. Inflation may initially boost output either if higher prices 'fool' producers into thinking there is more demand for their product or if selling prices rise faster than wage costs, thereby adding to profit margins. These beneficial effects will not prevail, however, and there is empirical support for the premise that inflation will eventually hurt output (Friedman 1977). The price mechanism cannot function well if prices become too unstable and, in the final analysis, resources will be diverted away from productive activity. For example, workers might insist on being paid multiple times a day and then leave work to spend the money immediately before it loses even more of its value. Such behaviour emerged in the latter stages of the great German hyperinflation after the First World War. Alternatively, people may quit their regular jobs to speculate on the massive short-run currency fluctuations, the Bolivian hyperinflation of the mid-1980s being a case in point. Ending such extreme inflationary episodes typically requires major institutional reforms to restore monetary and fiscal discipline, but regaining confidence in the money issuer will likely be an uphill task (Bernholz 2003).

Deflation may also hurt output. The short-run boost to output if prices rise faster than wages is reversed in a world where prices fall faster than wages. In this case profit margins fall and layoffs and unemployment are likely to follow. It is possible that these negative consequences could be eliminated over time if wage setting is adjusted to a new deflationary norm, but this would require acceptance of the idea of an annual cut in nominal wages (rather than an annual wage *increase*) and may not be easily achieved. Another concern with deflation is that the costs of servicing debt go up as the given debt is repaid with more valuable dollars. Fisher (1933) points to declines in goods prices being closely linked to declines in asset prices, with higher real debt burdens leading to rising default rates and bankruptcy. Collateral constraints could also come into play. In post-1990 Japan, for example, as land prices and share prices plunged, loan collateral was wiped out as well. Bank balance sheets also suffered from direct bank exposure to the stock market in this case, magnifying the developing bad debt problem and making banks still less willing to make new loans.

Deflation poses greater technical challenges for monetary policy-makers than inflation (Burdekin and Siklos 2004). In the case of inflation, policy-makers can tighten monetary policy and raise interest rates to higher and higher levels until the inflation is squelched. Thus, for example, the US Federal Reserve under Paul Volcker allowed interest rates to rise above 20 per cent in the early 1980s. While such a move may be costly for output and unemployment in the short run, as certainly seemed to be case with Volcker's experience, there is no limit to how high rates can be raised if the will to do so exists. On the other hand, fighting deflation requires loosening monetary policy and cutting interest rates. But here monetary policy-makers must confront the zero lower bound on nominal interest rates. Even if rates are cut to zero, as they were in Japan, borrowing costs can remain high in real terms in the face of deflation. Combined with the risk of deflation becoming partially self-sustaining through falling velocity and the postponement of spending, this means big concerns for policy-makers. Domingo Cavallo, who faced extremes of both inflationary and deflationary pressures as a policy-maker in Argentina, even remarked: 'I always thought that stopping falling prices would be easy....But I realize now that stopping hyper-inflation was the easy part' (Luhnow and Druck-erman 2001).

The Federal Open Market Committee meeting of 6 May 2003 gave official notice of the Fed's concern that 'the probability of an unwelcome substantial fall in inflation, though minor, exceeds that of a pickup in inflation from its already low level'. This represented, to say the least, a rather profound shift from the entire postwar focus on fighting inflation. It is true that falling goods prices could be triggered by any number of factors, including not only a drop in asset prices but also positive supply shocks that raise the economy's output level, thereby putting downwards pressure on prices even as production increases. Whether this really allows for the possibility of 'good' deflation rather than 'bad' deflation is debatable. But, in any event, sustained deflation is possible only when the rate of money growth falls behind the rate of growth of output and money demand. Fed Chairman Alan Greenspan (1998) agrees:

> While asset price deflation can occur for a number of reasons, a persistent deflation in the prices of currently produced goods and services – just like a persistent increase in these prices – necessarily is, at its root, a monetary phenomenon.

Japan's recent experience with deflation actually reveals abundant evidence of a chronic shortfall of aggregate demand, with the long-lived period of decline dating back to an abrupt tightening in Japanese monetary policy at the end of the 1980s. Using a quantity theory-based approach, Hetzel (1999) points to a sudden shift from excess money creation in the 1980s to an overly restrictive monetary policy that lagged behind growth in money demand in the early 1990s. China, like Japan, fell into deflation in the second half of the 1990s. In China the sharp tightening of monetary policy in 1994 led to disinflation that turned into outright deflation in

consumer prices in 1998. Although China's real economy continued to perform much more robustly than Japan's, the People's Bank of China, like the Bank of Japan, was criticized for initially responding too weakly to deflationary pressures. With inflation near zero in parts of the euro zone in 2003, the risk of deflation, particularly in Germany, also led to concerns that the European Central Bank had not been aggressive enough in cutting interest rates.

RICHARD C.K. BURDEKIN
CLAREMONT MCKENNA COLLEGE

References

Bernholz, P. (2003) *Monetary Regimes and Inflation: History, Economic and Political Relationships*, Cheltenham, UK.

Burdekin, R.C.K. and Siklos, P.L. (eds) (2004) *Deflation*, Cambridge, UK.

Burdekin, R.C.K. and Weidenmier, M.D. (2001) 'Inflation is always and everywhere a monetary phenomenon: Richmond vs. Houston in 1864', *American Economic Review* 91 (December): 1,621–30.

Cagan, P. (1956) 'The monetary dynamics of hyperinflation', in M. Friedman (ed.) *Studies in the Quantity Theory of Money*, Chicago.

Fisher, I. (1933) 'The debt-deflation theory of great depressions', *Econometrica* 1 (October): 337–57.

Friedman, M. (1977) 'Nobel lecture: Inflation and unemployment', *Journal of Political Economy* 85 (June): 451–72.

—— (1992) *Money Mischief: Episodes in Monetary Policy*, New York.

Greenspan, A. (1998) 'Problems of price measurement, remarks at the Annual Meeting of the American Economic Association and the American Finance Association', Chicago, IL, 3 January (available from http://www.federalreserve.gov/boarddocs/speeches/1998/default.htm).

Hetzel, R.L. (1999) 'Japanese monetary policy: A quantity theory perspective', *Federal Reserve Bank of Richmond Economic Quarterly* 85 (winter): 1–25.

Keynes, J.M. (1924) *Monetary Reform*, New York.

Luhnow, D. and Druckerman, P. (2001) 'Long hailed as hero, reformer in Argentina sees his dream sour', *Wall Street Journal*, 4 December.

SEE ALSO: macroeconomic policy; macroeconomic theory; stagflation; supply-side economics

INFORMAL/SHADOW ECONOMY

There is a widespread feeling that in many countries the underground economy is of substantial size and that it has been growing rapidly in comparison with the official economy. This holds in particular for developing and transition economies, but also for developed OECD economies. One major concern is that government revenue is lost, since these underground activities are not taxed. On the other hand, underground economies are value-creating and introduce a dynamic element into the economy.

The underground economy is variously defined, but on the most common definition it comprises all productive (i.e. value-adding) activities that should be part of gross national product (GNP), but which are not officially recorded at present. This definition excludes activities not included in the GNP (e.g. housework). Further, the informal economy is not identical to tax evasion (which is mostly redistributive) nor to illegal activities (some activities are legal but are not subject to taxes and therefore tend not to be recorded).

Economists have devised a number of approaches to measure the size of the underground economy. The direct approaches are based on surveys and the audit of tax returns. The indirect approaches analyse the discrepancies between what would be 'normal' and what is actually observed with respect to spending, employment, the use of money and physical input (such as electricity). A more refined approach constructs a model [DYMIMIC (dynamic multiple indicator multiple causes) method] identifying the incentives and disincentives of work in the underground economy: the burden of taxation and social security contributions, expected punishment and the moral cost of being active in the illegal economy.

In the twenty-one OECD countries, the size of shadow economies is estimated using either the currency demand method or the DYMIMIC method (see Schneider and Enste 2000, 2002). In the years 2000–1, Greece had the largest shadow economy, constituting 28.5 per cent of 'official' GDP. At the other end of the scale, the informal economy in the USA constituted 8.7 per cent of 'official' GDP. On average, the shadow economy constituted 13.2 per cent of GDP in the OECD states in 1989–90 and this average grew to 16.7 per cent in 2001–2. This average increase of 3.5 percentage points was significantly less than that in twenty-two transition countries, where the informal economy grew by 9.9 percentage points of official GDP over the same period. Moreover, the relative size of the shadow economy decreased slightly in fourteen of the twenty-one OECD countries, though the decline varied from country, and in some countries, including Germany, attempts to stabilize or to shrink the shadow economy were apparently not successful.

Rises in tax and social security contributions constitute one of the main causes for the increase in the shadow economy (Schneider and Enste 2000). Since taxes affect labour–leisure choices and also stimulate labour supply in the shadow economy, or the untaxed sector of the economy, the distortion of this choice is of major concern to economists. The bigger the difference between the total cost of labour in the official economy and after-tax earnings (from work), the greater is the incentive to avoid this difference and to work in the shadow economy. This difference depends broadly on the social security system and the overall tax burden, but even substantial tax reductions do not lead to a substantial decrease in the shadow economy. These measures may at best stabilize the size of the shadow economy and inhibit further growth. Social networks and personal relationships, the high profit from irregular activities and associated investments in real and human capital may make people reluctant to transfer to the official economy.

In neo-classical models the most important factor is the marginal tax rate. The higher the marginal tax rate is, the more significant the substitution effect and the greater the distortion of the labour–leisure decision. Especially when taking into account that the individual can also receive income in the shadow economy, the substitution effect is definitely greater than the income effect and, hence, the individual works less in the official sector. The overall efficiency of the economy is therefore generally lower and the distortion leads to a welfare loss (according to official GNP and taxation). However, welfare might also be viewed as increasing if the welfare of those who work in the shadow economy is taken into account.

The freedom of choice of individuals engaged in the official economy is further reduced by the increase in the intensity of regulations, often measured in the numbers of laws and regulations, like licence requirements. Regulations lead to a substantial increase in labour costs in the official economy. Since most of these costs can be shifted to the employees, they provide another incentive to work in the shadow economy, where they can be avoided (Johnson *et al*. 1998). Some governments nevertheless try to tackle the informal economy by introducing new laws and regulations, largely because this increases the power of bureaucrats and results in a higher rate of employment in the public sector.

There are many obstacles to overcome in measuring the size of the shadow economy (either in value added and/or in labour force units) and in analysing its consequences on the official economy, but some progress has been made. Research has shown that while it is difficult to estimate the size of the shadow economy it is not impossible, using methods such as the currency demand and the DYMIMIC approach.

FRIEDRICH SCHNEIDER
JOHANNES KEPLER UNIVERSITY OF LINZ, AUSTRIA

References

Johnson, S., Kaufmann, D. and Zoido-Lobatón, P. (1998) *Corruption, Public Finances and the Unofficial Economy*, Washington, DC.
Schneider, F. and Enste, D. (2000) 'Shadow economies: Size, causes, and consequences', *The Journal of Economic Literature* 38(1): 77–114.
—— (2002) *The Shadow Economy: An International Survey*, Cambridge, UK, and New York.

Further reading

Giles, D.E.A. (1999a) 'Measuring the hidden economy: Implications for econometric modelling', *Economic Journal* 109(456): 370–80.
—— (1999b) 'Modelling the hidden economy in the tax-gap in New Zealand', working paper, Department of Economics, University of Victoria, Canada.
Johnson, S., Kaufmann, D. and Shleifer, A. (1997) *The Unofficial Economy in Transition*, Washington, DC.
Johnson, S., Kaufmann, D. and Zoido-Lobatón, P. (1998) 'Regulatory discretion and the unofficial economy', *American Economic Review* 88(2): 387–92.
Lippert, O. and Walker, M. (eds) (1997) *The Underground Economy: Global Evidences of Its Size and Impact*, Vancouver, BC.
Schneider, F. (1994) 'Measuring the size and development of the shadow economy: Can the causes be found and the obstacles be overcome?' in H. Brandstaetter and W. Güth (eds) *Essays on Economic Psychology*, Berlin, pp. 193–212.
Tanzi, V. (1999) 'Uses and abuses of estimates of the underground economy', *Economic Journal* 109(456): 338–40.
Thomas, J.J. (1992) *Informal Economic Activity*, London.

SEE ALSO: national accounts; regulation

INFORMATION SOCIETY

The information society is a broad concept that has been used since the 1970s to refer to the growing centrality to social and economic development of equipment, techniques and know-how initially referred to as information technology (IT). This is associated with the convergence of computers, telecommunications and management science techniques, and highlights the increasingly pivotal role that electronic technologies play in the way individuals live, work, travel and entertain themselves. Since the 1990s, information society researchers have often added 'communication' to the term (from IT to ICT) to reflect the centrality of communication and networking issues, such as those stimulated by the diffusion of the Internet and World Wide Web (Castells 2000; Barabási 2002).

This concept is anchored in the work of many social scientists, including Fritz Machlup (1972) and Daniel Bell (1999). Bell posited information as the defining resource of the post-Second World War era, while raw materials were the core resource of the agricultural society and energy of the industrial society. In storing, processing, distributing and in other ways codifying information, ICTs were the defining technologies of Bell's postindustrial information society.

The use of the term information society has become so widespread that the concept cannot be understood as a reference to any specific thesis. Social scientists, politicians, journalists and futurists often use this term to denote a more ICT-centric society, in the same vein as others use such concepts as the network society, knowledge economy and the e-society.

The appropriation of this idea shows how important social science research on the information society has been in shaping policy and practice around the world. A view of the information society in terms of being a prescription rather than a forecast has influenced many governments to seek to anticipate and nurture the information sector in local, national and regional economies. For example, the information society vision inspired initiatives in the USA, Europe and elsewhere in the 1990s to build modern information and communication infrastructures – the so-called 'information super-highway'.

The promotion of the super-highway concept also indicated a key limitation of a focus on 'information'. The highway analogy reflected a growing awareness of the significance of the communication element in an integrated and increasingly convergent set of information *and* communication technologies, which reshape tele-access not only to information, but also to people, services and technologies (Dutton 1999). This broader conception of ICTs reconfiguring access (physical and electronic) to a wider array of resources has been furthered by the spectacular growth since the mid-1990s in the use of the Internet and Web (Barabási 2002).

Within this broader context, the information society remains a central idea for social scientists interested in the role of ICTs in social and economic development, particularly in relation to the trends in postindustrial society identified by Bell (Castells 2000). The most significant of these include the growth of employment in information-related work; the rise of business and industry tied to the production, transmission and analysis of information; and the increasing centrality to decision-making of technical experts, that is managers and professionals skilled in the use of information for planning and analysis.

The most significant trend associated with the information society is a shift in the labour force, defined by the growth in information work tied to creating, using, distributing or otherwise working with data, information or knowledge. The range of this 'information work' has grown to include an expanding array of jobs, ranging from new occupations like Web designers, software engineers and Internet service providers to traditional professionals, such as teachers and researchers. ICTs are also becoming more central to old as well as new jobs, and in every sector of the economy, including agriculture and manufacturing.

The information sector does not replace other sectors, but forms a new layer of economic and social development. In this respect, the occupational shifts associated with the information society do not necessarily imply a decline in the relevance of primary or secondary sectors to national or global economies. Instead, it indicates a diminishing need for labour within these sectors, as ICTs are used to redesign the business and organizational processes through which work is accomplished.

A second key trend identified in postindustrial information societies is the increasing importance of knowledge as being critical to forecasting, planning and managing complex organizations and systems, using theoretical knowledge and methodological techniques such as systems theory, operations research, modelling and simulation. According to Bell, the complexity and scale of emerging social and economic systems requires systematic forecasting and foresight based on such knowledge work, rather than the previous reliance on common sense or reasoning derived from surveys and experiments. For example, many national initiatives aimed at promoting advances in new forms of electronically enabled science ('e-science') using the Internet, high-performance computing and the powerful 'Grid' distributed computing approach are based on an assumption that scientific progress depends on increasing capabilities of electronic networks to support activities such as computation, visualization and collaboration.

A third set of trends involves power shifts, particularly the growing prominence of a professional and managerial class – the knowledge workers. These are the individuals and groups who understand and know how to work with information systems, the Internet and other digital media. According to Bell, the relative power of experts should rise with the emergence of an information society.

This trend has been challenged by empirical research that has found ICTs are adopted and used in ways that reinforce existing structures of power and influence, rather than systematically centralizing or democratizing power, or advantaging technocrats (Danziger *et al.* 1982). Social scientists maintain that individuals, organizations, nations and other actors can use ICTs to reconfigure access to information, people, services or technologies in ways that could enhance their 'communicative power', such as by changing the architecture of networks or undermining existing gatekeepers (Garnham 1999). However, the long-range impact of such strategies is not determined by the technology. Instead, it unfolds in often unanticipated ways from the choices of numerous actors co-operating and competing in a variety of separate but interdependent arenas or 'ecology of games' (Dutton 1999; Dutton *et al.* 2003).

These hypothesized trends identified with the information society have been of enduring significance in the social sciences, even though there has been controversy over the development, historical underpinnings and even meaning of an information society. Many critics of Bell's theory have focused on the deterministic view of social change derived from his identification of information technology as central to long-term changes in society at the macro-level (Miles and Robins 1992). Nevertheless, the information society idea has led to a valuable shift in the focus of social science enquiry to consider all the social, political and economic factors that have shaped the design and use of ICTs – and the myriad outcomes tied to these innovations.

WILLIAM DUTTON
UNIVERSITY OF OXFORD

References

Barabási, A.-L. (2002) *Linked: The New Science of Networks*, Cambridge, MA.

Bell, D. (1999) *The Coming of the Post-Industrial Society: A Venture in Social Forecasting*, New York.

Castells, M. (2000) *The Rise of the Network Society: The Information Age: Economy, Society and Culture*, Vol. 1, 2nd edn, Oxford.

Danziger, J.N., Dutton, W.H., Kling, R. and Kraemer, K.L. (1982) *Computers and Politics*, New York.

Dutton, W.H. (ed.) (1999) *Society on the Line: Information Politics in the Digital Age*, Oxford and New York.

Dutton, W.H., Gillett, S.E., McKnight, L.W. and Peltu, M. (2003) 'Broadband internet: The power to reconfigure access', *Forum Discussion Paper No. 1*, Oxford Internet Institute, Oxford.

Garnham, N. (1999) 'Information politics: The study of communicative power', in W.H. Dutton (ed.) *Society on the Line: Information Politics in the Digital Age*, Oxford and New York.

Machlup, F. (1972) *The Production and Distribution of Knowledge in the United States*, Princeton, NJ.

Miles, I. and Robins, K. (1992) 'Making sense of information', in K. Robins (ed.) *Understanding Information*, London.

Further reading

Duff, A. (2000) *Information Society Studies*, London.

Webster, F. (1995) *Theories of the Information Society*, London.

SEE ALSO: mass media; postindustrial society

INSTINCT

Instinct means different things to different people, and its connotations vary from context to context. For example it can refer to reflexive yet purposeful action carried out 'without foresight of the ends and without education in the performance' (James 1890); to compelling urges such as the parental imperative typical of mammals; to skills whose practice requires experience, such as the web-building of a spider; to genetically inherited propensities, such as hunting ability in a bloodhound. Bateson (2000) lists nine senses of the word, and more shades could be added. Everyday conversation usually accommodates this variation of meaning without much misunderstanding, but in scientific contexts the assumption that the several senses entail one another has been a recurrent cause of confusion (Beer 1983).

Darwin

Although ideas of instinct can be traced back at least to Thomas Aquinas, current accounts of their provenance are most likely to start with Darwin. In *On the Origin of Species* (1964 [1859]) Darwin began his chapter on instinct by dodging the question of definition since 'several distinct mental functions are commonly embraced by the term'. He used the word to refer to impulsions, such as that which compels birds to migrate; to dispositions, such as tenacity in a dog; to feelings, such as empathy in a person; and in other senses. However, he also argued as though 'instinct' stood for something that combined several of its connotations in a single concept, licensing inference from one meaning to another. For example, he tended to assume that if there was evidence of heredity, this meant that the trait developed independently of the effects of experience. Conversely, if there was evidence of learning, this ruled out the possibility that instinct was in play. However, he saw no contradiction in a bird's possession of an inborn migratory drive, while having to learn the fly-path to follow; or in the fact that you can breed dogs for sheep-herding, say, although they still require extensive training if they are to be useful in actually herding any sheep.

In *The Descent of Man* (1948 [1871]) and *The Expression of Emotion in Man and Animals* (1988 [1872]) Darwin focused on instinct as the basis of feeling, wanting and willing. Thus construed as impulse to action instinct manifests itself as behaviour directed towards a goal. Yet if the only evidence for instinct, in this sense, is the goal-directedness of the behaviour for which it is supposed to account, then to explain the behaviour as the product of an instinct will amount to circular argument. Unless there are independently identifiable indices of instinct, such as physiology might provide, the inventory of an animal's instincts will reduce to an inventory of the goals towards which the animal's behaviour can be seen to be directed. However, different observers can differ about what and how many kinds of goal govern an animal's actions. Also the assumption is questionable that all the behaviour involved in pursuit of a particular goal is driven by a single and unified motivational system. These difficulties did not present themselves as problematic to Darwin when he invoked instinct to support his case for psychological continuity between beast and human. They have, however, been points of contention for subsequent theories of instinct, such as those of Freud, McDougall and classical ethology.

Freud

Sigmund Freud wrote in German. That language has the word *Instinkt*. But the term that English translations of Freud have rendered as 'instinct' is usually *Trieb*. While *Instinkt* generally refers to automatic, unlearned, stereotyped response to a specific stimulus, and hence is close to the English 'reflex', *Trieb* connotes urge, impulsion, desire, and what in motivational psychology is called 'drive'.

Problems of translation aside, Freud clearly held different theories of instinct at different times. Early on he took the biological view that there are two basic instinctive forces governing life: the drives for self-preservation and reproduction. When he later abandoned his attempt to account for mental life in physiological terms, he argued as though there were a single supply of psychic energy, the libido, which fuelled the agencies of the id, ego and superego, with their rival imperatives of appetite, accommodation and morality (Freud 1953–74 [1923]). Alongside this he reconstituted a dual system consisting of contending instincts for life (*eros*) and death (*thanatos*) (Freud 1953–74 [1920]).

For Freud the manifest goals of overt action were false guides to the underlying instincts, since experience works through the ego to suppress or disguise their free expression, largely in accordance with social constraints. Only through

therapeutic analysis, utilizing free association, dream interpretation and transference, can the true inner dynamics of human action and mental life be uncovered.

Freud wrote at times as though instinct were a kind of blind energy, at least analogous to the energy of physics, and at other times as though it were an intentional agent employing strategies in the pursuit of ends. He also made little effort to obtain independent empirical evidence for his theories. Consequently, to some critics, psychoanalysis lacks sufficient empirical anchorage and conceptual consistency to count as serious science (e.g. Crews 1998). Others have contended that Freud's reliance on outmoded nineteenth-century biology (e.g. Haekel's biogenetic 'law' – ontogeny recapitulates phylogeny – and Lamarck's doctrine of the inheritance of acquired characteristics), anthropology and other life sciences undermined the foundations of much of his theorizing (Kitcher 1992; Sulloway 1992). Psychoanalysis itself has come to question the soundness and utility of instinct theories. Without denying the existence of biologically grounded forces affecting behaviour and mental life, analysis such as Horney (1937) and the British 'object-relations' theorists (e.g. Kernberg 1976) have emphasized the roles of society, culture and interpersonal relationships in the development, differentiation and dynamics of the psyche (Kurzweil 1990).

McDougall

In his *Introduction to Social Psychology* (1908) William McDougall defined instinct as:

> An inherited or innate psychological disposition which determines its possessor to perceive, and to pay attention to, objects of a certain class, to experience an emotional excitement of a particular quality upon perceiving such an object, and to act in regard to it in a particular manner, or at least experience an impulse to such action.

He identified the three aspects of instinct with the functional divisions of the nervous system, yet maintained a psychophysical conception of the relationship between the material and the mental: perception, emotion and impulse, as mentally manifested, are not epiphenomena – incidental by-products of causal mechanism as T.H. Huxley (1874) had argued – but are essential to and active in the instigation, control and direction of instinctive action.

Although McDougall, as an instinct theorist, is often represented as ignoring effects of experience, he did allow that instincts are capable of being modified through learning. But he maintained that such modification is restricted to the cognitive (perceptual) and conative (volitional) components; the emotional core was assumed to be immutable. Accordingly he argued that identification of the distinct primary emotions provides the means of determining what instincts an animal possesses, which is a necessary preliminary to understanding the dependent complexes and secondary drives patterning behaviour and mind. He listed the primary emotions and hence principle instincts of humans, and speculated about their adaptive significance and hence evolutionary basis.

The plausibility of McDougall's theory led to a fashion for instinct in psychology and adjacent fields (e.g. Trotter 1919; Veblen 1914). However, there was divided opinion on the inventory of instincts, and no agreed way of deciding among the different proposals. Also McDougall's conception of the psychophysical nature of instinct led him, like Freud, to vacillate between accounts in terms of cause and effects, and accounts in terms of intentions and actions, and his theory gave little purchase for empirical verification or experimental test.

Behaviourist critics were provoked into an 'anti-instinct revolt'. This was led by Dunlap (1919) who argued that McDougall's theory was scientifically vitiated by appeal to unobservable subjective purposiveness. Other attacks struck at the assumption of innateness, contending that wherever evidence was available it supported a role of experience in behavioural development. By and large the behaviourists get the better of the debate in their insistence on the primacy of hard fact and the requirement of experimental testability. Even McDougall lost confidence in the explanatory value of instinct. His theory has little following today (however, see Boden 1972).

Ethology

Behaviourism's dismissal of instinct was countered by ethology's espousal of it. This began in the 1930s with Lorenz's publications (e.g. Lorenz 1937) and culminated in Tinbergen's *The Study of Instinct* (1951). Lorenz drew on animal behaviour characteristics that are like morphological features in being correlated with taxonomic relatedness in their distribution and variation. Such evidence of genetic basis implied for Lorenz the other instinctive attributes: such behaviour must be unlearned, endogenously patterned, internally primed by 'action-specific energy'. This action-specific energy was also supposed to drive 'appetitive behaviour' seeking 'sign stimuli' necessary for 'release' of the instinctive act, and to which the mechanism controlling the act is innately tuned (Lorenz 1950). Tinbergen (1951) built the components of this conception into a more comprehensive and integrated theoretical model in which each of the major functional categories of behaviour – foraging, anti-predator behaviour, reproductive behaviour and so forth – is organized hierarchically, the underlying machinery consisting of control centres receiving motivational energy from above and distributing it to other mechanisms below depending on the sequence of alternative sign stimuli encountered through the consequent appetitive behaviour. For Tinbergen the whole of such a functional system constituted an instinct, and to it he connected his conceptions of sensory and motor mechanisms, behavioural evolution, development, adaptive function and social interaction to forge the classical ethological synthesis.

The next phase of ethology's history involved the dismantling of much of this theorizing. Both within and without ethology critics pointed out discrepancies between the quasi-hydraulic features of the models and what was known of how nervous systems actually work; the inadequacy of unitary motivational theories of the ethological sort to accommodate the full complexity of behavioural fact (e.g. Hinde 1960); and the fallaciousness of basing developmental and motivational inferences on evidence of hereditary transmission (e.g. Lehrman 1953, 1970). Tough-minded reaction to what was perceived as tender-minded speculation led to conceptual reform to meet empirical demands, methodological refinement to bring experimental testing to bear on theoretical implications, and quantitative rigour to bring precision to behavioural analysis. Tinbergen (e.g. 1963) himself warned of the ambiguity of 'instinct' and emphasized the necessity of distinguishing between different kinds of question raised by behaviour. The conception of instinct as a form of motivational energy has been undercut by evidence that control of behaviour involves numerous factors, related in complex ways, in multitiered networks, as represented by the motivational models of McFarland (1989) and Toates (1986). Indeed ethologists now rarely invoke instinct, except to reflect on past uses and abuses (Dawkins 1995; Bateson 2000).

Evolutionary psychology

Despite Tinbergen's (1963) insistence that ethology should give equal attention to the several different questions he singles out, developments since his time have witnessed a concentration on how behaviour can be understood in terms of evolutionary selection pressures, exemplified by the 'selfish gene' approach of Richard Dawkins (1989). A comparable emphasis on the genetic determination of behaviour marked the 'sociobiology' of E.O. Wilson (1975) and its offshoot, 'evolutionary psychology' (Barkow *et al.* 1992; Plotkin 1997). Evolutionary psychology opposes what it calls the 'Standard Social Science Model' – according to which the human mind is a unitary, general-purpose device constructed by culture – with the view that the mind consists of a number of innately based, relatively independent modules fashioned by evolutionary pressures that acted on our Palaeolithic ancestors. Although these modules are rarely referred to as instincts they obviously conform to one of the classical connotations of the term. Steven Pinker has explicitly recognized the connection in the title of one of his books: *The Language Instinct* (1994). Critics complain that the confusions which confounded the nature/nurture controversy in the past continue to plague the current version stirred up by evolutionary psychology, especially with regard to the interactive complexity of developmental processes (Gottlieb 1992; Elman *et al.* 1999; Rose and Rose 2000). Apparently the idea of instinct has proved useful at a rough level of discourse, but scientists who study animal and human behaviour should take warning from its history. The notion of instinct has thrived on blurred distinctions, but to the detriment of intellectual coherence and consistency.

C.G. BEER
RUTGERS UNIVERSITY

References

Barkow, J., Cosmides, L. and Tooby, J. (eds) (1992) *The Adapted Mind*, New York.
Bateson, P.P.G. (2000) 'Taking the stink out of instinct', in H. Rose and S. Rose (eds) *Alas Poor Darwin*, London.
Beer, C.G. (1983) 'Darwin, instinct, and ethology', *Journal of the History of the Behavioral Sciences* 19.
Boden, M. (1972) *Purposive Explanation in Psychology*, Cambridge, MA.
Crews, F.C. (ed.) (1998) *Unauthorized Freud*, New York.
Darwin, C. (1948 [1871]) *The Descent of Man*, New York.
—— (1964 [1859]) *On the Origin of Species*, Cambridge, MA.
—— (1998 [1872]) *The Expression of Emotion in Man and Animals*, New York.
Dawkins, M.S. (1995) *Unravelling Animal Behaviour*, Harlow.
Dawkins, R. (1989) *The Selfish Gene*, 2nd edn, Oxford.
Dunlap, K. (1919) 'Are there instincts?' *Journal of Abnormal Psychology* 14.
Elman, J.L., Bates, E.A., Johnson, M.H., Karmiloff-Smith, A., Parisi, D. and Plunkett, K. (1999) *Rethinking Innateness*, Cambridge, MA.
Freud, S. (1953–74 [1920]) *Beyond the Pleasure Principle*, London.
—— (1953–74 [1923]) *The Ego and the Id*, London.
Gottlieb, G. (1992) *Individual Development and Evolution*, New York.
Hinde, R.A. (1960) 'Energy models of motivation', *Symposia of the Society for Experimental Biology* 14.
Horney, K. (1937) *The Neurotic Personality of Our Time*, New York.
Huxley, T.H. (1874) 'On the hypothesis that animals are automata and its history', *Fortnightly Review* 22.
James, W. (1890) *The Principles of Psychology*, New York.
Kernberg, O.F. (1976) *Object Relations Theory and Clinical Psychoanalysis*, New York.
Kitcher, P. (1992) *Freud's Dream*, Cambridge, MA.
Kurzweil, E. (1990) *The Freudians*, New Haven, CT.
Lehrman, D.S. (1953) 'A critique of Konrad Lorenz's theory of instinctive behavior', *Quarterly Review of Biology* 28.
—— (1970) 'Semantic and conceptual issues in the nature–nurture problem', in L.R. Aronson, E. Tobach, D.S. Lehrman and J.S. Rosenblatt (eds) *Development and Evolution of Behavior*, San Francisco.
Lorenz, K. (1937) 'Über die Bildung des Instinktbegriffes', *Naturwissenschaften* 25.
—— (1950) 'The comparative method in studying innate behaviour patterns', *Symposia of the Society for Experimental Biology* 4.
McDougall, W. (1908) *An Introduction to Social Psychology*, London.
McFarland, D. (1989) *Problems of Animal Behaviour*, Harlow.
Pinker, S. (1994) *The Language Instinct*, New York.
Plotkin, H. (1997) *Evolution in Mind*, Cambridge, MA.

Rose, H. and Rose, S. (eds) (2000) *Alas Poor Darwin*, London.

Sulloway, F.J. (1992) *Freud: Biologist of the Mind*, Cambridge, MA.

Tinbergen, N. (1951) *The Study of Instinct*, Oxford.

—— (1963) 'On the aims and methods of ethology', *Zeitschrift für Tierpsychologie* 20.

Toates, F. (1986) *Motivational Systems*, Cambridge.

Trotter, W. (1919) *Instincts of the Herd in Peace and War*, New York.

Veblen, T. (1914) *The Instinct of Workmanship and the State of the Industrial Arts*, New York.

Wilson, E.O. (1975) *Sociobiology*, Cambridge, MA.

SEE ALSO: Darwin; evolutionary psychology; Freud; genetics and behaviour; physiological psychology

INSTITUTIONAL ECONOMICS

Institutional economics is concerned with the social systems that constrain the use and exchange of scarce resources. It attempts to explain both the emergence of alternative institutional arrangements and their consequences for economic performance.

By controlling the access of actors to resources, institutions affect economic performance in various ways:

1   Lack of control encourages wasteful attempts to accumulate wealth (consider open-access fisheries).

2   Credible controls lower the expectations of actors that their assets will be appropriated and reduce the expected transaction costs of protecting the assets, which in turn encourages specialization in production and long-term investments.

3   State controls shape the distribution of wealth.

4   Organization-specific controls influence the choice of economic organization (for instance, by outlawing certain ownership structures of firms).

5   Use-specific controls directly assign resources to particular activities, which may or may not be their most valued uses.

6   The structure of controls influences the long-term development of economic systems by affecting the relative value of investments and the nature of projects undertaken.

The social control of resources reflects the structure of institutions in communities. Institutions are human-made constraints that control and direct human interaction and consist of both formal rules such as laws and regulations and informal rules including norms and custom. Institutions are exogenous to individual actors, and the extent of social enforcement of the relevant rules determines the significance of particular institutions. The institutional structure varies both with people's social positions and with time, and in the long run actors may invest in attempts to alter their institutional environment.

The command that actors have over resources depends not only on the power granted them by social controls but also on power established through private controls (e.g. monitoring and enforcing contracts, fencing, or employing guards). These private efforts give rise to transaction costs, which are inversely related to the support provided by social controls. To further their ends, owners of resources contract to form organizations, but they are constrained by the institutional environment.

Until the 1980s standard economic analysis focused on exchange in secure markets. By limiting the enquiry to specific ideal type transactions – and by ignoring the complex factors of control, transaction costs, and incomplete information – economic theory could profitably deploy relatively simple mathematical methods and other powerful tools, particularly the rational choice model, assuming optimization subject to constraints, developing explanations of social outcomes in terms of individual behaviour (methodological individualism) and relying upon the concept of equilibrium.

Many institutional economists have long argued for the abandonment of standard economic method and analysis, but these critics have not developed a coherent alternative research programme for analysing economic performance and institutional change. However, attempts to use traditional economic analysis outside the setting of secure markets have frequently given misleading results, sometimes with serious consequences. Many scholars, not only in economics but also in other social sciences, have attempted to resolve the quandary by modifying and extending the traditional economic model to make it appropriate for general analysis of economic systems (Eggertsson 1990). Pioneering contributions were made by Alchian (1977 [1961]) on property rights, Coase (1937, 1960) on transaction costs, Coleman (1990) on social capital, North (1981) on historical institutional change, and Williamson (1985) on the logic of economic organization.

Attempts to develop a general economic theory of institutions, which gathered momentum in the 1980s, are still incomplete, but valuable lessons have been learned. An extended version of the standard economic approach, new institutional economics, which explicitly allows for incomplete information, transaction costs and property rights, has become a powerful tool for analysing transactions, economic performance and the logic of economic organization in various institutional environments. Increasingly, these modifications of the standard approach are recognized by mainstream economists, for instance in the field of industrial organization and contracts (Milgrom and Roberts 1992; Brousseau and Glachant 2002). Similarly, the economics of law has become a legitimate branch of economics (Cooter and Ulen 2004). New institutional economics has also had considerable success in analysing elements of institutional environments and institutional change. Transaction cost analysis and the rational choice model have provided important insights into the structure of democratic political organizations, such as legislatures, and the generation of formal rules (Alt and Shepsle 1990; Haggard and McCubbins 2001). Many studies have employed game theory to explore the nature, emergence and decay of informal institutions, such as norms and custom, giving special attention to explaining co-operation when enforcement by a third party is absent (Hechter and Opp 2001).

Yet it is particularly when it come to studying informal institutions that many scholars cast doubt on the usefulness of the new institutional economics. Informal institutions are closely related to the concept of preferences (tastes) in neoclassical economic theory, which builds on the core assumption of stable and exogenous preferences. The model of humankind and research methods employed in economics may be ill suited for explaining mentalities and the formation of social values. The concept of bounded rationality is an early attempt to modify the rational choice model, but in most applications bounded rationality is essentially equivalent to unlimited rationality with incomplete information and generates similar hypotheses. A more radical departure, and a logical extension of the information revolution in social science, attempts to explain the formation of shared mental models of the moral and physical world. Elements of new theories have emerged, in some instances drawing on evolutionary biology and cognitive science, but obvious breakthroughs and consensus on common approaches have yet to appear.

Institutional change can be either purposive or non-purposive. Usually changes in formal rules are purposive whereas informal institutions often emerge as unintended by-products of social interactions. One can envision a two-tier theory of institutional change for coping with both purposive and non-purposive change. The first level, the level of the individual, would apply theories of learning and of mentalities to explain how individuals perceive their environment, possibly employing findings in biology and the cognitive sciences. The second level, the social level, would treat mentalities as exogenous and apply some versions of the rational choice model and methodological individualism to analyse how actors respond to changes in their environments and how their responses are aggregated to produce social outcomes (Eggertsson 2004).

THRÁINN EGGERTSSON
UNIVERSITY OF ICELAND

References

Alchian, A.A. (1977 [1961]) 'Some economics of property rights', in *Economic Forces at Work*, Indianapolis, IN.

Alt, J.E. and Shepsle, K.A. (eds) (1990) *Perspectives on Positive Political Theory*, Cambridge, UK.

Brousseau, E. and Glachant, J.-M. (eds) (2002) *The Economics of Contract. Theory and Applications*, Cambridge, UK.

Coase, R.H. (1937) 'The nature of the firm', *Economica* 4.

—— (1960) 'The problem of social cost', *Journal of Law and Economics* 3.

Coleman, J.S. (1990) *Foundations of Social Theory*, Cambridge, MA.

Cooter, R. and Ulen, T. (2004) *Law and Economics*, 4th edn, Harlow, UK.

Eggertsson, T. (1990) *Economic Behaviour and Institutions*, Cambridge, UK.

—— (2004) *Imperfect Institutions. Limits and Opportunities for Reform*, Ann Arbor, MI.

Haggard, S. and McCubbins, M.D. (eds) (2001) *Presidents, Parliaments, and Policy*, Cambridge, UK.

Hechter, M. and Opp, K.-D. (eds) (2001) *Social Norms*, New York.

Milgrom, P. and Roberts, J. (1992) *Economics, Organization and Management*, Englewood Cliffs, NJ.

North, D.C. (1981) *Structure and Change in Economic History*, New York.

Williamson, O.E. (1985) *The Economic Institutions of Capitalism*, New York.

Further reading

Aoki, M. (2001) *Toward a Comparative Institutional Analysis*, Cambridge, MA.

Greif, A. (2004) *Institutional Theory and History: Comparative and Historical Analysis*, Cambridge, UK.

Libecap, G.D. (1989) *Contracting for Property Rights*, Cambridge, UK.

North, D.C. (1989) *Institutions, Institutional Change and Economic Performance*, Cambridge, UK.

Roland, G. (2000) *Transition and Economics: Politics, Markets, and Firms*, Cambridge, MA.

SEE ALSO: transaction costs

INTELLECTUALS

Why is the public so interested in intellectuals? Why the media profiles, the lecture series, the lionizing interviews, the outbreaks of character assassination? If an intellectual were simply someone occupationally involved in the creation or distribution of ideas, such celebrity-like attention would seem inexplicable. To explain it, we must consider the term 'intellectual' as standing less for a sociological category than for a normative ideal – an ideal whose empirical existence is always open to doubt.

It is generally agreed that the term 'intellectual' came into use in French in the 1890s as a result of the Dreyfus Affair. (The earlier development from the Russian 'intelligentsia' is a different if overlapping story.) Julien Benda, who participated in the defence of the falsely accused Dreyfus, proclaimed the heroic conception in *La Trahison des clercs* (1928 [1927]). The clerk or intellectual is defined in relation to power: he (as yet there is no she) speaks up heroically to and against power. But so immaculately idealistic an image calls out for its own defiling. Benda's title carries the swift and inevitable counter-charge: actually existing intellectuals are immediately held to acquiesce in and represent power. The evidence is there. Marxist intellectuals served Stalin; Macaulay served the British Empire. The clerk always betrays, as Regis Debray (1979) puts it. Some intellectuals have been real or aspiring political leaders, like Adam Mickiewicz in Poland, John Stuart Mill in Britain, Jose Rizal in the Philippines, and Leopold Senghor in Senegal. But viewed from an empirical, de-idealizing perspective, all intellectuals have access to at least some power, which is always the wrong kind of power. Thus they can always be seen as tainted by power.

Scholarship on intellectuals has grown increasingly impatient with the linked alternatives of idol-worship and desecration, the intellectual as a figure of (false) autonomy and of (too craven) servitude to power. Interest has shifted from figure to ground, from the 'free-floating' individual to the social landscape that surrounds him and anchors the meaning of his words, actions, postures, positions. What sort of power is it that the intellectual actually contests and/or possesses? When the novelist Emile Zola spoke up on behalf of Colonel Dreyfus, for example, he was seen as putting a reputation gained in the domain of literature to use in the very different domain of politics. In other words, it was against a backdrop of increased occupational specialization that the twentieth-century intellectual took on the role of one who crosses over – in Sartre's words, one who meddles in what is none of his business. In France, scholars have taken to mapping such transfers of cultural capital from field to field, as in Sartre's own case.

In Eastern Europe during the Cold War, on the other hand, the emergence of the intellectual-as-dissident presumed not so much an advanced division of labour as the opposition of an autocratic state. And so on. The whistle blower today presumes both a corporate bureaucracy and a more or less independent media. Michel Foucault's (1980) concept of the 'specific' intellectual and Antonio Gramsci's (1971 [1947]) concept of the 'organic' intellectual, though markedly different from each other, are both attempts to ground the intellectual in a distinctive and more precise vision of how modern power works. It is this new vision of the social field, rather than a simple retreat from grand universal claims, which gives both accounts of the intellectual their force.

Recent scholarship thus tends to affirm, with Didier Masseau (1994), that 'the man of letters doesn't exist outside of the institutions that form his social space'. For observers who cling to the heroic ideal, this sometimes implies that the intellectual or man of letters in fact does *not* exist – that the once-glorious figure has vanished along with Bohemia and the little magazines, absorbed into the banality of official institutions. In France, the institutional culprit is usually the media. In the USA, the institution most often blamed is the academy, which is said to have swallowed up all the would-be intellectuals and gently discouraged them from doing what true intellectuals must do: step outside their area of competence, write for more than one readership, worry about 'What is to be done?' Other observers claim that such activities persist, though modified to fit their contexts, in the university and even in the debased domain of corporate-owned and mass-mediated publicity. Moreover, they assert, such institutions have allowed for the emergence in significant numbers of intellectuals from previously under-represented constituencies. One such constituency is women, whose collective interest in the body and the constraints of biological reproduction had been excluded or downplayed by the ideal of the intellectual (associated with Benda, among others) as pure, disembodied spirituality. The recent success of the phrase 'public' intellectual, despite the apparent redundancy of the adjective, would seem to mark the recognition of new or previously unacknowledged forms of publicness – in the USA, for example, white majority acknowledgement of the large-scale presence of black intellectuals and of their valuable ability to define more capacious notions of racial identity for society at large.

Intellectuals frequently call upon other intellectuals to recognize and accept their 'responsibility'. The frequency with which this noun attaches itself to intellectuals is of course an index of their self-aggrandizement. For each call to responsibility, even in the form of severe self-chastisement, is also a claim that intellectuals possess a high mission or vocation, a significance beyond that of ordinary citizens. Controversy continues on the question of what authority this sense of mission rests upon. For many, an appeal to the authority of 'truth' (as in the formula 'speaking truth to power') has come to seem problematic. Can we assume that truth has the ability to compel power to *listen*? Can we assume that intellectuals have access, as politicians and media pundits do not, to a truth that is distinct from and higher than mere opinion? These assumptions seem unwarranted. Yet the word 'intellectual' continues to signify the demand for something like truthful speech, some way of being critical, distanced and oppositional, however paradoxical such a position may seem. The term confers honour, even if we cannot explain

how the social world we know permits such an honourable role to emerge or survive.

BRUCE ROBBINS
COLUMBIA UNIVERSITY

References

Benda, J. (1928 [1927]) *The Treason of the Intellectuals*, New York.
Debray, R. (1979) *Teachers, Writers, Celebrities: The Intellectuals of Modern France*, London.
Foucault, M. (1980) 'Truth and power', In C. Gordon (ed.) *Michel Foucault: Power/Knowledge: Selected Interviews and Other Writings 1972–1977*, New York.
Gramsci, A. (1971 [1947]) *Selections from the Prison Notebooks of Antonio Gramsci*, London.
Masseau, D. (1994) *L'Invention de l'intellectuel dans l'Europe du XVIIIe siècle*, Paris.

Further reading

Arac, J. (1990) 'Peculiarities of (the) English in the metanarratives of knowledge and power', in B. Robbins (ed.) *Intellectuals: Aesthetics, Politics, Academics*, Minneapolis, MI.
Jacoby, R. (1997) *The Last Intellectuals: American Culture in the Age of Academe*, New York.
Jennings, J. and Kemp-Welch, A (eds) (1997) *Intellectuals in Politics: From the Dreyfus Affair to Salman Rushdie*, London.
Mannheim, K. (1936) *Ideology and Utopia: An Introduction to the Sociology of Knowledge*, New York.
Said, E.W. (1994) *Representations of the Intellectual: The 1993 Reith Lectures*, New York.
Small, H. (ed.) (2002) *The Public Intellectual*, Oxford.

SEE ALSO: media and politics; public sphere

INTELLIGENCE AND INTELLIGENCE TESTING

The testing of intelligence has a long history (for psychology), going back to the turn of the century, when Binet in Paris attempted to select children who might profit from public education. Since that time the notion of intelligence has been the subject of considerable scrutiny, especially by Spearman in Britain in the 1930s, and of much and often bitter controversy.

The meaning of intelligence

Intelligence is defined as a general reasoning ability that can be used to solve a wide variety of problems. It is called general because it has been shown empirically that such an ability enters into a variety of tasks. In job selection, for example, the average correlation with occupational success and intelligence test scores is 0.3. This is a good indication of how general intelligence is, as an ability.

This general intelligence must be distinguished from other abilities such as verbal ability, numerical ability and perceptual speed. These are more specific abilities that, when combined with intelligence, can produce very different results. A journalist and engineer may have similar general intelligence but would differ on verbal and spatial ability. The illiterate scientist and innumerate arts student are well-known stereotypes illustrating the point (cf. Gardner's specification of seven types of intelligence (Gardner 1983)).

Intelligence tests

Most of our knowledge of intelligence has come about through the development and use of intelligence tests. In fact, intelligence is sometimes defined as that which intelligence tests measure. This is not as circular as it might appear: what intelligence tests measure is known from studies of those who score highly and those who do not, and from studies of what can be predicted from intelligence test scores. Indeed the very notion of intelligence as a general ability comes about from investigations of intelligence tests and other scores. Well-known tests of intelligence are the Wechsler scales (for adults and children), the Stanford–Binet test and the British Intelligence Scale. These are tests to be used with individuals. Well-known group tests are Raven's Matrices and Cattell's Culture Fair test.

The IQ (intelligence quotient) is a figure that makes any two scores immediately comparable. Scores at each age group are scaled such that the mean is 100 and the standard deviation is 15 in a normal distribution. Thus a score of 130 always means that the individual is two standard deviations beyond the norm, that is, in the top 2.5 per cent of the age group.

Modern intelligence tests have been developed through the use of factor analysis, a statistical method that can separate out dimensions underlying the observed differences of scores on different tests. When this is applied to a large collection of measures, an intelligence factor (or, strictly, factors, as we shall see) emerges that can be shown to run through almost all tests. Factor loadings show to what extent a test is related to a factor. Thus a test of vocabulary loads about 0.6, that is, it is correlated 0.6 with intelligence. Such loadings, of course, give a clear indication of the nature of intelligence.

The results of the most modern and technically adequate factor analysis can be summarized as follows (for a full description, see Cattell 1971). Intelligence breaks down into two components.

Fluid ability (g_f) is the basic reasoning ability that in Cattell's view is largely innate (but see below) and depends upon the neurological constitution of the brain. It is largely independent of learning and can be tested best by items that do not need knowledge for their solution. A typical fluid ability item is:

is to as is to...with a multiple choice of five drawings. An easy item (correct answer:).

Crystallized ability (g_c) is a fluid ability as it is evinced in a culture. In Cattell's view crystallized ability results from the investment of fluid ability in the skills valued by a culture. In Britain this involves the traditional academic disciplines, for example physics, mathematics, classics or languages. In later life, professional skills, as in law or medicine, may become the vehicles for crystallized ability. A typical Crystallized Ability Item is: Samson Agonistes is to Comus as Bacchae are to....A difficult item (correct answer: Cyclops).

Many social class differences in intelligence test scores and educational attainment are easily explicable in terms of these factors especially if we remember that many old-fashioned intelligence tests measure a mixture of these two factors. Thus in middle-class homes, where family values and cultural values are consonant, a child's fluid intelligence becomes invested in activities that the culture as a whole values (verbal ability, for example). Performance in education is thus close to the full ability, as measured by g(of the child. In children from homes where educational skills are not similarly encouraged there may be a considerable disparity between ability and achievement. On intelligence tests where crystallized ability is measured, social class differences are greater than on tests where fluid ability is assessed.

Thus a summary view of intelligence based on the factor analysis of abilities is that it is made up of two components: one a general reasoning ability, largely innate, the other, the set of skills resulting from investing this ability in a particular way. These are the two most important abilities. Others are perceptual speed, visualization ability and speed of retrieval from memory, a factor that affects how fluent we are in our ideas and words.

We are now in a position to examine some crucial issues in the area of intelligence and intelligence testing, issues that have often aroused considerable emotion but have been dealt with from bases of ignorance and prejudice rather than knowledge.

The heritability of intelligence

Positions on this controversial question polarize unfortunately around political positions. Opponents of the hereditary hypothesis were heartened by the evidence (now generally accepted) that Sir Cyril Burt had manufactured his twin data that supported this hypothesis. However, there are other more persuasive data, coming from biomentric analyses, which confirm this position.

First, what is the hereditary hypothesis? It claims that the variance in measured intelligence in Britain and the USA is attributable about 70 per cent to genetic factors and 30 per cent to environmental. It is very important to note that this work refers to variance within a particular population. If the environment were identical for individuals, variation due to the environment would be nought. This means that figures cannot be transported from culture to culture, or even from one historical period to another. This variance refers to population variance; it does not state that 70 per cent of the intelligence in an individual (whatever that means) is attributable to genetic factors. Finally, a crucial point is that interaction takes place with the environment; there is no claim that all variation is genetically determined.

These figures have been obtained from biometric analysis (brilliantly explicated by Cattell 1982) that involve examining the relationship of intelligence test scores of individuals of differing degrees of consanguinity, thus allowing variance to be attributed to within-family (found to be important) and between-family effects, as well as enabling the investigator to decide whether, given the data, assortative mating, or other genetic mechanisms, can be implicated. Work deriving from this approach is difficult to impugn.

Racial differences in intelligence

This is an even more controversial issue with potentially devastating political implications. Some social scientists feel that this is a case where research should be stopped, as for example with certain branches of nuclear physics and genetic engineering. Whether suppression of the truth or the search for it is ever justifiable is, of course, itself a moral dilemma.

The root of the problem lies in the inescapable fact that in the USA blacks score lower on intelligence tests than any other group. Fascists and members of ultra-right-wing movements have immediately interpreted this result as evidence of black inferiority. Opponents of this view have sought the cause in a variety of factors: that the tests are biased against blacks, because of the nature of their items – that blacks are not motivated to do tests set by whites; that the whole notion of testing is foreign to US black culture; that the depressed conditions and poverty of black families contribute to their low scores; that the prejudice against blacks creates a low level of self-esteem so that they do not perform as well as they might; that verbal stimulation in the black home is less than in that of whites. Jensen (1980) investigated the whole problem in great detail and many of these arguments were refuted by experimental evidence, especially the final point, for blacks do comparatively worse on non-verbal than verbal tests. But to argue that this is innate or biologically determined goes far beyond the evidence. Motivational factors and attitudes are difficult to measure, and may well play a part in depressing black scores (Steele and Aronson 1995). What is clear, however, is that on intelligence tests US blacks perform markedly less well than other racial or cultural groups, while these tests still predict individual success in professional, high-status occupations.

Importance of intelligence

Intelligence as measured by tests is important because in complex, technologically advanced societies it is a good predictor of academic and occupational success. That is why people attach great value to being intelligent. Cross-cultural studies of abilities in Africa, for example, have shown that the notion of intelligence is different from that in the West and is not there so highly regarded. Many skills in African societies may require quite different abilities. Thus as long as, in a society, it is evident that a variable contributes to success, that variable will be valued; and even though intelligence is but one of a plethora of personal attributes, there is, in the West, little hope that more reasoned attitudes to intelligence will prevail.

Two further points remain to be made. First, the fact that there is a considerable genetic component does not mean that the environment (family and education) do not affect intelligence test scores. It has clearly been shown that even with 80 per cent genetic determination, environmental causes can produce variations of up to 30 points in test scores.

Finally, the rather abstract statistically defined concept of intelligence is now being intensively studied in cognitive experimental psychology in an attempt to describe precisely the nature of this reasoning ability. Sternberg's (1982) analyses of analogous reasoning are good examples of this genre – the blending of psychometric and experimental psychology.

PAUL KLINE
UNIVERSITY OF EXETER

References

Cattell, R.B. (1971) *Abilities: Their Structure, Growth and Action*, New York.
—— (1982) *The Inheritance of Personality and Ability*, New York.
Gardner, H. (1983) *Frames of Mind*, New York.
Jensen, A.R. (1980) *Bias in Mental Testing*, Glencoe, IL.
Steele, C.M. and Aronson, J. (1995) 'Stereotype threat and the intellectual test performance of African-Americans', *Journal of Personality and Social Psychology* 69: 797–811.
Sternberg, R.J. (ed.) (1982) *Handbook of Human Intelligence*, Cambridge, UK.

Further reading

Gould, S.J. (1981) *The Mismeasure of Man*, New York.
Kline, P. (1992) *Intelligence: The Psychometric View*, London.
Neisser, U., Boodoo, G., Bouchard, T., Jr, Boykin, A.W., Brody, N., Ceci, S., Halpern, H., Loehlin, J., Perloff, R., Sternberg, R. and Urbina, S. (1996) 'Intelligence: Knowns and unknowns', *American Psychologist* 51: 77–101.
Resnick, R.B. (ed.) (1976) *The Nature of Intelligence*, Hillsdale, NJ.
Vernon, P.E. (1979) *Intelligence: Heredity and Environment*, San Francisco, CA.

SEE ALSO: problem-solving

INTEREST

The charge made (or price paid) for the use of loanable funds is called interest. The rate of interest is the amount payable, usually expressed as a percentage of the principal sum borrowed, per period of time, usually per month, quarter or year. Financial intermediaries such as banks will commonly both borrow and lend funds, their profitability being dependent on the difference between the rate that they are willing to pay depositors and the rate they charge borrowers. Interest rates may be calculated on a simple or a compound basis. Simple interest involves a percentage return on the principal per period, whereas compound interest involves a return based on both the principal and interest accumulated in previous periods. Interest rates may be fixed, in which case they stay constant throughout the period of the loan, or they may be variable, in which case they may be changed during the period of the loan. Some government or treasury ('index-linked') bonds pay interest linked to some measure of price inflation (e.g. a consumer price index) in order to protect the 'real value' or purchasing power of the interest paid.

The supply of loanable funds will depend on: the level of savings in the private sector; the rate of growth of bank lending; and, less commonly, on the size of the public financial surplus, which depends on the excess of government revenue over its expenditure. Demand for loanable funds can come from consumers, businesses and the government, due to the need to finance the Public Sector Deficit.

The charging of interest may be explained in a number of ways. First, the lender is entitled to a share of the profit resulting from the productive use of the loaned funds. Second, savers should be rewarded for abstaining from present consumption, which will probably be worth more to them than future consumption. Third, lenders should receive a fee for allowing someone else to borrow an asset that provides the service of liquidity. Fourth, lenders should be entitled to a risk premium, because they face the risk of non-repayment. These factors may also be used to explain the difference between lending and borrowing rates, and the fact that different types of financial assets bear different interest rates. In general, the shorter the term of the loan and the lower the risk, the lower the rate of interest.

There have been criticisms of the morality of charging interest in the form discussed above. Marx, for example, regarded interest as an element of surplus value, together with rent and profit, which accrued to finance capitalists and as such it stemmed directly from the exploitation of labour by capitalists. Marxist–Leninist regimes have typically had low interest rates, nominally to cover some of the costs of running banks and the payments mechanism. The charging of interest has also been condemned, at times, by followers of various religions, for example Christianity and Islam, the most reviled practices being those linked to private money lenders, usurers or Shylocks. Marxist objections, however, stem from social, rather than religious, ethics.

The growth of Islamic fundamentalism, in the 1980s and 1990s in Iran, Pakistan and Sudan, for example, revived criticism of Western-style interest charges. Islam clearly condemns usury, but there is some theological debate as to whether this means that interest rate charges in general should be prohibited. The reasons given for condemning such charges include their role in reinforcing the accumulation of wealth by the few, and thereby reducing people's concern for fellow humans; the fact that Islam does not permit gain from financial activity unless the beneficiary is also subject to risk of potential loss; and that Islam regards the accumulation of wealth through interest as selfish compared with that accumulated through hard work. These objections, especially the second, would rule out legally guaranteed regular interest payments. It would not, however, rule out equity investment, since this is subject to a return that varies with profit, and equity holders are subject to loss, although they are commonly protected through limited liability. In Pakistan attempts were made to develop an Islamic banking system in which returns are based on a profit and loss sharing principle, rather than regular guaranteed interest payments, and which are, therefore, akin to the returns on equities. Islamic financial instruments (e.g. mortgages) have become more widely available in the UK and elsewhere in recent years.

In Western economies with numerous financial assets there is a whole array of interest rates. These do, however, generaly tend to move up and down together (and they are related by a 'yield curve' – see below), and so it is possible to consider, in the abstract, the determination of the level of the rate of interest. Keynesian economists regard the interest rate as being determined by the equation of the demand for and supply of money. Classical economists claimed that it was determined by the interaction of the demand for funds, by investors, and the supply of funds, by savers. Keynes criticized this view, arguing that changes in national income were primarily instrumental in bringing about an equilibrium between savings and investment through their influence on the supply of, and demand for, loanable funds.

A distinction is often made between the nominal and the real interest rate. The real rate is the nominal rate less the expected rate of inflation; although it is sometimes approximated by subtracting the actual rate of inflation from the nominal rate or using the rate on the aforementioned 'index-linked' bonds. The concept of the 'natural rate' of interest is also often used. It is the rate of interest that would hold in an economy that was in a non-inflationary equilibrium. The rate of interest, being the contractual income expressed as a percentage of the nominal value of the security, is to be differentiated from the yield of a security, which is a percentage relationship of its income to its current market price. The 'yield curve' is used to depict the relationship between the interest rates (yields) of assets with different terms to maturity, that is, between short-, medium- and long-term financial assets.

Short-term interest rates are commonly set by the monetary authorities, increasingly in the form of an 'independent' central bank, such as the European Central Bank or the Federal Reserve System (Board of Governors) in the USA in pursuit of inflation and wider macroeconomic goals. 'Open-market operations' are required to maintain and effect changes in interest rates. These are normally conducted by buying and selling government or Treasury bills, and sometimes other securities (bills and bonds) with a short term to maturity (remaining life until redemption). Open-market operations can, however, be conducted in securities with a longer term to maturity, affecting the price and thus the interest rates of these 'longer dated' securities and thus the shape of the yield curve.

ANDY MULLINEUX
UNIVERSITY OF BIRMINGHAM

Further reading

Mishkin, F.S. (2001) *The Economics of Money, Banking and Financial Markets*, 6th (international) edn, Chapters 4 ('Understanding interest rates'), 5 ('The behaviour of interest rates') and 6 ('The risk and term structure of interest rates'), Boston.

SEE ALSO: capital, credit and money markets

INTEREST GROUPS AND LOBBYING

In broad terms interest groups (or pressure groups) are organizations that seek to influence public policy: that process of trying to achieve influence is 'lobbying'. US authors tend to use the term 'interest group' while the older British literature tended to 'pressure group'. There is no consensus as to whether these terms are describing discrete phenomena or whether they are synonymous.

The most important reason for studying interest groups relates to notions of democracy. The main contributions come from Dahl (e.g. 1989) who argued that interest groups are generally – though not necessarily – beneficial because they sustain a policy debate and influence political agendas. Of less theoretical significance, but of pioneering importance, was Truman's *The Governmental Process* (1951) in which he defined interests in terms of shared attitudes.

Interest group membership and the numbers of groups are generally thought to be on the increase, but the assumption that increased group competition results in a more open policy-making system has been contested. Gray and Lowery (1993) argue that whatever the *density* of group coverage, lack of *diversity* means a flawed contest.

Truman, Dahl and other pluralists regard the contribution of interest groups to the policy process more sympathetically. An important counter to Truman's work was Mancur Olson's *The Logic of Collective Action* (1965). Olson argued that to recruit members an organization had to supply *selective incentives* obtainable only by the membership and not rely on *collective goods* equally available to 'free riders' who did not join. Among explanations for group participation at levels higher than anticipated by the Olson argument are 'imperfect information' (the potential member is unaware of the irrelevance of their contribution); the avoidance of *collective*

bads; and the existence of an 'equity ethic' that drives individuals to make fair-share contributions (Walker 1991). Walker (1991) also points out that some groups rely on the contribution from patrons rather than membership subscriptions. Most importantly, there has been the extension of the rational choice approach beyond the simple economic cost–benefit analysis envisaged by Olson to include 'soft incentives' (Opp 1986).

Much attention has been given to the distinction between a party and an interest group, but this may not be the most interesting boundary area. One stereotypical notion of the interest group defines it as a voluntary association of individuals existing for the purpose of securing political goals, though some authors include associations of organizations as well as individuals. However, Salisbury (1984) showed that associations (especially of individuals) might be numerically few and politically marginalized in policy-making compared to state and local governments, corporations, think tanks, lobbyists, etc.

Authors who adopt a functional approach to the definition of an interest group include individual companies and bureaucratic units as such on the grounds that they attempt to influence policy. Such an approach is rejected by some authors who complain that sometimes every political institution acting politically is then seen as an interest group. Jordan *et al.* (1992) have suggested reserving the term interest group for multimember, politically oriented bodies and to use the term 'policy participant' for bodies such as a company acting politically.

If the collective (or otherwise) nature of the interest group has been controversial, another debate concerns the degree of organization. Those who accept the notion of the 'unorganized group' are operating in the same general area as those preferring the term 'social movement'.

Other important themes concern the relationship between the groups and government. In the 1980s this topic was dominated by the *corporatist* accounts of Schmitter and Lehmbruch (1979), and others who held that interest representation is organized in a formal way with the limited number of constituent units recognized by the state. In the 1990s more attention has been given in Britain to a *policy community* explanation that anticipates that there will be advantage to departments in co-operating over policy with specialist clienteles (Jordan and Richardson 1987).

The literature on lobbying echoes the same theme of mutual advantage between government and non-governmental bodies. The attention given to commercial or 'for hire' lobbyists (Jordan 1991), and lobbying of the legislature, should not obscure the direct and co-operative lobbying links between collective and corporate organizations, and the relevant sections of the bureaucracy. Lobbying is often not 'pressure' by external bodies on the executive, but the result of government looking for support and information among the affected groups.

Some commentators are critical of the involvement of groups in the policy process on the grounds that they threaten a public interest through biased mobilization or skewed resources. Berry (1984: 1) notes that interest groups constantly push government to enact policies that benefit small constituencies at the expense of the general public, which may appear to be anti-democratic. However, he suggests that, 'If the government does not allow people to pursue their self-interest, it takes away their political freedom.' A second argument about the usefulness of groups in democracy relates to the consequence of the act of participation *within* the group. The crude argument is that the 'habits of the heart' useful for democracies can be engendered in 'little democracies'.

Putnam argues that:

Civil associations contribute to the effectiveness and stability of democratic government....Internally, associations instil in their members habits of co-operation, solidarity, and public-spiritedness....Participation in civic organizations inculcates skills of co-operation as well as a sense of shared responsibility for collective endeavours....Externally, what twentieth-century political scientists have called 'interest articulation' and 'interest aggregation' are enhanced by a dense network of secondary associations.

(1993: 89–90)

Putnam's concern that group involvement is declining (hence *Bowling Alone*) was important in that this suggested a decline in the civic engagement underpinning democracy. The drop in memberships means, Putnam suggests, a drop in the opportunities for the development of social capital. Groups have perhaps in the past decade shifted from being objects of exaggerated normative suspicion to become instead bearers of unrealistic democratic expectations.

GRANT JORDAN
UNIVERSITY OF ABERDEEN

References

Berry, J (1984) *The Interest Group Society*, Boston.

Dahl, R. (1989) *Democracy and its Critics*, New Haven, CT.

Gray, V. and Lowery, D. (1993) 'The diversity of state interest group systems', *Political Research Quarterly* 46(1).

Jordan, G. (1991) *The Commercial Lobbyists*, Aberdeen.

Jordan, G., Maloney, W. and McLaughlin, A. (1992) *What is Studied When Pressure Groups Are Studied*, Working Paper no. 1, British Interest Group Project, Aberdeen University.

Jordan, G. and Richardson, J.J. (1987) *Government and Pressure Groups in Britain*, Oxford.

Olson, M. (1965) *The Logic of Collective Action*, Cambridge, MA.

Opp, K.-D. (1986) 'Soft incentives and collective action', *British Journal of Political Science* 16.

Putnam, R. (1993) *Making Democracy Work*, Princeton, NJ.

Salisbury, R.H. (1984) 'Interest representation: The dominance of interest groups', *American Political Science Review* 78(1).

Schmitter, P. and Lehmbruch, G. (eds) (1979) *Trends toward Corporatist Intermediation*, Beverly Hills, CA.

Truman, D.B. (1951) *The Governmental Process*, New York.

Walker, J.L. (1991) *Mobilizing Interest Groups in America*, Ann Arbor, MI.

Further reading

Baumgartner, F. and Leech, B. (1998) *Basic Interests*, Princeton, NJ.

Cigler, A. and Loomis, B. (eds) (2002) *Interest Group Politics*, 6th edn, Washington.

Dunleavy, P. (1991) *Democracy, Bureaucracy and Public Choice*, London.

Grant, W. (2000) *Pressure Groups, Politics and British Politics*, Basingstoke.

Heinz, J., Laumann, E., Nelson, R. and Salisbury, R. (1993) *The Hollow Core: Private Interests in National Policy Making*, Cambridge, MA.

Richardson, J. (ed.) (1993) *Pressure Groups*, Oxford.

—— (1999) 'Pressure groups and parties', in J. Hayward, B. Barry and A. Brown (eds) *The British Study of Politics*, Oxford.

Rothenberg, L.S. (1992) *Linking Citizens to Government*, New York.

Thomas, C. (ed.) (2001) *Political Parties and Interest Groups*, Boulder, CO.

Wilson, G.K. (1990) *Interest Groups*, Oxford.

SEE ALSO: public choice; representation, political

INTERNATIONAL INSTITUTIONS

Commonly known also as international organizations or international regimes, international institutions encompass such diverse entities as the United Nations, Greenpeace, and the international monetary regime. Although international institutions may be thought of conventionally only as international bodies that national governments agree to create and operate, practitioners and scholars have expanded the scope of the term to refer to both governmental and non-governmental organizations (NGOs), although some scholars prefer to call the former 'international institutions' and the latter 'international organizations'. The term international institutions, moreover, may include not only organizations that have well-defined rules, officers and physical office but also abstract rules and understandings that are shared among relevant actors. As recent scholarship demonstrates, the number and scope of international institutions have grown explosively since the 1940s (Boli and Thomas 1999; Sikkink and Smith 2002).

The study of international institutions has had its ups and downs throughout the past century, more or less reflecting the fate of the world it examines. The emergence of the League of Nations in 1919 sparked a creative burst of work on 'international government', but the initial optimistic phase was followed by a period of more cautious reassessment in the 1930s, only to gradually decline into obscurity thereafter. The study of international institutions re-emerged after the Second World War with renewed interest in formal institutions such as the United Nations (UN). Much research in the 1950s and 1960s continued to focus on the activities of formal organizations such as various UN agencies, and scholars were generally concerned with policy analysis and political commentary rather than with the development of theoretical insights. Interest in international institutions gained momentum in the 1970s when the issues of international political economy became more salient, challenging the then dominant paradigm of international relations: realism. In recent decades, the field's focus has moved away from a study of international institutions as organizational bodies, and research has addressed the under-lying causes of their existence and operation (Kratochwil and Ruggie 1986).

In the 1970s, as research increasingly came to focus on governing arrangements constructed by states to co-ordinate their expectations and behaviour, many researchers preferred the term international regimes, defined as the 'set of implicit or explicit principles, norms, rules, and decision-making procedures around which actors' expectations converge in a given area of international relations' (Krasner 1983: 2). Keohane, however, introduced the term international institutions, which became the term of choice for many scholars (Keohane 1986, 1988).

In recent years, divergent conceptions of international institutions have crystallized. On the one hand, international institutions are conceived of in behavioural terms, defined, for example, as 'explicit arrangements, negotiated among international actors, that prescribe, proscribe, and/or authorize behaviour' (Koremenos et al. 2001: 762). On the other hand, institutions are conceptualized in constitutive terms: they create actors and endow them with capabilities. Institutions are also characterized by some scholars as ideas that are shared by members of a collectivity. The different conceptualizations not only reflect the various ways in which international institutions affect international politics. They also indicate the particular theoretical orientations that scholars bring to their study.

The 1980s witnessed a sharp debate in the subfield of International Relations (IR) on whether international institutions really matter. This helped to clarify the differences between neo-realists, who emphasized the conflictual nature of international anarchy (i.e. the absence of an overarching authority that can make and enforce rules over states), and neo-liberals, who focused on the feasibility of co-operation under anarchy. Neo-realists argued that international institutions were a fleeting phenomenon, or at best a tool that a powerful state creates in its pursuit of its interest. Neo-liberals countered that institutions provided means with which states could overcome obstacles to co-operation. At the end of the decade scholars of both persuasions became more interested in delineating the conditions under which institutions would matter, instead of debating whether they matter (Baldwin 1993).

Following the sharp 'neo-neo debate' many researchers moved on to different theoretical questions. In what ways did these institutions matter? How did they relate to problems faced by states? The end of the Cold War raised new issues for the ongoing rationalist debate in IR, which once again pitted realists, who stressed the role of coercion, against liberals, who emphasized contractual relationships. It also opened up space for cultural and sociological perspectives (often referred to as constructivist) that emphasize the role of ideas and identity. Two broad theoretical tendencies emerged, their protagonists labelled rationalists and constructivists. The former rely on models drawn from game theory or on more broadly rationalist frameworks to explain the existence, forms or effects of international institutions in terms of an actor's calculation of the costs and benefits of choices made under a set of given constraints (Oye 1986). Constructivists focus on constitutive effects: the ways in which international institutions create actors, make possible certain actions or legitimize behaviour (Wendt 1999).

The kind of international institutions that receive scholarly attention is not completely dissociated from real-world events: the rise or salience of an international institution sparks academic enquiry, scholarly works sometimes serve as guides to future actions by the institution. Broadly speaking, four issue areas have preoccupied international institutions as well as scholars: political integration, international political economy, international security, and social and humanitarian issues. Political development in Europe in the early postwar period provoked a lively debate on the significance of political integration for the nation-state, as reflected in the famous question formulated by Hoffmann: 'obstinate or obsolete?' (Hoffmann 1966). Integration theory, as articulated by Haas, was dealt a severe blow in the 1960s when European efforts at regional integration stagnated after the Luxembourg Compromise and non-European efforts failed (Haas 1975). Empirical work on the European Community continued nevertheless, and with the acceleration of European integration in the past decade interest in the subject has revived (Checkel 2001; Hooghe 2001).

Institutions that govern international trade and finance have played a crucial role in international political economy, and organizations with a global reach like the World Trade Organization, World Bank and International Monetary Fund have received a great deal of attention. Studies of regional organizations such as the European Union, the North American Free Trade Agreement and the Asia-Pacific Economic Co-operation have also triggered a lively debate on the extent to which they facilitate or impede regional co-operation as well as on whether they represent a stumbling block or a building block of globalization.

Although realism initially allowed only a secondary role, if any, for international institutions in the issue area of security, international institutions are now recognized as an active agent in such diverse security operations as peacekeeping, non-proliferation, regional and global security. The continuation and expansion of security organizations in the post-Cold War world, for example NATO, has produced a lively debate among realists, liberals and constructivists about the causes of institutional persistence and adaptation (Walt 1997; Schimmelfennig 1998–9; Wallander 2000). Scholars have also begun to recognize the contributions that non-governmental organizations make to curtailing particular types of weapons or preventing or limiting conflicts (Finnemore 1996; Price 1998).

Social and human rights, and humanitarian issues represent the area in which non-governmental organizations have a prominent, and in some cases primary, role alongside governmental organizations. Many goals such as adequate nutrition, proper health care, women's rights and environmental protection are widely shared even if there are disagreements on specific programmes and implementation measures. The World Health Organization, the United Nations High Commissioner for Refugees, and the United Nations Conference on Environment and Development have all played a leading role in raising and addressing social and environmental concerns. Such NGOs as the International Committee of the Red Cross and Amnesty International have been working alone or in co-operation with governmental organizations to alleviate various forms of human suffering. Scholars have studied the ways in which NGOs contribute to social well-being and the extent to which NGOs and governmental bodies co-operate or compete (Risse-Kappen et al. 1999).

If progress has been made in understanding the ways in which institutions bring about positive effects that actors desire, some efforts are being directed at explaining unintended consequences or perverse effects of international institutions

(Gallarotti 1991; Barnett and Finnemore 1999). Yet although some international institutions, and notably the World Trade Organization (WTO), have been a focal point of global protest in recent years, the scholarly community has tended to avoid evaluative or normative assessment of these institutions (Held and McGrew 2002; Scholte and Schnabel 2002).

J.J. SUH
CORNELL UNIVERSITY

References

Baldwin, D.A. (1993) *Neorealism and Neoliberalism: The Contemporary Debate*, New York.

Barnett, M.N. and Finnemore, M. (1999) 'The politics, power, and pathologies of International Organizations', *International Organization* 53(4): 699–732.

Boli, J. and Thomas, G.M. (eds) (1999) *Constructing World Culture: International Nongovernmental Organizations since 1875*, Stanford, CA.

Checkel, J.T. (2001) 'Why comply? Social learning and European identity change', *International Organization* 55(3): 553–88.

Finnemore, M. (1996) *National Interests in International Society*, Ithaca, NY.

Gallarotti, G. (1991) 'The limits of international organization: Systematic failure in the management of international relations', *International Organization* 45(2): 183–220.

Haas, E.B. (1975) *The Obsolescence of Regional Integration Theory*, Berkeley, CA.

Held, D. and McGrew, A.G. (2002) *Governing Globalization: Power, Authority and Global Governance*, Cambridge, UK.

Hoffmann, S. (1966) 'Obstinate or obsolete? The fate of the nation-state and the case of Western Europe', *Daedalus* 95: 862–915.

Hooghe, L. (2001) *The European Commission and the Integration of Europe*, New York.

Keohane, R.O. (ed.) (1986) *Neorealism and Its Critics. The Political Economy of International Change*, New York.

—— (1988) 'International institutions: Two approaches', *International Studies Quarterly* 32: 379–96.

Koremenos, B., Lipson, C. and Snidal, D. (2001) 'The rational design of international institutions', *International Organization* 55(4): 761–99.

Krasner, S.D. (1983) *Structural Causes and Regime Consequences: Regimes as Intervening Variables. International Regimes*, Ithaca, NY.

Kratochwil, F. and Ruggie, J.G. (1986) 'International organization: A state of the art or the art of the state', *International Organization* 40: 753–75.

Oye, K.A. (ed.) (1986) *Cooperation under Anarchy*, Princeton, NJ.

Price, R. (1998) 'Reversing the gun sights: Transnational civil society targets land mines', *International Organization* 52(3): 613–44.

Risse-Kappen, T., Ropp, S.C. and Sikkink, K. (eds) (1999) *The Power of Human Rights: International Norms and Domestic Change*, Cambridge, UK.

Schimmelfennig, F. (1998–9) 'NATO enlargement: A constructivist explanation', *Security Studies* 8(2–3): 198–234.

Scholte, J.A. and Schnabel, A. (eds) (2002) *Civil Society and Global Finance*, London.

Sikkink, K. and Smith, J. (2002) 'Infrastructure for change: Transnational organizations, 1953–93', in S. Khagram, J. Riker and K. Sikkink (eds) *Restructuring World Politics: The Power of Transnational Agency and Norms*, Minneapolis, MN, pp. 24–44.

Wallander, C.A. (2000) 'Institutional assets and adaptability: NATO after the Cold War', *International Organization* 54(4): 705–35.

Walt, S.M. (1997) 'Why alliances endure or collapse', *Survival* 39(1): 156–79.

Wendt, A. (1999) *Social Theory of International Politics*, Cambridge, UK.

SEE ALSO: globalization; international monetary system; international relations; World Trade Organization

INTERNATIONAL MONETARY SYSTEM

International monetary relations developed in the early modern period – 1500 to 1700 – but there was no international monetary system (some set of rules more or less formally agreed upon by participants for effecting international payments) until after the emergence of the nation-state and national monies, together with the great growth of international trade and capital flows in the nineteenth century. It is therefore common and sensible to think in terms of the period from around the 1860s onwards when discussing the international monetary system.

Any international monetary system requires exchange-rate arrangements and perhaps some other institutions to facilitate payments, and a really good system will allow ready adjustment for balance-of-payments disequilibria. Various appropriate arrangements have emerged at different times. Sometimes these have been consciously designed, but more often they have simply appeared as the outcome of the forces at work. For example, it is obviously a short step from the use of commodity-based money to the acceptance of more formal rules and to a metallic standard, and then to the development of an international version of these mechanisms. Commodity money was used for a long period, and the later and more refined versions of this were bimetallic systems using both gold and silver. By the end of the nineteenth century most countries had adopted gold, a watered-down version of which lasted to the 1970s.

There are many accounts of the evolution of monetary regimes and of the determining factors in the transition from one to another. A regime can be thought of as a set of monetary arrangements and the public's reaction to them. In order to be sustainable, the arrangements should be internally consistent: monetary policy, fiscal policy and the exchange rate should be aligned with each other. They must also be credible to the public. Changes in the underlying conditions can produce the need for change in regimes.

In the period from the second half of the nineteenth century to the present time the international monetary system has had a number of different exchange-rate regimes, and there have been numerous deviations from the more commonly prevailing regimes. There were broadly five different regimes across the period. In the two decades before 1880 there was some competition between the bimetallic (gold and silver) standard and the gold standard. From about 1880 to the outbreak of the First World War the classical gold standard was supreme. That broke down on the outbreak of war, and was followed until the end of World War Two by a variety of attempts to cope in a world of turmoil. During the interwar period there was at first a free floating exchange system (1919–25/27); then came a restored but different gold standard – the gold exchange standard (1925–31/33); and finally there was a period of managed floating (1931/33–39).

These arrangements all had unsatisfactory features, and so an attempt was made to design a new system for the postwar years, which would draw on the strengths of the gold standard but would be more flexible. The Bretton Woods 'system' is usually said to have come into being in 1946, at least in its initial form, in which there was less than full convertibility of currencies. The essential idea was that the International Monetary Fund (IMF) would provide assistance to member countries to manage balance of payments in a way that was consistent with stable exchange rates. In fact the system did not get under way in the fashion that was planned, for the postwar world was not quite as the designers, working during the war, had anticipated. What did come into being was a pegged-rate dollar standard. This lasted until 1958, at which point currency convertibility was introduced. The new arrangements, with convertibility, broke down in 1971. Since the early 1970s the 'system' was essentially one of floating exchange rates, although periodic attempts have been made to escape what was seen as excessive volatility, involving the adoption of monetary unions, currency boards, dollarization and other measures.

Performance of regimes

How well have these different regimes performed? Some caution is needed in classifying the different regimes, and many different approaches to the question have been employed, though the broad classifications set out above should not provoke too much disagreement. Further, when performance assessment is done only in broad aggregate fashion there is less need for concern, although it should be borne in mind that the experience of particular countries may diverge significantly from the general trends. The three principal macroeconomic variables that are normally selected for investigation are exchange-rate variability, inflation and economic growth.

Unsurprisingly, there was greatest stability in the exchange rate under the classical gold standard, and during the Bretton Woods arrangements. That after all was essentially what these regimes did. They fixed exchange rates, and allowed other parts of the economy to take the strain. The period from 1914 to 1945 was one of political and economic turmoil. This was reflected in international economic variables and in these years variability in the exchange rate was greatest. In the years after 1971 there was initially high volatility but that has dropped to relatively moderate variability.

Inflation was lowest during the years of the gold standard and again during the second part of the Bretton Woods arrangements (1958–71). It peaked during the 1914–45 period, but after 1971 there were again phases of high inflation. Concerns about inflation led to a renewed search for a nominal anchor, particularly after the debacle of the European exchange-rate mechanism in the early 1990s. Inflation was brought down, and was then controlled by a variety of measures such as inflation targeting, central bank independence (the removal of political interference), greater openness in decision-making, and more accountability.

So far as economic growth is concerned, there is no evidence that any particular regime does better than another. This should not be surprising, since the exchange rate is simply a price reflecting relative national price levels. However, while low inflation is supposed to be good for growth, that does not show up in the statistics. The explanation is likely to be that there are many other factors at work that also influence growth.

International institutions

In recent years the phrase 'international financial architecture' has become popular. It is usually taken to refer to the structure of the international institutions that comprise the system. The principal institutions (in addition to the exchange-rate arrangements) are generally thought of as the International Monetary Fund (IMF), the Bank for International Settlements (BIS), established in 1929, and the World Bank. (There are some others; and there were others, some large, in the old Soviet Bloc.) These institutions came into being a long time ago and in spite of a changing world, and on occasions, an apparent loss of function, they have continued to grow. They have been subject to increased scrutiny in recent years. The IMF's role was originally to support the system of pegged exchange rates in the Bretton Woods period, but that role disappeared in the early 1970s when that system came to an end. The BIS's original role was to sort out German reparation payments after the First World War, but it evolved after 1950 to become part of the effort to provide stability. The World Bank was originally intended to promote recovery in industrial countries after the Second World War, but shifted its attention to the developing countries in the 1960s and 1970s. It has increasingly introduced commercial lending practices in place of subsidized lending.

International financial stability

After the sharp fluctuations in many variables in the 1970s talk of international financial stability began to be heard, but it was not always clear precisely what that implied. When economists think about the domestic economy, they consider the absence of financial crises and generally low volatility of financial variables to be important signs of financial stability. How do these factors translate to the international economy? What

does financial instability in the international economy mean? There are always likely to be all kinds of exchange-rate movements, some of them sharp, and these might cause difficulties of adjustment. On occasions, there will be debt problems where borrowing countries have difficulty servicing their foreign debt. But these are very different from the sorts of problems that may threaten the payments system in the domestic economy. In the domestic economy, if there are prudent banks and other financial institutions, and a lender of last resort to provide needed liquidity in times of crises, then stability is relatively straightforwardly achieved. In the international economy, matters are more complicated. For one thing, there is no single currency. The meaning of the lender of last resort is therefore cast into doubt, for there can be no provision of liquidity in its normal sense. There may be a contribution to be made by international institutions such as the IMF, but in a slightly different capacity, such as, for example, as a crisis manager. More generally their contribution is likely to come from the gathering and distribution of information, possibly the training of personnel, and as a forum for discussion.

Current and future

One major development in recent years has been the establishment of the European Monetary System. This has produced a monetary union with one currency and one central bank/monetary policy for most members of the European Union. Overall, the current international monetary system is a strange amalgam of different approaches to exchange-rates, and of institutions essentially designed for different purposes than those they are now carrying out. The current system is one of floating exchange rates. Some of these float freely while others are attempts at managing the float. A complaint that has often been heard is that there has been too much volatility in exchange-rate movement and that if left alone exchange rates will overshoot their true position, and that such overshooting can persist for long periods. It is sometimes claimed that such volatility damages trade and capital flows. Recommendations for improvement to the system have always been to hand and a popular move has been to adopt a target zone for the exchange rate, i.e. to allow it to fluctuate within some limits.

The vast majority of the roughly 200 countries in the world economy have floating rates. To be sure, there are only a handful of really important currencies: the US dollar, the Japanese yen, the euro and the pound sterling. These float against one another. Some commentators have suggested that the big three (the USA, Japan and now the euro) should fix their exchange rates against each other (based on some assessment of their purchasing power parity rate) and then pursue co-ordinated monetary policies to sustain these rates. A number of smaller countries choose to attach their currency formally or informally to one of these big currencies, sometimes by means of a currency board. Others attempt to escape from what they see as undesirable volatility by forming their own monetary unions. There can be no final settled outcome, because conditions are always changing. A continuing search is therefore likely, as changing conditions, objectives and interpretations of past experience emerge.

FORREST CAPIE
CITY UNIVERSITY, LONDON

Further reading

McKinnon, R.I. (1984) *An International Standard for Monetary Stabilization*, Washington, DC.
Mundell, R. (1983) 'International monetary options', *Cato Journal* (spring).
Williamson, J. and Miller, M.H. (1987) *Targets and Indicators: A Blueprint for the International Co-ordination of Economic Policy*, Washington, DC.

SEE ALSO: exchange rate; international trade; World Trade Organization

INTERNATIONAL RELATIONS

International relations (IR) emerged as a subdiscipline of political science in response to the transformation of international affairs during the nineteenth and early twentieth centuries, and took for its subject the analysis of interactions among states and other relevant actors in the global realm. It is multidisciplinary in character and draws traditionally from diplomatic history, political theory and international law as well as economics, and more recently from areas such as sociological, feminist or postmodern theory. IR is also a policy-oriented field, whose borders are increasingly challenged by the globalization of commerce and ideas.

By the end of the First World War, territorial entities competing with the nation-states (empires, city-states) had largely disappeared. States in the northern hemisphere had successfully monopolized external and internal means of violence and deployed military force in competition for regional and global power. The increasingly destructive and globalized force of war became the backdrop of the nascent social science of IR. The Second World War and the subsequent Cold War rivalry between two nuclear superpowers brought even greater focus on security issues, especially as the discipline evolved in the USA. IR scholarship focused on the following questions: What conditions cause or prevent interstate war? What are prudent actions for states in a world of anarchy?

In the same way that the nineteenth-century transformation of the international system led to the emergence of a state-centric view of international affairs, many of the post-Second World War developments in economic and political relations brought this focus on states and security into question. The challenge to state dominance emerged simultaneously from above (by intergovernmental organizations, IGOs) and from below (by non-governmental organizations, NGOs). The subsequent pluralization of IR generated new research in areas such as global trade and finance (international political economy, IPE), regional integration, or the global environment. Questions emerging from this perspective include: Under what conditions do states enter cooperative arrangements or even delegate control (sovereignty) to other entities? What are the domestic determinants of foreign policy? What is the role of transnational non-state actors? What forms of transnational governance emerge across the domestic, national and international spheres?

The new areas of enquiry further opened up IR to neighbouring fields (comparative politics) and disciplines (law, economics, sociology). Even as this development made the quest for a common methodological canon more elusive, it enriched IR as a field by integrating new and more critical voices into the mainstream. The following main sections use examples from three issue areas – security, welfare and governance – to illuminate this development. Mainstream theories such as neo-realism and rationalist institutionalism focus on interactions among rational and self-interested state actors at the systemic level. In contrast, liberal IR theorists (Moravcsik 1998) and foreign policy analysis dispute the unitary character of the state and explore the influence of various domestic actors (bureaucracies, societal interests) on international affairs. Finally, constructivism has recently questioned the analytical usefulness of 'objective' material conditions and state interests. Constructivists argue that material factors only become meaningful to actors when they are legitimized and reproduced in a social structure of shared understandings and expectations (Zehfuss 2002). On the basis of a more sociological version of institutionalism, constructivists see state actors frequently following a 'logic of appropriateness' (March and Olsen 1989) rather than a consequentialist logic of rational interest maximization.

Global security: war, peace and beyond

Until the early 1970s, IR in the USA was largely synonymous with security studies and (neo-)realism was the dominant theoretical perspective. Classical realism challenged idealist ideas of progressive international relations and developed a Hobbesian view to account for the persistence and brutality of interstate conflict (Morgenthau 1948). In 1979, Kenneth Waltz's *Theory of International Politics* developed a systemic analysis of international politics shaped by anarchy and different power capabilities of states. Anarchy creates a security dilemma for states, since any effort by one state to improve its security situation (by building armies or by entering an alliance) is seen as a direct threat to others. Within this neo-realist framework, scholars have debated the stability of uni-, bi- or multipolar international systems as well as the degree of co-operation possible under anarchy. Neo-realists debate whether states are more likely to maximize their autonomy or their influence under changing international conditions (Rittberger 2001).

The dominance of neo-realist theory created a fertile ground for alternative views (Keohane 1986). Sharing many neo-realist assumptions about states as unitary actors, a rationalist variant of institutionalist theory claimed that interdependence rather than anarchy was increasingly shaping international affairs (Keohane and Nye 1977). In the absence of a higher authority, institutionalists show how states are interested in developing rules and principles designed to facil-

itate collective action. International institutions (or 'regimes') play a crucial role by providing states with information, by lowering transaction costs for co-operation, and by monitoring compliance. Neo-realists either reject the idea that peace can be based on international institutions (Mearsheimer 2003), or refer any influence these institutions may exert to the interests of a hegemonic power like the USA. In the aftermath of the Cold War, the empirical challenges to neo-realism have grown as the international community continues to strengthen global and regional security institutions (e.g. the expansion of NATO and development of a EU foreign policy) and shows greater willingness to enforce shared standards (e.g. the increase in UN peacekeeping missions and humanitarian interventions). For institutionalists, the question is less whether or not institutions represent an independent force in international politics, but rather how they might become more efficient and effective.

Constructivist scholarship assigns even greater importance to institutions than do rational institutionalists. Constructivists do not take anarchy and power differences for granted, and explore how shared knowledge (as represented in international institutions) shapes the meaning of material factors as well as the interests and preferences of states (Wendt 1999). They point out that India and Pakistan feel more insecure as a result of their neighbour's development of nuclear weapons (as predicted by realists), but the same is not true for the relations between Great Britain and the USA. For constructivists, it is not the physical existence of nuclear weapons but their constructed meaning that drives international affairs.

There are other challenges to the state-centric and systemic view of international relations. A liberal view of international politics is expressed in the 'democratic peace thesis', which is based on the empirical claim that democracies do not go to war with each other (Huth and Allee 2003). Liberal IR theory focuses on the domestic realm (here: democracy/non-democracy) as the main explanatory variable for international outcomes. The eighteenth-century philosopher Immanuel Kant first suggested that a growing federation of republics with constitutional checks and balances would eventually create 'perpetual peace', because domestic economic and political interests would resist the disruptive force of war (Kant 1939 [1795]). More contemporary analyses focus on the greater transparency of decision-making processes in democracies and the recognition of another democracy as a part of the same in-group. Critics of the democratic peace thesis point to the ambiguous definition of the terms war and democracy, the willingness of democracies to attack non-democracies, and the possibility that simple random chance accounts for 'democratic peace'.

Foreign policy analysis follows the liberal preference for a domestic focus, but concentrates on the role of political leadership and bureaucratic politics. Allison's study of US decision-makers during the Cuban Missile Crisis undermined central neo-realist assumptions of states as unitary and rational actors. It drew attention to the decision-making process of policy-makers, bureaucratic infighting and the role of incomplete information and limited time (Allison and Zelikow 1999). Foreign-policy scholars have made important contributions to the study of international politics, by investigating the psychology and the perceptions of individual decision-makers (Jervis 1976), the role of group dynamics and the significance of interagency relations within the foreign policy establishment. In the past, the foreign-policy literature focused predominantly on the USA and produced mainly single-case studies. With the recent emergence of a more comparative perspective, synergies between foreign-policy analysis and IR are more likely to emerge (Hermann and Sundelius 2003).

Beyond interstate security, critical scholarship has focused attention on individual dimensions of security as well as the role of transnational non-state actors in fostering or undermining international peace. These challenges have emerged as the proliferation of small arms fuels a growing number of civil wars, which are today the main threat to the lives of innocent civilians (Holsti 1996). Moreover, outside of the USA, many states faced threats to their security from non-governmental agents such as terrorists or transnational crime long before 11 September 2001. On the other side of the spectrum, scholars have highlighted the influence of transnational peace and disarmament movements during the Cold War period (Evangelista 1999). Inspired by the constructivist turn in IR, scholars have shown how the social environment of states is affected by the principled mobilization of such activists and organizations.

Feminist scholars have also advocated a fundamental shift of perspective (Goldstein 2001). Mainstream feminists focus on the inclusion of women in all security areas, including combat, and are less concerned with using gender as a tool to change international politics. A competing, essentialist, view takes a more critical perspective on male practices in international affairs and argues that a greater participation of women would in itself contribute to more peaceful global conditions.

Finally, the growing influence of human rights issues in global affairs has led to the emergence of 'human security' as an alternative to national security. This concept is particularly relevant in the developing world, where the lives of millions are daily threatened by a lack of food and clean water. Such concerns have opened security studies to welfare and governance issues.

Welfare: global trade, economic integration and development disparities

The label economic globalization covers today not only international finance and trade, but also development disparities between rich and poor nations, issues that were traditionally treated separately but that nowadays are often brought together. The expansion of global trade has supported the claim of liberal institutionalists that international politics were increasingly shaped by economic interdependence. Institutionalists believe that free trade empowers domestic actors, increases global prosperity, spreads democracy and contributes to more peaceful interstate relations. Based on neo-classical economics (theory of comparative advantage), institutionalism and liberal IR theory identify domestic (economic) interests as the main force supporting or resisting international economic co-operation. For neo-realists (mercantilists), in contrast, economic development is subordinated to security concerns, and they take the view that trade is in the national interest only if it improves the security of the state (Krasner 1978).

Shifting the focus to the domestic realm increases the number of potential players and variables, but also creates the challenge of how best to bridge the domestic/international divide. Robert Putnam's metaphor of a 'two-level game' illuminates how state actors simultaneously bargain with societal interests at home and other state actors abroad (Putnam

1988). Other authors emphasize variation in domestic institutional arrangements to account for differences in the behaviour of states in foreign relations, investigating under what conditions interest groups are likely to become active, how institutional arrangements favour certain interests, and how particular demands may affect policy.

The challenge to neo-realism after the Second World War found its earliest and most significant empirical support in the economic integration of Western Europe. As one of the forerunners of constructivism, neo-functionalist and integration theories (Haas 1958) sought to identify the economic and social conditions shaping the interests of political actors. As the European integration process slowed in the late 1960s and other regions failed to follow, integration theories lost their appeal. After a resurgence of interest in the 1980s, current scholarship still debates the factors enabling the unique political development in Europe. While rational institutionalists highlight utility-maximizing decision-making in response to economic interdependence, constructivists claim that policy-makers were not primarily driven by considerations of economic interest, but were rather motivated by a powerful idea of a unified Europe (Parsons 2003).

The Marxist/Gramscian tradition has always rejected the artificial separation of politics and economics. Authors in this mould have proposed a structural analysis of capitalism bridging the domestic/international divide (Cox 1987), and argue that the diffusion of market ideas reinforces conditions of inequality and structural power between the rich and the poor nations (Strange 1996). Since the 1980s, these ideas have inspired transnational activists (Jubilee 2000, ATTAC) lobbying for a fairer global economic order. Major intergovernmental organizations such as the World Trade Organization (WTO) or the G8 summits are today regular staging grounds for global protests. Such activism has followed the internationalization of commerce by targeting multinational corporations on issues ranging from environmental destruction to unfair labour conditions (Brysk 2002). The issue has become a major focal point for the (re-)politicization of international economic relations and raises more general questions about the democratic legitimacy of global governance.

Governance issues: the state and its competitors

Despite – or perhaps even because of – the traditional state-centric view of IR, few mainstream scholars made the state (or governance issues more generally) a central object of analysis. However, scholars from developing nations have for some time pointed to the often fictitious character of state sovereignty and challenged assumptions of an international system populated by similar entities (Clapham 1996). A wave of state failures after the end of the Cold War has underscored the frailty of the international system and its constitutive units. The globalization of governance issues is also fuelled by the emergence of transnational NGOs and the growing autonomy of regional and global IGOs. Finally, developments internal to the discipline suggest strong links between governance and security issues. If democratic states are less likely to attack one of their own, for instance, then IR scholars can recommend the export of democracy as a high-priority foreign-policy goal.

Governance concerns issues that have previously been either off-limits (the domestic conduct of governments) or unthinkable (the delegation of sovereignty to higher authority) within a traditional IR framework. With regard to the domestic conduct of governments, the state has come under pressure from above and from below since the Universal Declaration of Human Rights established in 1948 a universal standard of norms shared by all member states of the United Nations. States are now answerable for their domestic conduct to both IGOs and domestic human rights activists. The most heinous crimes are universally condemned, and perpetrators may now be referred to the recently established International Criminal Court (ICC). While the international community has a far from perfect record, the post-Cold War increase in humanitarian interventions (Wheeler 2000) and United Nations peacekeeping missions indicates a growing willingness to enforce universally shared norms and principles.

In Europe, states have delegated significant parts of their sovereignty to supranational institutions like the European Court of Justice or the European Court of Human Rights. Democratic governance norms such as the civilian control of the military or the rejection of the death penalty are today undisputed requirements for each state aspiring to join the EU. In contrast to the pre-Second World War period, the domestic conduct of states is today a legitimate concern for the international community and the voluntary delegation of sovereignty no longer an inconceivable choice by a government.

IR research has focused on the role of both IGOs and transnational NGOs in shaping the emergence and implementation of international norms, and influencing domestic compliance with international norms (Klotz 1995). Scholars have focused here on the role of international institutions in representing and propagating certain ideals and models, which shape the identities and interests of state actors (Finnemore 1996). In addition, transnational non-state actors have been investigated for their ability to mobilize global public opinion as well as international institutions in the name of universal principles such as human rights (Keck and Sikkink 1998).

The future of IR

For decades, the disciplinary mainstream of IR, particularly in the USA, was shaped by (the threat of) global wars. In contrast, European IR as well as scholarship from the global South exhibited greater intellectual independence from the hegemony of the Cold War rivalry. The discipline evolved as a result of consecutive and increasingly bold challenges to the neo-realist paradigm. Rationalist institutionalism questioned the anarchic nature of international politics, liberal theory and transnationalism put in question the sharp divide between the domestic and the international realm, and constructivism highlighted the failure of traditional scholarship to take the social dimensions of global interactions seriously. As a result, the study of security, economics and governance has become more intertwined. IR today encompasses the study of both the domestic sources of international politics and the international as well as transnational factors shaping domestic outcomes. The future relevance of IR will depend on scholars' continued ability to embrace the interdisciplinary opportunities offered by the growing autonomy and influence of international institutions and non-state entities.

HANS PETER SCHMITZ
SYRACUSE UNIVERSITY

References

Allison, G.T. and Zelikow, P. (1999) *Essence of Decision. Explaining the Cuban Missile Crisis*, New York.

Brysk, A. (ed.) (2002) *Globalization and Human Rights*, Berkeley, CA.

Clapham, C. (1996) *Africa and the International System*, Cambridge.

Cox, R.W. (1987) *Production, Power, and World Order. Social Forces in the Making of History*, New York.

Evangelista, M. (1999) *Unarmed Forces. The Transnational Movement to End the Cold War*, Ithaca, NY.

Finnemore, M. (1996) *National Interests in International Society*, Ithaca, NY.

Goldstein, J.S. (2001) *War and Gender. How Gender Shapes the War System and Vice Versa*, Cambridge.

Haas, E.B. (1958) *The Uniting of Europe. Political, Social, and Economic Forces, 1950–1957*, Stanford, CA.

Hermann, M.G. and Sundelius, B. (eds) (2003) *Comparative Foreign Policy Analysis. Theories and Methods*, New York.

Holsti, K.J. (1996) *The State, War, and the State of War*, Cambridge.

Huth, P.K. and Allee, T.L. (2003) *The Democratic Peace and Territorial Conflict in the Twentieth Century*, Cambridge.

Jervis, R. (1976) *Perception and Misperception in International Politics*, Princeton, NJ.

Kant, I. (1939 [1795]) *Perpetual Peace*, New York.

Keck, M.E. and Sikkink, K. (1998) *Activists beyond Borders. Advocacy Networks in International Politics*, Ithaca, NY.

Keohane, R.O. (1986) *Neorealism and its Critics. The Political Economy of International Change*, New York.

Keohane, R.O. and Nye, J.S. (1977) *Power and Interdependence. World Politics in Transition*, Boston.

Klotz, A. (1995) *Norms in International Relations. The Struggle Against Apartheid*, Ithaca, NY.

Krasner, S.D. (1978) *Defending the National Interest. Raw Materials Investments and US Foreign Policy*, Princeton, NJ.

March, J.G. and Olsen, J.P. (1989) *Rediscovering Institutions. The Organizational Basis of Politics*, New York.

Mearsheimer, J.J. (2003) *The Tragedy of Great Power Politics*, New York.

Moravcsik, A. (1998) *The Choice for Europe. Social Purpose and State Power from Messina to Maastricht*, Ithaca, NY.

Morgenthau, H.J. (1948) *Politics among Nations. The Struggle for Power and Peace*, New York.

Parsons, C. (2003) *A Certain Idea of Europe*, Ithaca, NY.

Putnam, R. (1988) 'Diplomacy and domestic politics. The logic of two-level games', *International Organization* 42.

Rittberger, V. (ed.) (2001) *German Foreign Policy since Unification. Theories and Case Studies*, Manchester.

Strange, S. (1996) *The Retreat of the State. The*

Diffusion of Power in the World Economy, Cambridge.

Waltz, K.N. (1979) *Theory of International Politics*, Reading.

Wendt, A. (1999) *Social Theory of International Politics*, Cambridge.

Wheeler, N.J. (2000) *Saving Strangers. Humanitarian Intervention in International Society*, Oxford.

Zehfuss, M. (2002) *Constructivism in International Relations. The Politics of Reality*, Cambridge.

Further reading

Carlsnaes, W., Risse, T. and Simmons, B. (eds) (2002) *Handbook of International Relations*, London.

Elman, C. and Elman, M.F. (2003) *Progress in International Relations Theory. Appraising the Field*, Cambridge.

Hasenclever, A., Mayer, P. and Rittberger, V. (1997) *Theories of International Regimes*, Cambridge.

Katzenstein, P.J., Keohane, R.O. and Krasner, S.D. (eds) (1999) *Exploration and Contestation in Study of World Politics*, Cambridge.

SEE ALSO: conflict resolution; international institutions; international monetary system; peace studies; war studies

INTERNATIONAL TRADE

International trade is not intrinsically different from transactions in which commodities do not cross national boundaries. Nevertheless, the study of international trade has traditionally constituted a separate branch of microeconomics. It may be distinguished from other branches by its focus on situations where some but not all goods and factors are mobile between countries, and from international macroeconomics by its focus on real rather than nominal variables (trade flows and relative prices rather than exchange rates and money supplies), and by a tendency to examine medium-run issues using equilibrium analysis rather than short-run positions of disequilibrium.

One of the first and most durable contributions to the analysis of international trade is the principle of *comparative advantage* developed by David Ricardo in 1817. This is the antecedent of both the normative and positive strands of international trade theory. At a normative level, it postulates that an absolutely inefficient country will nevertheless gain from trade, and at a positive level, it predicts the direction of trade: each country will tend to export those goods that it produces relatively cheaply in the absence of trade. As an explanation of trade patterns, the principle has met with some success. However, in its classical form it is open to two objections: it assumes unrealistically that unit production costs are independent of scale or factor proportions; and it fails to explain why they differ between countries in the first place.

A theory that overcomes these deficiencies was developed in the first third of the twentieth century by the Swedish economists Eli Heckscher and Bertil Ohlin, who stressed international differences in *factor endowments* as the basis for comparative advantage and trade. Thus a country that is relatively capital-abundant will tend to export goods which are produced by relatively capital-intensive techniques. Largely through the influence of the US economist Paul Samuelson, a simplified version of this theory, assuming only two goods and two factors in each country, has come to dominate the textbooks. In this form it is a useful teaching device for introducing some basic concepts of general equilibrium theory but, not surprisingly, it is overwhelmingly rejected by the data. The most notable example of this is the so-called *Leontief Paradox*, an early application by Wassily Leontief of his technique of input–output analysis, which found that the presumably capital-abundant USA exported labour-intensive commodities, thus contradicting the theory. Nevertheless, for most economists the preferred explanation of trade patterns between countries at different levels of economic development is an eclectic theory of comparative advantage along Heckscher–Ohlin lines, allowing for many factors of production, some of them (such as natural resources) specific to individual sectors.

However, this theory fails to account adequately for certain features of contemporary international trade, especially between advanced economies with similar technology and factor endowments. Such trade is frequently *intraindustry*, involving both exports and imports of differentiated products within a single industry. Recent theories explain such trade in terms of imperfectly competitive firms producing under conditions of increasing returns. Attention has also focused on the increased international mobility of factors, in part through the medium of *multinational corporations*. The level of foreign direct investment, both in the form of 'greenfield' investment (building new plants) and cross-border mergers and acquisitions, has increased even more than that of trade in recent decades. The increased flows of goods, factors and ideas associated with these trends constrain domestic policy-makers, so posing a wide range of problems often grouped together under the catch-all term 'globalization'.

As well as attempting to explain the pattern of trade, positive trade theory also makes predictions about many aspects of open economies. Best known of these is the implication of the Heckscher–Ohlin model known as the *factor price equalization theorem*. This predicts that, under certain circumstances, free trade will equalize the prices of internationally immobile factors; more generally, it suggests that as more and more markets are opened to international trade, the remaining domestic markets become more exposed to foreign shocks and less to domestic ones. The theory also makes predictions concerning such issues as the effects of tariffs and international transfers on foreign and domestic prices, the effects of trade policy on domestic income distribution and the consequences of structural change.

Turning to normative trade theory, it has traditionally focused on the merits of free trade relative to autarky, stemming from a production gain (as the home economy specializes more according to its comparative advantage) and a consumption gain (as consumers are no longer constrained to consume only domestically produced goods). Similar arguments favour partially restricted trade relative to autarky, although the benefits of discriminatory trade liberalization (such as the formation of a customs union by a subgroup of countries) are not as clear-cut. Recent work on trade under imperfect competition has pointed towards additional sources of gain: trade may lead home firms to produce at lower cost and, by exposing them to foreign competition, at higher efficiency levels, and consumers may gain from increased diversity of choice.

Two exceptions to the case for free trade are normally admitted. The *optimal tariff argument* states that a country with sufficient market power can gain by behaving like a monopolist and restricting the supply of its exports. The *infant-industry argument* defends transitional protection to enable a new industry to benefit from learning and scale economies. (As with many arguments for trade restriction, the latter on closer examination is less an argument against free trade than against *laissez-faire*.) Recent work on *strategic trade policy* has added to these arguments the possibility that a government's ability to precommit to tariffs or subsidies may allow it to give an advantage to home firms competing against foreign rivals in oligopolistic markets. Notwithstanding these arguments for restricting trade, and the absence of conclusive empirical evidence in its favour, most economists subscribe to a pragmatic case for free trade, while recognizing that the benefits of rapid integration into the world economy may well be offset by the costs in the short run.

The persistence of protectionist sentiment, despite these theoretical arguments, may be explained by the fact that gains from trade accruing to the economy as a whole are not inconsistent with losses to individual groups, especially owners of factors specific to import-competing sectors. The textbook Heckscher–Ohlin model illustrates this principle with the *Stolper–Samuelson Theorem*, which predicts that (for example) increased imports of unskilled-labour-intensive goods will lower the wages of unskilled relative to skilled workers. Empirical evidence suggests that technological change rather than trade is the main culprit for the increased return to skills in developed countries. Nevertheless, organized workers and shareholders in import-competing industries, and other special interest groups, have incentives to lobby for protection, which may explain why trade remains considerably more restricted internationally than domestically.

Other special models have been developed to deal with important features of contemporary international trade. Thus, the growth of trade in intermediate goods (as opposed to goods for final consumption) has inspired the theory of *effective protection*, which builds on the insight that an industry benefits from tariffs on its outputs but is harmed by tariffs on its inputs. Changes in technology have made possible a process of vertical disintegration or *fragmentation* of production, as firms source their inputs from, or locate different parts of their production chain in, different countries. Falls in transport costs also appear to have encouraged *agglomeration* of economic activity, as firms locate near their competitors to benefit from lower input costs or improved access to consumers.

The enormous growth in world trade since the Second World War has been driven in part by steady declines in trade barriers. Some of these have taken place as a result of the formation of customs unions or free-trade agreements, such as the European Union (formerly the EEC) and the North American Free-Trade Agreement. However, most trade liberalization has resulted from multilateral negotiations under the auspices of the General Agreement on Tariffs and Trade (GATT), formally reconstituted in 1995 as the World Trade Organization (WTO). Successive rounds of negotiations have had to contend with new forms of trade restrictions, as the decline in importance of tariffs (at least between developed countries) has focused attention on the widespread use of *non-tariff barriers* (such as quotas, health and safety regulations, and government procurement policies) as methods of restricting trade.

J. PETER NEARY
UNIVERSITY COLLEGE DUBLIN

Further reading

Grossman, G. and Helpman, E. (2002) *Interest Groups and Trade Policy*, Princeton, NJ.
Grossman, G. and Rogoff, K. (eds) (1995) *Handbook of International Economics: Volume III*, Amsterdam.
Hoekman, B., Mattoo, A. and English, P. (eds) (2002) *Development, Trade, and the WTO: A Handbook*, Washington, DC.
Jones, R.W. and Kenen, P.B. (eds) (1984) *Handbook of International Economics: Volume I*, Amsterdam.

SEE ALSO: exchange rate; free trade; international monetary system; World Trade Organization

INTERVIEWS (QUALITATIVE)

An interview is literally an *inter view*, an exchange of views between two persons conversing about a theme of mutual interest (Kvale 1996). A research interview is a conversation with a structure and a purpose. It goes beyond the spontaneous exchange of views that occur in everyday conversations, and should be characterized by careful questioning and attentive listening, with the aim of obtaining thoroughly tested knowledge. A semi-structured life-world interview seeks to understand the world from the subjects' point of view, to unfold the meaning of people's experiences, and to uncover features of their lives as they understand and experience it.

Interviewing in the social sciences

Although conversation is a basic mode of human interaction, the interview is relatively new as a distinct method of obtaining knowledge. What was probably the first journalistic interview, conducted with the Mormon leader Brigham Young, was published in *The New York Herald Tribune* in 1859 (Silvester 1993). Qualitative research interviews were used in the social sciences throughout the twentieth century (Fielding 2003), in particular in anthropology and sociology. Interviews also provided significant contributions to psychological knowledge. Famous examples include Freud's psychoanalytic interviews, Piaget's interviews with children, the Hawthorne studies of human relations by way of qualitative interviews with more than 20,000 industrial workers, and the interviews carried out by Adorno and co-workers with authoritarian personalities (Kvale 2003). Interviews were, however, marginalized in textbooks on research methods. Only during the last quarter of a century have qualitative interviews been extensively discussed as a research method in the social sciences (Gubrium and Holstein 2002).

The increased use of interviews can be understood in relation to changes in conceptions of knowledge. Some social scientists came to favour phenomenological descriptions of experience and hermeneutical interpretations of meaning. More recently, constructivist approaches have emphasized the interrelational, conversational and linguistic aspects of knowledge. The widespread use of interviews is also linked to a consumer society, where systematic knowledge of the consumers' experiences, feelings, desires and lifestyles are essential for the manipulation of consumer behaviour by designing and marketing the meanings of consumer products. Qualitative interviews have long played a key role in marketing. 110,000 focus group interviews were conducted in 1990 alone (Greenbaum 1994).

Conceptions of the interview

We may distinguish two contrasting understandings of interviewing. In a *miner metaphor* knowledge is understood as buried metal and the interviewer is a miner who unearths the valuable metal to be processed. Nuggets of objective facts or essential meanings are uncovered from the subjects' interior, uncontaminated by the miner. An alternative *traveller metaphor* understands the interviewer as a traveller on a journey who wanders through a landscape and enters into conversations. What the traveller hears is transformed into stories to be told. The two metaphors relate respectively to empiricist conceptions of knowledge as given, and postmodern conceptions of knowledge as constructed, and each has different implications for how an interview investigation is conceived and carried out. In the first case, the interview is an instrument of data collection, and the crux is the later processing of the data that is collected. In the second case, the generation of meaning within the interview situation itself becomes the key issue.

The course of an interview investigation

Seven stages may be identified in the production of interviews. (1) *Thematizing* – formulate the purpose of an investigation and describe the conception of the topic to be investigated. The why and what of the investigation should be clarified before the question of how is posed and the method fixed upon. (2) *Designing* – plan the design of the study, and take into consideration all seven stages of the investigation before the interviewing starts. The design of the study is undertaken with a view to obtaining trustworthy knowledge, and takes into account the ethical implications of the study. (3) *Interviewing* – conduct the interviews on the basis of an interview guide and with a reflective approach to the knowledge sought and the interpersonal relation of the interview situation. (4) *Transcribing* – prepare the interview material for analysis, which commonly includes a transcription from oral speech to written text. (5) *Analysing* – decide, on the basis of the purpose and topic of the investigation, and on the nature of the interview material, which methods of analysis are appropriate for the interviews. (6) *Verifying* – ascertain the generalizability, reliability and validity of the interview findings. (7) *Reporting* – communicate the results of the study in a form that meets scientific criteria, and which provides a readable interview story.

Interviewing – twelve aspects of a semi-structured life world interview may be outlined. *Life world* – the topic of qualitative interviewing is the everyday lived world of the interviewee and his or her relation to it. *Meaning* – the interviewer registers and interprets the meaning of

what is said as well as how it is said. *Qualitative* – the interview seeks qualitative knowledge expressed in common language and does not aim at quantification. *Descriptive* – the interview attempts to obtain nuanced descriptions of different aspects of the life world. *Specificity* – descriptions of specific situations and action sequences are elicited, not general opinions. *Deliberate naiveté* – the interviewer exhibits openness to new and unexpected phenomena, rather than bringing ready-made categories and schemes of interpretation to the interview. *Focused* – the interview is focused on certain themes, but it is neither strictly structured, with standardized questions, nor entirely non-directive. *Ambiguity* – the statements of the interviewee may sometimes be ambiguous, reflecting contradictions in the world he or she lives in. *Change* – the process of being interviewed may produce new insights and awareness. In the course of the interview the subject may alter his or her descriptions and understandings. *Sensitivity* – different interviewers may produce different statements on the same themes, depending upon their sensitivity to and knowledge of the interview topic. *Interpersonal situation* – the knowledge obtained in an interview is produced through interpersonal interaction. *Positive experience* – a successful research interview may be a rare and enriching experience for the interviewee, who may obtain new insights into his or her life situation.

Interview forms

A diversity of interview forms exist, which vary with respect to structure, purpose, topic and subjects (see Flick 2002; Gubrium and Holstein 2002). A research interview may range from being firmly structured, using a questionnaire with a fixed wording and sequence of questions, to a non-directive interview, which after the opening question follows up the subject's answers. The most common form is a semi-structured interview, which follows an interview guide that sets topics to be treated and includes suggestions for questions and sequence, but which may be flexibly altered in the course of the interview. Research interviews may be exploratory and/or hypothesis testing. In therapeutic interviews, new knowledge may be gleaned as side-effects of helping patients to change. The interviews may primarily address the interviewees' experiences or their behaviours, or elicit narratives and life histories. Interviews may be with individuals or with groups, the latter often in the form of focus groups. Special considerations apply in interviewing certain groups, such as children and members of elites.

Interview quality

Given its deliberately flexible structure, the quality of a semi-structured interview depends on the knowledge and the interpersonal skills of the interviewer. The main measure of the quality of an interview is the extent of spontaneous, rich, specific and relevant answers elicited. In general, the shorter the interviewer's questions and the longer the subjects' answers the better, but the interviewer should follow up and clarify the meaning of the relevant aspects of the answers that are given. In an ideal 'traveller' interview, the interpretation is constructed in the course of the interview itself. The interviewer's interpretations of the subject's answers are verified in the course of the interchanges, and in the end the interview is a self-contained story that requires little more by way of commentary and explanations.

Analysing

Methods for the analysis of interview-produced texts include content analysis, categorization, meaning condensation, phenomenological analysis and hermeneutical interpretation, narrative analysis, discourse and conversational analysis. Novice researchers often ask, 'What method can I use to analyse the 1,000 pages of transcripts that I have collected?' The question is posed too late. Ideally, the mode of interviewing will follow from the mode of analysis that will later be applied. Quantitative content analysis and categorization will usually require more structured and probing interviewing techniques. Phenomenological and hermeneutical analysis, as well as narrative and discourse analysis, will allow for greater freedom and flexibility in following up the interviewees' statements.

Generalization, reliability and validity

Knowledge produced in interviews may be subjected to statistical generalization if a sufficient number of randomly selected subjects are included. Interviews may also be treated as case studies that nevertheless open the way to generalization. The researcher then provides arguments to suggest that the findings in a particular case can be extrapolated to other situations. In cases in law and psychiatry, in particular, a reader may be able to generalize to their own situations. *Reliability* refers to consistency of the results of an investigation. Interviews are sometimes discredited as unreliable because different interviewers come up with different results. On an alternative perspective, it may be regarded as a strength of qualitative interviewing that different interviewers, with specific knowledge and sensitivity, may bring out different aspects of the topic investigated. The controls then come from an explication of the interviewer's perspective and the documentation of the interview interaction. *Validity* refers to whether an interview study investigates what it is intended to investigate. Forms of validation will differ according to the type of knowledge sought, be it subjects' experiences of a topic, opinions and attitudes, behaviour in specific situations, life histories or oral histories. A distinctive feature of the qualitative research interview is the possibility of communicative validation *in situ*: following up the subjects' answers, clarifying and extending their meanings, cross-checking the results, including the deliberate use of leading questions to check the consistency of the subjects' answers. Validation may take place in conjunction with other methods, such as field observations and questionnaires. In the latter case, this may include pilot interviews in the course of the preparation of questionnaires, and also 'post interviews', that are designed to check the meaning of answers given by respondents. The validity of social science interviews may be improved by paying more attention to the linguistic medium of interview research, including the grammatical forms of an utterance, the use of metaphors and narrative structures, and the translation from oral to written language. Some positivist critics suggest that interviews lack scientific validity. However, the qualitative research interview offers privileged access to the interrelational, conversational and linguistic interactions that make up much of the human experience.

STEINAR KVALE
UNIVERSITY OF AARHUS, DENMARK

References

Fielding, N. (ed.) (2003) *Interviewing, Vols I–IV*, London.

Flick, U. (2002) *An Introduction to Qualitative Research*, London.

Greenbaum, T.L. (ed.) (1994) *The Handbook of Focus Group Research*, London.

Gubrium, J.F. and Holstein, J.A. (eds) (2002) *Handbook of Interview Research*, London.

Kvale, S. (1996) *InterViews*, London.

—— (2003) 'The psychoanalytic interview as inspiration for qualitative research', in P. Camic, J. Rhodes and L. Yardley (eds) *Qualitative Research in Psychology*, Washington, DC, pp. 275–97.

Silvester, E. (ed.) (1993) *The Penguin Book of Interviews: An Anthology from 1859 to the Present Day*, Harmondsworth.

SEE ALSO: ethnography; focus groups; questionnaires; sample surveys

INVESTMENT

Investment can be defined as the change in the physical capital stock over a period of time – normally a year for accounting purposes. It is not to be confused with financial investment, which involves the purchase (or additions to the stock) of financial assets, such as bonds and shares, and is, therefore, more closely connected with the analysis of saving. It is also commonly distinguished from inventory investment, which involves changes in stocks of finished goods, work in progress and raw materials.

Capital investment goods differ from consumption goods in that they yield a flow of services over a period of time, and these services do not directly satisfy consumer wants but facilitate the production of goods and services, or consumer goods. Although some consumer goods are perishable, a large number provide services over a period of time and are, therefore, akin to investment goods. Such goods are called consumer durables, e.g. cars. The existence of various goods that provide flows of services over time presents problems for national income accounting. This is because it is not always clear whether such goods should be classified as investment or consumer goods. Expenditure on land and dwellings by households is an example. In the UK such expenditures are treated as investment. Expenditure on plant and machinery is, however, clearly part of (capital) investment, since it either replaces worn-out machinery or adds to productive capacity. Gross investment is total expenditure on capital goods per year, and net investment is gross investment net of depreciation – which is the decline in the capital stock due to wear and tear.

A distinction is often drawn between public investment, which is undertaken by the public sector, and private investment. Foreign direct, or overseas, investment involves the purchase of financial or productive assets in other countries and should be distinguished from overseas portfolio investment. Foreign direct investment (FDI) is the net (i.e. the difference between a country's investment overseas and foreign investment in that country) inflow of investment from overseas and is a means by which a country can achieve a level of investment in excess of domestic savings rates.

A number of theories have been developed to explain the determination of investment demand. These commonly relate to private-sector investment demand, since public-sector investment may involve other considerations. The importance of investment lies in the fact that a rise in the capital stock of an economy may increase its productive capacity and potential for economic growth. It should be noted that the capital stock is one of a number of factors of production, along with labour and raw materials, which contribute to production and, therefore, that investment is not the sole determinant of growth. Additionally, investment is a major route through which technical progress can be made and thus productivity can be increased.

Public investment may be guided by principles other than narrow profit maximization, since the government should take account of social costs and benefits as well as pecuniary ones. Public investment might, consequently, be undertaken to alleviate unemployment in depressed areas or to encourage technical change. Keynesian economists have argued that public investment can be an important catalyst to economic development and may have a significant role to play in leading an economy out of recession. Modern 'endogenous growth theory' highlights the role of public infrastructural investment in the growth generation process. The attraction of FDI has increasingly been seen as a means of supplementing public investment targeted on economic regeneration of impoverished regions and subregions.

Economics literature postulates that there are two major determinants of private investment demand: the rate of interest, and the increase in national income. Other factors clearly influence investment as well: these include wage and tax rates, which affect the relative cost of capital and labour. Assuming that these other influences are constant, however, it is postulated that changes in the rate of interest or national income will cause a change in the desired capital stock and that this will lead to investment. Research and development, leading to innovation, can itself stimulate investment in the design of new products and the capacity to produce them, A change in the rate of interest will influence the desired capital stock by altering the expected profitability of various potential investment expenditures. This can be seen in various ways. Firms may be viewed as forecasting the revenues and costs over the life of the project in which the capital good is to be employed. To do this they must forecast the expected life of the project, the sales volumes and prices and various costs, in each year of the project. The expected project life will depend on both the physical life and the technological life of the capital good. A firm will not wish to operate with obsolete capital goods, since it will be at a cost disadvantage relative to its competitors. Having estimated the expected future flow of profits, and any scrap value that capital goods might have at the end of a project's life, the firm will then *discount* this expected income stream. If the firm discounts the stream using the appropriate market rate of interest, then it will caculate the gross present value of the project, and after subtracting the cost of the capital good it will have calculated the net present value. If this is positive, then the profit is acceptable given the risk involved and the attractiveness of alternative projects. A fall in the rate of interest will lead to a rise in the net present value of various projects and will, other things being equal, lead a number of firms to want to buy additional capital goods. In aggregate, the desired capital stock will rise. Keynes (1936) explained the influence of the interest rate on investment in a slightly different manner, based on the internal rate of return, or what he called the marginal efficiency of capital. This alternative suggests that firms will find the rate of discount that equates the (discounted) expected flow of returns to the cost of the capital good. If this rate is less than the appropriate market rate of interest, then the project is potentially profitable. A fall in the interest rate should, therefore, increase the number of poten-

tially profitable projects and hence the aggregate desired capital stock. If a firm is borrowing funds to finance investment, the interest rate represents the cost of borrowing. If it is financing investment from internal funds, the interest rate represents the *opportunity cost*, since it represents the revenue the firm could, alternatively, receive from financial, or some other, investment. Such explanations of the determination of investment demand are based on an assumption of fixed interest rates, throughout the life of the project. Financial institutions are, however, increasingly lending at variable rates, and this will further complicate the investment decision by requiring firms to form expectations of interest rates throughout the project's life. It is to be noted that expectations play a major role in determining investment demand, according to this analysis, and that, consequently, a government policy of trying to stimulate investment, by reducing the interest rate, might not have the desired effect in times of worsening expectations of future profits.

Implicit in the emphasis on the role of interest rates in determining investment is that investment will be, at least in part, externally financed by debt (bond issuance and bank loans). Since the early 1990s, however, there has been a rapid growth of the venture capital sector, which provides private equity finance aimed primarily at rapidly developing firms judged to have the potential for rapid and profitable growth.

In the late 1990s, for example, particularly in the USA, venture capital funds were instrumented in driving the communications and information technology investment boom.

A second major influence on investment demand is believed to be the change in national income. A rise in national income might increase expected sales and lead to a desire to increase productive capacity. The accelerator theory is a more formal explanation of the influence of a rise in national income on investment. It postulates a fixed ratio of capital to output, based on technological considerations, so that output growth should lead to an increase in the desired capital stock that in turn generates more growth in a virtuous circle. It seems unlikely that an economy's capital to output ratio is fixed over time, since many factors will influence this ratio, such as the relative cost of capital and labour, technical progress and changes in the relative importance of various sectors of the economy, which may have different capital/output ratios. In its crude form the accelerator theory does not perform well empirically, but in more flexible forms it is more successful at explaining investment.

It is, therefore, clear that a change in the rate of interest or in national income might influence the demand for capital goods and change the aggregate desired capital stock for the economy as a whole. The actual net investment that occurs each year in any economy depends on the rate of depreciation of capital stock, and on the extent to which the increased demand for capital stock is satisfied. This will in turn depend on the ability of the capital goods-producing industry to meet the increased demand; the extent to which the price of capital goods rises in response to the increased demand, thus raising the cost of capital goods and reducing the net present value of investment projects; and the extent to which

suitable capital goods can be purchased from and indeed funded from abroad.

ANDY MULLINEUX
UNIVERSITY OF BIRMINGHAM

Reference

Keynes, J.M. (1936) *The General Theory of Employment, Interest and Money*, London.

Further reading

Jorgenson, D.W. (1971) 'Econometric studies of investment behaviour: A survey', *Journal of Economic Literature* 9: 1,111–47.
Samuelson, P.A. (1966 [1939]) 'Interactions between the multiplier analysis and the principle of acceleration', *Collected Scientific Papers of Paul A. Samuelson*, Vol. 2, Cambridge, MA, Chapter 82.

SEE ALSO: accounting; profit; research and development (R&D)

J

JAMES, WILLIAM (1842–1910)

William James, eminent psychologist and philosopher, was born in New York City. He, his novelist brother, Henry, and his sister were the main recipients of an unusually unsystematic education supervised by their father that consisted largely of European travels and private tutors. After an interval in which he studied painting, James enrolled in the Lawrence Scientific School at Harvard in 1861. In 1864 he entered Harvard Medical School and received an MD in 1869. His life was marked by periods of acute depression and psychosomatic illnesses that occasioned solitary trips to Europe for rest and treatment. These periods, however, produced two benefits: they gave James first-hand experience of abnormal psychological states concerning which he was later to be a pioneer investigator; and they provided opportunities for extensive reading of science and literature in French, German and English. His marriage in 1878 appears to have been an important factor in improving his health and focusing his concentration on teaching and writing. His academic life was centred at Harvard where he became an instructor in psychology in 1875 and taught anatomy and physiology. Subsequently he offered courses in philosophy until his retirement in 1907.

James's work in psychology and philosophy was interfused and is not completely separable. His greatest effort and achievement was *The Principles of Psychology* (1890) that, some 10 years in writing, made him world famous and is now regarded a classic in both fields of study. James stated his intention to establish psychology as a natural science. By this he meant that metaphysical questions would be avoided and, wherever possible, explanations in psychology should be based on experimental physiology and biology rather than on introspective procedures that had dominated philosophic psychology since Locke and Hume. In contrast to a widely prevailing conception of mind as composed of ideas, like atoms, ordered and compounded by association, James proposed that mentality is a 'stream of consciousness' including in it feelings and interests. For James, the mental is to be construed in evolutionary and teleological forms; mental activity is evidenced where there are selections of means to achieve future ends. Darwinian theory had an important influence on James's psychological and philosophical views. Ideas and theories are interpreted as instruments enabling us to adapt successfully to, and partly transform, reality according to our interests and purposes of action.

In an address of 1898, 'Philosophical conceptions and practical results', James inaugurated the theory of pragmatism, which soon became the major movement in US philosophy. He also drew attention to the neglected work of Charles S. Peirce whom he credited with having originated pragmatism. The main thesis is that the value and significance of concepts, their meaning and truth, is determined not by their origins but by their future practical consequences. An application of this view is found in *The Will to Believe* (1896) and in James's Gifford Lectures (1901–2), *The Varieties of Religious Experience*; it is argued explicitly in *Pragmatism* (1907) and *The Meaning of Truth* (1909). In his later writings and lectures, James refined and defended his metaphysical doctrines of the pluralistic character of reality, indeterminism and 'radical empiricism' according to which the world is conceived as a growing continuous structure of experience.

H.S. THAYER
CITY UNIVERSITY OF NEW YORK

Further reading

Barzun, J. (2002) *A Stroll with William James*, Chicago.
Burkhardt, F. and Bowers, F. (eds) (1975–88) *The Works of William James*, 19 vols, Cambridge, MA.
Perry, R.B. (1935) *The Thought and Character of William James*, 2 vols, Boston, MA.
Skrupskelis, I.K. and Berkeley, E.M. (1992–) *The Correspondence of William James*, Charlottesville, VA.

JUDICIAL PROCESS

As studied by contemporary social scientists, focusing largely on liberal democracies, the judicial process is the complex of formal and informal operations by which tribunals adjudicate claims based on rules putatively authorized by the regime. The tribunals are differentiated and relatively autonomous from the rest of the polity, and typically do not initiate action, but respond when a claim fit for adjudication is presented to them through an adversarial presentation of evidence and argument. So defined, the judicial process is a relatively modern enquiry, dependent upon two intellectual developments: the emergence of the ideal concept of a distinct judicial function performed by a distinct institution; and the rise of a science of politics that emphasizes the informal processes over formal procedures of government and which, as applied to the study of the judiciary, questions the reality, attainability and intellectual sophistication of this conceptual ideal.

Although ancient and medieval political philosophers did distinguish a judicial function from other governmental functions, these distinctions were subordinated to a more fundamental one, that between legislation and politics. Legislation was regarded by the ancients as an extraordinary event, subject at most to rare and cautious amendment, while politics encompassed deliberations and actions within the framework of this legislation. Viewing God as the ultimate legislator, medieval thinkers regarded virtually all governmental functions as aspects of the judicial function.

Because the law was regarded as everlasting, yet the situations to which it was to be applied were ever-changing, the judicial function, both in ancient and medieval thought, included generous elements of practical wisdom and equity as essential supplements to the more literal terms of the law.

The more carefully defined and tightly circumscribed contemporary judicial function, performed by a specialized agency, arises concomitantly with the idea of law as the enactment of a sovereign legislator, or what students of political development call the shift of authority from a traditional to a constitutional basis. With authority to make law vested in a present institution having the capacity to change the law to meet new situations, the quasi-legislative character of the ancient and medieval judicial function would threaten to derange legislative authority and offend individual rights by effecting burdens and punishments retroactively. Ironically, this rigorous subordination of judgement to legislation also required the autonomy of the judiciary from the legislature, so that courts could be impartial to the parties before it and free from pressure to interpret the law other than as the legislature intended it at the time of enactment. From these conceptual and institutional developments there emerges, then, the idealized modern judicial function as one presupposing the existence of right answers at law, performed by a tribunal with sufficient autonomy to discern these answers in the resolution of disputes. We find numerous expressions of this ideal among theorists and jurists of liberal democracy; perhaps the most frequently quoted is that of Montesquieu, who held that judges were to be 'no more than the mouth that pronounces the words of the law, mere passive beings, incapable of moderating either its force or rigour'.

Influenced by evolutionary theory, jurists and social scientists during the late nineteenth and early twentieth centuries began shifting their focus from institutional forms and idealized purposes to the 'live forces' that were claimed to constitute the underlying reality. Those who called themselves realists provided the most radical onslaught on the ideal judicial function by dismissing the ontological claim of 'right answers'. In most instances, within wide boundaries, they maintained, there was no right answer to be discovered, no measure by which to assess the claims of one judge's opinion over another; what really constituted the law were the psychological traits of the judge. A distinct but related movement, sociological jurisprudence, emphasized not only the creative character of the judicial function, but also the need to consider both law and courts in the context of their larger political and social environments.

From this odd marriage of a judicial ideal, which is implicit in the theory and institutions of liberal democracy, and this realist assessment of that standard, is born the modern study of the judicial process. Bearing a greater likeness to its realist parent, it is predominantly an empirical enquiry. Central to its study are the following: the processes by which courts are staffed, the conditions of judicial tenure, and the effect of these on judicial decisions; how rules of procedure, both formal and informal, affect the definition and disposition of issues; the decision-making patterns of individual judges, the dynamics of collective decision making in juries and on appellate courts, patterns of interaction among the courts in appellate and federal systems; the impact and implementation of judicial decisions; and the comparative competence of judicial and non-judicial branches of government for effecting social change. Normative enquiries focus on modes of legal interpretation and, especially regarding constitutional law, the propriety of judicial activism and restraint.

In recent years, students of the judicial process have expanded their horizons to encompass processes of decision-making that are quasi-judicial in character, such as 'alternative dispute resolution', as an alternative to civil trials, and 'plea bargaining', as an alternative to criminal trials – each arising in part as a response to the cost, uncertainty and complexity of the formal judicial process. Another fruitful and expanding line of enquiry has been the comparative study of the judicial process, including legal systems in authoritarian and developing democracies, and the remarkable and nearly global phenomenon of growth in judicial power and independence.

STANLEY C. BRUBAKER
COLGATE UNIVERSITY

Further reading

Abraham, H.J. (1998) *The Judicial Process*, 7th edn, New York.
Rosenberg, G.N. (1991) *The Hollow Hope: Can Courts Bring about Social Change?* Chicago.
Segal, J.A. and Spaeth, H.J. (2002) *The Supreme Court and the Attitudinal Model Revisited*, Cambridge, UK.
Tate, C.N. and Vallinder, T. (eds) (1995) *The Global Expansion of Judicial Power*, New York.

SEE ALSO: law

JUSTICE, DISTRIBUTIVE

The best definition of justice remains that given by Justinian: a just distribution is one in which each person receives that which is his due. However, this relatively formal definition tells us very little, for it remains to be decided what is 'due' to each person. Moreover, 'What is due?' masks two questions: 'How much of the benefits and burdens of social co-operation should go to whom?' (the question of distribution), and 'What are those benefits and burdens?' (the question of *what* is to be distributed). In modern times, and particularly in broadly liberal societies, justice has been linked with two other concepts: desert and equality. What is due to a person is what is deserved by him. And, equals are to be treated equally. Like the formal idea of justice, these claims do not resolve the substantive issue of who gets what, but they constrain theorizing about justice.

Although justice is a virtue of individuals as well as of institutions, most political philosophy since the publication of Rawls's *A Theory of Justice* in 1971 has focused on 'justice as the first virtue of institutions' (Rawls 1971: 3). The focus has also been on justice within a particular state, although issues of international justice are of increasing importance in the literature. Four broad approaches to the distributive question can be distinguished: conventionalism, utilitarianism, justice as mutual advantage and justice as fairness. In addition, two accounts of the question of what is to be distributed have come to define the territory of the debate: welfarism and resourcism.

Conventionalists claim that what is due to whom is dictated by the norms, laws and conventions of particular societies. Its most sophisticated modern statement comes in the work of Michael Walzer (1983), who argues that each good ought to be distributed in accordance with the principle implicit in the community's understanding of the thing as a good. Thus, our understanding of the good of health care is such that once we think about why it is a good for us – it restores health – we see that there is an appropriate distributive principle: medical need. For Walzer, different communities have different social understandings of goods and so different distributive principles. The only universal principle is that these different shared understandings should be respected. Critics of conventionalism claim that there are few, if any, societies in which social goods have single unambiguous meanings (is abortion a response to medical need?). Moreover, they claim, conventionalism entails an unattractive and unconvincing relativism.

Utilitarians, who dominated moral and political philosophy for much of the twentieth century, argue that institutions are to be judged by how well (or poorly) they contribute to human welfare, happiness or 'utility'. Act utilitarians hold that the right act to perform is that act which will bring about the best consequences; rule utilitarians that the right act to perform is that act which falls under the relevant rule the adoption of which will bring about the best consequences. Critics of utilitarianism hold that it fails to respect people as moral equals. Thus, for example, a distribution that gave immense wealth to one group and enslaved another is in principle justifiable on utilitarian grounds if it so happens that the benefit to the wealthy outweighs the burden to the enslaved. The utilitarian reply is that such an outcome is very unlikely in the real world. This might be right, but even if it is, it seems to deliver the right answer for the wrong reasons. We object to slavery not simply because it causes unhappiness but because it is unjust and utilitarianism seems unable to accommodate this distinct sense of justice.

Theorists of justice as mutual advantage take seriously Rawls's claim that 'society is a co-operative endeavor for mutual advantage' and that rules of justice are needed to regulate that endeavour. If such rules are to be compelling then they must be in the interest of each co-operator. That is, each must be able to do better abiding by the rules of justice than he otherwise would do. On this account, the rules of justice will have to reflect the relative bargaining strengths of the co-operators, and, at the limit, those with nothing to offer the community of co-operators will 'fall beyond the pale' of morality (Gauthier 1986: 268). Some critics of such theories point to the difficulty of ensuring compliance given that the

reason for co-operation (advancing self-interest) may sometimes be a reason for free-riding. Other critics argue that any theory of justice that fails to protect the weak and vulnerable is not so much 'an alternative account of morality' as 'an alternative to morality' (Kymlicka 1991: 190).

Theories of justice as fairness, also, think of the rules of justice as regulating the co-operation of persons with different views of the good. What they add is the stipulation that such rules must respect and express the fundamental equal worth of moral persons. However, theorists of justice as fairness disagree on what such respect requires. For Robert Nozick, it requires only that persons are granted a set of absolute negative liberty rights (Nozick 1974). For Rawls (1971), it requires political rights with equal value to be given to all, and that social and economic inequalities be such that they arise from fair equality of opportunity and maximally benefit the least well off. Rawls's argument depends on the thought that to respect the equality of persons means putting to one side factors such as their natural talents and abilities that are undeserved and so 'arbitrary from a moral point of view'.

Rawls's insistence on the arbitrariness of talents and abilities sowed the seeds for the most interesting contemporary development within distributive justice theory: 'luck egalitarianism'. For luck egalitarians, the purpose of justice is to mitigate differences that result from chance while respecting differences that flow from choice. Precisely how this is to be done remains much contested, and, in the view of some critics, luck egalitarianism ignores the important egalitarian aim of responding to oppression (Anderson 1999).

These developments in the literature on distributive justice highlight the significance of the question of 'What is to be distributed?' Welfarists argue that if people are not responsible for their natural talents and abilities, then we should allow the possibility that some people will be bad at converting resources into welfare for reasons that are morally arbitrary. If so, in treating people as equals we should concentrate not on bare resources, but on what welfare those resources bring to their owners. Resourcists argue that welfarism leads to counter-intuitive results (for example, that a person with an unchosen expensive taste for fine wine should receive a public subsidy) and that we should concentrate on distributing resources (often widely understood so as to include rights and liberties as well as income and wealth). The 'equality of what? debate', as it has become known, has resulted in a 'college industry' producing new theories of what ought to be the 'stuff' of justice (see Clayton and Williams 2000).

MATT MATRAVERS
UNIVERSITY OF YORK, UK

References

Anderson, E.S. (1999) 'Egalitarian justice and interpersonal comparison', *European Journal of Political Research* 35: 445–64.
Clayton, M. and Williams, A. (2000) *The Ideal of Equality*, London.
Gauthier, D. (1986) *Morals by Agreement*, Oxford.
Kymlicka, W. (1991) 'The social contract tradition', in P. Singer (ed.) *The Blackwell Companion to Ethics*, Oxford, pp. 186–96.
Nozick, R. (1974) *Anarchy, State and Utopia*, New York.
Rawls, J. (1971 [rev. edn 1999]) *A Theory of Justice*, Cambridge, MA.
Walzer, M. (1983) *Spheres of Justice*, Oxford.

Further reading

Barry, B. (1989) *Theories of Justice: Volume 1 of a Treatise on Social Justice*, Berkeley, CA.
—— (1995) *Justice as Impartiality: Volume 2 of a Treatise on Social Justice*, Oxford.
Dworkin, R. (2000) *Sovereign Virtue: The Theory and Practice of Equality*, Cambridge, MA.
Hurley, S. (2003) *Justice, Luck, and Knowledge*, Cambridge, MA.
Matravers, M. (2002) 'Responsibility, luck, and the "Equality of What?" debate', *Political Studies* 50(3): 558–72.
Scanlon, T. (1999) *What We Owe to Each Other*, Cambridge, MA.

SEE ALSO: affirmative action; equality; Rawls; social choice; social contract

K

KEYNES, JOHN MAYNARD (1883–1946)

The son of John Neville Keynes, a Cambridge economist, philosopher and administrator, and Florence Ada (Brown), Cambridge's first woman town councillor and later its mayor, Maynard Keynes made contributions that extended well beyond academic economics. After an education at Eton and King's College, Cambridge (BA in Mathematics 1905), his first career was that of a civil servant in the India Office (1906–8). Although he soon returned to Cambridge to lecture in economics (1908–20) and be a Fellow of King's (1909–46), he never lost his connection with the world of affairs. He served as a member of the Royal Commission on Indian Finance and Currency (1913–14), was a wartime Treasury official eventually in charge of Britain's external financial relations (1915–19), a member of the Macmillan Committee on Finance and Industry (1929–31), a member of the Economic Advisory Council (1930–9), an adviser to the Chancellor of the Exchequer (1940–6) and a director of the Bank of England (1941–6). After 1919, he also had an active career in the world of finance as a company director, insurance company chairman and bursar of King's College, Cambridge. Moreover, under the influence of his Bloomsbury friends Vanessa Bell and Duncan Grant, as well as Lydia Lopokova of the Diaghilev Ballet whom he married in 1925, he played an active and important role in the cultural life of his time as a patron of the arts, founder of the Arts Theatre, Cambridge (which he gave to the city and university in 1938), trustee of the National Gallery, chairman of the Council for the Encouragement of Music and the Arts, and initiator and first chairman of the Arts Council of Great Britain.

Keynes's reputation as an academic economist arises from work that he started after his fortieth year and published after he was 47. Prior to that, he was much better known as a publicist and commentator on economic affairs, a career he began in 1919 after his resignation as the senior Treasury official at the Paris Peace Conference with his bestselling and influential indictment of the negotiation and terms of the Peace Treaty in *The Economic Consequences of the Peace* (1919). He continued in this popular vein with *A Revision of the Treaty* (1922), *A Tract on Monetary Reform* (1923), *The Economic Consequences of Mr Churchill* (1925), *The End of Laissez-Faire* (1926) and prolific journalism, notably for the liberal *Nation and Athenaeum* (1923–31) and the more socialist *New Statesman and Nation*, for both of which he was chairman of the board. This does not mean that he was unknown as an academic: he was editor of the Royal Economic Society's *The Economic Journal* (1911–45) and the author of *A Treatise on Probability* (1921), a philosophical examination of the principles of reasoning and rational action in conditions of incomplete and uncertain knowledge, the earliest ideas of which date after 1904 when Keynes was strongly influenced by G.E. Moore. Nevertheless, it would be fair to echo Sir Austin Robinson's comment (1947): 'If Maynard Keynes had died in 1925 it would have been difficult for those who knew intimately the power and originality of his mind to have convinced those who had not known him of the full measure of Keynes' ability.'

The bases for Keynes's academic reputation as an economist were his *Treatise on Money* (1930) and *The General Theory of Employment, Interest and Money* (1936). Both were stages in the development in theoretical terms of the principles that should underlie attempts by governments to achieve economic stability. In the *Treatise*, as in the more popular *Tract*, the main concern was with monetary and price stability, and the role that monetary policy alone could play in achieving them. As was common in contemporary monetary economics, Keynes dichotomized the economy into its monetary and real sectors, and, on the assumption that money was neutral in the long run, looked for the principles of monetary practice that would ensure price stability, in the *Treatise* case a monetary policy that made the long-term market rate of interest equivalent to the 'natural rate' at which savings equalled investment. This initial approach to the problem was found to be inadequate by Keynes's critics, who included R.G. Hawtrey, F.A. Hayek and D.H. Robertson, as well as a group of younger economists in Cambridge (R.F. Kahn, James Meade, Joan and Austin Robinson, and Piero Sraffa). When convinced of the inadequacies of the *Treatise*, Keynes began reformulating his ideas. The major breakthrough came in 1933 when, contrary to traditional theory, Keynes hit on the crucial role of changes in output and employment in equilibration savings and investment, thus providing the basis for a more general theory than his own or his predecessors' previous work. The new theory seemed to offer the possibility of equilibrium at less than full employment, something missing in previous work. From his 1933 breakthrough, which hinged on the consumption–income relationship implicit in the multiplier, after considerable further work, everything fell into place.

During the last 10 years of his life, although his activities were inhibited by a severe heart condition after 1937, Keynes devoted less time to defending and somewhat refining his theoretical views than to seeing them implemented. Even before the outbreak of war in 1939, he had started to influence Treasury thinking in Britain, while his students and his writings were becoming influential in such places as Washington and Ottawa. However, the problems of war finance and postwar planning appear to have been crucial in the spread of his ideas into day-to-day policy-making, for as he demonstrated in *How to Pay for the War* (1940) the new ideas when married to another contemporary development –

national income and expenditure accounting – provided a powerful new way of thinking about the economy and its management. The resulting 'new economics' put less emphasis than Keynes would have done on the roles of monetary policy and the control of public investment in the achievement of full employment, yet, along with a political determination to avoid the wastes of the interwar years, it led to widespread official commitments to postwar policies of high or full employment. By then, however, Keynes was less involved in such matters: the last years of his life saw him devoting much more of his efforts to shaping other aspects of the postwar world, most notably the international monetary order of the International Monetary Fund and the World Bank, and to securing Britain's postwar international economic position. Gaining these, or at least a semblance of them, finally exhausted him.

DONALD MOGGRIDGE
UNIVERSITY OF TORONTO

Reference

Robinson, E.A.G. (1947) 'John Maynard Keynes, 1883–1946', *Economic Journal* 57.

Further reading

Harrod, R.F. (1951) *The Life of John Maynard Keynes*, London.
Keynes, J.M. (1971–89) *The Collected Writings of John Maynard Keynes*, eds E. Johnson and D. Moggridge, 30 vols, London and New York. [Those approaching Keynes's ideas for the first time are advised to look at Vol. 9, *Essays in Persuasion*.]
Moggridge, D.E. (1992) *Maynard Keynes: An Economist's Biography*, Toronto.
Skidelsky, R. (1983–2000) *John Maynard Keynes*, 3 vols, London.

SEE ALSO: Keynesian economics

KEYNESIAN ECONOMICS

The Great Depression posed obvious difficulties for contemporary economic theory. With up to 30 per cent of the labour force unemployed, what sense could be made of the neo-classical notions of scarcity, opportunity cost, the decisive role of individual preferences, and the absence of unexploited gains from trade? The problem lay less in policy than in theory. Almost all economists of the time agreed that public works expenditure, financed by borrowing, was justified in severe depression. This, however, was inconsistent with their acceptance of Say's Law and the Treasury Doctrine, or 'full crowding-out' hypothesis, whereby each additional dollar of public spending would reduce private expenditure by a full dollar and every job created by the government destroyed a job in the private sector.

In *The General Theory of Employment, Interest and Money* (1936), John Maynard Keynes set out a new theory demonstrating that an economy could settle at a level of output well below that required to make full use of its productive capacity, and that no automatic, self-correcting mechanism could be relied upon to restore full employment. It was a *general* theory, he claimed, since it could also be used to analyse the special case of full employment, as he himself showed in *How to Pay for the War* (1940). It hinged on the principle of effective demand: output and employment are normally constrained by aggregate demand, not by the sum of individual supply decisions. Demand for consumer goods is limited by what Keynes termed the 'fundamental psychological law' that less than 100 per cent of each additional dollar in income is devoted to consumption; some of it is saved. In these circumstances the full-employment level of output will be produced only if investment demand is equal to the level of saving that would be generated at the full-employment level of income. But, Keynes argued, investment expenditure is restricted by entrepreneurs' expectations of future profitability, and these may be pessimistic, so that investment falls short of the required amount.

The link between investment and profitability could be severed by 'a somewhat comprehensive socialisation of investment' (Keynes 1936: 378). Failing this, the government would have to stimulate effective demand through loan-financed public works. Such an increase in government spending would have a multiplier effect on total income. Below full employment, there would be crowding-in, not crowding-out, with each additional public-sector job creating one or more extra jobs in the private sector.

Defenders of the orthodox or 'classical' theory that Keynes was attacking maintained that there were in fact two mechanisms that would tend to restore full employment without government intervention. One, the real balance effect (or Pigou effect), operates through a reduction in the price level, which increases the real value of the money stock and causes consumption to rise as people get rid of their excess money balances by spending them. The second mechanism is derived from the loanable funds theory of interest, and operates through the reduction in the rate of interest that occurs when savings exceed investment. Lower interest rates increase investment and reduce saving, until the full employment levels of output and employment are attained.

Keynes rejected both mechanisms. A falling price level would do more harm than good, he believed, since it would depress business confidence and encourage consumers to postpone inessential purchases in anticipation of yet further price reductions. And the rate of interest is determined in the market for money, not the market for goods; it depends on the liquidity preference of economic agents, not on the 'real' – that is, non-monetary – forces of productivity and thrift that are emphasized in loanable funds theory.

The *General Theory* lent itself to conflicting interpretations, and doubts were expressed from the outset about its revolutionary nature. Friendly critics like Roy Harrod and John Hicks claimed that Keynes had not broken fundamentally with classical macroeconomics, his own theory being only a special case – admittedly a very important special case – of conventional analysis. A second criticism concerned the static nature of Keynes's model. Joseph Schumpeter objected that he had omitted the central defining characteristic of capitalism, its ceaseless compulsion to innovate. This was no oversight: Keynes had deliberately restricted his analysis to the short period, in which both the capital stock and techniques of production remain unchanged. Marxists complained about Keynes's politics. He had ignored both the deep class division between capitalists and workers, and the class struggle over the distribution of income between wages and profits.

Keynes responded to the first of these criticisms, highlighting the role of uncertainty in the *General Theory* as his principal analytical achievement:

By 'uncertain' knowledge, let me explain, I do not mean merely to distinguish what is known for certain from what is only probable....The sense in which I am using the term is that in which the prospect of a European war is uncertain, or the price of copper and the rate of interest twenty years hence, or the obsolescence of a new invention, or the position of private wealth owners in the social system in 1970. About these matters there is no scientific basis on which to form any calculable probability whatever. We simply do not know.

(Keynes 1937: 213–14)

This, Keynes argued, was enough to discredit any theory that relied on automatic stabilizing tendencies to restore full employment.

For Keynes, economics was a policy science. Macroeconomics was worth doing only if it could be used to improve the operation of the economy. In a closed system this implied cheap money and functional finance: permanently low interest rates to encourage investment, and budget deficits or surpluses, depending entirely on the level of private-sector demand relative to productive capacity. Globally, it required an international monetary system geared to the promotion of full employment, with exchange rates, balance of payment adjustments and capital movements all controlled for this overriding purpose (Vines 2003). The age of *laissez-faire* was over.

One simple form of Keynesian macroeconomics entered the elementary textbooks in 1948 when Paul Samuelson's *Economics* introduced the celebrated 'Keynesian cross' diagram, in which the equilibrium level of output is set by the intersection of an aggregate expenditure function with a 45 degree line. At a more advanced level, the IS-LM model originated by Harrod, Hicks and others in the late 1930s became a cornerstone of the so-called neo-classical synthesis, in which Keynes's insights were merged with important elements of pre-Keynesian orthodoxy by means of simultaneous equations that can be solved for real output and the rate of interest to yield equilibrium in the markets for goods and for money. Disputes over theory and policy can then be resolved, or at least precisely formulated, in terms of the slopes of the two functions.

A second cornerstone of the neo-classical synthesis is the Solow–Swan growth model. In the short period, investment contributes to aggregate demand; in the long period, it also increases the capital stock and thereby increases potential aggregate supply. Harrod identified this long-period effect as a further source of instability, since there is only one rate of capital

accumulation that is consistent with the satisfaction of entrepreneurs' profit expectations. If the actual rate of growth differs from this 'warranted' rate, the outcome is growing unemployment or constantly increasing inflation. In the long period, the economy is poised precariously on a knife-edge. The neo-classical theorists Trevor Swan and Robert Solow restored stability by introducing an aggregate production function. Capital–labour substitution occurs in response to changes in the relative prices of the two factors of production, with the wage and profit shares in total income determined by marginal productivity.

Keynes rejected the Quantity Theory of Money in favour of a money wage theory of the price level, but what determines the rate of change of money wages? The third cornerstone of the neo-classical synthesis is the Phillips curve, which establishes an inverse relationship between unemployment (excess labour supply) and money wage growth. This carries important policy implications, since the Phillips curve can be interpreted as a menu for policy choice, with governments able to select the combination of the two economic 'bads', unemployment and inflation, which their electorates prefer.

No sooner had the neo-classical synthesis been perfected than it all began to fall apart. In the real world, unemployment and wage inflation rose together in the late 1960s, undermining the stability of the Phillips curve and eventually destroying the fixed exchange rate regime that had been established, with Keynes's support, in 1945. In the world of ideas, the Quantity Theory returned to prominence in the more flexible, 'monetarist' version that was tirelessly promoted by Milton Friedman as an alternative to Keynesian macroeconomics. In the 1970s an extreme variant emerged in the form of New Classical Economics, based on the postulates of 'rational expectations' and the full clearing of all markets even in the short period. All unemployment was viewed as voluntary, and the principle of effective demand was denied.

This intellectual challenge gave rise to two radically different reformulations of Keynesian ideas, Post-Keynesian and New Keynesian economics. The most important early influence on Post-Keynesianism was Michal Kalecki, who objected to the residual neo-classical elements in the *General Theory* and in particular to Keynes's neglect of class conflict and the power of oligopolistic corporations (Sawyer 1985). Joan Robinson (1956) took over many of Kalecki's ideas, and was also influenced by her Cambridge colleague Piero Sraffa in repudiating marginal productivity theory and the neo-classical analysis of capital, interest and profit. Also in Cambridge, Nicholas Kaldor developed a macroeconomic theory of distribution in which the wage and profit shares in total output are determined by the savings propensities of workers and capitalists, given the investment decisions of the latter.

In the USA, Hyman Minsky (1975) developed a distinctive Keynesian theory of the business cycle in which increasing financial fragility plays the central role in initiating recession. Sidney Weintraub and Paul Davidson criticized both the neo-classical synthesis and the monetarists for treating money as if it were an exogenous variable under the full control of the central bank. They proposed instead a model of inflation in which wage bargaining is central and an incomes policy is the least damaging solution. Davidson (2002) became the most prominent representative of the 'Fundamentalist Keynesian' strand in Post-Keynesian thought, insisting on the *General Theory* as the source of all wisdom in macroeconomics and stressing the unique properties of endogenous money in a radically uncertain world. A Marshallian in microeconomics, Davidson rejected the Kaleckian pricing and distribution theory that was influential with Kaldor, Robinson and many other European Post-Keynesians. All Post-Keynesians agree, however, that full employment should be the overriding goal of economic policy, and all reject monetarist and New Classical claims that monetary and fiscal policy is ineffective, at least in the long period (King 2002).

New Keynesian economics is much closer to the New Classicals in retaining rational expectations (thereby rejecting Keynes's analysis of uncertainty). It is also pre-Keynesian in asserting the neutrality of money and the operation of Say's Law in the long period (Mankiw and Romer 1991). In the short period, however, New Keynesians accept that markets fail to clear for several reasons, including imperfect competition between producers; union and government interference in the labour market; and informational asymmetries between borrowers and lenders. New Keynesians retain the neo-classical insistence on modelling the behaviour of representative economic agents who respond to risk but not to fundamental uncertainty. They acknowledge the need for government intervention in the short period to rectify the adverse macroeconomic consequences of market imperfections, but concur with the New Classicals in denying the ability of monetary or fiscal policy to influence output and employment in the long period. Their ideas can be regarded as 'Keynesian' only on a rather loose interpretation of that term.

J.E. KING
LA TROBE UNIVERSITY, AUSTRALIA

References

Davidson, P. (2002) *Financial Markets, Money and the Real World*, Cheltenham.
Keynes, J.M. (1936) *The General Theory of Employment, Interest and Money*, London.
—— (1937) 'The general theory of employment', *Quarterly Journal of Economics* 51(2) (February): 209–23.
—— (1940) *How to Pay for the War*, London.
King, J.E. (2002) *A History of Post Keynesian Economics Since 1936*, Cheltenham.
Mankiw, N.G. and Romer, D. (eds) (1991) *New Keynesian Economics*, 2 vols, Cambridge, MA.
Minsky, H.P. (1975) *John Maynard Keynes*, New York.
Robinson, J. (1956) *The Accumulation of Capital*, London.
Sawyer, M.C. (1985) *The Economics of Michal Kalecki*, London.
Vines, D. (2003) 'John Maynard Keynes 1937–1946: The creation of international macroeconomics', *Economic Journal* 113 (448) (June): F338–F361.

SEE ALSO: Keynes; macroeconomic theory

KINSHIP

Once deemed 'the central discipline of anthropology' (Fox 1967: 10), kinship was declared 'a non-subject' (Schneider 1972: 59) by the early 1970s, but it was unexpectedly raised again from the dead during the 1990s (Faubion 1996).

The invention of kinship

It has been argued kinship was 'invented' by the US lawyer, Lewis Henry Morgan, with the publication of his *Systems of Consanguinity and Affinity of the Human Family* in 1871, the year in which Darwin published *The Descent of Man* (Trautmann 1987). However, other scholarly lawyers (Bachofen, Maine, McLennan and others) with interests in antiquity and 'primitive society' also initiated debates between the 1860s and 1880s on such issues as forms of family and marriage, as well as kinship groups and terminologies. These writers assumed that all societies had to pass through the same series of stages of social evolution, and they speculated on the conjectural earliest stages of this development, postulating the ancient existence of promiscuous bands, in which incest was not prohibited. Morgan was, however, the first to use kinship terminologies as a tool for reconstructing the remote past, arguing that kinship categories could be decoded to reveal former systems of marriage. At the beginning of the twentieth century, W.H.R. Rivers renewed the evolutionist tradition by infusing it with history and diffusion. His name is still associated with the development of the 'genealogical method' for collecting information about terminologies and other aspects of kinship systems.

The classical tradition

After the demise of evolutionism, a new generation of British social anthropologists under the leadership of A.R. Radcliffe-Brown (and, to a lesser degree, B. Malinowski) redefined kinship studies within a structural-functionalist framework. It was now taken for granted that the family was universal, not a distinctive institution of higher civilizations (Malinowski 1929). Relationships, emotions and principles derived from family ties were then 'extended' to more distant relatives, creating a network of social relations. Particularly in their studies of African kinship systems, the students of Radcliffe-Brown and Malinowski investigated the ways in which kinship principles were central to the organization of political systems. 'Descent theory' identified a structural type of society, based on unilineal descent groups, and attempted to classify its components and variants.

'Alliance theory', associated with Claude Lévi-Strauss (1969 [1949]), presented an alternative approach to the classification of kinship systems, which focused on marriage instead of descent. Taking the incest taboo as his starting-point, Lévi-Strauss used the principle of reciprocity to explain both negative mating rules and positive marriage rules. His 'elementary structures of kinship' refer to marriage systems in which each young man and woman repeats the marriage of their parents or grandparents, all marrying into the same families and so creating alliances that are renewed in each generation. The three elementary structures – symmetric exchange, asymmetric exchange, patrilateral cross-cousin marriage – are based on different forms of cross-cousin marriage. Kinship systems that specify only who cannot be married, without identifying a particular category of relative who should be married, were described by Lévi-Strauss as complex structures.

Lévi-Strauss published his masterpiece on alliance systems in 1949. In the same year, Radcliffe-Brown's student Meyer Fortes published one of the most distinguished monographs on kinship in an African society organized on the basis of descent (Fortes 1949), and the US scholar George Peter Murdock published a comparative study, *Social Structure*, which combined a multilineal perspective of social evolution with statistical methods to arrive at a developmental typology of social structures. His typology of six types of kinship terminology, all but one of which were named after a North American linguistic group, continues to be used by many anthropologists, despite its analytical shortcomings. During the 1950s and 1960s, anthropological kinship studies continued to thrive. There were lively debates between supporters of descent and alliance theories, and new methods were borrowed from linguistics to represent and formalize kinship terminologies and kin relations.

The cultural critique and its aftermath

The period from the 1970s to the 1990s was marked by the cultural critique of kinship studies, primarily at the hands of David Schneider, though critical views about the autonomy and universality of kinship were also expressed by Leach, Needham and others. Schneider's initial contribution was to clear the way for the study of kinship as a cultural system, i.e. as a system of ideas and symbols, without reference to social behaviour or institutions. In *American Kinship* (Schneider 1968), he insisted that if kinship was a system of symbols there was no need to investigate norms and practices as previous researchers had done. Arguing that US kinship was based on two culturally constructed orders, the order of nature and the order of law, he provided not only an account of US ideas about relatives but also, more generally, a model for studying a particular kinship/cultural system without reference to the social system. In *A Critique of the*

Study of Kinship (Schneider 1984) he developed a frontal attack on the comparative study of kinship, arguing that the anthropological notion of kinship simply generalizes particular Western folk notions about the biology of reproduction. Since it was obvious that the Western model of the biology of reproduction is anything but universal, kinship could not be used as an analytical category in cross-cultural studies. (For assessments, see Feinberg and Ottenheimer 2001; Kuper 1999: Ch. 4.)

The immediate effect of Schneider's interventions was to discourage traditional studies of kinship and marriage. However, his work was also responsible for the revival of kinship studies in a new form. His insistence that local meaning and symbols should be given priority stimulated particularist accounts of kinship systems that were informed by a variety of perspectives ranging from symbolic anthropology (e.g. Witherspoon 1975) to feminist anthropology (e.g. Strathern 1992), a current that was itself concerned with many of the classical issues in kinship theory. Collier and Yanagisako (1987) issued a call for a unified analysis of gender and kinship, arguing that the study of both gender and kinship needed to be liberated from the straitjacket of supposed 'biological facts', a starting-point that led also to more recent studies of 'new reproductive technologies' (e.g. Franklin 1997) and other non-biological means of reproduction. At the same time, the study of kinship became intertwined with the investigation of cultural notions of sexuality.

The main benefit of the cultural critique was that it obliged anthropologists to confront the question: 'What is kinship *in a particular place, at a specific time*?' The classical tradition had assumed that kinship was a universal, biological given and had focused on the functions the institutions of kinship and marriage fulfilled in different societies. Nowadays, we have a variety of detailed cultural accounts of local meanings – and, sometimes, functions – of kinship.

The future of kinship studies

Kinship will surely remain an important subject as long as human groups phrase their thoughts and actions to a significant degree with reference to local notions of relatedness. Anthropologists traditionally paid most attention to the ramifications of kinship networks in non-Western societies, but the most fruitful new studies are as likely to address the nature and role of kinship in urban or transnational contexts, in new reproductive technologies and in adoption cases, in genetic research, and also in business and political dealings.

Although it has long been established that kinship is not (necessarily) predetermined by biology, anthropologists still often think about kinship separately from the other social forces that contribute to individual and group identities. Yet just as it surely makes sense to admit that kinship is quite easily recognized by ethnographers, wherever they go, so does it generally amount to more than a folk theory of relatedness, and more also than a network of domestic relationships, regulating some private matters. Kinship principles and ideologies can be relevant to social, economic and political contexts that have little or nothing to do with 'relatives'. Kinship networks often provide the only forms of social security. And while nepotism is formally condemned in some societies as conflicting with the principle that each person should be treated on his or her merits, it is widely regarded as a fine moral principle by probably the majority of people in the world. At the extreme, kinship may be used to build multinational family businesses, or to sustain some of the most long-lived dictatorships in the modern world. And as more and more anthropologists question Schneider's premise, that other peoples can be understood only in their own terms, the comparative aspect of kinship studies, which almost had been abandoned after the 1970s, might be due for rediscovery.

PETER P. SCHWEITZER
UNIVERSITY OF ALASKA FAIRBANKS

References

Collier, J. and Yanagisako, S. (eds) (1987) *Gender and Kinship: Essays Toward a Unified Analysis*, Stanford.

Faubion, J. (1996) 'Kinship is dead. Long live kinship: A review article', *Comparative Studies in Society and History* 38(1): 67–91.

Feinberg, R. and Ottenheimer, M. (eds) (2001) *The Cultural Analysis of Kinship: The Legacy of David M. Schneider*, Urbana, IL.

Fortes, M. (1949) *The Web of Kinship among the Tallensi*, London.

Fox, R. (1967) *Kinship and Marriage: An Anthropological Perspective*, Cambridge.

Franklin, S. (1997) *Embodied Progress: A Cultural Account of Assisted Conception*, London.

Kuper, A. (1999) *Culture: The Anthropologists' Account*, Cambridge, MA.

Lévi-Strauss, C. (1969 [1949]) *The Elementary Structures of Kinship*, London.

Malinowski, B. (1929) *The Sexual Life of Savages in North-Western Melanesia*, New York.

Morgan, L. (1871) *Systems of Consanguinity and Affinity of the Human Family*, Washington, DC.

Murdock, G. (1949) *Social Structure*, New York.

Schneider, D. (1968) *American Kinship: A Cultural Account*, Englewood Cliffs, NJ.

—— (1972) 'What is kinship all about?' in P. Reining (ed.) *Kinship Studies in the Morgan Centennial Year*, Washington, DC.

—— (1984) *A Critique of the Study of Kinship*, Ann Arbor, MI.

Strathern, M. (1992) *After Nature: English Kinship in the Late Twentieth Century*, Cambridge, UK.

Trautmann, T. (1987) *Lewis Henry Morgan and the Invention of Kinship*, Berkeley, CA.

Witherspoon, G. (1975) *Navajo Kinship and Marriage*, Chicago.

Further reading

Carsten, J. (ed.) (2000) *Cultures of Relatedness: New Approaches to the Study of Kinship*, Cambridge, UK.

Franklin, S. and McKinnon, S. (eds) (2001) *Relative Values: Reconfiguring Kinship Studies*, Durham, NC.

Parkin, R. and Stone, L. (eds) (2004) *Kinship and Family: An Anthropological Reader*, Oxford.

Schweitzer, P. (ed.) (2000) *Dividends of Kinship: Meanings and Uses of Social Relatedness*, London.

Stone, L. (ed.) (2001) *New Directions in Anthropological Kinship*, Lanham, MD.

SEE ALSO: family; Lévi-Strauss; marriage; primitive society